D0206683

Framing America

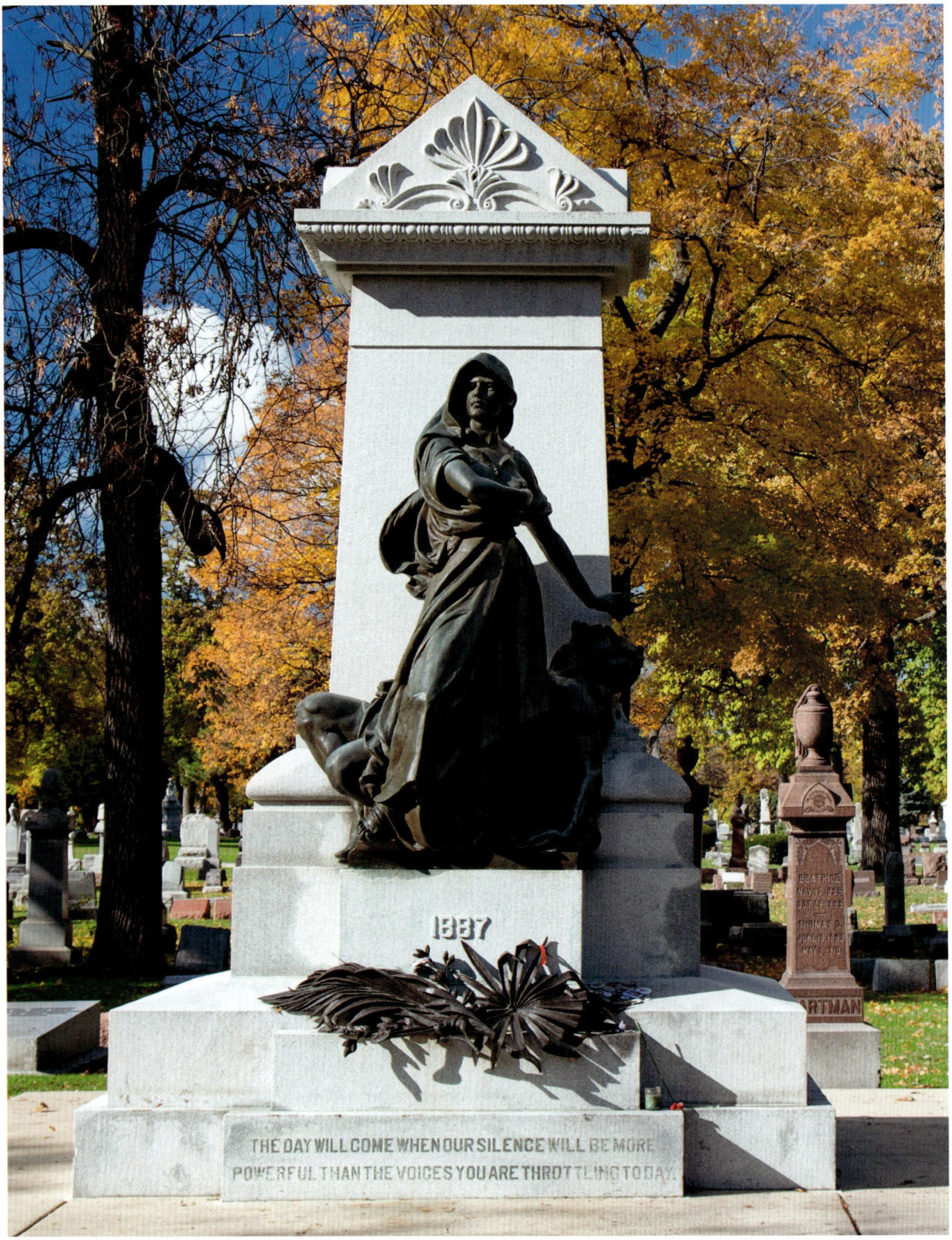
1887
THE DAY WILL COME WHEN OUR SILENCE WILL BE MORE
POWERFUL THAN THE VOICES YOU ARE THROTTLING TODAY.

Frances K. Pohl
Pomona College

Framing America

A Social History of American Art

Volume 1 *c.* 200 BCE – 1900

Fourth Edition

380 illustrations

Thames & Hudson

A Note on the Captions
Dimensions (except in the case of photographs) are given where known; h. = height, l. = length, w. = width. Full acknowledgments will be found on pp. 358–59.

On the cover
Front Erastus Salisbury Field, *Joseph Moore and His Family*, c. 1839 (see **2.7.12**; p. 141). Museum of Fine Arts, Boston, Massachusetts/Gift of Maxim Karolik for the M. and M. Karolik Collection of American Paintings, 1815–1865/Bridgeman Images
Back, left Arapoosh (Sore Belly), River Crow: decorated hide shield, early 19th century (see **3.8.4**; p. 151). National Museum of the American Indian, Smithsonian Institution, Washington, D.C.
Back, right E. Jane Gay, *Photographer*, after 1893 (see **5.17.22**; p. 316). The Schlesinger Library, Radcliffe Institute, Harvard University, Cambridge, MA

Frontispiece Albert Weinert, *Haymarket Monument*, 1893 (see pp. 274–76)
Granite and bronze, h. 16 ft. (5 m.)
Forest Home (formerly Waldheim) Cemetery, Forest Park, Illinois

© 2002, 2008, 2012, 2017 Thames & Hudson Inc.

All Rights Reserved. No part of this publication may be reproduced or transmitted in any form or by any means, electronic or mechanical, including photocopy, recording or any other information storage and retrieval system, without prior permission in writing from the publisher.

First published in 2002 in the United States of America by
Thames & Hudson Inc., 500 Fifth Avenue, New York, New York 10110

www.thamesandhudsonusa.com

Second edition 2008
Third edition 2012
Fourth edition 2017

Library of Congress Control Number 2017937578
ISBN 978-0-500-29295-2

Printed and bound in China by Everbest Printing Co. Ltd.

Contents

Preface 10

Map of North and Central America 15

Part 1 Art and Conquest *c.* 200 BCE–1821 CE 16

1 Visualizing the Conquest: Colonial Spain and Indigenous Mesoamerica (*c.* 1500–1580) 20
Tenochtitlan: Pyramids, Codices, and Monumental Sculpture 20
Christian Painting, Sculpture, and Architecture in New Spain 24

2 Art and Architecture in the Northern Territories of New Spain (*c.* 900–1821) 29
Early Explorations and Fortifications 29
The Pueblo Cultures 30
The Christianization of the Pueblos 33
Church Architecture in the Pueblos 34
Church Interiors and Adornments 36
Texas and Arizona in the Seventeenth and Eighteenth Centuries 40
Battle Scenes on Hide: Segesser I and II 43
The Californian Missions 45

3 New France: Contact Zones and Cultural Production (*c.* 200 BCE–1760 CE) 49
Material Exchange: The Impact of Trade on Indigenous Culture 49
France Bringing the Faith: Religious Instruction and Cultural Exchange 52
The Influence of Fashion: Painted Caribou-Skin Coats 55
Monuments to Death: Hopewell and Mississippian Burial Mounds and Effigy Funeral Vessels 57
Monuments to Life: Cahokia and the Grand Village of the Natchez 59
Indigenous America in Europe: The Comte d'Artois's Cabinet of Natural History 60

4 A Protestant Presence in America: The Arts of the British and Dutch Colonies (*c.* 1585–1772) 63
Picturing the "New World": John White and Theodore de Bry 63
Early Settlements: Jamestown and Plymouth 66
Art, Religion, and Politics in Seventeenth-Century New England 68
Displays of Status: Portraiture in New England 69
Displays of Status: Domestic Spaces in New England 70
The Dutch Influence in Architecture and Portraits 73
Aristocratic Pretensions in the South 75
Learning Their Stitches and Keeping Warm: Colonial Needlework 79
Doors to Eternal Peace: Carved Gravestones 81
Foreign Wars and Domestic Unrest: Benjamin West's *The Death of General Wolfe* and *Penn's Treaty with the Indians* 81

Part 2 Defining America *c.* 1765–1850 86

5 Representing the American Revolution and Its Leaders (*c.* 1765–1810) 88
Domestic Production and International Intrigue: The Portraits of John Singleton Copley 88
John Trumbull's Canvases of War 92
The Aspirations of Women: Post-Revolutionary Samplers 97
Money, Beauty, and Rank: Silver in the New Republic 98
Presidential Poses: Paintings and Statues of George Washington 100
Posthumous Portraits of Washington: The Mourning Picture 104
From Painting to Print to Embroidery: The History of an Image 106

6 Symbols of a New Nation: Architecture and Indigenous Histories (*c.* 1785–1827) 110
Home for a President: Thomas Jefferson's Monticello 110
Constructing a Capital: Washington, D.C. 112

The Louisiana Purchase: New Orleans and Plantation Architecture 113
An Architecture of Discipline: Shaker Communities 115
An Architecture of Discipline: Prisons 118
Nationhood and Native Americans: The Decoration of the Capitol Building 121
From Indian Queen to Greek Goddess 124
Narratives of Captivity 125
Portraits and Treaties 128

7 The Schooling of the Nation's Artists (*c.* 1820–1850) 131
Improving the Taste of the Nation: Samuel F. B. Morse and the National Academy of Design 131
The Entrepreneurial Spirit and the Production of American Culture: Rufus Porter and the "Valuable and Curious Arts" 135
A Plain Likeness: Itinerant Portrait Painters 140
Learning the "Sunbeam Art": The Daguerreotype 145

Part 3 Nature and Nation *c.* 1000–1863 148

8 Nature and the Sacred (*c.* 1000–1863) 150
Imagery of Creation and the Vision Quest 150
The Box that Speaks: The Integration of Form, Content, and Material 152
God's Nature as God in Nature 153
Landscape Tourism 154
Images of Niagara Falls 155
Thomas Cole, Federalism, and The Course of Empire 158
Successors to Cole 161
Edward Hicks and The Peaceable Kingdom 163
Frederic Edwin Church: From the Pastoral to the Sublime 166
Still and Troubled Waters: Luminist Landscapes 170

9 The Occupied Landscape (*c.* 1830–1863) 172
"A City May Rise": Albert Bierstadt's *The Rocky Mountains, Lander's Peak* 172
Native American Borders: Emanuel Leutze's *Westward the Course of Empire* 174
"The Looks and Modes" of Native American Life: George Catlin and His "Indian Gallery" 175
George Catlin and the Mandans 178
Photographic Portraits: Another Take on the Real 182
The Iconography of Progress: The City and the Train 183
Human Actors in the Landscape: Genre Paintings of the Yeoman Farmer 186
Human Actors in the Landscape: Genre Paintings of the Westerner 188

10 Domesticated Nature (*c.* 1818–1860) 192
Woman as Nature: The Nude, the Mother, and the Cook 192
The Fruits of Art: The Peale Family and Still-Life Painting 196
Tricking the Eye: Raphaelle Peale and the Art of Deception 199
Gender and the Art of Flower Painting 201
Ornithological Paintings as "Nature Morte": Alexander Wilson and John James Audubon 203

Part 4 A Nation at War *c.* 1830–1900 208

11 Images of Mexico and/as America: The Mexico-US War and Its Aftermath (*c.* 1848–1860) 210
Learning from the Past: Emanuel Leutze's *The Storming of the Teocalli* 210
Life on the Home Front 212
Life on the Front Lines 214
Mexican Culture as American Culture: The *Santeros* of New Mexico 214
The Local and the International: New Mexican Furniture and Textiles 218

12 A Nation Divided: Slavery and the Civil War (*c.* 1839–1865) 221
Prelude to the Civil War: Representing African Americans and Slavery 221
The Abolitionist Movement and the Challenging of Stereotypes 223
Paintings of Fugitives, Contraband, and Soldiers 229
Photographs of the War 233

13 Reconstruction and Shifting Images of African Americans (*c.* 1886–1900) 236
Winslow Homer's *Prisoners from the Front* and *A Visit from the Old Mistress* 236
Thomas Nast's "Grand Historical Paintings" 240
The Freed Slave: Edmonia Lewis's *Forever Free* and Thomas Ball's *Freedmen's Memorial* 241
Seated Generals, Standing Soldiers: Military Memorials to the Civil War 246

14 The Indian Wars and the End of the Ghost Dance (*c.* 1869–1900) 249
Native Americans in the Popular Press: *Harper's Weekly* and the Washita River Massacre 249
The Art of Incarceration: The Fort Marion Ledger Drawings 251
The Battle of the Little Bighorn 255
The End of the Ghost Dance 257
The Hampton Institute and Lessons in American History 260

Part 5 Art, Labor, and The Gilded Age *c.* 1865–1900 264

15 The Art of Industrial Labor (*c.* 1871–1890) 266

One Hundred Years of Independence: Taking Stock of America at the 1876 Philadelphia Centennial Exhibition 266
Factory and Foundry: Winslow Homer and Thomas Anshutz 269
Labor Unrest: Robert Koehler's "Strike" and Monuments to Justice and Liberty 272

16 The Art of Professional and Domestic Labor (*c.* 1865–1889) 278

Celebrating the New Male Professionals: Portraits by Thomas Eakins 278
Middle-Class Masculinity, Mass Production, and *Trompe l'oeil* Painting 283
Domestic Labor and Cultural Production 285
Helpful Women: The Evolving Image of the Domestic Servant 288
Spaces of Leisure and Labor: Domestic Architecture and Interior Design 292
Spaces of Leisure and Labor: Parks and Streets 295

17 Gender, the Ideal, and the Real (*c.* 1871–1900) 300

The Rise of Aestheticism 300
American Impressionism and Consumer Culture: William Merritt Chase's *In the Studio* 304
American Impressionism and the Nostalgic Landscape: J. Alden Weir and John Twachtman 306
American Impressionism and Portraiture 308
Performing Identity in Photographic Portraits 314

18 Art and Architecture at the End of the Century (*c.* 1885–1900) 318

Cultural Institutions and the Public Good: The Metropolitan Museum of Art 318
The Chicago School of Architecture and the White City 319
Women at the Fair: Allegories, Architects, and Artists 324
Race and Religion at the Turn of the Century: Henry Ossawa Tanner 332
Men at Sea: Albert Pinkham Ryder and Winslow Homer 335

Bibliography 338
Glossary 350
Acknowledgments for Illustrations 358
Index 360

Preface

Fifteen years have passed since the publication of the first edition of *Framing America: A Social History of American Art*. Although much has changed in the field of American art history during this time, much has also remained constant. The same is true of this edition. Readers will find the familiar works of art that filled the pages of the first three editions, together with the inclusive, continental approach to the subject, but the discussion now covers a number of new images and featured artists. In addition, while the order in which the material is presented remains chronologically based, some of the text has been reorganized in response to suggestions from faculty who use *Framing America* in order to make the content more digestible for students (for more details, see "New to This Edition," below). These changes will allow more flexibility for those teaching the history of American art over a number of semesters and will help students study the material in a more systematic fashion. The text has also been revised throughout, incorporating examples of the most innovative scholarship that has appeared in recent years. This scholarship points to the new approaches—for example, the rise of ecocritical art history—and new works of art that have helped ensure that the history of American art continues to be an engaging and meaningful area of study.

New to This Edition

- In response to instructors' suggestions, the text has been reorganized to offer teachers more flexibility when assigning sections for class discussion: what were previously long chapters are now nine overarching parts comprising thirty-two shorter chapters in total, split into two volumes tailored to two-term courses.

- Part-opener spreads featuring timelines and a succinct introduction to the chapters that follow give students a much clearer picture of how major events and movements relate chronologically.

- Brand-new review questions, designed to give students a chance to check their understanding of the material, conclude each chapter.

- More artworks (*c.* 470) are presented in color.

- New scholarship, including the work of Mary K. Coffey on the origins of Modernism in the Americas, Alan C. Braddock on ecocritical art history, and Shawn Michelle Smith on photography and critical race theory.

- The inclusion, in the introduction of Part 1, of a more detailed discussion of the significance of approaching the study of American art as part of a series of interconnected colonial enterprises undertaken by major European powers (most notably, Spain, France, and England) beginning in the sixteenth century.

- An expanded discussion in Chapter 17 of American Impressionism, with new material and detailed analysis of the impact of consumer culture and nostalgia for a pre-industrial landscape.

- New content, in Chapters 7 and 17, on the innovations and political significance of nineteenth-century photographic portraiture.

- New coverage of the work of Jean-Michel Basquiat, Edgar Heap of Birds, Mia Lehrer, and Lauren Bon in the twentieth and twenty-first centuries.

The following digital resources are also available to instructors:

- A test bank of more than one thousand questions, and teaching notes, all written by the author—a great help for novice and experienced instructors alike.

- All images presented in *Framing America* are obtainable as JPEGs and as PowerPoint art slides with captions.

- *Framing America* is also available as a single, complete e-book that contains all content from both volumes.

About This Book

The past fifteen years have not made writing a survey text on American art any easier. It is still both an exciting and frustrating process to visit museums, sift through books and articles, and select artists and art works that can enhance the narrative that I have already constructed, or shift this narrative in instructive ways. Some still question whether one should even attempt to create a text that claims to represent the history of American art when, in order to be manageable in the context of a college classroom and a publisher's budget, it necessarily has to leave out so much. Yet I believe that survey texts, no matter how selective, are still valuable as vehicles for the introduction of a broad range of creative expression, and for addressing the complexity of historical change.

This book is meant to be a starting point, not an end point, for those interested in learning about American art. Its format derives from my own experiences as a scholar and a teacher, while its content is heavily indebted to the scholarship of other historians in the field and to the comments of teachers and students who have used this book. Each new edition contains material shaped by such comments, ranging from alternative interpretations of images to requests for maps, timelines, a glossary, specific artists or media, or smaller chapters. The writing of art history has been, and always will be, an ongoing process in which many individuals offer sometimes competing arguments. For students of American art, the debate is often as instructive as any common ground that might be occupied.

I have arranged this book both chronologically and thematically, with an emphasis on developing a critical understanding of how artists, the work they produce, and the critical writings or debates surrounding that work function within specific communities at specific moments in history. In keeping with several earlier surveys of American art, this one includes examples of folk art as well as fine art, of architecture as well as furniture. Unlike many of those surveys, however, I have integrated this material into a single central narrative rather than isolating each medium or category of art into a separate section. I have done this in order to convey the interconnectedness of what has been variously described as fine art, folk art, popular art, and mass culture, and the built environment in which these cultural products circulate.

I have incorporated the work of Native American artists throughout the text as evidence of one of the many ongoing encounters between cultural traditions that have marked the history of this country. This work is presented as part of a series of regional cultures that often extend across national borders, whether north from Washington State into the Canadian province of British Columbia or south from New Mexico and Arizona into the Mexican states of Sonora and Coahuila. Other previously marginalized groups—white women, African Americans, Latinos/Latinas, Asian Americans—appear, as well, as active agents in the development of a national culture.

I have also chosen to vary the manner in which I treat the artists included in this text. Some are examined in depth, while others are dealt with briefly as part of a larger movement or historical event. I have done this in an attempt to highlight the different ways in which art historians have approached the study of American art—for example, through the use of biography, stylistic analysis, the study of patronage and/or the location of artistic production within struggles for political or personal power. I have included many individuals who have long been viewed as major American artists, such as John Singer Sargent and Jackson Pollock; but I have also treated lesser-known artists, such as the eighteenth-century needleworker Cynthia Burr, in comparable depth. My intent is not to create a new canon of "great" American artists, but to allow the reader access to the multiplicity of creative processes through which individuals or groups of individuals grapple with ideas and transform them into art forms that speak powerfully to particular groups at particular times. Those individuals who have gained reputations for greatness have done so for a variety of reasons, some having to do with their skills as artists, others with their connections to powerful or influential people or institutions. I hope this book will help students of American art recognize these institutional as well as personal factors at work in the creation and promotion of art and artists. The history of art is not simply the inevitable progression of styles and artists toward a predetermined goal in the present. Instead, it is an accumulation of tensions, crises, accidents, and insights, all embedded in a larger historical process that both forms and is formed by the workings and products of artistic activity.

A Social History of Art

The methodology I have briefly outlined above—the questions I have asked and the places where I have looked for answers—can best be described as a social history of art. In writing this book, I have drawn on, and am greatly indebted to, the work of early practitioners of such social history. First introduced to a broad public by the German scholar Arnold Hauser in his four-volume *The Social History of Art* (1951), this methodology positions artists and art-making firmly within history. For Hauser, artistic production was an integral part of social relations and was connected to particular social groups. In attempting to trace the connections between specific artistic styles and social groups, Hauser drew on Karl Marx's theory of ideology as the enactment, in the realm of ideas—legal, political, religious, aesthetic, philosophic—of the material conditions of production.

Many art historians have built upon the work of Hauser since the 1960s. They have often focused more intensely than he had on the fluidity of the connections between style and social groups, and on the social and cultural complexities of artistic production. T. J. Clark, one of the best-known of the second generation of social art historians, wrote in his book *Image of the People: Gustave Courbet and the 1848 Revolution* (1973) that the social history of art needed to cast its net wide, bringing into play "the connecting links between artistic form, the available systems of visual representation, the current theories of art, other ideologies, social classes, and more general historical structures and processes."

The rise of a social history of art was particularly important for historians of American art. In an overview of the field published in 1988, the art historian Wanda Corn noted that the study of American art began to flourish only in the late 1960s. Before this time scholars were primarily "self-trained, motivated by love for the work or curiosity about the development of the field." Many were artists turned historians, freelance writers, or librarians. Support for their work came largely from museums and galleries interested in verifying the provenance of works in their collections. There was little encouragement in graduate schools to work on American topics, in large part because American art was almost always seen as inferior in quality to European art. After World War II, American art appeared as a worthy competitor in the international arena in the form of such Modernist movements as Abstract Expressionism. Many of those who championed this art were interested in earlier work only insofar as it could be interpreted as a precursor to these movements.

In fact, American art as a field was initially defined as art produced before 1945. What came after was deemed "Modernist" art and thus the purview of Modernist art historians who may or may not have any knowledge of art produced in the US before 1945. The art historian John Davis comments on the limits of this division, noting how it "reifies the dichotomy of a provincial, attenuated national expression before 1945 and a more vigorous, international postwar art." Yet he also worries that ignoring this divide and claiming all art produced in the US as American risks "minimizing the global sweep of later-twentieth-century art and tying it down with nationalist baggage that prevents it from being seen as a participant in international forums." There is less of a risk of this happening, however, if American art is presented, as it is in *Framing America*, as having always participated in international conversations, whether with Britain during the late eighteenth century or Mexico in the early twentieth century, and as having always been informed to a greater or lesser degree by nationalist concerns.

Such nationalist concerns certainly marked the founding of the field of American art history. In the years surrounding World War I, a heightened concern about "Americanness" resulted in specialized subjects being established in the areas of American history, literature, art, philosophy, and so on. This self-conscious examination of the national mind and character led to the formation of American Civilization or American Studies programs in the 1950s and also helped legitimize the serious study of American art in the classroom. In this context, there was no need to apologize for its "quality."

This nationalist emphasis, Corn observed, brought into being most museum collections, wings, and galleries of American art. While these institutions provided much-needed economic and moral support for scholars, their existence led to the dominance of the documentary monograph in the scholarship of the 1950s and 1960s. Scholars were concerned, above all, with verifying authenticity, tracing ownership or provenance, and fleshing out the biographies of the artists. There was little interest in questions of iconography, patronage (which is different from provenance), and art criticism.

All this began to change when art historians trained in university programs replaced the self-tutored writers of the 1950s and 1960s. Many began engaging with feminist, Marxist, psychoanalytic, and poststructuralist scholarship, as well as the social history of art, often rejecting or supplementing the elite canon that privileged white male artists and "masterpieces." New artists and new media were examined and new attempts made to evaluate the relationship between American and European art. The populist politics of the 1960s and 1970s prompted a renewed interest in the art of the 1930s and a re-examination of the division between "high" and "low" art. Critiques of nationalism led to re-evaluations of such art movements as Abstract Expressionism in light of the Cold War politics of the late 1940s and 1950s. The demands of activist movements in the 1970s and 1980s led to a close consideration of the place of the visual arts within identity formation, a consideration informed by critical race, postcolonial, and queer theories. In the early twenty-first century, art historians have turned to the insights of legal scholars, media theorists, and environmental historians, among others, to understand how artists have grappled with the consequences of US involvement in what President George W. Bush defined in 2001 as a "war on terror," and with the impact of global warming.

While I have drawn on sources that exhibit a wide range of methodologies, I have chosen to call my study a "social history of art" because the social history of art, as I have come to understand it, is able to accommodate the many concerns I feel compelled to address. I want to examine how the meaning of a work is a function not only of its content, medium, and style, but also of where it is produced, where it is displayed, and the identity of the artist. I also want to examine how this identity is affected by race, ethnicity, class, gender, religion, and sexuality. I am concerned with the place of art within struggles for power in both the public and private realms, and with rethinking the category "art" itself. The best social history of art combines research on the institutions of art—academies, galleries, museums, journals, community art programs—with attention to the critical discourses surrounding these institutions. Such an approach leads to an understanding of larger political and aesthetic processes and of the tensions these processes ultimately create as change occurs.

Continental Perspective

Many practitioners of the social history of art are also concerned, today, with rethinking the processes of conquest and colonization that are such an integral part of American history. While Europeans explored the eastern coastline of North America in the eleventh through fifteenth centuries (for example, the Vikings and Portuguese cod fishermen), they did not establish permanent settlements until the early sixteenth century. Many different peoples inhabited the land they claimed. Some were organized into semi-nomadic chiefdoms, some into sedentary horticultural communities, and others into vast empire states. All had developed complex systems of communication, which drew heavily on images to express their identity, their place in the world, and their political power. The relationships that grew out of these early encounters were complex and are central to an understanding of the history of the United States—political, economic, and artistic. So, too, were those that developed as a result of the importation of vast numbers of slaves from Africa, beginning in the sixteenth century, in order to facilitate the colonization process.

In his book *Europe and the People Without History*, the anthropologist Eric Wolf argues that "the world of humankind constitutes a manifold, a totality of interconnected processes." Often, however, anthropologists and historians study only fragments of this totality and deny the complexity and interconnectedness and combativeness of human history. Wolf found standard versions of American history particularly problematic in this respect. They tended to present "the ever-changing boundaries of the United States and the repeated involvement of the polity in internal and external wars, declared and undeclared," as part of an inevitable progression of historical events. Such events were linked by the presumption that "thirteen colonies clinging to the eastern rim of the continent would, in less than a century, plant the American flag on the shores of the Pacific. Yet this final result was itself only the contested outcome of many contradictory relationships."

In other words, the current geographical borders and political organizations that mark this country are the result not of any inevitable historical progression (historicism) but of innumerable struggles, alliances, and accidents (historical materialism). The southwestern portion of the US could have remained part of Mexico; the British could have pressed their interests more aggressively in the northwest and created a border south of the forty-ninth parallel. The US evolved slowly over time, expanding in territory and, in the process, incorporating areas where artistic practices and cultural traditions were already well established. The Louisiana Purchase of 1803 did not cause the populace of New Orleans immediately to abandon their French ties. Neither did the Treaty of Guadalupe Hidalgo of 1848 erase the Mexican culture that was already firmly in place in what is now the American Southwest. And Native American cultures, while embattled as a result of wars and forced assimilation, did not disappear.

In the following pages I want to trace these ever-changing boundaries, to investigate how the cultural traditions that crossed and re-crossed them, or were divided and re-divided by them, survived to form a unique mix defined as American culture. In order to do so I will be looking at artistic developments in the US in part from a continental perspective. I will be examining the ways in which the visual culture of this country has been formed not only in relation to cultural practices in Europe, but also in relation to cultural practices that arose in the French and Spanish colonies that flourished along with the British and Dutch colonies on the North American continent, beginning with the arrival of the Spaniard Hernán Cortés in central Mexico and the Frenchman Jacques Cartier in the St. Lawrence River Valley in the early sixteenth century. As Caroline Levander and Robert Levine write in the introduction to their 2008 anthology *Hemispheric American Studies*, "moving beyond the nation does not mean abandoning the idea of nation but rather recognizing its dynamic elements and fluid, ever-changing, essentially contingent nature."

Including material previously absent from surveys of American art raises many challenges. Often both the objects themselves and the very processes by which they have been acquired by cultural institutions and come to be considered "art" must be analysed. For example, this country's major collections of Native American art were put together between 1860 and 1930 by such institutions as the Peabody Museum at Harvard University, the Smithsonian Institution in Washington, D.C., and the American Museum of Natural History in New York City. As a result of this collecting frenzy, more Northwest Coast Native American material ended up in the city of Washington than in the state of Washington, and the pottery-making traditions of Zuñi and Acoma pueblos were seriously destabilized. In her introduction to *The Early Years of Native American Art History*, the art historian Janet Berlo notes that over the past century these Native American objects have been organized and reorganized in constantly changing mosaics that have allowed us to construct "an image we claim represents Native American art and culture. We now realize that this image tells us at least as much about the collectors as it does about the materials collected." Any discussion of Native American art created or collected in the late nineteenth and early twentieth centuries must thus acknowledge the historical moment in which it was made and in which it was collected.

In writing this book, therefore, I am joining many other scholars in calling for a broadening of our understanding of the complex combination of traditions that make up this country's culture. Students in the twenty-first century need to be able to think both locally and globally, to understand both the separateness and the interconnectedness of nations throughout the world. As a Canadian living in the southwestern portion of the US, close to the Mexican border, I have experienced the benefits of grappling with these multiple relationships. In *Framing America* I attempt to present a paradigm or framework—hence the title of this book—for thinking in this broader, more complex, and comparative manner. Such a comparative analysis can help provide students in the US (and beyond) with a sense of this country's shared histories, with an understanding of common patterns of creative expression and cultural consumption, of exploitation and struggles for independence, of divisions and alliances.

At this point I need to say a word about the term "America." Since the 1970s many scholars and activists have taken issue with its use to describe only the United States of America. Some argue we need to speak of "the Americas," others that we need to refer to the country only as "the United States of America" or some other term or phrase that does not double for the continent or hemisphere as a whole. It is helpful to remember that the meaning of "America" has changed over time. In 1507 the German cartographer Martin Waldseemüller published the first map with the name "America" for the territory recently discovered by Europeans, after the Italian navigator Amerigo Vespucci. In 1776 rebellious colonists took on the name to describe their own particular part of the continent, the United States of America. Yet even there, "American" was at first used primarily to refer to indigenous peoples; only after 1815 was it adopted as a general term for more recent European arrivals. The anthropologist George Kubler points out that in the late eighteenth century the term was also "a name of opprobrium in Europe for returning colonials." The Spanish referred to their colonies in America as *las Indias* and the colonists as *Indios*.

For better or for worse, however, "America" has come to be associated today with the United States of America (Canadians traveling abroad are quick to point out that they are Canadians, not Americans). By using the term in a discussion of the personal, political, cultural, and economic processes involved in the production of the art of the United States of America, I hope to indicate the contingency of both the name and that which it describes—that the United States of America was, and is, not a stable entity, and that while the geographical boundaries may not change in the near future, the cultural mix will certainly continue to evolve. As early as 1990, *Time* magazine's culture critic, William A. Henry III, predicted that by 2056 most Americans will trace their descendants to "Africa, Asia, the Hispanic world, the Pacific Islands, Arabia—almost anywhere but white Europe." We do not have to wait until 2056 to grapple with the implications of this development and to find ways to ensure that the history of American art acknowledges the multiplicity of cultures that constitute this country's creative legacy.

Acknowledgments

This book emerged out of my years of teaching and research at Pomona College, and I owe a debt of gratitude to my students and colleagues for creating a stimulating intellectual environment and to the college administration for support in the form of research grants and release time. It also could not have been written without the many volumes and articles on American art that have appeared over the past four decades, in particular those that address the complex intersections of art and politics. The authors of these studies are too numerous to list here, but I have acknowledged as many as possible in the body of the text and in the bibliography. *Framing America* benefited from the support and guidance of Nikos Stangos, Peter Warner, and Emily Lane over the several years it took to complete the first edition, as well as from the insightful comments of Martin A. Berger, Patricia Hills, Robyn Roslak, and Mary K. Coffey on the original manuscript. Since then others at Thames & Hudson—Ian Jacobs, Priscilla McGeehon, Nicole Albas, Lucy Smith, and Hayley Maher, to name only a few—have ensured that the subsequent editions have maintained the high production and content standards of the first. I'd also like to thank the many faculty and students who have taken the time to talk with me about the book or email me their comments, pointing out small errors or indicating which sections worked particularly well in their classes and which did not. Finally, family and friends, in particular Gerald Ackerman, Leonard Simon, and Mary Kenon Breazeale, have provided much-needed intellectual and emotional support over the fifteen years since the first edition appeared.

The publisher would like to thank the following for their generous advice and feedback during the preparation of *Framing America*. Special gratitude goes to:

Janet Carpenter, City College of San Francisco
Susan Casteras, University of Washington
Anna Kamplain Dietz, University of Alabama
Wendy Katz, University of Nebraska–Lincoln
Karen Leader, Florida Atlantic University
Abigail McEwen, University of Maryland
Dennis Raverty, New Jersey City University
Sascha Scott, Syracuse University
Tanya R. Sheehan, Colby College

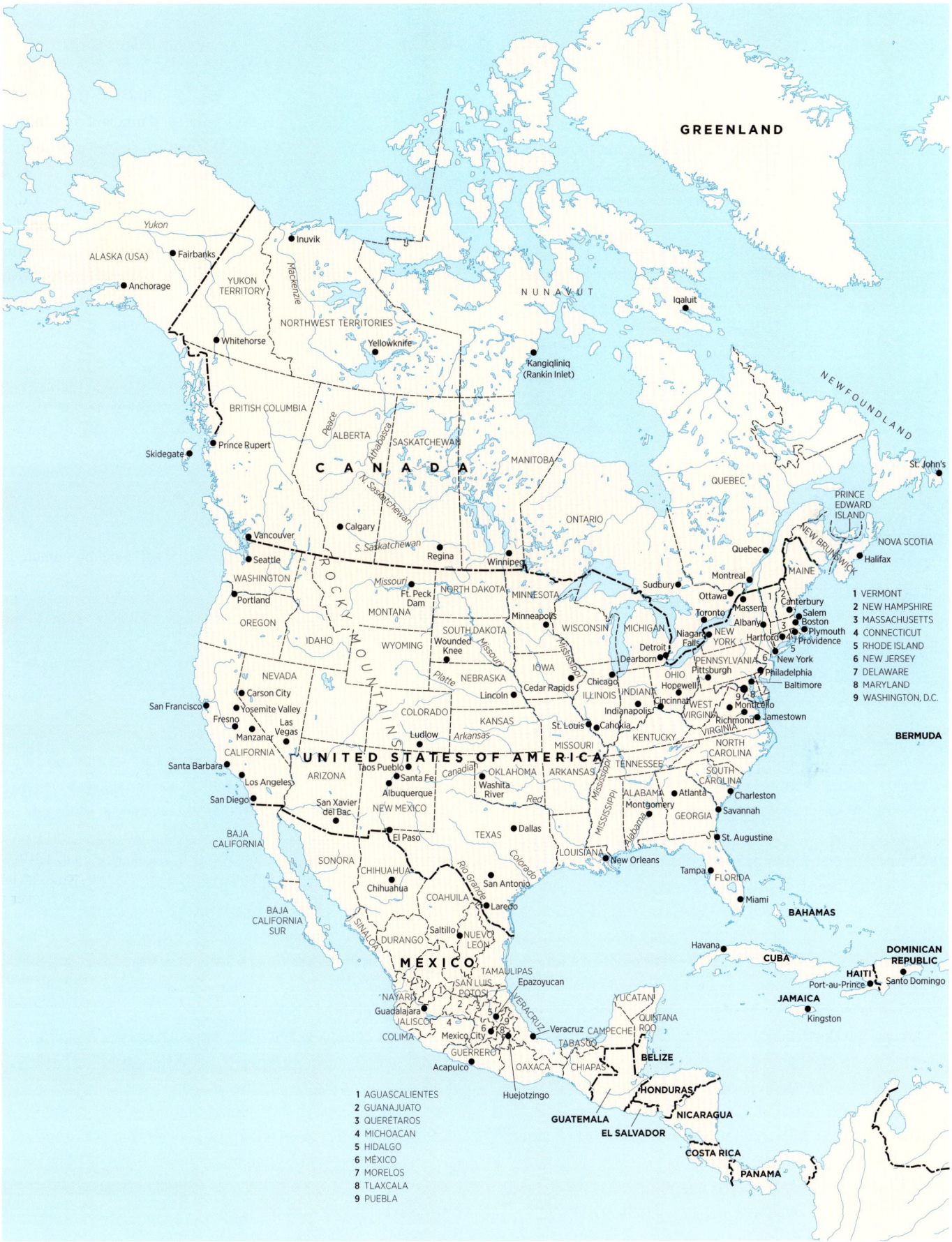
GREENLAND
Yukon
ALASKA (USA)
Fairbanks
Anchorage
Inuvik
YUKON TERRITORY
Mackenzie
NORTHWEST TERRITORIES
Whitehorse
Yellowknife
NUNAVUT
Iqaluit
Kangiqliniq (Rankin Inlet)
NEWFOUNDLAND
BRITISH COLUMBIA
Peace
ALBERTA
Athabasca
SASKATCHEWAN
Prince Rupert
Skidegate
CANADA
MANITOBA
N. Saskatchewan
QUEBEC
St. John's
PRINCE EDWARD ISLAND
ONTARIO
Calgary
Vancouver
S. Saskatchewan
Regina
Winnipeg
NEW BRUNSWICK
NOVA SCOTIA
Halifax
Seattle
Quebec
WASHINGTON
Missouri
Ft. Peck Dam
NORTH DAKOTA
MINNESOTA
Sudbury
Montreal
MAINE
Portland
ROCKY MOUNTAINS
MONTANA
Ottawa
Massena
Canterbury
Salem
Boston
Plymouth
Providence
OREGON
Minneapolis
SOUTH DAKOTA
WISCONSIN
MICHIGAN
Toronto
Albany
Niagara Falls
NEW YORK
Hartford
IDAHO
WYOMING
Wounded Knee
Missouri
Mississippi
Detroit
Dearborn
New York
PENNSYLVANIA
Pittsburgh
Philadelphia
NEVADA
IOWA
Platte
NEBRASKA
Chicago
OHIO
Hopewell
Baltimore
Carson City
Cedar Rapids
ILLINOIS
INDIANA
Cincinnati
Monticello
San Francisco
Yosemite Valley
Lincoln
WEST VIRGINIA
Jamestown
Fresno
Las Vegas
COLORADO
KANSAS
Indianapolis
Richmond
Manzanar
Ludlow
Arkansas
St. Louis
Cahokia
VIRGINIA
KENTUCKY
CALIFORNIA
MISSOURI
NORTH CAROLINA
UNITED STATES OF AMERICA
Santa Barbara
Taos Pueblo
Canadian
OKLAHOMA
ARKANSAS
TENNESSEE
SOUTH CAROLINA
Los Angeles
ARIZONA
Santa Fe
Washita River
Red
Mississippi
ALABAMA
Atlanta
Charleston
San Diego
San Xavier del Bac
Albuquerque
NEW MEXICO
Montgomery
GEORGIA
Savannah
BAJA CALIFORNIA
El Paso
TEXAS
Dallas
Alabama
St. Augustine
SONORA
LOUISIANA
New Orleans
Colorado
CHIHUAHUA
Rio Grande
San Antonio
Tampa
FLORIDA
Chihuahua
COAHUILA
Laredo
Miami
BAHAMAS
BAJA CALIFORNIA SUR
SINALOA
Saltillo
NUEVO LEÓN
DURANGO
Havana
CUBA
DOMINICAN REPUBLIC
MÉXICO
TAMAULIPAS
HAITI
Port-au-Prince
Santo Domingo
SAN LUIS POTOSÍ
Epazoyucan
VERACRUZ
NAYARIT
YUCATAN
JAMAICA
Kingston
Guadalajara
JALISCO
QUINTANA ROO
COLIMA
Mexico City
Veracruz
CAMPECHE
TABASCO
GUERRERO
BELIZE
Acapulco
OAXACA
CHIAPAS
HONDURAS
Huejotzingo
GUATEMALA
NICARAGUA
EL SALVADOR
COSTA RICA
PANAMA
BERMUDA
1 VERMONT
2 NEW HAMPSHIRE
3 MASSACHUSETTS
4 CONNECTICUT
5 RHODE ISLAND
6 NEW JERSEY
7 DELAWARE
8 MARYLAND
9 WASHINGTON, D.C.
1 AGUASCALIENTES
2 GUANAJUATO
3 QUERÉTAROS
4 MICHOACAN
5 HIDALGO
6 MÉXICO
7 MORELOS
8 TLAXCALA
9 PUEBLA

Puebloan Culture *c.* 700–1600

Mississippian Culture *c.* 800–1600

New Spain 1521–1821

New France 1541–1763

Virginia/New England

900–1150
Anasazi culture thrives in Chaco Canyon [1.2.4]

1050–1250
Height of Mississippian settlement of Cahokia [1.3.12]

***c.* 1345**
Founding of Aztec capital of Tenochtitlan [1.1.2]

1492
Christopher Columbus makes first of four voyages

1507
Cartographer Martin Waldseemüller publishes the first map with the name "America" for the New World

1519–21
Hernán Cortés arrives on east coast of Mexico; defeats Aztec Empire (1521)

1534–35
Jacques Cartier explores Gulf of St. Lawrence for France [1.3.1]

1535
First Spanish viceroy arrives in Mexico City

1539
Hernan de Soto explores Florida, South Carolina, Tennessee and eastern Oklahoma

1540
Francisco Vásquez de Coronado explores the Rio Grande region

1541
Cartier establishes the first French colony near Quebec City

***c.* 1550**
Formation of the League of the Iroquois

1565
Spanish massacre inhabitants of the French Protestant settlement of Fort Caroline, Florida (founded 1564), establish St. Augustine [1.2.1]

1585
John White accompanies the first short-lived British colony at Roanoke, off the coast of North Carolina, executes watercolors of Algonquian peoples [1.4.2 and 1.4.3]

1588
British fleet defeats the Spanish Armada off the coast of Calais

PART 1 Art and Conquest

c. 200 BCE–1821 CE

In 1590 the Franco-Flemish Protestant engraver Theodore de Bry (1528–1598) published the first of a thirty-volume series of illustrated accounts of European exploration throughout the world. Known collectively as the *Great Voyages* (the Americas, Oceania) and the *Small Voyages* (India, Japan, China, Africa), these were the first widely available illustrated narratives of cross-Atlantic travel (the first volume was published in Latin, German, English, and French; the rest appeared only in German and Latin). While other illustrated accounts had been circulated in the first half of the sixteenth century, they reached a very limited audience. Even fewer people had the opportunity to see the inhabitants and objects brought back to Europe.

Among the illustrations in De Bry's volumes were several that depicted scenes of Spaniards torturing and killing indigenous peoples of the Americas, such as *Hanging, by the order of Diego Ocampa, of rebellious Caribs*, from Part 4 of the Great Voyages [**1.0.1**]. In the foreground a Spaniard lights a fire under thirteen hanging Caribs (the peoples of the Caribbean islands or Taino), a reference to the persecution of Christ and the twelve apostles; another Spaniard readies himself to fling a young Carib child against a wall. In the background, Spaniards chase and club additional Caribs, while a Spanish ship rests at anchor in the harbor. The hanging men and women are sensitively depicted as suffering individuals rather than grotesque savages; indeed, the Spanish are portrayed as the savages, in actions if not appearance. De Bry based Part 4 of the *Great Voyages* on *The History of the New World* (1565) by the Italian adventurer Girolamo Benzoni. In turn, Benzoni relied heavily on descriptions from the accounts of earlier writers, in this instance the Spanish Dominican friar Bartolomé de las Casas's *A Short Account of the Destruction of the Indies* (1542). Such recycling of written texts was common, as was the recycling of figures or compositions from earlier prints and paintings.

Why is it appropriate to begin a social history of American art with such an image? In order to understand fully the history of the art and architecture of the United States of America, one must go back in time to the country's origins as one of a series of interconnected colonial enterprises undertaken by European powers beginning in the sixteenth century [**1.0.3**; p. 19]. The first Europeans to establish a permanent stronghold on the North American continent were the Spanish. By the early 1520s Spain had conquered much of what is now central Mexico and had

1590
Publication of *A Briefe and True Report* by Theodore De Bry

1598
Establishment of the first Spanish settlement in the northern territory at San Juan Pueblo

1607
John Smith establishes the first successful British colony, Jamestown (Virginia)

1608
Samuel de Champlain founds Quebec, New France [1.3.3]

1614
Dutch establish colony at Fort Nassau (Albany, New York)

1620
Pilgrims found New Plymouth (Massachusetts)

1620s
Arrival of Jesuits in New France [1.3.4]

1637
Pequot Massacre

1639
Arrival of Ursulines in New France

1642–49
Civil War in England

1680
Revolt of Pueblo peoples against the Spanish

1681
William Penn founds the colony of Pennsylvania

1682
Robert Cavelier, Sieur de La Salle, explores the length of the Mississippi, claiming the entire river basin for France

1708
Henrietta Dering Johnston arrives in South Carolina [1.4.27]

1710s
Ursuline nuns begin producing embroidered birch-bark boxes [1.3.6]

1744–48
King George's War between France and Britain

1759–60
British win Battle of Plains of Abraham, ending French and Indian War (begun 1754) [1.4.31]

1763
Treaty of Paris cedes French colonies in Canada to Britain

1769–1823
21 missions founded along coast of California [1.2.26]

1790
Unearthing of statue of Coatlicue in Mexico City [1.1.4]

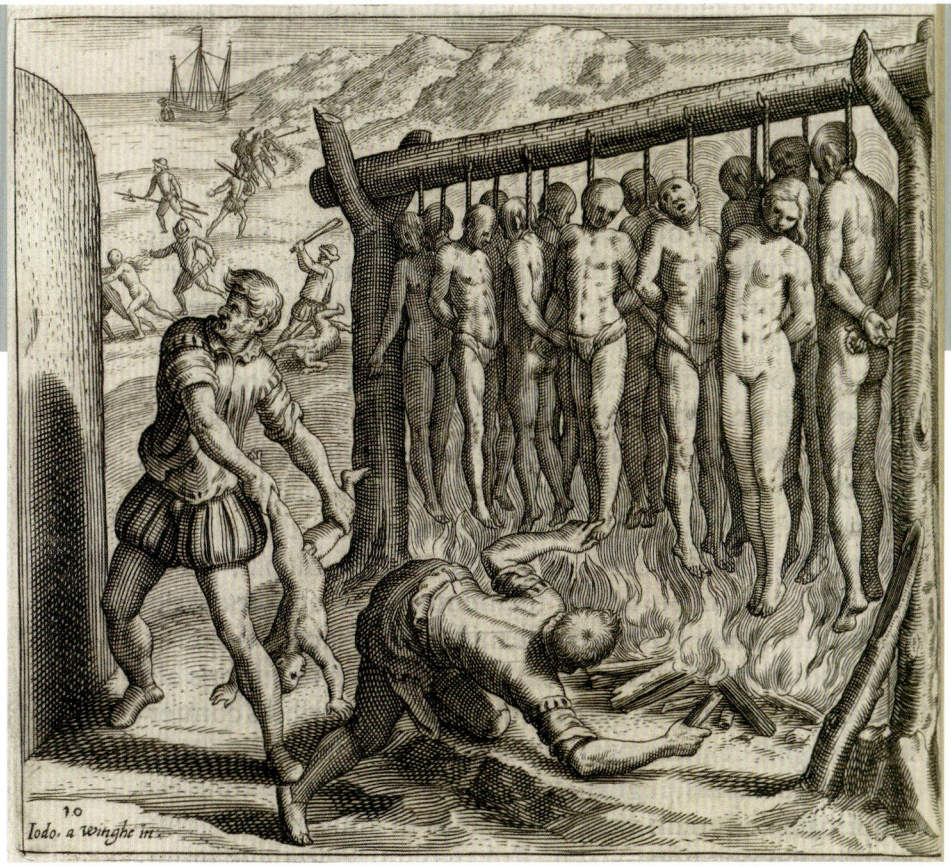

1.0.1 Engraving by Theodore De Bry: *Hanging, by the order of Diego Ocampa, of rebellious Caribs*, 1594. Beinecke Rare Book and Manuscript Library, Yale University, New Haven, Connecticut

begun exploiting the natural resources of the region and forcibly converting its indigenous peoples to Christianity. While Spain's power began to weaken at the end of the sixteenth century, allowing the English, French, and Dutch to gain a foothold in North America, Spain continued to be the most powerful political, economic, and cultural force on the continent until the end of the eighteenth century. Its wealth came from the mines, fields, and manufactories of New Spain, as well as the massive shiploads of Asian goods brought to the region on Spanish galleons from Manila beginning in the late 1560s. Some of these goods—

textiles, furniture, porcelain—made their way up the east coast to Boston and other commercial seaports, helping fuel a demand for Asian luxury items in the colonies on the Atlantic seaboard.

Spain's influence on the English colonies went beyond the facilitation of access to Asian goods. The historian Eliga H. Gould notes that the legal, religious, economic, and aesthetic justifications for Protestant Britain's colonial ventures were often formulated in opposition to the policies and practices of Catholic Spain. This was particularly evident in the ways in which the English drew upon the large body of anti-Spanish literature that had emerged in Europe in the sixteenth century and that was later described cumulatively as the Black Legend. This literature, in Gould's words, "identified Spain's overseas empire with everything that Britain's was not: indolence, superstition, backwardness, and tyranny." Whereas the brutal conquest of the Aztec empire was funded by corrupt Spanish monarchs and sanctioned by equally corrupt popes, the first English colonies were privately funded ventures and motivated by the desire to ensure religious freedom and to "liberate" land left uncultivated by indigenous populations. In keeping with the Black Legend, De Bry consistently presented the Catholic Spanish, in word and image, as more violent and less civilized than their Protestant counterparts. He often heavily edited accounts of their conquest to foreground this violence, or selected graphic passages from texts critical of the actions of Spanish conquerors by such authors as Benzoni and Las Casas.

In her book on De Bry's publications, the anthropologist Bernadette Bucher notes that they were "completely bound up with the emotional, financial, and political interests of the parties engaged in the struggle with the Spanish in America." These struggles were especially intense in the border areas of the regions claimed by the Spanish, French, and English. By 1700 the Spanish had explored almost every part of what is now the southern United States and traveled the full length of the Pacific coast. They left their imprint in various ways, in particular by establishing mission churches in the present-day states of New Mexico, Arizona, California, Texas, and Florida—New Spain's northern border. At the same time, the French (also predominantly Catholic) were moving west and south along the interconnected lakes and waterways that began with the St. Lawrence River and that continued along the Mississippi River to the Gulf of Mexico. They laid claim to this vast territory and thus controlled key commercial transportation networks.

The English had to adjust constantly to the pressures brought to bear by the French and the Spanish on their newly established settlements (just as they had to defend their home territory continually from attacks by the same powers back in Europe). Sometimes this meant engaging in military actions; other times it meant making concessions to settlers or indigenous communities in order to prevent them from shifting their allegiances to a rival nation, or to prevent African slaves, brought to the region in increasing numbers from the late seventeenth century onward, from seeking refuge in colonies with a less draconian racial order. On other occasions it meant advancing one's cause through the creation of images that demonized the enemy, be it indigenous or Catholic. Ultimately such adjustments shaped the very fabric of life in the English colonies.

De Bry's publications were extremely influential in establishing widespread notions of what people in the Americas were like, as well as the circumstances under which they came into contact with Europeans. The images and their accompanying texts were not, however, unbiased records of such encounters. They were informed not only by De Bry's anti-Catholicism, but also by the desire of the authors upon whom De Bry relied to ensure there was enough interest in this New World to fund further voyages. The inhabitants were variously presented as exotic, innocent, savage, mysterious, and almost always less civilized, indeed heathen, and thus in need of Christian instruction. Their settlements and modes of subsistence were documented in detail, providing evidence of the fecundity of the land and its suitability for colonization.

De Bry's representations of the indigenous peoples of the Americas did not go unchallenged. Alternative records can be found in the architecture, paintings, carvings, textiles, and other decorated objects created by the many different peoples who occupied North America prior to the arrival of Europeans [**1.0.2**]. After this arrival, indigenous artists often incorporated European visual conventions into their own images, representing themselves, their spiritual world, and Europeans in illustrated books, stone carvings, painted hides, beaded belts, and other carefully crafted works. At the same time, some Europeans engaged with indigenous styles, materials, and technologies. Both sets of representations reveal evidence of the conflicts that inevitably ensued as Europeans, in their drive to control this new territory and exploit its material resources, attempted to suppress indigenous artistic, social, and spiritual traditions or to incorporate them into Christian ones. The study of the art and architecture of the early period of conquest and colonization in North America thus provides an opportunity to explore how ideas about this region were constructed and made visible, and to examine how physical struggles for survival or dominance manifested themselves in the aesthetic realm.

1.0.2 (right) Overview of indigenous peoples in the area of the future United States and adjacent parts of Canada and Mexico, *c.* 1500. Within regions, peoples are listed roughly from north to south ("E" and "W" denote eastern and western parts of a region); those living in areas that span two or more regions are noted in one only.

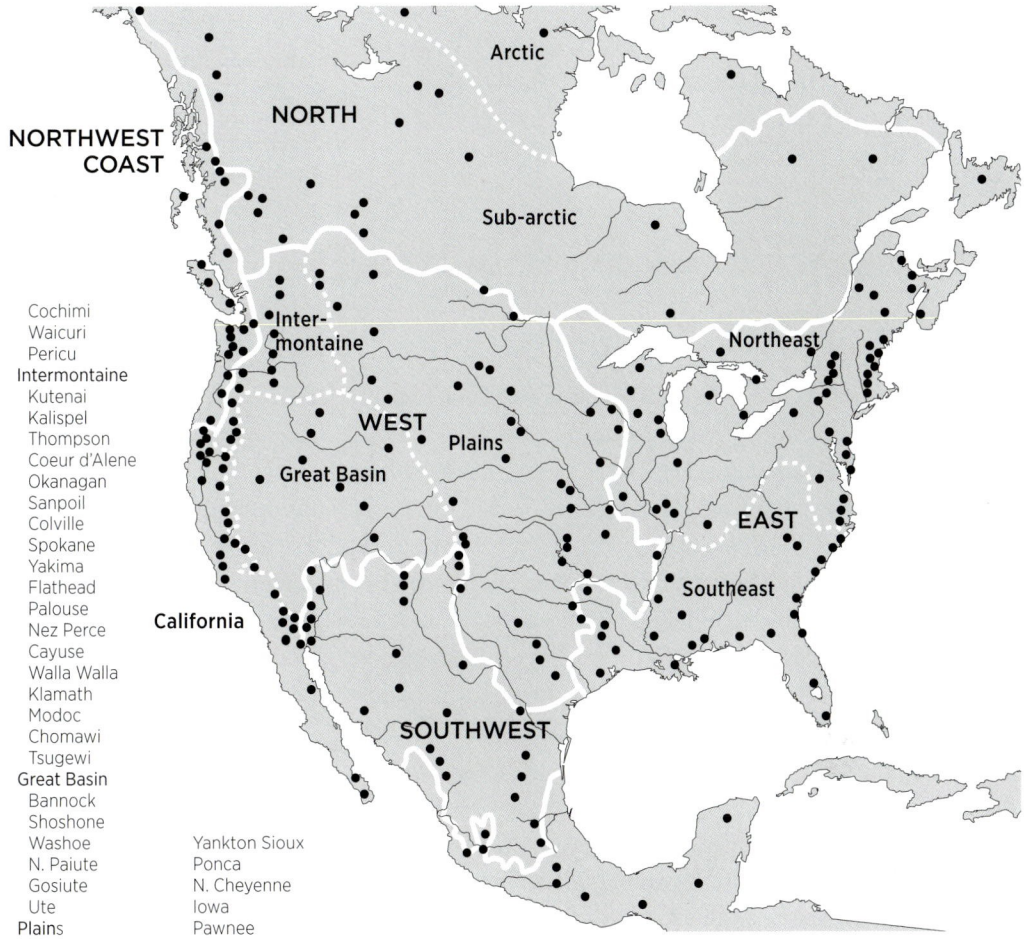

NORTH
Arctic
Bear Lake
Netsilik Inuit (E)
Arctic Quebec Inuit
Sub-arctic
Tutchone
Kaska
Tahltan
Dogrib
Yellowknife
Slavey
Chipewyan
Naskapi (Innu) (E)
Montagnais (E)
Beothuk (E)
Beaver
Carrier
Sekani
Sarsi
Siksika (Blackfoot)
Chilcotin
Cree
Kaigani
Shuswap
Ojibwa (Chippewa) (E)

NORTHWEST COAST
Tlingit
Gitskan
Tsimshian
Heiltsuk
Haida
Nuxalk
Oowekeeno
Bella Bella
Kwakwaka'wakw
Nuu-chah-nulth
Salish
Makah Puyallup
Nisqually
Chehalis
Chinook
Cowlitz
Tillamook
Klikitat
Molala
Kalapuya
Umpqua
Coos
Takelma

WEST
California
Karok
Yurok
Wiyot
Shasta
Hupa
Maidu
Yana
Mattole
Yuki
Pomo
Wintun
Miwok
Kawaiisu
Costanoan
Mono
S. Paiute
Yokuts
Panamint
Salinan
Chemehuevi
Chumash
Mohave
Serrano
Yavapai
Yuma
Cahuilla
Cochimi
Waicuri
Pericu
Intermontaine
Kutenai
Kalispel
Thompson
Coeur d'Alene
Okanagan
Sanpoil
Colville
Spokane
Yakima
Flathead
Palouse
Nez Perce
Cayuse
Walla Walla
Klamath
Modoc
Chomawi
Tsugewi
Great Basin
Bannock
Shoshone
Washoe
N. Paiute
Gosiute
Ute
Plains
Piegan
Plains Cree
Assiniboin
Atsina
Hidatsa
Mandan
Teton Lakota
Arikara
Crow
Santee Sioux
Yankton Sioux
Ponca
N. Cheyenne
Iowa
Pawnee
Omaha
Oto
Arapaho
Kansa
S. Cheyenne
Osage
Jicarilla Apache
Quapaw
Kiowa
Kiowa Apache
Mescalero
Apache
Tawakoni
Wichita
Comanche
Kichai
Waco
Tonkawa

SOUTHWEST
Pueblo
Navaho
Hopi
Zuñi
Kavasupai
Walapai
Pima
Maricopa
Papago
W. Apache
Lipan Apache
Opata
Seri
Concho
Karankawa
Tarahumara
Cahita
Coahuiltec
Yaqui
Acaxee
Tamaulipec
Huichol
Huastec
Totonac

[CENTRAL/SOUTH MEXICO]
Yucatan Maya (E)
Toltec
Tarascan
Otomi
Tlaxcalan
Aztec
Mixtec
Lacandon Maya
Zapotec

EAST
Northeast
Mi'kmaq
Malecite
Passamaquoddy
Abnaki
Penobscot
Pennacook
Mohawk
Ottawa (W)
Huron
Tobacco (W)
Menomini (W)
Oneida
Massachusett
Mahican
Wampanoag
Narragansett
Winnebago (W)
Potawatomie (W)
Sauk (W)
Fox (W)
Neutral (W)
Nipmuc
Pequot
Mohegan
Wappinger
Onondaga
Cayuga
Seneca
Erie
Susquehanna
Delaware
Nanticoke
Powhatan
Pamunkey
Missouri (W)
Wea (W)
Peoria (W)
Illinois (W)
Piankashaw (W)
Shawnee (W)

Southeast
Cherokee
Yuchi
Chickahominy
Mattapony
Tutelo
Pamlico
Nottoway
Tuscarora
Catawba
Tuskegee (W)
Choctaw (W)
Creek (W)
Yamasee
Guale
Alabama (W)
Chickasaw (W)
Timucuan
Hichiti
Caddo (W)
Natchez (W)
Apalachee (W)
Mobile (W)
Biloxi (W)
Tunica (W)
Chitimacha (W)
Alakapa (W)
Seminole
Calusa

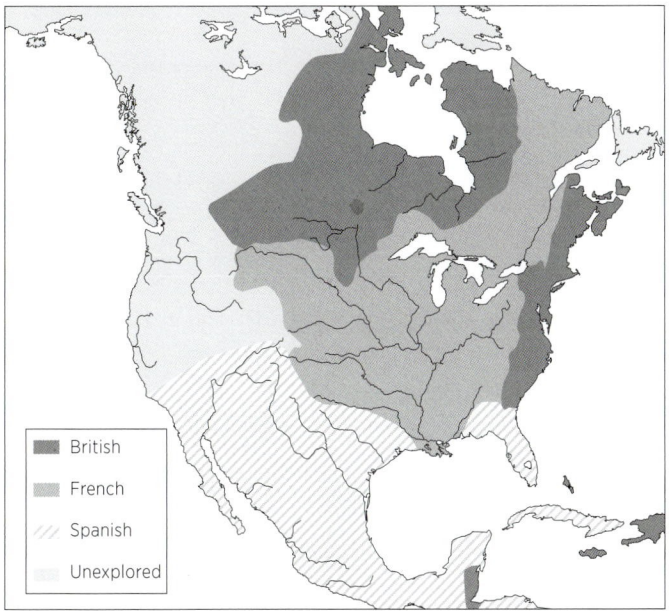

1.0.3 Colonial North America, *c.* 1750

CHAPTER 1

Visualizing the Conquest: Colonial Spain and Indigenous Mesoamerica (*c.* 1500–1580)

Tenochtitlan: Pyramids, Codices, and Monumental Sculpture

Shortly after the Spanish explorer Hernán Cortés (1485–1547) landed on the eastern coast of the Aztec empire in 1519 at a site he named Veracruz (the true cross), he advanced inland with an army of approximately five hundred men and twenty horses. At the head of his troops he displayed a banner bearing the image of the Virgin Mary within a crest and surrounded by the words "This is that which brought Don Fernando Cortés to the conquest of Mexico" [**1.1.1**]. Also present was a flag of white and blue flames with a cross in the middle and the Latin motto: "Friends, let us follow the cross and with faith in this symbol we shall conquer." This banner and flag proclaimed the religious justification for the military conquest of this new territory in the name of the Spanish monarchs. It also called to mind the successful expulsion in 1492 of Muslim forces from their final stronghold in the Iberian peninsula, which they had occupied since the eighth century. Thus, from the very beginning, images, both religious and secular, played an important role in the conquest of the Aztec empire. They conveyed not only specific objects or individuals, but also a way of viewing the world.

Cortés was not the first European to set foot in what soon came to be known as the Americas (named after the Italian navigator Amerigo Vespucci [1454–1512]). His most notable predecessor was the Genoese explorer Christopher Columbus. In 1492 he set out on what was to be the first of four trips across the Atlantic funded by King Ferdinand and Queen Isabella of Spain. Columbus and his royal sponsors were committed to spreading Christianity throughout the world. Yet they were also motivated by a desire to find a route to the Far East, with its commercial riches, that would bypass the Muslim traders who controlled the land route east from Europe to China and Japan.

When Columbus and his crew arrived in the Caribbean, they thought they had reached the outlying islands of East Asia, in particular Cipango, or Japan. As they explored various islands, they struggled to describe their impressions of the unfamiliar territory and peoples (the Taino), filling their notebooks with evaluations of both the wealth and beauty of the land and its inhabitants. Similar to those who came after them, they tried to fit the objects, peoples, and natural phenomena they encountered into the conceptual framework of Christian Europe in the late fifteenth century, fabricating an image of this "new world" that would convince the Spanish Crown to fund a second journey. Columbus described the "handsome bodies and faces" of the men who swam out to meet his ships, the clean and well-ordered houses, and wooden statues of female figures. Of these statues he commented: "I do not know whether they regard these as beautiful or for worship." He also described the landscape as a paradise or natural garden and the climate "like Valencia in April." Believing he was in the Indies, Columbus called the inhabitants "Indians" (*Indios*).

Cortés encountered a much more formidable indigenous presence than had Columbus—the massive Aztec empire under the leadership of Motecuhzoma II, the *tlatoani* or "speaker." The Aztec capital of Tenochtitlan was founded in *c.* 1345 on adjoining marshy islands at the southern end of Lake Texcoco in the central valley. It soon grew into the hub of an empire that, by the end of the fifteenth century, stretched from this valley to both coasts.

When the Spanish arrived, Tenochtitlan was the size of fifteenth-century London (approximately 150,000–200,000 people). It spread over 2,500 acres (just over 1,000 hectares) and was divided into four sections by two causeways that connected the island to the mainland and that intersected in a central walled plaza [**1.1.2**]. This plaza measured 525 × 590 feet (160 × 180 meters)

1.1.1 Unknown artist: banner of Cortés, 16th century. National History Museum, Chapultepec Castle, Mexico City

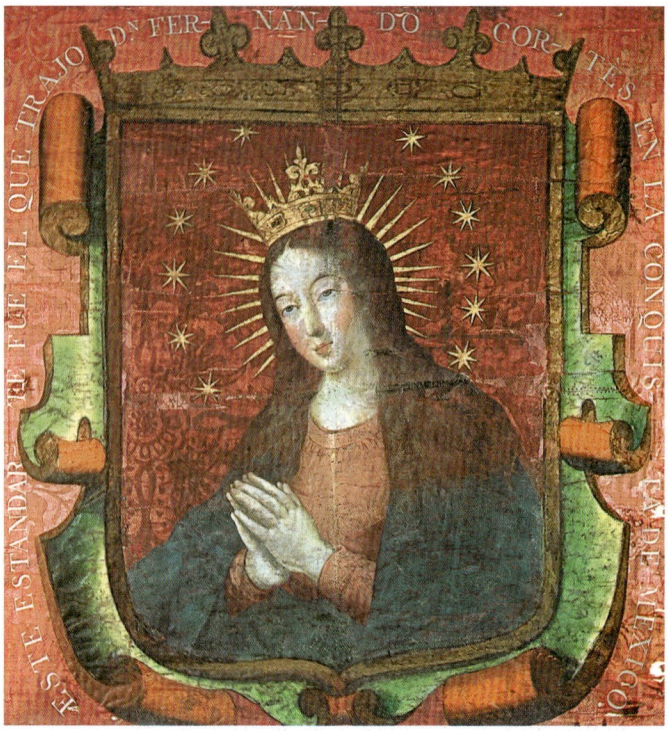

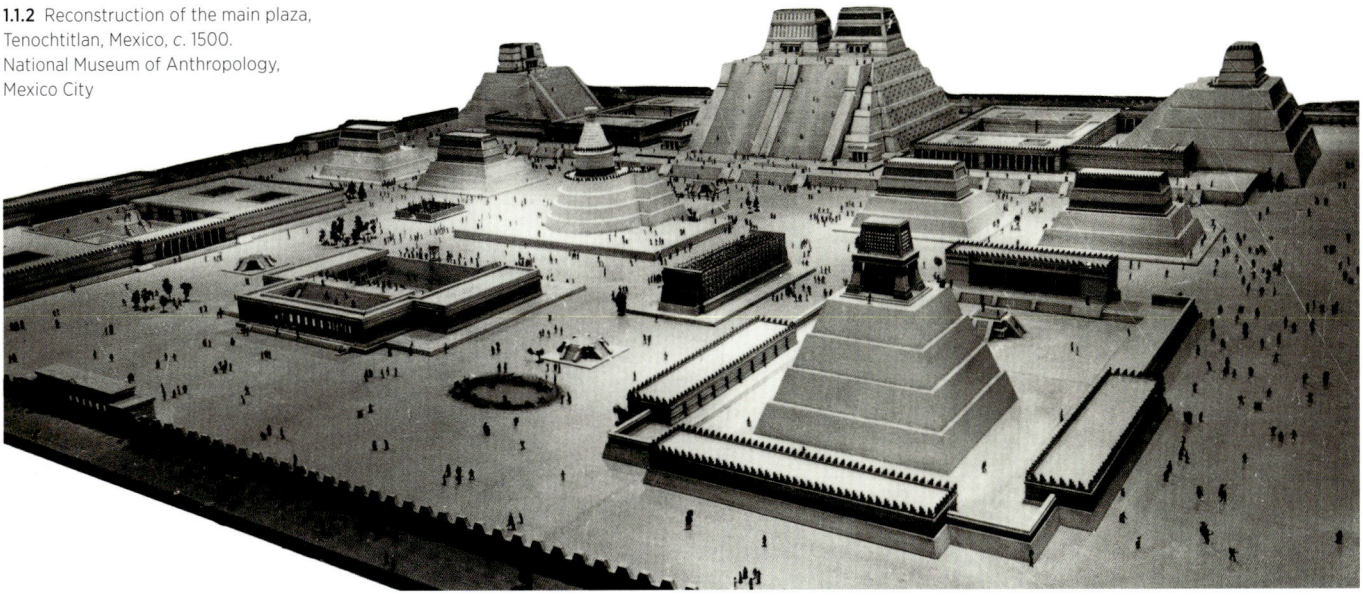

1.1.2 Reconstruction of the main plaza, Tenochtitlan, Mexico, *c.* 1500. National Museum of Anthropology, Mexico City

and included 70 to 80 palaces and temples. On the east was the palace compound of Motecuhzoma II, which contained administrative and residential buildings. Also on the east side, perched atop a truncated pyramid platform 200 feet (60 meters) high, were the twin shrines to the warrior god Huitzilopochtli and the rain god Tlaloc. During the rainy season the sun rose behind the blue shrine of Tlaloc, during the dry season behind the red shrine of Huitzilopochtli. On the two annual equinoxes, it rose between the two and shone on the round temple in front of the pyramid platform dedicated to the deity Quetzalcóatl, or Feathered Serpent. In form, the twin shrines and their pyramid platform echoed the volcanoes surrounding the central valley in which Tenochtitlan was located, in particular Popocateptl (Smoking Mountain) and Iztaccihuatl (White Woman). Lesser temples to the honored gods of subject peoples, as well as a ceremonial ball court, were also included in the main plaza.

The interiors of the shrines atop the pyramid platforms, which housed statues of the various deities, were modest in size. The main function of religious architecture was to define an exterior space, a setting for the massive public rituals that characterized Aztec society. The palaces of Motecuhzoma II, on the other hand, were described by Cortés as "befitting so great a ruler," with gardens, pools, balconies, patios, and "rooms nine feet high and as large as six paces square." The residences of the priests were also "very elegant...with very large rooms."

The Spaniards were greatly impressed by the architecture and organization of the city. Bernal Díaz del Castillo, who accompanied Cortés, later wrote:

> There were among us soldiers who had been to many parts of the world, to Constantinople, to the whole of Italy and to Rome, and they said they had never seen a market so well organized and orderly, so large, so full of people.

Others, because of the city's extensive canals, compared it to Venice. Cortés himself wrote that Tenochtitlan "was indeed the most beautiful thing in the world." The historian Stuart B. Schwartz notes that the plan of Tenochtitlan, with its four causeways and its neighborhoods organized in pairs of twenty communal corporate groups and temple-maintenance groups, represented the engineering ingenuity of the Aztecs. It also represented "the Mexica social and religious universe" (the Mexica, after whom Mexico was named, were the dominant ethnic group within the Aztec empire). The causeways embodied the four cardinal directions, the neighborhoods the twenty-day cycle of the 260-day Aztec ritual calendar. After the conquest, sections of the city, particularly the ceremonial plaza, were razed to make way for the capital of New Spain, Mexico City.

The Aztec also had a well-developed system of pictographic writing. It was found on low-relief and three-dimensional sculpture, murals, and codices—folding paintings usually made of bark paper or deerskin covered with a thin coat of calcium carbonate . The codices record genealogies, tribute systems, prophecies, divinations, calendars, religious rites, lists of merchandise, and conquests. The individual pictographs, or glyphs, are composed of a major figure, recognizable as human or animal or a combination of both, and abstract forms, such as dots and bars. The figures are two-dimensional and float in an undefined space, with broad areas of unmodulated colors defining clothing and architectural details. The majority of the preconquest codices were burned by the Spanish immediately after the defeat of the Aztecs. A small number, fewer than twenty, survived as gifts

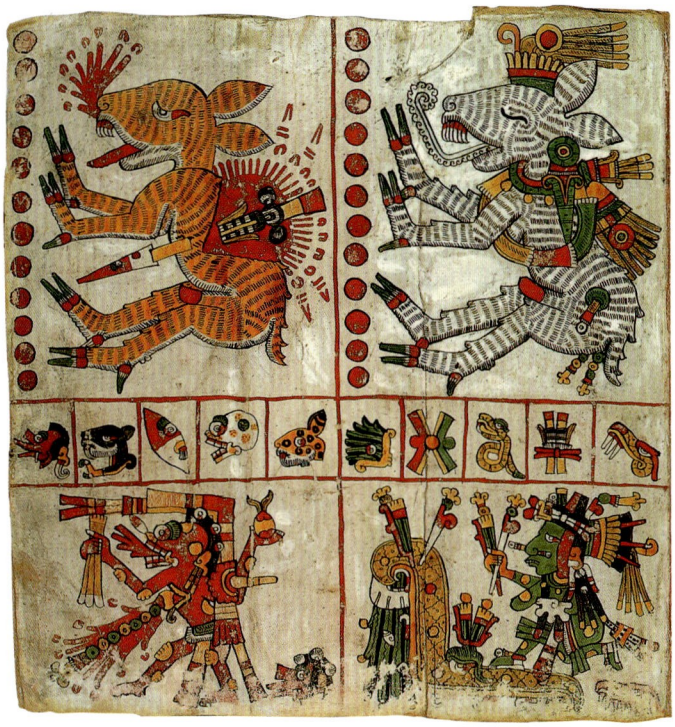

1.1.3 Unknown artist: a leaf from the *Codex Borgia*, pre-16th century. Biblioteca Apostolica Vaticana, Rome

or curiosities sent back to Europe, such as the one that ended up in the possession of the eighteenth-century Italian cardinal Stefano Borgia and that now resides in the Vatican [**1.1.3**].

The painters of the codices were known as *tlacuilos*, a Nahuatl term that meant both painter and scribe (Nahuatl was the language spoken by the Aztecs). *Tlacuilos* probably came from priestly or noble castes and were trained in special schools. They were powerful people in that they recorded and interpreted myths, rites, and genealogies. They possessed the ability to create the painted legends, as well as to decipher the meaning of codices through an interpretation of page layout, the scale of the symbols and their groupings, and chromatic variations. The concern was to record not the surface appearance of things or persons existing in a particular place and time, but the essence of a place, person, or object. In the words of the historian Serge Gruzinski, the images in the codices were meant to "render certain aspects of the divine world physically present and palpable."

The Aztecs and those who occupied territories controlled by them produced objects of finely worked gold, silver, jade, feathers, and stone. Peter Martyr of Anghiera, an Italian humanist scholar and teacher at the Spanish court who had been appointed to the Council of the Indies, wrote in 1520 of the gifts sent by Motecuhzoma II to King Charles V: "though I little admire gold and precious stones, I am amazed by the skill and effort making the work exceed the material....I do not recall ever seeing anything so appealing by its beauty to human eyes." The German artist Albrecht Dürer (1471–1528) saw the same objects in Brussels later that year, writing:

> Also I saw the things which were brought to the King from the New Golden Land: a sun entirely of gold, a whole fathom [approximately 6 feet, or 1.8 meters] broad; likewise, a moon, entirely of silver, just as big....I have never seen in all my days that which so rejoiced my heart, as these things. For I saw among them amazing artistic objects, and I marveled over the subtle ingenuity of the men in these distant lands.

Dürer and other Europeans would see few such objects, however, for most were melted down and recast into the coinage and art objects of European nations.

The Aztec pantheon of gods was occupied by a wide array of figures who assumed both animal and human guises. One of the most powerful was Coatlicue. A statue of Coatlicue [**1.1.4**], carved out of a massive basalt stone more than 8 feet (2 meters) high, was discovered in 1790 during a municipal excavation in the main plaza of Mexico City, which was situated on top of the old Aztec ceremonial center. It appears to have resided either on or near the twin-temple pyramid, for Coatlicue was the mother of Huitzilopochtli in Aztec myth. The art historian Mary Ellen Miller summarizes the story of Huitzilopochtli's birth as follows:

> According to legend, Coatlicue kept a temple shrine on a hill near Tula called Coatepec, or "hill of snakes." After tucking a ball of down feathers in her bosom, she became pregnant with Huitzilopochtli. Repelled by her condition, her children, especially her daughter Coyolxauhqui, plotted her death. When Coatlicue's enemies attacked her and sliced off her head, Huitzilopochtli rose from her severed trunk fully grown and armed. He banished the attackers and mutilated his evil sister, severing her extremities, so that she collapsed at the base of the shrine.

This myth was alluded to in the exterior decoration of the twin pyramid, the base of which was lined with serpents (serpent is an ideogram for Coatlicue). A large, flat, round stone with a carving of Coyolxauhqui, limbs severed, was discovered in the late twentieth century at the foot of the pyramid.

The statue of Coatlicue is carved in low relief on all sides—there is even a carving of the earth deity Tlaltecuhtli on its underside. Coatlicue, in addition to being the mother of Huitzilopochtli and of the moon and southern stars, was the goddess of earth and death. Her skirt is made up of intertwined serpents, with a human skull at the waistline; two profile serpent heads create her face. Some have suggested, in keeping with the legend of Huitzilopochtli's birth, that she has been decapitated and the serpents represent blood. Her arms are flexed upward, with serpents at her wrists; serpent heads form her feet, suggesting her hands and feet have been severed as well. A serpent descends between her legs, perhaps a reference to menstrual blood, and thus birth/life. Finally, Coatlicue wears a necklace of amputated hands and hearts. She was thus a symbol of everything the Spanish would find both fascinating and abhorrent in the New World, an embodiment of the power of the natural world and of the female as creator and destroyer. She was certainly a far cry from the Virgin Mary depicted on Cortés's banner [**1.1.1**; p. 20].

The history of the statue of Coatlicue from its unearthing to its present position of honor in Mexico City's National Museum of Anthropology reveals the complexity of attempts by the Spanish colonizers and their *mestizo* descendants (those of mixed racial background) to come to terms with the indigenous past. The Mexican writer Octavio Paz provides a brief account of Coatlicue's travels. After her discovery in 1790, the deity was placed among the plaster copies of Greco-Roman statues at the Royal and Pontifical University of Mexico. Meant to represent, in the words of the Spanish viceroy Revillagigedo, a "monument of America's ancient past," she proved too disturbing to the professors at the university, who had her reburied in the place where she had been discovered, lest she revive old beliefs. She was also seen as an affront to the very ideal of beauty embodied in the works of the ancient Greeks and Romans.

In 1804, the German naturalist Baron Alexander von Humboldt, on a visit to Mexico City, read of her discovery and requested that she be dug up again. Once his curiosity was satisfied, she was reburied, and permanently unearthed only after Mexico won its independence from Spain in 1821. From a corner of a courtyard at the university, she was moved to a hallway behind a screen and then to a more visible place to be studied as an object of historical and scientific interest. Finally, she was placed in the National Museum of Anthropology.

Paz tracks the statue's transformation "from goddess into demon, from demon into monster, and from monster into

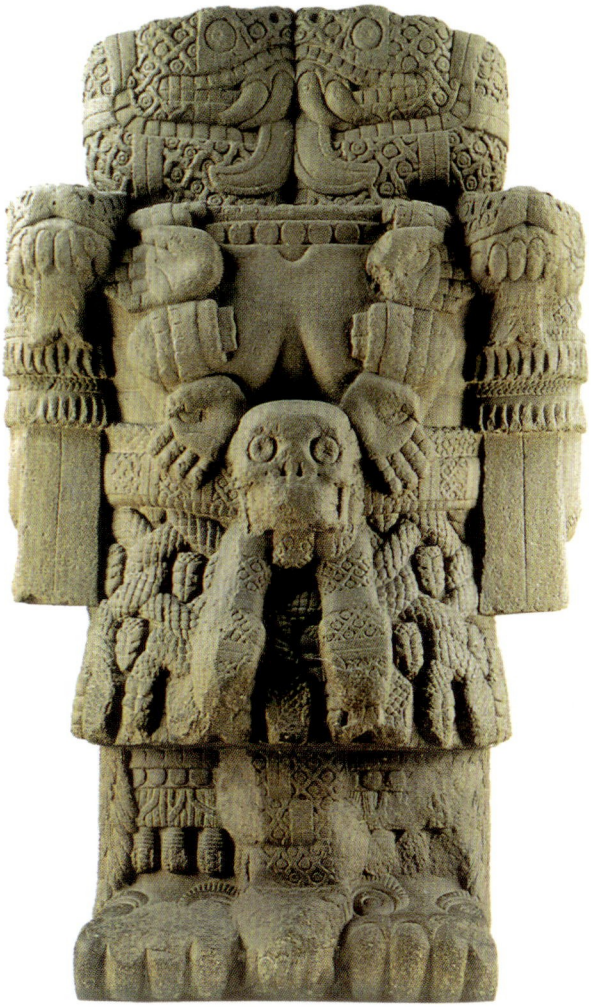

1.1.4 Unknown artist, Aztec: *Coatlicue*, late 15th century. Basalt, h. 8 ft. 3¼ in. (2.5 m.) National Museum of Anthropology, Mexico City

masterpiece," its move from the supernatural to the aesthetic and from the temple to the museum. He suggests that the unearthing of Coatlicue, and perhaps the encounters of modern museum-goers with the statue as well, are repetitions "on a reduced scale, of what the European mind must have experienced when confronted with the discovery of America." Instead of the polished marble and ideal human proportions of a Greek Aphrodite or the modest demeanor of a Virgin Mary, there was the massive, aggressive, part-animal, part-human goddess of life and death. What Europeans faced was

> not another reality but rather the other aspect, the other dimension of reality....By contrast to the cases of Persia, Egypt, or Babylonia, American civilizations were not older than that of Europe, they were different. And that difference was radical: it constituted a real "otherness."

In the mid-twentieth century Mexican artist Diego Rivera would exploit Coatlicue's ability to represent "otherness"—in this instance Mexican "otherness"—in murals he painted in the United States (see V. 2, 431–32).

The historian James W. Loewen also notes that the encounters with the indigenous peoples of the Americas created within Europe an increasing self-consciousness:

> In a sense, there was no "Europe" before 1492. People were simply Tuscan, French, and the like. Now Europeans began to see similarities among themselves, at least as contrasted with Native Americans. For that matter, there were no "white" people in Europe before 1492. With the transatlantic slave trade, first Indian, then African, Europeans increasingly saw "white" as a race and race as an important human characteristic.

Paz finds the key to the European conquest of the two American continents in their isolation and lack of substantial contact with significantly different peoples:

> Neither of the two civilizations of America [Incan and Aztec] had an experience that was common and constant among the societies of the Old World, that is, the presence of the other, the intrusion of foreign civilizations and peoples. That is why the indigenous peoples of America saw the Spaniards as beings come from another world, as gods or semigods.

The notion that Cortés was the reincarnation of an Aztec deity, in particular Quetzalcóatl, who had been banished from the earlier kingdom of the Toltecs and was predicted to return from the east, appears to have materialized after the conquest. Nahua informants may have created this story in order to explain Motecuhzoma II's vacillation in his dealings with the Spanish. This vacillation initially prevented the Aztec leader from understanding the motives and tactics of the newcomers.

The anthropologist Tzvetan Todorov adds three other factors that help explain how such a massively outnumbered group of Spaniards was able, by 1521, to defeat the powerful Aztec empire. First, Cortés allied with the Tlaxcalans and with several indigenous groups who had been subdued by the Aztecs, thus building up an army of sufficient size to overcome Motecuhzoma II's successor Cuauhtémoc (Motecuhzoma II died in 1520). Once victory was achieved, the Tlaxcalans were rewarded with many of the administrative positions in the new empire (much of the Aztec system of vassalage and taxes was maintained). Second, the Spanish possessed superior weapons. Their horses, crossbows, steel swords, and guns, though few in number, initially spread fear among the Aztec armies. Third, the Spanish were able to gather information about the Aztecs through an Aztec woman, whom they called "Doña Marina." She had been sold into slavery to the Maya and ended up with the Spanish as an interpreter (she was later referred to as "La Malinche"). It was she who translated the conversations between Cortés and Motecuhzoma II, helping Cortés devise military strategies that would outwit the Aztec armies.

Christian Painting, Sculpture, and Architecture in New Spain

One of the first tasks of the conquerors was to raze sections of the city of Tenochtitlan, destroy the religious images and architecture, and put in their place the symbols and structures of Christianity and New Spain. A new cathedral was begun close by the site of the twin pyramid, and the palace of the Spanish governors replaced the palace of Motecuhzoma II (the first viceroy, appointed in 1530, arrived in 1535). Objects of gold were melted down. While most of the codices were burned, the priests and friars who arrived after the conquest to convert the indigenous peoples to Christianity recorded their lives and customs in detail. They also encouraged local painters to produce pictographic texts similar to the preconquest codices, so that their traditional beliefs could be understood more clearly and thus countered more effectively. We can only wonder how accurate these chronicles are in depicting precolonial life. What they certainly do provide is a description of the process of colonization and its effects on both colonizer and colonized, as can be seen in the *Florentine Codex* [**1.1.5**] and *Telleriano-Remensis Codex* (*c.* 1562–63).

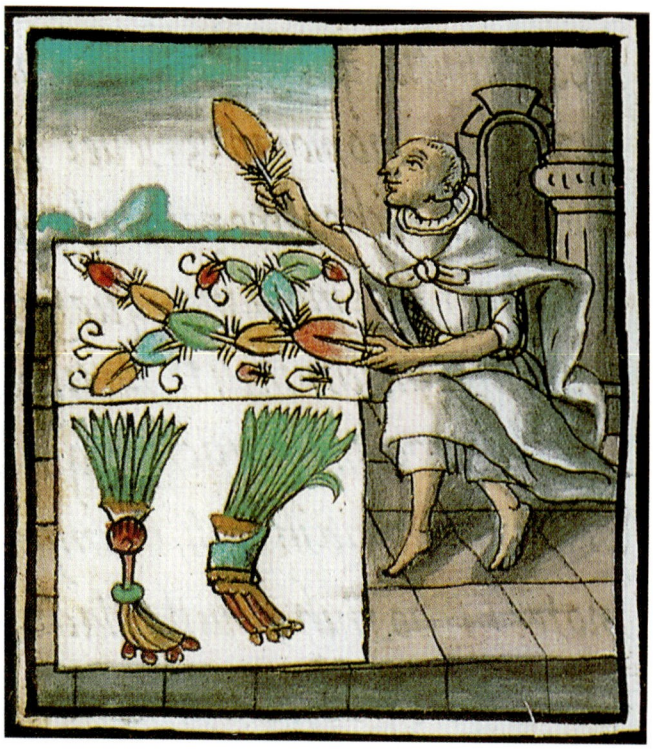

1.1.5 Unknown artist: the art of featherworking, illustrated in the *Florentine Codex*, 1570. Biblioteca Medicea Laurenziana, Florence

The first century of occupation had a devastating impact on the peoples of the Aztec Empire. The population decreased from approximately 25 million at the time of the conquest to less than 1 million by the mid-seventeenth century. Those who survived disease, massacre, or overwork in the mines and fields were incorporated into Spanish society as administrators, manual laborers, merchants, and artisans. Some were able to adapt relatively easily, in part because many of the new political, aesthetic, and commercial structures were similar to those of the Aztecs. Indigenous architects, painters, and carvers constructed and decorated the new religious and secular buildings. Others quickly mastered the languages of Europe, including Latin, and became part of the intelligentsia of New Spain, translating Christian and secular texts into Nahuatl.

The Europeans who took charge of teaching and training indigenous workers were primarily members of various Catholic orders who arrived shortly after the Spanish soldiers. The task of converting the peoples of the New World to Christianity had been set by King Charles V following the declaration of 1517, issued after debate at the University of Salamanca, that they were, in fact, rational beings and possessed souls. Pope Paul III confirmed this declaration in 1537 with a papal bull or letter; as rational beings, indigenous peoples could not be considered slaves based on Aristotelian categories of being, i.e. they could not be considered slaves "by nature."

Four major orders initially assumed this task of conversion. The Franciscans, Dominicans, and Augustinians were all mendicant orders who took vows of poverty, renouncing property and relying on begging (mendicancy) and the acceptance of alms to support their missionary endeavors. The Jesuits, or Society of Jesus, were not mendicants. They saw themselves as "soldiers of God" committed to the defence and propagation of the faith. The monopoly of these four orders was broken in the 1580s and 1590s, when other orders, for example the Benedictines, arrived. Many of these new arrivals focused more on the spiritual needs of the Spanish than on the needs of the indigenous population. Some participated directly in the defeat and subjugation of the indigenous peoples. Others, such as the Dominican friar Bartolomé de las Casas, while insisting they accept Christianity as the one true religion, championed their rights against repressive secular governments. In 1810, the Catholic priest Miguel Hidalgo y Costilla led the first revolution for independence against the Spanish (it failed and he was executed).

For most of the sixteenth century the church trained artists and supplied commissions. Friar Pedro de Gante set up one of the earliest workshops in the Chapel of San José de los Naturales (St. Joseph of the Natives). Many Spanish officials commented on how quickly indigenous peoples picked up European tools and skills. Bernal Díaz del Castillo wrote: "According to my judgment, that famous painter of ancient times, the renowned Apelles, or the modern ones named Michelangelo or Berruguete...could not with their subtle pencils equal the works which are done by three Mexican artists."

Similar to Europeans, the indigenous inhabitants of the newly conquered lands recognized the power of images. When the Tlaxcalans attempted to pressure the Spanish Crown in order to preserve control over their territories, they used images as part of their argument. To guarantee their claim, they produced, between 1550 and 1560, the *Lienzo de Tlaxcala*, a piece of cotton more than 23 feet (7 meters) long and 8 feet (2 meters) high, on which 87 scenes recorded the conquest as a glorious event, with the Tlaxcalans as Spain's allies. Before the arrival of the Spanish, codices had been used to record genealogies and land titles. Thus the Tlaxcalans continued a past visual tradition in using images to support their land claims.

The monks distributed countless pious images in the form of illustrated books, prints, paintings, statues, and tapestries that local painters and carvers copied. In the process, these artists assimilated a new iconographic and stylistic repertoire that they combined with earlier artistic forms. This syncretic art produced by indigenous artists in the service of Christianity was referred to as *tequitqui*, a Nahuatl word meaning "one who pays tribute."

The *Florentine Codex*, produced by indigenous converts from 1545 to 1590 under the supervision of the Franciscan friar Bernardino de Sahagún, is an excellent example of this new type of imagery. Its 2,400 pages are organized into 12 books, with more than 2,000 illustrations. As with many post-conquest codices, it includes text in both Nahuatl and Spanish, as well as incorporating European artistic conventions, such as three-dimensional rendering, along with Aztec iconography. For instance, in one of the scenes of the art of featherworking [**1.1.5**; p. 25], Aztec glyphs, which appear to float in a blank space, coexist with a figure dressed in European clothes. The figure is firmly grounded in a three-dimensional architectural space rendered through the somewhat awkward use of one-point perspective. The very activity depicted—the use of feathers by an indigenous man in a Christian school to create complex images—combined the practices of two cultures. The compositions of feather paintings were commonly based on Christian scenes derived from European prints and were seen as evidence of the success of the Church's conversionary efforts and of the technical skills of indigenous artists. Gruzinski includes such feather works in his description of the mixtures of visual traditions that appeared in rural parish churches: "fabrics and chasubles from Rouen, Castile and Holland, chalices and candelabra forged in local silver, crosses, shields and blazons made of tropical bird feathers showing Christ with crucifixion wounds, Michoacán flutes, Italian trumpets, pious images painted on morocco leather."

A sculptural example of *tequitqui* can be found in the stone carving of *La Virgencita del Nuevo Mundo* (*The Virgin of the New World*), created by an unknown Aztec artisan between 1521 and 1540 [**1.1.6**]. While much smaller than Coatlicue [**1.1.4**; p. 23], it is marked by the same low-relief carving, focus on repetitive, decorative patterns, and bilateral symmetry. The crescent moon beneath her feet identifies her as the Virgin of the Immaculate Conception. She also wears a crown surmounted by a cross, suggesting her role as the Queen of Heaven. According to the historian Linda Hall, the tassels on her cloak that frame her hands may be copied from a European source. Alternately, they could represent bells, a common motif in indigenous religious images and associated with Coyolxauhqui ("Bells-Her-Face"). The two large striated circles beneath the bells/tassels, with floral designs inside them, "are characteristic of Tezcatlipoca, the Smoking Mirror, the mysterious Aztec figure associated with the night wind, a trickster who introduced the random and the unexpected into the cosmos." The feather-like draping on the front of the gown suggests the Aztec god Quetzalcóatl, or Feathered Serpent.

Quetzalcóatl was paired with Tezcatlipoca in Aztec mythology. He functioned as the deity of the dawn, arts, knowledge, and order, in contrast to the darkness and chaos of Tezcatlipoca's realm. The two played major roles in creation myths, sometimes as collaborators and at other times as competitors. In one story, Coatlicue appeared alongside Tezcatlipoca as a key figure in the creation of the fifth Aztec world. The art historian Cecelia Klein summarizes this story as follows:

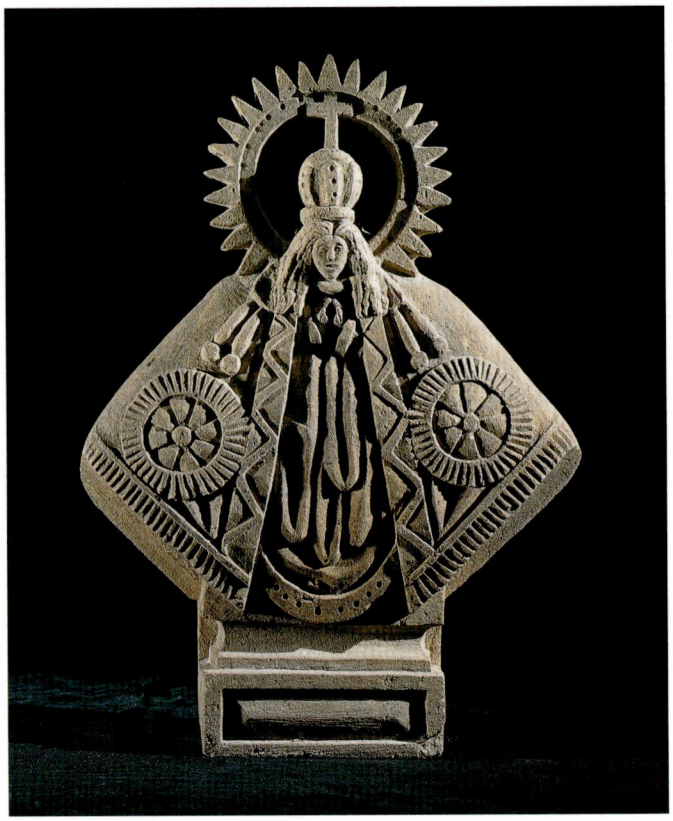

1.1.6 Unknown artist, Aztec: *La Virgencita del Nuevo Mundo* (*The Virgin of the New World*), c. 1521–40.
Cantera stone, 14¾ x 11 x 4½ in. (12.1 x 27.9 x 11.4 cm.)
Private collection

> when the earth was still in darkness, the god Tezcatlipoca created four hundred men and five women "in order that there be people for the sun to eat." The four hundred men died four years later, but the five women lived on for another twelve years before dying, according to the text, on "the day the sun was created."

Using this story and other colonial documents as well as pre-colonial sculpture, Klein argues that one of these five women was Coatlicue [**1.1.4**; p. 23]. She goes on to say that the large statue of this deity found at the base of the main temple of Tenochtitlan in 1790 represented the deity not in her role as the mother of Huitzilopochtli, an interpretation based primarily on a passage from the *Florentine Codex*, but as one of the five women who willingly sacrificed themselves in order to bring about the birth of the fifth sun.

Klein was prompted to question the earlier interpretation of the Coatlicue statue in part by the failure of the *Florentine Codex* passage to explain the detail and complexity of her skirt of braided serpents. In accounts of the creation of the fifth world involving Coatlicue, she and her four sisters "left behind only their *mantas*, or large rectangular panels of cloth used to make Mexica skirts, from which they eventually were resurrected." According to Klein, these *mantas* were thought to "contain the essence and powers of their original wearers," an important aspect of Aztec religious beliefs at the time of the conquest. The statue of Coatlicue, or "Snakes-Her-Skirt," therefore, with its elaborate serpent *manta*, represented the resurrection of the deity as creatrix. Similar attention is given to the cloak and gown of the small stone Virgin; thus, its carver calls up this *manta*/creatrix tradition, and brings together iconographic references to three major Aztec creator deities—Tezcatlipoca, Quetzalcóatl, and Coatlicue.

Another significant aspect of *La Virgencita* is the Virgin's open mouth, an indication that she is either speaking or singing, something seldom seen in European portrayals of the Virgin. Within Mesoamerican culture, speaking was a sign of authority, and powerful leaders were reputed to be eloquent orators. Speaking also implied a connection between the sacred and the human. That the Virgin Mary is shown speaking is quite appropriate, for she played a prominent role in the conquest of New Spain for both the Spanish and indigenous populations. As Hall writes, the Spanish brought the Virgin Mary

> as religious idea, psychological construct, and physical image to their New World....The idea and image of the Virgin appealed to indigenous populations as well, especially as a nurturer and a healer. So, in addition to being a comfort and a justification for those engaged in discovery and conquest, Mary became powerful in bringing indigenous peoples, at least in appearance, into the Roman Catholic faith.

At the same time that the Spanish brought the Virgin to the New World, however, they also brought the diseases and disasters that motivated the indigenous populations to appeal to her for relief. This created a certain ambivalence that may well be present in the iconographic complexity of *La Virgencita del Nuevo Mundo*. This small statue can be seen as embodying the tensions between dark and light, chaos and order, found in both the Spanish-dominated present and the Aztec mythological past. With its elaborate *manta*, it also points to the sacrifice—whether of Coatlicue or Christ—needed to bring a new world into being.

The majority of the religious objects produced by both Spanish and indigenous painters and sculptors were housed in mission churches, the most visible statement of the presence of Christianity in New Spain. By 1536 there were approximately forty Franciscan monasteries; by 1538, eight Dominican monasteries; and by 1559, forty Augustinian monasteries. Some were modest structures; others were built to accommodate massive numbers of converts, often with open chapels or a large courtyard (*atrio*). The historian Elizabeth Wilder Weismann tells of two missionaries at Xochimilco who baptized more than 15,000 people in one day by working in shifts. One monk complained: "It happened many times that they could no longer raise their arms to perform that function, and even though they changed arms, both were worn out."

The Augustinian monastery at Epazoyucan, Hidalgo, north of Mexico City [**1.1.7**], has such an outside chapel and courtyard. Its facade is marked by simple, geometric forms (rectangles,

1.1.7 Church and chapel of the Augustinian monastery, Epazoyucan, Hidalgo, Mexico, 16th century.

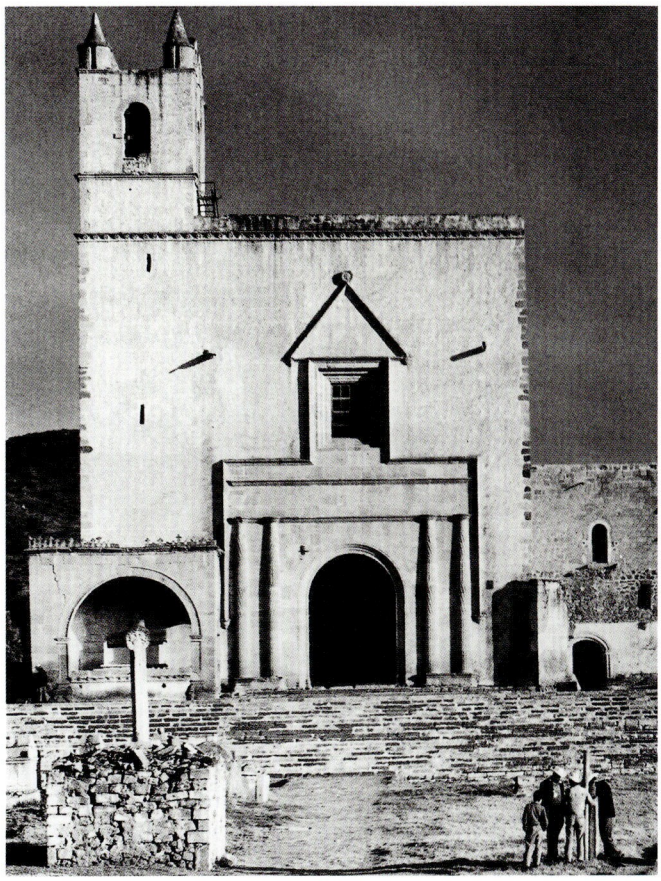

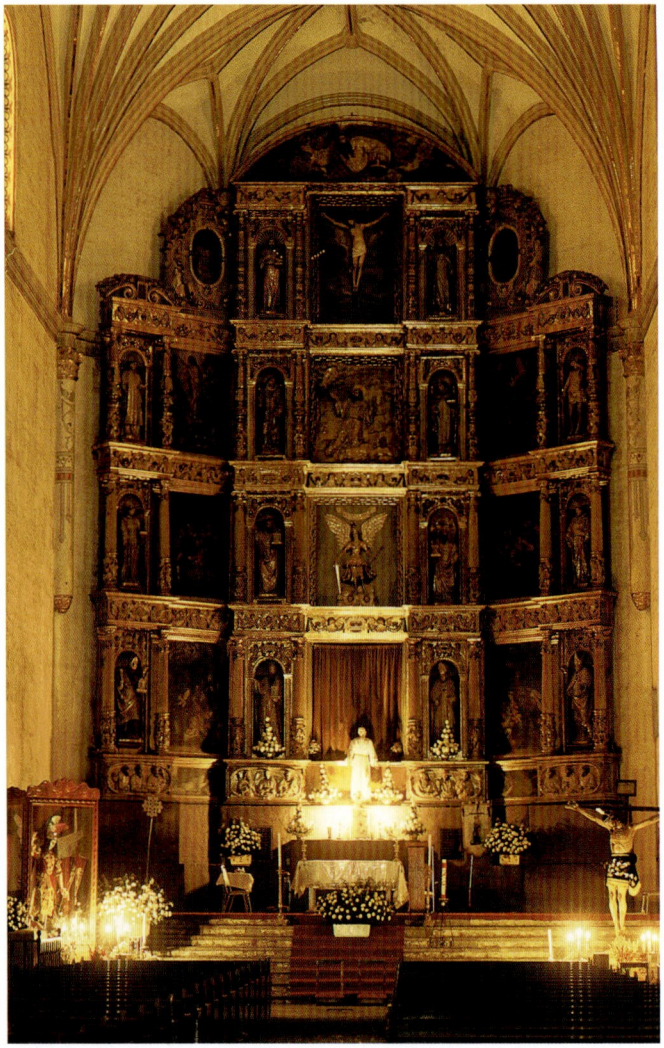

1.1.8 Simón Pereyns: *retablo*, Franciscan monastery church, Huejotzingo, Puebla, Mexico, 1580.

triangles) and Classical elements (columns, arches, a pediment). The architect may have been familiar with the revival of ancient Greek and Roman architectural motifs sponsored in Spain by King Charles V and his successor, King Philip II, and have wished to make a statement of allegiance to the King. The reference to a temple front around the entranceway, however, is somewhat idiosyncratic. The triangular pediment is shrunk to less than half its normal size. It is separated from the columns both by the suggestion of an architrave and frieze (the two horizontal flat areas outlined by slightly projecting stringcourses or moldings), as well as a rectangular window. The stark simplicity of the building suggests a shortage of funds. Yet in 1556 the Bishop of New Spain complained that Augustinians were making *retablos* (painted and/or carved altarpieces) that cost more than 6,000 pesos.

The elaborate *retablos* in these monasteries were the principal vehicle for the diffusion of style throughout New Spain. One of the earliest recorded examples is by the Flemish painter Simón Pereyns (*c.* 1540–1589), whose contract for the *retablo* at Huejotzingo [**1.1.8**] is dated 1580 (from the early 1500s to 1714, Spain was a significant political presence in Flanders, the approximate area of present-day Belgium). Pereyns arrived in Mexico in 1566 with the viceroy Gastón de Peralta. One of his first commissions was for a series of battle scenes for the viceregal palace. He then gathered around him an army of indigenous woodcarvers, assistant painters, joiners, and gilders and began furnishing *retablos* for the major monasteries. In the process, he introduced a new cadre of artists to the European Renaissance. Some European artists tried to form guilds that would give them exclusive control over major commissions, both civic and religious, but their efforts ultimately failed. A community of both indigenous and European artists and artisans would thus contribute to the shaping of the visual culture of New Spain.

Review Questions

1 Why start a history of the art and architecture of the United States of America with the art and architecture of the Aztec empire and New Spain?

2 What was the layout of the Aztec capital of Tenochtitlan, and why was it organized in this way?

3 Why were the Spanish forces led by Hernan Cortés, despite being massively outnumbered, able to conquer the powerful Aztec empire?

4 What was the role of art in the conquest and colonization of Mesoamerica?

5 What are some of the ways in which the content and style of the images and architecture of the Aztec empire and Spain came together to form a new set of visual traditions?

CHAPTER 2

Art and Architecture in the Northern Territories of New Spain

(*c.* 900–1821)

Early Explorations and Fortifications

Once the Spanish had secured control of Tenochtitlan and the surrounding region, they began moving northward. Few had ventured into this territory in the early sixteenth century. Those who did—Juan Ponce de León (1513, 1521), Alonso Álvarez de Piñeda (1519), Pánfilo de Narváez (1528)—were prompted primarily by a quest for gold, the intensity of which increased after the discovery of the vast treasures of the Aztecs. In 1539, Cortés set sail up the Pacific Coast, enticed by stories of large towns rich in gold and silver. The following year, 1540, a larger land expedition arrived in the Rio Grande region under the leadership of Francisco Vásquez de Coronado, only to discover that the stories of wealth had been exaggerated and that the villages he encountered in present-day western New Mexico were far from cities of gold. Exploratory parties were sent as far north as the Grand Canyon and east to a Wichita village on the banks of the Arkansas River, but no gold was found.

In addition to these expeditions, a few attempts were made to set up permanent communities. In the summer of 1526, five hundred Spaniards with one hundred African slaves led by the lawyer Lucas Vásquez de Ayllón established a short-lived settlement near the mouth of the Pee Dee River in what is now South Carolina. In 1565 a party under the leadership of Pedro Menéndez de Avilés made another attempt to colonize the northern region. Coming upon a settlement of French Protestants that had been established on the east coast of present-day Florida the year before, they massacred the inhabitants and set up their own fort, calling it St. Augustine. They also established a second settlement called Santa Elena on Parris Island, South Carolina. Santa Elena succumbed to attacks by the indigenous Guale, but St. Augustine survived. It became an important port, for it was located at the point where the Spanish treasure fleets turned offshore with the north-flowing Gulf Stream. A handful of friars was charged with the task of converting the local Timucuans.

In the early seventeenth century the British were stepping up their exploration of the region and establishing settlements to the north. To guard against attack by British forces, the Spanish enlisted indigenous and convict labor to build the Castillo de San Marcos from 1672 to 1687 [**1.2.1**]. Designed by Ignacio Daza, it was patterned after the latest fortifications in Europe, with thicker walls and other devices to protect against a relatively new military weapon—the cannon. The walls are *coquina*, or shell-limestone, which absorbs cannon balls rather than shattering like other stone. They are 25 feet (7.6 meters) high and 12 feet (3.7 meters) thick at the base, narrowing to 7 feet (2 meters) at the top. The fort itself is approximately 200 feet (61 meters) across, with triangular bastions at each corner. The enclosed courtyard was ringed by government offices, barracks, and store rooms. Two centuries later, these spaces would house Cheyenne, Kiowa, and other indigenous military leaders captured by the US Army during the Indian Wars of the 1870s (see pp. 251–55).

As before, the Spaniards subjugated the indigenous population, and then set about instituting systems of control through religious conversion, tribute labor, and intermarriage. As the archaeologist Brian M. Fagan notes, "the Spaniards integrated themselves physically with local populations, while still maintaining detailed, rigid, and highly legalistic classifications of people by race." This was in contrast to the pattern to be found in British colonies, where interactions were based on trade, warfare, slavery, and servitude, and much less on intermarriage. St. Augustine remained the capital of this region, called La Florida by the Spanish, until 1702, when the British attacked the town and forced its residents to flee. The region was eventually ceded to England in 1763, but not before it functioned for decades as a refuge for escaped slaves from the British plantations of South Carolina (see pp. 75–77).

While trade focused on St. Augustine, the center of missionary activity was Santa Catalina de Guale, on St. Catherine's Island off the coast of Georgia. By the mid-seventeenth century, 38 missions existed throughout La Florida, attended by 70 Franciscans who spread their faith among approximately 25,000 indigenous people. Because the buildings were made primarily

1.2.1 Castillo de San Marcos, St. Augustine, Florida, 1672–87.

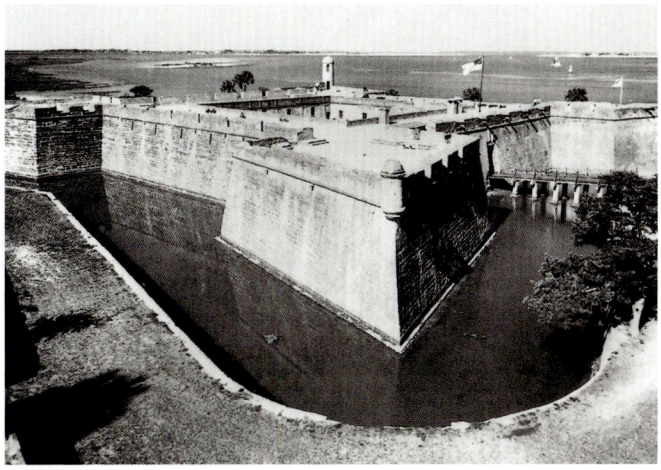

of mud, thatch, or thin boards, little remains of this architecture today. Excavations of the seventeenth-century mission at Santa Catalina revealed a single-nave church with a plaza in front and a friary complex across the plaza. Records show that Guale converts lived there and provided the labor necessary to keep it functioning.

The Pueblo Cultures

Little else was done to populate the northern frontiers of New Spain until the 1580s and 1590s, when Franciscans moved into what is now New Mexico. In the 1580s they explored the area, noting the types of cultures and planning how they were going to convert the local inhabitants to Christianity. The region was populated by descendants of three main groups who had lived there since approximately 300 BCE [**1.2.2**]. They were the Anasazi, in the northern part of Arizona and New Mexico and in Colorado; the Mogollon, in southeastern Arizona, southwestern New Mexico, and sections of northern Mexico; and the Hohokam, in the central region of Arizona to the Mexican border. In addition to hunting, all practiced various forms of agriculture, often utilizing canal-irrigated farmlands. Maize cultivation had arrived from central Mexico around 2000 BCE. All of the groups had highly developed ceramic traditions [**3.8.1**, **3.8.2**; p. 150], also thought by some to have originated in central Mexico. Their descendants, named by the Spaniards "Pueblo" peoples (*pueblo* is Spanish for town or village), would continue the development of these ceramic traditions through to the present (see V. 2, pp. 389–91).

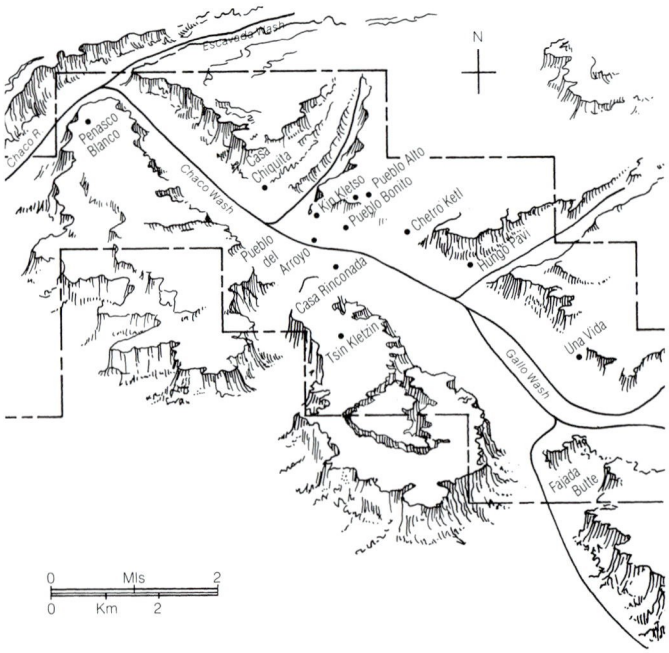

1.2.3 Main sites of Pueblo Bonito, Chaco Canyon, New Mexico, 900–1150 CE. (The stepped lines indicate the boundaries of the National Monument.)

1.2.2 Sites and major cultural divisions of the Southwest.

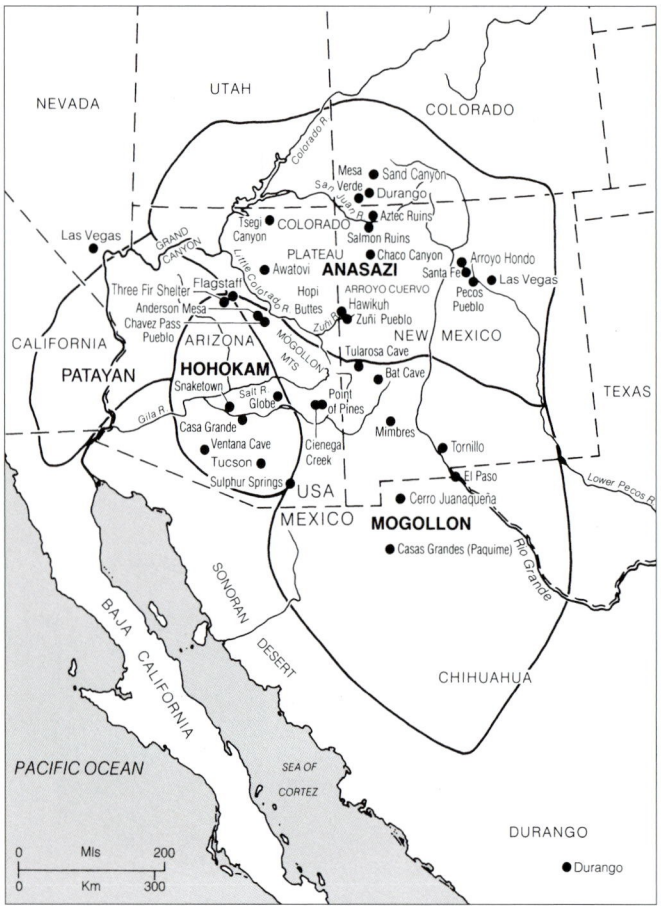

Of these three cultures, the Anasazi left the most extensive architectural remains. They mostly lived in small, scattered farming communities, but were associated in some way with larger multi-household complexes, some of which were built into vast natural indentations in the canyon walls. Chaco Canyon, in northwestern New Mexico, was the most ambitious of these complexes [**1.2.3**, **1.2.4**]. Flourishing from 900 to 1150 CE, it contained thirteen "towns" and several great *kivas*, or ceremonial buildings. The largest of these "towns" were built on the canyon floor, at the base of the cliffs. Thousands of elaborately carved or decorated items made of turquoise, macaw bones, clay, and copper have been found at these sites, suggesting that they functioned as significant trading centers. Another indication of their importance as a focus of either trade or religion or both is the elaborate network of more than 250 miles (400 kilometers) of roads that extend outward in all directions. Brian M. Fagan argues that the various settlements in the canyon housed fewer people than previously thought (current estimates for the period 1075–1115 are somewhere between 2,000 and 10,000),

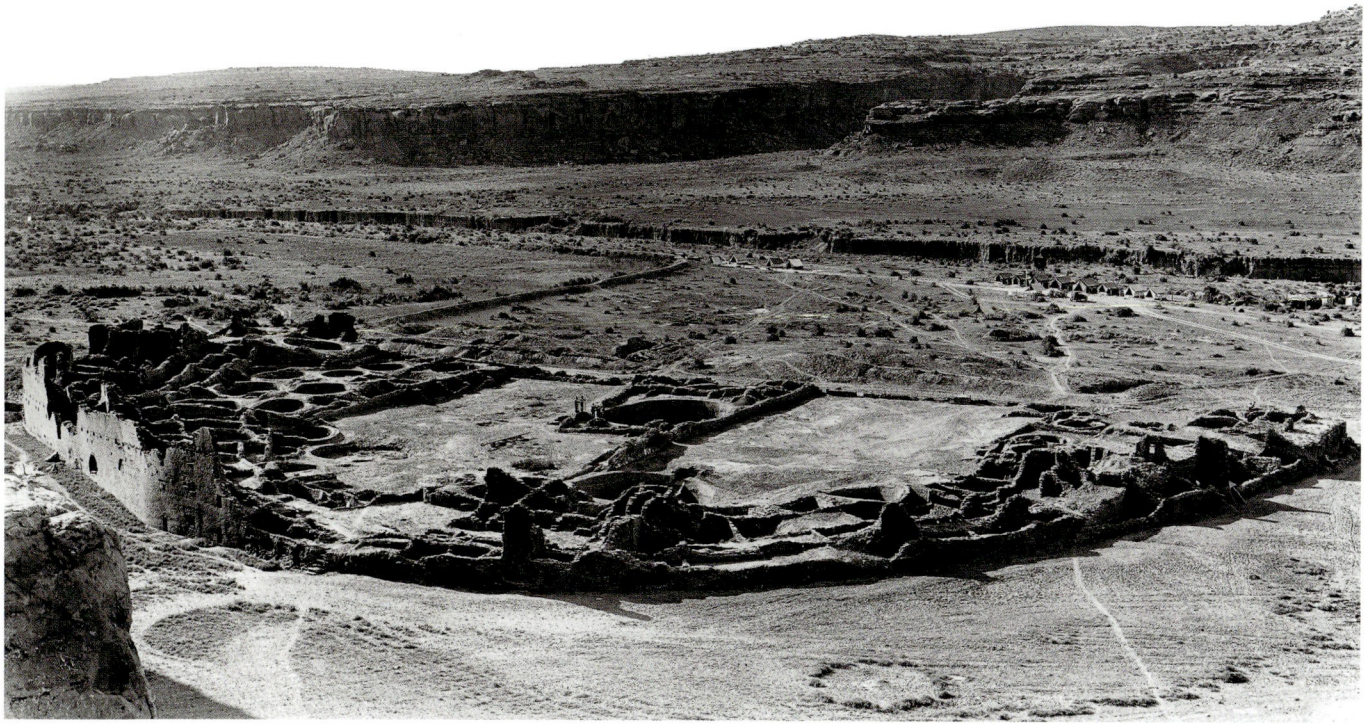

1.2.4 Pueblo Bonito, Chaco Canyon, New Mexico, 900–1150 CE.

and that these "towns" functioned more as ceremonial sites and storage centers for food, where people came together to trade, worship, and participate in the redistribution of resources in times of need. The construction of the buildings and roads would have required the cooperation of large numbers of people, suggesting that a relatively small elite must have possessed the power to orchestrate these projects. It is not clear, however, whether they formed a centralized authority based in Chaco Canyon, or were representatives of various communities who met at Chaco on ceremonial occasions to cement political and economic alliances.

The architectural historian Vincent Scully suggests that influences from the preconquest cultures of central Mexico can be seen at Chaco Canyon and at later Pueblo sites. One example is the location of ritual structures on top of cones of earth, which imitate temple platforms [**1.1.2**; p. 21]. Another is the focus on using architecture to define a ritual exterior space. In Pueblo architecture the primary ritual space is the plaza, framed by buildings with ledges and roof setbacks from which ceremonies could be watched [see V. 2: **6.21.13**; p. 388]. In 1540 Pedro de Castañeda, a member of Coronado's expedition, described Pecos Pueblo in north-central New Mexico as:

> square, situated on a rock, with a large court or yard in the middle, containing the steam rooms. The houses are all alike, four stories high. One can go over the top of the village without there being a street to hinder.

The plaza became more important in the Pueblo towns of the sixteenth century, as the size of the *kiva* diminished.

Around 1200–1250 CE the major Anasazi settlements, such as Chaco Canyon and Mesa Verde (in southwestern Colorado), were systematically abandoned, possibly because of a combination of soil erosion, drought, and political feuds. Many of the inhabitants moved south and west, forming the precursors of the contemporary Pueblo peoples, who developed a distinctive style of architecture [**1.2.5**; p. 32]. Archaeological evidence suggests that from 1250 to 1500 the Anasazi moved many times, building and abandoning numerous villages as they searched for fertile land and for a stable social system that would allow for the integration of different lineages. This nomadic existence is present in Pueblo origin myths, which often feature people forced to wander in search of water or away from disease and factionalism.

In the sixteenth century, the population of the region of New Mexico and eastern Arizona was approximately 100,000, with some 150 communities ranging in size from 200 to 3,000 persons. Seven different languages belonging to four families (Tanoan, Keresan, Zuñi, Uto-Aztecan) were spoken. In addition to the various Pueblo peoples, Athapaskan nomads migrated south from Alaska into the region in the second quarter of the

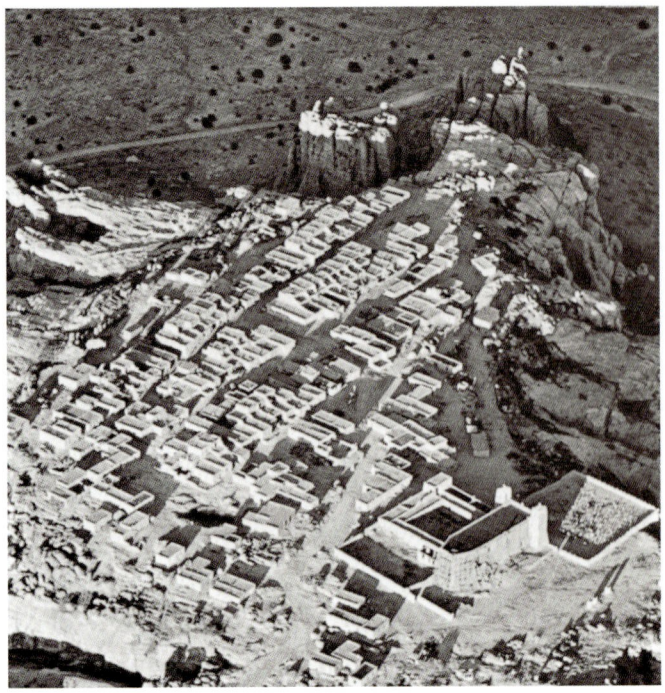

1.2.5 Acoma Pueblo, New Mexico. The mission church (see **1.2.8**), with its cloister and walled burial ground, is visible at the lower right.

century; they later became known as the Navajos and the Jicarilla Apaches. The competition for game posed by the Athapaskans forced the Pueblo peoples to rely more heavily on agriculture. In times of unrest, particularly after the arrival of the Spanish, groups or clans from certain pueblos would take refuge with the nomadic Navajos and Apaches.

Pueblo society was matrilocal (men moved to the homes of their wives when they married) and matrilineal (property was passed from mother to daughter). Men and women shared in the running of the communities. The main hierarchical division was generational, between the old and the young. In the mythological world of the Pueblo cultures corn was female and rain was male. Both were needed for survival. Men were responsible for hunting, protecting the community, spinning, and weaving. Women were responsible for the home and for building construction (although the men usually put the roof beams in place); they produced pottery, moccasins, ceremonial apparel, and turkey-down blankets. Sexuality itself was an important force within Pueblo cultures, being equated with fertility, regeneration, and the sacred. Sexual intercourse symbolized cosmic harmony, the balance of the masculine forces of the sky and the feminine forces of the earth.

Men controlled most of the ceremonial life of the pueblos, although the all-female Marau Society conducted ceremonies celebrating female fecundity, sexuality, and reproduction. There were four main male ritual associations, connected with warfare, curing, hunting, and rain-making. While warfare was necessary to protect the pueblos or to acquire goods in times of scarcity, the taking of human life through violence was not held in high esteem. Of greater value was a complex system of gifting, where the offering of food and hospitality to neighbors and travelers assured peace while setting up reciprocal obligations that tied the community together. In addition to the four ritual associations, there was also the primary chief, or "Inside Chief" (warrior association members were also referred to as the "Outside Chiefs").

Each of the ritual associations had its own *kiva* [**1.2.6**]. The main *kiva* was located in the center of the pueblo and was the preserve of the Inside Chief; he called together men from the other associations for major ceremonies. *Kivas* in the eastern pueblos were most often circular, while those in the western pueblos were rectangular. Most in both regions were set below ground level, with roofs constructed of wooden beams. Entrance was gained through a hole in the roof, which symbolized the place where the Corn Mothers, deities associated with corn, climbed onto the earth's surface, and down a pine ladder. In the center of the floor was a shallow hollow called the *shipapu*, representing the earth's navel or the place through which the people emerged from the underworld and through which they would return. The walls, usually made of coursed sandstone blocks covered with plaster, contained stone altars. A low ledge or bench covered with lion and bear skins ran around the room. The central *kiva* was situated at the core of the settlement and at the core of a spatial scheme that included the four cardinal directions, four levels or skies above, and the underworld. The ceremonies performed here or in the central plaza, if done correctly and joyfully, ensured cosmic harmony, i.e. the rising and setting of the sun, the coming of rain, and the change of seasons.

1.2.6 A Hopi *kiva*

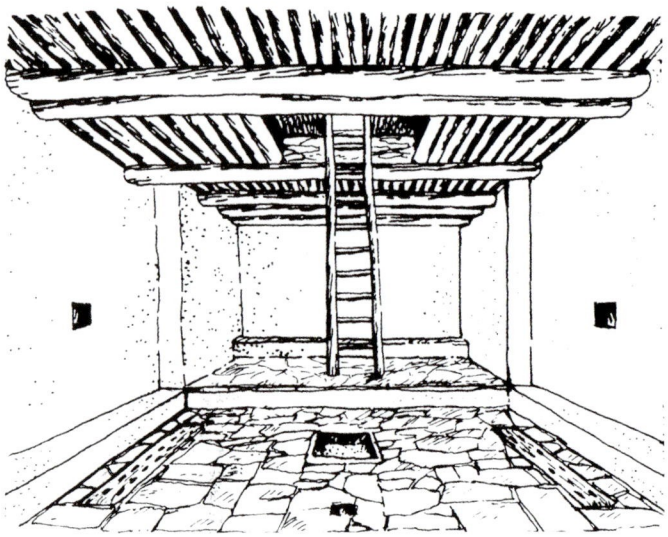

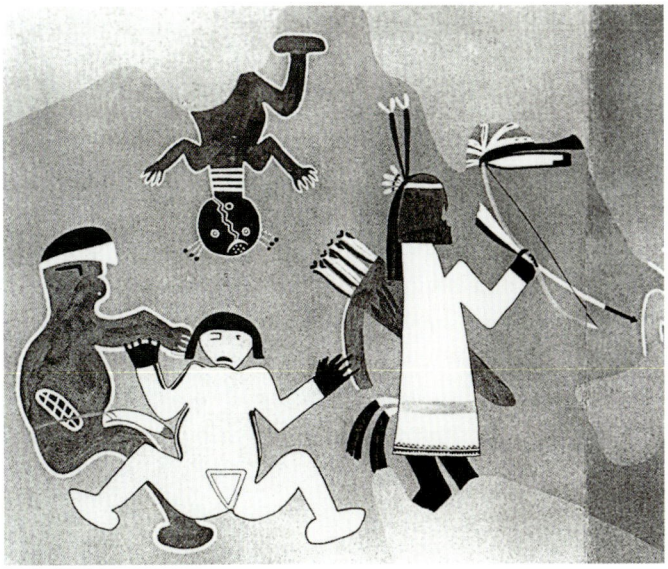

1.2.7 Unknown artist, Hopi: mural of Kokopelli and Kokopell Mana from Room 529, Awatovi Pueblo, Arizona, *c.* early 15th century (copy by Watson Smith).

The *kivas* also contained many ceremonial objects (for example, decorated wooden sticks, or prayer sticks, and masks) and several show evidence of murals. The latter included elaborate designs painted in a variety of colors [**1.2.7**] mostly derived from local minerals mixed with vegetable or animal oil and water. Excavations, most notably at the site of the Hopi pueblo Awatovi, which was abandoned around 1700, have revealed several layers, suggesting that murals were created for specific ceremonies, then plastered over and repainted. The earliest date from 900 to 1100 CE. Akin to the paintings of the Aztecs and their contemporaries [**1.1.3**; p. 22], the *kiva* murals are two-dimensional in style, with evenly applied colors, an absence of shading, and a tendency toward geometric forms.

Watson Smith, who led the excavations at Awatovi in the 1930s, suggests that the figures in the murals mirror those in the various ceremonies performed in the *kiva* or the plaza, most notably the katcina, which represent the forces of nature—clouds, rain, animals, and plants. They were invoked with dances and offerings of prayer sticks and other gifts. They lived underneath lakes and on mountain tops, and were called with puffs of smoke, representing the clouds it was hoped they would bring. The people believed that they themselves became katcina at death—indicating, once again, the reciprocal nature of Pueblo existence: in death there would be life. Katcina dancers wore distinctive costumes, which appeared on the numerous carvings or small dolls of the spirits found within Pueblo communities.

Smith lists the most common elements in the *kiva* murals: katcina, humans, plants (corn, beans, squash, cacti), animals (badgers, rabbits, deer, snakes, lizards, birds, fish, frogs), headdresses, prayer sticks, crooks, feathers, animal skins, bows, arrows, shields, clouds, and lightning. One mural from Awatovi [**1.2.7**] depicts the spirit-being Kokopelli on the left, characterized by his humped back and extended penis. To the right of him is the upside-down figure of his female companion Kokopell Mana, and a young female to whom Kokopelli is bringing the seed of life (he was known as a cosmic seducer of girls and bringer of babies). To the right of them is a fully outfitted warrior or hunter. Here, warfare and hunting, the domain of men; birthing, the domain of women; and sexuality, the domain of both, are combined in a continuous pictorial space, as in the Pueblo social order.

The Christianization of the Pueblos

The depiction of human sexual organs and the suggestion of sexual activity in the *kiva* murals undoubtedly troubled the celibate Franciscans who arrived in the late sixteenth century to convert the Pueblo peoples and establish missions. We know from written accounts that they were certainly concerned by what they saw as sexually provocative dances. The first permanent Spanish colony was set up in 1598 under the leadership of Juan de Oñate near San Juan Pueblo. Like Cortés, Oñate marched under a banner with an image of the Virgin. Also similar to Cortés, he was accompanied by a group of Tlaxcalan allies and brought with him a Pueblo woman, captured during an earlier expedition, as his translator. And, as was the case with Cortés, written accounts of the journey suggest that the Pueblo peoples thought Oñate might be a deity—in his case, a katcina—and thus greeted him, initially, with gifts and a cautious welcome.

The missionaries who accompanied Oñate attempted first to prove that their power to heal the sick, bring rain, and provide material sustenance to the community was greater than that of the Pueblo leaders. While some were suspicious of the friars, many who lived in the pueblos were impressed by their successes. Once established in the area, the Franciscans began to exploit the division between the young and the old to assist their conversion efforts. They encouraged the young to inform on their parents and attempted to impose a patriarchal order, in large part to control the sexuality of women. They were also aided in their efforts by the presence of Spanish troops close by.

Similar to their predecessors in central New Spain, the friars systematically confiscated and burned the ceremonial objects of Pueblo life—the katcina figures, ceremonial masks, and prayer sticks. They also destroyed many *kivas* or filled them in with sand. Sometimes they built their mission churches on top of them, at the same time conflating the Christian cult of the saints with the katcina cult. Certain formal similarities aided in this conflation. Many Pueblo prayer sticks resembled the Christian cross. Other similarities between the practices of Pueblo chiefs and Franciscan friars, such as flagellation and bloodletting, led to a more willing acceptance of certain Christian rituals.

This conflation resulted in a syncretism, or mixing, similar to that which occurred in central New Spain (see p. 25). Unfortunately, few artworks produced for the mission churches during the seventeenth century survived, for reasons that will become clear below, so evidence of the flowering of this combination of aesthetic and religious traditions is not readily available until the eighteenth century. Also, unlike their counterparts in Mexico City, the friars did not initially have the resources to train many Pueblo peoples in the creation of Christian imagery. Therefore, the majority of the work that adorned the early churches—altarpieces, paintings, chalices, freestanding statues, furniture—came from Mexico City or was made by the friars themselves. As much of the church decoration produced in Mexico City at this time was elaborately carved, polychromed, and gilded, the objects in missions probably evinced such traits. Where we do see the hand of the Pueblo artisan and evidence of the combining of cultural traditions is in the design of the buildings and the materials used.

Church Architecture in the Pueblos

Like the *kivas*, the mission churches were the physical symbols of the celestial community, containing sacred objects and providing the focus for sacred ceremonies. The friars adopted the adobe (clay mixed with water and a binder, such as straw or manure) that was such a distinctive part of Pueblo architecture. At the same time, they maintained the general layout established for missions in Mexico City in the middle of the sixteenth century—a single-nave church, a convent around a patio, and a large, walled atrium or churchyard, which might contain an open-air chapel and small corner chapels or *posas* [**1.2.10**]. The main variation was the inclusion of a transept, or crossing, in front of the high altar in many churches. To assist with the building, the Franciscans were given equipment from Europe. Every friar who set out from Mexico City received the following tools with which to build a church: 10 axes, 3 adzes, 3 spades, 10 hoes, 1 saw, 1 chisel, 2 augers, 1 plane, 1 latch, 2 small locks, a dozen hinges, some small latches, and 6,000 nails.

1.2.8 San Estevan, Acoma Pueblo, New Mexico, 1629–42. Seen from the southeast

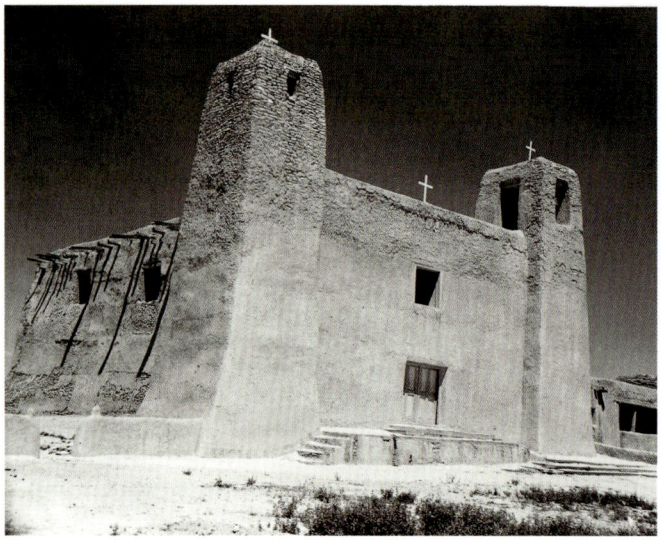

In his study of Southwestern churches, the architect Thomas Drain notes that by 1660 there were forty-five or fifty Franciscan churches in New Mexico; a century later the number had decreased to approximately thirty. While some were positioned within the pueblo, most were sited on its edge [**1.2.5**; p. 32]. This location was determined by at least three factors: mutual distrust between Pueblo peoples and Franciscans, considerations of defense (many mission churches were conceived of as fortresses), and future expansion.

For the most part the buildings were made of sun-dried adobe brick or field stone laid in adobe mortar. In many cases a final coat of clay or adobe was spread thickly over the walls to smooth out the surfaces. The roofs consisted of wooden beams (*vigas*) resting on decorated brackets [**1.2.9**], with smaller pieces of wood (*latias*) laid between the beams, which were then covered with adobe. The walls were extremely thick (often 3–5 feet/1–1.5 meters) and seldom rose beyond 35 feet (10.7 meters), thus making any kind of external wall reinforcement or buttressing unnecessary. The result was a more intimate, horizontal space, reflective of the tendency of the Pueblo peoples to construct their buildings in horizontal layers.

Unlike the churches elsewhere in the Spanish dominions, these adobe churches did not use arches and relied, instead, on post-and-lintel construction. The windows along the nave were few, small, and high. To create more dramatic lighting over the high altar, the sanctuary roof was sometimes raised to allow for a transverse clerestory window. Often there was a walled courtyard in front [**1.2.10**]. The exteriors were largely unadorned, a testament to the simplicity, humility, and poverty that formed the spirit of the Franciscan order.

As noted above, in Pueblo cultures the women were responsible for building (except for the roof beams) and maintaining the house. For their missions, however, the friars tried to enlist Pueblo men in the construction work (women were told they should spin and weave rather than build houses). Friar Alonso de Benavides lamented in 1630: "If we compel any man to work on building a house, the women laugh at him...and he runs away." Some took refuge with the Apaches and never returned to their pueblo.

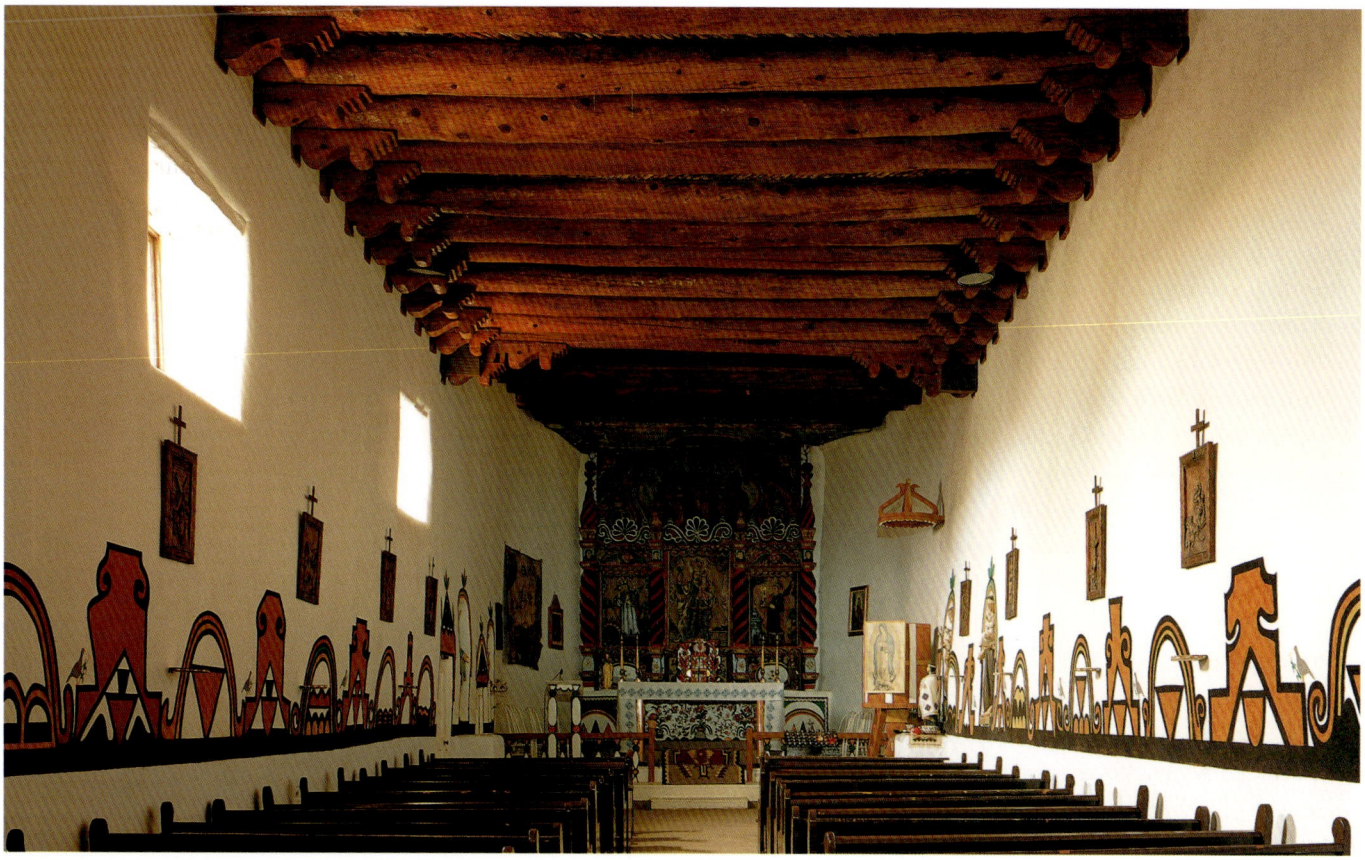

1.2.9 Nave, San José, Old Laguna Pueblo, New Mexico, *c.* 1760–1846.

The church of San Estevan at Acoma Pueblo is one of the best examples of seventeenth-century New Mexican mission architecture [**1.2.8**]. Built in 1629–42 at the edge of the pueblo, located on a high rock bluff [**1.2.5**; p. 32], it has a rubble core faced with adobe bricks and a smooth layer of adobe applied over the bricks. The two towers speak to the European element in the design, and also had a military function. The massing of the building is characteristic of seventeenth- and eighteenth-century missions. The absence of buttresses and the minimal size and number of windows result in the reduction of the external appearance to a block-shaped geometric form. This abstract massing is reinforced by the plain facade, marked only by the doorway, choir-loft window, and towers. With rounded and uneven edges and adobe surfaces, the church appears to grow organically out of the ground. While there is evidence that murals existed on the interior walls of the nave, little remains of the seventeenth-century decoration. The present decoration, combining European and Pueblo motifs, was probably painted in the eighteenth or early nineteenth century.

The many changes wrought by the Spaniards and their mistreatment of the local people did not go unchallenged. In 1680 the Pueblo peoples revolted, killing many of the friars and settlers from New Spain, and reestablishing the old social, religious, and economic order. Their revolt was fueled by a decade of famine and disease, as well as an ongoing rivalry between the clergy and the Spanish civil authorities that often rebounded on the indigenous population. The Keres at Acoma Pueblo had particular reason to revolt. In 1598 they had been appallingly punished after refusing supplies requested by a passing convoy of Spanish soldiers: all men and women over the age of twelve

1.2.10 San José, Old Laguna Pueblo, New Mexico, 1699–1706.
Looking from the east across the walled courtyard to the facade in 1881

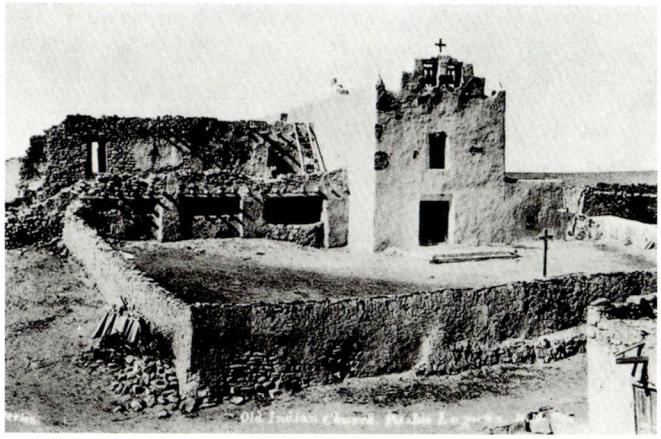

were sentenced to twenty years of slavery and all men over the age of twenty-five had one of their feet severed. Even one hundred years later they were among the most resistant (along with the Hopi and Zuñi) to Christianization, remaining matrilineal and refusing to abandon their traditional ceremonies.

During the Pueblo Revolt of 1680 most of the mission buildings were vandalized or burned, although many survived to be renovated later (the interior of San Estevan at Acoma was burned, but the building remained intact). At one church the statuary and the Holy Communion table were covered with excrement, the crucifix destroyed, and the arms of a statue of St. Francis cut off. At other missions images and altars were burned or paraded as trophies. Just as the Pueblo peoples' sacred objects and deities had been profaned by the Franciscans, so, too, did they profane and destroy Christian images representative of the new order. The revolt, however, was short-lived. By the 1690s the Spanish had reasserted control over the region.

In reconquering New Mexico, both the secular and religious authorities realized that the harsh treatment of the Pueblo peoples had contributed significantly to the unrest that led to the revolt. Under the new governorship of Cuervo y Valdez, Pueblo lands were protected with official royal grants. The Franciscans also became more tolerant of existing traditions, although not to such a degree that the old rituals could be performed in public. By the eighteenth century local craft practices began to develop to meet the demands of an increasing Spanish population, although in 1750 there were fewer than 4,000 Spaniards in New Mexico. The indigenous population was just over 10,000, having been decimated by famine and disease. This increase in the Spanish population was due in part to the encroachment of France and England on New Spain's northern borders. While the quest for new territories had lost its appeal for a Spanish Crown under duress in Europe, the king's representatives in New Spain were not about to lose the buffer zone that protected the valuable mineral resources in the territories just south of New Mexico from incursions by other European powers.

Constant raids on Spanish and Pueblo towns by Comanches and Apaches, continual bickering between the clergy and the secular authorities, minor local rebellions, and isolation from any central authorities prevented ambitious building and decorating projects from being undertaken in the eighteenth century. Several mission churches were constructed, however, most under the initiative of civil rather than religious authorities, the opposite of what had occurred in the previous century.

One of the first religious structures built after the Spanish reconquest of the region was the church of San José at Old Laguna Pueblo, constructed from 1699 to 1706 of fieldstone mixed with adobe [**1.2.10**; p. 35]. The building exhibits the same geometric massing and slightly undulating edges as San Estevan [**1.2.8**; p. 34]. The main difference is the use of a bell-screen rather than towers on the facade. This can be seen as an attempt to imitate the more ornate shapes of Spanish facade gables. This stepped form also corresponds to the Pueblo motif for clouds or the Pueblo universe prominent on pottery and female ceremonial headdresses. Like the architecture of San Estevan, San José uses post-and-lintel construction, with a roof of beams covered with branches, then adobe. And as at San Estevan, the rectilinearity of this post-and-lintel construction is offset by the organic lines and odd angles of the adobe building. These qualities make the church appear more fluid, as if in a state of transition.

Church Interiors and Adornments

The interiors of the eighteenth-century mission churches were also composites of Pueblo and European architectural and iconographic traditions. The painted and carved *retablo* behind the high altar at Old Laguna Pueblo is thought to have been created some time between 1760 and 1846 [**1.2.9**, p. 35; **1.2.11**]. It includes

1.2.11 Unknown artist, known as the Laguna *santero*: *retablo*, San José, Old Laguna Pueblo, New Mexico, *c.* 1760–1846.

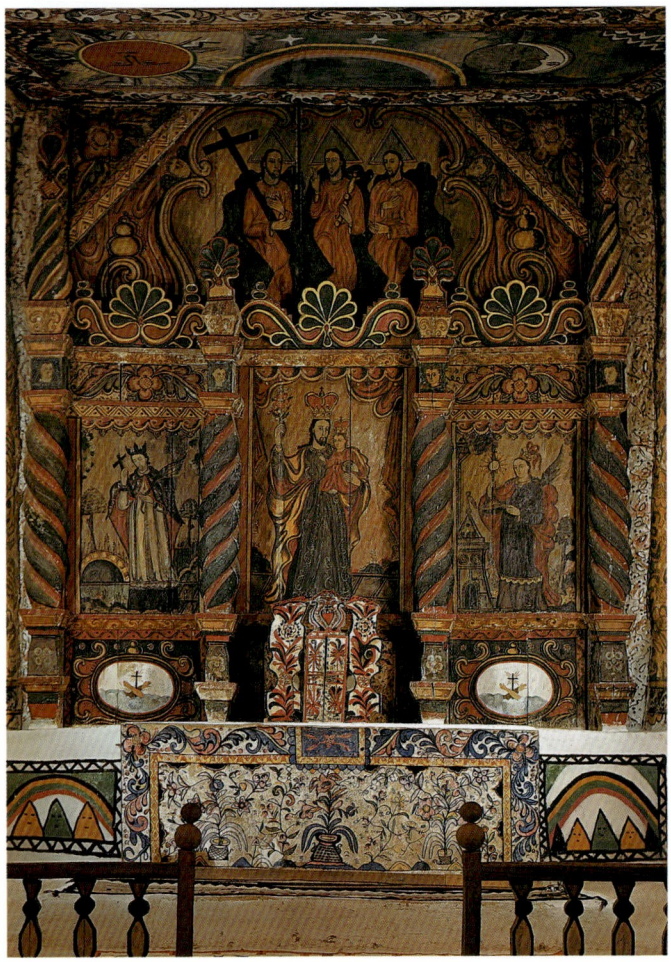

twisted Solomonic columns and biblical figures surrounded by floral frames and scrolls. In the top register the Holy Trinity is represented by three seated male figures: the one in the center holds a staff indicative of his authority to rule over both heaven and earth (God the Father); the one on the left holds a cross, a symbol of Jesus's crucifixion (God the Son); and the one on the right holds a dove (God the Holy Ghost). Below the Trinity is St. Joseph, the patron saint of the church, holding the Christ Child. To the right of Joseph is St. Barbara, protector against thunder, lighting, firearms, and sudden death; to the left is St. John Nepomuk, the patron saint of confession and secrecy. Attached to the ceiling is a painting on animal hide containing highly abstracted representations of the sun and the moon. Emanating from the former are zigzag lines ending in a triangular head, the mark of the Horned Water Snake, god of lightning and rain, an important Pueblo deity. Thus rain and thunder are represented by both Christian (St. Barbara) and Pueblo (Horned Water Snake) symbols.

A visitor to San José in 1846 described the interior as "painted with curious Indian ornaments, in which they have used the pure red, blue, and yellow." As late as the first half of the twentieth century, the walls to the immediate right and left of the altar were covered with floral motifs that replicated the elaborate woven tapestries found in more prosperous churches but out of the financial reach of the northern missions (these motifs have since been painted over). Along the nave walls the iconography is primarily Pueblo: cornstalks, sun, rain and thunder symbols, and terraced motifs [**1.2.9**; p. 35]. The birds perched on the stepped or terraced forms are thought to represent the souls of the people buried in the earth floor of the church.

The altar decorations reflect the lessons learned by Spanish and indigenous artists and artisans who studied in the Mexico City workshops set up by European artists, such as Simón Pereyns (see p. 28). They often included a mixture of local and imported work, as in the altarpiece of the Chapel of San Miguel in Santa Fe [**1.2.12**]. Erected in 1798, it contains paintings imported from central New Spain set within a frame carved and painted by the same individual who created the altarpiece at Old Laguna Pueblo [**1.2.11**], known as the Laguna *santero* ("saint maker" or artist who creates images of saints). The top register contains an image of St. Michael the Archangel—San Miguel, to whom the church is dedicated—flanked by St. Teresa of Avila on the left and St. Gertrude the Great on the right. Below St. Michael in the middle register stands Christ, with St. Francis on the left and St. Louis IX, King of France, and a member of the Third Order of St. Francis, on the right. The niche in the lower register contains a statue of St. Michael, possibly also from central New Spain, with further statues on either side made by local *santeros*.

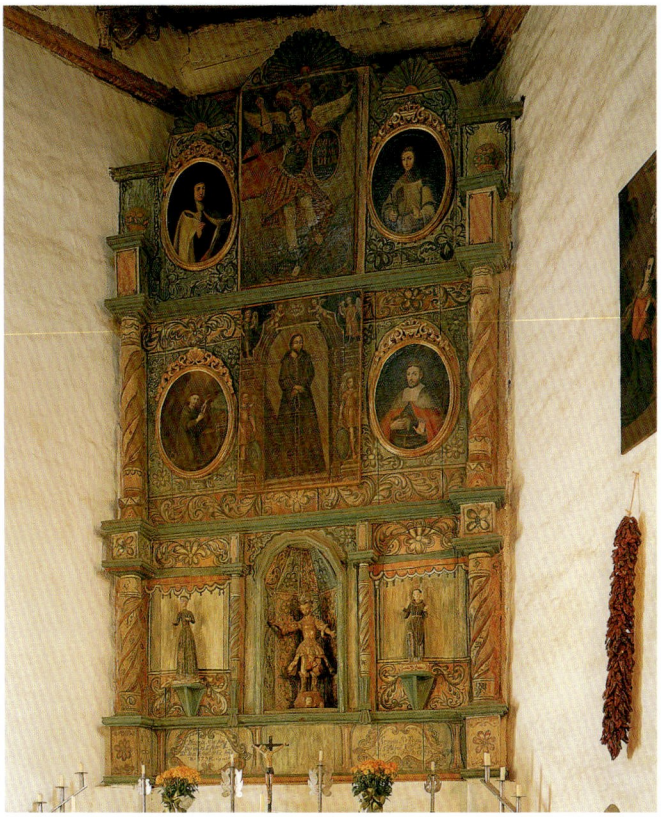

1.2.12 Unknown artist: high altar, Chapel of San Miguel, Santa Fe, New Mexico, late 18th century.

The walls and altars of eighteenth-century churches were also decorated with paintings on hide, which had the advantage of being both portable and durable. Unlike oil paintings on canvas, hide paintings did not include a gesso primer, which often cracked when rolled, causing the paint to flake off. Franciscan friars were often responsible for several missions and had to travel constantly. Perhaps the burning of church interiors during the revolt of 1680 also prompted them to favor religious images that could be easily removed in times of unrest. Technically, these paintings drew on the well-established tradition of Spanish leather work, introduced into Spain by Muslims as early as the twelfth century. Iconographically, they looked to the paintings of New Spain, which were often copied from book illustrations or prints from Europe. For example, a hide painting, *Christ on the Cross with an Angel* [**1.2.13**; p. 38], thought to have been created for the chapel of Captain Sebastián Martinez near San Juan Pueblo, is a traditional depiction of the Crucifixion with the Virgin Mary and the apostle John looking on, while Mary Magdalene grasps the bottom of the cross. A cityscape appears on the right in the distance. The figures are convincingly drawn in three dimensions.

The composition of this painting was probably copied from one of the numerous European woodcuts dating from the

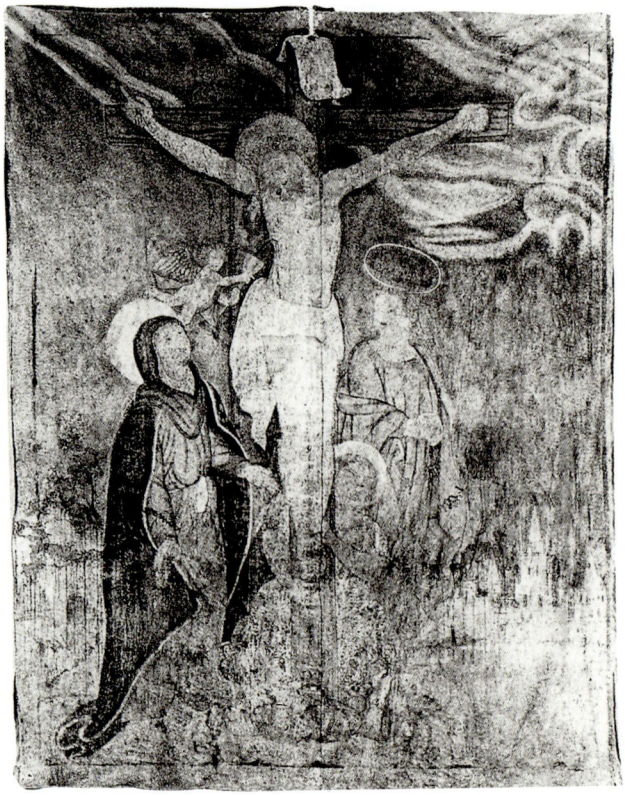

1.2.13 Unknown artist, probably from New Mexico: *Christ on the Cross with an Angel*, 18th century. Painting on hide, 78¾ x 65 in. (200 x 165.1 cm.) Museum of International Folk Art, Santa Fe, New Mexico

fifteenth and sixteenth centuries that depict the catching of the blood of the crucified Christ in chalices. The blood is a direct reference to the Holy Eucharist, through which humankind is offered heavenly redemption. As the art historian Thomas B. F. Cummins notes, such woodcuts, along with other printed materials, "were at the center of interactions between Spaniards and natives from the very beginning of exploration and they continued to be of critical importance throughout the colonial period." They were key sources for artworks—prints, murals, oil paintings, feather paintings—by both indigenous and Spanish artists in New Spain. Because of their number and portability, they also were able to "quickly create a common visual culture over a vast geographic area." Franciscans and their converts in northern New Spain "could imagine themselves participants in a single culture" that stretched from Madrid to Mexico City to Santa Fe. Such prints carried the authority of the Roman Catholic Church and the Spanish Crown. According to the art historian Kelly Donahue, both institutions attempted to regulate their content, production, and circulation, often with limited success. Found in every corner of New Spain, Christian-themed prints were both the focus of individual meditation and a vehicle for the creation of a new Christian community.

Another eighteenth-century hide painting contains an image of the Virgin Mary in the guise of Our Lady of the Assumption [**1.2.14**]. Donahue has identified the source of this image as an early eighteenth-century engraving: *Our Lady of the Assumption of Santa María la Redonda* by Antonio de Castro. The print refers to a statue of the Virgin in Mexico City that was said to have performed many miracles. In the hide painting, the figure is extremely schematic and two-dimensional. The position and attributes of the Virgin resemble the print. Yet the artist has added Pueblo motifs in the framing architecture, most notably the stepped pattern representing clouds or the Pueblo universe and the two pots perched atop columns that resemble cactus stalks. The artist has also added two angels on either side of the Virgin holding sticks to which are attached a sun and a moon, motifs that played a significant role in both Christian and Pueblo religions. Christine Mather, writing on the colonial art of New Mexico, suggests that the Pueblo motifs may have been added later, but the fact that other combinations of Christian and Pueblo imagery existed in the eighteenth century makes it possible that they were painted at the same time. At some point the picture was cropped and also torn in half.

Unfortunately, little is known about the individuals who created these hide paintings. The one of Christ on the cross appears to be the work of a friar who was well versed in the painting conventions of Europe. Donahue has dubbed him the

1.2.14 Unknown artist, from New Mexico: *The Virgin (Our Lady of the Assumption?)*, 18th century. Painting on hide, 33½ x 26 13/16 in. (85 x 68 cm.) Formerly in the L. Bradford Prince Collection

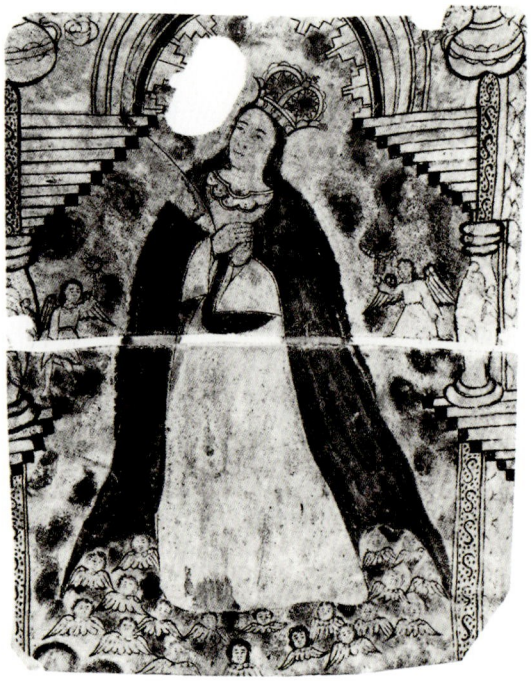

"Wavy Hem Painter," based on a common stylized treatment of the folds of drapery found in three eighteenth-century hide paintings. The hide painting of the Virgin could well be the product of a converted Pueblo artist, or of a friar less conversant with European visual conventions of three-dimensional rendering and aware of Pueblo symbols. The art historian Donna Pierce notes that there was a flourishing export trade in hides, both plain and painted, in New Mexico as early as the 1630s, when Governor Juan de Eulate set up a sweatshop in Santa Fe "where Indians, both Christianized and unconverted captives, were forced to labor for long hours under conditions of virtual servitude, weaving textiles and painting hides for export." Records reveal that the governor "usually had at least thirty Indians painting textiles and hides, several of whom are identified as Mexican Indians." The hides were acquired from the Apaches and other Plains peoples through trade, or as tribute from indigenous peoples within territory controlled by the Spanish.

The Pueblo Revolt of 1680 (see pp. 35–36) brought an end to the hide industry, but it was re-established after Spain reconquered the territory in 1692–93. Probate records and wills indicate that hide paintings were popular in the eighteenth century both in the mission churches and in the homes of the Spanish. Such paintings were condemned or destroyed in the mid-nineteenth century by the anti-Hispanic religious authorities installed after the conquest of the territory by US armed forces in 1848 (see p. 217). Many, however, were preserved by private citizens and made their way into museums throughout the Southwest in the twentieth century.

The eighteenth century also witnessed the appearance of single-panel paintings and carved wooden statues (*bultos*) of holy figures. While most that remain today are dated to the nineteenth century, a few survive from the eighteenth century. One of the most notable is the *bulto* of the *Santo Entierro* (Holy Entombment) [**1.2.15**]. It was carved by Father Andrés Garcia (active 1747–79) for the mission church of Santa Cruz de la Cañada, just north of Santa Fe. A new church was built in 1732–48, and in 1765 Father Garcia arrived and began decorating the interior.

1.2.15 Father Andrés Garcia: *Santo Entierro* (Holy Entombment), c. 1765–68.
Painted wood
Santa Cruz de la Cañada, New Mexico

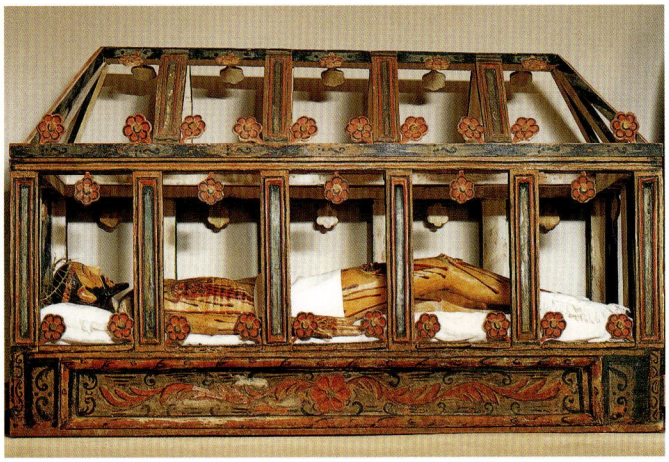

Over the course of three years Garcia created an altar rail, several carved images, a large *retablo* (probably for the high altar), an ornamented arch at the entrance to the sanctuary, and the *Santo Entierro*. In the latter, a life-size wooden figure of Christ lies in a coffin decorated with flowers. Poles at the base indicate that the carving was carried in the ceremonial processions marking Christ's burial, performed during Holy Week. Two fingers are missing from one hand; Drain notes that "*bultos* were considered to have miraculous powers, and local stories tell of pieces of statues being thrown into rising floodwaters to make them subside, or being burnt into ash for signing the faithful with a cross during an epidemic."

New Mexican *bultos* and *retablos* of the crucified Christ created in the eighteenth and nineteenth centuries were often marked by great displays of blood. Garcia's Savior is no exception, with blood streaming from his head, chest, and knees, and from under his loincloth. The historian Ramón Gutiérrez suggests that the blood may have been interpreted by Pueblo viewers "as rain fructifying the earth because blood had always been seen by them as a male nutrient of extraordinary fertilizing power," a meaning paralleled in Christian worship, where Christ's blood was seen as a nutrient.

In number, images of the Virgin Mary rivaled those of Christ in New Mexico. One of the most important was a small statue brought to Santa Fe from Mexico City in 1625 by Friar Alonso de Benavides, the newly appointed head of the missions of New Mexico [**1.2.16**; p. 40]. It was accompanied by its own gilded altarpiece with columns. During the Pueblo Revolt it was rescued by a Spanish woman, Josefa Sambrano de Grijalva, and taken to El Paso, where it came to be known as *La Conquistadora*, in honor of the Virgin's help in spiritual conquest. The statue was returned to Santa Fe in 1693 and housed in a special chapel, completed in 1717. Like *Santo Entierro*, *La Conquistadora* is made of wood, which was then painted. Her body, however, rather than being covered in blood as a sign of suffering and ultimate salvation, is clothed in an elaborate gown and jewels; her head is covered by a wig of long black hair. The Virgin Mary was the benevolent face of Christianity, the intercessor who would convey the prayers of rich and poor alike to her son Jesus and God the Father. *La Conquistadora* was attended with devotion, her costume replaced as it showed signs of age,

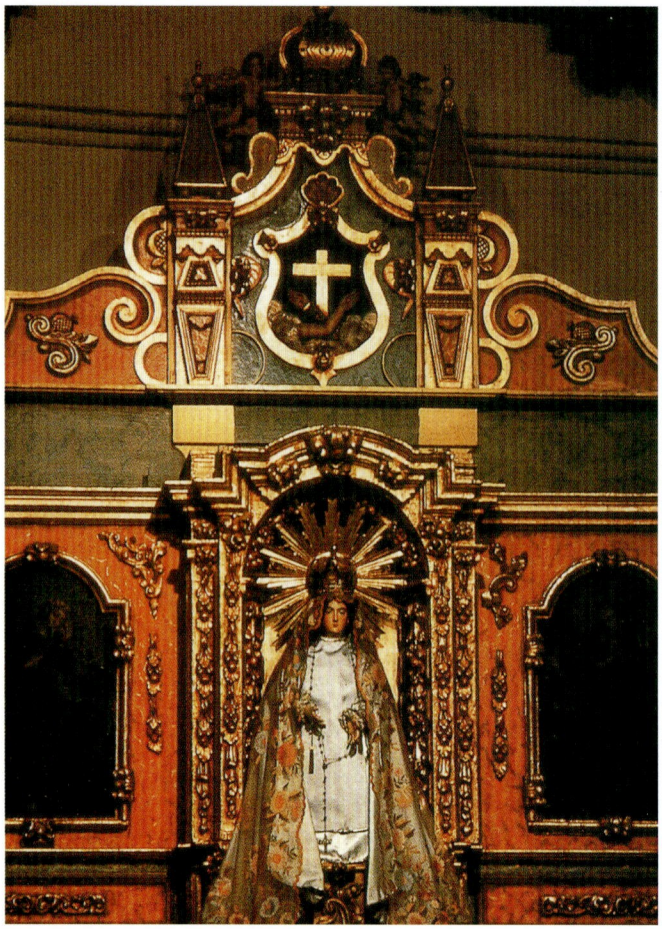

1.2.16 Unknown artist: *Virgin of the Rosary* known as *La Conquistadora*, c. 1625. Painted wood, in a setting completed in 1717
Cathedral of St. Francis, Santa Fe, New Mexico

an indication of the significance of clothing as a sign of power and prestige in both European and indigenous spiritual life (see p. 27). The chapel of La Conquistadora is now all that remains of the eighteenth-century parish church in the present-day Cathedral of St. Francis in Santa Fe.

Texas and Arizona in the Seventeenth and Eighteenth Centuries

The explorations of the French down the Mississippi River to its mouth, and their attempts to establish settlements on the Gulf Coast at the end of the seventeenth century, worried Spanish authorities. They responded by sending both soldiers and missionaries into the territory to the east of New Mexico, a territory that became known as *Tejas* or Texas. In 1690 Alonso de León, governor of the state of Coahuila, just south of Texas, and Friar Damián Massanet led an expedition that resulted in the founding of the San Francisco de los Tejas Mission. It was relocated several times before finding a permanent home in 1731 in San Antonio as the Mission of San Francisco de la Espada (St. Francis of the Sword). Construction of the church began in 1745 and was completed in 1756 [**1.2.17**].

The obvious difference between this church and its New Mexican counterparts [**1.2.8**, p. 34; **1.2.10**, p. 35] is the material out of which it is made—stone rather than adobe. The Coahuiltecans, who inhabited the area when the Spanish arrived, were nomadic and had no tradition of permanent building, living primarily in temporary brush shelters. Thus, those who designed the early Texas missions had no competing architectural models as did the designers in New Mexico. Stone was readily available, and was utilized to replicate the churches the missionaries had left in central New Spain or in Spain itself.

Other more subtle differences between Texan and New Mexican churches can be discerned by comparing the facades of San Francisco de la Espada and San José at Old Laguna Pueblo [**1.2.10**; p. 35]. Both are strikingly simple, marked primarily by a centrally placed door, a rectangular window above, and a stepped screen with openings for bells (three in the case of

1.2.17 Church of the San Francisco de la Espada Mission, San Antonio, Texas, 1745–56.

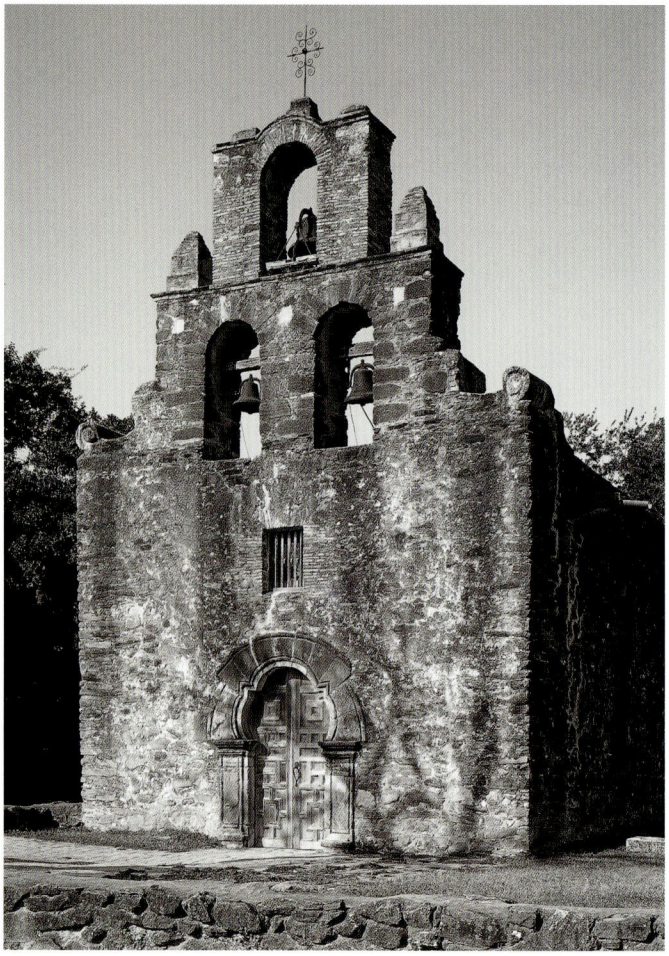

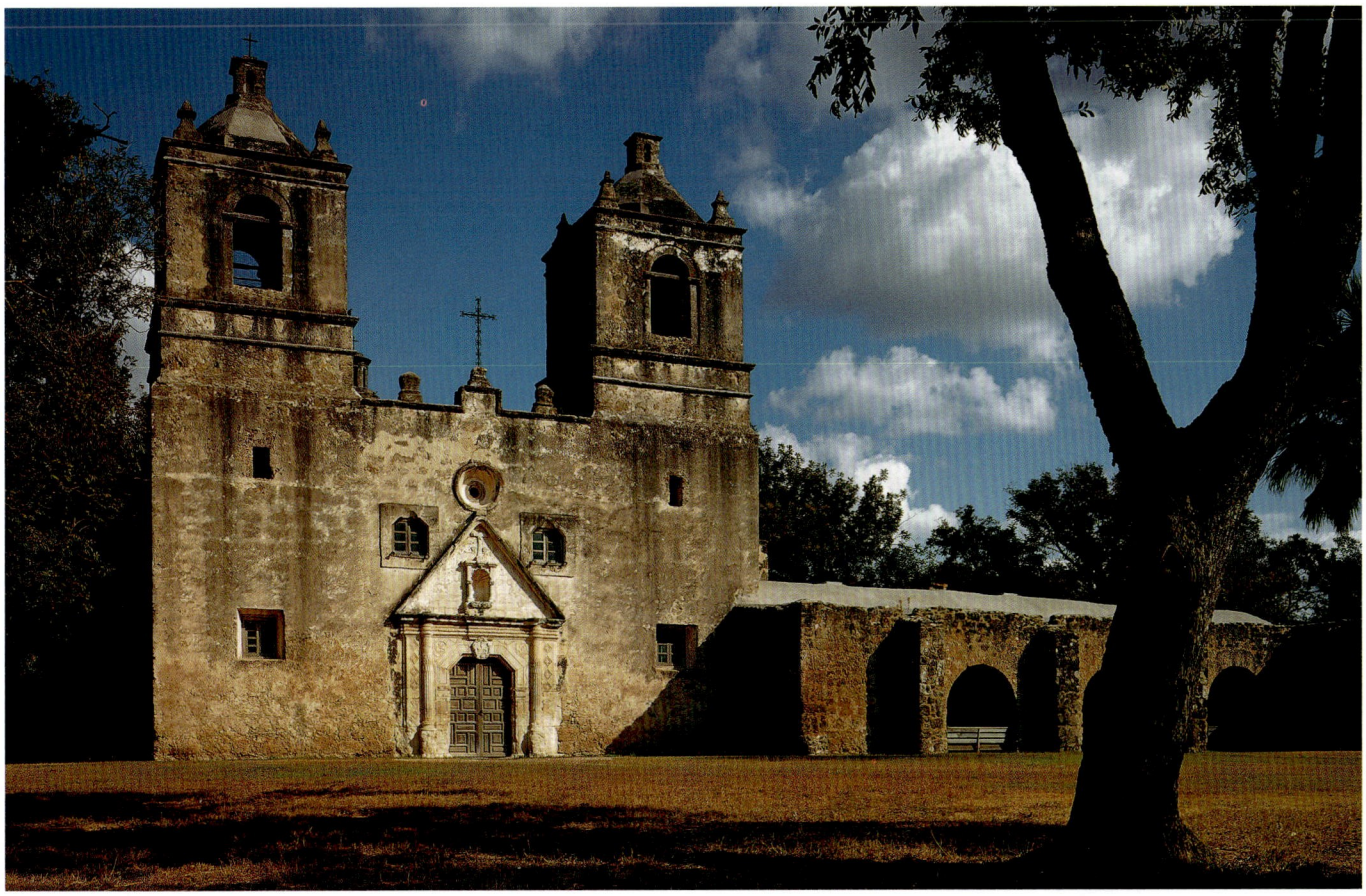

1.2.18 Church of the Nuestra Señora de la Purísima Concepción Mission, San Antonio, Texas, 1740–55.

San Francisco de la Espada, two at San José). The volutes (spiral forms) at the corners of Spanish bell-screens, only suggested at San José, are carefully carved in stone at San Francisco, and the bells are placed in arched, rather than rectangular, openings. The pinnacles on either side of the top bell could be the result of the continuing influence of Moorish architecture in both Spain and New Spain, despite the expulsion of Muslim forces from the Iberian peninsula in 1492 (see p. 20). The door is framed by an unusual trefoil (three-cusped) arch. Drain notes that a number of explanations have been put forward to account for this arch, including the theory that the larger stones at the top should have been on the sides instead. Yet the arch also resembles ones found in Moorish architecture and widely adopted by Spanish builders. The combination of arches and rectangles makes for a more complex facade, but the regularity of the stone and the exactitude with which the forms have been defined also results in a more rigid effect than that of the adobe churches.

An even more ambitious church was being built in San Antonio around the same time as the San Francisco de la Espada Mission. In 1740 the foundation was laid for the Mission of Nuestra Señora de la Purísima Concepción (Our Lady of the Immaculate Conception); the church was completed in 1755 [**1.2.18**]. The facade is marked by a combination of arches (angular-headed in the case of the doorway and two of the windows, Roman for the bell-tower openings), engaged columns, and a pediment that is reminiscent of the sixteenth-century Augustinian monastery at Epazoyucan [**1.1.7**; p. 27], although somewhat less idiosyncratic in its arrangement. The pediment frames a niche that once held a statue, probably of the Virgin Mary. At the apex is an oculus or round window. The entablature, columns, and area to either side of the door are carved with floral and geometric motifs. In addition, on the right side of the door in the upper corner is a representation of the Five Wounds of Christ. It is connected by a knotted Franciscan cord to the Franciscan coat of arms (the crossed arms of Christ and St. Francis, both with wounded palms) on the upper corner of the left side of the door. The two towers are topped by pinnacles at each of their four corners and four-sided pyramidal roofs, which are, in turn, topped by small rectangular structures. The rather understated look of the facade today is deceptive for, according to Drain, it

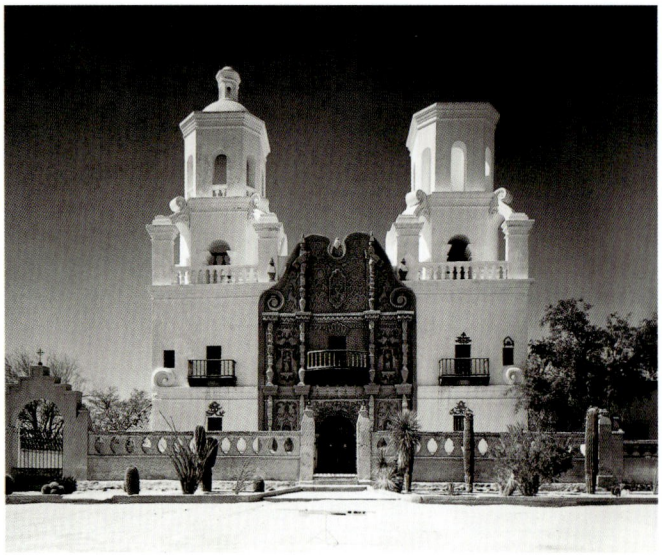

1.2.19 Church of the San Xavier del Bac Mission, Arizona, 1783–97.

1.2.20 Central part of the facade, San Xavier del Bac, Arizona, 1783–97.

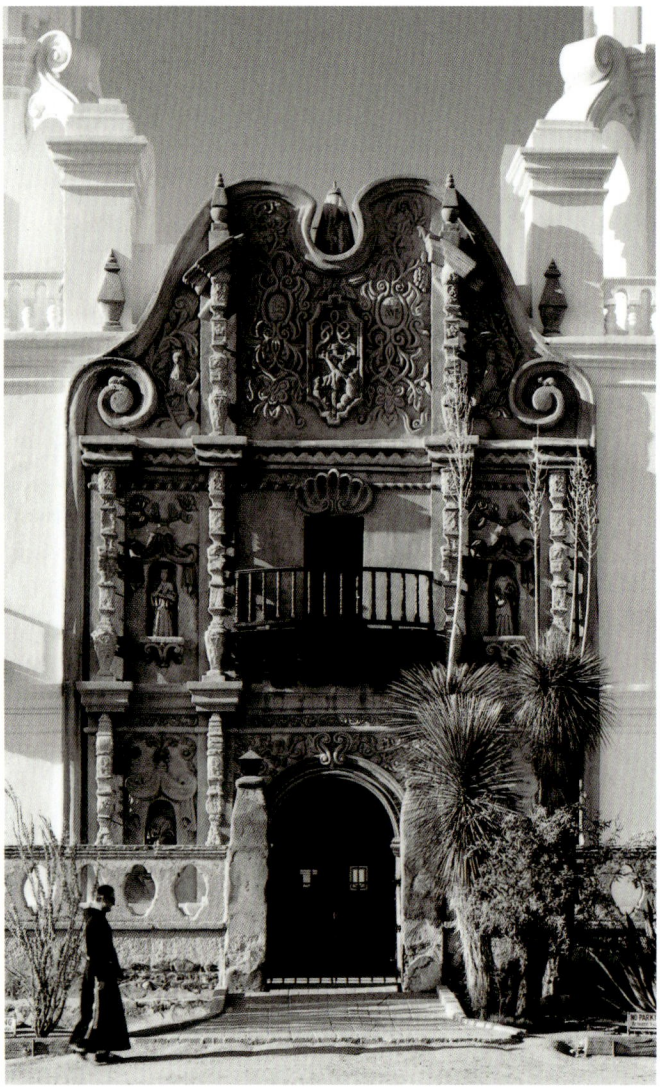

was originally painted, and each stone in the towers was ornamented with a cross-in-circle design.

Whereas the Franciscans were the key missionary force in New Mexico and Texas, the Jesuits laid claim to Arizona, sending the Italian Father Eusebio Kino into the region at the end of the seventeenth century. The most impressive of the missions he established is San Xavier del Bac, just south of present-day Tucson [**1.2.19–1.2.21**]. It was founded in 1692 in the center of the Tohono O'Ohdam (Papago) settlement along the banks of the Santa Cruz River. Father Kino had hoped to find an overland trail to California and to set up a series of missions along the way. While the foundation was laid in 1700, the church was not built until the end of the century (1783–97), well after the death of Kino in 1711. By this time the mission was controlled by the Franciscans. The Jesuits had been expelled from Spanish territories in 1767 by order of King Charles III (Pope Clement XIV suppressed the Jesuit Order in 1773, but it was restored in 1814). The church is composed of fired bricks covered with a lime wash. It incorporates domes, round-headed arches, and flying buttresses (semi-arch-shaped external supports) topped by volutes at the base of the upper bell towers. These forms were missing or very rare in the mission buildings of New Mexico.

The ornate portal, located between the two towers (one was never completed), contains the Franciscan emblem in the center of the top register. On either side of this emblem are the monograms of Jesus and Mary. In niches below are the figures of saints Barbara, Catherine of Siena, Cecilia, and Lucy [**1.2.20**]. Framing the niches are *estípites*, forms that stand in for the shafts of columns but are so extensively carved that their role as a support device is dissolved. This use of the *estípite*, along with the decorative volutes and low-relief vegetal carving, connects San Xavier del Bac to the elaborate ultra-baroque churches of seventeenth- and eighteenth-century New Spain. An example of this style in Mexico City is the Sagrario Metropolitano (1768), the parish church of the Cathedral of Mexico City, designed by Lorenzo Rodríguez (1704–1777) and located next to the Cathedral. The interior of San Xavier del Bac, particularly the high altar [**1.2.21**], also reflects the ornate and crowded interiors of ultra-baroque churches. As in the high altar or *Altar de los Reyes* (1737) of the Cathedral of Mexico City designed by Jerónimo de Balbás (*c.* 1680–1748), almost every square inch of surface is covered with carved and painted figures.

The architectural historian Robert J. Mullen notes that this style of architecture arose in New Spain as a result of the rapid accumulation of wealth by the political and religious elite in the eighteenth century. This increased wealth led to an escalation in competition for power between members of the religious orders (the Franciscans, Dominicans, and Augustinians) on the one

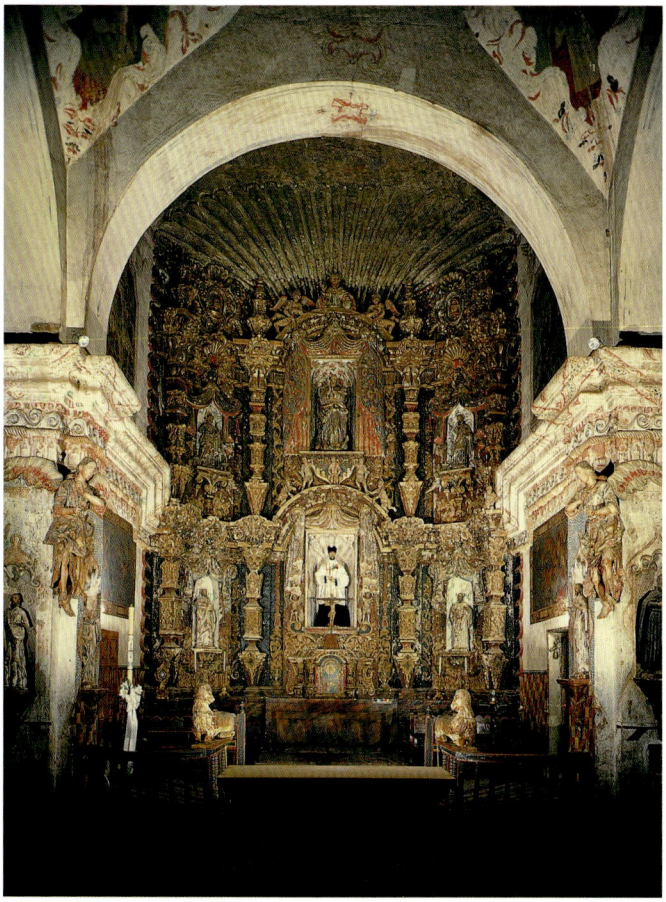

1.2.21 Looking toward the high altar, San Xavier del Bac, Arizona, late 18th century.

hand, who enjoyed considerable independence in the sixteenth and seventeenth centuries, and the bishops on the other. The bishops ultimately gained the upper hand, with elaborate cathedrals in urban centers standing as monuments to their religious authority. Yet the ultra-baroque style also spread eventually to churches in small towns in central New Spain and to the northern frontier.

Battle Scenes on Hide: Segesser I and II

After the death of Father Kino, another Jesuit, Father Philipp von Segesser von Brunegg, oversaw San Xavier del Bac from 1732 to 1735, before being transferred to a mission to the south in the region known as Pimería Baja (San Xavier del Bac was in Pimería Alta). In letters to his family in Switzerland, Father Philipp recorded indigenous uprisings involving the local Pimas and their enemies the Apaches, as well as the Yaquis and Seris to the south [see **1.0.2**; p. 19]. These attacks grew in frequency in the late 1730s and lasted until the 1760s (Father Philipp died in 1762).

Father Philipp also sent to his family in 1758 a box containing what he termed three "colored skins." Two have survived. Each is made up of three large, rectangular pieces of tanned hide, likely buffalo, sewn together with sinew. Gottfried Hotz, in a detailed study of the hide paintings, argues that their elaborate scenes represent battles between different groups of indigenous peoples and between Mexican, French, and indigenous soldiers. Through a careful analysis of geography, vegetation, costumes, hairstyles, and architecture, he has attempted to identify the subject matter.

In the case of the first, designated Segesser I [**1.2.22**], this identification is only tentative. It may, Hotz suggests, depict an unrecorded battle around 1700 that took place

> either on the Sierra Madre Plateau near Sonora... against Gila Apaches, traditional enemies of the Sonora Indians and of the Spaniards, or in the southeastern part of New Mexico, west of the Pecos River, against Faraon Apaches (later called Mescalero Apaches).

Hotz speculates that the attackers are probably "members of a southern nation—most likely Tarascans or Tarascan half-bloods." Soldiers from indigenous allied groups were used to strengthen the forces sent out during the reconquest of New Mexico (see p. 36). They were often outfitted with Spanish weapons and uniforms, yet maintained distinctive traits, such as hairstyles. This combination is seen here, where the short hair and types of headdresses recall those in carved reliefs and codices of central New Spain.

Hotz is more confident of his identification of the participants depicted in Segesser II [**1.2.23**; p. 44]. This hide painting, he argues, presents the surprise attack and defeat of the Spanish

1.2.22 Unknown artist: Segesser I, *c.* 1720–29: detail of battle scene. Painting on hide, overall size *c.* 19 ft. x 4 ft. 6 in. (6 x 1.5 m.) Palace of the Governors, Museum of New Mexico, Santa Fe

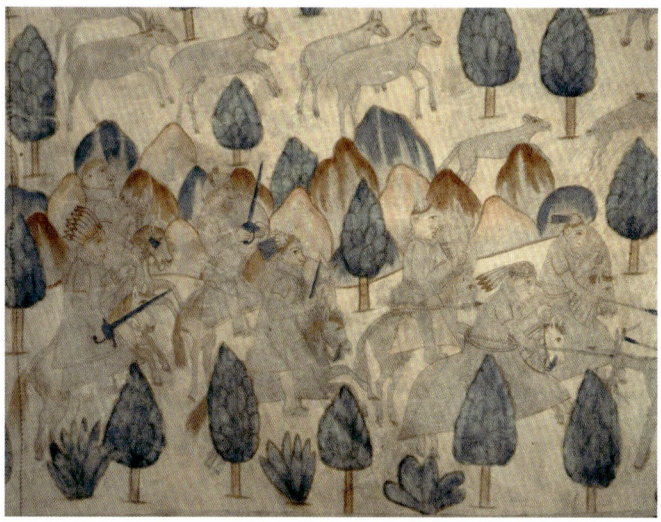

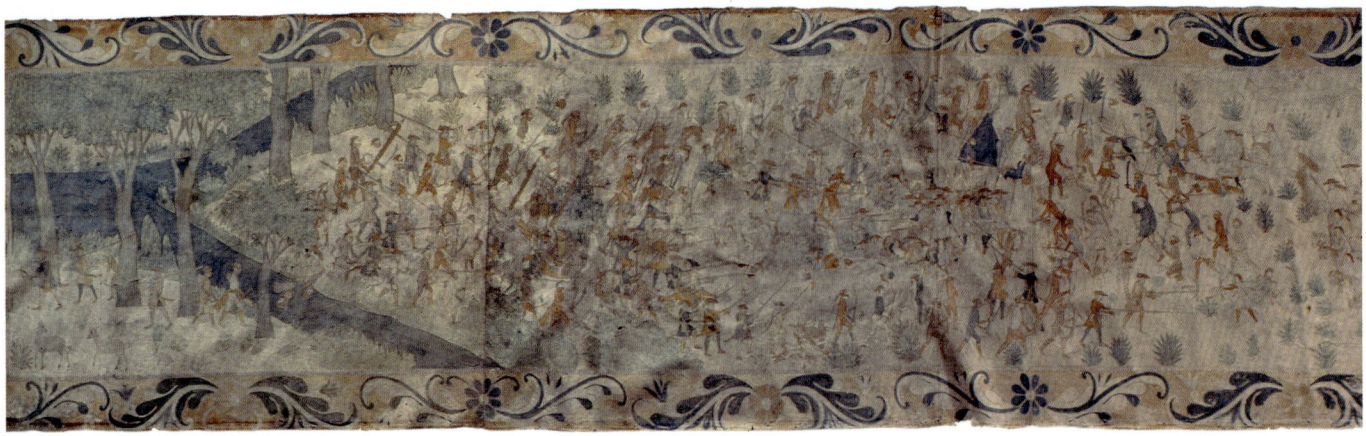

1.2.23 Unknown artist: Segesser II, *c.* 1720–29.
Painting on hide, *c.* 19 ft. x 4 ft. 6 in. (6 x 1.5 m.)
Palace of the Governors, Museum of New Mexico, Santa Fe

at the conjunction of the Platte and Loup rivers in Nebraska by the Skidi Pawnees and Otos. The Spanish troops numbered forty-five, with sixty Pueblo soldiers and a Spanish priest. Their leader was Pedro de Villasur, who had been sent northeast from Santa Fe in 1720 by Governor Antonio Valverde Cosio to determine the extent of the French presence in the region. Of this unit, sixty-three survived the attack. The painter includes several French soldiers with rifles among the attacking forces, perhaps in order to help Governor Valverde explain the defeat to the viceroy of New Spain. There is no hard evidence of French participation in the attack, although both the French and the Spanish spread rumors to this effect.

In attempting to determine who painted Segesser I and II, Hotz looked first at the tanning process, paint composition, and method of paint application. He found that all three resembled methods and materials used by Plains peoples, such as the Mandan. Yet when he looked at the style and iconography of Plains painted hides, he found significant differences. They tended to be marked by profile depictions of both animals and humans, with few facial features. There was also an absence of background or setting, an attention to outline with no highlights or shadows to give the illusion of depth, and geometric body parts (e.g. torsos, thighs). A Mandan buffalo robe from around 1800 contains many of these characteristics [**1.2.24**]. Stylistic similarities can be found between the Segesser hide paintings and the preconquest codices of the Aztecs and other peoples of central Mexico [**1.1.3**; p. 22]. Yet there are greater similarities between Segesser I and II and the post-conquest codices of New Spain, such as the *Florentine Codex* [**1.1.5**; p. 25], which contain the same mix of Spanish and indigenous peoples as well as two- and three-dimensional renderings of figures and landscapes.

Many scholars believe the hides were painted by Spanish-trained artists in New Mexico who had available eye-witness accounts of the battles. Hotz argues that an indigenous person or persons—Tlaxcalan, Tarascan or Pueblo—or someone of mixed heritage painted them, drawing on a tradition of image-making brought north from central New Spain. He also notes that the Spaniards in Segesser II have much more individuality than the French or Pawnees, suggesting further that the artist was a member of their camp. Whoever painted the hides drew inspiration from European prints depicting either battle or hunt scenes, and may also have had in mind the elegant tapestries that were popular in the royal courts of Europe.

The figures in Segesser II are rendered more convincingly than those in Segesser I, with a greater attention to three-dimensionality and accurate bodily proportions, and a greater ability to

1.2.24 Unknown artist, Mandan: buffalo robe, collected by Lewis and Clark in 1805.
Painted hide, l. 7 ft. (2 m.)
Peabody Museum, Harvard University, Cambridge, Massachusetts

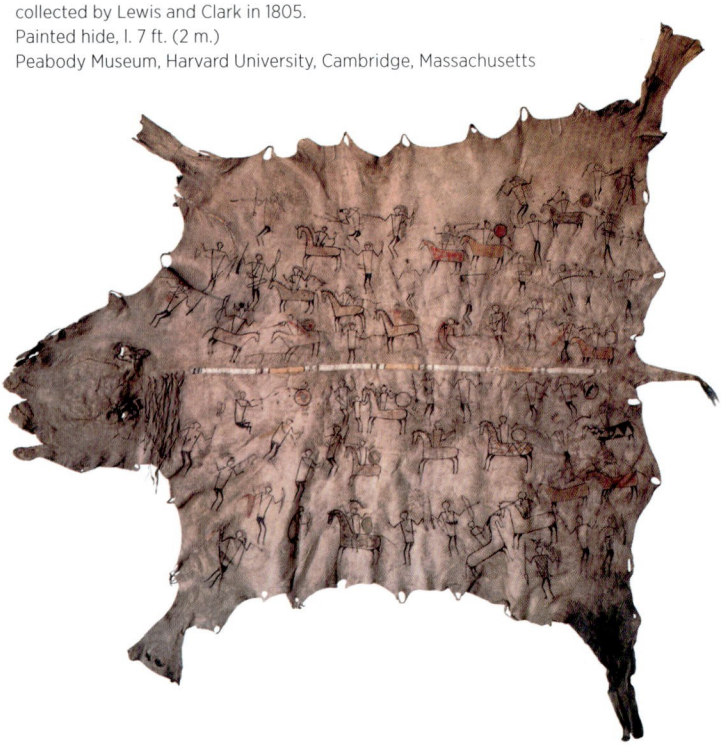

convey movement. Thus, if the same artist painted both works, then Segesser I was painted first, with Segesser II representative of a more developed, Europeanized style. Hotz suggests that Valverde may well have commissioned Segesser II as part of his defense of the Villasur expedition. Perhaps he commissioned Segesser I to commemorate another of his expeditions, for the two paintings appear to have been pendants. They are the same size and have similar borders. The fact that Father Philipp acquired both also suggests that they were in the possession of the same individual. Unfortunately, few such narrative hide paintings from the eighteenth century have survived, so it is impossible to tell if the general arrangement of Segesser I and II was common to many other works. What is clear, however, is that they provide another example of the interconnections of traditions and technologies that marked much of the art produced on New Spain's northern frontier.

The Californian Missions

As early as 1533 a small Spanish expedition explored the coast of Baja California, followed by a more ambitious venture by Juan Rodríguez Cabrillo in 1542. Commissioned by the Viceroy of New Spain to seek a water passage linking the Atlantic and Pacific, Cabrillo traveled at least as far north as present-day San Francisco and possibly to Cape Mendocino. He made contact with several groups of indigenous peoples, noting their physical features, dress, and weapons. In the latter half of the century many Spanish galleons passed along the coast on trading expeditions to the Philippines and China, although these were curtailed after 1588 due to attacks by the British under the leadership of Sir Francis Drake. Sebastián Vizcaíno was sent back up the coast in 1602 to produce detailed maps that would ultimately aid in the settling of this territory.

No attempt was made to establish permanent settlements, however, until the last half of the eighteenth century, with the first mission founded by Franciscans in the south at San Diego in 1769. Two years later another was established slightly north of San Diego, at San Gabriel. The historian Douglas Monroy opens his book *Thrown Among Strangers, The Making of Mexican Culture in Frontier California* with a look at the differing views of this second encounter between indigenous inhabitants and newcomers, as related by each side. According to interviews conducted in the early nineteenth century, the inhabitants of Yang-na (present-day Los Angeles) and other villages in the surrounding area at first thought the Spaniards were gods because of their ability to create fire. But when they saw a Spaniard kill a bird with a musket, they knew the Spaniards were men, because their own gods were givers, not takers, of life. They refused to eat the corn and beans proffered to them because each world had its own food, and theirs was acorns, deer, coyote, other small animals and birds, and roasted grasshoppers. According to the Franciscans' journals, friars who arrived in 1771 were met by

> a great multitude of savages [who] with frightful yells attempted to prevent the founding of the Mission.... One of the Fathers produced a canvas picture of Our Lady of Sorrows, [and] at the sight of it they became as if transfixed in wonderment, and all of them threw their bows and arrows on the ground, as "Tomeares" or Chiefs took from around their necks the necklaces they value so highly...and placed them at the feet of the Sovereign Queen of the Angels.

Father Junípero Serra, who led the Franciscans in founding the missions of California, provided another account of the transfixing effect of the image of the Virgin:

> As for the Indian women, when the Fathers showed them a beautiful painting of the Most Blessed Mary, artistically executed,...they were so taken with it that they could not tear themselves away from it. They went to their homes and came back loaded down with seeds and provisions, which they offered to the holy image....The very sight of how intent they were, and how much in earnest, touched one to the heart, and made one feel sure that they would pay even greater homage to the Great Queen when in the light of the faith they would come to know how exalted she was.

Men and women alike, the friars observed, were in awe of the Virgin Mary. According to the art historian Cynthia Neri Lewis, Serra was particularly fond of the painter José de Páez, who lived and worked in Mexico City. The friar imported several of Páez's paintings of the Virgin Mary and other Christian saints to adorn the missions of California. Images thus entered early on into the conversion and colonizing efforts of the Franciscans in this region, although their evaluation of the power of these images may well have been exaggerated. They would soon have to admit that paintings of the Virgin were not enough to gain the cooperation of the local peoples, and that more aggressive measures would have to be taken.

The great variety of environmental settings in the region encompassed by the current borders of California was matched in the eighteenth century by an equal variety of indigenous cultures. The precarious nature of food supplies in the desert areas resulted in small communities that shifted with the seasons. In the northwest, abundant marine resources allowed for larger, more complex social organizations, including villages with plank houses. In all there were approximately ninety different languages, with several hundred dialects, spoken. Estimates of the population of California at the time of the arrival of the Franciscans in 1769 range between 100,000 and 300,000.

The southern part of the present state was occupied by people who spoke Shoshonean, part of the Uto-Aztecan family of languages, or derivatives of Hokan stock (Chumash to the north, Yuman to the south) that had much older roots in the region. In contrast to the Pueblo economic and social order, they were patrilineal, with inheritance traced through the male line. They were also semi-nomadic, engaging in hunting and gathering. Their spiritual world was based on a belief that everything in nature—plants, animals, humans—had an existence or a "spirit," and that a careful balance had to be maintained between all parts of nature in order for humans to flourish. Social balance was also maintained through a system of gift-giving, where the power of a leader depended not only on his ability to amass wealth (stored foods or other consumables), but also on his willingness to give this wealth away. The various groups engaged in warfare with one another and also in trade. The Chumash in the Santa Barbara area would export steatite or soapstone, wooden vessels, beads, white pigment, and various dried fish, while importing black pigment, antelope and elk skins, obsidian, salt, and piñon nuts.

Villages in the south were composed of a series of round or conical huts of pliable poles supporting reeds, branches, and/or grasses, arranged in rows or clusters. The shape of the huts may have been related to the importance of the circle in spiritual life and of a cyclical view of time, determined most obviously by the seasons. The circle was also the distinctive shape of the baskets made by women that were used to gather, store, cook, and eat food as well as for ritual or everyday headgear. Basketry had a long tradition in the region, dating back to at least 5500–4800 BCE. Baskets functioned as important gift or trade items and as markers of special initiation rites. As the prized possessions of an individual, they were burned at the person's death or buried with him or her. They were also valued as prized possessions by the Spanish, as is indicated by the response of those who accompanied Juan Bautista de Anza, charged in 1774 with forging an overland route from Sonora north to Monterey. According to Christopher Moser in his book *Native American Basketry of Southern California*, "entire villages were depleted of baskets by the Spanish, who desired them as gifts for people in Mexico and Spain." There was a similar vogue among the French (and later British) for birch-bark boxes produced in the first half of the eighteenth century in New France [**1.3.6**; p. 54]. These early baskets were marked by abstract geometrical designs or stylized plant or animal motifs. Their symmetry may relate to the larger belief in the need for balance between humans and nature.

As in New Mexico, the Franciscan friars attempted to alter the social relations and spiritual beliefs of the local populations. In a series of twenty-one missions established along the coast a day's travel apart, a stone-and-adobe architecture of rectangles replaced a conical architecture of saplings, grasses, and mud. A life of stasis replaced one of movement and freedom. A fully clothed body replaced a naked or partially clothed body. Food produced at the mission supplemented or replaced the meat and plants acquired through hunting and gathering. Metal and porcelain dishes and storage containers joined baskets. People were renamed according to the names of their missions—e.g. Gabrielinos, Fernandeños, Luiseños, Diegueños, Obispeños. The German naturalist, explorer, and artist Ferdinand Deppe captures these contrasts between architecture and ways of life in a painting of around 1832. It depicts both the San Gabriel Mission in the background and a Chumash or Gabrielino conical grass house in the foreground [**1.2.25**]. Left to the viewer's imagination is the inevitable disruption to indigenous life that this coming together of two worlds entailed.

The friars found the indigenous peoples of southern California essential as converts and also as conscripted labor for the agricultural and commercial activities that turned the missions, by the early nineteenth century, into highly profitable enterprises. They were employed in construction, adobe brick making, candle making, hide cleaning and tanning, laundry, and cooking, and contributed to the decoration of the mission churches.

In 1792 twenty artisans arrived from Mexico City at the San Gabriel Mission to train the indigenous converts in masonry, carpentry, tailoring, and leatherworking. The church was constructed from 1800 to 1806, but suffered extensive damage during an earthquake in December of 1812 and had to be

1.2.25 Ferdinand Deppe: *San Gabriel Mission*, c. 1832.
Oil on canvas, 27 x 37 in. (68.6 x 94 cm.)
Santa Barbara Mission Archive Library, Santa Barbara, California

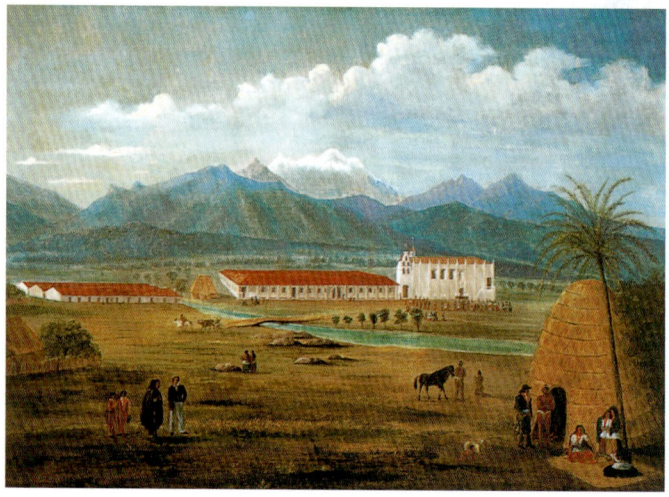

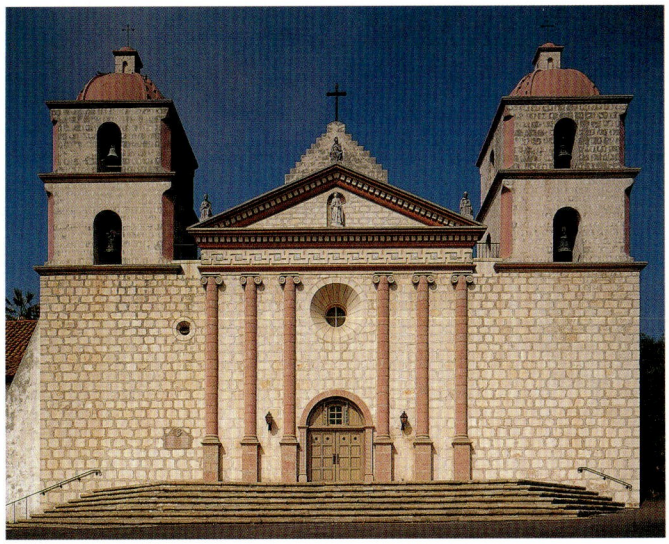

1.2.26 Church of the Santa Barbara Mission, Santa Barbara, California, 1815–20.

largely rebuilt. The new church was of adobe brick, with walls as much as 6 feet (1.8 meters) thick and 30 feet (9 meters) high. A far more elaborate church was built further up the coast at the Santa Barbara Mission [**1.2.26**]. Erected in 1815–20 by Chumash laborers around the remains of an earlier earthquake-damaged church, it draws heavily on the treatise of the ancient Roman architect Vitruvius (died 15 CE), an edition of which was present in the mission library. The church facade is dominated by a temple front, with thin, elongated Ionic columns (distinguished by the opposing volutes that make up the capital or top of the column), a decorated frieze, and pediment, to which is added a stepped gable. It is dedicated to St. Barbara (see p. 37), a Christian Roman virgin beheaded by her pagan father because of her faith. She is represented by the statue in the central niche and is joined by statues of the three theological virtues—Faith, Hope, and Charity—on the pediment above.

St. Barbara appears again, in much more colorful form, above the high altar, flanked by the Virgin and St. Joseph, with St. Francis and St. Dominic below [**1.2.27**]. The high altar also has four pairs of Ionic columns, painted to resemble marble, attached to the wall, as well as painted simulations of drapery and niches. This imitation of marble and other expensive materials (*trompe l'oeil* painting) is found throughout the Santa Barbara Mission and in other California missions. It can be seen, in part, as an imaginative response by the friars to the shortage of these materials and/or of skilled artisans.

While indigenous peoples were working on the construction and decoration of mission churches, they also continued to produce such items as baskets for their own use and for

1.2.27 Unknown artist: high altar, Santa Barbara Mission, Santa Barbara, California.

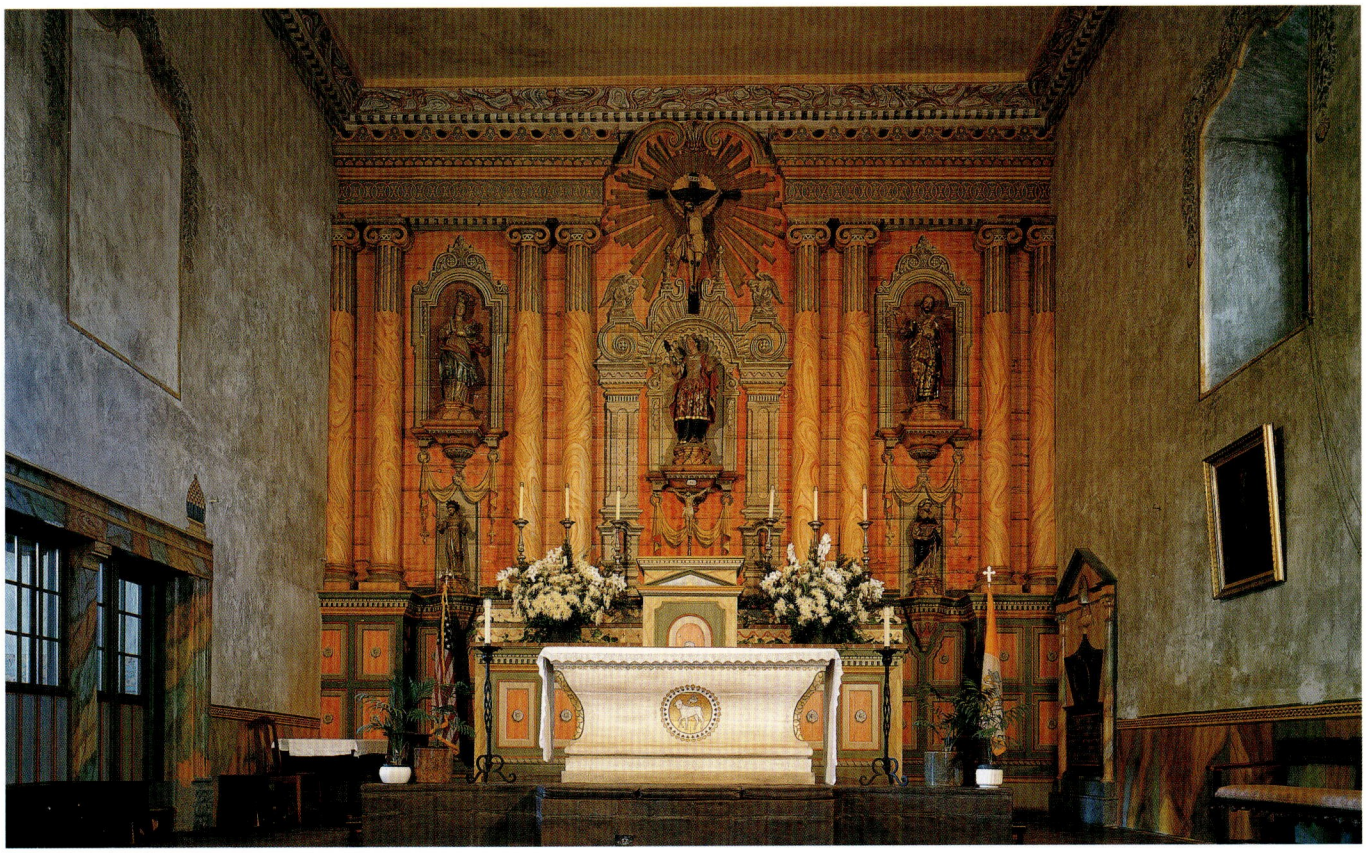

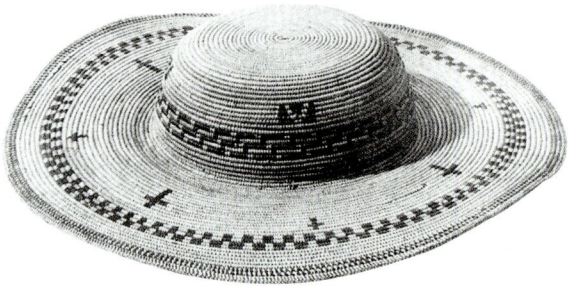

1.2.28 Unknown artist, Chumash: coiled hat, presented to George Vancouver at Santa Barbara, California, in 1793. Juncus reed, d. 15¼ in. (38.7 cm.) British Museum, London

trade. During his explorations of the West Coast in the 1790s, the British captain George Vancouver received, among other gifts, a coiled hat made by a Chumash woman that combined traditional geometric Chumash design motifs and the Christian cross [**1.2.28**]. Its shape, with a brim, is patterned after the sombreros worn by the friars (the hats of local peoples did not have brims). Special presentation baskets were also commissioned. In the early nineteenth century Maria Marta (born *c.* 1766) from the San Buenaventura Mission, whose indigenous name was Lapulimeu, created such a basket, with four repeating motifs derived from a colonial 8 reales or peso coin, showing the crown and shield of Spain flanked by the Pillars of Hercules [**1.2.29**]. On the rim she inscribed, in Spanish: "María Marta neofita de la mision de el Serafico Doctor San Buenaventura me hizo an," which translates: "María Marta, neophyte of the Mission of the Seraphic Doctor San Buenaventura, made me in the yr..." Scholars have posited that "an" was the beginning of the word "año" or "year," and that Marta ran out of space to complete the word and add the date. Between the four "coins" are vertical motifs that Moser suggests are some sort of masked figure or possibly clouds with rain descending. Regularly repeating geometrical designs complete the decoration. While a few other surviving baskets from the late eighteenth and early nineteenth centuries have inscriptions identifying the artist, the makers of most are unknown.

1.2.29 Maria Marta (Lapulimeu), Chumash: presentation basket made at the San Buenaventura Mission, California, early 1800s. Juncus reed, d. 15½ in. (39.3 cm.) Phoebe Hearst Museum, University of California at Berkeley

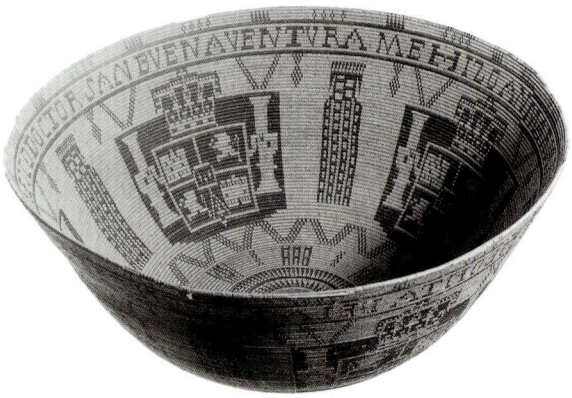

When the Franciscans arrived in California at the end of the eighteenth century, they were charged not only with converting the local people, but also with making them citizens of New Spain. The architectural historian Stanley Young notes:

> In theory each mission was a temporary institution that held all wealth and property in trust for the local Indians. Once the natives were appropriately civilized, the missions were to give up their stewardship of the land to create a pueblo for the Indians.

In practice, however, such a transfer never took place. With Mexican independence in 1821, the new government began the secularization of the missions, a process completed in the 1830s. All Spanish-born friars were expelled and the land theoretically became the property of those indigenous peoples who had converted to Christianity. Mexican settlers who had previously been unable to own land were now able to purchase it from these new owners. Most, however, simply took it, paying little if anything. The "Mission Indians" now worked as blacksmiths, *vaqueros* (cowboys), or servants on the new Mexican ranches for masters who often treated them as poorly as had the friars. They continued to contribute their labor to the creation of buildings and objects that would come to represent Mexican culture in the region in the first half of the nineteenth century.

Review Questions

1 What architectural and artistic influences did the Spanish missionaries bring with them to the northern regions of New Spain?

2 Why was the circulation of prints from Europe so important in northern New Spain?

3 How were the mission churches of New Mexico similar to those of Texas? How were they different?

4 What are some of the ways in which art historians have interpreted the iconography and style of the Segesser I and II hide paintings? Who do they think created them?

5 How is Mexico's colonial past still present in the US today?

CHAPTER 3

New France: Contact Zones and Cultural Production

(*c.* 200 BCE–1760 CE)

Material Exchange: The Impact of Trade on Indigenous Culture

When the French arrived in the northeastern portion of the North American continent they found no vast empire state with elaborate tribute systems, urban centers, and extensive agriculture as did the Spanish further south (see pp. 20–21). Instead, they encountered numerous relatively small communities with intricate alliance and trade networks. These communities engaged in horticulture, fishing, and hunting, and initially incorporated the trade imperatives introduced by the French into their existing social and economic worlds. Their relative mobility and adaptability to a rich but often harsh northern landscape, coupled with the small numbers of French colonizers that arrived in the late sixteenth and early seventeenth centuries, meant they were able to maintain their independence during the first century of contact.

The first Europeans to explore the territory that would become the colony of New France were Norse sailors, who came via Iceland and Greenland beginning in the eleventh century. While their settlements in Greenland lasted approximately five hundred years (982–*c.* 1500), those on the mainland of the North American continent were short-lived, due, historians speculate, to conflict with the indigenous inhabitants. The first person enlisted by the French government to explore this region was the Italian navigator Giovanni da Verrazzano, who sailed north from North Carolina to Newfoundland in 1524. The Frenchman Jacques Cartier arrived in 1534 and explored the Gulf of St Lawrence, returning to France with two indigenous Huron youths who acted as guides on his second voyage, which took place the following year.

On October 2, 1535, Cartier arrived at the Huron town of Hochelaga, the site of present-day Montreal. According to his account of the event, he was greeted by more than a thousand people with gifts of corn and bread. The town was composed of fifty multi-room houses made of sapling frames covered with sheets of bark (the basic building system in the region), grouped around a central plaza and surrounded by fortifications. Close by were fields of corn. A sketch made shortly after Cartier's arrival, and later engraved by the Italian Giovanni Battista Ramusio, combines abstracted and illusionistic renderings to convey his understanding of the organization of the town and its relationship to the surrounding landscape [**1.3.1**]. A later drawing, *c.* 1750, of the Mohawk town of Caughnawaga

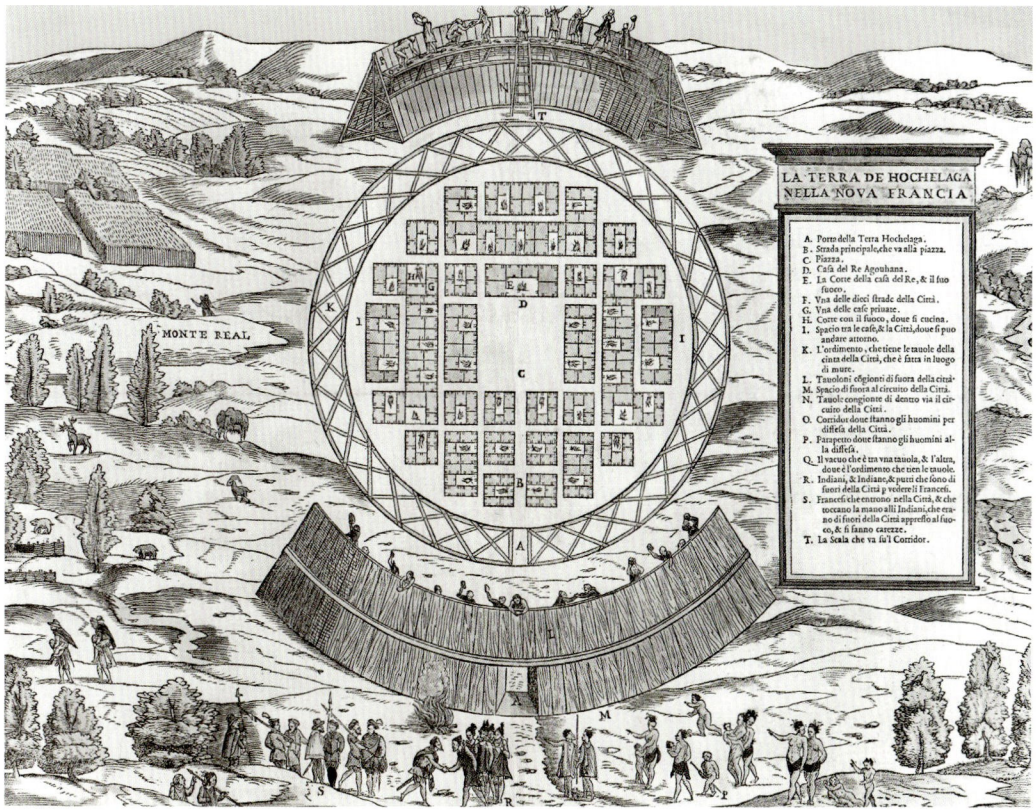

1.3.1 The Huron town of Hochelaga, *c.* 1535; the French appear at the lower left.
Engraving from Giovanni Battista Ramusio, *Navigationi et viaggi*, 1556.
Public Archives of Canada

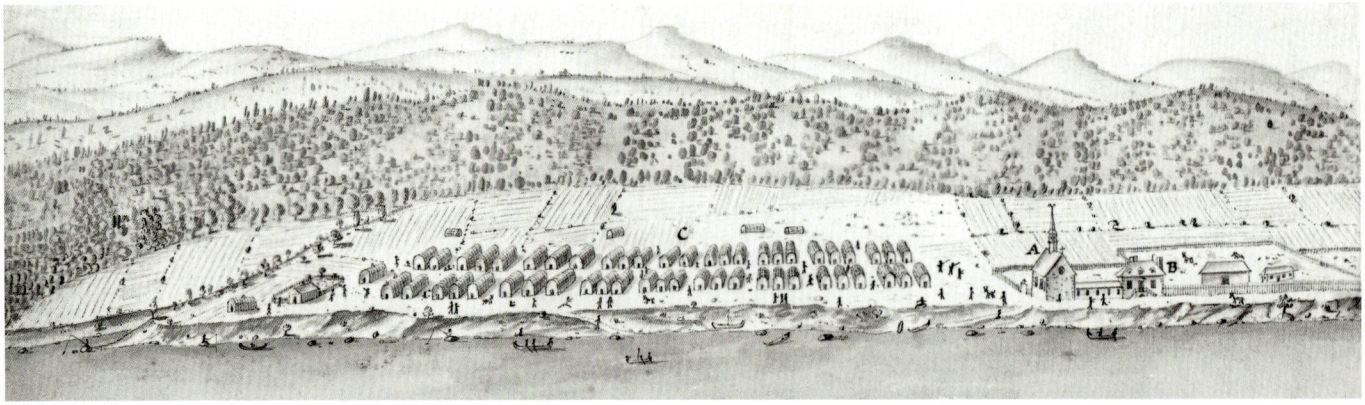

1.3.2 Unknown artist: the Mohawk town of Caughnawaga ("Sault St. Louis") on the St. Lawrence River, *c.* 1750. The key indicates: **a** church, **b** house of the missionary, and **c** "huts or village of the savages."
Drawing on paper (detail)
Bibliothèque Nationale de France, Paris

on the St. Lawrence [**1.3.2**] gives a clearer indication of the shape and arrangement of longhouses in Mohawk and Huron villages. They ranged from 40 to 400 feet (12 to 122 meters) in length and from 20 to 30 feet (6 to 9 meters) in width. The buildings of the Jesuit missionaries are shown to the right.

In the sixteenth century the eastern woodlands (southeastern Ontario and northern New York State) were occupied by two loose confederacies. The northwestern part of this region was home to the Huron, Erie, Tobacco, and Neutral; the southeastern portion to the League of the Iroquois, or Five Nations, made up of the Seneca, Cayuga, Onondaga, Oneida, and Mohawk. Each group sent representatives to ceremonial feasts and conferences to settle disputes, thus limiting blood feuding and warfare.

The League of the Iroquois was the strongest of the two confederacies. While feared as warriors, the Iroquois were also known for the quality of their social relationships, which focused on politeness and hospitality to both friends and strangers. They were matrilineal and matrilocal: children lived with their mother's clan, and men moved into their wives' longhouses at marriage. The women tended the children, made clothing and household goods, and took care of the crops (corn, beans, squash, sunflowers), which may have provided up to 80 percent of their diet. The men conducted wars, cleared land, hunted, fished, traded, carved ceremonial objects, and constructed the dwellings. The Iroquois conceptualized their League as a vast longhouse stretching from west to east. The Seneca were the "Keepers of the Western Door," the Mohawk the "Keepers of the Eastern Door," and the Onondaga both the "Keepers of the Council Fire" and the "Keepers of the Wampum Belts."

Wampum belts were significant objects in maintaining relations within and across indigenous communities in the region. They were composed of white and purple or black shells strung by women in various designs. According to the historian Daniel Richter, pre-sixteenth-century belts were made from the shells of whelks or marine snails (white) and quahog clams (dark purple). While the size and shape of the beads varied, most were disk-shaped. The type of wampum we are most familiar with—small tubular shell beads drilled for stringing—was a cross-cultural product made with iron tools obtained from Europeans. It was probably invented by peoples indigenous to the southern New England coast—the Pequot or Narragansetts—in the sixteenth century, and then introduced into Iroquois territory through traditional exchange networks.

The designs on wampum belts functioned as mnemonic devices, reminders of the terms of treaties or trade negotiations. The belts were carefully prepared for presentation at gatherings of indigenous leaders, or of leaders from both indigenous and European groups. As gifts, they were significant symbols of the power of the giver to enter into negotiations as a representative of his people. Within indigenous communities, the recipients often broke up the belts and distributed the beads to their followers. The beads would then enter into personal or community stores that would be drawn upon to construct more belts as occasion demanded. One of the most famous belts from the seventeenth century, said to have been given to the French explorer Samuel de Champlain in 1611, commemorates the Four Nations of the Huron with four highly abstracted human forms [**1.3.3**].

In their book *Native Americans: Five Centuries of Changing Images*, Patricia Trenton and Patrick Houlihan discuss the symbolism of the colors white and purple in wampum belts:

> Among the Northeastern Woodland Indians white shell was a metaphor for light and life, and in social rituals, such as treaties, for consensus, harmony, and peace. Purple bead strings and belts connoted death and mourning, and by the mid-18th century other matters of grave importance

> as well....The white field denotes a social context and connotes a peaceful message, while the figurative pictographs of purple beads carry the specific meaning.

There were, however, some exceptions to this use of white for the background and purple or black for the figurative elements, as seen in the Champlain belt. The use of dark beads for the background may indicate the gravity of the event commemorated.

The Dutch were the first to exploit wampum in their trade with the Iroquois. They purchased the belts from Algonquians in southern New England and then traded them to the Iroquois for furs. The Dutch had established a fur trading post called Fort Nassau on the Hudson River (present-day Albany, NY) in 1614, six years after they had sponsored the exploration of the river by its namesake, the British navigator Henry Hudson. This trade in wampum resulted in the production of unprecedented quantities of the beads, leading to a drastic decline in their value. Between 1641 and 1658 the value of wampum against specie fell 60 percent; in the 1660s it fell even further. In addition, the material composition of the belts began to change, as European glass beads replaced the original shell beads.

The arrival of French, Dutch, and British traders and settlers in the seventeenth century had a significant impact on the social order of indigenous communities in the Northeast. Not only did firearms give certain groups military advantage over their neighbors, but the emphasis on trading in furs and on warfare also gave men more power. Furthermore, acquiring food through trade reduced the energy devoted to agriculture. The availability of metal pots and dishes created less of a demand for, or interest in making, the watertight baskets formerly used for eating. Conversely, indigenous peoples also had an impact on European explorers and settlers. The French learned a great deal from them about the art of trapping, farming techniques, and the use of plants for medicinal purposes.

Initially the exchange between Europeans and indigenous peoples in the Northeast was on a relatively equal footing, with the superior firepower of the former offset by the larger numbers of the latter. The Europeans wanted furs, and the indigenous peoples wanted iron axes, beads, and guns. Often these metal and glass objects were incorporated into existing belief and value systems as yet another category of foreign objects with certain powers. Ultimately, however, the pressures brought to bear on indigenous peoples by the increasing numbers of Europeans eroded the stability of their communities and made it more difficult to maintain their own cultural traditions.

One of the major pressures came in the form of new diseases. As in New Spain, populations were decimated by such European ailments as smallpox and measles. Iroquois healers brought to bear all of their powers in attempting to cope with these new plagues. Healing in Iroquois communities was carried out primarily by members of the Society of Faces (or False Face Society). Its origin is recounted in a legend involving a contest between the Creator of the World and the first False Face spirit, also known as the Great Defender, over who would ultimately rule the world. Robert Ritzenthaler, in his study of Iroquois masks, relates it as follows:

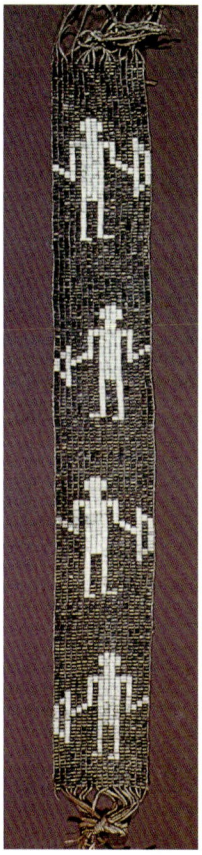

1.3.3 Unknown artist, Huron: wampum belt commemorating the Four Nations of the Huron, said to have been presented to Samuel de Champlain in 1611. Musée de l'Homme, Paris

> The False-face shook his giant rattle and commanded a mountain to come to him, but it moved only part of the way. Then the Creator summoned the mountain and it moved in back of False-face, who impatiently turned around and struck his face against it. He broke his nose and twisted his mouth in pain. The Creator then charged False-face with the task of driving disease from the earth. False-face agreed to give the Indians the power to cure by the blowing of hot ashes on a sick person. The Indians, in turn, were to carve masks in his image and make him offerings of respect, such as tobacco and corn mush.

The particular features of the False Face masks were said to appear to a man in a dream or vision (only men wore masks during the curing ceremonies). He then either carved it himself or commissioned another man to carve it for him out of a soft wood, such as basswood, magnolia, poplar, white pine, maple, or willow. The power of the mask was thought to be greater if it was carved from a living tree—the face is roughed out on the tree and then split off from the trunk, with the tree remaining alive.

Although the Society of Faces was unable to prevent the decimation caused by European diseases, its members continued to create masks and perform ceremonies down to the present day. Because of their ongoing religious significance to the Iroquois, and as a result of the passage of the Native American Grave Protection and Repatriation Act (NAGPRA) of 1990, and similar legislation in Canada, most masks in public collections have been repatriated or returned to contemporary Iroquois groups. Scholars have subsequently respected Iroquois requests not to reproduce them in their publications.

France Bringing the Faith: Religious Instruction and Cultural Exchange

The first French colony, established in 1541 by Jacques Cartier, was short-lived. In 1608, when Samuel de Champlain founded Quebec City, close by the site of Cartier's earlier settlement, the emphasis was on the acquisition of fur (French fishermen had been traveling annually to the shoals of Newfoundland for cod-fishing for years). Serious efforts to establish more substantial permanent settlements did not take place until 1663. At this time Louis XIV, recognizing France's tenuous hold on the region (there were only 700 colonists in 1650), decided to invest in New France the institutions of a province—governor, intendant, and sovereign council. French companies had been granted monopolies to process and ship both furs and fish to France, but the Dutch and the British were constantly challenging the borders of French territory.

Similar to the Spanish before them, the French played the various indigenous nations off against each other. They allied themselves with the Hurons, Montagnais, and Algonquians, who profited from trading furs, while the Dutch and British allied with the Iroquois League.

Religion arrived with the traders, and in the 1620s the Jesuits began the task of conversion, aided by nuns of the Ursuline Order, the first three of whom landed in 1639. Both groups created and commissioned paintings and carvings to adorn their churches and to help teach the ways of the Roman Catholic faith. *France Bringing the Faith to the Indians of New France* [**1.3.4**] aptly summarizes this use of images. The painting has been attributed to Frère Luc (1614–1685), a member of the Recollet Order, a reformed order of Franciscans, and dated around 1675; although some scholars now think it was painted in France around 1700 by an unknown Franciscan artist. Luc, born Claude François in Amiens, trained as a painter before joining the Recollets after his mother's death in 1644. He spent only fifteen months in Quebec, in 1670–71, and painted several religious canvases. On his return voyage to France in the company of Bishop Laval, who had been posted to Quebec in 1659, he helped lay out the designs for a proposed new Quebec seminary. He also sent several canvases to the French colony at the request of the Bishop. Around 1668, Laval founded an arts and crafts school at St. Joachim, 30 miles (48 kilometers) east of Quebec City along the St. Lawrence River, to encourage production of religious paintings, sculpture, and metalwork by French settlers.

France Bringing the Faith hung in the Ursuline convent in Quebec City (and still does today). It shows a scene that prefigures the one described a century later by Father Junípero Serra (see p. 45). An indigenous figure, clothed in a robe patterned with the French fleur-de-lis, kneels at the feet of a personification of France, said to have been modeled after a portrait of the Queen Regent Anne of Austria, mother of Louis XIV. Between the two is a painting showing the Trinity—God the Father (in the clouds), Son (seated on the throne), and Holy Ghost (the dove below God the Father). This central group is flanked by the Virgin Mary and her mother Anne on one side, and Joseph and Joachim (Mary's father) on the other. The kneeling figure looks in awe at France, indicating acceptance of the lesson presented in the painting by reaching for the canvas with one hand, while touching her heart with the other. The gestures of France indicate ownership and authority. Her right hand rests on the painting while her left hand points upward to a scene including the same cast of characters as in the painting. The authority of France comes from God and is conveyed, in part, through images.

In the scene in the clouds, God the Father hands to Christ the orb representing the world. Christ's left hand rests on the globe, while the dove of the Holy Ghost rests on Christ's hand. Religious and secular authority are thus combined into one. Those who sailed up the St. Lawrence River, shown in the background, had the political and religious authority to claim the land and convert the peoples who inhabited it into both Christians and citizens of France. In the process, they built their mission stations, seen on the left, and brought Christianity and European clothes, both of which connoted civilization, to those they encountered.

Yet this painting also contains evidence that all was not well in relations between Church and State in New France. As the art historian Joseph Monteyne has noted, King Louis XIV was concerned that the Jesuits, who had managed to establish themselves as the dominant religious order in the region, were wielding too much power in the secular realm. Monteyne argues

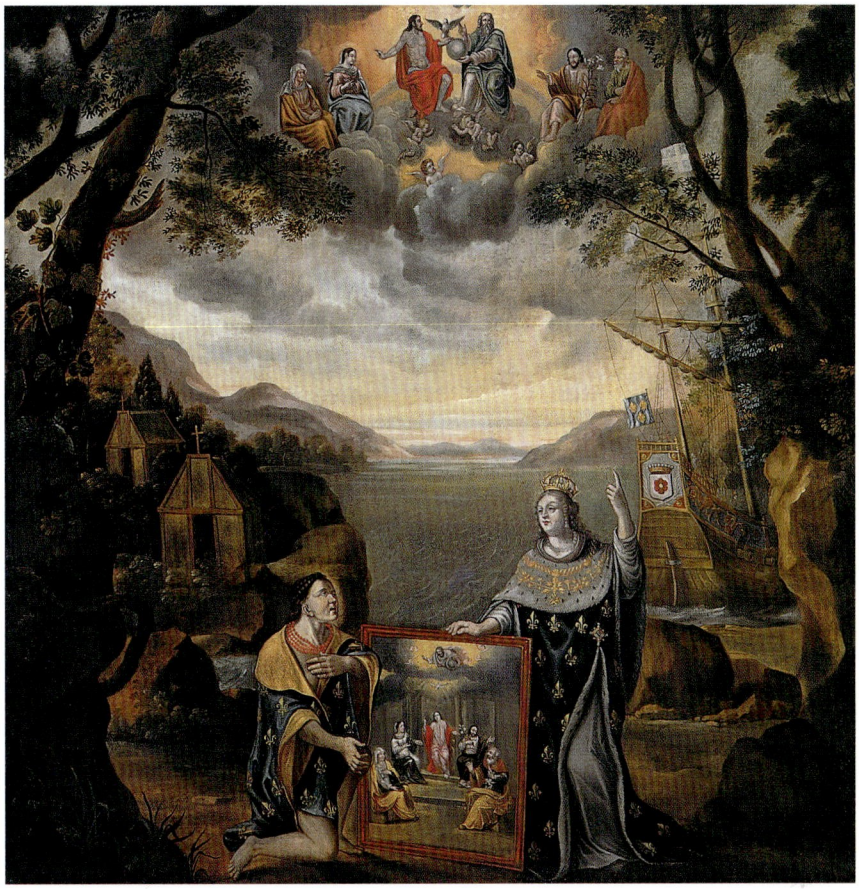

1.3.4 Attributed to Frère Luc (Claude François): *France Bringing the Faith to the Indians of New France*, *c.* 1675.
Oil on canvas, 86 x 86 in. (218.4 x 218.4 cm.)
Musée des Ursulines de Québec

that this tension between the Jesuits and the king is apparent in Luc's painting. There are no Jesuits occupying their mission stations on the left. Instead, the State, in the allegorical figure of France, is the dominant, divinely sanctioned force in this new French province.

This depiction of the willing acceptance of Christianity by the indigenous population was more wishful thinking, however, than an accurate record of what transpired after the arrival of the French. Relations between the French and the indigenous peoples were often peaceful, with several Jesuits moving to indigenous villages in order to convey more effectively to their inhabitants the value of a Christian life. Yet many French lost their lives when their settlements or trading parties were attacked. Even during peaceful times, only limited numbers of indigenous peoples converted to Christianity.

Nonetheless, the Jesuits and Ursulines did enjoy some success, due in part to their willingness to learn indigenous languages and, in the case of the Jesuits, to live in local villages. In the Ursuline convent in Quebec City, indigenous women were taught to read and write French, as well as to sing hymns in French, Huron, and Algonquian. In addition, they were taught European embroidery and painting. Mère Marie de l'Incarnation, one of the founders of the convent, wrote in 1640:

> They are so attentive to what they are taught....The girls sing with us in the choir, and we teach them what we wish, and they adapt themselves so well to it; I've never seen in French girls the disposition that I remark here.

She admitted, however, in 1663, that she had failed to convince a single girl to stay at the convent as a professed Ursuline.

According to art historian Gauvin Alexander Bailey, "the Ursulines were unique among female religious orders in the Americas in the degree to which the French colony relied on their arts production." The nuns, with their indigenous assistants, painted, carved, gilded, and embroidered most of the items necessary for religious services. One nun mentions in a letter after Mère Marie de l'Incarnation's death that a young indigenous woman had aided the convent's founder in her production of paintings for the altars of churches. The historian Natalie Zemon Davis suggests that some of the older pupils had probably already learned artistic techniques from their mothers and may have introduced certain indigenous motifs into the decorative work they did for the Church.

Bailey points to another influence present in the Ursuline embroideries in New France: that of Chinese visual traditions. For example, on altar frontals (embroidered textiles covering,

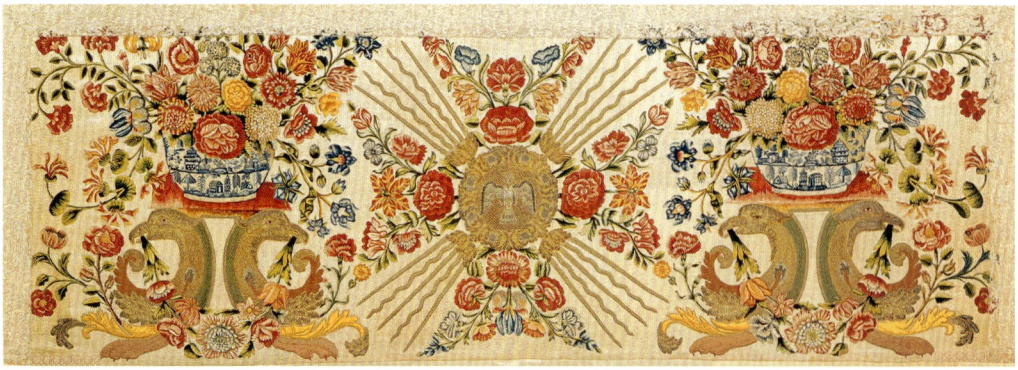

1.3.5 Ursuline workshop: *Dove of the Holy Spirit*, altar frontal, *c.* 1700. Embroidery with silk, wool, and gold and silk metallic threads, trimmed with needle lace, 37⅝ x 103⅞ in. (95.5 x 264 cm.) Musée des Ursulines de Québec

as the name suggest, the front of altars) one could find blue-and-white porcelains, pagodas, and birds of paradise alongside French floral designs and indigenous figures. The nuns may have had access to trade goods from China acquired through France or New Spain. Alternatively, they may have seen or owned decorative objects made by French artists who filtered the iconography, style, and media of Chinese art through European ideas of the whimsical and exotic East (a practice known as *chinoiserie* or "in the Chinese taste"). They could also have come across printed materials depicting such Chinese or French objects.

An altar frontal from about 1700 titled *Dove of the Holy Spirit* [**1.3.5**] is a fine example of this cultural mixing. It contains two blue-and-white Chinese-style vases brimming with cascading arrangements of flowers resting on tables supported by griffins. The vases frame the central image of the dove, which is surrounded by additional flowers and five-pronged symbols that represent the radiating golden light of the Holy Spirit. The scenes on the vases feature multi-story, pagoda-like structures, flowers, and birds, alongside longhouses [**1.3.2**; p. 50], wooden palisades [**1.3.1**; p. 49], and indigenous hunters. Bailey suggests that the Ursulines' choice of Asian-inspired colors and porcelain vases

> may have been inspired by Jesuit attempts to determine a palette that would appeal to Amerindians; the Jesuit missionary Charles Garnier noted in 1645 that the Hurons responded well to "a fine red and fine blue." The reds inspired by Chinese lacquers and the bright cobalt blues of porcelains—both Chinese and imitation-Chinese made at the Rouen kilns—would have fit the bill.

The Jesuits would have been quite familiar with Chinese porcelains and lacquer furniture as they were among the vanguard of Christian missionaries who traveled to India, China, and Japan in the mid-sixteenth century.

While indigenous and Chinese elements appeared in several examples of Ursuline embroidery, they were not as common as the floral motifs, birds, and Christian iconography that appeared with regularity in embroidered altar cloths and priestly vestments, as well as in Ursuline paintings. According to the ethnologist Marius Barbeau, these paintings followed the conventions of contemporary embroidery rather than painting. This combination of Christian iconography, flora, and fauna created a clear connection between Christianity and natural abundance. The colorful plants and birds would certainly have been a welcome sight during the long, cold winters in New France. Mère Marie de l'Incarnation wrote to the Ursuline convent in Tours: "Do not suppose that we could live long without returning again and again to the fireplace. Even I, who had never wanted to warm myself, am now reluctant to leave it."

Several of the Ursulines also turned to indigenous women for lessons in how to work with local materials, for imported goods were extremely scarce. As early as 1714 a nun from the settlement of Three Rivers had mastered the art of constructing birch-bark boxes and was showing the nuns of nearby Quebec City how to make them. They and their charges focused their attention on the production of particular types of containers, most often small and decorated with flowers, human figures, and/or animals embroidered in moose hair [**1.3.6**]. The general designs and techniques often matched those of the more traditional ecclesiastical objects made of thread and cloth imported from Europe; however, the narrative content differed.

1.3.6 Unknown artist, probably Quebec convent work: box, late 18th century. Bark embroidered with moose hair, l. 7⅞ in. (20 cm.), h. 3⅜ in. (8.5 cm.) Museum für Völkerkunde, Frankfurt

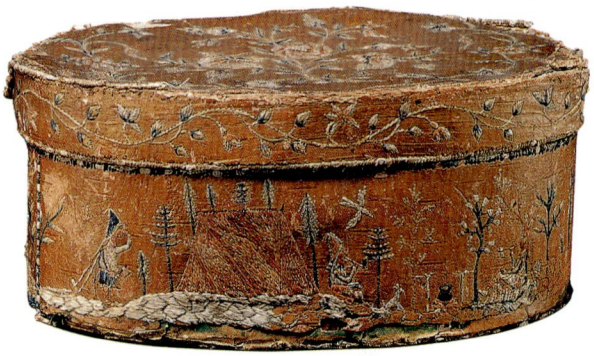

Indigenous peoples hunting, canoeing, or resting in the landscape often replace biblical figures or scenes.

Birch bark played an important role in the life of indigenous peoples in the region, who used it to make items ranging from canoes and dwellings to storage and cooking containers. Some, particularly the Huron, used moose hair to decorate clothing and other articles, but they did not embroider directly on the surfaces of bark containers. Neither did they create pincushions, wallets, boxes with lids, or any of the many other objects produced by the nuns. "The origin of these wares," writes the art historian Ruth B. Phillips, "was a true contact zone event that fused the technical knowledge of Aboriginal peoples with the entrepreneurship and artistry of Quebec nuns." The objects were often sent back to benefactors as gifts, much as the woven hats and baskets of the indigenous peoples of what is now the US southwest were purchased by the Spanish and British for shipment back home (see pp. 46–48). In addition, the sale of these birch-bark containers to visitors provided much-needed income. Phillips quotes the Ursuline embroiderer Mère Esther de l'Enfant-Jésus, who wrote in a letter of 1761:

> Despite all the troubles that have been visited on this country, one doesn't lack for the necessities of life if one has enough money; but we have nothing except what we earn from our little works in bark. As long as they remain in fashion the earnings that we get from them will be an important source of income, for we sell them really dear to Messieurs les Anglais.

The nuns' birch-bark products were popular with both the French and, after the British defeat of the French in 1759-60 (see p. 82), "les Anglais." For the former they functioned as "Indian curios," despite the fact that they were often made by French nuns. What made them "Indian" were the materials—birch bark, moose hair—and the scenes of indigenous peoples in the wilderness. These objects satisfied the desire of Europeans to see the peoples of the New World as "noble savages." The British also promoted this view of the "noble savage" and were enthusiastic customers. In fact, the English poet and dramatist John Dryden was the first to use the phrase in 1670, in a play about the New World entitled *The Conquest of Granada*:

> I am free as nature first made man,
> Ere the base laws of servitude began,
> When wild in the woods the noble savage ran.

"It is impossible, in effect," wrote Mère Esther de l'Enfant-Jésus, "despite our zeal for the work, to furnish this kind of merchandise to all the people who request them." The objects functioned for the British in a second way as well, as souvenirs of the "colorful" French population they had conquered. "Their purchases of moose hair and bark curios," writes Phillips, "were, thus, doubly romantic and exotic, acting as mementos not only of the Indians of North America, but also of the Catholic world of French Canada."

While the Ursulines had originally been charged with converting indigenous girls to Christianity, in 1720 they were officially released from this task. French settlers had increased in number and their spiritual needs replaced those of the indigenous populations. The nuns now turned their attention to educating the daughters of the wealthy French families in the region. After the British victory over the French, the nuns also began educating the daughters of the new British elite. The embroidery of birch-bark items was among the many lessons the girls received, which fostered a modest vogue for this activity among European women of the upper classes.

By the early nineteenth century, for reasons that are not clear, the nuns ceased production of these objects. The activity was subsequently taken over by the Huron, Mi'kmaq, and other indigenous groups in the region. Their motivation, too, was primarily financial, having had their traditional means of survival—hunting, fishing—severely circumscribed by the arrival of more settlers from both France and England. For many it proved a lucrative activity, as the nineteenth century saw a surge of travel by members of both the upper and the growing middle classes, who went in search of the primitive and the picturesque and who desired reminders of the indigenous settlements lining the more popular tourist routes. Paradoxically, financial success meant replicating the conventions of "Indianness" accepted and promoted by the foreign consumers. This was an exercise that, according to Phillips, "profoundly destabilized indigenous concepts of identity."

The Influence of Fashion: Painted Caribou-Skin Coats

French influence on indigenous cultures also appeared in the clothing designs of indigenous women. Early descriptions by secular and religious authorities in New France refer to painted clothing. For example, in 1616 the Jesuit Father Biard wrote of the people of Acadia (present-day Nova Scotia and part of New Brunswick): "They often curry both sides of elk skin, like our buff skin, and then variegate it very prettily with paint put on in a lace-like pattern, and make gowns of it." Father Paul Le Jeune observed the costumes worn in Quebec City in 1637–38 during religious ceremonies: "It was a beautiful sight to see a company of Savages marching behind the French, in their painted and figured robes, two by two, and very modestly."

The fashion historian Dorothy Burnham has studied painted caribou-skin coats produced by the Montagnais, Naskapi, and Cree, who inhabited the Quebec–Labrador peninsula (twentieth-century descendants of these peoples call themselves Innu). She found significant changes over the course of the eighteenth and nineteenth centuries. Just as Montagnais women helped embroider the vestments used in the masses celebrated within the Ursuline convents, so too did they translate the dreams of their men into abstract designs painted onto the coats worn during the caribou hunt. In the northern reaches of the peninsula, hunting was the main source of food. It was also viewed as a sacred activity, and Burnham suggests we consider these painted coats "holy vestments, one of the ritual elements that would ensure the success of the hunt." Men killed the caribou; women skinned the animal, prepared its hide, cut and sewed the coat, as well as painted the designs (it seems the men gave only general directions). The main colors used were yellow, red, and brown, with some black, blue, and green.

One of the earliest surviving coats, dated to *c.* 1700 [**1.3.7**], displays the complexity that is a feature of so many of these garments, with the various motifs organized symmetrically along a central axis. Most of the early coats contain an elaborately decorated triangular inset in the center of the back, which represented the Magical Mountain, home of the caribou. As seen here, bilateral symmetry governs both the overall arrangement of forms and almost all of the individual patterns. Two basic design types are used: a four-part layout, and a double curve, which can be found on the back of the coat illustrated. There are several circular and diamond shapes that contain a four-part design, while a series of double curves appear in both the collar and the horizontal decorative band in the lower section of the coat. Some of the elaborate patterns found on these coats may have been influenced by French embroidery brought to the area in the seventeenth century. Yet designs on Catholic vestments and altar coverings in New France tended to be much less abstract, more clearly representing vegetal motifs. They were also less likely to be segmented into individual units bordered by one or more lines. A comparison of an Ursuline altar frontal [**1.3.5**; p. 54] and the caribou coat makes this difference clear.

Burnham posits an interesting origin for the four-part design on the painted caribou coats, and its lace-like quality pointed out by Biard: the shapes produced by "the widespread and ancient art of biting a design into a thin piece of folded birch-bark." This art was practiced by indigenous women from Newfoundland to the Plains. Burnham describes the process:

> A small piece of bark is peeled down to a thin fine layer, which is folded in half, folded at a right angle in half again, and then folded diagonally from the centre to make eight thicknesses. The woman takes this small folded triangle of bark and moves it around while she bites it. She does not bite through to make a real hole but just squeezes the layers tightly together. When the piece of bark is unfolded, there, like magic, is a pattern of considerable complexity.

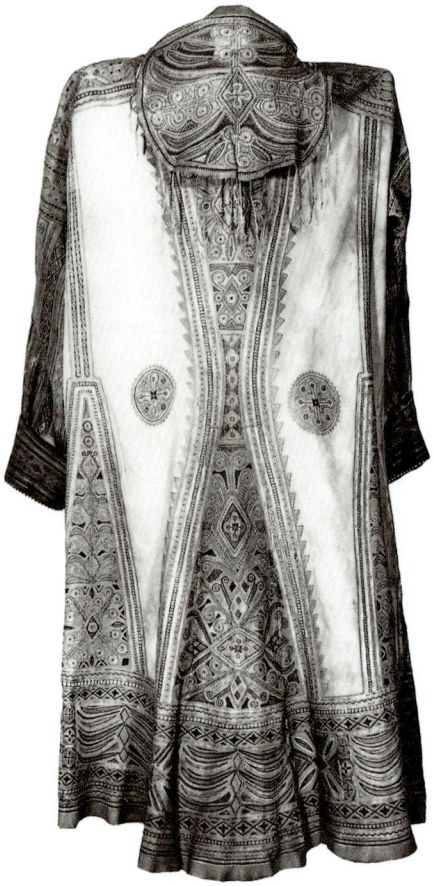

1.3.7 Unknown artist, probably Montagnais, from southwestern Quebec: painted caribou-skin coat, *c.* 1700.
Pitt Rivers Museum, Oxford

More folds might be added, to create complex floral motifs with stems and leaves, butterflies, bugs, or even animals, but most birch-bark bites were rosette designs based on the three basic folds [**1.3.8**]. The coat illustrated even contains tiny dots outlining much of the patterning, which suggest bite marks.

Burnham discovered, when making measured diagrams of the coats, that their shape changed from the seventeenth century onward following the evolution of European fashion. Early descriptions of garments worn by indigenous peoples along the St. Lawrence River note that they often had removable sleeves and that men and women wore the same type of clothing. Yet, by 1700, women were producing coats with permanent sleeves,

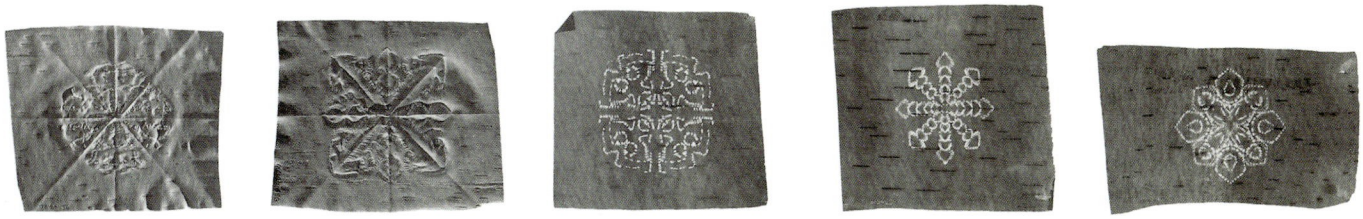

1.3.8 Angélique Merasty, Cree (1924–96): birch-bark bites, late 20th century.
Royal Ontario Museum, Toronto

which were worn only by men. Those from the early eighteenth century have a relatively straight cut, which corresponds to costumes worn by French men along the St. Lawrence at that time. By the second half of the eighteenth century a distinct flare marked the caribou coats, a feature also found in European fashion at that time. By the mid-nineteenth century the cut had slimmed down once again, as had European military apparel. This appearance of a special class of clothing worn only by men may have been one effect of the increasing pressure brought to bear on indigenous communities by the missionaries to adopt patriarchal social arrangements.

These changes in indigenous fashion were the result, in part, of the exchange of clothes as gifts between the French and indigenous male leaders. The son of one of the latter returned from France to Quebec in 1639 with six suits of clothes, three of which he gave away to other high-ranking men in his community. All were stored with the Jesuits and worn only during important processions honoring the king. The British too exchanged clothes as gifts with the Iroquois and other indigenous allies. Local women who saw the foreign coats may have been inspired by their design and symbolic significance in ceremonies marking special occasions. The products of these women's labor were also appreciated in Europe, whether as painted caribou-hide robes or as unpainted prepared caribou skins transformed into French high fashion.

Monuments to Death: Hopewell and Mississippian Burial Mounds and Effigy Funeral Vessels

While the majority of French settlers remained in the St. Lawrence River Valley around the towns of Quebec, Three Rivers, and Montreal, several pushed on to the Great Lakes and down the Missouri, Ohio, and Mississippi rivers. Robert Cavelier, Sieur de La Salle, worked his way down the length of the Mississippi in 1682 and claimed the entire river basin for France. In 1718 Jean-Baptiste Le Moyne, Sieur de Bienville, founded the city of New Orleans. Both ventures were challenges to Spain's claim to this territory and would lead to clashes between the two nations, such as the battle of 1720 celebrated in one of the Segesser hide paintings discussed earlier (see pp. 43–44).

In the course of their explorations, the French moved through territory filled not only with indigenous peoples, but also with the impressive archaeological remains of these peoples' ancestors. The most visible of these remains were large mounds of earth, most of which were used as burial sites. Archaeologists have identified a culture that flourished from *c.* 200 BCE to 400 CE, characterized by enormous earthworks—clusters of mounds and enclosures that sometimes extended over many acres—which they named Hopewell, after a farm in Ohio. While the Ohio River Valley was its center, Hopewell culture spread over much of the Midwest, with another focus in Illinois along the Mississippi. Through trade it influenced much of eastern North America. Within the mounds were objects made from a variety of materials, including marine shells, obsidian, shark and alligator teeth, and meteoric iron. There were also representational forms cut out of sheets of mica [**1.3.9**], copper ear spools, and figurines and pipes made of clay and stone. Some burials were much more elaborately decorated than those around them, suggesting Hopewell society was organized into small-scale chiefdoms.

1.3.9 Unknown artist, Hopewell: cut-out depictions of a human hand and the claw of a bird of prey, from an unknown location in Ohio, *c.* 100–500 CE.
Sheet mica, claw l. 11 in. (28 cm.)
Field Museum of Natural History, Chicago, Illinois

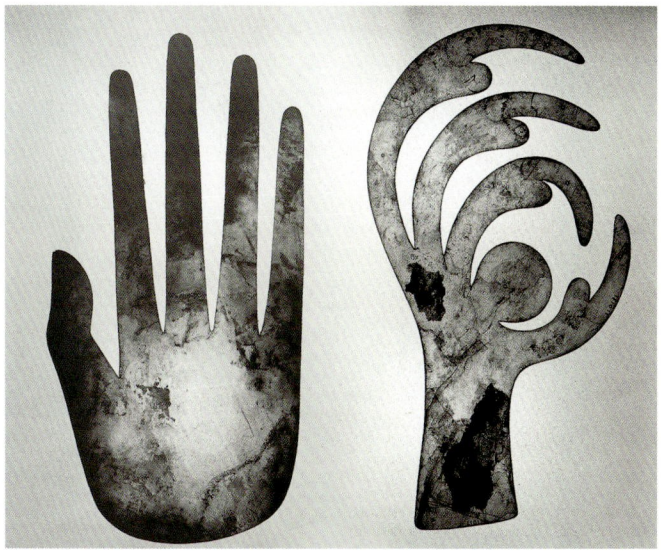

A distinctive form of ceremonial pottery was found in mounds throughout the lower Mississippi, in central Missouri, and in the lower Illinois Valley. Their pervasiveness suggests, according to the archaeologist Brian M. Fagan, "a decorative imagery that communicated a broadly similar ritual message in many different, widely separated areas." The pottery took the form of small, squat jars with a thickened vertical rim, decorated with bands of cross-hatched lines and curvilinear, geometric, or bird motifs [**1.3.10**]. Such avian motifs are also found on other objects made of stone, bone, copper, and shell.

It is not clear why Hopewell culture declined after 400 CE. What arose in its place, however, was a culture that produced much more impressive mound structures, an increased trade network, and objects of even greater technical and aesthetic complexity. This was the Mississippian culture, which flourished from 800 to 1500 CE throughout the Midwest and Southeast. The best known of these earthworks is the 1,254-feet- (382-meters-) long Great Serpent Mound in Ohio [**1.3.11**]. While originally classified by scholars as part of the Hopewell culture, recent carbon dating has suggested that the mound—which was not a burial site—may have been constructed later, around 1070 CE, making it a part of the Mississippian culture.

The larger centers of Mississippian culture were marked by a hierarchical political and social organization. Archaeologists speculate that the leaders of various communities oversaw the collection and redistribution of goods and foodstuffs, and that their prestige depended on this activity. Some of these stockpiles reached impressive proportions, as indicated in the travel accounts of the Spanish governor of La Florida and Cuba, Hernando de Soto. In 1539 he took a force of 622 men to the west coast of Florida and then pushed further inland than had previous Spaniards. He marched north into what is now South Carolina, then west through Tennessee and eastern Oklahoma, before turning south to Cuba in 1543.

1.3.10 Unknown artist, Hopewell: ceremonial vessel, found at Mound Group City, Ross County, Ohio, 1st century CE.
Clay, h. 6 in. (15.4 cm.)
Ohio State Museum, Columbus

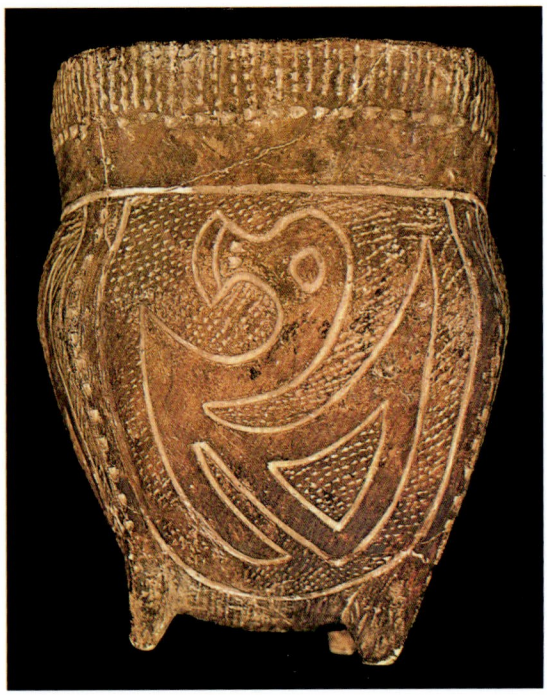

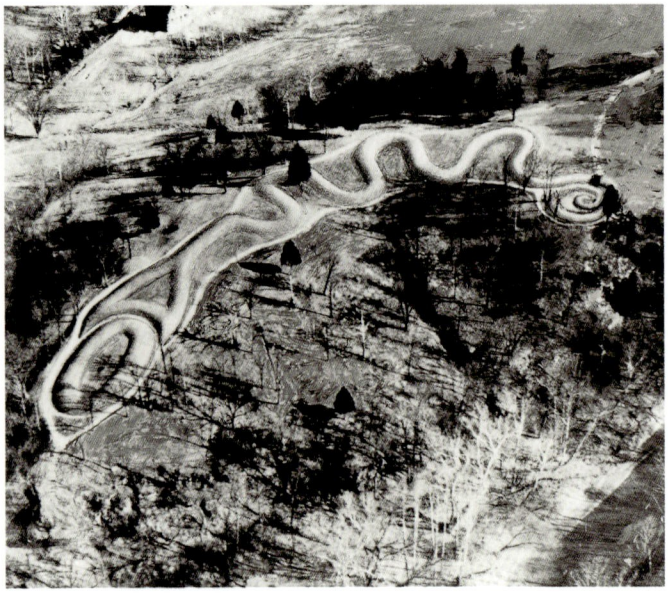

1.3.11 Hopewell or Mississippian: Great Serpent Mound, Hopewell, Ohio, *c.* 200 BCE–400 CE or *c.* 1070 CE.

The peoples De Soto encountered were organized into chiefdoms, and their villages were often marked by large earthen burial mounds, many of which were topped by temples. Both mounds and temples were filled with finely crafted objects made of mica, shell, pearls, wood, and many other materials. At Talomeco in South Carolina, the Spanish looted a large temple more than 100 feet (30 meters) long and 40 feet (12 meters) wide, situated on top of a large earthen mound. Its steep roof of reeds and split cane was adorned with seashells. Inside they found wooden statues decorated with pearls, bundles of skins and dyed cloth, copper-bladed ceremonial weapons, finely inlaid bows and arrows, and wooden and woven cane shields. Those who chronicled De Soto's expedition also described a scene in the village of Talomeco that was to become commonplace within the next few decades. Four of the houses contained hundreds of bodies, stacked and waiting to be either burned or buried. These bodies indicated that epidemics had already begun sweeping through the region, spread by earlier encounters with Europeans. De Soto's visit added to these epidemics; he himself died of fever before reaching Cuba.

Monuments to Life: Cahokia and the Grand Village of the Natchez

Despite the size of many Mississippian communities and the extent of their trade networks, most did not equal in political or economic power the state-organized empires of the Toltecs or Aztecs further south (see pp. 20–25). There are, however, a few Mississippian sites that indicate a more complex social, cultural, and political organization. The largest of these is Cahokia in Illinois, across the river from present-day St. Louis.

Cahokia was named after the people the French encountered living in the area in the eighteenth century. At the height of its power from 1050 to 1250 CE, it covered approximately 2,000 acres (about 800 hectares) with perhaps as many as 30,000 people at any one time [**1.3.12**]. While the residences were relatively simple pole-and-thatch houses, what marks the site as distinct is the number (more than one hundred) and size of the earthen mounds, many of which are located within a central walled precinct. The largest is called Monks Mound, after the Trappist monks who owned and farmed it in the nineteenth century. It covers 16 acres (6.5 hectares) and measures 1,037 × 790 feet (316 × 241 meters) at its base. Only the pyramids at Cholula (third century BCE–ninth century CE) and Teotihuacan (completed *c.* 100 CE) in Mexico are larger. Constructed in four terraces, rising to a height of 100 feet (30 meters), with a building on the highest terrace, Monks Mound faced a large plaza, which probably accommodated important civic and religious rituals.

Scholars have suggested that Cahokia was the site of a complex chiefdom, with several tiers of political hierarchy. One way in which leaders may have asserted their legitimacy is by possessing foreign objects obtained through trade. These objects represented their connection to supernatural powers and were linked to ceremonial architecture and land through use in rituals. There is little evidence, however, that the leaders were able to exert their control much beyond the outskirts of the site itself. Relationships with other communities appear to have been primarily ones of trade. Yet the existence of what look to be warrior figures carved in stone or clay and of walls surrounding the ceremonial precinct suggest that at least limited warfare played a role here, and thus in Mississippian society.

Cahokia's size was undoubtedly due to both its extensive exploitation of agriculture and its location near the confluence of several major waterways (the Mississippi, Missouri, Illinois, Meramec, and Ohio rivers). This allowed its inhabitants to travel with relative ease as far north as the Great Lakes and as far south as the Caribbean. The materials found in burial mounds suggest

1.3.12 Mississippian: reconstruction of the mounds at Cahokia, Illinois, *c.* 1100 CE. Monks Mound is in the center.

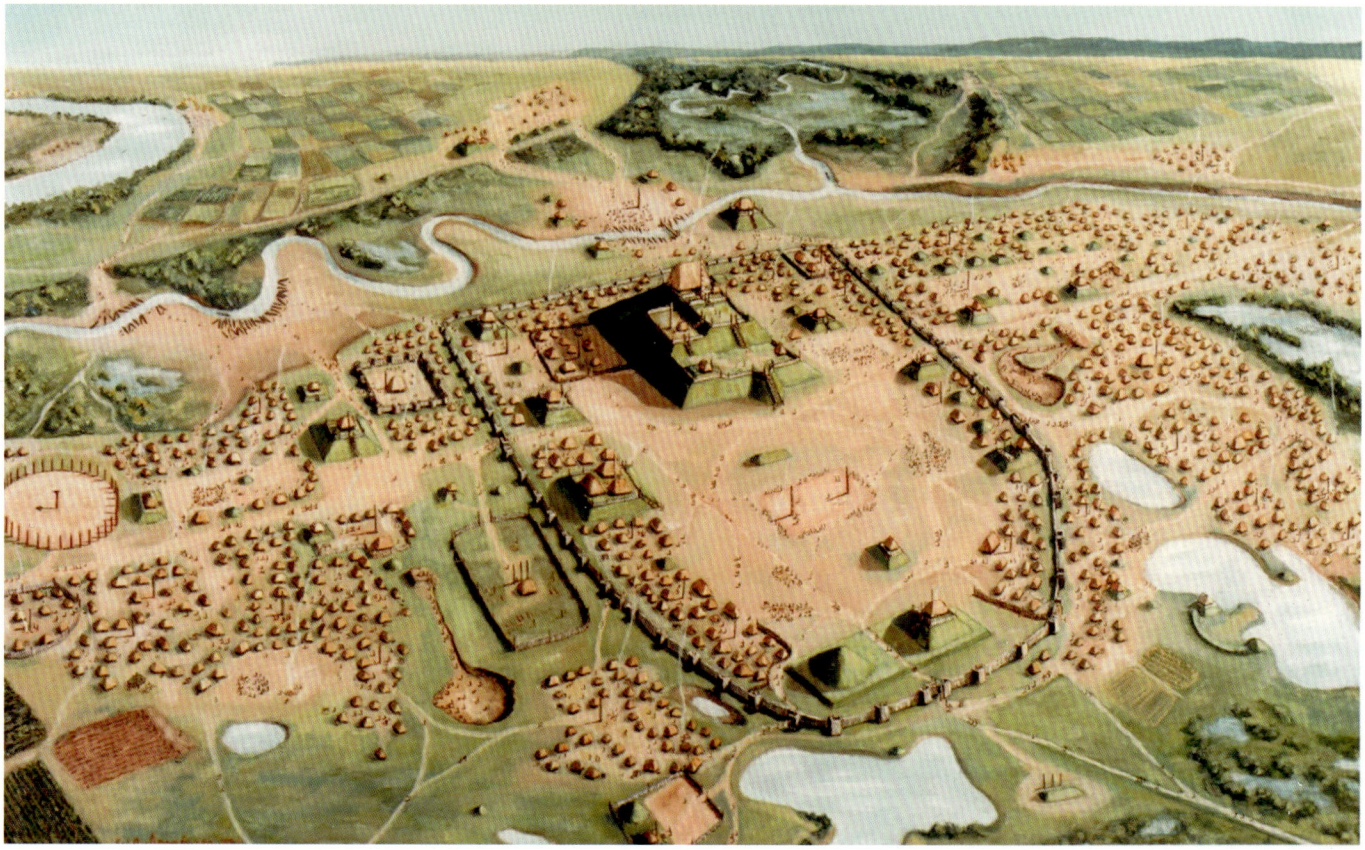

that they actually made such trips. These materials include rolled sheets of copper from the Great Lakes, arrowheads of black chert from Oklahoma and Arkansas, mica from North Carolina, and carved shells from the Gulf of Mexico. Cahokia also straddled three major language families, to the south, east, and west. Thus it may have played an important role as a mediator in matters of trade, information, and the regulation of social or political relations.

The shape of Monks Mound and the layout of the central plaza echo the ritual center of the Aztec capital of Tenochtitlan [**1.1.2**; p. 21]. Monks Mound, like the pyramid shrines of Tlaloc and Huitzilopochtli, was aligned with the position of the sun at the equinoxes, suggesting that astronomical factors played a role in its design and use. Many have argued that these parallels, plus iconographic and stylistic similarities in carved and painted objects, are strong evidence of contact, chiefly through trade, with cultures in central Mexico. Fagan contends, however, that local sources can be found for both architectural and sculptural styles, and that they are the result of trade within the Mississippian area.

One of the difficulties facing scholars today who study precontact cultures is amassing enough convincing evidence to make substantial claims about social and cultural patterns and influences. Adding to the difficulty in this case is the limited excavation of the Mississippian mounds and the fact that much of the early "excavations" took the form of indiscriminate looting, with little record of the original locations of the objects. As indicated in the Preface, scholars often make generalizations about cultures based on collections the very existence of which may be dependent on arbitrary circumstances. Speculation is often the best that can be offered, although such technological innovations as radio-carbon dating have made it possible to piece together more reliable sets of material facts. What always elude us, however, are the systems of thought of these peoples, whose material worlds we can partially reconstruct but whose reasons for doing or making things remain unknown.

When the French arrived, Cahokia had long been abandoned, but they encountered the heirs of Mississippian culture. In 1720 the Dutch historian Antoine Le Page du Pratz lived briefly among the Natchez, on the Lower Mississippi. Massive earthen mounds still marked the settlements, the largest of which the French christened the "Grand Village." Its ceremonial center contained three large platform mounds with structures on top. The central mound is thought to have been the residence of the Natchez leader Tattooed Serpent, while the southern mound held a temple.

Le Page du Pratz's account of his stay includes a description of the funeral of Tattooed Serpent, accompanied by an illustration that records the various stages of the event [**1.3.13**].

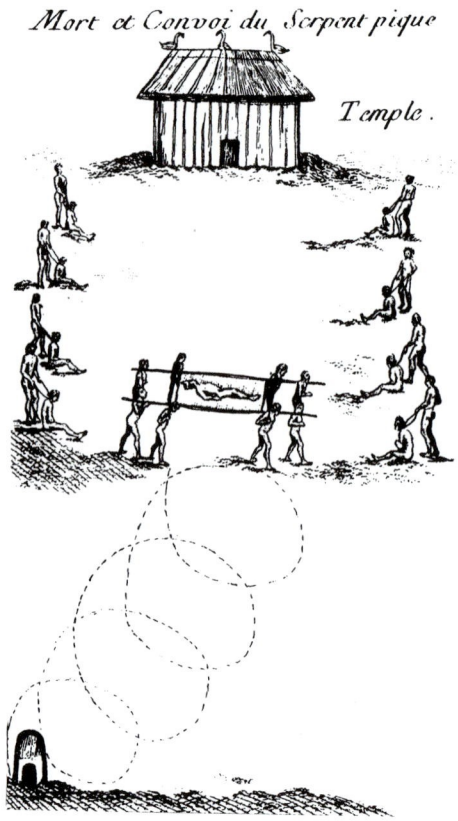

1.3.13 Antoine Le Page du Pratz: illustration depicting the funeral rites of the Natchez chief Tattooed Serpent in 1720, from Le Page's *History of Louisiana*, London, 1763.

The chieftain was placed on a litter and then the "whole procession went three times round the hut of the deceased, and then those who carried the corpse proceeded in a circular kind of march, every turn intersecting the former, until they came to the temple" atop the earthen mound. There he was to be buried with his wives and retainers, who were all to be strangled. The drawing is highly schematic, and does not indicate the physical features of the individuals. Instead, the emphasis is on the performance. The circular route from the leader's home to the temple is clearly indicated with a dotted line and the ropes around the necks of the seated figures leave little doubt about the manner of execution of those who were to be buried with Tattooed Serpent. All of the figures are represented unclothed, and Tattooed Serpent stands out from his bearers and retainers only by the slight suggestion of a crown or headdress.

Indigenous America in Europe: The Comte d'Artois's Cabinet of Natural History

Le Page du Pratz's description of his travels along the Lower Mississippi was published in Paris in 1758, when King Louis XV was losing interest in, and control over, his North American colonies. By the 1760s they were all gone, lost through war or sold to appease public opinion, which had turned against both the king and his commitments in the New World. When Louis XVI assumed the throne in 1774, however, there was a renewed interest in this world, sparked in part by such Enlightenment scholars as Jean-Jacques Rousseau. The philosopher promoted the investigation of a human history in which the stages of evolution included the "good savage, child of nature."

It was at this time that the Comte d'Artois, Louis XVI's brother, established a "Cabinet," or display, of natural history to aid in the instruction of his children. Included in it, along with seashells, minerals, and insects, was "the complete dress of a Canadian savage," arranged on a painter's mannequin [**1.3.14**]. Anne Vitart, in an essay on the Royal Cabinets, describes the mannequin as:

> dressed in a tunic made of animal hide, blue fabric leggings decorated with pearls, and moccasins, with a black feather headdress on his head, a knife in his belt, and an arrow and tomahawk "pipe" in his hands—the latter being a European-made item exchanged in alliance treaties. Above his head stood a sort of canopy with three painted hides, depicting birds, calumet feathers, tree branches, a buffalo, and a hunter.

1.3.14 The "Canadian savage" displayed in the Hôtel de Sérent, Versailles Musée de l'Homme, Paris.

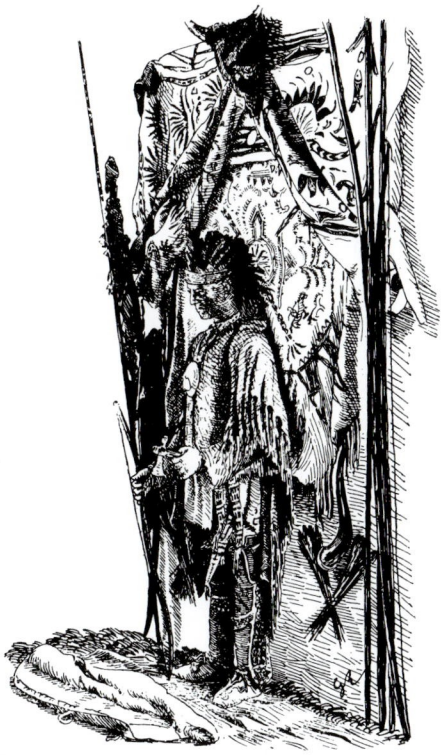

These items had been among a collection purchased by the Comte d'Artois from M. de Fayolle, formerly an official in the American colonies. The costume and canopy probably date to the first half of the eighteenth century.

The three hides that create the canopy above the "Canadian savage," now in the Musée de l'Homme in Paris, display a combination of geometric and pictographic forms. Vitart notes that the painted hides produced by women in the eighteenth century, used primarily as robes, were usually different from those produced by men. Women created hides with geometric, abstract designs [**1.3.7**; p. 56]—combinations of parallel lines, diamonds, and triangles, for example—while men utilized a more naturalistic, pictographic language, narrating scenes that included recognizable human and animal forms, notably horses and buffalo [**1.2.24**; p. 44]. Vitart offers two possible explanations for the combination of the styles on the canopy hides. First, they could have been painted by both men and women, with each contributing their own particular form of artistic expression. Robes were often used as trade items, and it is conceivable that the pictographic forms could have been added at a later date (an analysis of the paint would help resolve the question). Second, they could be the work of individuals who took on the clothes and duties of the opposite gender and who, according to Vitart, produced an intermediary style.

The majority of written accounts of such gender-mixing individuals, who existed in indigenous cultures throughout the North American continent, describe men assuming the roles of women. Yet the opposite also occurred. The Pueblo peoples called both "half-men/half-women." The Spanish referred to men taking on the roles of women as *putos* (male whores) or *mujerados* (literally, "made women"), indicating their disapproval. Nineteenth-century anthropologists, similarly disapproving, later settled on *berdache*, Arabic for male prostitute.

In 1711, on a mission in New France, the Jesuit Joseph-François Lafitau noted that such individuals took part in all major religious exercises and were looked upon with great respect. One of these exercises was the ritual of the calumet (a pipe the stem of which is decorated with feathers), which began among the Plains Pawnee in the seventeenth century before spreading east. The art historians Janet Catherine Berlo and Ruth B. Phillips note that in one version of the calumet ceremony the

> finely carved stone bowl, usually made of red catlinite, symbolizes the earth with its feminine regenerative powers, while the long stem, decorated with porcupine quills, paint, eagle feathers and other materials, symbolizes the male energizing powers of the sky world.

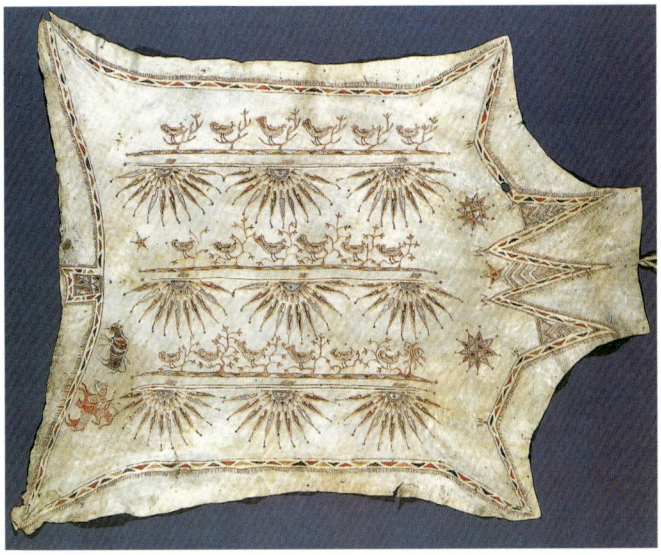

1.3.15 Unknown artist: robe with birds and calumet motif, 18th century. Painted hide, 50¼ x 35½ in. (127.5 x 90.3 cm.) Musée de l'Homme, Paris

One of the three canopy robes [**1.3.15**] includes three calumets one above the other, each paired with a pipe stem on which are positioned six birds that resemble those in European embroidery. It is possible that the person who painted the more geometric elements found in the decorative border and the calumets was trained in embroidery technique, perhaps at an Ursuline convent.

1.3.16 Unknown artist: robe with Louis XIV-style motif, 18th century. Painted hide, 41½ x 40 in. (105.6 x 101.9 cm.) Musée de l'Homme, Paris

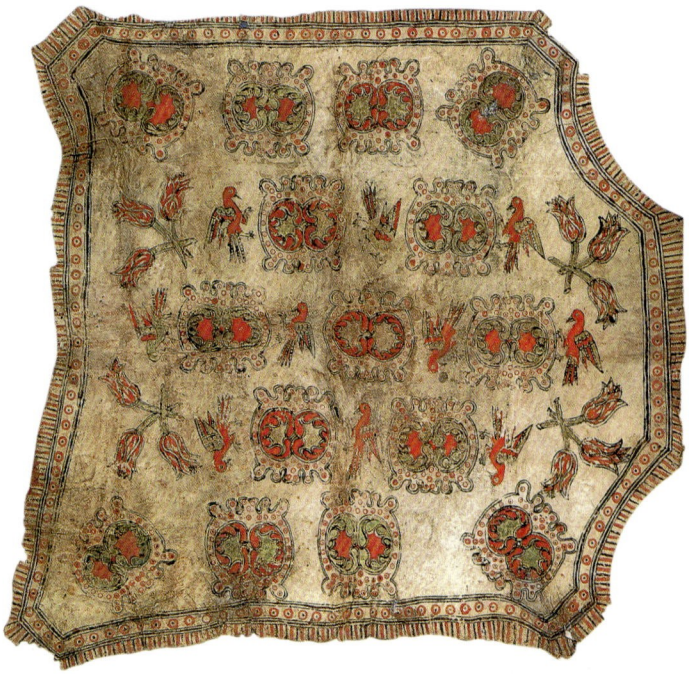

The inclusion of buffalo-hunt scenes on the canopy robe with calumets and on one of the others suggests they came from the eastern Plains region, just west of the Great Lakes, where the French were beginning their explorations of the Missouri and Mississippi river basins. This region was also, as the historian Richard White points out, a place of refuge for the Huron, Ottawa, and other indigenous allies of the French who survived the brutal Iroquois attacks of the late 1640s through 1660s. The calumet ceremony was particularly important here, as it bound individuals from different cultures together in peace and guaranteed safe passage, even if only temporarily.

Another eighteenth-century painted robe in the Musée de l'Homme [**1.3.16**] also provides evidence of this cultural mixing. Here the artist has combined tulips and parrots in a motif drawn from the era of Louis XIV. The border of lines and circles is the only reference to the geometric tradition of women's painted robes. Vitart suggests that this hide could have been bought west of the Great Lakes and transported back to the main French settlements on the St. Lawrence River, where indigenous women trained in European design painted its surface. From there it may have traveled across the ocean as a gift to an official or possibly to the king himself. If so, it would have continued a transatlantic trade in objects and ideas that had begun with the first voyages of Columbus.

Review Questions

1 How did the establishment of the fur trade by the French impact the lives of the indigenous peoples of New France?

2 What does the art historian Ruth B. Phillips mean when she describes the embroidered birch-bark boxes of the Ursuline nuns as representative of a "true contact zone event"? Are there other objects created in New France that can be described in this way?

3 What was the role of gender in the creation of art in both indigenous and French communities in New France?

4 What role did the Catholic Church play in shaping artistic production in New France?

5 What are some of the challenges art historians face today in discussing cultures that had declined, if not disappeared, by the time of the arrival of Europeans?

CHAPTER 4

A Protestant Presence in America: The Arts of the British and Dutch Colonies (*c.* 1585–1772)

Picturing the "New World": John White and Theodore de Bry

Most French settlements on the North American continent in the sixteenth and seventeenth centuries were Catholic and were sited along the St. Lawrence, Ohio, Missouri, and Mississippi river basins. In 1562, however, a small group of some 150 French settlers led by Jean Ribaut attempted to establish a Protestant, or Huguenot, colony on the east coast of Florida. Landing near the mouth of the St. John's River, they erected a column (one of five they had brought with them) establishing France's claim to the area before heading north and settling at a site they named Charlesfort, near present-day Beaufort, South Carolina. Ribaut returned home that year, but France's religious wars prevented his return to Charlesfort with supplies, and the settlement was abandoned.

In 1564 the French Huguenot explorer René de Laudonnière returned to the area and established Fort Caroline near the mouth of the St. John's River. He brought with him the artist Jacques Le Moyne de Morgues (1533–1588) to map the territory. Le Moyne executed a series of gouaches of the expedition after he returned to France. The Franco-Flemish engraver Theodore de Bry (see pp. 16–17) subsequently based several engravings on these gouaches. *René de Laudonnière and the Indian Chief Athore visit Ribaut's Column*, of *c.* 1570 [**1.4.1**], was once thought to have been the only one of Le Moyne's original paintings to survive, but several scholars now believe that it is a painting of approximately the same date not by Le Moyne, but by an unknown artist who copied one of De Bry's engravings.

Athore was the leader of the Timucuan people [**1.0.2**; p. 19] and is shown taking Laudonnière to see Ribaut's column. According to a written account left by the artist, this image describes a scene that took place shortly after Laudonnière's arrival. Le Moyne notes that when the French reached the column, they found the Timucuans worshiping it, having laid out offerings of food, flowers, and weapons. The column carries the emblem of the Valois kings of France composed of a shield containing three fleurs-de-lis surmounted by a crown. Festooned with vines and flowers, it is surrounded by various fruits and vegetables, some of which were not native to Florida, along with a bow and arrows. These objects and the people kneeling to the left of the column with their arms raised suggest that the Timucuans are worshiping not only the column, but also the French themselves.

Athore's costume and tattooing are carefully delineated, implying the accuracy of Le Moyne's observations. Yet the artist also utilized the stance and body type of ancient Greek and Roman statues of Apollo. In contrast to the sparsely clothed Timucuans, the Frenchmen are elaborately dressed, as well as armed. Athore places his arm around the shoulders of Laudonnière, indicating his acceptance of the Frenchman. Yet Laudonnière does not return this accepting gesture and, instead, extends his lance across the body of the Timucuan chief. What cannot be gained through diplomacy will be taken by force.

Laudonnière's colony was soon destroyed, however, by the Spanish under Pedro Menéndez de Avilés (the column was carried off to Havana). The territory did not remain under Spanish dominion for long, for the English had already begun making plans to extend their empire across the Atlantic. While they were motivated by a desire to exploit the still unknown resources of this new continent, they also wanted to establish a Protestant commonwealth to counteract the rapidly expanding territory of Catholic New Spain.

The Genoese navigator and explorer John Cabot had visited the northern reaches of North America in 1497 under the employ of the English king Henry VII, but England did not stake claim to this territory, in particular Newfoundland, until 1583. The claim was an attempt to control the cod fishing in the area, and no permanent settlements were founded. An effort was made in 1585 under the command of Sir Richard Grenville to establish a settlement on a small island off the northeast coast of North Carolina named by the settlers Roanoke. The larger territory claimed by

1.4.1 Jacques Le Moyne de Morgues: *René de Laudonnière and the Indian Chief Athore visit Ribaut's Column*, *c.* 1570.
Gouache and metallic pigments on vellum, 7 x 10¼ in. (17.7 x 26 cm.)
The New York Public Library, New York

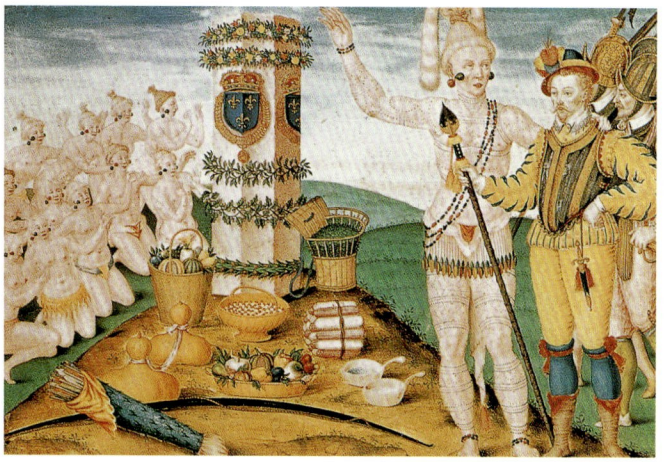

the expedition, occupied by Algonquian peoples, was designated "Virginia," after the Virgin Queen, Elizabeth I. The initial group of settlers returned to England in 1586 but was followed by another in 1587, which subsequently vanished without a trace.

The Roanoke expedition of 1585 included an artist, John White (active 1585–1593). White executed watercolors of the people, flora, and fauna of the new territory, and became the leader of the expedition in 1587. He had known Le Moyne, as the latter had left France for England around 1580 and entered the employ of Sir Walter Raleigh, who was responsible for sending the Roanoke expedition across the Atlantic. The scientist Thomas Harriot, another member of the first group in 1585, provided a written account to accompany White's watercolors. Similar to Le Moyne, White paid close attention to the physical appearance and costumes of the people he encountered, as well as their architecture. His images would provide valuable information for those in England who planned on increasing the number of settlers in Virginia.

One of White's watercolors is an overview of the Algonquian village of Secoton [**1.4.2**], located on the Pamlico River in North Carolina. It contains a clear indication of the carefully planted fields and the structure of the houses, with their barrel-shaped roofs, wood frames, and mat coverings. Resembling the Iroquois longhouse (see p. 50) only usually much smaller, such oblong or round dome-shaped huts were known as wigwams and were common among the peoples of the eastern woodlands and as far west as the Mississippi River. (In northern New England and southern Canada the term "wigwam" referred to a conical bark-covered structure framed with straight poles.) The ceremony depicted in the lower right-hand corner, which White reproduced in a separate drawing entitled *Indians Dancing* [**1.4.3**], also gives an indication of the type of artistic activities that took place in the village. The posts arranged in a circle around which people are dancing are carved at their tops with human faces.

White went back to England in order to obtain more supplies shortly after the second expedition arrived on Roanoke. He was unable to return to Virginia until 1590 because of the threat of the Spanish Armada, sent by King Philip II in 1588 to invade England (it was defeated by the English fleet off the coast of Calais). When he did manage to make it ashore on Roanoke, no one was to be found.

Interest in White's expeditions was kept alive by De Bry's publication in 1590 of *A briefe and true report of the new found land of Virginia*, the first volume of his *Great Voyages* series (see pp. 16–17). It included Harriot's narrative account illustrated by engravings after White's watercolours. The volume's frontispiece [**1.4.4**] contains several of White's figures. Here they are represented as sculptural forms decorating a clearly classical

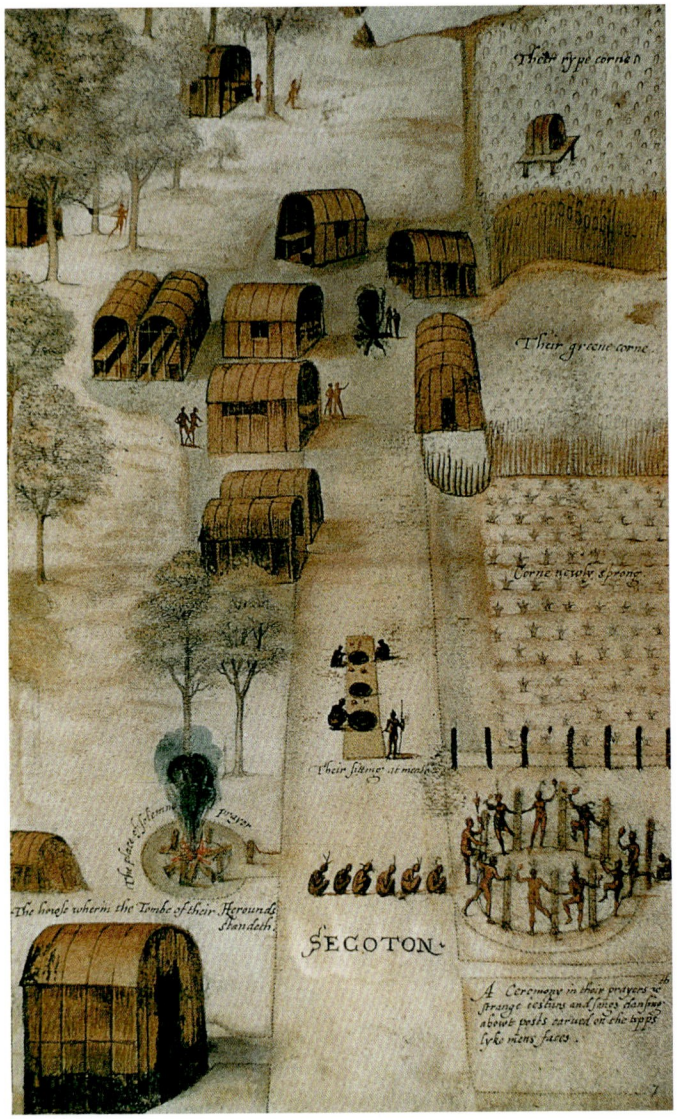

1.4.2 John White: *The Village of Secoton*, c. 1585. Watercolor on paper, 12¾ x 7¾ in. (32.4 x 19.9 cm.) British Museum, London

1.4.3 John White: *Indians Dancing*, c. 1585. Watercolor on paper, 10¾ x 14 in. (27.4 x 35.6 cm.) British Museum, London

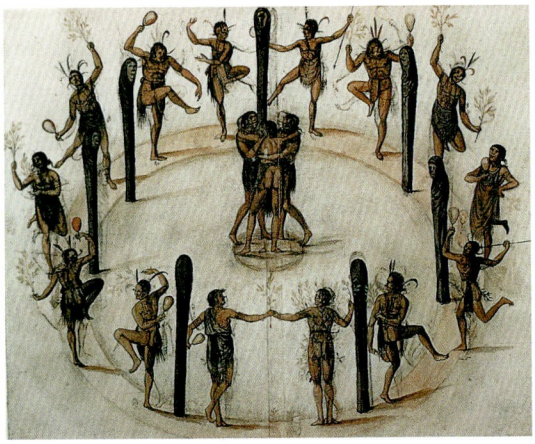

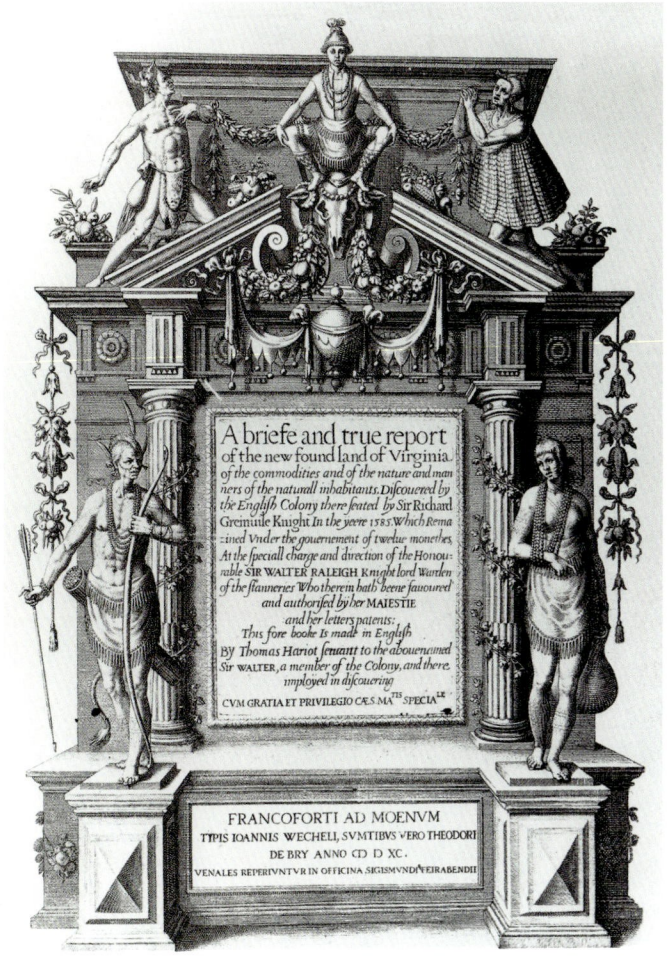

1.4.4 Frontispiece to Theodore de Bry, *A briefe and true report of the new found land of Virginia*, Frankfurt, 1590.

1.4.5 (below left) John White: *Theire Sitting at meate* (detail), *c.* 1585. Watercolor on paper, whole image 8¼ x 8½ in. (20.9 x 21.4 cm.) British Museum, London

1.4.6 (below right) After John White: "Theire sitting at meate" Engraving in Theodore de Bry, *A briefe and true report of the new found land of Virginia*, Frankfurt, 1590.

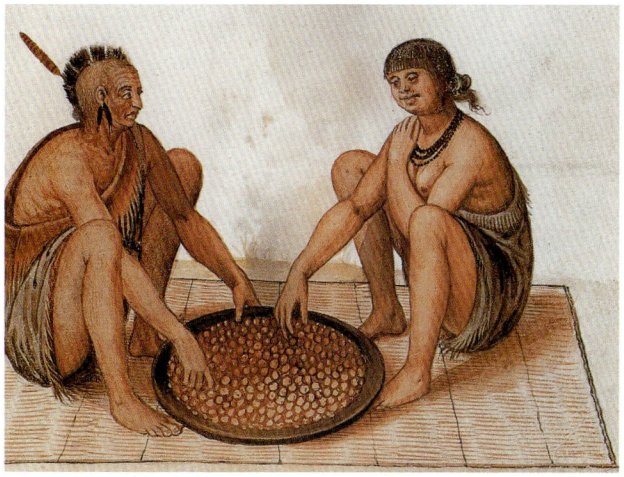

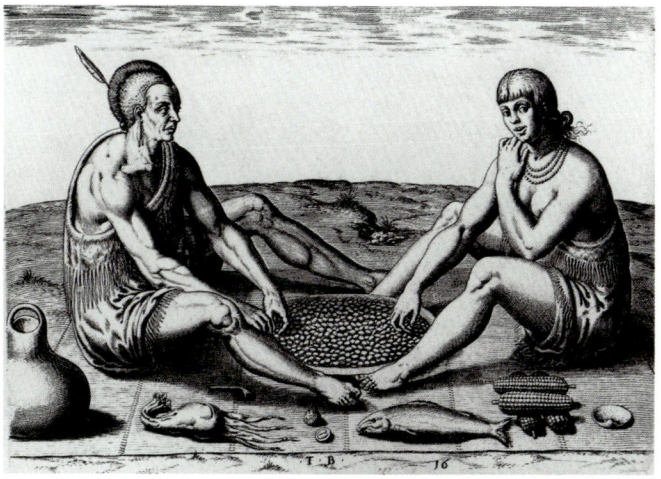

facade, with the requisite columns, entablature, and pediment, festooned with the floral and vegetal riches of the New World. The result is an image that is at once both familiar and exotic.

While De Bry's engravings are for the most part faithful to White's watercolors, there are certain significant differences. Paul Hulton, in *America 1585: The Complete Drawings of John White*, attributes some of these changes to De Bry's use of Le Moyne's drawings for certain background and costume details. For example, a Timucuan headdress appears on the Algonquian idol at the top of the pediment in the frontispiece. In at least one instance, De Bry altered the postures of the original figures. In White's watercolor of a man and woman eating a meal, the two sit on the ground in a squatting position, with their hands reaching out between their knees [**1.4.5**]. In the engraved version the legs of both figures are stretched out before them [**1.4.6**].

Hulton suggests that De Bry "could not accept" the squatting position because "it was outside his experience." Thus, he engraved the figures "with their legs stretched out before them in European fashion." But certainly much of what De Bry saw—and faithfully copied—in White's watercolors was "outside his experience." It is possible, instead, that his alterations were prompted by formal considerations, which had ideological implications. By stretching the legs outward, De Bry creates a more elongated and elegant composition. The torsos and the limbs of the figures are more clearly articulated, with the musculature on the male figure highlighted, in the exaggerated style of figuration popular at the time in Europe (De Bry does this in most of his engravings after White's watercolors). He has also changed the features and expression of the female figure. In the watercolor she looks with a smile at the plate of food, anticipating her own pleasure. In the engraving she looks seductively out at us, anticipating our pleasure in looking at her, a glance common in many European paintings of women, particularly those who are naked or partially naked.

White was concerned with recording as accurately as possible the physical characteristics, clothing, and customs of the Algonquians. De Bry was concerned with creating a set of images that would be inviting to look at and that would justify Protestant colonizing ventures (and condemn those of the Spanish) in the Americas (see pp. 16–18). The female Algonquian is rendered more in keeping with classical ideals of beauty. She becomes one of an endless stream of representations of naked or semi-naked indigenous women, often intended to symbolize the "New World" as a whole, who invite male European conquerors to take possession of their bodies and their resources.

Early Settlements: Jamestown and Plymouth

John Smith established the first successful English colony in 1607 at a site he named Jamestown after the King of England. Its funders, the Virginia Company, a joint-stock company set up by English merchants and gentry, intended it as a source of crops for export to England. Smith viewed it as a stop on the way to the Pacific Ocean (he was still searching for a northwest passage), while his men saw it as a source of immediate wealth, preferably gold or other precious minerals. None of these hopes would be realized in the early years of the settlement. Instead, Smith and his men faced the reality of backbreaking labor, disease, and hunger.

The site Smith had chosen for Jamestown was part of the territory controlled by an Algonquian-speaking confederacy of tribes known as the Powhatan, ruled by a patriarchal leader also known as Powhatan. The peoples of this confederacy belonged to the Mississippian culture. Their villages included temples that were closely associated with the treasure houses of ruling families and were filled with various decorated objects made of skins, copper, pearls, and beads. Smith observed that the leader's treasure house included at its four corners "4 Images as Sentinels, one of a Dragon another of a Beare, the 3rd like a leopard, and the fourth like a giantlike man." These images were probably carved on wooden poles, similar to the ones depicted in White's watercolor *Indians Dancing* [**1.4.3**; p. 64].

Smith's description has been used to help decipher the meaning of a finely decorated deerskin known as "Powhatan's Mantle" [**1.4.7**]. Four tanned hides of white-tailed deer have been sewn together and decorated with Marginella shell beadwork. The beads form several circles and three figures: a human in the center flanked by two animals. The animal on the right, with cloven hooves, could represent a white-tailed deer; that on the left, with round paws and a long tail, could be a mountain lion of the kind found in eastern Virginia. The mantle entered the "Cabinet" of natural history (see p. 61), also called a "cabinet of curiosities," of the two John Tradescants, father and son, in

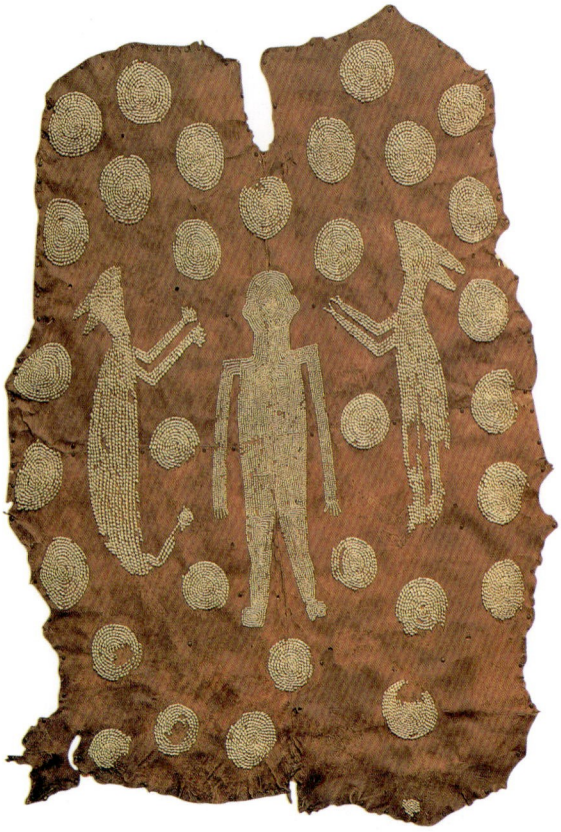

1.4.7 Unknown artist, Powhatan: "Powhatan's Mantle," before 1656. Hide, embroidered with shells, 92½ x 63 in. (234.9 x 160 cm.) Ashmolean Museum, Oxford

England not long after Smith's time. It was catalogued in 1656 as that of Powhatan. The art historian Christian Feest suggests that the feline and human figures could correspond to two of the four images found at Powhatan's treasure-house, although the connection is still tenuous. Nevertheless, the mantle does represent one type of ceremonial garment created by the Powhatan in the early seventeenth century.

The historian Gary Nash notes that from the very beginning in Virginia "some Indians lived among the English as day laborers, while a number of settlers fled to Indian villages rather than endure the rigors of life among the autocratic English." This was not what the Virginia Company had anticipated. According to the historian Eliga H. Gould, its decision to establish a settlement in the territory of the powerful and well-organized Powhatan confederacy was prompted by the hope that the colonizers could "replicate the indigenous labor and tributary systems of New Spain and Peru [and]...turn the colony into a sort of Protestant Mexico." There were, however, many differences between the Powhatan and the Aztec (see pp. 20–24). The head of the Powhatan confederacy had less power than Aztec leaders over their tributary subjects, while at the same time a greater ability to resist the small group of English who arrived with Smith. As a result, Smith was unable to create a Protestant version of the exploitative labor system of Catholic New Spain. Instead, the friendly, if cautious, relations that marked the first years of Jamestown did not last. Food shortages, illness, and internal dissension among the colonists led several to initiate attacks on the Powhatan and any colonists who sympathized with them. The Powhatan also became increasingly hostile toward the English, having already experienced the treachery of earlier Spanish visitors.

According to English accounts, peace was restored in 1614 after the president of the colony had held a young Powhatan girl named Pocahontas captive for two years. During the negotiations for her return, she decided to stay with the English, convert to Christianity, and marry the colonist John Rolfe. Her decision would be commemorated in numerous books, images [**1.4.9**; p. 68], and feature-length films and celebrated as evidence of the superiority of English culture and religion. Native American literary critic Paula Gunn Allen presents another account of what happened. Gunn Allen argues that rather than a captive, Pocahontas was a fledgling medicine woman sent to the English settlement by Powhatan in order to gather intelligence about the nature of this new people and the extent to which they constituted a threat to the Powhatan confederacy.

The Powhatan ultimately helped the Jamestown colony flourish. They offered Rolfe crucial assistance in the cultivation of a new cash crop—tobacco—which grew well in the Virginia climate. It was planted and harvested initially by indentured servants (individuals who worked for a set number of years to pay off their passage to the colony) and indigenous laborers. Later, African slaves would be the primary labor force. The first Africans were brought to Jamestown in 1619 on a Dutch ship as indentured servants; they subsequently arrived as chattel slaves, that is they were defined as property to be bought, sold, and inherited.

Ousted as president of Jamestown, Smith embarked on another voyage of exploration in 1614, this time along the northern Atlantic coast, a territory he named New England. This area would soon see its first permanent settlement at a site also named by Smith, Plymouth. The Puritans who established New Plymouth in 1620—they called themselves Pilgrims—were part of the Protestant Reformation that had spread throughout Europe in the sixteenth century. When King Henry VIII broke with Rome in 1534 and declared himself head of the Church of England, the church he established steered a middle ground between Roman Catholicism and Protestant reform movements, such as the Puritans. The latter were critical of what they saw as the extravagance of the Church of England and, as a result, suffered religious and political persecution.

The Pilgrims left England in 1608, traveling first to the Dutch Netherlands before continuing on to North America. The Dutch had flourished after wrenching control of their territory from Spain in the first half of the seventeenth century, and had become a successful manufacturing and trading Protestant nation. They had founded a colony in 1614 at Fort Nassau (Albany, New York) (see p. 51), and certain Dutch businessmen were interested in backing a group to establish a second trading colony on the island of Manhattan. The Pilgrims were not interested, however, in establishing a "New Amsterdam" (that colony would be founded in 1624). Instead, they accepted the backing of English merchants and a royal charter from the King of England, and arrived in New England in 1620 along with many non-Pilgrims (according to the historian James W. Loewen, approximately only 35 of the 102 settlers aboard the Mayflower were Pilgrims).

The expedition may have had in its possession a map of the site of Patuxet (Plymouth) drawn by Samuel de Champlain (see pp. 50–51) in 1605 [**1.4.8**], before the plague of 1617 that wiped out the village. The map shows an orderly arrangement of wigwams and planted fields. Upon their arrival, the Pilgrims found a fine harbor and an abundant supply of fresh water, as well as the remains of cleared fields recently planted in corn and local stores of corn and beans, which they raided to use as seed. These discoveries undoubtedly helped reconcile them to the fact that they had been blown off course and arrived not in Virginia, their intended destination, but hundreds of miles to the north. They also had the help of a Wampanoag named Squanto, who had been kidnapped and taken to England in 1614, but managed to make his way back to his village of Patuxet, only to find it decimated by disease. When the first English settlers arrived, he taught them local methods of planting and fishing and how to adapt to the new climate and geography.

1.4.8 Samuel de Champlain: map of Patuxet (Plymouth), 1605. From Champlain's *Les Voyages*, 1613

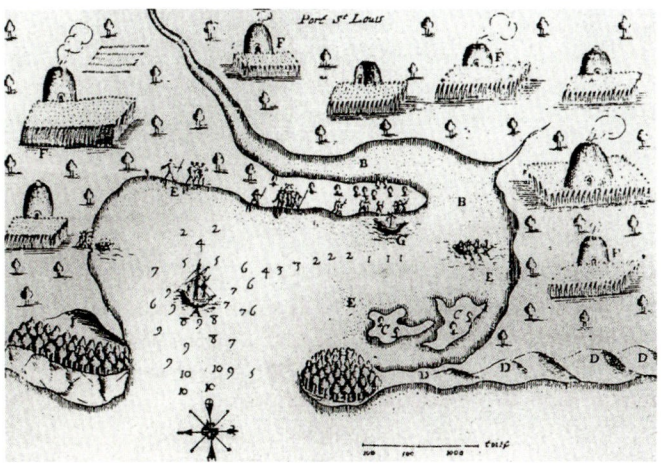

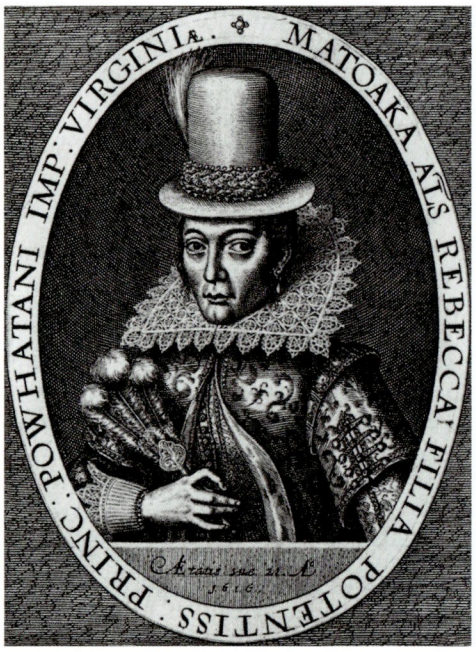

1.4.9 Simon van de Passe: *Pocahontas*, *c.* 1616. Engraving, 6⅝ x 4⅝ in. (17 x 11.7 cm.) British Museum, London

Most Puritans who formed the Plymouth Colony, and, in 1629, the Massachusetts Bay Company colony centered in Boston, came from medieval villages and cities, not from large Renaissance urban centers. They came as family units rather than single men as in Jamestown, and were a combination of homemakers, yeomen, middle-class merchants, intellectuals, and ministers. Initially ministers dominated the governing of the settlements, but soon merchants and farmers took control, a shift easily justified by a religion that advocated the importance of both individual freedom and material prosperity. A decisive blow to the power of Puritan clergymen came in 1691, when Massachusetts became a royal colony with an appointed governor and voting rights based on property rather than church membership.

The Puritan community itself also began to break up into competing factions that vied for both civic and religious authority. By the mid-eighteenth century, the colonies were home to several Protestant sects, including Congregationalists, Moravians, Quakers, Methodists, and Presbyterians, as well as Roman Catholics and a small number of Jews. In addition, colonists who were not Puritans seeking religious freedom, but individuals looking only to make their fortunes, continued to arrive. By the 1630s several new settlements were being established (for example, Providence, Newport, New Haven) to accommodate the increasing population, as well as diverging religious beliefs and economic ambitions.

This expansion into lands occupied by the Pequots and Narragansetts resulted in a series of armed conflicts and in one of the most infamous massacres in early American history. In 1637, after declaring war on the Pequots, troops from the Massachusetts and Connecticut colonies, led by Captain John Mason, surrounded the Pequots' coastal village at the mouth of the Mystic River. Some four hundred women, children, and old men had taken refuge there. The colonists burned it to the ground, killing all who tried to escape.

Art, Religion, and Politics in Seventeenth-Century New England

The relationship between religion and art in New England was very different from that in New Spain and New France. As Wayne Craven notes in his book *Colonial American Portraiture*, the focus of Protestantism was literary, not visual, expression. The chief means of religious teaching were the sermon and the reading of the Bible. The visual arts were condemned in the context of religious services, particularly images representing God, angels, or other spiritual beings. As the prominent Protestant sixteenth-century theologian and reformer John Calvin had written, "Only those things are to be sculpted or painted which the eyes are capable of seeing." This rejection of religious imagery was part of the larger Protestant critique of the opulence and corruption of the Roman Catholic Church. Thus, the word, not the image, was the primary tool used to meet the spiritual needs of New England communities, as well as to convert indigenous peoples to Christianity.

Protestants did not condemn the use of images in secular contexts, and even sometimes found historical biblical scenes acceptable in the home as inspirational aids and as testaments to the truth of the Bible. There was a certain amount of suspicion in England, however, of the art produced for the royal court under the reign of Charles I (r. 1625–49). Charles was an avid patron of the arts and turned increasingly to the European continent for artists to adorn the royal residences, commissioning works from such notables as the Flemish painters Anthony Van Dyck (1599–1641) and Peter Paul Rubens (1577–1640). In 1632 Van Dyck was appointed court portraitist and executed a series of elegant and full-bodied likenesses of the King and Queen. Queen Henrietta Maria was a French Catholic who sponsored extravagant theatrical displays, two facts that increased Puritan distrust of the royal court.

According to Craven, many within the gentry and merchant class supported an earlier and more subdued style of portraiture that marked the reigns of Queen Elizabeth I (r. 1558–1603) and King James I (r. 1603–25), known as the Elizabethan-Jacobean style. It was marked by minimal shading or other indications of physical depth, shallow spaces, and emphasis on detailed decorative patterning. The engraved portrait of Pocahontas of *c.* 1616 by the Dutch artist Simon van de Passe (*c.* 1595–1647) exhibits all of these characteristics [**1.4.9**]. Van de Passe spent many years working in England creating both portraits and maps. He executed the engraving of Pocahontas during her visit to London, when John Rolfe introduced her to the court of James I as an example of the success of the new colony of Virginia and of the efforts to convert the indigenous peoples of America to Christianity (see pp. 52–53).

There is little in Pocahontas's physical appearance, save perhaps the suggestion of dark skin, to indicate her identity as an indigenous woman from the Americas. Instead, she wears an English costume, with a high lace collar and an elaborate brocade dress with lace cuffs depicted with attention to the rich, decorative patterning. The feather fan and her tall hat, which was probably made of felted beaver fur, function as indirect references to the Americas. The text surrounding the image contains a more direct statement of her origins. It provides her indigenous name, Matoaka (Pocahontas was a nickname) and her English name, Rebecca, and indicates that she was the daughter of the Powhatan ruler. Pocahontas died in England of smallpox in 1617 before she was able to return to Virginia.

Displays of Status: Portraiture in New England

The Puritans who arrived in America in the middle of the seventeenth century brought with them, therefore, a rejection of art in the context of religious services. Many also preferred the Elizabethan-Jacobean style of portraiture. Painting in New England appears to have begun in the 1660s. Approximately forty portraits of merchants, ministers, civil officials, and their families remain from the seventeenth century. Craven points out that these were not the work of amateurish hacks, but of trained artists who came to New England, as did many others, to seek their fortunes. Because of the limited population in the English colonies, artists often had to supplement their income with more utilitarian tasks, such as the painting of signs for businesses.

As the art historian Margaretta M. Lovell notes, the family portraits that hung in New England homes, which used familiar European portrait conventions (the positioning of the figure, the inclusion of certain props, the styles of dress), helped shape and organize social life in the colonies. Their presence suggested "wholeness and completion and referentiality in a world which daily evidences disorder, incompletion, and the unravelling of yesterday's solutions."

Two of the best-known and best-studied portraits from the late seventeenth century are of John and Elizabeth Freake and their child Mary [**1.4.10, 1.4.11**; p. 70]. They were painted around 1671, with Mary added to Elizabeth's portrait in 1674, the year she was born. The complex and layered meanings of these two works are informed by the background of the Freake family and the political situation at the time. John Freake (1635–1675) was born in England and came to Boston around 1658. He soon prospered as a merchant and a lawyer, owning two houses, a brewhouse, a mill, land, and part interest in six ships. In 1661 he married Elizabeth Clarke (1642–1713), daughter of the Boston merchant Thomas Clarke.

The portraits were meant as celebrations of marital domesticity, family lineage, and social position. They also represented the piety of the Freakes and, in the process, the Calvinist doctrine of prosperity. Because of the ban on public religious imagery, one could not reveal one's devotion through the commissioning of altarpieces or other public religious works of art. Images of material wealth, however, could fill in as signs of piety, for, according to Calvin, God looked with favor on those who worked hard and kept the faith. In addition, as John Freake was among the merchants of Boston who were attempting to break the control of the ministers within the colony, he could use paintings as a way to justify on his own terms his rising prosperity.

Still, displaying one's wealth within a painting in New England was not that simple, for while Calvin preached that the devout would prosper, he also condemned lavish or ostentatious displays of this prosperity. There was much argument in the colonies over where the line should be drawn between moderation and ostentation. As the wealth of the merchant class grew, its members often got around or ignored the laws set by clergy, in particular those laws governing dress. In his portrait, John Freake is clothed in a refined, but not extravagant, manner. His coat is rich velvet brown, not the black of the Puritan garb. This rich brown sets off the fine lace collar and the white cuffs and gloves, as well as the gold ring, ornate brooch, and polished silver buttons. The background is also a rich brown, devoid of objects, so that our attention is drawn first to the bright white of the lace and cuffs, and then to the confident, self-satisfied expression of Freake himself.

Another important detail in this painting is the length of John Freake's hair. The Puritans considered long hair a sign of decadence and a mark of royalist sympathies. It was also associated with a suspect sympathy for indigenous peoples. Men in New England were regularly fined for sporting long hair. Short hair, on the other hand, was a mark of the Puritan clergy, and it was also imposed on the lower classes. Thus hair, like dress, was a sign of class. John Freake's shoulder-length hair is, like his dress, somewhere in between the two extremes.

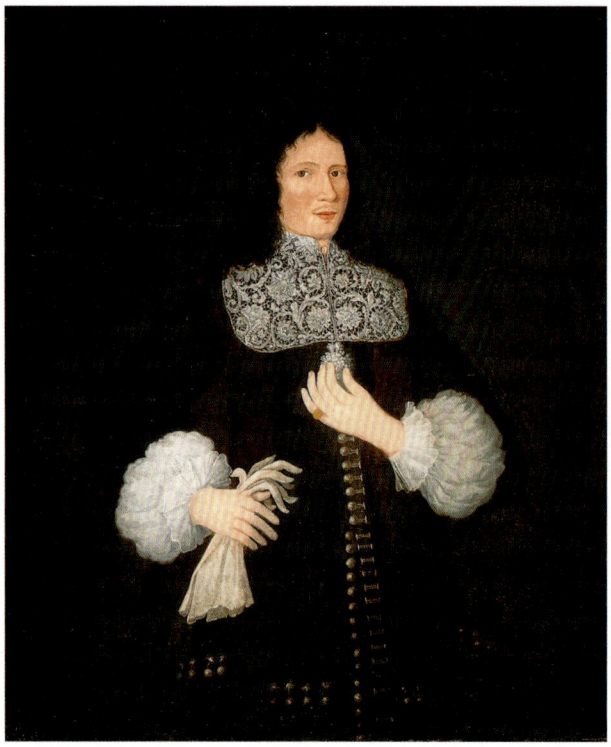

1.4.10 Unknown artist: *John Freake*, c. 1671 and 1674.
Oil on canvas, 42½ x 36¾ in. (108 x 93 cm.)
Worcester Art Museum, Worcester, Massachusetts

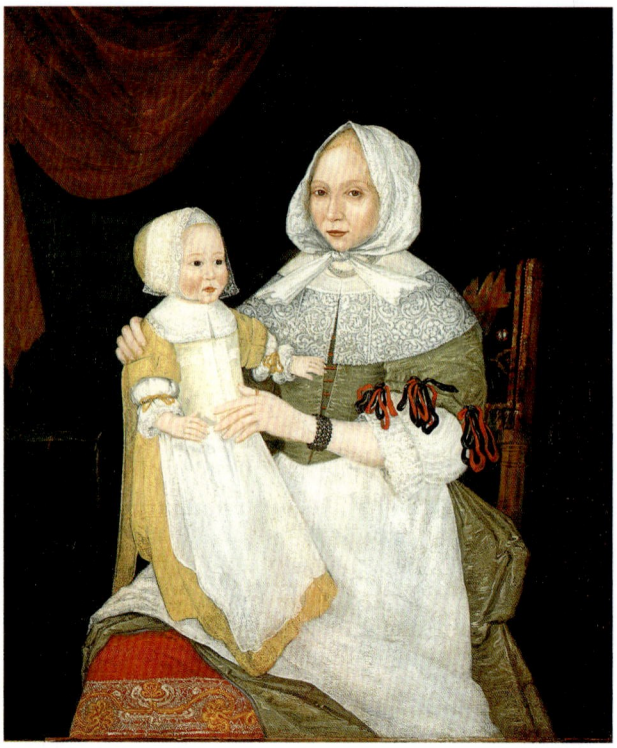

1.4.11 Unknown artist: *Elizabeth Freake and Baby Mary*, c. 1671 and 1674.
Oil on canvas, 42½ x 36¾ in. (108 x 93 cm.)
Worcester Art Museum, Worcester, Massachusetts

Elizabeth Freake and baby Mary are much more colorfully and elaborately clothed than John, as was often the case in double portraits of husbands and wives in both Europe and the American colonies. Elizabeth sports a triple strand of pearls, a four-strand garnet bracelet, and a gold ring. Her satin dress is decorated with fine lace and bows. The materials and jewels were probably imported; the satin from France, the lace from Spain, Venice, or the Netherlands, the brocade from England, the pearls from the Far East, and the garnets from India. Elizabeth sits on a Turkey-work chair, the upholstery of which imitates the patterns of Turkish carpeting. This chair was the most expensive type in the region at the time. Thus her costume and household furniture constitute a catalogue of merchant trade of the late seventeenth century, and a symbol of resistance to the limits the English crown was attempting to impose on its colonial traders.

The swag of drapery that appears in the upper left of Elizabeth's portrait is possibly an allusion to the elegant interiors of more aristocratic households. Yet it is more likely evidence of the influence of Dutch art in seventeenth-century New England portraiture. Swags of drapery are often found in seventeenth-century Dutch paintings of domestic interiors, where the drama of domestic bliss is enhanced by the presence of a theatrical curtain. In addition, this domestic harmony was often associated with national harmony in both New England and the Netherlands, thus creating another connection between domestic displays of material wealth and national aspirations. Another influence of Dutch painting can be found in the somewhat more naturalistic modeling of the faces of John, Elizabeth, and Mary Freake, which tempers the linear two-dimensionality, shallow space, and attention to detail of the Elizabethan-Jacobean style.

Displays of Status: Domestic Spaces in New England

The first permanent homes built by the settlers of New England were of timber post-and-beam construction with horizontal planks for the exterior. Most were a story and a half, with a loft accessible by steep stairs or a ladder. The main floor contained a single large room or two separate rooms, one for general activities and the other doubling as a "parlor" and master bedroom. Visitors would enter directly into one of these rooms from the outside. Smaller rooms were often added at the rear and the slope of the roof extended over them toward the ground, creating what came to be referred to as a "saltbox" house.

An example of a larger two-and-a-half-story structure from the late seventeenth century is the Parson Capen House of Topsfield, Massachusetts, built in 1683 by the community for the Reverend Joseph Capen [**1.4.12**]. An imposing, albeit plain, building for its time, it stood on the town common as a statement of the power of the clergy. Such houses were the products of carpenter-craftsmen rather than trained architects and were simple in form, with steeply pitched roofs and little exterior decoration—limited here to the deep overhangs of the second story and roof and the pendants beneath them. The design was reminiscent of many medieval merchants' houses in England.

The art historian Michael J. Lewis notes that Puritan towns were often laid out according to the model of the New Jerusalem, "the perfected city that would arise after the second coming of Christ, as described in the Book of Revelation." This city was rectilinear in plan, "recalling other gridded settlements in the Bible where divine order was expressed through right angles." This is not to say that all gridded European cities embodied the New Jerusalem. The grid had been used extensively for town plans throughout Renaissance Europe and in the Spanish American colonies, but, according to Lewis, most "lacked the religious theme of the Puritan town plan, which was a diagram of moral order and not merely a convenient system for the equable division of real estate." As such, the Puritan town paralleled the city of Tenochtitlan, the plan of which embodied the Aztec social and religious universe (see pp. 20–21).

Because Puritans viewed the entire community as holy, little emphasis was given to the design of the meeting house or place of worship, although it was often placed on high ground, like the Parson Capen House, to indicate the importance of events that took place within. The facades and interiors of these primarily wooden structures were plain, with the pulpit often located in the center of the hall.

Colonial homes required interior furnishings, which were made locally as well as imported. Almost all designs found in

1.4.12 Parson Capen House, Topsfield, Massachusetts, 1683.

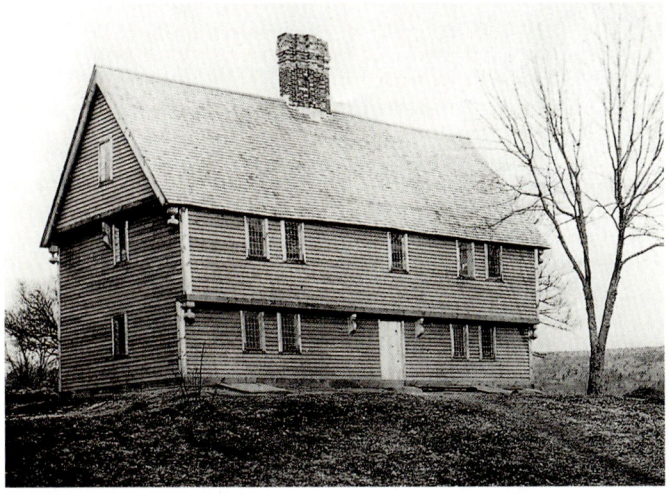

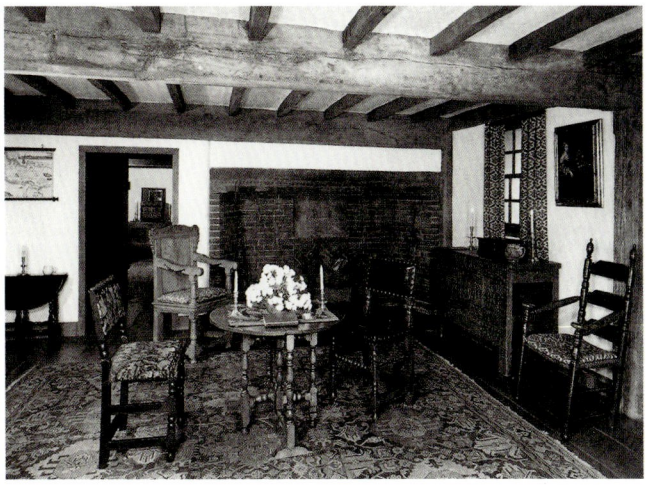

1.4.13 Oyster Bay Room, 17th century.
The Henry Francis du Pont Winterthur Museum, Winterthur, Delaware

New England furniture before 1680 were borrowed from Europe, in particular from London. But by the close of the century, with increased prosperity gained largely through international commerce, designs from other parts of the world began to appear, particularly in decorative detailing. They were often transformed by colonial craftspeople trained in medieval woodworking traditions into new syncretic forms specific to life and circumstances in the northeastern part of North America. According to the folk-art historians Robert Bishop and Jacqueline M. Atkins, two general schemes existed:

> high style (or that most akin to the imported prototypes), to which everyone with pretensions and financial ability aspired, and a popular style, or one that was based on a formal prototype and then simplified and modified by self-taught craftsmen, artists, and artisans.

The main hall of the Freake home may well have resembled the reconstruction of a seventeenth-century interior by the Winterthur Museum [**1.4.13**], with its Turkey-work chair, oak table, carved chest, and portrait on the wall. A fine piece made by a local furniture-maker in Northampton, Massachusetts is the Esther Lyman Chest (1712–22) [**1.4.14**; p. 72]. Much of its original red and black paint survives. Painting (often used to cover up inexpensive wood or rough construction) was particularly popular in conjunction with carving for chests in New England. Here the construction is quite simple and the bold decorative floral forms are carved in low relief. The name of the owner—Esther Lyman—is prominently carved across the front, while the name Erastus Banks, possibly the maker, appears on the bottom of the drawer and across the back.

The Esther Lyman Chest was probably meant to hold part of a girl's dowry, perhaps bed furnishings and clothing, to be taken to her new home once she married. It is an example of a type of early eighteenth-century carved furniture, known as Hadley, found throughout the Connecticut Valley between 1675 and 1740. These items share a decorative motif: a carved tulip-and-leaf pattern on the outer front panels. This motif may have been drawn from a late Elizabethan-Renaissance style of ornamental carving produced in Massachusetts by an immigrant Englishman named William Searle. Other craftsmen then picked up the design and created their own versions, adding scrolls, fleurs-de-lis, and meandering vines. Other chests had painted decoration only, which included buildings and landscapes as well as floral elements. Their legs are often more elegantly shaped and their edges more carefully finished, suggesting that their makers were more concerned with aspiring to the "high style" of furniture than the maker of Esther Lyman's chest.

Among this "high style" in New England in the first half of the eighteenth century was a type of furniture that had its origins in trade with Asia. This furniture utilized a technique known as "japanning", a painted imitation of Japanese lacquer work (objects with a clear or colored wood finish or lacquer that is applied in several layers and often carved or inlaid when dry). Japanning was found primarily on furniture and wall panelling. This practice was common in Europe and an indication of the spread of the taste for all things Asian among the political and cultural elite. During the eighteenth century, japanning spread in popularity throughout New England, New Spain, the Caribbean, and parts of South America, due in part to the importation of the style from Europe, and in part to the already flourishing direct trade between the Americas and Asia.

1.4.14 Erastus Banks (?): the Esther Lyman Chest, from Northampton, Massachusetts 1712–22.
Painted wood, 34 x 45 x 18¾ in. (86.4 x 114.3 x 47.6 cm.)
Private collection

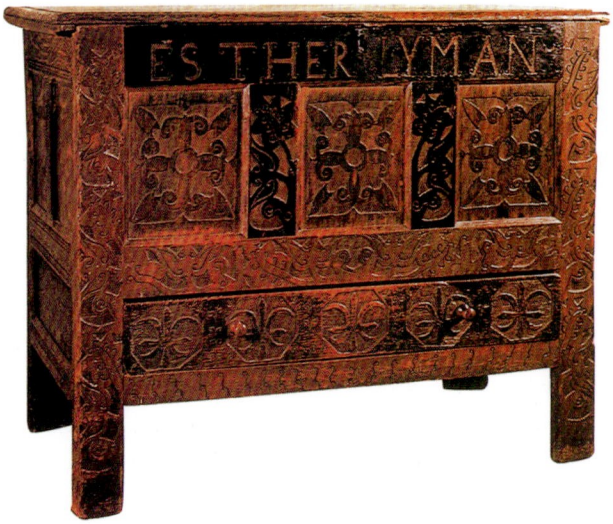

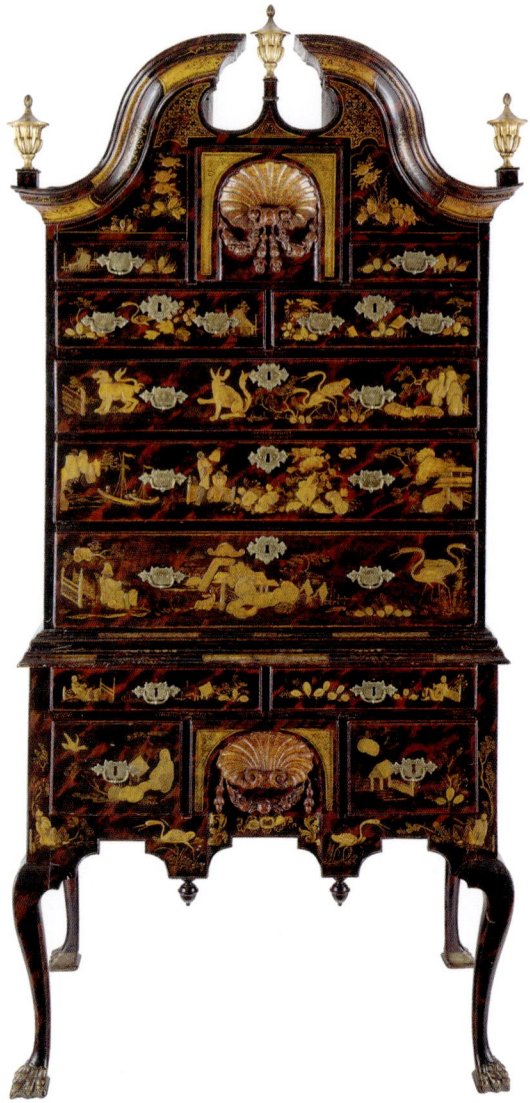

1.4.15 John Pimm, japanning attributed to Robert Davis: high chest, Boston, 1730–39.
Soft maple, black walnut, white pine, mahogany, with japanned decoration, 85¼ x 42 x 25¼ in. (216.5 x 106.7 x 64.1 cm.)
Winterthur Museum, Winterthur, Delaware

Furniture makers in New England had access to several European publications that provided information on japanning, such as Salmon's *Polygraphice*, which was available for sale in Boston as early as 1719. In fact, according to the art historian Dennis Clark, Boston emerged as a leading center for the production of japanned furniture in the early eighteenth century. A fine example is a high chest created some time between 1730 and 1739 by John Pimm (active by 1735, died 1773), with the japanning attributed to Robert Davis (died 1739) [**1.4.15**]. Clark describes the process used to create such chests:

> Boston japanning typically was painted directly on the wood substrate, usually locally available maple or pine.

> The painter started with a base of lampblack to simulate Japanese lacquer, or broad brushstrokes of lampblack (or dark brown paint) over a red ground to simulate tortoiseshell. Boston japanners often added raised figures in gesso, which were painted in oil paints and then highlighted with glazes and metallic powders, as seen in [the Pimm chest]. The powdered bronze, silver, or gold was sprinkled over a size, such as hide glue, to adhere it to the surface....The final step was to add "penwork," applied with a fine brush to give figures definition and detail.

The Pimm chest, with its shell decorations, metallic claw feet, golden lanterns, and scenes of pagodas, parasols, kimonoed figures, and cranes is reminiscent of the iconography of the Ursuline altar frontals [**1.3.5**; p. 54]. It functioned as an elegant testament to the worldliness of its owner.

The Dutch Influence in Architecture and Portraits

The Dutch influence in New England portraiture was not simply the result of the presence of Dutch paintings and engravings in New England. It was also due to the presence of the Dutch themselves in the New World. As indicated earlier (see p. 51), the first Dutch colony, Fort Nassau (Albany, New York), was established in 1614. It was followed by a second in 1624, New Amsterdam, which was intended to control the trade between Virginia and Plymouth. Its focus was profit, not religion, and those who prospered constructed homes and decorated the interiors with numerous prints and paintings. The town's architecture was marked by distinctive Dutch brick row houses with crow-stepped gables, seen in a lithograph made from a sketch by Adrian Danckers from 1679 [**1.4.16**]. The large stone building in the center is the Stadthuys or town hall, built in 1641–42.

1.4.16 View of the waterfront of New Amsterdam showing the Stadthuys of 1641–42.
Lithograph by George Hayward, after a sketch by Adrian Danckers of 1679, 19th century.
The New York Public Library, New York

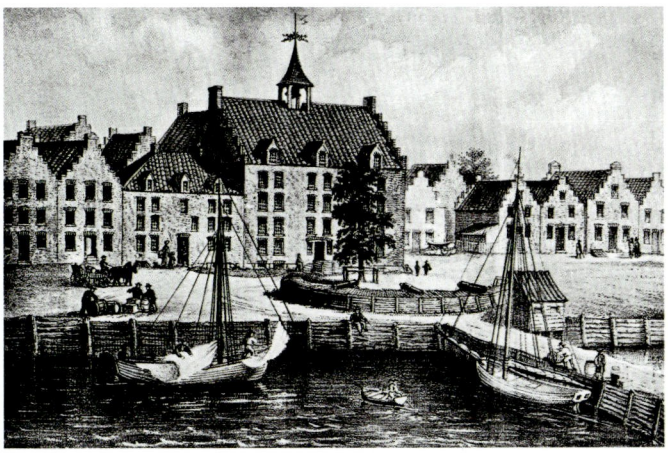

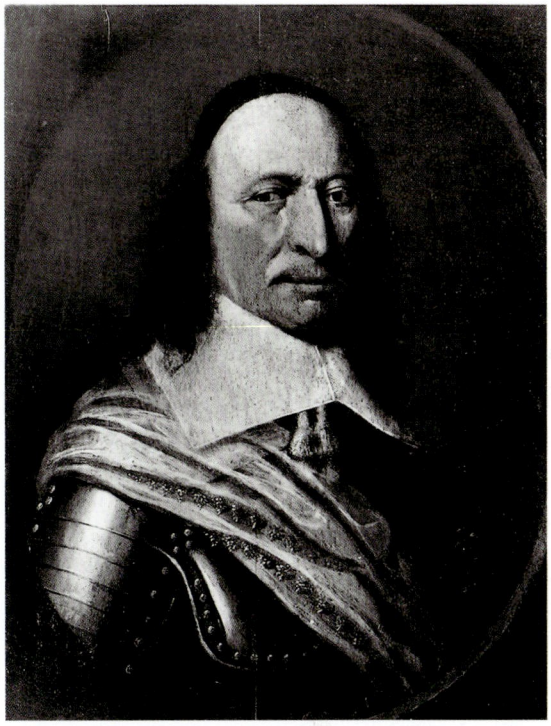

1.4.17 Attributed to Henri Couturier: *Governor Peter Stuyvesant*, c. 1663.
Oil on wood panel, 21½ x 17½ in. (54.6 x 44.4 cm.)
Courtesy The New-York Historical Society, New York

Few paintings from seventeenth-century New Amsterdam, survive today. One of the best-preserved is a portrait of Governor Peter Stuyvesant, painted around 1663 and attributed to the Dutch artist Henri Couturier [**1.4.17**]. Couturier immigrated to colonial America in 1660, living briefly in New Amstel (New Castle, Delaware) before moving to New Amsterdam. His portrait of Stuyvesant is certainly very different from the portrait of John Freake [**1.4.10**; p. 70]. The figure is fully modeled, positioned convincingly within a three-dimensional space, and wearing armor with a sheen that suggests the hardness of the metal.

If Stuyvesant looks somewhat concerned it was no doubt because of the seemingly impossible task that faced him as he took over the governorship of the colony in 1647. New Amsterdam was, by all accounts, highly unorganized, with everyone competing for profits and little interest in establishing communal organizations or defences. Alcohol flowed freely and trade with the Iroquois was haphazard. Stuyvesant controlled the sale of alcohol, organized trade with the Iroquois, and negotiated the Treaty of Hartford in 1650 with the English, who were encroaching on Dutch territory and who ultimately declared war in 1652 in an attempt to gain control of trade in the region.

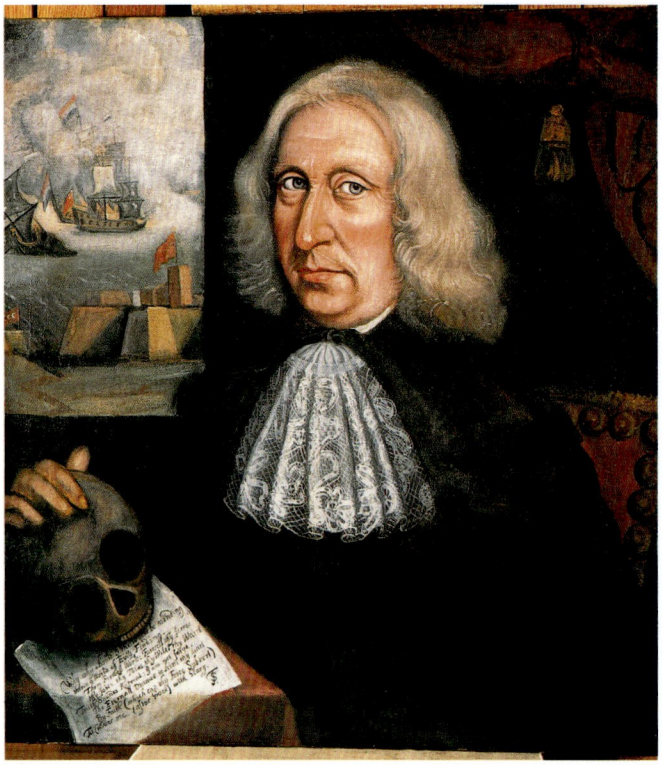

1.4.18 Thomas Smith: *Self-portrait*, *c.* 1680.
Oil on canvas, 24½ x 23¾ in. (62.9 x 60.4 cm.)
Worcester Art Museum, Worcester, Massachusetts

Skirmishes with the English to the north and the Swedes to the south continued over the next decade. New Amsterdam finally surrendered to the English in 1664 and the town was renamed New York.

Another portrait from the seventeenth century attests to this mix of Dutch and English in the New World, the *Self-portrait* painted by Thomas Smith (died *c.* 1691) in *c.* 1680 [**1.4.18**]. The image is much busier than those examined thus far. It includes not only a human figure modeled fully in the round, and evidence of the furnishings within the room, but also a seascape viewed out the window and a still life composed of a skull and a sheet of paper containing a poem. The art historian Roger Stein notes that despite its relatively small size, it has a commanding presence, due in no small part to the poem resting beneath the skull. To be more easily read, the poem is tilted up:

> Why, why should I the World be minding
> therin a World of Evils Finding
> Then Farewell World: Farewell thy Jarres
> thy Joies thy Toies thy Wiles thy Warrs
> Truth Sounds Retreat: I am not Sorye
> The Eternall Drawes to him my heart
> By Faith (which can thy Force Subvert)
> To Crowne me (after Grace) with Glory.

The melancholic tone of the poem, with its focus on aging and past glories, is reinforced by the presence of the skull (which appears to "speak" the words), turning the self-portrait into a *vanitas* or *memento mori* image with the message "remember that thou shalt die." Thus the conceptual, or the contemplation of death, outweighs the perceptual or worldly appearances.

Thomas Smith was a mariner who came to New England from Bermuda around 1650. A sailor by profession, he also painted and, at his death, was a wealthy man. His wealth did not prevent— and perhaps even encouraged—his philosophical ruminations on his eventual death, ruminations that appear both in the poem and in the painting itself. Smith presents his worldly self—his own full-bodied presence, the fine lace, and the naval exploits in which he took part. The ships in the distance are identifiable as Dutch and English; the fortress flag bearing the three crescents suggests that the scene may represent the joint English/Dutch attack on Cape Spartal on the African coast in 1670. At the same time he denies that self with the poem. Ultimately, he suggests that one can participate fully in worldly events and, in the afterlife, inhabit a spiritual world. The poem allows the religious elements of piety and transformation into the picture without representing saints or Christ himself, thus conforming to the Calvinist admonition not to paint what one cannot see.

Evidence of the Dutch presence in early eighteenth-century New England can also be seen in a large overmantel painting (a painting that hung above the mantel of a fireplace) of 1732–33 attributed to John Heaten and found in the Marten Van Bergen homestead in Leeds, Greene County, New York [**1.4.19**]. The rich detail of the picture, with the Catskill Mountains in the background, allows us access to both the architecture and the activities of the Van Bergen farm and its inhabitants. Heaten's overmantel documents members of the family as well as two white servants, four African slaves, and two indigenous figures, possibly members of the Catskill or Esopus peoples. Slaveholding was practiced in the Hudson Valley in the eighteenth century, and it is known that Mrs Van Bergen received a slave as a wedding present from her father. It is not clear whether the indigenous figures are also part of the farm's labor force, but their use as slaves as early as the 1630s in New England raises the possibility that they are.

The farmhouse is constructed of stone with a tile roof, building materials preferred by Dutch settlers over the wood used by the English (the roof of the kitchen addition is, however, made of wood shingles). The steep-pitched roof with dormer windows

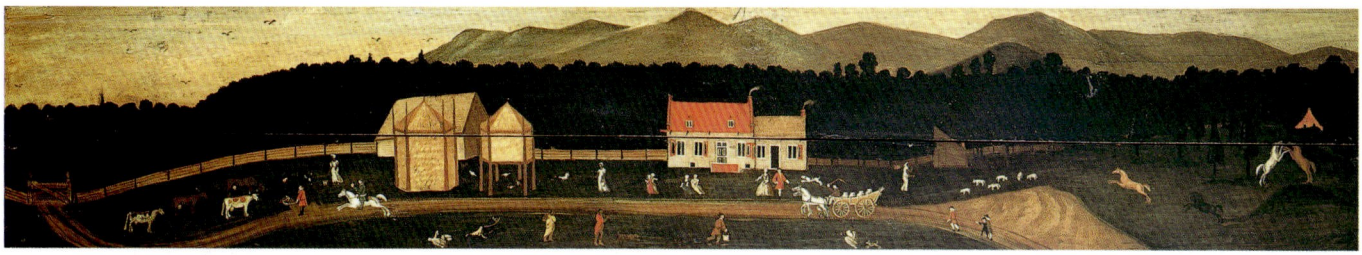

1.4.19 Attributed to John Heaten: overmantel from the Marten Van Bergen House, Leeds, Greene County, New York, 1732–33.
Oil on wood, 15¼ x 87½ in. (38.7 x 222.2 cm.)
New York State Historical Association, Cooperstown

and the chimneys in the end walls were also characteristic of Dutch farmhouse architecture. There is a barn and two hay barracks, of a kind distinct to this area, built so that the roof and floors could be lowered or raised to protect the hay (prototypes are known in Europe).

Aristocratic Pretensions in the South

In the seventeenth century, the southern colonies tended to be royalist and Episcopalian or Church of England, supporting the crown during the Civil War of 1642–51 in England (colonial Puritans backed the successful forces of the Puritan leader Oliver Cromwell). The charter of the Virginia Company made the Church of England official in the southern colonies. The distinctive architectural features of the churches that were constructed set them apart more clearly from domestic architecture than was the case with the meeting halls of Puritan New England (see p. 73). Most of the approximately fifty churches built in the seventeenth century were simple parish churches made of wood. The only one still standing, St. Luke's in Isle of Wight County [**1.4.20**], was built of masonry in 1632 and provides an indication of the architectural features that connected these churches to the religious architecture of medieval England—an entrance tower at the west end leading to a single nave, buttresses along the sides of the nave, and windows marked by pairs of pointed arches.

The plantation economy of the southern states was enabled by the large-scale importation of chattel slaves from Africa (the slave population numbered 15,000 in 1700 and rose to 100,000 in 1750). It produced a society in which the lifestyle and culture echoed that of the English aristocracy. The southern economy also included a significant number of indentured servants, who, as immigrants from England or other European countries, often assumed they had a right to participate in the political and economic order on an equal footing with the plantation owners once they had completed their agreed-upon terms of servitude. In 1676 Nathaniel Bacon led a rebellion of such laborers against those wealthy Virginians who resisted their participation (African slaves were also among Bacon's group). The rebellion failed, but not before causing serious distress among the local gentry.

While wary of political revolts carried out by what they perceived as the "lower orders" of society, Virginia aristocrats were not averse to fomenting their own revolution. As the historian Arthur Quinn points out, the generation that came out of the plantations in the middle of the eighteenth century—which included Patrick Henry, George Washington, Thomas Jefferson, James Madison, John Marshall, and James Monroe—would play a key role in the American Revolution. This elite would build residences patterned not after English village houses, as was the case in New England, but after English country manors.

One example of such a country manor is "Bacon's Castle" in Surrey County, used as a bastion by the followers of Bacon in 1676 [**1.4.21**; p. 76]. The home of Arthur Allen, it was constructed of brick around 1655. The fireplace and chimney are placed at the end, rather than in the center as in the Parson Capen House [**1.4.12**; p. 71]. This decision was determined in part by climate,

1.4.20 St. Luke's, Isle of Wight County, Virginia, 1632.

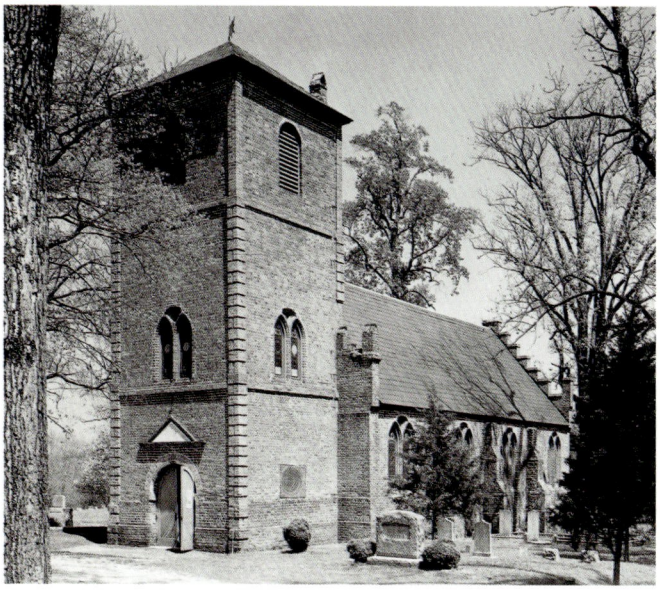

as having the chimney in the center provides more even distribution of the heat throughout the house during cold winters. The placement of the chimney at the end allowed for the use of its shape as a decorative element in the otherwise relatively plain exterior. The mass of the chimney rising through the two-and-a-half stories is topped by three chimneystacks set diagonally, which tower above the roof. Viewed from the end, the receding shapes of chimney, main house and projecting porches, along with the diagonally placed chimneystacks and the shaped gables (imported into England from Holland or Flanders in the late sixteenth century), create a play of forms that adds to the visual complexity of the building.

Bacon's Castle also included a molded brick pediment over the main doorway (not visible in the illustration), an early version of the classical detail found on the exteriors of most of the grander southern urban mansions and rural plantation houses in the following century (few the size of Bacon's Castle were built in the seventeenth century). One of the earliest of these eighteenth-century plantation houses was located on Mulberry Plantation in Moncks Corner, South Carolina. Thomas Broughton, an English planter and later Royal Governor of South Carolina, built the two-story brick structure in 1714 [**1.4.22**].

1.4.21 Bacon's Castle, Surrey County, Virginia, *c.* 1655.

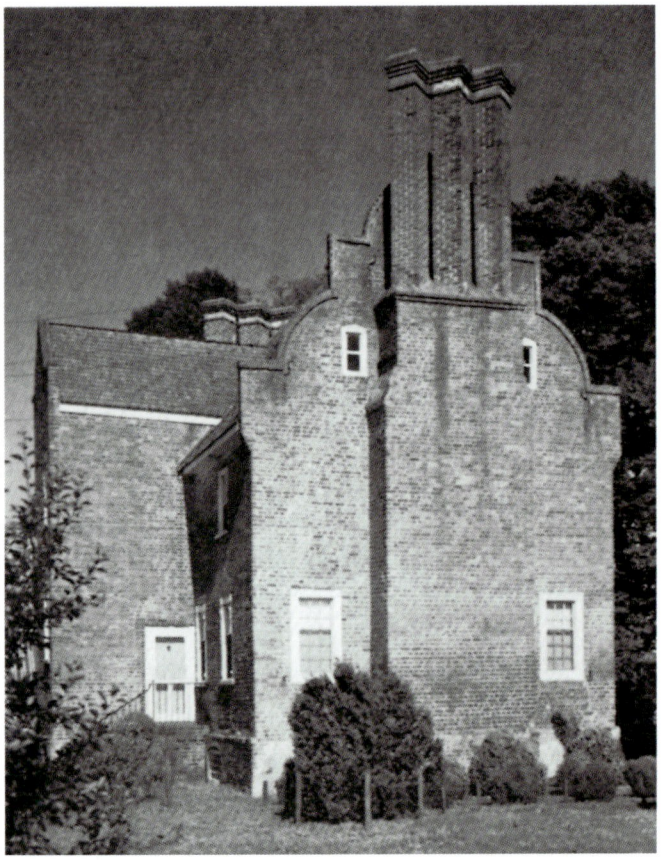

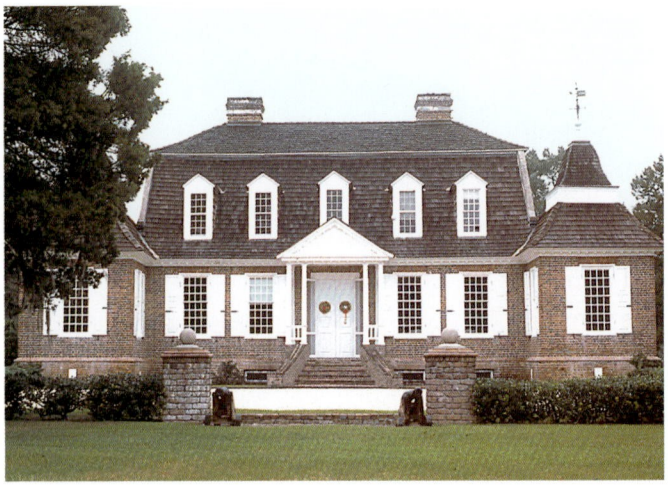

1.4.22 Mulberry Plantation, Moncks Corner, South Carolina, 1714.

1.4.23 Thomas Coram: *View of Mulberry, House and Street*, *c.* 1800. Oil on paper, 4⅛ x 6⅞ in. (10.4 x 17 cm). Gibbes Museum of Art, Charleston, South Carolina

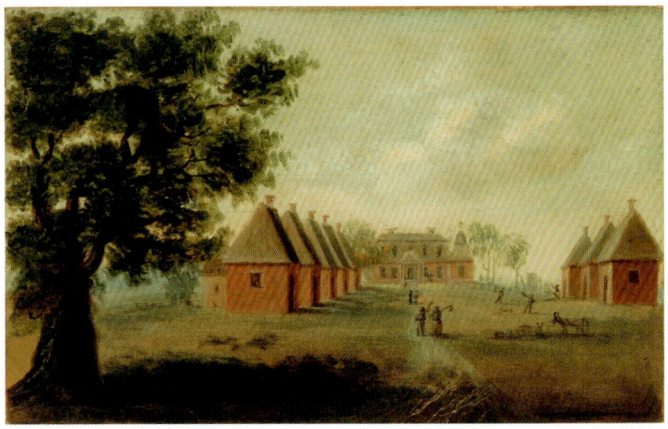

It is an imaginative architectural design, combining classical pediments over the entrance porch and second-story dormer windows in the central block with tower pavilions on either side. It also contains firing slits in the cellar's foundation walls, features that led to the nickname "Mulberry Castle." The building's references to a castle, or even fortress, were fitting, as a series of wars broke out in the region from 1711 to 1715 between the colonists and indigenous peoples over the expansion of English settlements. Several people took refuge at Mulberry Plantation during the war between the colonists and the Yemassee in 1715. South Carolina also experienced a major uprising of slaves in 1739, the Stono Rebellion, in which more than twenty white Carolinians and almost twice as many black Carolinians lost their lives.

Around 1800, the artist Thomas Coram produced an oil sketch of Mulberry Plantation [**1.4.23**], part of a projected book of "portraits" or engraved views of southern plantation mansions that was never completed. It shows a series of small huts with steeply pitched roofs that echo in design and color the tower pavilions of the main house. The huts are arranged in an orderly fashion along the road leading up to the main entrance of the plantation house in the distance. These huts housed the slaves, several of whom are shown on or beside the road. In his study of plantation architecture, the American Studies scholar and anthropologist John Michael Vlach notes that slave quarters were often located behind or away from the main house, as at Thomas Jefferson's plantation mansion Monticello (see pp. 110–12). Their presence alongside the major entrance road on some plantations, like Mulberry, served to reinforce the wealth of the planter and the size of the plantation. This might help explain why the slave quarters dwarf the plantation house in Coram's painting.

While the institution of chattel slavery affected the arrangement and types of buildings on southern plantations, the slaves themselves often created another, less visible, order on the land. They carved out landscapes to fit their own social needs. These included networks of trails through the woods and fields connecting plantations and clandestine meeting places. Large plantations with a hundred or more slaves often contained slave "towns," which were sometimes laid out by the planter in regular rows utilizing a grid plan that embodied, according to Vlach, the order and control that the planters imposed on the life of their slaves. Left to their own devices, slaves preferred irregularly placed buildings a considerable distance from the main house. One observer of rice plantations in Georgia commented that slaves, when allowed to build their own houses, "wanted their cabins in some secluded place, down in the hollow, or amid the trees, with only a path to their abode." The further away from the main house, the less subject the slaves would be to surveillance.

Vlach argues that despite the obvious limits placed on slaves' abilities to determine their own daily routines, they were able, in some instances, to claim at least a modicum of control through their arrangement of the spaces at the "back of the big house." They were able to create "plantation landscape ensembles" or "black landscapes" out of their own quarters and the various outbuildings (barns, stables, kitchens, storage sheds) that existed between these quarters and the plantation house.

Another way in which plantation slaves exerted a certain amount of control over their lives was through their knowledge of rice cultivation and the medicinal qualities of plants, as well as their skill in creating the baskets and the wooden mortars that were so central a part of the processing of the rice crop. According to the historian Peter Wood, the challenge for the eighteenth-century plantation owners of South Carolina, the major rice-growing region in the southern colonies, was not teaching African slaves how to plant and harvest their crops. Instead it lay in controlling the skills that Africans brought with them, skills that could easily be used against their masters. Many slaves came from West Africa where rice cultivation was common and where the climate and geography was similar to that of South Carolina. The English, on the other hand, often found the terrain foreign and difficult to manage. They relied on their African slaves to cultivate the fields and to transport them through the marshy shore lands in dugout canoes made by these slaves, which were similar to the ones they used in West Africa. These canoes, coupled with the intimate knowledge of the landscape, enabled some slaves to escape from plantations and to find refuge with various indigenous communities.

As the art historian Dale Rosengarten notes, the baskets made by African slaves for storing [**1.4.24**] or winnowing rice were different from the woven baskets of the indigenous peoples of the region. Like those in Africa, most African slave baskets in South Carolina were made using a coiling, rather than weaving, technique. Bundles of bulrush were bound together with thin oak splints or strips from the stem of the saw palmetto plant. Skilled basket makers were highly valued, and had a greater degree of autonomy than field hands; once they had finished the number of baskets they had been tasked with creating, they could make additional ones for themselves, which they could sell. While few baskets from the eighteenth century survive, the practice continues down to the present and is still a source of income for many African Americans in the South Carolina coastal regions.

The control that plantation owners exerted over their slaves had to be constantly reasserted, through both the surveillance and brutalization of slave bodies on the one hand, and the cultural assertion of the superiority of white Europeans on the

1.4.24 Unknown artist: covered work basket, South Carolina, possibly mid-18th century.
D. 17 ½ in. (44.5 cm.), Private collection

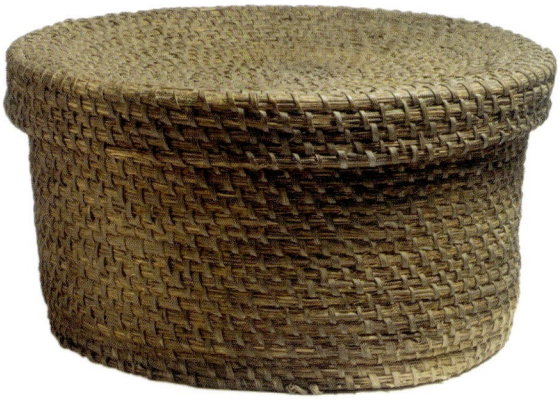

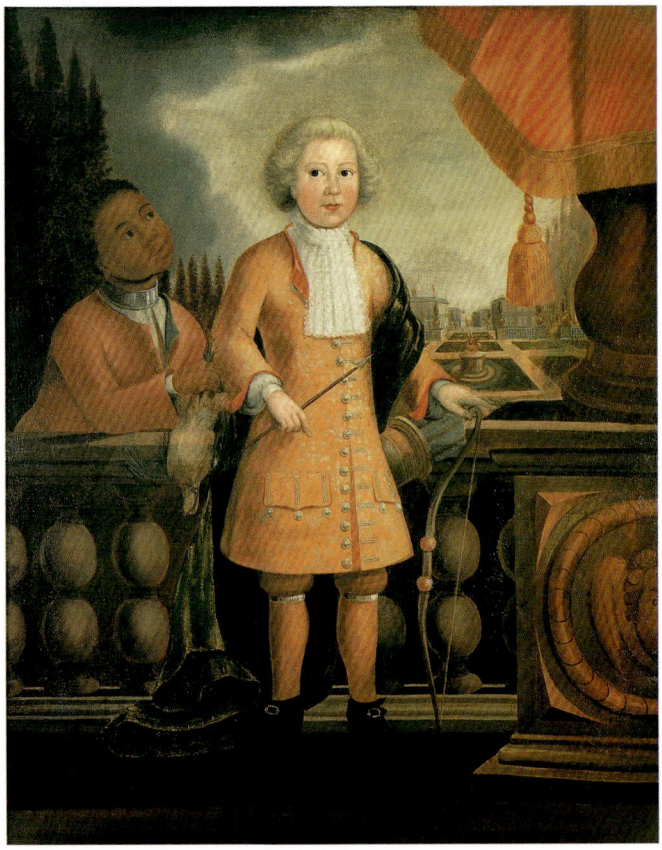

1.4.25 Justus Engelhardt Kühn: *Henry Darnall III as a Child*, c. 1710. Oil on canvas, 54¼ x 44¼ in. (137.8 x 112.4 cm.) Maryland Historical Society, Baltimore

other. This sense of superiority is embodied in the portraiture that developed in the southern colonies. For example, *Henry Darnall III as a Child* of *c.* 1710 [**1.4.25**], by Justus Engelhardt Kühn (died 1717), conveys the aristocratic pretensions of southerners through the elegant costume of the young figure and the elaborate formal gardens and palatial buildings behind him, references to the residences of English or Continental nobility. None of this magnitude existed in the colonies at this time, and Kühn may have copied the architecture and gardens from contemporary engravings. Henry's young African slave is another testament to the wealth and status of his family, one of the richest in the region surrounding Annapolis, Maryland. Wearing a silver collar as an indication of his slave status, he brings young Henry the results of the hunt. Both collar and bird are clear attempts to associate the young boy with a servile dog. His inferior status is further reinforced by his location behind and below Darnall, separated from the white boy by the balustrade and by the color of his skin.

In 1708, the year the German Kühn arrived in Annapolis, another artist stepped ashore in the southern colonies to ply her trade—Henrietta Dering Johnston (*c.* 1674–1728). Johnston had traveled to England from France with her Protestant parents in 1687. From there she moved to Dublin, Ireland, before coming to South Carolina as the wife of Gideon Johnston, a clergyman of the Church of England. She may have received some training in Ireland under the tutelage of Simon Digby, Bishop of Elphin, an amateur portraitist. At any rate, she brought with her pastels and paper and immediately began to supplement her husband's income (and pay off his debts) with pastel portraits of the leading citizens of Charleston.

It is instructive to compare the portraits Johnston executed of Colonel Samuel and Mary Prioleau in 1715 [**1.4.26, 1.4.27**] with those of John and Elizabeth Freake [**1.4.10, 1.4.11**; p. 70]. Just as the costumes of John and Elizabeth indicate their social standing as pious but prosperous merchants of Puritan Boston, those of Samuel and Mary link them to the high society of Charleston and, in particular, to the large French Protestant or Huguenot community of which they were members. Like Johnston and her parents, many Huguenots fled from France to Protestant Europe and America in the late 1680s, after Louis XIV revoked their religious and political freedoms in 1685.

Samuel wears the long, curled wig and high cravat of French court society, while Mary sports a décolletage that would have raised many a Puritan eyebrow, although by the late seventeenth century wives of successful merchants in New England were looking to the fashions of the European courts. Johnston is not concerned with meticulous, hard-edged detail, as was the painter of the Freake portraits. Instead, she renders Samuel and Mary with loose, painterly strokes and uses firm lines only around the eyes, which give them a particular prominence. And where the Freake portraits have somber backgrounds, the Prioleaus reside within light-filled, indeterminate spaces, qualities that are in keeping with an eighteenth-century style in France known as Rococo.

The medium chosen by Johnston is also significant, for pastels were only then being introduced into court society in Europe by another female artist, Rosalba Carriera (1675–1757) (the Freake portraits are done in oil). This medium was particularly popular in the court of Louis XV, for, in the words of the art historian Whitney Chadwick, it was "uniquely suited to the early eighteenth-century search for an art of surface elegance and sensation." The dry chalk pigments of pastels were also similar to those used in women's and theater make-up; pastel portraits were thus able to capture these enhancers of artifice so prevalent in aristocratic society.

Despite the difficulties of Henrietta Dering Johnston's life—a husband constantly in debt, hurricanes, mosquitoes, illness, the general hardships of colonial life, the antagonism between secular authorities and her husband, and the latter's death

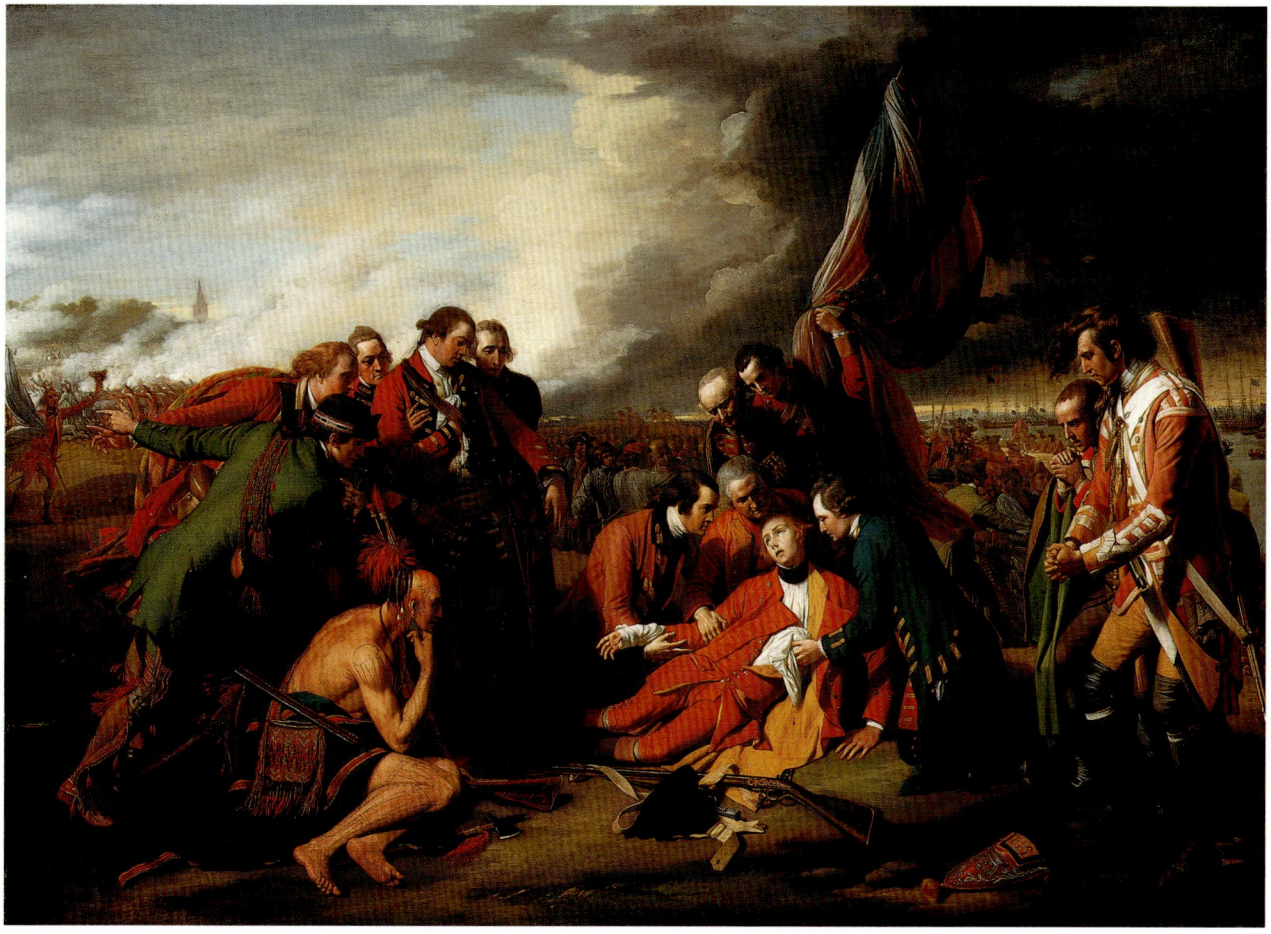

1.4.31 Benjamin West: *The Death of General Wolfe*, 1770. Oil on canvas, 59½ x 84 in. (151.1 x 213.4 cm.) National Gallery of Canada, Ottawa

secure the defeat of the French—the small figure on the left comes running with the news.

West took artistic license in his choice of the timing and location of Wolfe's death (he died in the first minutes of the battle after being wounded three times), the posing of the dying general's body, and the selection of those included in the painting. Only one of the onlookers, Lieutenant Henry Browne, who stands directly behind Wolfe holding the flag, was actually present at Wolfe's death. In fact, as far as can be determined, a mere four or five soldiers attended the demise of their general. A hint as to how the other figures made it into the painting can be found in a letter written several years later by the daughter of one of the officers who fought at Quebec, General John Hale. She notes that her father, who was not present at Wolfe's death, was not included in the painting because he refused to pay West £100 sterling. This implies that the others not present at the death did pay, including Brigadier General Robert Monckton, standing to the left clutching his chest wound, and Wolfe's Adjutant General, Major Isaac Barré, directly above the dying general's head. The art historian Susan Rather notes that West was often criticized in Britain during his life for a particularly "American" obsession with money.

The group surrounding the dying Wolfe also includes an Iroquois man, seated on the ground in a pensive position. Here West does allude to the classical past. The figure is modeled after classical prototypes found in Greek and Roman sculpture. His partial nudity provides West with an opportunity to demonstrate clearly his skill at rendering the human form. He is also the only figure who neither attends to the dying general nor shows distress at the event unfolding before him (West drew on the French painter Charles Le Brun's publication *Expressions of the Passions of the Soul* (1649) in formulating the specific facial expressions of the men surrounding Wolfe). He is present as a reminder of the locale of the battle—the North American colonies—and of the role indigenous peoples played in the wars between the British and the French. With his tattooed skin, sparse but finely decorated clothing, and elaborate hairstyle, he is evidence of the difference between these peoples and the British. He is shown passively contemplating an event that would have radical consequences for him and others like him in the near future.

Another figure reminds the viewer of the role of American colonists in the British Army. Directly behind and leaning over the head of the Iroquois is William Johnson, a New Yorker who had distinguished himself in earlier battles at Lake George and Fort Niagara but who was not present at the Battle of the Plains of Abraham. He wears moccasins and beaded breeches and has a beaded bag, similar to the one worn by the Iroquois, slung over his shoulder. As a superintendent of Indian affairs, Johnson had used his knowledge of indigenous customs and language (he had married a Mohawk woman) in gaining the cooperation of the Iroquois to ally with the British. He marks a transitional stage between the half-naked Iroquois man and the British officers in their full dress uniforms, just as the American colonies existed somewhere between the "untamed" lands and cultures of indigenous peoples and the elaborate courts of the British aristocracy.

Shortly after West finished *The Death of General Wolfe* he began another painting that dealt more directly with relations between European settlers and indigenous people, *Penn's Treaty with the Indians When He Founded the Province of Pennsylvania in North America* (1771–72) [**1.4.32**]. While ostensibly representing an event that took place in 1682, the year of William Penn's arrival, West's painting also addressed contemporary struggles for power between indigenous peoples and Europeans, and also between different groups of European settlers. Penn was an important member of the Religious Society of Friends, more commonly known as the Quakers, which had been founded in England in the late 1640s. One of its distinctive features was the belief that all members of the religious community were equal. The Quakers did away with the hierarchies that marked Catholicism and much of Protestantism as well. Puritans and Anglicans alike attacked Quakers, and Penn thus sought refuge, as the Puritans had before him, in the New World, hoping to build a community where Quakers could freely practice their religious principles. In 1681 he wrote a memorandum establishing the form of the new settlement of Philadelphia, its name indicating that it was to be the "city of brotherly love."

West's painting records the celebrated meeting between William Penn and the chiefs of the Lenni Lenape or Delaware peoples under an elm tree at Shackamaxon, where papers were signed marking the first legal agreement between Europeans and indigenous peoples. It also marked the first time the former paid the latter for land legally granted to them by the British government. Penn believed that sharing land and resources was necessary for the survival of the colony, but also that it was morally the right thing to do. Some now argue that the absence of contemporary written accounts of the meeting at Shackamaxon suggest that it never took place and that the painting is, instead, an allegory of colonial America: enlightened man of reason meets noble savage.

Even if the meeting did not take place at this location, Penn did manage to establish peaceful relations between the Quaker colony of Pennsylvania and the indigenous populations in the region, although they soon eroded as new settlers arrived and more land was needed. By 1737 Thomas Penn, William Penn's son, was appropriating indigenous lands protected by deeds signed by his father in order to satisfy the demands of these new settlers. Different tensions arose as well. By 1757 prominent Quakers were increasingly questioning both Thomas Penn's tax-exempt status and his desire to arm colonists against indigenous peoples. They initiated a "peace offensive" with local indigenous communities, holding gift-exchange ceremonies and recalling William Penn's legacy of peace without guns.

The art historian Ann Uhry Abrams argues that Thomas Penn commissioned West to paint *Penn's Treaty with the Indians* as an attempt to reassert the right of the Penn family to proprietorship of the colony of Pennsylvania. West was a particularly appropriate choice. He had grown up in Pennsylvania, the tenth child of an innkeeper in a Quaker community west of Philadelphia. His introduction to painting, he claimed, came from indigenous people in the area, who showed him how to mix the red and yellow earths with which they painted their faces. Like so many eighteenth-century artists, West then began copying engravings and portraits that hung in the homes of his family's friends. His talent was soon recognized, and at seventeen he entered Benjamin Franklin's College of Philadelphia as an honorary student. He gained the support of many of the town's leading citizens, including William Smith, an Anglican minister and ally of Thomas Penn.

When West left Pennsylvania in 1759, fighting had already broken out between indigenous communities and Quaker settlers. Many of his Quaker relatives were parting ways with Penn and Smith, whose power and fortunes depended on trade. By 1764 pacifist Quakers had lost control of the assembly and Thomas Penn's proprietary party took over. In 1768 Penn signed a series of new treaties that resulted in a temporary lull in the fighting.

West arranges the major historical and contemporary players in Pennsylvania into three overlapping groups—the Quaker political leaders, the merchants, and the indigenous peoples. The portly figure of William Penn stands slightly to the left of center. To reinforce the connection between this historical moment and the concerns of the 1760s, West clothes the Quaker men in eighteenth-century, rather than seventeenth-century, garb. He also includes his own half-brother and father among them (some think the figure at the far left leaning on a crate

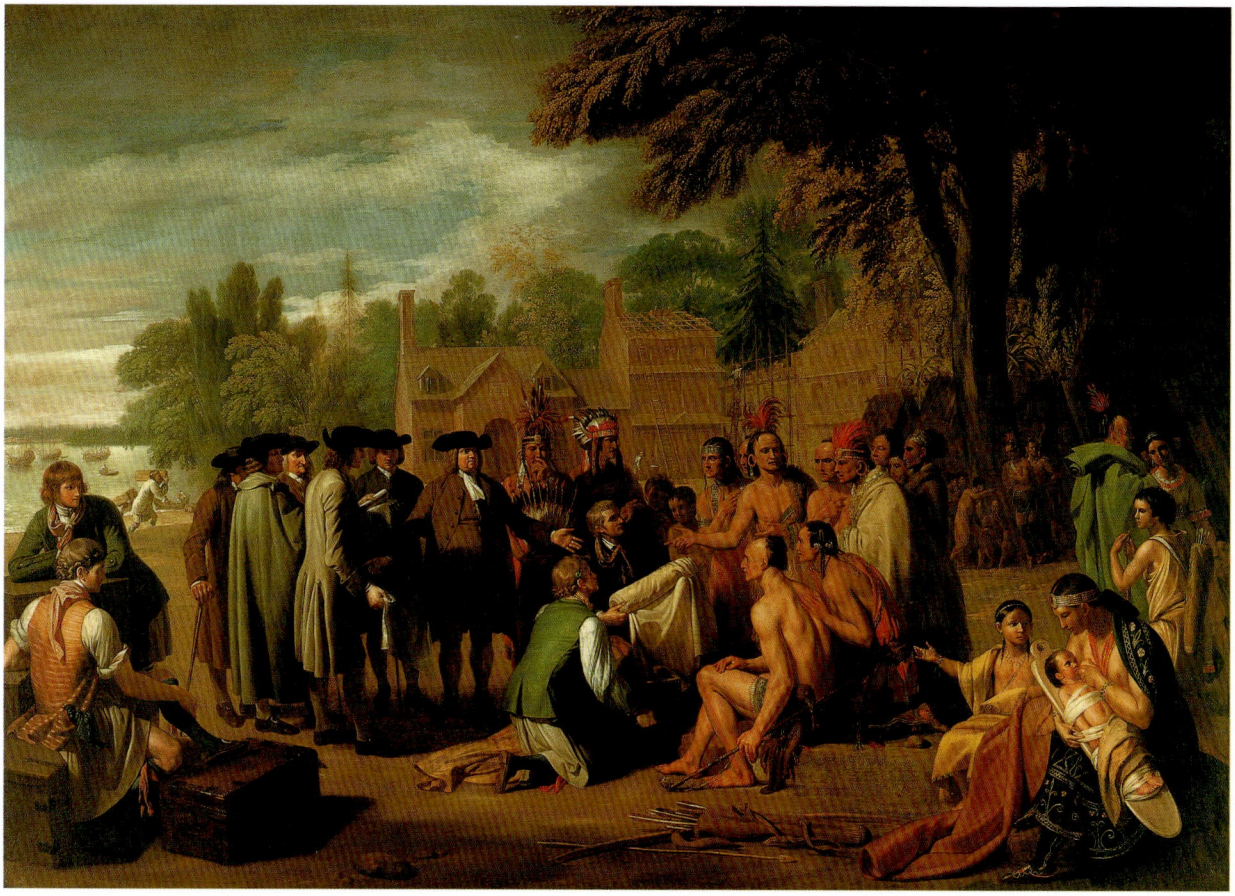

1.4.32 Benjamin West: *Penn's Treaty with the Indians When He Founded the Province of Pennsylvania in North America*, 1771–72.
Oil on canvas, 75½ x 107¾ in. (191.8 x 273.7 cm.)
The Pennsylvania Academy of the Fine Arts, Philadelphia

is a self-portrait). The Lenni Lenape or Delaware wear a combination of clothing, headgear, and ornaments drawn from the Lenni Lenape, Iroquois, and northern Algonquian peoples and borrowed from the collections of the Penn family and Matthew Clarkson of Philadelphia. The prosperity of the colony is indicated by the bustling harbour denoting trade and the large houses being constructed in the background. The indigenous peoples are placed closest to the forest, confirming their association with a land that has yet to be exploited by the settlers. As in *The Death of General Wolfe*, their bodies are modeled after classical nudes, such as *Apollo Belvedere*.

The calm of the scene was matched at the time West created his work by a momentary lull in the hostilities between indigenous peoples and colonists. This lull was soon broken, however, by a resumption of armed conflict between European colonists and indigenous peoples, and also between the colonists and the armies of the British king. The latter conflict would result in a radical shift in political power, the end of British rule, and the establishment of a new nation.

Review Questions

1 What were the written and visual sources used by Theodore de Bry in his *A brief and true report of the new found land of Virginia* (1590)? How did this publication influence European perceptions of the indigenous peoples of the Americas?

2 How did the relationship between religion and art in the British colonies differ from the relationship between religion and art in New France and New Spain?

3 How did the art and architecture of New England differ from that of the southern colonies?

4 Where did colonial painters look for sources of inspiration?

5 How would you describe the home of a seventeenth-century New England merchant? Where did the objects come from and what might they have said about the life experiences and status of the home's residents?

Federal Style (architecture) 1783–1815

US Capitol Building construction 1792–1865

Second Great Awakening

1770
Boston Massacre [2.5.2]

1773
Pope Clement XIV suppresses Jesuit Order; Boston Tea Party

1774
First Continental Congress in Philadelphia

1775–83
American Revolution

1776
July 4: Declaration of Independence

1776–77
John Singleton Copley paints group portrait after his family join him in London [2.7.14]

1785–89
Thomas Jefferson designs the Virginia State Capitol [2.6.1]

1786
Charles Willson Peale opens a museum of fine art and natural history

1787
Founding of the Free African Society

1788
US Constitution ratified [2.6.6]

from 1788
Rebuilding of the Vieux Carré in New Orleans

1789
George Washington inaugurated as first president of the United States [2.5.11]; French Revolution begins

1791
Pierre Charles L'Enfant completes plan of Washington, D.C. [2.6.3]

1792
Beginning of construction of the US Capitol Building; Moses Johnson completes Quaker Meeting House, Canterbury, NH [2.6.10]; Benjamin West elected president of the Royal Academy, London

1793
Passage of the Fugitive Slave Act, requiring return between states of escaped slaves

1800
Washington, D.C. replaces Philadelphia as the capital

1801–9
Thomas Jefferson (elected in 1800) serves as president

1802
Founding of the American Academy of the Fine Arts

1803
Louisiana Purchase

PART 2 Defining America

c. 1765–1850

The successful American Revolution (1775–83) may well have been a godsend for artists, for it created a series of dramatic events and heroic individuals ready to be celebrated in pictorial form. Here was a larger sense of purpose around which artists could rally. The new nation needed a history, and part of that history would be expressed visually. In addition to portraits and history paintings, the United States of America needed new buildings, state seals, stamps, flags, and monumental sculpture. While the creation of a national iconography was relatively easy, forming a national style was not. During the nineteenth century many debates would ensue over which style would express or embody most effectively the country's values and ideals. Artists and critics would also expend a great deal of energy debating the relative merits or patriotic value of history painting, landscape painting, portraiture, and genre painting.

The art historian Dell Upton writes that Thomas Jefferson used architecture as "a tool to remake himself, to declare his individuality, to transform himself from a colonial Virginian to a post-colonial American." Such was the case with many of the artists and architects who took up the challenge of producing an iconography for the new nation. They built new structures to house the growing population and reconfigured the image of the indigenous past to represent better the current political and economic world. In particular, they grappled with the incorporation of indigenous peoples into their representations of the nation's history located in new government buildings, such as the Capitol in Washington, D.C.

The US also needed new educational institutions to instill in its citizens the values and skills its leaders deemed essential for success. Among these institutions were academies of art, established not only to train artists but also to invest in the profession a sense of tradition harking back to classical times. Politicians and businessmen alike emphasized the country's newness and the endless opportunities available to all who ventured into its expanding territory. Yet they also were well aware of the need to associate their new state with the political powers of the past, thus endowing their own efforts with a sense of historical legitimacy. Artists struggled to produce images that would satisfy both demands—a celebration of the new and a respect for the old. The latter led, most notably, to a proliferation of classical forms—Greek costumes, temple fronts, columns—on everything from buildings and statues to tableware and needlework.

1805
Founding of the Pennsylvania Academy of the Fine Arts

1808
January 1: Importation of slaves prohibited by law

1812–14
War of 1812 between the US and Britain; Capitol burned and subsequently rebuilt [2.6.4] (completed 1865)

1816
Establishment of congregate prison system, Auburn, New York [2.6.16]

1817
John Trumbull commissioned by Congress to execute four paintings on the American Revolution for the rebuilt Capitol

1818
Northern boundary of US established at the 49th parallel

1819–21
Florida acquired from Spain

1821
Mexico gains independence from Spain; opening of Santa Fe Trail

1821–42
Charles Bird King completes some 143 portraits of Native Americans [2.6.26]

1822
Peale's Museum is incorporated as the Philadelphia Museum [2.7.4]

1825
Publication of Rufus Porter, *A Select Collection of Valuable and Curious Arts*, with instructions for, among other things, painted walls, floors, and furniture [2.7.7]

1826
Founding of the National Academy of Design

1827
Cherokee in Georgia draft constitution, declare themselves an independent nation; forcefully removed westward in 1838 (Trail of Tears)

1839
Samuel F. B. Morse introduces the daguerreotype, patented that year in France and England, to the US

1844
Samuel F. B. Morse [2.7.19] sets up telegraph line between Baltimore and Washington, D.C.

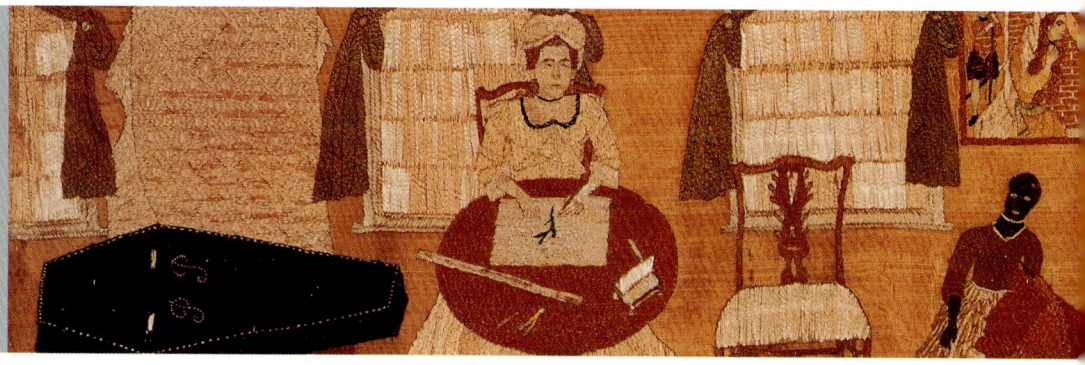

Prudence Punderson: *The First, Second, and Last Scene of Mortality*, before 1773, detail [2.5.17; p. 105].
Silk on silk, 13 x 17½ in. (33 x 44.4 cm.)
The Connecticut Historical Society, Hartford

Most artists settled in the major urban centers of the new nation and produced works for wealthy merchants and prominent politicians. Several, however, took to the road, helping both to fill and to encourage a growing demand in rural America for images among those of modest, as well as substantial, means. Some not only created their own works, but also taught others how to make art for themselves, whether decorative patterns on walls or floors or human profiles cut out of paper. Thus, while many painters in New York or Boston or Philadelphia bemoaned the lack of artistic patronage or taste in America, hundreds, if not thousands, of men and women busied themselves producing their own still lifes or portraits for the decoration of their homes. "Taste" may have been absent in early nineteenth-century America, but creativity certainly was not.

Visual artists of the new nation still relied heavily, as they had during the colonial era, on artistic conventions learned in the art academies of Europe or from copying prints of works that came out of these academies. In fact, the three most celebrated late-eighteenth-century American painters—Benjamin West, John Singleton Copley, and John Trumbull— spent the better part of their professional careers in London before, during, and after the American Revolution. One could argue therefore that, despite their American subject matter (portraits of Boston merchants, scenes of revolutionary battles) and birth in the colonies, they were more British than American.

Yet historians have claimed them as American artists, in part because the material conditions of colonial life informed the development of their early careers. These conditions included the limited patronage for paintings other than portraits, the tenuous connection between artists in the colonies and art institutions in London, and the close-knit kinship networks that supplied the bulk of artistic patronage. Ultimately, however, the worlds of Britain and the US could not be so easily separated. The American Revolution reframed, rather than severed, the relationship between Britain and its ex-colonies, and initiated a complex set of attempts by artists both to measure up to and distinguish themselves from their European forebears and contemporaries.

CHAPTER 5

Representing the American Revolution and Its Leaders

(*c.* 1765–1810)

Domestic Production and International Intrigue: The Portraits of John Singleton Copley

As Benjamin West was completing *The Death of General Wolfe* and *Penn's Treaty with the Indians* [**1.4.31**, p. 83; **1.4.32**, p. 85], another painter was recording the features of various New England residents who would figure prominently in the next military encounter to take place in the British colonies of North America: the American Revolution of 1775–83. John Singleton Copley (1738–1815) was born in Boston in the same year as West. He received training in the rudiments of art from his stepfather Peter Pelham, a mezzotint artist and dancing teacher. Pelham died when Copley was thirteen, increasing the young man's family responsibilities and prompting him to turn with determination to the practice of painting. He continued his training by copying as many engravings and portraits as possible.

Within a decade Copley had established himself as one of Boston's leading portraitists, known for the exactitude with which he rendered his sitters' features and their liveliness of character. He was also skilled at creating what the art historian Paul Staiti calls "centerpieces in the stagecraft of the eighteenth-century persona," portraits that claimed for their sitters a place "in the hierarchical and circumscribed social theater of colonial Boston." He accomplished this through the rendering of material wealth and also by capturing the gestures, objects, and dress appropriate to the social identity desired by the sitter, be it that of a successful merchant, a pious minister, a dutiful wife, or a studious child.

The art historian Margaretta Lovell points out that most of Copley's portraits, and eighteenth-century portraits in general, also functioned as reminders of the expected behaviour of family members in maintaining the hierarchical relationships that formed the basis of the patriarchal colonial family. They were most often viewed in the home of the sitter by networks of extended kin, the same networks that constituted Copley's main patrons. Portraits were commissioned to mark an individual's memorable achievements—marriage, birth of a child—and their elaborate furnishings, costumes, and other markers of wealth thus implied "the movement of family substance in an orderly, prescribed manner."

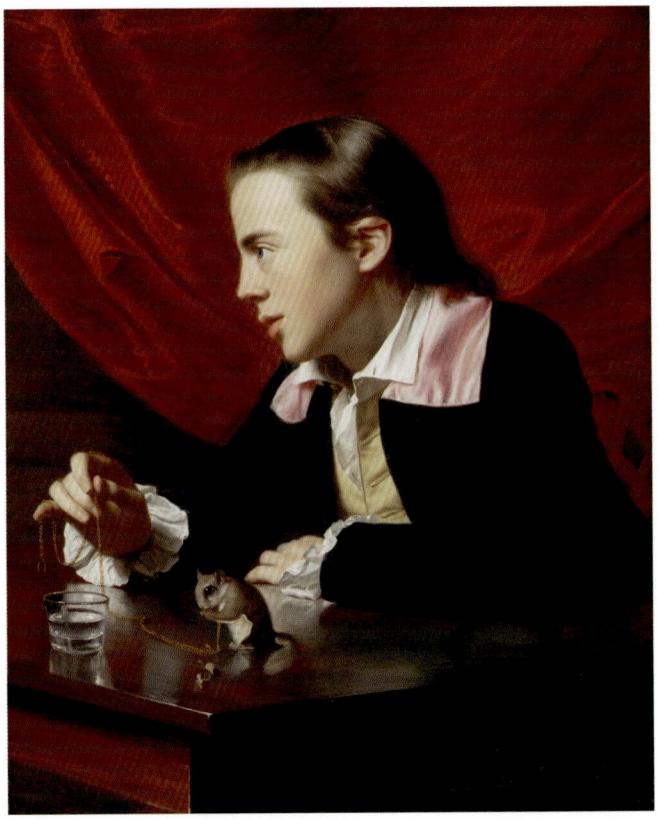

2.5.1 John Singleton Copley: *Henry Pelham* (*Boy with a Squirrel*), 1765. Oil on canvas, 30¼ x 25 in. (76.8 x 63.5 cm.) Museum of Fine Arts, Boston, Massachusetts

The painting that brought Copley to the attention of the London art world was of a member of his own family, the portrait he made in 1765 of his half-brother Henry Pelham [**2.5.1**]. In this work, Copley has captured the qualities of a wide variety of surfaces—skin, mahogany, glass, water, fur, metal, various textiles—with a verisimilitude that impressed those who viewed the painting in London. He has also created a carefully balanced composition that directs the viewer's gaze from the boy's face to his hand to the squirrel and back through his other hand and collar to his face again, prompting us to wonder what thoughts are occupying the boy's mind and whether the delicate chain attached to the squirrel is not some commentary on the fragile relationship between humans and nature in colonial America.

Henry Pelham (*Boy with a Squirrel*) was Copley's first non-commissioned work created specifically for a transatlantic art world audience rather than for domestic family consumption. He submitted the painting to the annual exhibition of the Society of Artists, an organization founded in London in 1761 to provide a venue for the exhibition of works by living artists. The art historian Jennifer Roberts argues that the painting's 2900-mile (4670-kilometers) transatlantic passage between Boston and London, which took one month to complete (and seven and a half weeks on the return voyage), is key to understanding Copley's compositional and iconographic decisions. In fact, she sees this painting as a "sea piece," not because it presents a recognizable image of a ship or body of water, but because it was created with the challenges and dangers of transatlantic travel in mind. For example, the chain draped above and across the drinking glass in the left foreground can be seen as a symbolic reference to the painting crossing the Atlantic Ocean. In addition, the squirrel, to which the chain is attached, while a fairly common symbol of diligence, patience, and proper education in colonial portraits (mostly of women and young girls), here has an additional meaning. As a flying squirrel, native to North America, it resonates with the idea of travel and movement (American ships in the 1760s and 1770s were sometimes named "Squirrel" or "Flying Squirrel"). When the squirrel's wings are stretched in flight, it resembles a canvas.

According to Roberts, Copley also needed to convey his understanding of the conventions of European portraiture, which he had learned from studying engravings, to his London audience. Many mid-eighteenth-century British portrait painters dressed their sitters up as allegories in order to present them as significant figures beyond their mere individual appearance. Copley chose, instead, to speak to the significance of his sitter by painting him in profile, a position associated in England with commemorative coins or ancient portrait medals. Coins also traveled well, retaining their value over long distances, an important consideration in the maintenance of a vast colonial empire. Thus, Copley used the profile pose to suggest prestige, as well as portability and reliability. The painting was, in Robert's words, the product of "a cultural moment that was actively exploring the agency of circulating objects in the process of binding together a far-flung empire."

2.5.2 Paul Revere: *The Bloody Massacre*, 1770.
Engraving with watercolor, laid on paper, 10¼ x 13¼ in. (25.8 x 33.4 cm.)
Library of Congress, Washington, D.C.

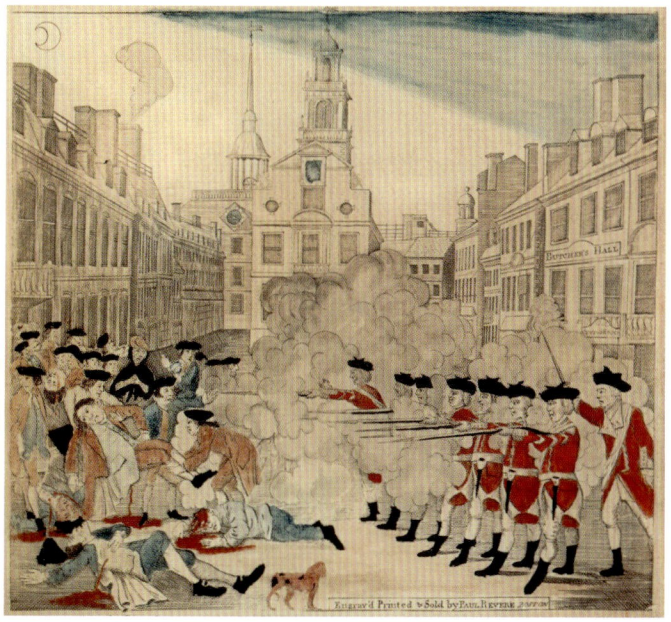

The need for such binding agents was particularly evident in the years surrounding the creation of Copley's painting. As a resident of Boston, he would have witnessed the eroding of the relationship between the colonies and the British crown. Boston, like other flourishing centers in the late eighteenth century, was chafing under the trade restrictions imposed by British authorities. Such restrictions were an integral part of a mercantilist system, where the health of the colonizing nation takes precedence over that of its colonies. Any economic exchange must benefit Britain. The colonies were thus instructed to trade only in certain goods and with certain trading partners. These instructions, however, were often ignored or subverted through the existence of a black market.

In 1765, the year Copley created his portrait, the British crown passed the Stamp Act, which authorized a direct tax on all sorts of printed materials to help pay for the French and Indian War (see p. 82). Many of the colonies protested and riots swept Boston, forcing the repeal of the act the following year. Yet other taxes were imposed, along with legislation interfering with the right of the colonies to govern themselves. This legislation was directed specifically at Massachusetts, the site of much of the most outspoken resistance. By the end of the 1760s British troops and ships of war were a common sight in Boston and its harbor.

From 1765 onward increasing numbers of prints, political cartoons, and broadsides critical of the British circulated throughout the colonies. One such print was *The Bloody Massacre* of 1770 [**2.5.2**], an engraving by the printmaker and silversmith Paul Revere (1735–1818). The composition was copied from an illustration by Copley's half-brother, Henry Pelham (1749–1806), who was also an artist. Revere then hired Christian Remick to add the color.

The engraving depicts the events of March 5, 1770, when crowds of Boston residents, mostly laborers, began taunting British troops stationed in the city. The troops then opened fire. Among the five men killed was Crispus Attucks, an African who had escaped slavery twenty years earlier and who was described by many witnesses to the massacre as a leader of the rebellion. Revere's print was issued three weeks after the fatal shootings. Its depiction of stony-faced soldiers shooting unarmed civilians at close range (not an accurate rendition of what actually happened), served to arouse even further resistance to the British. Several among the colonial elite of Boston feared the violence

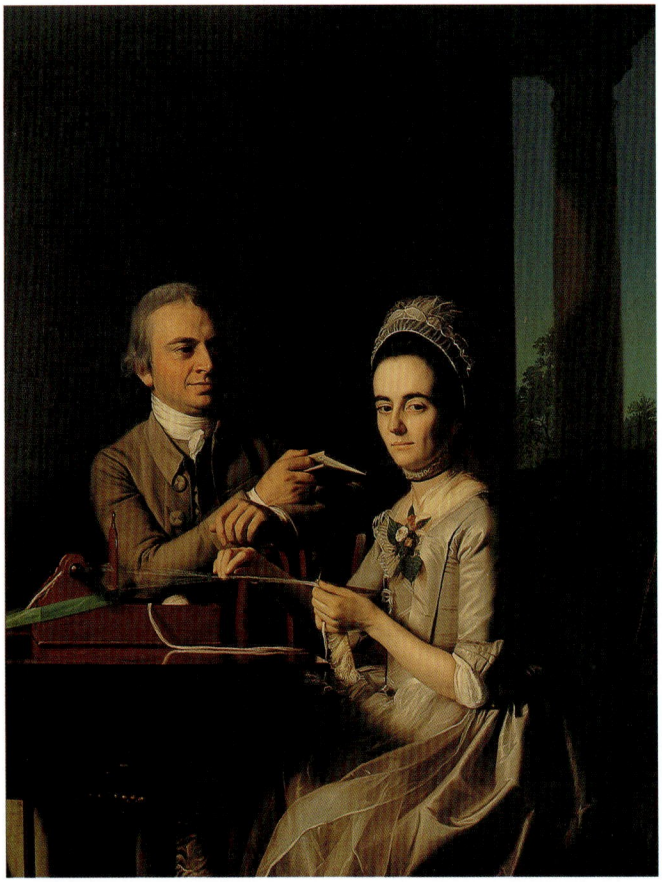

2.5.3 John Singleton Copley: *Governor and Mrs Thomas Mifflin*, 1773. Oil on bed ticking, 61½ x 48 in. (155 x 122 cm.) Historical Society of Pennsylvania, Philadelphia

of poor Africans and Irish Catholics more than the actions of an army of occupation, and defended the behavior of the soldiers as self-defense.

In 1773 Britain attempted to impose a tax on tea, as well as to remove the colonial middlemen in the marketing of tea. This would actually have lowered the final cost of the product for Bostonians, but in the process would have cut into the profits of the middlemen. In response, the leaders of Boston refused to let a shipment of tea be unloaded. Instead, a group of men descended on the harbor, many dressed as "Indians," wearing blankets or ragged clothing with faces blackened with lampblack or soot to hide their identities (what they were about to do was an act of treason). They dumped the tea in the harbor and their actions became known as the Boston Tea Party. The British responded by appointing a council to rule the colony in place of elected officials and closed the harbor. Twelve of the thirteen colonies (Georgia did not join in) met in 1774 in Philadelphia in the First Continental Congress and voted to support Massachusetts, agreeing to boycott trade with Great Britain, Ireland, and the British West Indies. Such boycotts were not new, and had been used effectively in the past.

Thomas Mifflin, a wealthy Philadelphia Quaker merchant, was a member of the group that met at the First Continental Congress. The year before this meeting Copley had created a double portrait of Thomas and his wife Sara [**2.5.3**]. The painting hung in the Mifflins' imposing Philadelphia home and may well have been witness to many of the conversations that preceded the Congress about the tactics to be used in resisting British interference in colonial affairs.

Much about this portrait suggests that it was composed with the economic and political tensions between Britain and its colonies in mind. While Thomas was a more important political figure than Sara, and the patriarch of his family, Sara seems to be the center of attention. Thomas looks at her and she, in turn, looks out at us with a confident and knowing gaze. Dressed in elegant attire, she has paused in the process of working threads of silk on a large wooden frame used to make fringes for carriage whips. Copley thus paints Sara Mifflin engaged in the home production of items that might normally be imported from England, calling to mind earlier boycotts of British goods. The spinning, weaving, and sewing expected of women as part of their regular daily routines now took on a patriotic meaning. As the art historian Lois Dinnerstein points out, Copley presents Sara as the industrious housewife, both a model of refinement and domestic virtue and an exemplar of revolutionary zeal.

Copley's own feelings about the impending revolution were ambivalent. By the early 1770s he had become a wealthy man, with three houses and twenty acres on Beacon Hill. In addition, his father-in-law was the principal agent in the colony for the East India Tea Company, and the owner of the ship from which cargo had been thrown overboard. Copley had friends on both sides of the political fence and had attempted to mediate between them before the Boston Tea Party occurred. His attempts failed, however, and he left New England on June 10, 1774, traveling first to Italy and then to London, and never returned.

The Congress that met in Philadelphia, with Thomas Mifflin in attendance, was not initially set on establishing an independent nation. Instead, it demanded that the colonies be allowed to govern themselves through elected officials, while at the same time maintaining certain political and economic ties to England. King George III refused these demands, and sent additional forces to defend his interests. The first battle between British and American troops took place on April 19, 1775, at Lexington and Concord, west of Boston. In May, the Second Continental Congress met in Philadelphia and formed a central government under the authority of the people of the colonies, with George Washington as commander in chief of the Continental Army. On June 17, British troops and rebel militiamen clashed at Breed's Hill, close to Boston (the battle was mistakenly named after neighboring Bunker Hill). While the British won the battle, they sustained heavy casualties. In July Washington laid siege to Boston from nearby Cambridge. The siege lasted until March 1776, when the British fled the city and set up their headquarters in New York.

On July 4, 1776, the Congress issued the Declaration of Independence. Those loyal to the crown (Loyalists) fled to Britain and Canada. The French entered the conflict on the side of the Americans against France's traditional enemy, Britain, and from 1777 onward supplied much-needed munitions. In August 1781 they sent part of their navy to help in the decisive victory at Yorktown, Virginia. By September 1783 the fighting was over and the final treaties signed, with the last of the British troops gone by the end of November.

Copley, as one of those who chose to relocate to England, now focused on building a new clientele to replace the one he had left behind in Boston. Shortly after his arrival in London, he began work on a painting that addressed a key issue in the political debates taking place on both sides of the Atlantic: that many who argued for freedom from oppressive colonial rule also supported the enslavement of Africans. *Watson and the Shark* [**2.5.4**], completed in 1778, was commissioned by the British merchant Brook Watson to commemorate a dramatic incident in which he lost a leg. But the art historian Albert Boime believes the painting is about much more. While the work contains a reconstruction of the attack on Watson, it also carries an indirect reference to the War of Independence.

When the shark attacked the young Watson in Havana harbor in 1749, nine men in a boat attempted his rescue. In his painting, Copley has treated this rather minor historical event in the manner of a grand history painting (the work is 6 × 7½ feet;

2.5.4 John Singleton Copley: *Watson and the Shark*, 1778.
Oil on canvas, 6 x 7½ ft. (1.8 x 2.3 m.)
Museum of Fine Arts, Boston, Massachusetts

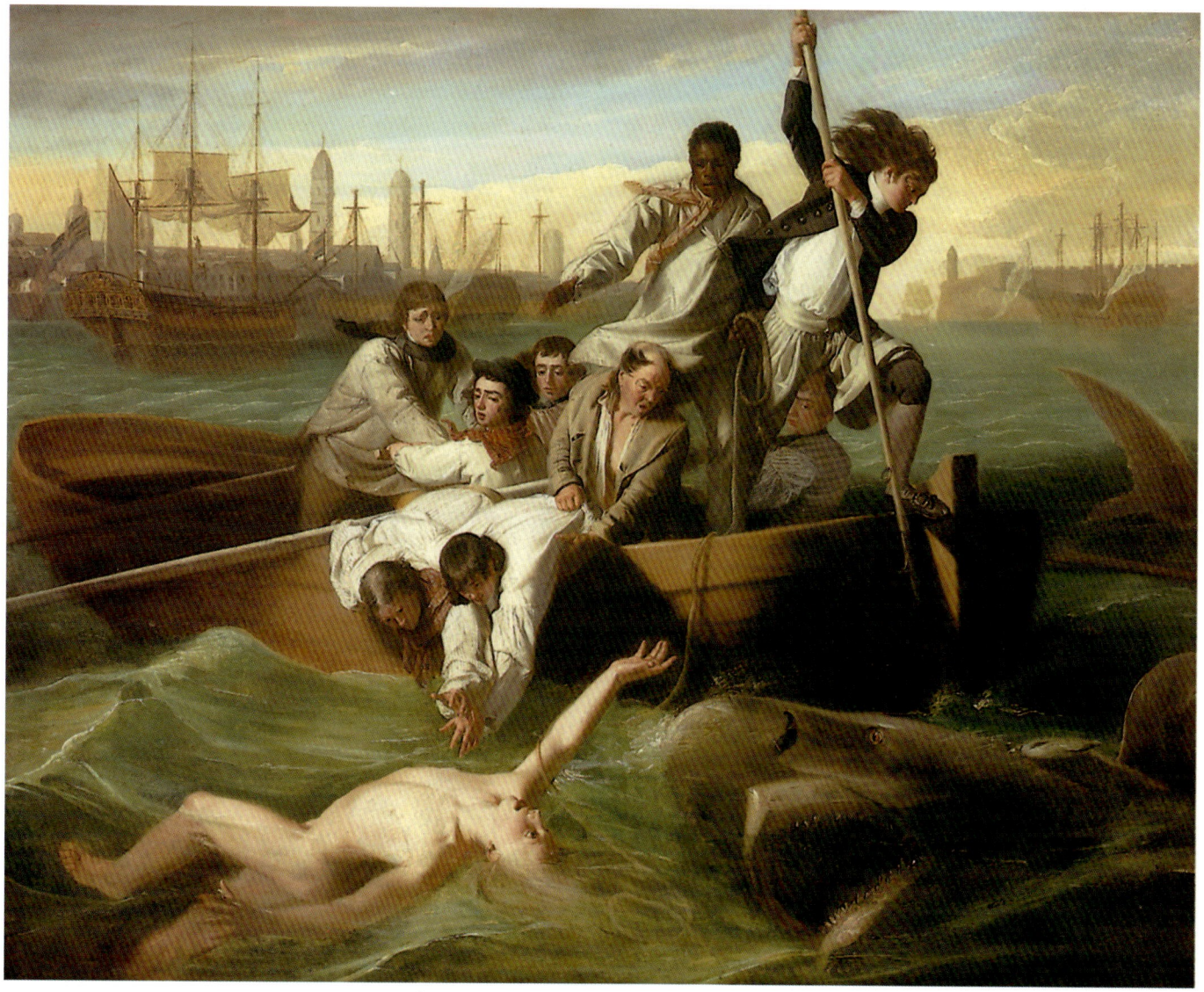

1.8 × 2.3 meters). He has organized the main actors in a pyramidal grouping in the center of the composition, with a black man close to the apex of the pyramid, a position usually reserved for important figures. All the other men are white. He has also placed in the black man's hand the rope that connects Watson, who occupies the base of the pyramid along with the shark, to the boat and that symbolizes his impending rescue. The large shark with its gaping mouth a mere arm's length from the naked body of Watson (and from the viewers of the painting) heightens the drama of the scene.

Many have read the black figure in Copley's painting as a servant waiting to hand the rope to the other men. Boime suggests a different interpretation, one connected to the debates over slavery. Watson had traveled to New England in the late 1740s to live with a relative who owned several ships that traded in the West Indies. Vessels regularly left Boston with timber, dried fish, and other goods, which were exchanged in Africa for slaves. These slaves were then transported to the West Indies and traded for sugar and molasses, which were brought back to Boston. It was on one such expedition that Watson lost his leg.

After his return to England, Watson rose to prominence as a wealthy merchant and a leading figure in the conservative Tory party. When he commissioned his painting from Copley, a heated debate was raging in Parliament over both the Declaration of Independence and the institution of slavery. Watson attacked the more liberal Whigs, who supported independence, and pointed out the hypocrisy of the Revolutionary leaders in calling for freedom from the British crown when they themselves were denying freedom to African slaves. While many in New England had begun arguing for an end to slavery, in 1778 it still existed in such places as Massachusetts. During the Revolution the British used slavery to divide the colonists, promising freedom for every runaway slave who joined the British army (seventeen of Washington's own slaves took the British up on their offer).

Copley's picture could therefore be read as a demonstration of Tory support for enslaved Africans, a key aspect of Tory opposition to the American Revolution. The shark-infested waters could also be seen as a metaphor for the colonies themselves, a breeding ground for dangerous revolutionary ideas, with the loss of Watson's leg a symbol of the loss of part of the British Empire. That the bodies of African slaves who died on the passage from Africa to the Americas were thrown overboard to the sharks provides a further connection between Watson, slavery, and the American colonies. While the black man might function within this complex set of references to slavery and revolution as a sign of emancipation, Copley still presents him as a servant awaiting orders, not a fully engaged participant in the rescue. Watson, argues Boime, may have realized the political advantage of condemning slavery but, in light of his own profitable involvement in the slave trade, could not wholeheartedly support its abolition.

The art historian Jennifer Roberts suggests another way to read this painting. She argues it is connected not only to the Boston Tea Party and the fragile status of the British Empire in America, but also to Copley's own involvement in the events leading up to the Tea Party. Before embarking on *Watson and the Shark*, Copley expressed in letters to his family his desire to create a memorial account of this momentous event. While he did not ultimately create such a painting, Roberts notes that the theme of *Watson and the Shark*—something going overboard in a harbor in the Americas and its immanent danger of disappearing—resonates with Copley's memory of the Tea Party. The gestures of the men reaching out to Watson parallel the gestures of men throwing crates of tea overboard as depicted in prints of the event. The frantic rowing of the men echoes Copley's own frantic rowing of a small boat back and forth between the Old South Meeting Hall, headquarters of those who wanted to ship the tea back to England, and the British fort of Castle William on an island in the harbor, where the tea merchants (including Copley's father-in-law) who wanted to keep the tea had taken refuge. The castle in the right background in the Watson painting reinforces this reading.

Copley's own failure in the face of this impending crisis is alluded to in the figure of the black man. He holds the key to Watson's salvation (the rope), but is unable to engage bodily in the rescue. The figure was white in Copley's preliminary sketches for the painting. Roberts suggests he changed it in order to deflect the idea of impotence or weakness (in particular his own) from a white to a black body. The change could also be a reference to the problematic nature of the transatlantic trade—in slaves, in tea, and in paintings—which was both the foundation of the British Empire in the Americas and one of the causes of its demise.

John Trumbull's Canvases of War

Many artists predicted that the greatest demand after the Revolution would be for portraits and battle scenes. One who moved to meet this demand was John Trumbull (1756–1843). The art historian Alexander Eliot suggests that Trumbull, born in Lebanon, Connecticut, was first attracted to art by the needlework of his sisters. In his autobiography, published in 1841, Trumbull also recalls that his "taste for drawing began to dawn early...and for several years the nicely sanded floors... were constantly scrawled with my rude attempts at drawing." In the nineteenth century women often scoured floors with sand and water, then, when dry, covered them with a thin layer of

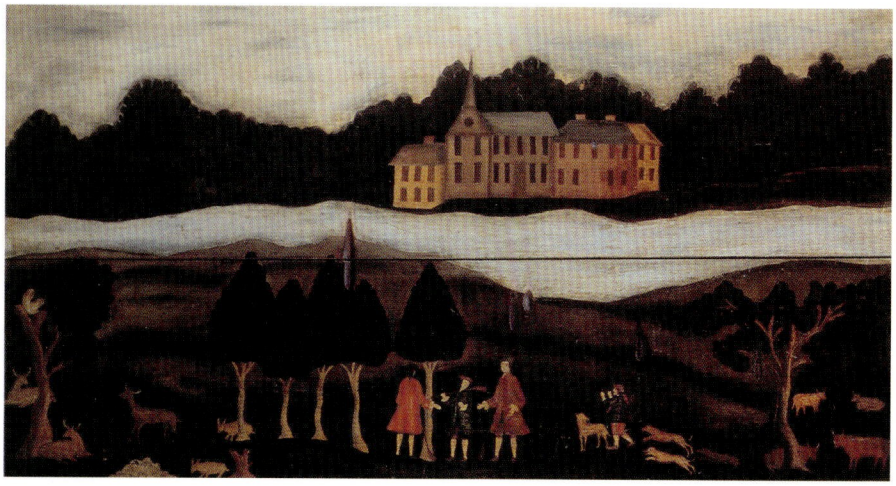

2.5.5 Sibyl Huntington May: *Hunting Scene*, overmantel, 1756.
Oil on board, *c.* 24 x 32 in. (61 x 81.3 cm.)
Brainerd Memorial Library, Brainerd, Minnesota

sand carefully swept into curved lines, scrolls, and herringbone patterns. He may also have been familiar with the work of Sibyl Huntington May (1734–?), who lived in the neighboring town of Haddam. Huntington May was well known for her skill as a painter and for such works as an overmantel painting of 1756 [**2.5.5**]. The painting depicts a hunting scene taken from early Haddam history, as well as the Congregational Church where her husband the Reverend Eleazar May had his pastorate. This work could be seen, in fact, as one of the first colonial history paintings.

Eliot writes that Trumbull's father, who was the governor of Connecticut, found his son's "odd attraction" to art "inappropriate on two counts: first, the boy had lost the use of one eye in a childhood accident, and second, he was a gentleman." While Governor Trumbull accepted picture making as "a fit diversion for young ladies and a profitable occupation for suitably skilled laborers," it certainly was not a calling for the sons of the elite. John was sent off to Harvard; but there, undoubtedly to his father's dismay, he met Copley, and embarked on an ambitious career as an artist. He served briefly in the Continental Army, where he made military maps, then departed for London in 1780, where, like so many painters from New England, he became West's student. With no art academies in the colonies, aspiring artists could only advance their skills so far on their own. England, and in particular London, was the inevitable destination for those who had both the talent and the financial resources.

Trumbull remained abroad for most of the next thirty-five years. In 1786 he began a series of Revolutionary War scenes. He planned thirteen, but only completed six by the end of the eighteenth century (two more would be realized in the first decades of the following century). He hoped to sell the paintings, as well as to have them engraved to sell as prints, thus increasing the financial returns on his artistic investment. Trumbull wanted them to contribute to the creation of a pantheon of national heroes that would help bind together the various factions that were already competing for political and economic power. In 1789 he clarified his reasons for undertaking these first pictorial icons of the new nation in a letter to Thomas Jefferson:

> The greatest motive I had or have for engaging in, or for continuing my pursuit of painting, has been the wish of commemorating the great events of our country's revolution. I am fully sensible that the profession, as it is generally practiced, is frivolous, little useful to society, and unworthy of a man who has talents for more serious pursuits. But, to preserve and diffuse the memory of the noblest series of actions which have ever presented themselves in the history of man; to give the present and the future sons of oppression and misfortune, such glorious lessons of their rights, and of the spirit with which they should assert and support them, and even to transmit to their descendants, the personal resemblance of those who have been the great actors in those illustrious scenes, were objects which gave a dignity to the profession, peculiar to my situation.

With these words Trumbull sets out the patriotic nature of his artistic enterprise. He also argues for the political significance of history painting for the new nation, as well as the significance of history and the new nation for painting.

Trumbull began his series of Revolutionary paintings in 1786 with *The Death of General Warren at the Battle of Bunker's Hill, 17 June 1775* [**2.5.6**; p. 94] and *The Death of General Montgomery in the Attack on Quebec, 31 December 1775* [**2.5.7**; p. 96]. One can see the influence of West in the compositions, in particular his *Death of General Wolfe* [**1.4.31**; p. 83]. In fact, Trumbull executed the first of his battle scenes in West's painting room in London.

All three canvases contain a group of soldiers in the foreground, a reclining wounded figure in the center, and smoke-filled skies in the background.

There are also differences between the battle scenes of Trumbull and West. Trumbull's pictures are much more dramatic and colorful. The figures are arranged along a dynamic diagonal that moves across the canvas, as opposed to the more static group of figures that dominates the center of West's works. While Trumbull undoubtedly relied on some of the same studies of facial expressions as West, such as those published by the seventeenth-century French court artist Charles Le Brun (see p. 83), the looser brushwork, red-tinged clouds, and wind-whipped flags heighten their intensity. Both West and Trumbull focus on the heroic deaths of individual men. Yet Trumbull's occur in the midst of battle, and the scene depicted in *The Death of General Warren at the Battle of Bunker's Hill* captures the moment after the wounding of not just one, but two officers. Finally, Wolfe's death alluded to the impending victory of the British over the French, but Montgomery's battle (also at Quebec) did not lead to victory, and the results of Warren's were not so clear-cut.

Trumbull had been nearby when the Battle of Bunker's Hill (which actually occurred on Breed's Hill—see p. 90) took place and observed it through field glasses. In his painting [**2.5.6**] he alludes to the battle's ambiguous end. Neither side is portrayed as entirely defeated or entirely victorious. Each has its mortally wounded, heroic leader surrounded by loyal comrades, General Joseph Warren—shot in the head with a musket—on the side of the Revolutionaries, Major John Pitcairn on the side of the British. In addition, Trumbull shows the British Major John Small grabbing the bayonet of a grenadier who is about to finish off General Warren. By placing Small's gesture in the center of the composition, the artist shifts the focus of the painting from the outcome of the battle to the enactment of noble deeds by noble men, both Revolutionary and British.

Trumbull's presentation can be explained in part by the nature of the battle, which the British won, but at great expense.

2.5.6 John Trumbull, *The Death of General Warren at the Battle of Bunker's Hill, 17 June 1775*, 1786.
Oil on canvas, 25 x 34 in. (62.5 x 85 cm.)
Yale University Art Gallery, New Haven, Connecticut

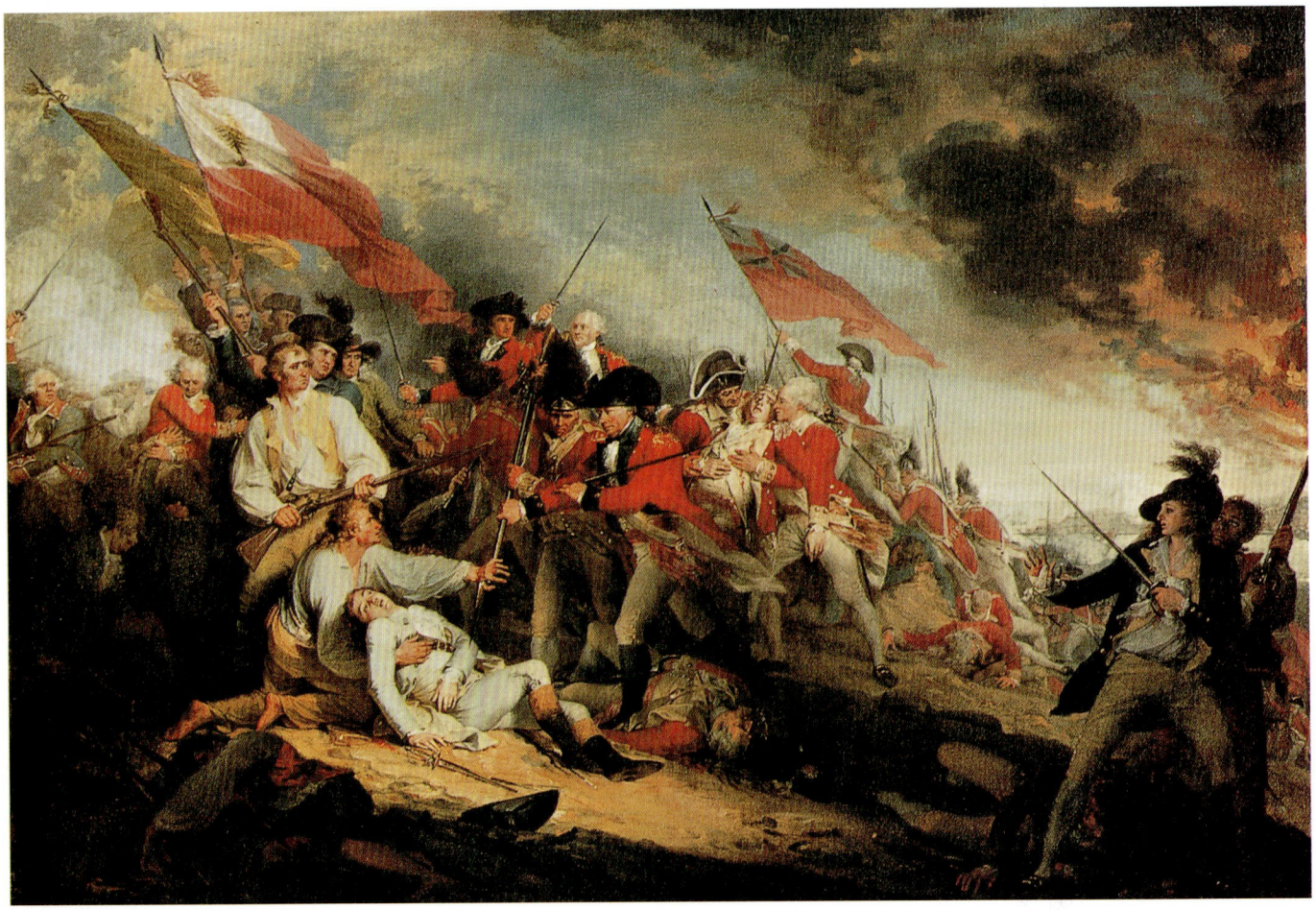

It can also be explained by his situation when he painted the work. As a resident of England, he could not be too pro-Revolutionary. He had already been arrested for treason in 1780 and forced to return to America upon his release in 1781. The sting of defeat was fresh in British minds when Trumbull arrived back in England in 1784. West himself had had to abandon plans for a series of paintings on the American Revolution for fear of offending George III, whom he served as court painter. Trumbull hoped to sell the engravings, if not the paintings themselves, in England as well as the United States, so he had to create a series that would appeal to buyers on both sides of the Atlantic.

Just as Copley included a black man in *Watson and the Shark* [**2.5.4**; p. 91], Trumbull includes two black figures among the otherwise white Revolutionary forces at Bunker's/Breed's Hill. Unlike Copley, however, and more in keeping with West's treatment of the indigenous figure in *The Death of General Wolfe*, Trumbull places them at the edges of the composition. One appears in the lower right-hand corner, accompanied by the white figure of Lieutenant Grosvenor. Trumbull himself described the pair as "a young American, wounded in the sword hand...attended by a faithful negro; but seeing his general fall, hesitates whether to save himself, or...return and assist in saving a life, more precious to his country than his own." The second black man appears on the opposite side, at the upper left, a mere head above the figure of a British officer and below the upraised arm of a chaplain. Again, as in Copley's painting, these black soldiers raise the issue of slavery and its place in a revolution dedicated to freedom from tyranny. Yet rather than highlight this issue, Trumbull marginalizes it, placing the most visible black man in an obviously subservient position behind Lieutenant Grosvenor.

Trumbull may also have included black soldiers in an attempt to be historically accurate. When the colonists gathered at Lexington and Concord in April 1775, black troops were included in their ranks. Approximately five thousand men of African descent served in the Continental Army (more fought on the side of the British). At least fourteen, known by name, participated in the "Battle of Bunker's Hill." The most famous of these men was Peter Salem. A firsthand account of the battle (recorded in 1787 by the New England historian Dr. Jeremy Belknap in his diary) includes the information that "a negro man, belonging to Groton, took aim at Major Pitcairne [sic], as he was rallying the dispersed British troops, and shot him through the head." The same event was described by another early chronicler of the battle, Samuel Swett: "Among the foremost of the leaders was the gallant Maj. Pitcairn, who exultantly cried 'the day is ours', when Salem, a black soldier, and a number of others, shot him through and he died."

Some scholars have identified the black man accompanying Grosvenor as Peter Salem. The art historian Patricia Burnham questions this, noting that Salem, a soldier from Massachusetts, would not have served under Grosvenor, an officer from Connecticut. If the other black man is Salem, he has been so carefully removed from the center of the action and distanced from Major Pitcairn, who has collapsed into the arms of British officers on the far right edge of the central grouping, that his participation in the death of the latter has been, for all intents and purposes, erased.

Peter Salem fought in battles before the encounter at Breed's Hill and continued to fight after. At the end of the war he returned to Massachusetts, built a cabin near Leicester, and wove cane for a living. He died in 1816 in a poorhouse in Framingham. He was among the first of many black men who would fight for their country hoping to improve their economic and political standing, and end up little better off than before.

There had been, in fact, a great deal of unrest within black communities in New England before the Revolution. Petitions were gathered demanding access to land and greater freedoms. While many were not slaves as in the South, they did not enjoy the same personal and economic freedoms as white Europeans. As John Adams was helping formulate the Declaration of Independence, his wife Abigail wrote to him regarding the protests of blacks: "It always appeared a most iniquitous scheme to me to fight ourselves for what we are daily robbing and plundering from those who have as good a right to freedom as we have." It would have been a very different painting, notes Burnham, had Trumbull "forecast ultimate victory...by showcasing Peter Salem killing Pitcairn."

In *The Death of General Montgomery* [**2.5.7**; p. 96], Trumbull followed West's precedent [**1.4.31**; p. 83] and placed an indigenous figure, the Oneida leader "Colonel Joseph Lewis," in the group surrounding the dying general. Unlike West's figure, he is more central and actively involved in the drama of the moment, as he turns with tomahawk raised. General Montgomery failed to take Quebec, and was killed by cannon fire; his troops laid siege to the city but were forced back in the spring with the arrival of British reinforcements. Trumbull had accompanied a regiment bound for Fort Ticonderoga in the spring of 1776 and had reported on the condition of the troops retreating from Quebec. "I did not look into tent or hut," he wrote, "in which I did not find either a dead or dying man."

Trumbull has taken the overall composition of his first painting and reversed it, with the diagonal now rising from the lower left corner to the upper right. Lord Grosvenor and the black soldier are replaced by three figures—Major Return Jonathan Meigs, Captain Samuel Ward, and Captain William

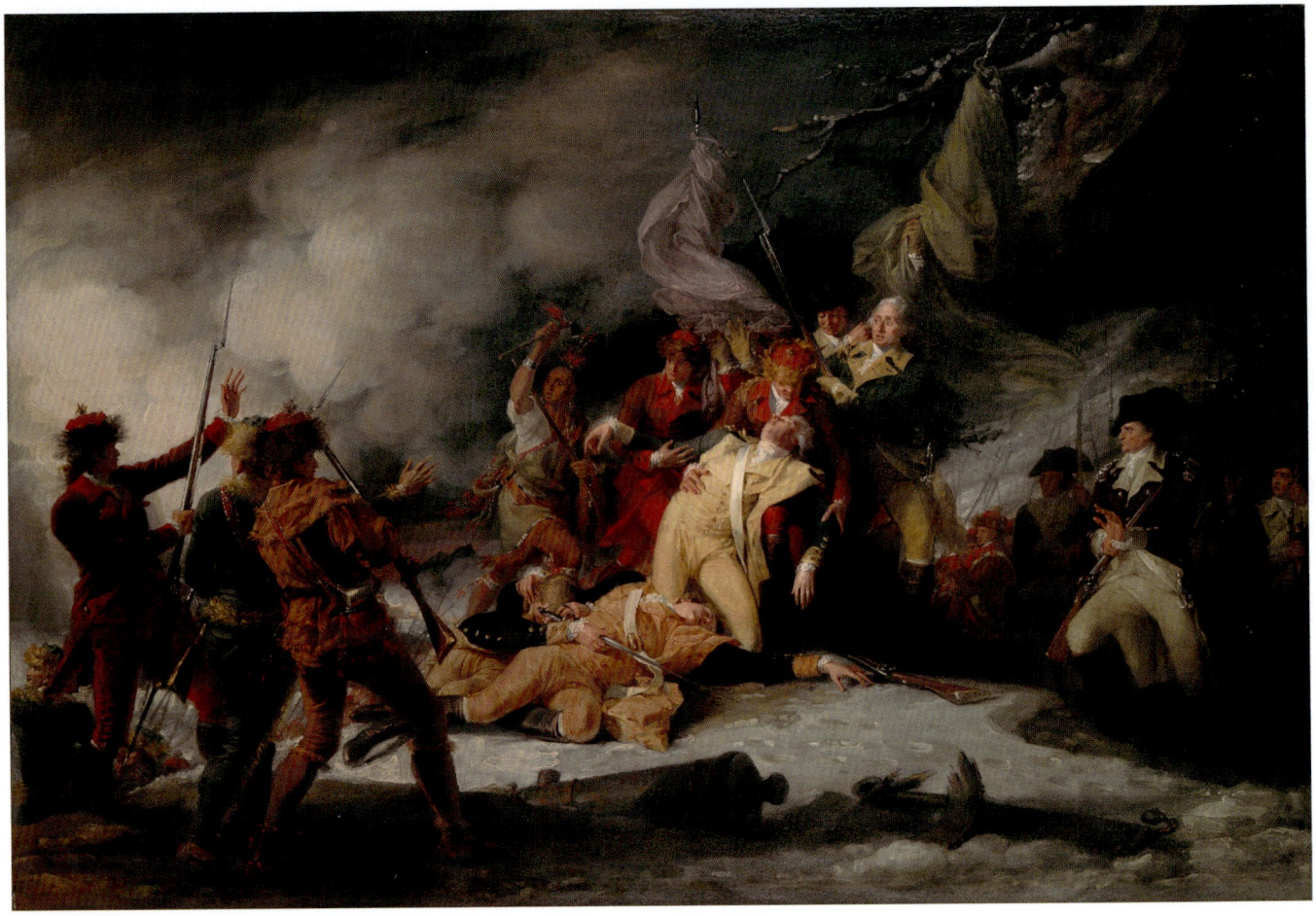

2.5.7 John Trumbull, *The Death of General Montgomery in the Attack on Quebec, 31 December 1775*, 1786.
Oil on canvas, 24⅝ x 37 in. (62.3 x 94 cm.)
Yale University Art Gallery, New Haven, Connecticut

Hendricks—who are similarly shocked at the death of their leader. The art historian Jules Prown suggests that their costumes were based on materials originally sent to West in 1783 by the Philadelphia artist Charles Willson Peale (see p. 135) to help him plan his proposed paintings of the war. Peale had obtained from an acquaintance

> a hunting shirt & leggens...such our Rifflemen usted [sic] to wear with Powder horn & shot pouch of the Indian fashion, with Wampum Belts, small Round hats of bucks tail and some times Feathers. Very often these shirts were dyed brown—yellow, pink and blue black colour according to the fancy of the companies.

Thus while the Oneida leader adopts the white shirt and rifle of European culture, two of the Continental Army officers wear the beaded pouches and moccasins of indigenous culture.

Subscriptions for engravings of Trumbull's paintings were offered for sale in the early 1790s, when his talents were being celebrated by at least a few people in the newly independent nation. The Reverend Timothy Dwight, president of Yale College, included a panegyric to Trumbull's works in "The Vision," Part VII of his poem of 1794, *Greenfield Hill*:

> On the bright canvas, see the pencil trace
> Unrivall'd forms of glory, and of grace!
> No strumpet, handed to perpetual fame,
> No scenes of lewdness, and no deeds of shame;
> Scenes, that would Envy of her snakes beguile,
> Deeds where fond Virtue loves to gaze, and smile:
> Such forms, such deeds, on Raphael's tablets shine,
> And such, O Trumbull! glow alike on thine.

Trumbull was the virtuous painter who would celebrate the successes of a nation the Calvinist Reverend Dwight viewed as "the favorite land of heaven; the greatest empire the hand of time ever raised up to view."

Unfortunately for Trumbull, not everyone shared Dwight's high opinion of his paintings. Neither the canvases nor the engravings were the success he had hoped they would be. While in America there might have been some desire for a national art, grandiose history paintings—despite being devoid of "strumpets" or other evidence of "lewdness"—were still connected in the minds of many to a corrupt aristocracy and a royal court. Some may also have seen Trumbull as unpatriotic for preferring residence in England. There, little interest was shown in images that reminded people of recent defeat; in fact, the artist admitted later that his Revolutionary War paintings "had given offence to some extra-patriotic people in England." Trumbull, like so many of his fellow artists, would have to turn to portrait painting to earn his living. Only later, in 1817, were his talents as a history painter recognized with a commission from Congress for four large canvases for the Capitol Rotunda in Washington (see pp. 121–22).

2.5.8 Cynthia Burr: *Let Virtue be A Guide to Thee*, 1786. Needlework sampler, 16½ x 14½ in. (42 x 37 cm.) Gift of Mrs. Murray S. Danforth. Museum of Art, Rhode Island School of Design, Providence

The Aspirations of Women: Post-Revolutionary Samplers

The same year Trumbull finished *The Death of General Montgomery* and *The Battle of Bunker's Hill*, another individual was recording her understanding of the state of the nation, its past and its future. On March 8, 1786, fifteen-year-old Cynthia Burr (1770–?) completed an elaborate needlework sampler [**2.5.8**] (for a discussion of samplers see p. 79). The central scene contains a two-story building, with wide steps leading up to a front door above which rises a pediment. Flanking the house are two couples, the one on the right appearing to be older than the one on the left, suggesting two generations of the same extended family. Each is located beneath a tree, the branches of which curve elegantly above them. A line of clouds traverses the area above the couples and house and frames the phrase "Let Virtue be A Guide to Thee." Above this phrase two more lines of text contain an alphabet (minus the "J" and "U") and the statement "Cynthia Burr was born May 21 1770." The lower edge of the central scene is marked by a brick wall, which encloses the two couples and two animals, one beneath each couple. Above the

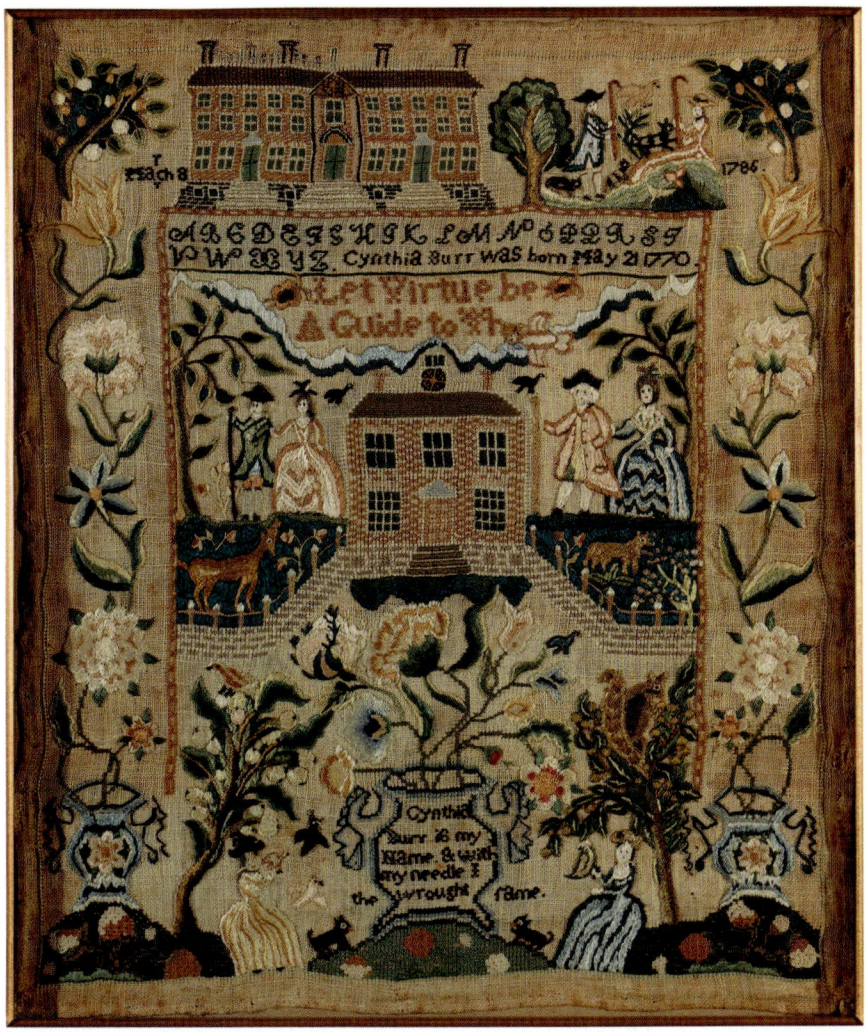

alphabet is a chain-like inner border, which extends down the sides but is open at the bottom, effectively linking the central scene to the subsidiary scene below.

The lower scene is at one and the same time separate and a continuation of the outer border of the sampler itself. It is composed of a large urn containing an elaborate array of flowers flanked by two women who each sit beneath a tree and are accompanied by two small animals, possibly cats. A large squirrel is perched in the tree on the right and a bird in the tree on the left. The woman on the right holds a small lyre or harp, while the one on the left holds what appears to be an artist's palette. These objects are common symbols of music and painting found in European prints and paintings of women as allegories of the arts. On the surface of the urn are stitched the words "Cynthia Burr is my Name and With my needle I wrought," with the last two words of the sentence—"the same"—located outside the parameters of the urn. Behind the two women are two additional urns, out of which grow the flowers that compose the right and left borders of the entire composition. At the top is another imposing building, this one suggesting a public edifice, possibly a school. To the right of the building is another couple, with crooks, who appear to be herding several animals, although they are quite elegantly dressed for the occasion.

Burr's sampler is similar in content and composition to several others produced at this time, in which the buildings have been identified as the University Hall at Brown University (at top) and the Old State House of Providence, Rhode Island (in the center). She may have attended Polly Balch's school for girls in Providence, for at least one other sampler of this type has been connected with a student there. While girls began with a similar pattern, each made her own additions in order to personalize her work. Burr's is much less crowded than some, with the various registers clearly separated from each other.

The emphasis on pastoral landscapes and strolling couples in many sampler patterns suggests a debt to eighteenth-century British landscape painting of country gentry surveying their estates, such as *Mr and Mrs Andrews* (*c.* 1749) by Thomas Gainsborough (1727–1788). Also common to both is the absence of any indication of the hard work involved in tilling the land or tending the animals (the couple in the top right of Burr's sampler seem to be playing at being shepherds). The presence of several couples also indicates one purpose of expertly stitched samplers: to provide evidence of a young woman's readiness for marriage.

Burr locates her name in two places. The line recording her name and birth date in the upper portion is associated with both learning (the alphabet) and virtue ("Let Virtue be A Guide to Thee"). This line is also in close proximity to the two couples below, suggesting she will follow their example in forming a virtuous marriage. By placing her name again on the surface of the urn, she suggests that she is, in fact, the source of fertility, be it as a mother or a needleworker. The abundance of flowers similarly points to the fecundity of both the prospective bride and the land itself. Her decision to place two words outside of the urn's borders may well have been a practical one—they just would not fit. But it also conveys the sense that the conventional frameworks that controlled or allowed for women's creativity were not sufficient to contain the artistic expression of the young Cynthia Burr. Her aspirations are tempered, however, by the misspelling of "March" in the top left-hand corner. Successful mastery of the alphabet and spelling would obviously require further study and hard work.

One detail in the sampler is rather puzzling. The faces and hands of all of the figures are embroidered with a bright white thread, except for the seated woman on the lower left. While her eyes and mouth are designated with black and red thread respectively, her skin remains the beige of the linen that forms the support for the embroidery. Perhaps it would be reading too much into this detail to see it as a reference to race in the new republic. Yet at least one prominent woman connected gender and race in the tumultuous years of the Revolution. Abigail Adams, who had encouraged her husband to consider the rights of Africans, both enslaved and free, when drafting the Declaration of Independence, also urged him to "remember the ladies." The rights of neither were directly addressed in the document. White women in the colonies, like black men and women, would have to wage their own battles for political and economic freedom. Both groups realized that the success of their efforts would depend largely on their access to education. They would need the skills necessary to press their demands in the courtroom, the schoolroom, the marketplace, and the art world.

Money, Beauty, and Rank: Silver in the New Republic

Both the revolutionary fervor of Trumbull's paintings [**2.5.6**, p. 94; **2.5.7**, p. 96] and the pastoral iconography of Burr's sampler [**2.5.8**; p. 97] can be found in silver objects created in the colonial era. The revolutionary fervor appears in a work by the most politically active, artistically innovative, and successful colonial silversmith, Paul Revere. Just two years before he produced his print of the Boston Massacre of 1770 [**2.5.2**; p. 89], Revere created his *Sons of Liberty Bowl* to commemorate both the radical Whigs whose names were engraved on the rim of the bowl and the ninety-two members of the Massachusetts House of Representatives who refused to rescind a letter sent to the legislatures of all the colonies in 1768 protesting the levying of taxes by the British crown. He also added homage to the radical English Whig and tax critic John Wilkes.

Revere also produced the Boston creampots and teapots on which pastoral iconography most often appeared. This iconography narrated, according to the art historian Patricia Kane, "the stories this class of colonial New England consumers told themselves, stories that reflect their concerns and interests," in particular about social status, land ownership, courtship, and sexual pursuit. These stories would have been reflected upon during teatime, a gathering Kane describes as at "the very core of family life, bringing together as it did the whole family once a day." Tea was also a time at which friends, acquaintances, and even strangers were welcomed into the home. At such moments, narratives about sexuality and courtship would have constituted a particularly salient aspect of the conversation, as young women of marriageable age were often responsible for serving at the tea table.

Tea sets were, in fact, among the most sought-after silver objects in the years immediately following the Revolution, one indication of what the museum curator Jeannine Falino describes as "a trend toward broad ownership of genteel goods." This trend had begun before the emergence of an independent republic, and increased at a rapid pace. A nascent wage-based economy was quickly replacing the subsistence and barter systems of an earlier era, enabling people from all walks of life to use their income to purchase goods. "Even in the colonies," writes Falino, "where currency problems were rife until the formation of the new republic, the power of the purse had an enormous impact upon the marketplace, where manufactured products at all price levels soon began to enter everyday life."

Revere's records of his silver commissions, along with other evidence relating to his customers, provide valuable accounts of purchasing patterns for silver in the second half of the eighteenth century. When his father died in 1754, Revere took over the family business. The customers he inherited came from a wide range of socio-economic groups—artisans, middling-income merchants, professionals, the business elite, and government appointees. Revere produced more low-end goods—flatware, shoe or knee buckles, buttons, harness fittings—than high-end, for the elite preferred to buy their more elaborate silver goods from England or other European countries. Much of his success after the Revolution, however, lay in his ability to respond to demands for specific kinds of more elaborate silver objects, in particular sugar bowls, creamers, and teapots. Falino notes that after the Revolutionary War, "Revere achieved near dominance of silver teapot production," taking advantage of a return to popularity of a beverage that had earlier symbolized a resistance to English taxes (see p. 90) and the consumption of which had thus diminished immediately prior to and during the hostilities.

Before the war, colonists had preferred to purchase silver as single pieces, slowly acquiring complete tea sets. After the war the purchase of larger tea services as a complete set became popular. Revere's production of such sets, or *en suite* tea services, was facilitated by the availability of rolled sheet silver, which was a more economical method of producing silver vessels. This was particularly the case for fluted teapots like the one at the center of the set he made for a wealthy Boston merchant and his wife, John and Mehitable Templeman, in 1792 [**2.5.9**]. The rolled sheet metal also made it easier to achieve the fluting and straight edges that mark these objects. Their clean lines and finely engraved designs of draped fabric and tassels recall the neoclassical forms that were then popular in much of Europe and associated with newly emerging republics on both sides of the Atlantic. These neoclassical attributes, found on all manner

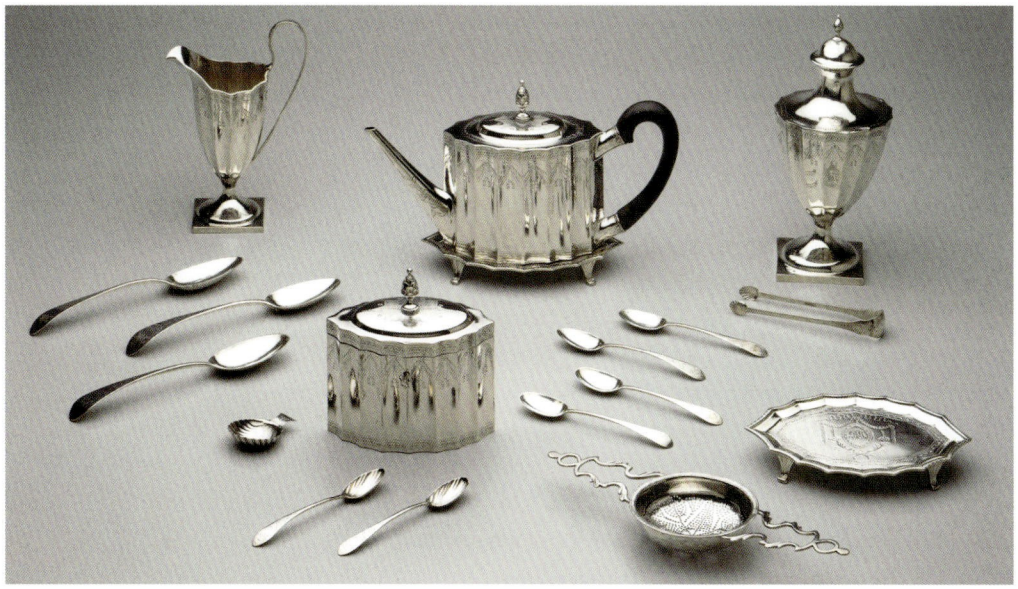

2.5.9 Paul Revere: Tea service, 1792. Silver and wood
Minneapolis Institute of Arts

of goods and buildings in the immediate post-Revolution or Federal period, were the hallmarks of what came to be known as the Federal Style. Revere engraved the Templemans' initials—JMT—on the spoon handles, stands, and sugar urn, reinforcing the association between these objects and their owners. These initials also served as a kind of insurance, making it easier to track down the owner if the item was stolen.

Much of the silver in the homes of the well-to-do in the eighteenth century took the form of coins that were often melted down and transformed into domestic objects, and sometimes re-melted to pay off debts or to fund revolutionary armies. This transference from craft to currency and back suggests the particular place that silver held in colonial and post-revolutionary America. According to the historian Richard Lyman Bushman, silver was "a powerful material for establishing identity and configuring hierarchical relationships....Everywhere, silver was used to command assent, to assert authority, or to claim respect." Silver's power lay in the fact that it could signify three things at once: money, beauty (also associated with divinity), and rank. In an era of dramatic fluctuations in paper currency, silver maintained its value and carried with it "the authority of British sterling and...the intractable worth of bullion."

Yet both its origins and its association with thievery and deceit tarnished the sheen of silver. Much American silver originated in mines in New Spain and Peru and was extracted through a system of forced indigenous labor marked by long hours and appalling conditions. These conditions were remarked upon in political treatises and literary tracts available to American colonists. Many of these colonists, through their participation in the slave trade, then acquired the coins created from this silver. Once acquired, owners of such silver had to worry about thieves who recognized the wealth and status associated with this valuable metal and who were not averse to counterfeiting as well as stealing. As Bushman writes, "silver figured in a complex and ambiguous narrative of power." As coinage or as teapots, it represented both elite status and a more democratic consumer revolution, while simultaneously pointing to the underbelly of the economic system that made both possible.

Presidential Poses: Paintings and Statues of George Washington

Burr's sampler [**2.5.8**; p. 97] and Revere's tea set [**2.5.9**; p. 99] attest to the presence of cultural traditions, often aristocratic, that originated in Britain and Europe in general. As much as leading citizens of the United States might espouse principles of liberty and equality, socio-economic hierarchies still marked the realms of culture and politics. These hierarchies are particularly evident in the portraits created after independence.

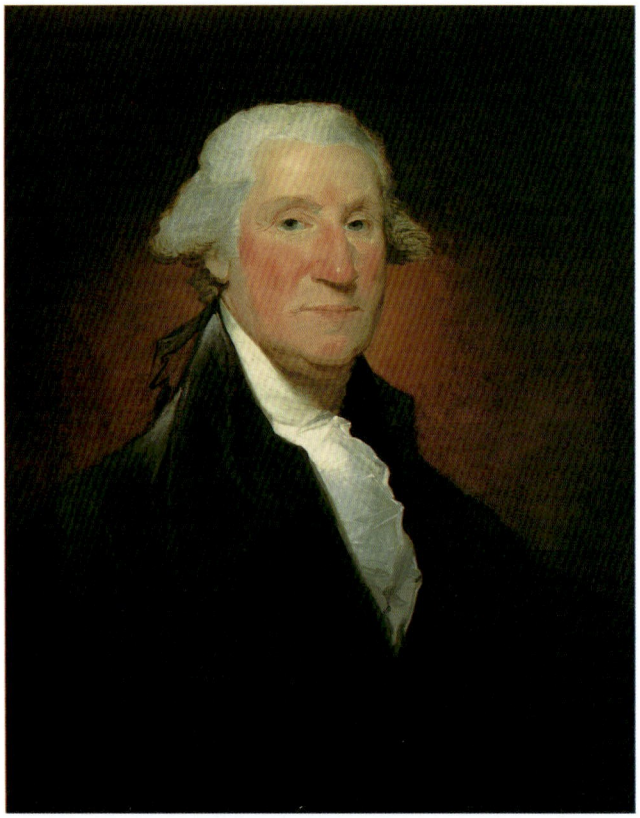

2.5.10 Gilbert Stuart: *George Washington* (the Vaughan Portrait), 1795. Oil on canvas, 29 x 23 in. (73.7 x 60.3 cm.) National Gallery of Art, Washington, D.C.

While portraits were most often seen as personal commemorations, those of important political or military leaders were also representations of the nation. George Washington was the most important political leader during the first years of American independence. Initially head of the Continental Army, he became the country's first president in 1789. While not an aristocrat by birth, he was a wealthy landowner, as were most of the men who led the colony into rebellion against Britain and who formed the Federalist Party. They believed that the new leadership must be drawn from the wealthy and well-educated citizenry. This conflict between elite rule and a more radical and leveling republicanism would mark the political debates in the United States throughout its early years of independence.

One artist who devoted much time to the depiction of the country's first president was Gilbert Stuart (1755–1828). Born in Rhode Island, Stuart studied in Scotland, England, and Ireland between 1772 and 1793, becoming a pupil of West's. Upon his return to the United States he met with great success as a portrait painter. One of his earliest paintings of Washington is the Vaughan Portrait of 1795 [**2.5.10**], in which the sitter gazes out at the viewer with confidence, a slight smile on his face. Stuart was a Federalist and, like most Federalists, was fearful of runaway populism, looking to strong leadership to keep the country's more "radical" elements in check. Yet he was also aware that lavish pictorial celebrations of the political or economic power of any single individual often met with disapproval in a country having only recently freed itself from British control. While Washington possesses an aristocratic bearing in Stuart's portrait, he appears as a statesman rather than a landowner, a man of republican rather than monarchical aspirations.

In another portrait, commissioned in 1796 by Senator William Bingham of Pennsylvania as a gift to the Marquis of Lansdowne [**2.5.11**], Stuart more self-consciously promotes Washington as the leader of a republic of elected representatives. His stance, with the upraised arm signaling public address, is that of a Senator of the Roman republic (the stance is found in many Roman statues from the first century BCE). The president is located not on the battlefield or on his estate but in his office. The books under the table, which include a copy of the Constitution and volumes of *The Federalist* and the *Journals of Congress*, indicate the dedication and studiousness of the country's new leader.

2.5.11 Gilbert Stuart: *George Washington* (the Lansdowne Portrait), 1796. Oil on canvas, laid to wood, 96 x 60 in. (243 x 152.4 cm.) Pennsylvania Academy of the Fine Arts, Philadelphia

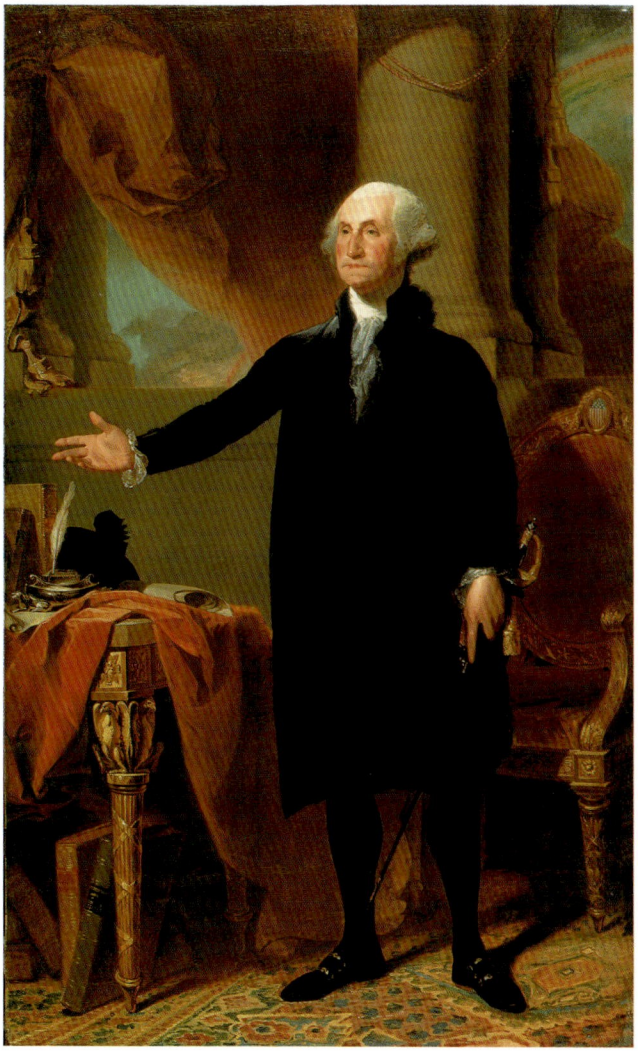

The chair and table in the Lansdowne Portrait also display the newly emerging iconography of the young nation—the stars and stripes on the back of the chair, the bald eagle carved on the leg of the table. These appeared on the country's seal, together with an olive branch and a bundle of arrows (representative of the combined strength of the colonies) clutched in the eagle's claws. The eagle and arrows were also symbols of the Iroquois League—an iconographic borrowing that may have represented a much broader, political appropriation. During the debates of the Continental Congress and the Constitutional Convention, speakers referred openly to Iroquois ideas regarding the unification of disparate units (peoples, colonies) into a league or confederation. Congress formulated a speech to the Iroquois in 1775 in which the Six Nations were referred to as a "wise people" who offered valuable counsel. In fact, for the first hundred years of independence, indigenous forms of political organization were acknowledged as one source of European American democratic institutions, along with British common law, the Magna Carta, Roman republicanism, and Greek democracy. This mix was evidence that the syncretic forms of both art and social organization that appeared shortly after the arrival of European colonists continued to evolve. Yet the political power and material circumstances of indigenous peoples in the new nation would rapidly deteriorate as the nineteenth century progressed (see pp. 175–77).

George Washington was also commemorated in carved portraits, although they were fewer in number than painted versions. Sculpture did not become a fully developed art form in the US until the early nineteenth century. Prior to that time it was viewed primarily as a craft, with its practitioners producing low-relief carvings on furniture (see p. 72) and gravestones (see p. 81) or wooden figures for commercial purposes. Sculpture was also more costly and time-consuming than painting and there were few buildings that required statues or carved decorations. Those who desired training as fine artists had to travel to Europe in order to study from either classical Greek and Roman statues or plaster copies and to gain access to supplies of marble.

Several skilled woodcarvers from Britain had set up shop in New England in the late seventeenth and eighteenth centuries to service both domestic and commercial needs and to train a new generation born in the colonies. One of the industries most in need of their skills was shipping. Almost every major community on the eastern seaboard had a shipyard, and carvers were enlisted to provide figureheads, sternboards, and other decorations for the ship's interior and exterior. Many successful carvers employed several apprentices. Designs were worked up, often from live models, and submitted to shipbuilders. A lengthy correspondence sometimes followed between the carver and the shipbuilder over the exact features of the figure.

An early example of a wooden figurehead is *Lady with Portrait Medallion*, dated to *c.* 1795–1805 and attributed to Samuel McIntire (1757–1811), an architect and carver from Salem, Massachusetts [**2.5.12**]. McIntire came from a family of carpenters and benefited from the prosperity that Salem enjoyed after the War of Independence, when shipbuilding and trade flourished. He designed several homes for Salem's wealthy merchants, often providing furniture and carved decorations. He also created the occasional wooden portrait bust. While *Lady with Portrait Medallion* may have been intended for a small sailing vessel or as a study for a larger figure, it was used as a shop sign. The portrait medallion may be of the captain of the vessel and the female figure, with her simple gown and broad shoulders, his wife. Captains of small whaling vessels often commissioned portraits of their wives or daughters who, similar to figureheads, constantly surveyed the seas, waiting for their husbands and fathers to return home.

2.5.12 (left) Attributed to Samuel McIntire: *Lady with Portrait Medallion*, figurehead, *c.* 1795–1805.
Painted wood, H. 26 in. (66 cm.)
Peabody Museum, Salem, Massachusetts

2.5.13 (right) Laban S. Beecher: *Figurehead of Andrew Jackson, from the US frigate "Constitution,"* 1834.
Painted wood, H. 142 in. (361 cm.)
Museum of the City of New York, New York

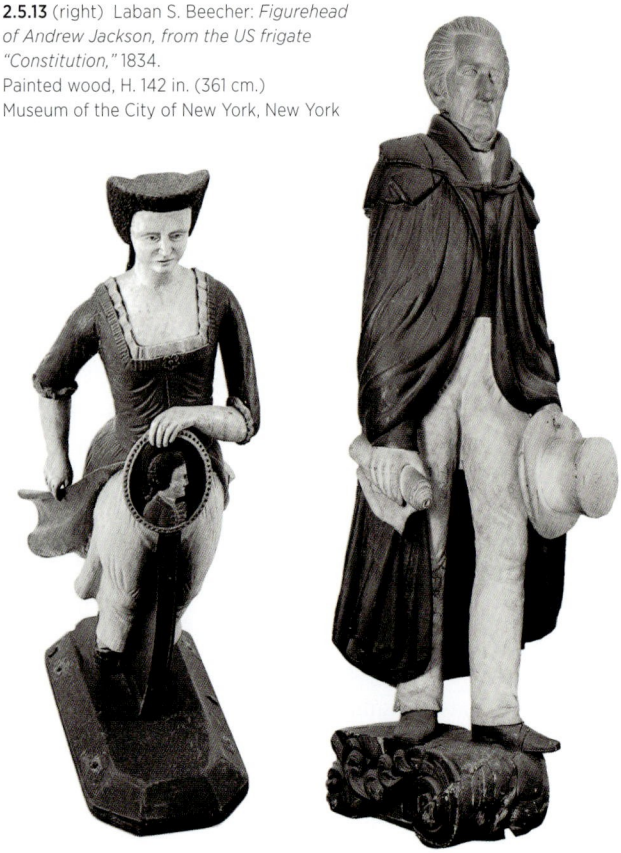

Different kinds of ships required different kinds of figureheads, ranging from the small, plain ones of the whalers to the larger, more elaborate women with billowing gowns and striding poses that graced the famous clippers. Not all figureheads, however, were female. Some ships displayed generic male sailors while others bore the likenesses of American politicians. The latter were most likely to be found on military vessels, such as the *Constitution*, which sported the Boston carver Laban S. Beecher's over-life-size figurehead of President Andrew Jackson [**2.5.13**]. Beecher's work was the *Constitution*'s third figurehead, the others having been damaged or worn beyond repair in military battles. Standing stiffly upright in a long dark coat, with a hat in one hand and the rolled-up Constitution in the other, President Jackson conveys not movement and dynamism but rigidity and intractability in the face of stormy waters. One person who objected to the new figurehead and the politics it represented proved his point by sawing off Jackson's head just below the nose shortly after the figure had been mounted on the ship. It was restored the following year.

At least one full-length wooden portrait of Washington was created around 1800 by the carver Joseph Wilson (1779–1857), who was well known for his ship figureheads. The commission came from Timothy Dexter, a wealthy merchant who resided in Newbury Port, Massachusetts. It was one of a group of forty-five life-size painted carvings that Dexter ordered from Wilson between 1799 and 1800, which were set atop the columns, fences, arches, and buildings located on the merchant's estate. The resulting display is recorded in a mezzotint from 1810, four years after Dexter's death [**2.5.14**]. The figures included not only Washington, but also Thomas Jefferson, John Adams, William Pitt, Napoleon Bonaparte, Dexter himself, and other luminaries with whom he wished to be associated (he took on the title of "Lord" as an indication of his own sense of self-importance). Washington can be seen atop the arch, flanked by Adams and Jefferson. Unfortunately, only the figure of Pitt and a few pieces from another carving survive.

Washington also came close to being memorialized in wax by the then well-known sculptor Patience Lovell Wright (1725–1786). Born in Bordentown, New Jersey, the daughter of an intensely religious Quaker farmer, Patience Lovell left home at the age of twenty and moved to Philadelphia, where she married the cooper Joseph Wright. She returned to Bordentown and spent the next twenty years raising a family, all the while continuing the modeling in clay that she had begun as a child. After her husband's death, Wright, along with her widowed sister Rachel Wells, set up a business modeling portraits in wax, a medium

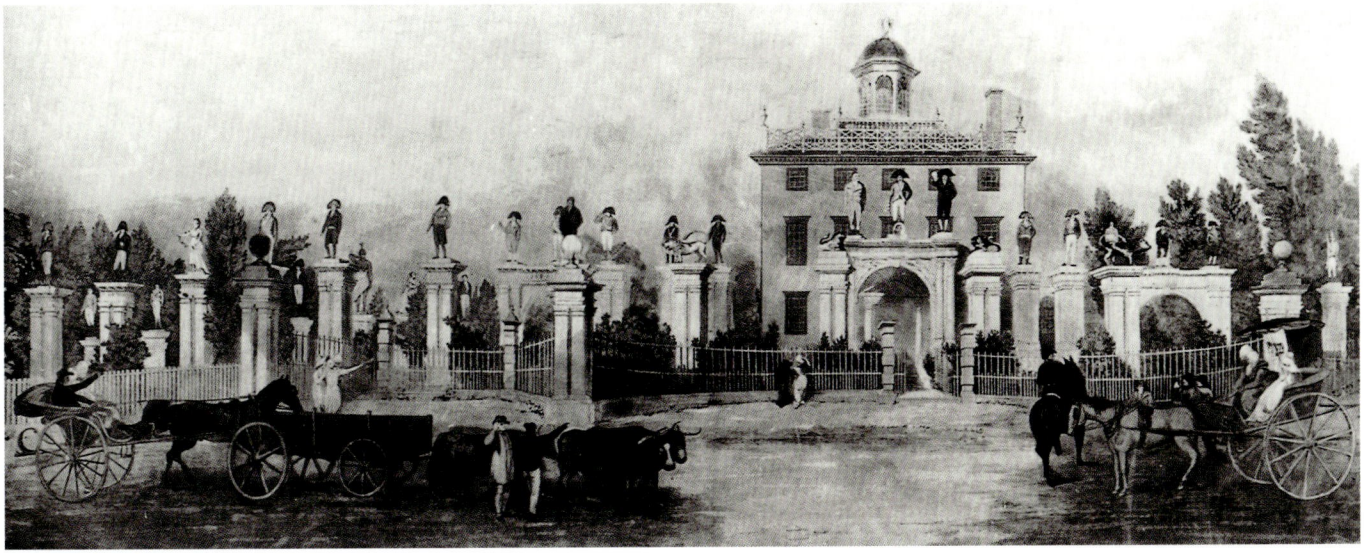

2.5.14 Unknown artist: *A View of the Mansion of the late Lord Timothy Dexter in High Street, Newbury Port*, 1810.
Mezzotint, 26½ x 16¼ in. (67.3 x 42.5 cm.)
Henry Ford Museum and Greenfield Village, Dearborn, Michigan

2.5.15 Patience Lovell Wright: *William Pitt, Earl of Chatham*, 1779.
Wax effigy, life-size
Undercroft Museum, Westminster Abbey, London

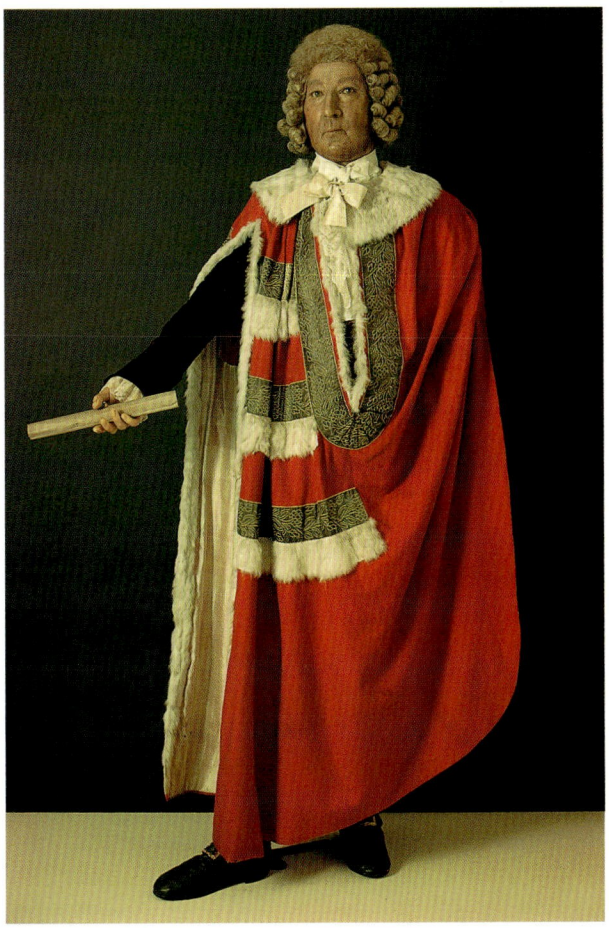

that extended back at least to Roman times in effigy portraits. It experienced renewed popularity in Europe at the end of the eighteenth century, particularly among women artists. Wright then moved to New York and became well known for her ability to sculpt accurate likenesses of her sitters, despite the fact that she was mostly self-taught. She created a waxworks show that toured the East Coast and completed portraits of many leading citizens, including Cadwallader Colden, Lieutenant Governor of New York. Her life-size figures were made more life-like by the addition of skin color, eyelashes, glass eyes, and real clothes. After a fire, which damaged many of her works, she left for England with her children in 1772 to make her fortune as an artist.

Once settled in London, Wright set up her waxworks show and began receiving some of the city's leading figures, as well as commissions to produce their portraits in wax. One of her few surviving works is a statue of the Prime Minister, William Pitt [**2.5.15**], dressed in his parliamentary robes and holding a scroll in his right hand. Created in 1779, it is a sympathetic portrait of someone Wright described as the "guardian angel" of America for his vocal support of the colonies. The art historian Charlotte Streifer Rubinstein reports that when the sculpture was cleaned in 1935 it was found that "the hands were veined and colored with underslips, and even showed hairs on the surface." She also summarizes Wright's working methods, known from contemporary accounts:

> To keep the wax malleable she modeled the bust under her apron, warming it with the heat of her body. At a certain point she would pull the head out from under the apron and put finishing touches on it under the astonished gaze of the sitter.

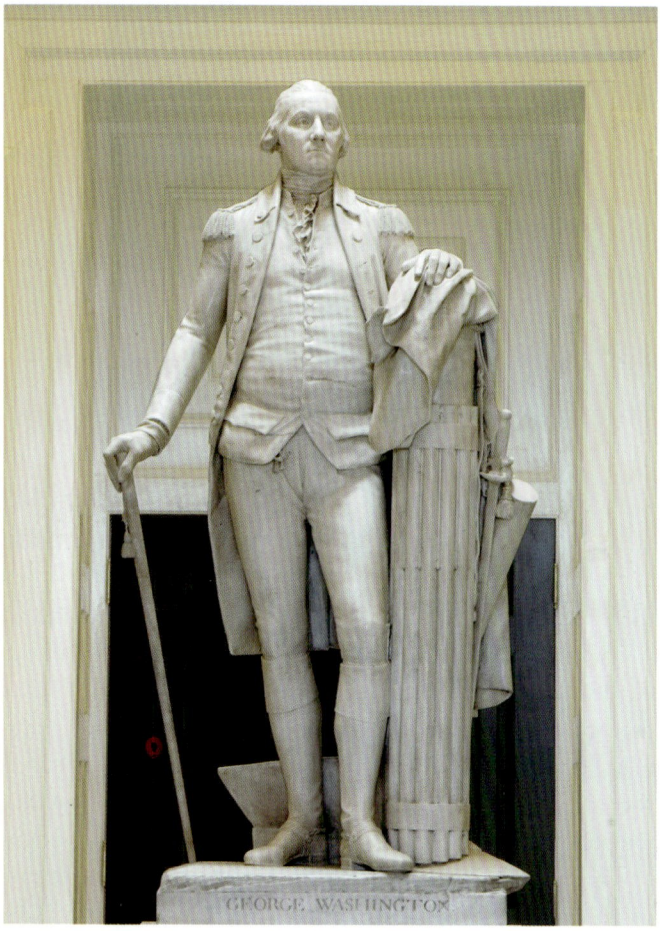

2.5.16 Jean-Antoine Houdon: *George Washington*, 1788.
Marble, life-size
Virginia State Capitol, Richmond

Widely known for her sharp wit and outspokenness, Wright undoubtedly enjoyed the allusions to childbirth that this working method entailed.

Wright was outspoken in her criticisms of the policies of George III, who had invited her to come to the palace and model his portrait. She advocated independence for the colonies and for women, and was said to have sent messages with political information home to her sister in the wax heads of her sculptures. Similar to her fellow expatriate Trumbull, Wright was inspired by the success of the Revolution and planned to create a series of monuments to the nation's new leaders. She wrote to George Washington, who replied that he would be honored to sit for her. Unfortunately, she died in 1786, before she was able to return to America and execute the portrait.

A year before Wright's death, the French sculptor Jean-Antoine Houdon (1741–1828) was commissioned to create a marble statue of Washington for the Virginia State Capitol at Richmond [**2.5.16**]. The piece was completed in 1788, the year before Washington's inauguration as president. It presents him in contemporary dress as a modern Cincinnatus, the Roman general who returned to farming after concluding his military service. The badge of the Society of Cincinnatus, a fraternal order founded in 1783 by several officers of the Continental Army who were returning to civilian life, projects from under Washington's waistcoat. Behind Washington is the proverbial sword-beaten-into-a-plowshare. Beside him is a bundle of thirteen rods, or fasces, a symbol of Roman political office. They, like the thirteen arrows in the eagle's claw borrowed from the Iroquois confederacy (see p. 101), represent the original thirteen states and the power to be gained through union. Upon these fasces Washington hangs the symbol of his military service, his sword. The battles he would now engage in would take place in the halls of Congress rather than the open countryside.

Posthumous Portraits of Washington: The Mourning Picture

After Washington's death in 1799 another type of portrait of the president was produced in great numbers—the mourning picture. Mourning pictures were created after the death of a loved one to aid in the mourning process. They appeared in late eighteenth-century America first in embroidered form and later as paintings or combinations of embroidery and painting (in the middle of the nineteenth century they would be replaced by hand-colored lithographs). As the death rate declined in the late eighteenth century, an earlier matter-of-fact approach was replaced by more elaborate and sentimentalized practices. Women played key roles in the rituals of death and mourning and were also the main creators of such pictures.

An early work by Prudence Punderson (1758–1784) provides a good example of the less sentimental treatment of death. Some time before 1773, the year she married Dr. Timothy Wells Rossiter, she created a needlework picture entitled *The First, Second, and Last Scene of Mortality* [**2.5.17**]. It depicts the various stages of the life of a white woman of comfortable means, from birth to middle age to death. On the right she comes into the world as a child, taken care of in her early years by a black female servant or slave. At the center she is a mature woman, busying herself with her embroidery (here the child serves a second function as an indication of the mature woman's role as a mother). On the left a coffin with the initials PP (those of the artist) rests on a drop leaf table. The black servant/slave at the edge of the composition is a common element in both painted and embroidered scenes by colonial women of their domestic interiors, indicating the extent of slavery or other forms of black servitude throughout the northern colonies in the eighteenth century. On the wall at the right is a painting of

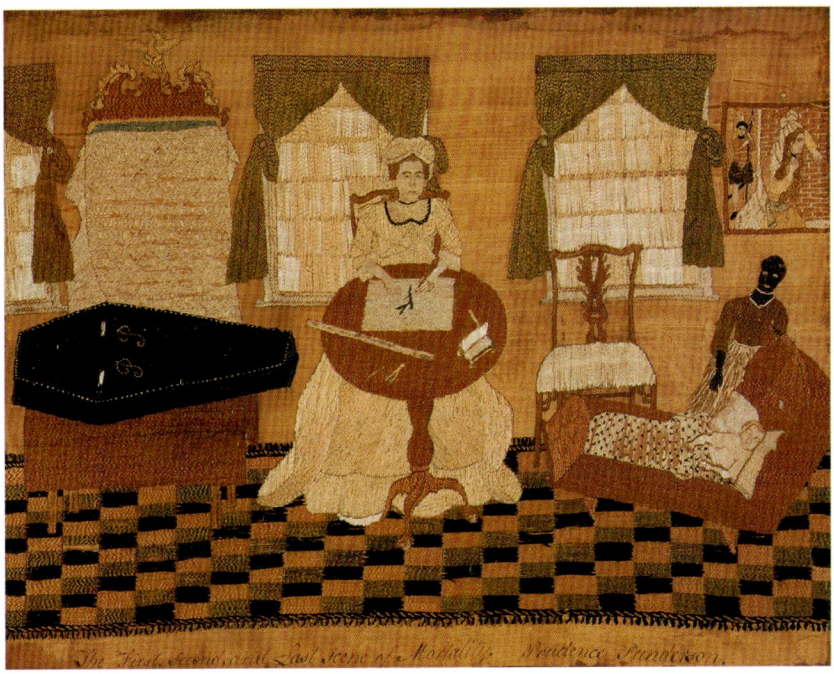

2.5.17 Prudence Punderson: *The First, Second, and Last Scene of Mortality*, before 1773.
Silk on silk, 13 x 17½ in. (33 x 44.4 cm.)
Connecticut Historical Society, Hartford

2.5.18 Hannah Punderson: *Mourning Picture for Prudence and Ebenezer Punderson*, completed *c.* 1822.
Pen and ink and watercolor on paper, 16½ x 20⅜ in. (42 x 51.4 cm.)
Connecticut Historical Society, Hartford

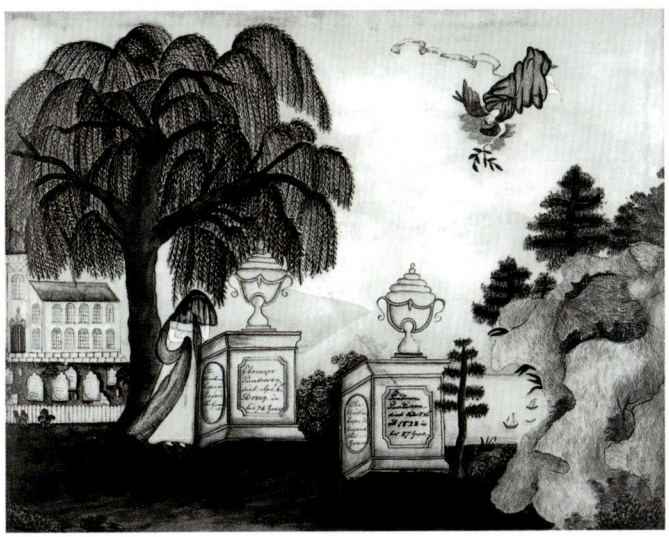

a woman elegantly attired and attended by a soldier in what appears to be medieval garb. The mirror behind the coffin is draped, a sign of mourning.

Early nineteenth-century mourning pictures were much more theatrical. They shared certain common features, noted by Kurt C. Dewhurst and Betty and Marsha MacDowell: "imaginary landscape settings, classical urns mounted on inscribed tombstones, weeping willow trees, and mourning figures, generally female, bowed in the classical posture of grief." The source of many of these elements was ancient Greek funerary art, and their increased use in embroidered and painted images was part of a larger revival of classical Greek forms in the US at the end of the eighteenth century. The American pictures were not drawn from the original Greek examples, however, but from engravings of the work of the British architect Robert Adam, the British ceramic manufacturer Josiah Wedgwood, and the Swiss painter Angelica Kauffmann, among others. They also contained new elements that set them apart from their European prototypes: churches, pine trees, villages, ships, angels, birds, and flowers. Thus the Greek and Roman past was combined with the American present and infused with Christian symbols.

Mourning Picture for Prudence and Ebenezer Punderson by Hannah Punderson (1777–1821), the sister-in-law of Prudence Punderson but a generation younger, is a fine early nineteenth-century example [**2.5.18**]. Painted in watercolor on paper, it commemorates the deaths of her husband's parents with the requisite urns, weeping willow, and mourning female figure (Ebenezer died in 1809; Prudence died in 1822, when the date was filled in on her urn). Punderson has added a church in the background, with its enclosed graveyard, and a curious upside-down angel. Perhaps the latter is descending to crown the tombs with laurel, although its rigid form gives little indication of movement. The stitching of the earlier embroidered works is replicated in the short, precise brushstrokes, a practice common in painted mourning pictures and a testament to their needlework origins.

One individual who capitalized on the demand for mourning pictures commemorating George Washington was the artist Samuel Folwell (1764–1813), who developed a stock design, "In Memory of the Illustrious Washington." Folwell would trace the basic composition on silk in *grisaille* (shades of grey), then give it to a student at the needlework school he and his wife ran in Philadelphia, who would stitch the design under the

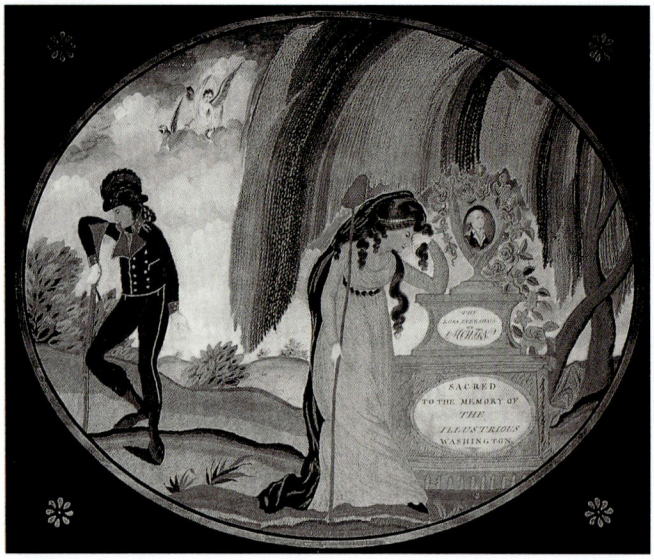

2.5.19 Attributed to Samuel Folwell and an unidentified needleworker: *Memorial to George Washington*, Philadelphia, *c.* 1805. Silk embroidery with ink and watercolor on silk, 16⅞ x 20¾ in.(43 x 52.7 cm.) Abby Aldrich Rockefeller Folk Art Center, Williamsburg, Virginia

supervision of his wife, Ann Elizabeth. He then traveled up and down the East Coast selling these needlework patterns, with the background already painted in. *Memorial to George Washington* [**2.5.19**] of *c.* 1805 is attributed to Folwell and an unidentified needleworker and closely resembles a memorial painted on silk signed by him five years earlier, except that the figure of a soldier leaning on his rifle has been added. Folwell would have executed the finishing painted touches, such as the portrait of Washington and the sky with an eagle and an angel blowing a trumpet and bearing a laurel wreath, signs of nationality and glory respectively. The mourning figure also holds a rod and cap that symbolize freedom (see p. 124), thus connecting her with representations of Liberty. The soldier speaks to Washington's role as leader of the Continental Army and thus his contribution to the successful struggle for freedom from colonial rule. Such images as this, framed and given a place of honor in the family parlor, helped spread patriotic sentiment and functioned as domestic counterparts to the marble statues and painted canvases that graced the nation's public buildings.

From Painting to Print to Embroidery: The History of an Image

Another image of the president that combines needlework and painting is *George Washington and His Family*, created around 1810 [**2.5.22**]. The painted portions include the hands, arms, and heads of the figures and the sky and water in the background. The needleworker and painter, who may have been the same individual, have not been identified, but the work itself is a copy of a print entitled *The Washington Family* [**2.5.21**], created by the American artist Edward Savage (1761–1817) in 1798, with the assistance of the English engraver David Edwin (1775–1841). Savage made the engraving after his painting of the same name [**2.5.20**]. Much can be learned by comparing the different manifestations of this scene.

Savage began his large group portrait in 1789. He took it with him to London in 1791, where he continued to work on it, and completed it in 1796, two years after he had returned to the United States. The engraved version proved extremely popular. Within three weeks of its initial appearance there were more than 430 subscribers and Savage estimated that it would earn him $10,000 within a year. Washington ordered four copies and was later presented by Savage with an example printed in color. A copy of the print hung over the mantel in the dining room of Washington's estate at Mount Vernon.

The painting shows George and Martha Washington, their two grandchildren Eleanor Parke Custis and George Washington Custis, and a black slave—a sign of wealth and privilege as in earlier paintings—whose identity is not certain. The figures are in a room in Washington's Mount Vernon residence. They are arranged around a table in front of two columns and a swag of drapery, elements often used as framing devices and to suggest both nobility and domestic harmony (see p. 70). On the table is a plan of the city of Washington, possibly patterned after the official engraving of Pierre Charles L'Enfant's design of 1791 for the new capital [**2.6.3**; p. 113], published in 1792. In the distance is a view of the Potomac River.

George Washington wears full military garb. His left hand rests on the table, on top of a set of papers and the plan and next to his sword and hat; Martha Washington points with her fan to one of the main streets of the city. The president's right hand rests on his grandson's shoulder. The grandson in turn rests his right hand, holding a compass, on a globe, and holds a piece of paper in the other. Eleanor Parke Custis also gestures toward the city plan. Thus, Savage has created an image of Washington as a military, civic, and family leader, a national patriarch ensconced in a learned environment and contemplating the future of the nation and its new capital. The artist has modeled the figures fully in the round, reinforcing the three-dimensionality of the setting through the use of a tiled floor pattern, the diagonal lines (orthogonals) of which emphasize its recession into the distance.

While the engraved version of Savage's painting differs little from its source, the needlework rendition contains significant changes. To begin with, the original format has been altered to produce an almost square picture, reducing the relative size of the figures in relation to the composition as a whole. The column

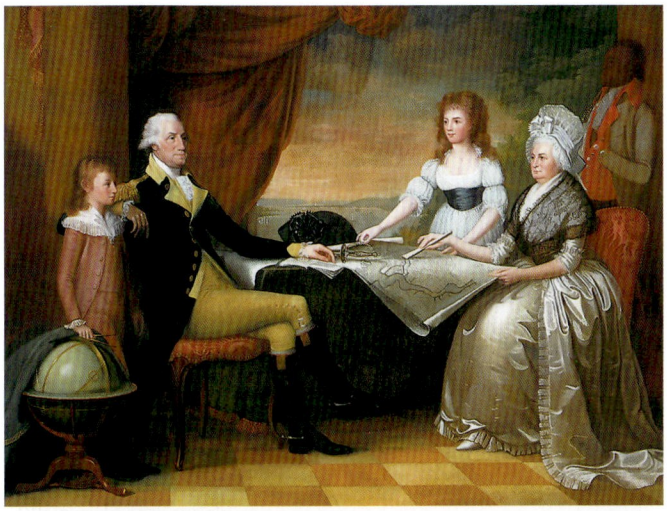

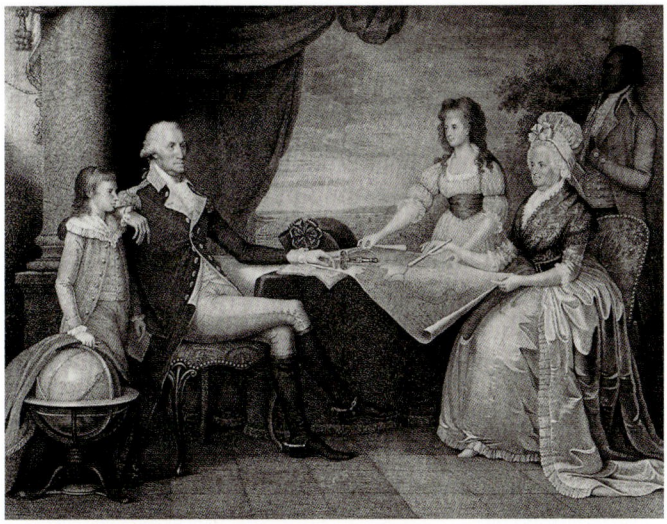

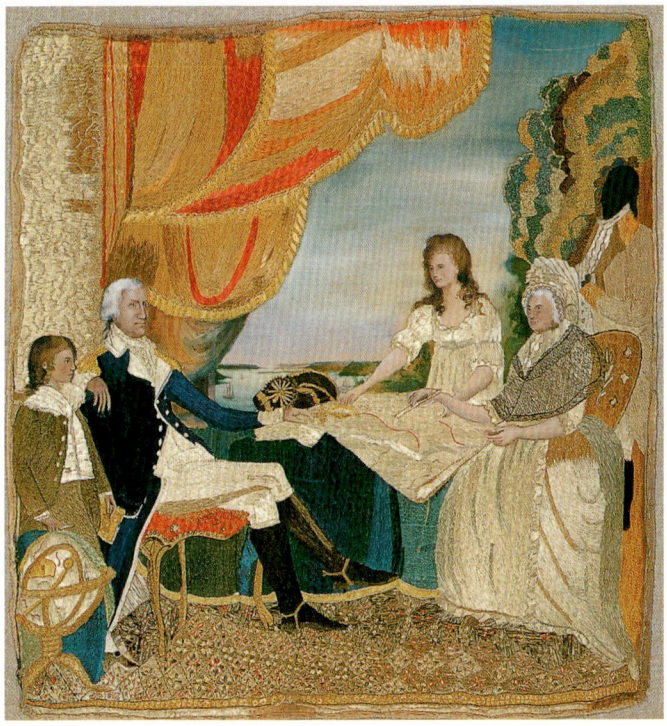

2.5.20 Edward Savage: *The Washington Family*, 1789–96.
Oil on canvas, 84⅜ x 111⅞ in. (213.6 x 284.2 cm.)
National Gallery of Art,Washington, D.C.

2.5.21 Edward Savage and David Edwin: *The Washington Family*, 1798.
Stipple engraving
National Portrait Gallery, Smithsonian Institution, Washington, D.C

2.5.22 Unknown artist, probably from New England:
George Washington and His Family, *c.* 1810.
Silk embroidery and watercolor on silk, 20¾ x 20 in. (52.7 x 50.8 cm.)
Abby Aldrich Rockefeller Folk Art Center, Williamsburg, Virginia

to the right has been omitted and the swag of drapery on the left extended further across the top section of the composition. The plain square floor tiles have been replaced by an elaborately embroidered carpet, which is tilted up, sacrificing the illusion of three dimensions for the clear display of the design. In fact, the needleworker seems to have taken the greatest pleasure—and exercised the greatest skill—in replicating the various types of textiles present in the composition, from the carpet and the swag of drapery to Martha's lace shawl and the green suit of the young boy. The trees in the upper right and the marble column on the left are less convincing as representations of plant matter and stone.

That a needleworker would take great pleasure in representing the qualities of different textiles is not surprising. Needlework played a major role in a woman's sense of herself, of her present and future prospects (see pp. 79–81). Public commentaries reinforced this identification, associating women with the textiles they produced and/or wore. This association was made in a review of the painting in the *New York Morning Chronicle* in 1802. Whereas the author admired Savage's rendition of George Washington for "the serene commanding aspect of a venerable man, whose presence alone calms the tempest," his commentary on Martha Washington focused on her clothing: "it is inexpressibly graceful—the small folds arise by the gentle gradation of an imperceptible curve from the grand and bold parts of the drapery, and are again dissolved in these parts with a noble liberty."

Martha Washington (1731–1802) was a skilled needleworker, as evidenced by her pinwheel patchwork quilt of 1785 [**2.5.23**; p. 108]. Indeed, in the needlework version of *George Washington and His Family*, the map on the table could almost be read as a work of embroidery or a quilt top. The quilt historian Cuesta Benberry provides a look into the nature of the textile production carried on at the Washington plantation, and quotes a description by Mrs. Edward Carrington in 1799 of the sewing room of Martha Washington:

> on one side sits the chambermaid with her knitting, on the other a little colored pet learning to sew, an old decent woman with her table and shears cutting out the negroes' winter clothes, while the good old lady directs them all, incessantly knitting herself, and pointing out to me several pairs of nice colored stockings and gloves she had just finished.

This intimate scene was not, however, the sum total of textile production at Mount Vernon, for Martha Stewart Wilson relates in another letter "Mrs. Washington told how it became necessary to make their own domestic cloth, a task at which sixteen spinning wheels were kept constantly busy."

Such ambitious facilities were common on large plantations, and many female slaves were taught needlework skills or bought in part for their sewing abilities. Several were able to use these skills to save enough money to buy freedom for themselves and members of their family and to support themselves once their freedom was gained. The importance of needlework in this regard was recognized by a number of slave-owners. In his will dated July 19, 1697, David Brown of Somerset County, Maryland, directed

> that Black Beetee be larned to read the bible and to Sowe with Needle well to have good Cloaths and two Cowes and Calves When set free Which I desire to be at the twenty Second yeare of her Age...

The will of Thomas Fluornoy of Powhatan County, probated in 1795, freed all his slaves and directed that the male youths be apprenticed to some mechanic until twenty-one to learn a trade, while the girls were to be taught to sew, spin, and weave until they became eighteen years of age. Unfortunately, few examples of the needlework of slaves from the eighteenth century have been preserved or identified.

George Washington stated in his will that all the slaves at Mount Vernon were to be freed after the death of Martha (although this did not stop his nephew, Supreme Court Justice Bushrod Washington, from selling twenty-five slaves to pay taxes on the estate). One of those slaves subsequently freed may have been Savage's model. In her essay on the painting, Ellen G. Miles notes that in an early study done before Savage left for London the slave was not present. He was added after Savage arrived in London and, according to one late nineteenth-century account, was modeled after John Riley, a freeman who was the personal valet of Thomas Pinckney, the American ambassador in London from 1792 to 1796. Another late nineteenth-century source identifies him as William Lee, a favorite slave of Washington's who had served with him during the Revolution. Lee was given the option, in Washington's will, of either accepting freedom or remaining at Mount Vernon because of accidents that had limited his ability to walk (he was known to have still been at Mount Vernon in 1804). Both men could, in fact, have served as Savage's model, for infrared reflectography has revealed a second, shorter figure underneath the taller one in the finished painting. Savage may have begun with Riley, and ended with Lee.

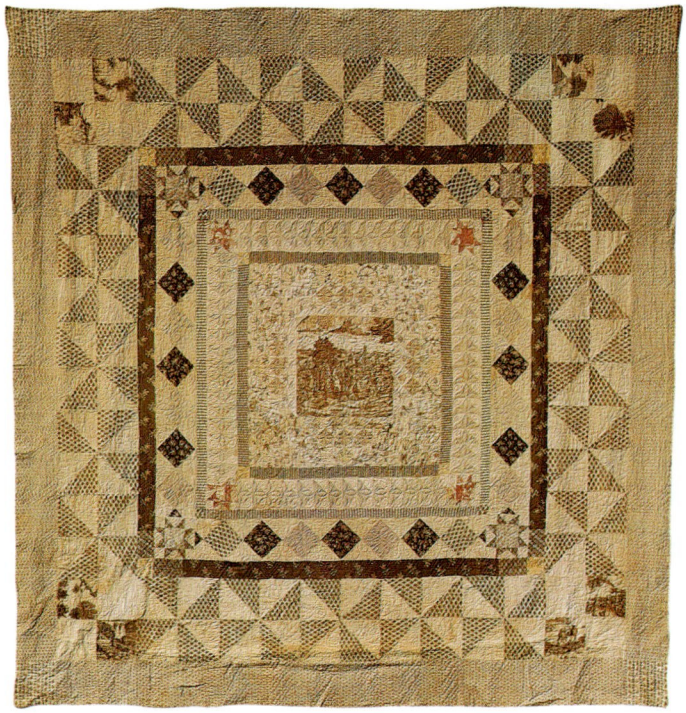

2.5.23 Martha Washington: pinwheel patchwork quilt, 1785. Linen and toiles, 100¾ x 100 in. (254 x 256 cm.) Mount Vernon Ladies' Association, Mount Vernon, Virginia

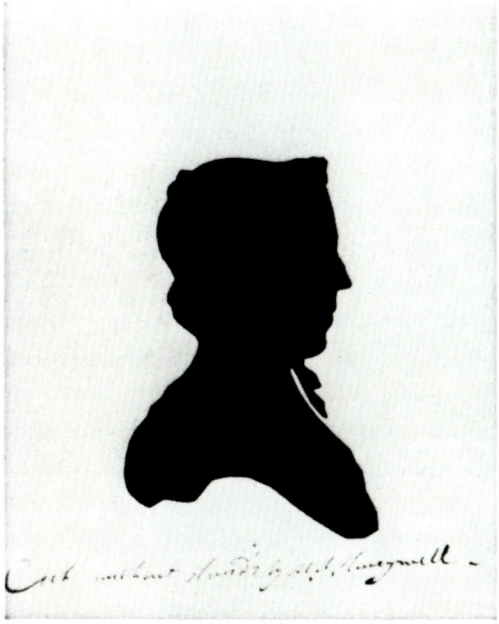

2.5.24 Martha Ann Honeywell: *Silhouette of a Woman*, early 19th century. Cut paper on paper background, 4 x 3 in. (10.2 x 7.6 cm.) Private collection

The slave in Savage's painting wears a fine red vest with a double row of gold buttons and a white shirt with lace front. The vest is almost the same color as the back of Martha's chair, while the lace front echoes the shirt worn by the president. Washington was very particular about the appearance of the slaves who worked in the house at Mount Vernon, dictating what they wore and how they styled their hair (he preferred it long). In fact, the physical appearance of a slave often determined the work he or she would do. Beauty and a dignified bearing often meant they would work in the house as opposed to the fields. In the needlework portrait, the vest of the slave is now muted beige (Martha's chair has also changed to a rust color). While he appears somewhat taller than in the painting, his head and hair are so darkly painted that his features are barely visible (unlike in both the painting and the engraving). In contrast, the faces of the Washington family are shown in exacting detail. These changes serve to diminish the presence and identity of the slave, although the general elegance of his costume and posture and his slave status continue to function as signs of the president's wealth and power.

The slave's dark profile in the embroidery is reminiscent of another type of portrait popular with women at the beginning of the nineteenth century: cut-paper profiles or silhouettes. These could be traced with mechanical aids, or cut free-form. Perhaps the most famous creator of cut profiles was Martha Ann Honeywell (1787–1848?), born in Lempster, New Hampshire [**2.5.24**]. Her fame was due both to her skill and to the fact that she had been born without arms and with only one foot, which required her to cut the profiles by holding the scissors in her mouth. Between 1806 and 1848 she traveled in the United States and in Europe, holding public exhibitions where she cut profile portraits of members of her audience. The twenty-five-cent admission charge included, according to one of her handbills, a "Profile Likeness (cut in a few seconds without hands by Miss Honeywell)."

Her parents, who orchestrated performances that often resembled circus freak shows, exploited Honeywell's talents. Yet she was able to support herself through the production of both silhouettes and other cut, painted, and sewn work. One of her more unusual offerings was the Lord's Prayer written in dime-sized spaces or cut from two-inch (five-centimeter) circles of paper. Honeywell often inscribed her work "cut without hands" or "cut with the mouth by Martha Ann Honeywell." She became one of a growing number of men and women who were able to support themselves with their artistic talents in a country where an increasing demand for images accompanied an unprecedented expansion in population and wealth, and where portraits of individuals from all classes and walks of life would join those of the nation's luminaries in filling out the iconography of the new nation.

Review Questions

1 Why were John Singleton Copley's portraits so popular?

2 How was race represented in depictions of the American Revolution and the events leading up to it?

3 How did women express a new sense of national identity through their needlework? To what extent did this needlework draw upon and/or diverge from the visual conventions of painting?

4 Why were engraved prints so important for American artists in the late eighteenth and early nineteenth centuries? How were they used?

5 How did transatlantic trade and travel impact the materials, styles, and content of the objects (paintings, needlework, silver) found in so many American homes both before and after the Revolution?

CHAPTER 6

Symbols of a New Nation: Architecture and Indigenous Histories

(*c.* 1785–1827)

Home for a President: Thomas Jefferson's Monticello

The building in which Jean-Antoine Houdon's statue of George Washington [**2.5.16**; p. 104] was installed was designed by Thomas Jefferson (1743–1826) and built between 1785 and 1789 [**2.6.1**]. A minister to the French court in Paris at the time, Jefferson firmly believed that architecture served an important symbolic function. Unlike the Federalists, who felt that England was still the cultural homeland of the new nation, Jefferson thought that the United States of America must not adhere strictly to British colonial architecture. Instead, it must draw more directly on the architecture of the ancient Roman Republic. Republican Rome would function as Jefferson's cultural and political patrimony as he argued against Federalist visions of a land of industry and commerce in favor of a democratic society of independent farmers. His Virginia State Capitol took classical revivalism a step further than most contemporary designs. Instead of simply adding a pediment, a series of columns, or applied decoration, Jefferson literally copied the Maison Carrée at Nîmes in southern France, a Roman temple from the first century BCE. The French architect Charles-Louis Clérisseau (1721–1820) helped Jefferson in the formulation of his design. Clérisseau was a strong supporter of the French neoclassical movement, and the author of a book on the Maison Carrée.

Just as Jefferson's Capitol building confirmed the neoclassical trend in official public architecture, his design for his own home, Monticello [**2.6.2a** and **2.6.2b**], ushered in new thinking in the realm of domestic architecture. The architectural historian Leland Roth observes that Jefferson's political convictions led him to reject not only English designs for government buildings, but also those for country houses. Yet the classical and Renaissance prototypes that inspired the designers of English country villas also inspired Jefferson, creating an unavoidable stylistic link between these homes and Jefferson's residence.

Monticello, located on a large estate outside of Charlottesville, Virginia, was built in two stages, the first from 1770 to 1782, the second from 1796 to 1809. During the first stage Jefferson was involved in the revolution against Britain and the drafting of the Declaration of Independence; during the second stage he assumed the positions of vice-president (1796–1800) and president (1800–1808) of the United States.

Jefferson departed from the colonial habit of locating the manor house near the edge of a river. Instead, he placed his home on top of a hill he called Monticello (Italian for "little mountain") in order to achieve a full view of the nearby Blue Ridge Mountains. The main plan of the complex was a broad "U" with the house at the center and arms made up of outdoor terraces stretching outward. In designing the house, Jefferson looked for inspiration to illustrations and treatises on the work of the sixteenth-century Italian architect Andrea Palladio (1508–1580). Palladio had been revived in Britain in the eighteenth century in

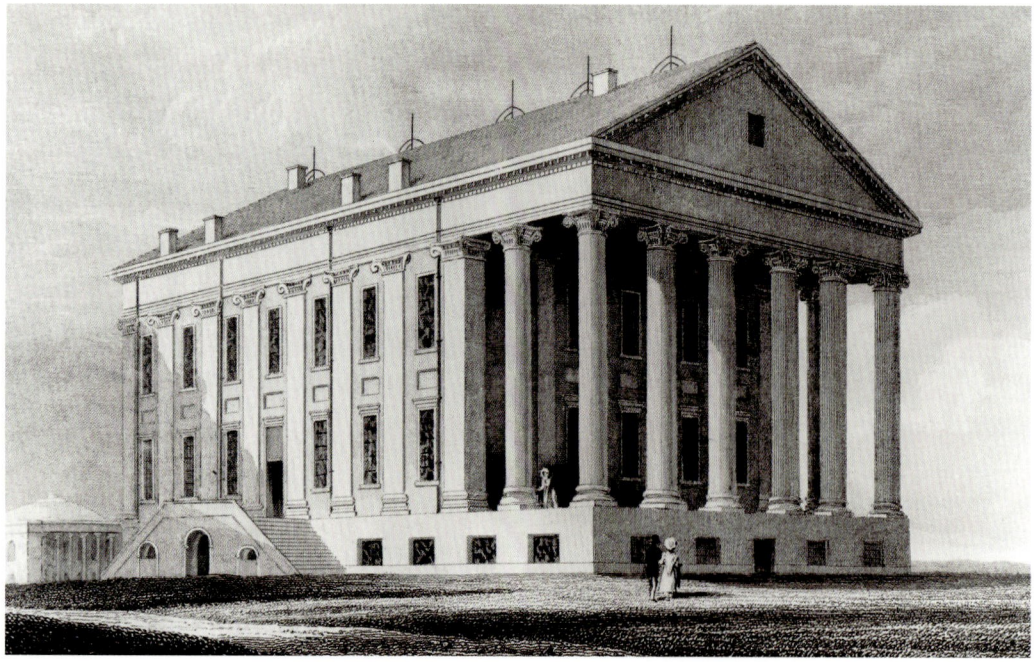

2.6.1 Thomas Jefferson: Virginia State Capitol, Richmond, Virginia, 1785–89.
This early 19th-century engraving shows the building as designed, before the later addition of wings.
Virginia State Library, Richmond

such buildings as Chiswick House, designed by Lord Burlington and completed in 1729. Palladio, in turn, had looked to ancient Roman buildings for inspiration for his own designs. Among the elements he borrowed—and which Jefferson subsequently adopted—were the porticos resembling temple fronts combined with a low dome.

Roth notes that Jefferson "pushed the dependencies at Monticello into the earth." The slave quarters were recessed into the hillside and the kitchen and storerooms were under the house. In the second phase of building Jefferson changed the proportions of the main pavilion so that its two stories would appear as one, adding a heavy Doric entablature that runs around the house. Jefferson also added a low dome to the garden front of the house, thus creating a third story. The effect of all these changes was, in Roth's words, "to press the house further into the hill," and thus to "preserve the view." The architectural historian Dell Upton offers another explanation for these changes. Upton argues that Jefferson's masking of the actual height of the building, making three stories and a basement appear as one story from the garden front, was part of a larger process of deception at work in Jefferson's life. He hid not only architectural stories but also "stories" or narratives dealing with the actual operations of the estate and the material conditions that underpinned Jefferson's ideology of the "Republican Man."

Jefferson represented himself as a scientist, a farmer, and a statesman. As president he forbade the use of his image on coins, cut military expenditures, and opened the president's house to any who chose to visit him, wanting to avoid any actions that might be interpreted as in imitation of the British monarch. He also wished to distinguish himself from the previous Federalist administration of John Adams, which had relished certain lavish ceremonial displays of authority.

Yet Jefferson, the man who coined the words "We hold these truths to be self-evident, that all men are created equal," owned eighty-three slaves, who were housed, as mentioned above, away from and lower than the main house (a location that may, in fact, have been preferred by the slaves themselves: see p. 77). Not only were their quarters out of view from his windows, but their bodies were also often out of view within his home through the use of dumb-waiters, which allowed the food to be moved from the basement kitchen to the main floor dining room. Jefferson also hid—or attempted to hide—his relationship with his slave Sally Hemings, the half-sister of Jefferson's deceased wife Martha (John Wayles was the father of both Martha and Sally; Sally's mother was Betty Hemings, one of Wayles's slaves). In 1802 the political journalist James T. Callender published the first of several charges that Jefferson kept a slave named Sally

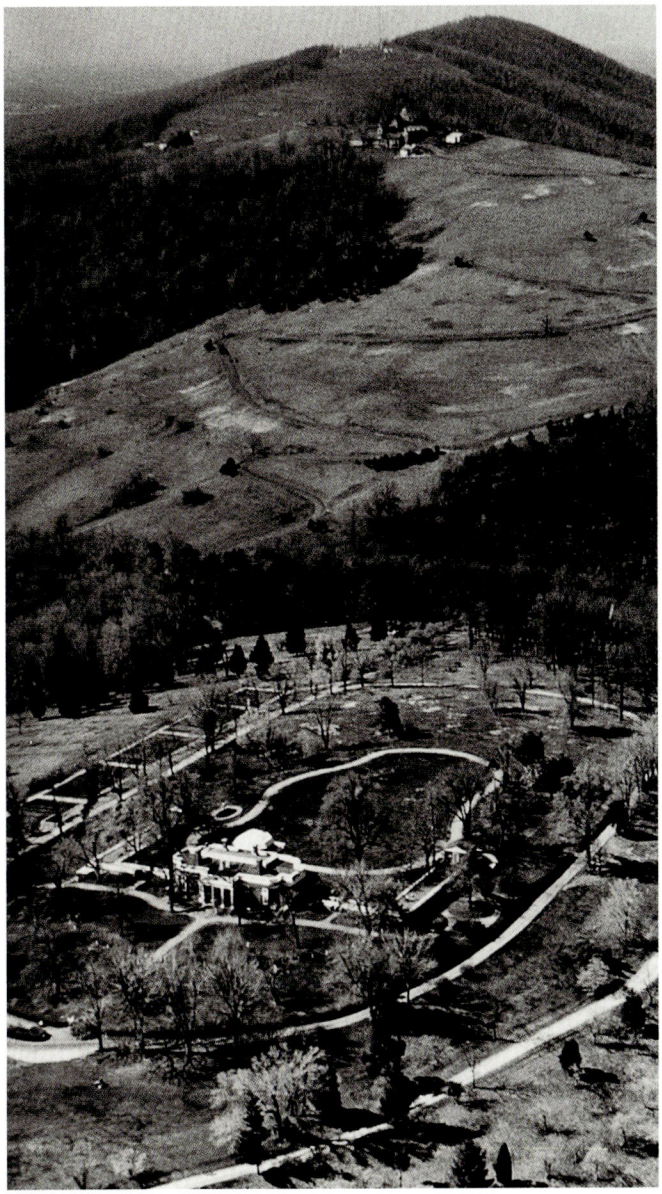

2.6.2a, 2.6.2b Thomas Jefferson: Monticello, Charlottesville, Virginia, 1770–82 and 1796–1809 (garden front facade).

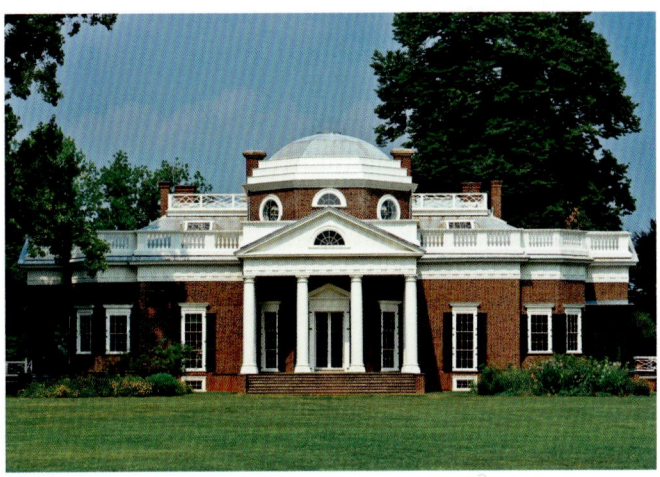

as his "concubine" and fathered several children by her, charges to which Jefferson refused to respond. The controversy continued into the twenty-first century, when the Thomas Jefferson Foundation and most historians decided that the claim was most likely true.

Jefferson opposed slavery, which he saw as contrary to the laws of nature. He believed, however, that the freeing of slaves should not be carried out by an act of the federal government. Instead, it would have to be part of a democratic process in which slave owners as a group willingly agreed to free their human property. This process would be gradual, beginning with the abolition of the transatlantic slave trade (achieved through legislation in 1807), the improving of the working and living conditions of slaves, the ending of slavery as an institution, and the return of freed slaves to Africa or the West Indies. Jefferson believed this removal was necessary because the experience of slavery would create a level of resentment among freed slaves that would endanger the safety of white Americans and risk a race war that would destroy the nation as a whole. At the same time, he felt that to leave slavery intact in a country divided between abolitionists and slaveholders risked a civil war that would also endanger the very existence of the nation, a prediction that ultimately came true in the civil war that erupted in 1861 (see Chapter 12).

Jefferson's beliefs about slavery informed his daily life. He rejected the blatant use of slaves as a sign of privilege, as shown in such paintings as Justus Engelhardt Kühn's *Henry Darnall III* [**1.4.25**; p. 78] and Edward Savage's *The Washington Family* [**2.5.20**; p. 107] and in the positioning of the slaves' quarters at Mulberry Plantation [**1.4.23**; p. 76], yet he did not give up ownership outright. In removing his slaves from view, he contributed to the creation of an image of himself as a self-sufficient man, a solitary hermit who sat on his hill pondering the monuments of the past and the political tasks of the future. In his refusal to play the role of the patriarch surrounded by his charges, he recast patriarchal authority as modern individualism. The library was the central room in Jefferson's private quarters, which were at the opposite end of the main floor of the building from the public quarters. Jefferson's cultivation of his inner self through his study of books reconciled the Republican dilemma of how to achieve a balance between Enlightenment concepts of individual liberty and social order. Jefferson could be alone, yet an active citizen; he could be a part of the public, yet not necessarily among it. Yet this self-sufficient "Republican Man" was a misrepresentation, for the evidence lying beneath the library told another story, one of reliance on slave labor to facilitate the intellectual and agricultural accomplishments of Jefferson's nation of "independent farmers."

Constructing a Capital: Washington, D.C.

The city where Jefferson took up residence as president was located on a triangular piece of land at the junction of the Potomac and Anacostia rivers (Philadelphia had served as the previous capital). In the early stages of its planning Jefferson had proposed a grid format, one he had promoted successfully in 1785, when Congress passed a land ordinance setting up the grid as the standard for all new communities. As a result, four-fifths of the US, writes the architectural historian Spiro Kostof, were subjected "to a regular system of land survey that answered the needs of an agricultural economy and could speedily be occupied in a democratic fashion" (for discussions of earlier uses of grid planning that also had symbolic meaning, see p. 71). President Washington was not impressed with such a modest proposal and called in Major Pierre Charles L'Enfant (1754–1825), a Frenchman who had been a volunteer with the engineering corps in the American Revolution and whose father was a court painter at Versailles, the French royal palace. L'Enfant produced a grandiose plan in 1791 modeled on the radiating avenues of Versailles, which he superimposed over Jefferson's grid [**2.6.3**]. Thus, the pretensions of absolute monarchy and, to a lesser degree, of the Federalists, were placed in tension with the democratic aspirations of Republican Jeffersonians. Just as these two political forces clashed throughout the growing nation, so, too, did the 78-foot- (24-meter-) wide radiating avenues and fine-meshed grid lead to endless urban complications as residents attempted to maneuver through a city filled with oddly shaped scraps of space.

The settlement of Washington proceeded at a slow pace. Few people wanted to move to the swampy, bug-infested site, and so the vast avenues and right-angle streets remained largely unoccupied throughout the early part of the nineteenth century. In 1842 the British author Charles Dickens visited, and noted that it was often dubbed "the City of Magnificent Distances." He, on the other hand, found "the City of Magnificent Intentions" a more apt appellation:

> for it is only on taking a bird's eye view of it from the top of the Capitol, that one can at all comprehend the vast designs of its projector, an aspiring Frenchman. Spacious avenues that begin in nothing, and lead nowhere; streets, mile-long, that only want houses, roads, and inhabitants; public buildings that need but a public to be complete...

The Capitol building from which Dickens was able to achieve his bird's-eye view was not the original structure designed by William Thornton (1759–1828) in 1792 and altered by Benjamin Latrobe (1764–1820), a disciple of Jefferson's. The Thornton/

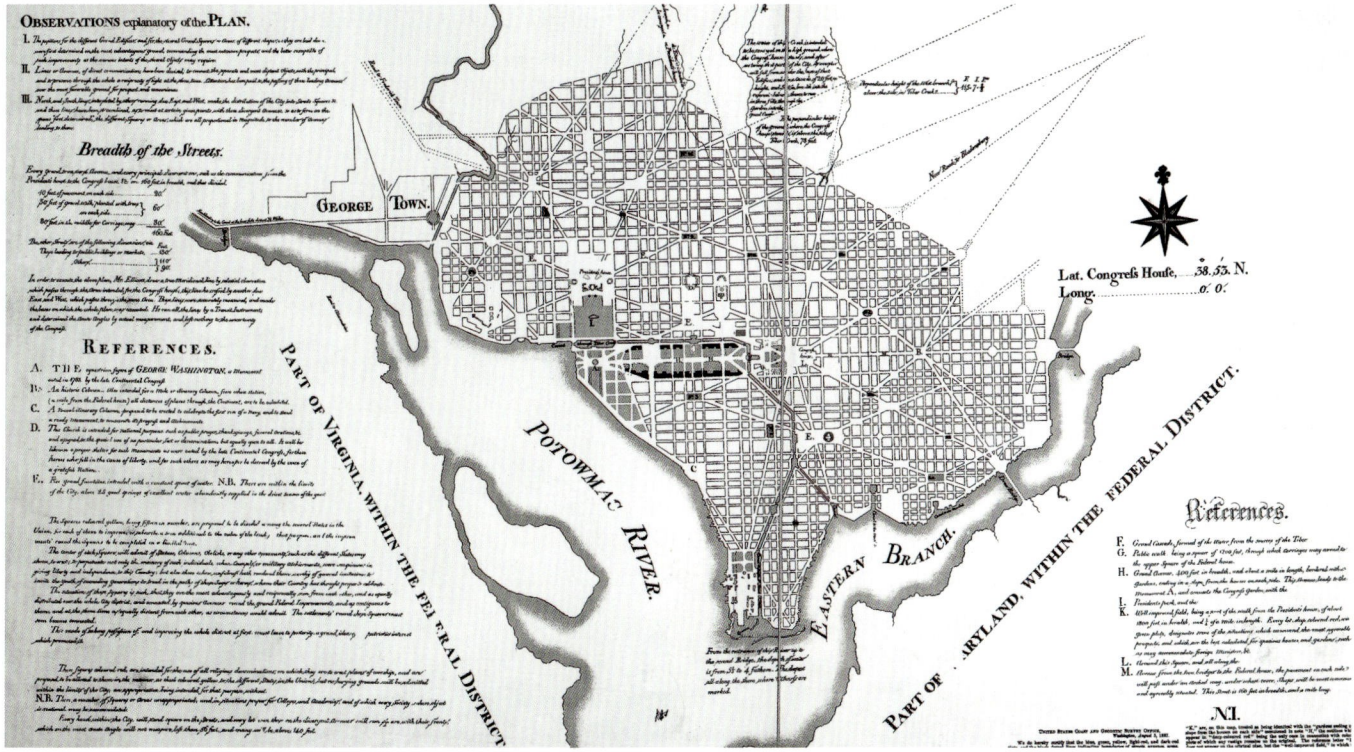

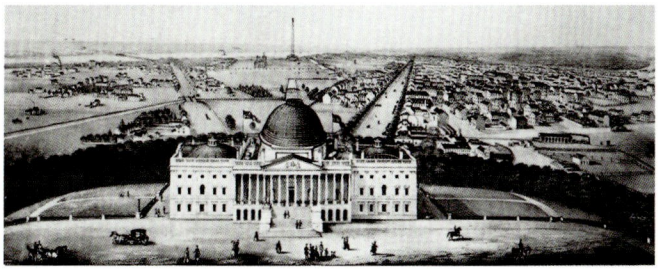

2.6.3 Pierre Charles L'Enfant: plan for Washington, D.C., 1791. Engraving of 1887 after the original drawing (detail) Library of Congress, Washington, D.C.

2.6.4 William Thornton, Benjamin Henry Latrobe, and Charles Bulfinch: United States Capitol, Washington, D.C., 1792–1850. Lithograph by R. P. Smith, 1850. Library of Congress, Washington, D.C.

Latrobe building had been gutted by fire when the British attacked the city in 1814, at the end of the War of 1812 (at the time of the fire the central portion was still unfinished). This war was a direct result of the outbreak of hostilities between Britain and France in 1803. Both countries began seizing American ships bound for each other's ports as part of an economic offensive intended to prevent the normal operations of trade. After a series of failed attempts at negotiations, the US declared war on Britain on June 1, 1812. The war lasted until December 1814, with several encounters between British and American troops, including the successful British attack on Washington that resulted in the burning of the Capitol.

The Capitol was rebuilt under the direction of Latrobe, who supervised the repair of the wings and the construction of a new rotunda and dome. While the building adhered to Jefferson's admonition to turn to classical models for inspiration, there were the occasional nods to local subject matter, such as the replacement of the acanthus leaves on the capitals of the Corinthian columns with corn cobs and tobacco leaves. Latrobe ran afoul, however, of the new commissioner of public buildings, Colonel Samuel Lane, and was relieved of his post as architect of the Capitol in 1817, replaced by Charles Bulfinch (1763–1844). Bulfinch oversaw the completion of the dome, replacing the original wooden framework with one of cast iron (which was painted gray to blend in with the stone building) [**2.6.4**]. The Capitol would undergo a final transformation in the 1850s, as it was enlarged to accommodate the entry of new states into the Union [**4.12.1**; p. 221].

The Louisiana Purchase: New Orleans and Plantation Architecture

In 1803, while architects and engineers were laying out the streets of the nation's new capital, President Jefferson was finalizing the purchase of the Louisiana Territory from the French leader Napoleon Bonaparte for $15 million. The Louisiana territory extended from the Mississippi west to the Rocky Mountains and from the Gulf of Mexico to British North America, thus effectively doubling the size of the US [**4.11.5**; p. 215]. It had not always been a French possession. Robert Cavelier, Sieur de La Salle, claimed it for France in 1682 (see p. 57), but it remained in French hands only until 1766, when it was ceded to Spain as part of the Treaty of Paris of 1763 (see p. 82). France was not too sorry to lose its colony, for Louisiana had been notably unsuccessful in producing any significant export materials and was constantly in need of funds. The Louisiana Territory returned to French control with Napoleon's conquest of Spain in the late 1790s.

Napoleon's willingness to sell the Louisiana Territory to Jefferson was the result of the successful rebellion of African slaves and former slaves on the French Caribbean island of Saint Dominique in 1803 (the independent republic of Haiti was declared in 1804). Louisiana functioned as a source of raw materials and strategic defence for the sugar plantations on the island, and when the French were expelled, the territory was no longer needed. The Haitian Revolution, along with several small-scale slave rebellions in the US, confirmed Jefferson's belief that enslaved or formerly enslaved Africans and whites could not peacefully coexist.

The historian Peter J. Kastor writes that the "Purchase came as an immense surprise to U.S. policymakers," as they had only sought to acquire "New Orleans and the Gulf Coast, in keeping with the plan to consolidate control of the Near West rather than expand into the Far West." They did not hesitate, however, to agree to the entire territory, but they subsequently celebrated the purchase as a benefit to the Near West, in particular through the control of the Mississippi River, rather than as an opportunity to expand beyond the Mississippi. While businessmen and landowners saw the immediate potential for land and profits, many in Jefferson's administration were nervous about the federal government's ability to administer such a large territory, particularly in light of the indigenous peoples and Spanish forces who laid claim to substantial sections of it. It would take another few decades before the federal administration would openly promote the advantages—if not the inevitability—of westward expansion into the newly acquired territory (see pp. 174–75).

In the early eighteenth century, few Europeans were interested in settling in the Louisiana Territory. The southern section (the approximate area of the current state of Louisiana) saw the greatest population growth. Some came to this region from Italy, Ireland, the Rhineland, and German-speaking cantons of Switzerland. Another group, French-speaking Catholic farmers known as Acadians, arrived in the late 1760s and 1770s after being expelled by the British from present-day Nova Scotia, New Brunswick, and Prince Edward Island. African slaves were imported into the area early in the century, primarily as

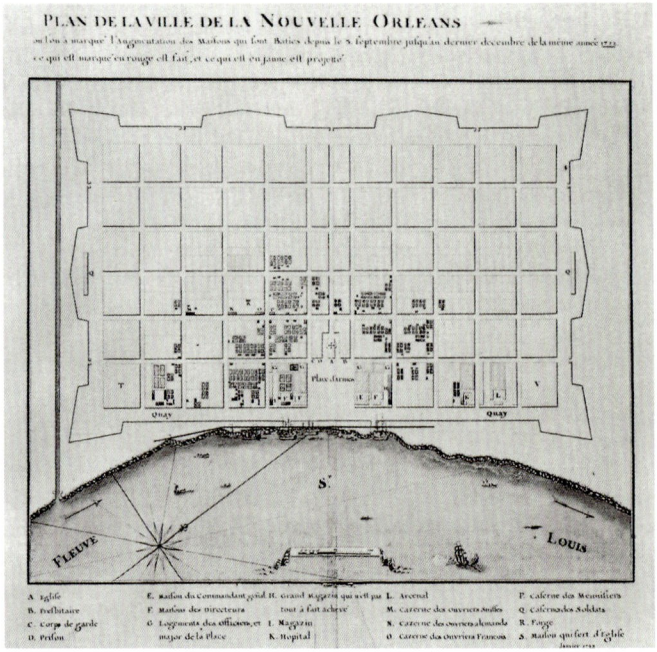

2.6.5 New Orleans, after the 1721 plan by Pierre Le Blond de La Tour, 1722.

2.6.6 Jackson Square, New Orleans, showing the Cabildo or town hall (1795–99), St. Louis Cathedral (1788–94), and the Presbytère or rectory (1788–1813), all by Gilbert Guillemard. The central tower of the cathedral was added by B. H. Latrobe in 1820.
From an early 19th-century lithograph

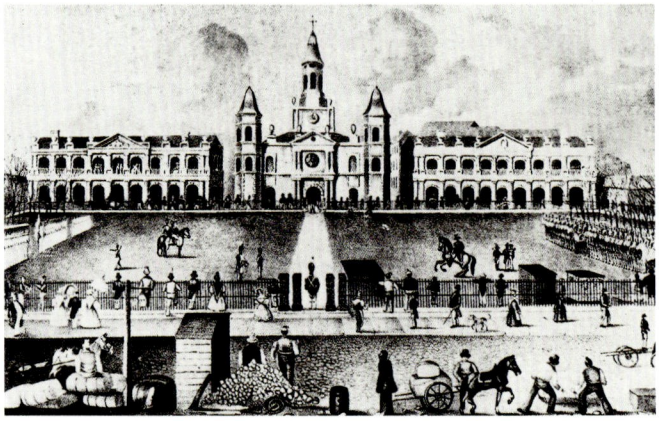

field hands, and composed a large percentage of the population. The indigenous peoples included the Natchez, Chickasaw, and Cherokee. Envious of the rich farmlands cultivated by the Natchez, the French began attacking their major settlements in the 1720s, culminating in a massacre in 1729. According to the historian Joel Gray Taylor, by 1730, a mere ten years after Le Page du Pratz had recorded the funeral of their leader Tattooed Serpent (see p. 60), the Natchez effectively ceased to exist as a people. Those who escaped took refuge with the Chickasaw and Cherokee, who were more effective in resisting French attacks.

Few Spanish actually settled in Louisiana during Spain's control of the territory. French culture—its language, religious practices, food, and entertainment—remained dominant. The main architectural project undertaken by the Spanish was the rebuilding of the *Vieux Carré* (French Quarter) in New Orleans after fires in 1788 and 1794. The "Old Quarter" had been designed by Pierre Le Blond de La Tour (*c.* 1670–1723), engineer-in-chief of Louisiana, and laid out in 1721 [**2.6.5**]. Its rigid gridiron form and fortifications, patterned after Roman military camps of antiquity, would certainly have appealed to Thomas Jefferson's aesthetic sensibilities. In the center facing the river is the *Place d'Armes* or military parade ground (later renamed Jackson Square after President Andrew Jackson).

Located around this large open area are several important religious and government structures, including the St. Louis Cathedral (1788–94) and, flanking that symmetrically, the Presbytère or rectory (1788–1813) and the Cabildo or town hall (1795–99) [**2.6.6**]. The French engineer Gilbert Guillemard (1746–1808) designed all three buildings. The Presbytère and Cabildo were two-story masonry structures with open arcaded ground floors. They were united in design with the Cathedral (rebuilt in 1849) through the use of classical elements—Roman arches, pediments, and applied columns. Thus, the classical revival in architecture at the end of the eighteenth century that embodied both the democratic aspirations of the newly founded United States of America and the absolutist dictates of the Spanish monarchs was already in place in Louisiana when it came under American control.

Outside the city, different models were invoked. The plantation house at Parlange, near New Roads [**2.6.7**], was built between 1785 and 1795. Its owner, the Marquis Claude Vincent de Ternant, had come from France to set up an indigo plantation. The double gallery surrounding the house, the high ceilings, and numerous large windows and doors were architectural devices utilized on the Caribbean islands to cope with the heat, and easily adapted to Louisiana mansions, which occupied a similarly hot and humid Gulf Coast climate.

2.6.7 Parlange Plantation, near New Roads, Louisiana, *c.* 1785–95.

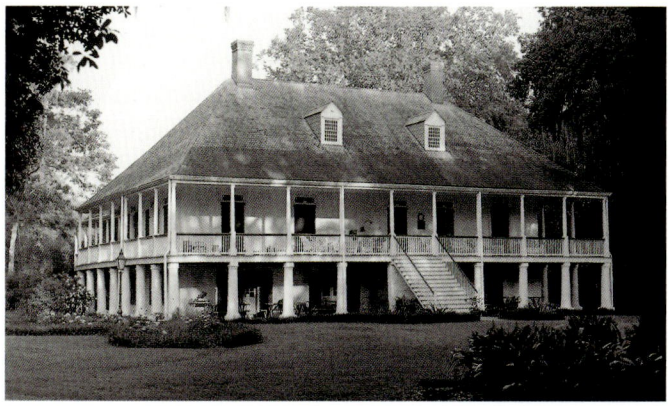

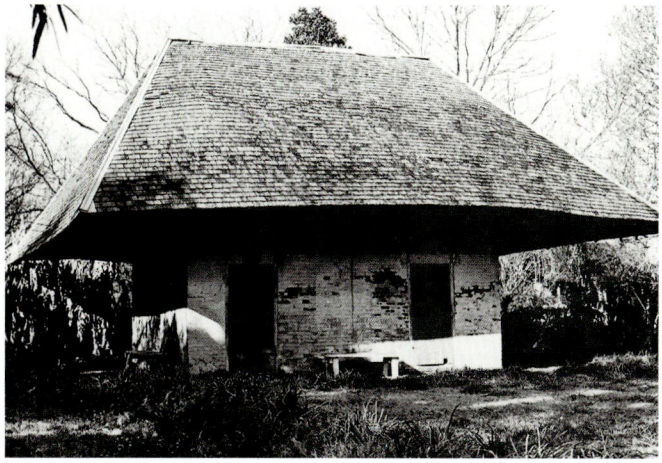

2.6.8 African House, Melrose Plantation, Natchitoches, Louisiana, late 18th century.

Plantation houses and city edifices alike relied on both skilled and unskilled African labor, both slave and free, for their construction. African slaves were brought into Louisiana, and into British and Spanish colonies in North America, not only to work the fields, but also to function as skilled craftsmen, such as ironsmiths, silversmiths, furniture-makers, and carpenters. African smiths were in particular demand for the production of grillwork and wrought-iron balconies. The art historian David Driskell notes that of the 3,085 skilled laborers registered in Louisiana in 1854, 2,668 were of African ancestry (470 were classified as black, 2,198 as mulatto). While these artisans most often worked from patterns or plans provided by European designers or architects, there is evidence, according to Driskell and others, of memories of African designs in some of their work. In the realm of architecture, this memory appears in several houses, for example the structure known as the African House near Natchitoches, Louisiana [**2.6.8**]. Built in the late eighteenth century by Marie Thérèse Quan Quan, a former slave who married the Frenchman Thomas Metoyer, it closely resembles certain rectangular houses with rammed-earth walls and sloping roofs common to the regions of contemporary Congo and Cameroon.

An Architecture of Discipline: Shaker Communities

Distinctive architectural styles also developed in certain religious communities in the late eighteenth century, such as those established by the Shakers. The United Society of Believers in Christ's Second Appearing originated in England in 1747; its members received their familiar name due to the trembling or agitated movement that many of them underwent during intense religious experiences (they were also referred to as the Shaking Quakers). They expanded under the effective leadership of Ann Lee. Persecuted because of her claim that she embodied

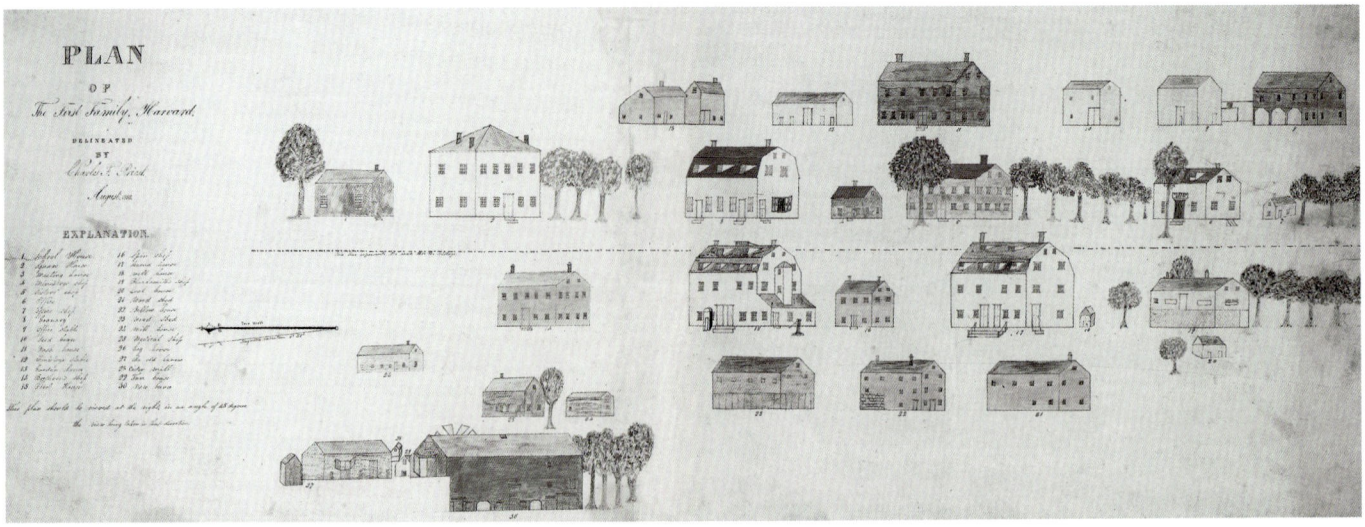

2.6.9 Charles F. Priest: *Plan of the First Family, Harvard*, 1833. The meeting house, with a dark gambrel roof, is just above the large "First House" in the center. Library of Congress, Washington, D.C.

the Christ spirit, she led a group of eight Shakers to America, arriving in New York in 1774 (she died in 1784). By 1826 nineteen Shaker communities were scattered throughout the states of Maine, New Hampshire, Massachusetts, Connecticut, New York, Ohio, Indiana, and Kentucky.

While many utopian religious communities were established in the US during the early years of its independence, none left as distinctive an aesthetic legacy as the Shakers. This legacy is particularly evident in their architecture. The architectural historian Julie Nicoletta writes that "the design, construction, building materials, and function of Shaker structures can be explored as components of a society that struggled to create a kingdom of heaven on earth." Shakers organized their lives around religious devotion and hard work. Ann Lee was said to have advised her followers: "Do all your work as though you had a thousand years to live, and as you would if you knew you must die tomorrow." Shakers practiced celibacy, lived communally, and believed in a deity that manifested both male and female natures. Men and women shared in the leadership of the community, and while the sexes were segregated and assigned particular tasks, neither was viewed as inherently weaker than, or inferior to, the other.

Joseph Meacham, one of Ann Lee's successors, set out clearer formal rules for worship, community property, and social behavior. He believed that spiritual salvation was attainable only through discipline in all aspects of life. He separated individual Shaker communities into "families" reflecting spiritual rather than blood lines. The First Family, known as the Church Family in the East and the Center Family in the Midwest, contained those who had achieved the highest spiritual development. They were the core of each village. Other families were named according to their geographical relationship to the First Family (for example, North Family) or according to the goods they produced (for instance, the Grist Mill Family).

Meacham also wrote down architectural rules. Nicoletta notes that the Shakers "came out of a long tradition of religious dissent and the Enlightenment belief that by controlling the environment, one could improve oneself and others." The architectural spaces within which they lived and worked were carefully planned. Meacham believed that architecture could help establish hierarchies among members and provide specialized spaces for both temporal and spiritual activities. Shaker communities were meant to be self-sufficient (although they were never entirely so) and, in addition to the meeting house, included dwelling houses, workshops, offices, and barns. Each family had its own set of buildings, but the meeting house was located on the property of the First Family.

A plan of the central structures of the Shaker settlement of Harvard, Massachusetts, drawn by Charles F. Priest in 1833, reveals the general outlines of the buildings and their relationship to each other [**2.6.9**]. Many are multi-storied, with the largest being the meeting house and the dwelling houses. While most of the buildings have gable roofs, the meeting house and two of the dwelling houses have gambrel roofs with dormer windows. Made primarily of wood, with stone foundations, the structures are marked by extremely plain facades, with window patterns providing the only decoration. Local roads often ran through the center of Shaker towns, allowing travelers to appreciate the well-kept grounds and simple but well-crafted buildings.

While Meacham set out general regulations, there was a certain amount of variation between communities and regions. Reliance on local materials meant that the majority of Eastern Shaker buildings were constructed of wood, while those in the

Midwest were more often made of brick or limestone. Eastern and Midwestern designs for particular types of buildings also often differed to a certain degree. The wood meeting house built by Moses Johnson in Canterbury, New Hampshire, in 1792 is distinguished by a gambrel roof and dormer windows, reflecting local Dutch traditions [**2.6.10**]. The brick meeting house built at Whitewater, Ohio, in 1827 has a gable roof, which allows for two full stories and an attic [**2.6.11**]. Both are simply and symmetrically designed, with two entrances: one for men and one for women. This symmetry and minimal ornamentation around doors and windows were also hallmarks of the Federal Style, a streamlined version of neoclassical architecture that flourished in both the East and Midwest in the late eighteenth and early nineteenth centuries. By the middle of the century, the exterior decoration had become somewhat more elaborate, with the addition of moldings, porches, shutters, and fanlights over the entrances.

The designs for meeting houses were also used for dwelling houses, which were usually larger and were the central structures in the daily lives of the Shakers, where they slept, ate, worked, and worshiped. Codes of behavior were enforced architecturally through separate entrances, sleeping and working areas for men and women, and limited space for each individual. Excess was to be avoided at all costs and in all areas of one's life—for example, conversation, belongings, dress, and food consumption. Work and religion could be included in this list as well, for a balanced life could not be achieved by a focus on one activity alone. As in architecture, however, the rules regarding personal behavior became less rigid as the century progressed and as membership in Shaker communities declined.

Shaker interiors are renowned for their efficient use of space, with built-in cupboards and drawers, and pegs along the walls for the hanging of everything from cloaks to chairs [**2.6.12**]. Regulations regarding the furnishing of sleeping rooms indicated that "bedsteads should be painted green" and that "blankets or comfortables [comforters] for out side [sic] spreads, should be blue and white, but not checked or striped." In addition, "no maps, Charts, and no pictures or paintings shall ever be hung up." The proscription against pictures extended to workshops and offices as well (and was also eroded by the last half of the nineteenth century). The exact type of furniture was not specified, but much of it was made by the Shakers themselves. It often incorporated ingenious features to make the work of its user easier, such as a yardstick marked off on the front edge of the top of a sewing table. This focus on labor-saving devices

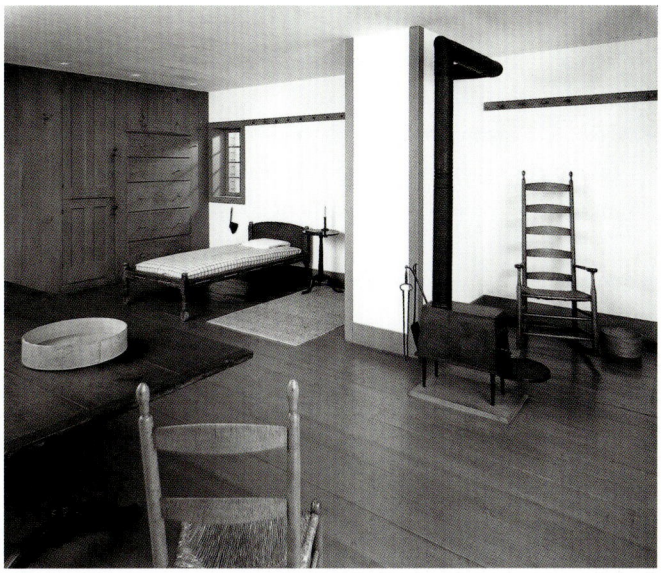

2.6.12 Shaker retiring room, 1830s.
Henry Francis du Pont Winterthur Museum, Winterthur, Delaware

2.6.10 (below) Moses Johnson: Meeting House, Canterbury, New Hampshire, 1792.

2.6.11 (right) Meeting House, Whitewater, Ohio, 1827.

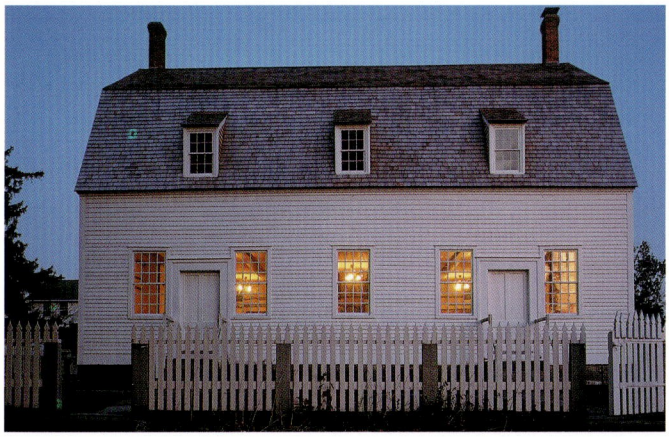

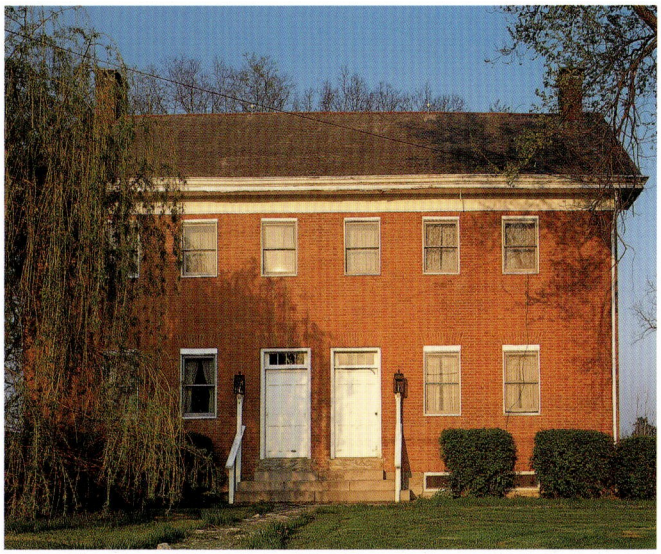

made Shaker interior design popular with mid-nineteenth-century writers on domestic reform.

Shakers also became well known for their sets of nesting boxes [**2.6.13**], which were made both for community use and for sale to customers on the outside. The American folk art historian Lynette Rhodes describes their construction:

> Oval boxes were made in the Shaker craft shops from thin, one-eighth-inch [3-millimeter] strips of maple that were steamed and wrapped around a mold; the top and bottom were made of pine. The tapered "fingers," fastened with copper rivets, were structural requisites, but also added to the visual appeal of this stark form. Although Shaker boxes were often stained red, yellow, blue, or green, the stylistic emphasis was always on the natural qualities of the wood and the shape of the box itself.

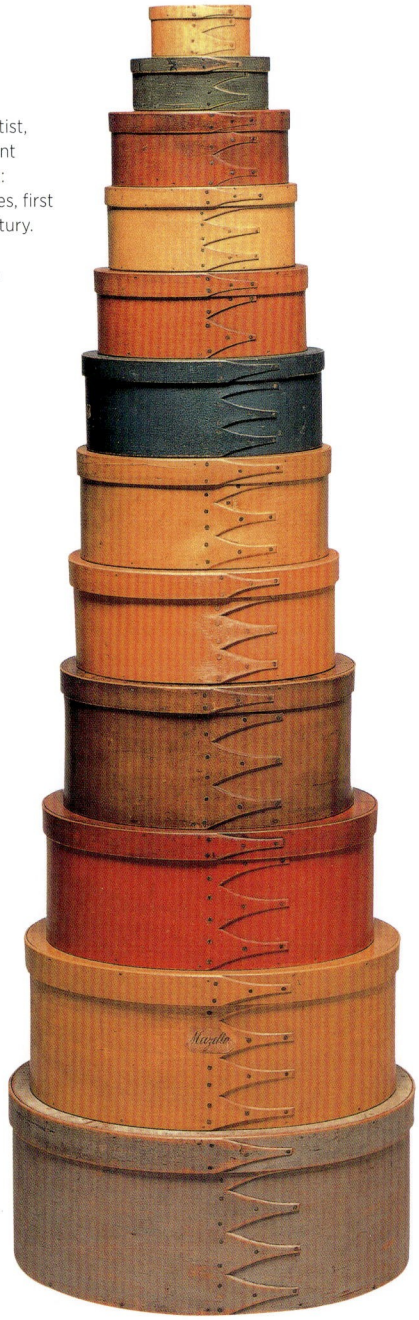

2.6.13 Unknown artist, probably from Mount Lebanon, New York: twelve nesting boxes, first half of the 19th century. Painted wood, various dimensions Private collection

Shakers stressed purity of design, which they saw as enhancing the object's "goodness" and its durability. This purity of design and high quality, evident in all Shaker products—boxes, furniture, architecture, seed packaging, and utensils—reflected a belief that creativity and work were forms of worship and a way of praising God.

An Architecture of Discipline: Prisons

Charles Dickens, in describing his visit to the Shaker community of Mount Lebanon, New York, in 1842 reveals one aspect of Shaker architectural and interior design that has received little attention. After failing to gain entrance to the meeting house, he wrote that "nothing was to be done but walk up and down, and look at it and the other buildings in the village (which were chiefly of wood, painted a dark red like English barns, and composed of many stories like English factories)..." Nicoletta notes that the resemblance between Shaker buildings and English factories was no coincidence. Both emphasized efficiency of function as a primary design priority. Nicoletta further points out that Shaker buildings also resembled early nineteenth-century prisons and asylums, institutions concerned not only with efficiency, but also with surveillance.

The American colonies had gained their independence at a time when prison reform was the focus of much debate in England. John Howard's *State of the Prisons*, published in 1777, exposed crowded, unsanitary living conditions, run-down buildings, and an almost total lack of supervision and control over inmates in England, Continental Europe, and Russia. This concern for the health and supervision of prisoners led to the development of a series of circular, polygonal, and radial schemes. The most famous is the Panopticon, conceived in 1790 by social philosopher and political economist Jeremy Bentham (1748–1832) [**2.6.14**]. Also well regarded as a criminal law reformer, Bentham's design for a circular prison resulted from a trip to Russia, where he witnessed the construction of a circular textile mill, which allowed for easy supervision of the workers. This surveillance, preferably unseen by those being watched, was a central element in Bentham's Panopticon. He believed that the key to disciplining inmates lay in convincing them that they were under constant observation, even if they were not. The architectural historian Norman Johnston describes the building as follows:

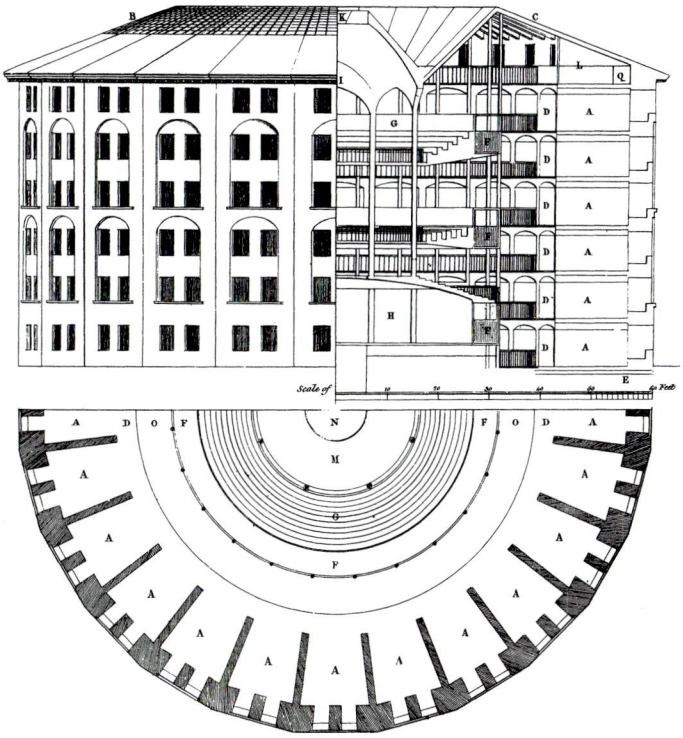

2.6.14 Jeremy Bentham: exterior, section, and half-plan of the Panopticon prison, 1791.
A cells; B–C annular skylight; D cell galleries; E entrance; F inspection galleries; H inspector's lodge; I dome of the chapel; K skylight of the chapel L store rooms with galleries; M floor of the chapel; N opening in the floor to light the inspector's lodge (open except at church times); O annular wall, for light, air, and separation

Bentham's scheme, remarkably advanced for the time, consisted of a very large circular building of cast iron and glass containing cells on several tiers around the periphery. The cells were to have barred fronts, and to be heated in winter and artificially cooled in summer by means of air forced over ice and directed through flues into the cells. Speaking tubes would connect each cell with the keeper's tower in the center. By these means the keeper in his louvered tower could carry out continuous, and unseen, surveillance both visual and auditory over the inmates.

The prisoners were not the only ones under surveillance. The keeper would be watched by the superintendents, who would themselves be watched by the public on unexpected visits. Thus, everyone would be disciplined through an atmosphere of constant watchfulness (Bentham also saw his plan as suitable for factories, asylums, hospitals, and schools.)

While Bentham's Panopticon was never built, it inspired several circular or semicircular buildings in other countries, including the Virginia Penitentiary in Richmond, built from 1797 to 1800 [**2.6.15**]. The penitentiary's plan was laid out by Thomas Jefferson and Benjamin Latrobe. The four-story horseshoe-shaped prison, with cells opening onto covered arcades on the first three levels, was originally closed by a wall joining the two ends of the horseshoe, with a warden's house in the center. The arcades reaffirm Jefferson's commitment to Roman architectural precedents (the Roman Colosseum immediately comes to mind) that appeared earlier in his Virginia State Capitol, also in the city of Richmond [**2.6.1**; p. 110].

The Virginia Penitentiary was one of several new prisons built in the US in the early nineteenth century, a time of rapid population growth and changes in ideas about how to treat those who were unwilling or unable to follow the new laws of the land. Prior to the end of the eighteenth century, few structures existed for the permanent imprisonment of either criminals or the insane. The latter were usually cared for by families or neighbors while the former were fined, whipped, placed in the stocks, banished, or executed. Such punishment was meted out

2.6.15 Thomas Jefferson and Benjamin Latrobe: Virginia Penitentiary, Richmond, 1797–1800, after the removal of the wall linking the ends of the horseshoe.

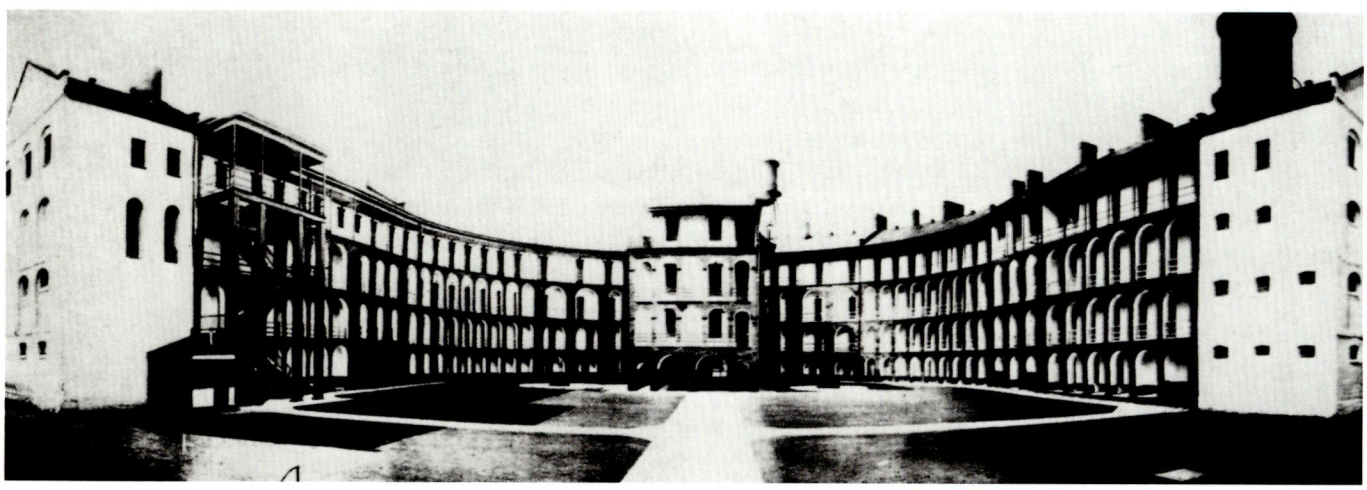

by local authorities. Jails were holding tanks for individuals awaiting trial. Imprisonment itself was not seen as a punishment or attempt at reform. Prisoners were placed together, did not have to wear uniforms, and were not supervised.

In America as in Britain, Quaker reformers played a leading role in instituting changes in the treatment of both criminals and the insane in the late eighteenth century. In 1786 the Pennsylvania state legislature abolished punishment by death, mutilation, or the whip. The following year a number of leading men of the city, including Roberts Vaux, a Quaker penal reformer, established the Philadelphia Society for Alleviating the Miseries of Public Prisons. The core belief of this new society was that criminals could be reformed through imprisonment, when they would be able to reflect on their sins. Their conditions of imprisonment were to be sanitary as well as supervised. Uniforms would be worn to maintain conformity and strict schedules would be followed to ensure discipline and control.

In the ensuing years one of the major debates in the area of prison reform centered around whether prisoners should be allowed to associate with one another or spend most, if not all, of their time in solitary confinement. The congregate system, established at the state prison at Auburn, New York, in 1816, was based in part on the earlier conception of prisons as domestic structures or houses. It allowed prisoners to eat and work together in silence, but isolated them at night. Thus, much space was devoted to communal eating, exercise, and work areas. Prison labor was seen as integral to the reform process and to the financial stability of the prison. Less space was devoted to a prisoner's individual cell. The Auburn cells were just over 7 feet long and almost 4 feet wide (about 2 × 1.2 meters), with 7-foot- (2.1-meter-) high ceilings. They were arranged back to back on five tiers in the center of a long cell building [**2.6.16**]. The African American Austin Reed left a written account of the effect of his imprisonment at Auburn in the 1840s and 1850s: "The high and noble mind which God had given to me [was] destroyed by hard usage and a heavy club."

An alternate system is represented by the Eastern State Penitentiary in Philadelphia, designed by John Haviland (1792–1852) and completed in 1829 [**2.6.17**]. Here prisoners were kept in solitary confinement around the clock. While Haviland had Bentham's Panopticon in mind, there are significant differences. The most important is that constant supervision of all cells in the single-story wings was not possible from the central guard tower. Similar to the Panopticon, however, each cell in Haviland's building was supplied with running water and a toilet to guarantee complete isolation. The cells were 8 × 12 feet (2.4 × 3.7 meters) with 16-foot- (4.9-meter-) high ceilings and an exterior yard measuring 8 × 20 feet (2.4 × 6 meters). The cell was used not only for eating and sleeping, but also for working and for spiritual contemplation (each contained a Bible). Haviland's fortress architecture, with its thick walls and crenellated Gothic towers, reaffirmed the function of the complex as a place of incarceration.

While many praised the Eastern State Penitentiary as an example of effective prison reform—discipline and supervision combined with healthful surroundings—others found the practice of continuous solitary confinement inhuman. Dickens described it in 1842 as "hopeless,...cruel and wrong" and added: "I believe that very few men are capable of estimating the immense amount of torture and agony which this dreadful punishment, prolonged for years, inflicts upon the sufferers." Auburn State Prison's congregate plan ultimately proved more popular—not, however, for humane reasons, but for financial ones. Each cell in the Eastern State Penitentiary cost ten times as much to construct as a cell in Auburn. The prison shops in the Auburn system were also more productive than the isolated cell labor of Eastern State. Isolation prevented inmates from engaging in housekeeping duties in the prison at large, which had to be done by an external labor force. Finally, many saw the relative idleness of prisoners in solitary confinement as going against the Protestant ethic of hard work that was so firmly in place by the early nineteenth century and that was seen as a central component of democratic communities.

In 1825, in order to accommodate New York's growing population of convicted criminals, a second prison was built on the Auburn plan at a nearby site on the Hudson River, the infamous Sing Sing. Just a year earlier, the Shakers at Mount Lebanon, a hundred miles (160 kilometers) up the river from Sing Sing,

2.6.16 Auburn State Prison, New York, 1816–35, interior showing cells.

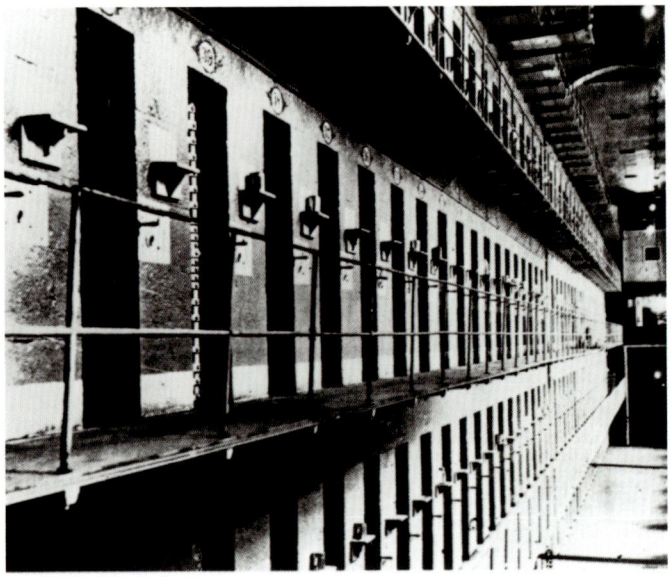

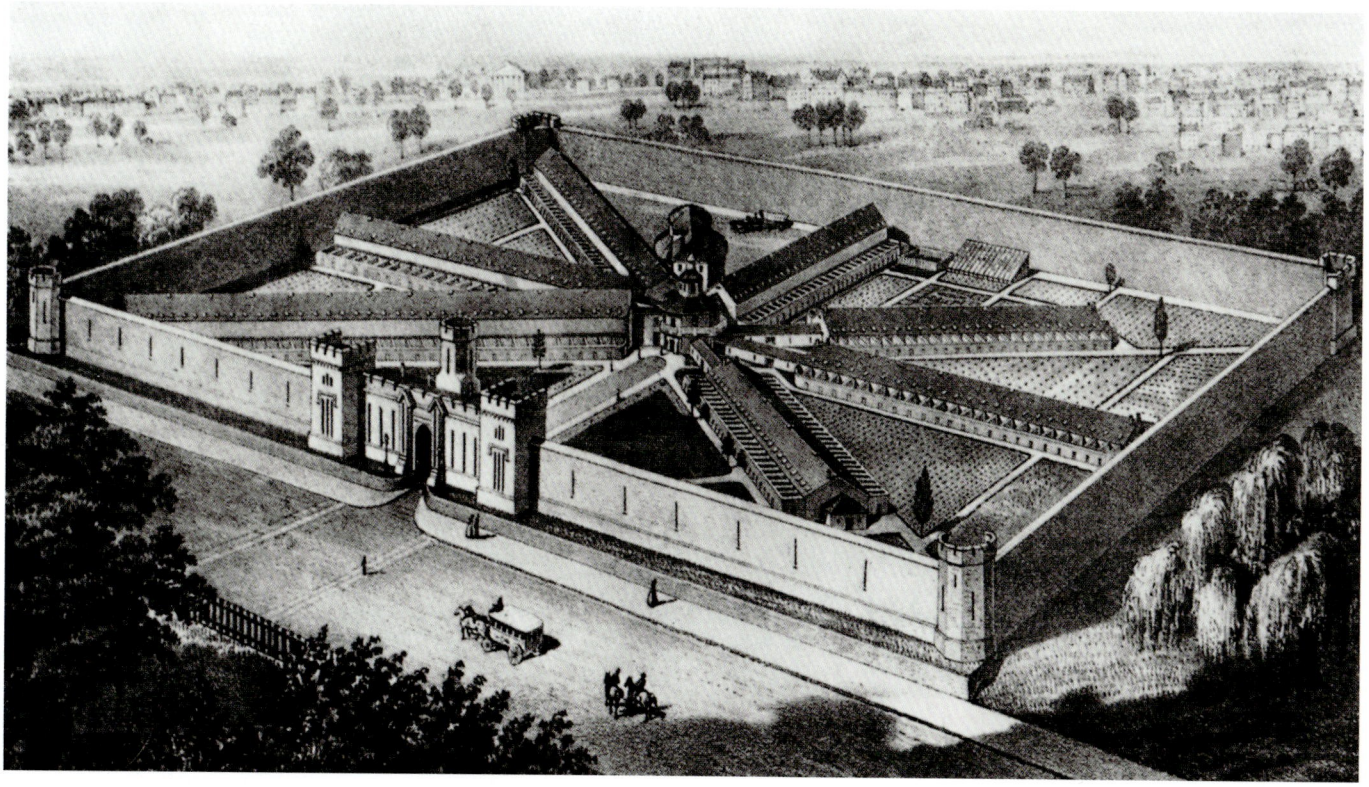

2.6.17 John Haviland: Eastern State Penitentiary, Philadelphia, Pennsylvania, completed in 1829.
From an early 19th-century lithograph

had finished a new meeting house to accommodate their own growing population. One cannot state whether Shakers influenced the prison system or vice-versa. Both certainly did know about each other, and both shared common concerns. Nicoletta writes:

> Shaker communities incorporated the values of religion, work, and silence introduced into prisons by the Quakers to induce moral improvement. The Shakers ate and worked in silence and according to strict schedules. They sought to enforce conformity through dress, behavior, and environment which stripped members of their individual identity.

The architectural forms adopted by the Shakers were also echoed in many state prisons, with their rows of endlessly repetitive windows and strict classification of interior space. Both prison reformers and Shakers, in their search for order, created an architecture of control that occupied a prominent place in the built environment.

In 2015 only one Shaker community remained, Sabbathday Lake, Maine, with four residents—two men and two women. Many Shaker buildings from other communities have been preserved, however, testaments to the fact that while the Shakers failed to achieve a permanent "kingdom of heaven" on American soil, they did create a striking and distinctive aesthetic that speaks to the power of their belief in an ordered and integrated world. The prison population, on the other hand, continued to expand, along with prison architecture. In 2015 the US had the largest prison population in the world, with more than 2 million incarcerated men and women, almost 1 percent of the nation's people.

Nationhood and Native Americans: The Decoration of the Capitol Building

Just as religious and moral commitments could be encoded in the design of a building, so too could a renewed sense of nationalism. Such was the case with the reconstruction and redecorating of the Capitol after the end of the War of 1812 and the departure of the British (see p. 113). The resurgence of nationalism and patriotism that accompanied this rebuilding was particularly fortunate for the artist John Trumbull, for it provided him with an opportunity to revive his earlier plan for a series of paintings documenting the Revolutionary War (see pp. 93–97). After the dismal reception of the first of the series in the early 1790s Trumbull had briefly turned to a career as a diplomat. In 1794 he accompanied Chief Justice John Jay to London as his secretary on the Jay Treaty Commission, intended to settle commercial and border disputes between Britain and the US.

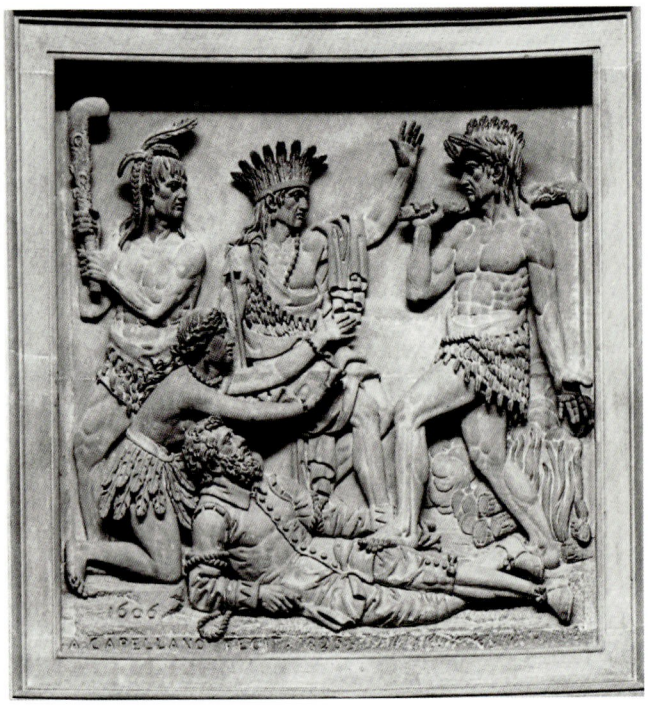

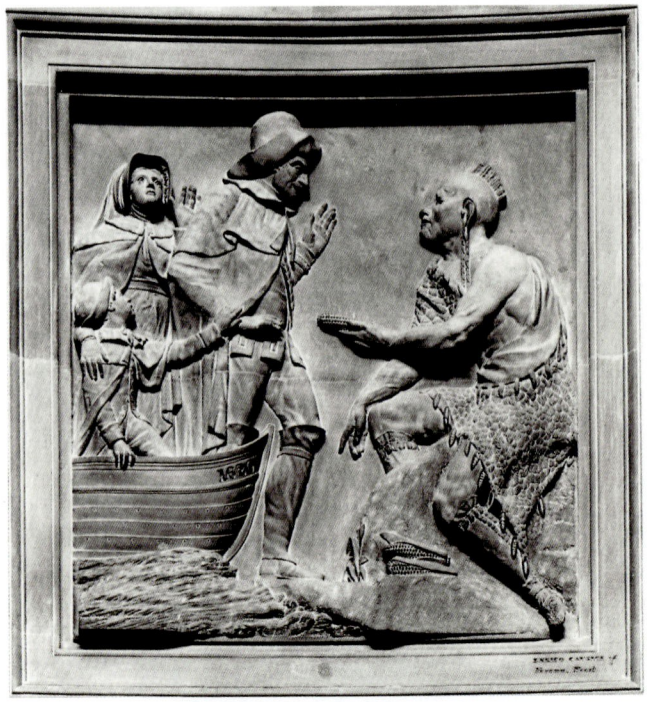

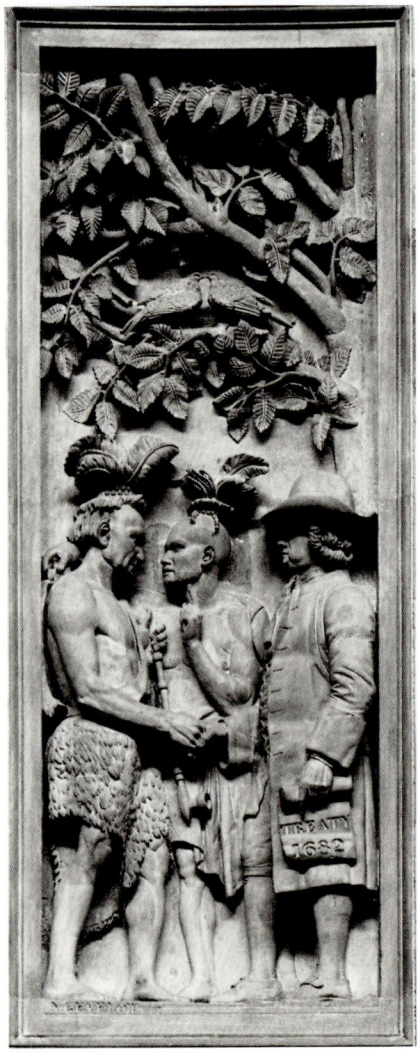

2.6.18 Antonio Capellano: *The Preservation of Captain Smith by Pocahontas*, 1825.
Sandstone
United States Capitol Rotunda, Washington, D.C., above the west door

2.6.19 Enrico Causici: *The Landing of the Pilgrims*, 1825.
Sandstone
United States Capitol Rotunda, Washington, D.C., above the east door

2.6.20 Nicholas Gevelot: *William Penn's Treaty with the Indians*, 1827.
Sandstone
United States Capitol Rotunda, Washington, D.C., above the north door

In 1800 Trumbull settled in New York City and began seeking portrait and history painting commissions, the new Capitol being the most likely location for the latter. He was in London at the beginning of the War of 1812 and was unable to return to the US until 1815, after hostilities had ceased.

In 1817 Trumbull was commissioned by Congress to execute for the rebuilt Capitol four paintings, each measuring 12 × 8 feet (3.7 × 2.4 meters), on the American Revolution. He based two of these—*The Surrender of Lord Cornwallis at Yorktown, 19 October 1781* (1787–1820) and *Declaration of Independence, 4 July 1776* (1787–1819)—on his earlier series, while the other two were new compositions—*The Surrender of General Burgoyne at Saratoga, 16 October 1777* (1822) and *The Resignation of General Washington, 23 December 1783* (1822–24). In these military scenes the high drama of *The Death of General Warren* and *The Death of General Montgomery* [**2.5.6**, p. 94; **2.5.7**, p. 96] is gone, replaced by a much more static representation of reconciliation between the leaders of the opposing forces, which suggested the future establishment of orderly economic, if not political, relations between Britain and its former colonies.

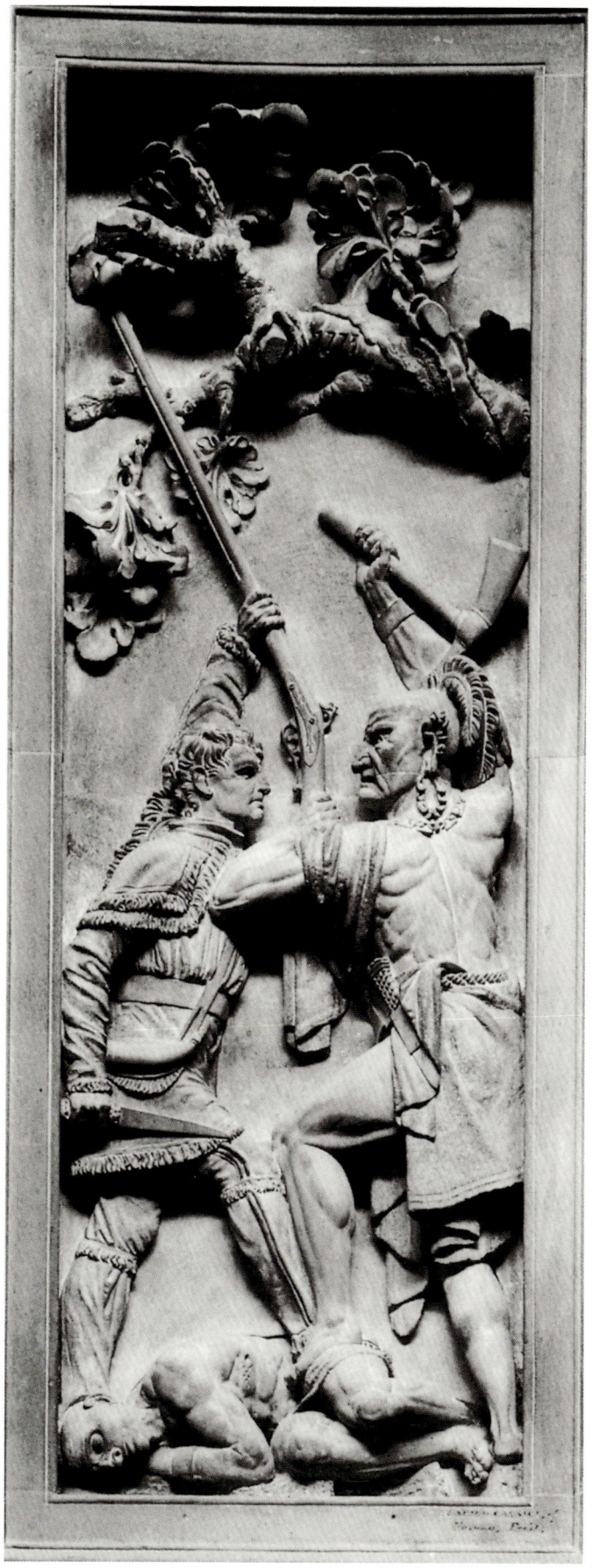

2.6.21 Enrico Causici: *The Conflict of Daniel Boone and the Indians*, 1826–27. Sandstone
United States Capitol Rotunda, Washington, D.C., above the south door

The art historian Vivian Green Fryd notes that nationhood was defined within the Capitol through a series of discoveries and battles in which indigenous peoples, now a part of the United States of America, often played a central role and which articulated "a remarkably coherent program of the early course of North American empire." Four relief panels appeared above the doorways of the Rotunda: *The Preservation of Captain Smith by Pocahontas* (1825) by Antonio Capellano (active 1815–?) [**2.6.18**]; *The Landing of the Pilgrims* (1825) [**2.6.19**] and *The Conflict of Daniel Boone and the Indians* (1826–27) [**2.6.21**] by Enrico Causici (active 1822–32); and *William Penn's Treaty with the Indians* (1827) by Nicholas Gevelot (1791–?) [**2.6.20**].

These four reliefs encapsulate a vision of European–Native American relations that had already assumed mythicohistorical proportions in the early nineteenth century through novels, poems, biographies, paintings, and memoirs. Pocahontas saves John Smith, foreshadowing her willing assimilation into English culture and conversion to Christianity. The Pilgrims accept the offerings of the Native American, whose crouching position indicates recognition of the superiority of the new arrivals. William Penn negotiates with the Delaware leader as an equal to ensure the peaceful acquisition of land. Daniel Boone, in facilitating colonial expansion westward, brings out the "true" savage nature of Native Americans, calling into question the civility represented in the other three reliefs. Robert Mills praised the Boone relief in a guidebook to the Capitol (1834) for effectively conveying "the ferocity and recklessness of the savage," and for having "more of the Indian character and costume represented in these figures than in any of the other sculpted pictures." The Native American as savage thus sat more easily with some visitors to the Capitol than the Native American as noble servant or political equal. Yet in May 1842 *Niles' Weekly Register* recorded the words of Henry Wise, a Whig representative from Virginia, who voiced a particularly astute summary of how Native Americans would undoubtedly read the messages contained in all four reliefs: "We give you corn, you cheat us of our lands: we save your life, you take ours."

These representations would be variously reinforced and challenged throughout the nineteenth century as territorial expansion and the continued struggle to define a national identity forced Native American and European American alike to rethink their relationships with one another. These relationships were caught up in what the historian Richard Slotkin has described as one of the oldest and most enduring national myths in the US, the myth of the frontier. Since colonial times,

European Americans had defined themselves as peoples engaged in a series of struggles to push the western frontier ever further back, a move justified with the rhetoric of pioneering progress, world mission, and eternal battle against the forces of darkness and subversion.

From Indian Queen to Greek Goddess

During the seventeenth and eighteenth centuries indigenous peoples were often portrayed as the very embodiment of the Americas. This geographic personification appeared most often in the guise of the classically rendered, semi-naked "Indian Queen." While this Indian Queen had earlier encompassed the whole of the New World—North, Central, and South America—after the successful American Revolution she was claimed as a symbol of the US alone. For example, she appears in a bronze medal of 1790 designed by the French artist Augustin Dupré (1748–1833) [**2.6.22**] and commissioned by President Washington. It was referred to at the time as the Diplomatic Medal and was awarded to two individuals, the Marquis de La Luzerne and the Count de Moustier. The obverse of the medal contains the figure of Mercury, the winged messenger representing Europe (the Old World), greeting the female personification of the US, wearing a feathered headdress and skirt (the New World). She is seated beside packaged objects, toward which she gestures with her right hand; in her left hand she holds a horn filled with fruits, which she extends toward Mercury. Thus, in exchange for manufactured goods from Europe, the US would provide food and raw materials. In order to connect the packages more clearly with Europe, an anchor is placed in the foreground, which alludes to the ship behind Mercury. And finally, in addition to the commemorative date on the lower portion of the medal—July 4, 1776—which marks this female figure as representing the US rather than the entire New World, the words "To Peace and Commerce" arch over the scene. On the reverse of the medal is the Great Seal of the United States.

2.6.22 Augustin Dupré: Diplomatic Medal, 1790.
Bronze, d. 2⅝ in. (6.7 cm.)
Division of Numismatics, Smithsonian Institution, Washington D.C.

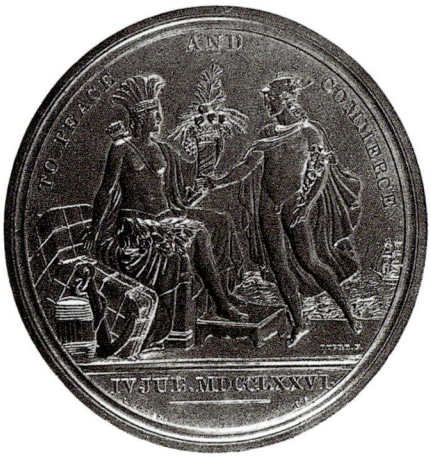

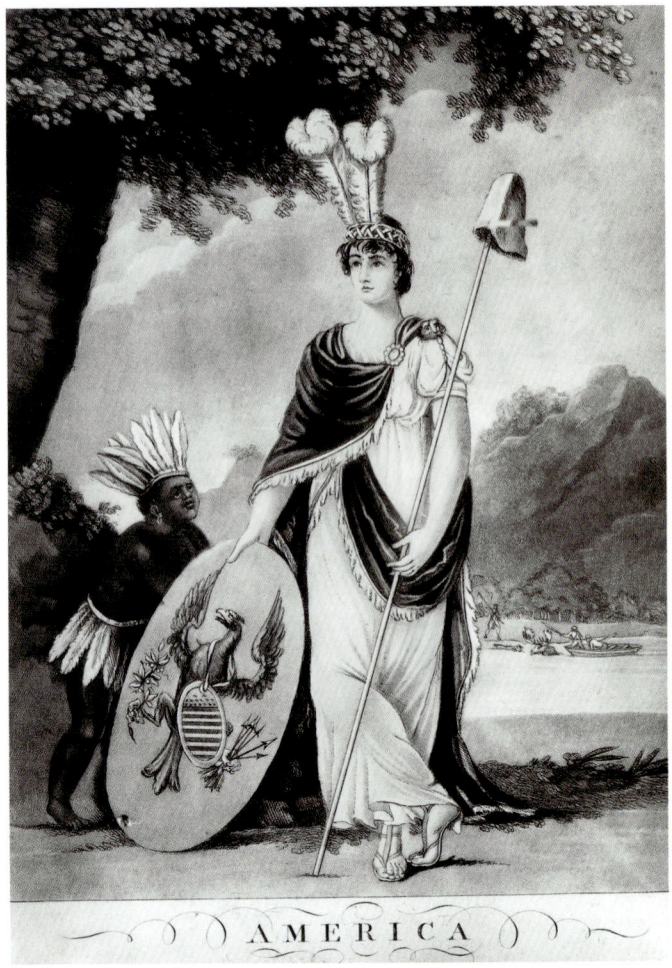

2.6.23 Unknown artist: *America, from The Four Continents*, London, 1804.
Engraving, 13⅝ x 9⅞ in. (34.6 x 24.6 cm.)
The Henry Francis du Pont Winterthur Museum, Winterthur, Delaware

The Indian Queen as a national symbol was soon joined by another female figure who was more decidedly European than Native American. Such a figure can be found in an anonymous engraving of 1804 entitled *America* [**2.6.23**]. The bared breasts and feathered skirt of the figure on the Diplomatic Medal are replaced by a simple gown reminiscent of the clothing worn by women in ancient Greece. Yet this figure also has a "contemporary" look to her. The Greek world was a major source in the early nineteenth century not only for sculptors, painters, and architects, but also for dress designers. "America" wears an elaborate cloak elegantly draped across her shoulders, and against her left arm rest a liberty pole and cap. The latter symbolize emancipation, a reference to both the American Revolution, which France entered on the side of the Continental Army, and the French Revolution of 1789.

The title of the engraving—*America*—might suggest that the figure represents the New World as a whole. Yet the liberty cap and the shield, on which is emblazoned an eagle festooned with a medallion containing the stars and stripes of the US flag, identify her as a representation of the United States of America. Her association with indigenous peoples is present in two ways. The ostrich feathers attached to her headband function, in the words of the art historian Barbara Groseclose, as "souvenirs of her Indian past." This past is more directly indicated by the dark-skinned, childlike figure of indeterminate gender beside her, who wears the feathered headdress and skirt of the woman in the *Diplomatic Medal*.

Groseclose suggests this shift from a strong central character bearing clear Native American referents to an ancillary child-like indigenous figure parallels the enforced dependency of indigenous peoples on the federal government during the nineteenth century. Indigenous physical features or clothing now refer to "condition, not geography—race instead of place." This dependency is borne out in the engraving by the placement of the child behind the shield and by his/her adoring gaze in the direction of America, a position and gaze that replicate those of the young African slave in Justus Engelhardt Kühn's portrait of Henry Darnall III [**1.4.25**; p. 78]. Indeed, the child can be seen as a mix of African American and Native American, for his/her skin is darker than many earlier and contemporary representations of indigenous peoples. The dependency of African Americans as slaves was already well established. They would continue to be subjected to the rhetoric of infantilization even after the Civil War of the 1860s brought an end to slavery.

The subservience of the indigenous/black figure in *America* is further evident if we compare the compositions of the Diplomatic Medal and the engraving. In the former the relationship between the US and Europe is presented as an exchange of gifts between equals. The enthroned Indian Queen is both Old World (classicized features) and New World (feathered skirt and headdress). She and Mercury are depicted within a horizontal composition as mutually interdependent. Both are shown with heads in profile and frontal torsos, approximately the same size and on the same level, and "dignified" by classical referents. The New World is gendered female and is associated with the land or nature; the Old World is male and will transform the products of nature offered to it into the products of culture, manufactured goods.

The relationship articulated in the engraving between European Americans and Native Americans/African Americans —domestic relations as opposed to foreign relations—is one of subservience, not equality. The composition itself is hierarchical. The child is located at the base of a triangle the apex of which is the head of America. Half the size of the statuesque figure, he/she leans inward and gazes up toward America, while the latter is erect and gazes off into the distance. The child is also more closely associated with the land in terms of skin color and costume, and is the compositional counterpart of the moose-hunting scene to the right (the place occupied by the ship in the medal—again, domestic production versus foreign trade). The message is that Native Americans/African Americans are children, to be protected by Mother America and by the shield of European American governance.

Narratives of Captivity

In 1804, the same year the engraving *America* appeared, John Vanderlyn (1775–1852) completed *The Murder of Jane McCrea* [**2.6.24**], a painting that drew on recent, as well as ancient, history in order to create a symbolic narrative of nationhood. Like *America*, it locates Native Americans as actors along an ever-changing frontier. In Vanderlyn's painting the classicizing elements appear not in references to Liberty figures, Greek architecture, or clothing, but in the physiques and poses of the two Mohawk warriors, who are about to scalp the young colonist

2.6.24 John Vanderlyn: *The Murder of Jane McCrea*, 1803–4. Oil on canvas, 32 x 26½ in. (81.3 x 67.3 cm.) Wadsworth Atheneum Museum of Art, Hartford, Connecticut

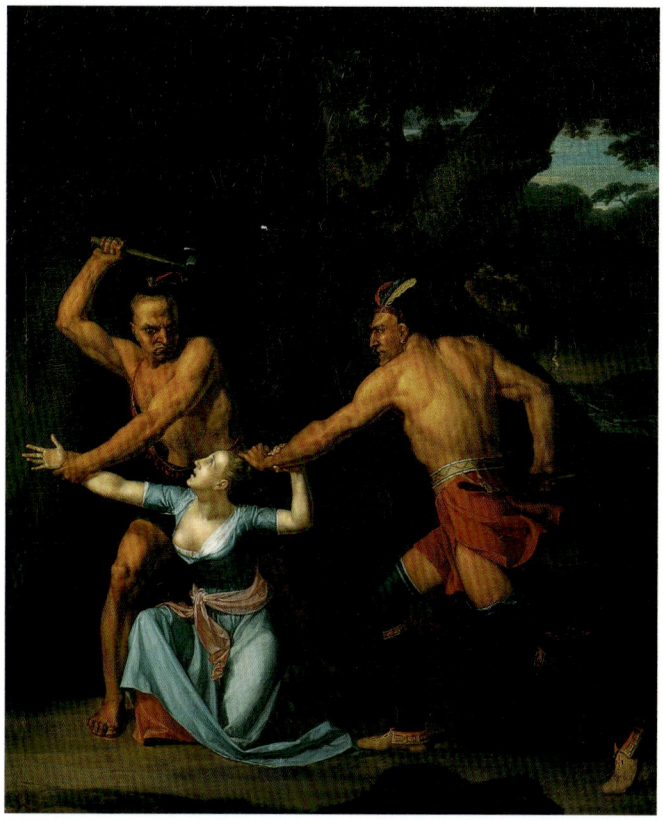

Jane McCrea. Such heavily muscled and dramatically posed men were particularly prevalent in sculpture created during the Hellenistic period in Greece (*c.* 323–30 BCE), and could also be found in abundance on later Roman sarcophagi (Causici drew on such prototypes for his *Conflict of Daniel Boone and the Indians* [**2.6.21**; p. 123]). They also appeared in many neoclassical history paintings produced in France in the late eighteenth and nineteenth centuries.

Vanderlyn's painting of Jane McCrea emerged out of a commission from Joel Barlow, President Jefferson's envoy to France, who had commemorated the event in his anti-British epic poem, *The Columbiad*. Barlow wanted Vanderlyn to provide illustrations for the poem, but the artist decided to create, instead, a large, dramatic history painting for submission to the Paris Salon of 1804 (Vanderlyn was in Paris at the time), leaving Barlow to find someone else to complete the illustrations. The painting depicts an incident that allegedly occurred in 1777, during the American Revolution. Jane McCrea, the orphaned daughter of a Presbyterian minister who was living with her brother in upper New York State, fell in love with a Loyalist. He left to join the British forces in Canada, but arranged for her to join him so they could marry. Against the wishes of her pro-Revolutionary brother, she left his home, but never arrived at her destination. On the way she was captured, killed, and scalped by Mohawks hired by the British to assist them in the war (the British offered bounties on the scalps of revolutionaries). Her death galvanized the residents of the area, who then defeated the British at the Battle of Saratoga, which marked a turning point in the war for the rebels.

Vanderlyn's painting was a success with the French art world and included in the Paris Salon of 1804. Despite this success, Barlow refused to purchase the work once the exhibition was over. It was subsequently bought by the American Academy of Fine Arts in New York. The art historian William H. Truettner suggests that the problem for Barlow may have been the intensity of the Indian-hating message of the painting. French audiences were used to seeing horrific scenes of conflict and death in history paintings (one of the reasons Vanderlyn chose such a scene) and would have appreciated the anti-British sentiment in Vanderlyn's work. Yet most paintings in the US depicting white–Native American relations up until this time, and for several decades after, were less violent (see **1.4.32**; p. 85), although written descriptions like Barlow's poem often did not mince words or details about Native American atrocities committed against white Americans. The purchase of such a violent scene might also have been particularly problematic for a US envoy at this time. In 1804 President Jefferson was courting various Native American leaders in his attempt to negotiate the removal of indigenous communities in the eastern regions of the nation west to the Ohio Country. He was also trying to establish cordial relations with the indigenous peoples of the recently purchased Louisiana Territory.

The historian June Namias points to another theme present in Vanderlyn's painting. She notes how McCrea, "a woman who had run off with a Tory soldier," was transformed not only into a martyred revolutionary heroine, but also a symbol of colonial women and of the nation at large. One common justification for killing indigenous people, in particular men, was the threat they posed to colonial women and, thus, to the nation's future.

The use of women in this way—as symbols of colonial vulnerability—is particularly evident in narratives documenting the experiences of European captives within indigenous communities, which appeared in written form at the end of the seventeenth century, and in engravings and paintings in the late eighteenth century. As the anthropologist Pauline Turner Strong has noted, in the captivity narratives promulgated by colonial clergymen (who often edited or wrote the accounts), the female captive "represents the vulnerability of the English colonies in the New World, where they are preyed upon by the brutish and diabolical forces of the wilderness which destroy domestic and civil order and threaten to seduce or devour them."

Notably absent from tales of captivity were accounts of the experiences of indigenous peoples, who formed the largest body of captives on the British colonial frontier and who were often treated as cruelly by the British as were those white captives depicted in tales authored by Europeans. The most famous indigenous captive, Pocahontas, was seldom represented as such. Instead, she appeared most often in texts and pictures from colonial times onward as a willing convert to Christianity and to the ways of the British [**1.4.9**; p. 68]. Such is the tenor of the painting *The Baptism of Pocahontas* of 1837–40 by John Gadsby Chapman (1808–89) in the Capitol Rotunda.

Vanderlyn's painting graphically illustrates the opposition described by Strong, and reiterated throughout the nineteenth century, between the indigenous male as diabolical force and the European female as vulnerable captive. Yet it also reveals the complex play between attraction and repulsion that marked so many paintings and that was present in some of the written captivity narratives as well. In the tales of men captured by "Indians" that appeared in the early nineteenth century (for example, that of Daniel Boone), the experience was presented as having toughened them, made them more manly. The men return to their own people, who appreciate the transformation. Yet not everyone returned. In the Reverend John Williams's earlier account of his own captivity and that of his family in 1704, he records that when they were freed, he was unable to "reclaim" his daughter Eunice, who was seven years old when they were seized. She eventually married a Mohawk, who had been converted to Catholicism by the French Jesuits, and remained in the community of Caughnawaga. Thus, in the eyes of her father, she was doubly lost—to Catholicism and to a "savage Indian."

Eunice's story was soon buried, however, among the more numerous accounts of female deliverance from diabolical indigenous forces through divine intervention or, as in Vanderlyn's painting, through death at the hands of these same forces. Vanderlyn's warriors are fearful savages threatening to "seduce or devour" Jane McCrea. The attraction of the Native American man is present in the painting's sexual charge, in the powerful physiques of the men and the almost fully bared breasts of the supplicant Jane McCrea. These elements, in conjunction with the impending blow from the tomahawk, worked simultaneously to enrage and arouse (in a sexual sense) and strike fear into the hearts of European American viewers, both male and female, who attended Vanderlyn's pay-as-you-enter exhibition of this painting and others in New York, Baltimore, New Orleans, and other cities across the nation. While federal officials may have found the painting's subject matter problematic, a broader audience would have been drawn to the high drama and sexual tension.

From the beginning of colonization, Europeans viewed indigenous peoples with an ambivalent attitude of acceptance and rejection, embodied in part by the noble/savage dichotomy. This ambivalence had an erotic element, and captivity narratives, according to Namias, "offer a body of work which depicts Indian–white relations on the sexual frontier as exciting, dangerous, potentially disastrous, sometimes fun, occasionally romantic." In Vanderlyn's painting, this ambivalence is fully conveyed. As if to emphasize the power of the indigenous men, European manhood is represented by the tiny, ineffectual figure in the distant right background, possibly McCrea's fiancé running vainly toward his loved one. The painting was also a warning to women who harbored what many men at the time viewed as a misplaced sense of independence. Had McCrea been an obedient sister, she would have heeded the advice of her brother and stayed home, thus avoiding a violent death.

Ten years after *The Murder of Jane McCrea*, Vanderlyn completed another painting in which a wayward daughter plays a central role. *Ariadne Asleep on the Island of Naxos* (1809–14) [**2.6.25**] depicts the daughter of Minos, the King of Crete, who betrays her father by rescuing the Greek sailor Theseus from the Minotaur. She then flees Crete with Theseus, who subsequently seduces and abandons her on the island of Naxos. While the story is from Greek mythology rather than recent American history, it contains, according to the art historian David M. Lubin, several possible references to contemporary political concerns, one of which involves relations between Native Americans and Europeans.

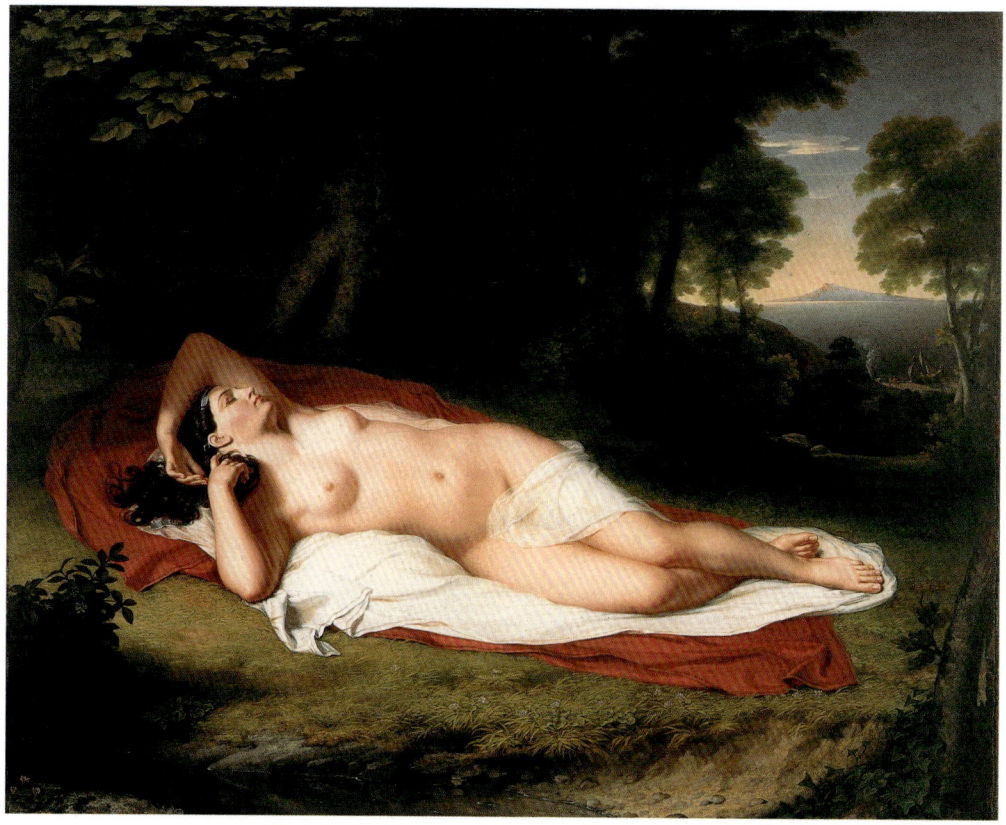

2.6.25 John Vanderlyn: *Ariadne Asleep on the Island of Naxos*, 1809–14. Oil on canvas, 68½ x 87 in. (174 x 221 cm.) Pennsylvania Academy of the Fine Arts, Philadelphia

The painting met with little critical success when it was first exhibited in the US, in large part because of its nudity. While reclining white female nudes appeared with regularity in exhibitions in Paris in the nineteenth century (Vanderlyn was still in Paris when he painted his Ariadne), they were rare in the US A conservative, if not Puritanical, American art-viewing public often saw them as inappropriate, even immoral. Yet female nudes had appeared with regularity in print media in the Americas since the sixteenth century. While these nudes were most often European in facial features and body types, they were meant to represent indigenous women, who symbolized the Americas in general, if not participants in specific historical events [**1.0.1**; p. 17]. Like the New World, they were there for the taking, embodiments of the natural resources that would be exploited for European material gain. The indigenous woman most closely associated with the Ariadne story was Pocahontas, who was also seduced and abandoned by a man she had recently saved, John Smith. In the account he wrote in 1624 of his encounter with Powhatan women, Pocahontas among them, Smith focuses on their nakedness and sexual availability.

While Vanderlyn's Ariadne has most often been read as white, Lubin argues that there are certain elements within the painting that suggest an indigenous heritage, in particular her headband and armband and her location in a landscape with plant life similar to that found in regions of the British colonies in the Americas. There is also a slightly red tinge to her skin, produced perhaps by the deep red cloth that surrounds her body or perhaps by her recent sexual encounter with Theseus, who is shown as a tiny figure in the background about to board his ship and sail away. The white cloth immediately beneath her also serves to heighten this red glow, which is echoed in reddish-brown areas in the grass slightly in front of Ariadne's body.

The seduction and abandonment of Ariadne and Pocahontas enabled the establishment of new political regimes—a revived Athens by Theseus and a successful British colony by Smith. While Smith's behavior might seem morally problematic as a founding narrative, John Rolfe provides the solution by marrying Pocahontas and facilitating her conversion to Christianity. She is thus saved and transformed from a "fallen woman" and a "savage" to a Christian wife and a model for appropriate indigenous behavior. Those who refused to follow her footsteps and recognize the superiority of the political, economic, and cultural ideals of a European settler society could thus be removed westward as the European population expanded and the desire for Native American territory grew.

Portraits and Treaties

While few Native Americans would have seen Vanderlyn's paintings of Jane McCrea or Ariadne, several did contemplate the representations of Native Americans created during the early nineteenth century in the nation's capital, in particular those images residing within the Capitol's Rotunda (see p. 121–23). Throughout the first decades of the nineteenth century, Native American delegates traveled to Washington to negotiate and finalize treaties. According to a guidebook to the Capitol written by William Force in 1848, a group of Wisconsin Winnebagos visited the building in 1832 after signing a treaty exchanging their land for land in Iowa. They responded to Causici's *Conflict of Daniel Boone and the Indians* [**2.6.21**; p. 123] in the following manner: after "scrutinizing and recognizing every part of the scene...they raised their dreadful war cry and ran hurriedly from the hall." Like Father Junípero Serra (see p. 45), Force celebrates the power of European images to convey the authority of the colonizers. He emphasizes the cultural superiority of European Americans by relating the ease with which Native Americans can be fooled by mere visual representations. Others, however, were unlikely to have been so easily deceived by Causici's rendering of Daniel Boone. During a set of treaty negotiations in the 1780s the Cherokee leader Old Tassel eloquently expressed his shrewd perception of the situation:

> Much has been said of the want of what you term "civilization" among the Indians. Many proposals have been made to us to adopt your laws, your religions, your manners, and your customs. We do not see the propriety of such a reformation. We should be better pleased with beholding the good effect of these doctrines in your own practices than with hearing you talk about them, or of reading your papers to us on such subjects. You say, "Why do not the Indians till the ground and live as we do?" May we not ask with equal propriety, "Why do not the white people hunt and live as we do?"

Old Tassel thus rejected a policy that dominated official thinking about Native Americans at the end of the eighteenth century: that they could and must be incorporated into a European way of life, giving up their own hunting, agricultural, and spiritual practices and their claim to vast tracts of land.

Old Tassel was right to question the intentions of federal negotiators. In 1802 the federal government told Georgia state officials that it would end its agreements with the Cherokee that allowed them to maintain their land holdings in Georgia in exchange for Georgia ceding its western land claims. When the governor of Georgia attempted to force the Cherokee to

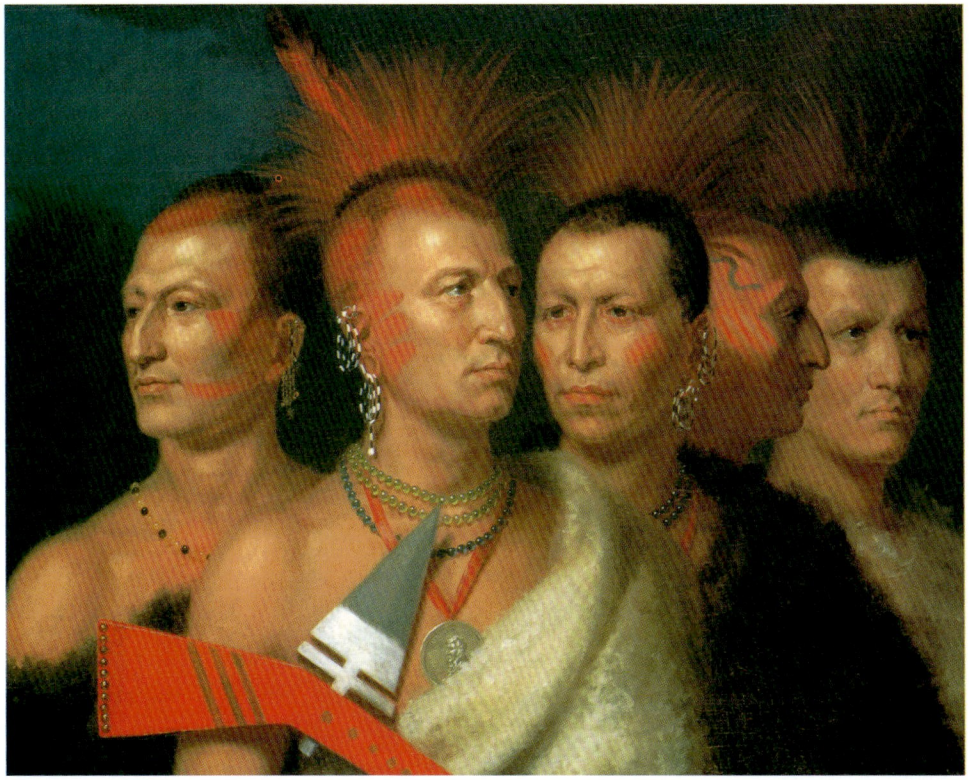

2.6.26 Charles Bird King: *Young Omawhaw, War Eagle, Little Missouri, and Pawnees*, 1822. Oil on canvas, 36½ x 28 in. (91.7 x 71.1 cm.) Smithsonian American Art Museum, Washington, D.C.

relinquish ownership in 1827, they drafted a constitution and declared themselves an independent nation with sovereignty over their lands. This indigenous resistance led federal officials to replace their policy of assimilation with a policy of removal. The governor of Georgia justified this removal by describing the Cherokee in the 1830s as, "ignorant, intractable, and savage people" who needed to cede to "civilized" people what was their right by the command of the Creator to possess.

Yet European American animosity toward the Cherokee was fueled in part by their very success at assimilating. A census taken among the Cherokee in Georgia in 1825 showed that they owned, among other things, 33 grist mills, 13 saw mills, 69 blacksmith shops, 2,486 spinning wheels, and 2,923 plows, sparking the envy of many of their less successful European American neighbors. Some of the more prosperous Cherokee also engaged in the buying and selling of African slaves. For example, according to the historian Tiya Miles, James Vann, the wealthiest man in the Cherokee Nation in the early 1800s, owned a large plantation in Spring Place, Georgia with approximately one hundred African slaves and a manor house surrounded by a cluster of slave buildings, possibly on the model of Mulberry Plantation [**1.4.23**; p. 76].

In the struggles over nationhood, therefore, Native Americans served as more than visual representations of the inevitable conflict between savagery and civilization. They actively questioned these very concepts, adopting agricultural practices that sometimes involved chattel slavery, writing a constitution modeled after that of the United States, and articulating their own demands for citizenship and nationhood. Ultimately, however, they were not strong enough to resist the relocation westward forced upon them by the US Government.

While negotiations between Native Americans and federal officials were taking place in Washington, D.C., Wisconsin, and Georgia, several artists were recording the appearance of those indigenous leaders who traveled to the nation's capital. One such artist was Charles Bird King (1785–1862). Born in Newport, Rhode Island, King studied in London at the Royal Academy and in the studio of West before returning to the US in 1812. He set up a studio as a portrait painter in Washington in 1819, and from 1821 to 1842 completed approximately 143 portraits of Native Americans. Many were commissioned by the federal government and included in the Department of War collection (the majority were lost in a fire in the Smithsonian in 1865). These portraits thus became part of a series of documents that recorded the transfer of the ownership of land from indigenous peoples to the federal government.

One of the earliest of King's portraits is *Young Omawhaw, War Eagle, Little Missouri, and Pawnees*, painted in 1822 to be sold privately [**2.6.26**]. The title suggests that it is an image of five different individuals, but they bear a striking resemblance to one another. The art historian Julie Schimmel suggests that all were based on the facial features of two Pawnee leaders,

Petalesharro, head of the Pawnee Loups, and Peskelechaco, head of the Republican Pawnees, whom King painted when they visited Washington with a delegation in 1821.

If Schimmel's suggestion is correct, King may have sacrificed the individuality of his sitters in order to create a facial composite that emphasized their nobility and that he hoped would be viewed favorably by a European American audience. At least one writer, the English traveler William Faux, who saw the 1821 delegation in Washington, voiced a similarly positive response to the features of the Pawnees. He noted that the men were "of large stature, very muscular, having fine open countenances, with the real noble Roman nose, dignified in their manners, and peaceful and quiet in their habits." Yet while the "Roman" noses and the peace medal around the neck of War Eagle in King's painting reinforce the nobility and peacefulness of the five men, the face paint, jewelry, hair styles, and war club (its blade pointed ominously at War Eagle's neck) signify their difference and their potential threat to European Americans. Many believed at the time that survival for indigenous peoples was possible only through the abandoning of such signs of difference and the subsequent adoption of the signs of civilization—the clothing and habits of European Americans.

While most contemporary viewers of King's multiple portrait would have read the costumes, facial paint, and hairstyles as evidence of a "noble savagery," late twentieth-century scholars have begun to read them, instead, as clues to a complex visual language used by many Native Americans. The art historians Patricia Trenton and Patrick Houlihan have noted in their research that the painted facial designs were related to certain religious rituals and often signified a personal protective medicine. The way in which a person's buffalo robe was positioned also carried a specific message. Nine message-conveying robe positions are currently known, two of which involve baring one shoulder, which was either a courtship sign or a message of admonition. Hairstyles among the Omaha and Pawnee peoples signified group affiliation.

At least two items in the painting attest to the syncretism at work in the formation of Native American cultural expression since the arrival of Europeans. The peace medals distributed by government officials were often prized possessions and signs of status and were worn on all formal occasions. The James Monroe peace medal worn by War Eagle included a profile bust portrait of the President on the obverse and a pair of shaking hands beneath a crossed tomahawk and peace pipe on the reverse. As was the case in the past, the European hand is indicated by an elaborate cuff, while the Native American wrist is bare. The knife-blade club held by War Eagle is derived in part from European culture, although in this instance the materials have

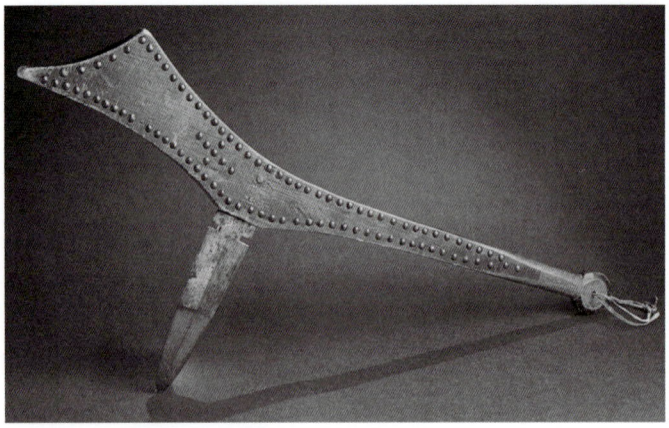

2.6.27 Unknown artist, Northern Plains?: gunstock club, before 1860. Painted oak, l. 33½ in. (86 cm.), double-edged blade l. 8¼ in. (21 cm.) Southwest Museum, Los Angeles, California

been refashioned. These clubs were also referred to as "gunstock clubs," due to the rifle-stock shape of the handle, and were recorded as early as the seventeenth century on the Great Plains [**2.6.27**]. The knife blades were often traded to Native Americans, and were subsequently fitted into wooden handles or attached to long sticks to use as spears.

Thus, while some contemporary art historians have questioned whether King's portrait contains accurate likenesses of five specific individuals, others have seen it, nevertheless, as providing valuable pieces of a historical puzzle. This puzzle is now being reconstructed by contemporary scholars in their attempts to understand the dynamics of nineteenth-century Native American cultures, even if only as filtered through the eyes of nineteenth- and twentieth-century European Americans.

Review Questions

1 What "stories" does the architecture of Monticello tell?

2 How is the early course of North American empire represented in the four relief sculptures above the doorways of the Capitol Rotunda in Washington, D.C.?

3 What did the religious beliefs of the Shakers and the philosophies of prison reformers have in common and how did these beliefs and philosophies influence the architecture that each produced?

4 How were gender and race enlisted in artworks of the late eighteenth and early nineteenth centuries to symbolize the new American Republic?

5 How and why did European American painters utilize classical Greek or Roman models or prototypes in their depictions of Native Americans?

CHAPTER 7

The Schooling of the Nation's Artists

(*c.* 1820–1850)

Improving the Taste of the Nation: Samuel F. B. Morse and the National Academy of Design

Most of those who assumed the task of interpreting and documenting America's history in the early nineteenth century were —like the artists Charles Bird King (1785–1862), John Trumbull (1756–1843), and John Vanderlyn (1775–1852)—trained in Europe. Calls soon arose, however, among artists and their supporters for a national academy that could take up this educative role and instill a sense of patriotism along with lessons in anatomy and perspective. One of the most vocal advocates for such a school was Samuel F. B. Morse (1791–1872) [**2.7.19**; p. 147].

Born in Charlestown, Massachusetts, the son of a Calvinist minister, Morse grew up in the midst of a religious upheaval known as the Second Great Awakening. The First Great Awakening, or period of religious revival, had begun in the 1730s and lasted through the 1760s. It was marked by the rise of itinerant evangelical preachers who, in emotionally charged sermons, challenged the control of the established religious authorities, whether Calvinist in the northern colonies or Anglican in the south. In advocating religious freedom and equality for all in the eyes of God, this evangelical movement attracted colonists of both modest and substantial means, as well as many African slaves. It spawned the popularity of other Protestant branches in America—for example, Baptist, Methodist, Presbyterian—and contributed to the emergence of a discourse of egalitarian democracy that helped lay the groundwork for the American Revolution. The Second Great Awakening that arose thirty years later and lasted through the 1830s was prompted by the concern of religious leaders over declining church attendance in the new republic. For Morse's father Jedidiah, a central figure within the movement, it was also, according to the art historian Paul Staiti, "an attempt to restore the political, moral, and social conventions of the colonial era that Calvinists felt had been undermined by the Revolution and the recently ratified Constitution."

Of particular importance for Morse's artistic and scientific, as well as religious, pursuits was the Second Great Awakening's adherence to millennialism, the belief that the thousand years of peace predicted in the Scriptures was imminent in America. This meant, for Morse, that America would be responsible for bringing peace to the rest of the world. Such an exalted task required not only theologians and politicians, but also artists fully aware of the significance and nature of their mission. Staiti aptly summarizes the parameters of Morse's and his father's often inflammatory evangelical crusade, a crusade that celebrated the economic and technological innovations of the early nineteenth century while at the same time drawing upon the centuries-old rhetoric of the anti-papist Black Legend (see p. 18). Staiti writes:

> they made their rhetorical leitmotif the ascent of American culture; they dreaded the influence of foreign artists, ideas, and governments; they believed that only an elite society could guide their country's destiny; and they saw the growth of industrial economy, technology, wealth, and mass communication as agents of freedom and progress and thus as tangible signs of God's favor.

Morse first began to paint while he was studying at Yale College (he graduated in 1810), inspired in part by the Reverend Timothy Dwight's celebrations of the redemptive qualities of painting (see p. 96). The year of his graduation he met the painter Washington Allston (1779–1843) in Boston, with whom he entered into his first directed study of anatomy, drawing, and art theory. Allston had traveled from his home in South Carolina to Harvard and then, in 1801, to England to study at the Royal Academy. From there he traveled to France and Italy, and honed his abilities to create elaborate historical or biblical scenes in the "Grand Manner," i.e. in the manner of Renaissance masters. When he returned briefly to America in 1808, however, what he introduced that was new in the fine arts was not this "Grand Manner," but a more subjective, romantic sensibility. This sensibility appeared most notably in his depictions of figures in landscapes, inspired by such artists as the Italian landscape painter Salvator Rosa (1615–1673). Allston painted not necessarily what he saw, but, as with the creators of many mourning pictures (see pp. 104–6), what he imagined, such as the scene in his *Moonlit Landscape* of 1819 [**2.7.1**; p. 132]. Here, clarity and heroics are sacrificed to gloomy spaces and a subtle foreboding, as dark shapes are chased by their shadows across the landscape.

Soon after commencing his study with Allston, and despite his suspicion of foreign artists and ideas, Morse felt compelled to travel to London with his teacher in order to further his training and career. Arriving in 1811, he was initially impressed by the encouragement artists received in England, as opposed to their relative neglect in America. By 1814, however, his millennialism reasserted itself and he proclaimed his belief that "the palm of painting still rests with America, and is, in all probability destined to remain with us." All that was needed was

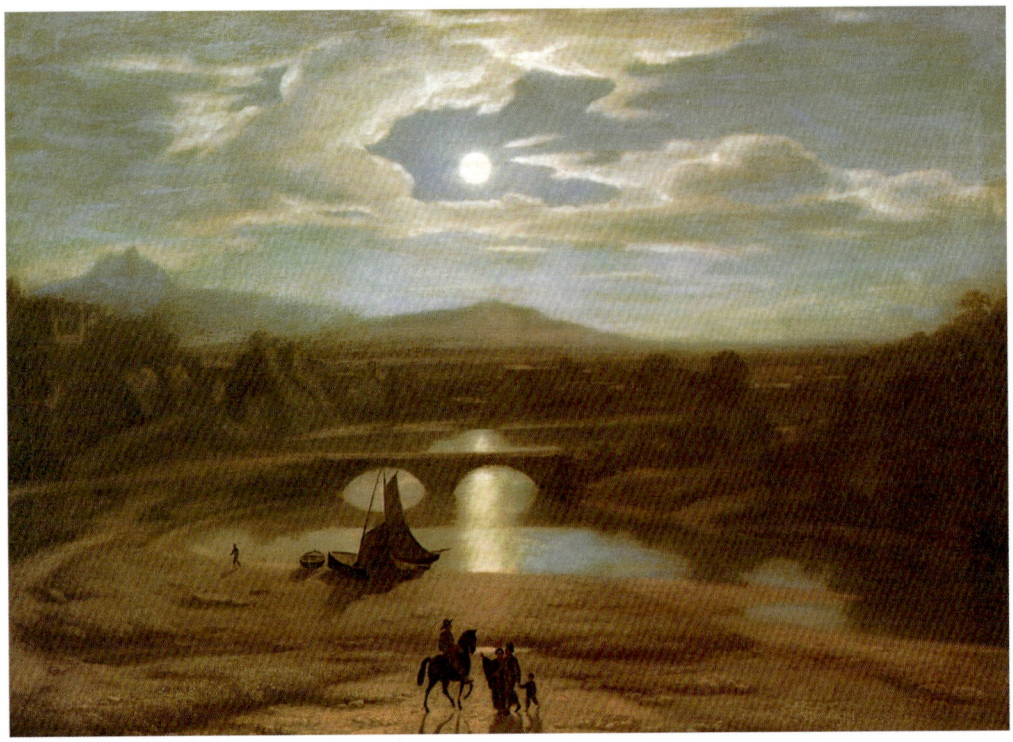

2.7.1 Washington Allston: *Moonlit Landscape*, 1819. Oil on canvas, 24 x 35 in. (61 x 89 cm.) Museum of Fine Arts, Boston, Massachusetts

"a taste in the country and a little more wealth." Morse could not directly affect the latter, but he did feel he could influence the former by introducing "first-rate pictures." He hoped that through the establishment of a national academy, perhaps in Philadelphia, already home to the Pennsylvania Academy of the Fine Arts, "Americans might remain at home and not, as at present, be under the painful necessity of exiling themselves from their country and friends."

Morse, like those academicians with whom he studied in London, believed that the only type of painting truly able to play the part of a national art form was history painting, for only it could "elevate and refine the public feeling by turning their thoughts from sensuality and luxury to intellectual pleasures." Yet Morse's mother's words in a letter of December 19, 1814, proved more prophetic, as she warned her son not to expect "to paint anything in this country, for which you receive any money to support you, but portraits." When Morse returned to Boston in 1815 he was unable to sell the history paintings he had produced in London and was forced to take up portraiture in order to survive. Even his efforts in this field failed until he moved to Charleston, South Carolina, in 1817, where he established a thriving practice painting the likenesses of the city's elite. Two years after his move to Charleston, Morse tried once again to stir interest in his work in Boston, where he put on display a portrait of Sarah Allston. But he fared no better than he had in 1815; the *New England Galaxy and Masonic Magazine*'s reviewer noted that "in ninety-nine instances out of a hundred" the wealthy people who attended the exhibition "admired the frame, in preference to the picture...and Mr. Doggett, the frame maker, gathered all the laurels at the expense of Mr. Morse the artist."

Morse, still not discouraged, decided to approach the problem in another way. He would paint a large history painting and take it on the road, displaying it for a fee in various halls throughout the country, thus achieving both financial gain and public edification. This entrepreneurial approach to art was not unprecedented. Trumbull's *Declaration of Independence* was shown to paying audiences in New York, Boston, Philadelphia, and Baltimore (at least 21,000 people paid a total of $4,000 to see it) before being installed in the Capitol Rotunda in Washington D.C., and several other artists had achieved financial success in the same way. Several had also failed, however, such as Vanderlyn. His panorama of Versailles, a series of 12-foot- (3.7-meter-) canvases pieced together to a length of 165 feet (50 meters) and covered with exterior views of the palace's garden facade and the gardens themselves, was displayed in the circular Rotunda on Chambers Street in New York City in the early 1820s. But the dignity of the classical building and the expansiveness of his canvas failed to draw the crowds that he had anticipated. This was also to be the fate of Morse.

Morse chose as his subject the House of Representatives, which he painted throughout 1822 and put on display in 1823 [**2.7.2**]. This was not a traditional history painting, however. Instead of privileging human figures and dramatic action, Morse presents a vast, largely empty, space peopled by eighty-eight figures engaged in, at most, relaxed conversation during a recess in Congressional debate while the candles of the large chandelier are being lit. Thus, despite its great size—over 7 × 10 feet (2 × 3 meters)—and the dramatic lighting created by the massive chandelier in the center of the room, the painting failed to arouse the interest of the general public.

Morse could have added more action and drama to his painting. Contemporary accounts often described sessions of Congress as resembling scenes in local taverns more than the peaceful, churchlike atmosphere depicted here. The inclusion of an increasing number of western states in the Union—Kentucky in 1791, Tennessee in 1796, Indiana in 1816, Illinois in 1818, and Missouri in 1821—brought to Washington individuals less attuned to the refined manners of the Federalist elite. Instead, they were more likely to attend sessions with their hunting dogs and to promote a form of democratic government that caused Federalists to shudder, such as abolishing property ownership as a prerequisite for voting.

As a Federalist, Morse believed that the moral and cultural progress of the nation required a centralized institution like the Federal Government led by a cultivated, god-fearing, materially prosperous elite. Thus, he wanted to present the House of Representatives in the best possible light. He even passed up the opportunity to record some of the heated debates over the shift from assimilation to removal in Native American federal policy that occurred in 1822. Instead, he merely included the figure of the Pawnee leader Petalesharro (see pp. 129–30) in the gallery at the far right. Jedidiah Morse had compiled a report, presented to Congress in 1822, arguing for the continuation of the policy of assimilation, in particular through religious instruction; he appears two figures to the left of Petalesharro in the gallery.

Morse's picture, as a whole, with its peaceable politicians and cavernous architectural space, is, in Staiti's words, "an antidemocratic gloss on the massive and disruptive shifts occurring in national politics." Intending to refine the aesthetic tastes of the populace at large and increase their knowledge of and

2.7.2 Samuel F. B. Morse: *The House of Representatives*, 1822–23.
Oil on canvas, 86½ x 130¾ in. (220 x 332 cm.)
Corcoran Collection, National Gallery of Art, Washington, D.C.

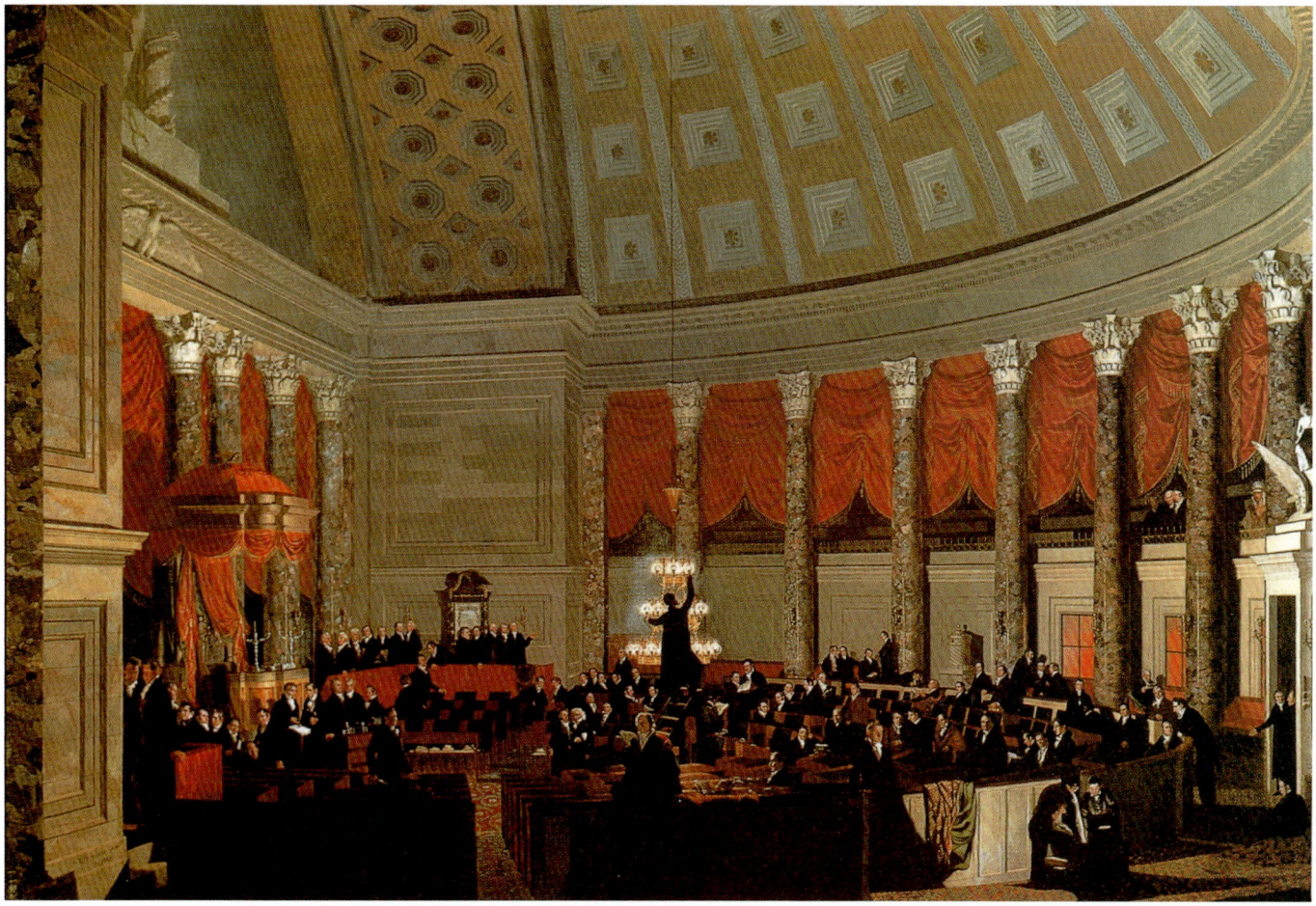

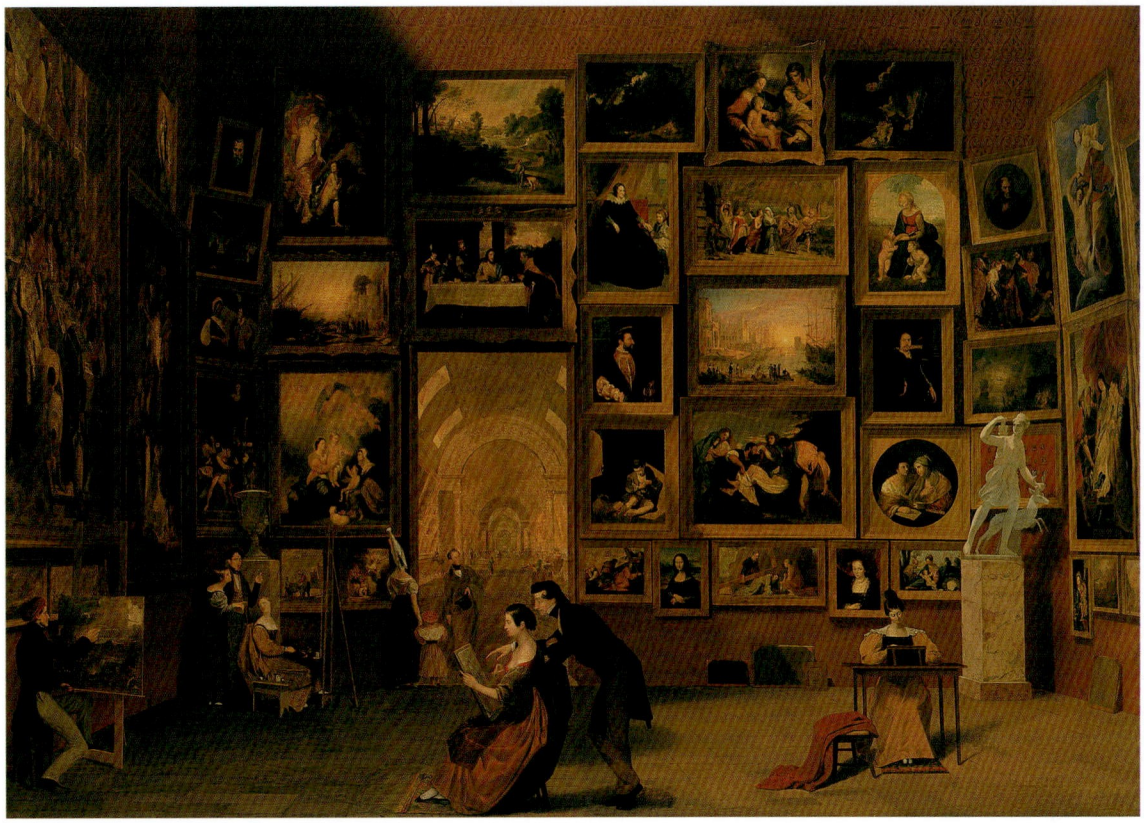

2.7.3 Samuel F. B. Morse: *The Gallery of the Louvre*, 1831–33. Oil on canvas, 73¾ x 108 in. (187.3 x 274.3 cm.) Terra Foundation for the Arts, Chicago, Illinois

faith in federal institutions, Morse omitted democratic debates, as well as anecdotal narrative content, and instead created a picture in which the symbolic commentary on the importance of centralized government was missed by most of the public, who simply found the painting boring.

Turning away from such public projects, Morse once again took up portrait painting. He was in great demand in New York City by 1826, when he achieved one of his life-long goals, the establishment of the National Academy of Design. The artist's first attempt at setting up a national academy had taken place in Charleston several years earlier. With the help of the state senator Joel Poinsett and the artist John Cogdell, he had founded the South Carolina Academy of Fine Arts in 1821. Unfortunately, the local economy took a turn for the worse in the 1820s, as cotton prices dropped and businesses failed. With little private or public support, the Academy closed its doors in 1830. In New York City, Morse's academy was preceded by many smaller teaching institutions, including the Columbian Academy, a private drawing school operated by Alexander and Archibald Robertson from 1792 to 1821. The Columbian Academy, and many others like it, catered to both male and female students, although it was often assumed by the instructors that women were there only to prepare for the genteel life of a refined wife and mother while the men were there to train for such professions as engineering and architecture.

The National Academy of Design was also preceded by the more prestigious American Academy of the Fine Arts, founded in 1802 and led in the 1820s by Trumbull. Yet by this decade many artists in New York found the American Academy wanting on all fronts—it lacked significant exhibitions, collections, and art classes, was controlled by wealthy collectors, and was too expensive for young artists to join. Morse led the call for a teaching academy run by artists, who would share responsibility with wealthy businessmen and politicians in defining the nation's artistic identity. As first president of the National Academy of Design, he drafted the constitution and by-laws of an institution for the training of American artists and the regular exhibition of their work, ensuring their control over their own professional development. He would play a significant role in the National Academy until 1837.

From 1831 to 1833 Morse tried, once again, to capture the public imagination with a large canvas entitled *The Gallery of the Louvre* [**2.7.3**]. The painting was a celebration of both the great masters of Europe and the talents of the American artist (Morse in particular) who would use these European greats as the foundation for a new and distinctly different national art. The painting also recorded the growing number of women who were engaging in the study of art, as three of the four students copying paintings are women. But, again, while appreciated by his colleagues, the painting drew few paying visitors from the general public, confirming Morse's low evaluation of the aesthetic tastes of the latter. This negative reception, combined with his failure to garner a mural commission for the Capitol Rotunda, led Morse to retire from painting and to devote the rest of his life to politics and to the scientific pursuits that had interested him for much of his adult life, in particular his work on the invention of the electromagnetic telegraph and the Morse code.

Some of those who viewed Morse's painting may have felt that the work gave too much emphasis to a European culture from which artists in the US were trying to distinguish themselves. The same could not be said of another gallery scene, produced by the Philadelphia artist Charles Willson Peale (1741–1827). Peale had been trained as a clocksmith, silversmith, and saddler in Annapolis, Maryland, before taking up the practice of portrait painting in the 1760s. He studied for two years with Benjamin West (1738–1820) in London and returned to Maryland to try his skills at rendering likenesses of local notables, transmitting his enthusiasm for art to many members of his family. In 1786, he opened a museum in a building next to his house that combined both fine art and natural history in a display meant to educate the general public in the wonders of both art and nature. It moved subsequently to the American Philosophical Society's Philosophical Hall in 1794 and, finally, to the Philadelphia State House, or Independence Hall, in 1802.

2.7.4 Charles Willson Peale: *The Artist in His Museum*, 1822. Oil on canvas, 103¾ x 79⅞ in. (263.5 x 203 cm.) Pennsylvania Academy of the Fine Arts, Philadelphia

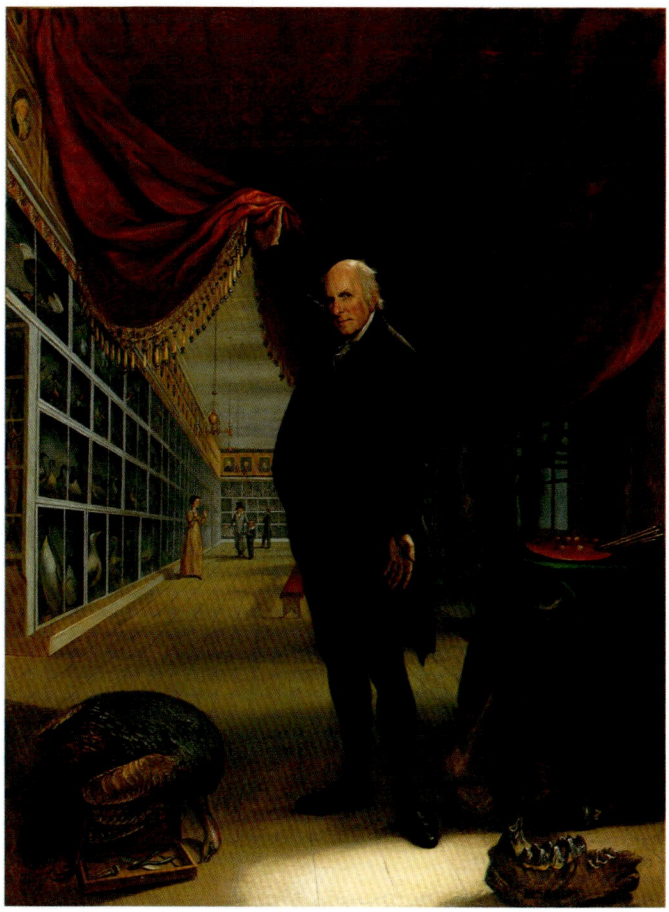

In 1822 Peale's museum was incorporated as the Philadelphia Museum. In honor of the occasion, the trustees commissioned a self-portrait from Peale, which resulted in *The Artist in His Museum* [**2.7.4**]. The painting presents a very different kind of institution from the one in Morse's work [**2.7.3**]. Rather than celebrating the masterpieces of European artistic achievement, Peale pulls back the curtain to reveal a mix of portraits of distinguished persons, stuffed specimens of American birds, and mastodon bones that Peale himself had excavated. In the left foreground an American turkey is draped over the tools of taxidermy, signaling its untimely fate, probably at the hands of Peale himself, who had mastered that art. To the right of Peale on a table are his palette and brushes. In the background are visitors, who take advantage of the lessons offered by the artist's museum. Peale takes his inspiration not only from other artists but also from nature, although nature once removed through the process of taxidermy. He thus presents a combination of science and art, imbued with nationalist sentiment, which Morse surely would have appreciated.

The Entrepreneurial Spirit and the Production of American Culture: Rufus Porter and the "Valuable and Curious Arts"

Samuel F. B. Morse spent much of the last part of his life attacking both Catholicism and capitalism, the former for undermining the spiritual and moral strength of the country, the latter for turning the fine arts into bourgeois commodities appealing to the lowest common denominator. He finally came to the conclusion that the nation would lead the world not in culture, but in commerce. But not everyone was so critical of the entrepreneurial spirit of American capitalism or of its effect on the production of American culture. Many artists willingly crafted their images according to the tastes of the average citizen of relatively comfortable means whose enthusiasm for the arts, even if not for the sort of arts Morse preferred, was very real. The art critic John Neal wrote in 1829: "you can hardly open the door of a best room anywhere, without surprizing [*sic*] or being surprized by the picture of somebody plastered to the wall, and staring at you with both eyes and a bunch of flowers."

Thus, there was fortune and fame to be had for those who possessed the willpower and talent to supply a growing demand for cultural commodities, from portraits and landscape paintings to stenciled chairs and clocks.

One such individual was Rufus Porter (1792–1884), who joined the growing ranks of artists traveling the back roads of the North to satisfy the demands of an expanding rural population for pictures [**2.7.5**; **2.7.11**, p. 140]. The Americanist David Jaffee describes Porter as an "artisan-entrepreneur" who, rather than accept the relatively insular and conservative tastes of such communities, aggressively promoted a more cosmopolitan model of culture and consumption: he thus played an important role in what Jaffee calls the "Village Enlightenment," when rural America was transformed "from a region resistant to change into one eager to embrace it." This transformation was part of a broader economic revolution that engulfed the whole of the country during the first half of the nineteenth century. A major spur was the growth of the southern cotton economy. As production boomed, aided by Eli Whitney's invention of the cotton gin in 1793, cities in the Northeast began to benefit in a number of ways. Bankers provided southern plantation owners credit, merchant seamen transported the cotton to Europe, and a textile industry emerged to take advantage of the ready supply of raw materials. This increase in wealth promoted a flurry of local projects including new roads, bridges, and canals. Railroads soon followed. The improvement in transportation made access to rural communities much easier for merchants and artists alike. It also made the urban centers of the East Coast more accessible from the country. One no longer needed to live on the coast and rely on the north–south water routes in order to move from place to place.

These improved systems of transportation and communication also brought more people into rural areas looking for land, increasing the pressure on an already short supply. Some moved westward. Those who remained found that they were being pulled out of their close-knit self-supporting communities and into a market economy that provided greater opportunities for both wealth and economic disaster. The influx of new people and new ideas also challenged local traditions of authority, with both sons and daughters now able to envision lives outside of the farm, as traveling merchants or workers in the growing textile industry. Thus, while Jaffee's "Village Enlightenment" opened up new possibilities that were eagerly embraced by many rural inhabitants of the Northeast, it also brought with it increasing anxieties, particularly for the local patriarchal authorities that had governed the old household system (see p. 88). It was into this mix of enthusiasm and anxiety that Porter and others like him arrived to hawk their artistic wares.

Porter was similar, in many ways, to Morse. While not having had the advantage of academic training or travel to Europe, he too believed that the arts needed to be accessible to, and appreciated by, the nation as a whole. As Morse was putting the final touches on his plans for a National Academy of Design, Porter produced his own pedagogical tool for the dissemination of the arts. In 1825, in Concord, New Hampshire, he published *A Select Collection of Valuable and Curious Arts, and Interesting Experiments Which are Well Explained, and Warranted Genuine, and May be Prepared, Safely and at Little Expense*, a text ranging widely over various topics in the arts, manufactures, and science (it went through five printings). The book was intended to help those country artisans who wanted to meet more effectively, if not help create, the growing demand for the "embellishment" of rural homes. It was filled with practical instruction rather than aesthetic speculation, providing precise measurements and rules for mixing colors, estimating the amounts of materials needed, and plotting out the designs for landscapes to be painted on walls. "In his work—both writing and painting—Porter placed repetition and rule at the very heart of the country vernacular," writes Jaffee.

In an advertisement in the *Providence Patriot* newspaper in 1822 Porter offered:

> to paint walls of rooms, in elegant fall colors, landscape scenery, at prices less than the ordinary expence [*sic*] of papering. Those gentlemen who are desirous of spending the gloomy winter months amidst pleasant groves and verdant fields, are respectfully invited to apply as above, where a specimen of the work may be seen.

Porter here identifies one of the central reasons for the popularity of painted walls—that they were less expensive than imported wallpaper. The results of his efforts can be found in the Holsaert House dining room in Hancock, New Hampshire, painted some time between 1825 and 1830 [**2.7.5**]. Here Porter provided those "pleasant groves and verdant fields" intended to distract the residents of the house during the long New England winters.

Some artists were more imaginative in their compositions. One is known as the "Bears and Pears" artist for his/her penchant for those subjects. On a wall in a home in Thornton, New Hampshire, between 1800 and 1825, this artist created an array of fantastic foliage, with giant pear and palm trees and a battalion of soldiers with pith helmets and swords [**2.7.6**]. Landscapes also decorated pieces of furniture, such as the mill complex depicted on the back of a Hitchcock-type armchair *c.* 1825 [**2.7.7**; p. 138], named after the furniture-maker Lambert Hitchcock.

2.7.5 (above) Rufus Porter: painted dining room, Holsaert House, Hancock, New Hampshire, *c.* 1825–30.

2.7.6 (below) Attributed to the "Bears and Pears" artist: wallpainting, from Thornton, New Hampshire, 1800–1825. The panel shown, *c.* 96 in. (244 cm.) high, is one of four that decorated the walls above the dado, as in ill. 2.7.5. Museum of American Folk Art, New York

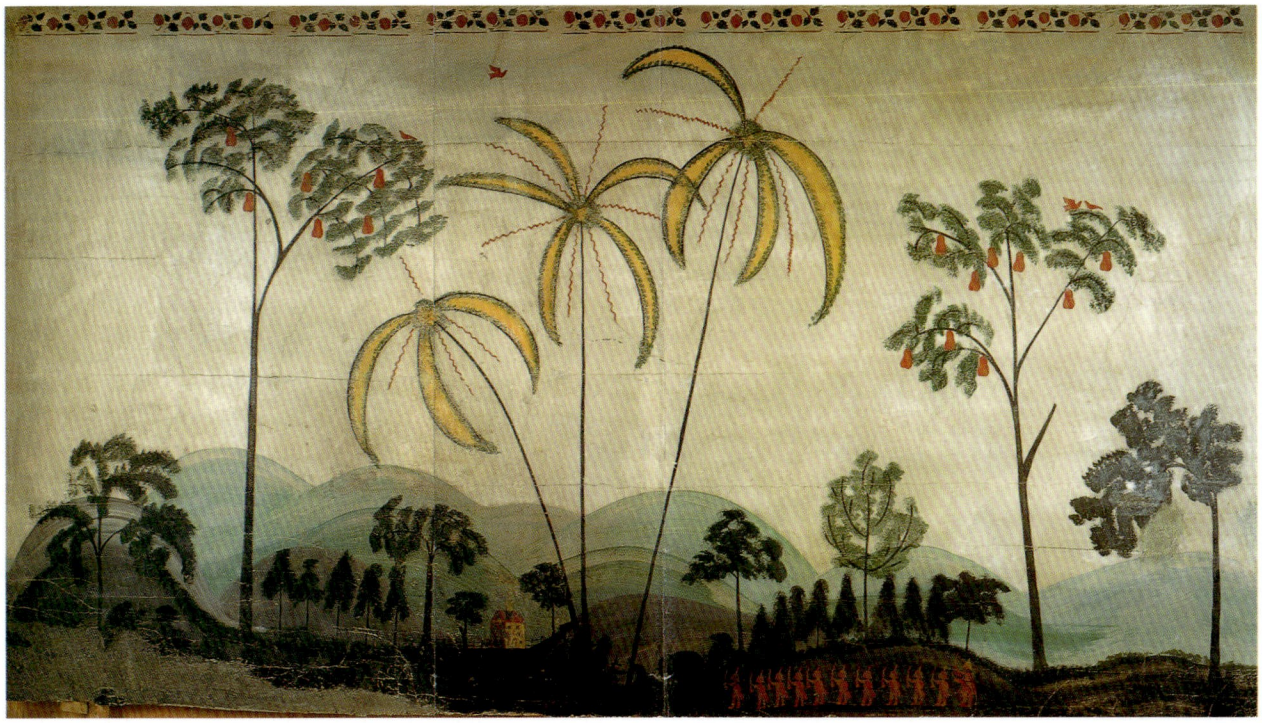

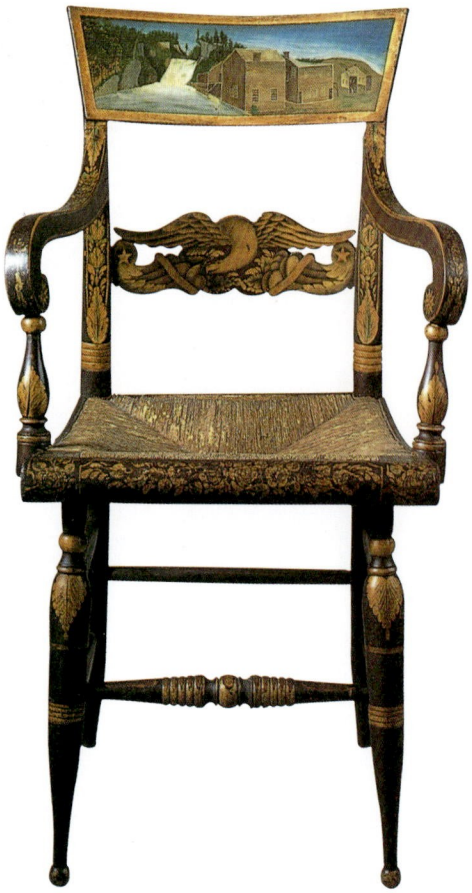

2.7.7 Unknown artist, from New England: Hitchcock-type armchair, *c.* 1825. Painted and stenciled wood and woven rush seat
Private collection

2.7.8 Unknown artist: stenciled wooden floor, in the Durant-Kenrick House, Newton, Massachusetts, *c.* 1790.

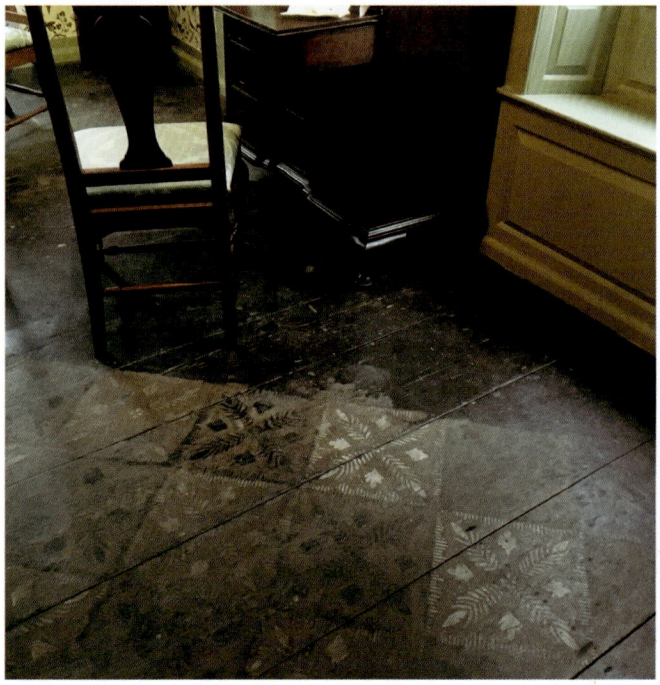

This chair also displays stenciled floral motifs and an eagle flanked by two stars, adding a patriotic element to the scene of industry above.

Porter's book could also have been used as a guide to the painting of floors or floorcloths. One of the few examples from the late eighteenth century that exist today can be found in the Edward Durant House in Newton, Massachusetts [**2.7.8**]. Here a variety of designs have been painted in repetitive patterns using stencils. Several written descriptions also add to our knowledge of this practice. Ruth Henshaw Bascom (1771–1848), who is known to have executed a number of pastel portraits, wrote in her diary in the early nineteenth century:

> 29 June Tuesday—fair....I began to paint my parlor floor in imitation of a striped carpet. 30 June Wednesday....I painted ¼ of my striped floor. 3 July Saturday....I finished painting my floor, at 6 p.m. Striped with red, green, blue, yellow and purple—carpet like.

An 1832 watercolor of the Talcott Family by Deborah Goldsmith (1808–1836) [**2.7.9**] suggests what such a striped floor might have looked like. As for floorcloths, Kurt C. Dewhurst and Betty and Marsha MacDowell quote a revealing passage from *The Autobiography of Lyman Beecher*, where he reminisces of his home in 1800–1801:

> We had no carpets; there was not a carpet from end to end of the town....Your mother introduced the first carpet. Uncle Lot gave me some money, and I had an itch to spend it. Went to a vendre [i.e. vendor], and bought a bale of cotton. She spun it, and had it woven; then she laid it down, sized it, and painted it in oils, with a border all around it, and bunches of roses and other flowers over the centre. The carpet was nailed down to the garret floor, and she used to go up there and paint.

Soon, however, painted floors and floorcloths were replaced by braided, hooked, or woven and embroidered rugs produced in the home or imported from abroad. One of the finest examples of such an embroidered carpet that has survived from the early nineteenth century was made by Zeruah Higley Guernsey Caswell in 1832–35 [**2.7.10**]. Composed of seventy-six embroidered squares, it measures more than 13 × 12 feet (4 × 3.6 meters) and is made of wool sheared, spun, and dyed by Caswell herself. To make it more adaptable to the seasons, Caswell created a removable rectangular section that covered the hearth in the summer months (on the left in illustration). The inclusion of a large basket of flowers and fruit on the edge of this removable section might refer to a custom common in the eighteenth century of placing a vase of cut flowers or boughs in an unused fireplace. The squares are filled with a wide variety of plants and animals plus a young man and woman, who gesture toward the main body of the carpet, as if to call our attention to the skill and imagination of its maker. Caswell predicted that this young couple would one day "keep house on her carpet."

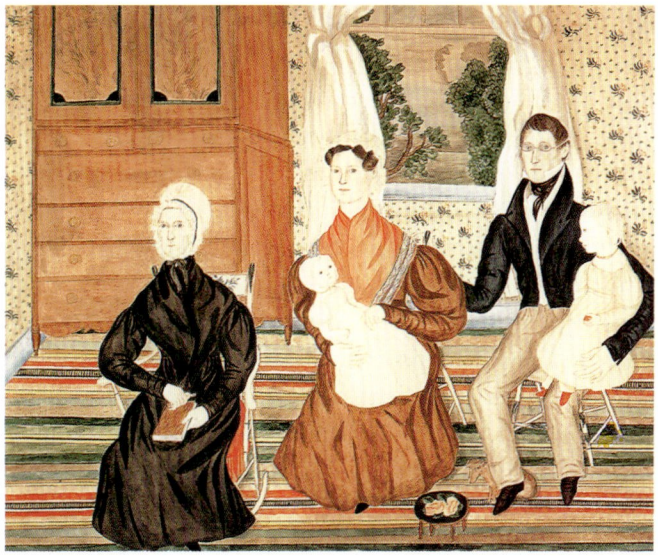

2.7.9 Deborah Goldsmith: *The Talcott Family*, 1832.
Watercolor on paper, 18 x 21 7/16 in. (45.7 x 54.6 cm.)
Abby Aldrich Rockefeller Folk Art Center, Williamsburg, Virginia

2.7.10 Zeruah Higley Guernsey Caswell: carpet, from Castleton, Vermont, 1832–35.
Wool embroidered on wool, 159 x 147 in. (400 x 373 cm.)
The Metropolitan Museum of Art, New York

A Plain Likeness: Itinerant Portrait Painters

Like Samuel F. B. Morse, Rufus Porter was an inventor as well as an artist (he founded the journal *Scientific American* in 1845). Unlike Morse, he was not averse to combining "art," "experiments," and "expense" in both his book and his daily practice. For example, he produced portraits with the aid of a profile machine and a camera obscura or "dark chamber." The latter is an artist's device in use since at least the fifteenth century composed of a light-tight box containing a small opening with a convex lens at one end and a screen that reflected the image at the other, allowing the artist to trace the image. These devices helped guarantee a "correct likeness" in a short period of time. The price of the portrait depended on the amount of detail (the more detailed the image, the higher the fee). Porter also made use of a copying machine or pantograph, thus producing a standardized product that gave his patrons, in the Americanist David Jaffee's words, "as much 'art' as they were willing to pay for." This use of mechanical aids, however, may account for certain odd combinations in Porter's portraits, such as profile ears attached to a head in almost full frontal view [**2.7.11**].

Those itinerant, or traveling, portrait painters who joined Porter on the back roads of New England to make their fortunes satisfying the growing demands of a rural population for images now had more opportunities than ever to refine their drawing and painting skills. They could study in New York as well as Paris or London, and could gain advice from manuals and pamphlets or from private tutors. Yet many continued to paint in a style reminiscent of their predecessors, one that emphasized flatness, minute detail, and frontality—"staring at you with both eyes," as art critic John Neal observed in 1824. Such characteristics can be found in the work of Erastus Salisbury Field (1805–1900), Ammi Phillips (1788–1865), and Joshua Johnston (1765–1830), among others. Several scholars have argued that, as with the painter of the Freake portraits at the end of the seventeenth century [**1.4.10**, **1.4.11**; p. 70], these characteristics cannot be seen as simply the result of ineptitude. Rather, they can be attributed, at least in some instances, to what the artist and folklorist Charles Bergengren calls "a social reticence in the presentation of self in egalitarian communities."

2.7.11 Rufus Porter: *Portrait of a Man*, c. 1820.
Watercolor and ink on paper, 4 x 3 in. (10.2 x 7.6 cm.)
Abby Aldrich Rockefeller Folk Art Center, Williamsburg, Virginia

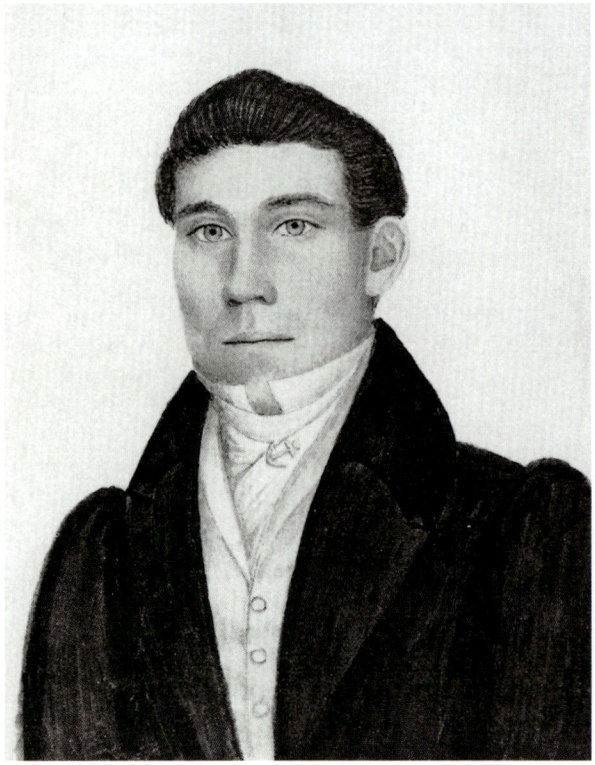

Bergengren, like Jaffee, suggests that we need to evaluate works like *Joseph B. Moore and His Family* of 1839 by Field [**2.7.12**] as part of a moment of rapid social change in rural America in the early nineteenth century, as an image "poised between forces of modernization at the hands of an upwardly mobile bourgeoisie and forces of a conservative morality drawn from a Puritan egalitarian lineage." Such patrons as Joseph Moore may have desired to be associated through portraiture with a wealthier, often urban class. Yet they were also restrained in their aspirations by earlier ideals based in more egalitarian religious or folk communities. The Reverend Timothy Dwight, who in his 1794 poem *Greenfield Hill* praised John Trumbull for banishing from his paintings the "strumpets" and "scenes of lewdness" found in the work of British artists (see p. 96), commended New England's rural people in similar terms. While England was "tinselled outside," a "painted tomb," and "foul harlot," New Englanders were "sunny geniuses," "plain," "frank," and "practical." It was this plainness and frankness that was captured in the portraits by Field and others.

Field was primarily self-taught, encouraged by his parents to explore his artistic talents while growing up in Leverett, Massachusetts. He did spend several months, however, studying with Morse in late 1824 and early 1825 in New York. Certainly he would have learned something of shading and perspective, but for this commission he chose, for the most part, to ignore these lessons. Field was living with his wife's parents in Ware, Massachusetts, and the Moore family lived across the street (he had already painted several portraits of Almira Moore's family, the Gallonds). Joseph Moore was a hatmaker in the winter, a traveling dentist in the summer, and a committed student of religion. Thus, he was a man of considerable means, but also of strong religious conviction.

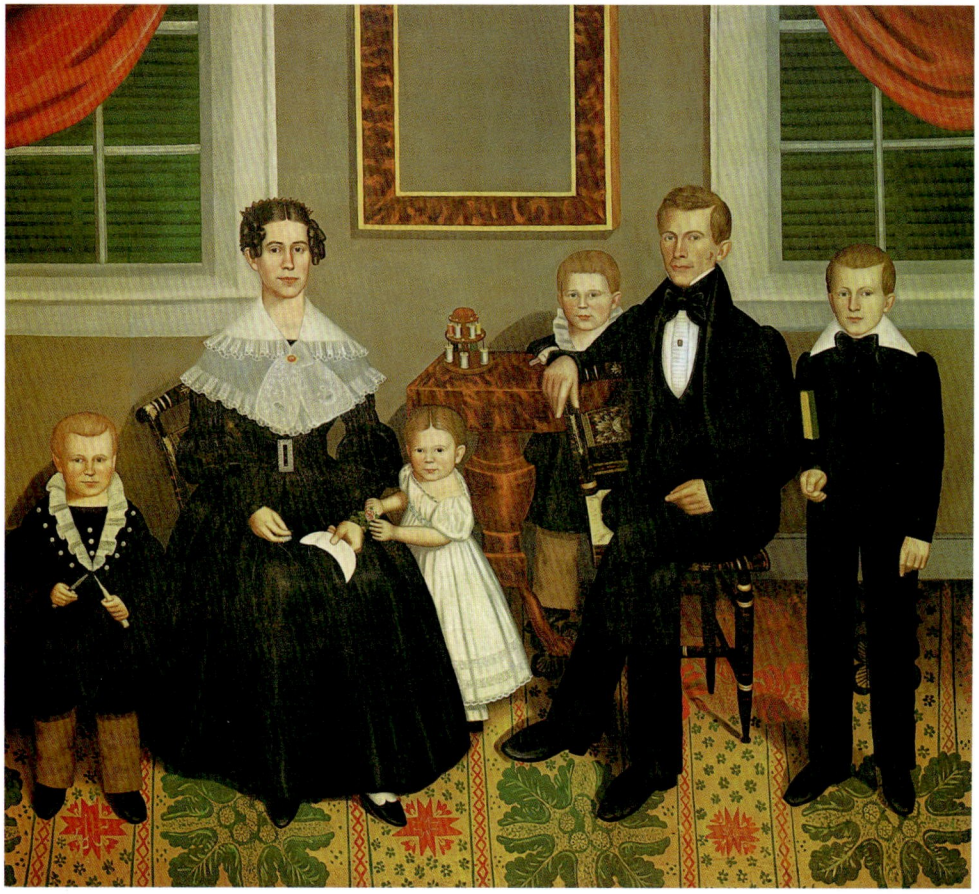

2.7.12 Erastus Salisbury Field: *Joseph B. Moore and His Family*, c. 1839.
Oil on canvas, 82¾ x 93¼ in. (210.2 x 237 cm.)
Museum of Fine Arts, Boston, Massachusetts

Field has organized the figures in the foreground of a shallow space, with the floor tipped up at such an angle that it continues the line of the wall, revealing the bright patterns of the carpet or painted floor (see p. 138). The shadows cast by Joseph and the boy beside him do little to break this flatness, which is emphasized also in the equal attention given to foreground and background detail and to the figures themselves, who all stare directly out at the viewer. This evenness of treatment applies to the surface as well, where there is little evidence of brushstrokes. Bergengren comments that such neutral lighting, undifferentiated space, and unmodulated paint surface "all contribute to the conservative effort to erase personality, to downplay aggressive 'presence' and to present instead a stable, permanent, even eternal image for posterity."

Yet personality is not totally absent from Field's portrait. The stiff poses are countered by the slight smiles on the faces of the figures, suggesting a certain sense of familiarity and family cohesiveness. Almira Moore is flanked by the two small children of her deceased sister Louisa; she holds a needle in one hand and a needlework form in another; behind her on the table is a small rack filled with spools of thread. The boy at her side holds a knife and a piece of whittled wood while the girl holds a flower. On either side of Joseph Moore are the couple's two sons, the older of whom holds a book under his arm. Industriousness is thus represented through personal objects symbolic of domestic work, creative play, and study. The dark clothes and shuttered windows suggest a somber mood, perhaps a reference to the death of Almira's sister. This mood is broken, however, by the colorful designs on the floor, chair back, table, and frame on the wall, and by the bright red curtains pulled back from the windows. Then again, the shuttered windows, in denying the viewer access to the world outside of the Moores' home, serve to focus attention on the figures, their modest prosperity and their industry.

Perhaps one can best appreciate the significance of Field's formal choices in conveying a certain impression of his sitters by comparing the painting to an earlier family portrait produced for a wealthy merchant in Boston, Joseph Blackburn's *Isaac Winslow and His Family* of 1755 [**2.7.13**; p. 142]. Blackburn (active 1752–1777) arrived in the colonies from England in 1752, spending two years in Bermuda painting portraits before traveling to Newport, then to Boston in 1755, the year he painted

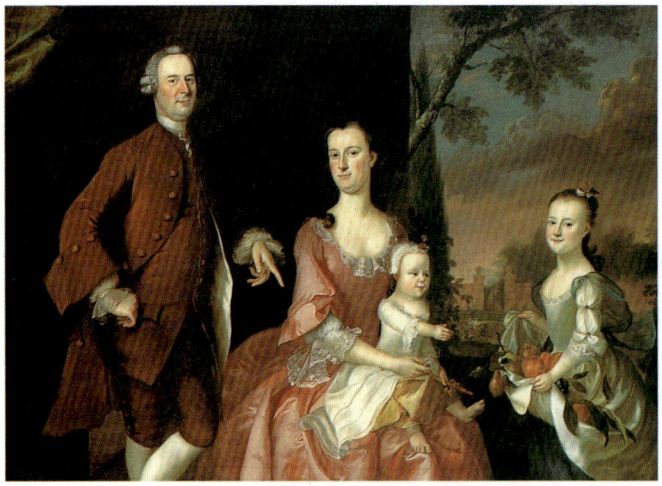

2.7.13 Joseph Blackburn: *Isaac Winslow and His Family*, 1755.
Oil on canvas, 54½ in. x 79½ in. (138 x 202 cm.)
Museum of Fine Arts, Boston, Massachusetts

the Winslow family. He portrayed Isaac and Lucy Winslow and their two daughters Hannah and Lucy in a manner and style common in English portraiture at the time. Whereas Field's portrait is marked by formality and restraint, Blackburn's is filled with informality and excess. Isaac stands in an exaggerated *contrapposto* (one leg bears the majority of the body's weight, while the other is slightly bent). One of his hands rests on his hip while the other points at his seated wife, who holds her young child on her lap. While Isaac's standing position connotes his authority as patriarch of the family, Lucy's central location within the painting and her close association with her children mark her importance in perpetuating the family line. The figures are located in a space on the border between the interior and exterior of the home, with a swag of drapery on the left and lush gardens extending into the background on the right, which increase the sense of depth in the painting. The low-cut bodices of the dresses of the wife and older daughter and their satiny texture add an element of sensuality to the scene. Rather than the single flower in the hand of the child in Field's portrait, the young Lucy Winslow carries an apronful of peaches and pears from the orchard. This is not a spare scene of propriety and industry, but a lushly painted representation of individuals proud of the wealth and status they have achieved.

An even greater contrast can be made between Field's painting and the self-portrait of John Singleton Copley (1738–1815) surrounded by his family of 1776–77 [**2.7.14**], which he painted just after they had joined him in London. While Blackburn's figures, like Field's, all (except for the small child) look out at the viewer, thus maintaining a certain degree of formality, many members of Copley's family ignore the viewer altogether, wrapped up as they are in shows of motherly or filial affection or lost in thought. Here the display of materials and textures is even more lavish; the brushstrokes even richer and more visible, particularly in the landscape in the distance; and the personalities of the sitters even more clearly displayed through the objects they hold and the clothes they wear, the expressions on their faces, and their poses. Copley, seated above his father-in-law and holding two sheets of paper in his hand, which appear to contain a faint drawing, looks out with confidence and satisfaction at the viewer, a mood undoubtedly caused in part by his recent reunion with his family after an absence of a year and a half.

The art historian Margaretta M. Lovell has noted that the focus on the mother-child relationship in paintings like those of Blackburn and Copley is evidence of a shift in beliefs about the nature of the family and the rearing of children during the eighteenth century. An authoritarian upbringing was replaced by a "gentler" attitude where mothers attempted to imbue their charges with a sense of self worth and self love rather than simply to control and counter what were seen as deeply rooted natural depravities. As a result, images of children at play and engaging in intimate exchanges with their mothers mark many of the family portraits of the late eighteenth century.

While New Englanders, both rural and urban, with adequate financial resources could well have commissioned family portraits in the manner of Blackburn's or Copley's, many chose not to. This preference for the flat, "plain" portraits of the itinerant painters allowed Ammi Phillips to support himself for fifty years, from 1810 to 1860, even though his travels extended over only a relatively small area composed of the western parts of Connecticut and Massachusetts and the bordering areas of New York. To date, approximately five hundred works have been attributed to him.

Phillips's *Mrs. Mayer and Her Daughter* of 1830–40 [**2.7.15**] shares with Field's work [**2.7.12**; p. 141] a flattened space, neutral lighting, attention to detail, and contrast between a predominantly somber mood and a bright flash of color, in this case the young girl's red dress, shoes, and necklace. Phillips has, however, created a much tighter, more integrated composition. He has effectively united the two figures by echoing the necklines of the two dresses; placing the girl to one side of the mother's lap so that the line of the child's shoulder repeats the puffed sleeve of the mother's other shoulder; and bringing the outside arms of both figures in line with each other through the flower in the mother's left hand, from which the child has just pulled a leaf. The intimate relationship between mother and daughter, while certainly more reserved than that between Susanna Copley and her young son as depicted in Copley's family portrait [**2.7.14**], is still convincingly conveyed (Mrs. Mayer may have only partially

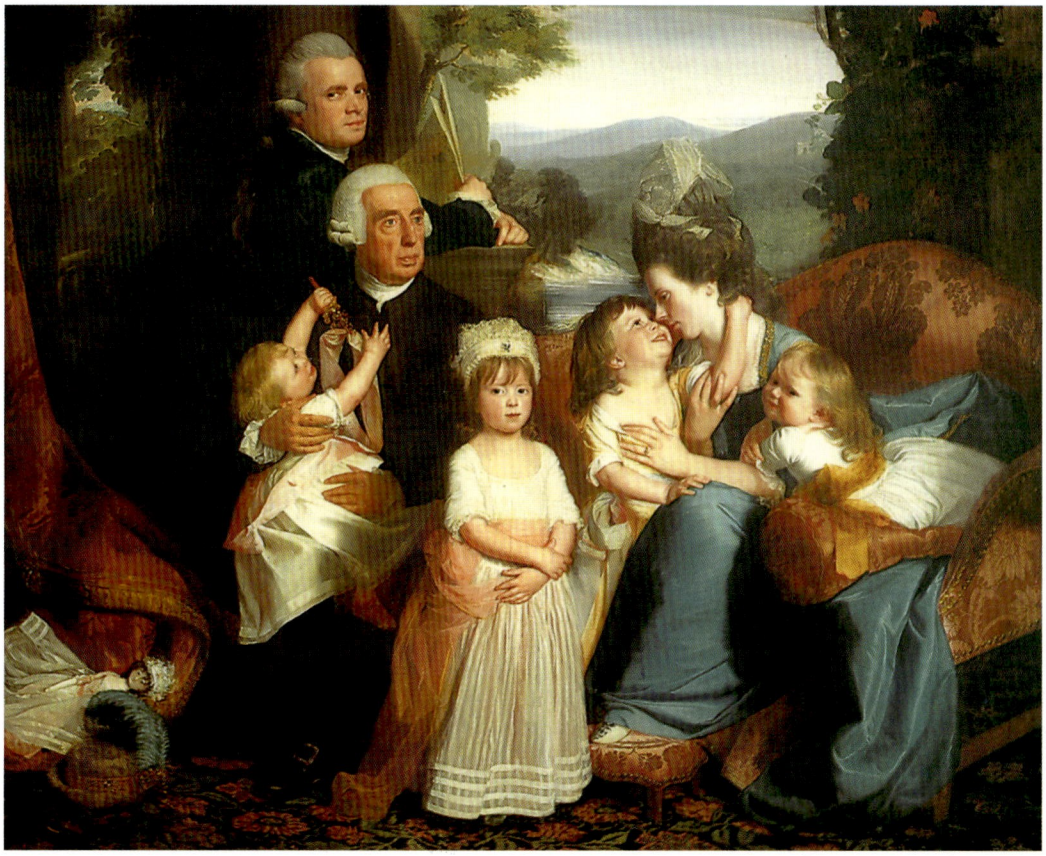

2.7.14 John Singleton Copley: *The Copley Family*, 1776–77.
Oil on canvas, 72½ x 90¼ in. (184 x 229.2 cm.)
National Gallery of Art, Washington, D.C.

2.7.15 Ammi Phillips: *Mrs. Mayer and Her Daughter*, 1830–40.
Oil on canvas, 37⅞ x 34¼ in. (96.2 x 87 cm.)
The Metropolitan Museum of Art, New York

adopted the new "gentler" practice of childrearing). In addition, small details—the necklace, the strawberry in the child's other hand, the intricate pattern on the lace cap—are set against broad areas of color or light, adding an element of dramatic contrast to the work.

Such a taste for "plainness" in portraiture was not limited to the states of New England. For example, the likenesses of many of the leading families of the South were captured for posterity in the work of the Baltimore artist Joshua Johnston. The artist had been born a slave but had gained his freedom by 1796, when he was recorded in the city directory as a portrait painter (he appears in several Baltimore directories from 1796 to 1824, in two specifically listed as a freeman). There is no record of where Johnston received his training, although scholars think he may have studied with the American artist Charles Peale Polk (1767–1822) or at least known of his work. In an advertisement he placed in the December 19, 1798, issue of the *Baltimore Intelligencer* Johnston claimed to be "a self-taught genius deriving from nature and industry his knowledge of the Art" and able "to execute all commands, with an effect, and in a style, which must give satisfaction" [**2.7.16**, **2.7.17**; pp. 144–45].

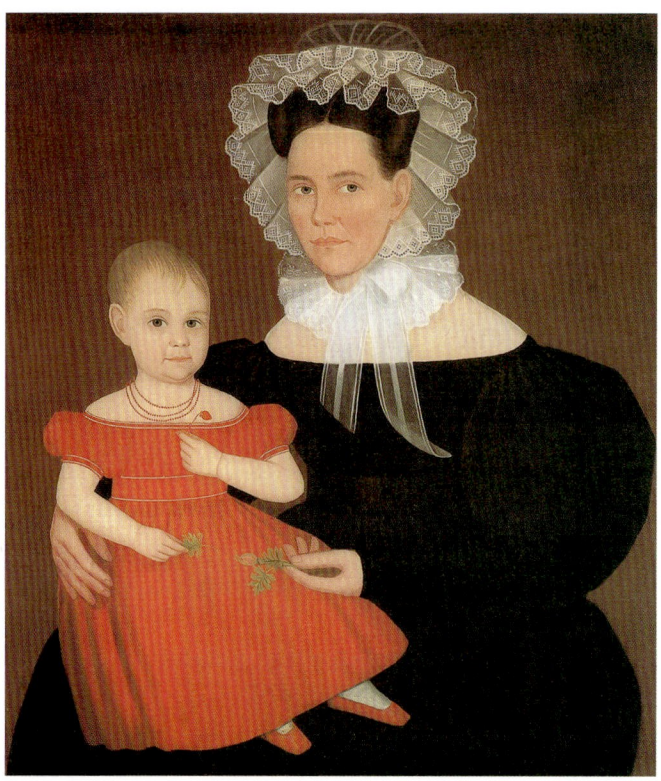

Johnston was not the only African American painter working in the US at the end of the eighteenth century. In 1794 and 1795 a large group of French refugees fled the slave insurrection in Santo Domingo (Haiti) (see p. 114), bringing with them to the US African slaves, several of whom were known to be silversmiths and painters. Evidence of other free African American painters can be found in such advertisements as the one in the January 7, 1775, edition of the *Boston Newsletter*, which offers the services of an African man who "makes portraits at the lowest rates" and who "has worked with the best masters in London." In addition, the poet Phyllis Wheatley, a slave in the Boston household of John Wheatley, mentions the work of an African painter named Scipio Moorhead (active 1770s) in a collection of her poems published in London in 1773. Moorhead may have been a slave in the household of the Reverend John Moorhead of Boston, and may have learned to draw and paint from the Reverend's wife, Sarah, who was an art teacher.

As the art historian Sharon Patton points out, Johnston was not an itinerant artist in the same sense as Phillips or Field, for he spent most of his career near his home city of Baltimore. "Itinerancy among black artisans and artists," writes Patton, "was ill-advised because slave-traders were active, and patrols and slave auctions routine." The Fugitive Slave Act of 1793, which provided for the return between states of escaped slaves, "rendered all African Americans potential escapees." This Act was particularly important for slave owners after the transatlantic slave trade (although not slavery itself) was abolished by law in the US on January 1, 1808 (*c.* 40,000 Africans were brought into the country between 1808 and 1861 via a black market in slaves). Johnston found ample work, however, in Baltimore, home to the Maryland Abolitionist Society, as well as to 25,000 free blacks (as compared to 3,000 slaves) in the early 1800s.

All but two of the approximately thirty paintings currently known to be by Johnston are of members of prosperous white families, some of whom sympathized with the goals of abolitionism. *Portrait of a Cleric* [**2.7.16**], of *c.* 1805, is one of two images of individuals of African descent. The portrait of the James McCormick family, of *c.* 1805 [**2.7.17**], is a representative example of the rest of his work. It is obvious from these paintings that Johnston was capable of working in at least two different styles. The head of the cleric is carefully modeled, his distinctive features convincing us that this is, indeed, a portrait. The McCormick family, on the other hand, is depicted in the "plain" style described by Bergengren—neutral lighting, undifferentiated space, formulaic faces, particularly among the children, and a rigid frontality.

While the identity of the cleric is unknown, there is ample information about the McCormick family. James McCormick came to Alexandria, Virginia, from Ireland soon after the Revolution and then moved to Baltimore, where he became a prosperous merchant and married Rachel Ridgely Lux. They had four children, three of whom are shown in order of their age from left to right—William, Sophie, and John. There is little in the painting to indicate the extent of their wealth, except for a general sense of ease and the modest stylishness of the clothing. The bodies and/or clothing of the figures overlap, creating an impression of a single familial unit. In addition, the gestures of the outside pair of figures echo each other—William's hand on his mother's shoulder, John's on his father's chest. Finally, Johnston uses the arching line of brass tacks at the top edge of the Sheraton sofa to literally link four of the figures, with the fifth positioned directly beneath the crest of the arch (his penchant for this element earned him the nickname "the brass-tack artist"). Like Phillips [**2.7.15**; p. 143], Johnston uses accents of red, most notably the slippers of Sophie and the strawberries she holds in her basket, to contrast with the otherwise predominantly white and black/brown color scheme. John, who stands rather awkwardly between the legs of his father, is also

2.7.16 Joshua Johnston: *Portrait of a Cleric, c.* 1805.
Oil on canvas, 28 x 22 in. (71 x 55.8 cm.)
Bowdoin College Museum of Art, Brunswick, Maine

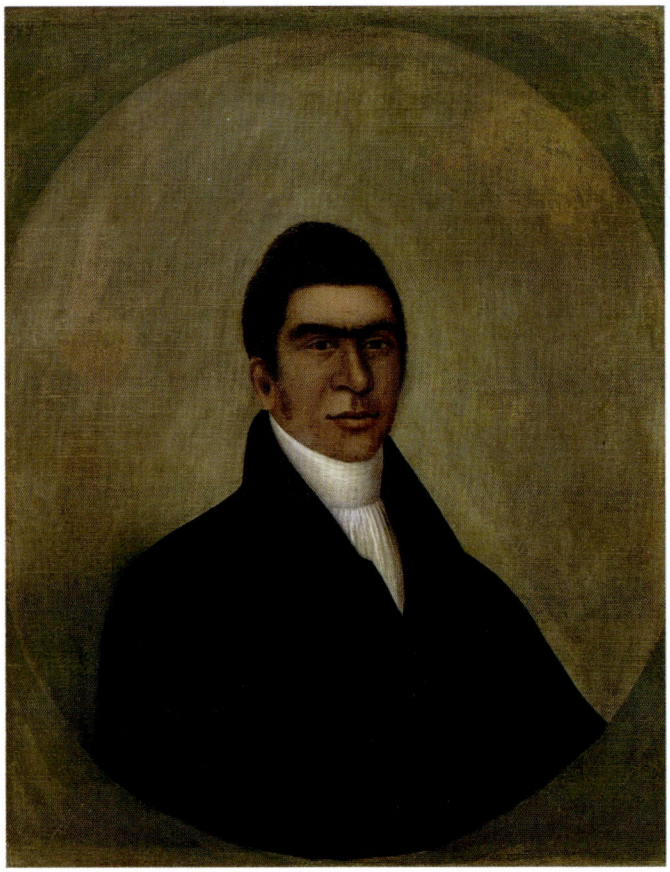

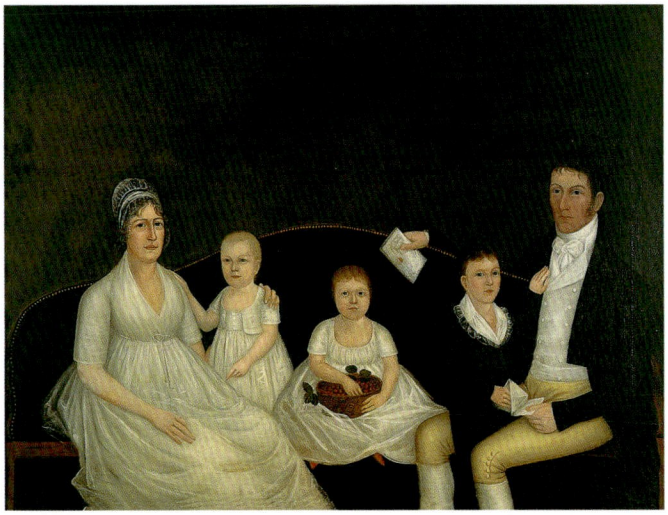

2.7.17 Joshua Johnston: *The James McCormick Family*, c. 1805.
Oil on canvas, 50 13/16 x 69 7/16 in. (129 x 176.5 cm.)
Maryland Historical Society, Baltimore

connected to the elder man through the piece of paper that each grasps with one hand, possibly a letter. The father holds another document, marked with a small red seal, in the hand resting on the back of the sofa. While the contents of these documents are unknown, they could suggest connections to a larger extended family or to business contacts, both of which would have significance for the future of the young John as oldest son and heir to the family fortune.

Learning the "Sunbeam Art": The Daguerreotype

The demand for portraits by such itinerant painters as Joshua Johnston, Ammi Phillips, and Erastus Salisbury Field declined in the 1840s and 1850s with the arrival of the daguerreotype. This early form of photography was developed in France in the 1830s by Joseph-Nicéphore Niepce (1765–1833) and Louis-Jacques-Mandé Daguerre (1789–1851) and in England by William Henry Fox Talbot (1800–1877). It was introduced in 1839 to the US by none other than Samuel F. B. Morse. While a student at Yale, Morse had experimented with the camera obscura (see p. 140). He wanted to capture the reflected image produced by this device on a light-sensitive surface, but was only able to create a negative of the image on paper dipped in a solution of nitrate of silver. Daguerre succeeded where Morse had failed, using light-sensitized metal plates. Morse did not see the daguerreotype as "the ruin of art" but, rather, as an aid for both artists and critics in learning how to look at nature, which could be captured in all its detail.

The photography historian Gisèle Freund notes that while the daguerreotype was extremely successful throughout Europe, "it was in America that it took hold and developed into a prosperous business." The rapid development of this medium in the US was due in no small part to Daguerre himself. He sent fellow daguerreotypist François Gouraud to America to organize exhibitions, lecture about the daguerreotype process, and promote the sale of a camera and accessories made by the Paris firm of Alphonse Giroux and Company under Daguerre's supervision. The US was undergoing rapid industrialization thanks to technical advances in the areas of agriculture, mass production, and transportation, and photography came to be seen by many as "an ideal way to preserve and promote its accomplishments." It could celebrate the people who facilitated these advances or whose lives were transformed for the better.

The extent of the popularity of the daguerreotype is revealed in a quote from T. S. Arthur's temperance tract *Ten Nights in a Barroom*, published in 1850:

> If our children and children's children to the third and fourth generation are not in possession of portraits of their ancestors, it will be no fault of the Daguerreotypists of the present day;...there is scarce a county in any state that has not one or more of those industrious individuals busy at work catching "the shadoe" ere the "substance fade." A few years ago it was not every man who could afford a likeness of himself, his wife, or his children;...now it is hard to find a man who has not gone through the "operator's" hands from once to a half-a-dozen times....Truly the sunbeam art is a most wonderful one, and the public feel it a great benefit.

Thus, the same public that had become accustomed to obtaining increasingly inexpensive likenesses through the efforts of painters like Phillips and Rufus Porter, who presented their clients through stiff poses and limited color schemes, was now drawn to this new black and white medium. Daguerreotypes were able to capture an even greater degree of likeness for even less money, with a stiffness of pose guaranteed by the long exposure time. By the early 1850s there were reportedly some 2,000 daguerreotypists plying their trade in the US. Some set up shop in cities and towns, while others took to the road in wagons and to the rivers in flatboats. And while they turned their cameras on landscapes (see p. 297) and cityscapes (see p. 299), portraits remained the most popular subject matter among Americans at mid-century.

Among these thousands of daguerreotypists were hundreds of women, who placed advertisements in local papers throughout the country or built a clientele through word of mouth. As the historian Martin W. Sandler notes there is little information about most of these women. Yet several of their images remain as testament to their mastery of the medium and to their persistence in establishing themselves in a business that, while still new, was overwhelmingly male. One example of such an image is a framed portrait from the 1840s of an unidentified woman wearing an elaborate bonnet and staring confidently at the viewer [**2.7.18**]. The daguerreotypist was Lydia B. Webb White (dates unknown) of Providence, Rhode Island. White established her own studio, L.B. White and Company, in Providence in 1854 and was joined the following year by her husband, Joseph, who had given up engineering to learn photography. Maureen Taylor, writing on the history of the daguerreotype in Providence, makes an observation that is unfortunately all too common in accounts of these early women photographers. After noting that Joseph White headed up his own company from 1856 to 1861, she adds: "Nothing else is known about Lydia."

Many daguerreotypists learned the trade through lectures like those given by Gouraud or by reading pamphlets or apprenticing in established businesses. Others learned from people who had experimented early on with the technique, including Morse. One of the first to learn the daguerreotype method from Morse was Mathew B. Brady (*c.* 1823–1896), who studied art at the National Academy of Design before becoming a daguerreotypist and opening a studio on lower Broadway in New York City in 1844. Around 1845 Brady captured his former teacher in a three-quarter-length image, his left hand resting on his newly invented telegraph [**2.7.19**]. On May 24 of the previous year Morse had successfully transmitted his first message from Washington to Baltimore. It was fitting that the seemingly magical transmission of sound over wire was commemorated through a process often perceived as equally magical.

2.7.18 Lydia B. Webb White: *Unidentified woman*, 1840s. Private Collection

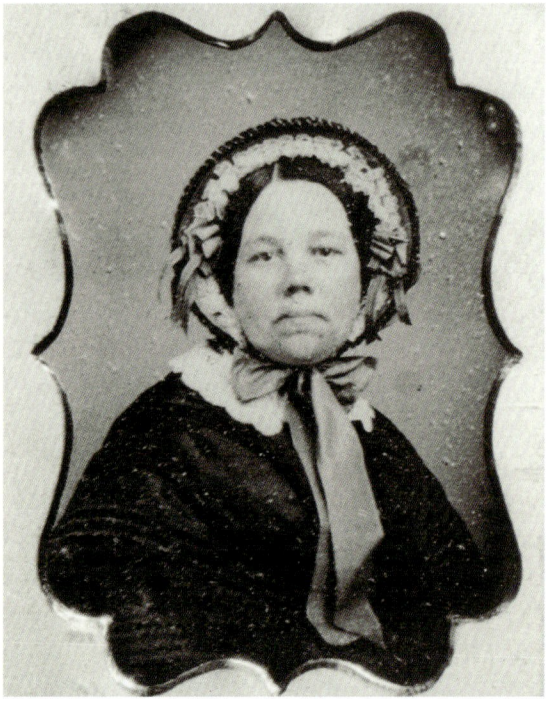

In fact, according to the cultural historian Alan Trachtenberg, from the beginning photography had "aroused contradictory responses. Pictures seemed both reassuringly familiar and disconcertingly new, recognizable as pictures, but with a difference." While the mechanical apparatus suggested a scientific or more "truthful" way of perceiving the world, the composition of the images followed well-established conventions of portraiture or landscape painting. At the same time, these conventions, and the exact mirroring of the details of the sitter or landscape, were achieved not through knowledge of drawing or manual dexterity, but through mechanical means. Photographers used the exactitude of this mirroring to establish their legitimacy as portraitists. They could produce a likeness of a sitter, they argued, much more accurately than any painter. And while early daguerreotypes required the sitter to hold still for several seconds, a painter would take days, if not weeks or months to achieve a comparable likeness.

This relationship between painting and photography can been seen through a comparison of Brady's photograph of Morse and Charles Willson Peale's *Artist in His Museum* [**2.7.4**; p. 135]. Both men stand with their body slightly turned to one side; the heads of both are shown in three-quarters view; each is associated with an object or objects indicative of his profession; each is located close to the front of the picture plane; both wear modest but fashionable dress. While Peale looks out at the viewer, Morse looks off to his right, two gazes common in portrait painting.

Peale's painting is significantly different from the portrait of Morse, however, in its setting. Morse's three-quarter-length figure is located in a shallow space in front of a blank backdrop while Peale's full-length figure is located in his museum, pulling back a curtain on its exhibits and visitors. Yet according to Trachtenberg, the painting "depicts the conceptual world of art into which photography would appear seventeen years later—a world in which art seems comfortable in its task of providing exact copies of visible nature." Peale presents himself as both an artist and an impresario. His museum is both a workshop and a stage, the tools and other objects in the foreground connected to the displays in the background. By choosing "a theatrical mode—the proscenium, the curtain, his gestures," Peale projects "the image of the artist as a responsible citizen sharing his skills and serving the cause of truth." This is also how photographers would present themselves, as individuals performing a civic role that involved bringing together art and craft in order, through exact imitation, to make knowledge sensible.

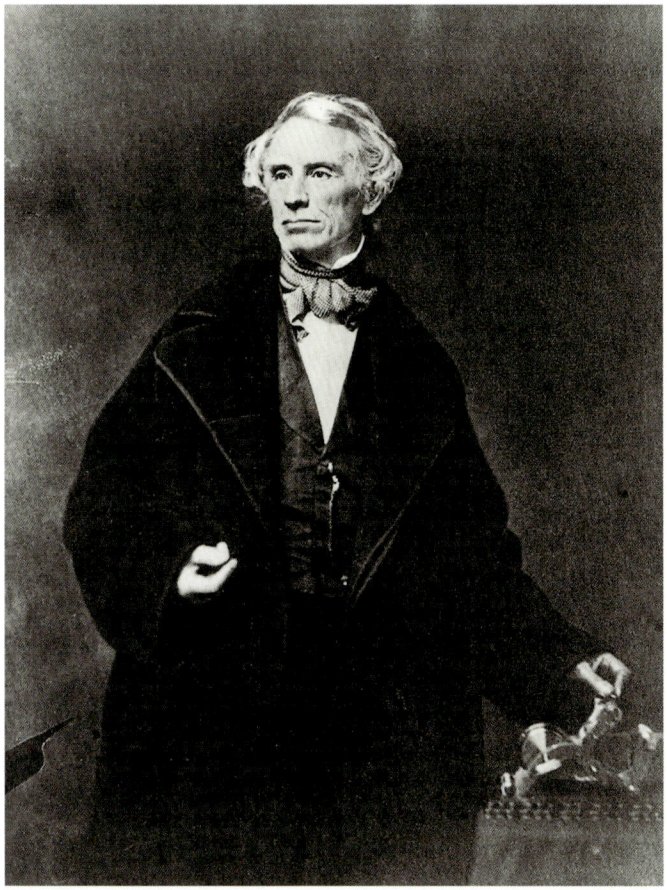

2.7.19 Mathew B. Brady: *Samuel F. B. Morse*, c. 1845.
Daguerreotype
Library of Congress, Washington, D.C.

Yet there is more than truthfulness in Peale's painting. What, for example, is the source of the light that shines so brightly on the head of the artist? According to Peale, he achieved this effect by placing the mirror he used to paint his self-portrait facing a window through which a strong light shone; this reflected light illuminated his face and head. In the painting , however, what is behind Peale is the darkest part of the curtain. "The light we see," notes Trachtenberg, "has no demonstrable source in the picture; seeming to emanate from the artist's head itself, light deceives, is a trick of mirrors." Thus, "the 'mirror of nature' implied by the painting's overt theory of imitation coexists with a magician's mirror which conjures illusions and distorts appearances." Is this artist in "a place of rationalist enlightenment, or in a theatre of illusions?" Photographers would also occupy a similarly ambiguous social space, hailed as truth-telling scientists by some and condemned as charlatans by others.

The development of glass negatives in the 1850s allowed for sharper and more stable images and the printing of several positive images from the same negative. This marked the demise of the daguerreotype (which was a unique object) and ensured the further proliferation of photographic reproductions at all levels of American society. The US was now embarked on an era of vast social and economic transformation fueled by rapid technological change, which painters, sculptors, printmakers, and needleworkers, along with photographers, attempted to record, accommodate, advance, or resist as best they could.

Review Questions

1 How are the educational projects of Samuel F. B. Morse, Charles Willson Peale, and Rufus Porter similar and/or different? Who were their intended audiences, and how did both artists and audiences understand the place of art in the newly emerging American Republic?

2 What are the characteristics of the "plain" style of portrait painting and why was it so popular in rural New England in the early nineteenth century?

3 How do such works as *The Talcott Family* (1832) by Deborah Goldsmith and *Joseph B. Moore and His Family* (1839) by Erastus Salisbury Field help us understand both home decoration and domestic life in the early Republic?

4 What role did race play in the lives and careers of itinerant portrait painters in the early nineteenth century?

5 How, according to Alan Trachtenberg, did painting inform the practice of early photography?

Hudson River School 1825–50s

Height of genre painting

1000–1130
Classic Mimbres pottery [3.8.1]

1770s
Arrival of Russia, England and Spain in the Pacific Northwest

1804–6
Lewis and Clark Expedition maps Louisiana Territory

1808–13
Publication of Alexander Wilson's nine-volume *American Ornithology*

1810s
Raphaelle Peale first American to focus on still-life painting [3.10.8]

1820s
Growing division in Quaker communities between Orthodox and Hicksites leads to Separation of 1827

1820s–49
Edward Hicks paints *Peaceable Kingdoms* [3.8.22]

1820s–60s
More than 30,000 miles (48,280 kilometers) of railway track laid

1824
Catskill Mountain House opens, becomes favorite retreat for landscape artists

1825
John Trumbull discovers the early landscape paintings of Thomas Cole [3.8.9], beginning the Hudson River School; opening of the Erie Canal; signing of The Friendship Treaty between Apsáalooke (Crow) leaders and the US government

1828
Formation of the Democratic Party, election of Andrew Jackson as first Democratic President of the United States; publication of *Metamora: or, The Last of the Wampanoags; An Indian Tragedy in Five Acts*, by John Augustus Stone

1828–38
Publication of John James Audubon's *Birds of America* [3.10.17]

1830
Passage of the Indian Removal Bill

1830–36
George Catlin makes five trips to the territory west of the Mississippi to paint Native Americans [3.9.4]

1831
Revolt of African slaves led by Nat Turner, Southampton County, Virginia

PART 3 Nature and Nation

c. 1000–1863

From the moment Europeans first set foot on the North American continent, their attention was drawn to the landscape before them. Many, like Christopher Columbus, struggled to describe the strange plants and animals they saw, and drew on mythic tales of monsters and paradises that had circulated in Europe in the fourteenth and fifteenth centuries. The English artist John White (active 1585–1593) took a more direct approach, attempting to delineate the features of plants and animals, as well as peoples and architecture, without resorting to such myths (see pp. 64–65). Columbus wanted to explain what he saw, White simply to describe it.

Yet White's mind was not a clean slate; he had been trained as an artist in Europe and brought with him a set of skills and presumptions about how the exterior world appeared to the human eye. His artworks, and those of the numerous European artists who followed him, were very different, stylistically and compositionally, from the images produced by many of the peoples who already occupied the North American continent. These differences were due, in part, to different perceptions of the world and of the place of humans within this world. The development of one-point perspective in the fifteenth century in Europe—a mathematical division of the flat painting or drawing surface into a grid that allowed for the creation of the illusion of a three-dimensional space—positioned the human viewer as the center of the world, as the originator of meaning. In much of the narrative art of indigenous peoples, humans and animals and their surroundings are viewed as if from above, with no horizon line to locate them within a definable space and no privileging of human over other life forms. As these two world views—humans as organizers and controllers of nature versus humans as one element within a complex and carefully balanced world—collided, each side struggled to maintain and adapt their beliefs and behaviors, using both rhetorical persuasion and force.

The opening up of the continent west of the Mississippi with the Louisiana Purchase in 1803 (see pp. 113–14) intensified these struggles and drew artists into a public debate that tested their moral as well as artistic mettle. This westward expansion raised questions not only about the treatment and depiction of Native Americans and European Americans and the land they occupied, but also about relationships between humans and those supernatural beings that helped them understand or come to terms with the joys and hardships they encountered in their

1832–34
Karl Bodmer accompanies Prince Maximilian of Wied-Neuwied on a journey up the Missouri River, makes sketches for the Prince's travel account

1834–36
Thomas Cole paints the *Course of Empire* series [3.8.11] for Luman Reed

1835
Thomas Cole publishes "Essay on American Scenery"

1839
Publication of Prince Maximilian of Wied-Neuwied's *Travels in the Interior of North America in the Years 1832 to 1834*, with illustrations by Karl Bodmer [3.9.9]; George Catlin leaves for London

1840s
Rise in popularity of flower still-life paintings [3.10.13]

1841
George Catlin publishes *Letters and Notes on the Manners, Customs, and Conditions of North American Indians* [3.9.6]

1842
Founding of the American Art-Union in New York (successor to the Apollo Association, founded 1839), which publishes *Bulletin* and *Transactions*

1847
Hiram Powers's *The Greek Slave* (1843) [3.10.1] tours the US

1848
Seneca Falls Convention and "Declaration of Sentiments"

1852
Publication of Harriet Beecher Stowe's novel *Uncle Tom's Cabin*

1853
Frederic Edwin Church makes the first of two trips to South America (he makes a second trip in 1857) [3.8.25]

1854
Founding of Cosmopolitan Art Association, which commissions paintings from such artists as Lilly Martin Spencer [3.10.2] to be reproduced as prints

1856
Henry Rowe Schoolcraft publishes *Historical and Statistical Information Respecting the History, Condition and Prospects of the Indian Tribes of the United States*

1859
Albert Bierstadt makes the first of several trips out West [3.9.1]

1869
May 10: Completion of the transcontinental Union Pacific Railway

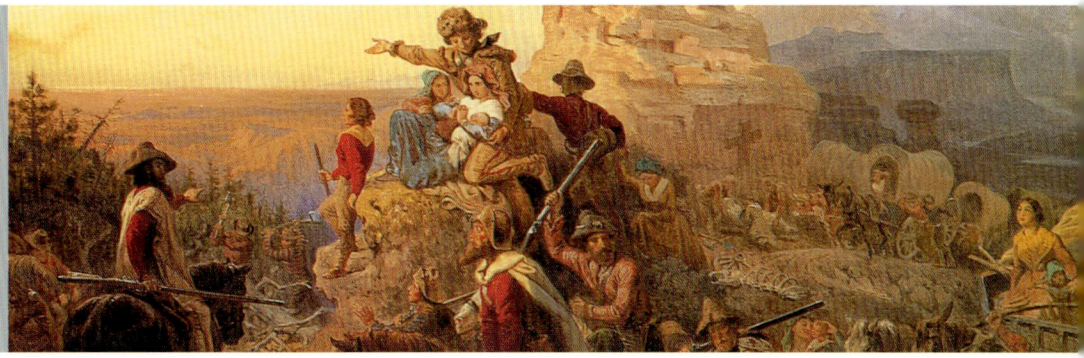

Emanuel Leutze: study for *Westward the Course of Empire Takes Its Way* (*Westward Ho!*), 1861, detail [**3.9.3**; p. 174]. Oil on canvas, 33¼ x 43⅜ in. (84.5 x 110.2 cm.) Smithsonian American Art Museum, Washington, D.C.

daily lives. Many European Americans saw their move westward to settle and farm the land as divinely sanctioned; God called on humans to make the land fruitful through hard work and to populate the earth and bring the word of God to all they met. Such a set of beliefs informed the mid-century ideology of Manifest Destiny—that Christian European settlers were destined to redeem and remake the western lands.

These Christian beliefs informed depictions of the American landscape. Sometimes the landscape was shown devoid of human presence, God's primordial wilderness. At other times it was a backdrop for the industrious actions of farmers and merchants. In other instances it appeared in still lifes and domestic genre scenes in the form of produce from locally cultivated fields and gardens, about to be transformed into nutritious meals as part of women's patriotic (the food was home-grown rather than imported) and Christian duties as wives and mothers. Through displays of the heroic wilderness, the cultivated landscape, or the bounty of nature in the domestic sphere, European American artists attempted to formulate an image of nationhood that accommodated religious, scientific, and commercial concerns. This image celebrated God's wonders while at the same time promoted the expropriation and exploitation of the land crucial to the expansionist plans of America's political and industrial elite.

This dual task—the celebration of both the spiritual and the commercial aspects of the American landscape—became more complicated as the population of the country increased dramatically in the first half of the nineteenth century, from 4 million in 1790 to 31 million in 1860 [**3.9.2**; p. 173]. By the 1860s half lived west of the Atlantic states, many on land previously farmed or hunted on by Native Americans [see **1.0.3**; p. 19]. This explosive population growth put further pressure on Native Americans and their cultural traditions, significantly diminishing their presence in the physical and cultural landscape of the United States. Their demise was often presented as inevitable, by both politicians and artists, while Native Americans themselves used what little power or prestige they had to preserve both their cultural practices and their claims to their spiritual and material worlds.

CHAPTER 8

Nature and the Sacred

(*c.* 1000–1863)

Imagery of Creation and the Vision Quest

In describing two large Mimbres pots from southwestern New Mexico, created around 1000–1130 CE, the artist and architect Rina Swentzell of Tewa-Santa Clara Pueblo wrote:

> Po-wa-ha ("water-wind-breath") is the creative energy of the world, the breath that makes the wind blow and the water flow. Within Mimbres pots, several world levels are usually depicted, showing the human, animal, and plant realms. Around them are the mountains and surrounding everything is the breath that flows completely around. That's why they're so enormous and all-encompassing—because they suggest the breath that flows around the whole world.

In one bowl [**3.8.1**], this integrative, creative breath appears in the swirling cloud forms and the play between light and dark areas. In the other [**3.8.2**], the integration is present in the overlapping of human and bear figures, with a diamond-shaped form common to both. This form, writes Swentzell, suggests "the rhythmic motion of the heart that both the man and the bear share. The intertwining of the human and animal is a central theme in Mimbres pottery."

Swentzell's words echo earlier accounts by Native Americans of the symbolic meaning of their imagery. Such words reaffirm the strong connection between humans and the natural world and the powerful role of a creator spirit or spirits in bringing order to this world. Creation myths are often the source of Native American iconography and reveal the universe as a layered structure composed of sky, earth, and underworld. In these myths the realms of sky and underworld are personified by supernatural beings, the former often in the shape of a celestial bird or thunderbird, the latter in the form of an underwater panther or water serpent. A highly abstracted thunderbird appears on a painted hide collected by French Jesuits in the Great Lakes region in the eighteenth century [**3.8.3**] (for more on painted hides, see pp. 44, 61–62, 179, 181). The thunderbird created thunder through the flapping of its wings and lightning through the blinking of its eyes.

Another source of Native American iconography is the vision quest. According to Apsáalooke (Crow) teacher and storyteller Joseph Medicine Crow, young people embark upon these quests in order to obtain *baxbe* or sacred power. This power comes from the First Maker or Creator and is granted through an animal emissary—for example, an owl, eagle, or butterfly. After a person has spent long periods of fasting and doing without physical comforts, the Creator has mercy and confers some of its power. The individual then creates shields or medicine bundles or other objects containing representations of the sacred animal. Only their owner knows the full story behind these symbols.

One such object, a shield, belonged to Arapoosh, also known as Sore Belly (*c.* 1795–1834). In the early 1800s Arapoosh was the leader of the River Crows, who lived along the Big Horn,

3.8.1 Unknown artist, Mimbres: bowl, *c.* 1000–1130 CE.
Painted clay, d. 10½ in. (27 cm.)
National Museum of the American Indian (Smithsonian Institution, Washington, D.C.)

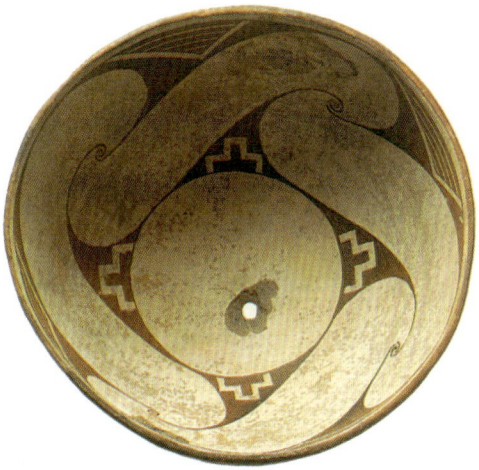

3.8.2 Unknown artist, Mimbres: bowl, *c.* 1000–1130 CE.
Painted clay, d. 10½ in. (27 cm.)
National Museum of the American Indian (Smithsonian Institution, Washington, D.C.)

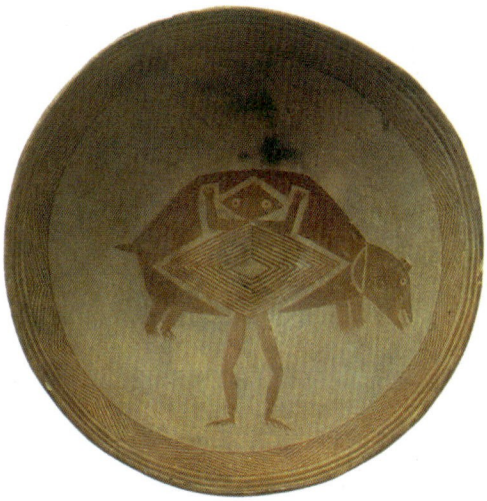

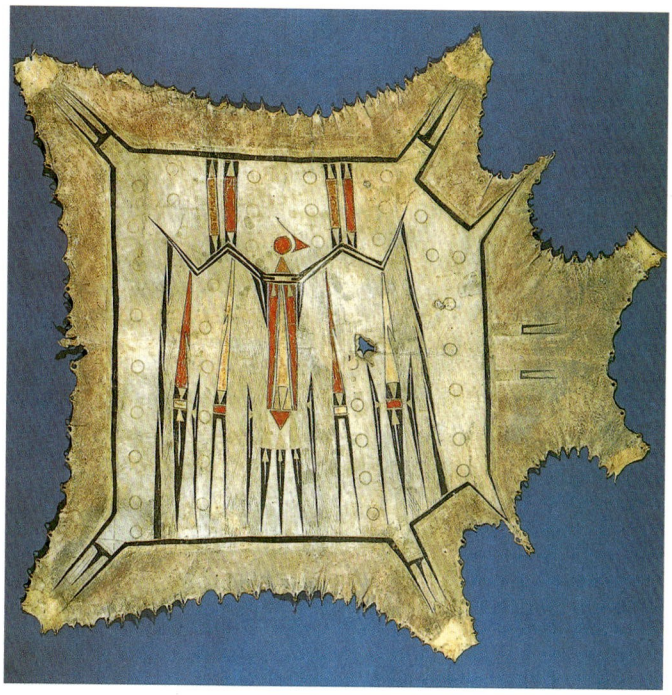

3.8.3 Unknown artist: robe with an abstract thunderbird motif, 18th century. Painted hide, 47¾ x 42½ in. (121.3 x 107.6 cm.)
Musée de l'Homme, Paris

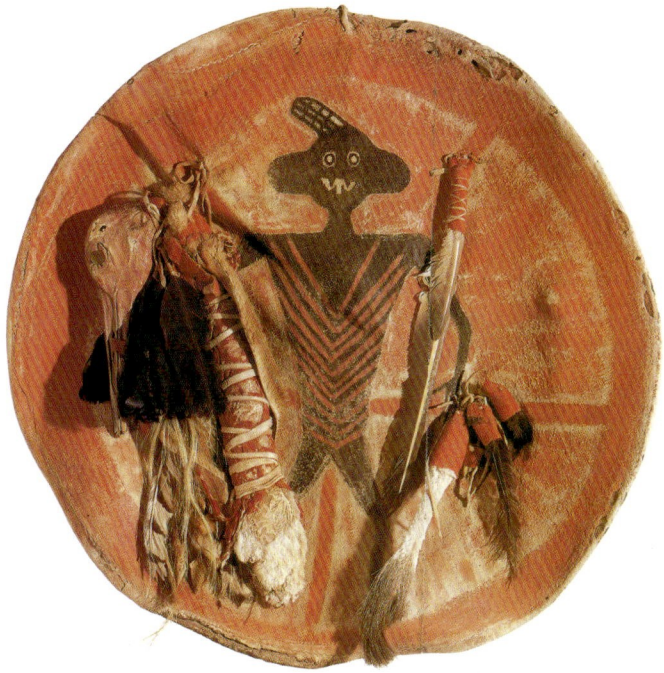

3.8.4 Arapoosh (Sore Belly), River Crow: decorated hide shield, early 19th century. d. 24¼ in. (61.5 cm.)
National Museum of the American Indian (Smithsonian Institution, Washington, D.C.)

Powder, and Wind Rivers in present-day northern Wyoming and southern Montana. The shield is made of buffalo hide and deerskin, and has an undecorated outer cover and an elaborately decorated inner cover [**3.8.4**]. The buffalo hide used for such shields often came from the thick hump section, which was particularly impervious to arrow points and even, according to some accounts, musket balls. Arapoosh believed his shield possessed magical powers of prophecy, and stories have been handed down over the years containing evidence of these powers. For example, the historian John C. Ewers relates an incident where Arapoosh made his decision to lead a war party against the Cheyenne by rolling the shield, "promising that if it fell painted side down he would not proceed. It stopped painted side up, and Arapoosh led his people to a great victory on the Arkansas River."

The central figure on the inner cover, who appeared to Arapoosh in a vision and presented him with his shield, has been interpreted as either the moon or a twin named Thrown into the Spring, who disappeared into the sky and was rescued by his brother with the help of cranes. The torso of the figure is presented in full frontal view and marked by thin red lines in a chevron pattern, suggesting either ribs or a protective covering; the legs are in profile. This mix of frontal torso and profile legs is common in early nineteenth-century Plains figural art (see p. 44). The outer edge of the shield is outlined in dark red, with five red lines radiating out from the center of the figure's body to the outer edge, suggesting the spokes of a wheel. This may be a reference to the medicine wheel, an important sacred symbol within many Native American cultures that embodies the four directions, as well as the sky, earth, and spirit tree or axis at the center of the world, the focus of ceremonial life.

Many monumental medicine wheels were created out of boulders arranged on the ground in the Plains region centuries before contact with Europeans. Such sites were probably used as ceremonial spaces for the performance of rituals, including the Sun Dance, which helped celebrate the place of humans in the universe. An example of a large medicine wheel, measuring 80 feet (24 meters) in diameter, can be found in Apsáalooke (Crow) territory in northern Wyoming. Known as the Big Horn Medicine Wheel, this site is marked out in stones on the ground and dates to *c.* 1200. Its twenty-eight spokes are thought to symbolize the days in a lunar month. In the center is a small raised circle or cairn made out of stones, with six other cairns arranged around the outside edge of the wheel, which align with the rising and setting of the sun and several stars, allowing for a reaffirmation of the vital links between humans, earth, and sky.

To the left of the figure on the shield are attached the head and neck of a crane, the feathers of a hawk and crow or raven, and a narrow length of otter fur. A deer's tail and eagle feathers are fixed to the right of the figure. These multiple references

> God has promised us a renowned existence, if we will but deserve it. He speaks of this promise in the sublimity of Nature. It resounds all along the crags of the Alleghanies. It is uttered in the thunder of Niagara. It is heard in the roar of two oceans, from the great Pacific to the rocky ramparts of the Bay of Fundy. His finger has written it in the broad expanse of our Inland Seas, and traced it out by the mighty Father of Waters! The august TEMPLE in which we dwell was built for lofty purposes. Oh! that we may consecrate it to LIBERTY and CONCORD, and be found fit worshippers within its holy wall!

Artists, in interpreting the face of nature/God in their paintings, became spiritual leaders of sorts, and participants in the creation of a national iconography. The art historian Barbara Novak notes that in "painting the face of God in the landscape so that the less gifted might recognize and share in that benevolent spirituality, they were among the spiritual leaders of America's flock." Nature became a text, like the Bible, to be read and interpreted. Artists attuned to the visual world, thus had the powers of both creation and revelation. Nature and art became routes to spiritual understanding and, through that understanding, to the creation of community, both local and national.

Yet this celebration of God in/as nature was accompanied by the increasing desecration of nature as a result of conquest and settlement. This created a serious conflict among those who concerned themselves with the spiritual, if not material, well-being of the nation. If God resided in nature, then what was to become of this God as increasingly large portions of nature fell to the ax? How could human cultivation be reconciled with God's primordial wilderness? Was not the garden of paradise the place where humans fell from grace? Thus there arose a conflict between piety and ambition, between the desire to remain devout Christians and the desire to exploit God's vast wilderness for material gain. This conflict appeared over and over again in the paintings and writings of American artists.

One of the first actively to promote and to excel in the field of landscape painting was Thomas Cole (1801–1848). His awareness of the connection between God, nature, and nation is evident in "Essay on American Scenery" (1835), in which he argues that America's wilderness is its most distinctive feature:

> because in civilized Europe the primitive features of scenery have long since been destroyed or modified.... And to this cultivated state our western world is fast approaching; but nature is still predominant, and there are those who regret that with the improvements of cultivation the sublimity of the wilderness should pass away; for those scenes of solitude from which the hand of nature has never been lifted, affect the mind with a more deep toned emotion than aught which the hand of man has touched. Amid them the consequent associations are of God the creator—they are his undefiled works, and the mind is cast into the contemplation of eternal things.

The role of the artist was, in Cole's mind, a moral one—to present to the viewer the perfection of God's creation, a perfection often unseen by those of a lesser moral standing.

Landscape Tourism

Thomas Cole's reasons for creating landscape paintings were not solely moral. Painting was his chosen profession and, like any working man, he had to support himself and his family. Cole was born in Bolton-le-Moors, a small town in Lancashire, England. His father James, a small-time woolens manufacturer, was a member of the "middling class"—shopkeepers, professionals, and artisans whose numbers grew in the early decades of the nineteenth century. James was not a very good businessman and constantly struggled to keep the family out of the poorhouse. Thomas went to work as an engraver at a calico printworks and continued in this field after the family moved to the US in 1818. The art historian Alan Wallach suggests that Cole's early interest in the arts and his criticism of what many celebrated as industrial or technological progress were prompted in part by a desire to distance himself from the industrial world of his father and the financial insecurity that accompanied it.

In the early 1820s Cole decided to dedicate himself to painting, and methodically went about teaching himself the necessary skills. Rather than attending classes at the Pennsylvania Academy of the Fine Arts or other art schools, Cole did what many before him had done—he traveled as an itinerant portrait painter while copying paintings and prints and reading as many books as he could on the subject of art. One very important book for him was William Oram's *Precepts and Observations on the Art of Colouring in Landscape Painting*, published in London in 1810. With its sections on tonal gradations, aerial perspective, and the setting of palettes for various situations, this book provided him with a firm grounding in the basics of landscape composition and coloring. Once Cole had settled on landscape painting—a decision some claim he made because of his inability to draw human figures—success came relatively quickly. The artist John Trumbull (1756–1843) noticed his work in 1825, and immediately began introducing him to a circle of people who proved important as future patrons. In 1829 Cole traveled to London, Paris, and Florence, studying the landscapes of the British artists John Martin (1789–1854), John Constable

(1776–1837), and J. M. W. Turner (1775–1851), as well as the work of the earlier French artists Claude Lorrain (1600–1682) and Nicolas Poussin (1594–1665). While in Florence Cole produced many Italian landscapes for his American patrons. Thus, he was able to explore the full range of landscape traditions available to him through the study of European art, and to create his own unique adaptations.

Cole's success was due, in large part, to an existing taste for landscape in the 1820s. This taste was still, however, the domain of a relatively small group of wealthy individuals who had access to education in aesthetic theory. These individuals examined paintings, prints, and aesthetic treatises (usually British) and traveled extensively throughout the north-eastern US, engaging in what Wallach calls "landscape tourism." "To put the matter somewhat differently," writes Wallach, "acquiring a taste for landscape in the early 1800s depended upon being part of the genteel subculture in which landscape was valued as a form of aesthetic experience." Not all landscapes produced aesthetic experiences, however. As is the case today, when national parks are dotted with signs pointing out particularly "scenic" views for camera-toting tourists, the places visited in the early nineteenth century were often those that had already been celebrated by Cole and other painters. Thus, a complex reciprocal relationship was set up between the landscape itself and visual representations of it.

Images of Niagara Falls

Perhaps the most dramatic landscape vista that captured the imagination of artists and tourists in the early nineteenth century was Niagara Falls, located between Lake Ontario and Lake Erie on the border between Canada and the US. John Trumbull had produced a series of early views of the falls in 1807 and 1808. The difference between Thomas Cole's work and that of his mentor is apparent when one compares two of their Niagara scenes [**3.8.7**; **3.8.8**, p. 157]. Also apparent are the similarities, the continuities between what Trumbull attempted and what Cole then developed further, continuities that undoubtedly help explain Trumbull's positive response to Cole's early work.

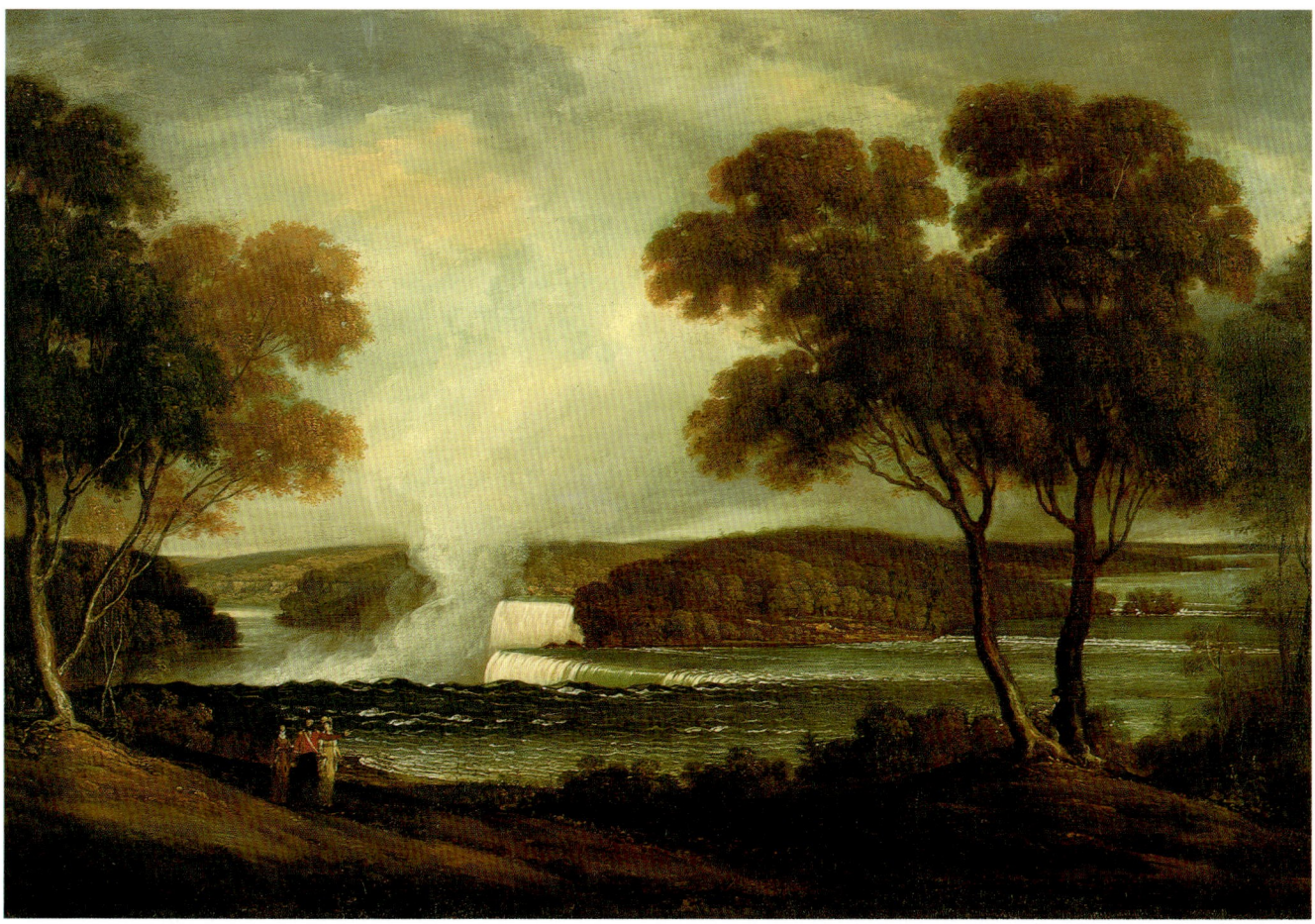

3.8.7 John Trumbull: *Niagara Falls from an Upper Bank on the British Side*, *c.* 1808.
Oil on canvas, 24⅜ x 36⁹⁄₁₆ in. (61.9 x 93 cm.)
Wadsworth Atheneum Museum of Art, Hartford, Connecticut

While Trumbull devoted most of his time to the production of portraits and history paintings, between 1804 and 1808 he executed several paintings of the American landscape, most notably four views of Niagara Falls. Although few in number, these works represent, according to the American Studies scholar Bryan Wolf, "the first sustained effort at landscape painting by an American artist." They also participated in the formulation of an iconography of nationalism, in which natural landmarks, such as Niagara Falls, gained particular prominence. In his Niagara paintings, especially *Niagara Falls from an Upper Bank on the British Side* [**3.8.7**; p. 155], Trumbull shows a clear reliance on the "picturesque" tradition popular in England in the second half of the eighteenth century, a tradition that had its roots in the previous century in the work of the French landscape painters Claude Lorrain and Nicolas Poussin. Wolf describes the picturesque as an artistic "middle ground" between the "terror and limitlessness" of the sublime and the "closed perfection" of the beautiful: the sublime and the beautiful being two opposing categories set up by the British writer Edmund Burke in his *Philosophical Inquiry into the Origins of Our Ideas of the Sublime and the Beautiful* (1757). The picturesque, Wolf goes on,

> combines an emphasis on novelty and discontinuous states of being with a celebration of the capacity to frame: to take a random view of nature and compose it according to recognizable aesthetic conventions. The picturesque thus assimilates the strange and uncanny into traditional and familiar form. It employs its conventions in an effort to establish interpretative control over its material.

In Trumbull's view of Niagara, three figures stroll along the river's edge, with a fourth person resting between the trees at the far right, sketching the scene (perhaps a self-portrait). The falls, visible in the middle ground, thus become a backdrop to the human activity in the foreground. A balance is achieved in the composition through the placement of the two pairs of trees in the foreground, which frame both the figures and the falls and direct our gaze into the central portion of the painting. They also anchor the horizontal planes into which the composition has been divided. The falls themselves are small in scale; their power is diminished by the calm waters of the Niagara River, which flow on either side, and the vast expanse of sky above. Thus, even the most powerful of natural phenomena is presented as if tamed by human hands. Trumbull, according to Wolf, "is not interested in the falls per se, but in the process of socialization by which natural wealth is translated into human abundance, and both then come to be associated with an emerging national destiny."

Trumbull painted the falls from the British—i.e. Canadian—side and included a British soldier as the central one of the three figures. He did so, perhaps, to increase the painting's appeal in England, where he hoped to sell it along with his other three Niagara views (he planned to use two as the basis for a large panorama). His hopes were dashed, however, and he had to ship all four back to the US, where they were later sold. The reasons for the lack of interest in England may well have included the increasing political tensions that led to the War of 1812 (see p. 113). In 1807, as Trumbull was sketching at Niagara Falls, the British opened fire on the frigate Chesapeake off the coast of Virginia and killed three Americans.

Though he did not explore it fully in his own landscape painting, Trumbull was also interested in another landscape tradition, Burke's "sublime," exemplified by the work of the Italian painter Salvator Rosa (see p. 31). Here the focus is the unrestrained power of nature, expressed in dramatic contrasts rather than pastoral order. This interest may have drawn Trumbull to the early canvases of Cole when he first saw them in the window of a New York framemaker in 1825. He introduced Cole's work to his artist friends and to the wealthy Baltimore merchant Robert Gilmor, one of Cole's earliest patrons.

Cole painted the falls in *Distant View of Niagara Falls* of 1830 [**3.8.8**], a work that draws on the tradition of the sublime. Here the viewer, rather than standing on a gentle rise of land as in Trumbull's work, is perched on the edge of a cliff above the falls, thus devoid of easy access to the water's edge. Dark clouds fill most of the horizon and contrast with the small patch of blue in the upper right and the bright white spray. The falls occupy a dominant position in the center of the composition and are painted straight on rather than in profile. The park-like grounds of Trumbull's painting are replaced by untamed wilderness, with any evidence of the numerous tourist facilities that had clustered around the site by the 1830s removed. Thus, the viewer is overwhelmed by the vastness and power of the natural world. The only humans visible are two Native Americans in the foreground, one standing and one sitting, identified as such by the feather headpiece and fringed jacket of the standing figure. Such indigenous figures were often used to represent the "wildness" of the territory and its still pristine state. Yet the standing figure holds a rifle, an indication that this wilderness, and the indigenous figures who represent it, had already felt the impact of European exploration and trade, if not settlement.

In his *Distant View of Niagara Falls* Cole also adopts what Albert Boime has termed "the magisterial gaze," that panoramic view from above that grants access to the wonders of God's creation, as well as to the future real estate and industrial wealth of the nation. Boime has traced the insistent use of this "view

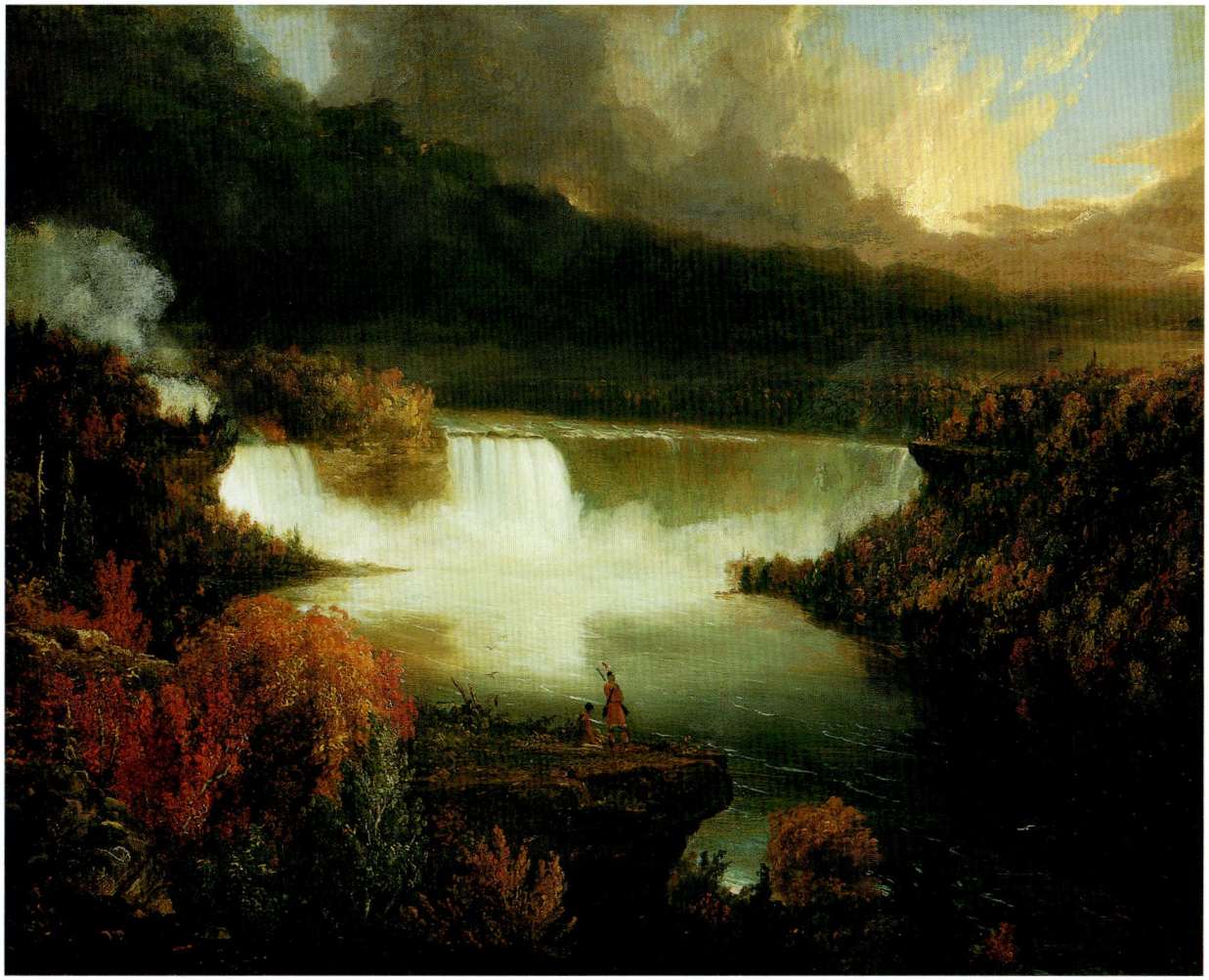

3.8.8 Thomas Cole: *Distant View of Niagara Falls*, 1830.
Oil on panel, 18⅞ x 23⅞ in. (47.9 x 59.3 cm.)
Art Institute of Chicago, Chicago, Illinois

from on high" in both the literature and visual arts of America in the early nineteenth century to rationalize the ongoing expansion of territory and exploitation of natural resources. In some instances the land that artists and writers celebrated was also the land in which they invested financially. It was no coincidence, writes Boime, that Cole, the artist who would gain fame for his views of the Hudson River Valley, first came to the attention of the New York art world in 1825, the same year the Erie Canal, which connected the Hudson River at Albany to Lake Erie at Buffalo, was opened. The canal gave the Hudson River increased importance as the main water route between the East Coast and the Midwest via the Great Lakes. It thus increased profits for those who controlled the territory and businesses along its shores, all the way to New York City. Among Cole's patrons was Philip Hone, Mayor of New York, who purchased two of the artist's Hudson River views.

Cole was particularly fond of the area around the town of Catskill on the Hudson, approximately halfway between Albany and New York City. He was not the only one to choose this particular locale, for in 1824 the Catskill Mountain House opened on a high bluff overlooking the river and became the favorite retreat of many of the elite on the East Coast and of a number of landscape artists who, along with Cole, would come to be known as the Hudson River School. In one of his first paintings of this region, *The Falls of Kaaterskill* [**3.8.9**; p. 158], Cole locates the viewer not above the waterfalls but below, entangled in the dense undergrowth of the forest. Again, the stormy clouds on the horizon move slowly to reveal a patch of blue sky to the right. And, as in his view of Niagara, a Native American with feather headpiece stands on a rock in the center of the image, a further indication of the wildness of the landscape (here he holds a bow rather than a rifle); all evidence of the popularity of the site with tourists that might interfere with the sublime, primordial quality of the scene—a wooden viewing tower, steps, handrails—has been omitted.

Thomas Cole, Federalism, and *The Course of Empire*

Thomas Cole's East Coast patrons, while a varied lot, came from two general economic groups: wealthy landowners and businessmen who formed the core of the Federalist Party and whose roots in the US went back to before the Revolution; and a new middle class made up of individuals profiting from the nation's phenomenal growth in population, technology, and productivity. The old elite was slowly losing its political clout, as first President Thomas Jefferson and then President Andrew Jackson attacked Federalist resistance to the expansion of democratic rights. At the same time, the newly rich were gaining political and economic influence. Each group made different demands on Cole. The former were more certain of their aesthetic tastes and thus dictated more closely what they wanted from Cole. The latter attempted to emulate the cultural practices of their "betters," but experienced a certain sense of inferiority. Thus they were more willing to listen to the artist, whose knowledge they viewed with greater respect.

In the late 1820s Cole began to move away from depicting the untamed landscape and to create, instead, what he called "historical landscapes," which included scenes most often drawn from ancient Greek or Roman history or from the Bible. Certain of Cole's Federalist patrons were willing to support this work. For example, in 1827 Daniel Wadsworth, the son of an important Hartford financier and member of the Connecticut elite, commissioned *Scene from "The Last of the Mohicans": Cora Kneeling at the Feet of Tamenund*, an episode from James Fenimore Cooper's historical novel *The Last of the Mohicans* (1826). Cole argued that such works, with their incorporation of historical or biblical themes, were "a higher style of landscape," closer to the status accorded history painting. Wadsworth and other of his Federalist patrons were not willing, however, to underwrite his proposals for pairs or series of paintings on a single theme, which would allow him to convey a larger moral message, not limited to any specific locale. When he attempted a pair on his own, *The Garden of Eden* (1828) and *The Expulsion from the Garden of Eden* (1827–28), he was unable to find buyers.

Cole was able, nevertheless, to convince at least a few of his bourgeois patrons to support these more ambitious projects, most notably Luman Reed, who commissioned Cole's most complex series of paintings, the five-part *Course of Empire* (completed in 1836). Reed was a self-made man, having risen from a store clerk to a successful merchant in the wholesale grocery business. His success was so great that he was able to retire at the age of forty-eight, yet he was a modest man, unwilling to flaunt his wealth. Art patronage was, for him, a way to gain entrance into a world of culture and attain a greater degree of respectability. He focused his collecting on the work of living American artists and opened his art gallery once a week to a select audience. Cole met Reed in 1833 and, that same year, convinced him to commission *The Course of Empire*.

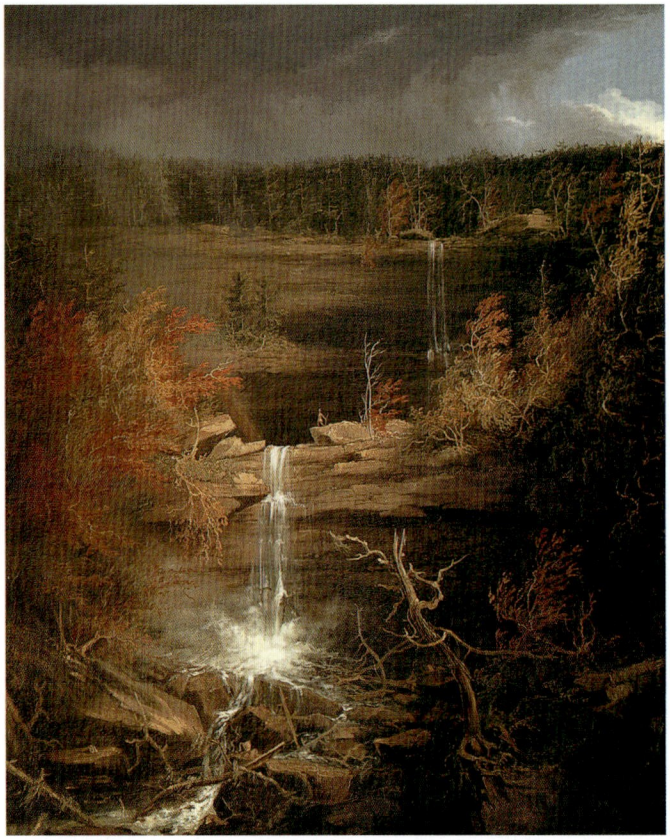

3.8.9 Thomas Cole: *The Falls of Kaaterskill*, 1826.
Oil on canvas, 43 x 36 in. (109.2 x 91.4 cm.)
The Warner Collection, Gulf States Paper Corporation, Tuscaloosa, Alabama

In *The Course of Empire*, Alan Wallach observes, Cole "set forth in allegorical form his pessimistic philosophy of history and his agrarian-republican critique of Jacksonian democracy." Like Jefferson, Cole worried about the destructive aspects of technological progress. In his "Essay on American Scenery" of 1835, he denounced the clearing of the land for roads, railways, and canals: "the ravages of the axe are daily increasing—the most noble scenes are made destitute, and oftentimes with a wantonness and barbarism scarcely credible in a civilized nation." Cole promoted, instead, a form of Jefferson's agrarian ideal where farmers resided in relative harmony within nature, the scene displayed in *The Pastoral or Arcadian State* [**3.8.11**]. Yet, in keeping with the Federalists and many Jeffersonians, Cole was also concerned about the potentially destructive effects of the spread of democracy and the resulting lawlessness and mob rule that would bring down the republic.

Cole's concerns, and the five paintings, are linked through a cyclical theory of history, based on the view that moral law governs all history, engendering endless cycles of rise and fall caused by the inherent sinfulness of humans. This theory was popular with many Federalists, who hoped that their decline in power was only temporary. Jacksonian democrats may have believed that democracy would halt this historical cycle and prevent the political corruption that led to downfall. This view was taken by at least one critic, who wrote of the series:

> The climax in the course of man's progress, which Mr. Cole has here represented, is that which has been and was founded on the usurpation of the strong over the weak: the perfection which man is hereafter to attain, will be based upon a more stable foundation: political equality; the rights of man; the democratick [sic] principle; the sovereignty of the people.

In 1833 Cole provided Reed with a sketch that showed how the paintings would be displayed [**3.8.10**]. *The Savage State* began the series at the upper left, drawing upon the conventions of the sublime landscape tradition to convey the power of nature in its untamed state. Next, below it, came *The Pastoral or Arcadian State* [**3.8.11**], a picturesque view suggestive of the benign rule of the Federalist or Jeffersonian landowner, with limited cultivation and a harmony with nature. In the middle, *Consummation* [**3.8.12**; p. 160], while seemingly calm, also suggests, in its crowded streets and the almost total absence of nature, the inevitable chaos conveyed in *Destruction* at the upper right. In the final painting, *Desolation*, the ruins of a once mighty empire give way to nature.

Each scene is shown at a different time of the day, beginning with dawn. To reinforce this passage of time, three small panels above show the rising and setting of the sun. The general locale

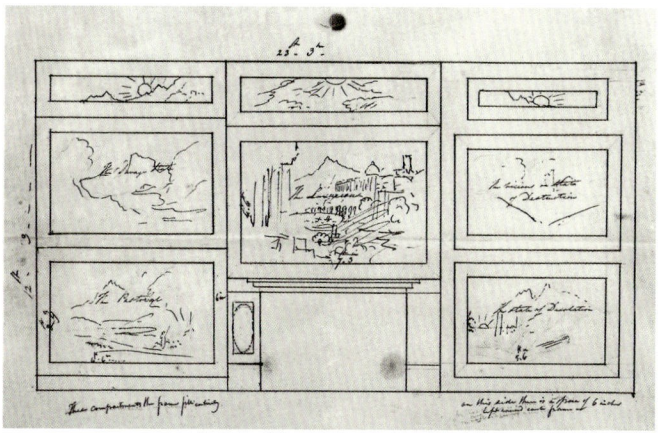

3.8.10 Thomas Cole: installation plan for *The Course of Empire*, 1833. Pen and brown ink over pencil on paper, w. 13⅛ in. (33.4 cm.) Detroit Institute of Arts, Detroit, Michigan

3.8.11 Thomas Cole: *The Course of Empire: The Pastoral or Arcadian State*, 1834. Oil on canvas, 39¼ x 63¼ in. (99.7 x 160.6 cm.) Courtesy The New-York Historical Society, New York

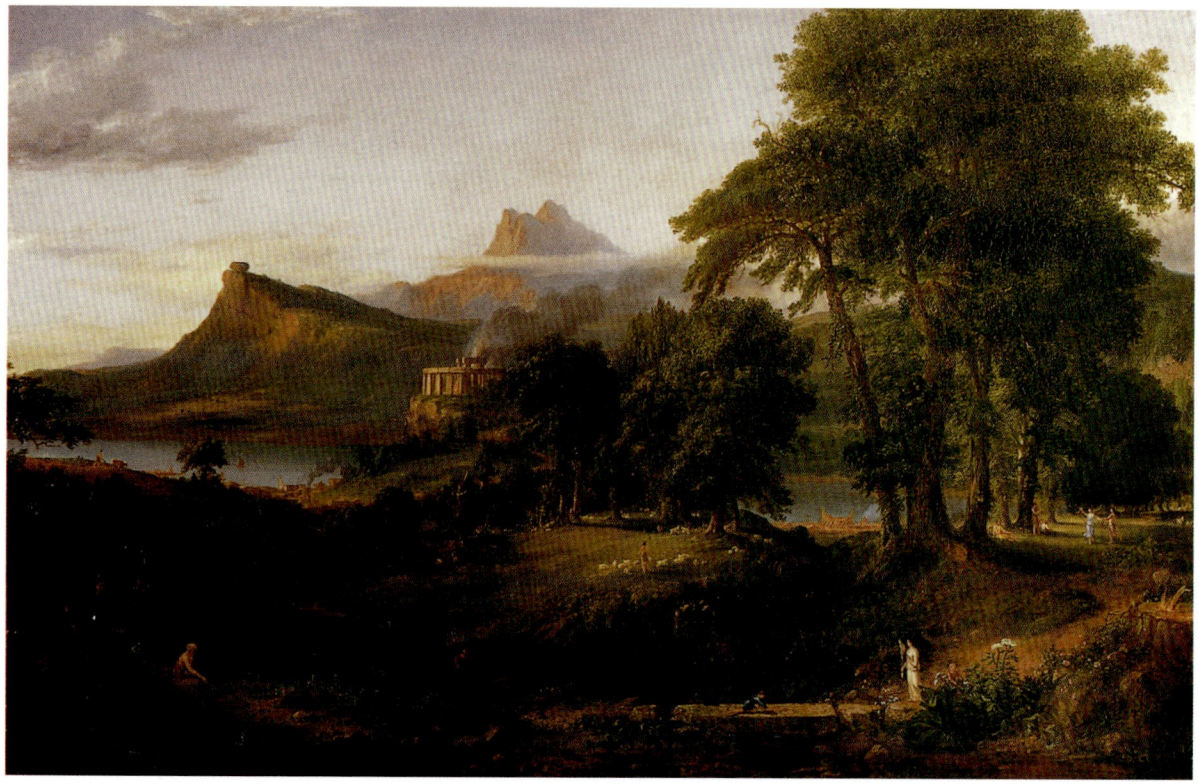

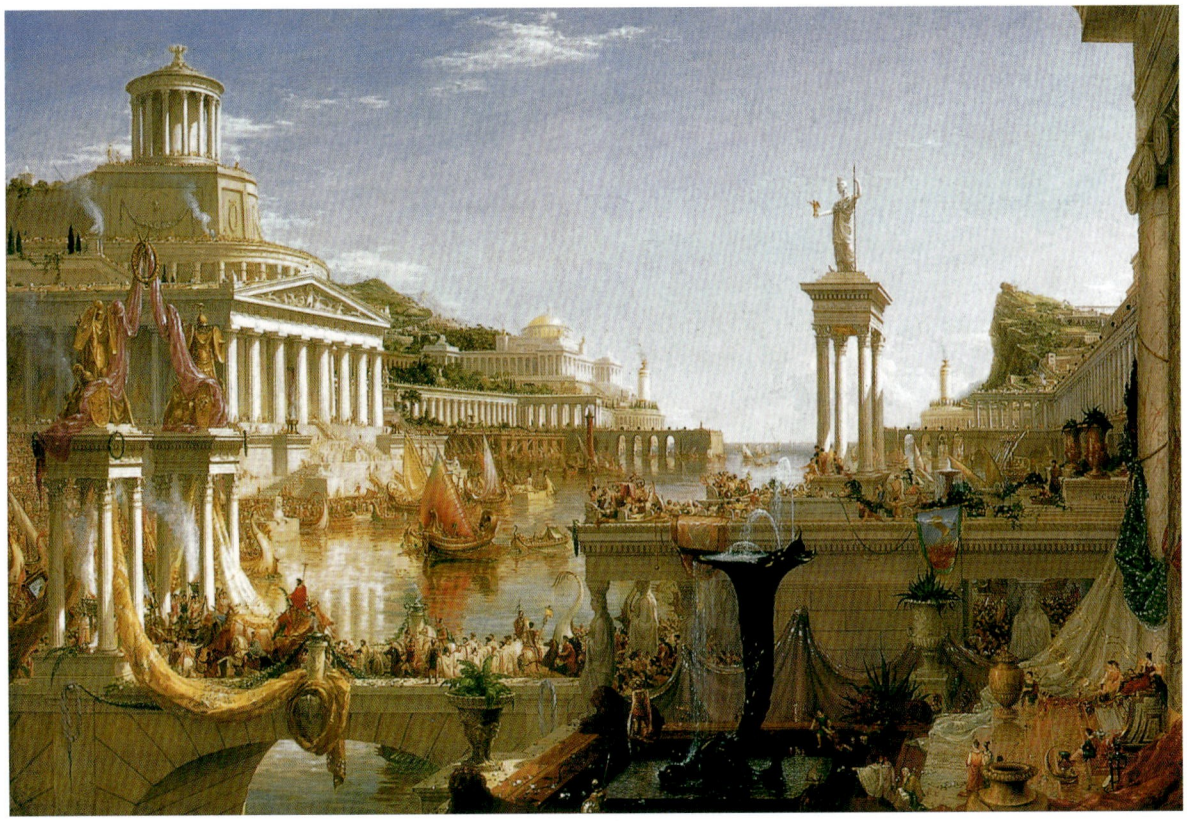

3.8.12 Thomas Cole: *The Course of Empire: Consummation*, 1835–36. Oil on canvas, 51¼ x 76 in. (130.2 x 193 cm.) Courtesy The New-York Historical Society, New York

in all five paintings is kept the same, distinguishable by the mountain in the distance. The height of civilization displayed in *Consummation* is represented through a combination of Greek and Roman architectural and cultural motifs. Despite their historical specificity, Cole, like many other artists and architects, used these classical motifs to imply that his series referred not to one specific empire but empires in general; it was a universal statement about historical inevitability. Yet some saw a more specific reference, not to ancient Greece and Rome but to contemporary America. The art historian Angela Miller writes that Cole's series would easily have been understood as a Whig allegory (the Federalists had transformed themselves into the Whig Party in the late 1830s) critical of Andrew Jackson. The Whigs believed that Jackson's "imperious and arbitrary style of leadership made him a modern-day Caesar, prepared to manipulate the citizens of the republic for his own corrupt and self-serving ends," thus setting the stage for "the triumph of faction, the concentration of power, and the rise of the corrupt imperial state."

Cole's *The Course of Empire* met with great success when exhibited in 1836. Those who wanted to see the US as an exception to this general theory of rise and fall could easily do so, arguing that democracy would prevent, rather than foster, despotism and mob rule. Not surprisingly, the series was also well received by aging Federalists, who saw their era—*The Pastoral or Arcadian State*—celebrated and their demise mourned. Yet there is a certain tragic irony, as Wallach points out, in the fact that "a self-made merchant paid a small fortune [$5,000] to a self-taught artist for paintings that elaborately mourn the passing of an aristocracy to which both merchant and artist aspired and to which neither could ever belong."

While Reed might be able to match the wealth of the Federalist elite, he could never challenge its cultural authority. And although Cole achieved a reputation as America's foremost landscape painter, he found only the occasional sympathetic patron, such as Reed, to support his grander artistic schemes. Despite his reputation as a landscapist, Cole longed to succeed as a history painter, admired as much in Europe as the US. At the end of his life he issued a lament that could well have come from the pen of Samuel F. B. Morse (1791–1872) or any number of other early nineteenth-century American artists: "I am not the artist I should have been, had taste been higher. For instead of indulging myself in the production of works such as my feelings and fancy would have chosen—in order to exist I have painted to please others."

Successors to Cole

Thomas Cole's untimely death in 1848 was met with much mourning and praise of his talent and genius. It also prompted speculation as to who would succeed him as the leader of American landscape painting. Several candidates identified themselves by producing of memorials to Cole. In 1849 Asher B. Durand (1796–1886) exhibited *Kindred Spirits* [**3.8.13**], which had been commissioned by Jonathan Sturges, the business partner of Luman Reed. In this work Cole, on the right, surveys the Catskill Mountains with his friend and fellow nature-lover the poet William Cullen Bryant (Sturges presented the painting to Bryant as a gift). Bryant had delivered the eulogy at Cole's funeral and had highlighted the significance of the Catskills in the painter's life and art: "To us who remain, the region of the Catskills, where [Cole] wandered and studied and sketched and wrought his sketches into such glorious creations, is saddened by a certain desolate feeling when we behold it or think of it."

As the president of the National Academy of Design, Durand seemed the logical choice to succeed Cole. Having begun his career as an engraver, he had turned to painting in the mid-1830s and had soon risen to prominence among landscape artists on the East Coast. Yet he was challenged by several younger artists, including Jasper F. Cropsey (1823–1900). Cropsey's *Ideal Landscape: Homage to Thomas Cole* (1850) [**3.8.14**] appeared two years after Cole's death. It presents the landscape as an ideal or holy place, the site of God's glory as captured through the eye and skill of the prophet/painter. This focus on art as a moral force was reiterated in 1851 by the Reverend Samuel Osgood who, in commenting on the virtues of landscape painting, made a toast to "Art, the Interpreter of Nature; Nature, the Interpreter of God."

Cropsey continued to produce moralizing historical landscapes similar to those of Cole's later years. For example, his *The Millennial Age* of 1854 [**3.8.15**], with its luminous cross positioned just below the carved lion on a classical altar, presents the triumph of Christianity over the forces of paganism. Cole's celebrations of Christian progress were praised, yet Cropsey's works did not receive the same positive reviews. Many were troubled

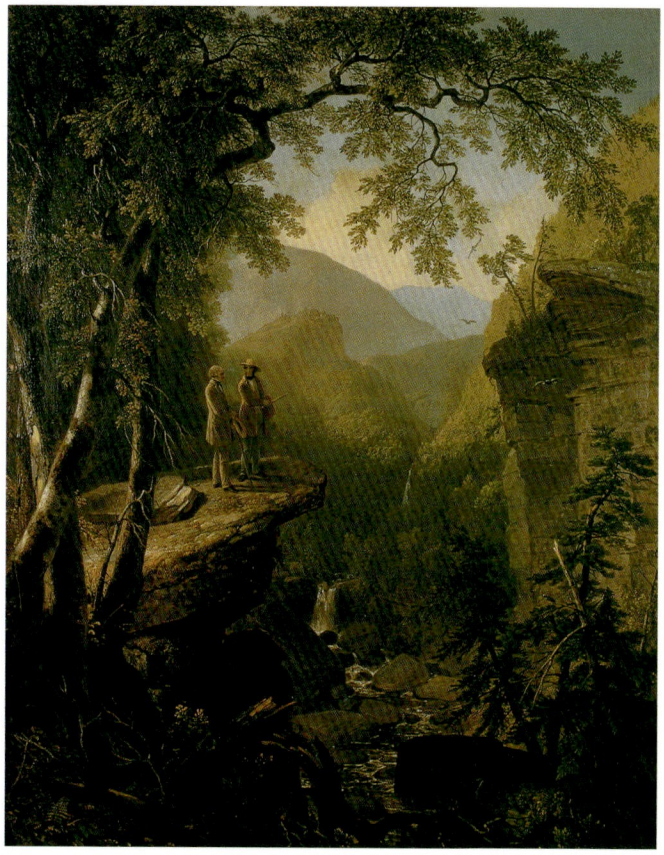

3.8.13 Asher B. Durand: *Kindred Spirits*, 1849.
Oil on canvas, 44 x 36 in. (111.8 x 91.4 cm.)
Crystal Bridges Museum of American Art, Bentonville, Arkansas

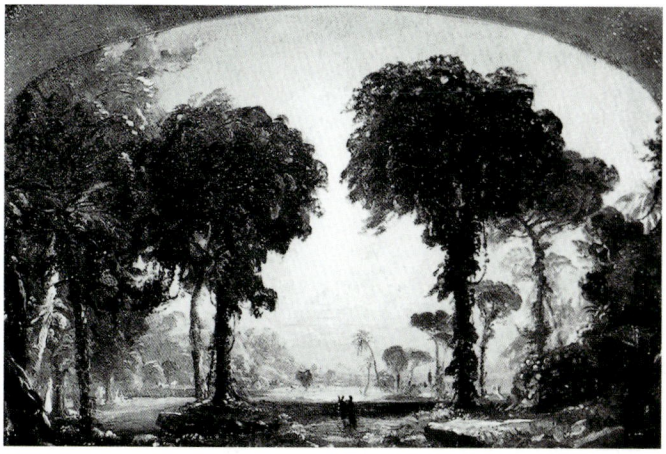

3.8.14 Jasper F. Cropsey: *Ideal Landscape: Homage to Thomas Cole*, 1850.
Oil on canvas, 8⅛ x 12¼ in. (20.7 x 31 cm.)
Thyssen-Bornemisza Foundation, Lugano, Switzerland

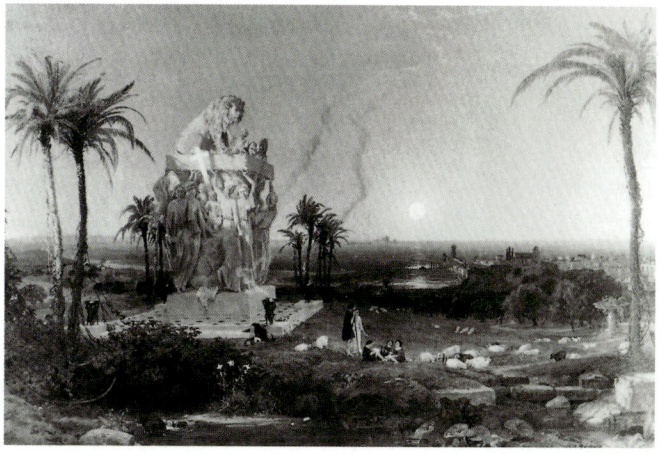

3.8.15 Jasper F. Cropsey: *The Millennial Age*, 1854.
Oil on canvas, 38 x 54 in. (96.5 x 137.2 cm.)
Newington-Cropsey Foundation, Hastings on Hudson, New York

by his reliance on the older artist, evident in *The Millennial Age* in the cross, taken from Cole's last series, *The Cross and the World* (left incomplete at his death), and the allusions to *The Pastoral or Arcadian State* [**3.8.11**; p. 159] from *The Course of Empire* series. In 1852, a critic for the *Literary World* wrote:

> Cropsey is commonly considered an imitator of Cole....That he willfully imitates Cole we do not think; but that he has been influenced by him to too great a degree is evident, and to a greater extent than is consistent with his own originality.

Even Cole's own historical work was coming under attack by the mid-1850s, with one critic noting in 1856 that the "office of painting is with the visible world" and that "the success of [Cole's] allegories, generally, has been as injurious to the ideal of Art, as instrumental to his own success in life." Painters should focus on recording the visible world rather than making art "the servant either of ethics or theology." This view was also being promoted by the contemporary British art critic John Ruskin, whose writings would become influential in the US in the second half of the nineteenth century (see p. 300).

Some artists, including Robert S. Duncanson (1821–1872), continued to champion Cole's more fantastical historical landscapes while at the same time attending to the close recording of the American landscape seen in Cole's earlier works. Duncanson was born in New York State into a family of free African Americans whose primary trades were house-painting and carpentry. After moving to Monroe, Michigan with his family in the late 1820s, he worked briefly as a house- and sign-painter before moving again, around 1840, to Mount Healthy, a small town north of Cincinnati, to embark on a career as an artist (he settled in Cincinnati itself in 1850; see pp. 184–85).

As did others before him, Duncanson began with portraits, executing the likenesses of the members of wealthy families in both Cincinnati and Detroit and of various political notables, including Lewis Cass, Michigan's abolitionist senator, and James G. Birney, editor of the abolitionist newspaper *The Philanthropist*. Nicolas Longsworth, a Cincinnati lawyer, provided Duncanson with his first major landscape commission in 1848: requested

3.8.16 Robert S. Duncanson: *Blue Hole, Little Miami River*, 1851. Oil on canvas, 29¼ x 42¼ in. (74.3 x 107.3 cm.) Cincinnati Art Museum, Cincinnati, Ohio

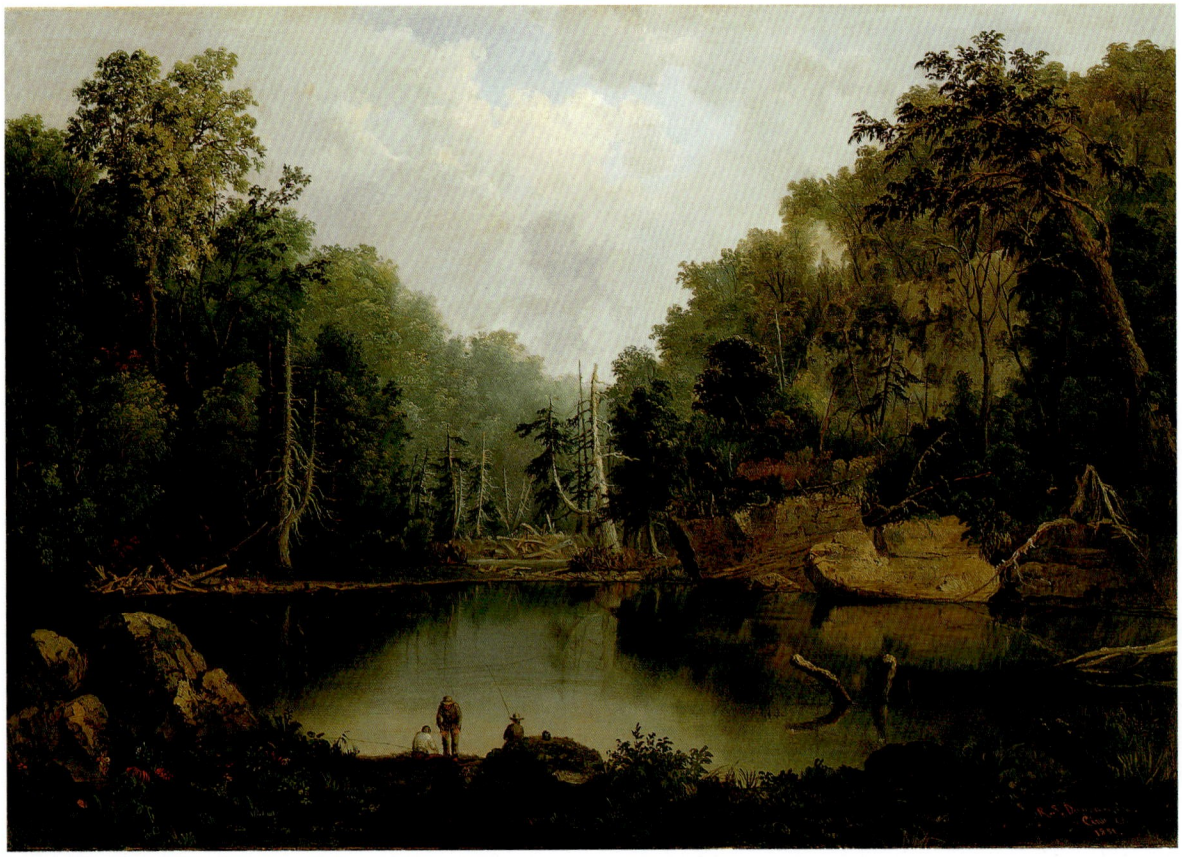

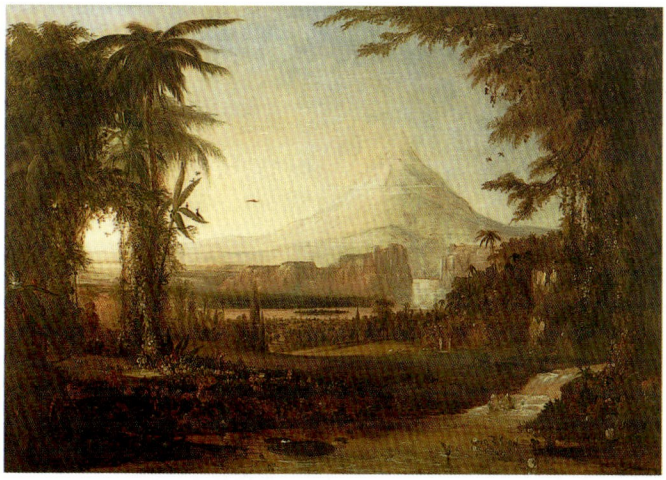

3.8.17 Robert S. Duncanson: *The Garden of Eden*, 1852.
Oil on canvas, 32¾ x 48 in. (83 x 121.9 cm.)
West Foundation, on loan to the High Museum of Art, Atlanta, Georgia

to paint a series of eight "wall decorations" for Longsworth's mansion (now the Taft Museum), he produced a series of idealized landscapes (classical pastoral scenes, picturesque rural landscapes) heavily indebted to the work of the French painter Claude Lorrain. Subsequently, however, he turned to the particularities of the American scene, as in *Blue Hole, Little Miami River* of 1851 [**3.8.16**], a painting more in keeping with Cole's wilderness landscapes. Cole's influence on Duncanson in the realm of historical or biblical landscapes is also clearly evident in *The Garden of Eden* of 1852 [**3.8.17**], which was based on a print of Cole's own painting (1828) of the same name.

Edward Hicks and The Peaceable Kingdom

The artist who most consistently situated a biblical narrative within an American landscape was Edward Hicks (1780–1849), a Quaker minister and sign-painter from Bucks County, Pennsylvania. The Quakers, or Society of Friends, like many other Protestant sects, did not encourage the arts. Prohibitions against music, dancing, and theater were clearly written down. Yet there seem to have been no written proscriptions against painting or drawing. Thus, while Hicks was visited on at least one occasion by a committee of Quakers who protested his public defense of art, there was no formal attempt to prevent him from painting. The art historian Eleanore Price Mather observes that Hicks's initial painterly efforts would have been considered craft rather than art, and thus a useful, and therefore acceptable, activity. The Quaker respect for craft resulted in the presence of many skilled potters, silversmiths, cabinetmakers, and needleworkers in Quaker communities across America.

Hicks was born to Anglican parents, but his mother died when he was only eighteen months old and he was raised by a Quaker friend of hers. He began work as a coach- and sign-painter, and did not convert to Quakerism until his early twenties, by which time he had tasted the pleasures not only of painting, but also of music, dancing, and theater. In 1812 he was recognized as having a special gift for voicing the Inner Light, or Holy Spirit, and was accorded the title of minister. As such, he joined other ministers in local meetings and traveled to neighboring towns carrying the word of Truth.

Hicks was certainly aware of the potential conflicts between his role as a Quaker minister, with its commitment to sobriety and simplicity, and his activities as a painter of colorful commercial coaches and signs. He briefly gave up painting in the 1810s in favor of farming, but his agricultural skills left much to be desired, and he soon returned to the painting that he loved. What allowed Hicks to take up his former profession without any pangs of conscience was his discovery of the theme of "the Peaceable Kingdom" in a Bible engraving after the British artist Richard Westall (1765–1836) [**3.8.18**]. This illustrates the sixth verse of the eleventh chapter of Isaiah: "The wolf also shall dwell with the lamb, and the leopard shall lie down with the kid; and the calf and the young lion and the fatling together: and a little child shall lead them." Mather posits that Hicks may have been drawn to this theme by his love of children, animals,

3.8.18 Charles Heath after Richard Westall: *The Peaceable Kingdom of the Branch Engraving in The Holy Bible* (London, 1815).
Free Library of Philadelphia, Philadelphia, Pennsylvania

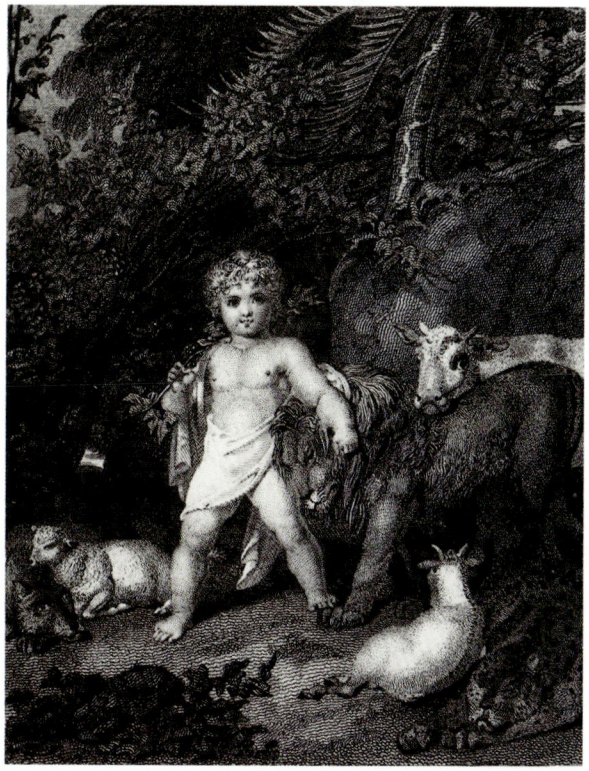

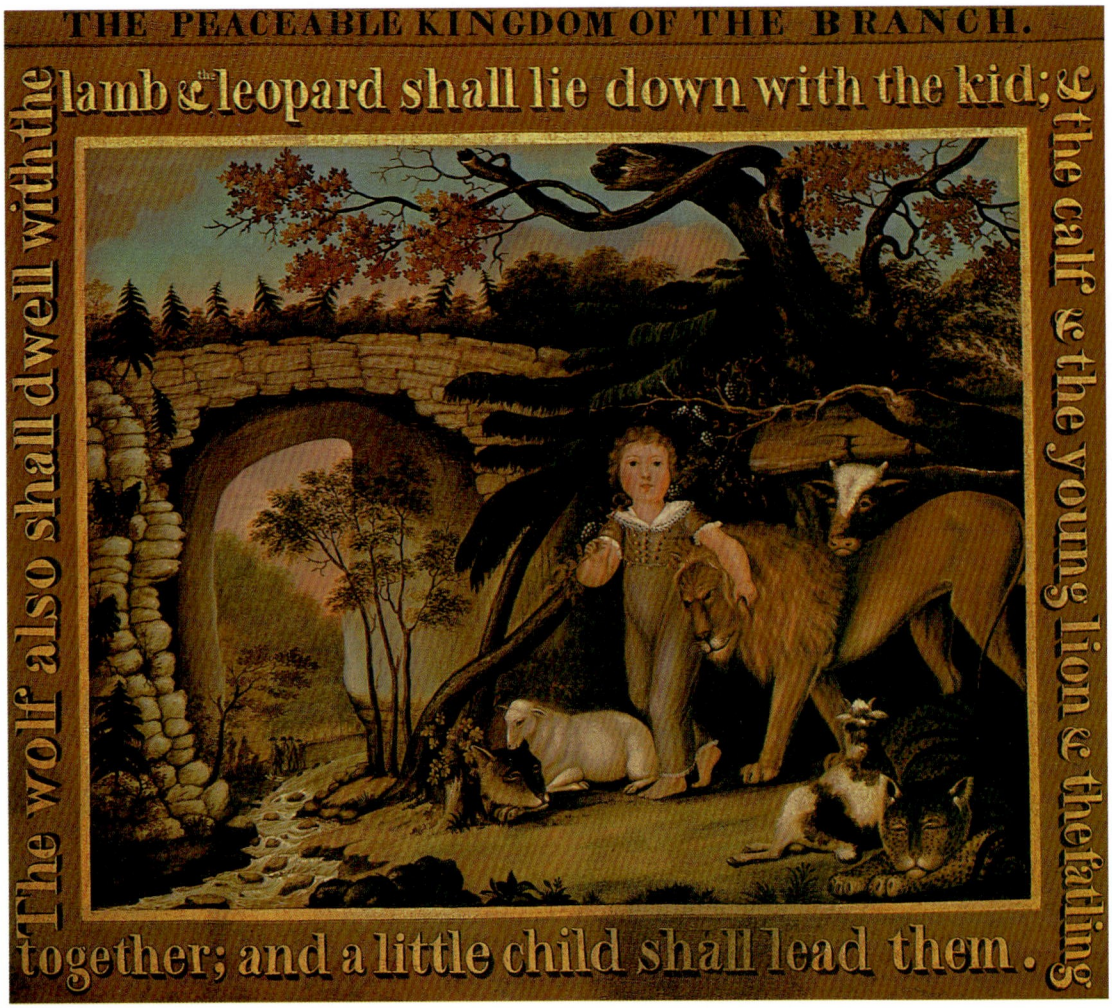

3.8.19 Edward Hicks: *The Peaceable Kingdom of the Branch*, c. 1825–30.
Oil on canvas, 32¼ x 37¾ in. (81.9 x 95.9 cm.)
Abby Aldrich Rockefeller Folk Art Center, Williamsburg, Virginia

3.8.20 Vignette from *A Map of North America* by Henry S. Tanner, Philadelphia, 1822.
Library of Congress, Washington, D.C.

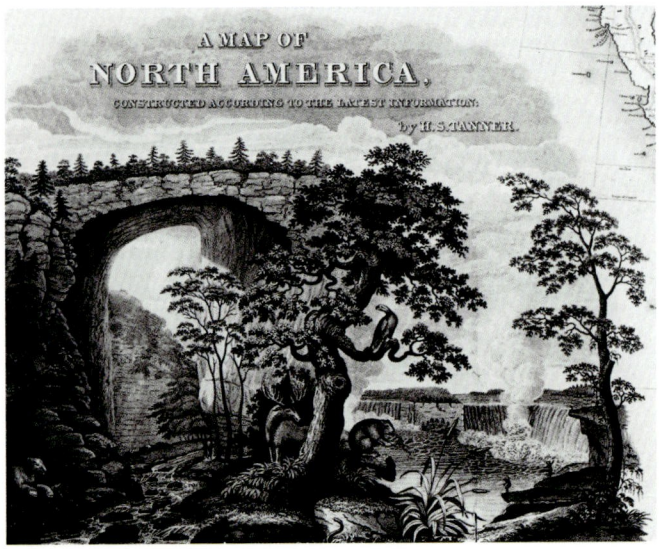

3.8.21 Germantown Print Works: handkerchief with motif after an engraving by John Hall of Benjamin West's *William Penn's Treaty with the Indians* (detail), 1824.
Printed linen, w. 14½ in. (36.8 cm.)
Swarthmore College Peace Collection, Swarthmore, Pennsylvania

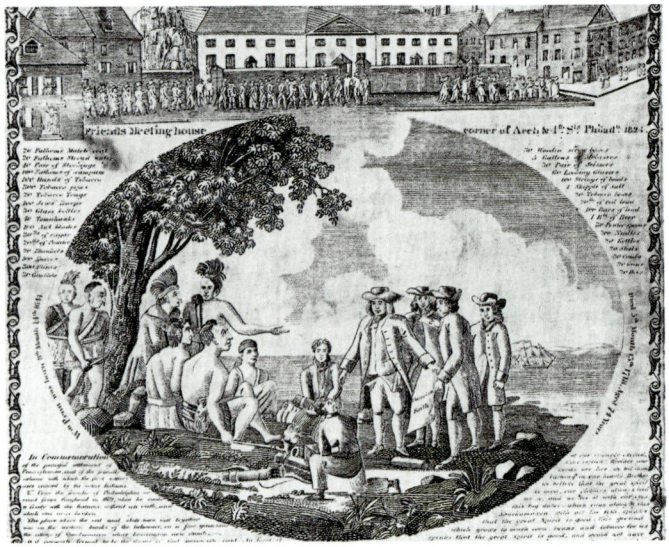

and the Scriptures themselves. Or he simply may have "correctly perceived in the biblical engraving a sermon on salvation that would justify the pictorial work he inwardly craved." The appropriateness of his choice of subject matter is attested to by the fact that many of his paintings were purchased by fellow Quakers.

In one of his first paintings on this theme, *Peaceable Kingdom of the Branch* (*c.* 1825–30) [**3.8.19**], Hicks added to Westall's general grouping of figures a distinctly American setting. At the left is the Natural Bridge of Virginia, taken from a vignette on a popular map of 1822 by Henry S. Tanner [**3.8.20**]. Below its arch is the central group of figures in Benjamin West's *Penn's Treaty with the Indians* [**1.4.32**; p. 85], with the positions of the Quakers and the Native Americans reversed. Hicks may have seen an engraving of the painting, or perhaps a version of it on a printed linen handkerchief [**3.8.21**] manufactured by the Germantown Print Works in 1824. Hicks was thus in agreement with at least one well-known academic artist, Samuel F. B. Morse, in situating the impending millennium on American soil. His inclusion of William Penn is an obvious tribute to the Quaker leader and his attempts to initiate a more immediate and pragmatic peace on earth in America through treaties with its indigenous peoples. The child in this early *Peaceable Kingdom* carries a grape branch (hence, the title of the work), a symbol of the redemptive blood of Christ. The painting also includes a border with the title of the painting at the top in black and the verse from Isaiah rendered in gold lettering. Such narrative borders appear in many of Hicks's paintings and recall his early practice as a sign-painter, where image and text were often combined. They also reinforce his role as a Quaker minister, where the word, rather than the image, carried ultimate authority.

Over the course of some thirty years Hicks painted many *Peaceable Kingdoms*, at least sixty of which have survived. In tracing the changes in these paintings, Mather argues that they address "the nature of man and his relation to the Divine," as well as Hicks's own inner conflicts and the growing divisions within the ranks of Quakers as a whole. The community suffered a serious split in the 1820s between the Orthodox Quakers, who promoted a greater reliance on a "correct" interpretation of biblical texts and increased attention to the life and death of Christ, and the Hicksites, who resisted such a move in favor of an emphasis on individual revelation, or the Inner Light, as one's primary spiritual guide. One of the most famous leaders of the latter group was Edward's cousin Elias Hicks, whose name became synonymous with rebellion against the Orthodox. While Edward allied himself with Elias, he had misgivings about the severity of some of his cousin's pronouncements and regretted the split in the Quaker community, which was finalized on April 21, 1827 at the Philadelphia Yearly Meeting.

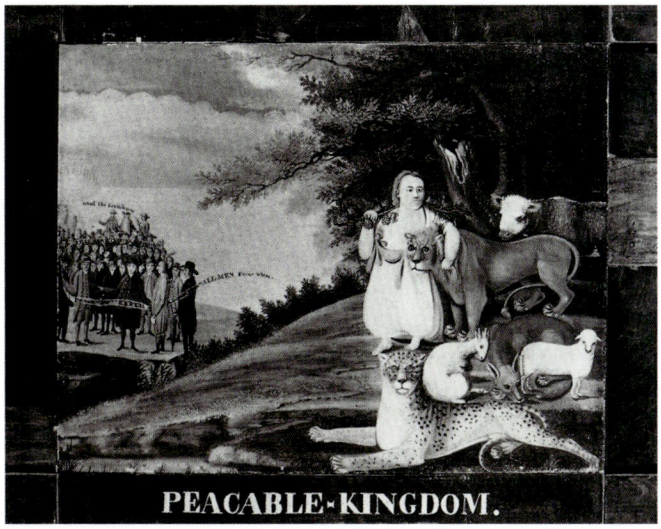

3.8.22 Edward Hicks: *Peaceable Kingdom with Quakers Bearing Banners*, *c.* 1827–32.
Oil on canvas, 17¾ x 23¾ in. (45.1 x 60.3 cm.)
Holger Cahill Collection, New York; on extended loan to Smith College, Northampton, Massachusetts

Some time between 1827 and 1832 Hicks painted the first of a series of *Peaceable Kingdoms* in which a pyramid of Quakers replaces the scene of Penn and the Indians [**3.8.22**]. These works, with their harsh landscapes and worried looks on the faces of the animals, are direct references to the Separation of 1827. The banner weaving through the Quakers includes the Hicksite doctrine—"Mind the light within"—and the angel song from the Gospel of Luke announcing the birth of Christ—"it is glad tideing [sic] of Grate [sic] Joy peace on earth good will to all men Everywhere." Elias Hicks is shown hatless in profile at the front of the group, with the banner circling behind him; at the apex are, right to left, George Fox, the founder of Quakerism, Penn, and Robert Barclay, theological defender of Quakerism.

In subsequent *Peaceable Kingdoms*, Hicks would convey his alliance with the Hicksites in more subtle terms. The pyramid of Quakers disappears, and is replaced once again by Penn and the Indians, larger than ever and located not beneath the Natural Bridge of Virginia but in front of a view of the Delaware River. Elias Hicks's promotion of the doctrine of the Inner Light is expressed in these paintings by the absence of the grape branch, symbol of Christ's death on the Cross, which had appeared in the child's right hand in earlier versions of the scene. Hick's original inclusion of the grapes may have been due more to his copying of the Westall engraving than to any particular doctrinal concern. But in the midst of the Quaker controversy, grapes and what they symbolized took on a new meaning. They stood for "the blood of Christ," a phrase that, during the split, had become a badge of Orthodoxy.

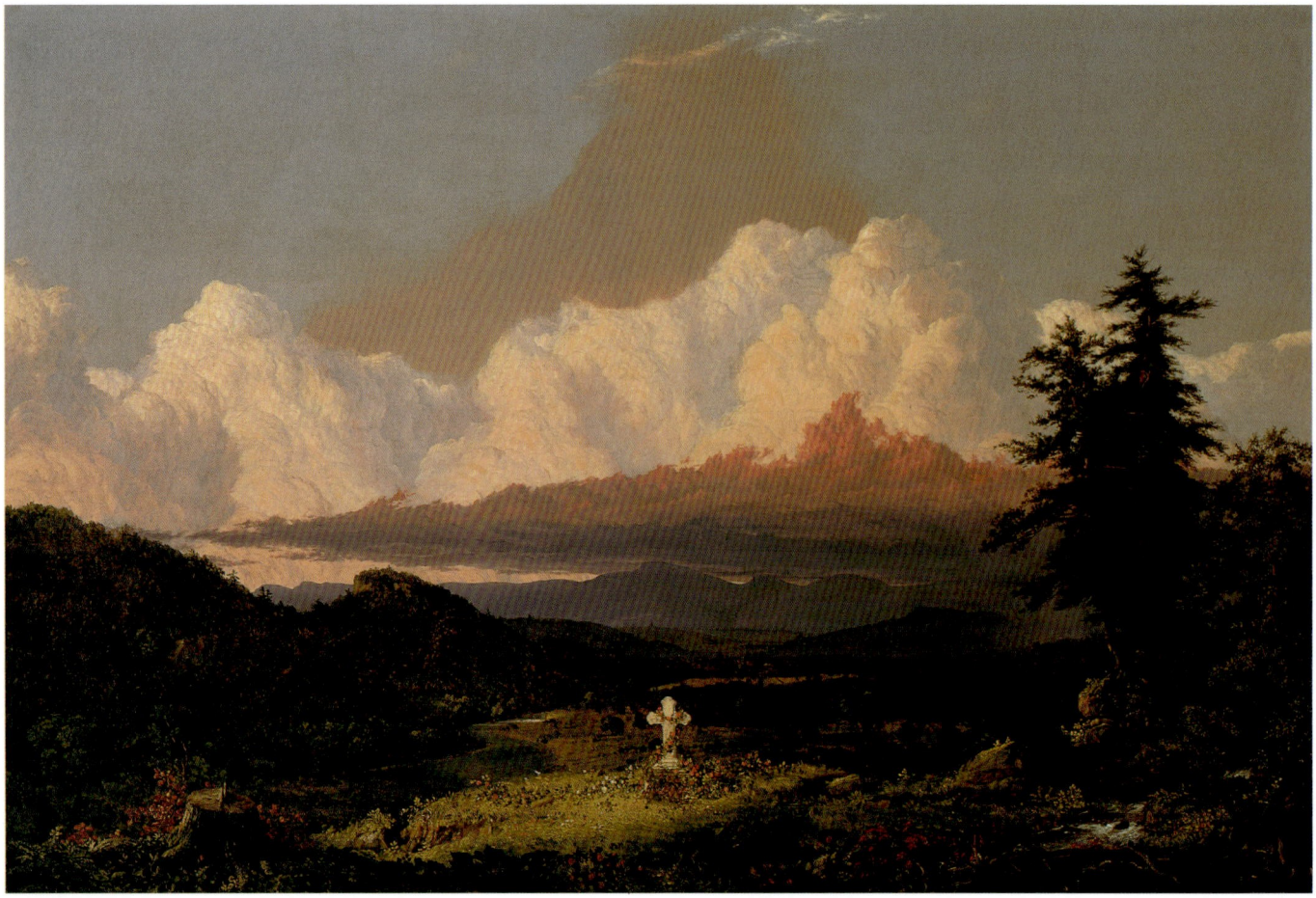

3.8.23 Frederic Edwin Church: *To the Memory of Cole*, 1848. Oil on canvas, 32 x 49½ in. (81.3 x 125.7 cm.) Courtesy Sotheby's, London

Frederic Edwin Church: From the Pastoral to the Sublime

In 1848, the year of Thomas Cole's death, another young landscape painter, Frederic Edwin Church (1826–1900), produced a tribute entitled *To the Memory of Cole* [**3.8.23**]. While Church, like Jasper F. Cropsey [**3.8.14**; p. 161], presents the landscape as an ideal or holy place, he also includes mountains in the background that are recognizable as the Catskills. Church may well have been the true successor of Cole. He not only created a series of early works that emulated Cole's historical landscapes, such as *Hooker and Company Journeying through the Wilderness from Plymouth to Hartford, in 1636* (1846), but he also, and more importantly, continued Cole's deliberate attempts, according to the art historian Franklin Kelly, "to infuse realistic landscape with deep and profound content." In so doing, he brought together, in a way Cole was never able to, science and religion, the real and the ideal.

Church came from the kind of background to which Cole aspired. The son of a wealthy and influential family in Hartford, Connecticut, he had access to whatever was needed to achieve his desired goal—to become a great landscape painter. Having overcome his father's initial resistance to his chosen profession, he gained unprecedented access to the master himself, becoming Cole's first and only pupil in 1844, for which his father paid the considerable sum of $600. Church was a quick pupil, exhibiting his first works at the National Academy of Design in 1846.

In his paintings of the late 1840s and early 1850s Church focused on the pastoral vistas of Cole's *Arcadian State* [**3.8.11**; p. 159]. Yet Church was not depicting the picturesque as a memorial to a past era. While certainly aware of Cole's mixed feelings regarding the effects of human industry on the landscape, he opted for a more celebratory presentation of the picturesque, of nature as altered by civilization. In his *New England Scenery* of 1851 [**3.8.24**] he includes the requisite cultivated fields and small town with church spire, but also a saw mill, a sign of the clearing of the land and the utilization of new technology in the process. His inclusion of saw mills rather than the more traditional grist mills in several of his landscapes may well have been due to his own family's financial investments in the products of the forest (his father and uncle owned a paper mill and had interests in other mills). Saw mills also signified a more positive view of the clearing of the land than tree stumps, often included in the foreground of landscape paintings to indicate an ambiguous attitude toward the arrival of civilization [**3.9.18**; p. 185].

New England Scenery was different from Church's earlier topographical landscapes in that it did not record a specific site. Rather, it was a compilation of many different scenes, brought together in order to make a broader statement. It was, in Kelly's words, "an ideal of what New England—and, by extension, the nation—should be." It moved from a mere record of the details of reality to a thoughtful and consciously manipulated image of reality, a manipulation that moved the painting, in the minds of contemporary art critics, into a higher category of art. Its symbolism placed it in the realm of Cole's historical landscapes, except that biblical narratives are replaced by an account of everyday life in America. The bridge and road indicate the expansion of transportation networks, the mill technology, the cleared fields agriculture, and the church religion. There is a harmonious balance between humans and nature. The Conestoga wagon in the foreground symbolizes the export of these industrious New Englanders and their political, religious, and economic ideals westward across the Great Plains and beyond.

In the middle of the 1850s Church's work began to shift from the pastoral landscape to the dramatic wilderness, from the picturesque to the sublime. This shift was prompted in part by a trip to South America with his friend Cyrus Field. Field was interested in exploring the commercial possibilities of this new territory and welcomed the painter along as both companion and recorder of the landscape. Church's interest in South America had already been piqued by the writings of the German naturalist Alexander von Humboldt, in particular his multivolume treatise on science and nature, *Cosmos*, the first volumes of which became available in the US in the late 1840s. In writing of the different climate zones throughout the world, Humboldt displayed his widespread knowledge of geology, botany, chemistry, archaeology, geography, mathematics, metallurgy, and landscape painting. In a chapter on the latter he praised the art for its ability to reveal "the external world in all its rich variety of forms" and also to take these forms and transform them, through an "inward process of mind," into something more than a simple record of facts—into, instead, "heroic landscape painting." That Church had already engaged in such a transformation with his *New England Scenery* shows the extent to which he empathized with Humboldt's thinking. Now he was to try his hand at a similar synthesis in new territory—South America.

3.8.24 Frederic Edwin Church: *New England Scenery*, 1851.
Oil on canvas, 36 x 53 in. (102 x 145 cm.)
George Walter Vincent Smith Art Museum, Springfield, Massachusetts

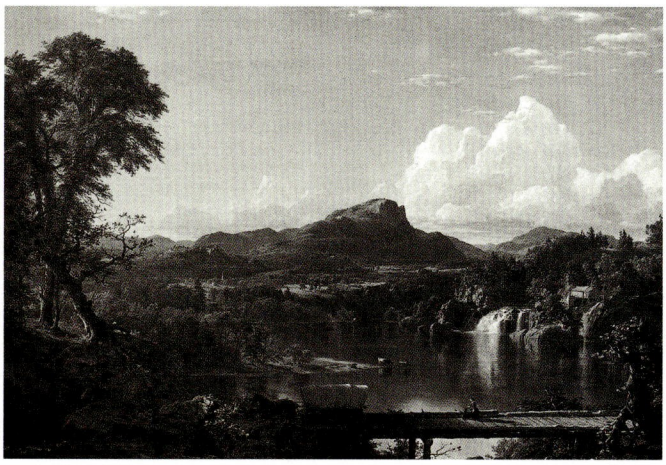

Church spent six months traveling with Field and made extensive sketches and notes. The first canvases he produced upon his return to the US drew on the same pastoral formula he had used in his New England landscapes, with palm trees replacing elm trees. In the mid-1850s, however, he moved away from pastoral scenes and began a long series of dramatic images that were dominated not by the marks of civilization and progress, but by the features of rugged, vast, and largely uninhabited lands.

Church was not the only one turning his attention to uninhabited lands. By the mid-1850s many intellectuals on the East Coast were calling for the preservation not of the picturesque but of America's disappearing wilderness. In 1853 the writer Henry David Thoreau issued a call for "national preserves...not for our own idle sport or food, but for inspiration and our own true recreation." Two years later Asher B. Durand wrote in the newly founded journal *The Crayon* that instead of focusing on foreign subject matter aspiring painters should concentrate on

> the "lone and tranquil" lakes embosomed in ancient forests, that abound in our wild districts, the unshorn mountains surrounding them with their richly textured covering, the ocean prairies of the West, and many other forms of Nature yet spared from the pollutions of civilization.

In 1858 New York City began construction of Central Park in recognition of the belief that access to nature was morally uplifting. At the same time, Frederick Law Olmsted, the park's designer, pushed forward with his campaign to create a series of national parks to preserve the most spectacular and sublime of the nation's wilderness areas (see pp. 295–96). Church appears to have shared the concerns of Thoreau and Olmsted, and heeded Durand's call for the depiction of nature "spared from the pollutions of civilization."

Church made a second trip to South America in 1857, spending all of his time in Ecuador. Two years later he produced *The Heart of the Andes* [**3.8.25**], the sublime equivalent to his picturesque *New England Scenery* [**3.8.24**; p. 167]. Like that work, *The Heart of the Andes* records no single location, but a composite of elements intended to represent the essence of South America, its geography and climate. While, as in *New England Scenery*, there is evidence of human presence (the small figures located next to the cross in the foreground, a village in the middle distance), this presence is overwhelmed by the overarching drama of the mountains, forests, and river. Unlike in *New England Scenery,* transportation networks and technology had yet to open this vast territory to large-scale settlement and commercial exploitation, although, as Cyrus Field understood, there was great potential for such exploitation.

With this painting Church also entered into a new, more entrepreneurial phase of exhibiting his work. He did not show the 10-foot- (3-meter-) wide canvas at the National Academy of Design, as he had previous works. Instead, he followed the example of earlier painters of large-scale canvases (see p. 132), and exhibited *The Heart of the Andes* on its own as a paid-entrance attraction. By displaying the painting in a darkened room surrounded by tropical plants, Church was able to heighten its dramatic effect and attract increased public attention.

Perhaps Durand's call to paint national rather than foreign locales also prompted Church to create two of his best-known images of the American wilderness, *Niagara* (1857) and *Twilight in the Wilderness* (1860). In his depiction of Niagara Falls [**3.8.26**], Church departs from the conventions utilized by both John Trumbull and Thomas Cole. He provides no stable, cultivated ground upon which to stroll, or high cliff from which to gaze upon the falls in the distance. Rather, the viewer appears to be literally standing in the falls, or precipitously perched on their edge, the driftwood in the foreground about to be carried over suggesting the fate of anyone who takes a wrong step. This sense of imminent danger serves to heighten the experience of the sublime. The painting was also read, like the works of Trumbull and Cole, as a symbol of nationhood and of the unlimited power of American empire. That Church painted the view from just above Table Rock overlooking Horseshoe Falls on the Canadian side did not interfere with such a reading. Church's works had already been consistently interpreted in a nationalistic light, and would continue to be seen this way, even when the landscapes, as in this case, depicted foreign locales. *Niagara* toured successfully in both the US and Britain, gaining the approval of the British critic John Ruskin.

3.8.25 Frederic Edwin Church: *The Heart of the Andes*, 1859.
Oil on canvas, 66⅝ x 119¼ in. (168 x 303 cm.)
The Metropolitan Museum of Art, New York

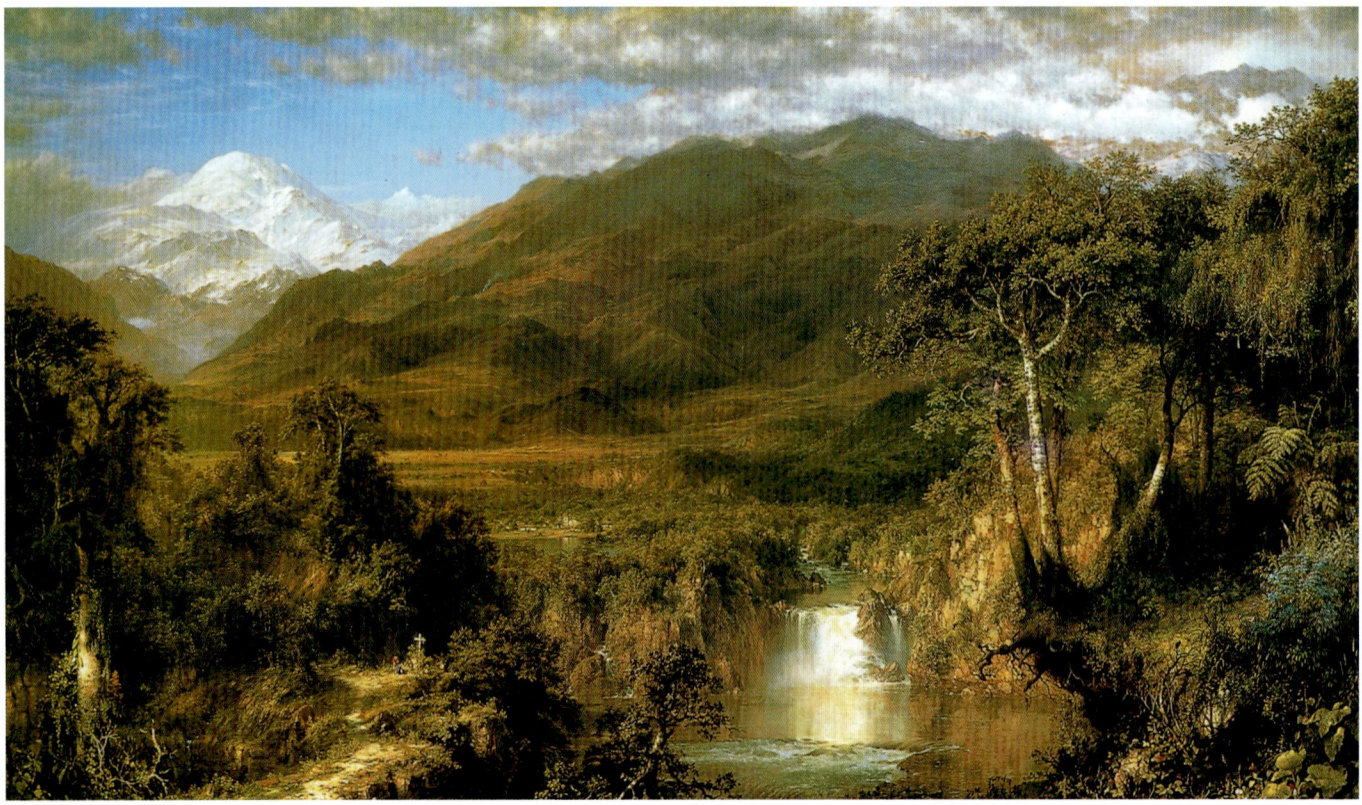

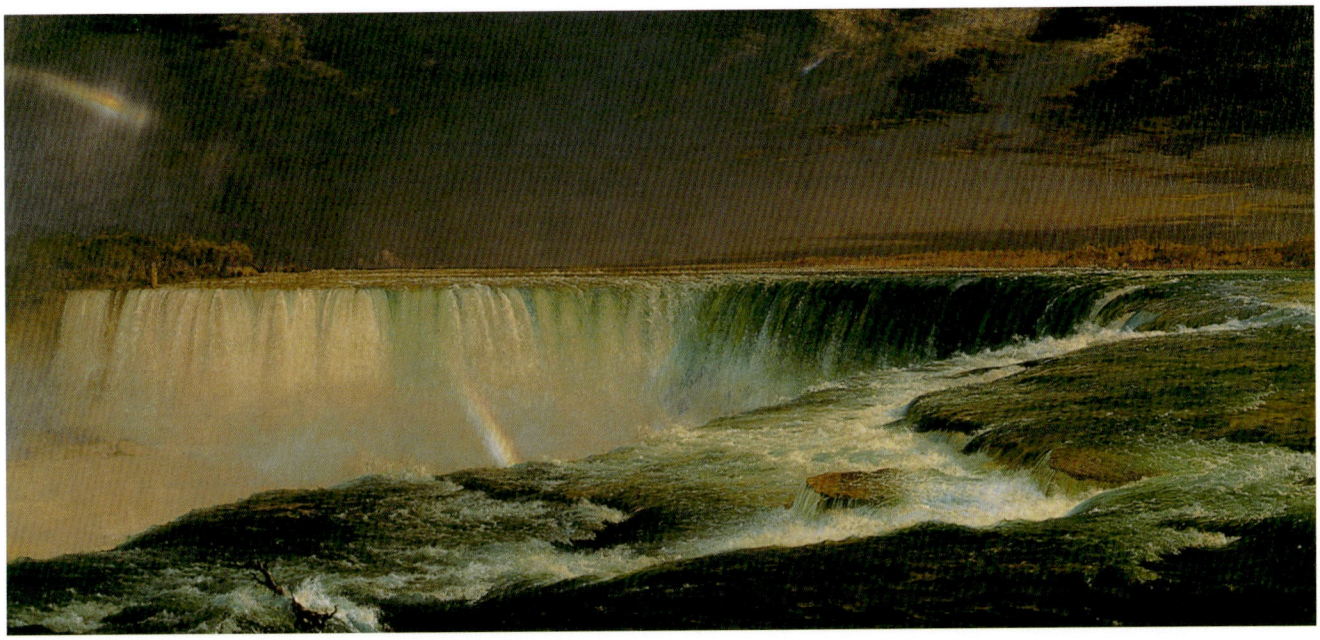

In *Twilight in the Wilderness* [**3.8.27**], Church has banished all evidence of human habitation. In addition, rather than the bright sunlight of midday, he has portrayed a brilliant autumn sunset. Read symbolically, Kelly suggests, this is not an optimistic vision of the future of the nation, but a more troubled image of uncertain times ahead, particularly in the western regions where the sun is setting. Increased expansion westward had

3.8.26 Frederic Edwin Church: *Niagara*, 1857.
Oil on canvas, 42¼ x 90½ in. (107.3 x 229.9 cm.)
Corcoran Collection, National Gallery of Art, Washington, D.C.

3.8.27 Frederic Edwin Church: *Twilight in the Wilderness*, 1860.
Oil on canvas, 40 x 64 in. (101.6 x 162.6 cm.)
Cleveland Museum of Art, Cleveland, Ohio

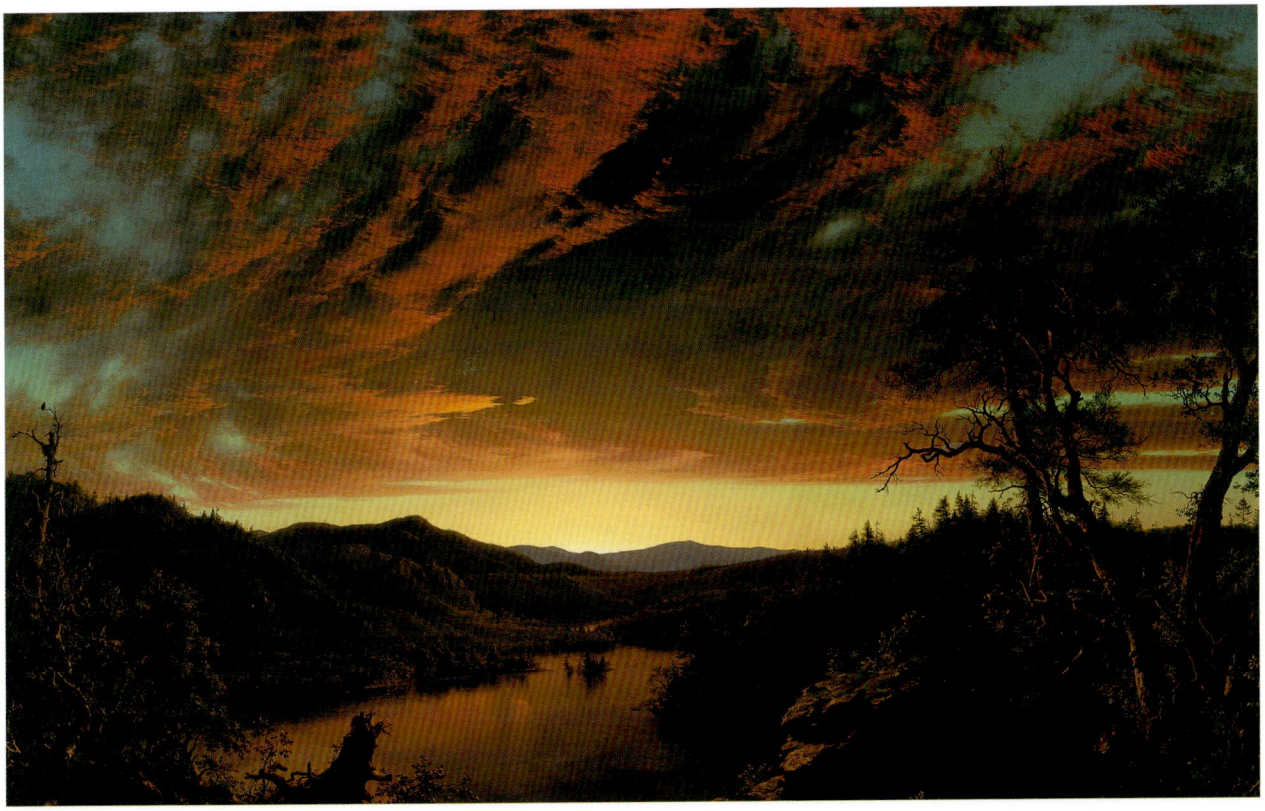

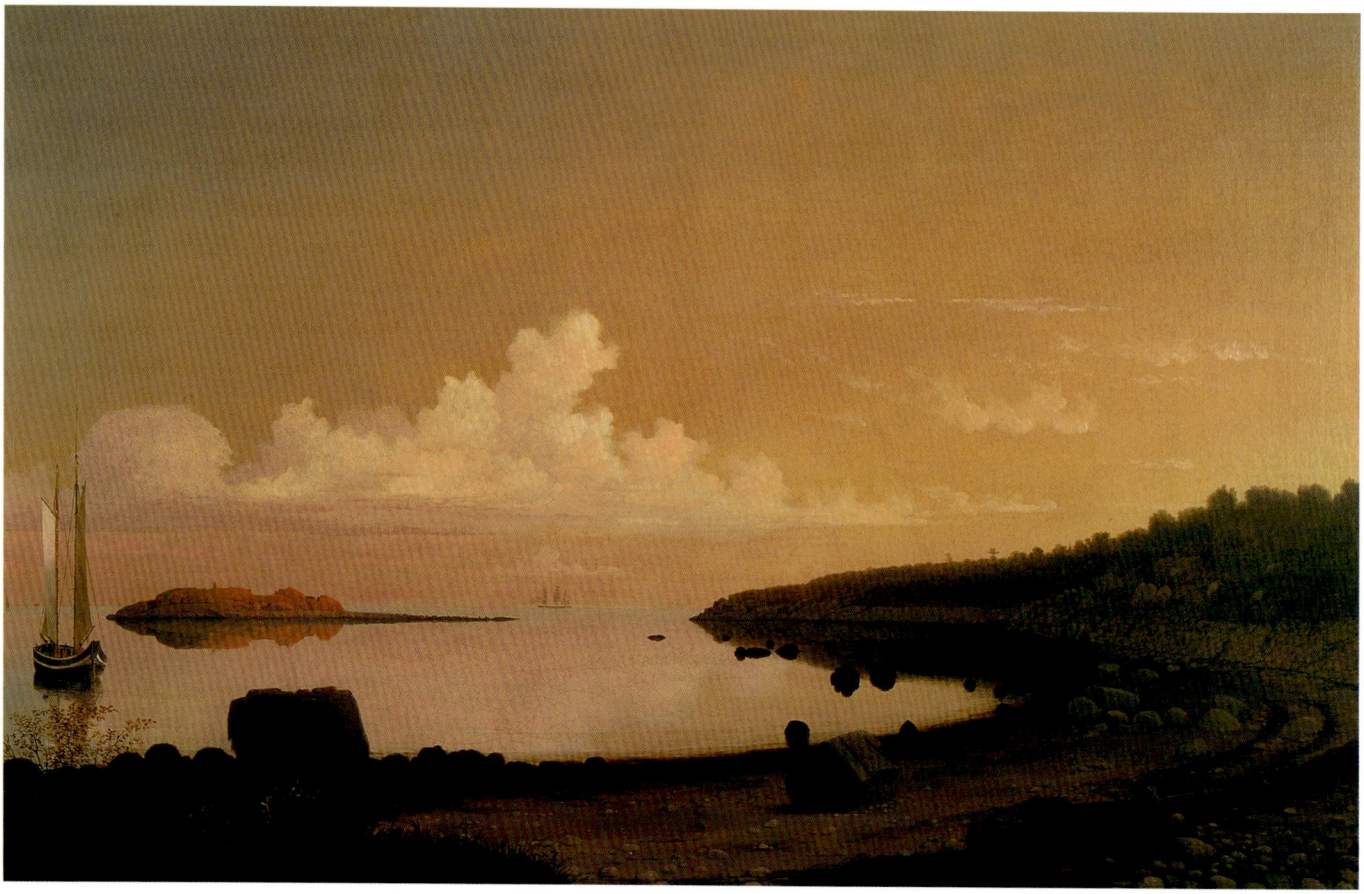

3.8.28 Fitz Henry Lane: *The Western Shore with Norman's Woe*, 1862.
Oil on canvas, 21½ x 35¼ in. (54.6 x 89.5 cm.)
Cape Ann Historical Association, Gloucester, Massachusetts

pitted East Coast preservationists against western settlers, who saw no need to "preserve" what appeared as an endless wilderness and source of income to them. It had also brought into heightened relief the issue of slavery. Were the new territories, once admitted to the Union, to be free or slave states? Would the Union, itself, survive the factionalism that was increasingly surfacing in state and national assemblies? The outbreak of the Civil War the following year would make it more difficult for artists to produce optimistic expressions, via depictions of the American landscape, of inviolable truths about the nation.

Still and Troubled Waters: Luminist Landscapes

In contrast to the large, dramatic vistas of Frederic Edwin Church, several East Coast artists were producing relatively small, intimate depictions of the American landscape, many of which focused on the Atlantic coastline or the shores of New England's lakes. The distinctive quality of the light in their paintings, which often enveloped the entire scene in a uniform glow, led to their being dubbed "Luminists" in 1954 by the art historian John I. H. Baur. Among this group of artists were Fitz Henry Lane (1804–1865), John Frederick Kensett (1816–1872), and Martin Johnson Heade (1819–1904). In Lane's *The Western Shore with Norman's Woe* of 1862 [**3.8.28**], Kensett's *Beacon Rock, Newport Harbor* of 1857 [**3.8.29**], and Heade's *Thunder Storm on Narragansett Bay* of 1868 [**3.8.30**] one senses not the bravura of a nation whose future lies to the west, but the reflectiveness of a nation whose past lies to the east and whose future is not yet resolved. Here one finds not paint-laden brushstrokes, reminders of the artist's presence, but smooth surfaces, devoid of evidence of artistic labor to distract the viewer. "The impersonality of many luminist paintings," writes the literary scholar David C. Miller, also "derives from the simplification and abstraction of forms" and an evenness of treatment over the entire composition that verges on "a democratization of the picture plane." These qualities distinguished Luminist works from the pastoral, allegorical, and sublime landscapes of Church, Thomas Cole, and others, where select areas of the canvas are highlighted through, among other things, contrasts of light and dark.

Barbara Novak has noted the quiet, spiritual qualities of these paintings (even Heade's *Thunder Storm* is marked by calm waters and a clear golden light in the foreground), and has posited a connection with the American Transcendentalist

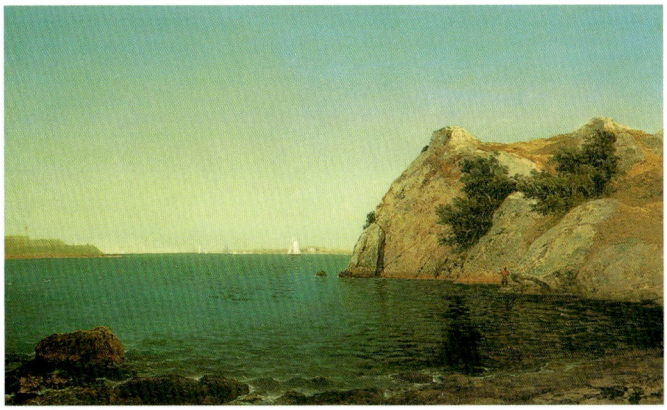

3.8.29 John Frederick Kensett: *Beacon Rock, Newport Harbor*, 1857.
Oil on canvas, 22½ x 36 in. (57.2 x 91.4 cm.)
National Gallery of Art, Washington, D.C.

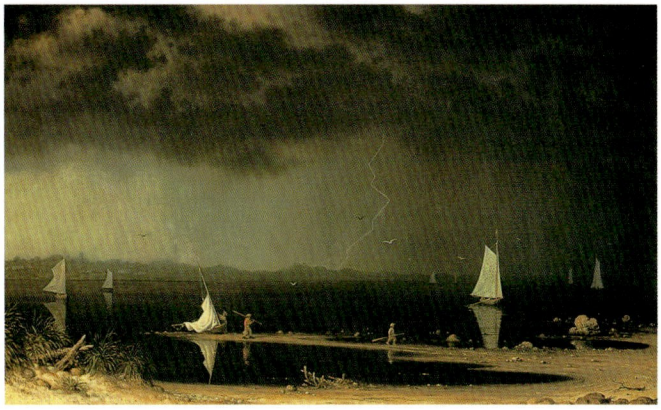

3.8.30 Martin Johnson Heade: *Thunder Storm on Narragansett Bay*, 1868.
Oil on canvas, 32 x 54 in. (81.3 x 137.2 cm.)
Amon Carter Museum, Fort Worth, Texas

movement led by such figures as Ralph Waldo Emerson and Henry David Thoreau. Transcendence is achieved not through immersion in the awesome sublime, representative of God's terrible power, but through repose within the silence of nature (Emerson's "wise silence" of the Over-Soul). Cole himself noted this alternative experience of nature, which he also equated with a certain kind of sublime. In his "Essay on American Scenery", published in 1835, Cole writes that in encountering two lakes in Franconia Notch, he was

> overwhelmed with an emotion of the sublime such as I have rarely felt. It was not that the jagged precipices were lofty, that the encircling woods were of the dimmest shade, or that the waters were profoundly deep; but that over all, rocks, wood and water, brooded the spirit of repose, and the silent energy of nature stirred the soul to its inmost depths.

While Luminist paintings refrained from high drama, they were not always restful. The foregrounds of several, such as Heade's *Thunder Storm*, contain evidence of unease, a silence that suggests emptiness and barrenness as much as oneness with nature. Transcendentalism also had its less optimistic side, a sense of alienation that often appeared in representations of "desert places." The foregrounds of both *Thunder Storm* and Lane's *The Western Shore with Norman's Woe* could stand in for those desert places, with their rocky, vacant terrain. These are not plentiful landscapes; even the boats give little evidence of the bounty of the sea. Instead, the shorelines are, in Miller's words, liminal spaces, "where values constantly turn into their opposites, where the moment confronts eternity, where flux and stasis endlessly trade places."

Miller suggests that Luminism is perhaps best understood "as a quality of vision its practitioners unconsciously expressed which bore a profound affinity to the contemporary cultural climate." Luminist paintings deeply touched people who were "confronting a world whose underlying assumptions were giving way to an unprecedented degree during the years around the Civil War." Perhaps the stasis in these paintings is a symbolic attempt to arrest both land and history, to stop the inevitable escalation of political turmoil and commercial development that was so apparent on the Eastern seaboard in the late 1850s and that ultimately led to armed conflict.

Review Questions

1 Compare the ways in which the shield of Arapoosh and the *Peaceable Kingdom* paintings of Edward Hicks convey a connection between nature and the spiritual.

2 The celebration of God in/as nature in the early nineteenth century created a serious conflict in the minds of those who concerned themselves with both the spiritual and material wellbeing of the new American Republic. What was the source and nature of this conflict and how was it represented in landscape paintings?

3 What are the main characteristics of the picturesque and the sublime?

4 What is the cyclical view of history that informs Thomas Cole's *The Course of Empire* series?

5 How did the landscape paintings of Frederic Edwin Church and the Luminists (Fitz Henry Lane, John Frederick Kensett, Martin Johnson Heade) both build on and depart from the work of earlier landscape artists, such as Thomas Cole and Robert S. Duncanson?

CHAPTER 9

The Occupied Landscape

(*c.* 1830–1863)

"A City May Rise": Albert Bierstadt's *The Rocky Mountains, Lander's Peak*

Frederic Edwin Church was not the only artist creating grandiose depictions of the American landscape [**3.8.25–3.8.27**; pp. 168–69]. He was joined by Albert Bierstadt (1830–1902), who focused not on New England but on the expansive vistas of the American West. Like Church, Bierstadt relied on his entrepreneurial skills as well as artistic talents to promote his career. Bierstadt came from a much more humble background than Church. In 1832 his family moved from Prussia to New Bedford, Massachusetts, the capital of New England's whaling industry, where his father worked as a cooper to support a wife and six children. It is not clear exactly when Bierstadt decided he was going to become a painter, but once he did, he went about teaching himself the necessary skills. In 1850 he felt confident enough in his accomplishments to advertise himself as a drawing instructor.

Unable to accumulate much income from his drawing lessons, Bierstadt worked with fellow artist George Harvey (1801–1878) on Harvey's "Dissolving Views" of American scenery, in which landscapes painted on glass were projected in a theater (such projected scenes anticipated the technology of turn-of-the-century motion pictures). The success of this traveling show allowed Bierstadt to finance a trip to Düsseldorf in 1853. The city's academy had already attracted a number of American artists, but, unfortunately, he was not able to enroll. The American artists Emanuel Leutze (1816–1868) and Worthington Whittredge (1820–1910) welcomed him, however, into their studios and provided him with his first sustained lessons in painting. After exploring Germany, Switzerland, and Italy, Bierstadt returned to New Bedford in 1857.

While he drew a certain amount of attention with his European paintings, Bierstadt soon realized that depictions of America's landscapes were in much greater demand. He made his first of multiple trips out West in the spring of 1859. Upon his return in the fall, he moved to New York City and began the production of a series of western landscapes that would gain for him a firm footing as perhaps *the* major American landscape painter.

The Rocky Mountains, Lander's Peak of 1863 [**3.9.1**] was among the first of Bierstadt's paintings to be exhibited publicly as a paid-entrance piece, with an accompanying pamphlet for sale that described the significance of the work. The art historian Linda S. Ferber attributes the success of Bierstadt's

3.9.1 Albert Bierstadt: *The Rocky Mountains, Lander's Peak*, 1863.
Oil on canvas,
73½ x 120¾ in. (186.7 x 306.7 cm.)
The Metropolitan Museum of Art, New York

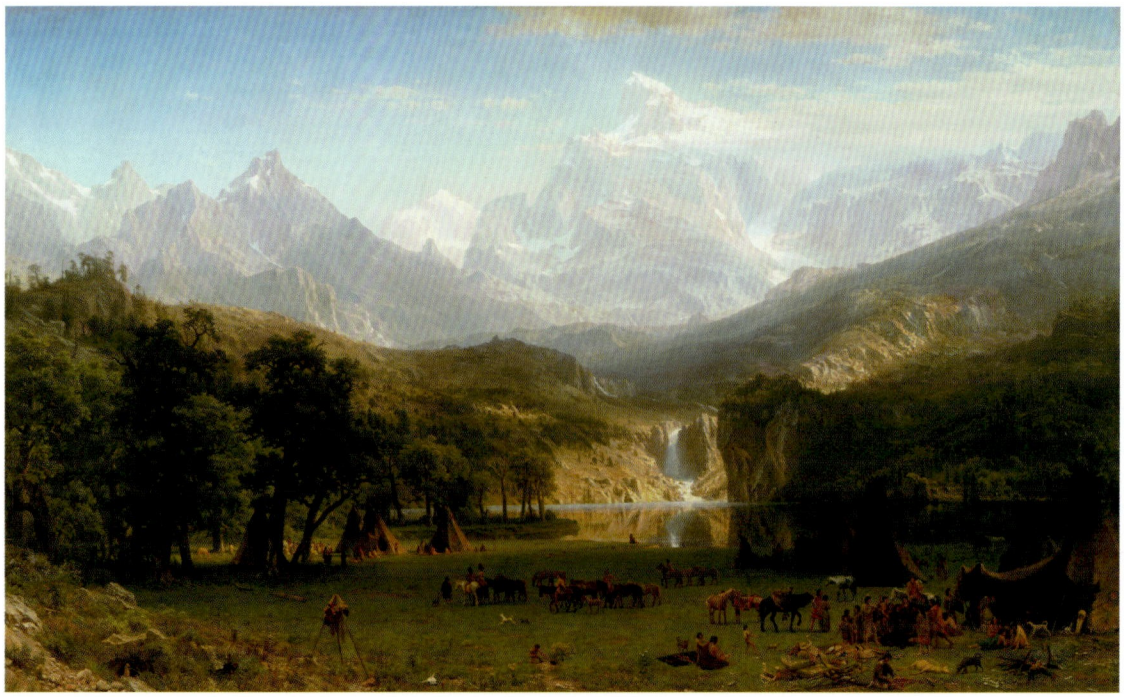

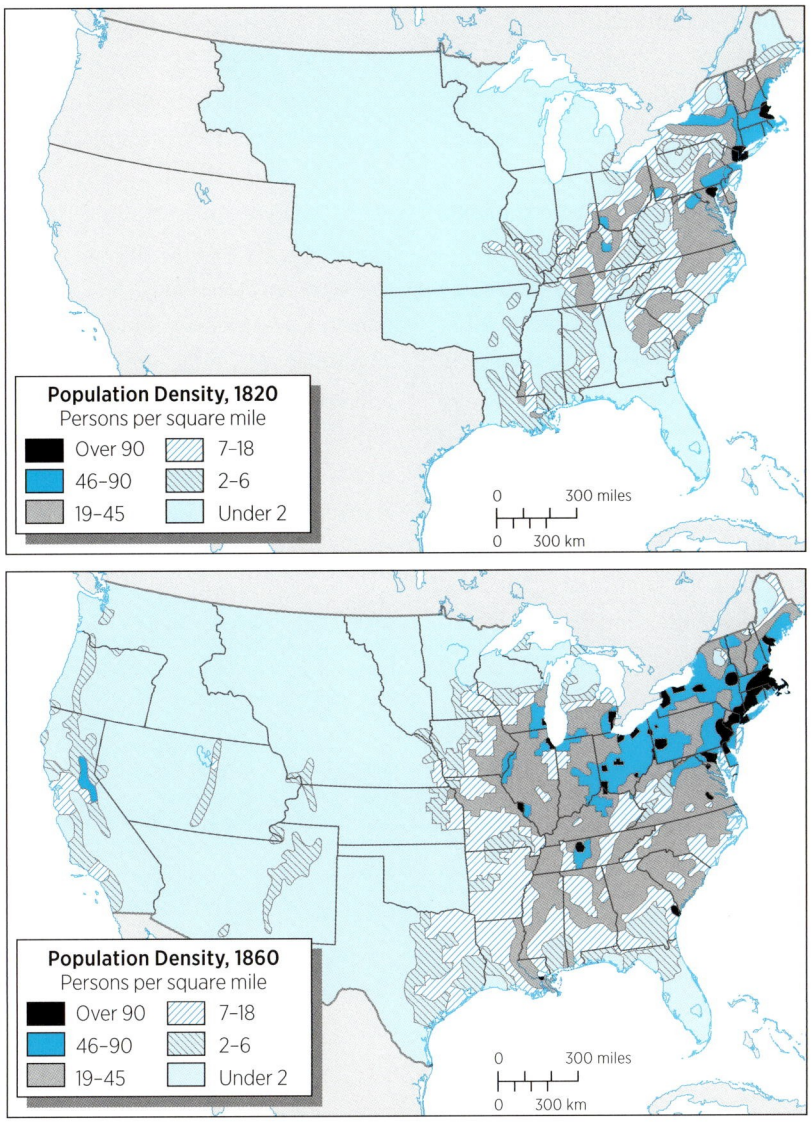

3.9.2 Population density in the United States in 1820 and in 1860.

western paintings to "public curiosity and excitement about these remote national territories" and to "the powerful idea of Manifest Destiny." This idea had gained currency in the 1840s and implied the inevitability of the continued territorial expansion of the US to the west and south, an expansion made more attractive in the early 1860s by anxieties about the future of the Union (see Chapter 12). The groundwork for the popularity of Bierstadt's paintings had also already been laid by the painted panoramas of the early nineteenth century, many of which were slowly unrolled in theatrical settings to the thrill of the audience. The art critic and collector James Jackson Jarves observed in 1864: "The countryman that mistook the *Rocky Mountains* for a panorama, and after waiting a while asked when the thing was going to move, was a more sagacious critic than he knew himself to be." Like panoramas, Bierstadt's paintings were large and thrilled not only with their size but also with their comprehensiveness and detail. *The Rocky Mountains* toured the US and Europe and was purchased by James McHenry, an Englishman who profited financially from the building of the railroads in the US that helped open the West to further settlement and commercial ventures.

In the pamphlet Bierstadt produced to accompany *The Rocky Mountains, Lander's Peak* he wrote that, in the area mapped in the foreground of the painting, "a city, populated by our descendants, may rise, and in its art-galleries this picture may eventually find a resting-place." Yet this foreground plain in Bierstadt's painting is not devoid of humans: it includes a Shoshone camp, with tipis and horses, as well as individuals engaged in the daily activities necessary for survival. Their presence, in combination with Bierstadt's comment, points to the widespread belief that Native Americans were destined to make way for the increasing waves of white settlers moving across the continent in the second half of the nineteenth century who would occupy and transform the landscape [**3.9.2**].

Native American Borders: Emanuel Leutze's *Westward the Course of Empire*

Most Europeans who settled in North America believed that the key to prosperity and a new life lay in the acquisition of land. For much of the nineteenth century, the richest land yet to be exploited by European settler colonists and their descendants lay west of the Mississippi River. This was the area most commonly conjured up in people's minds when they heard the phrase "the West." The Louisiana Purchase of 1803 (see pp. 113–114), and the simultaneous exploration of the northwestern reaches of the continent by Captain Meriweather Lewis and Second Lieutenant William Clark quickened the pace of westward expansion and the demand for land by a rapidly growing population. It also stimulated the interest of artists and writers in this new territory. These individuals, knowingly or not, would help formulate justifications for confiscating the land from its current inhabitants while, at the same time, celebrating the humanity of indigenous peoples and the value of their cultural practices.

The Louisiana Purchase was quickly seen as a solution to "the Indian problem." Those who refused to give up claim to their lands would simply be "relocated" west of the Mississippi River. In 1830, two years after he was elected president, Andrew Jackson secured the passage of the Indian Removal Bill. By 1838, 70,000 Native Americans had been forcibly removed to the Plains area west of the river, despite treaties guaranteeing them the right to their lands. Thousands died during these forced marches, and many would suffer several subsequent relocations as participants in the ever-westward-moving stream of settlers and entrepreneurs cast covetous eyes on the newly established Indian territories. And in each case, the confiscation of land would be accompanied by pronouncements of the savagery of Native Americans and, increasingly, of their inevitable demise.

3.9.3 Emanuel Leutze: study for *Westward the Course of Empire Takes Its Way* (*Westward Ho!*), 1861.
Oil on canvas, 33¼ x 43⅝ in. (84.5 x 110.2 cm.)
Smithsonian American Art Museum, Washington, D.C.

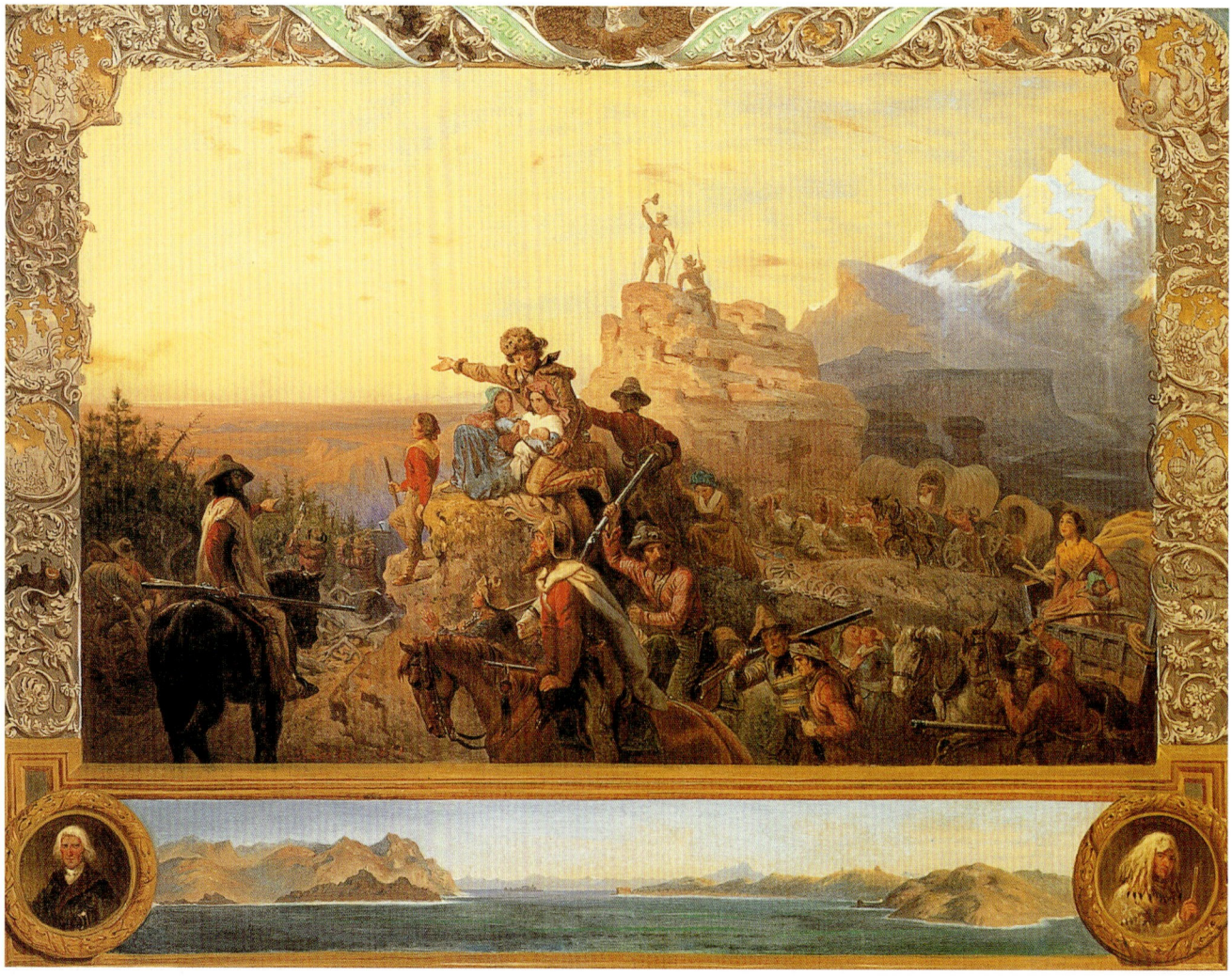

As early as 1824 John C. Calhoun, US Secretary of War, declared that Native Americans as a race were approaching extinction, despite the fact that their numbers, while greatly diminished, were still significant.

One highly visible image of this seemingly inevitable push by European Americans was Emanuel Leutze's *Westward the Course of Empire Takes Its Way (Westward Ho!)* painted in 1861–62 for the Capitol Building in Washington, D.C. [**4.12.2**; p. 222]. An oil study of 1861 [**3.9.3**] shows the artist's overall conceptualization of the scene. The title of the work is drawn from a poem by the Irish idealist philosopher Bishop George Berkeley entitled "Verses on the Prospect of Planting Arts and Learning in America" (1752), inspired by Berkeley's efforts in 1726 to establish an experimental college in Bermuda to convert America's indigenous peoples to Christianity. Its final stanza reads:

> Westward the course of Empire takes its way;
> The four first Acts already past,
> A fifth shall close the Drama with the day;
> Time's noblest offspring is the last.

Housed in the Capitol Building, along with the images of Native Americans discussed earlier [**2.6.18–2.6.21**; pp. 122–23], Leutze's painting articulated the belief of Europeans and European Americans since the sixteenth century that they had a Christian duty and an inalienable right to expand their territory and influence. This belief was codified in the US in the nineteenth century in the doctrine of Manifest Destiny. In conquering the West, the final New World frontier, European Americans would bring to culmination the progress of civilization.

The sun-bleached bones and burial scene in the center of the painting [**3.9.3**; **4.12.2**, p. 222] attest to the hardships that the pioneers endured in crossing the vast continent, whose natural power and beauty are evoked by the towering, snow-capped mountains, the broad expanse of plateau land, and Golden Gate Bay, the port of San Francisco, shown in a separate scene at the bottom. Yet Leutze chooses to downplay one of the most written-about hardships encountered during the journey across the continent: attacks by Native Americans. The only possible reference to these attacks in the oil study is the bandaged head of the young man in the center foreground (the final composition [**4.12.2**; p. 222] also includes a small boy clutching a bow and arrows). Instead, Leutze places Native Americans, along with wild animals, in the decorative plant forms that border the top and sides of the main composition, implying that both groups, like the land itself, must be conquered and subdued. Thus, Native Americans are literally marginalized, functioning as a framing device for the exploits of the American pioneers.

Also included in the painting's border are roundels containing biblical and classical scenes such as Moses leading the Israelites through the desert, the spies of Eshcol bearing the fruits from Canaan, and Hercules dividing Spain from North Africa. Yet these Old World figures are not presented as the equals of the indigenous figures or even as occupying the same world. Rather, they occupy their own separate worlds contained within the leafy borders of the roundels instead of being caught up among the vines like the animals and Native American figures. These Old World men serve to reinforce the sanctity and significance of the main scene and the preordained mission of the US to expand westward. Like them, the settlers are embarked on a momentous, heroic journey marked by trials and tribulations.

There is one other, more indirect, reference to Native American life in Leutze's painting. It appears in the medallion portrait of Clark, in the lower right-hand corner of the oil study [**3.9.3**]. Unlike Daniel Boone on the left, who is dressed in recognizably European clothes, Clark wears a buckskin jacket and animal-fur headdress, clothing that would have been immediately associated with the dress of the mountain men and trappers who were but one step removed from Native Americans and who, by facilitating the trade in furs, laid the groundwork for the arrival of settlers. These medallion portraits were transferred to the vertical frame segments in the final composition. In their stead in the lower border, framing Golden Gate Bay, Leutze placed symbols of mining, agriculture, and hunting—activities that would transform the land from a state of wilderness into one of civilized productivity.

"The Looks and Modes" of Native American Life: George Catlin and His "Indian Gallery"

While US Secretary of War John C. Calhoun and others engaged wholeheartedly in the condemnation of Native Americans as savages and heathens, some felt more conflicted about the destruction of these peoples, as well as about the continuing exploitation of the land. One way in which they expressed these views was through dressing up as "Indians." For explorers like William Clark, wearing Native American clothes and learning Native American ways was often essential for survival. For white men living in urban centers, dressing up as Native Americans was often a way to express symbolically a dissatisfaction with the material results of the government's expansionist policies—the decimation of indigenous peoples and of the forests in which they lived—or with the very idea of progress itself. This form of dissatisfaction was acted out in various plays throughout the nineteenth century, one of the most popular of which was *Metamora: or, The Last of the Wampanoags; An Indian Tragedy in Five Acts* (1828) by John Augustus Stone. Indigenous peoples represented a time of innocence and nobility before the development of urban centers and industrialization.

There were certain European American men, however, who were not satisfied with simply donning the clothes of Native Americans; they also wanted to examine Native Americans themselves and to define through pictorial representation what it meant to be or look "Indian." They were encouraged to do so by both government and non-government agencies, which issued calls for artists to capture the "look" of the indigenous peoples before they disappeared from the face of the earth. As the editor of the art magazine *The Crayon* wrote in 1856:

> It seems to us that the Indian has not received justice in American art....It should be held in dutiful remembrance that he is fast passing away from the face of the earth.... Absorbed in his quiet dignity, brave, honest, eminently truthful, and always thoroughly in earnest, he stands grandly apart from all other known savage life. As such let him be, for justice sake, sometimes represented.

Charles Bird King (1785–1862) had met this challenge in Washington, painting Native American delegations to the nation's capital [**2.6.26**, p. 129; **3.9.13**, p. 182]. George Catlin (1796–1872), on the other hand, left his position as a successful, largely self-taught, portrait painter in Washington and Philadelphia in 1830 and headed for the frontier city of St. Louis. Over the next six years he would make five trips into the territory west of the Mississippi, recording his observations of Native American dress and ways of life.

This was not the first time, however, that Catlin had turned his attention to this subject matter. In the late 1820s he had visited Iroquois reservations in New York State and painted several portraits. But Catlin, like some of his contemporaries, was not satisfied with simply recording the consequences of federal assimilationist policies—Native Americans living in log houses and wearing suits and dresses patterned after European fashions and made out of cloth purchased from local stores. Instead, he wanted to convey an image of indigenous peoples devoid of evidence of contact with European civilization, declaring: "it is for these uncontaminated people that I would be willing to devote the energies of my life." In 1832 he explained his reasons for wanting to paint such Native American life:

> I have, for many years past, contemplated the noble races of red men who are now spread over these trackless forests and boundless prairies, melting away at the approach of civilization. Their rights invaded, their morals corrupted, their lands wrested from them, their customs changed, and therefore lost to the world; and they at last sunk into the earth, and the ploughshare turning the sod over their graves, and I have flown to their rescue—not of their lives or of their race (for they are "doomed" and must perish), but to the rescue of their looks and their modes, at which the acquisitive world may hurl their poison and every besom of destruction, and trample them down and crush them to death; yet, phoenix-like, they may rise from the "stain on a painter's palette," and live again upon canvass [sic], and stand forth for centuries yet to come, the living monuments of a noble race.

While Catlin sympathized with the plight of Native Americans, and harshly criticized government policies that had resulted in their degradation if not demise, he also ultimately accepted the proposition that they were "doomed and must perish." He does not attempt to rescue "their lives or...their race"—it would be hard to imagine how he could have done so in the face of federal policies and the market imperatives of both real estate and the fur trade—but only "their looks and their modes." Catlin thus engages in what the anthropologist Renato Rosaldo calls "imperialist nostalgia," a yearning for that which one has directly or indirectly participated in destroying, a preservation of "looks and modes" in the face of the "unfortunate but necessary" destruction of a people.

When Catlin arrived in St. Louis he met Clark who had been made Superintendent of Indian Affairs for the western region. Clark was impressed by Catlin's portfolio of Iroquois paintings and agreed to help him visit various Native American settlements in the West. Catlin produced over five hundred scenes of indigenous life. *The Last Race, Part of Okipa Ceremony (Mandan)* of 1832 [**3.9.4**] and *Mah-To-Toh-Pa (Four Bears), Mandan Chief* of 1832–34 [**3.9.5**] represent the two general categories within which Catlin's images can be placed: multi-figure scenes set in natural landscapes or village settings and studio-type portraits of single individuals. The former are more loosely painted and often have the appearance of field sketches. The latter tend to be much more carefully worked up and utilize poses familiar to portrait painters back in the East.

Having spent six years in the field, Catlin returned to the East Coast in 1837 and organized his paintings, along with costumes and a collection of Native American objects, into an "Indian Gallery," which toured the US from 1837 to 1840. The year Catlin began his tour the Mandans, a people whose "looks and modes" Catlin had "rescued," were nearly completely wiped out by a plague of smallpox (see p. 51). The Mandans, with whom Meriweather Lewis and Clark had stayed during the

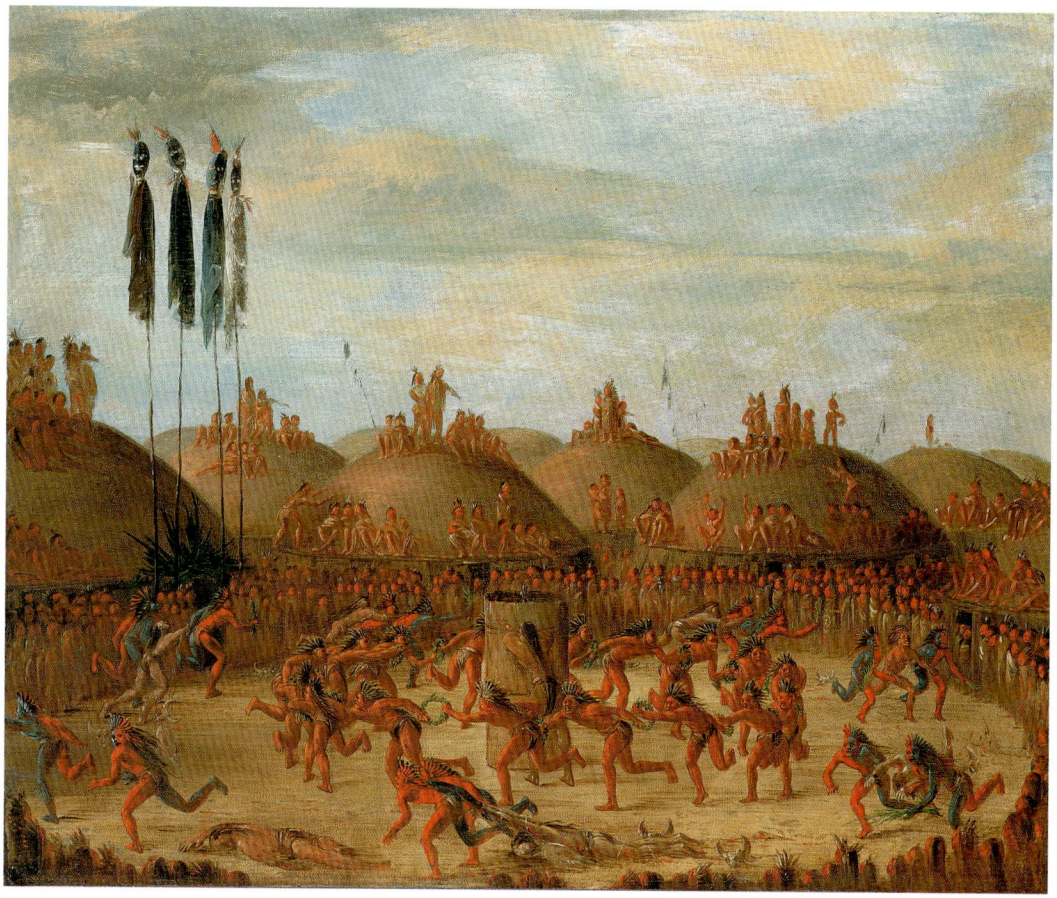

3.9.4 George Catlin: *The Last Race, Part of Okipa Ceremony (Mandan)*, 1832.
Oil on canvas,
23⅜ x 28⅛ in. (58.8 x 71.3 cm.)
Smithsonian American Art Museum, Washington, D.C.

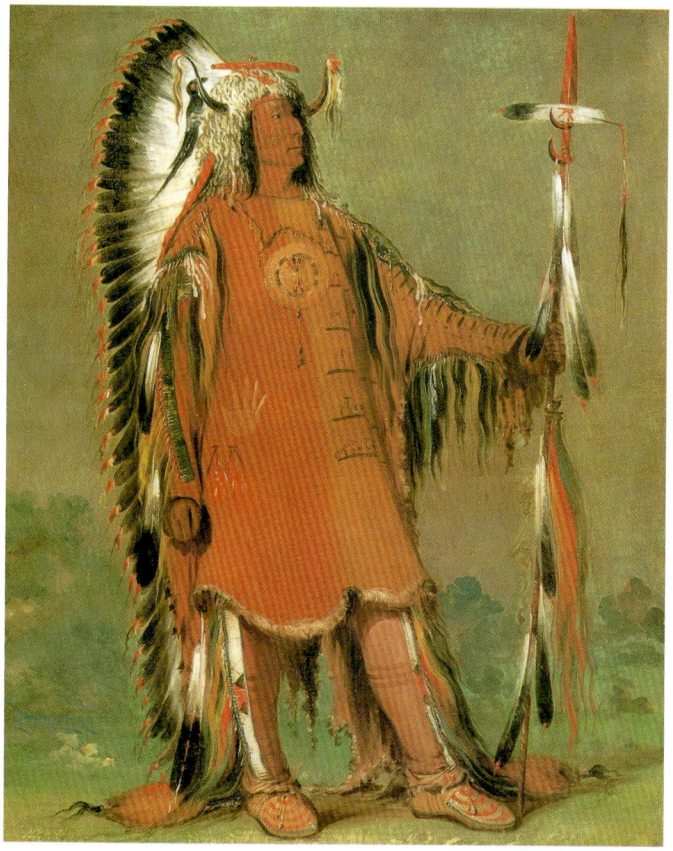

3.9.5 George Catlin: *Mah-To-Toh-Pa (Four Bears), Mandan Chief*, 1832–34.
Oil on canvas,
29 x 24 in. (73.7 x 61 cm.)
Smithsonian American Art Museum, Washington, D.C.

winter of 1804–5, had been at the center of a Northern Plains trade network in foodstuffs and fur that ranged from the Pacific Northwest and the Hudson Bay to Florida, the Gulf Coast, and the Atlantic Seaboard. Catlin's father wrote to him and commented that this devastating plague would greatly increase the value and importance of his son's works, for they would be one of the few reminders of a once flourishing people.

Catlin also took his "Indian Gallery" to London and Paris in the 1840s. Its success there was due in no small part to the fact that what Catlin presented was an affirmation of an already well-established conception of the Native American as "noble savage" popularized initially by writers such as John Dryden (see p. 55). Dryden's presentation of "noble savagery" in a positive light at the end of the seventeenth century was taken up again in the eighteenth century by Jean-Jacques Rousseau, Voltaire, and other French Enlightenment thinkers in their criticisms of what they viewed as corrupt contemporary French morals and practices. While Catlin's images attended to the details of costumes, landscapes, and daily life, they still participated in a larger, more generalized discourse about an innocence and purity that, while desirable in many ways, were part of a past that ultimately could not be re-created. The "noble savage," untainted by civilization, was destined to make way for civilization's inevitable arrival.

Catlin's paintings have often been praised for providing a wealth of information about the "manners, customs, and conditions of North American Indians" in the early nineteenth century—manners and customs that had already been altered by contact with Europeans. Catlin himself went to great pains to verify the accuracy of his depictions. He included in his *Letters and Notes on the Manners, Customs, and Conditions of North American Indians* (1841) written statements attesting to this accuracy by various government officials, traders, and scholars familiar with the peoples he was painting. These statements of authenticity are accompanied in Catlin's book by his constant laments about how others had misrepresented Native Americans, and how these misrepresentations fed an antagonism toward these peoples that was unfounded or exaggerated. Those searching after truth would be most likely to find it, according to Catlin, in his own text and images.

George Catlin and the Mandans

While most art historians admit that Catlin's text and images add to our knowledge of Native American life, some have gone on to question certain aspects of his visual representations. Catlin sometimes intentionally left out elements of a scene or individual he was painting or altered the scene itself. The art historian Kathryn Hight points out one example of this in the frontispiece to *Letters and Notes* [**3.9.6**]. Catlin would like us to believe that he has recorded a scene that actually occurred. Captioned "The Author painting a Chief at the base of the Rocky Mountains," it shows sitter and artist outdoors, surrounded by a crowd chiefly of men, in front of two tipis. In the text of the book, however, Catlin describes painting the individual in question—Mah-To-Toh-Pa (Four Bears), second chief of the Mandan—in the Mandan village of Metutahanke on the upper Missouri River, indoors, surrounded by women and children. He also adds a detailed description of the chief's costume, which included a belt containing a tomahawk and scalping knife, a painted robe, and a bear-claw necklace. In the single-figure painting on which the figure in the frontispiece was based [**3.9.5**; p. 177], these specific items are already not in evidence.

What is the significance of these changes? How do they alter the meaning of the images? In his text, Catlin tells his readers how much time the chief had spent getting ready for his portrait, indicating that the Mandan leader had a very clear idea how he wanted to be represented. Catlin then goes on to justify the omissions: "Such was the dress of Mah-To-Toh-Pa when he entered my wigwam to stand for his picture; but such I have not entirely represented it in his portrait; having rejected such trappings and ornaments as interfered with the grace and simplicity of the figure." Removing several symbols of the chief's power as a warrior and spiritual leader—the tomahawk, scalping knife, and bear-claw necklace—may, indeed, simplify the composition. Yet it also makes Mah-To-Toh-Pa appear less threatening, both to the painter within the image itself and to the reader of Catlin's memoirs. Moving the scene outdoors allows an increase in the size of the audience, and this larger number, which now includes men as well, attests to the importance of the event and the significance of Catlin's artistic achievements. The expressions of fear and wonder on the faces of the spectators attest additionally to the accomplishments of European artistry in general. Catlin depicts his ability to capture the physical likeness of the chief on canvas as an act of magic in the eyes of the Mandan villagers. While the frontispiece is rendered in a reductive graphic style, with little shading or other attempts to create a convincing three-dimensional space, Catlin, Ma-To-Toh-Pa, and the other figures are still much more life-like than the elementary stick figures on the sides of the tipi that represent Mandan artistic expression.

Catlin's familiarity with the pictorial art of the Mandans is recorded in his memoirs. In fact, Mah-To-Toh-Pa gave the artist a replica of his own painted buffalo-skin robe on which he had recorded his military exploits and which he wore to have his portrait painted (and which the artist did not show). While the whereabouts of Catlin's robe are unknown, another Mandan

3.9.6 George Catlin: "The Author painting a Chief at the base of the Rocky Mountains," frontispiece to *Letters and Notes*, 1841.
Engraving, 9½ x 6 in. (24.1 x 15.2 cm.)
Henry E. Huntington Library and Art Gallery, San Marino, California

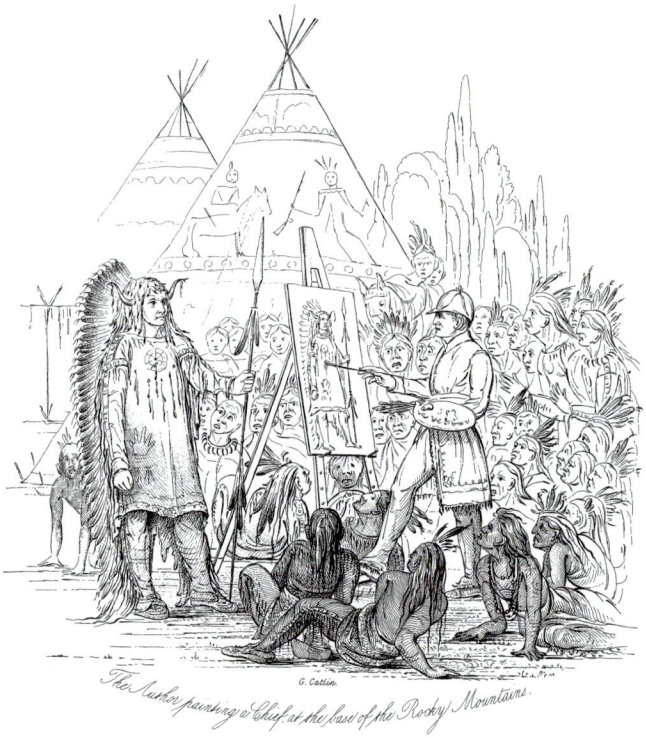

robe [**3.9.7**], collected in 1837, has scenes that closely resemble his written and pictorial descriptions of it, and may in fact have belonged to Mah-To-Toh-Pa. The horses and human figures are certainly two-dimensional and highly schematic. Yet they are much more sophisticated in their rendering and design than the stick figures on the tipi. These latter figures, with their triangular torsos and frontal heads, more closely resemble the designs on an earlier Mandan buffalo robe sent to President Jefferson by Lewis and Clark in 1805 [**1.2.24**; p. 44]. The later example reveals an increasing sureness in the handling of human and animal bodies and a greater concern with decorative patterning.

The indigenous peoples of the Plains had already had extensive contact with Spanish, French, and English traders and/or soldiers before the arrival of Catlin (see Chapters 1–3) and some had undoubtedly been exposed to European images through reproductions or contact with European artists who accompanied these trading expeditions. Native American artists would continue to develop the narrative art forms found in hide paintings throughout the nineteenth century and use them as a means of pictorial communication, incorporating knowledge they had gained from observing the work of artists like Catlin while maintaining aspects of their own distinctive style and iconography. A major change in materials also occurred in the middle of the century with the widespread introduction through trade of paper and new pigments (see pp. 251–57).

The tipis in Catlin's frontispiece [**3.9.6**] may have been included for compositional reasons. The central one not only provides a surface for the display of Native American imagery but also connects the figures of Catlin and Mah-To-Toh-Pa. The lines of its sides link their heads, anchoring them within the pyramidal composition and suggesting they are, to a certain extent, equal. The easel echoes the shape of the tipi, reinforcing the comparison between the stick figures behind and the mimetic portrait that it supports, between the "childlike" record of gun-toting exploits and the European celebration of noble individuality.

The inclusion of the tipis in this particular scene is puzzling in view of the fact Catlin knew quite well that the distinctive dwellings of the more sedentary, horticultural Mandans were not portable bison-hide tipis but hemispherical earth-covered lodges. The roofs of these lodges were popular places for socializing and watching ceremonies in the plaza below. The buildings also covered cache pits filled with corn that the Mandans grew in their extensive fields and then dried. According to the historian Elizabeth A. Fenn, the irregular placement of these dwellings in Mandan villages (there were no right-angled streets) was a way to disorient attacking war parties.

This distinctive Mandan architecture is evident in Catlin's painting *The Last Race, Part of Okipa Ceremony (Mandan)* [**3.9.4**; p. 177], where overlapping layers of domed buildings covered with seated and standing Mandans recede into the distance. The circular shape of the dome is echoed in the circular plaza in the foreground, which contains Mandan men performing the last part of the annual four-day Okipa Ceremony. Many scholars have connected this ceremony, with its fasting, gift exchange, and self-piercing, to the Sun Dance common among Plains peoples (see p. 151). According to Fenn, the Okipa ceremony, "restored balance...evinced love for the spirits...affirmed female ascendancy...brought bison herds near...[and] helped gardens grow. It transmitted history, power, and wisdom from one generation to the next. It was the very essence of being Mandan." The circular plank structure around which the men move contains a cedar post that represents Lone Man, the son of First Creator in one of the Mandan origin stories, who saves the Mandans from a flood by building a plank corral around the town.

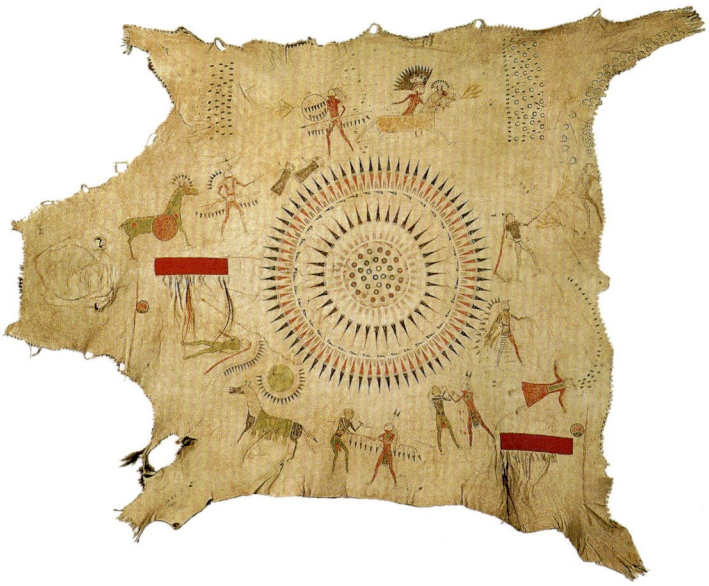

3.9.7 Unknown artist, Mandan: buffalo robe, collected in 1837. Painted hide, w. 82¾ in. (210 cm.), Historisches Museum, Bern

By locating the Mandans in front of tipis, the dwelling type of nomadic Plains peoples, Catlin participates in the creation of a generalized view of Native Americans, one that erases their differences (the tipi soon became a sign for "Indian"), even as he claims to be recording these differences. This generalized view was particularly appropriate for the frontispiece of a book that included a vast array of Native American peoples too complex to be captured in one image, although the numerous illustrations contained in the book allowed the reader access to this complexity.

It is interesting to compare the frontispiece of *Letters and Notes* with a later picture based on it, *Catlin Painting the Portrait*

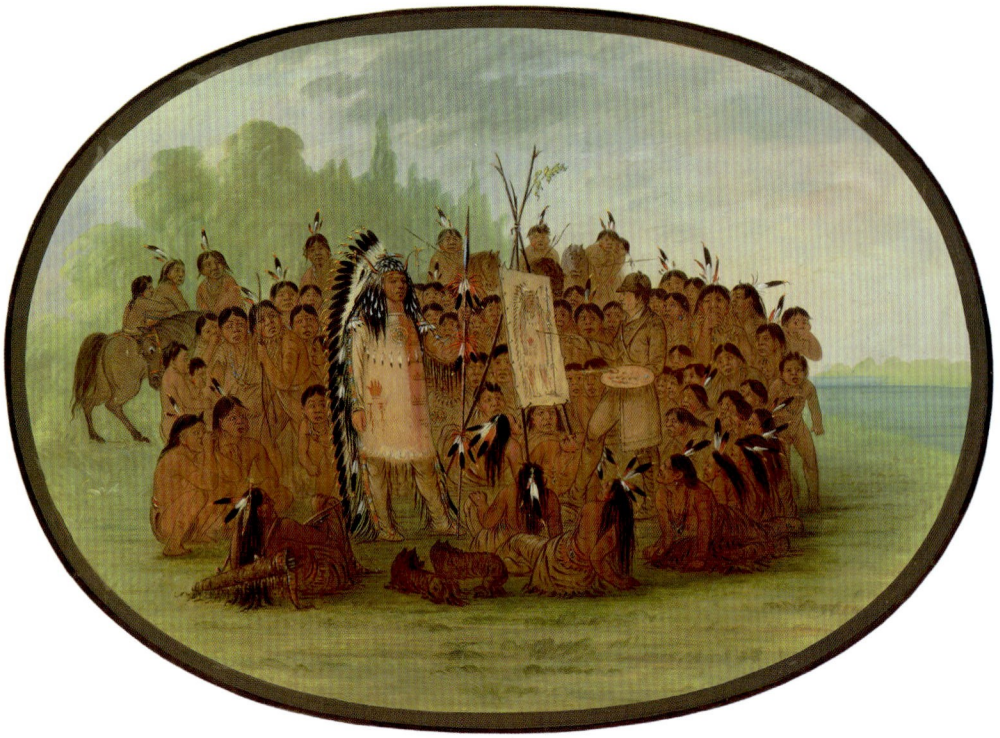

3.9.8 George Catlin: *Catlin Painting the Portrait of Mah-To-Toh-Pa—Mandan*, 1857–69.
Oil on board,
15⅜ x 23⅞ in. (39 x 60.6 cm.)
National Gallery of Art, Washington, D.C.

3.9.9 Karl Bodmer: *Mató-Tópe (Four Bears), Mandan Chief*, 1833–34.
Watercolor on paper,
16½ x 11⅝ in. (41.9 x 29.2 cm.)
Joslyn Art Museum, Omaha, Nebraska

of Mah-To-Toh-Pa—Mandan of 1857–69 [**3.9.8**]. Catlin has removed the tipis and shifted Mah-To-Toh-Pa closer to the center of the composition, increasing the number of Mandans located behind the chief. He has also replaced the European easel with a makeshift structure of branches tied together like the frame of a tipi. In addition, he shows the canvas only roughly attached to this frame, suggesting the loosely attached hide coverings of the tipi. Thus, the tipi and easel of the engraving have been collapsed together in the painting. The effect of these changes is to heighten the presence of the Mandan chief in the composition and the connection between the Mandans and nature, and to locate Catlin more clearly within the Mandan world. Yet he is still present as artist and creator, and perhaps even more so than in the engraving. In the painting, Catlin presents himself as literally repainting the surfaces of the "Indian" tipi/easel, which once held Mandan pictographs. He thus redefines the significance of the Mandan leader-as-artist and of pictorial representation in general in Mandan culture.

Catlin described his painting of the Mandan leader:

> No tragedian ever trod the stage, nor gladiator ever entered the Roman Forum, with more grace and manly dignity than did Mah-To-Toh-Pa enter the wigwam, where I was in readiness to receive him. He took his attitude before me, and with the sternness of a Brutus and the stillness of a statue, he stood until the darkness of night broke upon the solitary stillness.

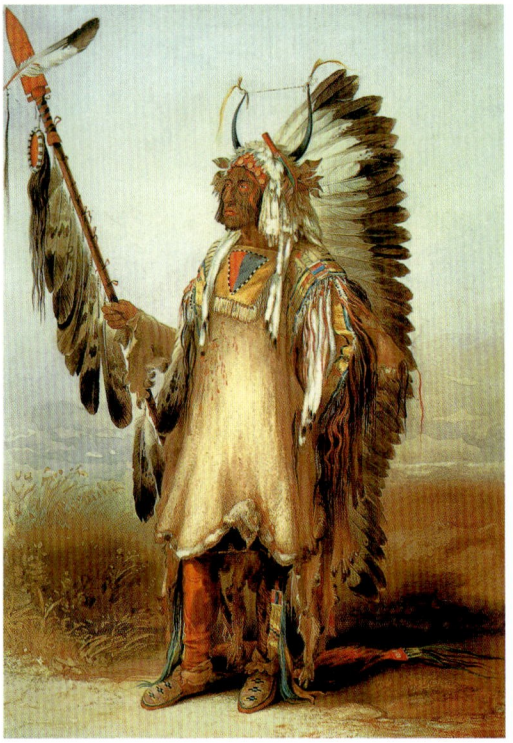

Catlin meant these Roman references as praise for the nobility and bravery of Native American leaders. Yet, combined with a belief in their inevitable demise, these references located Native Americans even more firmly in the past, as noble precursors of a present and future society in which they would have little control over their own destiny.

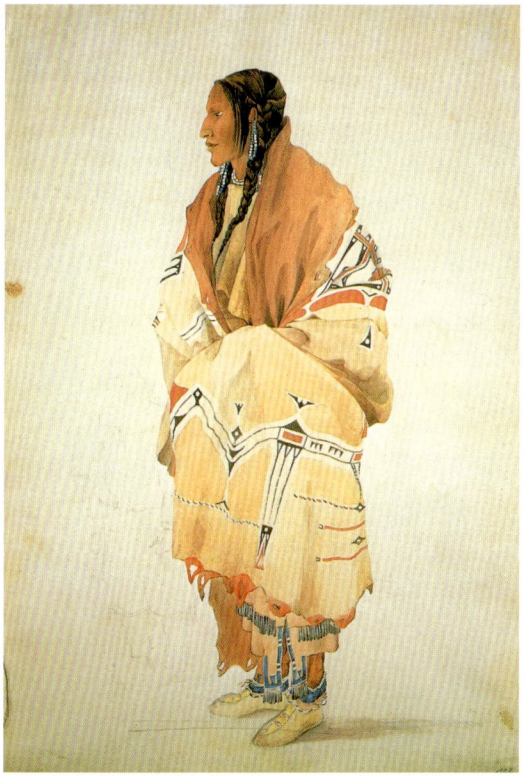

3.9.10 Karl Bodmer: *Chan-Chä-Uiá-Teüin, Teton Sioux Woman*, 1833–34.
Watercolor and pencil, 17 x 11⅞ in. (43.2 x 30.4 cm.)
Joslyn Art Museum, Omaha, Nebraska

Catlin's vision of Mah-To-Toh-Pa as Brutus does not seem to have been shared by the Swiss artist Karl Bodmer (1809–1893), [**3.9.9**] who also visited the Mandans in the early 1830s. Bodmer accompanied the German Prince Maximilian of Wied-Neuwied on a two-year journey up the Missouri River through the northern Plains territory. He was commissioned to execute watercolors of Native Americans that would be used to illustrate Maximilian's *Travels in the Interior of North America in the Years 1832 to 1834*, published in 1839. While Bodmer's portrait of Mah-To-Toh-Pa exhibits certain similarities in costume and facial features to that of Catlin, the relative sizes of warrior and spear suggest a much smaller man than appears in Catlin's painting [**3.9.5**; p. 177]. Perhaps Bodmer, as illustrator of another man's narrative, had less of an investment in dignifying Mah-To-Toh-Pa through Roman allusions.

Bodmer's paintings are often much more precise in their rendering of costumes and facial features than Catlin's, due probably to his more extensive training as an artist. For example, Bodmer presents a careful depiction of a Teton Sioux woman's costume in his portrait *Chan-Chä-Uiá-Teüin* of 1833–34 [**3.9.10**]. As mentioned earlier (see p. 61), women's robes tended to display abstract, geometric patterns, while men's contained narrative scenes. Five generalized geometric patterns were most often used, and the one in Bodmer's painting appears to be the border-and-box pattern [**3.9.12d**]. An example of a Plains robe from the eighteenth century provides a clearer view of this design [**3.9.11**], which is thought to derive from the splayed outline of a skinned-out large animal, such as a buffalo, with the "box" representing the animal's viscera.

3.9.11 Unknown artist: robe with arrowhead and broken diamond motif, 18th century.
Painted hide, 49¾ x 40¼ in. (126.3 x 102.2 cm.)
Musée de l'Homme, Paris

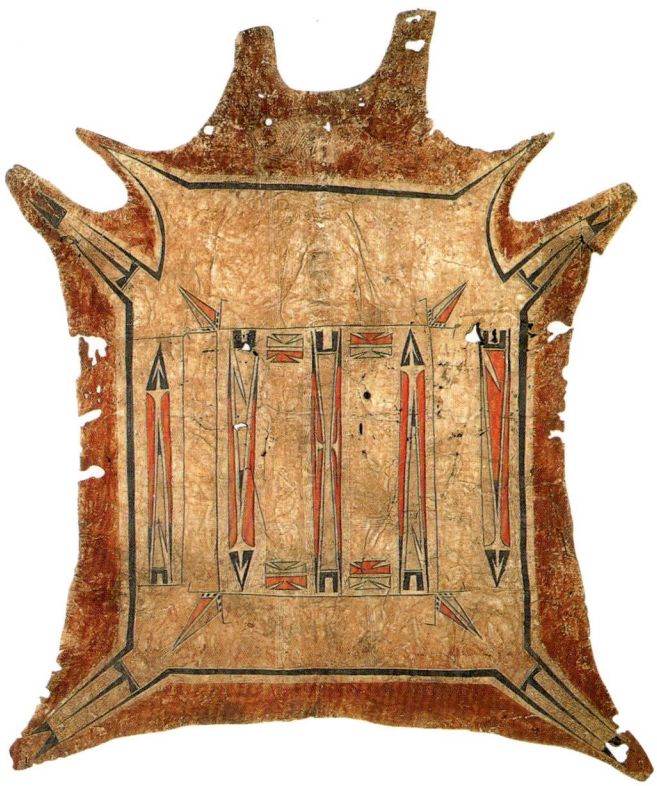

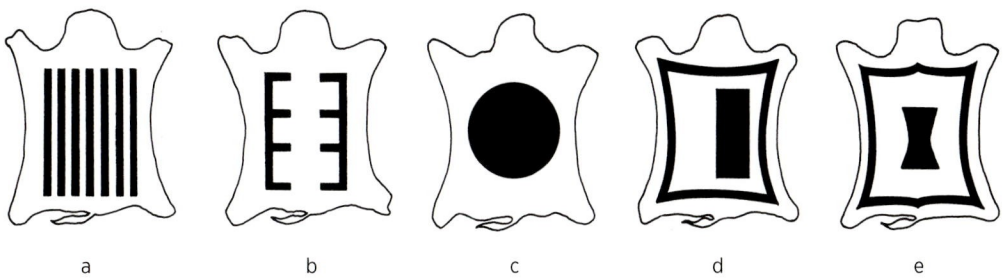

3.9.12 Styles of painted designs for Plains women's buffalo robes:
(a) horizontally striped,
(b) bilaterally symmetrical,
(c) feathered circle,
(d) border-and-box,
(e) border-and-hourglass

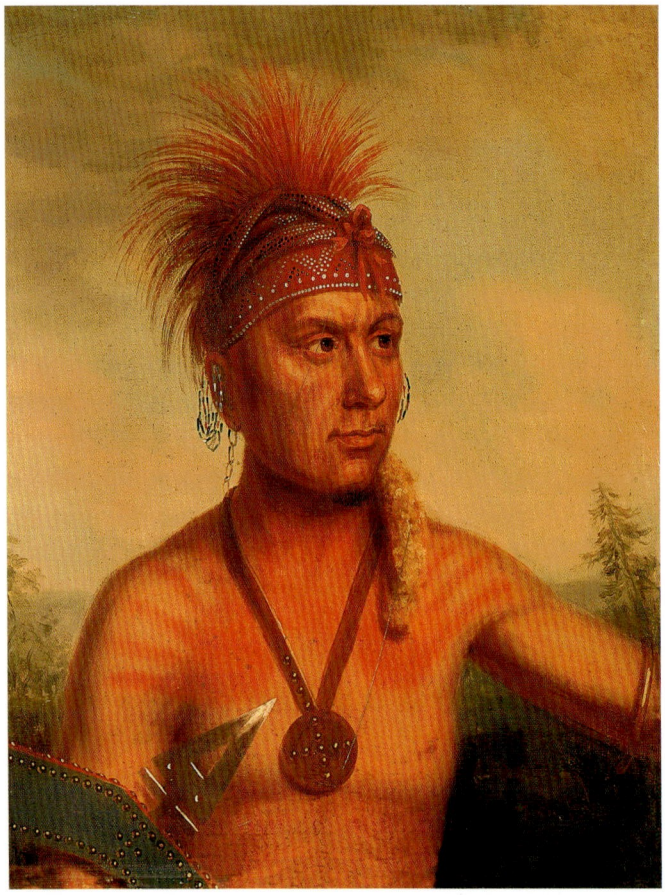

3.9.13 Charles Bird King: *Keokuk, Sac (Watchful Fox)*, 1827.
Oil on panel, 17½ x 13¾ in. (44.4 x 34.9 cm.)
National Museum of Denmark, Copenhagen

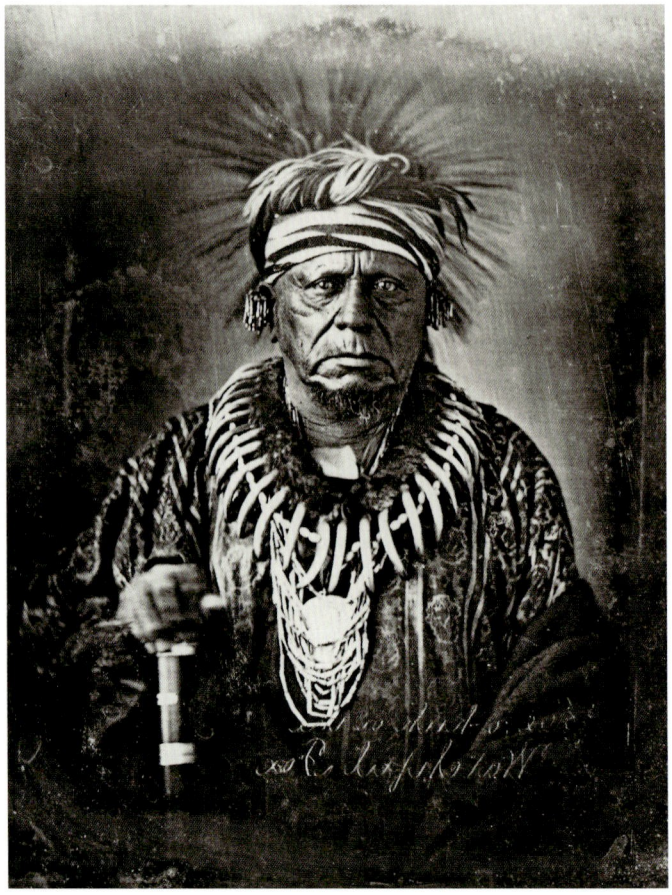

3.9.14 Thomas Easterly: *Keokuk, or the Watchful Fox*, 1847.
Daguerreotype, copied in 1868 (reproduced here with original orientation)
National Anthropological Archives, National Museum of Natural History, Smithsonian Institution, Washington, D.C.

Photographic Portraits: Another Take on the Real

While George Catlin and Karl Bodmer used paint to create their images of Native Americans, others turned to a different medium, one they claimed was better able to render accurately the faces of the frontier, albeit in black and white—photography (for a brief history see pp. 145–47). In 1847 Thomas Easterly (1809–1882) produced a daguerreotype of the Sauk and Fox leader Keokuk, or the Watchful Fox [**3.9.14**], who was well known for his diplomacy in negotiating with government officials. In 1837 he succeeded in protecting Sauk and Fox claims to their Iowa land holdings against counterclaims by the Sioux. Easterly presents Keokuk in a stark interior setting, eyes staring straight ahead, impassive and stony-faced, rendered in sharp detail yet emotionally inaccessible. These pictorial qualities had much to do with the mechanics of the daguerreotype—for example, the long exposure time that required the subject to sit completely still for several seconds. They can also be traced to the unfamiliarity of the medium, which resulted in an awkwardness or discomfort in front of the camera.

Daguerreotypists, like painters, made choices concerning costume and setting, and invested their images with their own understanding of the frontier and the peoples who inhabited it. These choices are apparent when one compares Easterly's image with an earlier painted portrait of the same man. In 1824 Keokuk traveled to Washington, D.C. with a delegation of Sauk, Fox, Iowa, and Piankashaw leaders. During this visit, he had his portrait painted by Charles Bird King, a copy of which was made by the artist in 1827 [**3.9.13**]. Here Keokuk is at ease, a slight smile on his face, his gaze directed beyond the picture frame, allowing the viewer's eye to wander freely over his body, stopping to examine his costume or facial features. He wears a simple medallion on his bare chest, reminiscent of the peace medals distributed to indigenous leaders [see **2.6.26**; p. 129], and his war club with its knife blade is given a secondary position in the lower left-hand corner. There is a sense of complicity between the viewer/painter and the sitter, a willingness on the part of Keokuk to expose himself to scrutiny. The trees and sky locate the Sauk and Fox leader in an ill-defined landscape, belying the fact that the portrait was painted in King's studio.

Easterly engages in no such illusionism and his photograph of the massive, fully clothed older man creates little sense of willing complicity. Keokuk sits in front of a grey/black backdrop, directly engaging the viewer with his gaze. His head is partially framed by an imposing bear-claw necklace, a symbol of his physical and spiritual power, which creates a distinctly more imposing image than the boy-like figure in King's painting.

It is difficult to imagine that the painted Keokuk is the same young man that the ethnologist Henry Rowe Schoolcraft met in 1825. Schoolcraft, the author of a six-volume history of Native Americans entitled *Historical and Statistical Information Respecting the History, Condition, and Prospects of the Indian Tribes of the United States* (1856), described him as "like another Coriolanus," "a prince, majestic and frowning. The wild, native pride of man, in the savage state, flushed by success in war, and confident in the strength of his arm, was never so fully depicted to my eyes." The Roman analogies are similar to those used by Catlin in his description of Mah-To-Toh-Pa. Schoolcraft had been an early admirer of the work of Catlin; indeed, a testimony by him is included in *Letters and Notes* verifying the artist's accuracy. He later questioned, however, the truthfulness of some of Catlin's descriptions—a questioning that, according to the painter's granddaughter, prevented the sale of Catlin's collection to the French government. Yet one can also question the accuracy of Schoolcraft's description of Keokuk, in light of King's painting. Both painter and author saw what they wanted to see, King focusing on the exotic but rather passive Keokuk and Schoolcraft emphasizing the discourse of the noble savage. Perhaps Easterly presents us with the most accurate of the three descriptions, capturing in his daguerreotype an aging man whose bearing and costume (he does not remove the bear-claw necklace as did Catlin) reflect his military and spiritual power without recourse to a romanticized classical past.

The Iconography of Progress: The City and the Train

George Catlin's memoirs included not only descriptions of the "manners, customs, and conditions" of the indigenous peoples of North America, but also detailed descriptions of the land they inhabited:

> Soul melting scenery that was about me!...I mean the prairie...whose thousand thousand velvet-covered hills, (surely never formed by chance, but grouped in one of Nature's sportive moods)—tossing and leaping down with steep or graceful declivities to the river's edge, as if to grace its pictured shores, and make it "a thing to look upon."

Just as Catlin participated in defining how the nation would understand the lives and customs of indigenous peoples, so too did he join in the pictorialization of the American landscape, its transformation, through both written description and painted canvas, into "a thing to look upon." And just as his respect for Native Americans was combined with an acceptance of their inevitable demise, so too was his appreciation of the beauty of the untamed landscape tempered by an acknowledgment of its inevitable transformation through cultivation and settlement by Europeans. A page after exulting over the wild prairie, Catlin anticipates the words of Albert Bierstadt (see pp. 172–73) when he writes:

> I...roamed from hill-top to hill-top, and culled wild flowers, and looked into the valley below me, both up the river and down, and contemplated the thousand hills and dales that are now carpeted with green, streaked as they will be, with the plough, and yellow with the harvest sheaf; spotted with lowing kine—with houses and fences, and groups of hamlets and villas.

By the mid-nineteenth century several artists were producing images of this transformation of the natural landscape into farms, towns and cities, building on the pastoral vistas of the first half of the century. In 1853, before he issued his call to artists to paint the American wilderness (see p. 167), Asher B. Durand produced *Progress* [**3.9.15**], a clear representation of the inevitable march of progress, from the wilderness foreground, with its Native Americans in the lower left corner looking on, to the bustling city on the banks of the river in the valley below, with its church spire, train, and steam boats. "The wild Indian is seen taking a last look at the land of his fathers," one reviewer

3.9.15 Asher B. Durand: *Progress*, 1853.
Oil on canvas, 48 x 72 in. (121.9 x 182.9 cm.)
The Warner Collection, Gulf States Paper Corporation, Tuscaloosa, Alabama

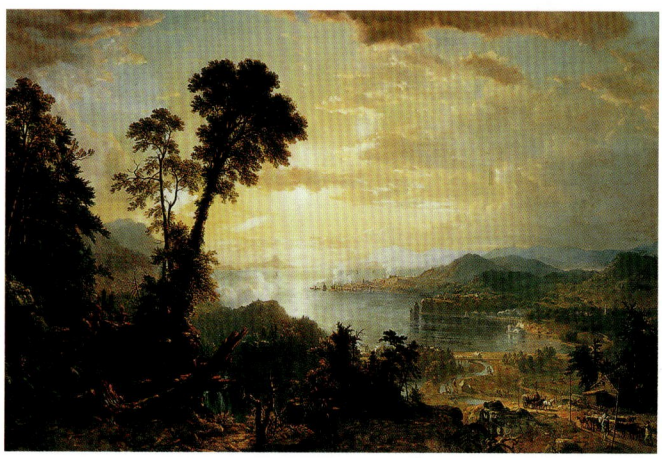

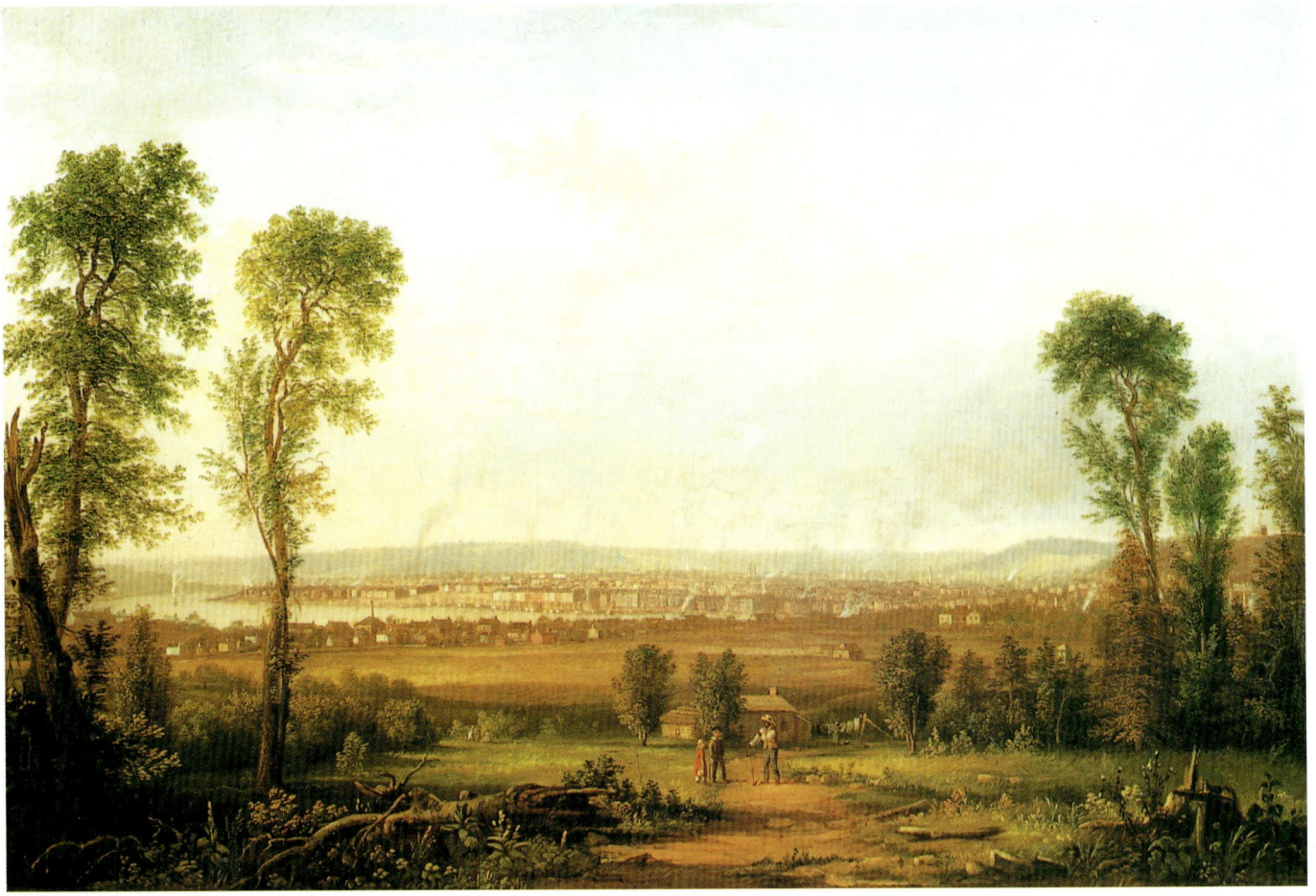

3.9.16 Robert S. Duncanson: *View of Cincinnati, Ohio, from Covington, Kentucky*, 1858.
Oil on canvas, 25 x 36 in. (63.5 x 91.4 cm.)
Cincinnati Historical Society, Cincinnati, Ohio

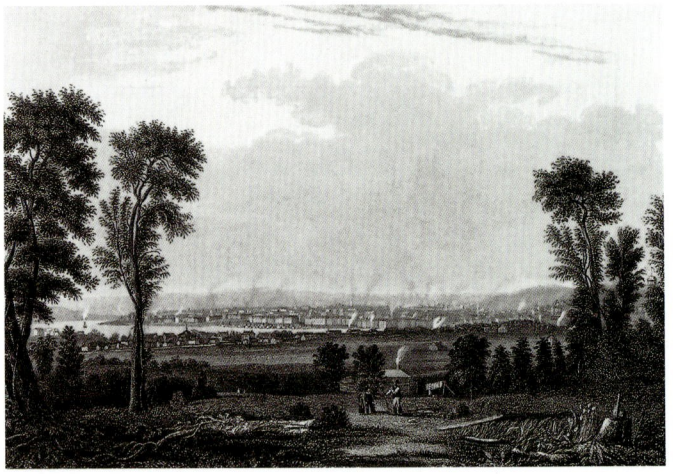

3.9.17 Unknown artist: *View of Cincinnati, Ohio*, 1848.
Engraving from *Graham's Magazine*, June 1848

wrote, "and for the last time treading those mountain glades, so beautiful in their wild scenery, but soon to change and disappear before the white man's resistless march of improvement."

Robert S. Duncanson also directed his attention to the landscape transformed in his *View of Cincinnati, Ohio, from Covington, Kentucky* of 1858 [**3.9.16**]. Here the foreground is occupied not by displaced Native Americans but by African American farmers, whose rural life in Covington is contrasted with the bustling commercial center of Cincinnati. Unlike Durand's *Progress*, which offers a symbolic landscape, Duncanson's work focuses on the specifics of a particular site, from the Mitchel (Mount Adams) Observatory on the hill at the far right to the boats moored at the Cincinnati Public Landing. His painting is based on a daguerreotype that appeared in engraved form in *Graham's Magazine* of June 1848 [**3.9.17**]. Yet, as the art historian Joseph D. Ketner has pointed out in his study of Duncanson, the artist has changed the white man in the foreground of the engraving speaking to two white children to a black farmer and the woman hanging out laundry from white to black. This black man and woman might well represent 2 of the 50 free African Americans who, in addition to 15,000 whites and 100 slaves, made up Covington's population at the time. The theme of freedom is further reinforced by the fact that African

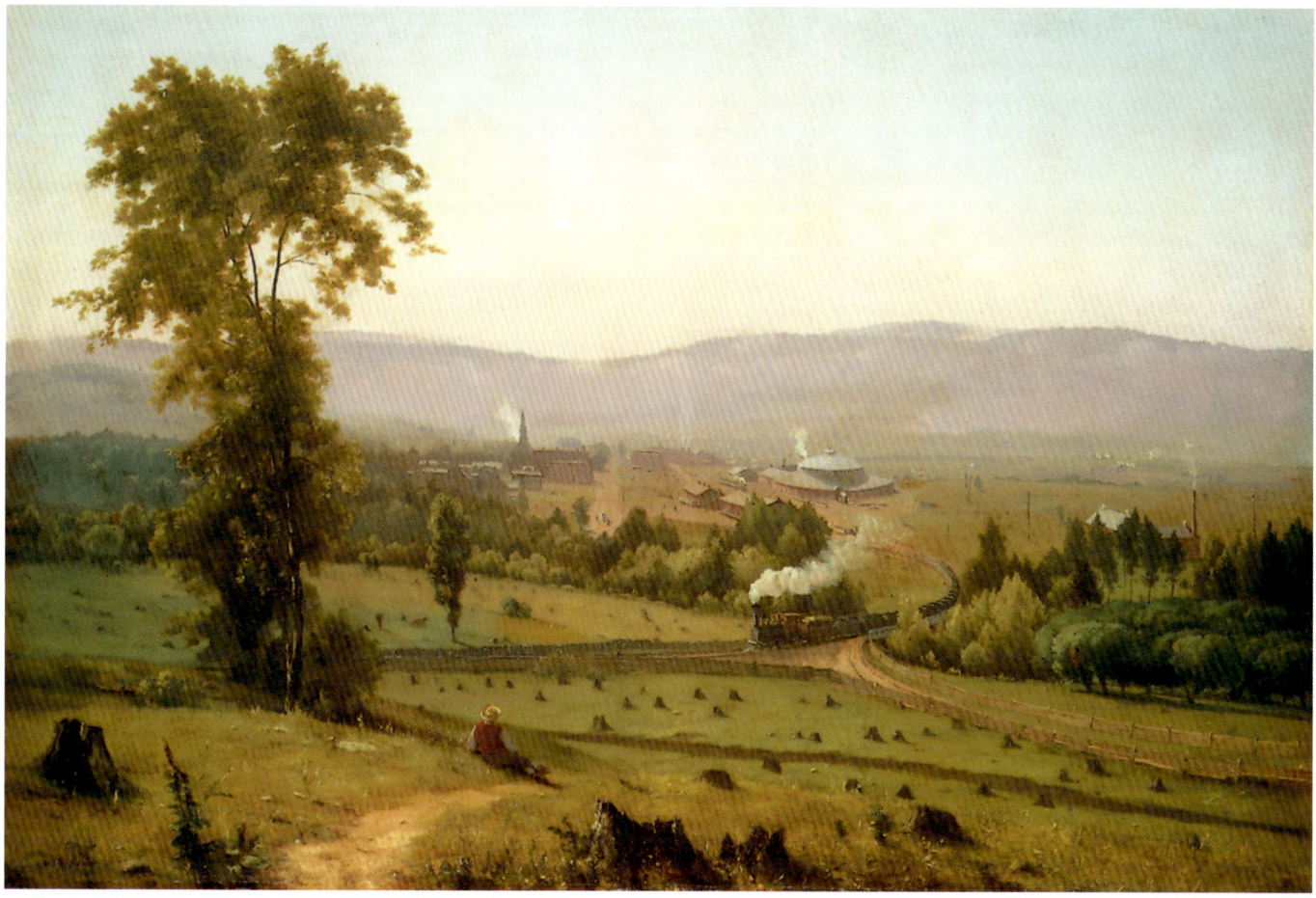

3.9.18 George Inness: *The Lackawanna Valley*, c. 1855. Oil on canvas, 33⅞ x 50¼ in. (86 x 127.5 cm.) National Gallery of Art, Washington, D.C.

Americans in Kentucky often escaped slavery via Covington in the winter when the Ohio River froze over.

The art historian David M. Lubin also argues that the bodies of water that play a dominant role in Duncanson's landscape paintings—*View of Cincinnati* [**3.9.17**], *Blue Hole, Little Miami River* [**3.8.16**; p. 162], and *The Garden of Eden* [**3.8.17**; p. 163] being only three examples—functioned as a "trope of freedom itself." The writings of African Americans often included references to crossing bodies of water to freedom, be it the passage over the Great Lakes to Canada or over the Ohio River to Ohio. Duncanson's residence in both Detroit and Cincinnati would have made him particularly aware of the symbolic dimensions of these two bodies of water.

Probably the most famous description of its time of such a crossing appeared not in the writings of an African American, however, but in the European American Harriet Beecher Stowe's popular novel *Uncle Tom's Cabin; or, Life Among the Lowly* (1852). In Stowe's novel, the Kentucky slave Eliza, faced with the icy Ohio River, "vaulted sheer over the turbid current by the shore, on to the raft of ice beyond," stopping only when, "as in a dream, she saw the Ohio side, and a man helping her up the bank." Stowe lived in Cincinnati in the 1840s and patterned this episode after a news item describing a similar winter crossing of the Ohio by a slave woman with her child in her arms. Duncanson was certainly aware of Stowe's book. The year after its publication, he painted two of its characters, Uncle Tom and Little Eva, in a landscape containing, not surprisingly, a large body of water [**4.12.5**; p. 225].

Another landscape artist concerned with the specific topography of a particular location was George Inness (1825–1894). In 1855 he was commissioned by the first president of the Delaware, Lackawanna, and Western Railroad to depict its new roundhouse complex at Scranton, Pennsylvania, for the princely sum of $75 (Frederic Edwin Church received $5,500 for *Niagara* in 1857) [**3.9.18**]. Some scholars date Inness's painting to the end of the 1850s, noting that the roundhouse complex was not completed until 1856. Others defend the 1855 date, saying he could have included it on the basis of designs to which he undoubtedly had access.

Here, once again, a tiny foreground figure, this time a young white boy, directs our gaze down the gently sloping hill to the train, the roundhouse, and the town of Scranton. In place of a wilderness foreground, Inness depicts a field of stumps, evidence of the axe's progress in pushing back untamed nature to make way for the technology of civilization most aptly represented by the train. Unlike Durand's *Progress* [**3.9.15**; p. 183], the train occupies the center of the composition as it emerges out of the settled landscape into the intermediate space of the freshly cleared field. The train and the railroad buildings are framed by the church on the left, its spire rising above the town, and the factory on the right, its chimney emitting a stream of smoke. The factory itself is almost totally hidden by trees, thus appearing as if part of nature rather than of the urban landscape.

Inness's privileging of the train and the roundhouse complex could be read as a celebration of this appearance of technology in the American landscape. Indeed, alongside the promotion of the sublime aspects of the American wilderness there had also emerged effusive praise of what the art historian Barbara Novak terms the "technological sublime," a sense of awe in the face of the vast power of machines. But the celebratory aspects of the painting are undercut by Inness's use of the tree stumps, which had long since come to represent mixed feelings regarding the destruction of the pristine wilderness. If God-as-nature is destroyed, would God-as-organized-religion, represented by the church, be able to survive? By pairing the church spire and the factory chimney, is Inness suggesting divine sanction of American enterprise, or is he suggesting that both, to survive, must keep their distance?

That Inness places so many tree stumps in such a prominent position in the painting suggests his awareness of the massive destruction of forests necessitated by the construction of the railways. Companies were often given the right to fell a broad section on either side of the railway bed to prevent trees from falling on the track. Between 1820 and 1860 more than 30,000 miles (48,000 kilometers) of track were laid, with the final spike linking the Atlantic and Pacific coast lines driven on May 10, 1869, at Promontory, Utah. Trees were also used for railroad ties, fuel, and in the building of the cars. The existence of railroads facilitated the transportation of lumber, which, in turn, led to more trees falling to the ax. The limits of these forests would not become apparent for at least another century, although far-thinking individuals at the time predicted their inevitable demise if measures were not taken to rein in their destruction. These protests, however, were drowned out by the more insistent declaration of America's boundless opportunities and unlimited natural resources.

Human Actors in the Landscape: Genre Paintings of the Yeoman Farmer

The transformation of the land also appeared in another series of images, ones in which the small figures in the foreground of many earlier landscapes began to take center stage and to form the basis of what came to be known as genre paintings. In her study of American genre paintings, Elizabeth Johns notes that critics consistently celebrated these scenes of "everyday life" during the antebellum period, from 1830 to 1860. Two of the most common characters were those of the yeoman farmer and the Westerner. Why, Johns asks, were these particular subjects so popular at this time? What are the ideologies that inform these images, the social assumptions that are not necessarily apparent at first glance, but which provide the interpretive framework upon which the figures and settings are hung? Who exactly found them so appealing?

While the genre paintings discussed by Johns were often celebrated as distinctly American, she argues that their popularity was the result of their appeal to a particular region of the country—New York City. It was here that the majority of the paintings were either produced or exhibited or both. It was here that the political, economic, and cultural forces of the nation were coalescing, particularly after the opening of the Erie Canal in 1825. It was here, also, that the most intense upheavals and challenges to the social cohesion of the nation were felt, upheavals that contributed to the popularity of genre paintings.

The thirty years of genre painting's heyday were years of increased opportunities for a broad segment of the white male population, opportunities that were accompanied by increasing tensions surrounding changes in economic and social status. One response to such tensions was the creation of "types," characters who embodied these changes and upon whom others could project their anxieties. Two issues of particular significance during the 1830s and 1840s were democracy and citizenship—who was a citizen, how were citizens supposed to conduct themselves, what were the implications of the spread of individual sovereignty? Such questions and the anxieties they produced were not new, but they became of increasing concern to the political and financial elite of the East Coast after 1828 when Andrew Jackson, a Westerner and a Democrat, was elected to the presidency.

The yeoman farmer as a type had roots in the British yeoman, an individual loyal to the landowning class as well as aware of his inferior station. In the US, the farmer who worked the land was seen as the fundamental productive force of the new nation, a nation made up of small landholders who would guarantee the moral and economic wellbeing of the country through their productive labor. But American yeomen did not

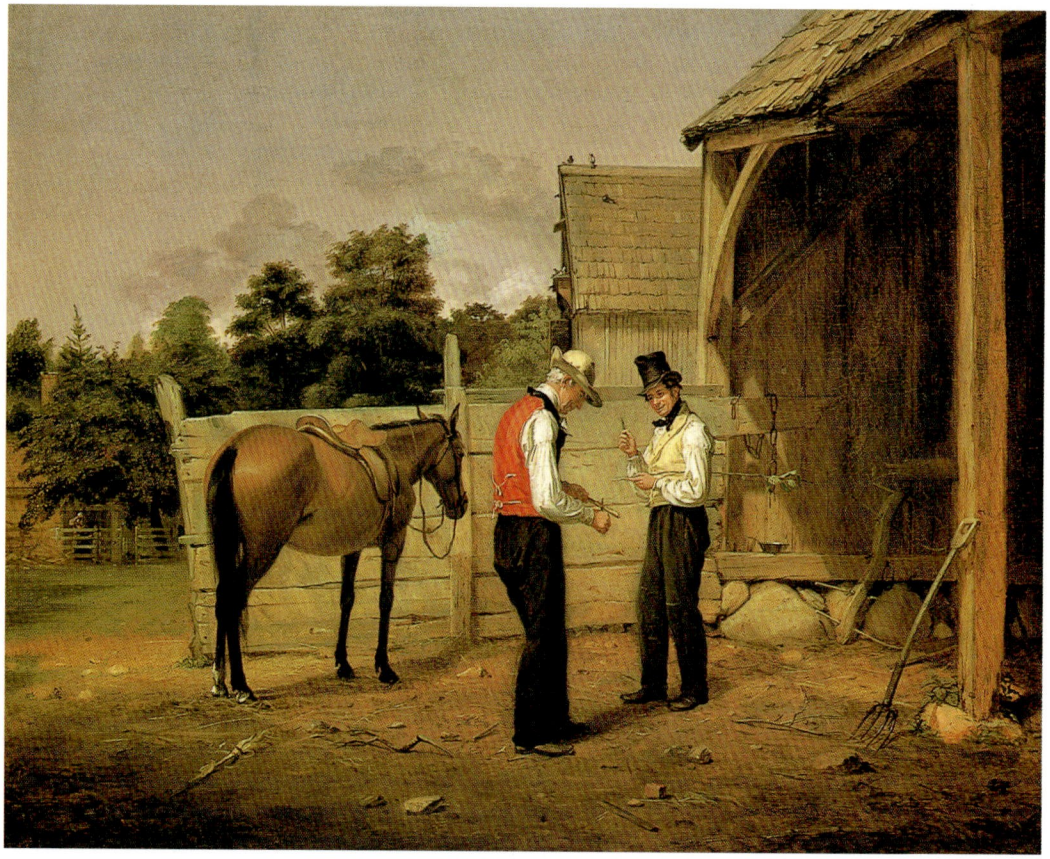

3.9.19 William Sidney Mount: *Bargaining for a Horse*, 1835. Oil on canvas, 24 x 30 in. (61 x 76.2 cm.) Courtesy The New-York Historical Society, New York

"know their place." Those large landholders who formed the founding fathers and who dominated the political scene into the early nineteenth century were constantly complaining of the uncitizen-like actions of many new property owners. These newcomers were often portrayed in literary publications and theatrical venues as lower-class, ignorant, and concerned only with individual gain rather than the betterment of the community at large. New Yorkers further refined this image into the "Yankee" farmer, a reference to New Englanders upon whom New Yorkers could project all of their anxieties about their own drive to amass wealth. Thus while the country's rural origins were celebrated, actual farmers were often mocked and ridiculed.

One artist who tapped into these mixed emotions was William Sidney Mount (1807–1868). Born into a comfortable, landowning family on Long Island, Mount was apprenticed to his brother Henry, a sign-painter, in 1824. After enrolling in lessons at the National Academy of Design, he began his career as a painter at the end of the decade, exhibiting his first history painting in 1828. Meeting with little success with his history canvases, in 1830 he hit on the portrayal of the nation's rural life, creating scenes of dances and general country life. But the proliferation of caricatures of the Yankee farmer after the election of Jackson in 1828 must have struck a chord with Mount, for he began a series of images of this much-maligned character that gained him considerable critical attention.

Mount's first significant work in this vein was his painting *Bargaining for a Horse* of 1835 [**3.9.19**]. The work was commissioned by Luman Reed, a self-made merchant from a rural background in upper New York State who, two years earlier, had charged Thomas Cole with executing his five-part *The Course of Empire* (see pp. 158–60). Interestingly, just as Cole's series recorded a cyclical view of history that captured the anxieties of an elite cultural world of which Reed would never be a part, *Bargaining for a Horse* mocks a general social type—the ambitious, materialistic individual—to which Reed could easily be seen as belonging.

Bargaining for a Horse depicts two men, one considerably older than the other, engaged in a business transaction. One wears a straw hat, identifying him as a farmer, while the other wears a black top hat, suggesting the city—though Mount's original title, *Farmers Bargaining*, identifies both as farmers. The process of negotiation is accompanied by whittling, which adds a certain nonchalance and goodwill to the scene. The open shed in front of which the figures stand, however, is run-down and empty, suggesting a lack of productivity. "In their devotion to getting a good deal," Johns proposes, "the yeomen have abandoned the productive work of plowing, sowing seed, harvesting, stacking hay, and even maintaining their property." Here are the results of subordinating production to deal making, a message that would undoubtedly have added meaning in 1835, the year in which a frenzy of land speculation and gambling took hold in New York.

Mount also makes use of verbal metaphors in his painting. "Horsetrading" was a term recently applied to the practice of promising material benefits in exchange for votes, a practice identified with the Democratic Party. The whittling also brought to mind two other colloquialisms, "coming to the point" and "shaving" or being duplicitous. In addition, the birds located on the roof of the far shed above and between the two men, are probably pigeons (note the loft on the end wall of the shed beneath the peak of the roof). This suggests, according to Johns, "that a 'pigeon'—a term ubiquitous in the anxious vernacular of the period—is about to be plucked." At least one reviewer perceived the intended vernacular wordplays when the work was exhibited in 1835. After noting that the painting was "an image of pure Yankeeism and full of wholesome humor," he added that "both of the yeomen seem to be 'reckoning,' both whittling, both delaying." When the painting was engraved in 1839 for the annual publication *The Gift of 1840*, the publisher Edward L. Carey changed the title from *Farmers Bargaining* to *Bargaining for a Horse*, thus making it easier for the engraving's broader audience to perceive the horsetrading metaphor.

Human Actors in the Landscape: Genre Paintings of the Westerner

If the wheeling and dealing of the New England farmer caused certain New Yorkers some anxiety about the demise of the nation's agrarian ideal, the seemingly uncontrollable egalitarianism and entrepreneurship of the Westerner caused them even greater concern. At least the Yankee was a known entity, whereas the Westerner was somewhere "out there," in a landscape that was both intimidating and profitable beyond many Easterners' wildest dreams. Just as the Yankee farmer served as a figure on which New Yorkers could project their anxieties about citizenship and materialism, so the Westerner provided them with a site for the projection of their dreams of classlessness and individualism. As the urban and industrial centers of the East Coast expanded and immigration from Europe increased, creating more glaring class and ethnic divisions, the West appeared refreshingly devoid of these social and economic complications. If the agrarian life of the past provided a nostalgic vision of social balance, the West functioned as a present and future promise.

One of the best-known painters of the West in the antebellum period was George Caleb Bingham (1811–1879). Bingham first gained attention as a portrait painter in the 1830s, but soon turned to the landscape and daily activities of the West, and in particular of the Missouri and Mississippi Rivers (he had moved to Missouri at the age of eight). While the majority of his paintings depict the presence of white settlers, Bingham produced a few early images that served to highlight the transitions this landscape was undergoing through the use of the figure of the Native American. In 1845 he painted *The Concealed Enemy* [**3.9.20**], in which an Osage warrior (recognizable by his headdress and body paint) crouches behind a rock, rifle in hand. The dark foreground adds to the drama of the scene, made even more sinister by its contrast to the bright sky at the upper right. This Osage is obviously waiting for his prey, some riverboatmen who hoped safely to navigate the waters shown at the base of the cliff below.

By the 1840s the Osages had disappeared from much of the Missouri landscape, having been forced to relocate to territory further west. Bingham's painting most likely refers to a time some twenty years earlier, when they were still numerous in the region. He may have come across some Osages in the 1820s in the town of Arrow Rock where he grew up. He also may have learned about them through talks with his father, who had kept a diary of his travels that contained descriptions of the various indigenous peoples he had encountered along the way. Or he may have gotten his ideas from the growing number of illustrated books being published about the West, which favored dramatic renditions of dangerous warriors rather than picturesque portraits of noble leaders.

3.9.20 George Caleb Bingham: *The Concealed Enemy*, 1845. Oil on canvas, 29¼ x 36½ in. (74.3 x 92.7 cm.) Stark Museum of Art, Orange, Texas

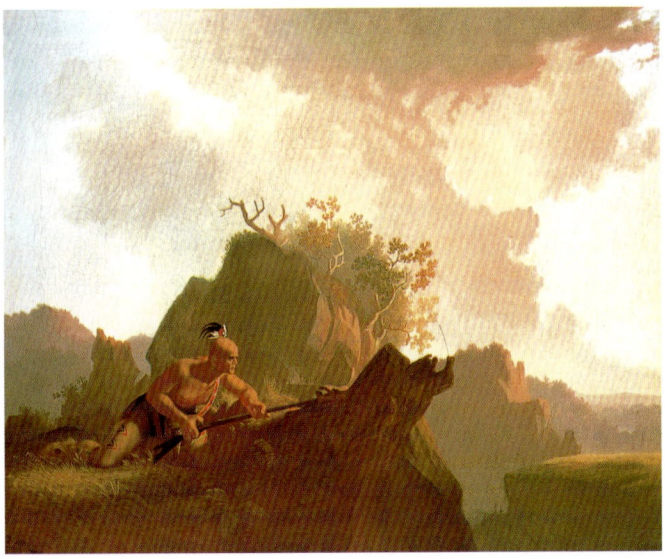

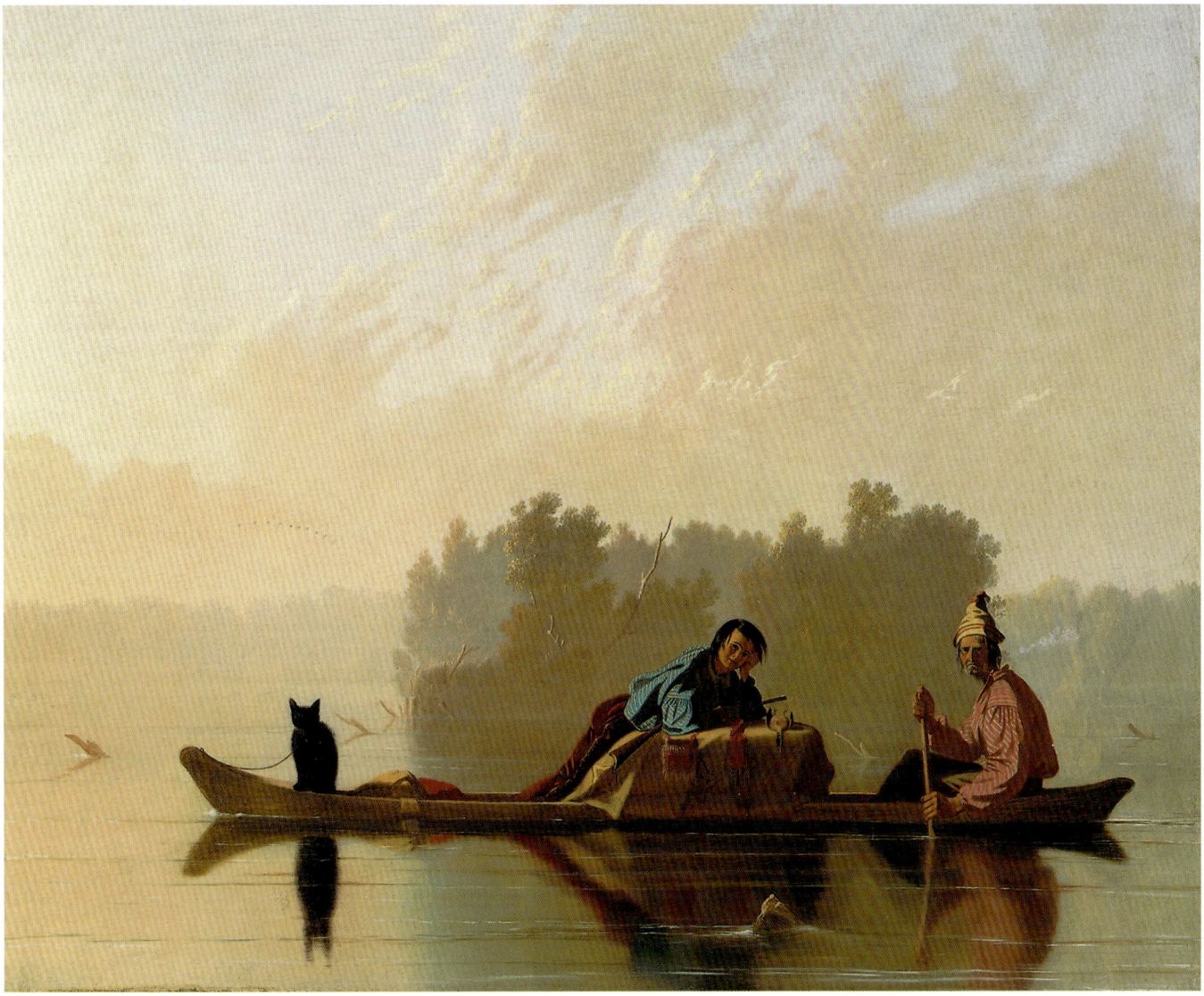

3.9.21 George Caleb Bingham: *Fur Traders Descending the Missouri*, 1845. Oil on canvas, 29¼ x 36¼ in. (74.3 x 92.1 cm.) The Metropolitan Museum of Art, New York

Bingham painted another work in 1845 that many consider a companion piece to *The Concealed Enemy: Fur Traders Descending the Missouri* [**3.9.21**]. George Catlin's writings give us insight into the situation of fur traders in the Missouri region in the 1830s and 1840s. He was accompanied during much of his travel up and down the river and its tributaries by two French Canadian trappers, Ba'tiste and Bogard, who appear to have done most of the paddling while he steered. Catlin describes them as hardy, somewhat comical men who were skilled in the arts of navigating rivers and shooting or trapping game. The men were members of a much larger group of French Canadian *voyageurs* who first opened up the region's fur trade in the late eighteenth century and who continued to work the area in the early nineteenth century. But the expansion of American settlements and the arrival of the steamboat and other larger vessels put many of them out of business or forced them even further west. Indeed, Catlin includes an account in his memoirs of how he rescued Ba'tiste from the difficult conditions of a "free trapper"—constant debt to the fur companies, constant attacks by Native Americans who stole his furs—by offering him a job as boatman, which Ba'tiste quickly and gratefully accepted.

The French Canadian trappers often had as companions Native American women, who bore them children. This situation is referred to in the original title of Bingham's painting, *French Trader and His Half-Breed Son*. Unlike the Osage in *The Concealed Enemy*, the young boy wears pants and a shirt, rather than body paint and feathered headdress. His hair has been cut short rather than shaved off and his rifle lies at rest beneath him rather than ready for attack. He leans on the pile of furs and looks out at us, as does his father, rather than toward the river.

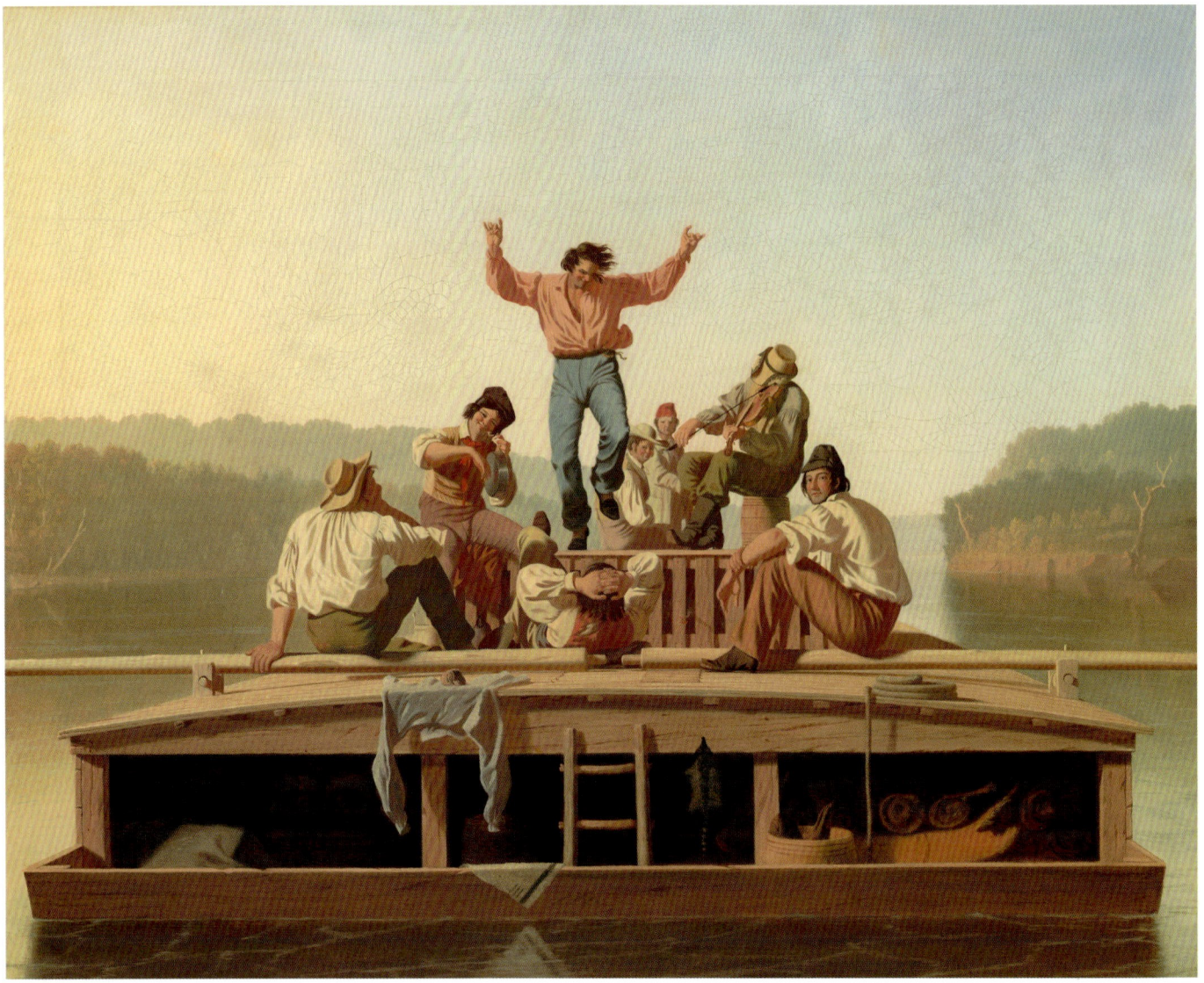

3.9.22 George Caleb Bingham: *The Jolly Flatboatmen*, 1846. Oil on canvas, 38⅛ x 48½ in. (96.8 x 123.2 cm.) National Gallery of Art, Washington, D.C.

The atmosphere is calm rather than foreboding, with the glassy surface of the river reflecting the figures in the boat.

Thus the two paintings are both parallel and different in their subject matter. *The Concealed Enemy* suggests the presence, although diminishing, of the threat of Native Americans to westward expansion, while *Fur Traders Descending the Missouri* represents the beginning of European American commerce on the rivers of the Midwest and the resultant taming of both the indigenous peoples and the wildlife that inhabited the region (the species of the furry animal chained to the front of the boat—cat, bear cub—is still the subject of much debate).

Bingham did not limit his activities to those of an artist. In 1839 he became involved in the founding of the Whig Party in Missouri and served as a state representative in the late 1840s. He also produced painted banners for various Whig campaigns, the iconography of which, according to the art historian Nancy Rash, provided inspiration for a later series of riverboat paintings, such as *The Jolly Flatboatmen* of 1846 [**3.9.22**]. One of the major Whig goals of the 1840s was to obtain federal funding for the clearing of the Missouri and Mississippi Rivers. The Democratic Party argued, however, for territorial expansion, including the annexation of Texas, rather than internal improvements, and felt that states should pay for river projects. Bingham's paintings of commerce on Missouri's rivers, therefore, were the products of an avid Whig politician, who made several speeches in the 1840s in support of facilitating such commerce. The snags of wood which appear in *Fur Traders* and several of his riverboat paintings are reminders of the dangers that face traffic, both large and small, along these waterways (a few paintings also include steamboats that have run aground).

Fur Traders and *The Concealed Enemy* were among a group of four of Bingham's paintings purchased in December 1845 by the American Art-Union (the other two were rural scenes, the agricultural counterpart to scenes of commerce on the river). The Art-Union had been founded in 1842 as an outgrowth of New York City's Apollo Association. It was organized as a lottery and was open to anyone who paid the membership fee. The prizes were the paintings it had purchased. All members received an engraving each year made after a popular painting. In its calls for submissions, the organization encouraged landscapes or scenes of daily life in all parts of America. Thus, through the circulation of engravings of works by contemporary American artists, the Art-Union hoped to develop a taste among Americans for American art dealing with American subject matter, while at the same time providing financial support for artists. It was enormously successful, distributing some 150,000 engravings and 2,400 paintings by more than 250 artists in the 10 years that it existed. Its two publications, *Bulletin* and *Transactions*, sent to members, were among the first journals of art in this country. In a way, its success was its downfall. Other art organizations, such as the National Academy of Design, and artists not favored by the Art-Union helped initiate a legal suit against it, which resulted in a court decision outlawing it as a lottery. After its demise, its role was taken over by its successor, the Cosmopolitan Art Association.

The fact that *Fur Traders* received the highest price of the four paintings undoubtedly encouraged Bingham to continue with his riverboat subject matter. *The Jolly Flatboatmen (1)* was subsequently purchased and distributed in engraved form by the Art-Union. The popularity of these paintings was part of a growing interest in western scenes among audiences in the East, an interest undoubtedly encouraged by Catlin's "Indian Gallery" (see pp. 175–78). Bingham's paintings differed from Catlin's, however. They celebrated not the nobility of a dying race, but the commercial and agricultural progress of a European-based civilization in the western regions.

The American Studies scholar Bryan Wolf suggests two additional levels of meaning in Bingham's paintings. *Fur Traders Descending the Missouri* re-affirmed in Missouri viewers their pride in their state and also appealed to the specialized knowledge of some—if the animal is a bear cub, it would refer to the state symbol; the canoe would call to mind the state's name, Missouri, which is a Native American word that means "people who use canoes." This same painting, and the later riverboat paintings, appealed to Eastern audiences faced with increasing incidents of labor unrest in their cities, the result of the demise of the independent artisan and the rise of a system of wage labor. They allowed such audiences to convince themselves that the world of artisan and free laborer, the bulwark of republican values, still existed, in the West if not in their own back yard. Thus, the West provided a solution not only to the "Indian problem" but also to the "labor problem." Unemployed workers could go west to start a new life, rather than remain in the East and foment rebellion against those whose wealth depended on an acquiescent wage-labor force. Yet, as Catlin's description of Ba'tiste's situation indicates, one would have to travel much further west than the Missouri River to retain one's independence in the face of market forces that encouraged the consolidation of industries and the spread of wage labor. One would also have to travel much further west to find a landscape that had not been impacted by these economic developments.

Review Questions

1 What was the ideology of Manifest Destiny and how was it represented visually?

2 How were the portraits of Native Americans by Charles Bird King, George Catlin, and Thomas Easterly similar? How were they different?

3 How was the idea of "progress" represented in the paintings of Robert S. Duncanson, Asher B. Durand, and George Inness?

4 During the antebellum period (1830–60), while the country's rural origins were celebrated, actual farmers were often mocked and ridiculed. Why was this so? How did this appear in the genre paintings of this era, such as William Sidney Mount's *Bargaining for a Horse* (1835)?

5 Both George Catlin and George Caleb Bingham created genre scenes of life in the American West. What did each choose to focus on, and why?

CHAPTER 10

Domesticated Nature

(*c.* 1818–1860)

Woman as Nature: The Nude, the Mother, and the Cook

As the art historian Elizabeth Johns notes, women seldom appear in the genre paintings of George Caleb Bingham (1811–1879), William Sidney Mount (1807–1868), or other men who became famous in this category of painting during the antebellum period. When they do appear, they are most often tiny figures in the background, as in Mount's *Bargaining for a Horse* [**3.9.19**; p. 187]. They certainly do not congregate in groups and exhibit the camaraderie of Bingham's boatmen. Instead, in the world of art, as elsewhere, women were seen not so much as occupying nature, but as embodying nature. They were grounded in the materiality of their bodies (most clearly in the process of childbirth) and in the realm of the senses. Thus, they were seen as unable to engage in the life of the mind—the worlds of art, science, and industry—that marked the realm of culture.

Paintings from continental Europe, in particular France and Italy, often included female nudes reclining in lush landscapes, with the fecundity of their bodies symbolizing the fecundity of the land. Few such nudes appeared in the US in the first half of the nineteenth century, a testament to the ongoing influence of Puritan sentiments and British painting traditions in the art world (depictions of nudes were rare in Britain as well). A notable exception, discussed in Chapter 6, was John Vanderlyn's *Ariadne Asleep on the Island of Naxos* (1809–14) [**2.6.25**; p. 127].

One genre painter who reconfigured this connection between women and nature in the antebellum period was herself a woman—Lilly Martin Spencer (1822–1902). In her paintings of domestic scenes, the nation's natural resources often appear as fruits and vegetables, freshly picked and awaiting further transformation by the women of the household into the nutritious meals that were to sustain their families, the nation's present and future citizens. Yet the women in Spencer's paintings are more than competent wives, mothers, daughters, and servants. They also exude a sense of confidence and forthrightness absent from most contemporary images of women in the home.

Spencer's parents were French socialists, who traveled first to England, then to the US in 1830, settling near Cincinnati. Their goal had been to form a utopian colony of families, and while they never achieved this goal, they became strong supporters of women's rights, the temperance movement, and the abolition of slavery. Spencer received encouragement from her parents in her artistic pursuits in Cincinnati (she was largely self-taught) and, after 1848, in New York. During her first year in New York she sold several paintings to the American Art-Union (see p. 191), which became her most dependable patron, creating for her a national reputation through the circulation of prints of her works. This reputation was vital for Spencer, for she had to support not only herself, but also her husband and their seven children (she gave birth to thirteen, but only seven survived to adulthood). After the demise of the Art-Union, she found another patron in its successor, the Cosmopolitan Art Association.

Spencer worked at a time when many women's lives were being transformed by the emergence of an organized movement focused on gaining greater political, social, and economic rights for women. This movement also influenced the ways in which female bodies and female sexuality were discussed and represented. The same year Spencer moved to New York City, approximately three hundred men and women gathered in Seneca Falls, New York under the leadership of Elizabeth Cady Stanton and Lucretia Mott. Stanton and Mott were prominent advocates of women's rights and organized the meeting to initiate a campaign for the political, social, civil, and religious rights of women.

At the end of two days, 100 people (68 women and 32 men) had signed the Declaration of Sentiments, a document written largely by Stanton and modeled upon the Declaration of Independence. It proclaimed, among other things, that all men and women are created equal and marked the beginning of a women's rights movement that mobilized both sexes across the nation and culminated in the passage of the Equal Suffrage (Nineteenth) Amendment to the Constitution in 1920 granting women the right to vote. It was also closely aligned with the abolitionist movement. The African American author and activist Frederick Douglass, then editor of the *North Star* in Rochester, New York, was one of the signatories of the Declaration of Sentiments.

The women's rights, or suffrage, movement created heated and widespread debates over women's place in society. Should women have the right to vote and own property? Should they be allowed to attend institutions of higher education? Should they be allowed equal access to all professions and trades? Many opposed the extension of the rights of women by arguing that while morally superior to men, women were too delicate to enter the public sphere. The Declaration of Sentiments challenged this assumption, asserting that if women were, indeed, morally superior, then they needed to exercise that moral superiority in religious and other public assemblies, as well as in the home. The Declaration also criticized the double standard often adopted by men in their criticisms of women who

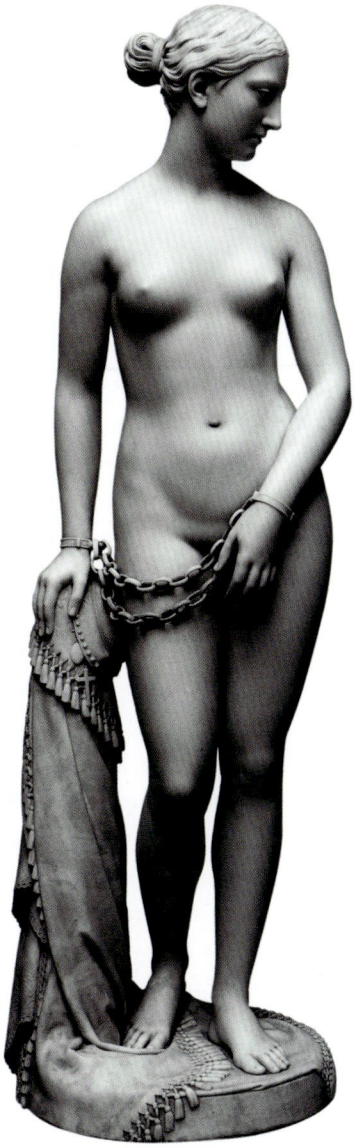

3.10.1 Hiram Powers: *The Greek Slave*, 1846.
Marble, after the original plaster of 1843, h. 66 in. (168 cm.)
Corcoran Collection, National Gallery of Art, Washington, D.C.

dared to assume a public life: "Resolved, That the objection of indelicacy and impropriety, which is so often brought against woman when she addresses a public audience, comes with a very ill-grace from those who encourage, by their attendance, her appearance on the stage, in the concert, or in feats of the circus." This resolution addressed another aspect of the debates regarding women's place in society, one that was particularly relevant in the art world: what was the relationship between women's moral and sexual natures? How was the female body to be displayed and viewed?

These questions can be addressed by examining an artwork created five years before the Seneca Falls Convention that gained national notoriety in subsequent years for its display of the naked female body: *The Greek Slave* (1843) by the Vermont-born artist Hiram Powers (1805–1873). The statue was exhibited not only in the United States, but also in Powers's studio in Florence, where he spent most of his professional career, and in London at the Great Exhibition of 1851. The artist made six full-size replicas of the work [**3.10.1**] as well as several smaller versions and busts.

The art historian Joy Kasson has thoroughly documented the extent of and reasons for *The Greek Slave*'s widespread popularity, particularly in a country still resistant to the public display of nudity. While there is, indeed, a prurient side to the statue, Powers was able to make the nudity acceptable by emphasizing the woman's powerlessness, and thus her lack of responsibility for her own downfall. The image, therefore, becomes one of pathos and violence, given a contemporary meaning by the recently ended Greek and Turkish war (1821–32). Powers described the figure as the only surviving member of a Greek family from an island invaded by the Turks. (According to Kasson, few in the US publicly connected *The Greek Slave* with slavery in America, although many may well have done so in private.) Here was a pious Christian woman, her cross hanging on the draped support to her right next to a locket suggesting a lost husband. Her head is averted and her chained hand covers her genital area in an attempt at modesty.

When *The Greek Slave* went on tour to several US cities in 1847, it was accompanied by a pamphlet containing numerous texts—press notices, poems—that instructed audiences on how to view the work properly, i.e. how to perceive the moral rather than sensual elements. Perhaps the most influential of these texts was a review by a Unitarian minister, the Reverend Orville Dewey. He compared *The Greek Slave* favorably with the famous first century BCE Greek statue *Venus de' Medici* (the obvious model for Powers's statue), and affirmed that "there is no sentiment in the Venus, but modesty." Thus, the meaning of Powers's work lay not in the sensuality of the female body but in the higher moral purpose it inspired. The artist was able, writes Kasson, "to make the spiritual reign over the corporeal; to sink form in ideality; in this particular case, to make the appeal to the soul entirely control the appeal to the senses."

The numerous love poems inspired by the statue revealed, however, that not all viewers chose the spiritual route in their response to the work. Many of these poems, and some of the commentaries made by both male and female viewers, revealed a play between purity and eroticism that spoke to an ambivalence regarding the naked body and female sexuality in particular. The 1840s saw an increased concern about the dangers of sexuality and the threat that modern life posed to the delicate constitutions of women. This concern was fueled in part by the rise of dance halls and other places of popular entertainment where partially clothed female bodies, and thus female sexuality, were on display. *The Greek Slave* epitomized this endangered female body, while providing it safe haven in an idealized moral narrative. Yet viewers often saw the statue as representative of the disruption of domestic harmony, a disruption that could only partially be compensated for by the woman's spiritual purity and resignation to her fate.

Others saw a revolutionary potential in *The Greek Slave*. While a slave herself, she had the power to inspire resistance to enslavement. She was able to subdue the gallery audience, to create a respectful silence as her condition was contemplated. Women were empowered to view her openly and to take away lessons specific to their own situation. The popularity of *The Greek Slave* can accordingly be found in the many narratives embedded within it. Such narratives, writes Kasson,

> told the story of the female body as their authors understood it—vulnerable, dangerous, and endangered, representing beauty and shame, attractive in its self-absorption but threatening to overwhelm the viewer. By extension, they told the story of the body politic, which was undergoing transition to a commercial culture amid contemplation of unsettling changes in gender roles and family life. The contradictory meanings embodied in *The Greek Slave*—eroticism indulged and denied, passion and passionlessness, power and powerlessness—were the meanings with which its viewers themselves struggled in a rapidly transforming culture.

Women were thus expected to fill a complex role. They were to be both pure and seductive, powerful and powerless, moral guardians of the home yet ruled by their emotions. Their influence was allowed to extend outside the home primarily in the carefully reared bodies of their sons and daughters, the former as active citizens and wage earners and the latter as future caretakers of their own homes. The movement that coalesced in Seneca Falls in July 1848 would systematically challenge this ideology of domesticity, creating new opportunities for women as political and cultural actors on the stage of history. At the same time, those opposed to the suffrage movement would insist even more forcefully that woman's "natural" place was in the home, that women were the moral center of the nation, and that the preservation of their virtue depended upon their domestic locale. The creation of a safe domestic space presided over by a loving, virtuous wife and mother was seen as an essential antidote to the materialistic and self-interested pursuits of men in the world outside of the home.

Spencer's work addressed many of these tensions surrounding the representation of the domesticated female body and female sexuality. During the 1850s she produced several scenes of women in the home preparing food that combine the domestic and the sexual, such as *Kiss Me and You'll Kiss the 'Lasses* of 1856 [**3.10.2**]. The painting was commissioned by the Cosmopolitan Art Association, which recognized the potential popularity of an image where sexuality is playfully suggested yet safely ensconced in a domestic setting. Like Mount, only more forthrightly, Spencer includes a play on words in the title. Having just tasted a spoonful of molasses ('lasses), the young woman, smiling suggestively, warns her guest of what is in store for him (nineteenth century viewers would assume she was addressing a man) if he kisses her (the lass). Like Vanderlyn, Spencer connects the fertility of nature, evident in the abundant produce in the baskets on either side of her, with the sexuality of women. Here, however, the woman is standing, not lying down. She is awake, not asleep. She confronts the viewer rather than averting her head. And she actively takes pleasure in her awareness of her own sexual attractiveness.

As the art historian Annelise K. Madsen points out, the "domestic angel" who presided over the home was most often represented in the visual arts and literature as decidedly middle-class. She was also most often white. She adhered to the proper etiquette laid out in the numerous etiquette books that were appearing during the 1840s and 1850s, such as *Beadle's Dime Book of Practical Etiquette for Ladies and Gentlemen* (1859). She was a sign of status for the urban man who could afford to maintain a family on his own income in relative comfort. As will become clear in a later chapter (see pp. 285–92), this domestic angel was most often portrayed at rest, and while she might oversee the activities of servants, she would seldom be shown engaging in cooking or housecleaning herself. In addition, women who worked outside their own homes were seldom celebrated as guardians of virtue.

Spencer presents the young woman in *Kiss Me and You'll Kiss the 'Lasses* in a middle class domestic interior, with elegant rugs on the floor and a silver pitcher on the table. She is appropriately attired in a rich green gown, with gold earrings in the shape of fruit baskets. She appears to be in an intermediary space between the kitchen and the parlor. The materials on the table, floor, and chair (various fruit, molasses, sugar cubes) suggest she is in the process of making jam, hence engaging in a form of domestic labor. Yet there is no stove or fireplace to cook the fruit or boil the water to sterilize and seal the jars. Her attention is focused outward and is accompanied by a flirtatious expression that acknowledges her power as a sexual being. The overflowing basket of cherries, a fruit that symbolizes virginity, love, fertility,

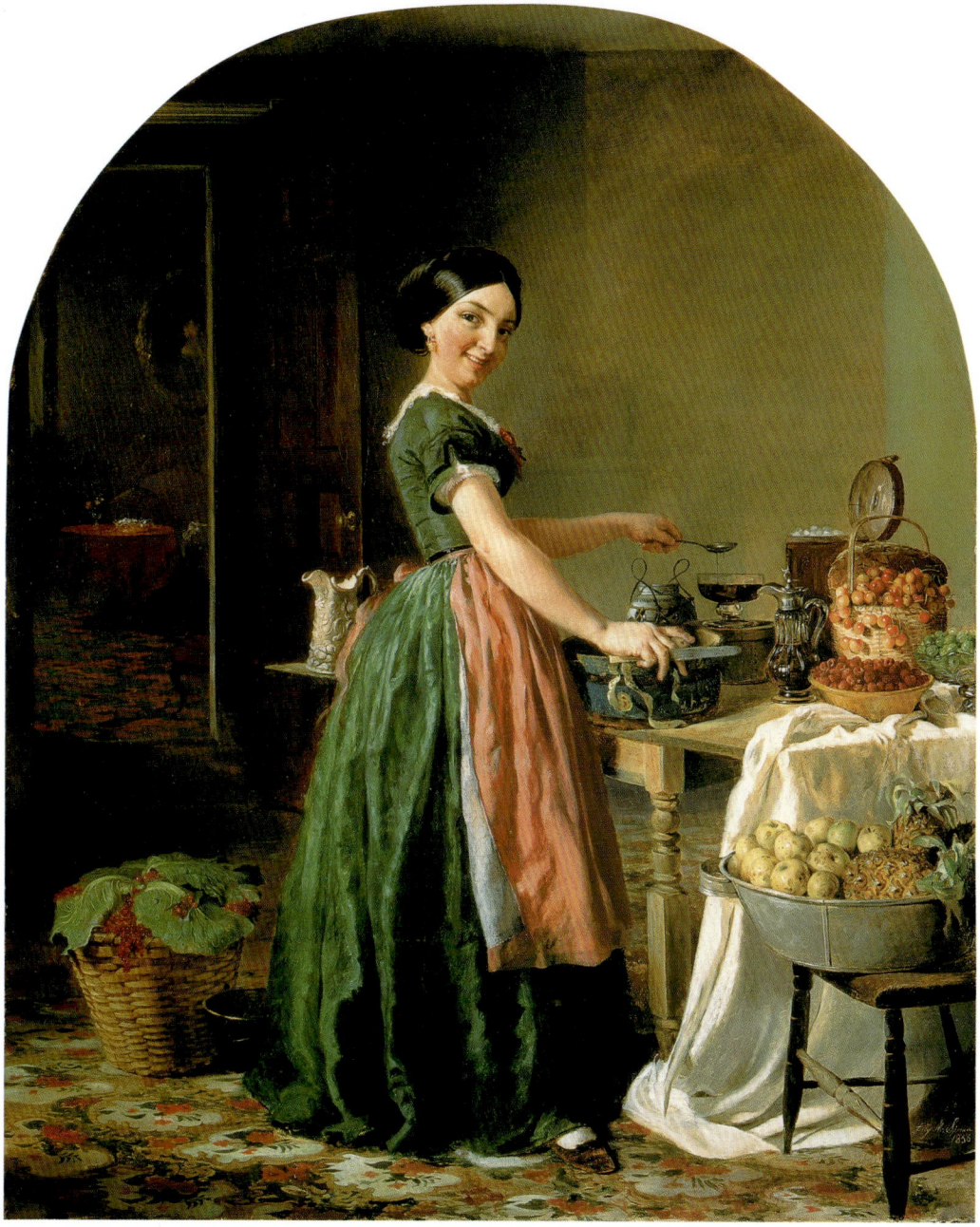

3.10.2 Lilly Martin Spencer: *Kiss Me and You'll Kiss the 'Lasses*, 1856.
Oil on canvas, 30⅙ x 25⅙ in. (76.5 x 73.8 cm.)
Brooklyn Museum of Art, New York

and merriment in Christian iconography, reinforces this sexual theme, along with the metal bin full of bruised apples on the chair, a nod to the Garden of Eden. The pineapples alongside the apples add an exotic tropical element to the scene.

Thus, while Spencer locates her women in middle class domestic settings, they are often not as virtuous as many viewers, particularly men, might have wanted. They are a little too forward, a little too "lower-class" in their manners. There is a tongue-in-cheek quality to *Kiss Me and You'll Kiss the 'Lasses* that both acknowledges and transgresses the rules of etiquette for a respectable middle class woman. Such a transgression would have been particularly meaningful to many of the middle-class women who bought prints of such paintings and who, like Spencer, experienced both the demands of household labor and the difficulties of living up to the vision of the virtuous domestic angel.

While Spencer's husband, unable to find steady employment, stayed home to help with the family and with the book-keeping aspects of her painting career, she still had to rely on her own domestic skills to ensure the smooth running of her

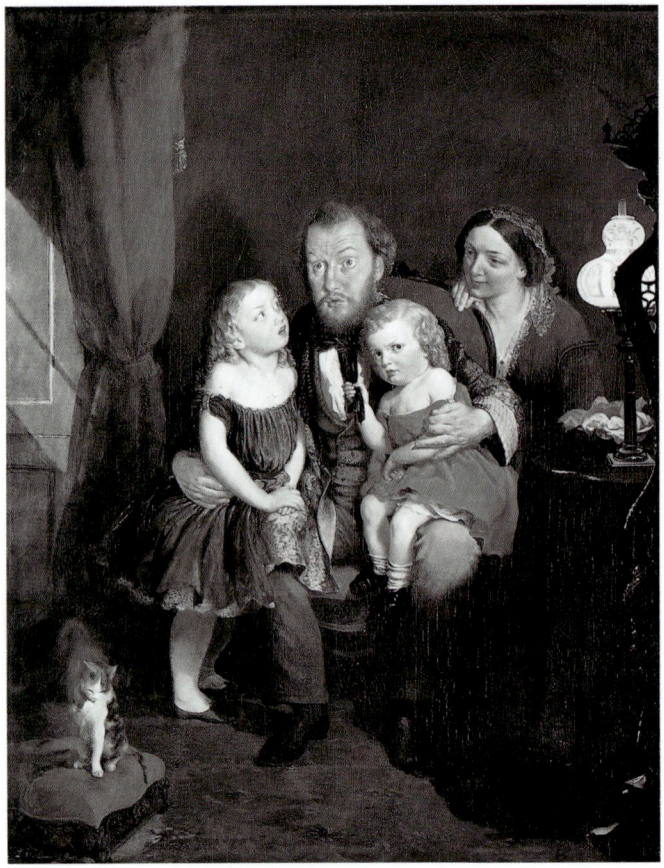

3.10.3 Lilly Martin Spencer: *Fi! Fo! Fum!*, 1858. Oil on canvas, 35⅞ x 28⅝ in. (91.4 x 72.4 cm.) Private collection

household. She was thus torn between maintaining her responsibilities as a wife and mother on the one hand, and succeeding as a professional artist in an art world that assumed that women could not be major painters on the other. It was expected that if women did paint, they must paint appropriate subject matter, that is, domestic scenes or still-life paintings.

While Spencer accepted certain assumptions about the proper roles for women, she also subscribed to many of the more radical demands being made by women for greater individual freedom outside of the home and for changes in the social relations within the home itself. Utopian socialists and feminists like Spencer's parents attacked the patriarchal family model, which assumed an unquestioned male authority figure who meted out punishment and showed little open affection. They advocated instead more communal family arrangements, with fathers as companions, and women as both workers and mothers. Others did not want to get rid of the patriarchal family altogether, but to humanize the father figure, allowing him to dispense both discipline and affection.

Spencer celebrated this middle version, known as the sentimental family, in paintings such as *Fi! Fo! Fum!* of 1858 [**3.10.3**]. Here the father entertains his children while the mother looks on. While he is the center of attention, he is also presented in a humorous, somewhat vulnerable manner. In telling the story of Jack and the Beanstock he creates considerable anxiety in his two children, the younger of whom grabs hold of his cravat; at the same time, he reassures them with his firm embrace. The art historian David M. Lubin suggests that when Spencer created this painting, she may have been thinking of a larger economic anxiety, one that swept the nation in the face of the Panic of 1857. In this context Jack, who exchanges the family cow for magic beans on the chance that he might make it rich, becomes the epitome of the Yankee trader, ever willing to risk his family's well-being in search of an easy fortune.

The Fruits of Art: The Peale Family and Still-Life Painting

Lilly Martin Spencer also excelled in another category of painting that commented on nature transformed—the still life, or *nature morte*. As the demand for genre paintings declined in the 1860s, she found a lucrative market in the production of fruit and flower paintings [**3.10.4**] which, like her genre scenes, were reproduced in lithographic form and sold to a wide audience. They did not increase her reputation as an artist, however, for in the hierarchy of subject matter determined by academies of art, still life occupied the lowest position. As early as 1669 the critic and theorist André Félibien lectured to students at the French Royal Academy:

> those that do landscape perfectly are above those who only create fruits, flowers and shells. Those who paint living animals are more worthy than those who represent only dead things without movement; and as the figure of man is the most perfect work of God on earth, it is thus certain that he who acts in imitation of God in painting human figures is much more excellent than all others.

A century later, in 1770, Sir Joshua Reynolds, so prominent a figure in London's Royal Academy and an influential authority in the development of art institutions in the US, praised still life but affirmed that, no matter how expert one might become in the production of this type of art, it should never be one's primary focus of attention:

> Even the painter of still life, whose highest ambition is to give a minute representation of every part of those low objects which he sets before him, deserves praise in proportion to his attainments; because no part of this excellent art, so much the ornament of polished life, is destitute of value and use. These, however,

are by no means the views to which the mind
of the student ought to be primarily directed.

The texts of Reynolds and Félibien clearly indicate why still life was relegated to the bottom rung of the aesthetic ladder: because it dealt with "low objects" and "dead things" and because it neglected the most perfect of God's creations, the human form. Thus, the disparate array of objects included in still-life paintings—fruit, flowers, vegetables, tableware, dead game, cheese, bread, armor, shells, ceramic and glass containers—are brought together as a coherent category by the fact that they are all part of what guardians of high culture viewed as a lower plane of reality. This reality was above all that of the domestic sphere, the locus of the repetitive and mundane activities necessary for the maintenance of daily life, rather than the site of the heroic exploits of a larger History. It is little wonder, therefore, that women found an accepted place as still-life painters, for the home or domestic sphere was their acknowledged realm. Yet in the middle of the nineteenth century, even in this lowliest of art forms, those who tended to garner the greatest reputations as still-life painters were men, and among the best known were Raphaelle and James Peale.

Raphaelle Peale (1774–1825) was the son of Charles Willson Peale (see p. 135) and the nephew of James Peale (1749–1831). While fruit and flowers had appeared as prominent items in the portraits of artists like John Singleton Copley (1738–1815), Benjamin West (1738–1820) and the elder Peale, Raphaelle Peale was the first fine artist in the US to focus on the category of still-life painting, taking it up in the 1810s. He was followed in the next decade by his uncle James. Their work was influenced, in both style and composition, by seventeenth- and eighteenth-century French, Dutch, and Spanish still-life paintings. It also contained the sort of allusions to the abundance of a burgeoning economy or to the transience of life that marked those European paintings.

According to the art historians Judith A. Barter and Annelise K. Madsen, it is not surprising that still-life painting began in Philadelphia, the home of the Peale clan. The city was experiencing a surge of interest in horticulture in the early nineteenth century, an interest that may have been due to the strength of the city's Quaker community. Shunning displays of material wealth, Quakers "focused on the bounties and blessings of the natural world, believing that nature provided a direct route to a relationship with God."

The cultivation and consumption of home grown fruits and vegetables were also, according to Barter and Madsen, "points of pride that linked the varying members of the young democracy." As early as 1768, Thomas Jefferson wrote that "[g]ardens

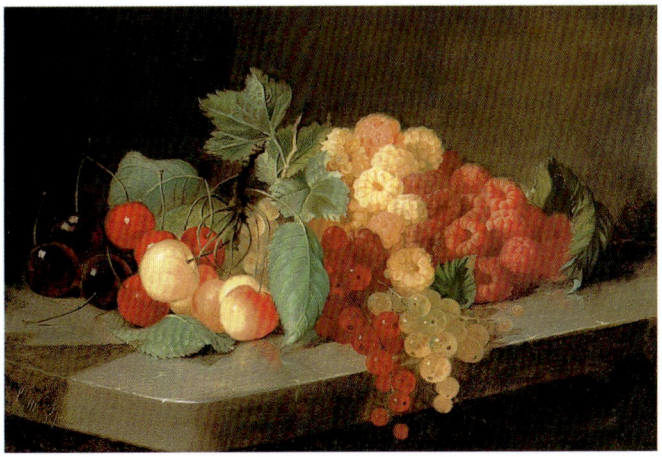

3.10.4 Lilly Martin Spencer: *Still Life with Berries and Currants*, c. 1859–60. Oil on panel, 8 x 12 in. (20.3 x 30.5 cm.) Ira Spanierman Gallery, New York

[are]...worthy of the attention of an American, because it is the country of all others where the noblest gardens may be made without expense. We have only to cut out the superabundant plants." Many of the gardening books of the early nineteenth century reiterated this connection between home grown products and democracy. Barter and Madsen quote a particularly enthusiastic horticulturalist who praised gardening in 1829 as a practice "which furnishes us with delicious but wholesome luxuries, and with cheap but splendid ornaments: May it never want encouragement in a Republican and economical country." Thus, patriotic Americans, while practicing the virtues of frugality and industriousness, could also enjoy "delicious but wholesome luxuries."

Fruit and vegetables dominated the still-life paintings of the first half of the nineteenth century, with flower paintings gaining popularity in the 1840s, paintings of game and fish in the 1860s, and paintings of compilations of manufactured objects at the end of the century (see pp. 283–85). Raphaelle Peale's *Still Life* of 1818 [**3.10.5**; p. 198] and James Peale's *Vegetables with Yellow Blossoms* of 1828 [**3.10.6**; p. 198] are representative of the first phase. Each records a selection of the foods found in the majority of homes on the eastern seaboard—apples, peaches, dried plums, nuts, squashes, eggplants, tomatoes, and beets. In both works the various fruits and vegetables are painted in a precise manner, with great attention to detail. They are brightly lit from one side and are located within a shallow space, between the edge of a plain shelf visible in the foreground and a blank wall behind. This meticulous detail, bright light, and shallow space force the viewer to pay attention to objects that would normally not be noticed in daily life. Pushed to the foreground, they are there for us to reach out and take. The pictures reproduce the atmosphere of the table and allude to the process of eating.

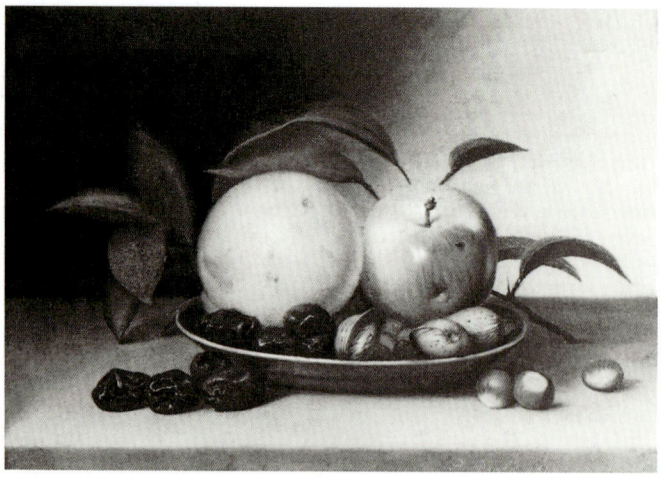

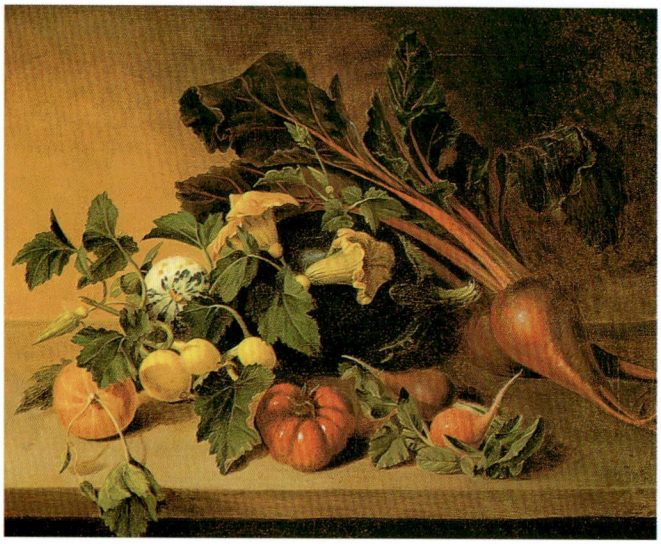

3.10.5 Raphaelle Peale: *Still Life*, 1818.
Oil on board, 10¼ x 15¼ in. (26 x 38.7 cm.)
Collection of Edith and Robert Graham

3.10.6 James Peale: *Vegetables with Yellow Blossoms*, 1828.
Oil on canvas, 19 13/16 x 25⅜ in. (50.2 x 64.7 cm.)
The Henry Francis du Pont Winterthur Museum, Winterthur, Delaware

While the still lifes of Raphaelle and James Peale have many common characteristics, they also differ in certain important ways. Raphaelle tends to choose fewer objects. He organizes them horizontally along the shelf in a way that creates a restrained, self-contained, and contemplative mood, and that reduces associations with the world outside of this carefully constructed pictorial space. James's paintings show a greater abundance of fruits and vegetables, allowing him to display a more wide-ranging virtuosity. The occasional leaf or branch often extends over the edge of the shelf, providing a small bridge to the space of the viewer. He also tends to reveal blemishes or wormholes, evoking a sense of transience. In addition, James's works tend to be larger than Raphaelle's, ranging upward from 18 × 24 inches (45.7 × 50.8 centimeters). Raphaelle's are more often approximately 10 × 14 inches (25.4 × 35.6 centimeters).

In looking at these paintings filled with tantalizing fruits and vegetables, one might experience feelings of comfort and satisfaction. Yet one might also feel a slight anxiety, if not alienation. The viewer is close to the fruit and vegetables, but the edge of the shelf or table clearly divides her or his space from that of the objects desired. The harsh light, while allowing one to recognize the objects in all their characteristic detail, also creates a feeling of unfamiliarity, for few are used to seeing them in this particular way. In his study of still-life paintings, the art historian Norman Bryson notes that many contain a "feeling of impassiveness, of a protocol of distance." The celebration of the mundane, of the food that allows us to live, is simultaneously reassuring and disturbing. The paintings counter the sense of conviviality usually associated with food and the table by denying human fellowship, consequently prompting reflections on the nature of one's membership in civil society, as well as on one's own mortality. A sense of anxiety was also in the air in 1818, the year Raphaelle painted his *Still Life*. According to Barter and Madsen, President James Madison, in a lecture at an agricultural society meeting in Charlottesville, Virginia, "decried the destruction of once-fertile soil, stripped of its nutrients and subjected to erosion." To counter this destruction he "espoused better methods of fertilization, plowing, and other improvements that would nurture American soil and conserve resources." Scientific approaches would thus be necessary to ensure that the "noble gardens" of America would survive in the coming century.

One of James Peale's daughters, Margaretta Angelica Peale (1795–1882), was also a still-life painter. She produced a type that falls somewhere between the work of her father and her cousin in content and composition. In *Still Life with Watermelon and Peaches* of 1828 [**3.10.7**] Margaretta creates a certain quietness of mood and humbleness of form that recall Raphaelle's work. The subject matter, carefully delineated, is limited to a slice of watermelon, a plate of peaches, and a bunch of grapes. Watermelons were an African gourd brought to the Americas by the Spanish in the seventeenth century. The one in Margaretta's painting, along with the peaches and grapes, may have been grown on the Peale family farm, Belfield, near Philadelphia (Charles Willson Peale had created a greenhouse and heating system that allowed him to cultivate fruit year-round). Yet Margaretta does not include all of the grapes within the space of the canvas, suggesting an abundance that is more in keeping with the work of her father; she invites viewers to partake in a feast that shares the space in which they are located. Also, several of the seeds of the watermelon appear to be captured in the act of falling onto the table. The still life as a whole is, therefore, not a passive, distanced

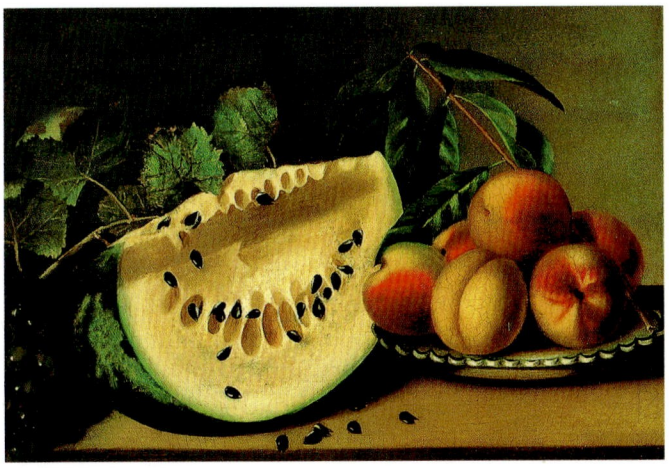

3.10.7 Margaretta Angelica Peale: *Still Life with Watermelon and Peaches*, 1828. Oil on canvas, 13 x 19½ in. (33 x 49.5 cm.)
Smith College Museum of Art, Northampton, Massachusetts

representation of human sustenance, but a work alive with the potential for conviviality, as seeds drop and hands reach out for the grapes just beyond the edge of the picture.

The sense of calm that marked Raphaelle's still lifes could well have resulted from a trip he made to South and Central America in 1793 in order to collect specimens of birds and mammals for his father's museum [**2.7.4**; p. 135]. While in Mexico he may have come across Spanish still lifes of the *bodegón* type, in which the harsh light, shallow space, and limited number of forms create a sense of monastic discipline involving the contemplation of one's daily bread in an attempt to transcend its function as earthly sustenance.

Raphaelle was neither a monk nor an overly religious person, yet he did capture this mood of ascetic contemplation or abstinence, a mood reinforced by the fact that both his works and *bodegón* paintings usually present the prelude, rather than the aftermath, of a meal. The greatest difference between them is that his paintings often include items indicative of the life of Philadelphia's comfortable middle class: China trade porcelain, silver spoons, cut-glass decanters and wine glasses, or pearl-handled knives with silver blades. Yet even when these items are included, they are never present in such abundance that excessive wealth is suggested. Rather, they indicate a restrained display that recalls early Puritan proscriptions against pride in one's material prosperity (see pp. 69–73).

Tricking the Eye: Raphaelle Peale and the Art of Deception

Several scholars have celebrated Raphaelle Peale's work as the first significant body of still-life painting to appear in America. Yet few have attempted to explain exactly why he chose this much-denigrated category of painting, one that had yet to find an audience large enough to support him and his family (in 1817 two of his still lifes were purchased by the Pennsylvania Academy of the Fine Arts for $24). Some argue that it was lack of ambition that led him to fail as a portraitist, others that he succumbed to the overbearing will of a tyrannical father. Raphaelle himself left no explanation and few letters or other written records—what we know of him comes primarily from the correspondence of his large extended family.

The historians Daniel C. Ward and Sidney Hart have taken up this question, looking more closely at Raphaelle's relationship with his father. Charles had high hopes for his eldest son as a portrait painter, particularly after retiring from his own career in 1794 to devote himself to his natural history museum and mechanical inventions (he developed a new type of stove and innovative bridge designs). But Raphaelle did not live up to his father's expectations. "He paints in portraits the striking likeness," Charles wrote to Benjamin West in 1815, "but does not give them dignity and pleasing effects."

Raphaelle could never totally break away from his father's world, as he was forced to remain financially dependent on him. He did, however, resist his father's agenda, and also refused to adhere to the staunch Enlightenment principles that informed the elder Peale's scientific and artistic pursuits. Charles was an ardent advocate of the powers of observation and reason. Raphaelle, on the other hand, took pleasure in the powers of deception and illusion. He became an expert ventriloquist and developed a coded language that he used in his correspondence with his brothers. Ventriloquism, or "biloquism," as Ward and Hart point out, was not simply an innocent parlor trick in America in the early nineteenth century:

> Rather, it was seen as a subversive action that undermined Enlightenment epistemology concerning the accuracy of the informing senses. In terms of the political culture of the early Republic, ventriloquism was seen as an attack on the notion of an informed and virtuous citizenry capable of making intelligent decisions based on observation.

Thus, deception, illusion, and coded meaning were hallmarks of both ventriloquism and much of Raphaelle's art. Such qualities represented a "rejection of his father's world," a world that also represented the mainstream of American art at the time.

Raphaelle Peale's penchant for deception can be seen most clearly in two paintings, *Fruit Piece with Peaches Covered by a Handkerchief (Covered Peaches)* of *c.* 1819 [**3.10.8**; p. 200] and *Venus Rising from the Sea—A Deception (After the Bath)* of *c.* 1822 [**3.10.9**; p. 200]. "Deception" was the word used to describe a category of painting better known today as *trompe l'oeil*. "Deceptions" were paintings that "tricked the eye" into believing

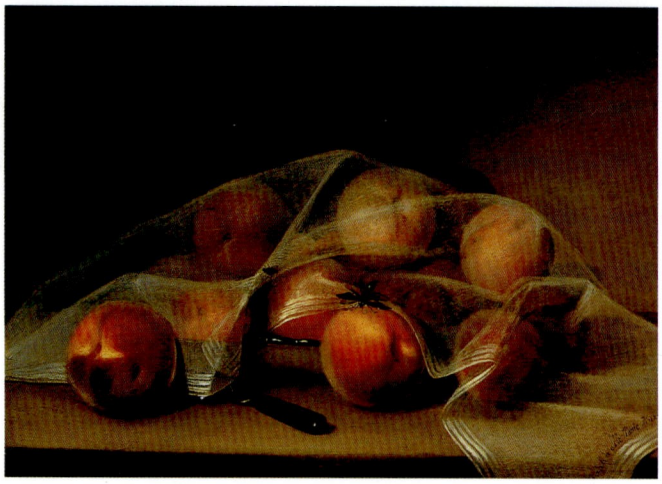

3.10.8 Raphaelle Peale: *Fruit Piece with Peaches Covered by a Handkerchief (Covered Peaches)*, c. 1819.
Oil on panel, 12½ x 18⅛ in. (31.8 x 46 cm.)
Private collection

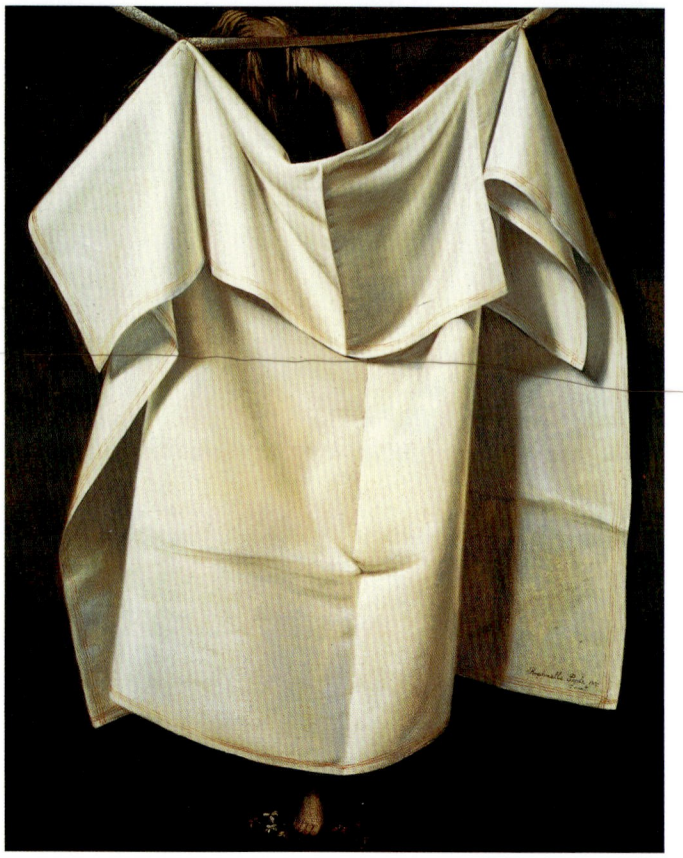

3.10.9 Raphaelle Peale: *Venus Rising from the Sea—A Deception (After the Bath)*, c. 1822.
Oil on canvas, 29¼ x 24⅛ in. (74.3 x 61.5 cm.)
The Nelson-Atkins Museum of Art, Kansas City, Missouri

that what one saw was real, not a painting—the visual equivalent of ventriloquism. One of the earliest references to *trompe l'oeil* painting can be found in ancient Greece, in a competition between two artists recorded in the first century CE by the Roman author Pliny the Elder in his *Natural History*:

> Parrhasios and Zeuxis entered into competition, Zeuxis exhibiting a picture of some grapes, so true to nature that birds flew up to the wall of the stage. Parrhasios then displayed a picture of a linen curtain realistic to such a degree that Zeuxis, elated by the verdict of the birds, cried out that now at last his rival must draw the curtain and show his picture. On discovering his mistake he surrendered the prize to Parrhasios, admitting candidly that he, Zeuxis, had deceived only the birds, while Parrhasios had deceived himself, a painter.

In his *Covered Peaches* [**3.10.8**], Raphaelle paints a wasp crawling onto one of the peaches and a fly resting on one of the folds of the cloth, thus creating two levels of deception: if the viewer recognizes the peaches as painted, she or he may still mistake the wasp or fly as real. In *Venus Rising* [**3.10.9**], he adds to Parrhasios's linen curtain the arm, foot, and hair of a woman. In so doing, he gives the viewer an additional, prurient reason for wanting to pull back the curtain and see what is behind. However, by naming the woman Venus in the title, Raphaelle shifts the subject from the material world of the lascivious to the realm of ideal beauty where, according to the academy, a higher level of aesthetic contemplation can be pursued. Yet while apparently embracing this mythological subject, Raphaelle simultaneously rejects the subject, and the academic canon it represents, by not painting Venus. He may also have been commenting wryly on a gradual increase in the number of prints and paintings of naked women in the homes of prosperous Americans, who passed off their presence as a sign of cultivation rather than as an opportunity to indulge in more sensual viewing pleasures. Indeed, Raphaelle's Venus looks back to an engraving by Valentine Greene after James Barry's *Venus Rising from the Sea* of 1771 [**3.10.10**]. This engraving is thought to have been the source for a 1774 painting of Venus by Raphaelle's father. Unfortunately Charles's painting, commissioned by his Maryland patron the plantation owner Edward Lloyd, no longer exists.

Moreover, Ward and Hart suggest that in *Venus Rising*, Raphaelle rejects the academic system upon which his father based his whole career as an artist, as well as the corruptions of an art market his father wanted him willingly to join. The art historian Roger Stein also points out that Raphaelle's painting stands in stark contrast to his father's *The Artist in His Museum* [**2.7.4**; p. 135], executed around the same time. While Charles

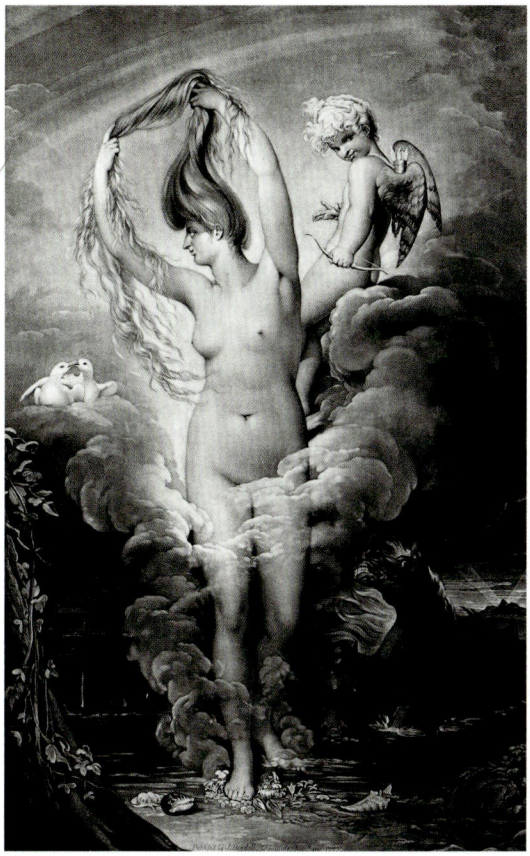

3.10.10 Valentine Greene after James Barry: *Venus Rising from the Sea*, 1771. Mezzotint, 24⅙ x 15⅝ in. (61.1 x 39 cm.)
Ackland Art Museum, The University of North Carolina at Chapel Hill

pulls back the rich, red, gold-tasseled curtain to reveal the results of his scientific and artistic endeavors—nature transformed through the tools of painting and taxidermy—Raphaelle leaves his curtain in place, a curtain that oddly resembles an unfolded linen napkin. In fact, the painted curtain is the actual size of such a napkin, and so provides another instance of *trompe l'oeil*, one that serves to shift Venus from the realm of the ideal to that of the domestic sphere, where Greene's engraving of Venus would have hung.

In organizing his painting in this way and in titling it *Venus Rising from the Sea—A Deception (After the Bath)*, Raphaelle indicates to viewers that all is not what it seems. He draws them in with the promise of another scintillating image of a nude woman, yet denies them access to such an image. At the same time, he seemingly effaces evidence his own painterly skills and therefore calls into question the feasibility of a successful artistic career. Yet he is also diminishing the efforts of his father to define him—literally—for on the canvas beneath this painting of Venus lies Raphaelle's copy of his father's 1822 half-length portrait of him (the barely visible segment of a framed still life at the upper right and a palette and brushes at the lower left show through from the original portrait). While he initially simply covered his face and shoulders with the cloth, he ultimately turned his rejection of this father's image of him into a wry and complex critique of his father's world and of the art world in general in the early nineteenth century.

Gender and the Art of Flower Painting

By the 1840s the fruits and vegetables so popular in the canvases of the Peales were joined by all manner of flowers, artfully arranged in vases or spilling over onto the surfaces on which the vases were set. Representations of flowers were already present in abundance in American homes as part of larger compositions found on painted fireboards and furniture and in the needlework of women [**1.4.28**; **1.4.29**, p. 80; **2.5.8**, p. 97]. Now they assumed center stage on canvases hung in parlors and dining rooms. One example of this mid-century floral abundance is an album quilt of 1848, made up of several blocks or sections each containing its own "picture," attributed to Mary Heidenroder Simon (1810–?) of Baltimore, Maryland [**3.10.11**]. What distinguishes her work from that of earlier quilters is the integration of the world of commerce and technology in both subject matter and method of execution. Her procedure, the quilt historian Elaine Hedges writes:

3.10.11 Attributed to Mary Heidenroder Simon: album quilt, 1848. Appliquéd cottons, with ink work, 108 x 108 in. (274.3 x 274.3 cm.)
Collection of Linda Reuther, Julie Silber/Mary Strickler's Quilt

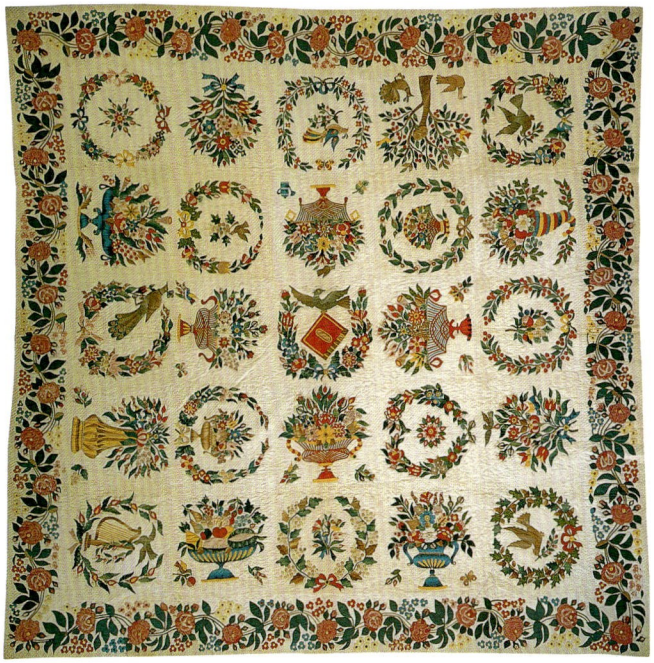

of supplying prefabricated blocks for which she received payment (and also of signing those blocks in a standardized script with their donors' names) suggests both the specialization of work of the new industrial world and the commercial methods of the urban merchants who were proliferating in Baltimore at the time.

Often blocks purchased from Simon would be combined with blocks made by women in the family, integrating the prefabricated and the homemade. In addition, this combination of the industrial and the preindustrial worlds appeared in the subject matter of several quilts. While most album quilts were composed of floral wreaths, cornucopias, and baskets of fruit and flowers, these items were now supplemented by ships, steam engines, and urban buildings and monuments.

The flower paintings of the 1840s and 1850s were also connected to a long history of botanical illustrations. Since the arrival of John White (see pp. 64–65), European naturalists had been recording the flora and fauna of North America in carefully worked drawings and watercolors, which were reproduced and widely circulated in books and pamphlets. Their American descendants continued this work. In the early nineteenth century another type of publication appeared: sentimental flower books, usually written by women, that combined illustrations of specific flowers with poetry, such as Sarah Edgerton Mayo's *The Flower Vase: Containing the Language of Flowers* (1848). Several of these publications included scientific descriptions and/or histories of each flower, but most were concerned with the symbolic aspects of their subject. For example, the anemone symbolized frailty, the carnation pride, the daisy innocence, and the violet faithfulness. These books were particularly popular from the 1830s through the 1850s and provided broader access to the combined efforts of science and art.

The art historian William H. Gerdts doubts that these flower books influenced many of the flower painters of the mid-nineteenth century. Rather, he argues, these painters looked to models from France or the Netherlands. One early flower painter, however, who was certainly aware of the books was George Harvey (see p. 172). In 1843 he exhibited five paintings in a one-man show in New York City, two of which were described in the catalogue as "A Complimentary Letter from Flora" and "For Eulogy Conveyed by Flowers." Each entry lists the flowers in the picture and their symbolic references. The first image contained hollyhock ("Aspiring"), mignonette ("Worth and Liveliness"), convolvulus ("Worth Sustained by Affection"), scarlet lily ("High Souled"), white and blue periwinkle ("Pleasures of Memory" and "Early Friendship"), and yellow jasmine ("Grace and Elegance"). Taken together, the message was: "The pleasures of memory of our early friendship, when grace and elegance were to be seen by the side of high souled worth and loveliness, causes [sic] me to aspire in all my actions to be worthy of your affections." Harvey's later works, including *Still Life* of 1865 [**3.10.12**], were seldom accompanied by such clear explications of their symbolic characteristics, but one can assume that he never completely forgot the lessons he learned from his early exposure to sentimental flower books.

One of the most successful flowers painters of the 1850s was Severin Roesen (active 1845–1872), who fled to the US from Germany in 1848 to avoid prosecution for fraudulent bankruptcy (he had been a porcelain dealer). He exhibited two floral still lifes at the American Art-Union that same year and another five paintings the following year. He lived in New York City until 1857, and then abandoned the city and his wife and two children and moved to Pennsylvania, living in various towns until he finally settled in Williamsport. Nothing is known of him after he left Williamsport in 1872.

Three to four hundred works by Roesen are known today. Unfortunately, only some twenty are dated. All of his known works are still lifes, filled with fruit or flowers or combinations

3.10.12 George Harvey: *Still Life*, 1865. Watercolor on paper, 15 x 9¼ in. (38.1 x 23.5 cm.) Private collection

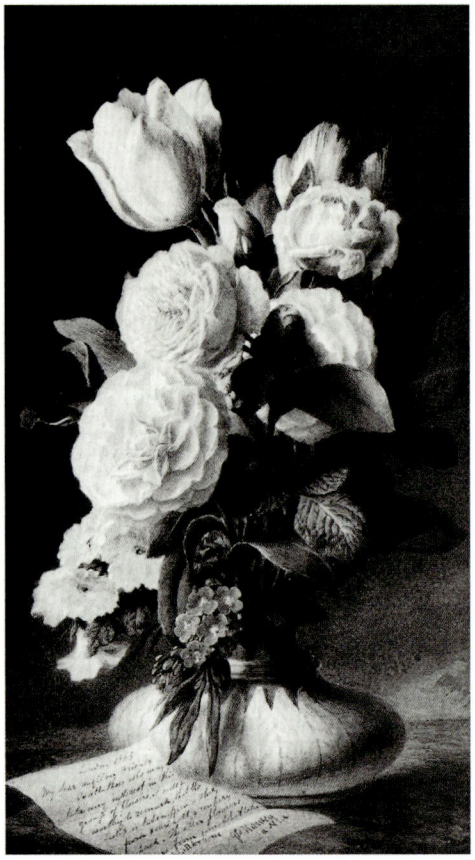

of both. His canvases tend to be large, like *Flowers in a Glass Pitcher with Bird's Nest and Fruit* [**3.10.13**], and filled with a profusion of items. "While these often gigantic paintings of literally hundreds of objects have been interpreted as standard Victorian horror vacui," Gerdts notes, "they are also the ultimate embodiment of mid-century optimism, representing the richness and abundance of the land, the profusion of God's bounty in the New World, his blessing upon the American Eden through this cornucopia of plenitude."

The size of Roesen's paintings may have contributed to their popularity. Rather than adding a subtle highlight to a dining room or parlor, these works dominated the room, providing both a visual and a conversational focus. His New York and Williamsport patrons may have been intrigued by his enlargement of a type of painting traditionally modest in size. In order to facilitate the continuous production of these large canvases it seems Roesen resorted to the use of templates; individual flowers or pieces of fruit, or even whole arrangements, are often repeated in several paintings.

3.10.13 Severin Roesen: *Flowers in a Glass Pitcher with Bird's Nest and Fruit*, c. 1867.
Oil on canvas, 50 x 36 in. (127 x 91.4 cm.)
Reynolda House, Museum of American Art, Winston-Salem, North Carolina

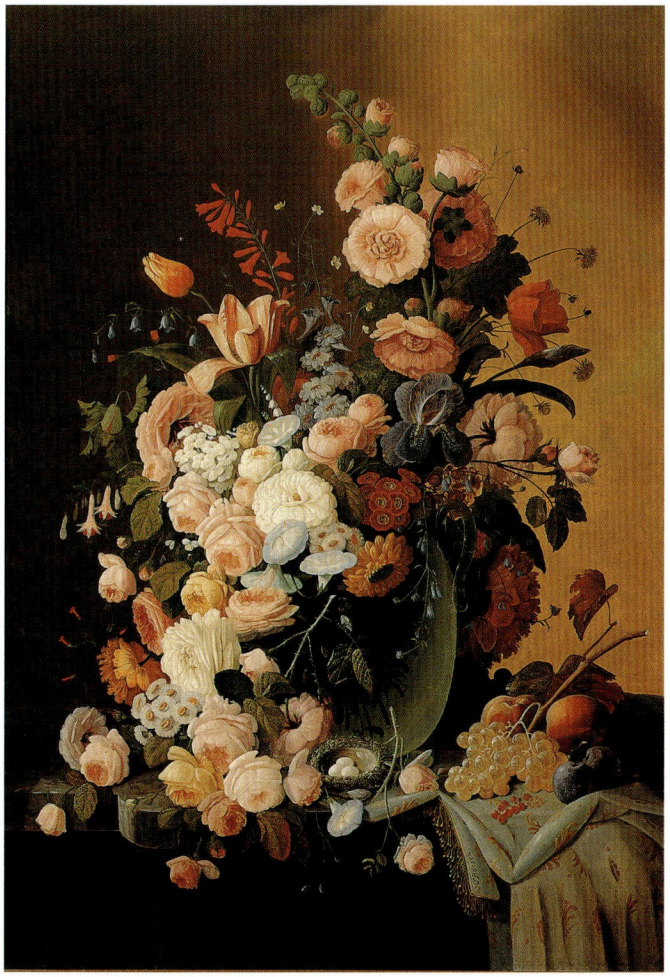

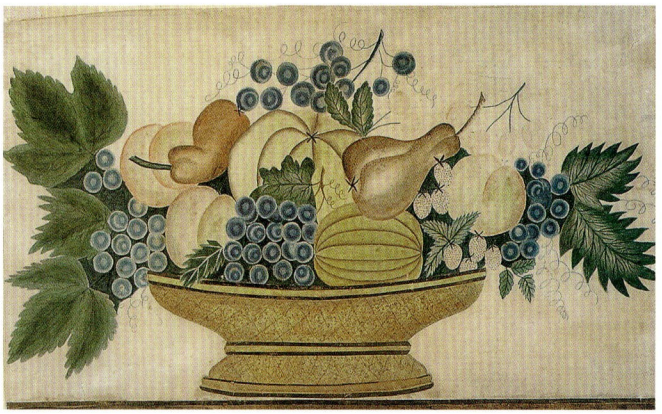

3.10.14 Mary R. Wilson: *Fruit in Yellow Bowl*, c. 1840.
Watercolor and gold-foil collage on paper, 10⅛ x 17½ in. (25.2 x 44.4 cm.)
Abby Aldrich Rockefeller Folk Art Center, Williamsburg, Virginia

Templates were essential to the practice of theorem or stencil painting, which was carried out primarily by women for the decoration of their homes. The technique came into fashion in America soon after its introduction into England from China at the end of the eighteenth century. Similar stencils were used to decorate walls, floors, and furniture in the early nineteenth century [**2.7.8**; p. 138]. Theorem painters would use several stencils to outline the basic shapes of their compositions, typically still lifes of fruit or flowers, and then add various details. *Fruit in Yellow Bowl* [**3.10.14**], painted c. 1840 by Mary R. Wilson, is executed in watercolor and gold foil on wove paper, the foil embellishing the dish holding the fruit and simulating the top of a table. Wilson has added a diamond pattern to the dish and has shaded the pears and painted in the spaces between the fruit to add depth. Such pictures provided symbols of nature's abundance and beauty for those who could not afford to purchase an oil painting or watercolor by a professional artist. And even for those women who could, many continued to produce their theorems, as they did their needlework, for the pleasure and sense of accomplishment such work gave them.

Ornithological Paintings as "Nature Morte": Alexander Wilson and John James Audubon

While bird paintings from the early nineteenth century are seldom categorized as still lifes in art history texts, they are included here because they represent, for the most part, *nature morte*, or "dead nature." The "founder of American ornithology," the English gentleman Mark Catesby, who taught himself etching so as to be able to produce his two-volume *Natural History of Carolina, Florida and the Bahama Islands* (1731–43), drew most of the 109 illustrations of birds from life. His successors, Alexander Wilson and John James Audubon, did not. Instead, they relied on lifeless specimens to produce their lifelike representations.

The Scottish poet and artist-naturalist Alexander Wilson (1766–1813) found inspiration not only in nature but also in the natural history museum of Charles Willson Peale, who was also particularly fond of birds. In his study of early American naturalists, literary scholar Christoph Irmscher notes that there was a marked preoccupation in the eighteenth century with birds. This preoccupation had one of its roots in the assumption that, although "birds were in their superficial anatomy the animals most different from humans...their social habits often had something to teach us." Thus, observing birds could, in some manner, provide lessons for the human observer, if not a mirror image of his or her own basic assumptions about right and wrong actions. A bird building a nest was a model for human industry; a hummingbird tearing a flower or a fellow bird apart a warning of human destructiveness.

Peale's penchant for birds was also due, however, to the fact they were easier to handle than larger mammals and more effectively preserved for museum display. He ultimately gathered together a collection of over 1,600 species, many of them exhibited in the Long Room of his State House museum quarters [**2.7.4**; p. 135] in identical cases with painted backgrounds of the habitat appropriate to each bird. Wilson used Peale's collection to create drawings for his nine-volume *American Ornithology*, published in 1808–13 (three volumes were later added by Charles-Lucien Bonaparte). His *White-Headed Eagle* of 1811 [**3.10.16**], shown here in a hand-colored print engraved by Alexander Lawson (1772–1846), was based on Peale's white-headed or bald eagle, one of the few birds that have survived to this day from the artist's museum [**3.10.15**]. The differences between the stuffed specimen and the bird in the print are obvious. In an attempt to bring his subject to life, Wilson has opened its mouth, placed a fish under one of its claws, and given it a more sinister expression. He has also positioned it on a bank with Niagara Falls in the distance, thus connecting two national symbols. Yet while the viewer would undoubtedly accept as accurate the descriptive aspects of Wilson's work, he or she would also recognize the contrived nature of the image, that the eagle was most likely not drawn in this exact location.

While Wilson relied on Peale to be the executioner of the birds he drew for his *American Ornithology*, John James Audubon (1785–1851) did the honors himself. Irmscher notes that the poet Robert Penn Warren, in response to an inquiry as to what inspired his *Audubon: A Vision*, stated: "Audubon was the greatest slayer of birds that ever lived....He destroyed beauty to create beauty." Audubon was born Jean Rabin in Les

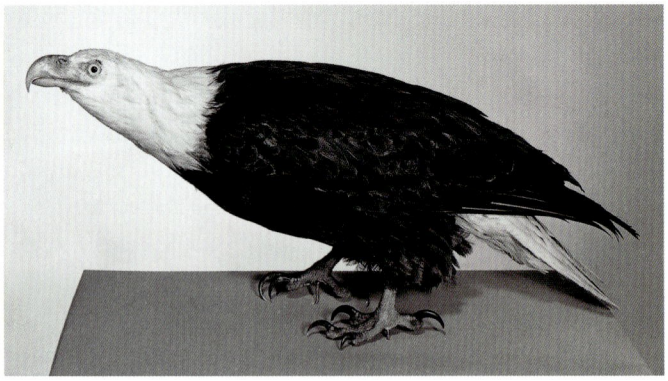

3.10.15 White-headed or bald eagle, from Peale's Museum, *c.* 1810.
Ernst Mayr Library of the Museum of Comparative Zoology, Harvard University, Cambridge, Massachusetts

3.10.16 Alexander Lawson after Alexander Wilson: *White-Headed Eagle*, from Wilson's *American Ornithology*, 1811.
Hand-colored engraving and etching, 10⅞ x 14½ in. (27.9 x 36.8 cm.)
Academy of Natural Sciences of Philadelphia, Philadelphia, Pennsylvania

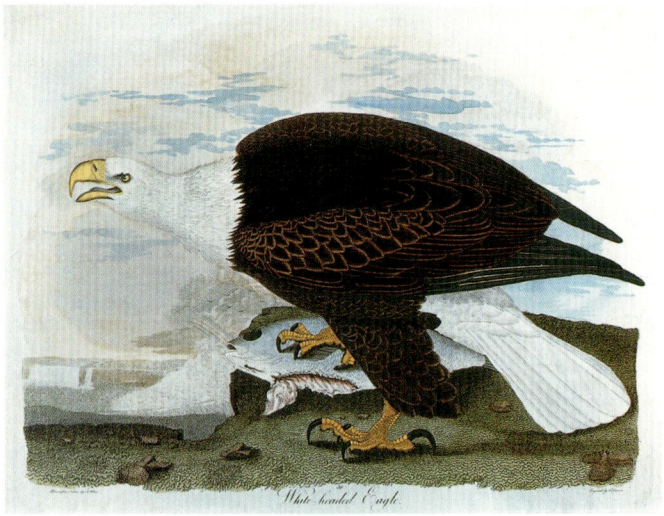

Cayes, Haiti, in 1785, the illegitimate son of the trader, plantation owner, and slaveholder Captain Jean Audubon and Jeanne Rabin, a chambermaid from Les Touches, France. His mother died shortly after giving birth. His father, troubled by the early signs of slave insurrection on the island (see p. 114), took Jean back to France in 1788, subsequently adopting him. By 1803 the young man had Anglicized his name, becoming John James Audubon, and left France for Philadelphia in order to avoid being drafted into Napoleon's army and to manage his father's nearby estate, Mill Grove.

In 1807 Audubon moved west to Louisville, Kentucky and became a merchant, transporting to the city much-desired goods from the East Coast and Europe, making the arduous 800-mile (1,287-kilometer) land and water voyage between Philadelphia and Louisville once or twice a year. Unfortunately, his position as one of the richest men in Kentucky came to an end after the Panic of 1819. This widespread financial crisis began in 1818 when the national bank called in its loans to other banks. Regional banks, like those in Kentucky, had printed copious amounts of paper currency well beyond the value of the specie capital in their vaults, thus extending credit beyond their ability to repay. Audubon, like many businessmen, was unable collect on his own loans to pay his creditors, and so was forced to declare bankruptcy.

It was at this moment of financial ruin that Audubon turned to what he called his first love, ornithology. The art historian Jennifer Roberts notes that Audubon often drew and observed birds during his trips hauling merchandise and "was especially interested in their ability to traverse in an instant what for Audubon himself was a laborious, crawling process of earth-bound movement." This laboriousness marked the circulation of Audubon's extremely large prints as well, which he personally transported, along with the drawings on which they were based, four times back and forth across the Atlantic. He then traveled throughout the US, Britain, and continental Europe with his cumbersome portfolios in search of subscriptions. Roberts argues that this artistic project was Audubon's attempt to "rebuild his own shattered economic life and to imagine a form of representation, exchange, and distribution that would be immune to the ills of the market as he knew it." He created a form of art that in its "size, weightiness and immediacy," countered "the instabilities of modern monetary culture."

Audubon claimed to have studied drawing with the French painter Jacques-Louis David (1748–1825), a claim many historians now question. No other evidence of professional training exists, so one might assume that he, like many American artists, was largely self-taught. He was obviously an excellent teacher, for his unrivaled masterpiece, *The Birds of America*, issued in 87 parts between 1828 and 1839, was an instant success, bringing him material rewards (full sets sold for more than $1,000), election as Fellow of the Royal Society in London, and membership in the American Philosophical Society.

In his essay "My Style of Drawing Birds," Audubon describes how he arrived at his own particular method of acquiring and posing his models:

> I continued for months together, simply outlining birds as I observed them, either alighted or on the wing, but could finish none of my sketches. I procured many individuals of different species, and laying them on the table or on the ground, tried to place them in such attitudes as I had sketched. But, alas! they were dead, to all intents and purposes.

In order to breathe life back into them, he mounted the dead birds on wooden boards with wires so that he could pose them:

> I pierced the body of the fishing bird, and fixed it on the board; another wire passed above his upper mandible held the head in a pretty fair attitude, smaller ones fixed the feet according to my notions, and even common pins came to my assistance. The last wire proved a delightful elevator to the bird's tail, and at last—there stood before me the real Kingfisher...This was what I shall call my first drawing actually from nature, for even the eye of the Kingfisher was as if full of life whenever I pressed the lids aside with my finger.

As the birds were not preserved, Audubon had to work quickly, before they decomposed. His work was made more arduous by the fact that he insisted on rendering his feathered specimens life-size, using the largest paper available to him at the time (38 × 25½ inches/96.5 × 64.8 centimeters). Those birds too large to fit upright were painted in a variety of ingenious poses. Audubon completed 435 watercolors containing 1,065 birds representing 489 species, which served as models for the even larger plates executed by the English engraver Robert Havell, Jr. (1793–1878), who utilized a complex process of engraving, etching, and aquatint. Each plate was hand-colored in London under Audubon's watchful eye (copper sheets large enough for the engravings were unavailable in the US). Subscribers received the prints in sets of five as they were completed; they were later bound into four volumes.

In his depictions of birds, Audubon often focused on the more violent aspects of their lives. Many of his works deal with death, meted out by the birds on each other or on their unsuspecting prey, as in his watercolor *Golden Eagle Female Adult* of 1833–34 [**3.10.17**; p. 206]. Here one can see how Audubon's method far surpassed that of Wilson in presenting the illusion of "realness." The eagle has a fleshiness and flexibility impossible to achieve when working from a stiff museum specimen.

Irmscher suggests that Audubon's *Golden Eagle Female Adult* includes a portrait of Audubon himself in the lower left-hand corner, as the man making his way across a fallen tree with a dead bird under his arm and a gun strapped to his back (the figure was omitted from the engraving). Yet in an essay in his *Ornithological Biography*, Audubon tells a different story about how he came to possess the eagle depicted: he bought it alive in 1833 from Nathan E. Greenwood, a subscriber to *Birds of America*. Both attracted and irritated by the bird's noble and haughty demeanor, its "bright unflinching eye," Audubon considered letting it go, yet ultimately decided a portrait was in order.

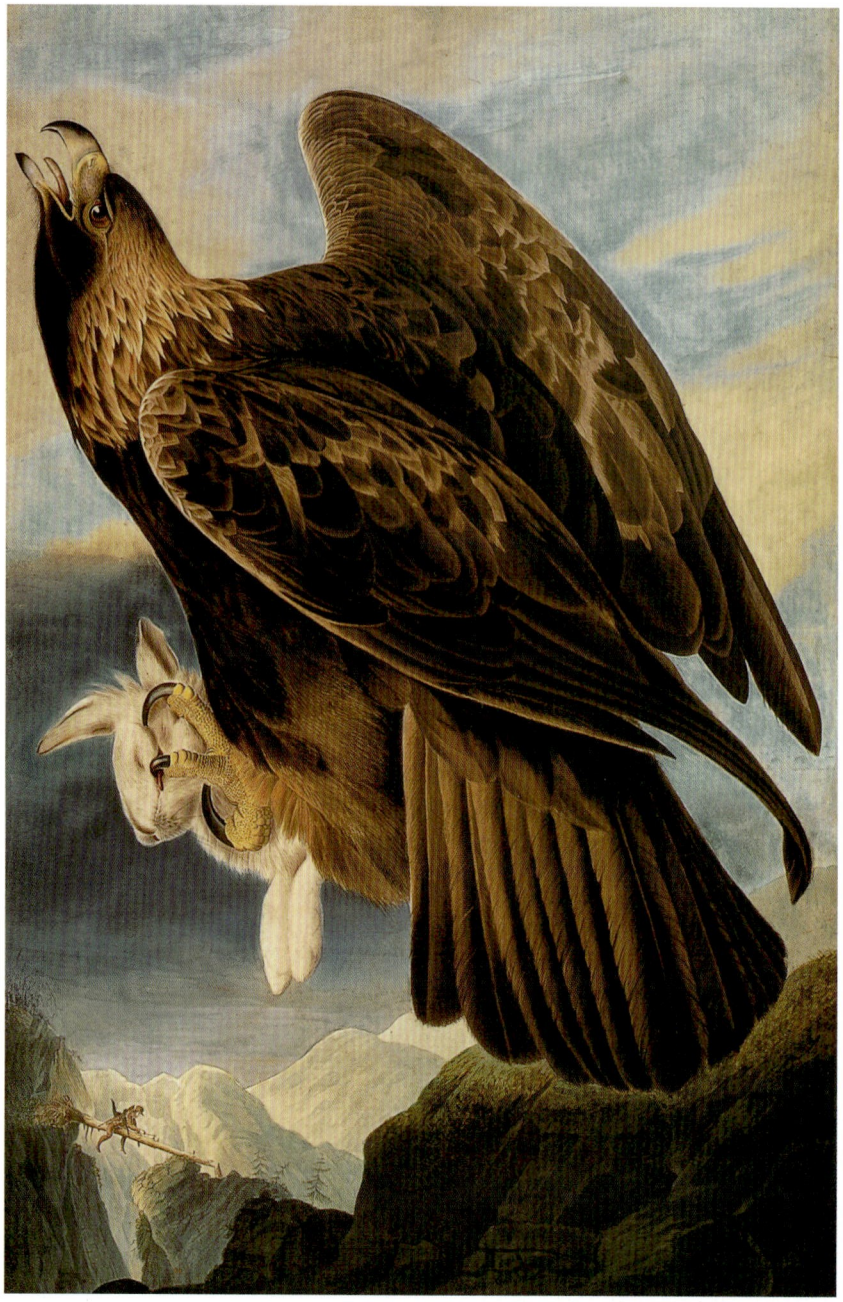

3.10.17 John James Audubon: *Golden Eagle Female Adult*, 1833–34.
Watercolor, graphite, pastel, and selective glazing on paper, 38 x 25½ in. (96.6 x 64.7 cm.)
Courtesy The New-York Historical Society, New York

Rather than shooting it, he attempted to suffocate it by placing it in a sealed room with a pan of burning charcoal. When the charcoal didn't work, he added sulfur, and when even that failed to kill the bird (although it almost killed Audubon and his son), he pierced its heart with a long piece of steel. He then spent a fortnight, much longer than usual, drawing the bird, claiming that he "worked so constantly at the drawing, that it nearly cost me my life."

In Audubon's painting both human and animal are shown having successfully killed their prey. While the artist identified the bird in an inscription on the painting as female, he transforms it in his written account into a male, "casting the encounter," according to Irmscher, "in the terms of a heroic struggle between males." Yet the bird and the man in the watercolor are certainly not presented as equals. The bird is life-size, where the man clearly is not. The eagle ascends with her prey, calling out her victory; the man balances precariously as he descends the log, head down, the corpse of a bird under his arm, caught in "a laborious, crawling process of earthbound movement." Both have their prey, but the eagle appears also to have maintained her dignity. Irmscher notes that this watercolor, with its tiny man and life-size bird, is "an ironic counterpoint to Charles Willson Peale's life-sized self-representation at the very center of his famous painting *The Artist in His Museum*" [**2.7.4**; p. 135].

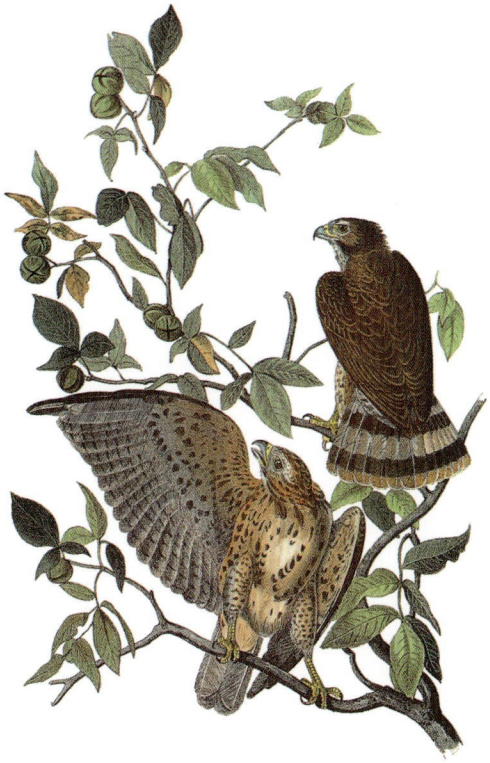

3.10.18 Robert Havell, Jr., after John James Audubon: *Broad-winged Hawk*, from Audubon's *The Birds of America*, 1828–38. Hand-colored aquatint, 39½ x 29½ in. (100.3 x 74.9 cm.) British Library, London

The inclusion of the male figure struggling in the wilderness in the composition may be a reference to the struggles Audubon engaged in to create this work, which, in his own words, "nearly cost [him] his life."

In his *Ornithological Biography*, Audubon describes another encounter with a female bird, a broad-winged hawk, only this time he managed to capture her alive. The bird did not resist when taken from her nest, and when brought to Audubon's studio seems to have willingly assumed the poses desired by the artist, as if he had already killed her and strung her up with wires [**3.10.18**]. The attitude of the hawk, as perceived by Audubon, was also very different from that of the golden eagle, although it achieved a similar disquieting effect: "Its eye," writes Audubon, "directed toward mine, appeared truly sorrowful, with a degree of pensiveness, which rendered me at that moment quite uneasy." According to Irmscher, the bird, in "playing her own birdness, at least the kind of birdness Audubon wants for his lifelike, life-sized paintings," survived her own representation and was finally set free by the artist.

If humans were to learn lessons applicable to their own lives from the actions of birds, then the message for women embedded in these two encounters between man and female bird was clear. One could argue that the women who met at Seneca Falls in 1848 to initiate a movement to expand the rights of women (see p. 192) heeded the message. Some would choose to resist male authority openly, risking their reputations, if not their lives. Others would choose to work within the system, to frame their demands within the rhetoric of patriarchy (for example, women needed more education to be better wives and mothers) in order to ensure their own survival.

Review Questions

1 The painters Lilly Martin Spencer and Raphaelle Peale both faced obstacles to the pursuit of their chosen profession and/or subject matter. What were some of these obstacles and how did each artist overcome them?

2 What do the works of Lilly Martin Spencer, Severin Roesen, and Mary R. Wilson tell us about the domestic sphere in the early nineteenth century?

3 How does the world of horticulture in the early nineteenth century help us understand the significance of still-life paintings?

4 How do the works of Raphaelle Peale and James John Audubon engage with the tension between illusion and reality?

5 Both James John Audubon's *Golden Eagle Female Adult* (1833–34) and Arapoosh's *Decorated Hide Shield* (*c.* 1825) [**3.8.4**; p. 151] contain depictions of interactions between humans and birds. What motivated each to create his work? What stories do they tell and how do they tell them (for example, what materials do they choose and how do they arrange their compositions)?

Abolitionist Movement *c.* 1787–1865

Community of Female Sculptors in Rome 1852–1900

The Civil War 1861–65

1839
Rebellion of African slaves on the ship *La Amistad*, led by Cinque [4.12.4]

1845
Texas becomes the 28th state

1846
Territory comprising Washington, Oregon, and Idaho acquired by treaty with Britain; establishment of the Smithsonian Institution in Washington, D.C.

1846–48
War between the United States and Mexico [4.11.1]

1848
California Gold Rush; Chinese immigration begins

1850
Compromise allows California to enter the Union as a free state in exchange for strengthening of the Fugitive Slave Act

1851
Arrival of French-American priest Jean-Baptiste Lamy as first Bishop of Santa Fe, who condemns sculptures and paintings by local *santeros* [4.11.8]

1852
Harriet Hosmer leaves for Rome, founds colony of women artists [4.13.5]

1857
Supreme Court issues the Dred Scott decision, confirming that a slave's arrival in the North did not automatically result in freedom

1859
John Brown leads a raid on the arsenal at Harper's Ferry, West Virginia, as part of a planned slave revolt; mixed response to John Rogers's *Slave Auction* [4.12.7]

1861
Winslow Homer begins work for *Harper's Weekly* as artist-reporter [4.12.12]; Civil War begins

1862
Publication of Matthew Brady's *Photographic Views of the War*

1863
January 1: President Lincoln issues Emancipation Proclamation; Navajo forced to move to eastern New Mexico in the "Long Walk" (allowed to return to northwestern New Mexico/northeastern Arizona in 1868)

PART 4 A Nation at War

c. 1830–1900

The middle decades of the nineteenth century in the United States were marked by heightened military conflict. Up until the 1830s, expansion westward meant battles with Native Americans, who were seen as having little legitimate claim to the territories they inhabited. But coveting the land of the newly independent nation of Mexico was another story. Here was a territory occupied not only by indigenous peoples but also by descendants of Spanish settlers. To claim it meant engaging in armed conflict with a sovereign nation. Some in the US argued against such action, worried about the expansion of slavery or the inclusion within the country of a Catholic mixed race (Spanish and indigenous) population. Pro-war forces won out, however, for the appeal of acquiring the remaining territory between the Louisiana Purchase and the Pacific Ocean was too great.

Artists had been celebrating war in their work since the colonial period, and they continued to paint and draw the battles on the western frontier. But they were joined now by a new group of individuals who claimed they were able to bring to the public more truthful images than those of the fine artist. These individuals drew on photography and on the development of what came to be known as the penny press to promote their careers and their version of the key events in American military and political life.

Those who created images for this new penny press often utilized the conventions of fine art in composing their images. At the same time, many fine artists were attracted to this world of newspapers, popular prints, and magazines. In fact, several artists who came to prominence in the fine art world in the US in the second half of the nineteenth century began their careers as commercial artists. Some continued to create illustrations for popular magazines after their reputations had been established. They did so for financial reasons or for political reasons, believing that making fine art more accessible to a larger, non-art-world audience would improve the aesthetic and moral character of the nation. In addition, the meaning of a particular image often depended upon where it appeared and by whom it was viewed. For example, an illustration in *Harper's Weekly* of a military encounter between US and Mexican forces may have meant one thing when seen by a resident of New York City and quite another when seen by someone living in Santa Fe, New Mexico. Acknowledging the significance of context and audience thus

Reconstruction Period 1865–77

Gilded Age 1877–1900

1865
Thirteenth Amendment to the US Constitution abolishes slavery [4.13.6]; President Abraham Lincoln assassinated; Andrew Johnson becomes president; Civil War ends

1866
Publication of Alexander Gardner's *Photographic Sketch Book of the War* [4.12.18]; founding of the Ku Klux Klan

1867–68
Reconstruction Acts passed dividing the South into five military districts

1868
Massacre of Cheyenne by US Army at Washita River; founding of the Hampton Institute to educate freed blacks

1870
Fifteenth Amendment to the US Constitution grants African American men the vote

1875
Passage of Civil Rights Act outlawing discrimination in use of public facilities

1875–77
Creation of ledger books by Plains Native leaders imprisoned at Fort Marion, Florida [4.14.4]

1876
Defeat of General George Armstrong Custer at the battle of the Little Bighorn

1877
Federal troops withdrawn from the South, ending Reconstruction; Hampton Institute admits Native Americans

1883
US Supreme Court voids the Civil Rights Act of 1875

1889–90
Ghost Dance movement [4.14.10]

1890
December 29: Defeat of Lakota at the Battle of Wounded Knee, South Dakota [4.14.8]

1896
US Supreme Court upholds the "separate but equal" doctrine of segregation

1897
Augustus Saint-Gaudens creates memorial to Colonel Robert Gould Shaw and the all-black 54th Massachusetts Regiment [4.13.11]

1899–1900
Frances Benjamin Johnston produces photographs of the Hampton Institute [4.14.14]

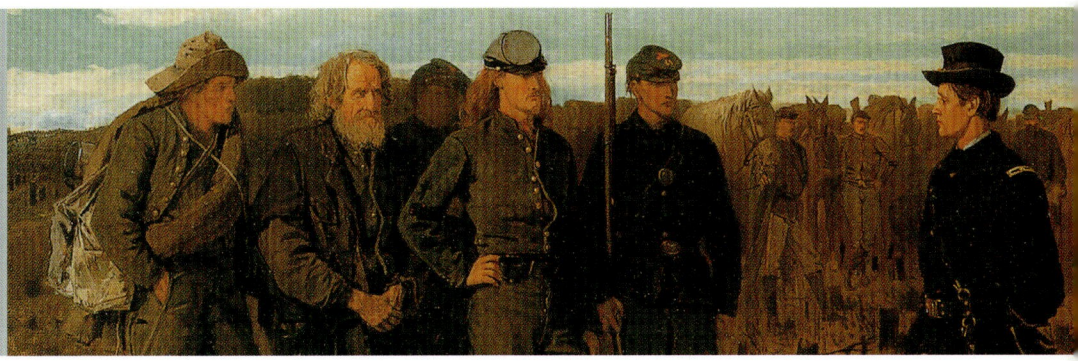

Winslow Homer: *Prisoners from the Front*, 1866, detail [**4.13.1**; p. 237]. Oil on canvas, 24 x 38 in. (61 x 96.5 cm.) The Metropolitan Museum of Art, New York

helps us understand the wide-ranging and varied impact of pictorial representations.

The conflicts of the mid-century included battles not only with foreign nations and indigenous peoples but also with fellow-citizens over political and economic independence and the institution of slavery. These battles led ultimately to a bloody and devastating civil war, one that created new challenges for artists. How were they to use the conventions of battle painting meant to glorify the victors and humiliate the vanquished when both the victors and the vanquished were citizens of the same nation? Where was the romance in brothers slaughtering brothers? And how were white artists to represent the role of African Americans in ensuring victory for the North, and thus in helping to bring about an end to slavery? Several rose to the occasion, creating images that acknowledged the complexity of the Civil War. Photographers also roamed the battlefields, recording the bloody aftermath of the military campaigns, sometimes adding items or repositioning bodies in order to create more dramatic compositions.

While African Americans appeared in the photographs of the Civil War, black bodies were strikingly absent from most of the public monuments that commemorated this war in the second half of the nineteenth century, particularly in the South. It wasn't until the end of the century that the black soldier would appear as a fully individualized standing figure in the *Shaw Memorial* by Augustus Saint-Gaudens [**4.13.11**; p. 247].

The end of the Civil War led to the intensification of military campaigns to rid the country of the remaining pockets of Native American resistance to European American demands that they relinquish their territory and abandon their way of life. Images would circulate throughout the country in the penny press, supplementing the written rationales for the rightness of these campaigns. Native Americans would create their own images of these battles, ones that drew on traditional indigenous styles while adopting certain visual conventions from their European American counterparts. Their images would reveal much about their changed circumstances, as they were imprisoned and forced onto reservations. They would also reveal much about their strategies of accommodation and resistance to these new circumstances.

CHAPTER 11

Images of Mexico and/as America: The Mexico–US War and Its Aftermath

(*c.* 1848–1860)

Learning from the Past: Emanuel Leutze's *The Storming of the Teocalli*

In 1848, thirteen years before his grandiose *Westward the Course of Empire Takes Its Way* [**3.9.2**, p. 174; **4.12.2**, p. 222], Emanuel Leutze completed a large and dramatic history painting entitled *The Storming of the Teocalli by Cortez and His Troops* [**4.11.1**]. The work is marked by an obsession with detail and a tight, naturalistic rendering of both figures and setting that implies an accurate depiction of what actually occurred. Chaos appears to reign over the mass of writhing bodies arranged on the steps of the teocalli or sacred pyramid. Yet Leutze has, in fact, divided the figures into two groups, with Cortez and most of his troops massed on the left, in an S-curve that moves from the dead soldier in the center foreground to the soldiers on the top level of the pyramid. The Aztec leader and most of his followers are pressed together on the right. While the dead and dying include both Aztecs and Spaniards, the impending Spanish victory is indicated by their greater numbers (the soldier in the lower far right corner suggests the Aztecs are surrounded) and by the Spaniards waving the flag on the top of the pyramid. The bravery of the Aztec warriors and the sacrificial offerings of the Aztec priest will not be enough to stave off disaster.

Leutze patterned his painting after an episode in William H. Prescott's *History of the Conquest of Mexico*, published in 1843. Prescott was a close friend of Amos Binney, the physician and businessman who commissioned the painting. Leutze's rendition of the scene differs, however, from Prescott's account. As the art historian Ron Tyler has pointed out, Leutze problematizes the "savage Aztec/civilized Spaniard" stereotypes promoted by Prescott. While the Aztecs are shown sacrificing a young child in a religious ritual, they are also portrayed as handsome and heroic. Leutze, a Protestant, continues the pictorial tradition begun by Theodore de Bry, presenting the Spaniards as just as savage as the Aztecs in their actions, despite their civilized dress and weaponry. A Spaniard atop the pyramid is about to throw a young Aztec child over the edge, his action echoing that of the Spanish soldier in De Bry's *Hanging, by the order of Diego Ocampa, of rebellious Caribs* [**1.0.1**; p. 17]. His action also functions as a visual counterpart to the sacrifice of the child by the Aztec priest, yet in this instance there is no religious justification. A dying Aztec at the extreme left refuses the last rites offered by a friar, while a Spanish soldier behind him steals a necklace from the body of a dead Aztec, thus bringing together the two major rationales for Spanish conquest—to convert the indigenous peoples to Christianity and to acquire wealth (see p. 20). The behavior of the victors caused contemporary critics to view the picture as somewhat problematic. If neither side was morally superior, then what would justify the vicious acts being committed by both?

Leutze's painting referred not only to the invasion of the Aztec empire by the Spanish but also to the more recent conflict between the United States and Mexico, that began in 1846 and was brought to a close in 1848, the year of the work's completion. It also may have been informed by the revolutions taking place in Europe in 1848, particularly in Germany. Leutze, who was born in Germany but raised in the US, supported these uprisings of peasants, workers, and small businessmen in their quest for a constitutional government and national freedom. He was also a strong proponent of democracy as it had been achieved in the US. His presentation of the victorious Spaniards engaged in acts of barbarism may have been intended as a reminder to his American audience that victory in the battle with Mexico must be accompanied by democratic institutions and just treatment for those who would now become citizens of the US.

US expansion into Mexican territory began prior to the war of 1846–48 [**4.11.5**; p. 215]. New Spain's northern regions—the present states of California, Utah, Nevada, Arizona, New Mexico, parts of Colorado, Texas, and Florida—had always been the most difficult for Spanish armies to defend. These regions were isolated from Mexico City, the center of political, cultural, and economic life; they became even more so after New Spain gained its independence from Spain in 1821 and formed the sovereign nation of Mexico. The decades following 1821 were fraught with political unrest and economic crisis, and the financial support given to the northernmost territories became sporadic at best. General Antonio López de Santa Anna Perez—often known as Santa Anna—was president eleven times between 1833 and 1855 (there were thirty-six presidents during this period). His corruption led the country to near bankruptcy, a crisis complicated by war with France.

The survival of the northern territories was facilitated in part by the Mexican government's removal of the bans on trade with outside nations, leading to the opening of the Santa Fe Trail in 1821, which allowed trade with the US. In addition, as the residents of New Spain were about to gain independence, the Spanish crown gave permission to Moses Austin, a US citizen, to colonize Texas. The main conditions were that the settlers were to be of good moral character, accept the Roman Catholic faith,

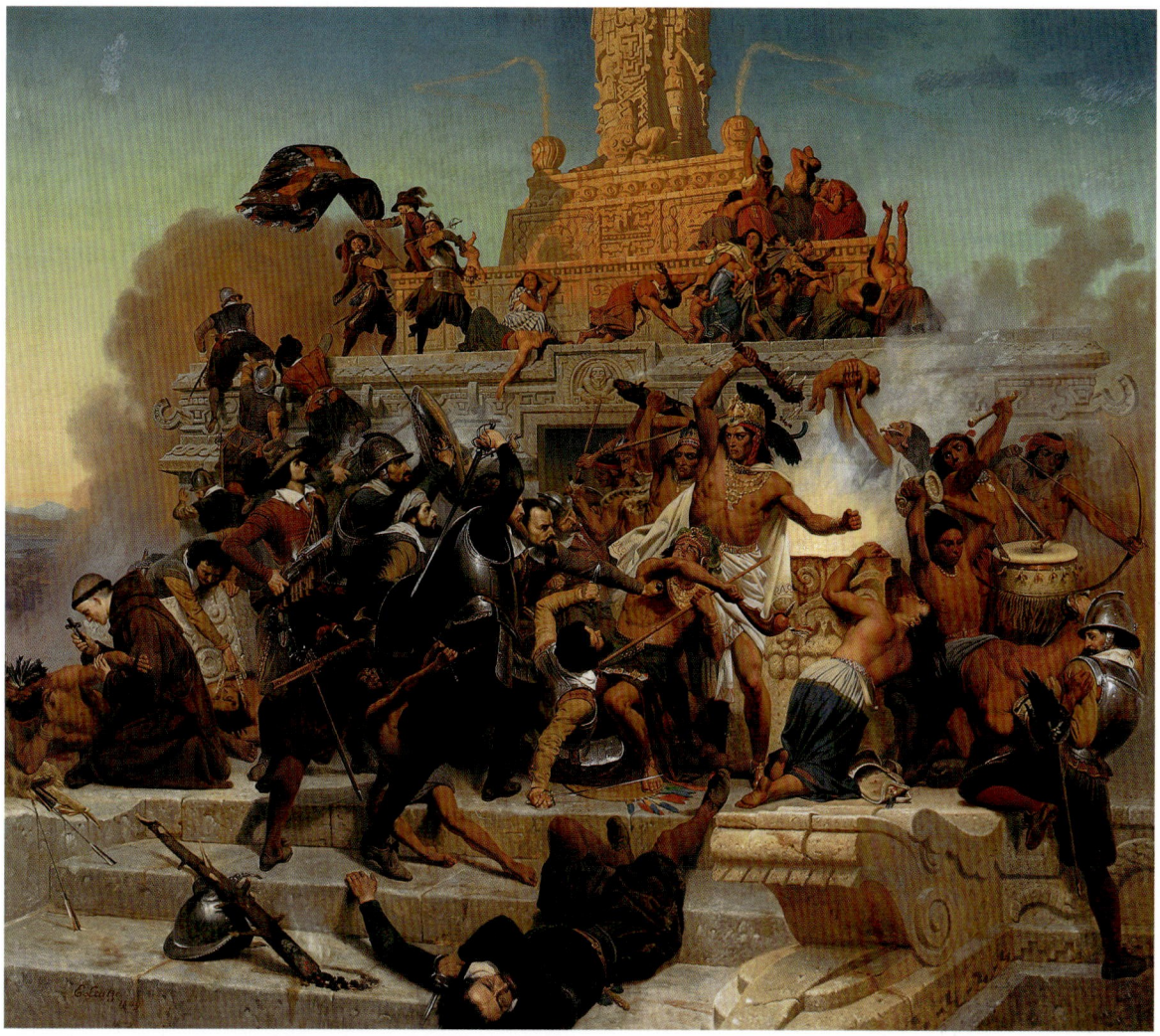

4.11.1 Emanuel Leutze: *The Storming of the Teocalli by Cortez and His Troops*, 1848. Oil on canvas, 84¾ x 98¾ in. (211.9 x 246.9 cm.)
Wadsworth Atheneum Museum of Art, Hartford, Connecticut

and abide by the laws of Mexico. Land was to be sold for ten cents an acre, with each male colonist allowed 640 acres (260 hectares) for himself, 320 for his wife, 160 for each child, and 80 for each slave. It was not long before the immigrant population outnumbered the Spanish missionaries and civilians. With the support of the majority of this new population, and with the help of the US Government, Texas broke away from Mexico in 1836 and became the Lone Star Republic. It was brought into the Union as a state in 1845.

President James Polk was not satisfied, however, with simply annexing Texas; he had his sights set on California. A Washington newspaper echoed Polk's ambitions in 1845:

> Let the great measure of annexation be accomplished, and with it the questions of boundary and claims. For who can arrest the torrent that will pour onward to the west? The road to California will be open to us. Who will stay the march of our people?

Shortly after, John O'Sullivan, the editor of the *Democratic Review*, commented: "Our manifest destiny is to overspread the continent allotted by providence for the free development of our yearly multiplying millions." Thus was coined the phrase—"Manifest Destiny"—that would be used time and again over the course of the nineteenth century to justify with religious fervor what was carried out through diplomacy or force.

With such pronouncements from the White House and media in Washington, D.C., it was only a matter of time before war erupted between Mexico and the US, with the first encounter occurring on April 25, 1846, in the lower Rio Grande Valley in far south Texas. Not everyone in the country was in favor of war. Abolitionists were concerned that it would provide a means to extend southern slave territory, a concern justified in light of the slaveholding policies of Texas. Many condemned this imperialist adventure as inimical to the legacy of the Revolutionary generation. Others were worried that the addition of large numbers of former Mexican citizens, many of whom were *mestizos* or mixed race and most of whom were Catholics, would "pollute" the US population. Yet those who ultimately won out saw the war, instead, as an occasion to extend the blessings of liberty and the opportunities for material prosperity.

Life on the Home Front

Ambivalence regarding the war can be found not only in *The Storming of the Teocalli* by Emanuel Leutze, but also in *Old '76 and Young '48* of 1849 [**4.11.2**] by Richard Caton Woodville (1825–1855). Here the Revolution of 1776 and the war between the US and Mexico (often referred to in Mexico as the American War) are brought together in the form of two individuals. The old man seated next to the fireplace, his gaze directed downward in contemplation, represents the "Old '76", while the young wounded soldier gesturing excitedly relates tales of the military glory of the "Young '48" to his parents, sibling, grandfather, and black household servants (the latter, as is so often the case, relegated to the edge of the composition). The old man's connection to the Revolutionary War can be found in three elements with the painting: his oval portrait as a youthful member of the Continental Army, toward which the young soldier gestures; a bust of George Washington; and a framed print of John Trumbull's *Declaration of Independence* (see pp. 122 and 132) above the fireplace. Thus, Woodville summarizes the various ways in which this war and its aftermath had been celebrated artistically. The art historian Gail Husch notes of the troubled old man that this "link to the glorious Revolutionary past does not, by carriage or expression, affirm victorious American exploits in Mexico." It seems Woodville hesitated to replicate the pictorial celebrations of the American Revolution in his treatment of a war whose revolutionary goals many had called into question.

Woodville produced another painting that addressed the conflict between the US and its southern neighbor, *War News from Mexico* of 1848 [**4.11.3**], exhibited at the American Art-Union in 1849. Here he focuses not on the ambiguity felt by many toward this campaign, but on how most Americans came

4.11.2 Richard Caton Woodville: *Old '76 and Young '48*, 1849. Oil on canvas, 21 x 26⅞ in. (52.3 x 68.2 cm.) Walters Art Gallery, Baltimore, Maryland

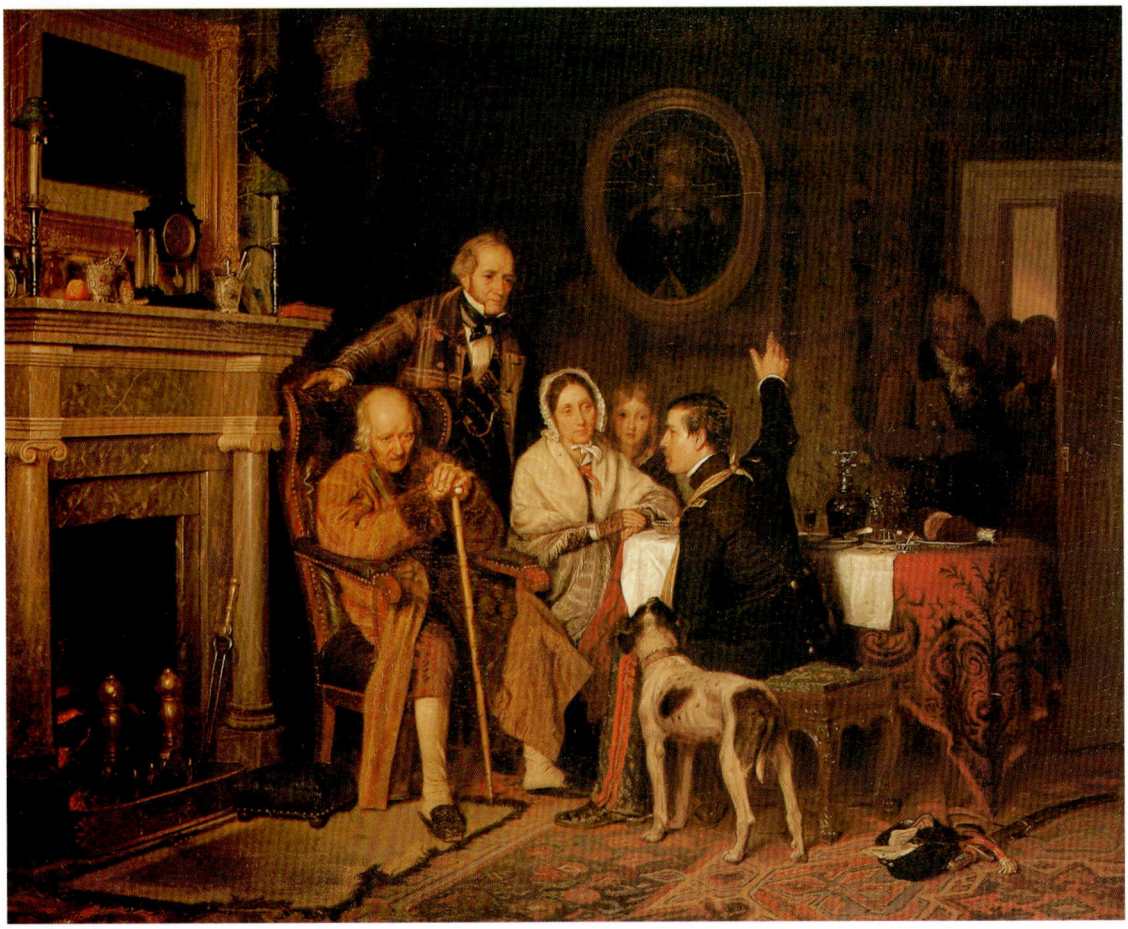

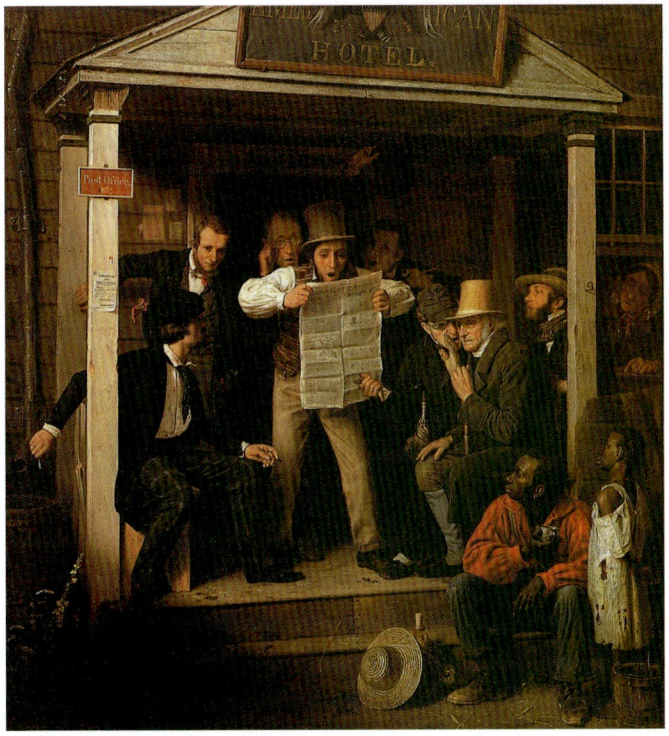

4.11.3 Richard Caton Woodville: *War News from Mexico*, 1848.
Oil on canvas, 27 x 24¾ in. (67.5 x 61.9 cm.)
Private collection. On loan to the National Gallery of Art, Washington, D.C.

to understand what it was all about—through reading the penny press, or inexpensive mass-produced newspapers. The war with Mexico was the first foreign war to be covered extensively by US correspondents, and it soon became clear that private news-gathering institutions were more efficient than the military itself (President James Polk often relied on newspapers rather than official dispatches for his information). The "eye-witness" accounts of the penny press were distributed across the country, competing with stories in local publications and creating in the process a national audience hungry for its news.

The mass-production of newspapers grew out of advances in technology that took place in the 1830s and 1840s, most notably the development of the steam engine. James Gordon Bennett, editor of one of the first penny-press newspapers, the *New York Herald*, made use of ocean steamers to gather news from around the world and of steam-driven rotary presses to print his newspaper. He also introduced crude woodcuts based on drawings of battles. In addition, the spread of literacy in the US and the constitutionally protected freedom of the press ensured a growing role for newspapers in American life.

News was now becoming big business and was marketed with an eye to providing readers with accounts that could be relied upon to tell the "truth" in an objective fashion, unlike party publications whose articles were filled with political bias. Illustrations added to the sense of truthfulness of the accompanying article. The penny press presented itself as the "voice of the people" and the "defender of the public good" against growing business monopolies. In doing so, it helped define the parameters of the war with Mexico and other events of national importance, while at the same time growing in size. Of course, newspaper accounts were not completely objective; rather, they were filtered through the sensibilities of those who owned the presses and circulation networks. The news reporter and editor, like the artist, became interpreters of the news.

Woodville places in the center of his painting not a soldier or a politician but a newspaper. Almost all eyes are focused on this paper, the source of information/truth that is then relayed to those not close enough to read its print. The group of men gathered around the central figure is framed by the portico of the "American Hotel," a not so subtle indication of the symbolic dimension of the painting. Woodville also repeats the connection between the past and the present found in his *Old '76 and Young '48*. The knee breeches worn by the seated old man identify him with the Founding Fathers and the American Revolution. The business of news and politics in the US is also clearly represented as a white man's world, an accurate depiction of democratic practices in America at mid-century. At the right edge of the composition is a woman leaning out of a window (her place is within the home), and on the steps sits a black man, with a young black girl standing beside him. All are outside of the portico and gaze at the group of white men, making us aware that, while marginal to the main action, their lives will be transformed by the events recorded in the newspaper. Slavery would become a flashpoint in the politics of territorial expansion, while the political rights of women in the country as a whole would find a voice at the Seneca Falls Convention, held the same year the war ended and Woodville created his painting (see p. 192).

Notices attached to the porch post and front of the hotel announce calls for volunteers to fight in Mexico, while another advertises a horse sale. The post on the left also contains the sign "Post Office," indicating a key means by which news was distributed throughout the country, in particular via letters between soldiers and their families. The multiple creases in the newspaper suggest that it may well have been folded up and sent via the postal service. These reference to business dealings and to systems of transportation and circulation call attention to what this war was all about—the acquisition of land and the expansion of business opportunities (most newspapers promoted the Government's expansionist policies). Thus, Woodville's painting is a celebration not of the glories of battle, but of the business of war and of the patriotism of US entrepreneurism.

Life on the Front Lines

Newspapers were not the only media making information about the war widely available. With the invention of lithography in the late eighteenth century in Europe, and its subsequent spread throughout the US in the nineteenth century, hundreds of prints could be made with relative speed and little expense from a single stone. This was a drastic departure from the time-consuming processes of engraving and etching (see p. 286). Most of the important events of the war with Mexico were recorded in oversize colored lithographs. While many were patterned after stock European prints of battles or earlier published images of Mexico, several were based on eye-witness accounts, for artist-soldiers were among the first troops sent into Mexican territory.

Major Joseph Horace Eaton (1815–1896), General Zachary Taylor's aide-de-camp, was one of these artist-soldiers. Several of his sketches were published, most notably his *Battle of Buena Vista* of 1847, which was turned into a hand-colored lithograph by Frances Bond Palmer (1812–1876) [**4.11.4**]. Eaton has carefully arranged the troops and recorded the distinctive characteristics of the terrain, with its flat mesas and looming mountains, indicating that his picture was as much a topographical military record as a work of art. In addition, he has positioned the viewer well above the battle, thus suggesting a full understanding, if not control, of the situation. Yet the orderliness of the soldiers and lack of casualties give little indication that Eaton portrayed the prelude to one of the bloodiest days of the conflict (February 23, 1847). While the US ultimately won the battle, victory seemed far from inevitable.

W. M. Albin, a reporter in Saltillo, Mexico, just north of Buena Vista and south of Laredo, Texas, wrote to a friend in 1846 of his frustration with the license taken by those who created illustrations for US newspapers:

> One image represents Gen. Taylor mounted on a fierce, prancing steed, in full military suit, with towering plume, huge epaulettes....Those who for the last five or more years have seen Gen. T. every day, and never mounted on any other but "that same old white horse," with that same old long coat on, and glazed cap, and common soldier's light blue overalls, will be forcibly struck with the faithfulness of this picture.

That readers of the penny press expected greater accuracy or truthfulness in printed images than in painted scenes is not surprising, since those who promoted the press promised such accuracy. It is also not surprising that this promise often was not fulfilled, for those who founded the early mass newspapers soon became aware of the power they wielded in constructing a national understanding of events in keeping with their own interests. While Albin was able to detect the inaccuracy of General Taylor's representation, few had the advantage of his inside information. Those far from the battlefield relied primarily on the lithographs and news stories (supplemented for some by letters from the front) for their understanding of the war between Mexico and the US.

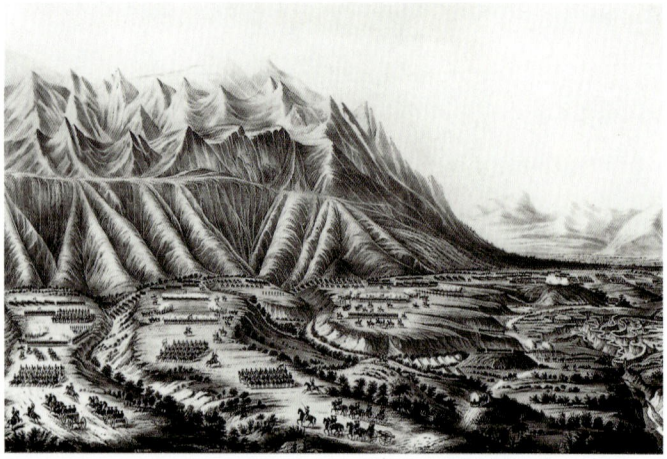

4.11.4 Frances Bond Palmer after Major Joseph Horace Eaton: *Battle of Buena Vista*. View of the Battle-Ground of the "Angostura" Fought Near Buena Vista, Mexico February 23rd. 1847 (Looking S. West), 1847.
Hand-colored lithograph, 19¼ x 29½ in. (48.9 x 74.9 cm.)
Amon Carter Museum, Fort Worth, Texas

The heroic image of General Taylor that Albin found so questionable was just part of an outpouring of visual, oral, and written praise for the victorious general that buoyed his reputation. In 1848, the year of the signing of the Treaty of Guadalupe Hidalgo ending the war, Taylor was elected president of the US. The man who conquered Mexico would now lead the country into the second half of the nineteenth century, a sure sign that Manifest Destiny and territorial expansion were the order of the day.

Mexican Culture as American Culture: The *Santeros* of New Mexico

In July 1848, shortly after the end of the war with Mexico, the New York newspaper *The Home Journal* carried the following challenge:

> We vanquish in order to elevate....It is a divine, rather than a mortal trait, thus to exert superior force—not to appropriate a triumph, but to diffuse a blessing....The duty of maintaining uninjured... this matchless establishment, which God and our forefathers have given us, is of infinite responsibility.

Mortal rather than divine concerns, however, guided postwar US policies in the vast new territory that had been added to the still-fledgling nation—present-day California, Nevada, Utah, the majority of Arizona, and parts of Colorado and New Mexico (the current states of Washington, Oregon, and Idaho were acquired by treaty with Britain in 1846) [**4.11.5**]. This territory was already populated by individuals who, prior to 1848, had been Mexican citizens. Most chose to remain in their homes, hoping they would be treated fairly as part of the "matchless establishment" that constituted the American democratic experiment. Their hopes were often dashed by corrupt and intolerant US Government officials and settlers; by 1858 almost 90 percent of New Mexicans had lost their land. Yet they managed to keep a presence in the region, working what was left of their farms, ranches, and businesses, as well as maintaining their cultural and religious practices.

As indicated earlier, religion played a central role in the lives of those who colonized the northern frontier of New Spain (see pp. 33–48). Roman Catholicism, unlike Protestantism, thrived on lavish visual displays, and sparsely populated communities were often brought together through the numerous celebrations honoring Christ, the Virgin Mary, and various saints. Family life was also organized around daily religious rituals, with images of saints and Jesus adorning family altars. While the paintings and sculptures created for these ceremonies and altars were modest compared to their counterparts in Mexico City, they embodied the region's attempt to continue both the religious traditions of Spain and Mexico and the unique visual tradition that had begun to take shape in the region in the seventeenth century.

While the territory ceded to the US in 1848 had been part of Mexico, it was so distant from the cultural and political center that it developed and maintained a strong sense of separate identity. This isolation, according to the art historian Keith McElroy, led to the emergence of a local art tradition that was more than simply the awkward copying of the art of Mexico City by untutored craftspeople. Paintings, prints, and sculpture from Mexico and Spain provided the models for much of what was produced locally. Yet the *santeros*, the artists who produced the numerous images of saints used in religious ceremonies, also made conscious choices to reject or add elements to their work. In particular, they maintained a certain lack of finish and abstraction of the human body that is in marked contrast to the highly naturalistic religious art of Mexico's urban centers.

The subject matter chosen by the *santeros* reflected the tastes of both Mexico City and regional communities. Most popular were single figures of saints in landscape or interior settings. In accordance with the mandate of the Council of Trent, convened by the Roman Catholic Church in the mid-sixteenth century in response to the Protestant Reformation, depictions of the Holy Family and the humanity of Christ were emphasized. This resulted in the creation of numerous images of the Virgin, the Crucifixion, the Christ Child, and St. Joseph. John Nepomuk [**1.2.11**; p. 36], canonized in 1729, was also a popular subject because he was the patron saint of confession and secrecy (he was martyred for refusing to reveal the secrets of the confessional). He was favored by the numerous lay confraternities,

4.11.5 Territorial growth of the United States from 1776 to 1912.

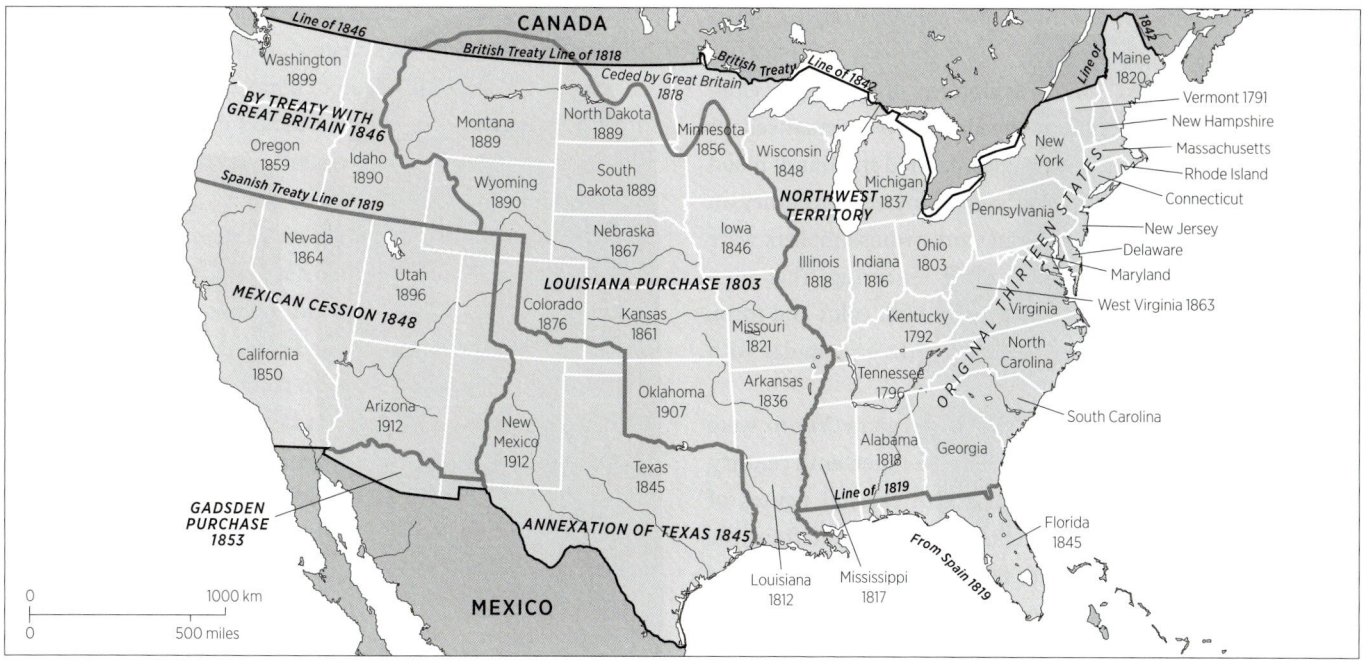

Mexicans, that no amount of condemnation and ridicule could destroy their power. Many hide paintings were removed from churches and preserved in private homes and *moradas*, and while the *santero* school declined after Lamy's arrival, it did not disappear, thanks in large part to the confraternities.

The Local and the International: New Mexican Furniture and Textiles

The Mexicans who inhabited the Southwest also had a rich and fully developed secular culture, marked by imaginative furniture design and textiles. As with the religious imagery, the furniture remained relatively unaltered in form over several centuries, relying on Spanish prototypes from the sixteenth century. Change is found primarily in the carved decoration. The pieces were simple in design and highly portable, consisting primarily of boxes, chests, chairs, benches, tables, cupboards, and shelves. Chests were by far the most common item: families often owned several, using them for storage, as supports for boards for dining or sleeping, or as surfaces on which to write or sit. In New Mexico the only wood readily available for furniture-making was local pine, which imposed certain restrictions. Pine tends to split in straight lines along the grain, so pieces are typically rectilinear, with simple carved decoration.

Three main types of chest were constructed in the eighteenth and early nineteenth centuries: board chests, made of six boards fitted together with dovetail joints and pegs; more complicated framed chests, consisting of panels set into a framework of rails and stiles with pegged mortise-and-tenon joints; and false-framed chests—the first type disguised as the second by applied strips of molding. One late board chest from the eighteenth or early nineteenth century [**4.11.11**] is covered by painted geometric designs, which include the stepped-fret motif. This motif is a reference to either the Pueblo Indian cloud-terrace motif or the Moorish stepped and bracketed designs found on Mexican and Spanish furniture from the sixteenth through nineteenth centuries. Families also imported furniture from Mexico, in particular from the area of Michoacán. Many examples of the latter were brightly painted with elaborate floral designs [**4.11.12**].

Visitors arriving from the eastern United States after 1846 frequently remarked upon the lack of furniture in people's homes. Yet often what was lacking was furniture of a familiar type. In *El Gringo, or New Mexico and Her People* (1856) W. W. H. Advise writes of New Mexican interiors:

> Few chairs or wooden seats of any kind are used, but in their stead mattresses are folded up and placed around the room, next to the wall, which, being covered with blankets, make a pleasant seat and serve the place of sofas. This is an Eastern custom, and was undoubtedly borrowed from the Moor....The females in particular, prefer the easy *colchón*—folded mattress—to the straight

4.11.11 Unknown artist, from New Mexico: board chest, late 18th–early 19th century. Pine, gesso, water-based paint, iron hardware, w. 29 in. (73.7 cm.)
Spanish Colonial Arts Society Collection, Santa Fe, New Mexico

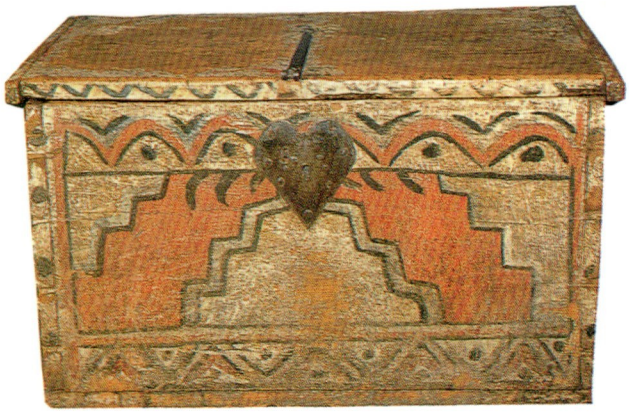

4.11.12 Unknown artist, from Mexico, probably Michoacán: writing chest, 18th century. Hardwood, gesso, paint, gold leaf, iron hardware, w. 31 in. (78.7 cm.)
Spanish Colonial Arts Society Collection, Santa Fe, New Mexico

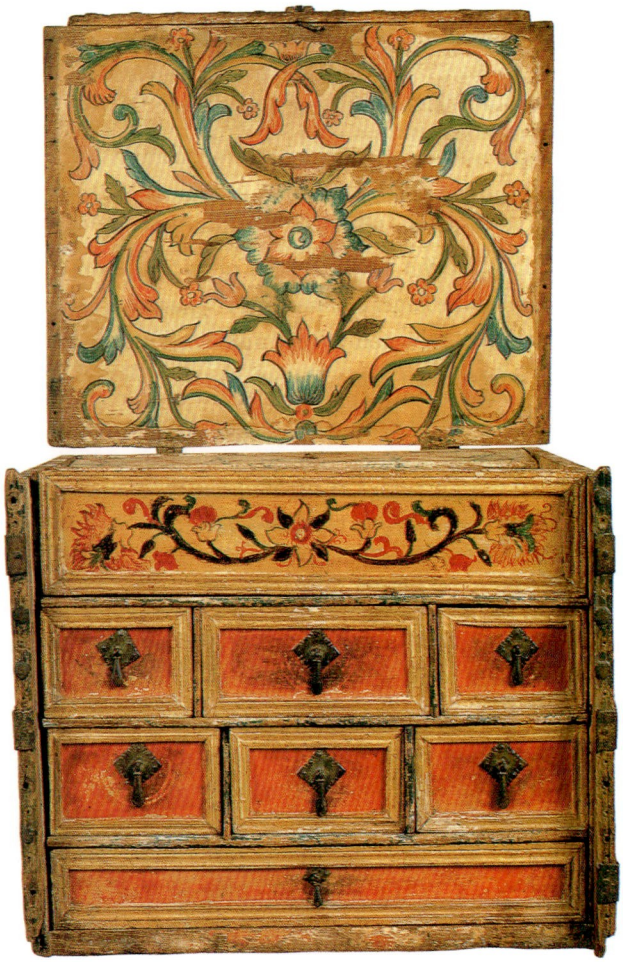

> and stiff-backed chairs and settees; and frequently they spread a single blanket in the middle of the floor, upon which they sit at work and receive visitors.

The mattresses often functioned as couches by day and beds by night. Another Anglo-American, Susan Magoffin, described the Santa Fe home of the wealthy Gaspar Ortiz family in 1846 as "one of the best in the city....The long salon to the front is the sitting room. This is furnished with cushions, no chairs, two steamboat sofas, tables, a bed, and other little fixtures."

A wide array of textiles, made locally or imported from Mexico or Asia, provided a wealth of color in New Mexican homes. Blankets and shawls were found in abundance, draped over cushions and mattresses. Sometimes even the floors, particularly in the *salón de recibo* or parlor, were covered wall-to-wall with a cloth known as *jerga*, roughly woven most often in a checkerboard pattern using natural white and brown combinations or vegetal dyes. During the 1860s commercial dyes were introduced, resulting in brighter colors. Such *jergas* are reminiscent of the painted floor cloths of New England homes in the early nineteenth century (see p. 138).

When the first Spanish settlers arrived in New Mexico, they found the Pueblo peoples weaving fine cloth of cotton and vegetable fibers on vertical looms. The Spanish brought their own textiles and, more importantly, herds of churro sheep, which adapted well to the high desert terrain. By the early nineteenth century, hundreds of thousands of these sheep existed throughout the Southwest and wool replaced cotton among the Pueblo peoples and the Navajo, except for certain ceremonial attire.

While indigenous peoples had their own weaving traditions, the friars who came into the area also trained those who lived near the missions to use European treadle looms. The friars then set up several workshops using a mixture of forced indigenous labor and Spanish workers to produce textiles for trade within the territory of New Mexico and with neighboring Mexican states to the south. Many of the woven and embroidered *colchas* or bed coverings produced in the region came from these workshops. The elaborate floral patterns of some [**4.11.13**] reflect the influence of textiles imported from India.

The blankets and *sarapes* or ponchos in New Mexican homes were often marked by a series of zigzag stripes and diamonds, a pattern popular with Navajo weavers [**4.11.14**]. This design had appeared earlier in Navajo basketry patterns and was then adapted to woven blankets. The Navajo are thought to have taken up weaving in the latter half of the seventeenth century, adopting the wide upright loom of their Pueblo neighbors. Yet in Navajo culture the women did the weaving, while in Pueblo culture it was the men. Navajo weavings soon became part of a vast trade network that stretched south into Mexico and east into the Great Plains. Art historians often describe the period between the 1820s and the 1860s as the Classic period in Navajo weaving, which was brought to an end in 1863 by

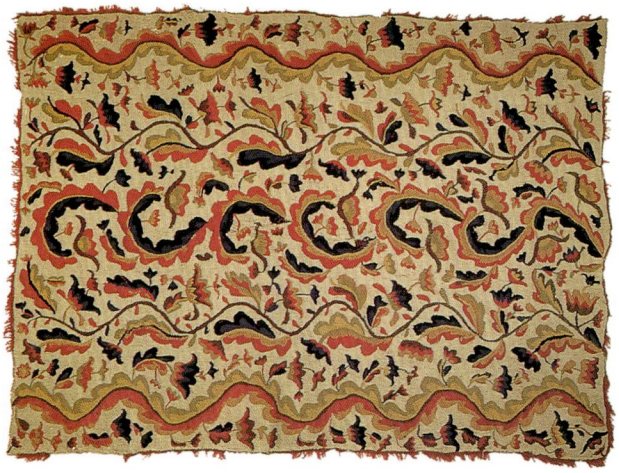

4.11.13 Unknown artist, from New Mexico: *colcha*, late 18th–early 19th century. Hand-spun, handwoven sabanilla cloth with undyed and vegetal-dyed wool yarn and possibly Manchester yarn
Spanish Colonial Arts Society Collection, Santa Fe, New Mexico

4.11.14 Unknown artist, from Navajo: *sarape*, *c.* 1825–60. Hand-spun undyed and vegetal-dyed wool, 69⅜ x 52½ in. (176 x 133.4 cm.)
National Museum of the American Indian, Smithsonian Institution, Washington, D.C.

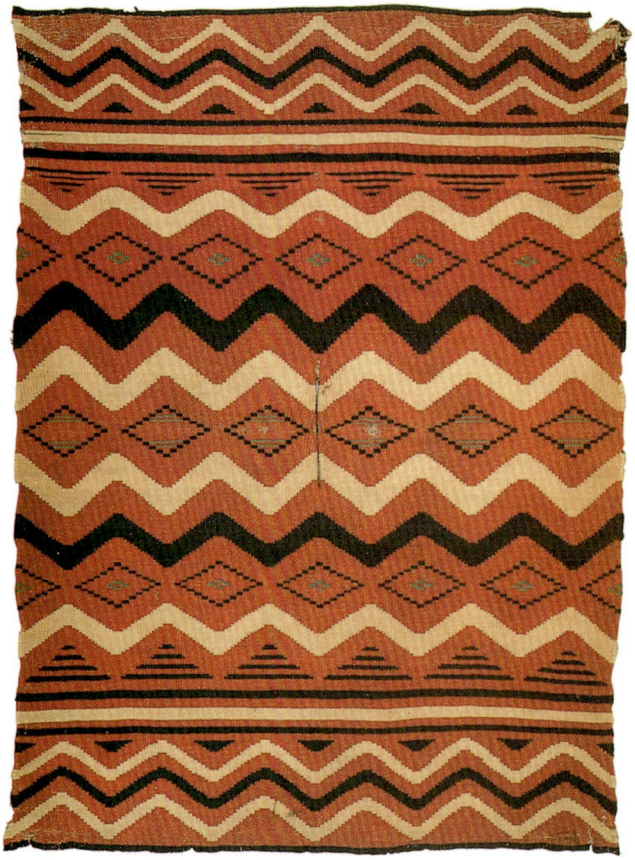

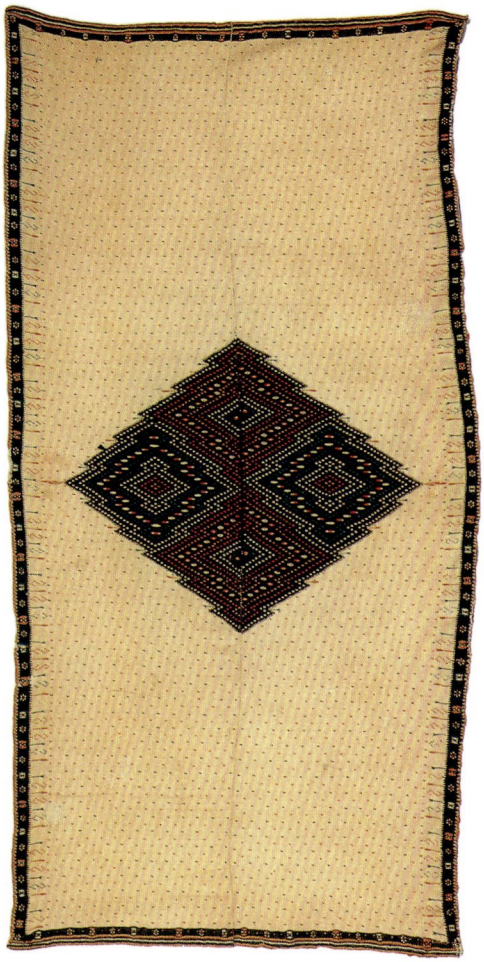

4.11.15 Unknown artist, from Saltillo, Coahuila, Mexico: *sarape*, late 18th–early 19th century.
Hand-spun undyed and vegetal-dyed wool
Spanish Colonial Arts Society Collection, Santa Fe, New Mexico

what became known as "The Long Walk." In order to counter indigenous attacks on settlers moving onto indigenous lands, the US Government forced thousands of Navajo to march to Bosque Redondo in eastern New Mexico. Five years later they were allowed to return to a much smaller territory within their original homelands in northeastern Arizona and northwestern New Mexico. With their herds of sheep destroyed, they were forced to adapt to a new economy of factory-processed yarns and chemical dyes.

Sarapes from the town of Saltillo in northern Mexico were also in great demand in New Mexico, prized for their beauty and high quality. Woven in two matching vertical panels, then sewn together, they were often marked by a central diamond shape composed of smaller diamonds surrounded by serrated concentric bands, with a decorative border echoing the colors and motifs of the central diamond [**4.11.15**]. Many who produced Saltillo *sarapes* in the nineteenth century were descendants of the Tlaxcalans, allies of the Spaniards in their war against the Aztecs (see p. 24). They were sent into the region in 1591 to help subdue hostile indigenous peoples and enable the establishment of silver mines. They settled in the town of Saltillo and were granted a special *barrio* or neighborhood, San Estebán de Nuevo Tlaxcala. Tlaxcalan men had already gained a reputation as skilled weavers among the Spanish in central Mexico (they had been taught the craft by the Otomí, with whom they had intermarried). They continued this activity in their new northern home, combining their old practices with new Spanish designs, materials, and technologies.

The form of the *sarape*—a rectangular blanket with a vertical slit for the head and open at the sides—may have originated in the indigenous *manta* (see p. 27), for such garments did not exist in Spain. After Mexico gained independence from Spain in 1821, the *sarape* became a prominent nationalist symbol, a requisite part of the costume of the *vaquero*, the Mexican counterpart of the American cowboy.

New Mexican homes might also contain embroidered silk shawls from China and the Philippines alongside the Navajo blankets, Saltillo *sarapes*, and textiles from the friars' workshops. These shawls were evidence of a cosmopolitan taste that would soon expand to include the new textiles and furniture brought into the area from the US by tourists and businessmen. New dyes and tools would also aid in the transformation of local traditions of textile production, while the designs of Navajo and Mexican weavers and embroiderers would find their place in drawing rooms throughout the nation in the following century.

Review Questions

1 How is Emanuel Leutze's painting *The Storming of the Teocalli by Cortez and His Troops* (1848) a commentary on the 1846–48 war between Mexico and the US?

2 What new technologies appeared in the 1830s and 1840s that influenced the creation and distribution of images of military conflicts?

3 What are some of the distinctive characteristics (style, iconography) of the religious imagery created in New Mexico in the first half of the nineteenth century?

4 What impact did the incorporation of New Mexico into US territory have on religious life?

5 What can we learn about the lives of the residents of New Mexico in the first half of the nineteenth century by examining the furniture and textiles found in their homes? How does this material compare to the furniture and textiles found in the homes of their contemporaries in New England?

CHAPTER 12

A Nation Divided: Slavery and the Civil War

(*c.* 1839–1865)

Prelude to the Civil War: Representing African Americans and Slavery

In the 1850s Thomas Ustick Walter (1804–1887) enlarged the Senate and House wings of the United States Capitol Building in Washington, D.C. to accommodate the eighteen new states that had joined the Union by mid-century, increasing the size of the dome to offset the increased size of the wings [**4.12.1a**]. Thomas Crawford (1813–1857) was approached in May 1855 to create a statue for the top of the dome. He proposed *Freedom Triumphant in War and Peace.* The plaster model for the 19½-foot- (6-meter-) tall bronze statue depicted a heroic female in flowing robes, with the right hand on the hilt of a sheathed sword. The left hand held a laurel wreath and rested on the Shield of the United States. Placed on the figure's head were a crown and a liberty cap, the latter a Roman symbol of the emancipated slave.

US Secretary of War Jefferson Davis was in charge of the expansion and decoration of the Capitol building from 1853 to 1857. According to the art historian Vivien Green Fryd, this slaveholder and future president of the Confederacy objected to the liberty cap because "its history renders it inappropriate to a people who were born free and would not be enslaved." Davis ordered Crawford to remove it; Crawford acquiesced. When the finished statue was hoisted to the top of the dome in December of 1863, it wore a military helmet, its rim circled by stars and its crown topped by the head of an American eagle festooned with additional feathers [**4.12.1b**]. As Fryd notes, the liberty cap caused few objections in images of the new republic in the early nineteenth century [**2.6.23**; p. 124]. Its virtual absence, however, in the Capitol decoration in the two decades before the Civil War, along with the absence of any other reference to slavery, was "no accident, but instead resulted from conscious efforts to avoid the very issue that threatened national unity."

Yet when Emanuel Leutze's *Westward the Course of Empire Takes Its Way* was installed in the western staircase of the House of Representatives chamber in December 1862 [**4.12.2**; p. 222], things had changed, not only in the political climate, but also in the mural itself. The oil study of 1861 [**3.9.3**; p. 174] did not include the symbols of mining, hunting, and agriculture found in the final composition. Also not present in the study was the black man in the center foreground of the finished mural leading a white woman and child on a mule.

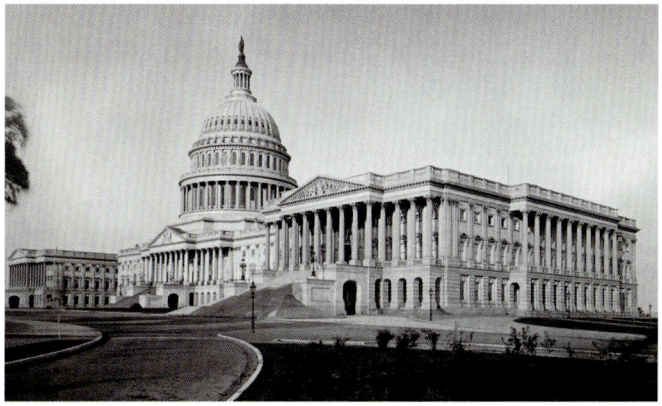

4.12.1a United States Capitol, Washington, D.C., as enlarged by Thomas Ustick Walter, 1851–65.

4.12.1b Thomas Crawford, *Freedom Triumphant in War and Peace*, US Capitol, Washington, D.C. Perspective view looking to the right side of statue. Photo taken in 1993 during restoration work.

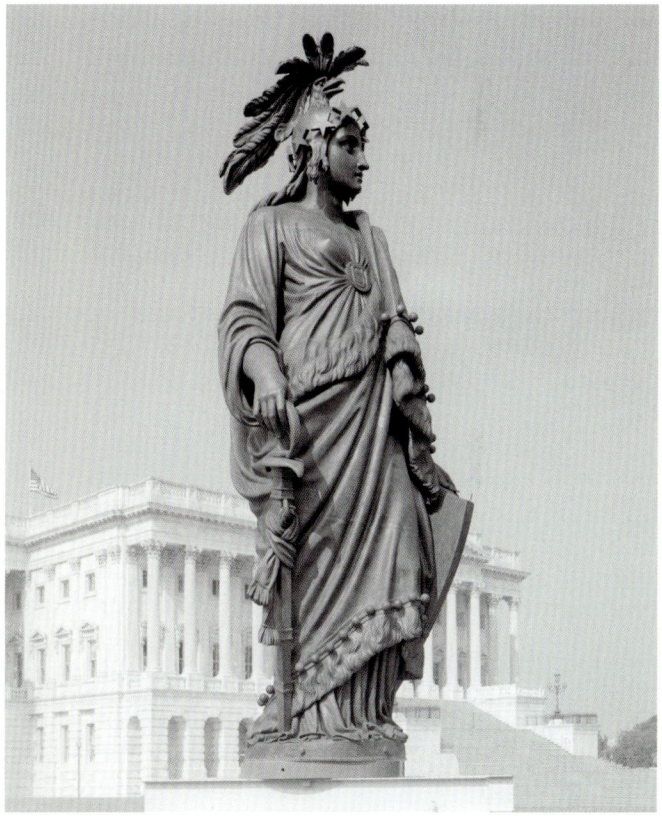

Leutze had received his Capitol commission in June 1861, shortly after the opening salvo of the Civil War. One hotly debated issue at the time was whether or not slavery should be extended into the new territories. Secretary of War Simon Cameron was then in charge of the decoration of the Capitol building and approved Leutze's initial study. While Cameron was an expansionist opposed to the emigration of blacks into the western territories, he did not force Leutze to remove the black figure. By including a black man in such a prominent position, Leutze (whose pro-abolitionist sentiments were well known) suggests that blacks, as well as whites, might experience a new freedom in the West. The presence of the woman and child on a mule creates a parallel between the flight of the Holy Family from persecution at the hands of Herod and the opening up of the West. Leutze thus provides another gloss on the theme of Manifest Destiny (see p. 149), one marked by the morally charged arguments of the abolitionist movement.

As the historian Lerone Bennett, Jr., has noted, "America, contrary to the generally accepted view, is an African as well as a European invention." African slave labor enabled the growth of a plantation economy in the South in the seventeenth and eighteenth centuries, while African American wage labor aided the expansion of industrialization in the second half of the nineteenth century. Some European Americans attempted to justify the enslavement and exploitation of Africans and African Americans through representations of them as either childlike and in need of care, or savage and in need of disciplining (they were not, however, like Native Americans, "doomed to perish," for their labor was central to the country's economy).

Yet the Civil War, and the abolitionist movement that preceded it, forced a re-evaluation of the image of black men and women in American culture. Prior to the 1860s the dominant stereotypes of black men were silent servants, situated on the margins of the composition [for example, **4.11.2**; p. 212], or high-stepping, banjo-playing "darkies," happy and childlike, who, when not working contentedly in the fields, performed either for their families or for their white owners. Black women were "mammys," protective of their white charges and proud of their place as servant, maid, and nanny within the white household. Enslavement was seen as good for Africans, for it domesticated inherently savage people: to free them would actually do them a disservice, for they would lose their childlike innocence (whether acquired or innate) and revert to savagery.

Such stereotypes appear in John Lewis Krimmel's *Quilting Frolic* of 1813 [**4.12.3**]. Krimmel (1786–1821) was born in Germany and studied with the genre painter Johann Baptist Seele

4.12.2 Emanuel Leutze: *Westward the Course of Empire Takes Its Way (Westward Ho!)*, 1861–62.
Mural, 20 x 30 ft. (6 x 9 m.)
United States Capitol, Washington, D.C., House wing, west stairway

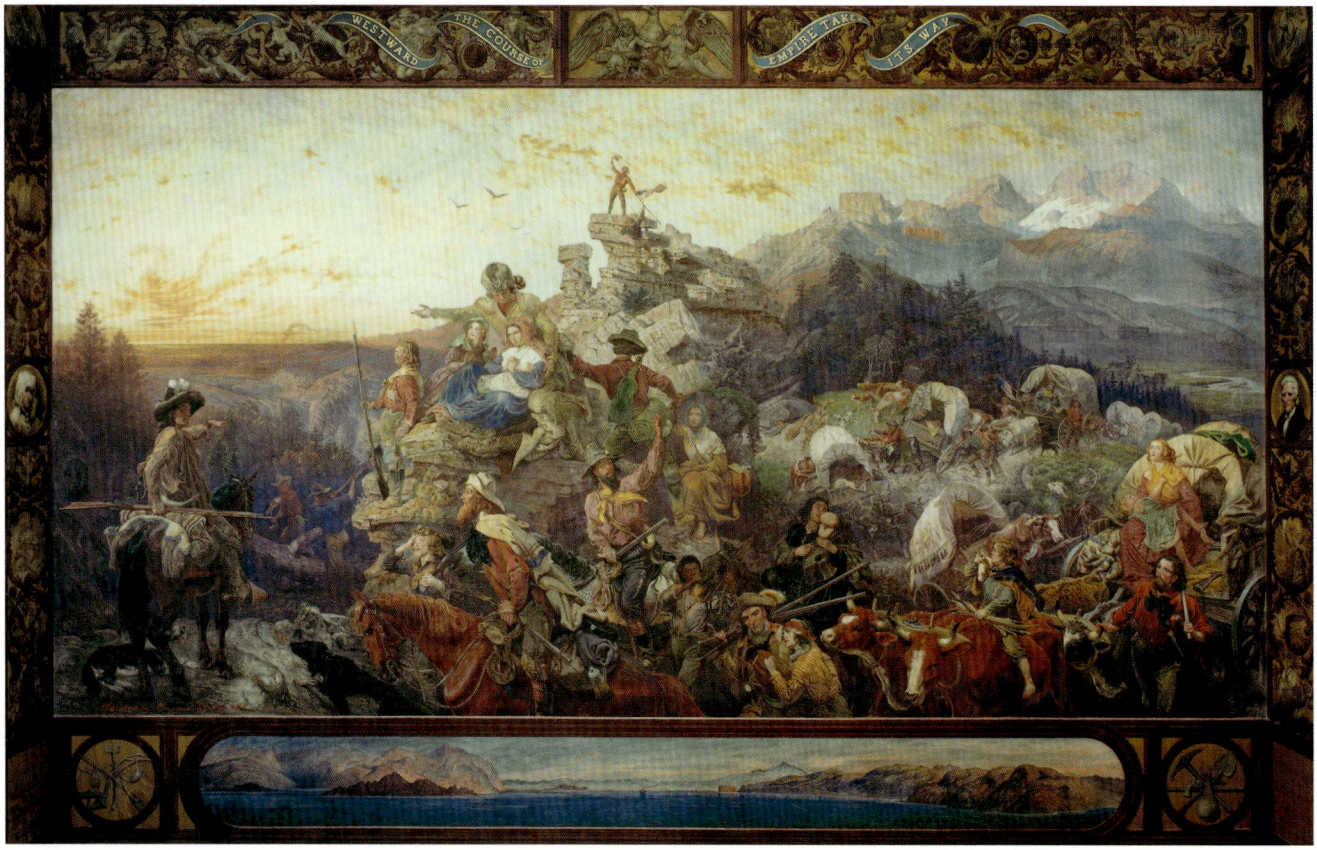

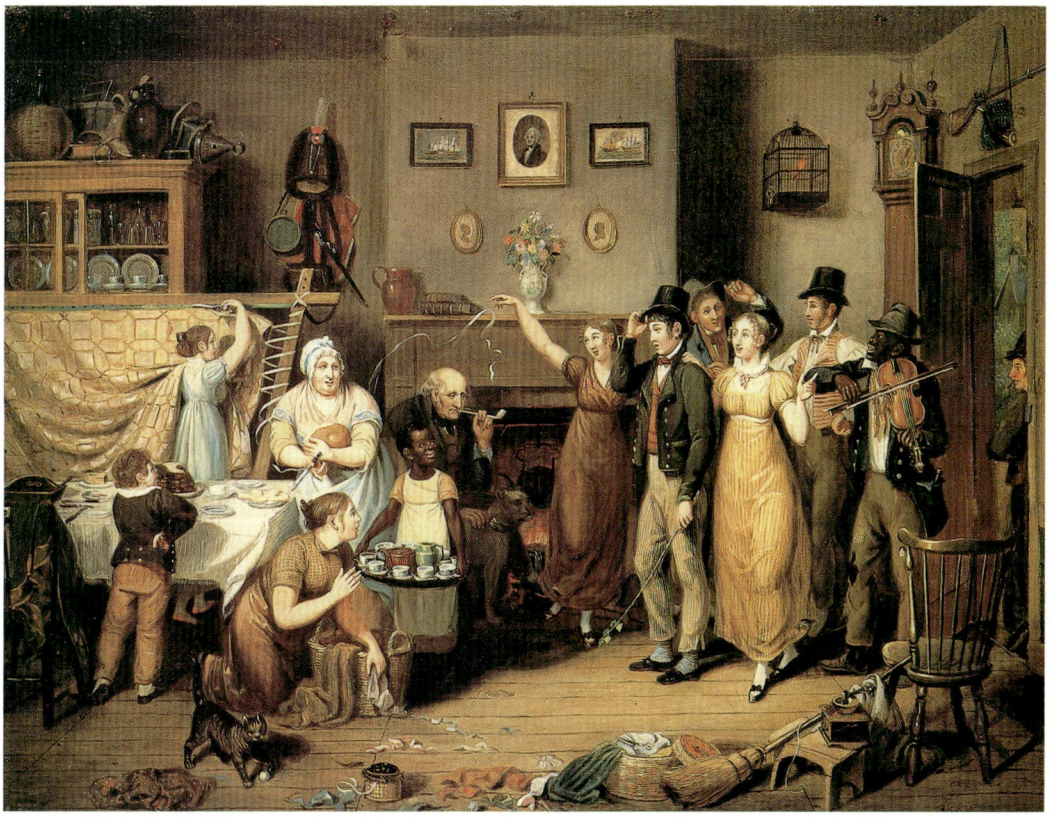

4.12.3 John Lewis Krimmel: *Quilting Frolic*, 1813.
Oil on canvas,
16⅞ x 22⅜ in. (42.8 x 56.8 cm.)
The Henry Francis du Pont Winterthur Museum, Winterthur, Delaware

(1774–1814) before coming to the US in 1810. He was also an admirer of the works of the British artists William Hogarth (1697–1764) and David Wilkie (1785–1841) and, like them, recorded the looks and foibles of the peasant, merchant, and artisanal classes. *Quilting Frolic* depicts the preparations for an evening of merriment after a day of quilting and contains a detailed inventory of the belongings of a middle-income household. The paintings on the wall—a portrait of George Washington flanked by two maritime scenes, one of which involves a battle—attest to the cultured and patriotic character of the inhabitants. Other objects on the walls or on the tops of cupboards indicate the social status and lineage of the family. The black slave or servant girl and the black fiddler underline this social status, the girl through her role as a slave or servant and the fiddler through his shabby clothing, which contrasts so markedly with the finery of the white figures next to him. According to the art historian Guy C. McElroy, Krimmel was among the first

> to utilize physiognomical distortions [toothy grins, oversized lips] as a basic element in the depiction of African-Americans; his comic portrayal was probably meant to establish a good-natured humorous scenario, but it profoundly reinforced developing ideas regarding the humorous, even "debased" appearance of African-Americans.

The Abolitionist Movement and the Challenging of Stereotypes

While the stereotypical depictions of African Americans produced by John Lewis Krimmel and others dominated the art world in the first half of the nineteenth century, they did not go unchallenged, particularly after the establishment of the American Anti-Slavery Society in 1833. Led by both African Americans and European Americans, it joined such African American anti-slavery organizations as the Free African Society, founded in 1787, and the General Coloured Association, founded in 1826. It became one of the key organizations in the American abolitionist movement, flooding the Southern slave-holding states with literature and lobbying throughout the country for an end to slavery.

The abolitionist movement was fuelled in part by the Second Great Awakening of the 1810s and 1820s (see p. 131). Members of this evangelical revival, which included many African Americans, criticized declining morals and an increase in sinful practices. Abolitionists also took up the charge of political hypocrisy leveled by the British at the end of the eighteenth century: how could the American revolutionaries claim independence in the name of freedom and liberty while enslaving a whole race of people? Many artists belonged to the abolitionist movement or were inspired by its efforts, and translated its messages into painted form.

One such artist was Nathaniel Jocelyn (1796–1881). Initially trained as an engraver, he turned to painting in 1820 and became well known as a portraitist in the New Haven area of Connecticut. He returned to engraving at the end of his career after a disastrous studio fire. In 1839, the black abolitionist Robert Purvis commissioned Jocelyn to produce a large oil portrait entitled *Cinque* [**4.12.4**]. Cinque was one of fifty-three men and women captured in the Mendi region of Africa in 1839 and purchased by Portuguese slave traders, in violation of treaties prohibiting the international slave trade. They were then sold to Spaniards in Havana. While they were being transported to Puerto Rico, Cinque led a rebellion on the ship *La Amistad*. The rebels demanded that the ship return to Africa, but the crew altered its course at night and brought it ashore on Long Island. Local authorities freed the crew and arrested the mutineers, who were held in New Haven while awaiting trial. Abolitionists came to their defence. The case went all the way to the Supreme Court, which in March 1840 ruled that the Africans had been illegally seized. Cinque and his compatriots were released and toured the Northeast, appearing at numerous anti-slavery meetings, before returning to Africa in 1841.

In place of the physiognomic distortions used by Krimmel in his depiction of the black fiddler [**4.12.3**; p. 223], Jocelyn has produced a noble portrait of an African man. Jocelyn's abolitionist sympathies no doubt played a role in his decision to depict Cinque in this manner. He was also undoubtedly influenced by the numerous accounts of Cinque's activities in the popular press that included descriptions of him as "of magnificent physique [and] commanding presence." Phrenologists had carefully analyzed Cinque's head in an attempt to understand his daring behavior. They reported that its shape indicated "great vigor of body and mind...ambition, independence...love of liberty." Such curiosity suggests that, despite numerous rebellions on board slave ships, many European Americans still assumed that ambition, independence, and the intelligence needed to plan a successful revolt were anomalies among Africans. Their obsession with his physical features, recorded in Jocelyn's portrait, also suggests they thought his intelligence could be due to the fact that he did not "look like an African": in other words, he did not look like the stereotype of Africans that had been created by European American artists in the US.

4.12.4 Nathaniel Jocelyn: *Cinque*, 1839.
Oil on canvas, 30¼ x 25½ in. (76.8 x 64.8 cm.)
New Haven Colony Historical Society, New Haven, Connecticut

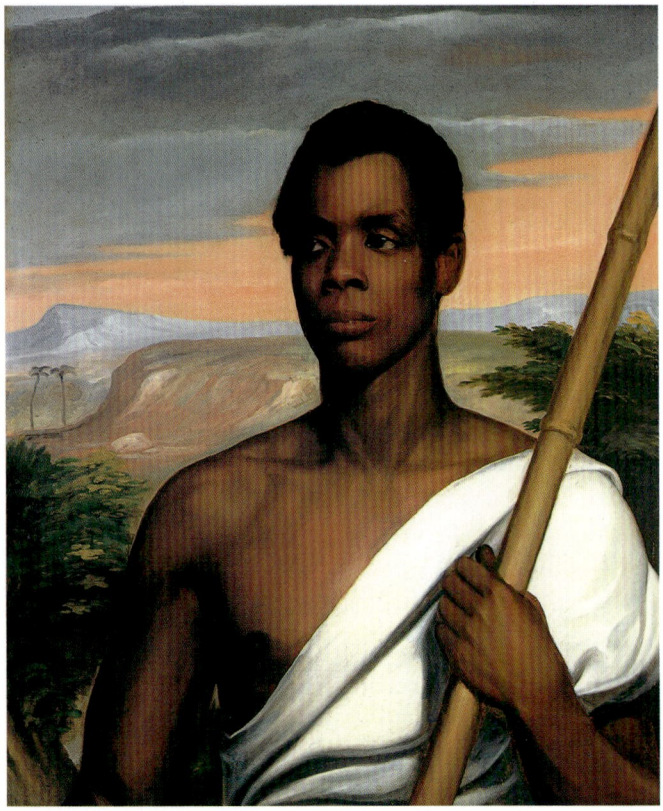

Jocelyn has also rejected the ragged clothing of Krimmel's fiddler and has clothed Cinque in the white toga of ancient Greece and Rome. The palm trees in the background evoke his exotic origins, and the stalk of cane he holds refers to the sugarcane fields of the Caribbean where he and his fellow rebels were to have labored. By using conventions from European neoclassical painting—the pose, the toga, the cane held like a staff of office—Jocelyn creates a parallel between Cinque, and African slaves in general, and the ancient Greeks and Romans with whom many European Americans traditionally identified.

The abolitionist movement led to growing support for the education of African Americans, and several artists received both financial and moral backing. Robert S. Duncanson, best known as a landscape painter (see p. 162), produced two paintings dealing directly with African American subjects: *View of Cincinnati, Ohio, from Covington, Kentucky* [**3.9.16**; p. 184], and *Uncle Tom and Little Eva* (1853) [**4.12.5**]. In the latter, two characters in Harriet Beecher Stowe's popular abolitionist novel, *Uncle Tom's Cabin; or, Life Among the Lowly* (1852), are set within a landscape that combines a luminous harbor scene with an overgrown arbor. Duncanson's composition was patterned after a wood engraving by Hammatt Billings (1818–1874) from the illustrated edition of the novel (1852). The engraving had also appeared on the coversheet of the popular song *Little Eva; Uncle Tom's Guardian Angel* by John Greenleaf Whittier [**4.12.6**]. Stowe's book sold more than 300,000 copies in its first year of publication, and was subsequently translated into several languages. The 116 engravings after designs by Billings certainly increased sales of the novel, yet its ability to touch the emotions of a wide range of readers with a powerful abolitionist message was the main cause of its popularity.

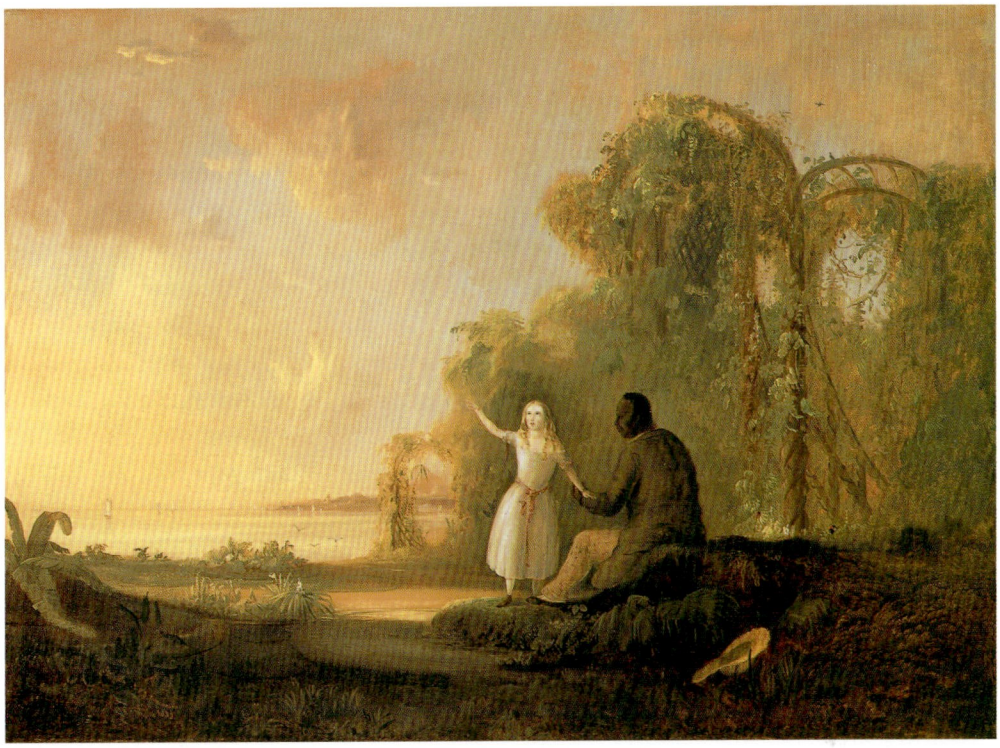

4.12.5 Robert S. Duncanson: *Uncle Tom and Little Eva*, 1853.
Oil on canvas,
27¼ x 38¼ in. (69.2 x 97.2 cm.)
Detroit Institute of Arts,
Detroit, Michigan

4.12.6 Baker and Smith after Hammatt Billings: *Uncle Tom and Litte Eva*, 1852.
Wood engraving, 3½ x 5½ in. (8.9 x 14 cm.), on a song sheet cover

Billings's engraving illustrates a scene at the opening of Chapter 22 at the St. Clare family's summer home, "on a little mossy seat, in an arbor, at the foot of the garden" on the shores of Lake Pontchartrain, outside of New Orleans. It is sunset on a Sunday evening and Little Eva is reading from the Bible to her humble and faithful servant and friend Uncle Tom, who had earlier saved her from drowning. The scene illustrates her commitment to educating the family's black slaves and, ultimately, to using her inheritance to buy a home in one of the free states so they could all be liberated. It also attests to Little Eva's (and thus Stowe's) belief that both spiritual and physical salvation for African Americans would be found through devotion to the Christian God. The little blond Eva thus represents the best of abolitionist sentiment and Christian love, although she dies shortly after the scene by the lake, leaving the task of freeing slaves to those who have been inspired by her example.

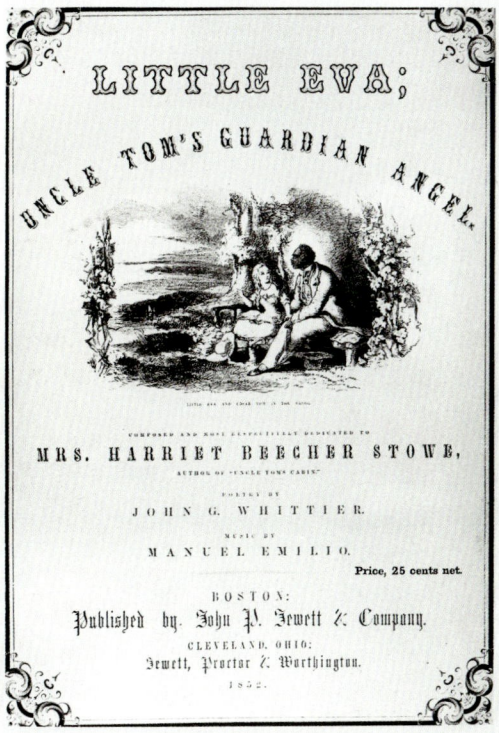

The patronizing tone of both the written passage and the engraving are unmistakable: the blond, white child will lead the old black man out of darkness and ignorance into salvation and light. Duncanson's painting maintains this tone; he has made the scene more dramatic, however, by placing Little Eva in front of Uncle Tom, standing and gesturing toward the setting sun with eyes turned upward. There is a sense of Christ-like prophecy in her pose, suggesting her impending death, and an equal sense of religious devotion on the part of Uncle Tom. This interpretation of the scene draws, once again, upon Stowe's text: "[Uncle Tom] loved her as something frail and earthly, yet almost worshipped her as something heavenly and divine. He gazed on her as the Italian sailor gazes on his image of the child Jesus—with a mixture of reverence and tenderness."

White abolitionists saw the passivity and devotion of Uncle Tom as evidence of his humanity and of the rightness of their efforts to free him. While such portrayals may have helped the movement make political headway, many African Americans found them unacceptable. "Uncle Tom" eventually became a derogatory label used to criticize those who felt their salvation lay in working with, rather than against, white people and their interests. Stowe reaffirmed her commitment to the "Uncle Tom" approach to liberation in her second anti-slavery novel, *Dred* (1856), in which she condemns the idea of African Americans achieving freedom through retaliation against whites.

The character of the rebel in *Dred* is patterned after the slave Nat Turner, who led a rebellion in 1831 in Virginia. That rebellion resulted in the killing of fifty-five whites before it was crushed and Turner caught and hanged. His was only the latest in a series of revolts or planned insurrections that had increased the tension between Southern plantation owners and their growing slave population. Indeed, the rebelliousness of Southern slaves had forced the federal government to confront the possibility that an end to slavery might come about through a massive uprising, which could spread to an attack on the enslavers and the privileged classes in general. While the Civil War is connected in the minds of many to the liberation of African American slaves, it was also about controlling the way in which this liberation was to take place.

Rebellious slaves often managed to escape from Southern plantations and find freedom in the North or in the new western territories, where the Fugitive Slave Act of 1793 was seldom enforced. The treatment of escaped slaves became a particularly volatile political issue in 1850, when California applied for statehood. There were then fifteen free states and fifteen slave states, and the addition of California threatened to tip the balance in favor of the free states. A compromise was worked out between the North and the South. California would enter the Union as a free state, but a more stringent Fugitive Slave Act would provide for the return of escaped slaves to the South. This Act was reinforced by the Supreme Court's Dred Scott decision of 1857, which confirmed that a slave's arrival in the North did not automatically result in freedom. The majority opinion also held that an African American descended from slaves had no rights as a citizen and therefore no standing in court. Not until the Emancipation Proclamation of 1863 and the repeal of the fugitive slave laws in 1864 would arrival in the North signify freedom.

Two years after the Dred Scott decision the possibility of a massive slave revolt was again brought home to the southern states. That year the sixty-year-old white man John Brown led a group of twenty-two men, five of whom were African American, in an attempt to seize the federal arsenal at Harper's Ferry, West Virginia and then set off a revolt of slaves throughout the South. His plan failed and he was executed. Many in the South were convinced that northern abolitionists and politicians were behind Brown's actions and that the North was committed to depriving them of their property and prepared to do so, if necessary, through the arming of Southern slaves.

The critical reception of two works produced in 1859 gives an indication of the tensions surrounding the issue of slavery at this time. John Rogers (1829–1904), a Yale-trained engineer who turned to sculpture in the late 1850s, created many small genre scenes that were reproduced in plaster and sold in great numbers. The first work he mass-produced and offered for sale on a mail-order basis was *Slave Auction* [**4.12.7**]. The small sculpture was put on the market only a few weeks after the execution of Brown. The group includes a white auctioneer in the center, calling for bids, and a slave family below the podium. The male slave assumes an angry and aggressive stance, arms crossed, a scowl on his face. The woman cradles one child in her arms while another hides behind her skirt. The message of the piece is twofold: slavery is an affront to the dignity and humanity of African Americans, and African American men are not going to accept this fate passively. The work did not sell as well as Rogers had expected, prompting him to comment at the end of the

4.12.7 John Rogers: *Slave Auction*, 1859.
Plaster, h. 13¼ in. (33.7 cm.)
Courtesy The New-York Historical Society, New York

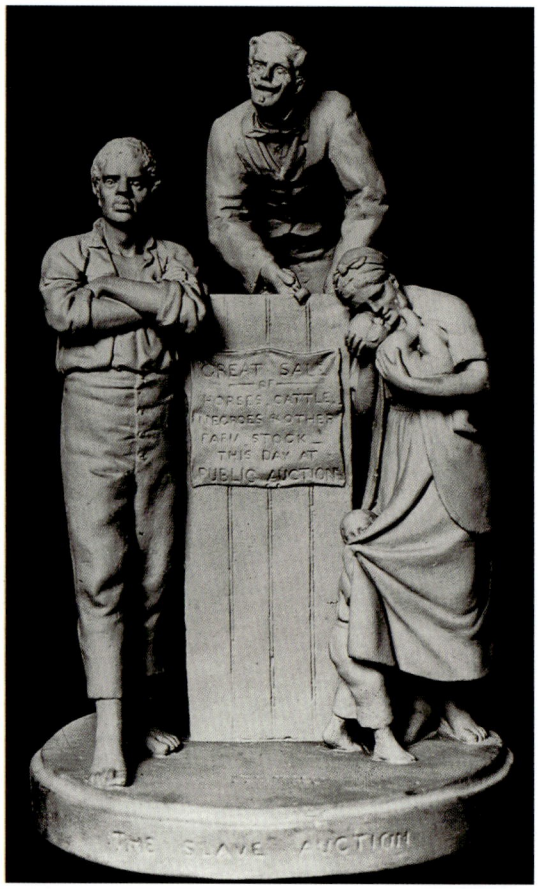

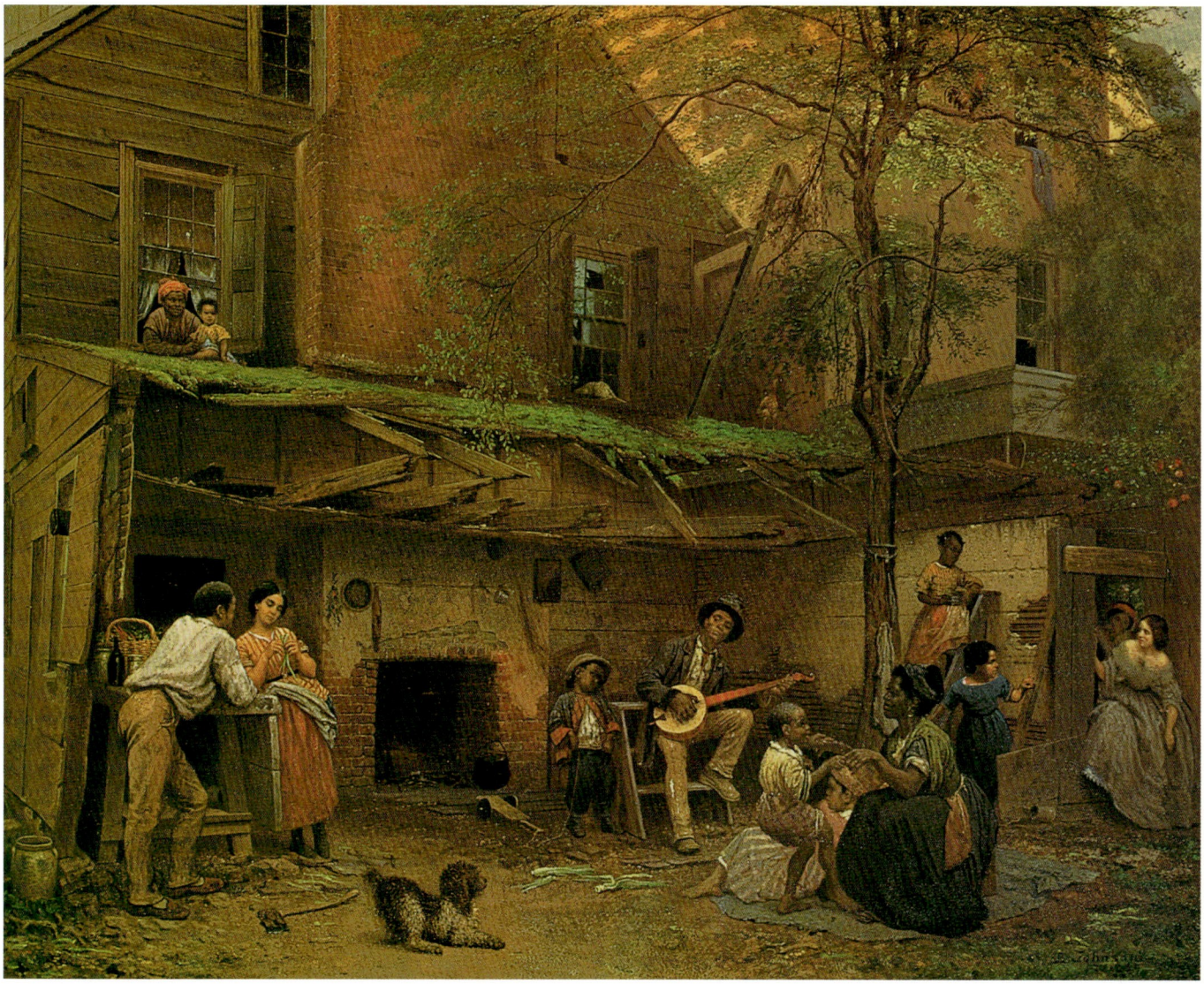

4.12.8 Eastman Johnson: *Negro Life in the South (Kentucky Home)*, 1859. Oil on canvas, 36 x 45 in. (91.4 x 114.3 cm.)
Courtesy The New-York Historical Society, New York

year: "I find the times have quite headed me off...for the Slave Auction tells such a strong story that none of the stores will receive it to sell for fear of offending their southern customers."

The second work produced in 1859, which received a much more positive response, was a painting by Eastman Johnson (1824–1906) entitled *Negro Life in the South* (also referred to as *Kentucky Home*) [**4.12.8**]. Shown at the 1859 spring exhibition of the National Academy of Design in New York, it portrays African Americans engaged in a variety of leisure-time activities—playing the banjo, dancing, socializing, and playing with children. In style and subject matter it shows the influence of Johnson's studies in Düsseldorf and Holland from 1849 to 1855. While there he had been impressed by the minutely detailed paintings of peasant and small-town life that had been recorded by Dutch artists, particularly in the seventeenth century.

The figures are arranged for the most part in discrete groups in front of a ramshackle house. A woman and child look out of the top window at the scene below. But they are not the only ones gazing upon these activities. Stepping through a hole in the fence between the slave quarters and the slave-owner's house is a young white girl, dressed in finery that, as in the Krimmel painting [**4.12.3**; p. 223], contrasts sharply with the ragged clothing of the slaves. Two young girls, one with much darker skin than the other, acknowledge her presence. Their varying shades of skin color could reflect the varying skin colors of West Africans themselves. Yet it was more likely the result of the rape of black female slaves by their white male owners, whose offspring were always considered African Americans. "One drop" of black blood was all it took, by law, for an individual to be considered black, and thus a slave.

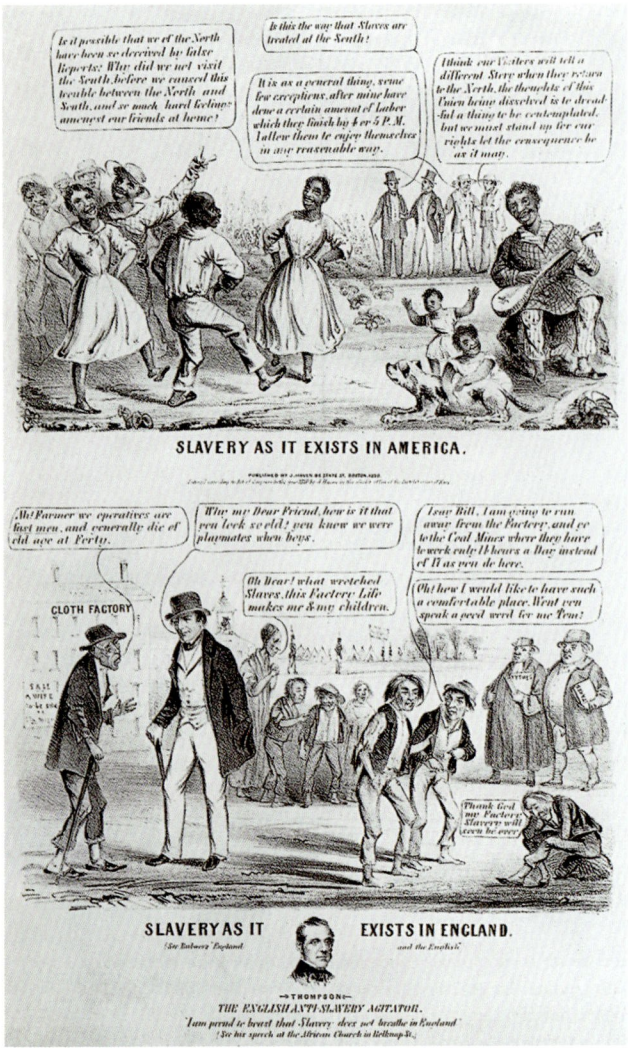

4.12.9 Unknown artist: *Slavery As It Exists In America; Slavery As It Exists In England*, 1850.
Lithograph published by J. Haven, Boston
Library of Congress, Washington, D.C.

The painting was an instant success, due both to its style and to its content. The scene was painted in painstaking detail, achieved in part through Johnson's use of his father's Washington house and household servants as models. This detail engaged viewers and convinced them of the artist's consummate talents. The painting was also noncommittal on the issue of slavery. Abolitionists in the North interpreted it as a condemnation of the dismal living conditions in the South, while slaveholders were confirmed in their belief that, despite somewhat "uncomfortable" living conditions, Southern slaves were basically a happy lot. The contrast between the dilapidated slave quarters and the home of the owners could also be read as evidence of the peaceful coexistence of master and slave.

Several of Johnson's black figures bear a certain resemblance in their arrangement and activities to an 1850 lithograph that defended slavery by comparing it to the lives of British factory workers. In *Slavery As It Exists In America; Slavery As It Exists In England* [**4.12.9**], black slaves are portrayed as happy and carefree, while white wage laborers long to escape a bondage that turns them into old men before their time. (It would not take much of a stretch of the imagination to connect the British factory system to a similar system emerging in the northeastern US at the time.) Neither group is shown engaging in work: rather, labor is represented in the text. In the American scene, two Southern slave-owners describe for their northern visitors how truly easy are the lives of their slaves, whose work usually ends around four or five o'clock in the afternoon, while in the English scene the factory workers bemoan their seventeen-hour work days. Significantly the slaves, unlike the factory workers, do not speak for themselves, buttressing the argument that they are childlike and need the protection of their masters.

What was the relationship between Johnson's image [**4.12.8**; p. 227] and others like it showing happy, dancing slaves on the one hand, and the material conditions of slave life in the South on the other? John Little, a slave who escaped to Canada, provides us with a partial answer in a passage from his description of his life prior to his escape, as told to the Boston school principal and journalist Benjamin Drew in 1855:

> They say slaves are happy, because they laugh, and are merry. I myself and three or four others, have received two hundred lashes in the day, and had our feet in fetters: yet, at night, we would sing and dance, and make others laugh at the rattling of our chains. Happy men we must have been! We did it to keep down trouble, and to keep our hearts from being completely broken: that is as true as the gospel! Just look at it,—consider upon it,—must not we have been very happy? Yet I have done it myself—I have cut capers in chains!

But the singing and dancing could not keep down trouble in the South. After Abraham Lincoln's election to the presidency in the fall of 1860, six southern states seceded from the Union, with five more joining them later. Their goal was to set up a separate, sovereign nation that would allow them to control their agricultural economy, which relied for its success on slave labor. The northern industrial states wanted economic expansion, wage labor, a free market economy, and high protective tariffs for manufactured goods, all of which the southern states opposed. Lincoln's main aim during the early months of the Civil War, which began in April 1861 with the bombardment of Fort Sumter in South Carolina, was to preserve the Union, even if it meant assuring the southern states that he would not dismantle the institution of slavery. As late as September 1862, when he issued his preliminary Emancipation Proclamation, he promised to leave slavery intact in the states that came over to the North. The Emancipation Proclamation of January 1, 1863 declared slaves free in areas still fighting the North, but said nothing about those behind Union lines. Abolitionist forces pushed for a more all-encompassing declaration and, in April 1864, the Senate adopted the Thirteenth Amendment declaring an end to slavery. The House of Representatives followed with a vote of approval in January 1865.

Paintings of Fugitives, Contraband, and Soldiers

Many of the paintings of African Americans during and immediately after the Civil War focused on the flight of slave families to the North (some, such as Robert S. Duncanson, escaped the war by going to Canada). These paintings were often based on events artists had witnessed while serving in the army or accompanying Union forces. Two examples are Eastman Johnson's *A Ride for Liberty: The Fugitive Slaves* of *c.* 1862–63 [**4.12.10**] and Theodor Kaufmann's *On to Liberty* of 1867 [**4.12.11**; p. 230]. Johnson's *A Ride for Liberty* is strikingly different from his earlier *Negro Life in the South* [**4.12.8**; p. 227]. In place of a meticulously rendered anecdotal scene of slave families contentedly enjoying themselves, one finds a sketchily rendered nighttime scene of flight away from slavery and toward the safety of the Union lines, indicated on the left by the reflections off the barrels of the soldiers' rifles. The faces of the family on the horse, along with the horse itself, are mere dark silhouettes against a gray, smoke-filled sky. The scene counters the Southern claim that slave families were happy with their life on Southern plantations. This fleeing family, like the group in Emmanuel Leutze's *Westward the Course of Empire* [**4.12.2**; p. 222], also contains Christian connotations, suggesting a parallel with the flight of Mary, Joseph, and the baby Jesus to Egypt. Johnson had accompanied Union troops on several occasions in 1862 and 1863, and on the back of the canvas he identifies the source of the painting: "A veritable incident in the civil war seen by myself at Centerville on the morning of McClellan's advance toward Manassas, March 2, 1862."

Kaufmann (1814–after 1877) enlisted in the Union Army in 1861 and advocated the Union cause in his writings, lectures, and paintings. German-born, he received his artistic training in Munich and Hamburg before coming to the US in the early 1850s. In *On to Liberty* [**4.12.11**; p. 230] he creates a dramatic scene of the flight of African American women and children, although it is much more anecdotal in its detailed rendering of costumes and facial features than Johnson's painting. Emerging out of a dark forest, the group heads toward Union lines visible in the distance. While the scene is filled with tension, Kaufmann provides some comic relief in the group of children to the right, the older boy dragging the younger one along by the back of his shirt. Such comic relief accommodated earlier stereotypes

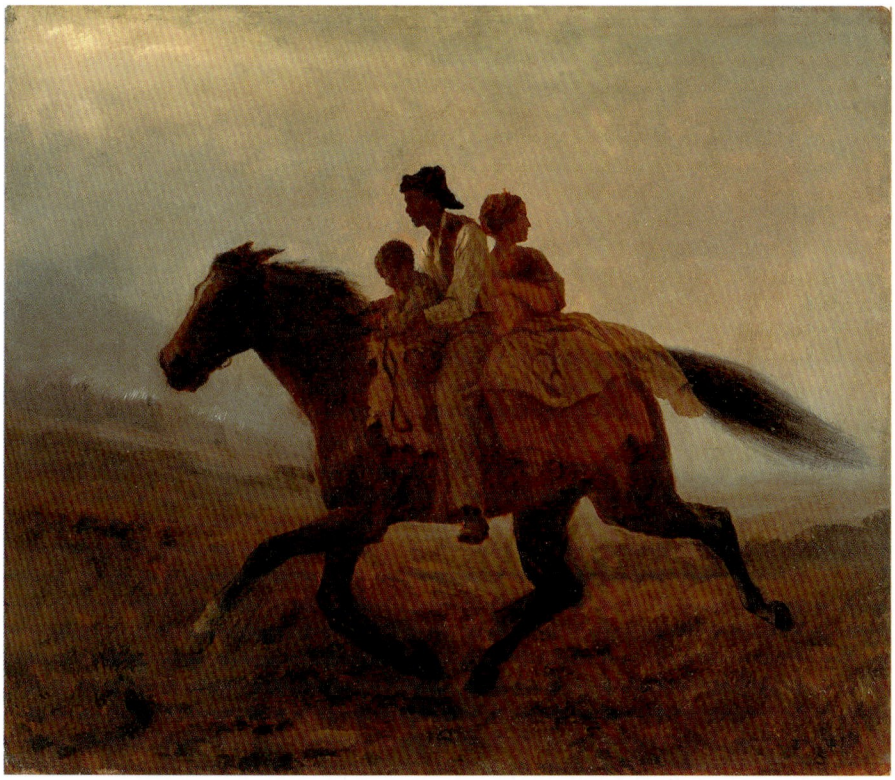

4.12.10 Eastman Johnson: *A Ride for Liberty: The Fugitive Slaves*, *c.* 1862–63.
Oil on board, 22 x 26¼ in. (55.8 x 66.6 cm.)
Brooklyn Museum of Art, New York

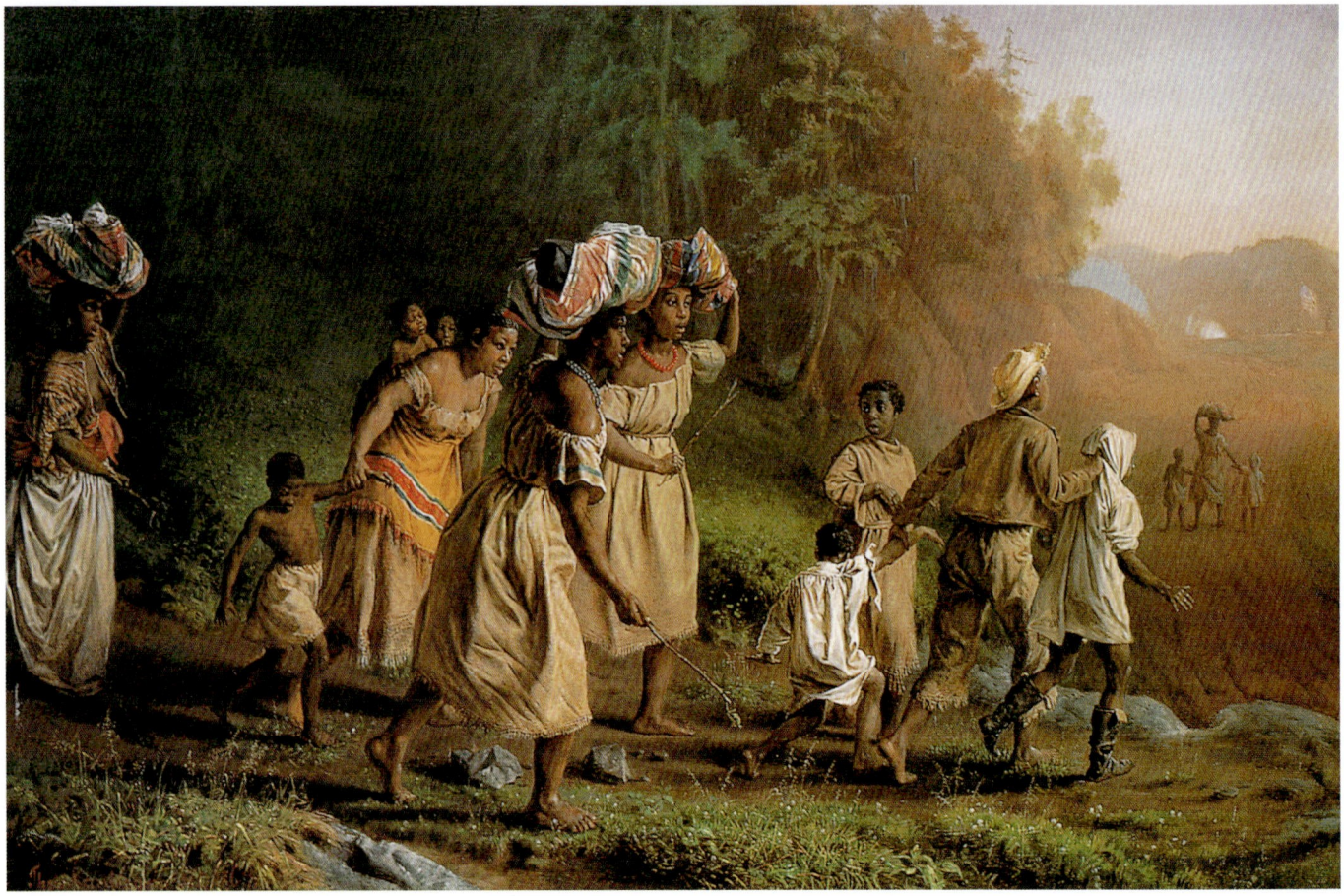

4.12.11 Theodor Kaufmann: *On to Liberty*, 1867. Oil on canvas, 36 x 56 in. (91.4 x 142.2 cm.) The Metropolitan Museum of Art, New York

of African Americans found in such paintings as John Lewis Krimmel's *Quilting Frolic* [**4.12.3**; p. 223]. Kaufmann also adds an element of voyeurism, undoing the blouse of the female slave to the far left so that her breasts are partially revealed. The absence of adult men in the group reflects the fact that they were often conscripted by the Confederate Army to work behind the lines and thus were less likely to be fleeing with their families.

Many African Americans joined in the war effort on the side of the North. They found their way into the ranks of the Union Army as enlisted soldiers or as "war contraband" (escaped slaves, considered property by their owners, were viewed as "confiscated" property by Union officers). In both capacities they carried out the more menial tasks of the war effort, including cooking for the troops, building roads, driving mule teams [**4.12.13**, p. 231; **4.12.16**, p. 233] and burying the dead [**4.12.18**, p. 234], while, at the same time (until 1864), being paid less than white soldiers. Their lives were portrayed in the paintings and graphic work of the artist Winslow Homer (1836–1910).

Homer was born in Boston and grew up at a time when the city was filled with abolitionist debates and controversy. He was apprenticed in a lithography shop in the mid-1850s before taking up work as a freelance illustrator. He then trained as a fine artist in 1859 at the National Academy of Design, where he exhibited his first work the following year. After the outbreak of the Civil War, Homer joined the Union campaign as an artist-reporter for *Harper's Weekly*. He was also commissioned by the publishers Louis Prang and Co. in 1863 and 1864 to design sets of campaign sketches, which were reproduced in lithographic form.

A Bivouac Fire on the Potomac, one of Homer's earliest wartime scenes, appeared as a wood engraving in the December 21, 1861, issue of *Harper's Weekly* [**4.12.12**]. It focuses on camp life, as did most of his war images, rather than the battlefront. It is evening, and an African American dances around the fire for the pleasure of the white Union soldiers. Homer has used two of the stereotypes then in place for the depiction of African Americans: the shabbily clothed high-stepping dancer with corkscrew curls, and the grinning, fat-lipped fiddler sitting at the edge of the fire playing for the dancer.

An attempt to move away from such stereotypes—a direction he would increasingly follow—can be found in his small

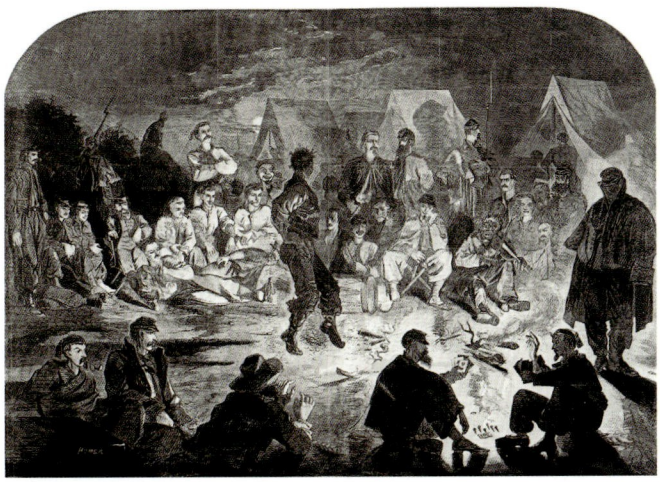

4.12.12 Winslow Homer: *A Bivouac Fire on the Potomac*, in *Harper's Weekly*, December 21, 1861.
Wood engraving, 13¾ x 20 in. (34.9 x 50.8 cm.)
Sterling and Francine Clark Art Institute, Williamstown, Massachusetts

painting *The Bright Side* of 1865 [**4.12.13**]. It depicts five mule drivers, four of whom are asleep, resting against the sunny side of a tent. Only the head of the fifth man is visible. Homer claimed to have sketched the scene from life, with the fifth man appearing out of the opening in the tent just as he had finished drawing the first four. When the work was shown in 1865, first at the Brooklyn Art Association's Spring Exhibition in March and then at the National Academy of Design Annual Exhibition in April, it received favorable critical and popular reviews. These reviews were at least in part responsible for Homer's acceptance into the Academy in May of that year.

Critics praised *The Bright Side* both for its truthfulness and for its humor. One wrote: "The lazy sunlight, the lazy, nodding donkeys, the lazy, lolling negroes, make a humorously conceived and truthfully executed picture." For this critic, and for many others, a "truthful" depiction of African Americans was, inherently, humorous. African Americans were also "inherently" lazy, despite ample record of the often brutal labor that was involved in their work. Teamsters were frequently compared with the mules they drove, animals regularly described as unintelligent, stubborn and lazy, despite, again, evidence to the contrary.

The art historian Marc Simpson points out, however, that "if a seemingly racist humor can be found in Homer's painting of the teamsters, complicating elements are also there that require more than a chuckle in response." The direct gaze of the central figure is one such complicating element. The depiction of all five men as closely observed individuals rather than stock characters is another. Homer abandons the physiognomic stereotypes of African Americans. Yet he still places the mule drivers in a setting and in poses that allowed most viewers to ignore their individuality in favor of the generalizing stereotypes.

Another artist who covered the Civil War for *Harper's Weekly* was Thomas Nast (1840–1902), best known for his scathing political cartoons of the late nineteenth century. Born in Germany,

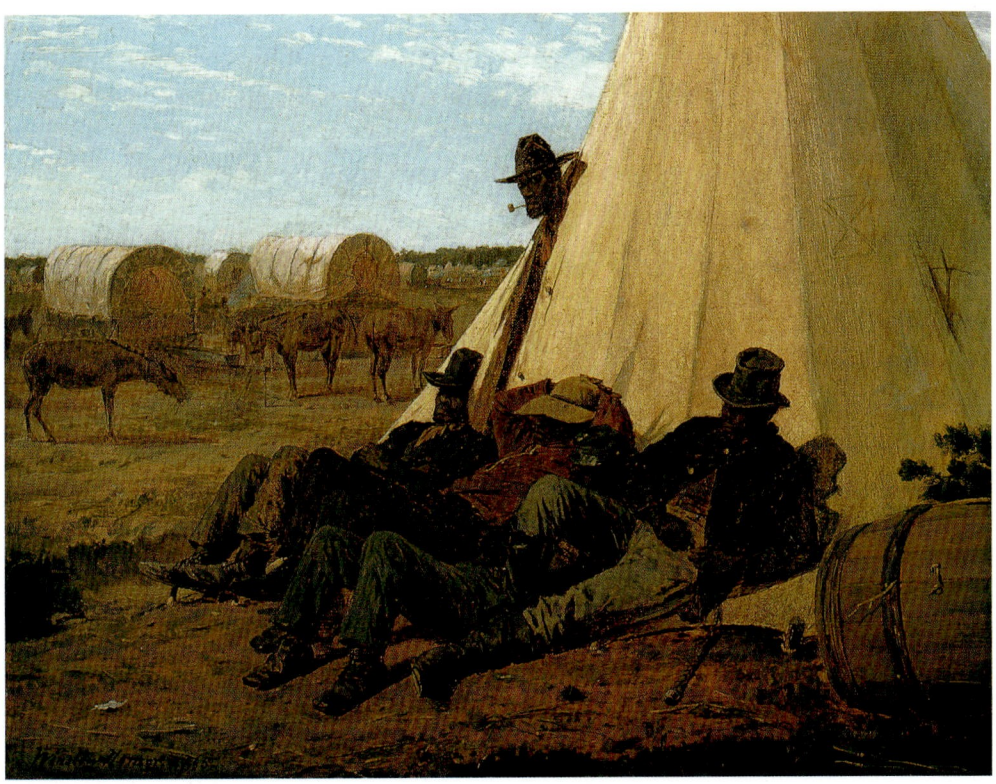

4.12.13 Winslow Homer: *The Bright Side*, 1865.
Oil on canvas,
13¼ x 17½ in. (33.7 x 44.4 cm.)
Fine Arts Museum of San Francisco, San Francisco, California

he came to the US in 1846 and studied with Kaufmann, later entering the National Academy of Design. After working for *Frank Leslie's Illustrated Weekly* and the *New York Illustrated News*, Nast was engaged by *Harper's Weekly* in the summer of 1862. In 1865 he produced an image that was strikingly different from the majority of portrayals of African Americans during the war. *Entrance of the 55th Massachusetts (Colored) Regiment into Charleston, South Carolina, February 21, 1865* [**4.12.14**] shows the volunteer all-black regiment triumphantly entering the Southern city. It is one of a limited number of pictures that acknowledge the presence of African Americans as active Union soldiers who fought in many of the major battles of the Civil War. The image would have had added significance for black soldiers and abolitionists. Less than two years earlier Colonel Robert Gould Shaw, the white officer who headed the first all-black Union regiment, the 54th Massachusetts, had died along with almost half of his troops in an attempt to capture Fort Wagner near Charleston (see p. 246).

According to the historian David W. Blight, after the fall of Charleston those who remained in the city, mostly freed slaves, decided to turn the Washington Race Course and Jockey Club, the site of a prison camp for Union soldiers (more than 250 died and had been buried in a mass grave), into a monument to these soldiers. They reburied the dead in individual graves, and then built a fence and erected an archway at the site. On May 1, 1865 a procession made its way to the racecourse led by 3,000 African American children carrying armloads of roses and hundreds of black women with flower baskets, wreaths and crosses. Next came black men, Union infantry soldiers and more citizens of Charleston, both black and white. Once at the racecourse, the crowd listened to prayers, speeches, and music and then picnicked together. Thus took place the first Memorial Day celebration marking the Independence Day of the Second American Revolution.

Once Abraham Lincoln's initial resistance to the enlistment of African Americans ended, the numbers joining up increased throughout the war. Official records indicate that approximately 185,000 joined the Union Army, and more than 200,000 civilians worked in Union camps. Historians now agree that the presence of such large numbers of African Americans in the northern forces turned the tide against the Confederate Army in 1864 and 1865. The African American in the center foreground of Nast's drawing can be seen as dancing not for the pleasure of the white officers but in joy at the arrival of the black regiment and at the coming end of the Civil War.

4.12.14 Thomas Nast: *Entrance of the 55th Massachusetts (Colored) Regiment into Charleston, South Carolina, February 21, 1865*, 1865.
Pencil, neutral wash, and oil, heightened with white, on board, 14¼ x 21¼ in. (36.2 x 53.9 cm.)
Museum of Fine Arts, Boston, Massachusetts

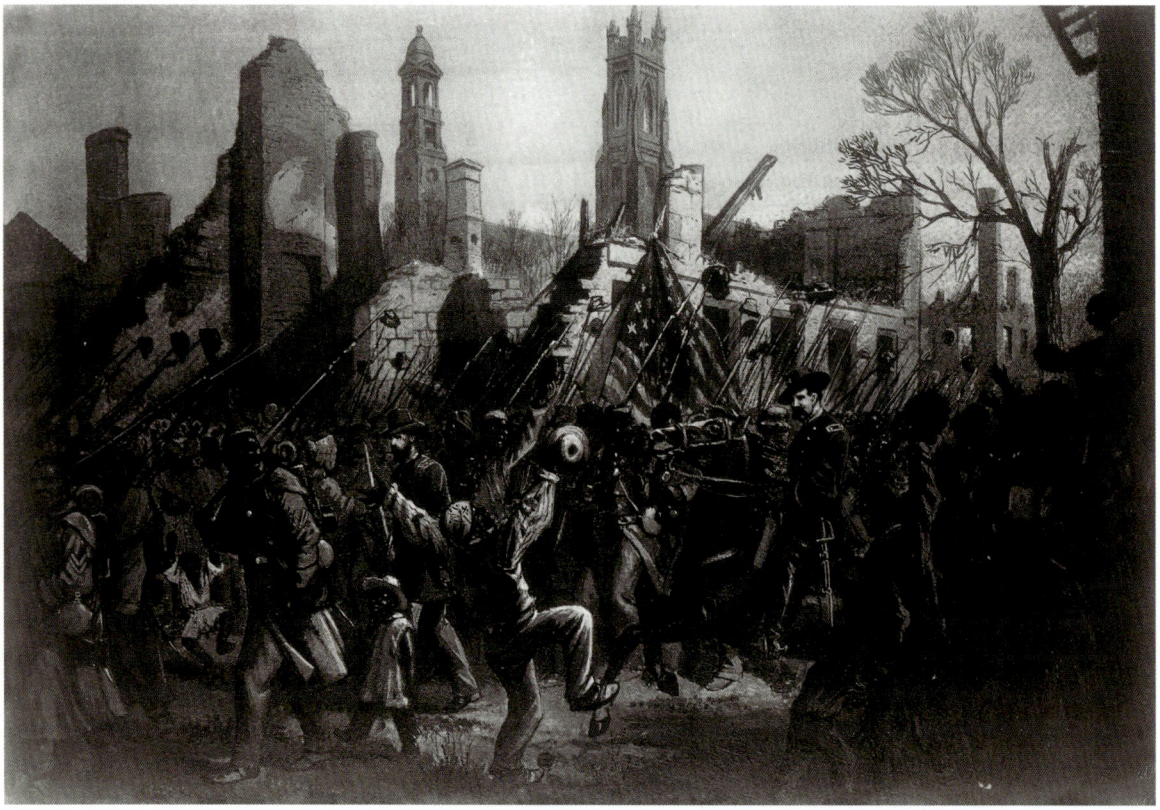

Photographs of the War

The price of the Union victory at Charleston depicted in Thomas Nast's image [**4.12.14**] is graphically told in the ruins towering over the scene, ruins that recall the many burned-out buildings featured in photographs taken at the end of the war. A view of 1866 by George P. Barnard (1819–1902), *Ruins in Charleston, S.C.* [**4.12.15**], shows the same city; some think that Nast's work was based, at least in part, on such a photograph.

The Civil War was extensively documented by photographers. Photographic technology at the time required the subject to remain still for long periods of time—anywhere from five to thirty seconds—so most of the scenes were of camp life or the aftermath of fighting. Thus, they presented war not as a grand, heroic activity, in the style of Benjamin West or John Trumbull [**1.4.31**, p. 83; **2.5.6**, p. 94; **2.5.7**, p. 96], but as episodes of daily life or as gruesome scenes of corpse-strewn battlefields.

Among the thousands of images produced were sets of stereoscopic views, in which two identical photographs are looked at through a device containing two lenses, giving the impression of depth to a picture. The results were miniature panoramas, three-dimensional experiences undertaken within the comfort and safety of the home. In many cases stereographs were accompanied by written explanations, thus providing a more directed "educational" experience for the viewer. One such stereograph is *A Group of "Contrabands"* [**4.12.16**], produced by the War Photograph and Exhibition Company between 1861 and 1865. It shows a group of African American teamsters lined up in front of a wagon and a shack, which is described as their home. Their eclectic clothing indicates their "contraband" status (see p. 230), and their solemnity and placement in the middle ground of the composition suggest both a physical and a psychological distance between them and the viewer. The image is a far cry from the happy, dancing slaves of prewar times and from the sleeping mule drivers of Winslow Homer's painting *The Bright Side* [**4.12.13**; p. 231].

4.12.15 George P. Barnard: *Ruins in Charleston, S.C.*, 1866.
Photograph, from George P. Barnard, *Photographic Views of Sherman's Campaign*, 1866

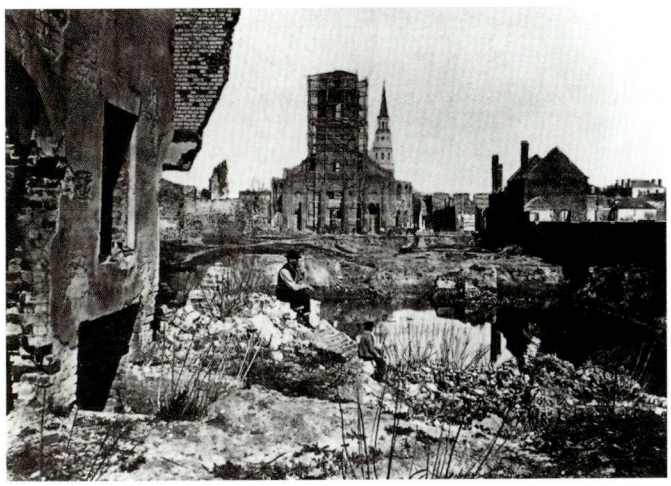

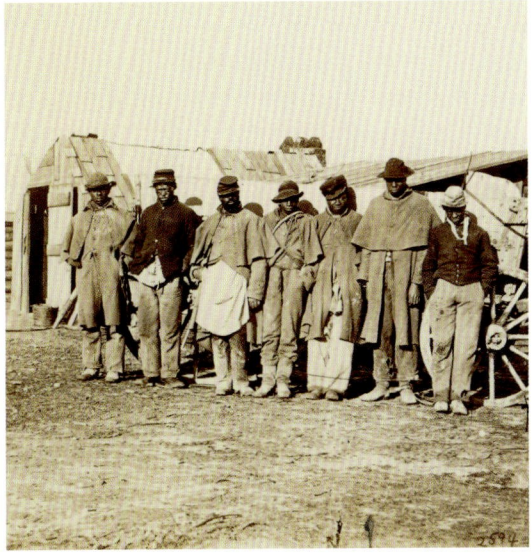

4.12.16 War Photograph and Exhibition Company: *A Group of "Contrabands,"* c. 1861–65.
Albumen silver print stereograph (one image of two)
Library of Congress, Washington, D.C.

A stereoscopic view by Taylor and Huntington Publishers that appeared in 1864, *Execution of a Colored Soldier* [**4.12.17**; p. 234], shows the fate of an African American in the Union Army accused of having "attempted to commit a rape on a white woman" near Petersburg, Virginia. The soldier, whose name was Johnson, was tried by court-martial, found guilty, and hanged. All this information is given on the back of the image. In the photograph he is shown hanging from the scaffold, his face covered by a white cloth. Union soldiers rest in the shade of a tree to the right, and the text on the back tells us:

> A request was made of the Rebels, under a flag of truce, that we might be permitted to hang Johnson in plain sight of both armies, between the lines. The request was granted, and this is a photograph of him hanging where both armies can plainly see him.

The educational value of the stereograph lay in its assurance that freedom for African Americans would not be achieved at the expense of "white womanhood." While the description suggests that Johnson was fairly tried, few, if any, black men were ever acquitted when charged with a crime against a white woman. As the art historian Ellwood Parry has noted in a discussion of this image, the public display of his hanging also suggests that

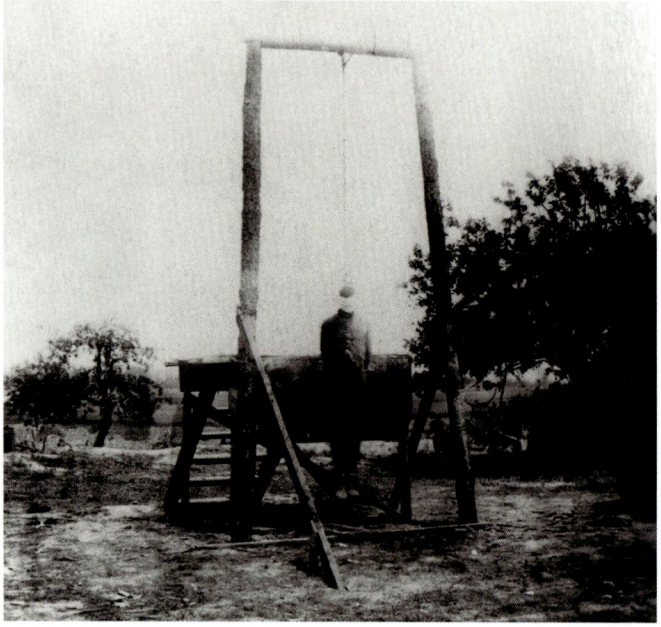

4.12.17 Taylor and Huntington Publishers: *Execution of a Colored Soldier*, 1864. Stereograph (one image of two)
Courtesy The New-York Historical Society, New York

white men on both sides of the war saw this as an occasion for a shared racist entertainment.

Photographs also appeared in books about the war. Mathew B. Brady (see p. 146) and Alexander Gardner (1821–1882) were actively involved in the production and distribution of war imagery in the form of stereographs, album cards, and large mounted photographic prints. They also published a number of books of prints, including *Brady's Photographic Views of the War* (1862) and *Gardner's Photographic Sketch Book of the War* (1866). The American Studies scholar Alan Trachtenberg notes that such books constituted attempts "to organize a rapidly accumulating mass of war and war-related images, to present, even as the war progressed and images piled up, the entire mass as a single whole, an emergent totality." As did the narratives accompanying stereographs, these books presented the war "as if from the grand perspective of Providence."

But there were fissures, at times, in these narratives, claims Trachtenberg. One appears in the text accompanying a photograph by the Civil War photographer John Reekie (active 1860s), *A Burial Party, Cold Harbor, Virginia, April 1865* [**4.12.18**], in *Gardner's Photographic Sketch Book*:

> This sad scene represents the soldiers in the act of collecting the remains of their comrades, killed at the battles of Gaines' Mill and Cold Harbor. It speaks ill of the residents of that part of Virginia, that they allowed even the remains of those they considered enemies, to decay unnoticed where they fell. The soldiers, to whom commonly falls the task of burying the dead, may possibly have been called away before the task was completed. At such times the native dwellers of the neighborhood would usually come forward and provide sepulture for such as had been left uncovered.

This commentary speaks of soldiers, who then turn out to be missing, of native dwellers, who both bury and do not bury the remains of their enemies. Yet the fact that African American soldiers are doing the actual burying is never mentioned. "In a gesture so simple that it eludes the author of the text," writes Trachtenberg, "the two grand invisibilities of the war become palpable here: the dead in their state of utter decomposition and dissolution; blacks in the posture of field laborers whose performance of the task of sweeping the battlefield clean of its grim refuse prefigures a history we still inhabit."

The dead soldiers in Reekie's photograph of 1865 had been reduced largely to bones and bits of uniforms by the time they were buried, with the skulls stacked in the cart in the foreground reminiscent of those found in *memento mori* paintings and carvings [**1.4.18**, p. 74; **1.4.30**, p. 81]. That same year another photographer, Thomas C. Roche (1826–1895), captured a Confederate soldier soon after he had been killed during the last great battle of the Civil War, when Union forces overtook the Confederate Fort Mahone near Petersburg, Virginia [**4.12.19**]. The recognisability of the figure—he could be one's son, father, brother, or husband—makes the reality of his death more immediate.

4.12.18 John Reekie: *A Burial Party, Cold Harbor, Virginia, April 1865*. Photograph, from Alexander Gardner, *Gardner's Photographic Sketch Book of the War*, 1866
Library of Congress, Washington, D.C.

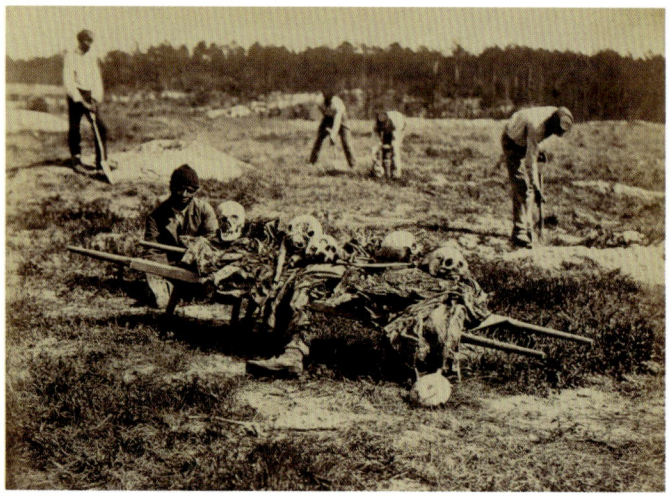

Roche was working for E. & H. T. Anthony, the country's largest purveyor of stereoscope views, when he took *Rebel Artillery Soldiers, Killed in the Trenches of Fort Mahone, Called by the Soldiers "Fort Damnation," at the Storming of Petersburg, Virginia, April 3, 1865* [**4.12.19**]. The caption on the back of the stereograph included both the title and the following two sentences: "The one in the foreground has US belts on, probably taken from a Union Soldier prisoner, his uniform is grey cloth trimmed with red. This view was taken the morning after the fight." While the text says nothing about the second body, the reader assumes that it too is a soldier, as the title uses the plural noun. Yet close inspection of the photograph reveals that the second figure is an African American man in civilian clothes, and thus certainly not a Rebel soldier in a scene depicting the capture of a Confederate fort.

The historians David Lowe and Philip Shiman note that this was the last of three photographs that Roche took of the same dead Confederate soldier. The gun sponge in the lower right corner of the third photograph is present in the second image but not the first. Roche may have added it in order to reinforce the fact that the victim was an artilleryman. In neither of the first two images, however, is there a second body. After examining Roche's negatives from that day and the next, the two historians discovered that the African American was actually the photographer's teamster. He appears in the same clothes, alive, in the negative of a photograph taken later that day or the next in the town of Petersburg. The horse and wagon in the rear of the photograph also probably belonged to Roche.

We do not know why Roche added the second body. Perhaps he thought it increased the sense of loss and devastation. Or perhaps he felt that the combination of a white Confederate soldier and an African American slave would point to one of the key causes of the Civil War. His manipulation of the scene, however, was not uncommon, for while photographers could not create images of soldiers in action, they did their best to construct engaging photographs of these same soldiers' gruesome demise.

During the Civil War more than half a million slaves fled the South. Four million remained, yet it was only a matter of time before many of them would also escape to the North. The African American activist and scholar W. E. B. Du Bois later wrote of these events in *Black Reconstruction* (1935):

> Either the south must make terms with its slaves, free them, use them to fight the North and thereafter no longer treat them as bondsmen; or they could surrender to the North with the assumption that the North after the war must help them to defend slavery as it had before.

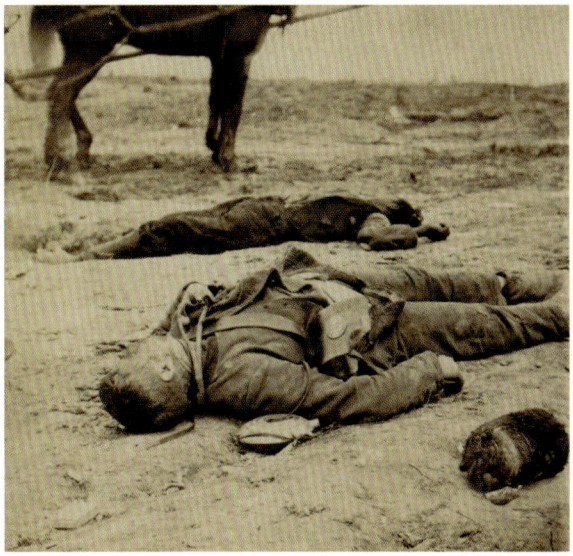

4.12.19 Thomas C. Roche: *Rebel Artillery Soldiers, Killed in the Trenches of Fort Mahone, Called by the Soldiers "Fort Damnation," at the Storming of Petersburg, Virginia, April 3, 1865.*
Albumen silver print stereograph (one image of two)
Library of Congress, Washington, D.C.

General Robert E. Lee chose the latter route, surrendering to General Ulysses S. Grant at Appomattox on April 9, 1865. The war was at an end. Five days later, President Lincoln was assassinated. While slavery was never officially restored in the South, white politicians in the North did, in fact, collude with their counterparts in the South to reinforce in new ways the subservience of African Americans.

Review Questions

1 What were some of the stereotypes used to depict African Americans in the first half of the nineteenth century?

2 How did some artists challenge the stereotypes referred to in the previous question?

3 Why did John Rogers's *Slave Auction* (1859) not sell well the year it was produced? Why was Eastman Johnson's *Negro Life in the South (Kentucky Home)*, painted the same year, so successful?

4 What kind of challenges did the American Civil War present to painters and graphic artists? How did they attempt to meet these challenges?

5 How did the photographs taken during the Civil War differ from paintings and prints? What were the causes of these differences? Were there any similarities between the three media?

CHAPTER 13

Reconstruction and Shifting Images of African Americans

(*c.* 1866–1900)

Winslow Homer's *Prisoners from the Front* and *A Visit from the Old Mistress*

In the decade after the end of the Civil War, known as the Reconstruction Period, education was opened to African Americans in the South, and African American men were given the vote and allowed to run for political office. Many were elected to local, state, and federal positions. The Civil Rights Act of 1875 outlawed discrimination in the use of public facilities. Most Southern whites did not accept these new laws, however, and organized groups, such as the Ku Klux Klan (founded in 1866), to terrorize African Americans and prevent them from exercising their new freedoms. As long as the Union Army remained in the South, they were protected to a certain degree from these attacks. But in 1877 troops were withdrawn as part of a larger political deal. Republicans agreed not to interfere with the undoing of the civil rights gains for blacks in the South if southern Democrats would give the Republican presidential candidate Rutherford B. Hayes enough electoral college votes to become president. In 1883 the Civil Rights Act was nullified by the Supreme Court, which found it unconstitutional. The act was replaced in 1896 with a Supreme Court decision allowing railroads, and thus, by precedent, all other public services, to segregate black and white if the segregated facilities were "equal." By 1900 all southern states had written into law the disenfranchisement and segregation of blacks.

Winslow Homer (1836–1910) produced several paintings addressing the tensions and accommodations produced by the end of the war and by the attempt to "reconstruct" the South. One such painting is *Prisoners from the Front*, completed in 1866 [**4.13.1**]. This work draws upon the well-established compositional conventions of confrontation scenes between the vanquished and the victor after a battle. The identification of the two groups is usually clearly marked. The vanquished kneel or dramatically bow down on the left, guarded by members of the victorious army. The victor stands to the right surveying the vanquished, often surrounded by his military retinue.

Homer maintains the general outlines of this compositional scheme. To the left of center stand three Confederate soldiers who have just surrendered. Two Union soldiers stand to the right and just behind this group. Facing the Confederate soldiers is a Union officer. He is alone, although behind him at a distance are more Union soldiers with their horses and a Division flag. They are all located in a barren landscape, the young trees and bushes having been cleared by the advancing armies for firewood and to facilitate the movement of troops.

The Confederate soldiers have indicated their surrender by placing their rifles on the ground. They do not, however, bow down in submission. The prisoner closest to the Union officer assumes a defiant pose, hand on hip, staring directly at his Union counterpart, his flowing locks contrasting with the other man's short hair. Both appear to be in their twenties or thirties. The remaining prisoners are of markedly different ages. The old man in the middle sports a full white beard and white hair and is the most submissive of the three, standing with his hands clasped in front of him. To the left of the old man is a very young man, probably in his teens, with his hands in his pockets, the slightly worried expression on his face belying his attempt at nonchalance. It is the defiant Confederate soldier who dominates, however. He occupies the center of the painting. Yet none of the figures—the prisoners, their two guards, and the Union officer—is positioned above the others. They are all arranged on the same level in a horizontal band across the front of the picture plane, the high horizon line cutting through the head of each figure, locking them in place.

The picture was well received when it was shown at the National Academy of Design Annual Exhibition in 1866 and, along with *The Bright Side* [**4.12.13**; p. 231], at the Paris World Exposition of 1867. As the art historian Patricia Hills has noted, the American section of the Paris Exposition that year included at least fifteen (out of eighty-two) works referring to the Civil War or to African Americans, indicating a strong interest on the part of artists and the section's organizers in addressing the significance of this conflict, particularly for African Americans (this interest declined sharply by the end of the 1860s as political support for the reforms of Reconstruction waned).

While Homer's works received a positive reception in New York and Paris, critics had some difficulty categorizing *Prisoners from the Front*. Was the artwork a figure painting, a genre painting, or a history painting? The latter usually contained symbolic representations of lofty ideals or permanent truths or, at the very least, commemorations of particular victories or heroes. *Prisoners from the Front* does none of these things. The taking of prisoners was usually only accorded the privilege of being commemorated in paint if the prisoners were high-ranking and well-known figures. The Union officer is recognizable as General Francis Channing Barlow, Homer's distant cousin whom he had visited at the front early in the war, but the identities of the Confederate soldiers are unknown.

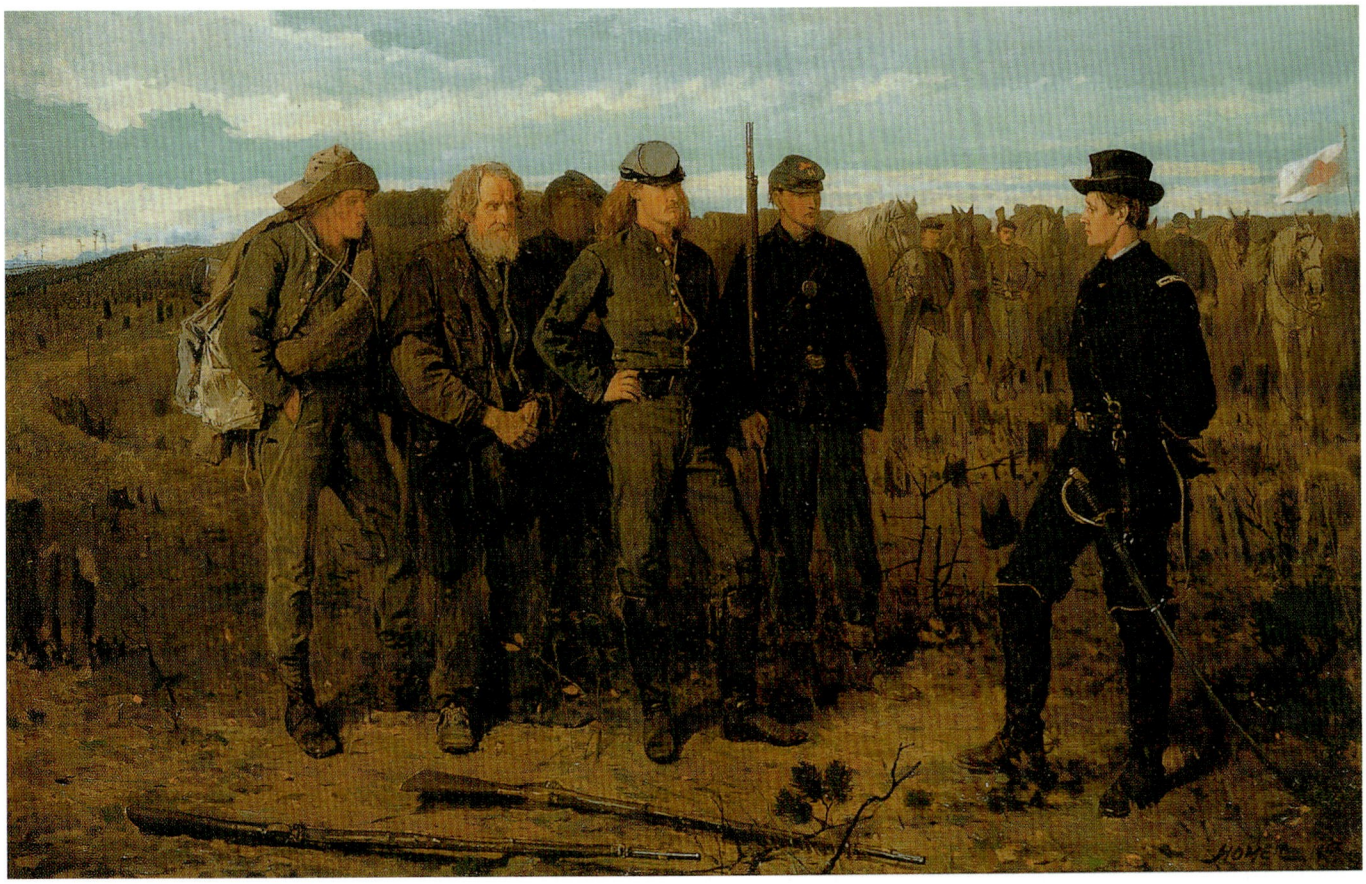

4.13.1 Winslow Homer: *Prisoners from the Front*, 1866.
Oil on canvas, 24 x 38 in. (61 x 96.5 cm.)
The Metropolitan Museum of Art, New York

Some critics did see *Prisoners from the Front* as a symbolic commentary on the Civil War as a whole, not simply a factual account of one event. In this sense it was a history painting rather than an anecdotal genre painting. It was seen as a history painting for other reasons as well. In an article entitled "Historical Art in the United States" (1869), the art critic Eugene Benson argued that history painting should not be about events before the painter's lifetime but should deal with events that are contemporaneous. History painting should "give us art that shall become historical; not art that is intended to be so." He saw *Prisoners from the Front* as a perfect example of such history painting.

What, then, is Homer's commentary on the Civil War in this painting? Earlier, in an issue of the *New York Evening Post* (April 1866), Benson—using the pseudonym Sordello—wrote:

> On the one side the hard, firm-faced New England man, without bluster, and with the dignity of a life animated by principle, confronting the audacious, reckless, impudent young Virginian, capable of heroism, because capable of impulse, but incapable of endurance because too ardent to be patient; next to him the poor, bewildered old man, perhaps a spy, with his furtive look...; back of him "the poor white," stupid, stolid, helpless, yielding to the magnetism of superior natures and incapable of resisting authority. Mr. Homer shows us the North and South confronting each other, and looking at his facts, it is very easy to know why the South gave way. The basis of its resistance was ignorance, typified in the "poor white," its front was audacity and bluster, represented by the young Virginian—two very poor things to confront the quiet, reserved, intelligent, slow, sure North, represented by the prosaic face and firm figure and unmoved look of the Union officer.

The main characters were thus read more as types than as individuals and, as types, they were "keys" to the meaning and causes and, ultimately, the outcome of the Civil War. The defiant Confederate soldier in the center of the painting represented the defiance of the South in the face of defeat by the North. The Union officer's contemplative gaze, in turn, represented the North's evaluation of how best to deal with this implacable southern defiance. According to one critic, "the men are both young; they both understand each other." In 1888 another wrote: "the influence of [Homer's] picture was strong on the side of brotherly feeling." It was this understanding and brotherly feeling that ultimately led to the deal struck between the North and the South that allowed Hayes to become president. A new Union would be created that allowed southern whites to maintain political and economic control through concessions to northern industrialists and politicians. Those who lost out in this deal were those in whose name the Civil War was supposedly fought—black slaves. As early as 1865 and 1866, the years in which Homer was creating *Prisoners from the Front*, vagrancy and apprenticeship laws were being passed by southern legislatures (the Black Codes), which restricted the rights of freedmen.

Does Homer represent this aspect of the Civil War—the betrayal of African Americans—in his painting? The one element that could possibly carry this message is the shadowy dark-skinned figure of a Union soldier standing behind the three prisoners. Unlike the rest of the foreground figures, his facial features are only faintly suggested (those of the figures in the distant right background are more clearly discernible). His boots are not completely sketched in and the bottom half of his left leg is missing. So unfinished is the presentation that it is possible, at first glance, to read this figure as a white soldier in shadow. But the bodies of the Confederate prisoners are the only possible source of shadow, and their positioning makes the necessary blocking out of the sun impossible. Is this soldier, therefore, African American?

X-radiographs have shown that the soldier was absent from Homer's original composition. He was added after the Confederate prisoners had been laid in and the brown ground filled in around them. Then, rather than being worked up in the same detail as the rest, his face was left marked by the color of the brown ground. An infrared photograph reveals Homer painted the face in and scraped it off at least once, if not several times; but rather than restoring it, he simply smoothed over the traces of the scrape marks and added the brim of the cap. Perhaps he had intended to create another obviously white Union guard. Yet in the painting he submitted as "finished" to the National Academy of Design in 1866, the soldier behind the prisoners remained dark-skinned and only faintly articulated.

None of the critics who commented on *Prisoners from the Front* mentioned this dark-skinned soldier. Yet Homer's support for the abolitionist cause and his increased awareness of the contributions of African Americans to the war effort both as soldiers and as support personnel may well have prompted him to include a reference to black soldiers, and thus to slavery, in his symbolic commentary on the Civil War. Having laid in the devastated landscape and included the figures of the Confederate soldiers and General Barlow, he may have turned to his earlier depictions of contrabands and banjo-playing African Americans [**4.12.12–4.12.13**; p. 231]. Should he include one of these figures, or was there a better way to represent the presence of African Americans in the Cicil War? But how does one represent an African American as an active subject, as an alert soldier rather than a sleeping teamster or a banjo-playing entertainer? How would the critics respond to the inclusion of a black soldier in his painting? While black and white soldiers may have fought side by side in the heat of battle, they were organized in segregated units and would not have been found together in the kind of post-battle scene recorded in *Prisoners from the Front*.

Perhaps Homer's awareness of the potential resistance of critics, and the public in general, to the inclusion of a black soldier may have caused him to back away from presenting a fully realized figure. Yet he did not omit the soldier altogether, nor did he make him recognizably white. In the end, he may have decided simply to leave intact the ghostly presence of an African American soldier behind the Confederate prisoners as another, more subtle, "key" to understanding the nature of the Civil War and its aftermath: that African Americans functioned as both soldiers and slaves, the former helping win the war for the North on the battlefield, the latter providing the war's moral justification. The soldier also represented those who had the most to lose as a result of the brotherly postwar negotiations between the North and the South that had begun even as the paint dried on Homer's canvas.

A second painting by Homer that addresses the aftermath of the Civil War is also a confrontation scene. Here, however, the confrontation is located indoors and takes place between a white woman and three African American women who were once her slaves. In *A Visit from the Old Mistress* (1876) [**4.13.2**] the white woman is dressed, like the Union officer in *Prisoners from the Front* [**4.13.1**; p. 237], in dark clothes. She assumes a stance similar to the officer's as she confronts three adult figures. The former slaves, like at least two of the Confederate prisoners, are dressed in ragged clothing. Homer's manner of execution is even more unfinished in this painting than in *Prisoners from the Front*, although the greatest finish appears in the face and upper costume of the white woman. This is particularly evident if we compare her to the African American woman closest to her, whom she confronts directly and whose features, in an echo of those of the Union guard in the earlier painting, are only barely articulated. Indeed, this woman resembles the guard not only in the schematic manner in which she is rendered, but also in the shape and positioning of her head. If the African American has emerged from the shadows of the Confederacy, therefore, it is as a woman in the home rather than a man on the battlefield.

What is the nature of the confrontation depicted here? Who is the victor, who is the vanquished? The title of the painting suggests the women on the left are the victors. The white woman is, after all, the "old" or former mistress. Yet, in compositional terms, she is located in the position of the victor. She has a slight smile on her face and looks directly at the women in front of her. As in *Prisoners from the Front*, however, there is no show of obeisance by the others. Rather, there is a distinct sense of suspicion and mistrust, particularly visible in the gesture and facial expression of the seated woman on the far left. In historical terms, they are the victors. This was 1876, more than a decade since the end of the Civil War and the institution of slavery. That the black woman on the left remains seated rather than rising at the entrance of the white woman signals the changed relations between mistresses and their former slaves. Yet the next year northern and southern politicians struck their deal to put Hayes in the White House, effectively ending Reconstruction. From this point on, the gains made by African Americans over the previous ten years would be systematically dismantled.

Thus, as in *Prisoners from the Front*, there is no clear-cut victory or defeat. Even the visit of a white woman to her former slaves' quarters cannot be read as an act of capitulation. Such visits were common in the earlier slave-holding period and often depicted in engravings in the popular press in the 1870s as examples of "the good old days" when slaves knew their place and welcomed the benevolent gestures of their masters and mistresses.

In creating an enclosed, almost claustrophobic, space for the four women (the painting is almost half the size of *Prisoners from the Front*), Homer acknowledges the intimate nature of the contact between white women and the African American slaves who worked for them in the plantation mansions. While white men had personal servants, most of their contact with black slaves occurred in the fields or other places of work separate from the home. White women maintained control in the domestic sphere—over their children and over their African American slaves. These slaves engaged in tasks that directly involved the well-being of the family—cooking, cleaning, and raising the children. As is suggested in *Uncle Tom's Cabin*, household servants often became the friends of their young white charges, if not of

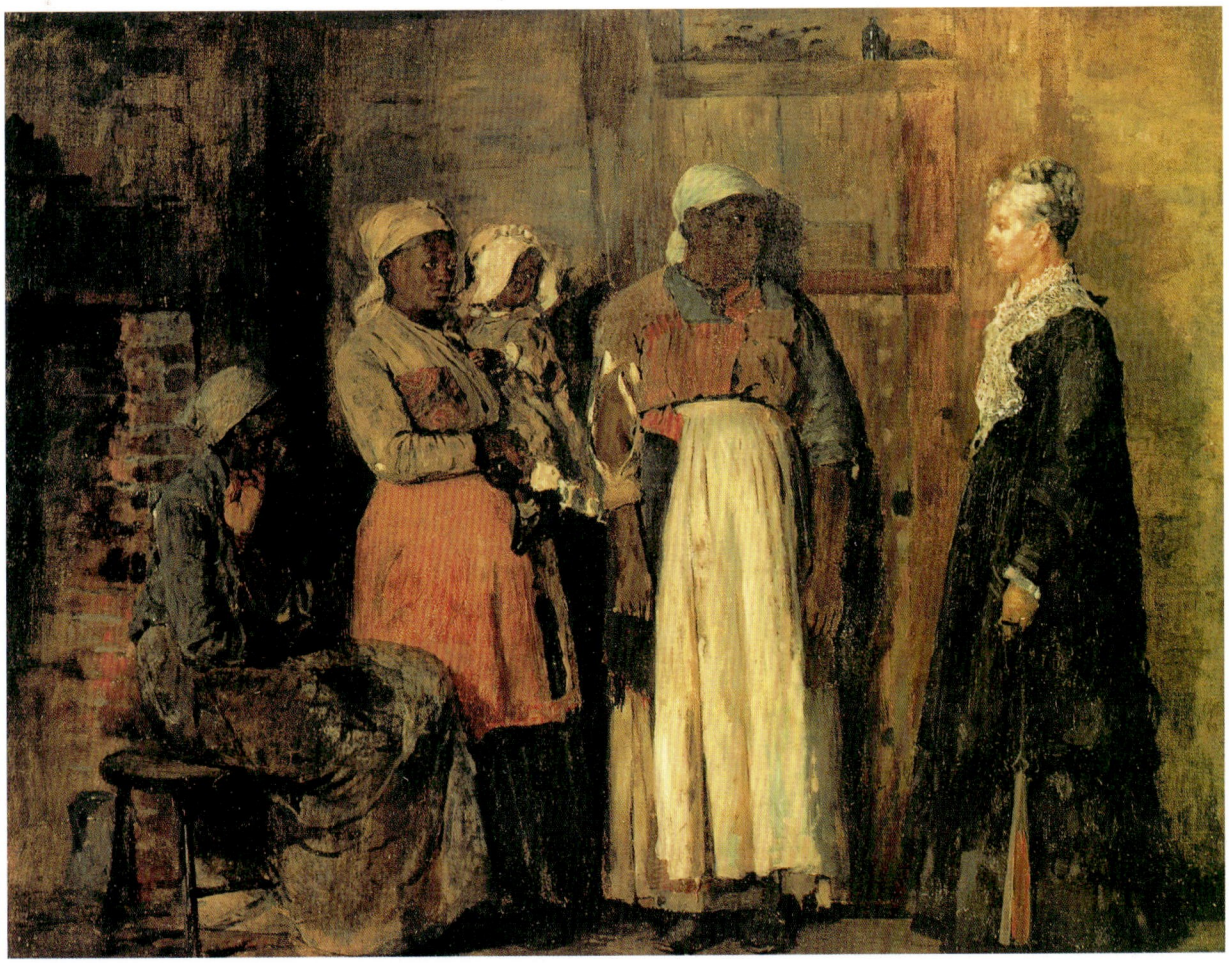

4.13.2 Winslow Homer: *A Visit from the Old Mistress*, 1876. Oil on canvas, 18 x 24⅛ in. (45.7 x 61.3 cm.) Smithsonian American Art Museum, Washington, D.C.

the older members of the household. Such friendships created the basis for an understanding of the inequities of slavery and a willingness to end slavery as a whole. The potential for understanding between the two races appeared to be greater in the female sphere of the home than in the male spheres of business, politics, and war.

Yet the potential for violence was also great in the home, as indicated by the beatings of household slaves and the attempts by these same slaves, sometimes successful, to murder their masters and mistresses. The work of household slaves was generally lighter than that of field slaves, but was accompanied by constant surveillance that forced the continuous wearing of a public mask. Yet, as Lerone Bennett, Jr. notes, court records of the mid-nineteenth century "yield ample evidence that a large number of slaves refused to play the game of slavery: they would neither smile nor bow. Other slaves bowed but would not smile." Others bowed and smiled, but sabotaged the system from within, breaking utensils or staging slowdowns. The close proximity of the women in Homer's painting and their demeanors suggest both the potential for understanding and the potential for harm. The physical and psychological distance between the white and black women, while filled with tension and mistrust, is also bridgeable by a single gesture.

Thomas Nast's "Grand Historical Paintings"

Thomas Nast joined Winslow Homer in recording the limits of Reconstruction. Nast, however, used the sharp tongue of political caricature rather than the more muted voice of Homer's symbolic narratives. The historian Morton Keller points out that Nast had "no rich tradition of American graphic satire or caricature" upon which to draw, so turned to transatlantic sources, such as the French artist Honoré Daumier (1808–1879), whose commitment to liberty and justice was echoed in Nast's works. Stylistically, he was more indebted to the British caricaturist Sir John Tenniel (1820–1914), whose work appeared in the British publication *Punch*. *Harper's Weekly* would be the major venue for Nast's graphic commentaries.

In 1867, Nast produced his "Grand Caricaturama," thirty-three pictures—each approximately 8 × 11 feet (2.4 × 3.4 meters)—that he described as "Grand Historical Paintings." While Homer created a subtle commentary on the conventions of history painting in *Prisoners from the Front* [**4.13.1**; p. 237], Nast challenges these conventions through open ridicule. Nast also plays

4.13.3 Thomas Nast: *The Massacre at New Orleans*, from Nast's "Grand Caricaturama," 1867.
Monochrome painting, h. 94¾ in. (240.7 cm.)
Library of Congress, Washington, D.C.

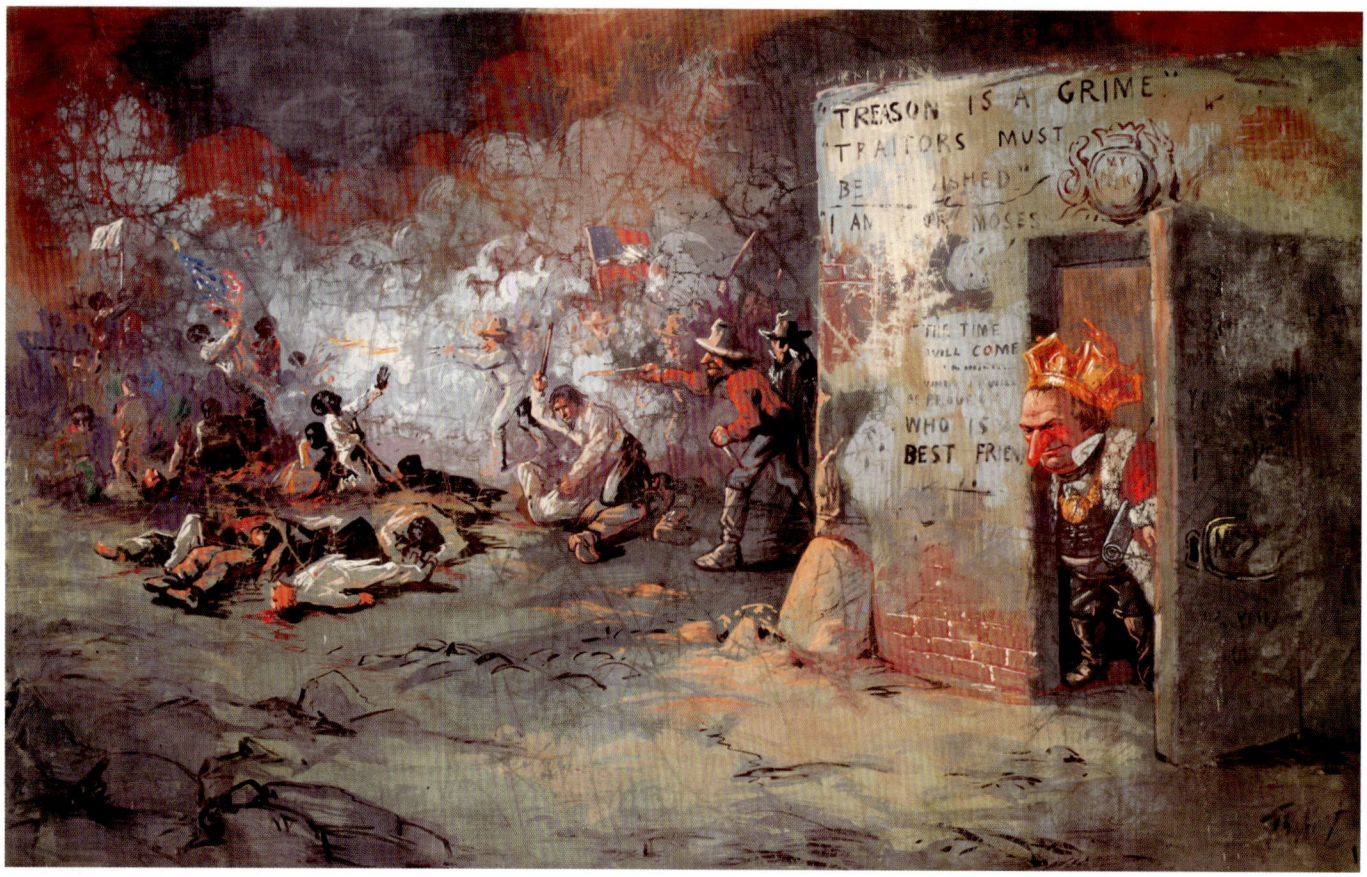

with the conventions of the panorama, where images on a vast scale were meant to transport the viewer to another world for a vicarious experience of the drama of exotic scenery or epic battles. Nast transports his viewers to a place from which they would want quickly to escape, all the while directing their viewing through a lecture by a hired speaker accompanied by music.

The "Grand Caricaturama" was meant as a scathing criticism of President Andrew Johnson. Johnson's predecessor, Abraham Lincoln, was unwilling to allow unregenerate white southern politicians to resume power after the end of the war, and committed the federal government to protecting the rights of freed slaves. When Johnson assumed office in 1865 after Lincoln's assassination, he did not continue Lincoln's hard-line policy toward the defeated South. Instead, he argued for States' rights and white supremacy, and was ready to abandon freed slaves to their former masters. Only the strong presence of Radical Republicans in Congress prevented him from fully realizing his pro-South policies. As a Radical Republican and popular illustrator, Nast was influential in helping to bring about Johnson's demise within the Republican Party (Ulysses S. Grant was the Republican candidate in the 1868 presidential election).

Only five of the works that made up the "Grand Caricaturama" still exist today. One of these, *The Massacre at New Orleans* [**4.13.3**] depicts President Johnson on the right, wearing a crown and looking out the door of a building at the scene on the left. His crown and the coat of arms above the door refer to what Radical Republicans claimed were Johnson's royalist aspirations. On the left is the massacre by the city's white police of Radical Republicans, most of whom were black, who had gathered for a constitutional convention in New Orleans on July 30, 1866.

Nast's work is patterned after the painting *The Third of May, 1808* (1814) by the Spanish artist Francisco de Goya (1746–1828). In Goya's painting men are about to be shot at close range, with one in the middle ground raising his arms in a pleading gesture. In the foreground are the bodies of those who have already been killed. This reference to Goya reinforces the suggestion of royalist aspirations on the part of Johnson; Napoleon's invasion of Spain, which led to the massacre of May 3, 1808, took place after he had declared himself emperor.

"King" Johnson is a mean-spirited man, with a run-down brick building for a castle. His lackeys are murdering unarmed people (thirty-seven black delegates and three white sympathizers were killed). One of these unarmed men holds up a white flag of truce. Thus, Nast uses history painting to convey a moral message. This massacre, and other racially motivated massacres that followed, could have been stopped, suggests Nast, had Johnson been less allied with racist Southerners and more willing to prosecute those responsible for such lawless actions.

The Freed Slave: Edmonia Lewis's *Forever Free* and Thomas Ball's *Freedmen's Memorial*

In 1867, the same year Thomas Nast produced his "Grand Caricaturama" [**4.13.3**] and a year after Winslow Homer completed *Prisoners from the Front* [**4.13.1**; p. 237], Edmonia Lewis (*c.* 1845–after 1909) presented another testimony to the end of slavery. Like Robert S. Duncanson, she had benefited from the encouragement and support of white abolitionists. Born in upstate New York of a Chippewa mother and an African American father, Lewis—originally named Wildfire—was orphaned at four and raised by her mother's people until she was twelve. At thirteen, with the help of her brothers and various abolitionists, she entered the Young Ladies Preparatory Department at Oberlin College in Ohio, adopting the Christian name of Mary Edmonia Lewis. While there, she was accused of attempting to poison two of her white schoolmates and of stealing. Lewis was defended at trial by the well-known African American lawyer John Mercer Langston, and acquitted of all charges, yet was not allowed to graduate. With the help of the abolitionist William Lloyd Garrison, she settled in Boston and met the sculptor Edward Brackett. He lent her sculpture fragments to copy and, with the sculptor Anne Whitney, helped her develop her skills as an artist.

Lewis's first works were busts and medallions of various abolitionist leaders and heroes, including Garrison, Charles Sumner, Maria Weston Chapman, and Colonel Robert Gould Shaw (see pp. 246–48). Lewis's posthumous portrait of Shaw, completed in 1865, impressed his family, who organized a group of friends to buy one hundred copies at fifteen dollars each. This money, and the help of her benefactors the Story family, allowed Lewis to finance a trip to Italy in 1865. There she joined the women gathered in Rome around the American sculptor Harriet Hosmer (1830–1908). These women went to Europe in search of good marble, collections of classical Greek and Roman sculpture, and trained carvers who would teach them. They were encouraged by liberal parents or, as with Lewis, friends who could support them financially. Almost all remained single and devoted their lives to their artistic endeavors. The success of those like Hosmer and Lewis was notable for two reasons: the difficulty for women of becoming a recognized artist in any medium in the nineteenth century; and the special physical challenges produced by sculpture, which resulted in even stronger prejudices against women taking it up.

Hosmer provided Lewis with both a supportive environment within which to work in Rome and examples of images that addressed the issues of slavery and rebellion. Born in Massachusetts, Hosmer traveled to St. Louis to study anatomy and to explore the Far West before proceeding on to Rome in

1852, where she remained for the rest of her professional career. Success came quickly. By the end of the decade she was selling her work directly from her studio (a common practice in Rome and Florence), and receiving regular visits from artists and collectors including the Prince of Wales and the Russian Czar.

In 1857 Hosmer carved the reclining *Beatrice Cenci* [**4.13.4**], an Italian noblewoman who, with her mother Lucretia, killed her abusive and tyrannical father Francesco in the late sixteenth century. Both women were condemned to death and beheaded, despite many pleas for clemency. Hosmer shows Beatrice asleep the night before her execution, having come to terms with her actions and fate through prayer. Two years later Hosmer produced *Zenobia in Chains* [**4.13.5**]. Zenobia, a queen of Palmyra in Syria, was defeated and captured by the Romans in the third century. Hosmer has modeled Zenobia on antique prototypes, presenting her as noble and resolute in her defeat; she gathers up her chains along with her robe, grasping them firmly in her hand as she contemplates her future. When the statue was exhibited in the US in 1863, it was received with great enthusiasm as an example of moral rectitude and resistance to defeat, a fitting symbol for a country in the throes of a civil war.

While Hosmer focused on the political and personal struggles of women against men and male-defined institutions, Lewis turned her attention to the struggles of African Americans against the institution of slavery. She created two works on this subject while in Rome, *The Freed Woman and Her Child* (now lost), and *Forever Free*, (1867) [**4.13.6**]. The latter, originally titled *The Morning of Liberty*, attempts to capture the emotional impact on African American slaves of President Lincoln's proclamation, on January 1, 1863, that all persons held as slaves (in those areas still fighting the North) "are, and henceforward shall be, free." A woman, the manacle still around her ankle, kneels and clasps her hands in thanksgiving while a man stands above her, one hand on her shoulder, the other raised and holding the manacle and chains that previously had been attached to his ankle. Another manacle remains attached to his wrist, however, indicating that freedom has yet to be fully achieved. Both gaze upward, acknowledging the existence and help of a higher power (it was around this time that Lewis converted to Catholicism).

Lewis fully intended the figures to be read as African American slaves. Yet there is little in their appearance that identifies them as such, save the curly hair and the slightly broader features of the man. One might argue that, as in Eastman Johnson's *Negro Life in the South* [**4.12.8**; p. 227], Lewis acknowledges the varying

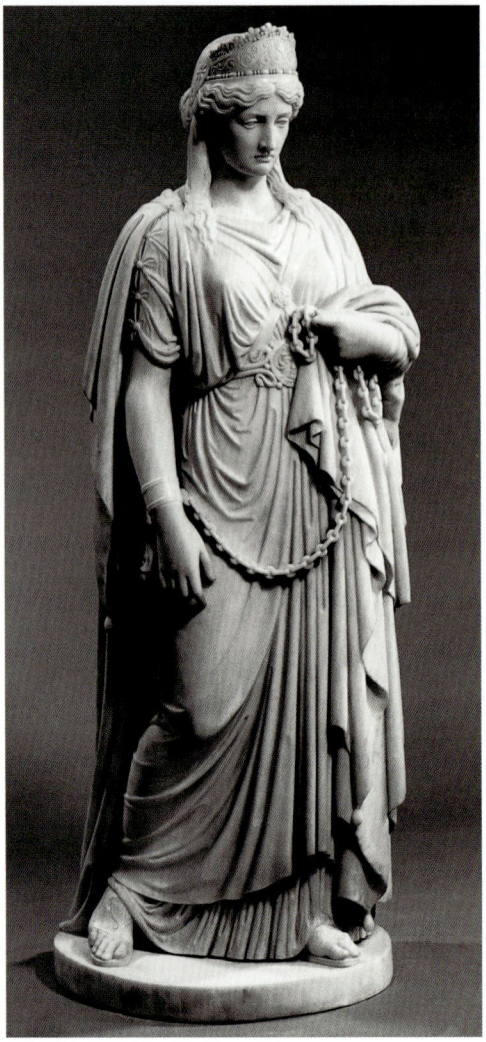

4.13.5 Harriet Hosmer: *Zenobia in Chains*, 1859.
Marble, h. 84¾ in. (215.3 cm.)
Wadsworth Atheneum Museum of Art, Hartford, Connecticut

4.13.4 Harriet Hosmer: *Beatrice Cenci*, 1857.
Marble, 17⅛ x 41⅛ x 17 in. (43.8 x 104.7 x 43.1 cm.)
St. Louis Mercantile Library, St. Louis, Missouri

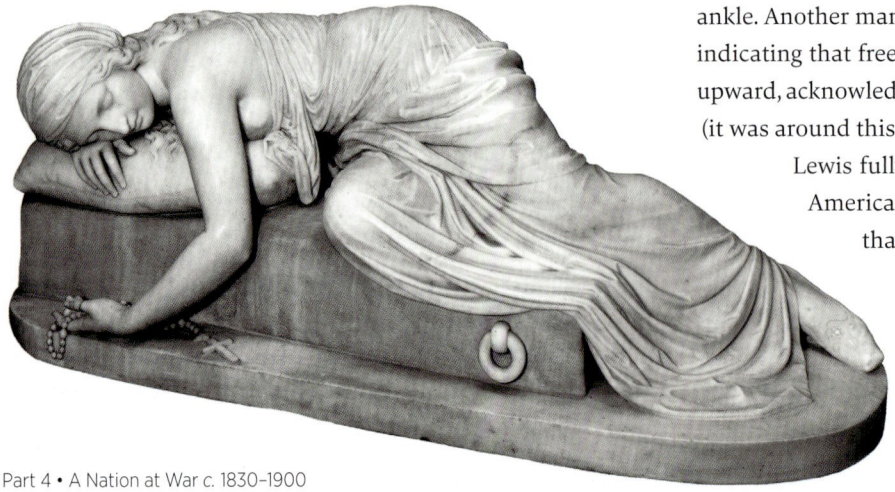

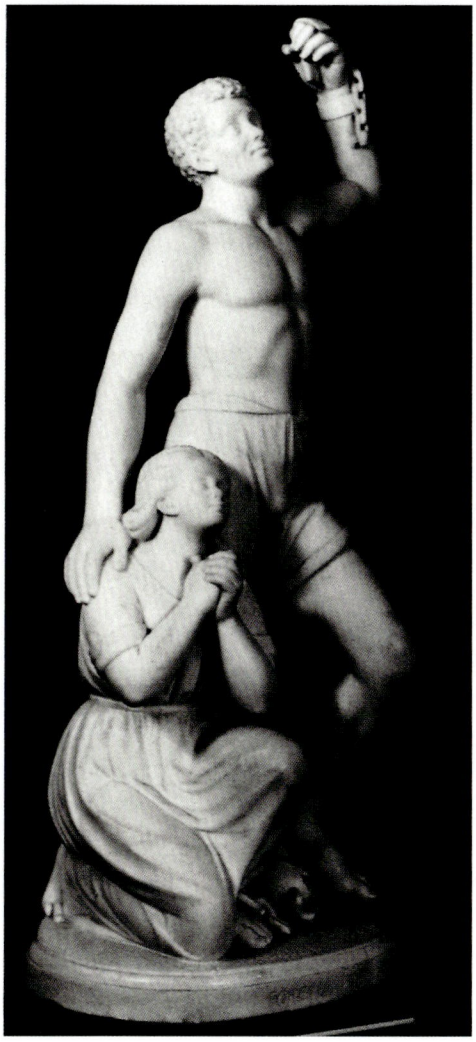

4.13.6 Edmonia Lewis: *Forever Free*, 1867.
Marble, 41¼ x 11 x 7 in. (104.8 x 27.9 x 17.8 cm.)
James A. Porter Gallery of Afro-American Art, Howard University, Washington, D.C.

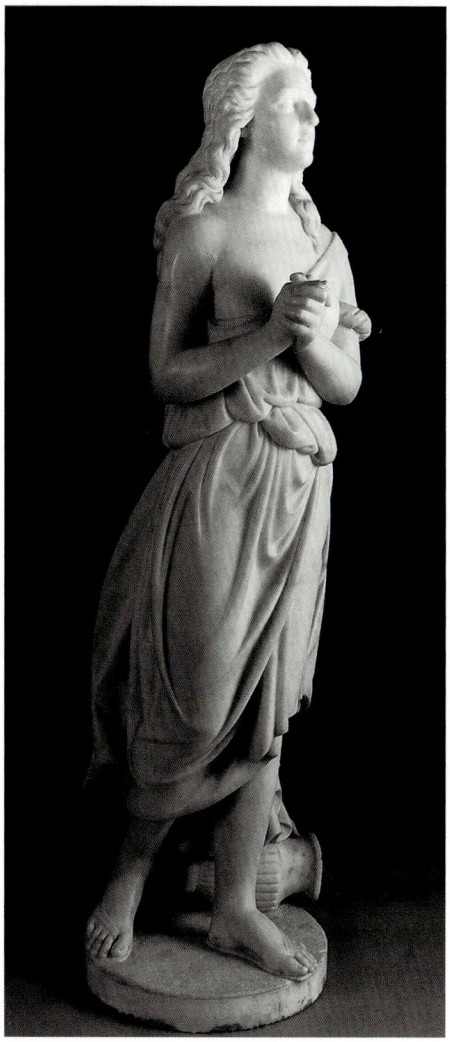

4.13.7 Edmonia Lewis: *Hagar in the Wilderness*, 1868.
Marble, 52⅝ x 15¼ x 17 in. (133.6 x 38.8 x 43.4 cm.)
Smithsonian American Art Museum, Washington, D.C.

physical features of African American slaves, who were often, like Lewis herself, a mix of African and European or African and Native American descent. The art historian Kirsten P. Buick also suggests that Lewis's decision to Europeanize the features of the black woman in *Forever Free* was an attempt to prevent the work from being read as autobiographical, as a "self-portrait" rather than a statement about black women as a whole. Unlike Johnson, however, Lewis could not use her chosen material of marble to render the subtle variations in skin color of African American slaves. A tension is thus created between the (absent) dark skin and the whiteness (of the marble) against which darkness is always measured and found wanting. Marble, the famed material of Greek and Roman artists, gave aesthetic and historical legitimacy to the two freed slaves, while at the same time erasing the visual signifier of race and thus of servitude.

A year after completing *Forever Free*, Lewis created *Hagar in the Wilderness* (1868) [**4.13.7**], a tribute to the Old Testament Egyptian maidservant of Abraham's wife, Sarah, who was cast into the desert to escape the rage of Sarah after having borne Abraham a child. The parallel to the situation of African American female slaves in the US is clear (according to Buick, "Egypt was coded as black Africa among abolitionists and colonizationists in the nineteenth century"). Lewis wrote, in reference to another work representing Hagar, "I have a strong sympathy for all women who have struggled and suffered."

Lewis remained in Rome throughout the late 1860s and early 1870s, making only brief visits to the US to promote her work. In October 1869, she visited Boston to present *Forever Free* to the Reverend L. A. Grimes at Tremont Temple. In 1873 she traveled to California where five of her works were exhibited at the San Francisco Art Association. She was in Boston around the time of the Philadelphia Centennial Exposition of 1876, which included her *Death of Cleopatra* of the same year.

Lewis's financial success attested to her skill at producing the type and quality of work expected by the American art-buying public in the later nineteenth century. Yet, even in Rome, she was continually confronted by the prejudices of an art world accustomed to acknowledging only white, male members. She was often viewed as a novelty, as "exotic" because of her gender and her dress, which was sometimes described as "mannish" (the novelist Nathaniel Hawthorne visited Hosmer in 1858 and described the upper half of her clothing as "precisely that of a young man").

Lewis was also subject to comments about her race. The author Henry James described her as "a negress, whose colour, picturesquely contrasted with that of her plastic material, was the pleading agent of her fame." In other words, her success was the result not of her artistic talent, but of her novelty, which James sees in terms of a contrast—between her dark skin and the white marble in which she worked. The critic Laura Curtis Bullard wrote in 1871:

> Edmonia Lewis is below the medium height, her complexion and features betray her African origin; her hair is more of the Indian type, black, straight and abundant.... Her manners are child-like, simple and most winning and pleasing. She has the proud spirit of her Indian ancestor, and if she has more of the African in her personal appearance, she has more of the Indian in her character.

At the time this description was written Lewis was in her mid-twenties and an accomplished artist. Yet she was still seen as childlike, winning, and pleasing, attributes that made her success and independence as an artist and single woman less threatening to men and to those women who believed in the need to maintain their "femininity" even as they entered professions previously closed to them. Bullard also combines two stereotypes—the "proud" Native American and the "childlike" African American—in her description of the artist.

Little is known of Lewis's career after the mid-1880s. She disappeared from exhibition records and art journals, and the last printed reference to her appears to be in the *Catholic Rosary* magazine, which noted in 1909 that she was aging but "still with us."

Lewis was one of the first American artists to commemorate black Americans in sculpture. Her work, however, had a limited audience. And while John Rogers's *Slave Auction* [**4.12.7**; p. 226] reached many more people, its small size and multiple copies deprived it of the moral legitimacy of "fine" art. The art historian Kirk Savage notes that several artists did attempt to create monumental public sculptures marking the emancipation of slaves. Few succeeded, however, and those who did created commemorations that reinforced, as much as undermined, the traditional relationship between master and slave.

The task these artists faced was similar to the one Homer may well have faced as he worked on *Prisoners from the Front* [**4.13.8**, p. 237]: how to create an image of a black person as a free agent, as a heroic individual representative of the new united nation that Northern politicians claimed had emerged from the bloodshed and devastation of the Civil War. Prior to that conflict, calls for an end to slavery were often accompanied by an image of a kneeling, chained slave surrounded by the words "Am I Not a Man and a Brother." This image was derived from a small, low-relief, Wedgwood ceramic medallion designed in England in 1786, which functioned as an emblem of the British abolitionist movement. It appeared in the US in the early nineteenth century in popular prints [**4.13.8**] and on a variety of household objects. Once slavery ended, one would assume the kneeling slave would stand, as in Lewis's work, celebrating his newly found freedom. Yet it appears sculptors and their audiences found it difficult to envision a freed slave in a public place in anything but a kneeling position.

Savage suggests that sculptors were faced with a challenge not faced by painters: how to create a heroic representation of a free black person in a medium that had come to be "embedded in

4.13.8 Unknown artist: *Am I Not a Man and a Brother*, 1837. Woodcut, 10½ x 9 in. (26.7 x 22.8 cm.) Library of Congress, Washington, D.C.

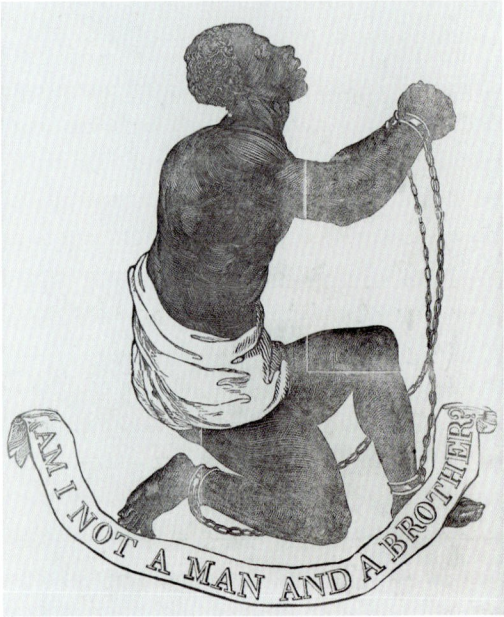

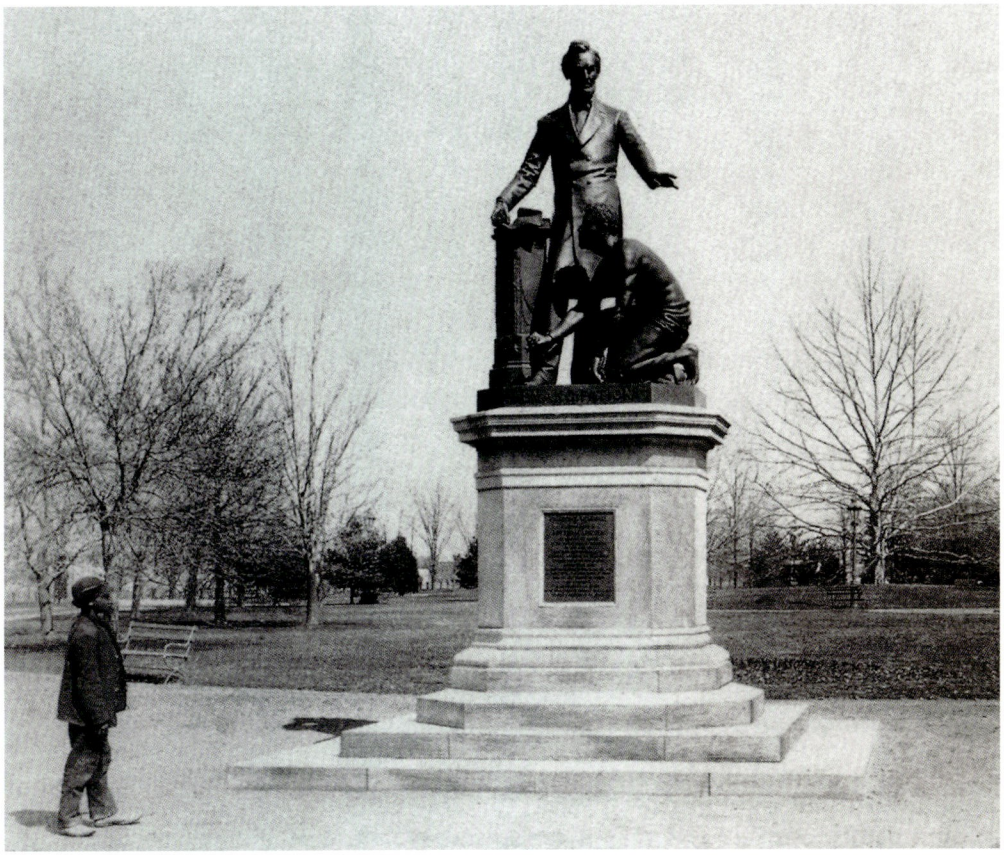

4.13.9 Thomas Ball: *Freedmen's Memorial to Abraham Lincoln (Emancipation Monument)*, 1876. Lincoln Park, Washington, D.C.

the theoretical foundations of racism that supported American slavery and survived long after its demise." Racism, in Savage's words, "centered on the analysis and representation of the human body." And in the central nineteenth-century texts articulating racist theory, such as *Types of Mankind* (1854) by J. C. Nott and George R. Gliddon, the ideal body type was often represented by classical Greek or Roman sculpture. Thus, classical sculpture came to signify not simply antiquity, but whiteness. "Natural philosophers used classical sculpture," writes Savage, "to visualize and articulate a new racial construct, but the resulting theory transformed the understanding of classical sculpture by racializing it." The body of the black person signified the antithesis of both whiteness and sculpture, for "classical sculpture still served as the benchmark of the sculptural and thereby defined what was not sculpture." This helps explain the tension that exists in Lewis's work, as she tries to reconcile the classical and the black body.

One of the few monuments to the emancipation of black slaves that materialized in the decade after the Civil War was the bronze and stone *Freedmen's Memorial to Abraham Lincoln* or *Emancipation Monument* of 1876 in Washington, D.C. [**4.13.9**] by Thomas Ball (1819–1911). As a public monument located in the nation's capital, it had to be both conservative and progressive; it had to commemorate an event—emancipation—that had not yet been fully realized in a manner acceptable to both abolitionist and former slave- owner. The solution arrived at by Ball, and other sculptors, was to commemorate emancipation not through the bodies of independently acting freedmen, but through the body of Abraham Lincoln.

Ball's monument is dominated by the relationship between the standing Lincoln, who holds a scroll representing the Emancipation Proclamation, and the kneeling black man, who gazes at the scroll in recognition of its significance for him (the latter was modeled after a former slave named Archer Alexander who had escaped the South in 1863). This configuration speaks to the limits of emancipation and to the continuance of the link between master/benefactor and slave/freedman. The presence of a white man and a black man together on a public monument was thus made acceptable through the visual hierarchy of standing and kneeling and its coding of the master/slave (servant) relationship. The semi-nude body of the black man, which by itself would have referred to the heroic realm of classical sculpture, here comes to represent the less civilized, less human contrast to the fully clothed Lincoln. It is a far cry from Homer's *Visit from the Old Mistress* [**4.13.2**; p. 239], where the black women hold their ground in the presence of their former mistress. Yet a small painting did not have to carry the ideological load of a public sculpture.

African Americans paid for Ball's monument through a public subscription. Yet a group of white men, members of the Western Sanitary Commission of St. Louis, a war relief agency, collected the money and decided on its design and character. (They rejected a design by Hosmer that included four standing African Americans, along with four allegorical figures and a portrait of Lincoln.) The resulting work inserted the sculpted black body into a national monument for the first time, yet negated the freedom it claimed to celebrate. Its ultimate failure to celebrate emancipation made it an apt commemoration of Reconstruction, which also failed to emancipate blacks from the political and social structures underlying slavery. And even this compromised reference to emancipation in Ball's sculpture disappeared after 1876. Subsequent portraits of Lincoln were devoid of kneeling (or standing) freedmen or even of scrolls that had earlier symbolized the Emancipation Proclamation. Instead, Lincoln came to be depicted on his own, celebrated as the Savior of the Union rather than the Liberator of Slaves.

Seated Generals, Standing Soldiers: Military Memorials to the Civil War

Not surprisingly, emancipation also failed to materialize in public monuments in the deep South. There the Civil War was commemorated in the body of another famous man, General Robert E. Lee. Just as Abraham Lincoln monuments came to focus on union rather than emancipation, Lee monuments commemorated the battle to protect States' rights rather than to preserve slavery. The most famous of these monuments is the equestrian statue by the French sculptor Antonin Mercié (1845–1916), with a pedestal designed by the architect Paul Pujol (1848–?), erected in Richmond, Virginia, in 1890 [**4.13.10**]. The Southern cause had to be dissociated from slavery after the war in order to situate the region as a full partner within the new Union. This precluded the appearance of any black figure, kneeling or standing, soldier or slave, on the monument. The very absence of African Americans in public monuments in the South, however, combined with their very real presence on the streets of southern cities, was a constant reminder of the racial domination that had formed the basis of slavery. This domination continued to determine interracial relationships once the institution of slavery was abolished.

The standing black soldier in full military garb would not appear in a public monument in the North until the end of the century. The *Shaw Memorial* of 1897 on Boston Common [**4.13.11**] by Augustus Saint-Gaudens (1848–1907) celebrates Colonel Robert Gould Shaw and the all-black 54th Massachusetts. Nearly half of the regiment had been killed, along with Shaw, in 1863 while attempting to take Fort Wagner near Charleston.

Joshua B. Smith, a former slave living in Boston, proposed the idea for the commemoration in 1865 and donated $500 of his own money. The project was eventually taken over by a group of individuals from the white cultural elite of Boston that included many active participants in the abolitionist movement and supporters of the political and economic rights of freed slaves. This group was aware of the injustice of excluding black soldiers from Civil War monuments and hoped to rectify this situation with the *Shaw Memorial*. As Kirk Savage points out, they were also motivated by a strong antipathy toward the proliferation

4.13.10 Antonin Mercié and Paul Pujol: *Lee Memorial*, 1890, seen at its unveiling Monument Avenue, Richmond, Virginia.

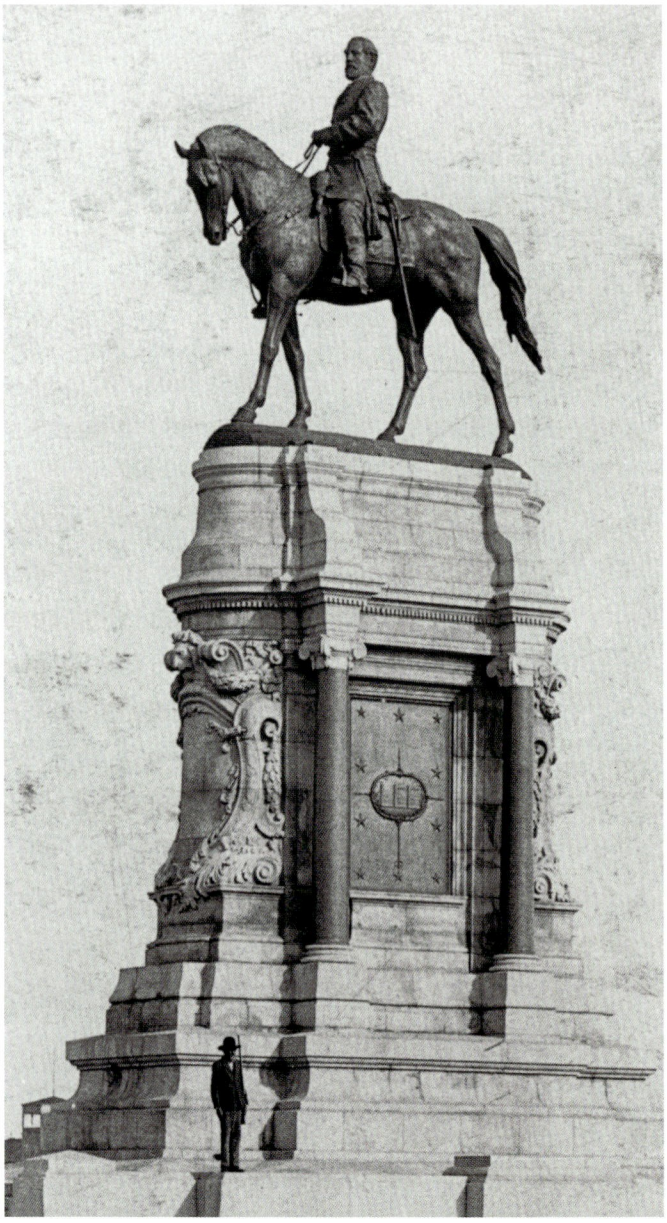

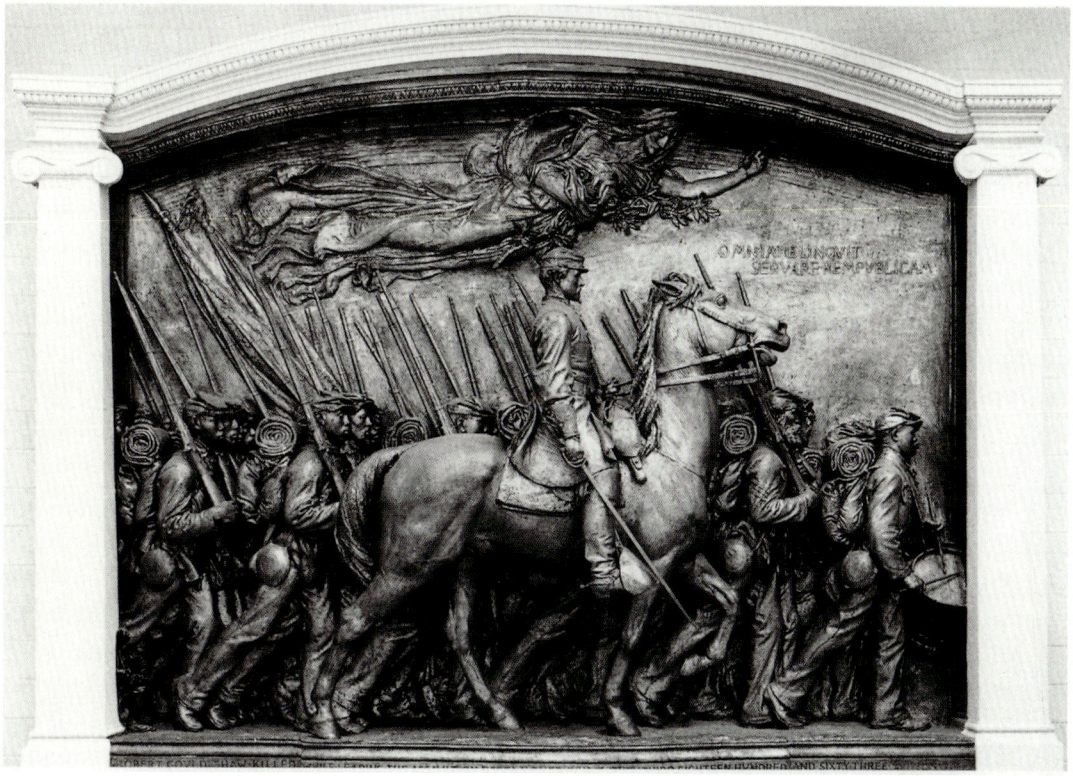

4.13.11 Augustus Saint-Gaudens: panel of the *Memorial to Robert Gould Shaw and the 54th Massachusetts Regiment*, 1897. Boston Common, Boston, Massachusetts

of standardized, made-to-order, "common soldier" monuments. These endless individual white soldiers ("common" could never be represented by a black soldier) stood at parade rest on top of pedestals in public squares throughout the country, promoting the nationalist ideology of the citizen-soldier and restoring a sense of individual initiative and personal agency to the many survivors of the Civil War. Yet for the organizers of the Shaw commission, they were a "cultural disaster." They degraded what was viewed as the noblest of art forms. True art was unique; its value resided not in its repetition, but in its difference. What could be more different then, than a monument commemorating the role of black soldiers in the Civil War?

Saint-Gaudens had established a national reputation as a sculptor with several public monuments, including two of Lincoln in Chicago. He was also closely connected to those responsible for the *Shaw Memorial*. His high-relief bronze monument to Shaw, set into a stone frame designed by the architect Charles Follen McKim (1847–1909), combines the traditional equestrian portrait of the military leader/hero with the more recent form of the standing "common soldier." Shaw and his horse are placed beside the foot soldiers, suggesting a certain level of camaraderie. Shaw is also located between the black soldiers under his command and the Angel of Death, who hovers above them all bearing the symbols of victory (laurel) and sleep (poppies). In his depiction of the members of the 54th Regiment, Saint-Gaudens departs from the "common soldier" monuments in at least two ways: the soldiers are moving rather than standing at parade rest, marking them more clearly as historical agents; and each soldier has been portrayed with distinct, individual features, rather than as a generic stereotype.

Yet some see Shaw's monument as containing certain elements that worked against the celebration of African American soldiers. The art historian Albert Boime argues, for example, that the clear association between the black troops and the horse downplays the individuality and humanity of the troops by reaffirming the common racist equation between African Americans and animals. The legs of the troops echo those of the horse, the troops (many are obscured by the animal's body) are on the same level as the horse, and both troops and horse follow the direction of Shaw.

Boime supports his reading of the Shaw monument, in part, by citing Saint-Gaudens's correspondence surrounding the commission, which reveals a view of African Americans as childlike, ignorant, "difficult," and lacking initiative. This view was certainly not that of Shaw and his family, who were leaders of the abolitionist movement in Boston. When Saint-Gaudens initially proposed a conventional equestrian statue, family members encouraged him to consider, instead, a plan including Shaw's troops, for it was the latter's role as leader of an African American regiment that was of greatest significance for them. The extent of this significance is evident in their response to Union General Quincy Adams Gilmore's suggestion that Shaw's body be exhumed from the common grave on the battlefield where he had been buried along with his African American troops (Gilmore had been in charge of the attack on Fort Wager where Shaw died). The family rejected the idea, preferring the unity of black and white symbolized by this common grave.

Savage agrees that Saint-Gaudens "shared the common racial prejudices of the white elite." Yet he also argues that these prejudices were overcome in the monument by artistic imperatives, in particular by the artist's desire to create a work marked by individuality rather than repetition, an individuality that set the work apart from common soldier monuments.

> Saint-Gaudens's sympathetic portrait studies of black men do not imply a special sympathy for black men in the mind of the artist, nor does the lack of sympathy he showed in his memoirs invalidate the visual evidence of the sculpture. It was the self-imposed demands of art, not racial ideology, that compelled the sculptor to portray these men as he did. The artistic imperative of difference over repetition was so powerful that it drove Saint-Gaudens to humanize his models in ways he had never originally intended.

The impact of these artistic imperatives is suggested in a passage from Saint-Gaudens's memoirs, where he states that "through my extreme interest in it [the project] and its opportunity, [I] increased the conception until the rider grew almost to a statue in the round and the Negroes assumed far more importance than I had originally intended."

This tension between African Americans as individuals and as stereotypes, between the white commander and his black troops, led to differing responses to the monument. Many white critics ignored the individuality of the troops, referring to them as an undifferentiated "mass" and seeing the work, instead, as a celebration of the heroism of Shaw. Others, however, remarked upon the significance of these troops to the monument's larger meaning—the participation of black soldiers in the eradication of the institution of slavery.

Much of the emotional power of the monument came from the fact that those who viewed it were fully aware of the symbolic and pragmatic significance of the entrance of African American soldiers into the Civil War and of the tragic fate of the regiment and its leader. The location of the monument reinforced this awareness. John A. Andrew, governor of Massachusetts, had presented the colors to the regiment on Boston Common on May 28, 1863, before it set off to join the Union forces in South Carolina. Saint-Gaudens depicts the soldiers as they moved forward across the Common and on toward Boston Harbor. In his publication *Emancipation and the Freed in American Sculpture* (1916), the black writer Freeman Henry Morris Murray commented on this movement and on the destination of the troops:

> The scene is evidently the departure of the colored troops; the leader a young man of noble mien who recognizes the significance of the fateful day. With head square set upon the broad shoulders and sad eyes unflinching, he rides steadily to his fate. The fiery horse is a splendid sculptural achievement, clean cut and magnificently wrought, but, conspicuous as he is, easily dominated by the presence of the silent rider. Then, behind and across the entire background, march with swinging tread the black men, their muskets over shoulders which bend under the burdensome knapsacks. They are equipped for a long journey from which not many will return. The movement of this great composition is extraordinary. We almost hear the roll of the drums and the shuffle of the heavy shoes. It makes the day of that brave departure very real again.

Murray celebrates the strength and commitment of the soldiers at the same time as he mourns their impending deaths. The monument held special personal significance for him, for his father had served under Shaw at Fort Wagner and had survived. In the early twentieth century, such visual recognition of their accomplishments would increase as African Americans like Murray came together in major urban centers of the North to form their own distinct cultural movement (see V. 2, pp. 393–401).

Review Questions

1. What makes Winslow Homer's *Prisoners from the Front* a history painting?
2. How is Winslow Homer's *Visit from the Old Mistress* different from his *Prisoners from the Front*? How is it similar?
3. How did Edmonia Lewis's biography inform her choice of subject matter? How did it inform the critical response to her work?
4. What, according to Kirk Savage, were some of the challenges sculptors faced that painters did not in creating representations of freed African American slaves?
5. How do Albert Boime and Kirk Savage differ in their interpretation of Augustus Saint-Gaudens's *Shaw Memorial*?

CHAPTER 14

The Indian Wars and the End of the Ghost Dance

(*c.* 1869–1900)

Native Americans in the Popular Press: *Harper's Weekly* and the Washita River Massacre

During the 1870s Edmonia Lewis (*c.* 1845–after 1909) often participated in western fairs, setting up booths in the form of wigwams to emphasize the links between the West and her Native American heritage. She also created several small marble works directly addressing this heritage, such as *Old Indian Arrowmaker and His Daughter* (1872) [**4.14.1**], based on Henry Wadsworth Longfellow's poem "The Song of Hiawatha," published in 1855. Although, as in *Forever Free* [**4.13.6**; p. 243], the daughter's facial features are decidedly Europeanized, here Lewis conveys a sense of the interrelationship between the activities of Native American men and women. The older man creates the arrows to kill the forest animals, whose hides the young woman will prepare for clothing and whose meat she will cook. It is a tranquil scene, yet it is not self-contained, for the two figures both gaze outward, perhaps at Hiawatha, who offered Minnehaha a deer as part of his marriage proposal.

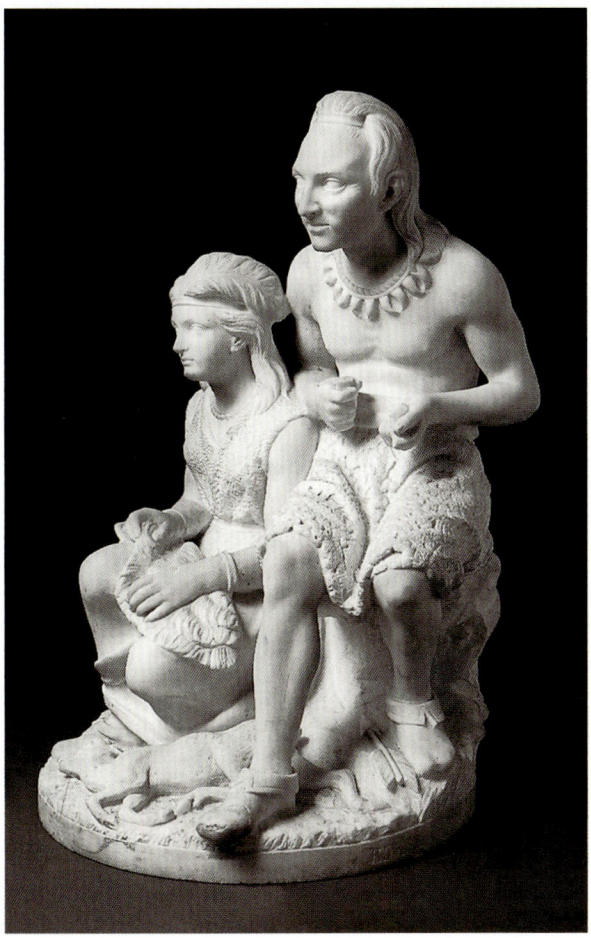

4.14.1 Edmonia Lewis: *Old Indian Arrowmaker and His Daughter*, 1872. Marble, h. 27 in. (68.6 cm.)
Carver Museum, Tuskegee Institute, Alabama

The last quarter of the nineteenth century was far from tranquil for Native Americans. Once the Civil War was over, the army turned its attention to the final eradication of indigenous resistance to westward expansion and to the ongoing confiscation of the land granted to Native Americans under earlier treaties. Artists continued to play a role in representing these developments through paintings, drawings, and photographs. Many of the photographs taken by such individuals as Thomas Easterly [**3.9.14**; p. 182] appeared in sets of stereoscopic views, similar to those produced of the Civil War. Photographs were also added to official government records of transactions between Native Americans and government representatives and often were translated into illustrations that appeared in popular magazines and novels. Sometimes they provided only general inspiration for the illustrations; other times they were literally copied. This was also the case with certain paintings and drawings. Sometimes the magazine illustrator utilized general painterly conventions in creating his or her image; other times he or she copied specific paintings or drawings in detail.

Page 41 of the January 16, 1869 issue of *Harper's Weekly* [**4.14.2**; p. 250] contains a series of images from the worlds of both drawing and photography. It is part of a larger article titled "The Indian War" recounting the latest success for the US Army. This success included General George Armstrong Custer's surprise attack and victory over the Cheyenne Chief Black Kettle at Washita River, Oklahoma, on November 27, 1868. After killing the chief and 102 of his warriors, Custer and his troops proceeded to the undefended village. There they killed all males over eight years old and many of the women and younger children. The lodges, winter stores of food, and ammunition were then destroyed, leaving the survivors to die a slow death from starvation or exposure to the cold. Custer also destroyed 875 Indian ponies.

The three wood engravings that take up most of the page are meant both to illustrate and to justify what came to be known as the Washita River Massacre. The top and bottom images are engraved versions of drawings produced by Theodore R. Davis (1840–1894), a well-known illustrator-reporter on the staff of *Harper's*. While Davis had spent six months with Custer out West in 1867, he had been back East for at least a year when the massacre occurred. His experience with Custer probably contributed to the decision to assign him the task of illustrating the article.

The detailed nature of Davis's drawings gives the impression that he had been present at Washita River. The phrase "Sketched by Theo. R. Davis" included in parentheses after the caption for each image also implies that they were quickly executed while the artist was looking at the events as they unfolded. Davis does not portray the actual battle, but instead shows two events that happened immediately afterward. The top engraving is captioned "Custer's Indian Scouts Celebrating the Victory Over Black Kettle." The opposition between the civilized white soldiers and the savage Indian scouts is spelled out in the wild gestures, face paint, and costumes of the group of Osage and Kaw scouts who perform by firelight, and the impassive faces and poses of the white soldiers who watch. The tails that form part of the scouts' costumes reinforce their demonic appearance. This sketch also suggests that Native Americans, as much as European Americans, were responsible for the massacre at Washita River. The US Army took advantage of existing rivalries between indigenous peoples and played one group off against another, promising them land or weapons in exchange for cooperation.

The bottom image shows Custer's soldiers engaged in an activity that the caption describes as "shooting down worthless horses." Again, there is an opposition between the agitated horses and the calm soldiers who shoot them in the head at close range. Thus, the horses—representing nature partially tamed—and Native Americans are visually equated. This would not be the first time that the destruction of animals was seen as parallel to the destruction of Native Americans. The animal in question, however, was usually the buffalo. Just as the destruction of the Cheyenne horses (certainly not "worthless" to them) was part of the military strategy of the 1868–69 campaign, so too was the destruction of buffalo part of a larger military strategy. "Kill every buffalo you can," advised one army officer. "Every buffalo dead is an Indian gone."

The frantic activity contained in the upper and lower sketches contrasts sharply with the stasis of the central image. The words in parentheses after its caption, "The Scalped Hunter," explain this contrast—"Photographed by Wm. S. Soule." As indicated earlier (see p. 233), photographic technology was not yet able to depict objects in motion clearly. While the sketch could capture the action of war, even if only as conceived of in the imagination of the artist, the photograph could capture only its mundane preliminaries or its more deadly aftermath.

This wood engraving after a photograph by William S. Soule contains the one dead person on the magazine page. But this

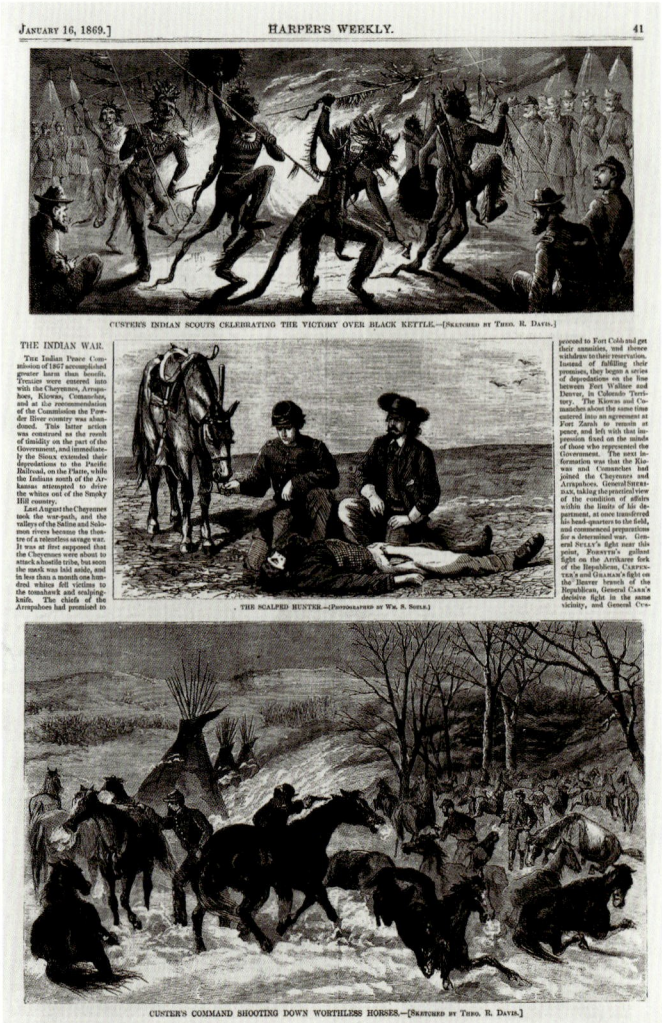

JANUARY 16, 1869.] HARPER'S WEEKLY. 41

CUSTER'S INDIAN SCOUTS CELEBRATING THE VICTORY OVER BLACK KETTLE.—[SKETCHED BY THEO. R. DAVIS.]

THE INDIAN WAR.

THE Indian Peace Commission of 1867 accomplished greater harm than benefit. Treaties were entered into with the Cheyennes, Arrapahoes, Kiowas, Comanches, and at the recommendation of the Commission the Powder River country was abandoned. This latter action was construed as the result of timidity on the part of the Government, and immediately the Sioux extended their depredations to the Pacific Railroad, on the Platte, while the Indians south of the Arkansas attempted to drive the whites out of the Smoky Hill country.

Last August the Cheyennes took the war-path, and the valleys of the Saline and Solomon rivers became the theatre of a relentless savage war. It was at first supposed that the Cheyennes were about to attack a hostile tribe, but soon the mask was laid aside, and in less than a month one hundred whites fell victims to the tomahawk and scalping-knife. The chiefs of the Arrapahoes had promised to proceed to Fort Cobb and get their annuities, and thence withdraw to their reservation. Instead of fulfilling their promises, they began a series of depredations on the line between Fort Wallace and Denver, in Colorado Territory. The Kiowas and Comanches about the same time entered into an agreement at Fort Zarah to remain at peace, and left with that impression fixed on the minds of those who represented the Government. The next information was that the Kiowas and Comanches had joined the Cheyennes and Arrapahoes. General SHERMAN, taking the practical view of the condition of affairs within the limits of his department, at once transferred his head-quarters to the field, and commenced preparations for a determined war. General SELLY's fight near this point, FORSYTH's gallant fight on the Arikaree fork of the Republican, CARPENTER's and GRAHAM's fight on the Beaver branch of the Republican, General CARR's decisive fight in the same vicinity, and General Cus-

THE SCALPED HUNTER.—[PHOTOGRAPHED BY WM. S. SOULE.]

CUSTER'S COMMAND SHOOTING DOWN WORTHLESS HORSES.—[SKETCHED BY THEO. R. DAVIS.]

4.14.2 Theodore R. Davis and William S. Soule: illustrations in *Harper's Weekly*, January 16, 1869.

white man did not die before or during the Washita River battle referred to in the caption to the image directly above. The source of the photograph is included in the *Harper's* article. The hunter Ralph Morrison was murdered and scalped by Cheyenne warriors less than a mile from Fort Dodge, Kansas, on December 7, 1868. Soule, stationed at the fort, "availed himself of the opportunity to benefit science and gratify the curiosity of...readers by taking a counterfeit presentment of the body, literally on the spot."

Soule's photograph was, according to the author of the article, "the only picture ever taken on the Plains of the body of a scalped man, photographed from the corpse itself, and within an hour after the deed was done." The author continues:

> The pose of the remains is delineated exactly as left by the savages, the horrible contortion of the ghastly features, the

> apertures left by the deadly bullet, the reeking scalp, the wounds, the despoiled pockets of the victim, all are true to life anomalous as the presentment of death may seem.

The gruesome detail of this description both titillates the reader and reinforces the veracity of the visual account. This aspect of truthfulness is further guaranteed by the scientific method used to capture the scene—photography—despite the fact that the written description includes elements not readily visible, or not visible at all ("horrible contortion"), in the engraving. The dead body may well have been photographed exactly as it had been found. Yet the two figures behind it, Lieutenant Reade of the Third Infantry on the left and the fort's head scout, John O. Austin, on the right, were obviously posed to create a connection between the dead man and the soldiers who would avenge his death.

The death of one white hunter thus functions visually as a justification for the actions at Washita River as captured in the images at the top and bottom of the page, despite the fact that the hunter was killed ten days after the massacre had occurred. There is, however, a connection between the two locations and the two events. Custer had camped near Fort Dodge with his troops and scouts before heading out on November 12 toward Washita River. After the massacre, he returned to the fort with fifty-three women and children as captives. The Cheyenne attack on the hunter near Fort Dodge, therefore, may well have been retribution for Custer's attack on Washita River.

The Art of Incarceration: The Fort Marion Ledger Drawings

The battles between Native Americans and the US Army continued throughout the late 1860s and early 1870s. In the spring of 1875, at the end of the Red River War, seventy-two Southern Plains chiefs and warriors were imprisoned at Fort Marion (the renamed Castillo de San Marcos [**1.2.1**; p. 29]) in St. Augustine, Florida. These Cheyenne, Kiowa, Arapaho, Comanche, and Caddo were deemed dangerous criminals by the US Government for their wartime aggressions. They were held at Fort Marion to ensure that their people would adjust more peacefully to the reservation life that had been imposed upon them in the aftermath of the recent battles.

During their three years of incarceration, from 1875 to 1878, many of these men filled drawing books with brightly colored images of Native American life on the Plains and of the world of white men and women within which they were forced to live. Such drawings had appeared earlier in the century, after the introduction of the necessary materials to Native Americans by white traders and soldiers. Indeed, the Mandan Mah-To-Toh-Pa [**3.9.5**, p. 177; **3.9.8**, p. 180] was given such materials by Karl Bodmer (1809–1893) during the artist's visit in 1833–34. By the last third of the century this "ledger art," so-called because the paper often came from accountants' ledgers and was thus lined, was a significant presence alongside the traditional painted buffalo hides within indigenous culture. (Often the ledgers already contained entries by their previous white owners, over which Native Americans drew their images.) Because it evolved during a time of radical transition within southern Plains culture, ledger art also functioned as a testimony to the changes and adjustments being made by Plains peoples.

One example of a Cheyenne ledger drawing from the early 1870s was discovered in the papers of Captain John Gregory Bourke, an aide-de-camp to General George Crook of the 3rd US Cavalry in Wyoming Territory [**4.14.3**; p. 252]. The work, datable to 1871–76, shows Last Bull, Head Chief of the Kit Fox Society (he is identified by his shield and his Kit Fox Society bow lance), capturing a horse. This capture occurs during a battle, indicated by the bullets that fly past Last Bull but do not stop him. As is typical of ledger art, and of its antecedents found on the animal hides examined in earlier chapters [**1.2.24**, p. 44; **3.9.7**, p. 179], the figures are two-dimensional, with clear, dark outlines that are carefully filled in with flat areas of color. Human figures and animals are shown in profile and the action proceeds from right to left. This arrangement is common in most ledger art depicting battles or hunting scenes (when two individuals face each other, the victor is almost always positioned on the right).

The exploits of warriors and hunters, along with scenes of courting, were the most common subject matter of ledger art. Books of drawings produced by men were powerful autobiographical statements and were often taken along into battle. In all three categories of images the horse played a key role, whether as a warrior's mount, war booty, or an indication of a man's status. The introduction of horses by the Spanish in the seventeenth century transformed the lives of Native Americans on the Plains, enhancing their ability both to hunt buffalo and to wage war. Horses connoted power, both military and personal, and were key to a male warrior's identity. It is little wonder, then, that horses played such a dominant role in the pictorial art of Plains peoples throughout the nineteenth century.

In the last quarter of that century, however, as Native Americans were increasingly confined to reservations, the horse came to symbolize not only the personal exploits of individuals, but also the ethnic identity of Plains peoples as a whole. As the art historian David W. Penney has pointed out, reservation life offered little opportunity for men to distinguish themselves in battle, or in the hunting of buffalo, the herds of which had been depleted by the 1880s. Yet men and women continued to produce images of mounted warriors and hunters in their

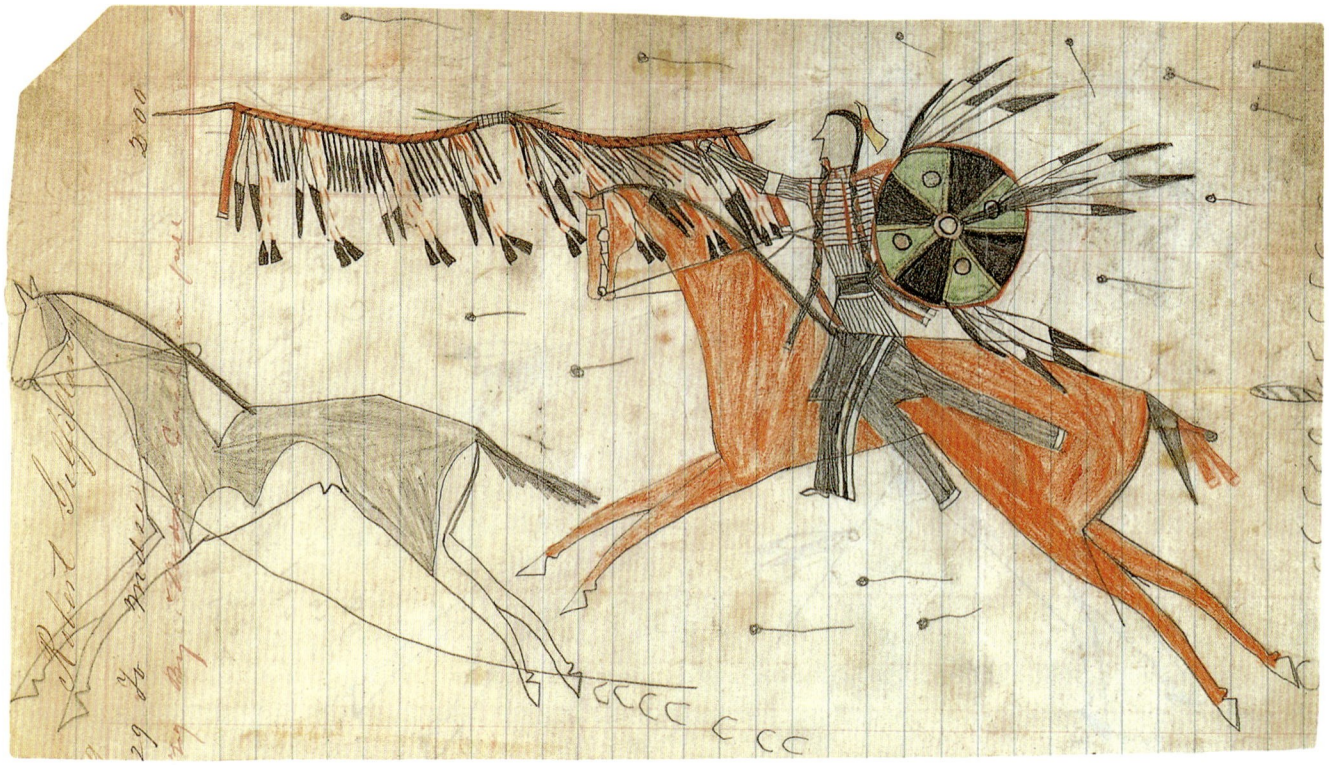

4.14.3 Unknown artist, Cheyenne: *Last Bull Captures a Horse*, 1871–76. Pencil and colored pencil on paper, 6⅞ x 10½ in. (17.7 x 26.7 cm.) United States Military Academy Library, West Point, New York

paintings and beadwork. These figures "gave testimony to the great accomplishments of that earlier generation whose memory was thus kept alive" and became symbols of "solidarity and difference in relation to others."

Captain Bourke acquired his books of drawings as did many other US soldiers, either by ransacking Indian camps and battlefields or by purchasing them from their makers, other military men, or traders (his collection contained more than a thousand drawings). Bourke presented a large display of these drawings in Omaha in 1881, catering to a growing public interest in works by Native Americans.

Another military officer, Colonel Garrick Mallery, had contributed to this public interest. In 1877 he had published an article on a Winter Count, or calendrical history, covering the period 1800 to 1876 by the Lakota (Sioux) Lone Dog. Each year is represented by one or two pictographs recording a notable event of that year. The article caught the attention of the federal government. The US Geological and Geographical Survey then hired Mallery to conduct research on the indigenous peoples of North America. Five years later the Bureau of American Ethnology devoted its entire annual report to his 822-page *Picture-Writing of the American Indians*. In this work Mallery noted that these pictographs were made "with intention and care—seldom for mere amusement. Even when the labor is undertaken merely to supply the trade demand for painted robes or engraved pipes or bark records, it is a serious manufacture."

This was certainly true of the works produced at Fort Marion. Captain Richard H. Pratt encouraged the artistic efforts of his prisoners by providing them with drawing materials and allowing them to sell their books of drawings for two dollars each to the tourists who often visited the fort (the prisoners also sold bows, arrows, fans, and pottery). The books were part of Pratt's larger attempt to reform his Native American charges through education, religious instruction, and hard work. This effort had obvious connections to the broader penal reforms that were under discussion throughout the nation (see pp. 118–21). The material produced was soon in great demand. One might argue, in fact, that the popularity of the Fort Marion work helped spur the vogue for ledger drawings and other objects decorated with indigenous designs among European Americans in the last decades of the nineteenth century. The art historian Janet Catherine Berlo notes that in the 1890s in particular, a "brisk commerce in beadwork, basketry, pottery, and many other goods swept across the nation. Of special interest were small items and miniatures that could be displayed in a Victorian parlor or in an 'Indian corner.'"

There was thus a new audience for the products of these Native American artists—white tourists rather than fellow warriors or members of the artist's village or the occasional soldier or trapper. This new audience, along with the fact of the artists' imprisonment, had a decided effect on the subject matter of the drawings. Scenes from the train journey to Fort Marion and from daily life at the fort now appeared, leading to new representations of encounters between European Americans and Native Americans. At least one of the artists, the Cheyenne Howling Wolf, also had extensive contact with European artistic traditions during a trip to Boston for medical treatment. This trip resulted in certain stylistic changes in his work, notably an increased use of landscape elements and a painterliness that countered the two-dimensionality of his earlier ledger art.

In *Fort Marion Prisoners Dancing for Tourists* (1875–77) [**4.14.4**] the Cheyenne warrior Cohoe presents his own interpretation of the theme of the "savage" Indian entertaining "civilized" European Americans that had been represented by Theodore R. Davis approximately six years earlier in his *Harper's* sketch [**4.14.2**; p. 250]. There are striking differences between the two images. While Davis places the viewer at eye level, within the circle of army officers, Cohoe presents a double perspective. The viewer is simultaneously on the same level as the group (the figures are represented as if the viewer is standing in front of or behind them) and above it. The overall feeling is of distance or removal, as opposed to the inclusiveness of Davis's piece. Davis creates a sense of three-dimensionality through the use of shading and perspectival conventions (for example, the overlapping of figures or their decreasing size as they recede into the background). Cohoe, on the other hand, creates a two-dimensional image through the use of flat areas of color and clearly outlined figures of equal size placed in a space devoid of ground lines or other orientational markers.

Davis pays great attention to the costumes of the dancing scouts, while Cohoe pays equal attention to the costumes of the white tourists, particularly those of the women. The identities of his figures appear, indeed, to lie in their clothing rather than their facial features, for their faces are left completely blank. One of the effects of the adoption of paper and pencil or watercolor on Native American imagery was an increase in detail. Such detail was more readily produced with pencils or pens or manufactured brushes than with the stick and bone brushes used earlier to paint on hide. The only man dressed in a soldier's outfit, standing to the right of the dancers, may well

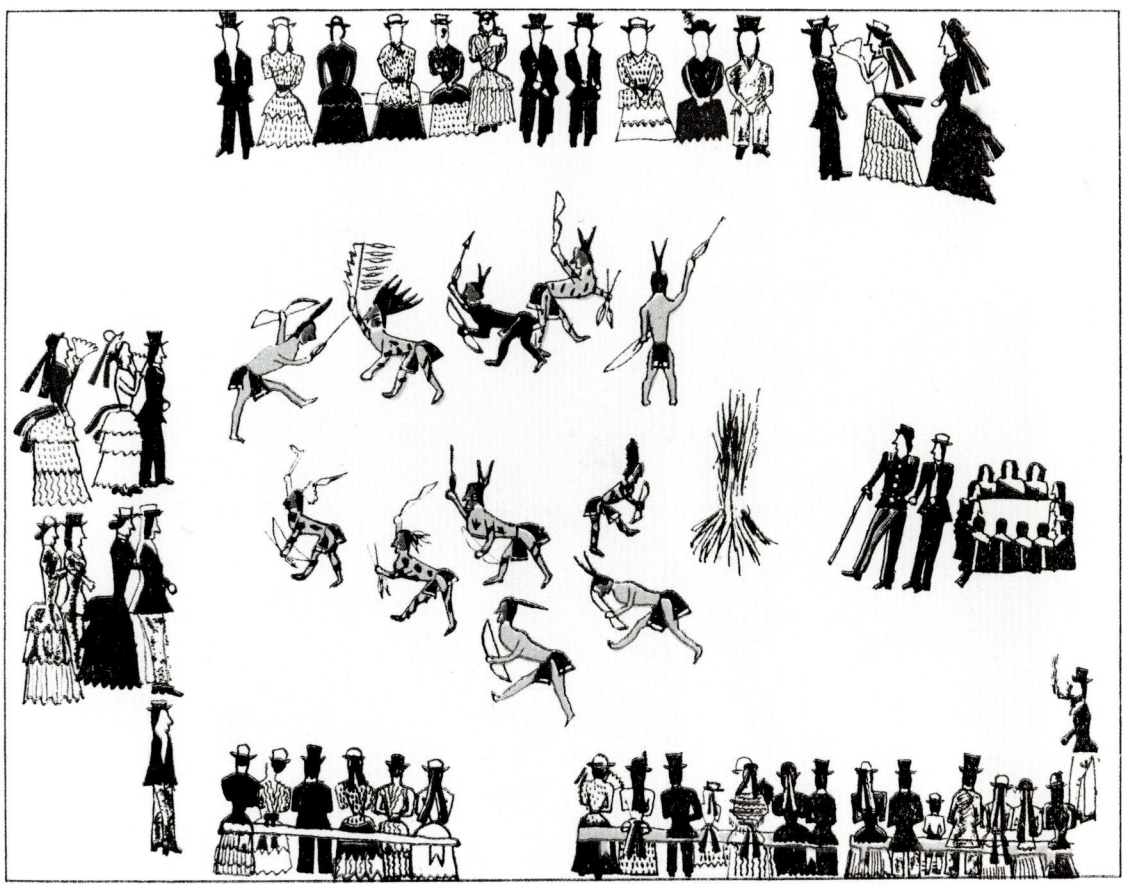

4.14.4 Cohoe, Cheyenne: *Fort Marion Prisoners Dancing for Tourists*, 1875–77. Pencil and colored pencil on paper
Private collection

have been Captain Pratt, while the circle of Native American figures behind the two standing men could represent drummers or chanters (or both).

Both Davis and Cohoe were creating for white audiences, but from strikingly different positions. The European American artist Davis was creating within the conventions of Western art for an employer committed to the sensationalizing of information. He was also creating for an audience eager to experience—vicariously, of course—some of the drama of the frontier, an audience that, for the most part, had accepted the distinction between savage and civilized that is embedded in Davis's image. The Cheyenne prisoner Cohoe was drawing upon the conventions of Plains hide painting to create images primarily for white tourists. These tourists wanted to take with them a souvenir of their trip to what Berlo describes as an "idealized penal colony, where a miniature but representative society of Plains warriors enacts scaled-down and sanitized simulacra of warfare for their captors' pleasure." The three-dimensionality and mimetic nature of Davis's work read as real to the white viewer; the two-dimensionality of Cohoe's work read as childlike and naive. The tourists who left Fort Marion thus took with them, in Berlo's words, "a memento of their voyeuristic experience, secure in their privileged insight into 'the Indian Problem' and its solutions."

Cohoe's fellow prisoners would have read his image differently. Having experienced, themselves, the indignity of having to don traditional dress to perform for tourists, or having watched others do so, they may well have read the scene as one of humiliation rather than pleasurable entertainment. The two-dimensional style would have signified not "childlikeness" but their own art traditions. The tourist audience, arranged in rigid order around the dancers, would have conveyed a sense of the dancers' own entrapment, both literally at Fort Marion and figuratively within a foreign culture. In fact, the rectilinear positioning of the tourists around the circular arrangements of Native Americans suggests the importance of the free-flowing circle in Native American life as opposed to the box-like architectural forms and the penchant for order, symmetry, and conformity so ever-present at Fort Marion.

Yet the continuation of their ceremonies and their visual arts traditions, in however compromised a form, may also have functioned as a means of resistance to the imposed white order. Through their drawings, the imprisoned chiefs and warriors represented their experiences at Fort Marion not only for themselves and for white tourists, but also for their own people. They often sent drawings to their families as "letters" and received similar pictographic responses in return.

The Kiowa prisoner Wo-Haw (1855–1924) also created an image that spoke to the entrapment of Native Americans within white culture. In *Classroom at Fort Marion* (1875–77) [**4.14.5**] he depicts, again in the flat, two-dimensional Plains style, a schoolroom scene where nine warriors, in Western suits with

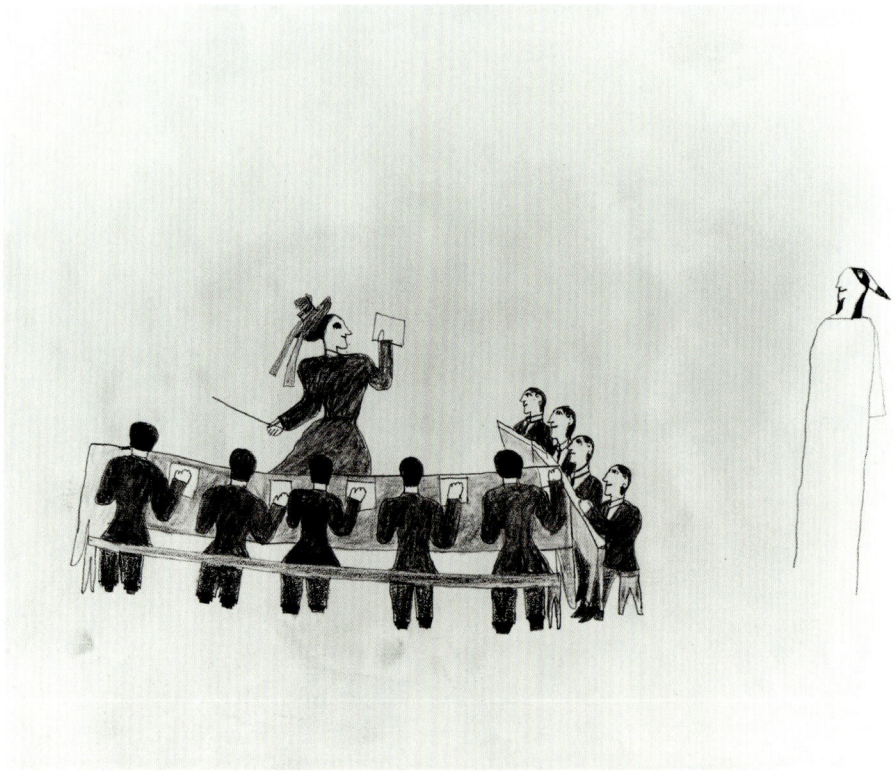

4.14.5 Wo-Haw, Kiowa: *Classroom at Fort Marion*, 1875–77.
Pencil and crayon on paper, 8¾ x 11¼ in. (22.2 x 28.5 cm.)
Missouri Historical Society, St. Louis, Missouri

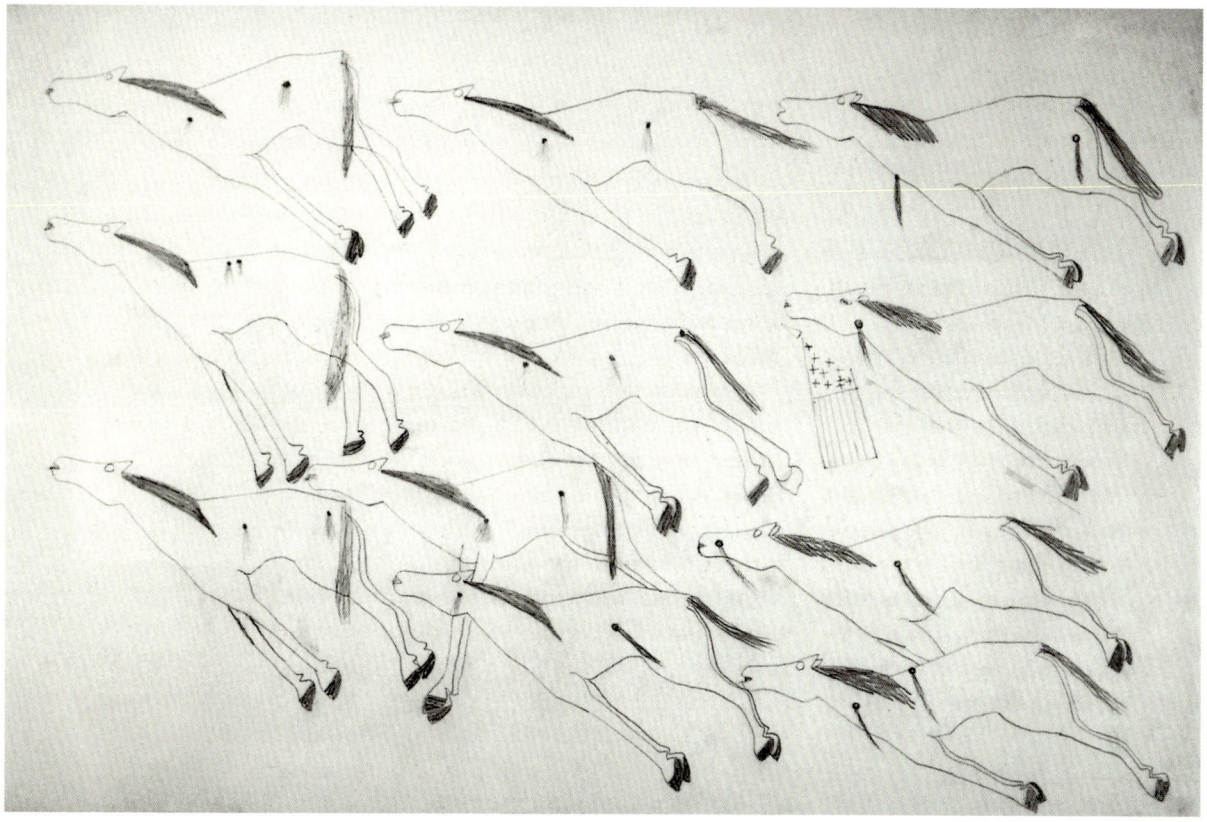

4.14.6 Red Horse, Minneconjou Lakota: *Dead Cavalry Horses*, 1881. Pencil and colored pencil on paper, 8¾ x 11¼ in. (22.2 x 28.5 cm.) National Anthropological Archives, National Museum of Natural History, Smithsonian Institution, Washington, D.C.

hair shorn, attentively watch the female teacher in the center. Wo-Haw has also absorbed certain Western artistic conventions, positioning the teacher behind the long table and placing a shorter table at right angles to suggest a three-dimensional space. While the students turn their attention to the teacher in front of them, they are, at the same time, being watched, not by another white teacher or soldier but by the spectral form of a Native American with a feather in his long hair. Here is the ghostly presence of that culture from which these warriors have been forcibly removed, a culture that their white captors want them to forget or to replicate only for the amusement of tourists.

The Battle of the Little Bighorn

Throughout the nineteenth century two solutions had been proposed to the "Indian problem": extermination and assimilation. The need for a solution became even greater after the defeat of General George Armstrong Custer and his troops on June 25–26, 1876, at the Battle of the Little Bighorn in southeast Montana. Coming upon an encampment of more than 7,000 Lakota, Cheyenne, and Arapaho on the Little Bighorn River, Custer underestimated its size. He thought his 700 men of the 7th Cavalry could destroy it as easily as they had the village of Native Americans camped along the Washita River eight years earlier (see p. 249). He was sorely mistaken, losing not only the battle, but also his own life and the lives of 258 of his men.

The Battle of the Little Bighorn was recorded five years later in a series of forty-two large drawings by one of the participants, the Minneconjou Lakota Red Horse. In a poignant testimony to its aftermath, Red Horse depicts a field of dead horses [**4.14.6**]. Given the high regard in which horses were held by Native Americans, it is not surprising that Red Horse resists the sensationalizing engaged in by Theodore R. Davis, who showed the frantic horses in the act of being slaughtered at Washita River [**4.14.2**; p. 250]. Instead, through an economy of means, he presents us with horses whose physical weight has dissolved. Their bodies appear to float in a timeless space, anchored to the historical moment only by the small American flag positioned in front of the only horse whose eyes have not yet closed, whose last breath has yet to be taken.

The Cheyenne Hehúwésse or Yellow Nose (*c.* 1852–1914) provides a more dramatic rendition of the actual encounter at the Little Bighorn in four drawings produced around 1885. In one [**4.14.7**; p. 256] he shows himself riding into the enemy camp and performing his most famous exploit of the battle, the capture of a US flag and his subsequent use of it to "count coup,"

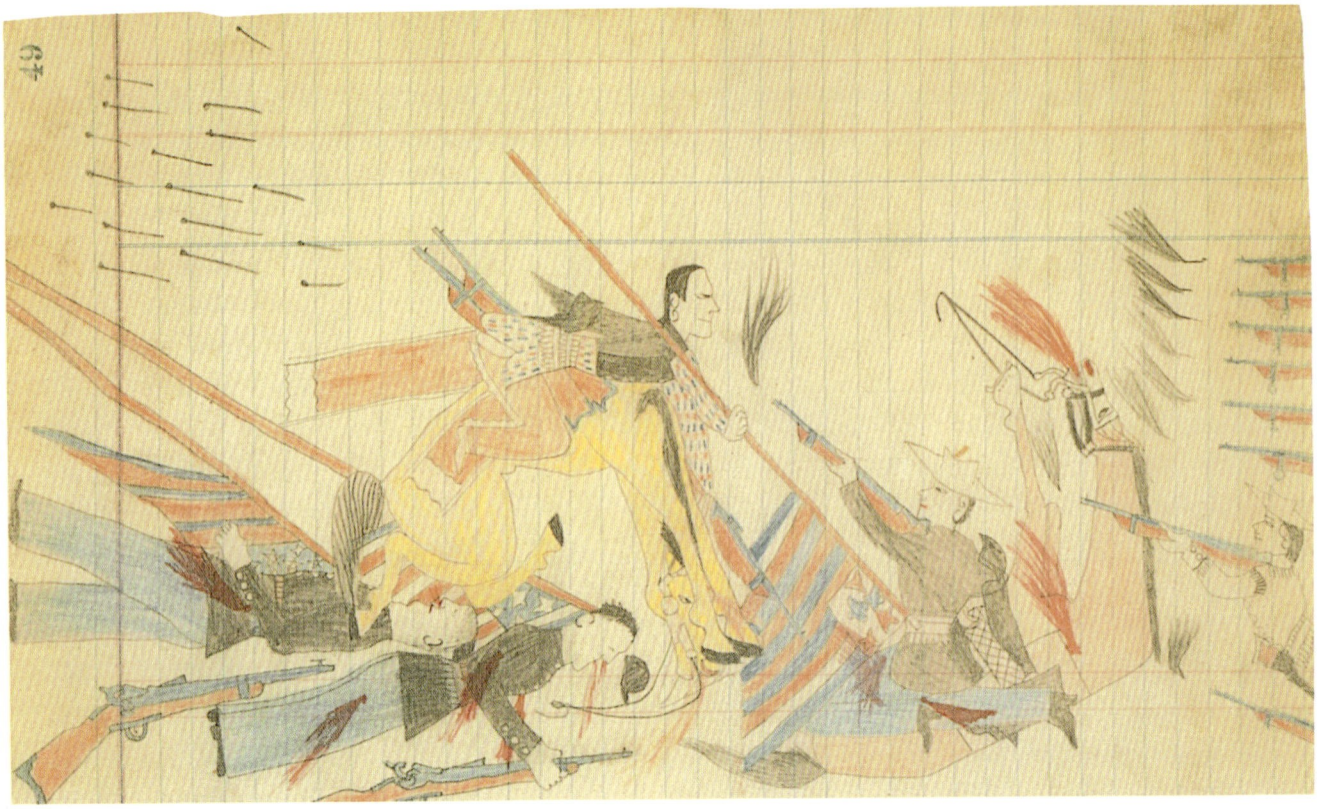

4.14.7 Yellow Nose (Hehúwésse), Cheyenne: *Drawing of the Battle of the Little Big Horn*, c. 1885.
Pencil and colored pencil on paper, 12½ x 7¼ in. (31.7 x 18.4 cm.)
National Anthropological Archives, National Museum of Natural History, Smithsonian Institution, Washington, D.C.

i.e. to touch the enemy. The drawing shows him counting coup on a soldier whose mount has collapsed beneath him. Yellow Nose's drawing is a far cry from the pictographs of riders found on hides in the first part of the nineteenth century [**1.2.24**, p. 44; **3.9.7**, p. 179]. While the figures are still formed of clear outlines and filled in with flat areas of color, Yellow Nose's horse, almost doubled in half as it charges, is without precedent in its presentation of energy and movement.

Custer's defeat provided ammunition for those assimilationists who argued against the policy of creating reservations for Native Americans. Their objections were not that the policy deprived indigenous peoples of land that was rightfully theirs, but that such peoples, despite being on reservations, still remained a threat to surrounding white communities and to European Christian ways. An article in an issue of *Frank Leslie's Popular Monthly* (September 1876) suggested that not only reservations, but also the entire Indian way of life should be abolished; Indians should be given trousers and shirts instead of blankets. Such an approach was also promoted a decade later by the Friends of the Indians, which included many wealthy philanthropists and Protestant clergymen. They felt that Native Americans should be given membership in American society in exchange for a repudiation of their culture. The Friends lobbied in support of the Dawes Act, passed by Congress in 1887, which offered an allotment of land and eligibility for full citizenship to every Native American male who willingly cut his ties with his people and adopted the habits of European American life.

Yet the author of the article in *Frank Leslie's Popular Monthly* also acknowledged that there had been greater success in assimilating Africans and Chinese than Indians. This was due largely to the fact that the former had been removed from their homelands and cultures, making their immediate survival in this new country more dependent upon assimilation. It was not a new country for Native Americans, and their sense of entitlement to their ancestral lands and ways of life was strong. Assimilation was successful only after a large percentage of Native Americans had been killed, and then only partially successful. The land on which they lived, and continue to live, functioned as a reminder of their culture and their history, as did their ledger drawings. Janet Catherine Berlo fittingly describes the ledger books as "encyclopedias of experience," records of both spiritual and individual history that "depict the comprehensiveness of the Plains Indian worldview in the second half of the 19th century." The art historian Anna Blume adds:

> In the turbulent years at the end of the nineteenth century, there was an interconnected web of killing and writing, drawing and photographing on the Great Plains. Ledger books, with their drawings by Native Americans, exist in the interstices between writing, drawing, and violence; their production is a metaphor for history in the Great Plains itself.

While the production of ledger art declined after the early 1890s, its stylistic influence remained and played a strong role in a revival of Plains painting in the 1920s and 1930s (see V. 2, pp. 409–411).

The End of the Ghost Dance

Despite being outnumbered, Native Americans continued to engage in armed resistance against the US Army until 1890, when this resistance was finally broken in a battle between the Lakota and the US Army at Wounded Knee Creek, South Dakota, on December 29. More than two hundred Lakota men, women, and children died. Their burial in a mass grave was delayed two days by a blizzard. On January 1, 1891, George E. Trager (1861–after 1895) recorded the scene in a photograph entitled *The End of the Ghost Dance* [**4.14.8**]. US soldiers stand, weapons in hand, by the large hole in the ground, stacked high with the frozen bodies of the dead. They assume the position of proud hunters, the Native American bodies equated with the Indian ponies and buffalo that met a similar fate at the hands of these same soldiers or their counterparts [**4.14.2**; p. 250; **4.14.6**, p. 255].

The title of Trager's photograph refers to the Ghost Dance movement, begun around 1889 in the Nevada region by Wovoka, a Paiute visionary. Wovoka prophesied that a time would come when white people would be no more, the land would be returned to indigenous peoples, and peace would reign. The beginning of this new era would be marked by the appearance of a messiah or savior figure, and the transformation would be non-violent: whites would simply disappear, along with persecution, hunger, and disease. All generations, both living and dead, would then coexist together in a perfect world. The similarity to the Christian Last Judgment narrative is not surprising, for many such combinations of Western European and indigenous cultural and religious traditions existed in the US by the end of the nineteenth century. Despite the non-violent aspect of Wovoka's prophecy, it instilled fear in many European American settlers and prompted the army to step up its attacks on the final pockets of Native American resistance.

The Ghost Dance movement is among the best known of several such millenarian movements, which evolved out of the extreme hardships endured by Native Americans in the

4.14.8 George E. Trager: *The End of the Ghost Dance*, 1891. Photograph
Nebraska State Historical Society, Lincoln

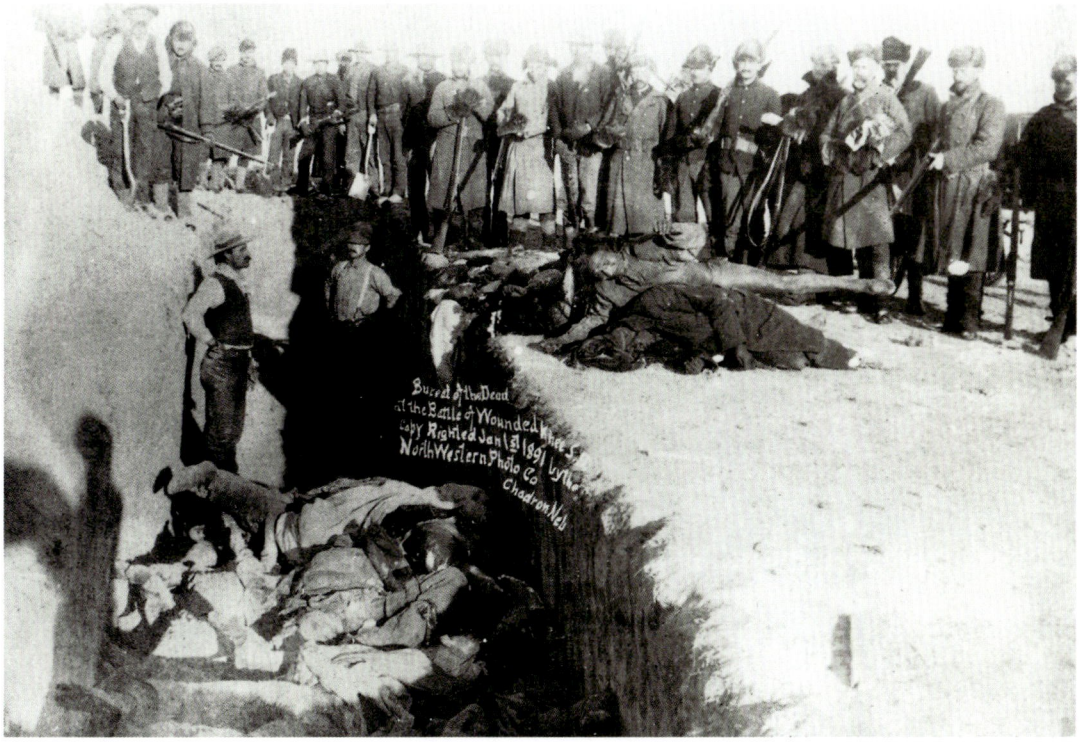

early years of the reservation period. It represented a form of resistance to the social, political, and economic orders being imposed upon these peoples, and spawned its own ceremonies and ritual objects. The movement extended throughout the Plains. While regional variations existed in the ceremonies and the decoration of ritual objects, all those who adopted the Ghost Dance performed a distinctive circle dance, which was meant to hasten the arrival of the new era. In many Plains areas, men and women took part together, a practice unprecedented in earlier dance ceremonies. Individuals would often go into a trance and collapse while the dancing continued around them.

In 1891 Yellow Nose was commissioned by the anthropologist James Mooney to depict a Ghost Dance ceremony on a deer hide [**4.14.9**]. Here the circle of men and women follows the edges of the hide. Arapaho women are distinguished from Cheyenne women by their hairstyles (the former have loose hair, while the hair of the latter is braided). The costumes of the dancers are rendered with the same attention to detailed patterning as the attire of the white women in Cohoe's drawing [**4.14.4**; p. 253]. At least two people have fallen to the ground in a trance. One woman on the lower edge holds a stuffed crow, a bird associated with the Ghost Dance, while others hold handkerchiefs and a hoop or baqati wheel.

While Yellow Nose records several aspects of the dancers' costumes, such as stripes, dots, and belts containing disks of German silver, he does not show the detailed imagery that characterized Ghost Dance shirts and dresses. Fortunately, several of these items of clothing still exist. Two Arapaho dresses from *c.* 1890 provide a glossary of Ghost Dance symbols. Those on the first dress [**4.14.10**] are primarily astral. The yoke contains two forms representing stars—the two rows of circles at the top and the two rows of Maltese crosses (all four arms of the cross are of equal length) at the bottom. The latter represent the morning star, which may allude to the coming of a new era. In the center of the yoke is a crescent moon. The eagle feathers may refer to the belief that eagles carried Ghost Dancers to the other world, where they met their ancestors and tasted the world of peace and prosperity that was to come. Thus the symbolism on this dress firmly locates its wearer within the cosmic universe of a spiritual and cultural revival.

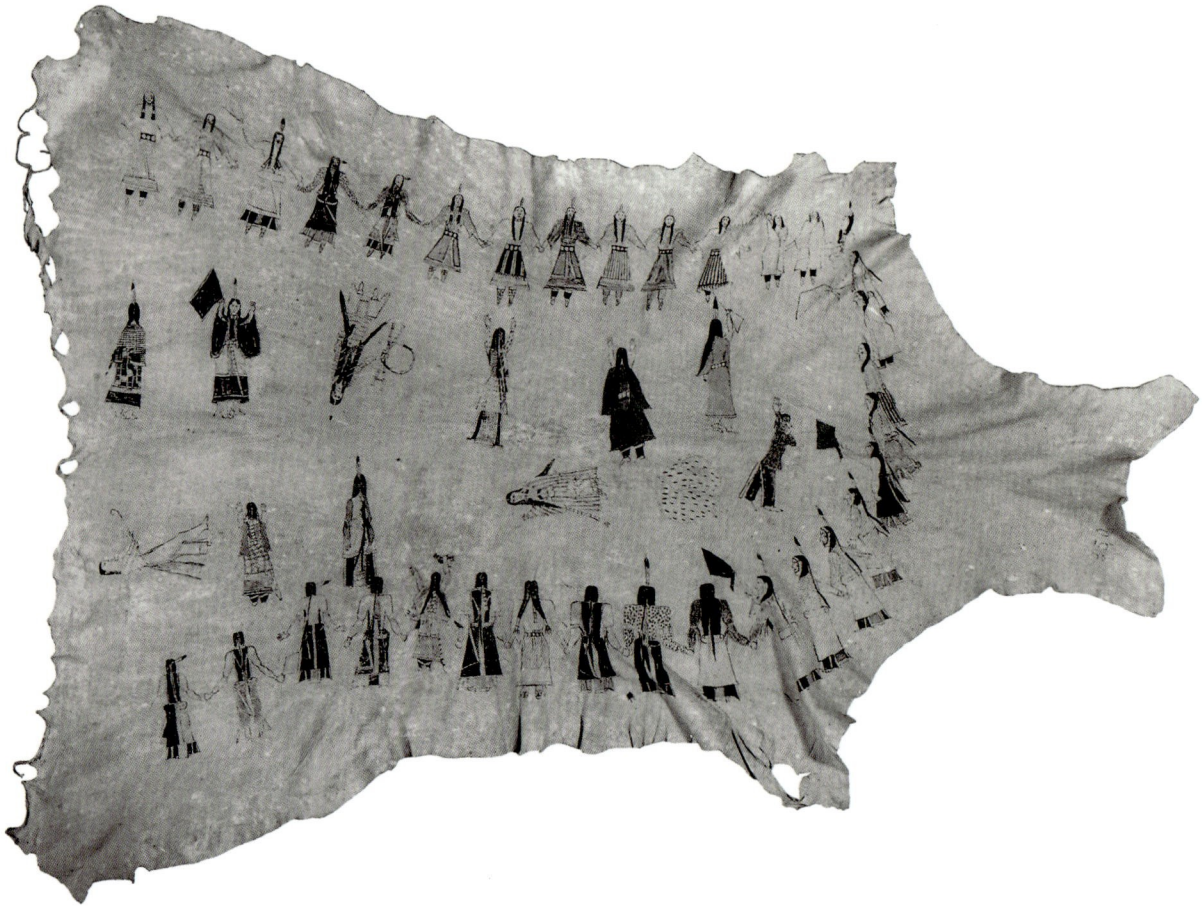

4.14.9 Yellow Nose (Hehúwésse), Cheyenne: robe depicting the Ghost Dance, 1891. Colored ink on deerskin, 39 x 49⅝ in. (99.1 x 125.7 cm.)
National Museum of Natural History, Smithsonian Institution, Washington, D.C.

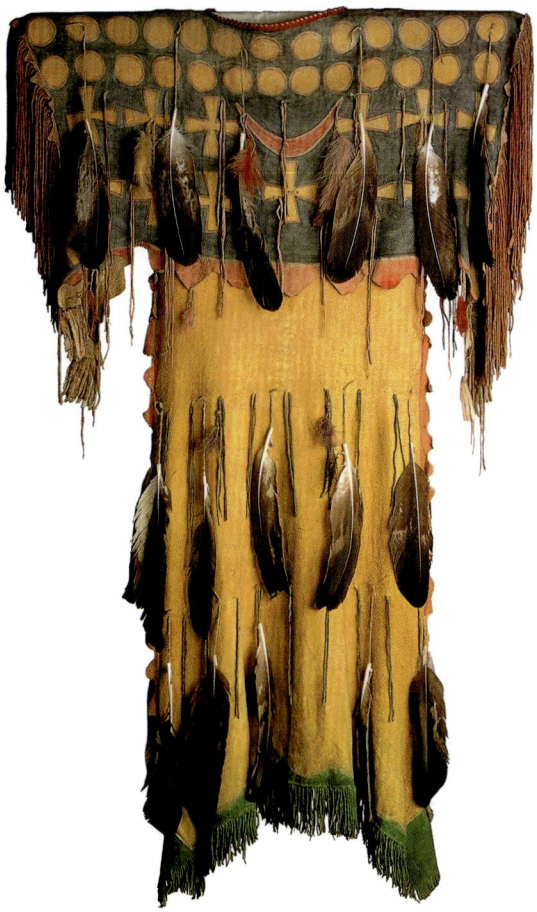

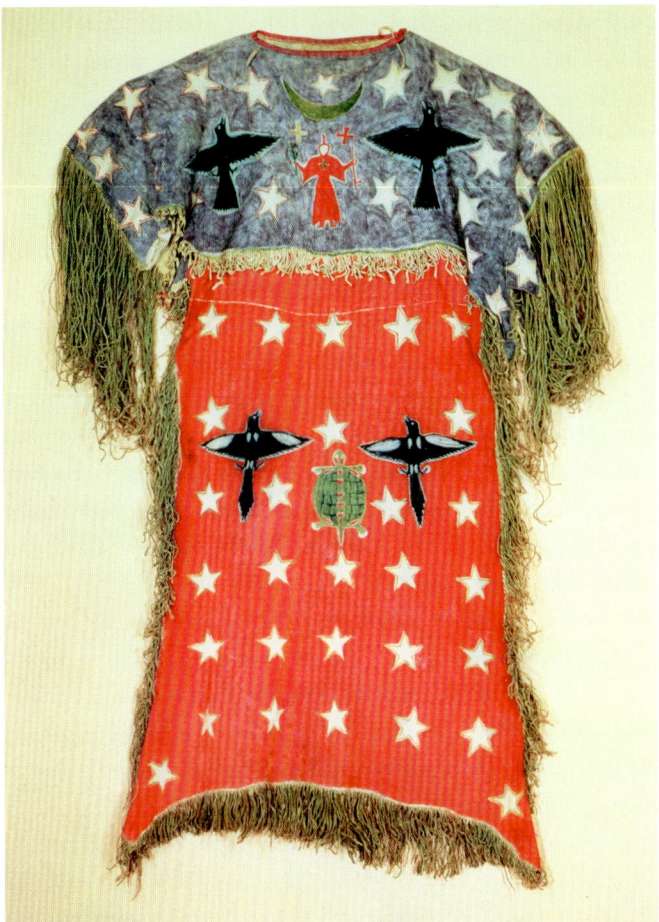

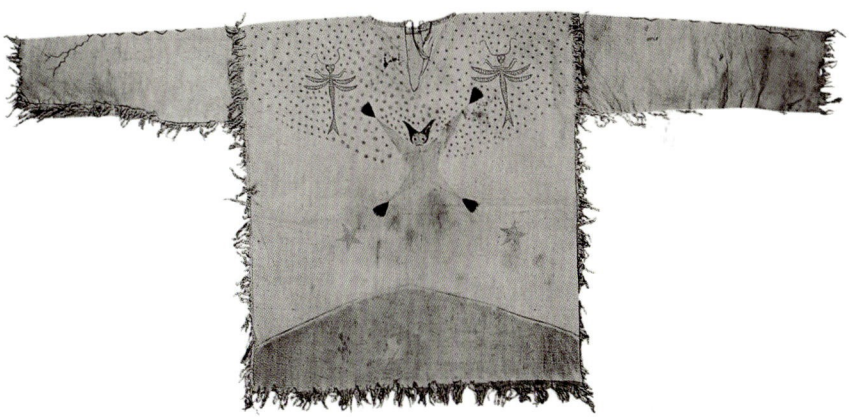

4.14.10 Unknown artist, Arapaho (Inuna-ina): Ghost Dance dress, *c.* 1890. Hide with pigment and eagle feathers, 57½ x 35 in. (146.1 x 89 cm.) Logan Museum of Anthropology, Beloit College, Beloit, Wisconsin

4.14.11 Unknown artist, Arapaho (Inuna-ina): Ghost Dance dress with painted design of birds, turtle, and stars. Buckskin, 21½ in. (55 cm.) long Museum of the North American Indian, New York

4.14.12 Attributed to Little Wound, Oglala Lakota: Ghost Dance shirt, 1890–91. Cotton muslin, pigment, and commercial leather, 34¼ x 32½ in. (87 x 82.6 cm.) University Museum, University of Pennsylvania, Philadelphia

The second dress [**4.14.11**] also includes astral symbols, this time in the form of five-pointed stars, suggesting a source in American flags and military paraphernalia. The yoke, however, contains the figure of a woman flanked by two eagles. In her left hand she holds a pipe, symbolic of peace, and in her right hand a branch, perhaps a sage bundle. Above her are two Maltese crosses, as well as a crescent moon, and in her hair is a feather. The turtle in the center of the dress is a symbol of the creation of the earth and is flanked by two magpies. These birds were admired for their swift flight and iridescent feathers.

Many Plains people believed that Ghost Dance clothing performed a protective function, like a shield, preventing the wearer from being harmed by bullets or other weapons. Some dancers even referred to the painted bib area or yoke of dresses and shirts as the "shield." This protective function was also associated with another group of Ghost Dance symbols, several of which are found on an Oglala Lakota Ghost Dance shirt from 1890–91 that has been attributed to Little Wound [**4.14.12**]. The yoke is marked by a dot pattern representing a hail of bullets. Among the dots are two dragonflies, known for their quick, darting movements, thus allowing them to dodge the hail of bullets. A head has been added to the large four-pointed star in the center of the shirt, thus anthropomorphizing it and turning it into a five-pointed star. The back of the shirt also contains a cluster of bullets around the neck and a splayed eagle with jagged lines of power or lightning coming from its claws.

Imagery, however, was not able to protect the wearers against the onslaught that descended on Native Americans at Wounded Knee or at other battles of the last decade of the nineteenth century. With little hope now of the arrival of a new era, the Ghost Dance movement slowly disappeared. The notion of a return to an earlier time survived, however, and prompted additional revivals of older cultural forms that had fallen into disuse. Such revivals would take on a new dimension in the early twentieth century under the guiding hand of European American entrepreneurs (see V. 2, pp. 389–93).

Several European American artists also produced images of the Ghost Dance. One of the most dramatic of these representations is a life-size bronze statue by Paul Wayland Bartlett (1865–1925) entitled *The Indian Ghost Dancer* (1888–89) [**4.14.13**]. Bartlett produced the work while he was in Paris, and the plaster model, from which the bronze statue was cast, was exhibited at the Paris Salon of 1889. Through a highly textured surface, intense facial expression, and exaggerated pose, he conveys the trance-like state of exhaustion experienced by a Ghost Dancer. Of course, these dancers wore elaborate costumes rather than performing in the nude. As a young sculptor attempting to establish himself in the art worlds of France and the US, however, Bartlett needed to prove his ability to model the human form. The expressiveness of his figure contrasts with the staid and dignified poses of Harriet Hosmer's *Zenobia in Chains* [**4.13.5**; p. 242] and Edmonia Lewis's *Forever Free* [**4.13.6**; p. 243]. This expressiveness is testimony to Bartlett's apprenticeship with Auguste Rodin (1840–1917), the leader of sculptural innovation in Paris. He was an assistant in Rodin's studio in the late 1880s and early 1890s.

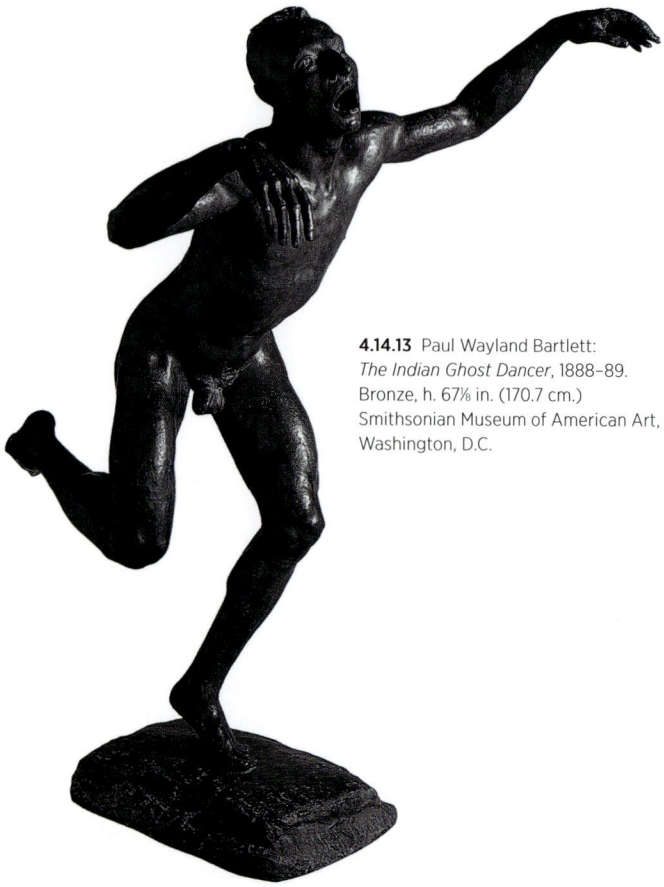

4.14.13 Paul Wayland Bartlett: *The Indian Ghost Dancer*, 1888–89. Bronze, h. 67⅞ in. (170.7 cm.) Smithsonian Museum of American Art, Washington, D.C.

Nonetheless, Bartlett did not support many of the artistic movements flourishing in Paris under the general rubric "Modernism" in the late nineteenth century. Rather, he saw the self-absorption, sensuality, and lack of rigorous training evident in the life-styles and work of these artists as "subversive." In 1913 he spoke of Modernist artists as having "the mentality of epileptics" and as gathering in studios "where painting is only a vicious daubing, and where deformities, holes and humps pass for sculpture." The art historian Thomas P. Somma argues, in fact, that *The Indian Ghost Dancer* is not only a statement about the practice of Ghost Dancing and, by association, the barbaric nature of Native Americans, but it is also a reference to the irrational, undisciplined, and irresponsible world of the Modernist artist. In this world, self-absorption and trance-like states prevent artists from acquiring the qualities of industriousness, rationalism, and competition that traditionally were perceived as the hallmarks of true artistic genius. Such attacks on Modernist art would multiply in the early twentieth century as the formal innovations of European Modernism made their way across the Atlantic (see V. 2, Chapter 19).

The Hampton Institute and Lessons in American History

Debates over the character of European artistic vision and practice were certainly far from the minds of Native Americans in the 1880s and 1890s. This did not mean, however, that they did not take part in discussions about the nature of education in general and the continuation of their own cultural practices in particular. Many who survived the battles and deprivations of the time ended up in educational institutions established specifically for Native Americans and/or freed African Americans. One of these was the Hampton Institute, a co-educational normal school set up in 1868 for freed blacks, with a program for Native Americans added in 1877. Its founder, Samuel Chapman Armstrong, was born in Hawaii, the son of missionaries. His father, as the Minister of Public Instruction at Honolulu, viewed

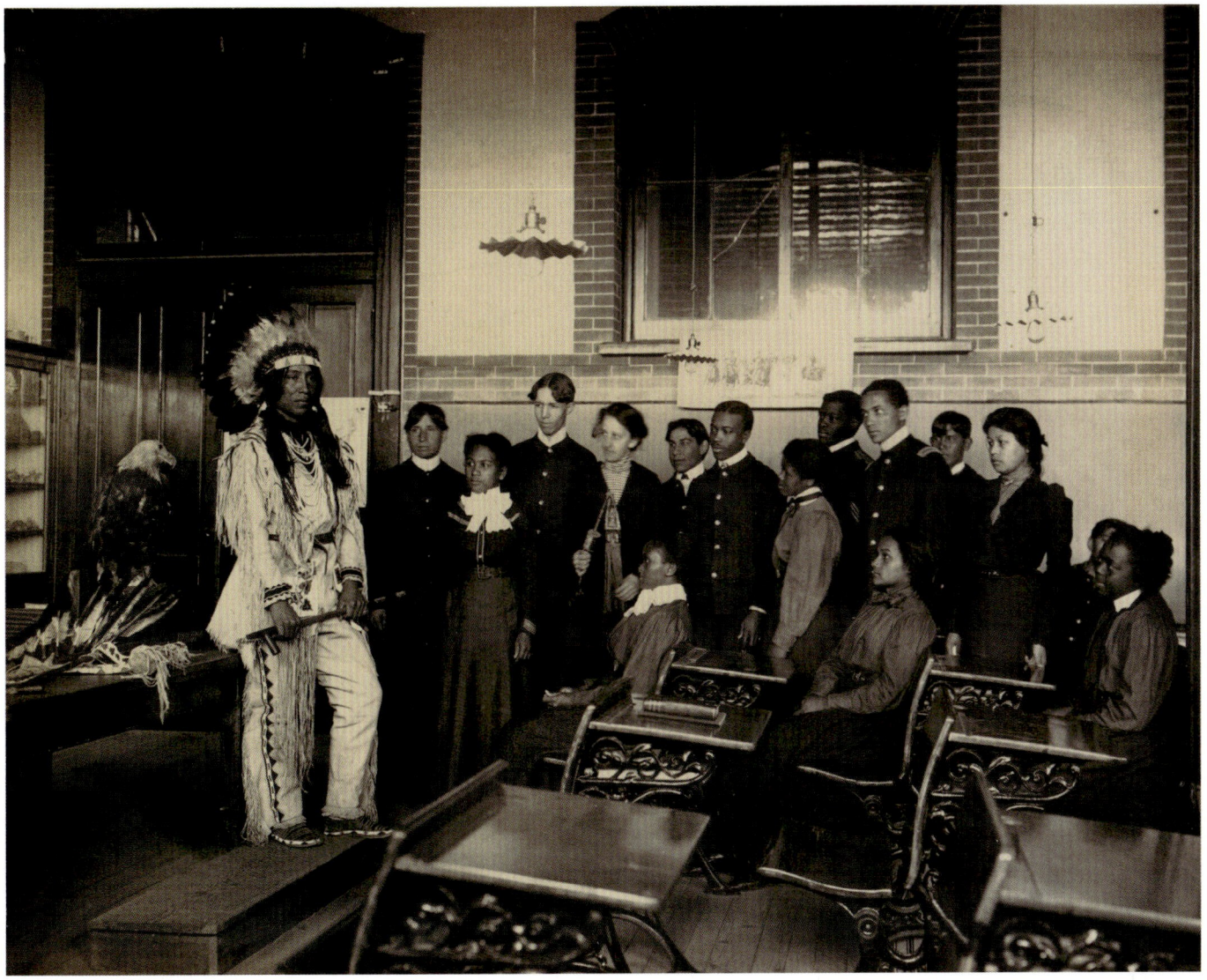

4.14.14 Frances Benjamin Johnston: *Class in American History*, 1899–1900. Photograph
Library of Congress, Washington, D.C.

indigenous Hawaiians as "lazy people" and believed that their education must include physical labor if they were truly going to become civilized. Samuel Armstrong maintained this commitment to physical labor and practical skills at the Hampton Institute. He also inherited some of his father's mistrust of dark-skinned people, writing in 1862, after having joined the Union Army, "I am sort of an abolitionist, but I have not learned to love the Negro." Even after having led a regiment of black soldiers for the final two years of the war, he noted in 1865 that he felt "the colored soldier had not done enough" to have proved himself the equal of the white soldier.

Upon leaving the army, Armstrong was granted a position with the Freedmen's Bureau as superintendent of the Ninth Subdistrict of Virginia. In this capacity, he gathered around him a group of individuals committed to his cause of educating future African American teachers and leaders, helping them to adapt to existing social and political norms. The same goal was later set for Native Americans. They were to receive vocational and religious training at his institute and then return to their reservations to pass on the knowledge they had gained.

In the late 1890s the Washington photographer Frances Benjamin Johnston (1864–1952) was commissioned by the Hampton Institute to create a series of photographs marking its success. This series was shown at the Universal Exposition in Paris in 1900 as part of an exhibit tracing the rapid progress of African Americans since the end of the Civil War. One of the photographs was *Class in American History* [**4.14.14**]. As in Wo-Haw's drawing [**4.14.5**, p. 254], Native Americans in European garb with cropped hair (here joined by African Americans) are pictured with a Native American in "traditional" dress. He is not a ghostly presence, however; nor is he evidence of a living

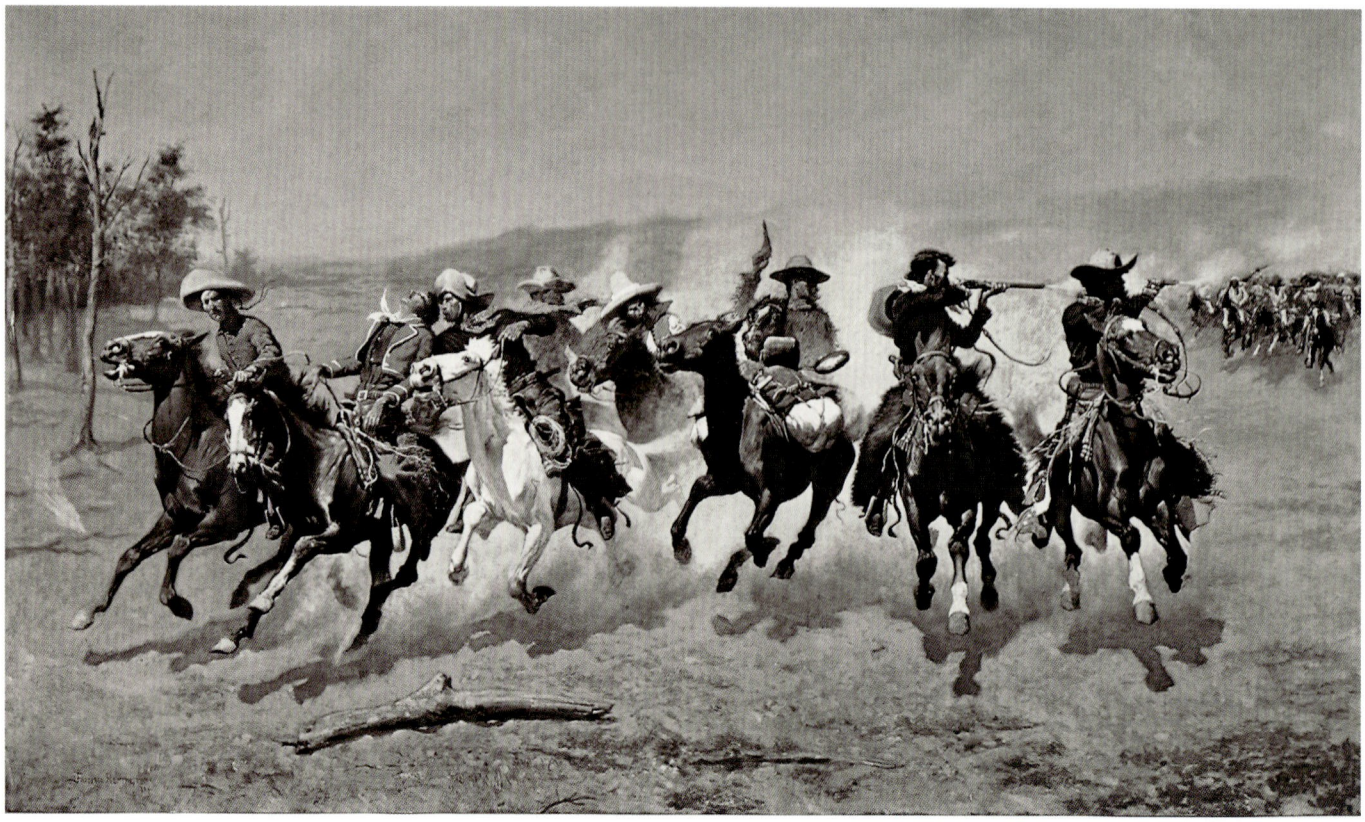

4.14.15 Frederic Remington: *A Dash for the Timber*, 1889. Oil on canvas, 48¾ x 84⅜ in. (123.8 x 214.6 cm.) Amon Carter Museum, Fort Worth, Texas

culture. Rather, he is present in flesh and blood as "history" and as artifact, a symbol of a noble yet savage culture destroyed by the inevitable march of progress. This progress is embodied in the print of gun-slinging cowboys or cavalry above the heads of the children and in the very clothes and hairstyles of the children themselves.

The print on the wall refers to a contrast that was central to the imagery of the West in the late nineteenth century, that between the cowboy and the Indian. An artist who became famous for his depictions of these two figures was Frederic Remington (1861–1909), whose *A Dash for the Timber* (1889) [**4.14.15**] could well have been the model for the print in Johnston's photograph. Remington had begun his artistic career in the early 1880s as an illustrator for *Harper's Weekly*, providing images of the West to accompany the magazine's articles (later he also wrote and illustrated his own articles). By 1888 he was submitting paintings to the annual exhibition of the National Academy of Design, where they received favorable reviews. Soon prints after several of these paintings began circulating throughout the country, available for anywhere from ten cents to two dollars. Remington was one of several artists depicting the West in the last decades of the nineteenth century. Unlike most of the others, however, he appeared in a popular and widely circulated magazine, and in a promotional campaign begun by *Harper's Weekly* in 1890. This campaign presented him as both a true Westerner and one who "draws what he knows and knows what he draws," thus ensuring him a place in the public imagination.

What Remington knew about the West, and how that knowledge affected his paintings and drawings, has come under scrutiny, however. The art historian Alexander Nemerov quotes Remington: "I sometimes feel that I am trying to do the impossible in my pictures in not having a chance to work direct but as there are no people such as I paint it's 'studio' or nothing." While Remington made several trips to the West (sketching, photographing, and collecting clothing, guns, and other artifacts for his paintings), the works themselves were created primarily in his studio in the East. The accuracy of costume and setting ensured that many would read his images as truthful accounts. Yet what gave his works even greater power was the belief that this place and time of charging horses, brave men, and threatening Indians was over, and that the civilized life of the East—with its factories, cities, and increasing numbers of immigrants—had pushed the West of adventure and excitement off the map.

Several of the Native American prisoners at Fort Marion went to the Hampton Institute after their release. One of them, the Cheyenne Bear's Heart, captured the collision of cultures embodied in Wo-Haw's drawing and Johnston's photograph in a speech he made in English in May 1880, in Virginia. The audience included President Rutherford B. Hayes and Governor John D. Long:

> Before Indians went to school, Capt. Pratt he gave Indians clothes just like white men, but Indians not want hair cut. Sunday Indians go to church St. Augustine: down from head, Indians same as white men; but heads, long hair just like Indians. By and by after Indians go to church, they say I want my hair cut; my teachers very good. Two years I stay at St. Augustine, then come Hampton. At Hampton I go to school and work.

The historian Donal F. Lindsey writes in his study of Native Americans at the Hampton Institute that most evidence "shows not only whites but many Indians and blacks verbalizing Eurocentric themes. At a school whose educational philosophy was among the nation's most accommodationist, independent thinking by blacks and Indians was usually unwanted and thus its expression rarely preserved." Lindsey also notes that such independent thinking did occur at times, and forced changes in the Institute's policies. Bear's Heart does not openly criticize the policies of either Fort Marion or the Hampton Institute. He may well have found, however, that what was most valuable in the education that he and his fellow prisoners and classmates received were lessons in the advantages of accommodation as a mechanism of survival.

All three individuals—Bear's Heart, Wo-Haw, and Johnston—present, in their words and images, the coming together of two worlds that was so crucial a part of the development of visual culture and of a sense of national identity in the US in the nineteenth century. Bear's Heart conveys, in halting words, the gradual process of Native Americans' accommodation to the ways of their captors, although he leaves much unsaid about what motivated this accommodation. Wo-Haw presents Native American culture as a living presence (albeit a ghostly one) in the daily lives of his people at Fort Marion [**4.14.5**; p. 254]. Johnston presents this same culture exhibited as a curiosity, an example of what needs to be left behind as a lived experience. Yet, at the same time, it had to be kept alive as a memory and a symbol of the US, like the stuffed eagle on the table, through endless pictorial representations. This living memory was, and still is, necessary, according to the historian Richard Slotkin, in order to assuage a national conscience trying to reconcile the near-destruction of a people with the establishment of a democratic nation.

Wo-Haw's image, and others like it, however, also need to be brought to the fore in order to remind us that Native American culture did not die in the nineteenth century, but remained a resilient and dynamic force in Native American life. Recognizing this allows us to read the many images of this life and of the American frontier critically, not as records of unchallengeable facts or truths, but as the products of individuals perpetuating or resisting the material and ideological processes of conquest and colonization.

Review Questions

1. What are the differences in style and content between Theodore R. Davis's sketch of "Custer's Indian Scouts Celebrating the Victory Over Black Kettle" (1869) and Cohoe's *Fort Marion Prisoners Dancing for Tourists* (1875–77)? Who were the audiences for each work and how would they have interpreted the images?
2. How is Yellow Nose's *Drawing of the Battle of the Little Big Horn* (*c.* 1885) different from the Mandan hide paintings of the early nineteenth century [**1.2.24**, p. 44; **3.9.7**, p. 179]?
3. What was the Ghost Dance, and what were some of the symbols used in its ceremonies?
4. Why did Paul Wayland Bartlett depict his male figure naked in his *The Indian Ghost Dancer* (1888–89)?
5. What does the Native American figure at the head of the classroom represent in Frances Benjamin Johnston's *Class in American History* (1899–1900)?

1834
Nathaniel Currier begins producing lithographs (joined by James Merritt Ives in 1852)

1844
Founding of Philadelphia School of Design for Women

1854
Treaty of Kanagawa opens Japanese ports to trade with US

1857
Beginning of the construction of Central Park, New York, designed by Frederick Law Olmsted, with the assistance of Calvert Vaux [5.16.23]

1864
Yosemite Valley, California, becomes a state park (becomes a national park 1890) [5.16.25]

1869
Publication of *American Woman's Home* by Catherine Beecher and Harriet Beecher Stowe; founding of the American Women's Suffrage Association

1870
Founding of The Metropolitan Museum of Art, New York [5.18.1], and the Museum of Fine Arts, Boston; John D. Rockefeller forms the Standard Oil Company of Ohio; the first train travels from Boston to San Francisco

1871
Great Chicago Fire

1873
December 13: Winslow Homer's *The Old Mill* (*The Morning Bell*) (1871) [5.15.4] appears in *Harper's Weekly*; publication of *The Gilded Age* by Mark Twain and Charles Dudley Warner

1874
James Parton publishes *The Triumph of Enterprise, Ingenuity and Public Spirit*, hailing chromolithography as "oil painting by machinery"; Charles Eliot Norton appointed at Harvard to the first chair in fine arts at an American university

1875
Thomas Eakins's *The Gross Clinic* [5.16.3] rejected by the Philadelphia Centennial art jury (it appears in the medical section)

1876
Centennial Exhibition, Philadelphia; founding of the Philadelphia Museum of Art; invention of the telephone by Alexander Graham Bell

1879
Founding of the Art Institute of Chicago; Thomas Alva Edison invents the incandescent light bulb

PART 5 Art, Labor, and The Gilded Age

c. 1865–1900

With the end of the Civil War, the United States turned its attention to rebuilding its political and economic infrastructure, asserting a new national unity as well as a growing international presence. The last quarter of the nineteenth century came to be known as the "Gilded Age," after a popular book by Mark Twain and Charles Dudley Warner, published in 1873, that cast a critical eye on post-Civil War America as a time when "the air [was] full of money, nothing but money, money floating through the air." American industrialists and financiers, unfettered by anti-trust, health, labor, and income tax legislation, were able to amass vast fortunes, gaining control over large segments of the US economy. Artists and architects were often the beneficiaries of these wealthy individuals, who constructed and decorated elaborate mansions, as well as cultural institutions such as libraries and museums.

But the amassing of wealth by these "Robber Barons" did not go unchallenged, as workers organized and fought back against oppressive working conditions in factories and low wages. The strikes and labor protests that rocked the country in the last quarter of the nineteenth century were grounded in the ever-swelling ranks of manual laborers arriving from countries throughout the world. The population of the US more than doubled between 1860 and 1900 (from 31 million to 76 million), with the fast pace of industrial development that resulted from the material needs of the Civil War continuing apace in the postwar decades.

The growing popularity of photography also resulted in the establishment of mini-factories staffed by groups of individuals assigned one of several tasks that went into the production of a photograph. Oliver Wendell Holmes described the inside of the photography studios of Messrs E. and H. T. Anthony of New York City [**4.12.19**; p. 235] in 1863, where "[a] young person who mounts photographs on cards all day long confessed to having never, or almost never, seen a negative developed, though standing at the time within a few feet of the dark closet where the process was going on all day long." "As an account of fragmented and alienated labor," writes Alan Trachtenberg, "this could hardly be improved upon."

Artistic labor was also changing. By the mid-nineteenth century photographs were increasingly being used as preliminary "sketches," allowing, for example, for more accurate renderings of humans or animals in motion. The invention of collapsible

Tonalism c. 1880s–1915

Chicago School of Architecture 1880s–90s

American Renaissance c. 1885–1920

1880
Rookwood Pottery in Cincinnati, Ohio founded by Maria Longworth Nichols Storer [5.18.11]

1882
Chinese Exclusion Act

1883
Thomas Eakins collaborates with Eadweard Muybridge on a project documenting locomotion for the University of Pennsylvania

1884–92
Monadnock Building, Chicago [5.18.5], by Daniel H. Burnham and John Wellborn Root

1886
Robert Koehler paints *The Strike* [5.15.8]; founding of the American Federation of Labor; national strike for eight-hour work day; Haymarket Riot in Chicago; installation of Auguste Bartholdi's Statue of Liberty in New York harbor [5.15.10]

1887
Eadweard Muybridge publishes *Animal Locomotion* [5.16.1]; passage of Dawes Act dividing Reservation lands into individual allotments

1888
Exhibition of John Singer Sargent's *Isabella Stewart Gardner* [5.17.14] at Boston's St. Botolph Club

1889
Completion of Frederic Edwin Church's home, Olana [5.16.19]

1890
Publication of *How the Other Half Lives* by Jacob Riis [5.16.22]; publication of *The Gentle Art of Making Enemies* by James Abbott McNeill Whistler [5.17.1]

1893
Hawaii becomes a US Protectorate; World's Columbian Exposition, Chicago [5.18.2]; Frederick Douglass and Ida B. Wells denounce segregated admission policies at Exposition

1898
US annexes Hawaii; Puerto Rico becomes a US Territory and Guam and the Philippines ceded to the US by Spain after Spanish-American War

1900
Exhibition of W. E. B. Du Bois's four portfolios of photographs at the American Negro exhibit at the Paris Exposition [5.17.23]

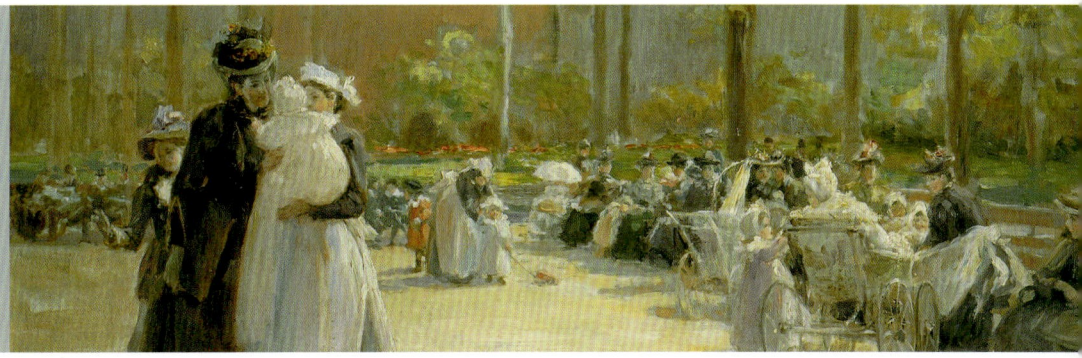

Alice Barber Stephens: *A Spring Morning in the Park*, 1892, detail [5.16.17; p. 292]. Oil on canvas, 18 x 26 in. (45.7 x 66 cm.) Private collection

tubes for paint in 1841 by the American artist John G. Rand, freed painters from hours of preparation and allowed them much greater mobility. And mass production techniques cut the cost of prints and sculptures while mass distribution systems facilitated the appearance of these objects in thousands of homes across the nation.

The changing world of work inside studios, photography shops, and factories was also marked by another crucial factor— gender. As more women were forced, or chose, to enter the wage-labor force, their jobs echoed the types of labor they had performed in the home—domestic service, teaching, textile production. At the same time, middle-class women were increasingly subjected to what came to be known as "the cult of domesticity," which anchored women's identity in their ability to manage their homes and raise their children. Many paintings appeared at the end of the century in which well-dressed women sit in lavish interiors or have tea in overgrown gardens, while waited on by domestic servants.

Women were also increasingly identified as the preservers, not creators, of culture. Yet many did paint and sculpt and played an important role in the creation of fine ceramics, metalwork, and needlework. They were emboldened by a growing women's movement and assumed active roles in the re-examination of the political, social, and artistic norms of the end of the nineteenth and beginning of the twentieth century.

The increasing association of women with culture also facilitated the development of a new critical art language and a new style. John Ruskin's emphasis on "truth" and "nature" was replaced by James Abbott McNeill Whistler's focus on "beauty" and "art." Detailed realism and smooth surfaces were abandoned by many artists for hazy landscapes and paint-laden brushstrokes, the clearly drawn narratives of the former now nudged aside by the moods and vague sentiments of the latter. The decorative was celebrated in painting and the subject matter best suited for such a decorative emphasis was women, whether naked or clothed, whether residing in comfortable interiors or misty landscapes. Men occupied the recognizable world of economics, women the ideal world of aesthetics. This move away from the narrative and toward the decorative or abstract would continue in the first part of the twentieth century and would spawn increasingly heated debates over which styles of art were truly representative of the US in a new, "modern" era.

CHAPTER 15

The Art of Industrial Labor

(*c.* 1871–1890)

One Hundred Years of Independence: Taking Stock of America at the 1876 Philadelphia Centennial Exhibition

The one hundredth anniversary of independence from Britain in 1876 was, for many, a major landmark, proof of the country's coming of age. A civil war had been weathered, ensuring the unity of the nation. Technological advances had taken place that drastically altered the lives of Americans, sometimes for the better, sometimes for the worse. In 1870 the first train traveled from Boston all the way to San Francisco. Brokers could exchange news in seconds via Samuel F. B. Morse's telegraph (see pp. 146–47). Middle- and upper-class families could read their daily magazines and newspapers by gaslight. Many farmers now had automatic reapers, and women were aided in their daily needlework tasks by the sewing machine. At the same time the continually deteriorating conditions in factories and the lack of safety devices on much of the new machinery took the lives and limbs of increasing numbers of men and women. This same new machinery also created unemployment for many skilled laborers. Slums expanded to accommodate the waves of people pouring into cities in search of work, setting up stark contrasts between the homes of the wealthy and the poor.

The Philadelphia Centennial Exhibition of 1876 focused, however, on the glories rather than the tragedies of progress. The nature of this celebration, and the framework of historical progress within which it was encased, were eloquently captured in an illustrated engraved stock certificate issued in 1875 to shareholders in the Centennial Corporation [**5.15.1**], set up to facilitate the funding and organization of the Fair. Its overall iconography was probably established by a committee of the Centennial Board of Finance, with the project then given to Felix O. C. Darley (1811–1888) and Stephen J. Ferris (1835–1881) of Philadelphia, who created the final engraving.

The stock certificate is divided into three registers, each containing groupings of figures that, together, frame the text in the center. The main characters in the top register are women—not historical characters, however, but allegorical representations of continents and concepts. America, dressed in the classical garb of Liberty and wearing a liberty cap, stands in the center, her arms extended in a welcoming gesture to either side. At her feet sit personifications of Fame, with her laurel wreaths, and Art, with her palette and brush. To the right of Art stand women bearing gifts. They are recognizable—through their physical features, gifts, and clothing—as representations of the lands of India, Africa, and the Far East. To the left of Fame stand Europe, Central America, and South America, similarly identifiable by their features and what they wear. In front of this group of women are busts of George Washington on the left and Ulysses S. Grant on the right. (Their two seats of office, the Philadelphia State House and the Capitol in Washington, float faintly above them in the background.) The two presidents, whose terms of office mark the two ends of the country's hundred years of independence, are connected by a bald eagle carrying a US flag, the pointed staff of which is directed somewhat ominously at the head of Grant.

Thus America as hostess welcomes nations from around the world to the Centennial International Exhibition. Her handmaidens, Fame and Art, sit ready to judge and commemorate the best that this world has to offer, represented by the agricultural gifts carried by the women to either side. Yet agricultural products were not the primary focus of the Centennial Exhibition. Instead, center stage was occupied by the kinds of objects carried by the pairs of men faintly sketched in the background on either side—inventions relating to trade and commerce. National progress was to be measured not by agricultural wealth, but by advances in industry and technology.

In the central register, to the right, appear two men presenting a sewing machine and a schooner—real, not symbolic, images of trade and commerce. Below them are four men—a black man engrossed in a book, a Yankee mechanic, a Union soldier, and a Continental soldier. The book represents the educational opportunities opened to African Americans after the end of slavery and their assimilation into European American culture. Yet the man's isolation heralds the "separate but equal" legislation that was soon to take away much that had been gained in the decade after the end of the Civil War (see p. 236).

The group of men on the left side of the central register represent the various geographical sections of the West and South. A California miner offers a piece of gold to America, while behind him a Southern plantation owner holds a boll of cotton and talks to a Midwestern farmer, with his sheaf of wheat. A mountain man who carries furs from the Rocky Mountains ignores a Native American behind him, who turns away from the central group as he glances at them over his shoulder. There is no place for him, with his indigenous clothing and weapons, in this celebration of Western expansion. In addition, the representation of the South and West as suppliers of natural resources—food, minerals, furs—is a subtle reminder of the political and commercial primacy of the Northeast, for no one character represents this region of the country. Rather, the

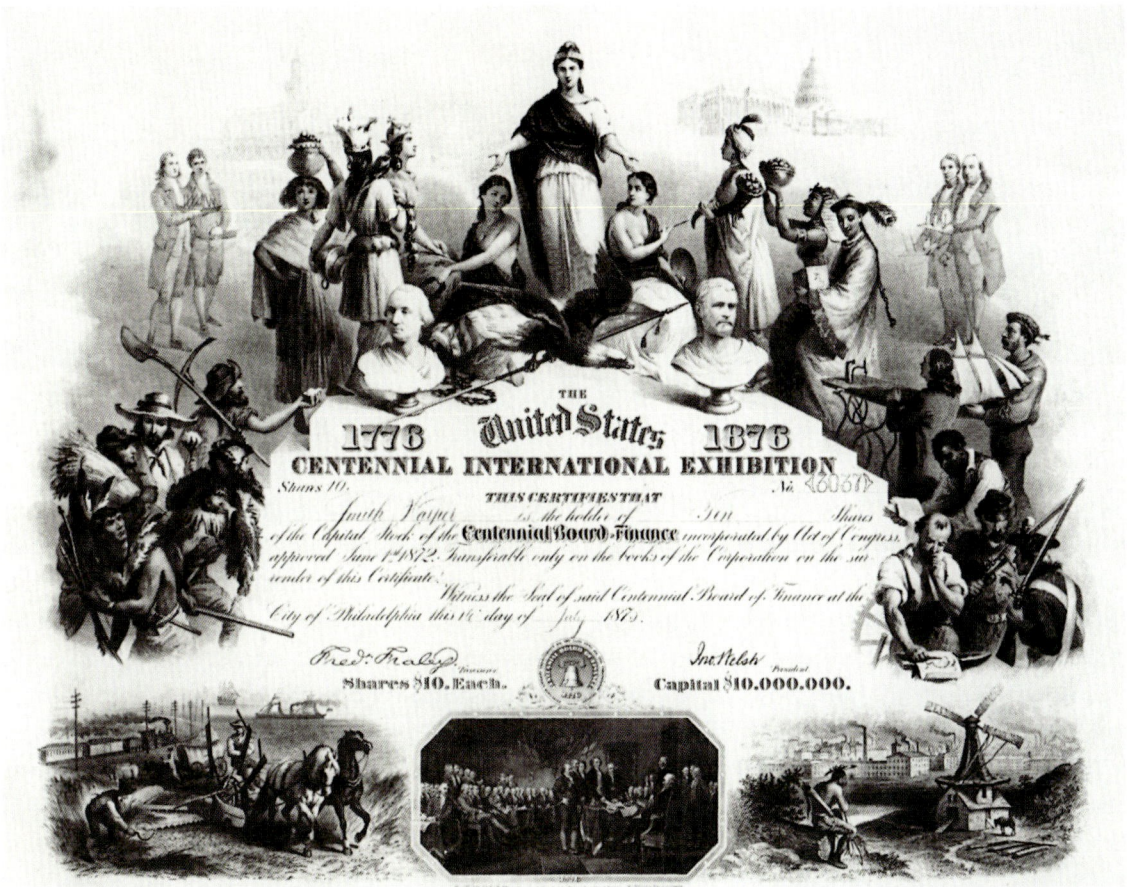

5.15.1 Felix O. C. Darley and Stephen J. Ferris: *Centennial Stock Certificate*, 1874–75. Engraving, 18½ x 22½ in. (47 x 57 cm.)
Courtesy Professor and Mrs Ellwood Parry III

industry and commerce and political rule represented throughout the stock certificate are presumed to reside there.

The three vignettes at the bottom repeat the themes above. In the center is a reproduction of John Trumbull's painting *Declaration of Independence* (see pp. 122 and 132). Beneath the farmers, miner, trapper, and Native American are images of what made westward expansion possible. Settlers came first by Conestoga wagon, then by train. They harvested the land, once home to massive herds of buffalo, first with a sickle, then with a reaping machine. They kept in touch with eastern relatives first by mail rider, then by telegraph. The ships that transported people and goods were powered first by wind, then by steam engines. Such was the nature of progress over the past hundred years. The vignette on the lower right reiterates this theme of past and present, with the farm and windmill in the foreground contrasted to the factories and smokestacks in the background. The Native American reappears here not in the act of turning away, but in the act of pondering what lies ahead, having resigned himself to the inevitable advance of "progress."

The pensive pose of this indigenous figure is similar to a marble statue of *The Dying Indian Chief* (1856) by Thomas Crawford (1813–1857), which appeared on the right side of his sculptural program for the pediment of the Senate wing of the Capitol [**5.15.2**; p. 268]. Crawford had learned his lessons well as a student of the Danish neoclassical sculptor Bertel Thorvaldsen (1770–1844). His heavily muscled, perfectly proportioned figure is Native American only in his headdress. The pediment, like the stock certificate, contains a celebration of western expansion, industry, and commerce—a settler chopping down a tree, a soldier, a merchant sitting on bales of goods, a mechanic leaning on a cogwheel—all presided over by a female figure of America holding a laurel wreath and accompanied by a bald eagle. In this instance, Crawford was not instructed to remove the liberty cap from the figure's head, as was the case with his sculpture *Freedom Triumphant in War and Peace* for the top of the Capitol dome [**4.12.1b**; p. 221]. The dying chief is included, along with a Native American woman and child, as a reminder of what had to disappear in order for this particular version of progress to be achieved. Titled *The Progress of Civilization*, the pediment echoes the content of Asher B. Durand's painting *Progress* (1853) [**3.9.14**; p. 183], with the same indigenous figures looking on as industry and commerce fill the landscape.

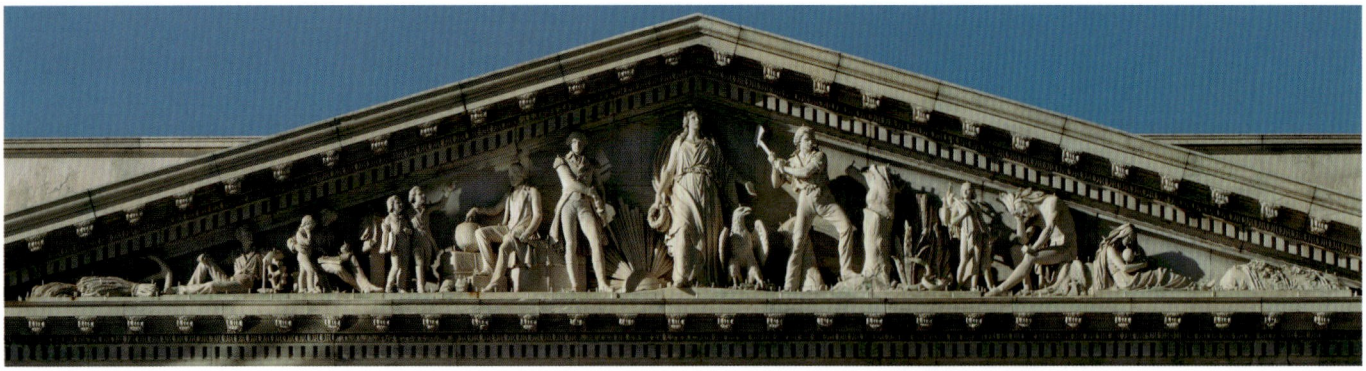

5.15.2 Thomas Crawford: *The Progress of Civilization*, 1851–63. Senate pediment, United States Capitol, Washington, D.C.

The Centennial Stock Certificate thus encapsulates the advance of civilization over the past hundred years through the exploitation of natural resources on the one side, with the inevitable exclusion of Native Americans, and the development of industry and commerce on the other, with the necessary assimilation of African Americans after the end of slavery. Here, then, are the material elements of progress—the minerals, the wheat, the machines. Only in the lower left-hand corner do we see the actual processes of labor involved in the development of agriculture, industry or commerce, and nowhere are there any indications of the inevitable conflict that accompanied this development—no massacres of Native Americans, no striking workers, no slaves. Instead, what occupies the center of the composition is a description of the particular type of economic organization into which these resources and developments were increasingly channeled: the corporation.

As Alan Trachtenberg points out in *The Incorporation of America*, corporations prior to the mid-nineteenth century were usually of a religious or communal nature, guilds, monasteries or boroughs established through an act of sovereign authority. The general assumption was that the incorporated body would act in the interest of the public good. By the mid-nineteenth century, however, incorporation in the US increasingly had become a private enterprise. This development was fueled by the rapid economic growth that took place during the second quarter of the century. This growth was accompanied by the extension of the railroads westward, the rise of the factory system, and the development of a national market.

Selling shares directly to a general public allowed for the quick and efficient raising of capital necessary for the corporation's expansion. Thus, corporations pushed more and more small individual or family-owned enterprises out of business. The increase in capital enabled the integration of industries, bringing the total process, from the extraction of raw materials to the making and sale of the final product, under the umbrella of a single corporation. Business magnate John D. Rockefeller incorporated the Standard Oil Company of Ohio in 1870; by 1880 he controlled approximately 90 percent of the oil trade, from extraction to transportation and sale. Stockholders benefited from the company's success (or suffered from its failure) without having to take responsibility for its operations, which would be the purview of its board of directors. They also would not be liable for actions taken by or against the corporation.

The Centennial Corporation was more akin to the earlier incorporated bodies. It sold stock not to make a profit, but to fund a patriotic venture that was to benefit the nation as a whole, hence the elaborate imagery on the stock certificate. Yet investment in the Centennial Corporation would, ultimately, serve American businessmen well, for the Centennial Exhibition was primarily a trade fair, a place for nations to exhibit their commercial and technological might. Such a reassuring display of economic prosperity was sorely needed in the US. Three years earlier, in 1873, the country had been hit by a severe economic downturn, with bankruptcies and business failures affecting all sections of the economy. This crisis, which would persist to varying degrees for more than twenty years, created widespread market uncertainties and increasing competition both at home and abroad. Many businesses were unable to move their inventory, while prices declined worldwide. Credit for farmers tightened, wages were cut, layoffs increased, and many families were forced to the brink of starvation.

Thus, a sense of economic gloom hung over the Machinery Hall at the fair, with its profusion of power looms, presses, sewing machines, toolmaking machines, locomotives, telegraphs, and the first version of Alexander Graham Bell's telephone. Yet even the most economically deprived visitors to the Hall may have forgotten their cares and been overcome by awe and wonder in the face of the two most impressive machines on display, the 30-foot- (9-meter-) high Corliss double walking-beam steam engine and a 7,000-pound (3,175-kilogram) electrical pendulum clock, with twenty-six lesser "slave" clocks dispersed around the building. "Unstinted but channeled power, and precisely regulated time: that combination," writes Trachtenberg, "seemed to hold the secret of progress."

Yet, as Trachtenberg also notes, the image of the machine in the latter half of the nineteenth century was "increasingly charged with contradictory meanings and implications." The other side of the awe and wonder expressed in the face of mechanical prowess appeared within a year of the closing of the Centennial Exhibition. Railroad workers on the Baltimore and Ohio line, hit with a 10 percent pay cut in July 1877, went on strike. The strike quickly spread to other lines across the country and quickly escalated into violent confrontations between local police and militia on the one hand, and strikers on the other. The latter took over railroad yards and smashed equipment. More than one hundred strikers were killed, and millions of dollars of property destroyed. Thus, the US embarked on its second hundred years of independence with a fierce battle over who would reap the economic benefits of this thriving democracy.

Factory and Foundry: Winslow Homer and Thomas Anshutz

From the time of its emergence as an independent republic the United States was celebrated as a land of opportunity, where individuals could succeed through initiative and hard work. This idea is expressed in John Neagle's *Pat Lyon at the Forge* of 1826–27 [**5.15.3**]. Lyon, a successful blacksmith, asked Neagle (1796–1865) to portray him in his work clothes at his forge, rather than lounging in his study in his Sunday best. He was proud of having risen to his position of wealth and prominence through hard work rather than inherited privilege. This rise occurred despite having been falsely accused and imprisoned in his youth for bank robbery (the tower seen through the window is that of Philadelphia's Walnut Street Jail in which he was incarcerated). The positioning of the young man behind Lyon suggests that he, too, will have the opportunity to make his own fortune through hard work.

Yet not all who came to the new republic, or to the British colonies that preceded it, were able to profit from their own labor. The wealth of the British colonies was not in the abundant gold and silver that the Spanish found further south (see pp. 21–22), but in the potential for agricultural and commercial goods. In the face of intransigent resistance by indigenous peoples to enslavement, the British colonists in the New World had to acquire workers by whatever means possible. Indentured servants and convicts were soon followed by African slaves, while many skilled craftspeople also struck out for the New World with hopes of making their fortunes.

Organized resistance to exploitation accompanied the arrival of these indentured servants, slaves, and tradespeople. Strikes or uprisings occurred in both the North and the South in the seventeenth and eighteenth centuries (see p. 75). Slave rebellions before the Civil War also took place (see pp. 76 and 226). These strikes and rebellions tended to be localized and small in scale. It wasn't until the second half of the nineteenth century, with the expansion of industrialization and the development of large corporations, that strikes assumed a national scale.

The new forms of industrial labor emerging in the latter half of the nineteenth century and their social ramifications did not attract the interest of many painters or sculptors. An abundance of imagery appeared, however, in the popular press. Winslow Homer (1836–1910) created some of the earliest visual commentaries on industrial labor in the fields of both fine and popular art before moving to Prout's Neck, Maine, in 1883, where he spent the rest of his life and produced a series of dramatic seascapes. For example, a variant on his painting *The Old*

5.15.3 John Neagle: *Pat Lyon at the Forge*, 1826–27. Oil on canvas, 93 x 68 in. (236.1 x 172.6 cm.) Museum of Fine Arts, Boston, Massachusetts

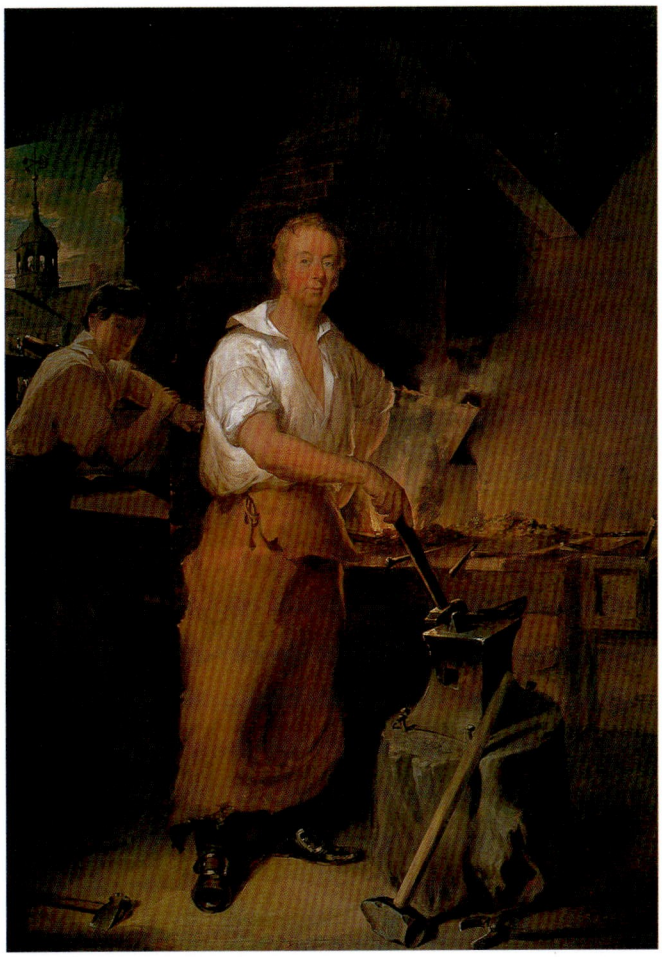

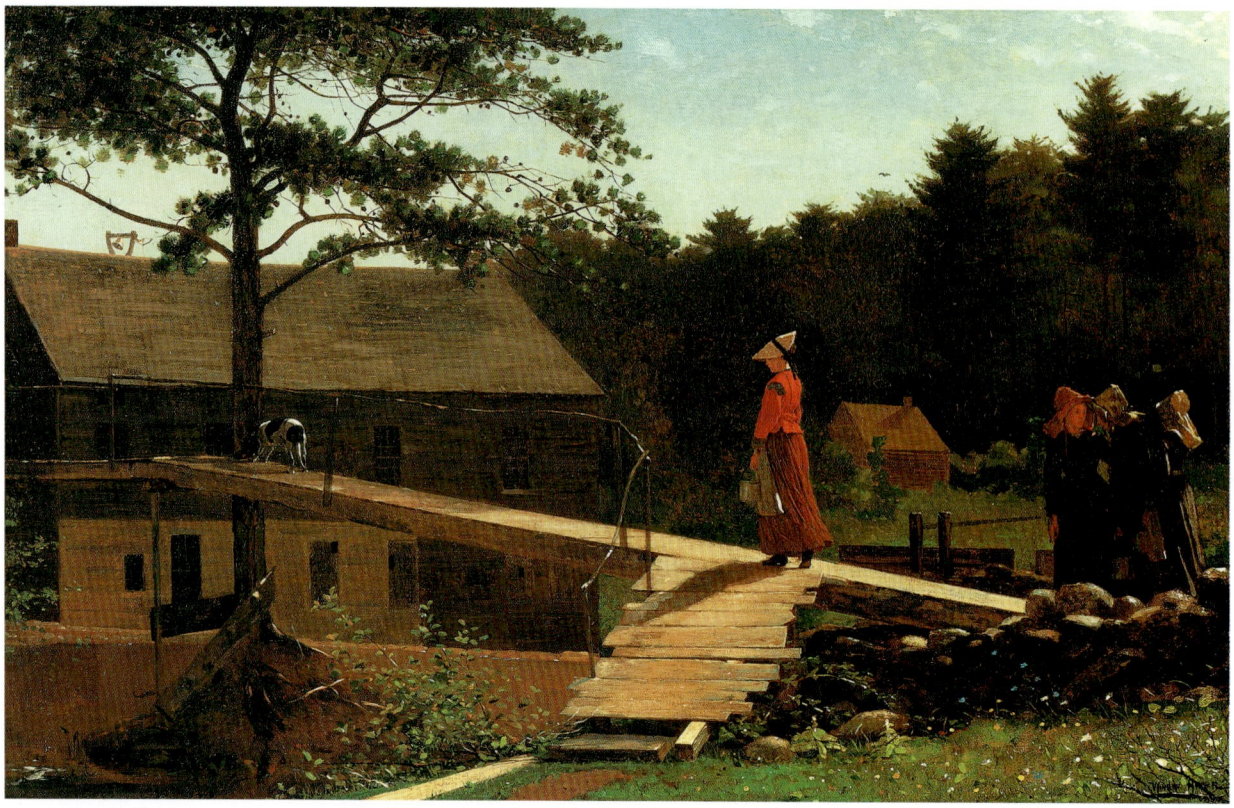

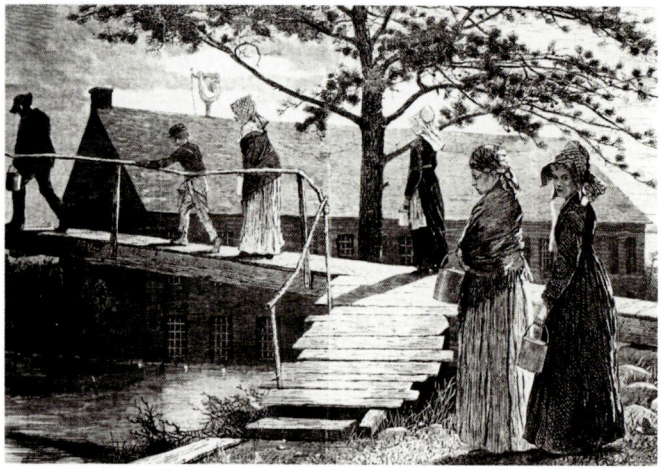

5.15.4 Winslow Homer: *The Old Mill* (*The Morning Bell*), 1871. Oil on canvas, 24 x 38¼ in. (61 x 97.2 cm.) Yale University Art Gallery, New Haven, Connecticut

5.15.5 Winslow Homer: *The Morning Bell*, in *Harper's Weekly*, December 13, 1873. Wood engraving, 9⅛ x 13½ in. (23.4 x 34.3 cm.)

Mill or *The Morning Bell* (1871) [**5.15.4**] appeared as an engraving in *Harper's Weekly* in 1873 [**5.15.5**]. The differences between the two images are telling. In the painting, the factory, probably a textile mill, is located in the middle distance and is surrounded by trees, the one in front of it dwarfing the building. The young woman advancing on the bridge walks upright, although her gaze is cast downward. She is more fashionably dressed than the three women behind her, who stop in conversation, just as the dog in front of her stops to sniff the trunk of the tree. The women's hats catch the glint of the morning sun. There is little, except perhaps their lunch pails and a slight reluctance on their part to continue across the bridge, to suggest that they are off to a long day's labor. Indeed, a writer for the April 20, 1872, issue of the *New York Evening Telegram* read the painting as "an old school house, with a group of country girls, dinner buckets in hand going over the lonely wooden path." Even the bell calling them to work is not a major presence in the painting, located as it is beneath one of the lower branches of the tree.

In the engraving, however, which appeared in the December 13, 1873, issue of *Harper's Weekly*, the factory has grown considerably in size and the lone tree functions not as a pastoral setting but as the last vestige of a forest quickly being replaced by industrial architecture. The four women have been rearranged, with two placed in the foreground close enough for us to discern their unhappy expressions. Two women now occupy the bridge, with the one closest to the factory bent over as if already anticipating the long day ahead. In front of her is a young boy and between the two of them a much-enlarged bell. A man with bent head precedes them all across the bridge. The bell and the factory clearly indicate the changes in both the location and rhythm of work that were taking place, while the women, man, and child provide a catalogue of the generations and genders of factory workers in the late nineteenth-century. Thus Homer, like many artists, reserved his pointed commentaries on the effects of industrialization for his commercial work, maintaining a more palatable, pastoral narrative in his paintings.

Several artists working in the last quarter of the nineteenth century, however, did feel compelled to comment in their paintings on changes in the nature and organization of work and the distribution of wealth. Thomas Anshutz (1851–1912) grew up in Wheeling, West Virginia, in a family that owned and operated iron mills. In 1880–81 he produced a small painting entitled *The Ironworkers' Noontime* [**5.15.6**] in which he pays close attention to the anatomy of the male workers he has chosen as his subject matter. The figures are arranged across the full width of the canvas and also recede into space. All occupy different poses, with their various gestures working off of one another. Anshutz made numerous drawings (in 1880 he began sketching Wheeling's ironworkers) in his attempts to discover the exact combination of figures and poses that would produce, for him, a perfect compositional balance.

Like Homer, Anshutz has located his figures in front of the building in which they work. Yet there are no trees intervening between the workers and the ironworks, no picturesque river to cross. Instead, the carefully arranged interlocking figures convey a sense of both group identity and individual isolation. They are set against a massive angled building in a landscape devoid of vegetation. Only the two pairs of children engage in anything that could be described as communication. Two men to the right of center may be talking to one another, but the arm of the man in front of them stretches across their faces, preventing the viewer from knowing for sure if a conversation is taking place. The majority of the figures look off into the distance or are absorbed in a particular task or self-reflection. The short, staccato movements marked by the bare arms of the men create a sense of dislocation. This is not an image of the work that these men do, but of the effects of that work on their bodies and their minds. The blank stares create a sense of exhaustion; the contrast between the bright sun and the dark windows reminds the viewer that this is but a momentary break in a long day of heavy labor. A contemporary critic described Anshutz's painting as follows:

> At the stroke of noon the toilers at forges and furnaces emerge into the cinderous outer precincts of the foundry

5.15.6 Thomas Anshutz: *The Ironworkers' Noontime*, 1880–81. Oil on canvas, 17⅛ x 24 in. (43.5 x 61 cm.) Fine Arts Museums of San Francisco, San Francisco, California

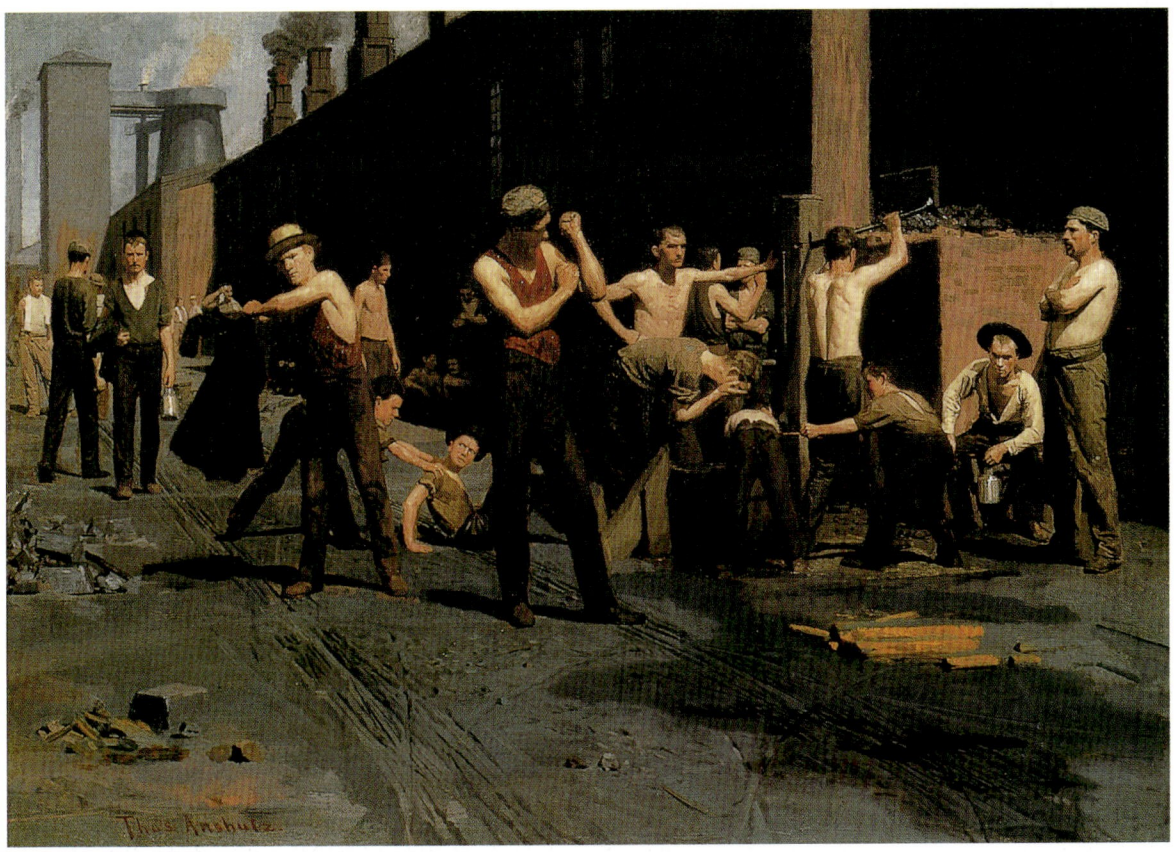

for a brief respite from labor, and refreshment against labor yet to come. Utter weariness and the robust strength of abundant manhood are seen in contrast. One young giant stretches his powerful limbs, as if shaking off his chains. Some seek refreshment in drenching their hot, grimy bodies with water, while others sink listlessly into supine repose.

The painting was also seen as a marked departure from previous depictions of work, which tended to be much more idealized versions of individual craftspeople, such as Neagle's *Pat Lyon at the Forge* [**5.15.3**; p. 269], or group labor on family farms. Unlike Neagle's painting, *The Ironworkers' Noontime* contains no tools to mark the various tasks performed by ironworkers. They are connected to their work through the architecture of the mill behind them and through the brown used to delineate both the building and the men's clothes. In addition, the hours of the men are not regulated by the needs of the body—independent artisans ate when hungry or rested when tired—or by the rising and setting of the sun, or the passage of the seasons. Instead, work routines were set by factory owners and organized around the clock or the bell to achieve optimal productivity from both workers and machines. The imposition of standard time across the nation by the early 1880s aided the efforts of industry and commerce to regulate both the production and the sale of commodities.

Paintings like Neagle's were ultimately more popular in the late nineteenth century than those depicting factory workers, for few art patrons wanted to be reminded of the current or potential labor unrest that had spread throughout the country. Instead, they wanted to be reminded of President Thomas Jefferson's dream of an ideal nation of citizen-farmers and small businessmen who would labor with the best interests of the country, as well as the individual, at heart.

Anshutz received little encouragement to continue his immortalization of industrial workers in paint, despite the reproduction of the painting in *Harper's Weekly* on August 30, 1884 (which prompted the soap and candle company Proctor & Gamble to use it as the basis for an ad to sell their new brand of floating soap called Ivory), so he turned to the production of portraits and genre scenes. *The Ironworkers' Noontime* was bought in 1883 by Thomas B. Clarke, a merchant collector and later an art dealer. Clarke was interested in encouraging the development of figure painting in the US as a marketable item to place in competition with European imports. The same year that he bought Anshutz's work he also instituted a cash prize to be awarded at the annual exhibition of the National Academy of Design for the best figure painting by an American artist who was not a member of the Academy.

Labor Unrest: Robert Koehler's "Strike" and Monuments to Justice and Liberty

The historian Richard Slotkin writes that the motif of "the last stand" so common in artistic depictions of the western frontier came to function in a new way in the late nineteenth century as a powerful allegory of the plight of capitalism in an era of increasing labor unrest. Workers and immigrants were shown pitted against factory owners or their armed guards, as in the stand-offs between Native Americans and the US Cavalry. In newspaper descriptions of these confrontations, protesting workers were often described as "savages" or "redskins." The art historian Alexander Nemerov notes that Frederic Remington (1861–1909) was sent to Chicago by *Harper's Weekly* in 1894 to cover the Pullman strike. Just as he portrayed Native Americans and the cavalry engaged in close combat, so too did he show the coming together of strikers and soldiers in such images as *Giving the Butt* (1894) [**5.15.7**], where soldiers attack strikers with the butts of their rifles. Remington describes the strikers for *Harper's* readers as "vicious wretch[es] with no blood circulating above [the] ears," a description buttressed by his visual depiction of them as scruffy and ill-dressed. Considering himself of pure Anglo-Saxon stock, Remington blamed the country's increasing labor unrest on "the malodorous crowd of anarchistic foreign trash."

Remington was right in one respect. The growing number of immigrants entering the country contributed to the ranks of striking workers. But he was wrong in thinking that this unrest would have disappeared had the workers all been Anglo-Saxon immigrants. Workers of all nationalities hired for a wage by factory owners were quickly replacing the self-sustaining mechanic, merchant, or farmer of the first half of the nineteenth century.

5.15.7 Frederic Remington: *Giving the Butt* (published in "Chicago under the Mob" in *Harper's Weekly*, July 21, 1894).
Pen and ink on paper
Frederic Remington Art Museum, Ogdensburg, New York

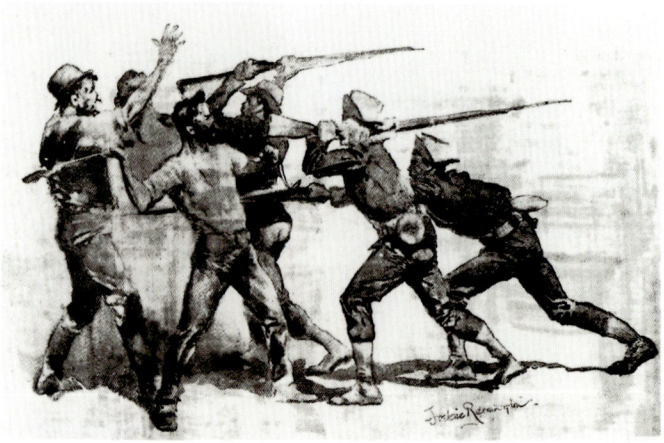

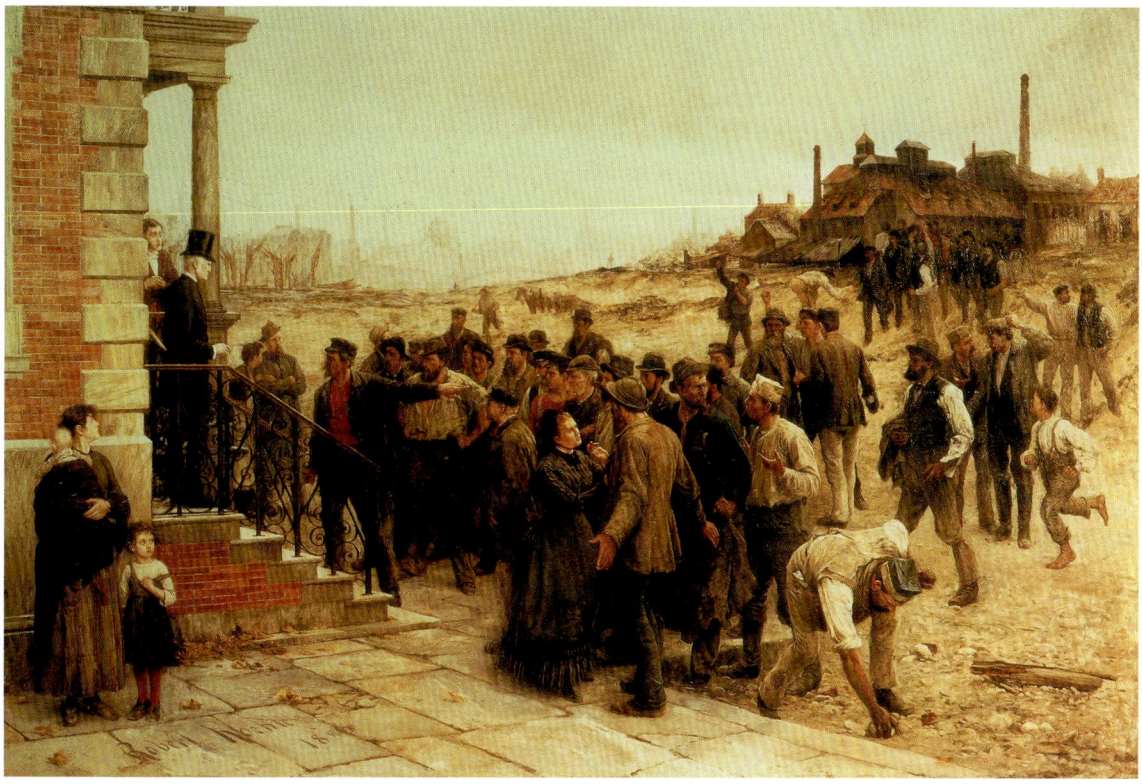

5.15.8 Robert Koehler: *The Strike*, 1886. Oil on canvas, 71⅝ x 108⅝ in. (182 x 276 cm.) Deutsches Historisches Museum, Berlin

Child labor was also common nationwide in the late nineteenth century, as indicated in both Winslow Homer's *The Old Mill* [**5.15.4**; p. 270] and Thomas Anshutz's *The Ironworkers' Noontime* [**5.15.6**; p. 271]. In 1880 there were more than one million between the ages of ten and fifteen in the wage-labor force; by 1900 there were over two million. Another painting that makes reference to child labor is *The Strike* (1886) [**5.15.8**] by Robert Koehler (1850–1917). Koehler was born in Germany but grew up in a working-class family in Milwaukee. He studied art in the US, Paris, and Munich before he was appointed director of the Minneapolis School of Fine Arts in 1886.

The Strike was the first major work exhibited in the US in which the struggle between workers and employers was openly addressed. Men and boys cross a barren landscape separating the factory and the home of its owner, reminiscent of the setting in Homer's *Prisoners From the Front* [**4.13.1**; p. 237]. The men are angry; one addresses the employer, gesturing at his companions behind him. The worried look of the owner's assistant is echoed in the worried gaze of the girl below him in the left-hand corner. The factory owner shows no such emotion.

There are three adult women in the painting. One stands in the lower left-hand corner, holding a baby and accompanied by the young girl. She and her children can be seen as the justification for the men's actions: they need a living wage in order to support themselves and their families. The second woman stands just below the factory owner, next to one of the strikers. She appears to be talking to the latter, her hand resting on his arm. Her white apron suggests she is a servant in the owner's house. The third woman stands in the middle foreground. She is on the edge of the paving that signifies the ordered space of the city, with its classical porticos, as opposed to the devastated landscape occupied by the men and the factories. She engages in a heated discussion with one of the men, who holds his arms out as if saying, "But, what else can we do?" This woman could be a relative of one of the men, or a middle-class reformer (see p. 295). She appears to be trying to interject a voice of reason into the emotionally charged scene. Her central position suggests the importance Koehler gave to women in their role as peacemakers. Koehler described the evolution of the painting in an issue of the *Minneapolis Journal* (March 23, 1901):

> *The Strike* was in my thoughts for years. It was suggested by the Pittsburgh strike (of 1877). Its actual inception was in Munich and there the first sketches were made. I had always known the working man and with some I had been intimate. My father was a machinist and I was very much at home in the works where he was employed. Well, when the time was good and ready I went from

> Munich over to England and in London and Birmingham I made studies and sketches of the working man—his gestures, his clothes. The atmosphere and setting of the picture were done in England, as I wanted the smoke. The figures were studies from life, but were painted in Germany. Yes, I consider *The Strike* the best, that is the strongest and most individual work I have yet done.

In contrast to *The Ironworkers' Noontime* [**5.15.6**; p. 271], the response was enthusiastic when *The Strike* was shown at the National Academy of Design in 1886. A *New York Times* critic wrote on April 4:

> Mr. Koehler has done well to show the earnest group of sweating workmen, quite possibly with justice on their side, but ready, some of them, to take the law into their own hands. He has contrasted with them fairly well the prim capitalist. But in trying to rouse our sympathies with a beggar woman his moral gets heavy...All the same, *The Strike* is the most significant work of this spring exhibition.

This review indicates why Koehler's work was so well received and Anshutz's not. First, in Anshutz's work, the laborers are at rest. There is no moral or narrative with which the viewer can engage. Second, Koehler's work is large—approximately 6 × 9 feet (1.8 × 2.7 meters)—which allows for a dramatic presentation of the moral message concerning failed justice. Art viewers were used to large dramatic paintings. While most depicted historical scenes or military exploits, French artists had painted at least two large strike scenes in the early 1880s in Europe. *Coal Miners' Strike* by Alfred-Philippe Roll (1846–1919) had been exhibited at the Paris Salon of 1880; *The Iron Workers' Strike* by Paul Soyer (1823–1903) appeared in 1882. Koehler was in Europe during the early 1880s and may have seen one or both of these works, as did possibly several other American artists, for many studied with Soyer.

A third reason for the positive reception of Koehler's work can be found in the way in which the artist acknowledges the reality of the strike, yet presents it as a personal confrontation between the capitalist and the workers, with the suggestion that a solution can be reached through personal negotiation or the efforts of the woman in the center foreground. In reality, such personal meetings seldom occurred. Strikers were met, instead, by the military or private police forces, not by those who owned the factories. In fact, the absence of a boss in Anshutz's *The Ironworkers' Noontime* more effectively represents, according to the historian John Gladstone, "the corporate 'they,' absent but omnipresent." Koehler, on the other hand, ignores the fact

> that the age of the trust, the corporate monopoly, is already upon us, that the boss will no longer be a clearly identifiable character, a paternalistic individual, but will metamorphose into an anonymous corporate octopus, that he will become a faceless "they," and, as in *Ironworkers*, will be remote from the shop floor.

By the 1880s the public was familiar with striking workers and with the reasonableness of much of what they were demanding. Many began to feel that they might well have "justice on their side." Out of this feeling grew the social reform movement of the last quarter of the nineteenth century, with reformers, both men and women, arguing for shorter hours, improved working conditions, and a minimum wage to diffuse the potential for violence. The fear of violence was strengthened by events in 1886. Labor leaders across the country had designated May 1 as the target date for achieving the eight-hour workday, calling for a nationwide strike wherever the eight-hour day was refused. Chicago, with its anarchist/socialist Central Labor Union and its large population of radical German labor activists, became a major center of activity.

The Strike was reproduced as the center spread in the May 1, 1886, issue of *Harper's Weekly*; on the same day more than 300,000 workers went out on strike, with 40,000 in Chicago alone. The city's railroads ground to a halt and most of its industries were paralyzed. On May 4 a rally was called near Haymarket Square to support striking workers at the McCormick Reaper Works. At the end of a day of peaceful assembly, the police moved in and demanded the crowd disperse. As they advanced, a bomb was thrown into their midst. Seven policemen and several civilians were killed and many others injured. Only one individual, a policeman, could be shown to be a victim of the bomb; the others were killed when the police opened fire on the unarmed crowd after the bomb was thrown. No official count of the civilian dead was ever made. The bomb thrower was never found, but eight labor leaders, the backbone of the anarchist labor movement, were arrested and charged with inciting the act. They were found guilty and seven were condemned to death. The eighth received fifteen years in the penitentiary. Four were hanged, and one was killed in jail under suspicious circumstances. Three were later pardoned by Illinois Governor John Peter Altgeld. Thus, after May 4, it would have been impossible to look at Koehler's work and not confront the reality of the national strike and the violence that followed.

Two monuments appeared in Chicago to commemorate the Haymarket incident, one dedicated to the police who tried to disperse the demonstrators, the other to the condemned labor leaders. The first was commissioned in 1888 by a committee

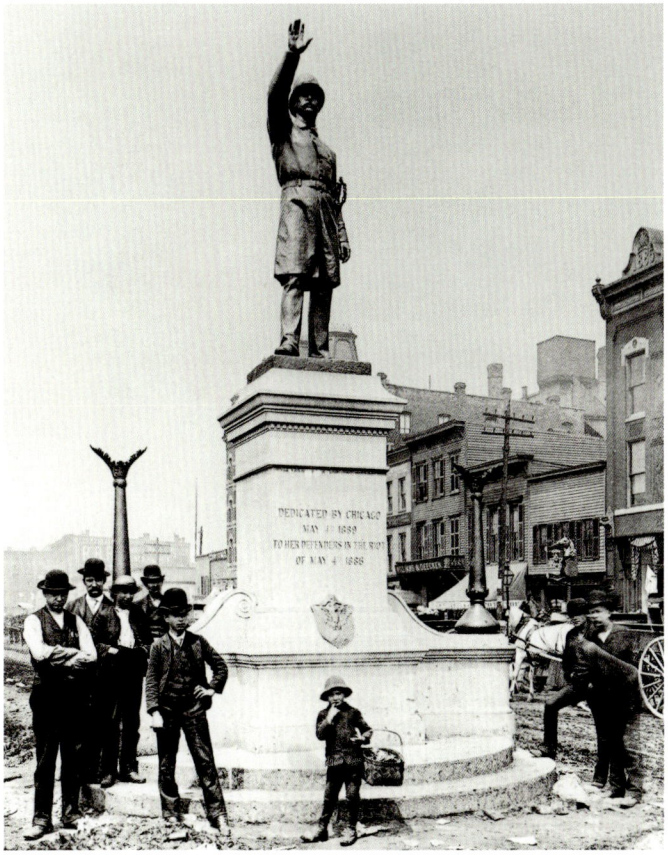

5.15.9 Johannes Gelert: *Police Monument*, 1889, in its original location in Haymarket Square, Chicago.
Chicago Historical Society, Chicago, Illinois

of twenty-five businessmen and civic leaders and completed in 1889 by the Danish sculptor Johannes Gelert (1852–1923) [**5.15.9**]. The bronze life-size figure was erected in Haymarket Square on May 31, Memorial Day. Gelert had arrived in the US in 1887 after studying art in Copenhagen and Paris. The *Police Monument* was his first major commission. Intended to represent Captain William Ward, who had called out for the crowd to disperse, it was modeled after another police officer, Thomas Birmingham, whom Gelert had spotted directing traffic in Chicago. The static figure, legs spread and arm raised, his costume and features portrayed with detailed realism, embodied male institutional authority in contemporary Chicago.

Gelert's initial design for the monument showed an allegorical female figure of Law holding an open book over her head. The selection committee favored, instead, a decidedly male and down-to-earth commemoration of the event and of the authority that was to preserve civic order. The anarchist sympathizers who organized a monument to the "Haymarket Martyrs," however, did choose a female allegorical figure. This large bronze and stone sculpture was also the first major commission of a recent immigrant (this time from Germany), Albert Weinert (1863–1947). The *Haymarket Monument* [ill. p. 4] was erected in Waldheim Cemetery (now Forest Home) outside of Chicago, where the executed labor leaders were buried.

The art historian Melissa Dabakis points out the contrast between these two monuments and the manner in which they "display a gendered coding that both reinscribed and subverted power hierarchies." Unlike the decidedly static and male figure of the *Police Monument*, the female who dominates the *Haymarket Monument* strides forward, one foot extending off her stone base. With one knee bent, she twists her torso to one side as she stares resolutely forward, her drapery billowing behind her and her hood casting deep shadows across her face. With one bare arm she pulls up her cape and with the other she holds a laurel wreath over the head of the dead martyr stretched out behind her.

While her classical features mark her as allegorical, she is different from the allegorical female figures at the top of the *Centennial Stock Certificate* [**5.15.1**; p. 267]. She not only assumes an active pose, but also wears a recognizable peasant smock and apron. This clothing brings her out of the realm of the ideal and into the material world of fields and factories. The bare arms, resolute gaze, and pose also mark her as "masculine," and thus dangerous. While the curls of hair and noticeably swelling breasts add a traditional feminine touch to the work, they cannot completely erase the marks of masculinity.

Weinert was undoubtedly aware of the use of such earthy and aggressive Liberty and Justice figures to both mock and celebrate revolutionary struggle and resistance, particularly in France in the years surrounding the Paris Commune of 1871. Supporters of traditional structures of power found revolutionary women, even if in allegorical guise, non-women: everything that women were not supposed to be. For many revolutionaries, however, such women were admirable figures who symbolized the overthrow of the existing social order.

Weinert also reworks another well-known figural group, that of Mary cradling the dead body of Christ. The reclining pose of the martyr suggests the many painted and sculpted representations of Christ taken down from the cross. Yet the female figure in Weinert's work does not cradle the dead man in her lap. Instead, she sets out to continue the work begun by him and to live out the challenge issued by the condemned anarchist August Spies just before he was hanged, which is carved into the base of the monument: "The day will come when our silence will be more powerful than the voices you are throttling today." Here, the usual gender roles are reversed: the motionless reclining man is contrasted to the standing active woman.

As Dabakis points out, the "complex relationship between universal and political meaning" in the *Haymarket Monument*—the allegorical versus the historical—informed its production and reception. The mainstream Chicago press viewed the work with apprehension if not outright disgust. The woman was described as expressing "contempt," "fearlessness," "defiance," and "resolution." Identified variously as Justice, Anarchy, or Revolution, she was seen as "a female figure in an attitude of defiance," and thus as a figure to be feared and condemned. Yet for anarchist sympathizers she was a "warrior woman," a symbol of revolutionary struggle to be emulated. "At Waldheim Cemetery over the graves of the martyred anarchists," writes Dabakis,

> the *Haymarket Monument* has functioned as a site where anarchists, socialists, and their sympathizers interacted with the image of an unruly woman and envisioned a world where power relations were not fixed. To this community, woman served as the sign of that liberatory space.

The *Haymarket Monument* has fared much better over the years than the *Police Monument*, becoming a gathering place for those attempting to keep alive the struggle for justice for working people. The *Police Monument* on the other hand has suffered both relocation and mutilation. In 1900 it was moved to Union Park, and on May 4, 1927 was knocked off its base by a streetcar that jumped its tracks. That this occurred on the anniversary of the riot led to speculation that it was not an accident. In 1958 the statue was moved back to Haymarket Square, and in 1968 (again on the anniversary of the riot) it was partially painted black by Vietnam War protesters. The following year, its legs were blown off. The statue was repaired, bombed again a year later, repaired once again, and placed under twenty-four-hour surveillance. In 1972 it was moved to the lobby of the central police headquarters, and finally, in 1976, to the courtyard of the Chicago Police Training Center, where it can be viewed only by special appointment. "Commemorating an historical event in Chicago police history," writes Dabakis, "the monument constructs a social memory at once sacred to those upholding political order and reviled by those seeking to change it."

Another highly symbolic public monument was put in place in 1886, the year of the Haymarket riot: the *Statue of Liberty* (1875–84) by the French sculptor Auguste Bartholdi (1834–1904) [**5.15.10**]. The statue, an engineering wonder, was a gift from France to the US in commemoration of the countries' alliance during the Revolution of 1776, as well as their economic ties. Approximately 151 feet (46 meters) in height, it was composed of beaten copper sheets riveted together and suspended by steel and iron struts from an inner pylon. Its design was begun by the architect Eugène-Emmanuel Viollet-le-Duc (1814–1879) and completed after his death by the engineer Gustave Eiffel (1832–1923). This design allowed the statue to be

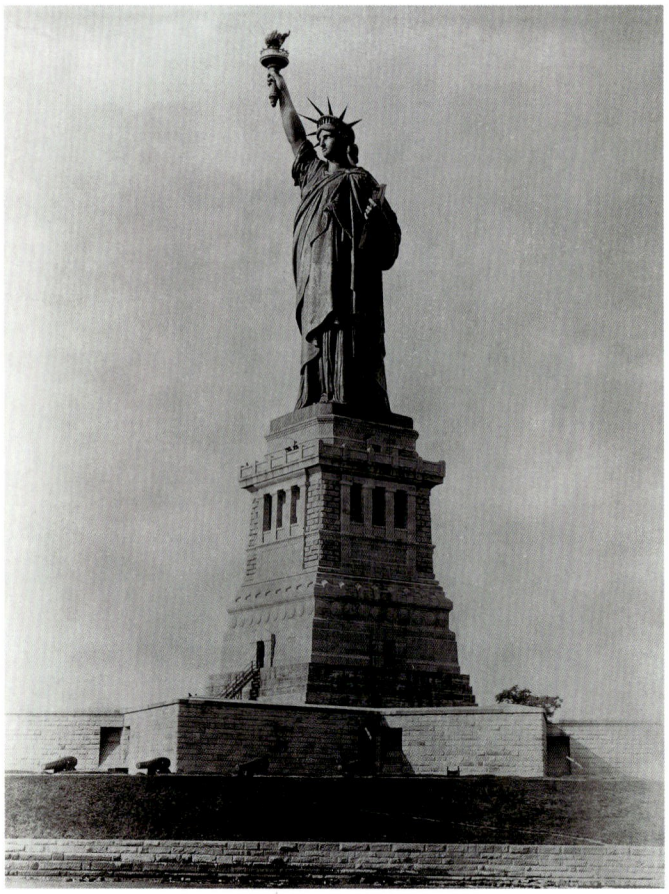

5.15.10 Auguste Bartholdi: *Statue of Liberty* (*Liberty Enlightening the World*), 1875–84, set up in 1886 on the pedestal by Richard Morris Hunt. Copper sheeting over iron armature, h of statue 151 ft. 6 in. (46.2 m.) New York harbor

assembled in France, then taken apart to be shipped to the US and reassembled. Located on Bedloe Island in New York harbor, the *Statue of Liberty* stands on an elaborate multi-tiered neoclassical pedestal designed by the American architect Richard Morris Hunt (1827–1895).

Not surprisingly, much of the public discussion evoked by this sculptural project in the year of its dedication focused on the nature and meaning of the concept of liberty. For the conservative French republican intellectuals and politicians who initiated and promoted this artistic gift to the US (it was funded by public subscription), "liberty" was a stabilizing force, a guarantee against the excesses of both monarchy and anarchy. For French socialists and communists, however, "liberty" was more of a revolutionary force that brought disruption in the name of freedom. A similar split occurred in the US. The wealthy businessmen and politicians courted by Bartholdi, who facilitated the acceptance of the French gift and the raising of funds for the pedestal (a public subscription also played a role in this endeavor), preferred to view Liberty as a beneficent rather than revolutionary figure. At the dedication, President Grover Cleveland commented: "Instead of grasping in her hand the thunderbolts of terror and death, she holds aloft the light that illumines the way to man's enfranchisement." The railroad magnate Chauncey M. Depew added that the struggles for universal suffrage, equality under the law, freedom of religion and speech, as well as "the problems of labor and capital, of social regeneration and moral growth, of property and poverty, will work themselves out under the benign influences of enlightened lawmaking and law-abiding liberty, without the aid of kings and armies, or of anarchists and bombs."

The last phrase in Depew's comment can only be read as a reference to the recent trial of the Haymarket Eight. Indeed, Lucy Parsons, the wife of one of the condemned anarchists and an ex-slave, was in New York two weeks prior to the dedication of the *Statue of Liberty* raising money for an appeal against the guilty verdict. In her presentation she called into question the talk of liberty circulating within the nation at that time:

> Is it American liberty when poor working men cannot talk for their rights; when seven men are doomed to die because they are socialists and a number of children are about to become fatherless and women made widows to die of broken hearts?

The talk that filled the mainstream newspapers and political speeches was of liberty "for the rich and not for the poor."

Middle-class women would also have to fight doggedly for their share of the liberty that was so openly touted as the hallmark of American democracy. At the Centennial Exhibition of 1876 women were not only denied a space in the Main Exposition Hall for a display of work (after a committee of women had raised $125,000 for the Exhibition), but were also excluded from the platform of dignitaries at the Fourth of July ceremonies. And at the dedication of the *Statue of Liberty*, the New York State Woman Suffrage Association was refused a place in the naval parade to Bedloe's Island. In response, the women moored their boat in a prominent position near the island. They then invited the public on board to hear the president of the Association, Lillie Devereux Blake, assert "that in erecting a Statue of Liberty embodied as a woman in a land where no woman has political liberty men have shown a delightful inconsistency which excites the wonder and admiration of the opposite sex."

Bartholdi embodied in the design of his statue the conservative republican notions of liberty espoused by his American and French backers, which he himself shared. Unlike the *Haymarket Monument* [ill. p. 4], which depicts a determined woman with sleeves rolled up and robes billowing behind her, Bartholdi's Liberty assumes a more subdued *contrapposto* stance, at rest yet ready to move. Her heavy gown anchors her in place and her raised arm with torch continues the static, vertical pose. The original title of the work was *Liberty Enlightening the World*, a theme reinforced by the crown of rays on her head and the torch in her hand. In selecting this crown Bartholdi rejected the more politically charged Phrygian bonnet, or liberty cap, which, since 1792, had increasingly become a symbolic reference to popular uprisings. Felix O. C. Darley and Stephen J. Ferris used it on the figure of America in their stock certificate design of 1874–75 [**5.15.1**; p. 267] to refer to the American Revolution. By the 1840s and 1850s, it had also come to represent liberty for African American slaves (see p. 221). Many of the millions of immigrants arriving in the latter half of the nineteenth century would engage in repeated protests, if not uprisings, as they struggled to achieve the liberty and enlightenment promised to them by Bartholdi's statue.

Review Questions

1. How does the Centennial Exhibition of 1876 stock certificate by Felix O. C. Darley and Stephen J. Ferris compare with the narrative of nationhood in the relief sculptures of 1825–27 [**2.6.18–2.6.21**; pp. 122–23] above the doorways in the Capitol Rotunda in Washington, D.C.?
2. How did the rise of corporations in the US reshape the country's economy, and how is this reshaping visible in Thomas Anshutz's *The Ironworkers' Noontime*?
3. Why was Robert Koehler's painting *The Strike* so well received? How does it differ in its depiction of workers from Thomas Anshutz's *The Ironworkers' Noontime*?
4. What role did gender play in the designing of the *Police Monument* by Johannes Gelert and the *Haymarket Monument* by Albert Weinert, as well as in the reception of the two monuments?
5. How did Auguste Bartholdi represent the concept of liberty in his *Statue of Liberty*? Why did he decide to represent this particular understanding of liberty?

CHAPTER 16

The Art of Professional and Domestic Labor

(*c.* 1865–1889)

Celebrating the New Male Professionals: Portraits by Thomas Eakins

The last half of the nineteenth century saw not only a drastic increase in the number of industrial and factory workers, but also the development of new professions. Medical doctors, engineers, scientists, architects, and lawyers trained in Europe or in the fledgling educational institutions of the United States were now replacing their earlier largely self-taught counterparts. These predominantly white men celebrated reason, order, and self-discipline as the hallmarks of the modern professional and of progress, in general, in their fields—a progress closely connected with technological advances. They also engaged with what the art historian Martin A. Berger describes as "the complex and contradictory dictates of masculinity," as work in offices or laboratories replaced physical labor, often seen at the time as the hallmark of male identity. Contemporary critics often recommended strenuous physical exercise or sport as an antidote to the emasculating effects of too much mental labor.

5.16.1 Eadweard Muybridge: *Female Figure Hopping*, 1887.
Sequence photography, from *Animal Locomotion*, Philadelphia, 1887
Library of Congress, Washington, D.C.

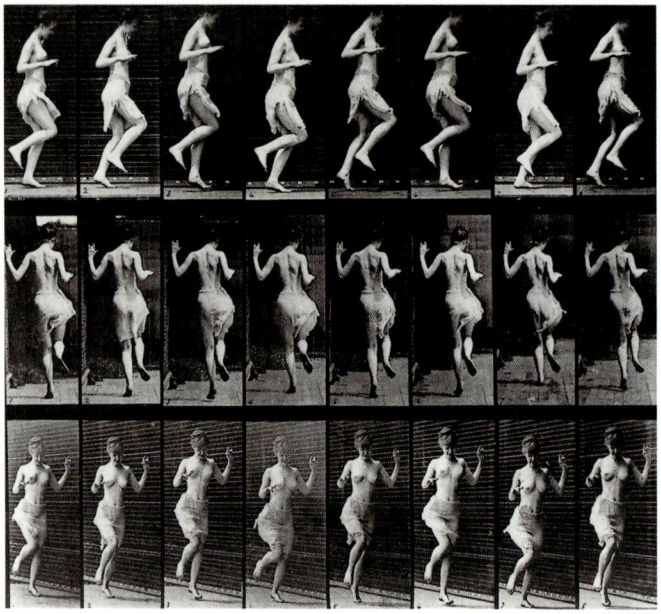

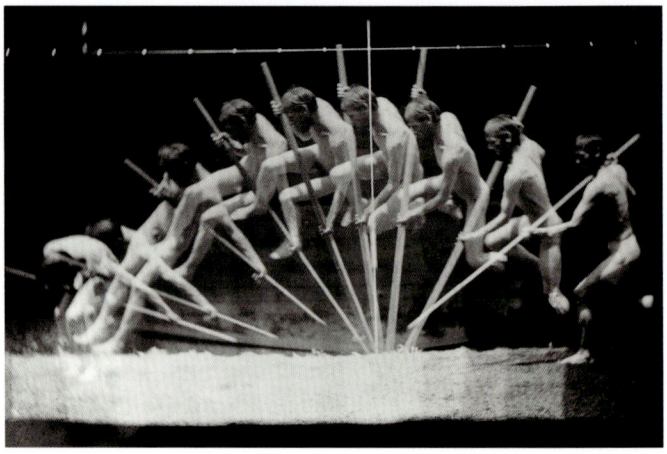

5.16.2 Thomas Eakins: *Motion study: George Reynolds, nude, pole-vaulting to left*, 1885.
Copy from a dry-plate negative
The Pennsylvania Academy of the Fine Arts, Philadelphia

An artist who excelled in the representation of members of this new class, and whose often heroic images may have helped reassert their masculinity, was the painter Thomas Eakins (1844–1916). Eakins studied first at the Pennsylvania Academy of the Fine Arts and later in France with Jean-Léon Gérôme (1824–1904). He was particularly interested in the human body—how it functioned and how it moved through space. This interest led him to both the dissection room and the photography studio. It also led to his resignation in 1886 from his teaching position at the Pennsylvania Academy, where he had been criticized for his use of a nude male model in a class containing both men and women.

In 1883, Eakins collaborated with the photographer Eadweard Muybridge (1830–1904), who had moved from England to America in the 1850s, on a project documenting locomotion for the University of Pennsylvania. The results of the project were published in 1887 in a book by Muybridge entitled *Animal Locomotion*. In his own motion studies, Eakins relied not on Muybridge's methods, but on those of the French scientist Étienne-Jules Marey (1830–1904). While Muybridge captured movement in a series of separate frames using several cameras [**5.16.1**], Eakins combined several positions of the same figure in a single frame, using a single camera in front of whose open lens spun a disc containing a small hole. This allowed for successive exposures on a single plate [**5.16.2**]. Muybridge's images had the advantage of being able to be projected serially onto a screen using a device he invented called a zoopraxiscope. His shows for both scientists and general audiences provided a taste of what was to come in the field of "motion pictures."

Eakins devoted most of his career, however, to painting portraits, producing more than two hundred (only approximately

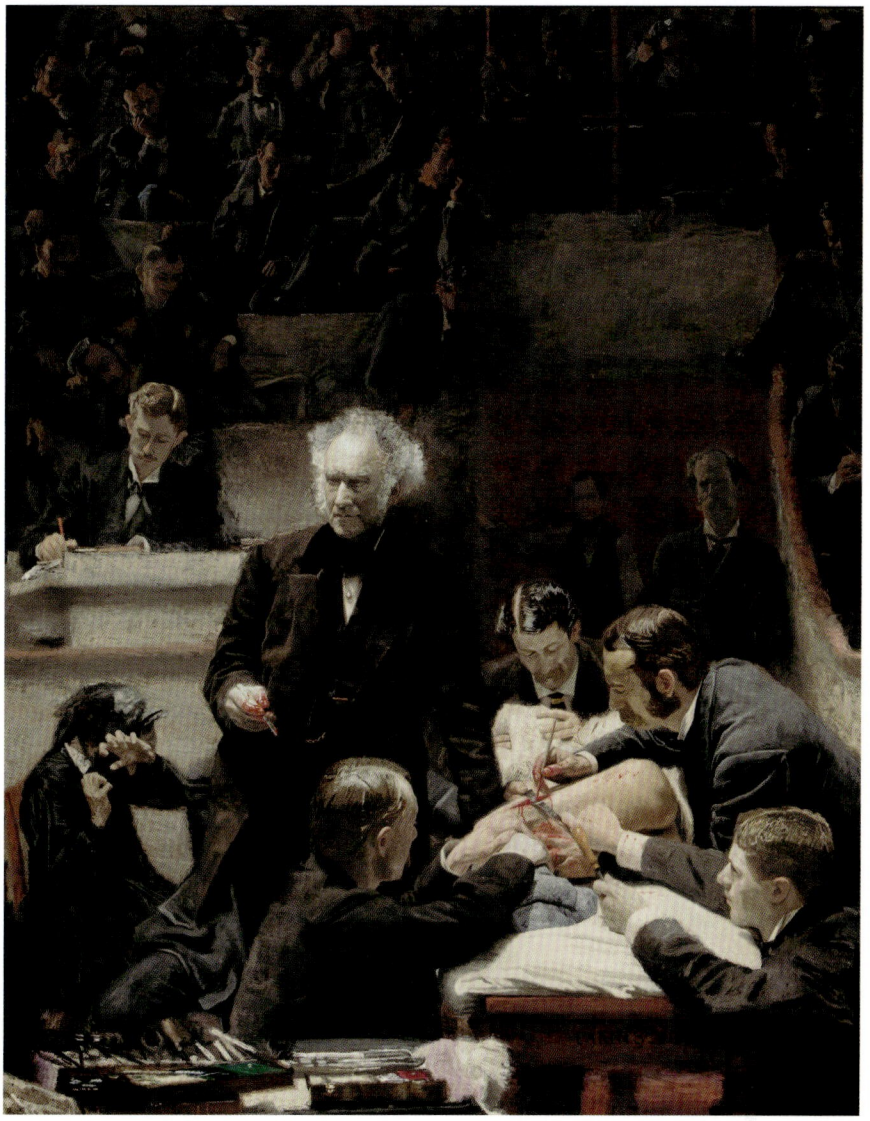

5.16.3 Thomas Eakins: *The Gross Clinic (Portrait of Professor Gross)*, 1875. Oil on canvas, 96 x 78 in. (244 x 198 cm.) Jefferson Medical College of Thomas Jefferson University, Philadelphia, Pennsylvania

twenty were commissioned). Eakins was particularly interested in depicting white middle-class professional men engaged in either work or leisure time pursuits. For example, he created images of surgeons in the midst of operations and men rowing or sculling on the Schuylkill River in Philadelphia (his women appeared primarily in domestic interiors).

One of Eakins's earliest portraits of a professional man, and certainly his best known, is *The Gross Clinic* or *Portrait of Professor Gross* of 1875 [**5.16.3**]. In this painting he portrays the Philadelphia surgeon Dr. Samuel D. Gross pausing in the midst of performing an operation in an amphitheater filled with medical students. He is assisted by an anesthesiologist and four surgeons (one is hidden behind him), and holds in his hand a bloody scalpel. The patient lies on the operating table, the incision in his left leg clearly visible. The only woman in the room, probably his mother, recoils in horror, her hand covering her face at the sight of the scalpel, providing an emotional counterpart to the surgeon's calm. Gross towers over the figures in the foreground, his high forehead bathed in light as he gathers his thoughts before speaking. Light also bathes the hand holding the scalpel and the thigh of the patient, highlighting the three major elements of Eakins's narrative: the intellectual power and technical skill of Gross, which come together in the thigh of the man to produce a successful operation.

Among the figures seated in the amphitheater is Eakins himself, at the far right, holding a pad of paper and pencil. Eakins had studied anatomy at Jefferson Medical College where Gross taught, as well as in Paris at the Ecole de Médicine, going on to teach anatomy and dissection himself. He was thus familiar with the life of the medical clinic and with the skills of Gross. He was prompted to undertake this ambitious portrait by the upcoming Centennial celebration in Philadelphia. The city's reputation as the center of advanced medical research had spread not only within the US but also in Europe.

The art historian Elizabeth Johns argues that Eakins's choice of Gross as the subject of the portrait was ideal in that the surgeon represented not just an individual, but also a larger community, both locally and internationally. Gross was "a man of humble origins, trained in the French clinical—the scientific—tradition, an untiring worker, and a brilliant researcher and writer." As such, he "was at the center of a community—a community of people, of values, of techniques, of history."

Surgical training in the US in the nineteenth century was dominated by two schools. The first was based in British practice, which often focused on assigning students to work individually with a surgeon. The second drew on French practice, which depended largely on instruction via clinics like the one shown in Eakins's painting. British surgery was seen as more elitist, with entrance into medical schools thought to depend more on personal connections than individual talent, while French surgery had about it a democratic aura. Clinics and lectures in early nineteenth-century Paris were free and open to anyone with a passport. Jefferson Medical College, founded in 1825 by the surgeon George McClellan, also offered white men equal access to a medical education and adopted the clinical method of teaching (African Americans and white women were not accepted until the early twentieth century). By the 1860s the college had produced more than one-quarter of the medical graduates in the country. Thus, *The Gross Clinic* celebrated the clinical method of teaching and the democratic character that was attached to it.

The painting also emphasized Gross's role as a teacher, one he valued highly. Eakins respected Gross's insistence on a dignified and solemn atmosphere in the clinic as opposed to the more dramatic and flamboyant demonstrations adopted by many of his colleagues. Such demonstrations may have aggravated the still common belief that the medical profession was in large part "quackery." "The operation is proceeded with, slowly, deliberately, and in the most orderly, quiet, and dignified manner," wrote Gross in his *System of Surgery* (1882). Certainly he is the epitome of quiet dignity in Eakins's portrait.

Eakins also alluded to another aspect of Gross's medical philosophy in his choice of the particular operation being performed, the removal of a piece of dead bone, the final stage in the treatment of osteomyelitis. This infection of the long bones of the body was found primarily in individuals between the ages of five and twenty-two. Until the nineteenth century, amputation of the limb above the infection was the usual treatment. Gross was a strong believer in "conservative" surgery; to remove a limb or part of a limb was seen as failure. He performed many operations for osteomyelitis, and took great satisfaction in restoring young bodies to health.

The Centennial art jury rejected Eakins's painting. Its members were offended by the presence of so much blood. Nevertheless, the painting appeared at the Centennial Exhibition in the medical section under the sponsorship of Gross, along with medical texts and the latest developments in medical care. It was admired by many of the approximately seven hundred physicians and surgeons who attended an international congress held in conjunction with the exhibition.

Fourteen years later Eakins created another work in which a surgeon pauses in the midst of an operation, *The Agnew Clinic* (1889) [**5.16.4**]. Dr. D. Hayes Agnew's students commissioned this painting in honor of his retirement in 1889 from the University of Pennsylvania. The students paid $750 for a single portrait, and Eakins added all of the other figures at no extra charge. Here one can see the changes that had taken place in the field of surgery. White gowns replace the dark street clothes of 1875. While not evident by looking at the picture, Agnew and his assistants also would have been operating with sterile instruments, the practice of asepsis having been adopted by then to control the spread of germs. The lighting is different, reflecting the shift from natural daylight as it entered the clinic through skylights to a much brighter and more evenly dispersed artificial light. In addition, as Johns points out, "the pyramidal structure of the Gross clinic scene is transformed into a horizontal format that shows the teamwork more characteristic of recent surgery, which had to some extent replaced the individual heroism of Gross."

A final difference can be found in the solemn uniformed nurse, who replaces the emotional relative in *The Gross Clinic*. She is an indication of the emergence of the new profession of nursing. While earlier in the century women had functioned as doctors in their roles as midwives and healers, they now were largely denied the option of practicing medicine as full-fledged professionals (few medical schools accepted them). Instead, women were channeled into the position of assistants to male doctors. Agnew strongly opposed the education of women in regular medical classes, and thought that teaching them anything more than "housekeeping, hygiene and belles-lettres" was a waste of time.

Just as we know the names of Agnew and his male assistants, so too do we know the name of the nurse. She is Mary V. Clymer, the top woman in her nursing class. What makes her presence particularly significant is the shift in the sex of the patient in the Agnew painting from male to female, and of the operation from the removal of a piece of bone to the removal of a cancerous breast. In an essay on the painting, the American Studies scholar Judith Fryer writes that Clymer assumes a problematic position. She is not a spectator like the male students. Rather, she is a member of the medical team performing the operation.

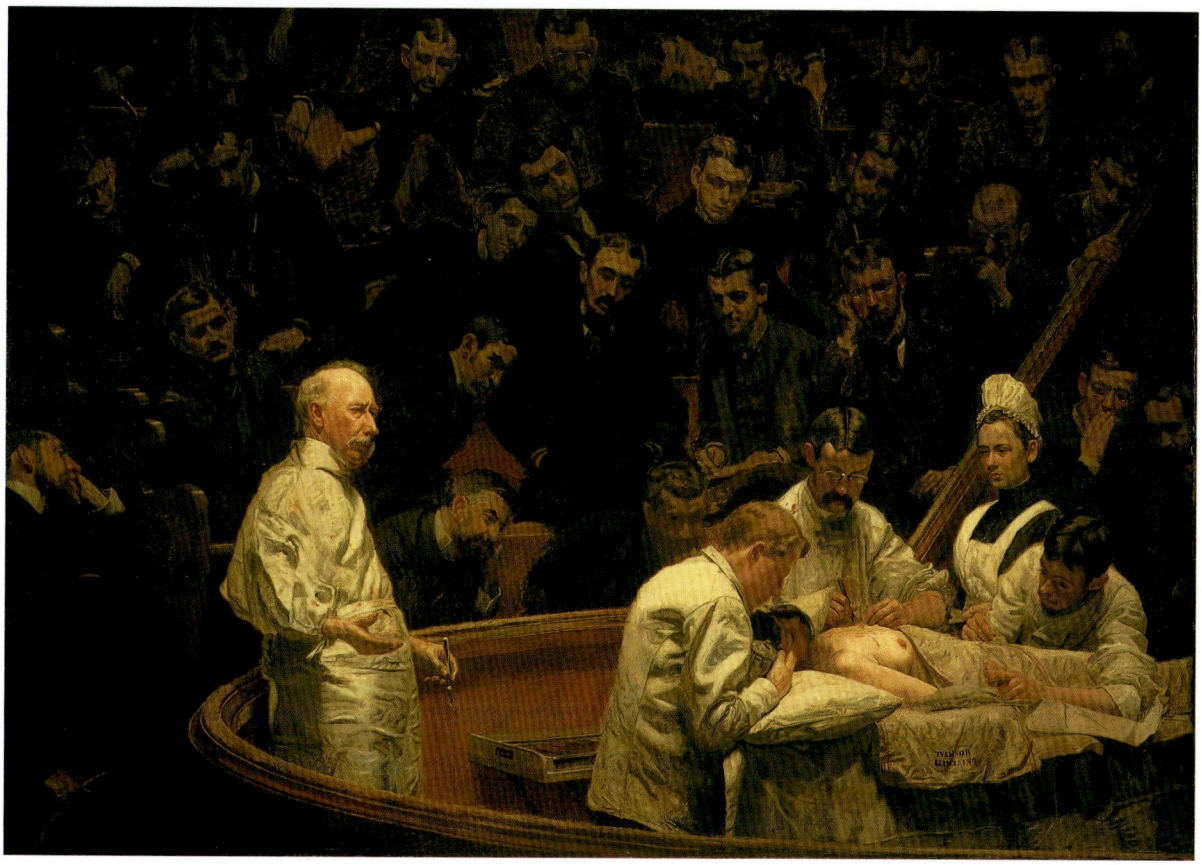

5.16.4 Thomas Eakins: *The Agnew Clinic*, 1889.
Oil on canvas, 74½ x 130½ in. (189.2 x 331.5 cm.)
University of Pennsylvania Art Collection, Philadelphia

Yet she is not a doctor. Instead, she is "hierarchically inferior even to the medical students whom she might one day assist. With whom does she identify—the doctors or the unconscious and mutilated woman?" Unlike the woman in *The Gross Clinic*, however, and unlike the unconscious woman with breasts bared on the operating table, Clymer is actively looking on. She thus functions as a surrogate for the female viewer of the painting, a means of entry into the male medical world of Agnew's clinic. She also functions as a chaperone, making "proper" the actions of the three doctors who physically press upon the body of the patient. She also chaperones the male students, who gaze in rapt attention at the spectacle of a woman's breast being cut open.

Eakins again includes himself, at the right edge of the canvas, directly behind Clymer. She blocks his view of the patient's body, making it necessary for the action to be described to him by his neighbor, Dr. Fred Milliken. Eakins is thus included in the medical community through words rather than sight. But, of course, the real Eakins had full access to the patient's naked body in the act of painting her, something viewers of the painting would have understood. The same is true of Clymer. While she blocks Eakins's view of the patient, she is also, writes Fryer, "subject to the doctors who employ her, and to the artist who paints her, and who views her—in the painting—from behind and—before his easel—from the front." Hence, Eakins, like Agnew and Gross, has "mastered" the female body. He has come to know it through both scientific study and artistic representation.

Fryer also addresses the way in which socio-economic class enters into Eakins's paintings of both clinics. The doctors are part of a newly emerging professional middle class while the patients on whom they operate are from the lower classes. Poor men and women from almshouses were regularly offered medical care in exchange for allowing their bodies to be used in medical instruction. No self-respecting middle- or upper-class woman would have her body displayed in the manner of the patient in *The Agnew Clinic*. Also, the use of chloroform as an anesthetic and the surgical procedure of breast removal (mastectomy) were still in an experimental phase, and who better to experiment on than the poor? Thus, while Eakins's painting is certainly a portrait of Agnew in his role as surgeon and teacher, it is also a statement about how gender and class operated within the medical profession at the end of the nineteenth century.

In 1891 the directors of the Pennsylvania Academy of the Fine Arts refused to include the painting in an exhibition because, suggests Fryer, "it violated museum standards of decorum." For a society that celebrated feminine beauty and refinement within a well-appointed home, the representation of the cancerous, mutilated body of a poor woman would have been unacceptable. Yet this mutilated body is only intimated, not revealed, in Eakins's painting, for, unlike in *The Gross Clinic*, the viewer is not given access to the actual incision. Rather, he or she is presented with a complete healthy breast, which, combined with the large number of men looking on, gives the painting a sexual charge that may well have been more of a reason for the academy's rejection of the painting.

Also largely absent from the painting is the blood that covers the hands of Gross and his assistants in Eakins's earlier work. Instead, blood is limited to some spatters on the gowns of Agnew and Dr. J. William White, who completes the operation, and a few drops on their hands, despite the fact that breast cancer surgery was marked by an inordinate loss of blood. The art historian Bridget L. Goodbody notes that Agnew actually insisted that there not be a lot of blood in the painting, and she posits that this insistence may have been a response to "the public's equation of surgery with butchery."

Goodbody also suggests that the absence of blood was an attempt to hide the medical profession's inability to cure breast cancer patients or even prolong their lives. Agnew estimated that 1 in 10 patients died during surgery due to loss of blood, while others estimated 1 in 6. Shortly before his death, Agnew stated in a lecture that he performed breast cancer surgery solely for the "moral effect" on the patients and that the operation shortened rather than prolonged their lives. White referred to this operation as "the present opprobrium" or shame of surgery. Another of Agnew's colleagues, Dr. S. Weir Mitchell, wrote in 1893 that, despite advances in medical science, doctors were doomed to be "defeated by a woman's breast." This defeat is erased in the painting, however, not only by the absence of blood and the mutilated breast, but also by the clear presentation of the healthy breast which, in Goodbody's words, "generates the feeling that the patient is whole." This feeling creates a corresponding sense of confidence in the doctors' powers to cure her.

Eakins received a much more positive response to his depictions of healthy middle-class women at rest or of men at play. Even when at play, however, Eakins's men exhibit the qualities of reason, order, and self-discipline that often marked their working lives. This is certainly true of his rowing paintings. *Max Schmitt in a Single Scull* of 1871 [**5.16.5**] was his first major painting on this theme (he created nineteen in all). In it he depicts his friend Max Schmitt, champion rower, having just won a major race in Philadelphia on the Schuylkill River on October 5, 1870. As with *The Gross Clinic* and *The Agnew Clinic*, Eakins includes himself in the painting, to the right of

5.16.5 Thomas Eakins: *Max Schmitt in a Single Scull*, 1871. Oil on canvas, 32¼ x 46¼ in. (81.9 x 117.5 cm.) The Metropolitan Museum of Art, New York

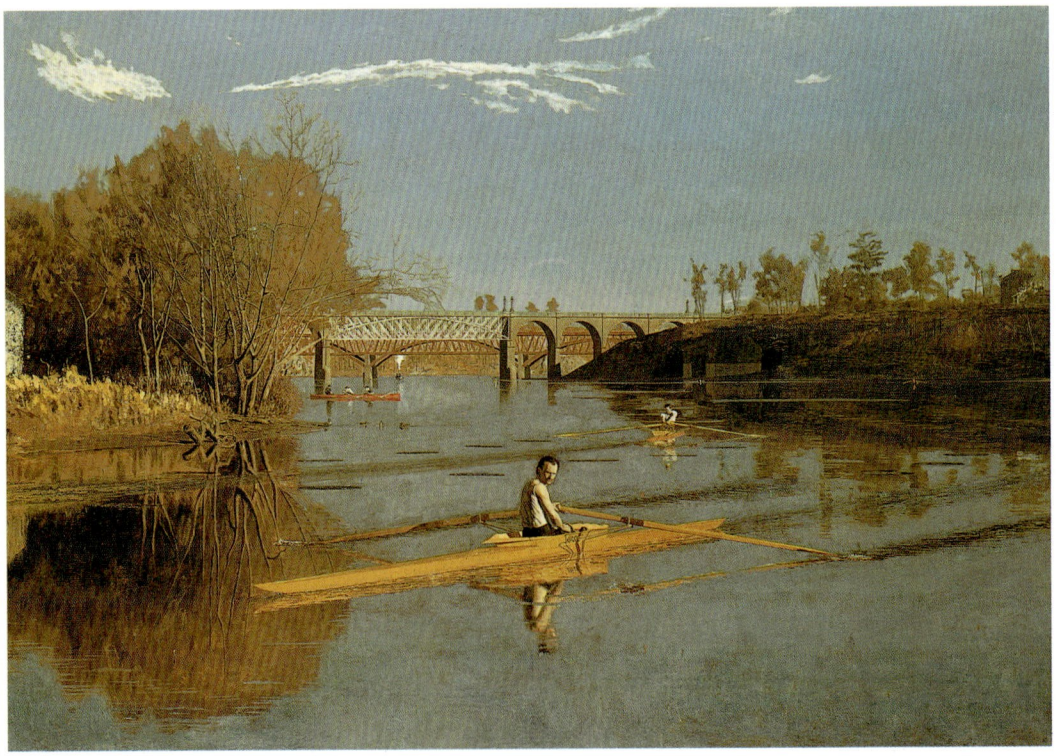

center in the middle distance rowing away from the viewer. The scene is one of healthful outdoor activity, engaged in on a clear fall day, the rust colors of the leaves and the boat reflected in the calm water. The painting's verisimilitude—the convincingly rendered trees, water, figures, boats, and bridges—call to mind photographic records of the landscapes and human figures that Eakins himself often used in composing his paintings.

From the 1860s to the 1880s rowing enjoyed heightened popularity among middle-class professionals. Eakins himself was an avid rower, as were his parents and sisters. Many viewed the sport as improving both one's mental and physical capabilities, for it required concentration as well as strength. Some even argued that it helped people meet the challenge of modern life. As more and more men were confined indoors during the workday, such sports as rowing allowed them to develop mental, physical, and moral discipline in a setting reminiscent of an earlier, more robust working environment (fewer women took up rowing). This, theoretically, applied to those who worked in factories as well as those who worked in offices, for rowing was celebrated as a "democratic" sport, available to all for the cost of a boat rental.

Eakins's rowing paintings, however, are not simply accurate renditions of the leisure time activities of Philadelphia's professional class. According to the art historian Alan C. Braddock, during the 1870s, when Eakins was executing his rowing paintings, "newspapers and public health reports repeatedly rang alarm bells about the effects of industry and population growth on the sanitary condition of the city's water supply, especially the Schuylkill River." Different species of wildlife were disappearing and the death toll from typhoid was rising (Eakins's sister Margaret died of the disease in December 1882). By 1876, writes Braddock, a city known for "good government, scientific progress, and clean water" was now "infamous for pollution." Eakins did not depict this environmental disaster. Instead, he created "a celebratory civic vision, neither strictly empirical nor overtly critical in its realism."

Middle-Class Masculinity, Mass Production, and *Trompe l'oeil* Painting

Concerns about middle-class masculinity can also be found in the emergence of a new type of *trompe l'oeil* still life painting in the late nineteenth century. Its detailed realism was intended to "trick" the viewer into thinking that he or she was viewing the "real" thing rather than a painted image, even if this perception was only momentary. *Trompe l'oeil* artists often arranged their material on or in front of a wall, thus increasing the illusionism of the work, as the painted wall blended easily into the wall upon which the painting was hung.

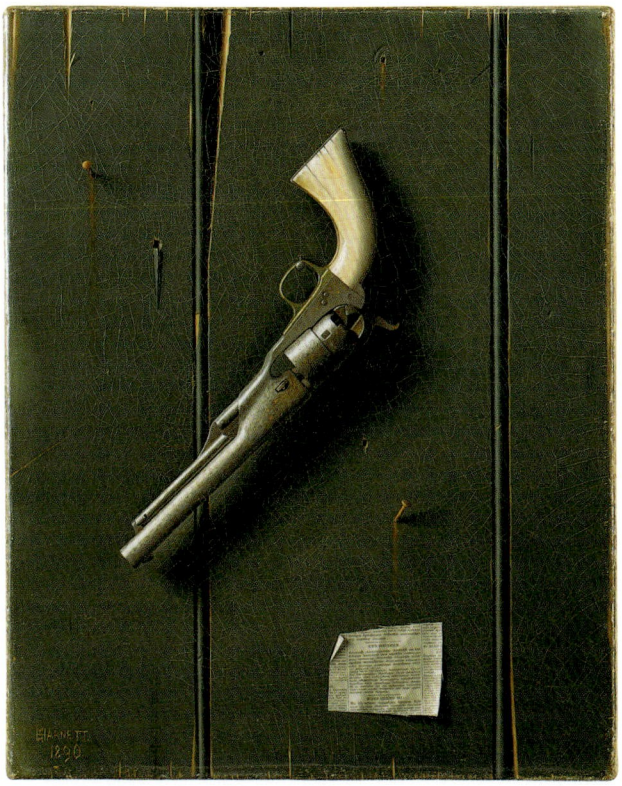

5.16.6 William Michael Harnett: *Faithful Colt*, 1890.
Oil on canvas, 22½ x 18½ in. (57 x 47 cm.)
Wadsworth Atheneum Museum of Art, Hartford, Connecticut

These *trompe l'oeil* still lifes are different from their early-nineteenth-century counterparts by such artists as Raphaelle Peale, which include the fruit, dishes, and silverware of traditional still life paintings [**3.10.8**; p. 200]. Instead, the objects are well-worn, much-handled items from everyday life—books, pipes, guns, hats, newspaper clippings, money. They are cracked and rusted and chipped or torn. One of the best-known painters in the genre was William Michael Harnett (1848–1892), and his *Faithful Colt* (1890) [**5.16.6**] is characteristic both in the detailed illusionism and in the aged objects featured. Harnett enjoyed widespread popularity and, unlike Peale, was able to make a comfortable living through the sale of his paintings.

The art historian David M. Lubin has looked closely at the work of Harnett and attempted to explain his popularity and that of his fellow *trompe l'oeil* painters. Lubin describes the typical patron as "the self-made, geographically mobile, urban middle-class bureaucrat, businessman, or career professional." Such men played a crucial role in the dissemination of art beyond museums, galleries, and private mansions and into men's clubs, hotel lobbies, and department stores. Works that refused to follow the hierarchies of academies and critics were

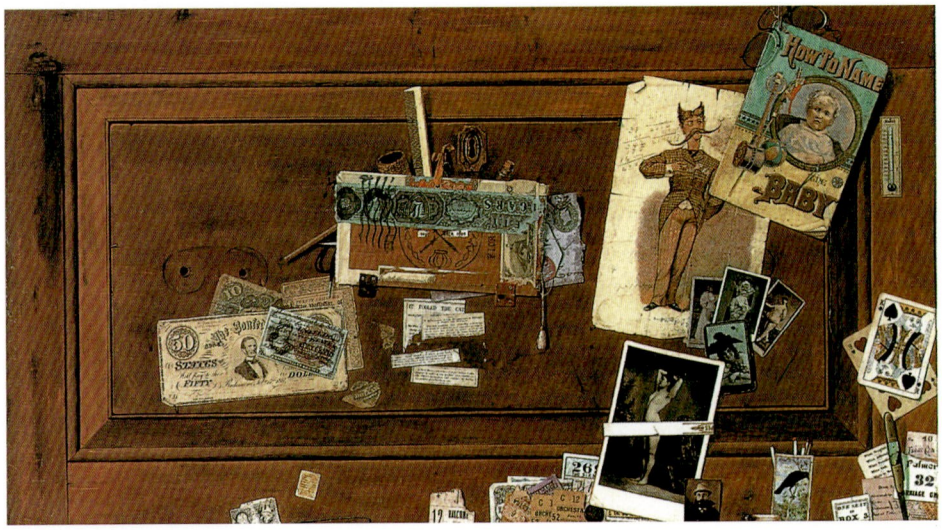

5.16.7 John Haberle: *A Bachelor's Drawer*, 1890–94.
Oil on canvas, 20 x 36 in. (50.8 x 91.4 cm.)
The Metropolitan Museum of Art, New York

5.16.8 William Michael Harnett: *After the Hunt*, 1885.
Oil on canvas, 71½ x 48½ in. (181.6 x 123.2 cm.)
The Fine Arts Museums of San Francisco, San Francisco, California

often welcomed. The academician placed still life at the lower end of the hierarchy of genres (with history painting still assuming a prominent place at the top), and was likely to dismiss *trompe l'oeil* illusionism as lacking in that crucial element of great art—imagination. The department store shopper and middle-class traveller, however, followed his or her own tastes. And these tastes were increasingly being guided by the same men who marketed other objects with persistence in their stores and saloons.

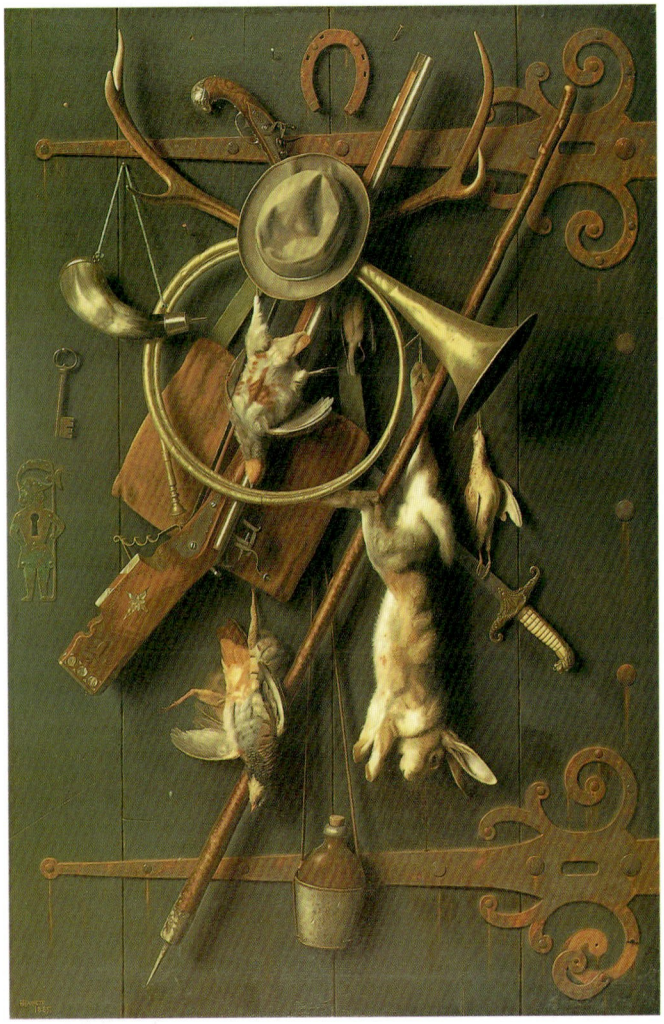

It is not surprising that the subject matter of most late nineteenth-century *trompe l'oeil* paintings was seen as masculine by both male and female viewers. Harnett's *Faithful Colt* celebrates the trusty gun with which a man defended himself and his family. *A Bachelor's Drawer* (1890–94) [**5.16.7**] by John Haberle (1856–1933) evokes the world of single men, marked by playing cards and female nudes and an understandable discomfort with such tasks as naming babies. Harnett's *After the Hunt* (1885) [**5.16.8**] hung in Theodore Stewart's Warren Street saloon in New York. For the businessman or professional who was now married and seldom trod the backwoods, gun in hand, in search of game, it carried a reassuring reminder of the markers of masculinity. Lubin argues that these images served "a psychologically affirmative function" for many men, as well as women, by aesthetically demarcating gender identities at a time when they were being challenged.

Lubin also notes that virtually all of the objects "seemed distinctly different from modern, urban, factory-made consumer goods." While they had obviously once been new commodities, they are shown in their worn states, suggesting that their economic value has been replaced by use and sentimental value. They certainly differed greatly from the shiny objects that filled the ever-increasing numbers of advertisements and shop windows. They also differed in that manufacturers and department store owners clearly targeted women as their audience, for women had become, among their other various roles, the ultimate consumers. This implied dissimilarity "must have made the viewers who admired these paintings feel, by contrast, more manly—or, this is to say, less like a woman."

In at least one important respect, however, *trompe l'oeil* pictures were similar to mass-produced commodities. Their visual style, their precision, and the erasure of the hand of the artist—one seldom sees the trace of a brushstroke on the surface—imitated the erasure of the hand of the laborer in the very processes of mass production. While critics may have been impressed by the skill of such artists as Harnett, they often criticized their work as impersonal or imitative, qualities easily attached to mass-produced items. Yet these qualities also allowed the paintings to counter their associations with a past realist tradition by partaking of a distinctly "modern" machine aesthetic. "Old and worn objects provided appealing subject matter," writes Lubin, "but just so long as the portrayal of them, the painting itself, had the look of an object good as new." In the end, Harnett's paintings softened these associations with mass production through a tender and referential treatment of old and worn objects, suggesting that traditional ways of life could coexist with the new machine age. This was a message welcomed by many caught up in the psychological and material dislocations of an urbanizing and industrializing era.

Domestic Labor and Cultural Production

In their roles as mother and keeper of the home, women were expected not only to cook and clean, but also to engage in the work of educators, providing their children with a sense of "culture." This culture came in two forms. The first embodied the general values, habits, and structures of thinking, feeling, and acting shared by a particular community. The second involved an elite realm of refinement, aesthetic sensibility, and higher learning—a realm that could also operate as a social and political force. The more "cultured" an individual in the latter sense, the more likely this person was to succeed as a businessman or politician or professional if male, and as a wife if female. Working-class women could provide their children with the first sense of culture—the values of a working-class, and often immigrant, community—but seldom the second. Social commentators often pointed to this as evidence of the unsuitability of members of this class for political leadership, although, as will be seen below, some felt mass production would provide many working-class families with access to some of the benefits of "high" culture.

In the latter half of the nineteenth century much was written about the importance of environment on character development. The home was presented as both the breeding ground for future citizens and also as an escape from the harsh workaday world for those who had already graduated to citizenship. It provided a dose of civilized culture as an antidote to the cut-throat norms of the marketplace. Thus, the decoration of the home took on particular importance. Popular guides were published to help instruct women in this endeavor. One of the better-known of these guides was *American Woman's Home* by Catherine Beecher and Harriet Beecher Stowe, published in 1869. The authors encouraged wives and mothers to "renovate degraded man and clothe all clime with beauty." They recommended setting aside $80 for the purchase of "tasteful" and "beautiful" objects, such as wallpaper, tablecloths, curtains, pictures, and plaster groups. Of this sum, $20 was designated for the latter two categories of objects. If one couldn't afford original paintings, one could always buy chromolithographs, which, "when well selected and of the best class, give the charm of color which belongs to expensive paintings." The authors suggested *The Little Scrapbook Maker* by Miss Oakley ($7.50) or *The Barefoot Boy* by Eastman Johnson ($5.00), reproduced by Louis Prang and Co. [**5.16.9**]. And if one couldn't afford store-bought picture frames, then one could make them out of twigs, demonstrating both frugality and creativity.

5.16.9 Louis Prang and Co. after Eastman Johnson: *The Barefoot Boy*, 1867. Chromolithograph, 12¾ x 9¾ in. (32.7 x 25.1 cm.) Boston Public Library, Boston, Massachusetts

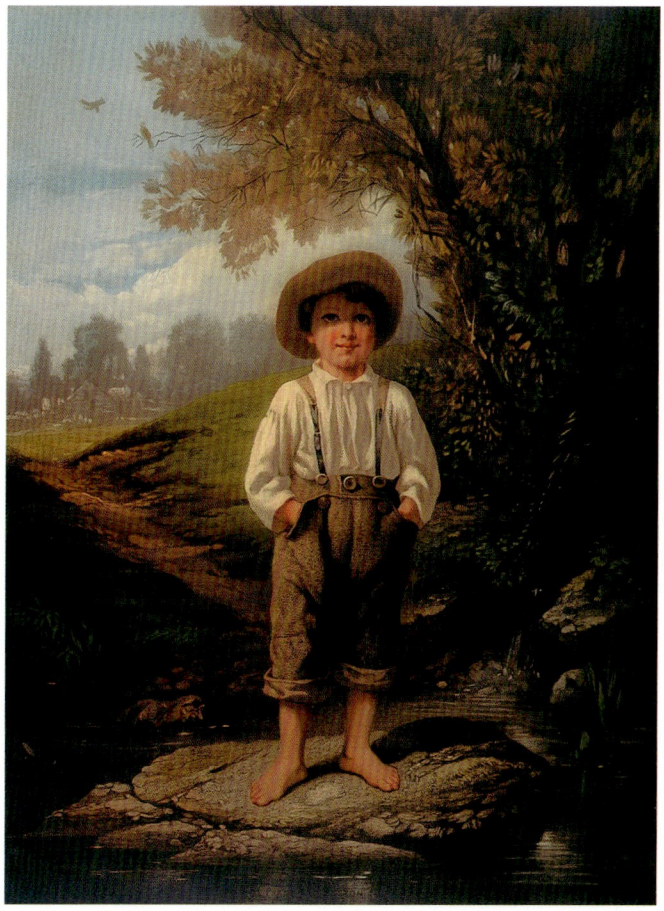

In setting out to purchase their color lithographs, many women would have turned to the firm of Currier and Ives, the best-known and most successful lithography firm in the US in the last quarter of the nineteenth century. Nathaniel Currier began producing lithographs in 1834 and was joined by his brother-in-law James Merritt Ives in 1852. At their height in the 1860s, 1870s, and 1880s, their name was almost synonymous with the category of popular lithography itself.

The success of Currier and Ives was due in large part to effective marketing rather than superior quality, although the two men prided themselves on producing as high a quality print as was possible through the lithographic process. They did not, however, have any "artistic" pretensions: they presented themselves as "publishers of cheap and popular pictures," not of "fine" art. The smaller 3- × 5-inch (7.6- × 12.7-centimeter) prints sold for from 15 to 25 cents retail, while the larger folio images [**5.16.10–5.16.11**] cost several dollars. The primary outlet was the Currier and Ives store on Nassau Street in New York City, where the wares were stacked on long tables in the center or in bins around the walls. Framed and unframed prints and a few original paintings hung on the walls. Outside were additional tables offering items at bargain prices. If people did not want to come down to the store, they could purchase prints from the numerous peddlers who wheeled their carts through the streets of the city. Currier and Ives also had agents across the country and a London office to facilitate distribution throughout Europe.

The main factory for the production of Currier and Ives lithographs was on Spruce Street in New York. Here the stones were prepared, images transferred, and printing done. A drawing was made in reverse with a grease pencil on a slab of limestone. The grease in the ink penetrated the stone, allowing the surface drawing to be washed off. The stone was then kept moist and subsequently inked with a roller (the ink adheres only to the area saturated by the grease pencil) and passed through a press, thus transferring the ink from the stone to the paper and creating a positive image. Lithographs were much easier to produce than engravings or etchings and were more economical, for several hundred prints could be taken from a single stone.

As with mass-produced photographs (see p. 264), the production of lithographs involved a complex division of labor, also marked by gender as well as race. Artists were hired under a variety of contractual arrangements, but three categories were particularly important. In the first were the individuals commissioned to create the works to be copied. Some well-known artists

5.16.10 Frances Bond Palmer and James Merritt Ives: *Across the Continent: "Westward the Course of Empire Takes Its Way,"* 1868. Hand-colored lithograph, 17⅝ x 27⅛ in. (43.8 x 68.7 cm.) Private collection

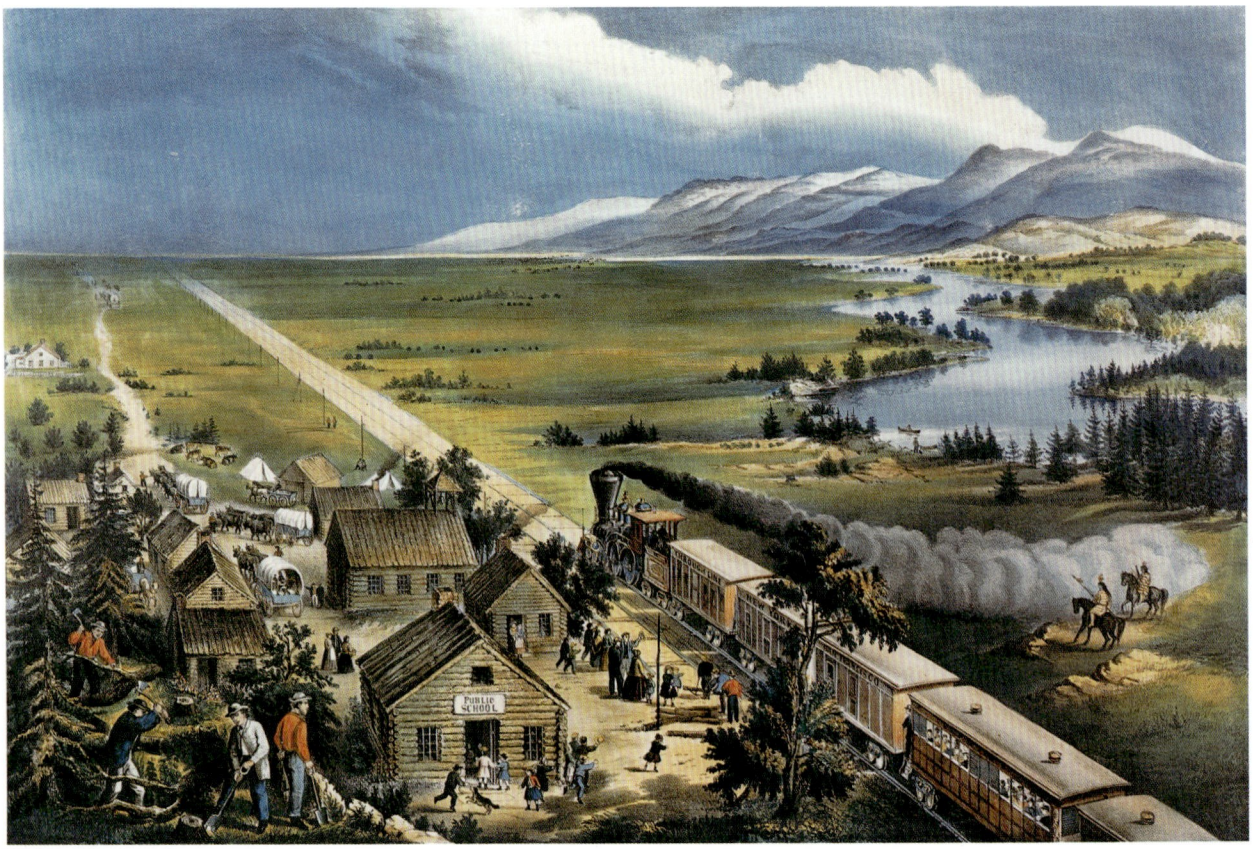

appear in this group, but most were lesser-known ones, who often became associated with particular types of scenes, and most were white men. Frances Bond Palmer was one of the few white women (or women of any race) employed by Currier and Ives in this category. She was in demand not only for still lifes but also for rural views and scenes of westward expansion, such as *Across the Continent: "Westward the Course of Empire Takes Its Way"* (1868) [**5.16.10**], a less lofty take on Emanuel Leutze's piece for the Capitol Rotunda [**4.12.2**; p. 222]. In the second category were shop hands and printers, responsible for copying the designs onto the stones and printing them. Most, if not all, of these individuals were also white men. The third category included the countless white women hired to color the prints by hand in assembly-line fashion.

Rather than producing true chromolithographs by using separate stones for each color, Currier and Ives printed only the black and white drawing, which was then colored by hand on the fifth floor of the Spruce Street factory. The women, mostly of German descent, sat around a table, in the center of which was propped a fully colored print to serve as a model. Each would apply one color, then pass the new image on to her neighbor. When the print had made a complete round, another woman, known as the "finisher," would add the final touches. Currier and Ives used only the finest Austrian colors in an attempt to prevent fading from exposure to light. The names of the colorists, and of the shop hands and printers, are mostly unknown, subsumed under the name of the artist who produced the painting that was copied, and the company itself.

The women who colored lithographs were trained either at Currier and Ives or at the numerous art schools that were springing up around the country. One of the best-known of these schools was the Cooper Union in New York City. Founded in 1859 by the wealthy iron master Peter Cooper, it provided free instruction for working-class men and women. This training included the coloring of lithographs and photographs, and seven rooms were devoted to the female school of design.

The cultural historian Russell Lynes argues that Currier and Ives were successful because they understood public taste and provided people with what they wanted, such as idyllic depictions of snow-covered parks, quaint country scenes, and seascapes. But Currier and Ives prints also contributed to the formation of public taste, including the reinforcement of contemporary prejudices. Middle-class homes acquired images of Native Americans as noble savages, African Americans as childlike or comic figures [**5.16.11**], and the urban landscape devoid of the harsh reality of slums and factories.

The popular essayist James Parton remarked upon the function of such prints in constructing particular social norms

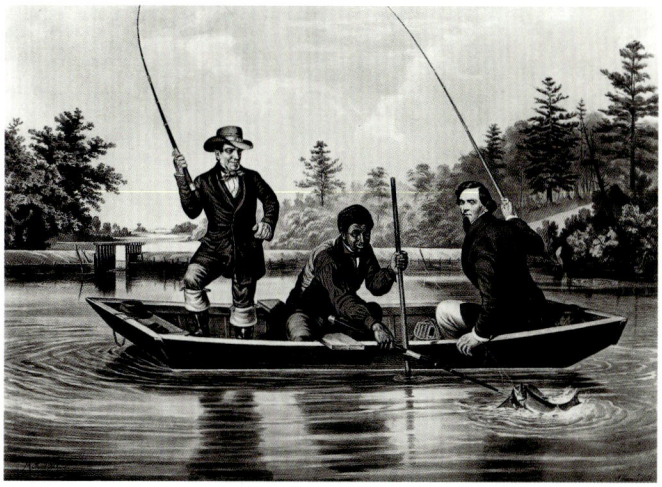

5.16.11 Otto Knirsch after Arthur Fitzwilliam Tait: *Catching a Trout. "We hab you now, sar,"* 1854.
Lithograph, published by Nathaniel Currier, 18¼ x 25¾ in. (46.4 x 65.4 cm.)
Museum of the City of New York, New York

and values in *The Triumphs of Enterprise, Ingenuity and Public Spirit*, published in 1874. Lithographs and chromolithographs, which he hailed as "oil paintings by machinery," were able to do the "special work of America at present." They were able to help in the conversion of the influx of immigrants from Europe's underclasses, "as well as the emancipated slaves from the South," into "thinking, knowing, skillful, tastefull [sic] American citizens." Parton recognized that some might not be able to afford their own prints (in 1890 the annual wages for railroad laborers totaled $124, with brakemen making $212). Yet they could still view them in the shop windows of Currier and Ives or other printsellers.

Parton's linkage of machinery and culture, as well as his linkage of both to social change, was significant. The mass production and dissemination of culture were made possible by mechanization and the development of a market economy. This same mechanization, and the division of labor that accompanied it, were responsible for the erosion of older cultures of work and shared pleasure, which were then replaced by the mechanically produced new cultures. Thus, the same processes that created insecurities in people's daily lives, both at work and at home, also created new images of security for the home environment in the form of cultural goods.

This connection between security, consumption, and culture was articulated perhaps most eloquently by the economist Simon Patten in his essay "The Consumption of Wealth" (1889). Patten's solution to the gap between the standards of living of the laboring classes and employing classes did not lie in any reordering of social relations or redistribution of wealth. Instead, it lay in providing the laboring classes with more opportunities to consume a greater variety of goods. Patten argued that people worked not simply to satisfy material needs but also to satisfy desires. As existing desires are satisfied, new ones will take their place, thus creating the need for a wider variety of goods to satisfy these new desires.

Unfortunately, notes Patten, the satisfying of desires through consumption had yet to raise the poor from their state of poverty. This was because the goods they could afford appealed to their more "primitive" desires—drinking, smoking—and thus did not challenge them to strive for higher personal and professional goals. What was needed, therefore, was to make goods that appealed to a person's more "refined" senses—fine music, painting—cheaper, and those that appealed to their "primitive" senses more expensive. With a higher level of refined taste would come a greater consumption of goods (both facilitated by a shorter work day and inexpensive education) and a greater social harmony. The ultimate gain for society would be the widespread coexistence of both peace and production. High culture would thus guide consumption and promote a society of equals. Who would have thought that so much would result from the cheap reproductive processes that made "the beautiful within reach of all"? Even advertisements, remarked Patten, would allow beauty into the homes of the very poorest. Beauty is thus transformed into a commodity, and the walls of the domestic sphere into billboards.

Helpful Women: The Evolving Image of the Domestic Servant

As middle-class women participated in this new commodification of culture and inculcation of new social norms and values, they also struggled with the material transformation of labor within the home, particularly as manifested in the presence of household servants. The employment of servants was nothing new in the nineteenth century. As the art historian Elizabeth O'Leary points out, approximately half of the immigrants who came to the American colonies from Europe in the seventeenth and eighteenth centuries arrived as bound servants. "In every colony," she writes, "white servitude preceded black slavery." Yet while it was possible for white servants to work their way out of servitude, this was not an option for the majority of blacks who, by the end of the seventeenth century, had become slaves, not servants (the first Africans arrived in Jamestown in 1619 as indentured servants—see p. 67).

The lives of servants, both white and black, during the colonial period were hard. Many died of overwork and illness before they were able to pay off those who had financed their trip to the colonies. The American Revolution's rhetoric of liberation from the tyranny of bondage thus struck a chord with those who had experienced bondage in their early years in the colonies and who feared their hard-won freedom might be taken away from them should the rebellion against England be crushed.

Following the revolution, indentured servitude among whites quickly disappeared and the portrayal of white servants in paintings and prints, rare during colonial times [**1.4.19**; p. 75], became even rarer in the new republic. Even the term "servant" fell out of use as a term for white household workers (it remained in effect for blacks, along with "slave") and was replaced by the less offensive term "help." Much of the "help" employed in early nineteenth-century homes was composed of the sons and daughters of neighbors or relatives, thus blurring the authoritarian boundaries between employer and employee. Also, at this time the home was still an important site of economic production, so that the members of the household often worked side by side with their help.

These social and economic relations of production within the home changed in the middle of the nineteenth century. As factories multiplied and increasingly took over the task of producing many of the necessities of life, many women were forced out of the home and into these factories to provide the currency necessary to purchase manufactured goods. Women also entered domestic service, especially those arriving in large numbers from Europe. Ireland was a major source of immigrants, particularly after the potato blight of 1846–49. Some ten years later, Irish men and women constituted almost half of the country's foreign-born population.

By 1850, from 15 to 30 percent of urban households employed live-in domestics, many of whom were recent female immigrants. Paid domestic labor had come to be regarded by women born in the colonies or in the new nation as one of the least desirable forms of employment. It involved heavy, backbreaking labor and was also associated with low morals (though the suspect morals of young female servants were often the result of the unwanted sexual attentions of the men of the house). While factory labor could also be backbreaking, it allowed women greater independence, for domestic workers often lived with their employers and were on call twenty-four hours a day.

As more and more foreigners took over the duties of domestic help, a greater distinction was made between them and family members, and the word "servant" came back into popular usage. In addition, many middle- and upper-class women, who employed the majority of domestic workers, began complaining increasingly of the "servant problem." Even Lilly Martin Spencer (1822–1902), who had produced sympathetic images of household workers, such as *Shake Hands?* (1854) [**5.16.12**], began

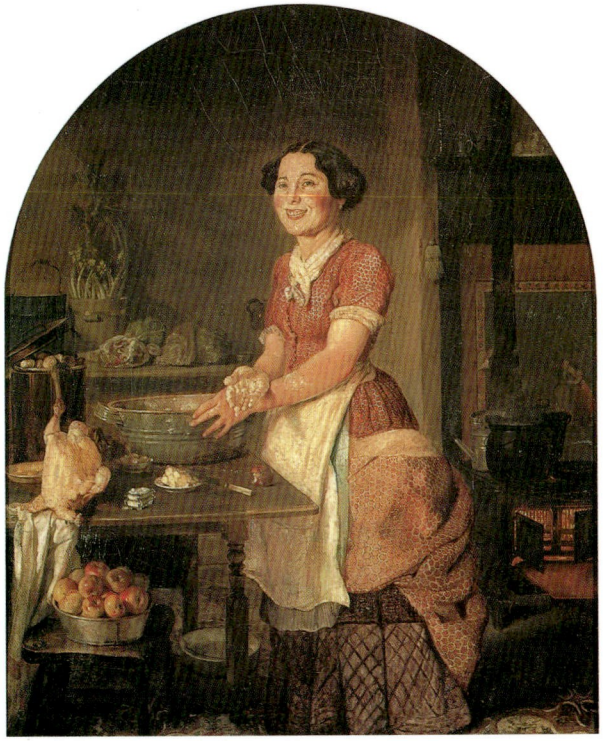

5.16.12 Lilly Martin Spencer: *Shake Hands?*, 1854.
Oil on canvas, 30⅛ x 25⅝ in. (76.5 x 63.8 cm.)
Ohio Historical Society, Columbus

to complain at the end of the 1850s of the difficulty of finding good servants and of their laziness and dishonesty. This less sympathetic attitude can be found in her painting *The Fruit of Temptation* (*c.* 1857), known from a lithograph by Jean-Baptiste-Adolphe Lafosse for the French firm Goupil [**5.16.13**]. Here, instead of an industrious woman pausing in her work to offer her flour-covered hand playfully to the viewer (another instance of a slight transgression of the rules of etiquette; see pp. 194–95), we have an irresponsible servant, concerned more with her own appearance than with the household labor and childcare tasks assigned to her. Her feckless nature was often attributed to her foreignness. She was "Bridget," the Irish Catholic immigrant whose laziness was matched only by her surliness.

Household disarray had a broader symbolic meaning as well. A well ordered and prosperous home was seen as indicative of both a stable family and a well-ordered and prosperous nation. Many pinpointed the waves of new immigrants as the cause of disruption within both the home and the nation, despite the fact that their labor enabled the massive expansion of industry, which led to the increasing accumulation of wealth within the US. Many working-class men and women born in the US saw these new immigrants as a threat to their jobs. Middle- and upper-class men and women also saw them as swelling the ranks of the working class and spreading revolutionary ideas about socialism and workers' rights.

African American women were also found in large numbers among the ranks of household servants. In fact, the animosity between African American and Irish workers intensified in the last half of the nineteenth century as both groups competed for the lowest-paying jobs in urban centers. African American female servants had a long history of being represented in paintings and prints at the margins of compositions (for example, Prudence Punderson's *The First, Second, and Last Scene of Mortality* [**2.5.17**; p. 105] and Richard Caton Woodville's *Old '76 and Young '48* [**4.11.2**; p. 212]). When they were foregrounded, they often were shown as comic or irresponsible figures.

One example of the comic portrayal of African American servants is *Her Mistress's Clothes* (1848) [**5.16.14**; p. 290] by Harriet Cany Peale (1800–1869), the second wife of the artist Rembrandt Peale. O'Leary points out how the painting alludes to the pseudosciences of phrenology and physiognomy. Such pseudosciences promoted racial comparisons and hierarchies, with the Anglo-Saxon body always presented as occupying the highest rung on the evolutionary ladder. By juxtaposing the

5.16.13 Jean-Baptiste-Adolphe Lafosse after Lilly Martin Spencer: *The Fruit of Temptation*, *c.* 1857.
Lithograph, published by Goupil, New York, 24½ x 20⅛ in. (62.2 x 51 cm.)
Ohio Historical Society, Columbus

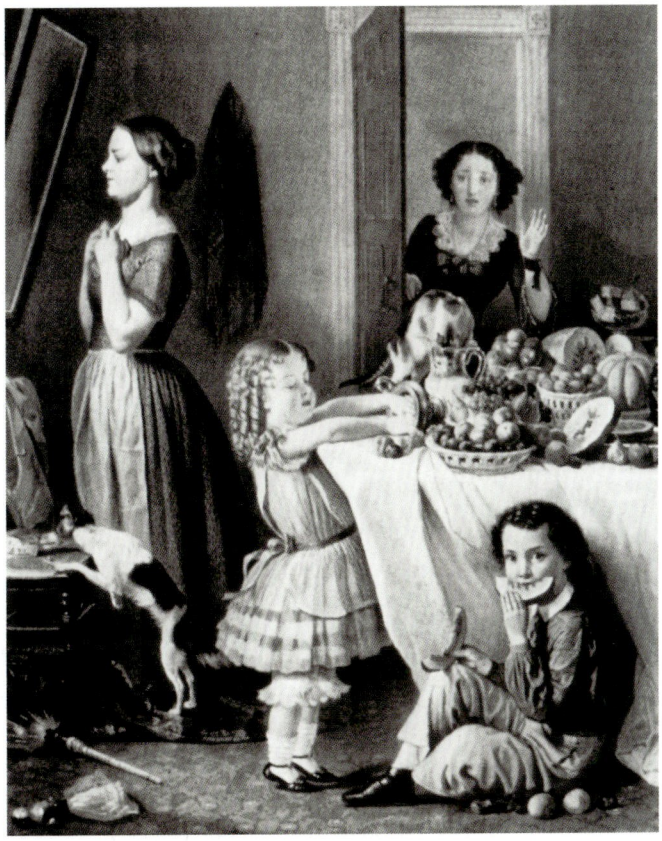

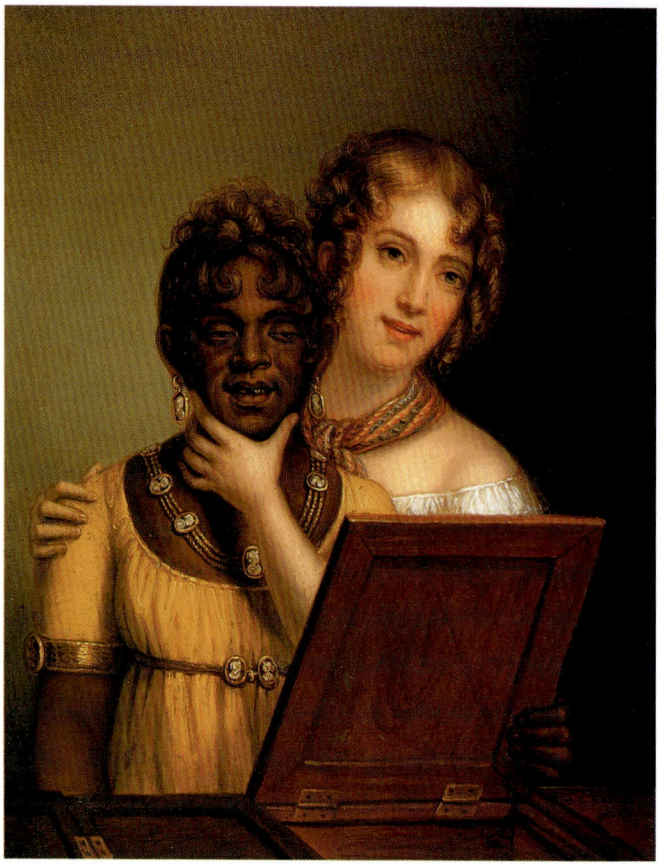

5.16.14 Harriet Cany Peale: *Her Mistress's Clothes*, 1848.
Oil on panel, 10⅞ x 8¼ in. (25.7 x 21 cm.)
The Charleston Renaissance Gallery, Robert M. Hicklin Jr., Inc., Charleston, South Carolina

heads of the young white girl and her even younger African American servant, Cany Peale sets up an obvious contrast, in which the oval face, aquiline nose, light skin, and small lips of the white girl are inevitably seen as superior. Furthermore, a difference is made between the dresses worn by the two young women. The painter, who was employed in a fancy-goods business in Philadelphia before her marriage, would have been very knowledgeable about women's fashion. The African American girl may be wearing "her mistress's clothes," but the neoclassical Empire-style gown and cameo necklace, earrings and belt, while valuable, were long out of fashion. The latest style was the simple, off-the-shoulder dress and plaid scarf worn by the white girl. The viewer is invited to smile at the servant's naiveté, as she is obviously pleased by her reflection in the mirror.

Perhaps the oddest aspect of the painting, however, is the position of the white girl's hand on the black girl's neck. The artist probably intended it to be read as the white girl directing the black girl's gaze toward the mirror, but it ends up looking as if the white girl is strangling her young servant. Cany Peale created this painting at a time of heightened racial tension in Philadelphia, a city that contained the largest population of free African Americans of any northern city. Three years earlier a Jamaican Emancipation Day parade had been followed by riots, where white mobs attacked the black paraders and then went on to destroy black homes and churches. These events led not to the punishing of members of the white mob, who were primarily Irish, but to the passage of ordinances limiting African American assembly. "A local audience having grown uneasy with its large black community," writes O'Leary, "might have found Peale's portrayal of a domesticated African American reassuring." They also might have been further reassured by the white girl's seemingly firm grip on the black girl's throat, a suggestion that any dissatisfaction with this domesticated status would be met with swift punishment.

Older African American female servants appeared in paintings and popular media primarily in the roles of cooks or nursemaids. These figures, commonly referred to as "Mammy" or "Dinah," were most often represented as large and sexless, with

5.16.15 Unknown artist: trade-card advertisement for Edward Chamberlin & Co.'s "Concentrated Leaven," 1860.
Lithograph, published by John H. Bufford, Boston, Massachusetts
Courtesy The New-York Historical Society, New York

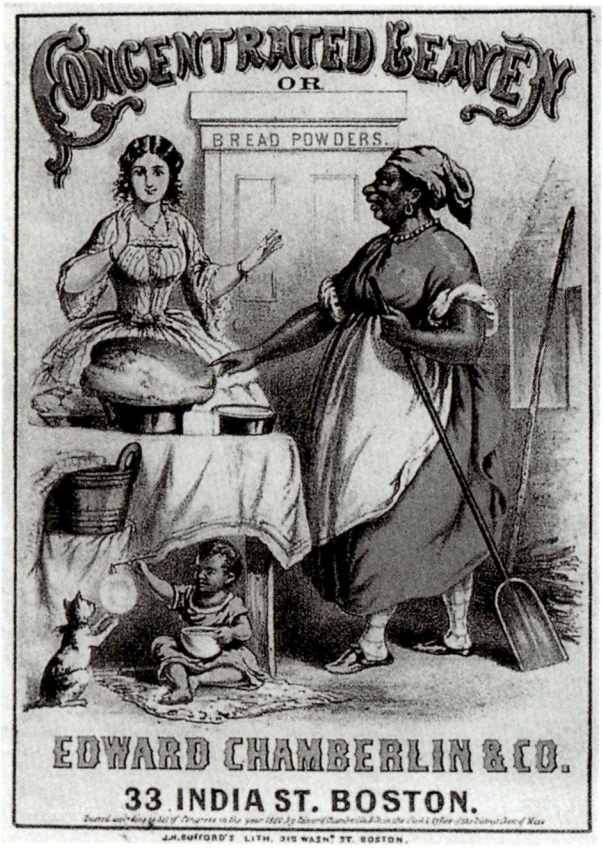

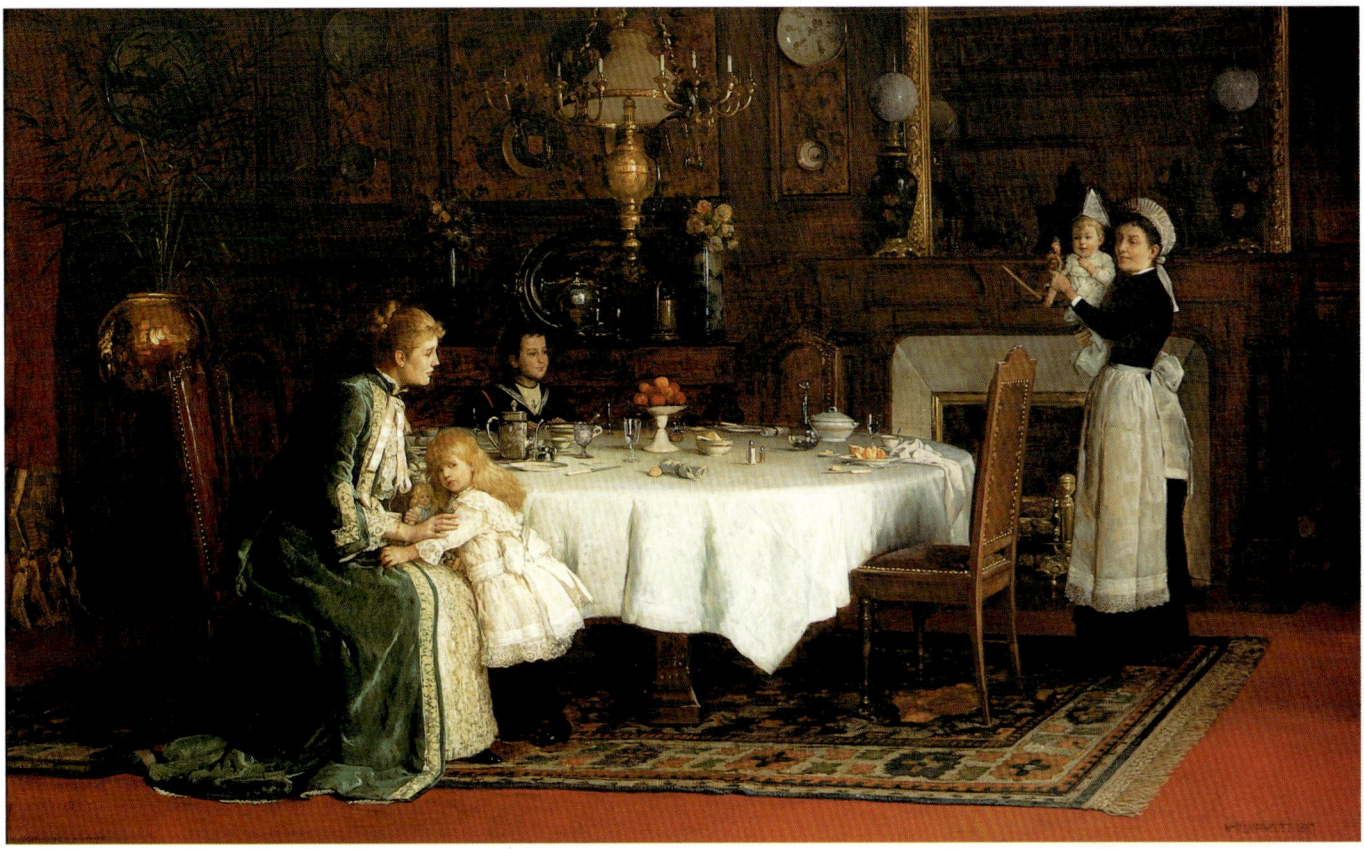

5.16.16 William Henry Lippincott: *Infantry in Arms*, 1887. Oil on canvas, 32 x 53¼ in. (81.3 x 135.3 cm.) The Pennsylvania Academy of the Fine Arts, Philadelphia

heads covered by kerchiefs. They were fiercely independent, but ultimately kind, loyal, and devoted to their white charges. This Mammy/Dinah character appears in an 1860 trade card advertisement for Edward Chamberlin & Co.'s "Concentrated Leaven" [**5.16.15**], a precursor of the ubiquitous Aunt Jemima pancake advertisement [see V. 2, pp. 527–28] that made its debut in 1893 at the World's Columbian Exposition in Chicago. What is most striking is not the magical effect of the leaven, but the contrast between the slender, well-dressed, small-featured white woman and the large-featured, buxom, plainly dressed African American woman. The latter is a powerful character physically and she appears fully at home in her kitchen. She nurtures all the members of the household, and because of this nurturing commands a certain degree of respect. But no one would mistake her physical presence and control of the kitchen for any real social or economic power.

As the economy continued to grow in the last quarter of the nineteenth century, with an ensuing expansion of an urban-based middle class, the demand for household servants also grew. O'Leary notes that "by the end of the 1870s, one-fourth of all urban and suburban households employed at least one servant." The wealthier households now looked to European-trained help, and began insisting on a more rigid formal relationship. "Servants were increasingly set apart by special uniforms, titles, duties, and stations," writes O'Leary. "As never before in the nineteenth century, an American servant class became clearly visible."

This visibility was particularly apparent in the numerous paintings of the domestic interiors of the upper class. Here servants were not portrayed as surly and/or homely Irish "Bridgets" primping in front of a mirror or elbow-deep in flour. Instead, they appeared as beautiful women who functioned, along with their mistresses, as decorative objects testifying to the wealth of the man of the house. And in the Gilded Age, an era of conspicuous consumption and growing number of millionaires, decorative objects abounded (there were only three millionaires in the US in 1861; by 1900 there were more than four thousand).

William Henry Lippincott (1849–1920) produced several paintings of upper-class households, including *Infantry in Arms* (1887) [**5.16.16**]. Lippincott had studied in Paris in the studio of Léon Bonnat (1833–1922) and upon his return went to New York City and became an instructor at the National Academy of Design. *Infantry in Arms* portrays a lavish dining room marked by leather chairs, an oriental carpet, various silver, brass, and

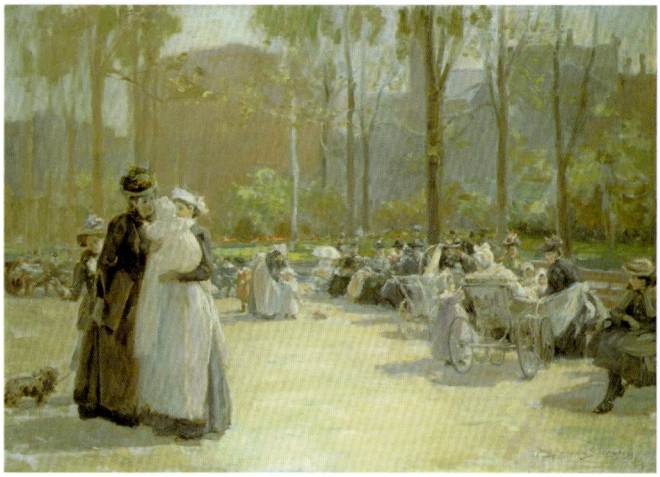

5.16.17 Alice Barber Stephens: *A Spring Morning in the Park*, 1892.
Oil on canvas, 18 x 26 in. (45.7 x 66 cm.)
Private collection

gold leaf objects, and a liveried nursemaid attired in the traditional dark dress, white apron, and hat. She stands with a child both "in her arms" and "in arms" (dressed in military costume), while the child's mother sits opposite her. The latter's seated pose and the former's uniform make it perfectly clear who is the servant and who is the mistress. Despite the nursemaid's smile, the young blond girl clings to her mother's dress, unwilling to leave her side, in fear of her "armed" sibling.

Liveried nursemaids also changed the look of major urban parks, as is shown in *A Spring Morning in the Park* (1892) [**5.16.17**] by Alice Barber Stephens (1858–1932), with its numerous women in the requisite dress of their occupation. Stephens was a well-known professional illustrator who studied painting in the late 1870s at the Pennsylvania Academy of the Fine Arts under Thomas Eakins. She subsequently joined a large number of American artists who traveled to Paris after the Civil War. Women were not allowed to study at the Parisian Academy of Fine Arts, so Stephens attended the privately-run Académie Julian and the Académie Colarossi. While in Paris, she, like most of her fellow American students, was exposed to the works of the French Impressionists. The effects of this art movement, with its loose brushwork and concern with light and atmosphere, can be seen in Stephens's rendition of Rittenhouse Square in Philadelphia in the spring (for more on American Impressionism see Chapter 17). While at first glance a scene of upper-class leisure, it is also a scene of work, as the several uniforms testify. Indeed, the figures at work function to heighten the leisured status of the standing woman in the flowered hat in the left foreground, who is being shown the young child by a nanny while another child hovers behind her and plays with a dog.

Spaces of Leisure and Labor: Domestic Architecture and Interior Design

While uniforms made servants more visible in parks and paintings of upper-class parlors, architects worked to ensure that they were seen within the home only when necessary. Just as President Thomas Jefferson utilized dumbwaiters and subterranean kitchens to keep his house slaves out of view (see p. 111), so too did late nineteenth-century architects construct elaborate mansions patterned after the homes of the wealthy in Europe, which included separate service wings, entrances, and stairways. A design of 1878–82 by George B. Post (1837–1912) for a New York mansion for the socialite and businessman Cornelius Vanderbilt II shows a service staircase and servants engaged in various tasks [**5.16.18**].

Post's drawing suggests not only the palatial size of many of the houses of late nineteenth-century "Robber Barons" but also the intricate and varied nature of the items found within these homes—for example, the exquisitely carved fireplace mantels and the wall filled with oil paintings. In the second half of the century, the earlier preference for austere classical architectural forms [**2.6.2b**, p. 111; **2.6.4**, p. 113; **2.6.15**, p. 119] was supplanted

5.16.18 George B. Post: presentation drawing for the house of Cornelius Vanderbilt II, New York (detail), 1878–82.
Ink and watercolor on paper, 30 x 50 in. (76.2 x 127 cm.)
Courtesy The New-York Historical Society, New York

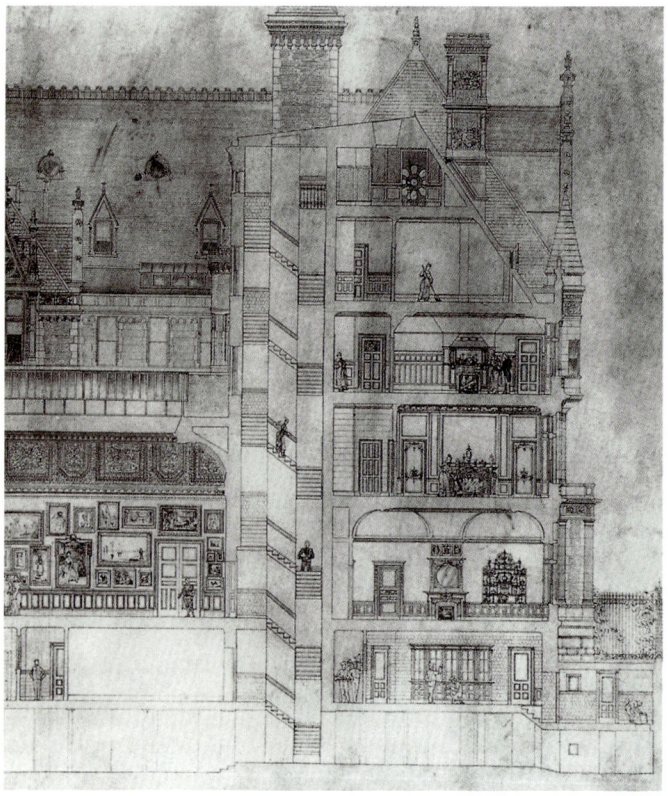

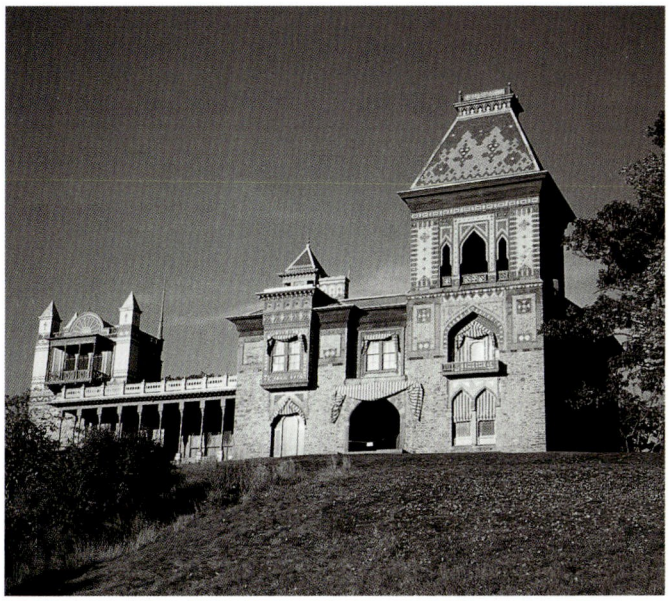

5.16.19 Calvert Vaux and Frederic Edwin Church: Olana, Hudson, New York, 1870–72 and 1888–89.

by a series of more elaborate and decorative revivalist styles in both exterior and interior design. These included the luxuriant and naturalistic Rococo, the elegant and uplifting Gothic, the stately and lavish Renaissance, or an imaginative combination of several period styles. The architectural historian Spiro Kostof describes the decades after the Civil War as ones of "exuberant eclecticism and a lawless, energetic, architectural laissez-faire. Unmindful of even the pretense of archaeological accuracy, buildings were composed as if to prove that all human culture was fair quarry for this triumphant nation."

Calvert Vaux (1824–1895) and the painter Frederic Edwin Church (see pp. 166–170) designed one of the most eclectic residences of this period, Olana (Arabic for "our place on high"), which served as Church's home overlooking the Hudson River near Hudson, New York (1870–72, 1888–89) [**5.16.19**]. Church was inspired by the architecture of Egypt and the Near East, having traveled in those regions in the late 1860s. As a veteran showman and entrepreneur, he was undoubtedly pleased with this unique architectural statement, with its multicolored tiles, glazed brick, and carnivalesque roofline.

The economic boom that followed the Civil War brought new wealth and new homes to entrepreneurs on the West Coast as well. The lumber magnate William M. Carson constructed an elaborate home in Eureka, California, in 1884–86 [**5.16.20**] in which the source of his wealth—wood—was excessively displayed. The structure was designed in the High Victorian style by Samuel Newsom (1854–1908) and Joseph Cather Newsom (1858–1930), brothers who traveled to California from Ontario, Canada, and who soon established a flourishing business. This mansion was, in Kostof's words, one of those "gaily painted houses with irregular silhouettes, jutting elements and projections, crests, brackets, scrolls, and finials; oversized public monuments of stone and aggregates of curdled ornament, building up to tall mansarded roofs and contumacious towers." Conspicuous consumption was the rule of the day, and homes like Carson's would appear with regularity in the urban centers of California throughout the late nineteenth century.

An obsession with decoration also marked the interiors of these elaborate homes, beginning in the mid-century. Sometimes one house would contain rooms in different period styles, or rooms that combined elements from many different periods. In a reconstruction of a Rococo Revival parlor of around 1852 [**5.16.21**; p. 294] one can see the characteristic elements that mark the Rococo style in the delicately carved fruit and vegetal ornament of the rosewood furniture by the well-known New York cabinetmaker and manufacturer John Henry Belter. Naturalistic designs also mark the tapestry velvet rug, gilded mirrors, window coverings, and chandelier. The overall opulence of the room suggests the wealth of its inhabitants. One can also well imagine what faced the servants who were required to maintain it in pristine order. The sweeping, dusting, and polishing of the furnishings of even a modest urban mansion, along with the washing of household linens and clothing, would keep several women busy from dawn to dusk.

5.16.20 Samuel Newsom and Joseph Cather Newsom: William Carson House, Eureka, California, 1884–86.

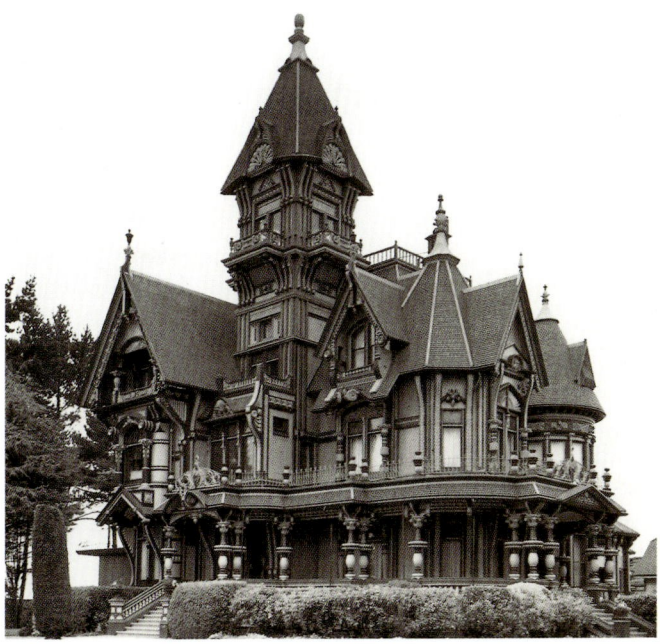

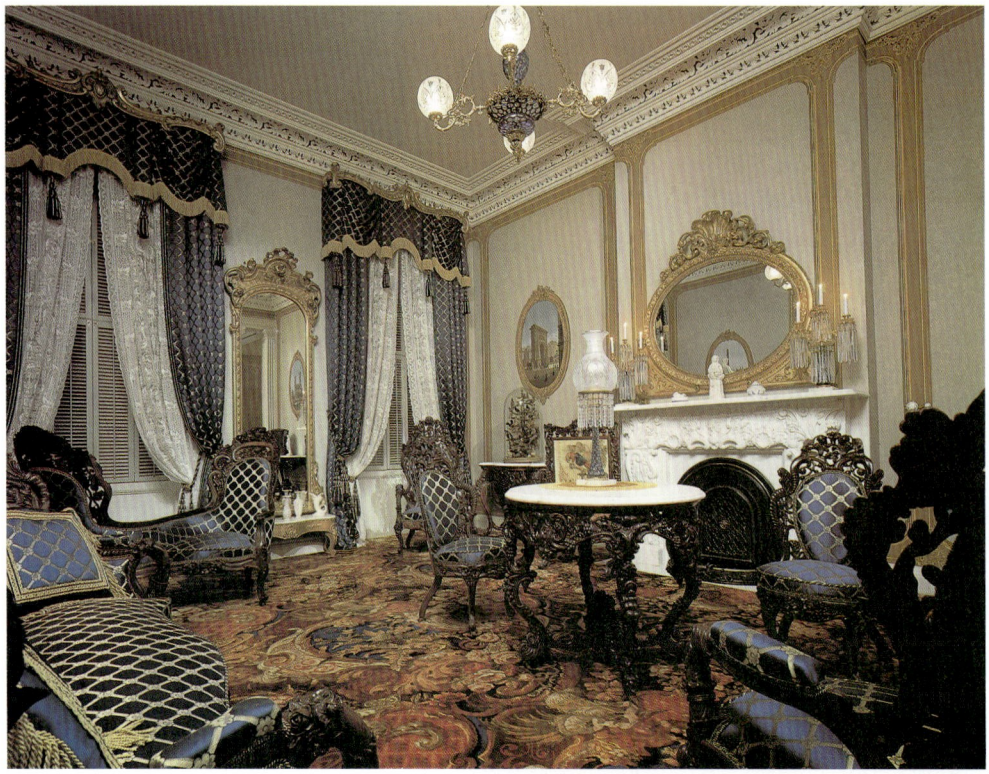

5.16.21 A Rococo Revival parlor, with architectural elements from a house at Astoria, New York, of *c.* 1852, and rosewood furniture by John Henry Belter. The Metropolitan Museum of Art, New York

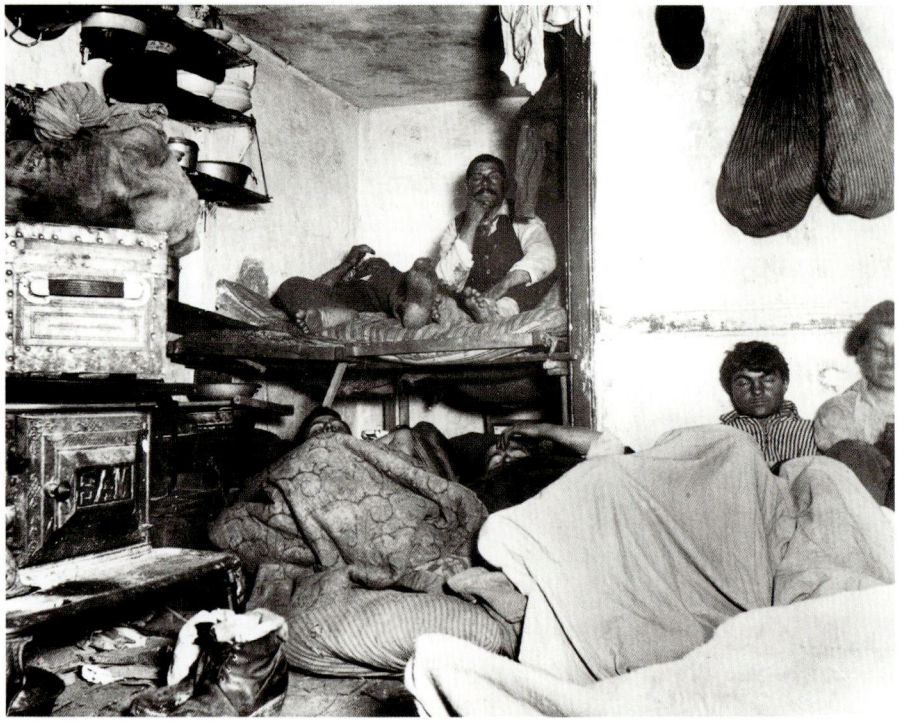

5.16.22 Jacob A. Riis: *Five Cents a Spot*, 1889. Photograph
Museum of the City of New York, New York

Not everyone, however, enjoyed the luxurious interiors of these elaborate mansions. Many lived in more modest homes, while even more lived in crowded urban slums. Such slums were recorded in the photographs of Jacob A. Riis (1849–1914). Riis was born in Denmark in 1849 and came to the US in 1870. He worked primarily as a writer and a reporter for various newspapers and magazines. In the late 1880s and early 1890s, however, he used his camera to take photographs of a New York tenement district, which were included in several books, the most famous of which is *How the Other Half Lives* (1890). *Five Cents a Spot* (1889) [**5.16.22**] shows a small room in a house on Bayard Street. Riis described the scene:

> In a room not thirteen feet [4 meters] either way slept twelve men and women, two or three in bunks set in a sort of alcove, the rest on the floor. A kerosene lamp burnt dimly in the fearful atmosphere, probably to guide other and later arrivals to their "beds," for it was only just past midnight.

Those passing the night in this room paid 5 cents for their spot. The men and women attempt to maintain a semblance of order. Their belongings are gathered into bundles that hang on the wall or sit on top of a trunk, and the dishes are stacked neatly on the shelves.

At the time of his death Riis was celebrated as a social reformer, but no mention was made of his photographs. Today he is celebrated, instead, as one of the first photographers to direct his attention to the urban poor [see V. 2, **6.19.13**; p. 347], and his images are seen as a historical record of a particular moment in time. These photographs, however, like those taken in studios, were often posed in order to achieve the desired effect. Sometimes the posing created a nobler image of the sitters, as they pulled out what few prized possessions they owned for display. Other times a more sinister or destitute atmosphere was created. Yet despite these alterations, Riis's photographs provide as close an image as we are ever likely to have of the living conditions of that "other half."

Riis's photographs were meant to aid in the clearing of New York's worst slums and in the construction of more sanitary housing for the city's working class. Sometimes, however, the slums were replaced by housing for the city's wealthier residents, thus compromising the efforts of well-meaning reformers. These reformers came primarily from the educated middle class, with women among the most visible. In their attempts to better the lives of the country's urban poor, they lobbied for laws requiring sanitary and safe working and living conditions and limits on the use of child labor. They also set up community centers or settlement houses where people could come for physical and cultural nourishment. Culture, as mentioned earlier (see pp. 287–88), was drawn into the battle against poverty and political unrest. While helping immigrant communities retain a sense of cohesiveness, social reformers also worked to assimilate the members of such communities into a broader "American" culture, the parameters of which were still being formed.

Spaces of Leisure and Labor: Parks and Streets

The harmonious interaction between servant, young charge, and wealthy mistress displayed in Alice Barber Stephens's *A Spring Morning in the Park* [**5.16.17**; p. 292] contrasts with the battles that were taking place around and within urban parks not only over wages and working conditions, but also over access. New York's Central Park is a case in point [**5.16.23**; p. 296]. An early example of the "City Beautiful" movement that swept the country in the last quarter of the century, it was designed in the late 1850s by Frederick Law Olmsted (1822–1903), with the assistance of the architect Calvert Vaux—who would later help Frederic Edwin Church design his residence Olana (see p. 293). Their design drew more heavily upon the British pastoral and picturesque traditions than the formal garden designs common in France. Thus, rather than broad avenues and elegant fountains (the formal Bethesda Fountain and area to the south being the main exception), one finds carefully placed winding paths, open fields, groves of trees, lakes and streams, and buildings which appear unexpectedly as one rounds a corner. Olmsted ordered the natural environment in a manner similar to many landscape painters, utilizing artificial conventions to make sure that his constructed landscape looked "natural."

While wealthy New Yorkers wanted the park primarily as their own cultural preserve dotted with museums and other educational institutions, working-class men and women wanted a place for sport and amusement. Olmsted managed to steer a course between these two competing camps. The eldest son of a wealthy New England merchant, he shared with many late nineteenth-century intellectuals a concern for the creation of a unifying national culture. One way in which it could be created, he thought, was through environmental planning or "ecological engineering." Olmsted believed that the American democracy that had developed in a rural environment now had to be adapted to an urban environment. What needed to be maintained was the sense of community of the village. Since the home and the workplace had become increasingly separated, this required a new physical locale, and that locale could be the city park.

Olmsted's concern with order, despite the look of randomness, was closely connected to this vision of the park as a social experiment. Central Park, a vast natural space in the midst of a rapidly growing city, was to be an educational environment where poor immigrants could mingle with members of the middle and upper classes, many of whom occupied the townhouses and mansions then bordering its southern end. These immigrants would therefore learn the "proper" way to comport themselves. Thus, the park became both a release valve of sorts—a place to go to escape the cramped and unhealthy quarters at work and at home—and a "schoolroom." To ensure it retained its educational character, strict regulations regarding behavior within the grounds were established and enforced by the police, ranging from the types of vehicles allowed to the types and numbers of commercial vendors granted licenses. In addition, four sunken "parkway" roads helped prevent cross-town traffic from impinging on the peaceful strolls of the park visitors.

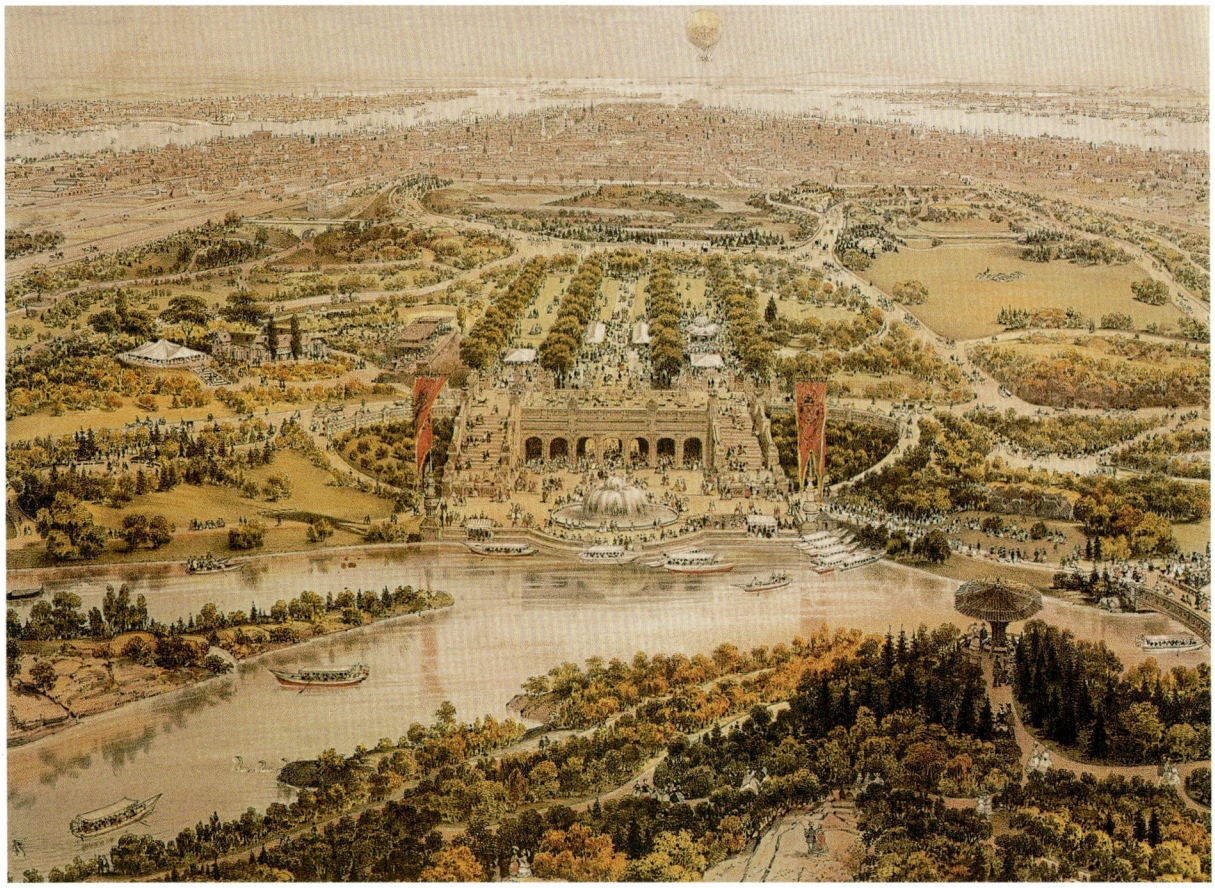

5.16.23 Frederick Law Olmsted and Calvert Vaux: Central Park, New York, begun 1857.
This bird's-eye view by John Bachman of *c.* 1870 shows about one-third of the park, looking south toward the formal Bethesda Fountain in the center of the much more extensive informal landscape, with the crowded city beyond.
Courtesy The New-York Historical Society, New York

Olmsted also applied his ordering skills to a more unruly landscape, Yosemite Valley, a large expanse of territory on the eastern edge of California. He traveled to the region in 1863 to take up the job of director of the Mariposa Mining Estates, a gold mining enterprise on the edge of Yosemite controlled by Eastern interests. This enterprise and other mining, farming, and lumber ventures had been facilitated by the forced removal of the indigenous Ahwahneechee, a branch of the Southern Sierra Miwok, from the region by federal troops in 1851. Olmsted's concerns were with the physical plant of the mining operations, as well as the homes and public facilities being built for the miners and their families.

The year after Olmsted arrived in California, the lobbying efforts of those devoted to preserving sections of what they saw as the nation's pristine wilderness paid off. In 1864 Yosemite Valley became a state park (it became a national park in 1890). A commission was established, and Olmsted was appointed its first president. Upon visiting the valley, Olmsted was immediately struck by its potential as a place for recreation and scientific study. He oversaw the mapping and surveying of the site and drafted a report outlining management policy for its maintenance and preservation. Visitors were met by a series of carefully laid-out roads and trails determined in large part by geological formations. Yet these trails were also conditioned by Olmsted's vision of the sublime (see p. 156). In due course, many arrived with a preconceived image of the dramatic landscape acquired through commercial brochures or through such paintings as Albert Bierstadt's *Looking Down Yosemite Valley, California* (1865) [**5.16.24**].

Photographers also joined painters in preparing the visitor for his or her wilderness experience. Often their work relied on the same artistic conventions used by such painters as Bierstadt (1830–1902). For example, in 1863, the same year Bierstadt painted *The Rocky Mountains, Lander's Peak* [**3.9.1**; p. 172], the San Francisco photographer Carleton E. Watkins (1829–1916) captured a view of Yosemite in his *Best General View, Mariposa Trail* [**5.16.25**]. As in Bierstadt's painting of Yosemite Valley, the landscape recedes into the distance in overlapping layers of hills and rock. In both works mountains and hills take up three-quarters of the picture plane, with a thin band of sky at the top.

5.16.24 Albert Bierstadt: *Looking Down Yosemite Valley, California*, 1865. Oil on canvas, 64 x 96¼ in. (162.6 x 244.5 cm.) Birmingham Museum of Art, Birmingham, Alabama

5.16.25 Carleton E. Watkins: *Best General View, Mariposa Trail*, 1863. Photograph Library of Congress, Washington, D.C.

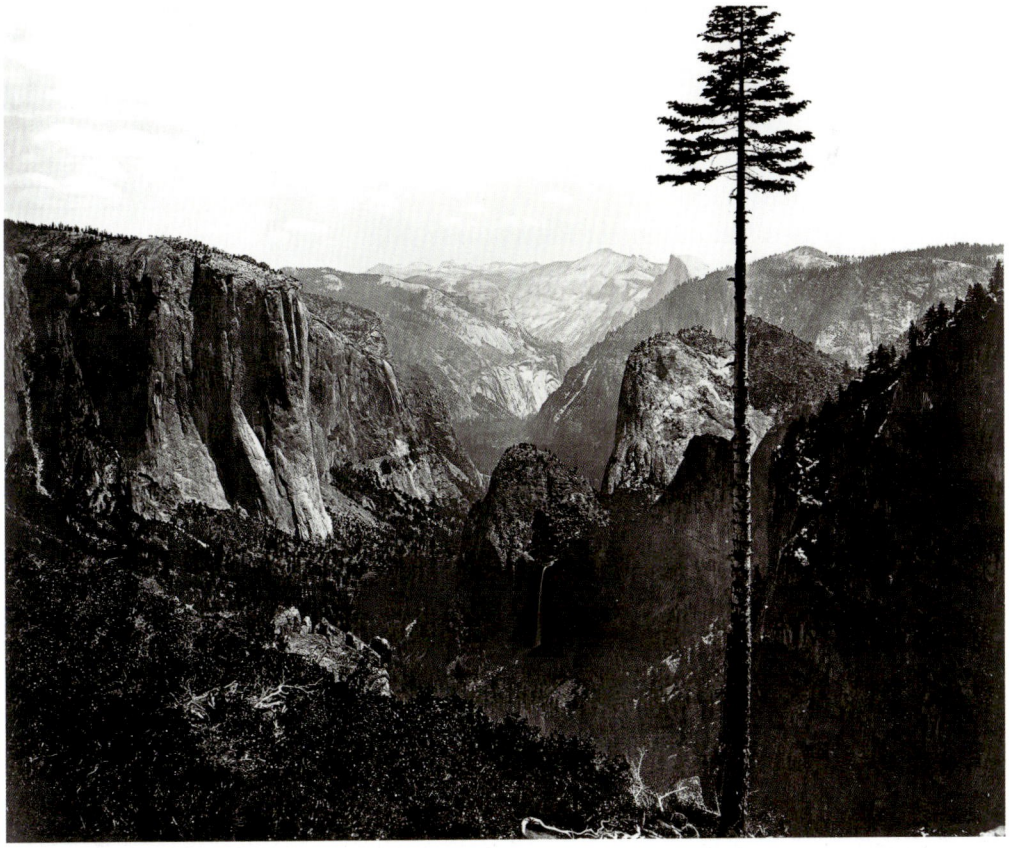

Watkins's Yosemite views were widely distributed as prints and stereographs and helped create for the park a reputation as one of America's most stunning pristine landscapes. Twenty-four of his photographs were also included in Josiah Dwight Whitney's *The Yosemite Book* (1868), which was intended to help those who could not visit the valley themselves, as well as those who could. Like Olmsted's trails, it guided the viewer from place to place, ensuring a common experience of the site.

Watkins later accompanied a government team headed by the geologist Clarence King. The team was charged with making a geological and topographical survey of the territory between the Rocky Mountains and the Sierra Nevada in the area of the 40th parallel, following the transcontinental railway. King's was one of four surveys of the western territories initiated in the late 1860s as part of an ambitious post-Civil-War collaboration between politicians and businessmen to promote private enterprise. As urban parks were constructed to relieve the pressures of urban life, and sections of wilderness set aside for national parks, vast tracts of land and money were appropriated by Congress to help create a privately owned national railroad system.

While Watkins's photographs for the US Government can be seen as landscapes, with all of the painterly conventions that the term "landscape" implies, their main purpose was to provide information. They were meant, in the words of the art historian Alan Trachtenberg, to "examine and describe the geological structure, geographical condition and natural resources of a belt of country." They contained detailed depictions of "rock formations, mountain ranges, detrital plains, mines, coal deposits, soils, minerals, ores, saline and alkaline deposits" and anything else caught within the camera's lens. They were produced for government publications rather than for wide distribution. As compilations of images, they were meant to be read as empirical, objective information, despite the fact that the views described are those of interest to the government and the businessmen who were intent on transforming the land with their mining ventures and railways.

This survey aesthetic marked many of the pictures of the cities of the West as well, including Watkins's place of residence, San Francisco. The discovery of gold in California in 1848 and the region's entry into the Union in 1850 (see p. 226) led to an explosive population growth. The city was the port of arrival for many of the workers who went on to the gold fields and railroad construction sites throughout the state. Among these workers were large numbers of Chinese men, who had begun arriving in the US in the 1850s in search of employment as laundrymen, cooks, gardeners, miners, railroad workers, and other forms of manual labor. As with immigrants to New York City [**5.16.22**; p. 294], many congregated in temporary quarters in a small section of San Francisco near the waterfront, sharing rooms and resources until they could move on to the gold fields or other parts of California. This area soon came to be known as Chinatown.

According to the art historian Anthony W. Lee, European American businessmen and politicians in San Francisco in the second half of the nineteenth century tended to view Chinatown as a colony or a clearly circumscribed area in a thriving port city "that belonged not to the Chinese but to Californians. The Chinese made up a servant class, an undifferentiated mass whose work in the fields or on the tracks served the interests of the new state and its people." This view denied the fact that the Chinese were increasingly becoming a permanent part of the immigrant population of the state. Yet it facilitated a series of discriminatory legal and social practices that ensured, as is customary in colonies, the racial domination of one group over another.

The survey aesthetic contained in photographs of Chinatown in the 1870s and 1880s reaffirmed this notion of Chinatown as a colony. The images were presented as containing information about an urban landscape that was going to be transformed at some future point into a more productive, and thus civilized, space by European American businessmen.

The photographer who created the greatest numbers of images of the streets of Chinatown in the 1870s and 1880s and who adopted this survey aesthetic was Isaiah West Taber (1830-1912), who had arrived in San Francisco from the East Coast in 1864. According to Lee, San Francisco was a highly competitive place for photographers, and Taber's rise to prominence was accompanied by Watkins's fall. "In 1875 Taber purchased (some would say stole) the entire stock of Carleton Watkins's prints and negatives, which were sold at auction without Watkins's knowledge or consent." Watkins was unable to recover professionally from the loss of his archive. What Taber gained was not only a collection of negatives, but also a pictorial tradition—that of the survey photograph.

By 1872 Taber's studio had expanded to sixteen rooms and he employed nearly a dozen people. He sold his own photographs, as well as the paintings and prints of others. He also hired painters to retouch the photographs produced by his firm. Among the images that emerged from Taber's studio were hundreds of scenes of Chinatown. An untitled view [**5.16.26**] surveys an intersection and captures all its particularities—unfurled awnings, boxes of merchandise, brick facades, a horse and cart, cobblestone streets, men wearing various styles of hats. The extent to which the economic dealings of the area had extended out into the streets in the 1870s was an indication of an increasing congestion connected to the completion

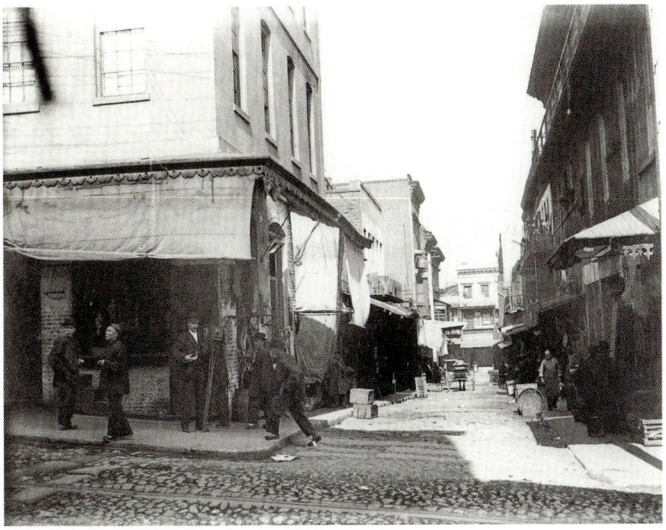

5.16.26 Isaiah West Taber: *Untitled* (*Taber in Chinatown*), c. 1870s–80s. Photograph
California Historical Society, San Francisco

of the transcontinental railways in 1869. With their jobs now at an end, Chinese railroad workers poured into San Francisco's Chinatown, swelling the population to 12,000 by 1870, six times what it had been a decade before.

While the street scene utilizes the conventions of survey photography, it also functions as a portrait of Taber, standing beside his tripod, and provides insight into his working method. As Lee notes, Taber employed a number of assistants, each of whom had their own camera. He would position them on opposite corners of an intersection and have them point their cameras "straight down the middle of the street, rather than seeking harsh oblique views or focused shots of the sidewalks." This was "a far more industrial manner of photography than would be practiced by anyone else in San Francisco until perhaps the 1910s." By putting himself in the crowd, Taber "acknowledged his mediating presence, freely mixing the empirical attitude of the western view with a new kind of photographic subjectivity."

Taber's willingness to join the Chinese men on the street and to document their neighborhood at close quarters can be attributed, at least in part, to his search for new clients. Many Chinese men came to his studio to have their portraits made, but Taber understood that the physical location of Chinatown itself held great economic potential for him. Taber's photographs of the storefronts and streets capture a common element in the representations of Chinatown at this time. As Lee writes, "they register not only the commercial climate of 1870s Chinatown but also the desire by non-Chinese to take possession of the quarter's economy."

The influx of Chinese laborers into San Francisco also created tension and increased competition with non-Chinese workers in the city. This tension led to a series of ordinances making access to jobs more difficult (for example, by legislating a minimum amount of space for a lodger, thus removing already scarce housing) and limiting their business ventures (for instance, by charging launderers high city fees). Ordinances were also passed prohibiting certain cultural practices, including the use of gongs in theaters. Finally, in 1882 the Federal Government passed the Chinese Exclusion Act prohibiting immigration of all laborers from China for the next decade and excluding current Chinese residents from US citizenship (the law was extended in 1892 and made permanent in 1902; it was not repealed until December 1943). Thus, Taber's photographs also recorded the street life and economy of a community under duress, one that managed to survive despite concerted attempts to undermine it.

Review Questions

1 How did Thomas Eakins celebrate the accomplishments of Dr. Gross and Dr. Agnew in his portraits of the two surgeons? How are they different, and what does this difference reveal about the medical profession?

2 How, according to Simon Patten, could mass-produced prints help solve some of the social and economic problems of the second half of the nineteenth century? What roles did women play in the creation and consumption of such prints?

3 How did the idea of the household servant or help change over the course of the nineteenth century, and why? How did artists represent these workers?

4 Why did Jacob A. Riis take photographs of New York tenement buildings and their inhabitants? How did he represent these spaces and people?

5 What is the "survey aesthetic" in the field of photography? How was it used by both Carleton E. Watkins and Isaiah West Taber?

CHAPTER 17

Gender, the Ideal, and the Real

(*c.* 1871–1900)

The Rise of Aestheticism

As the interiors of the homes of the nation's wealthy became more profusely decorated, many of the paintings that hung within them became more decidedly decorative. The late 1870s and 1880s saw the return of a generation of young artists who had gone to Europe to take advantage of the more extensive art training offered there, especially in the cities of Paris and Munich. A shift in emphasis had taken place in the European art world, particularly in the academies and ateliers of Paris. The heroic male ideals and masculine virtues celebrated in the early part of the century in the paintings of Jacques-Louis David (1748–1825) and Baron Jean-Antoine Gros (1771–1835) had been replaced by the feminine ideals of beauty expressed in the female nudes of William-Adolphe Bouguereau (1825–1905), Alexandre Cabanel (1823–89), and Jean-Léon Gérôme (1824-1904), three artists with whom many American painters studied. Thus, the focus of much of their training was the female figure.

When these artists returned to the US they continued this emphasis, which marked a notable shift from the earlier focus on men in American painting (see pp. 186–91). It also marked what many saw as the growing cosmopolitanism of the American art world. The new female figures were not, however, women taking part in a nationalist narrative of westward expansion or economic transformation. They were, on the contrary, often in groups but seldom conversing. They did not engage in any apparently meaningful activity, not even domestic work. Sometimes the female figures were naked or dressed in classical garb; more often they appeared in contemporary dress. But almost always they were situated in interior spaces or vaguely defined landscapes, and most often, if not always, they were white. When the interior spaces were recognizably of the nineteenth century, they were also recognizably middle- or upper-class.

Just as "culture" had been elevated to a position above and separate from the materialism of everyday life, so too were women. They were an ideal force, allotted a role outside of this materialistic world, even as they were simultaneously charged with countering its effects within the home (see p. 285). Culture and women were both portrayed in lengthy commentaries by learned men—and several learned women—as refining and civilizing forces. In order to perform these functions, women—and culture—needed to be protected and isolated, ensconced in a world of ideal truth and beauty. This world, not surprisingly, was full of references to middle- and upper-class lifestyles, thus conflating women, art, and the economic elite. As the art historian Bailey Van Hook writes, these idealized women "could fulfill the artists' prescriptions for art...because their flesh-and-blood female counterparts were perceived as occupying a position analogous to art itself." The definition of art, she continues, as well as culture in general, "coincided with the construction of the feminine gender in the Gilded Age, making the resulting imaging of women inevitable."

Accompanying this movement from male-dominated history and genre scenes to female-dominated interiors and landscapes was a shift in artistic discourse. The British critic John Ruskin (1819–1900), with his emphasis on moral narrative and truth to nature, was particularly popular in the third quarter of the nineteenth century in the US. He was a strong supporter of a group of artists in England who called themselves the Pre-Raphaelite Brotherhood, and whose narrative paintings were based on historical or contemporary literary texts (by such authors as William Shakespeare, John Keats, and Alfred Lord Tennyson). Among the most notable of these artists were Dante Gabriel Rossetti (1828–1882) and Edward Burne-Jones (1833–1898).

Many American painters were familiar with the work of the Pre-Raphaelites, and admired its decorative qualities. They tended to reject, however, its anecdotal, sometimes moralizing, narratives (also found in many American genre paintings of the mid-nineteenth century [**3.9.19**; p. 187]). Instead, they favored more generalized scenes that could be categorized in terms of formal or aesthetic considerations rather than content. Many artists, according to Van Hook, "had consciously shifted the language of their written and pictorial discourses to substitute beauty for Ruskin's emphasis on truth, art for nature, and aesthetics for morality."

One of the leading proponents of the attack on Ruskin, and on narrative realism in general, was the American expatriate artist James Abbott McNeill Whistler (1834–1903). Whistler's work was well known in the US by the end of the nineteenth century, particularly after the exhibition of his *Symphony in White No. 1: The White Girl* (1862) [**5.17.1**] in New York City at The Metropolitan Museum of Art and the Union League Club in 1881. Whistler also gained notoriety as a result of a much-publicized lawsuit. In referring to Whistler's painting *Nocturne in Black and Gold: The Falling Rocket* of *c.* 1874, Ruskin had commented that the artist had flung "a pot of paint in the public's face." Whistler sued for libel and won, but was awarded only a farthing. His legal expenses forced him into bankruptcy. This legal victory, and the publicity it generated, helped spread his opinions, which quickly supplanted those of Ruskin in the US.

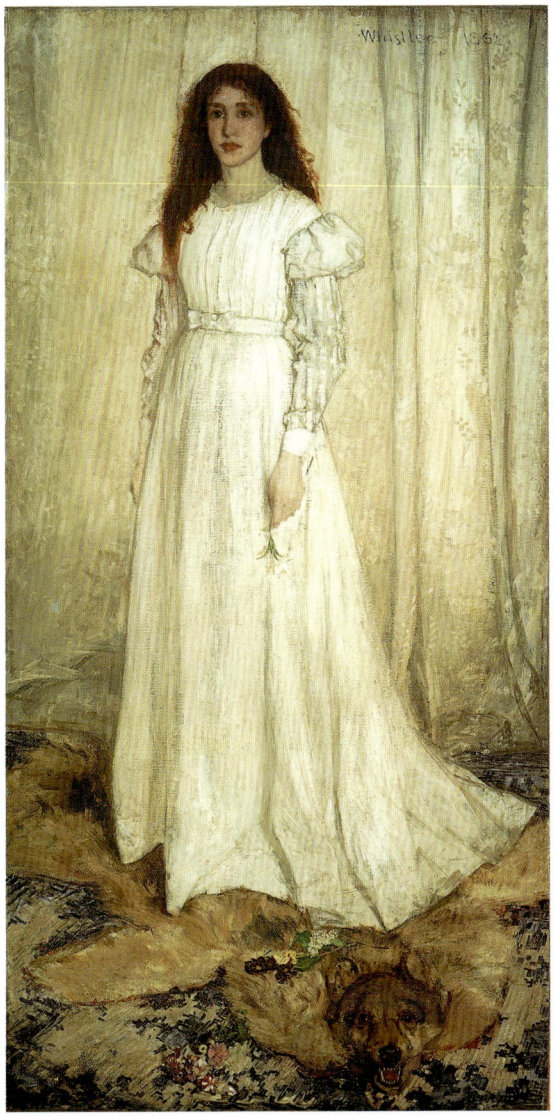

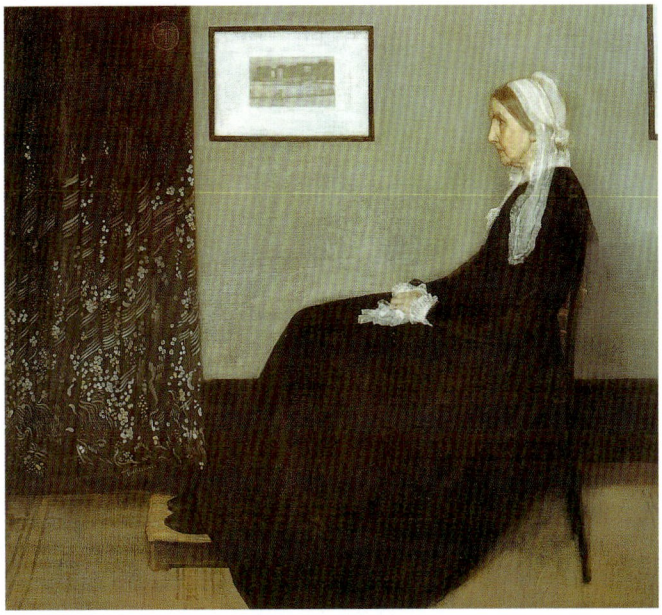

5.17.1 (left) James Abbott McNeill Whistler: *Symphony in White No. 1: The White Girl*, 1862.
Oil on canvas, 84½ x 42½ in. (214.7 x 108 cm.)
National Gallery of Art, Washington, D.C.

5.17.2 (above) James Abbott McNeill Whistler: *Arrangement in Grey and Black No. 1: The Artist's Mother*, 1871–72.
Oil on canvas, 57 x 64½ in. (144.6 x 163.8 cm.)
Musée d'Orsay, Paris

In a collection of essays entitled *The Gentle Art of Making Enemies*, published in 1890, Whistler wrote that art

> should be independent of all clap-trap—should stand alone and appeal to the artistic sense of ear or eye, without confounding this with emotions entirely foreign to it, as devotion, pity, love, patriotism and the like. All these have no kind of concern with it, and that is why I insist on calling my works "arrangements" and "harmonies."

The best-known of the former is a painting exhibited in 1872 at London's Royal Academy under the title *Arrangement in Grey and Black No. 1: The Artist's Mother* [**5.17.2**]. While it is a portrait of his mother, the identity of the woman, according to Whistler, should be of no interest to the viewer, only the formal arrangement of grays and blacks. Art was not about moral instruction or storytelling but, instead, about formal perfection—the flat areas of gray and black, the echoing of the picture frame in the framed print on the wall, the contrast between the delicate patterning of the curtain and the stark black of the woman's dress.

According to Whistler, to use art as a morally uplifting device in the service of social reform would only result in it succumbing to the materialistic concerns of an industrial, consumer society. Artists should produce not what they see in nature but their emotional response to it. Their work should be filled with sentiment, not sentimentality. Art should be about art, not the world around it. These ideas formed the basis of the Aesthetic Movement of the 1870s and 1880s in Europe and influenced several American artists then studying there.

While many returning from Europe turned their attention to the female nude, their nudes were much less voluptuous than those of the academic painters with whom they had studied, for the subject in general still met with a cool reception. As late as 1906 Anthony Comstock, secretary of the New York Society for the Suppression of Vice, ordered a raid on the offices of the *American Student of Art* because the publication included illustrations of nudes. When Americans did paint nudes, they attempted to downplay the sexual implications by making the women more youthful and thus more "innocent," as well

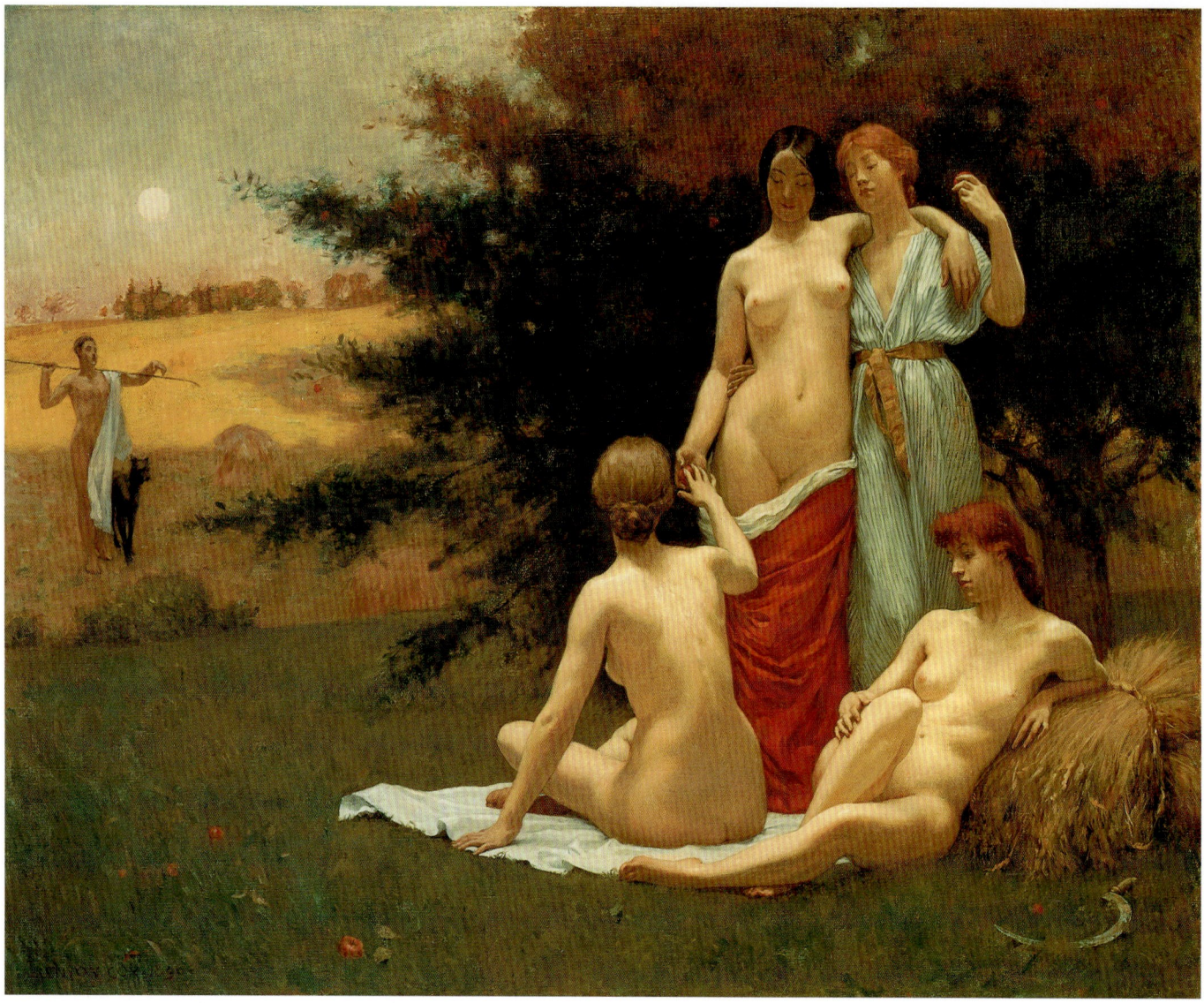

5.17.3 Kenyon Cox: *Eclogue*, 1890.
Oil on canvas, 48 x 60½ in. (121.9 x 153.7 cm.)
Smithsonian American Art Museum, Washington, D.C.

as more idealized, as can be seen in *Eclogue* (1890) [**5.17.3**] by Kenyon Cox (1856–1919). Cox had studied with Cabanel and Gérôme in Paris in the late 1870s and early 1880s, before returning home in 1882. An eclogue is an idyllic pastoral poem, and he has arranged his figures in poses reminiscent of classical prototypes, although this does not totally remove the erotic charge of the painting. He also adds a male figure and his dog in the background, both looking in the women's direction, confirming the purpose of this display of female flesh.

Despite his attempt at idealization through the adoption of classical poses, Cox's inclusion of the individual features of his live models inserts a touch of naturalism, as does the striped dressing gown of the standing woman on the right. This combination of the ideal and the real also appears in works of Abbott H. Thayer (1849–1921) such as his *Angel* (*c.* 1889) [**5.17.4**], for which his daughter Mary posed. Thayer studied under Gérôme, and chose to seek the feminine ideal in the world of Christianity rather than the classical world. His figures were often described as exuding a divine or spiritual beauty, in addition or opposed to a mere physical beauty. Thayer insisted that he was searching for a transcendent beauty, one that would impart to the physical body a moral quality. For the art historian Ross Anderson, Thayer perceived "woman as a being whose purity was constantly menaced, who if not enshrined by art might easily fall into an abyss of materialistic degradations." Thayer saw himself as a transformative agent, taking the real female body in front of him and, through the processes of artistic creation—the addition of wings or a white gown—turning her into a purer, higher creature.

Critics sometimes interpreted the youth and innocence of the female figures of Cox and Thayer as particularly "American" qualities. They contrasted them not only with the more voluptuous, and thus more lascivious, nudes and semi-clothed women in paintings by Europeans, but also with the very real female immigrants entering the US at this time, whose poverty and foreignness marked them as less than ideal. By the end of the century an image of the "American Girl" emerged that functioned, in the words of Van Hook, both at home and abroad as a symbol of "national innocence, independence, and naiveté... a child compared to her European forebears, uncorrupted by jaded European decadence." The American Girl was decidedly white, if not necessarily Anglo-Saxon, and decidedly pure, despite her increased visibility in the public sphere. Her ascendancy would be short-lived, however, for at the beginning of the twentieth century culture and femaleness would part company and new, more masculine ideals would displace the feminine qualities of purity and beauty (see V. 2, p. 339).

Thomas Wilmer Dewing (1851–1938), like Cox, was also known in the 1880s for painting female figures draped in classical garb.

5.17.4 Abbott H. Thayer: *Angel*, c. 1889.
Oil on canvas, 36¼ x 28⅛ in. (92 x 71.5 cm.)
Smithsonian American Art Museum, Washington, D.C.

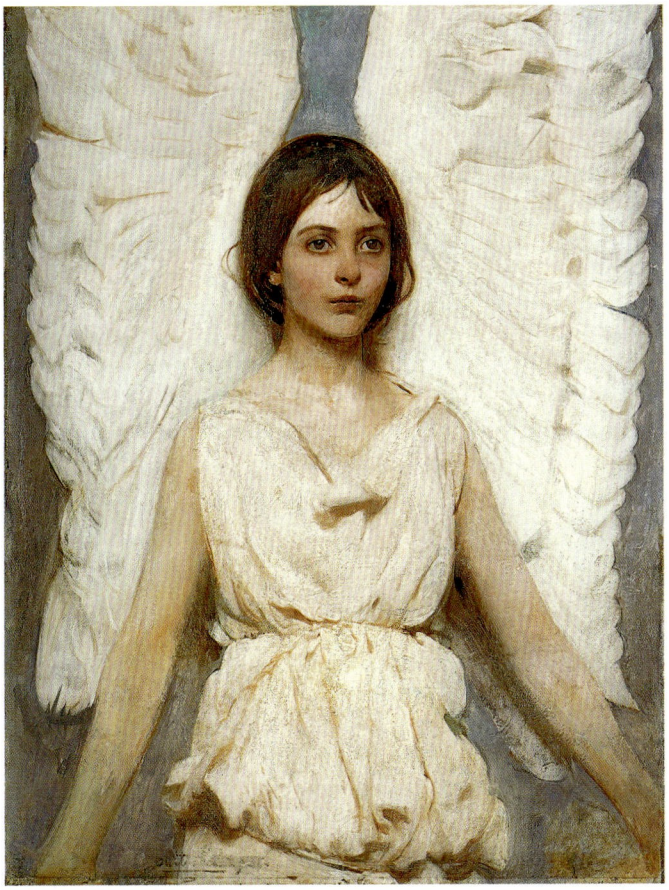

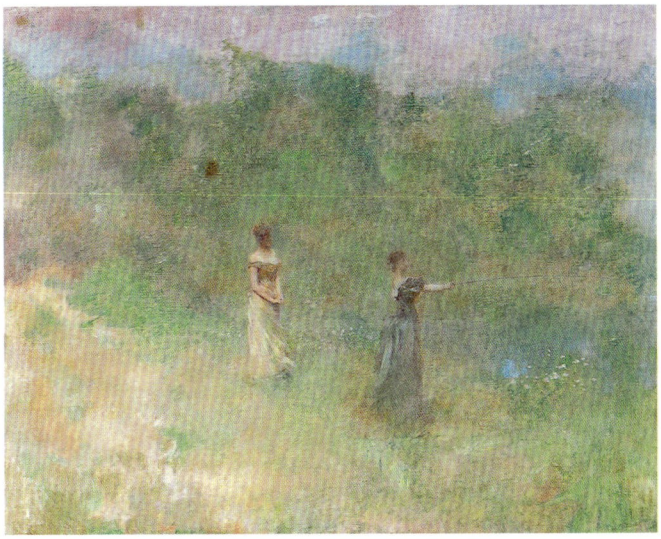

5.17.5 Thomas Wilmer Dewing: *Summer*, c. 1890.
Oil on canvas, 42⅛ x 54¼ in. (107 x 138 cm.)
Smithsonian American Art Museum, Washington, D.C.

The influence of his studies in Paris at the Académie Julien, with Jules-Joseph Lefebvre (1836–1911) and Gustave-Rodolphe Boulanger (1824–1888), is evident in the artworks he created in the decade after returning to Boston in 1878. In the 1890s, however, his stylistic approach changed in favour of compositions filled with subtle tonalities and mists or hazes (he would later be categorized as one of a group of landscape artists known as Tonalists). These works were populated by figures who were decidedly contemporary, yet still anonymous and idealized.

Summer of c. 1890 [**5.17.5**] reflects Dewing's new style. Here, two elegantly dressed women move through a vaguely defined landscape; one extends a long, slim pole in front of her, suggesting the act of fishing, or perhaps butterfly-catching. Their actions and identities are not important to Dewing: what he wants to convey is a mood, one suggested by the title *Summer*. Indeed, artists often gave their paintings emblematic or evocative titles—Morning, Spring, Summer, Lilies—that denied the specificity of the setting and the figures, thus encouraging the viewer to focus on the aesthetic aspect of the work.

The art historian Kathleen Pyne argues that the women in Dewing's paintings "encapsulated the late 19th-century definition of America as an Anglo-Saxon nation that promised to be the culmination of world civilization." Dewing was one of many in the US who subscribed to the theories of the British philosopher Herbert Spencer, who offered a more palatable alternative to Charles Darwin's seemingly grim, survival-of-the-fittest theory of evolution. In Pyne's words, Spencer "held that nature advanced harmoniously in an inherently moral universe toward higher forms of life. In his scheme, evolution impelled human life toward a peaceful, utopian state." This theory was particularly popular with those of Anglo-Saxon descent, who felt embattled and threatened by the latest waves of immigration. Within Spencer's theory, they could envision themselves as the most advanced state of life. Spencer also believed that environment played a key role in evolution. Hence, "cultured" environments would civilize "darker" immigrants, and advance those of lighter complexion even further in their progression toward utopia. Furthermore, Spencer's emphasis on unity, harmony, and repose fit well with the new aesthetic theories espoused by Whistler and his supporters.

Dewing's paintings, according to Pyne, present the idea of evolutionary self-refinement in two ways. The first "centered on the turning inward of the self to the nurturing world of the psyche and the imagination; the other involved the release of the self into the sustenance and boundlessness of nature." Thus the women in his paintings who dissolve into nature and/or into self-reflection are furthering the progress of civilization. They are, in Pyne's words, "distillations of intellect and aesthetic sensibility; their physical bodies have been devalued and sloughed away." Yet these bodies are of a decidedly Anglo-Saxon cast, with their elongated limbs, pale skin, and aquiline facial features: they are simultaneously not of this world in their aesthetic contemplation, and very much of it in their upper-class physical and cultural characteristics.

This utopian world of long-necked women in elegant attire baffled most art viewers, who still wanted "the facts." The more such works were criticized as unintelligible, the more their creators pointed to the need to maintain a distance between their art and the undiscerning public, be it conservative art critics or the person in the street. Having to compete with a proliferation of image-makers, from producers of popular prints to portrait photographers, many felt compelled to distinguish themselves clearly from this mass-produced culture. They created paintings marked by formal effects that mechanical reproduction had yet to master—visible brushstrokes, subtle gradations of color, fog-shrouded hills. Photographers like William B. Post (1857–1925), though, easily replicated their subject matter and mood, if not their color [**5.17.6**]. While the idealized women would soon almost disappear, the emphasis on formal innovation and the disdain for mass culture and mass audiences would continue apace into the twentieth century.

5.17.6 William B. Post: *Summer Days*, 1895. Photograph
George Eastman House, Rochester, New York

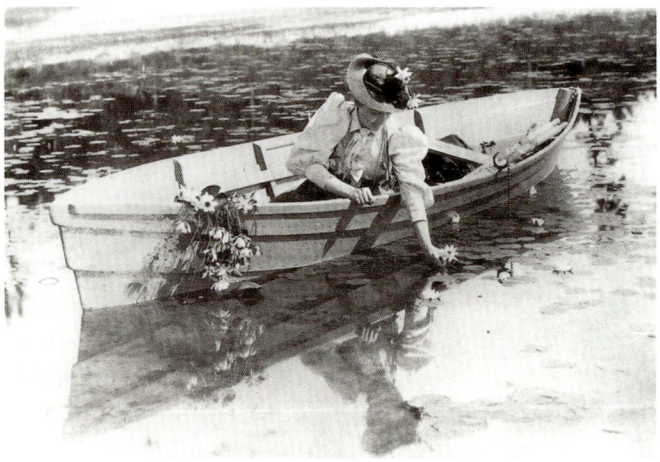

American Impressionism and Consumer Culture: William Merritt Chase's *In the Studio*

While some of the artists who returned from Europe depicted women in clothing or settings evoking the worlds of ancient Greece or Rome, others rejected this vision and instead portrayed the female figure dressed in contemporary garb and located in urban spaces, domestic interiors, gardens, or landscapes. In subject and style, their paintings echoed the work of the French Impressionists (for example, Edgar Degas [1834–1917], Camille Pissarro [1830–1903], and Claude Monet [1840–1926]), and because of this they came to be known as American Impressionists. Their works received the greatest critical attention in the 1890s and the first decade of the twentieth century.

According to the art historians H. Barbara Weinberg, Doreen Bolger, and David Park Curry, Impressionism resisted "established hierarchies of subject, order and finish." Rather than clear narratives, it favoured the spontaneous and the trivial. It "empower[ed] the ordinary viewer, insisting on his or her engagement with and esteem for fragments of familiar—specifically local and national—experience." In 1892 Childe Hassam, a member of the American Impressionist circle, commented on Impressionism's focus on the present. Instead of "always depicting the manners, customs, dress and life of an epoch of which he knew nothing," a "true historical painter, it seems to me, is one who paints the life he sees about him, and so makes a record of his own epoch." Hassam's words echo those of the art critic Eugene Benson who, in a review of Winslow Homer's *Prisoners from the Front* of 1866 [**4.13.1**; p. 237], argued that history painting should give us "art that shall become historical, not art that is intended to be so."

One of the most popular American Impressionists was William Merritt Chase (1849–1916). While most within this group studied in Paris, Chase instead chose Munich. The heavy, visible brushstrokes and dark tones in his early paintings reflect the influence of this training (the tones and paint application are generally much lighter in the work of Paris-trained artists). These

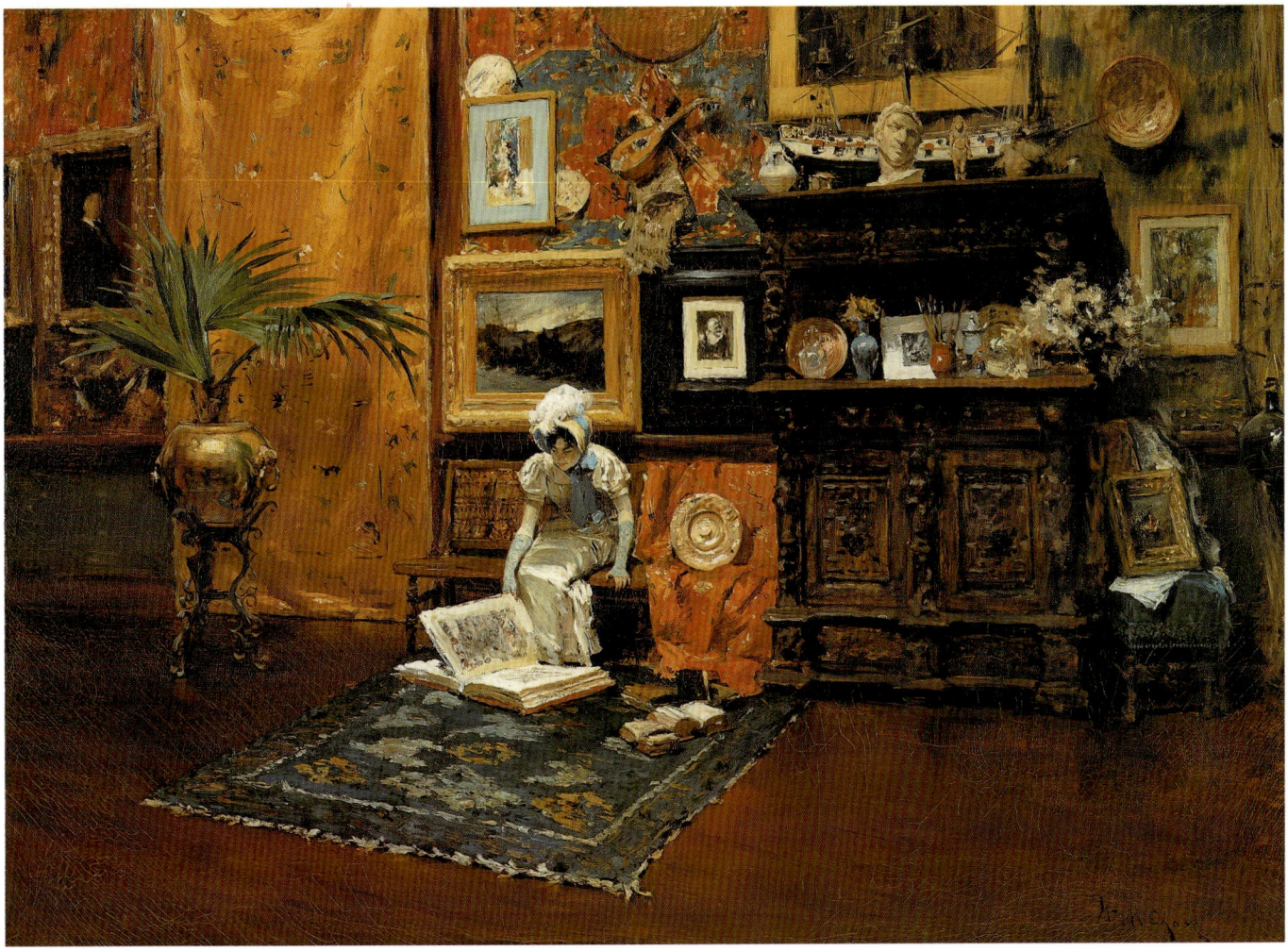

5.17.7 William Merritt Chase: *In the Studio*, 1880. Oil on canvas, 28⅛ x 40⅙ in. (71.4 x 101.8 cm.) Brooklyn Museum of Art, New York

qualities can be found in Chase's *In the Studio* (1880) [**5.17.7**]. The painting is dominated by the deep browns of the floor and furniture and the rich golds of the silk hanging and picture frames. The paint-laden brushstrokes are visible in the clothing of the elegantly dressed woman sitting on the bench, the portfolio she examines, and the rug on which the portfolio rests. In fact, the woman is painted as another of the richly textured objects that adorn this artist's studio—the Japanese fabrics, brass plant-holder, and ornately carved Renaissance-Baroque credenza. The woman both looks at art and is presented as art by the painter.

Chase's painting is one of several by the artist and his contemporaries that locate women within lavish artists' studios. While these works may speak to the material success of their creators, the art historian Sarah Burns suggests that they, and the women within them, represent a more complex change in the material world of the late nineteenth century. They represent, she argues, part of the emergent consumer culture that was displacing the Victorian moralities of work, thrift, and self-denial with a focus on self-gratification through the acquisition of material goods. In this context, the elaborately decorated artist's studio is a salesroom intended to display the artist's wares "and to create desire among potential clientele by seducing their senses through the romantic associations of the aesthetic commodities on show." The emphasis of Chase and others on the surface quality of paintings, and on the experiencing of emotion or sentiment, increased the association between the object being viewed and the immediate visual pleasure. This association was effectively used to sell not just artworks, but also commercial products in the new palaces of consumption of this era—department stores.

This merging of the displays of art and commerce (department stores also often included art galleries) created an ambivalence and anxiety among artists and critics, writes Burns. Older celebrations of art's "elevating moral and ideological functions" now came up against new, market-driven discourses, which directly addressed "the commercial dimensions of artworks produced as luxury consumer goods promising individual self-gratification, both sensual and spiritual."

In both realms—the department store and the studio—gender played a crucial role. Women had been identified early on in the development of the department store as its major customers; they were the ones who perused the goods on display and made the family purchases. According to contemporary accounts, women also constituted the majority of visitors to the open houses held by artists, such as Chase, in their studios. Thus, Burns suggests that the women in paintings of studio interiors may be read as "cultural shoppers," "engaged in a drama of cultural consumption."

At the same time, women were seldom the nominal purchasers of major artworks (their fathers or husbands would assume this role). Rather, they functioned as "mediators between raw money from the arenas of commerce and capital and the pure, transcendent spheres of art." Their presence aided in the feminizing of the studio, inserting a passive, yet sensual quality into a world ultimately dependent on industrial or commercial wealth, which was coded inevitably as male. By the early twentieth century many male artists were stripping their studios of opulent clutter in an attempt to reassert their masculinity and distance themselves from the excesses of material consumption.

The prominence of objects from Japan in Chase's painting reflects a well-established association between the Far East and the exotic or sensual. It also indicates an increased interest in the region in both America and Europe after a US Navy expedition led by Commodore Matthew C. Perry forced Japan to open trade with the West in 1854, thus ending the country's 220-year-old policy of national seclusion. In 1856, Perry published a report on his journey that contained facsimiles of Japanese prints; by 1860 prints by Katsushika Hokusai (1760–1849) were circulating in major cities in the eastern US, just as Japan was setting up its first embassy in New York City.

Painters began featuring objects from Japan (*Japonaiserie*) in their work and adopting the formal qualities of Japanese prints, with their shallow spaces and large areas of unmodulated color (*Japonisme*) (Whistler did both). Wealthy individuals also began acquiring Japanese art objects (for an example of Japanese influence in colonial American homes see p. 72). The railroad magnate William H. Vanderbilt, one of the richest men in the US in the late nineteenth century, had a Japanese Room constructed in which to display his collection [**5.17.8**]. It was marked by red-lacquered beams, ebonized wood cabinets, gold brocade wall-hangings, and a woven bamboo ceiling. In addition, Japanese motifs were taken up in the decorative arts [**5.18.11, 5.18.12**; p. 326]. This fascination with the artistic products of Asia was accompanied by an interest in the region's potential for economic investment. Soon the US would become a neighboring colonial power, with the expulsion of Spain and the US occupation of the Philippines in 1898 as a result of the Spanish-American War.

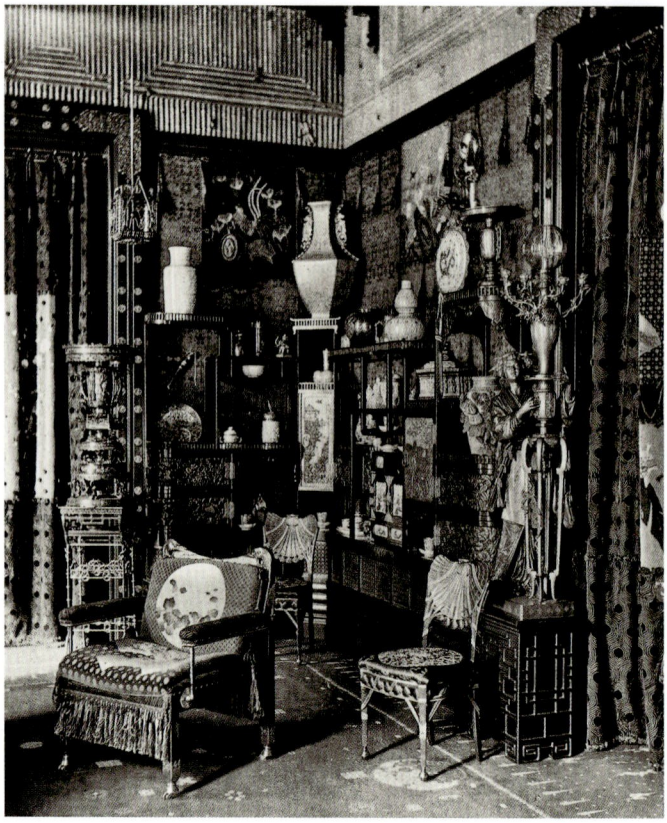

5.17.8 The Japanese Room in the house of Cornelius Vanderbilt II, New York; From Edward Strahan (Earl Shinn), *Mr. Vanderbilt's House and Collection*, New York, 1883–84.
Morris Library, University of Delaware, Newark

American Impressionism and the Nostalgic Landscape: J. Alden Weir and John Twachtman

Impressionist painters were interested in capturing, through exacting observation, the transient aspects of the contemporary world, in particular the qualities of light, color, and atmosphere. As did many American artists before them, American Impressionists turned to the landscape for subject matter. Their approach, however, was radically different. The art historian William H. Gerdts sums up the history of American landscape painting during the nineteenth century "as a shift from the solid and substantial to the ephemeral, from forests and mountains to light and atmosphere, from the timelessness of classical art to the transience of Impressionism." While the American Impressionists, like their Hudson River School predecessors (see p. 157), were committed to depicting the American landscape, they used a cosmopolitan visual language grounded in the experiments of contemporary French artists. They also tended to paint more personal spaces—the family farms or small villages in New England where many of these artists settled.

Like Kenyon Cox and Thomas Wilmer Dewing [**5.17.3**, p. 302; **5.17.5**, p. 303], several American Impressionists combined women and landscape in their paintings. One case in point is *Obweebetuck* (*c.* 1908) [**5.17.9**] by J. Alden Weir (1852–1919), who spent several years studying in Paris before returning to the US and settling in New York City. The title of this painting refers to the mountain in the background located in the northeast corner of Connecticut, near the village of Windham ("Obweebetuck" is an Algonquin word meaning "the place you see the river"). His wife's family owned a country home near Windham, and the artist often painted there during the summer. According to the art historian Anne E. Dawson, the building visible in the upper right, with the three women located on or near the porch, is the lye house on the Baker family's property. The painting is filled with bright greens, yellow, and lime green, with the blue-gray mountain in the background set off against an almost white sky. The leaves and branches of the trees to the left and right provide a canopy of shade to protect the house and the figures from the strong rays of the sun, which fall on the white picket fence and trees in the middle distance.

The mountain and lye house indicate the specific locale of the painting (although Weir moved the mountain to the right to achieve what he felt was a more pleasing composition). The women lack such specificity. While we can surmise that they are Weir's daughters, the quick paint-laden brushstrokes that make up the figures provide no evidence of their individual identity.

5.17.9 J. Alden Weir: *Obweebetuck*, *c.* 1908.
Oil on canvas, 19½ x 23¼ in. (49.5 x 59.1 cm.)
Private collection

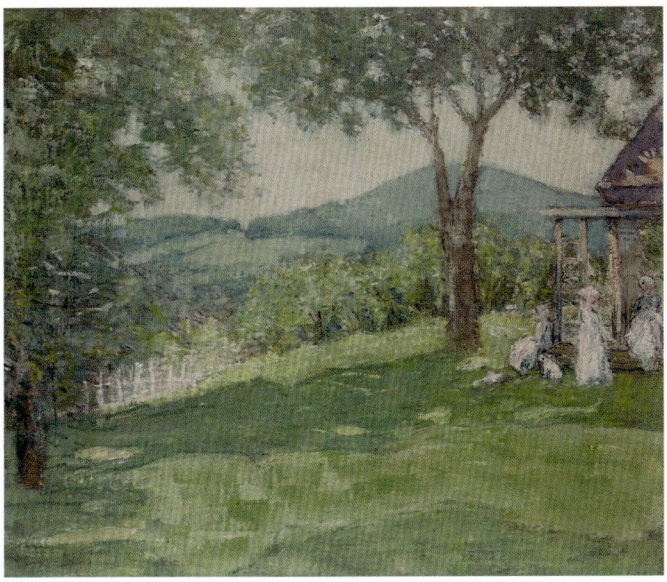

They are primarily compositional devices that allow Weir to capture the quality of the light and the relaxed mood, while also unifying the work. The white of the fence is echoed in the white of the women's dresses and their small dog; the posts of the lye house porch mimic the fence's pickets.

Weir also locates the three female figures in a liminal space between the domestic sphere and the world of nature. The lye house was initially a place of labor (lye was used to make soap), yet had been transformed into a playhouse by his daughters. The women do not engage in labor; instead they survey a landscape that has been marked by the labor of others. Originally the home of the Algonquin peoples who named the mountain in the distance, the land was claimed, cleared, and marked off with white picket fences by European settler colonists for their farms.

The inclusion of the large framing trees and the forested area in the background indicate not only Weir's desire to create a contemporary pastoral landscape, but also his commitment to preserving what tree cover remained in the surrounding area (the region around Windham had been largely deforested to accommodate agricultural pursuits). He was known to buy trees near his farm in Branchville, Connecticut in order to prevent them from being cut down. The area near Windham was also home to the Willimantic Linen Company, which Weir painted in a similar pastoral manner, nestled in the tree-filled small town with no factory workers in sight. Other textile factories were also located in the valley, drawn by the rivers and the ready access to the railroads. As H. Barbara Weinberg, Doreen Bolger, and David Park Curry note, the landscapes of the American Impressionists often "appealed to a new American audience that increasingly valued landscape because its beauty was at once threatened and made more accessible by progress."

Weir's friend, John Twachtman (1853-1902), also located his women in such a liminal space in his *On the Terrace* of *c.* 1897 [**5.17.10**; p. 308]. In Paris from 1883 to 1885, he studied at the Académie Julian with Jules-Joseph Lefebvre and Gustave-Rodolphe Boulanger. Here, we know for certain that the figures are Twachtman's wife Martha and their three children, and that the setting is the Twachtman farm in Greenwich, Connecticut. Once again, however, the identity of the figures is not the focus of the artist, for their faces are only vaguely demarcated. Instead, as in Weir's painting, they stand out because of their bright white dresses, which allow Twachtman to capture certain reflective qualities of light. These dresses, in fact, serve to hide rather than demarcate the bodies, which seem to float in space. As in *Obweebetuck*, they are not situated in bright sunlight, but in a soft light, the top left corner of the farmhouse in the background catching the stronger rays of the sun. The cultivated garden, with its flowerbeds and arbor, encloses the figures.

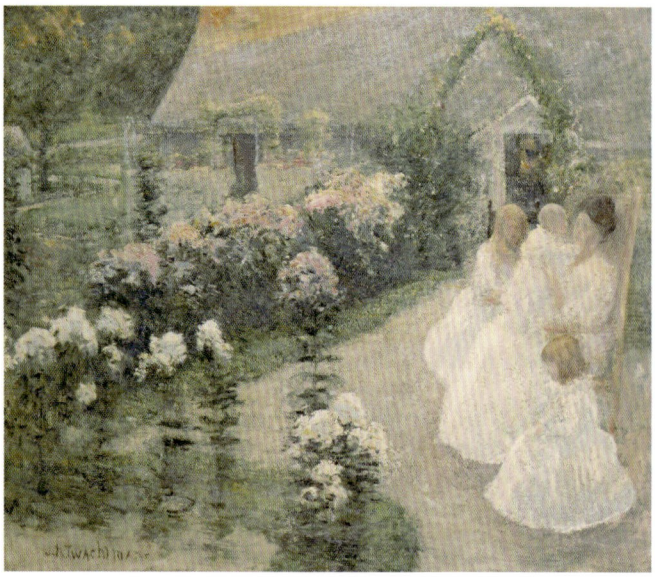

5.17.10 John Twachtman: *On the Terrace*, c. 1897.
Oil on canvas, 25 x 30⅛ in. (63.5 x 76.5 cm.)
Smithsonian American Art Museum, Washington, D.C.

While a scene of contemporary life, it is imbued with a strong sense of the romantic and nostalgic.

This presentation of the Twachtman farm as an idyllic rural hideaway is what brought increasing numbers of New Yorkers the short distance by train to Greenwich and the nearby fishing village of Cos Cob. As the fishing industry declined, the region became the site of summer homes or vacation stays for wealthy city residents, with recreational yachts replacing fishing boats. When not staying at his farm, Twachtman often commuted between New York City, where he taught, and Cos Cob. Many of the American Impressionists who worked and exhibited with Twachtman in the city joined him in these picturesque country retreats. They preferred, in the words of Weinberg, Bolger, and Curry, to escape the "social and visual ills" of the urban environment in order to be "close to the memories of bygone days and far removed from the realities of modern life." When these realities intruded, they were made more palatable through insertion into light-filled pastoral landscapes.

American Impressionism and Portraiture

One category of Impressionist painting where the distinctive features of human figures come into focus is that of portraiture. This is evident when William Merritt Chase's *In the Studio* [**5.17.7**; p. 305] and his *Portrait of Miss Dora Wheeler* (1883) [**5.17.11**] are compared. Each depicts a woman seated in an interior. Each is marked by rich silk Japanese fabrics, elegant dark furniture, and finely decorated ceramics. In each the artist has unified the composition through the use of color. The deep browns and golds that permeate *In the Studio* are broken up by the brilliant whites of the woman's dress, the pages of the portfolio she examines, the mattes of the pictures on the credenza, and the paper or cloth under the painting on the chair to the right. In *Portrait of Miss Dora Wheeler*, the muted brown floor is overwhelmed by the brilliant yellows of the silk and flowers, and the striking blues of the vase and Wheeler's gown.

Yet there are also significant differences between the two paintings. While *In the Studio* is dominated by horizontals and verticals, *Portrait of Miss Dora Wheeler* is organized around two intersecting diagonals. One is composed of Wheeler's relaxed body, while the other begins with the cat in the upper left and runs through the yellow daffodils and the blue ties of Wheeler's gown that hang over the edge of the chair. One figure looks down, absorbed in the portfolio, whereas the other looks directly at the viewer. The strong design, shallow composition, and careful placement of yellows and blues together enhance the decorative quality of Chase's portrait. Yet the viewer's eye is continually drawn to the least decorative element—the self-confident gaze and strong features of Dora Wheeler, an artist who had studied at the Académie Julian in Paris. In composition and subject matter Chase's painting also echoes that of James Abbott McNeill Whistler's *Arrangement in Grey and Black No. 1: The Artist's Mother* [**5.17.2**; p. 301]. Yet in Chase's work the woman turns to confront the viewer, making it next to impossible to ignore her identity in favor of the formal aspects of the composition.

5.17.11 William Merritt Chase: *Portrait of Miss Dora Wheeler*, 1883.
Oil on canvas, 62½ x 65¼ in. (158.7 x 165.8 cm.)
The Cleveland Museum of Art, Cleveland, Ohio

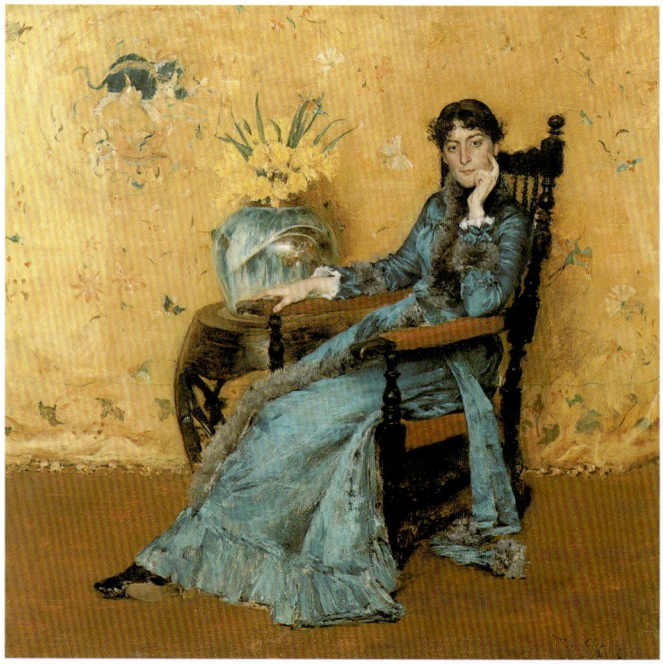

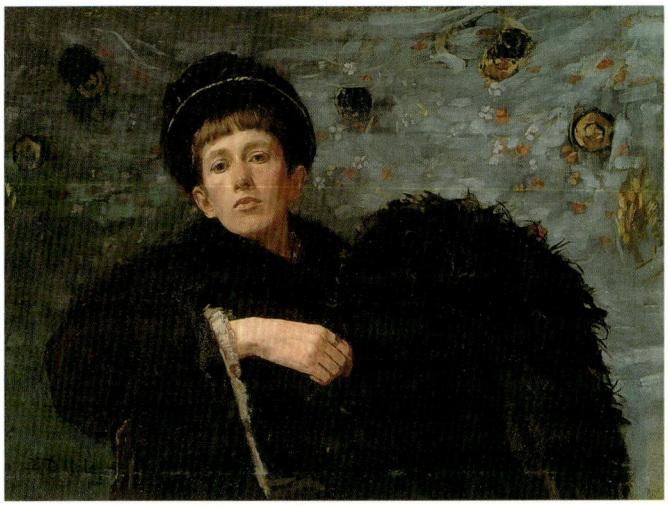

5.17.12 Ellen Day Hale: *Self-Portrait*, 1885.
Oil on canvas, 28½ x 38¾ in. (72.4 x 98.4 cm.)
Museum of Fine Arts, Boston, Massachusetts

This self-confident gaze also appears in *Self-Portrait* of 1885 [**5.17.12**] by the American Impressionist Ellen Day Hale (1855–1940). Hale came from a prominent Boston family whose lineage included Nathan Hale the patriot, Lyman Beecher the preacher, Harriet Beecher Stowe the author, and Catherine Beecher the educator. Many of her living relatives were also authors and painters, and her art instruction began early in Boston, culminating in several trips to Europe in the early 1880s to study with various artists and at the Académie Colarossi and the Académie Julian. In her self-portrait, Hale adopts the floral patterned backdrop and shallow space that mark so many of the interior scenes painted by Impressionists and artists of the Aesthetic Movement. Again, however, the gaze and strong personality of the artist are striking. Hale has increased the emphasis on her face and hand by portraying herself in dark clothing; even her ostrich-feather fan is dark. Her prominence in the painting—she is located at the front of the picture plane and takes up almost half of the canvas—ensures that her presence and her identity will take precedence over, and be enhanced by, the formal qualities of the work.

Two American artists well known for their portraits of elegant middle- and upper-class women were John Singer Sargent and Cecilia Beaux. Born in Florence of American parents, Sargent (1856–1925) spent most of his life in Europe, particularly in Paris and London. He was closely associated with the Aesthetic Movement in England in the 1880s and 1890s, but has also been viewed by art historians as an American Impressionist. Unlike Whistler, he believed that rendering the "appearance" of things was an honorable goal for an artist, but he also believed that appearances needed to be refined and intensified for the viewer. His friend Edmund Gosse wrote that Sargent thought "the artist ought to know nothing whatever about the nature of the object before him...but should concentrate all his powers on a representation of its appearance." Thus, the less one knew about the subject, the freer one was to concentrate on its formal qualities.

Sargent was most concerned with creating form through the manipulation of light and shadow, and produced brilliant paintings marked by luscious skin tones, accents of rich color, and subtle plays of light across surfaces. His visible and seemingly effortless brushstrokes provided texture to the surface of the canvas. He had learned his lessons well in the Paris studio of Emile-Auguste Carolus-Duran, an artist who encouraged his students to strive for virtuosity and flair in their work.

These qualities—feathery brushwork, subtle plays of light—are clearly apparent in one of Sargent's more decorative works, *Nonchaloir (Repose)* of 1911 [**5.17.13**]. Like Whistler's *Arrangement in Grey and Black No. 1: The Artist's Mother* [**5.17.2**; p. 301], the painting is both a portrait and a study in form and color. Sargent's niece Rose-Marie Ormond was the model for the painting, yet her personality does not dominate the composition. What dominates is the mood of repose or relaxation. The woman is integrated into the interior through the green and gold tones that permeate everything, from table to sofa to dress to skin.

In contrast to this, Sargent's portrait of 1888 of the wealthy Bostonian art patron Isabella Stewart Gardner [**5.17.14**; p. 310] is above all about the sitter's personality and presence. Yet there is a certain tension in the painting between Sargent's commitment to decorative form and his need to capture the features and

5.17.13 John Singer Sargent: *Nonchaloir (Repose)*, 1911.
Oil on canvas, 25⅛ x 30 in. (63.8 x 76.2 cm.)
National Gallery of Art, Washington, D.C.

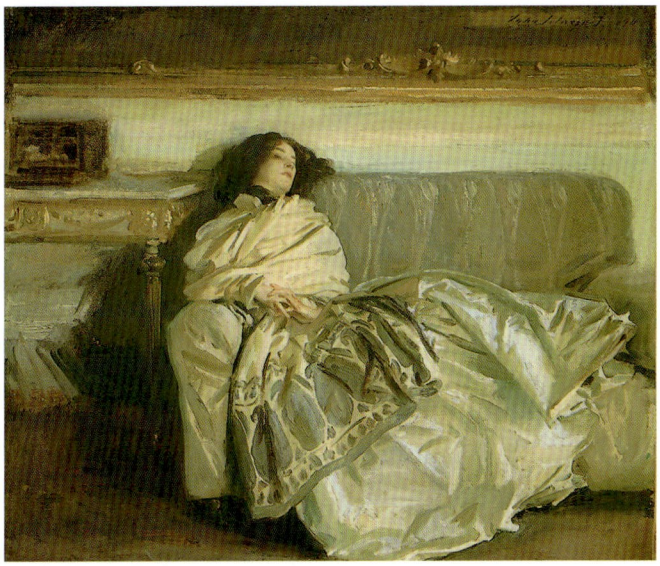

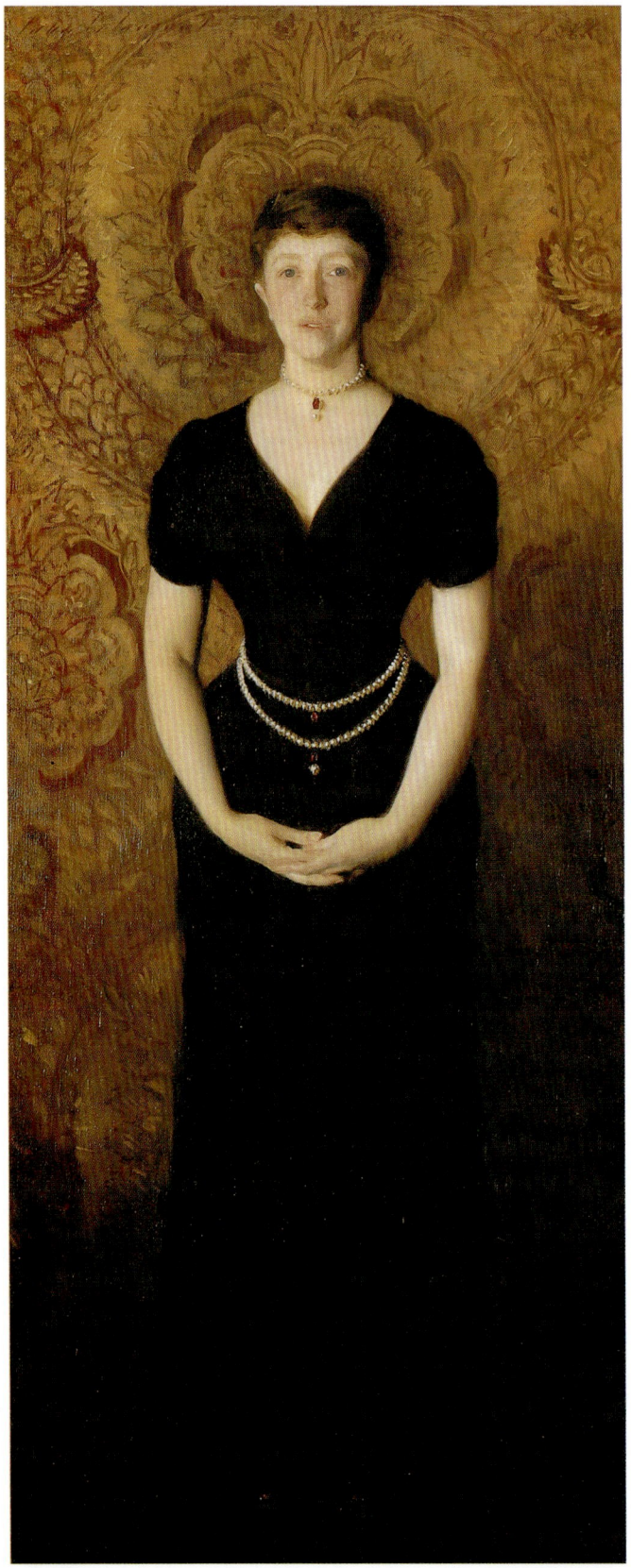

5.17.14 John Singer Sargent: *Isabella Stewart Gardner*, 1888. Oil on canvas, 74¾ x 31½ in. (189.9 x 80 cm.) Isabella Stewart Gardner Museum, Boston, Massachusetts

personality of a subject about whom he must, of necessity, know something. Sargent has emphasized the decorative through the placement of the figure in front of an Italian cut-velvet brocade from the sixteenth century owned by the sitter. By placing her head in the center of one of the pomegranate motifs, he adds a subtle religious connotation, the concentric rings radiating outward like a pulsating aura or halo. In fact, the author Henry James described the painting as a "Byzantine Madonna with a halo." At the same time, the design directly above her head resembles a crown, adding a more secular suggestion of authority. The curved lines of the design are also echoed in the pearls around Gardner's neck and waist and in the position of her arms. Yet, unlike the woman in *Nonchaloir*, Gardner does not dissolve into her interior. She stands proudly in the center of the image, as if waiting to accept the offerings of her admirers.

The painting created a considerable stir when it was exhibited in 1888 at Boston's St. Botolph Club. Many thought Gardner had been depicted as a goddess. Others debated the significance of her pose: was it a flattering likeness or a generic image of woman as enigma, much as Ormond was representative of woman as repose? Perhaps the most complex response came several years later in the French writer Paul Bourget's *Outre-mer (Notes sur l'Amérique)*, published in 1895. Bourget calls Sargent's portrait the "American Idol" and goes on:

> Rubies, like drops of blood, sparkle on her shoes... The head, intellectual and daring, with a countenance as of one who had understood everything....The rounded arms...are joined by the clasped hands—firm hands... which might guide four horses with the precision of an English coachman. It is the picture of an energy at once delicate and invincible, momentarily in repose, and there is something of the Byzantine Madonna in that face, with its wide-open eyes. Yes, this woman is an idol, for whose service man labors, whom he has decked with the jewels of a queen, behind each of whose whims lie days and days spent in the ardent battle of Wall Street. Frenzy of speculation in land, cities undertaken and constructed by strokes of millions of dollars, trains launched at full speed over bridges built on a Babel-like sweep of arch, the creaking of cable cars, the quivering of electric cars, sliding along their wires with a crackle and a spark, the dizzy ascent of elevators in buildings twenty stories high... these are what have made possible this woman, this living orchid, unexpected masterpiece of this civilization.

The art historian Albert Boime sees this passage as indicative of male anxieties surrounding the emergence of the "new woman" at the turn of the century. Here was the "femme fatale" that populated the work of British and French followers of Aestheticism, the counterpart to the more passive and sexually available female nudes. While she is made possible by men's accomplishments—Gardner's father was a wealthy New York merchant and her husband a prominent Boston banker—she also makes them possible. She exerts power over men, urges them on in their acquisition of wealth, and directs the spending of their fortunes. She will banish the pure and innocent American Girl from her position as national icon, and take her place as the more aggressive New Woman of the early twentieth century, more apt to be criticized than celebrated in painting.

The American Impressionist Cecilia Beaux (1855–1942) created another version of the New Woman in her portraits. Beaux began her art training in the Philadelphia home of her maternal grandparents and aunts (her mother died shortly after giving birth to her, and her grief-stricken father returned to his native France). While recently having suffered financial setbacks, they instilled in her the attitudes of the well-to-do, in particular an appreciation of the various arts.

Beaux started her art training by copying lithographs and later studied with a relative, the history painter Catharine Ann Drinker. She also supplemented her income by painting nearly life-size heads of children on porcelain plates. Her biographer Tara Leigh Tappert notes that these were so successful that "parents nearly wept over them;" by the early 1880s her reputation as a china painter had spread to "mothers in the Far West." Fortunately, a few of these early portraits survive, such as *Clara Hoopes* (1882) [**5.17.15**]. The image of Clara, the daughter of a neighbor of Beaux's in West Philadelphia, was based on a daguerreotype of about 1853, when she was eight years old, and the stiff pose reflects this origin. Beaux updated the portrait by including brown-flowered wallpaper and geometrically patterned wainscoting in the background, marks of the Aesthetic-style interior decoration of the 1870s and 1880s. Tappert notes that Beaux proudly sent her china portraits to the annual exhibitions at the Pennsylvania Academy, but later denounced them as the "lowest depth I ever reached in commercial art."

After several years of further study in Philadelphia, Beaux traveled to Paris in the late 1880s and attended the Académie Julian, returning to the US in 1889. While in Paris she met Sargent, with whom she remained close friends. The stylistic similarities between them, and their common focus on portraiture, caused many critics to compare their work. For example, one reviewer wrote of *Sita and Sarita* (1893–94) [**5.17.16**; p. 312] when it was shown in 1895 at the Society of American Artists in New York: "I am going to say that I don't see how even Mr. Sargent could paint a portrait with more distinction than that of the woman with a black cat by Miss Beaux in the present exhibition."

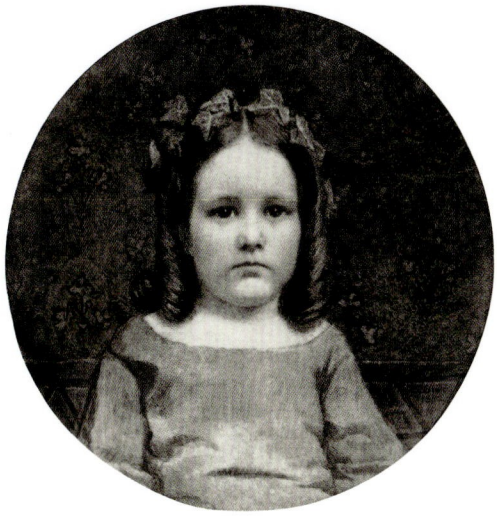

5.17.15 Cecilia Beaux: *Clara Hoopes*, 1882. Oil on porcelain, d. 12½ in. (31.8 cm.) Elizabeth Arthur

Beaux quickly became a much-sought-out portrait painter after her return from Paris, building on the reputation she had already made for herself. By the turn of the century her clientele came not only from Philadelphia, but also from Boston, New York, Washington, and many towns in between, causing her to move to New York to be more centrally located. Beaux was interested in the same problems as many of her male contemporaries—how to create a sense of quick execution through heavily laden brushstrokes while still maintaining the structural integrity of the figure, and how to give an overall decorative unity to the composition. She also focused on similar subject matter—women and girls in interior settings or generalized landscapes.

Beaux knew most of her sitters and was successful not only in capturing their personalities, but also in devising overall unified compositions. In *Sita and Sarita*, a portrait of her cousin Sara Allibone Leavitt with a black cat, the young woman's body dissolves into a series of white slashes and folds (this is one of a series of "white" paintings from the 1890s). These markings reinforce the shallowness of the space that is initially suggested by the dark background. The billowing lines of the sleeves are echoed in the curved forms of the upholstery and its vegetal designs.

The most compelling elements in the painting, however, are the pairs of eyes that echo each other and continually draw the viewer's own gaze. While the woman stares off into the distance, the cat stares directly out. It is so close to her head that it blends

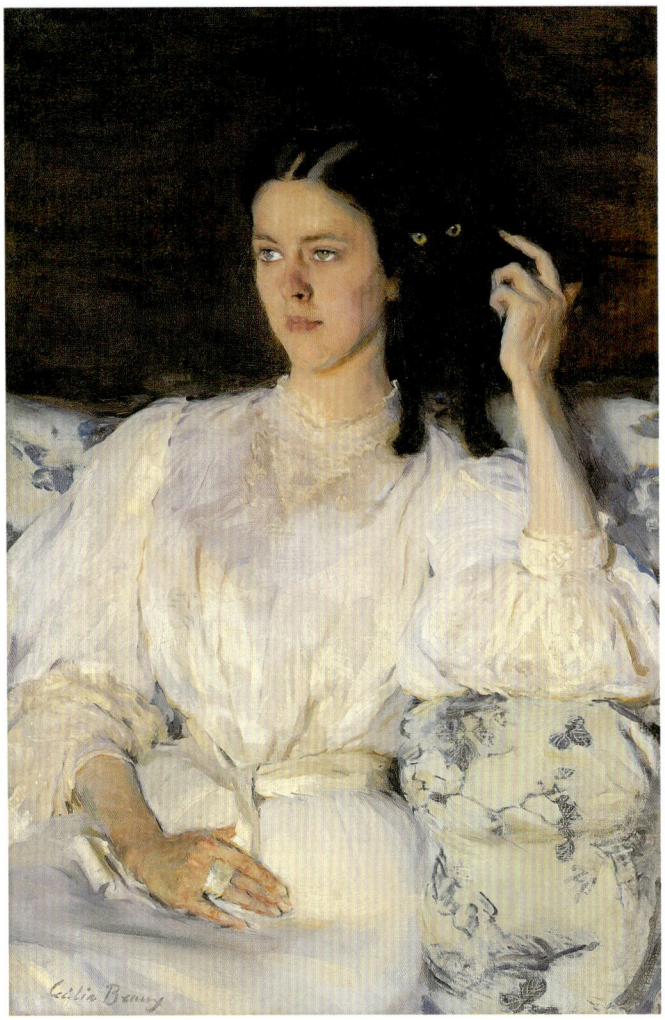

5.17.16 Cecilia Beaux: *Sita and Sarita*, 1893–94.
Oil on canvas, 37 x 25 in. (94 x 63.5 cm.)
Musée d'Orsay, Paris

into her black hair, suggesting it is somehow a manifestation of her or her animal "familiar." While in Paris, Beaux had met Edouard Manet (1832–1883), a pivotal figure in the emergence of Impressionism, and was undoubtedly aware of his painting *Olympia* (1863) [**5.17.17**] and the furore it caused when it was exhibited at the Paris Salon of 1865. The frankness of Olympia's nudity and her confrontational pose caused many to see her not as an inviting nude but as an urban prostitute, whose nakedness was an affront to respectable society. The black woman with flowers and the black cat at the end of the bed functioned as signs of Olympia's sexual availability, the former associated with "savage" Africa, the latter with the unholy world of witches.

Beaux's cat, which assumes the same arched pose and direct stare as the cat in *Olympia*, is associated with a fully clothed woman, one whose respectability and purity are symbolized by her white dress. Yet just as the cat in *Olympia* darkens the light-colored shawl beneath it with its shadow, so too does Beaux's cat darken the white shoulder upon which it is perched. In addition, the sheer material in the top of the bodice provides a glimpse of the skin beneath, just as a slight blue shadow suggests the cleavage between her breasts. These details suggest a sexual energy behind the reserved exterior. So, too, does the figure's hand that, as in *Olympia*, is placed firmly over her pubic area. The threading of her sash under the first finger of this hand, over the next two, and under the fourth creates an additional sense of restrained composure. Thus, Beaux's painting works against the denial of sexual feelings in "respectable" women, a denial that was a key part of gender discourse at the end of the nineteenth century and that was undoubtedly drilled into her by her grandmother and aunts, who were of good Puritan New England stock. It comments subtly on the connections so often made between "uncontrolled" female sexuality, evil witches (with their animal "familiars"), and darkness.

An interesting comparison can be made between *Sita and Sarita* and another portrait in which a figure is paired with a cat, that of Beaux's brother-in-law *Henry Sturgis Drinker* (1898) [**5.17.18**]. Normally, her portraits of professional men show figures in dark suits seated in simple wooden chairs with little else to identify the location. Drinker, a corporate railroad lawyer, is indeed seated in a Windsor chair and located in a shallow space, but it is clearly a domestic space, with shutters and curtains visible in the background. The use of an overall color scheme of white, green, and gold adds a decorative quality, most often associated with images of women. Drinker wears a white, not black, suit, which catches the light coming in through the window. Again, white clothing is usually worn by women, not men, although contemporary viewers would undoubtedly have interpreted the white here as an indication of the casualness of the moment, rather than the purity of the sitter.

5.17.17 Edouard Manet: *Olympia*, 1863.
Oil on canvas, 51¾ x 74¾ in. (130.5 x 190 cm.)
Musée d'Orsay, Paris

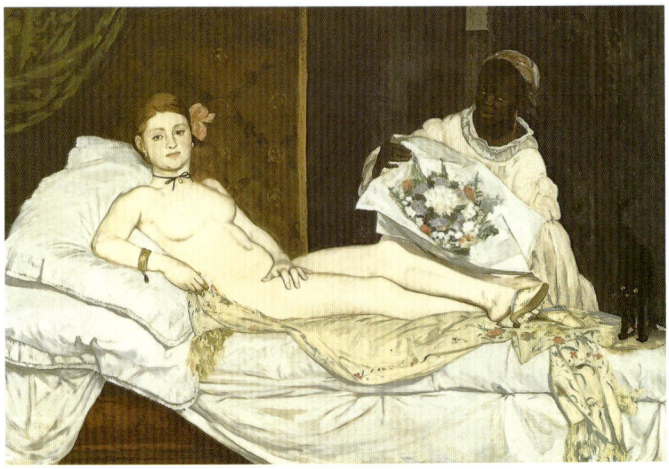

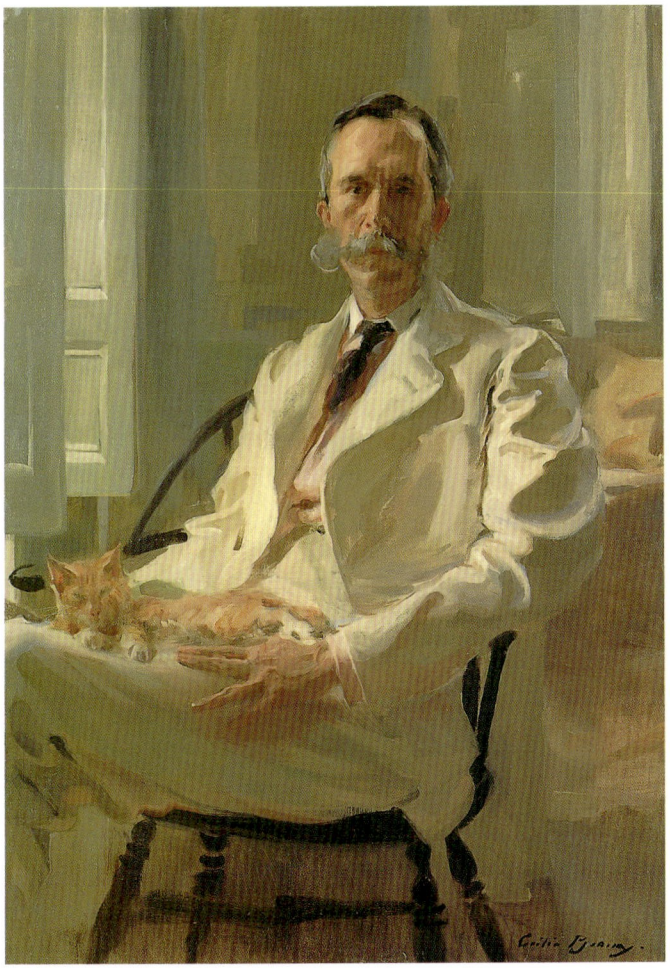

5.17.18 Cecilia Beaux: *Henry Sturgis Drinker (Man with a Cat)*, 1898.
Oil on canvas, 48 x 34 in. (121.9 x 86.4 cm.)
Smithsonian American Art Museum, Washington, D.C.

The attitudes of cat and human are reversed from those in *Sita and Sarita*, where the cat confronts us and the woman looks away. The man gazes out, while the orange tabby cat rests with eyes half-closed in his lap. The two bound fingers of Sara's right hand are replaced by the spread fingers of Henry's left hand. The open and unself-conscious manner in which Henry presents himself to his artist sister-in-law suggests his comfort in her presence and his own sense of self-confidence. Yet the self-confidence is not total, for the slightly knitted brow and darkened left eye suggest a possibly troubled soul. Tappert describes Drinker as a man who loved his wife, Beaux's sister Etta, "in a distracted and somewhat distant manner...a strong-willed patriarch who occupied a distinctly male world and firmly believed that only men shaped destiny." Beaux has, in Tappert's words, "domesticated" and "tamed" this distant patriarch, bringing him out of the world of law and high finance and into the more subdued, female-controlled world of the home.

Beaux also created several portraits of women using the conventions commonly adopted for male portraiture—sombre palettes, dark and nondescript backgrounds. Such conventions were appropriate, for these women occupied important positions in that male world outside of the home. The subject of *M Adelaide Nutting* (1906) [**5.17.19**] was superintendent of nurses and principal of the training school for nurses at Johns Hopkins University Hospital in Baltimore. Just as Dr. Agnew's students commissioned Thomas Eakins to create a portrait of their teacher (see p. 280), so, too, did Nutting's students, along with the alumnae association, commission Beaux to commemorate the retirement of their beloved teacher in paint. The mottled green background lightens somewhat the dark foreground marked by Nutting's black dress. The white hat, collar, and cuffs draw attention to the sources of her success—her sharp mind and skilled hands. In these hands she holds the red notebook that she constantly carried with her on her rounds. She gazes past the viewer with assurance, reflecting on her many years of work and on what lay ahead for women in the field of medicine.

5.17.19 Cecilia Beaux: *M. Adelaide Nutting*, 1906.
Oil on canvas, 37 x 24 in. (94 x 61 cm.)
Johns Hopkins Hospital, Baltimore, Maryland

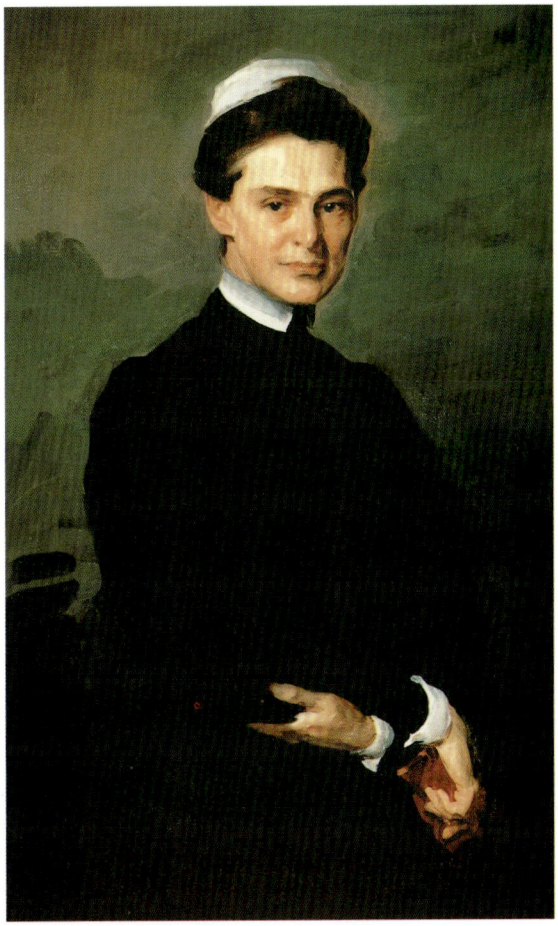

Performing Identity in Photographic Portraits

While the oil portraits of the American Impressionists filled the homes of wealthy Americans, photographic portraits proliferated in the domestic spaces of both rich and poor. In 1850, as T. S. Arthur writes, it was "hard to find a man who has not gone through the [daguerreotypist's] hands from once to a half-a-dozen times" (see p. 145). By the end of the nineteenth century it was even more difficult to find such an individual, male or female, who had not accumulated a sizable archive of photographs of him- or herself, family and friends. These family collections joined other photographic archives—those of government agents, criminologists, sociologists, eugenicists—that created hierarchical narratives based on race, gender, and class. At the same time, however, photography allowed individuals to challenge these hierarchies by disrupting the dominant photographic narratives circulating within and outside of the home.

The popularity of photographic portraits resulted in an explosion of photographers and studios after the Civil War. As mentioned earlier, photographers in San Francisco in the 1870s and 1880s faced stiff competition for customers (see pp. 298–99) and had to increase their advertising to draw attention to their products. One form of publicity that emerged in the 1860s was the cabinet-card advertisement. Cabinet cards were similar to *cartes-de-visites* (small photographic portraits on cardstock given out on social occasions as gifts or used as calling cards), only larger at approximately 4 × 6 inches (10.16 × 15.24 cm). A precursor of the postcard, they were often mailed to friends. The fronts of many of these cards included the name and location of the photographer, and thus functioned as a form of publicity.

Photographers also created cabinet cards specifically to advertise their businesses (rather than simply adding their names and addresses at the bottom of a commissioned portrait). The San Francisco studio of Thomas Houseworth and Company produced one such card in the 1880s, titled *The Masquerade* [**5.17.20**]. A woman stands in the center of the composition in front of a wall marked on the right by an engaged pier decorated with vaguely classicizing forms. She faces to her left (the viewer's right). She holds a fan in her left hand, which covers her face below her eyes. To her dress are attached multiple photographic portraits of various sizes, and on her head sits a camera. The large photographs located at the bottom of her skirt contain, at their lower edges, the text "Houseworth's Celebrities."

Thomas Houseworth (1828–1916) began as an optical-instrument maker on the East Coast. He arrived in California in 1849 along with many others looking to make their fortunes in the Gold Rush. After two years with little success, he teamed up with the optometrist George Lawrence and opened up an optician's office in San Francisco. They also sold camera lenses, and, after 1859, stereoscopic photographs. In 1860 the pair began producing their own stereoscopic views of the West, for which they soon became famous. They also added urban street scenes and society portraiture to their portfolio. Houseworth oversaw the Western landscape aspect of the business, and hired a team of photographers, including Eadweard Muybridge [**5.16.1**; p. 278]. Lawrence retired in 1868, leaving the business to Houseworth. In the 1880s, as the demand for western scenery began to wane, the studio began to offer celebrity portraiture, as advertised in the lower portion of the woman's dress in *The Masquerade*.

The literary critic Shawn Michelle Smith's description of a cabinet card containing a similar woman covered in photographs applies equally well to the Houseworth card:

> The photograph presents us with a strangely literal image of the body as tabula rasa, representing the body itself as a kind of archive. The figure of the woman... becomes a living display case, a physical frame for the images of others....Indeed, her exterior is mapped almost entirely by other personages; her face exists as one among many. The woman's body becomes a backdrop on which the photographic process and its results are displayed, as she inhabits both the studio and the products of the studio advertised.

5.17.20 Thomas Houseworth and Company: *The Masquerade*, *c.* 1880s. Cabinet card advertisement
Private Collection

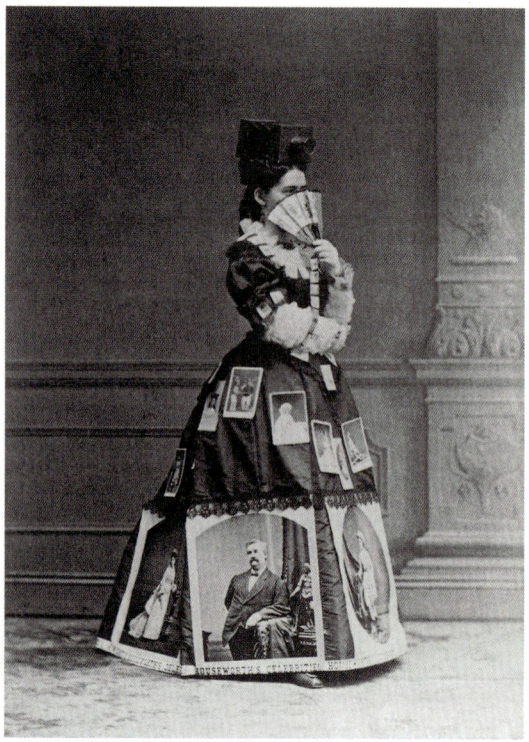

At the same time, Smith continues, while the woman's identity appears to have been overridden by the presentation of her body as archive, "one might also imagine that an individual identity has been protected from 'the gaze of the curious' here, hidden by the almost unnerving effect of reflection."

The title of the photograph—*The Masquerade*—also deflects the viewer's assumption that he or she could "know" the woman beneath the photographs and behind the fan. In fact, it also suggests that photography itself participates in this masquerade. With the camera on top of her head, the woman, as Smith notes, embodies "the whole of the photographic process, symbolically occupying at once all of the positions engendered by photography: photographer, photographed, and viewer." The fan, the symbol of masquerade, draws the viewer's attention to the camera. While the camera is celebrated for capturing the "real person" through its scientific information-gathering process—displayed fulsomely in the photographs attached to the woman's dress—the fan short-circuits that process. While the masquerade performed by the woman denies us access to her identity, her own vision "remain[s] unimpaired, bettered, in fact, by her photographic prosthesis. Indeed, the model, in her slightly alarming visage as cyclops, might unnerve the viewer with her usurpation of the gaze."

George Fiske (1835–1918), one of the photographers employed by Houseworth, created a different image of female resistance to gendered identities with his image of Kitty Tatch and Katherine Hazelston of *c.* 1895, waitresses at hotels in Yosemite National Park [**5.17.21**]. The two women have strayed from the paths carefully laid out throughout Yosemite Valley by Frederick Law Olmsted (see pp. 296–98). Instead, they stand on Overhanging Rock, legs raised in an "unladylike" pose holding hands. The precipitous 3,000-foot- (914-meters-) drop into the valley below shown in Fiske's photograph emphasizes the daring nature of their act. In the American West, it seems, anything is possible.

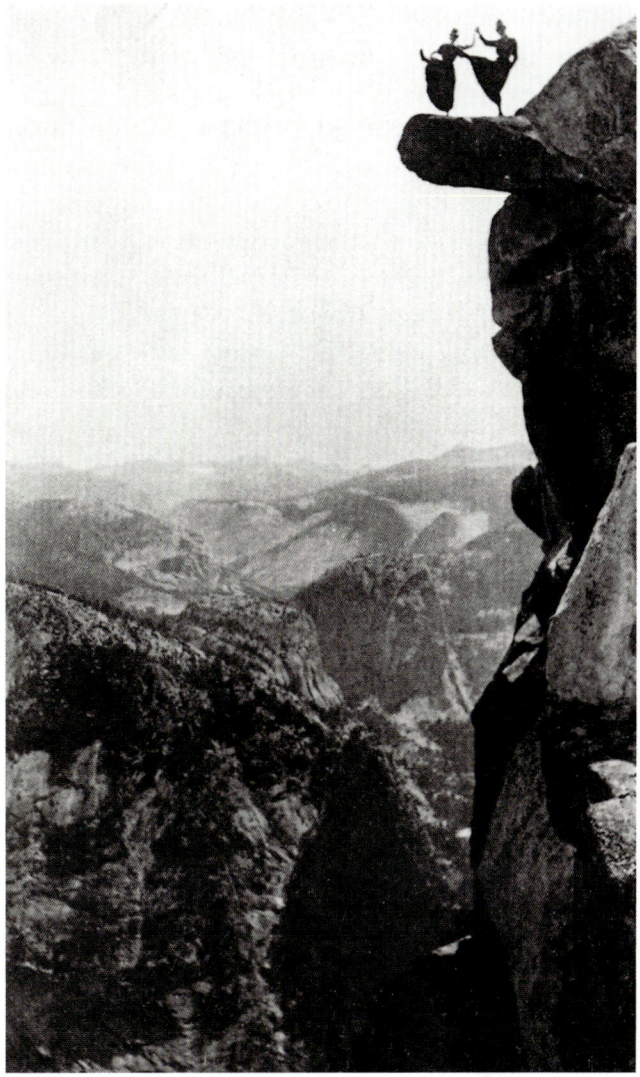

5.17.21 George Fiske: Kitty Tatch and a friend at Yosemite National Park, *c.* 1895. Photograph
National Park Service

Fiske has combined the conventions of two visual traditions in this image, landscape and portraiture, while simultaneously undermining both. In landscapes, small human figures are often placed safely in the foreground to provide a sense of scale or of human control over the land [**3.8.8**, p. 157; **3.8.9**, p. 158; **3.9.1**, p. 172]. Here, the two figures perch precariously in the top right corner of the composition, providing the viewer with a vicarious thrill. In portraiture, the person is usually close to the front of the picture plane, available for inspection by the viewer, who is looking for information about the subject's identity or social position. In Fiske's composition, the women are a considerable distance from the photographer, and thus from the viewer. Their identities lie not in the details of their facial features or their costumes, but in their audacious act. They are performing their gender in a way that marks them as alternatives to the narratives of proper female comportment. They are also performing for a broad public. Fiske's image was transformed into a best-selling postcard, which circulated widely. Such alternative performances would increase as the century ended and the women's rights movement gained momentum.

Another image that resists the conventions of both portraiture and female comportment is E. Jane Gay's self-portrait *Photographer* (after 1893) [**5.17.22**; p. 316]. Gay (1830–1919) began her adult life as a schoolteacher and school administrator before becoming a nurse for the Union Army during the Civil War. After the war she worked as a children's tutor and then a clerk in the Washington, D.C. Dead Letter Office. She was also an expert cabinetmaker, seamstress, gardener, and gourmet cook. Throughout her life she lived with a series of female friends and never married. In 1888 she met her old friend Alice Fletcher, an anthropologist and agent for the US Department of the Interior's Bureau of Indian Affairs, who had just completed fieldwork among the Omahas of Nebraska. Looking for a way out of her clerking job, Gay volunteered to accompany Fletcher on her future trips in the field as her companion, photographer, and cook. Fletcher agreed, and Gay began to teach herself photography.

Fletcher's next government assignment was to implement the Dawes Act of 1887 (see p. 256) among the Nez Perce people of Idaho. Reservation lands were to be divided into 160-acre (67-hectares) parcels or allotments assigned to individual Nez Perce in exchange for abandoning indigenous culture and taking up the ways of the American citizen-farmer. During the summers of 1889 to 1892, the two women traveled to Idaho to take part in the government-sponsored inventorying, surveying, and reshaping of the American West.

The literary scholars Susan Bernardin, Melody Graulich, Lisa MacFarlane, and Nicole Tonkovich comment on how Fletcher and Gay's project represents the contradictory and entangled nature of many government and scientific agendas. While government policies promoted the assimilation of Native Americans to white Christian ways, the newly emerging field of ethnography focused on the study and recording of the indigenous traditions being destroyed. Fletcher and Gay also presented a paradox to those they encountered in the field: two single middle-aged women doing work normally associated with men. Yet women were welcomed into the emerging disciplines of anthropology and ethnology by its primarily male founders as assistants, in part because their "natural nurturing abilities" were assumed to make them suitable for the study of infancy and the development of humankind, while "their womanly patience and tolerance for repetitive and detailed work qualified them to collect ethnographic [data]." Many, however, moved beyond the role of helpmeet and distinguished themselves through their own independent research. Photography had also become a profession open to more women as new technology made cameras lighter and easier to operate. This was particularly important for women like Gay, who wanted to travel to regions a considerable distance from towns or cities where supplies and technical assistance were readily available.

5.17.22 E. Jane Gay: *Photographer*, after 1893. Photograph
The Schlesinger Library, Radcliffe Institute, Harvard University, Cambridge, Massachusetts

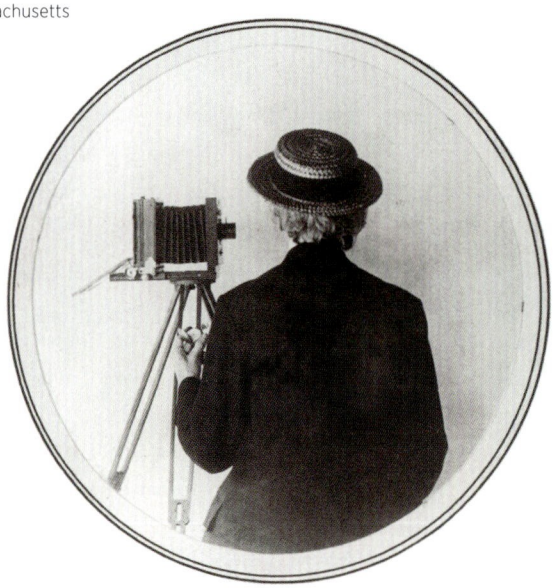

Photographer is one of Gay's few self-portraits. It was created after the conclusion of the summer trips to Idaho, and thus can be seen, in part, as a reflection on her first experience as a photographer. For Bernardin, Graulich, MacFarlane, and Tonkovich, it functions as a self-conscious critique of the "nexus of camera, subject, image, consumer, and viewer." Gay intentionally chose a circular format, rejecting the more common linear, rectangular frame. She also rejects the frontal gaze and instead presents the act of portrait making through an ambiguously gendered subject seen from behind. The pocket watch in Gay's left hand introduces a temporal element into the image—the time one had to sit still for a photograph, the time it took to develop and print it, the time it took to view it. The circular format of Gay's photograph also replicates the lens of the camera, reinforcing the position of the viewer as photographer and causing us to wonder who, in fact, took the photograph. Who is the "photographer" referred to in the title?

As with *The Masquerade*, the woman in *Photographer* resists the viewer's gaze, but not by covering her face with a fan and diverting her head. Instead, she turns her back. The camera perched on the model's head in the Thomas Houseworth and Company photograph positions the woman as photographer rather than subject. *Photographer* was taken by a woman, yet the gender identity of the person in the photograph is complicated by the hat and jacket, usually worn by men.

In her written accounts of her travels with Fletcher, Gay created a series of personas: Her Majesty, The Allotting Agent, and Miss F. for Fletcher; The Photographer, The Cook, The Friend, and I for herself. As Tonkovich notes, she used the persona of the Photographer, who is gendered male in her writings, when referring to herself in her official capacity as an agent of the government. She did not always support the project in which she and Fletcher were involved. The Photographer often functioned as the voice of the philosopher/critic, pointing out the serious flaws in the Dawes Act and its negative impact on the

Nez Perce. This criticism also, writes Tonkovich, informed her photographs, which "challenge[d] photography's claims to documentary realism, often by parodying the conventions of realism through emphasizing the banal" or foregrounding "the complicity of image making and image taking with US enterprises of imperial expansion in the late nineteenth-century West." Thus, The Photographer in Gay's self-portrait may embody a critique of the medium itself and its ability to provide any meaningful evidence of a racial or gendered identity.

Questions of race and gender also inform a series of photographic portraits compiled by the sociologist and civil rights activist W. E. B. Du Bois for the American Negro exhibit at the Paris Exposition of 1900. The names of the photographers are unknown, but as Du Bois was the individual responsible for collecting, organizing, and presenting the images, they have come to be associated with him.

As Smith notes, these albums included formal studio portraits, "informal snapshots of groups outdoors, children playing, and people working, images of homes and business establishments, and interior views of elaborately decorated middle-class parlors." Du Bois arranged the photographs into four albums: *Types of American Negroes; Georgia; USA;* and *Negro Life in Georgia, USA*. They were intended to counter claims that African Americans were an inferior race. He commented that those people who visited the American Negro exhibit would find "several volumes of photographs of typical Negro faces, which hardly square with conventional American ideas."

Formal individual portraits introduced each volume. Each individual sat for two photographs, a frontal and profile or semi-profile image, as can be seen in the head-and-shoulders photographs of an African American girl [**5.17.23**]. The girl is dressed in fashionable attire, attesting to a certain level of material prosperity. In the frontal image she looks out confidently at the viewer. She sits in front of a plain dark-gray background.

Such photographic pairings and setting echo the poses and setting of scientific photographic archives created in the nineteenth century that attempted to codify the racial "other" through repeated images of similar bodies, often naked from the waist up. Yet there is no sameness in the clothed bodies of the individuals in Du Bois's albums. As Smith writes, by "[r]eproducing the variations of 'color, hair and bone' that were legally encompassed by 'one drop' of blood identity laws at the turn of the century, Du Bois's albums confront white America's obsession with the color line." They do so by taking apart stereotypes of African Americans in popular culture [**5.16.11**, p. 287; **5.16.15**, p. 290], creating instead multiple "types." They "dispute the notion of racial purity upheld by eugenicists and white supremacists, and the anti-miscegenation laws that prohibited legal, mutually desired unions between whites and blacks, but not the rape of African American women by white men."

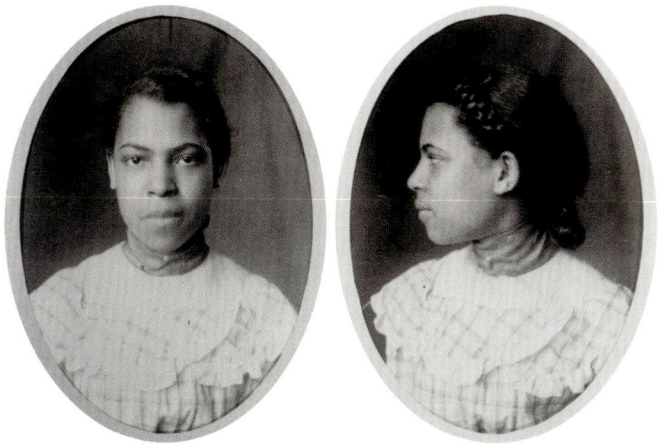

5.17.23 W. E. B. Du Bois: *African-American girl, head-and-shoulders portrait, facing front and facing left*, 1899.
Photograph, Library of Congress, Washington, D.C.

Smith argues that Du Bois's images do not intend to represent any "real" or "true" blackness. Neither do they attempt to record—as did Frances Benjamin Johnston, whose photographs of the Hampton Institute were also displayed in 1900 in Paris [**4.14.14**; p. 261]—the transformation of Africans into "Americans." Instead, they are an attempt to enable white viewers "to see the cultural logics and privileged practices that reproduce racism." In selecting photographs of people who directly engage the viewer, Du Bois creates an archive that individualizes and particularizes American identity and places it "squarely back on the terrain of negotiation, conflict, and 'race.'"

Review Questions

1 What were the characteristics of the Aesthetic Movement, and how did its practitioners contribute to a new image of American women?

2 How is William Merritt Chase's painting *In the Studio* a commentary on the rise of consumer culture in the US?

3 What types of landscapes drew the attention of American Impressionists and why?

4 What are the similarities and differences between Cecilia Beaux's portraits of her cousin Sara Allibone Leavitt and her brother-in-law Henry Sturgis Drinker?

5 How did E. Jane Gay's *Photographer*, Thomas Houseworth and Company's *The Masquerade*, and W. E. B. Du Bois's *African-American girl* both utilize and undermine photographic conventions and narratives of race and/or gender?

CHAPTER 18

Art and Architecture at the End of the Century

(*c.* 1885–1900)

Cultural Institutions and the Public Good: The Metropolitan Museum of Art

"High" culture came to play a particularly prominent role in the education, assimilation, and pacification of urban immigrant populations. It was seen as a key element in combating social and political unrest, and was often rhetorically coupled with social reform legislation. Its promotion created some strange bedfellows. Middle-class reformers bent on improving the lives of working people and wealthy philanthropists who effectively benefited from the low wages and poverty of these same people came together in the last quarter of the nineteenth century to establish major cultural institutions—libraries, museums, concert halls, universities. The Metropolitan Museum of Art in New York and the Museum of Fine Arts in Boston were founded in 1870, the Philadelphia Museum of Art in 1876, and the Art Institute of Chicago in 1879.

The buildings constructed to house these early museums often drew on Gothic and Renaissance architecture. These styles served to associate this most recent phase in the development of American culture with either the spiritual cohesiveness and idealism of Gothic England or the artistic and scientific revolutions of the Italian Renaissance. For Charles Eliot Norton, the first professor to teach art history at Harvard University (he was appointed to the first chair of fine arts in any American university in 1874), medieval England was the high point of civilization. It was a time (he imagined) when Christianity unified all social classes. This unity was embodied in the architecture of churches and cathedrals. The Renaissance, on the other hand, celebrated a mix of secular and sacred forces. It marked the beginning of the rise to prominence of the former at the expense of the latter, with market economies replacing those based on feudal allegiances. So extensive was the use of Renaissance forms in all areas of the visual arts that the last decades of the nineteenth century and the first decade of the twentieth century came to be referred to as the American Renaissance.

One of the best-known of the new museums by the end of the century was The Metropolitan Museum of Art in New York City [**5.18.1**], which utilized both architectural styles. Its original building of 1880 by Calvert Vaux (1824–1895) drew on the pointed arches of Gothic cathedrals. Its later Fifth Avenue facade by the architect Richard Morris Hunt (1827–1895) turned to the Italian Renaissance, with its Corinthian columns and massive Roman arches. Like its many sister institutions, its interior was marked by monumental staircases and hallways, and its rooms were filled with casts and originals of ancient Greek and Roman statues and European paintings from more recent eras, all donated by wealthy patrons. The museum was meant to function as a democratic enterprise, diffusing knowledge, taste, and refinement. Yet it also reminded those of modest means who entered its halls that high culture was not a part of their daily lives but resided, rather, in objects from foreign lands and earlier times. It was something to be admired, but at a distance.

The founding of the Metropolitan Museum was also meant as a statement of American prestige on an international level. It was intended, in part, to put the lie to the country's reputation in Europe as a materialistic, uncultured nation, and to proclaim

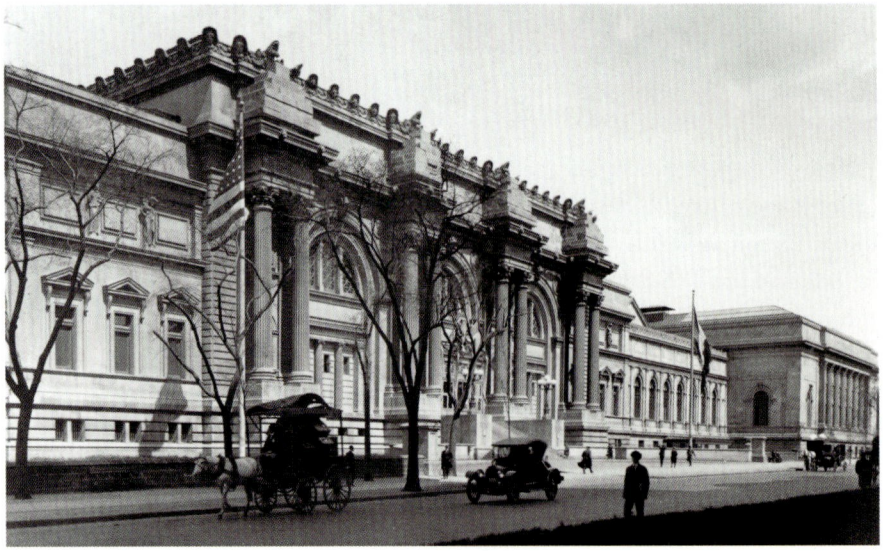

5.18.1 Richard Morris Hunt: Fifth Avenue facade of The Metropolitan Museum of Art, New York, 1902.

its readiness to assume a prominent position in the development of Western civilization. The idea for the museum was first broached by the lawyer John Jay in Paris in 1866 at a gathering of men filled with pride in the triumph of Northern industrialists in the Civil War. Three years later, three hundred wealthy New Yorkers gathered to hear the poet William Cullen Bryant, in his role as the president of the organizing committee, summarize why a major museum of art was needed:

> Our city is the third greatest city in the civilized world. Our Republic has already taken its place among the great powers of the earth; it is great in extent, great in population, great in activity and enterprise of her people. It is the richest nation in the world. [With a museum of art] we might have, reposited in spacious and stately buildings, collections formed of works left by the world's greatest artists which would be the pride of our country.

Thus, national pride was a central issue in the founding of the Metropolitan. By proposing to bring into existence a museum to rival the Louvre in Paris, Bryant and those for whom he spoke—the Rockefellers, the Carnegies, the Morgans—asserted their cultural, as well as economic, power. They also asserted their concern with the public good through their association with a public institution. Yet the relationship between public and private with regards to the museum was a complicated one, embedded in the manner in which it was to be owned and administered. The building would be located on city land and owned by the city, with tax-payer money used to cover maintenance costs. The collection would be owned and controlled by those wealthy individuals who made up the museum's Board of Trustees. Thus private individuals would determine which art would best serve the educational needs of the nation and how that art would function as a reinforcement of already established economic and social, as well as cultural, hierarchies.

The Chicago School of Architecture and the White City

The biggest cultural event of the nineteenth century in the United States was also the biggest economic event of the century: the World's Columbian Exposition of 1893 in Chicago [**5.18.2**]. This exposition marked the four hundredth anniversary of the arrival of Christopher Columbus in the Americas and was intended to provide proof to both the nation and the world of the quality of US achievements in the realms of industry, technology, agriculture, and the fine arts. The grounds were laid out by Frederick Law Olmsted (1822–1903), in what was his last major urban design project. The fair's primary architectural statement

5.18.2 World's Columbian Exposition, Chicago, 1893.
The Court of Honor or "White City" is in the left foreground; the Midway Plaisance runs back from upper center to beyond the ferris wheel.

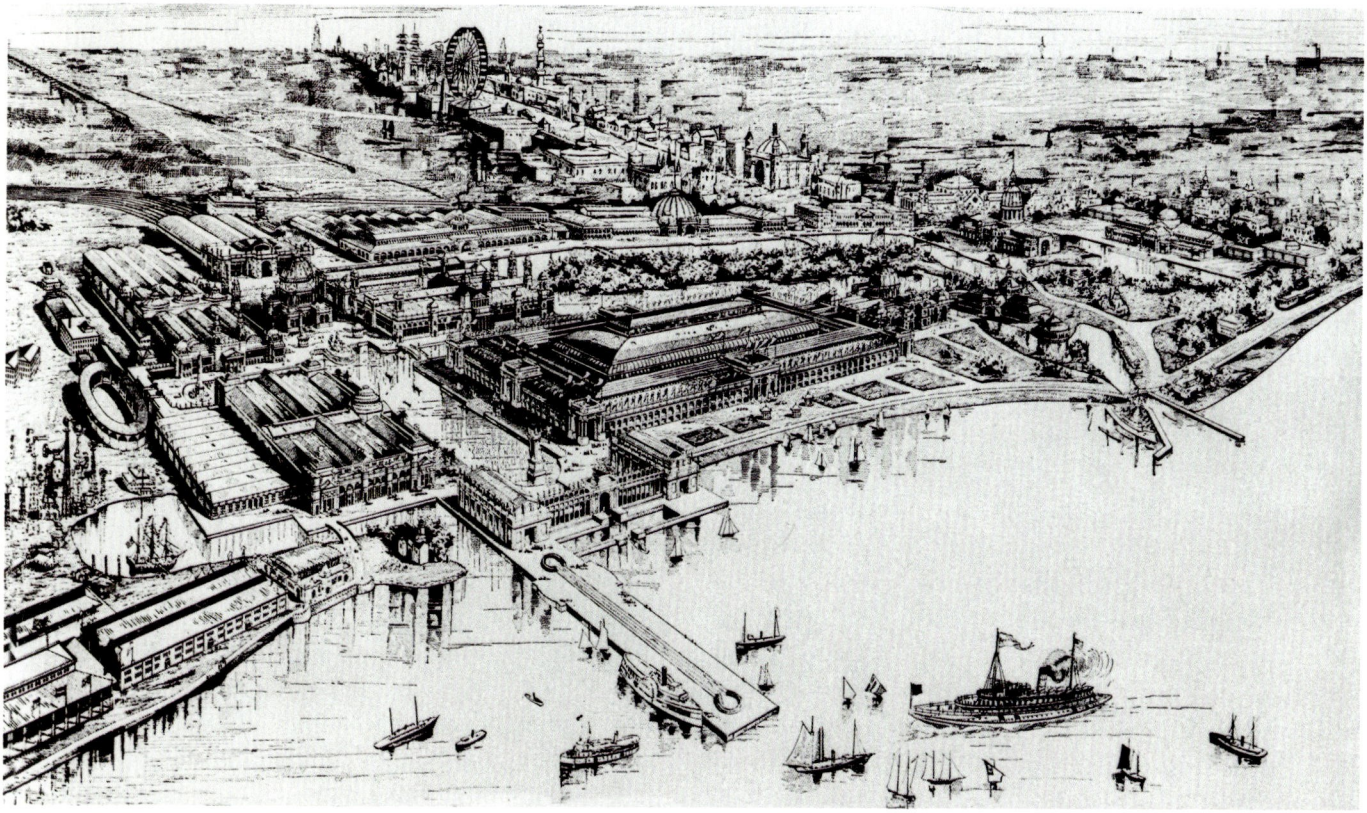

was its central Court of Honor, which featured an elaborate display of white neoclassical facades [**5.18.8**; p. 323]. Nicknamed the "White City," it captured the visitor's imagination through its unity, its overwhelming size, and its festive atmosphere. Yet the strength of these classical forms was illusory, for the plaster exteriors, with their references to the authority of ancient Greece and Rome, hid steel frames that provided the structural support for the buildings. And the festive atmosphere was, if not illusory, then certainly temporary. Like the Centennial celebration of 1876, Chicago's Exposition took place in the midst of a severe economic depression. It functioned, in part, as an attempt to restore faith in national institutions at a time when such faith was being seriously eroded by economic crisis and labor unrest.

In choosing a neoclassical style for the main court, the fair's organizers turned their backs on a revolutionary development in building design taking place in the city of Chicago itself. Ironically, the man given the task of overseeing the architectural elements of the fair, Daniel H. Burnham (1846–1912), was a key player in this new development, which led to the rise of the modern skyscraper.

Several factors prompted the appearance of radical architectural change in Chicago. As a major railroad hub and gateway to the Far West, the city had grown rapidly throughout the third quarter of the century. In 1871 fire destroyed a large portion of the downtown area. Speculation was intense; the price of land rose by 700 percent between 1880 and 1890. In order to make the most efficient use of this limited and expensive space, buildings began to rise upwards, a movement facilitated by new technological developments, including Bessemer steel, the passenger elevator, and the telephone.

As architects designed taller buildings and utilized new technologies, several also considered abandoning the elaborate historical decoration that had adorned earlier commercial exteriors. They began to develop an aesthetic that celebrated "truth to materials," taking its cue from engineers, who claimed a greater concern with forms that expressed the present function of a building. This move away from historical decoration can be seen in the eleven-story Home Insurance Building (1884–85) [**5.18.3**] by William Le Baron Jenney (1832–1907). The first six stories made use of cast- and wrought-iron columns and cast-iron girders; steel girders supported the remainder. This proved historically significant, as it was the first use of that material in a building. The internal structural systems thus spoke to the new technologies available to architects. Jenney clad them in a conventional stone veneer and included familiar decorative elements such as columns, capitals, and cornices. Yet he used these elements sparingly and in a way that emphasized both the height of the building (the corner piers and central pilasters) and the grid structure of its internal framework (the window patterns).

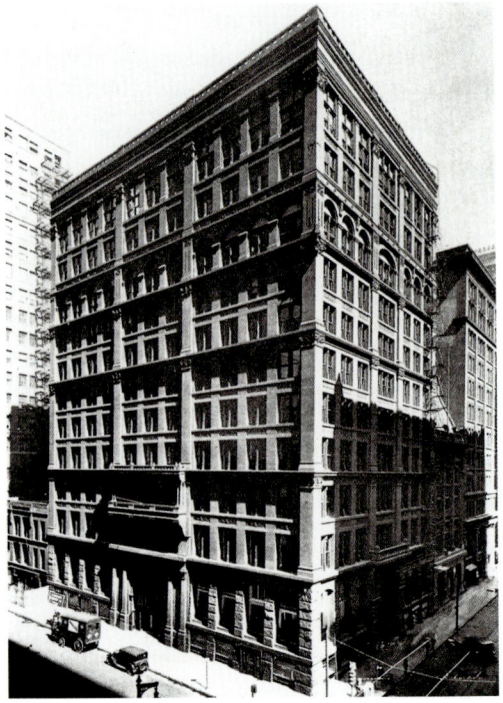

5.18.3 William Le Baron Jenney: Home Insurance Building, Chicago, Illinois, 1884–85 (destroyed).

William Holabird (1854–1923) and Martin Roche (1855–1927) worked in Jenney's office. They left separately in the early 1880s and, in 1883, set up their own partnership. Three years later they began the design of the twelve-story Tacoma Building [**5.18.4**], making use of improved riveted metal frame construction. Here, the exterior exploited the enclosing wall's new-found freedom from its supporting function. The continuous succession of bays runs the full height, thus maximizing exposure to light and air. While the metal frame is still hidden, Holabird and Roche used a brick and terracotta sheathing, creating a much lighter effect than in the Home Insurance Building. In addition, traditional exterior ornamentation is eliminated and the large plate-glass windows are exposed with a greater frankness. Thus, lightness rather than monumentality is the dominant impression conveyed by the building.

A further simplification of the exterior of the Chicago office building can be found in the Monadnock Building (1884–92) [**5.18.5**] by Burnham and John Wellborn Root (1850–1891). It was completed after Root's death and shortly before the opening of the World's Columbian Exposition. The emphasis here is not on lightness but on weight and monumentality. This is due in large part to the fact that the Monadnock is not a steel-frame building. Rather, the brick walls still serve as supporting elements for the sixteen stories and are 17 feet (5 meters) thick at

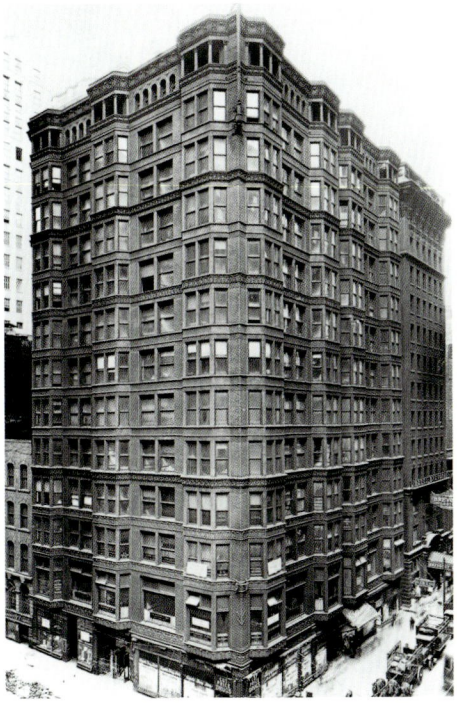

5.18.4 Holabird and Roche: Tacoma Building, Chicago, Illinois, 1887–89 (destroyed).

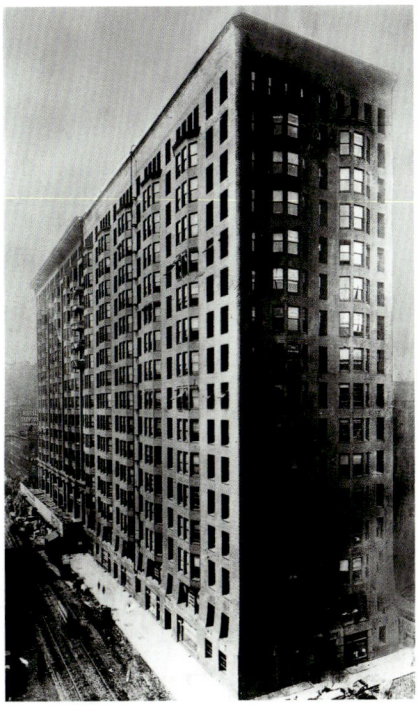

5.18.5 Burnham and Root: Monadnock Building, Chicago, 1884–92.

5.18.6 Adler and Sullivan: Wainwright Building, St. Louis, Missouri, 1890–91.

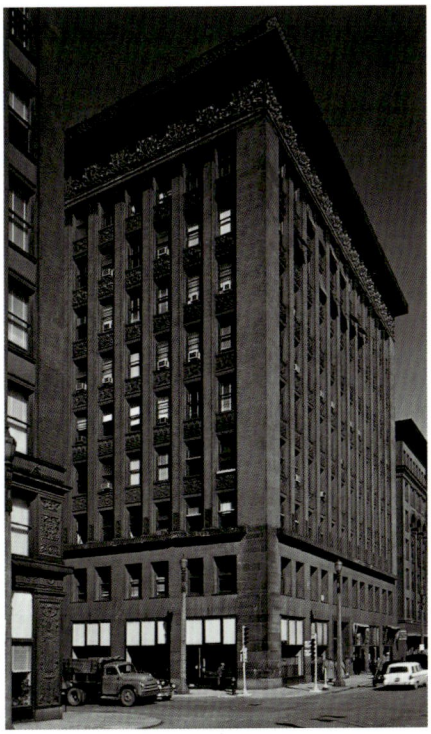

the base (they flare out slightly to facilitate their load-bearing function). Soon, however, load-bearing walls would become a thing of the past, and the steel frame combined with the absence of exterior decoration would become the distinctive features of Modernist architecture.

Residing somewhere between the architecture of the tall, undecorated office building and the neoclassical architecture of the World's Columbian Exposition is the work of Louis Sullivan (1856–1924). Another student of Jenney, Sullivan left in 1874 to study at the Academy of Fine Arts in Paris before returning to Chicago and entering the practice of Dankmar Adler (1844–1900). He later became a partner in the firm of Adler and Sullivan.

Sullivan was a proponent of the new tall building with all its technological advances, yet did not eschew ornamentation outright. What he rejected was historicist ornamentation, that which self-consciously harked back to an earlier time in order to lend legitimacy to the building, or at the very least to create an aura of nostalgia. Sullivan's preferred decorative motifs were drawn from geometry and nature. In the Wainwright Building in St. Louis, Missouri [**5.18.6**], of 1890–91, verticality is emphasized. The corner piers run unobstructed almost the full height from ground level to the elaborate projecting cornice. While the building is faced with stone, the exterior articulation of piers and windows echoes the metal frame within. The most striking decoration can be found on the cornice, which establishes the Wainright's presence on the St. Louis skyline. Minor decorative elements can also be found in several places: the horizontal areas (or spandrels) separating the vertical banks of windows; the bases and capitals of the intermediate piers in the central

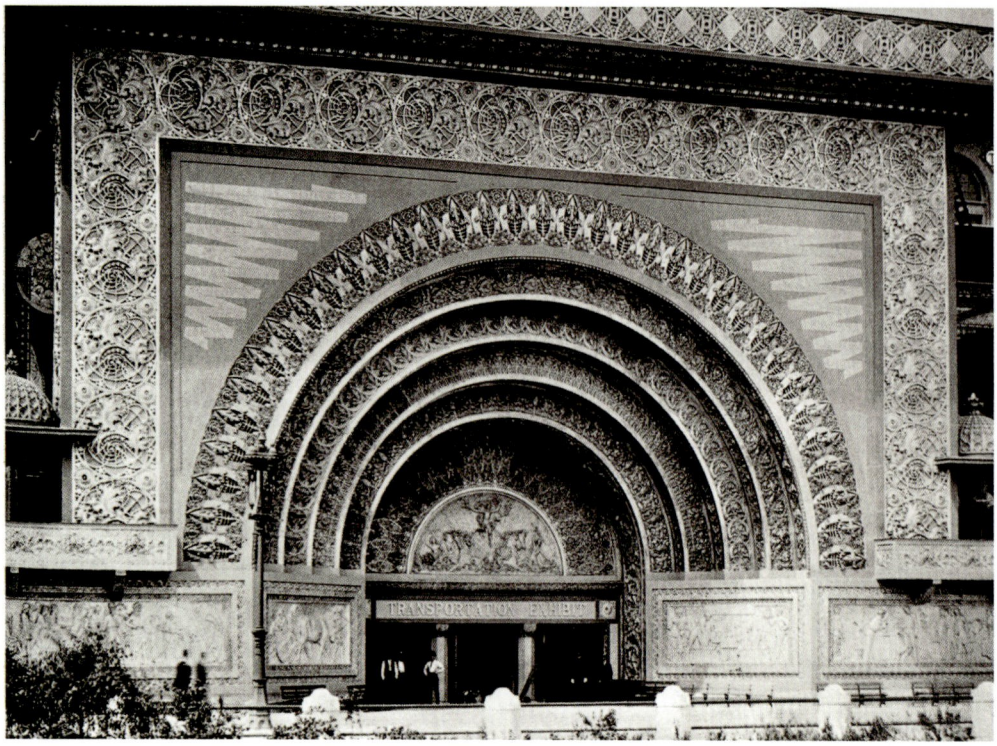

5.18.7 Adler and Sullivan: entrance to the Transportation Building, World's Columbian Exposition, Chicago, Illinois, 1893 (destroyed).

section of the building; the face of the belt course that marks the division between the lower and central sections; and a narrow frame around the main entrances on the ground floor. In all cases the designs are drawn from nature and are composed of repetitive and intricate foliate motifs.

Sullivan was present at the World's Columbian Exposition, having been given the task of designing the Transportation Building. Its location outside the central court allowed him to depart from the dominant neoclassicism and produce, instead, an imaginative facade composed of geometric forms—the rectangle, the semicircle—with elaborate foliate decoration that framed, and thus highlighted, these forms. The entrance [**5.18.7**] was marked by a series of receding rounded arches and the foliate ornamentation was covered with bright gold leaf. In fact, the exterior combined red, orange, blue, yellow, and green.

Sullivan criticized the neoclassical architecture of the fair [**5.18.8**] as "snobbish and alien to the land." Instead, as early as 1885 he had called for an architecture that spoke to the aspirations and desires of the many, not the few. Yet one could argue that the Court of Honor was more familiar and more accessible to the general public than Sullivan's imaginative Transportation Building, with its elaborate, gilded facade. Hundreds, if not thousands, of neoclassical public buildings had been constructed in cities and towns across the country. While Sullivan still gives a nod to classical forms in his use of the Roman arch and broken colonnades, his building more readily conjures up associations with the Middle East rather than Middle America.

In the process of creating a national architecture that spoke to the general population, Sullivan also wanted to create buildings that celebrated American business enterprise as a heroic, individual effort. Yet his golden doorway can also be seen as a celebration in part of the corruption and excess that marked many of the business ventures of the Gilded Age. Immediately inside this doorway was a miniature replica of the town of Pullman, just a few miles south of the fairgrounds, which had been created for the employees of the Palace Car Company. It was a model workers' town, with clean, tree-lined streets, green lawns, varied architecture, and elegantly furnished library. But this beautiful environment was also accompanied by close control over workers' lives and by low wages.

A year after the fair, the nation witnessed a bloody strike between the American Railroad Union and the Pullman Palace Car Company over successive wage cuts. In fact, the completion of the fairgrounds had been delayed by strikes over wages and working conditions by many of the 16,000 workers employed at any one time during the construction of the White City. The historian David Silkenat points out that as at Pullman, these workers were closely watched, and the fairgrounds where they both lived and worked were fenced off to prevent labor leaders from trying to organize them. In addition, John Bonfield, commander of the police force in the Haymarket Riot (see p. 274), headed the Secret Service contingent of the guards that had been hired to police the perimeter of the grounds. The Haymarket Monument itself [ill. p. 4] was dedicated in Chicago during the fair, with a crowd of three thousand marching through the streets and thousands watching.

Sullivan's inclusion of non-classical elements in his facade was part of a larger architectural variety found outside of the fair's Court of Honor. In fact, the further one moved away, the more varied the styles became, until one found oneself on the Midway Plaisance, a mile-long strip of land that extended out from the main body of the fair. The content of the Court of Honor and of the Midway Plaisance, and their relationship to each other [**5.18.2**; p. 319], shed light on contemporary notions of progress and racial and ethnic hierarchies.

In celebrating Columbus's landing, the exhibition was celebrating the bringing of European civilization to the Americas. Housed in massive, white, neoclassical buildings in the Court of Honor were the achievements of that civilization, chiefly its American representatives. These were tacitly accepted as the standard by which the achievements of all peoples were to be measured. The Midway, on the other hand, officially classified under the Department of Ethnology, contained various replica villages, restaurants, marketplaces, etc., of non-white, non-Western, and a few marginal European groups. The exhibits were organized culturally and racially, from the far end, as follows: Africa/Native American; Mohammedan world; West and East Asia; Teutonic and Celtic races. The literary critic Denton J. Snider observed at the time that the best way of viewing these groups and their exhibits was "to behold them in the ascending scale, in the progressive movement; thus we can march forward with them starting with the lowest specimens of humanity, reaching continually upward to the highest stage."

By emphasizing the superiority of the white race not only in the Midway, but also throughout the fair, its organizers provided white Americans with a sense of shared racial identity and national pride, one buttressed by scientific concepts of progress and evolution. While Africans and African Americans were on display in the Midway Plaisance and elsewhere during the entire run of the fair (including a woman dressed up as Aunt Jemima, a character developed by the Quaker Oats Company to sell breakfast food products [see V. 2, pp. 527–28]), African American visitors were allowed admittance only on select days. In a publication entitled "The Reason Why the Colored American Is Not in the World's Columbian Exposition," the black writers and abolitionists Frederick Douglass and Ida B. Wells denounced the segregated admission policies and the exhibition of "the Negro as a repulsive savage." They also connected such displays to the growing imperialist ambitions of the US—ambitions that would lead to the Spanish-American War and US intervention in the Caribbean and the Philippines in 1898.

5.18.8 Court of Honor, World's Columbian Exposition, Chicago, looking west to the Administration Building, 1893 (destroyed).
Seen from the back is Daniel Chester French's *Republic*; in the distance is Frederick William MacMonnies's *The Triumph of Columbia*

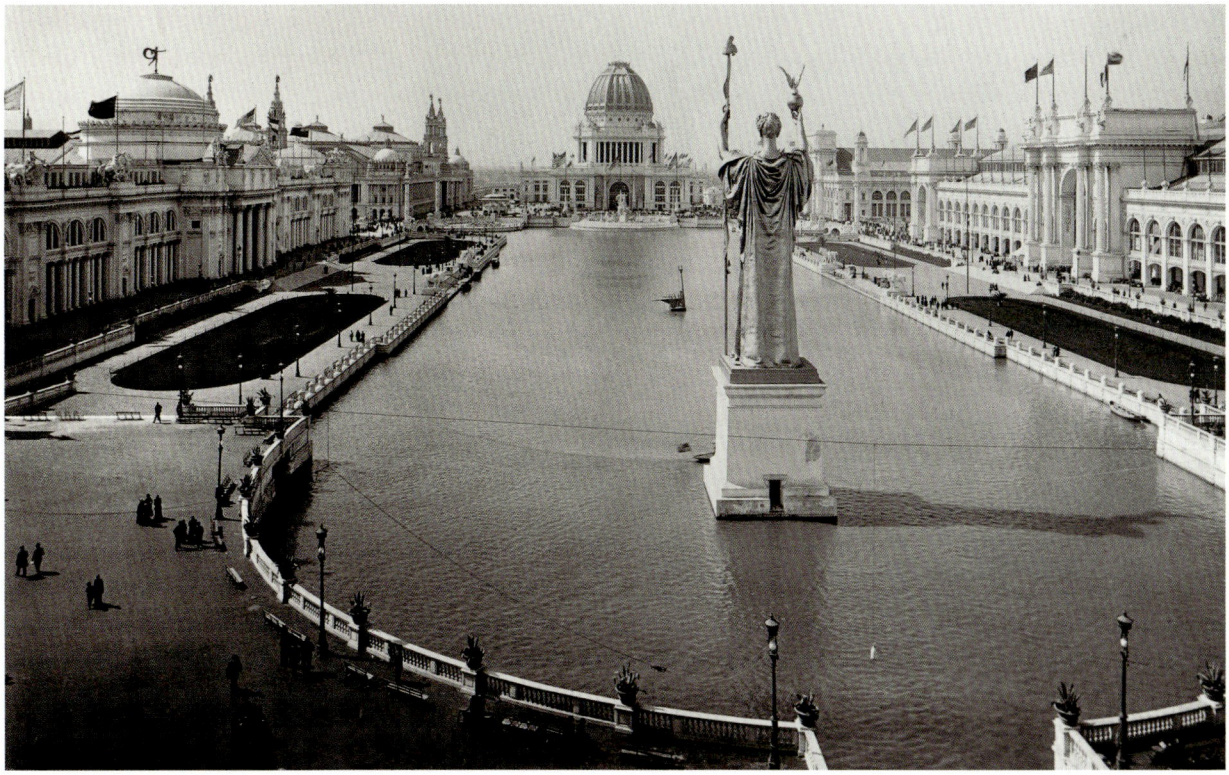

Women at the Fair: Allegories, Architects, and Artists

In celebrations of the white race at the World's Columbian Exposition, men appeared as actors on the stage of history, while women functioned as they had at the earlier 1876 Centennial Exhibition—as allegorical representations of continents or concepts [**5.15.1**; p. 267]. The Court of Honor embodied this division. At either end of the great lagoon stood two large sculptural works, a figure of the *Republic* by Daniel Chester French (1850–1931) [**5.18.8**; p. 323], and *The Triumph of Columbia* or *The Barge of State* by Frederick William MacMonnies (1863–1937) [**5.18.9**].

Augustus Saint-Gaudens (1848–1907) had been charged with overseeing the sculptural program of the court and gave both French and MacMonnies an indication of the types of works he would like to have in the lagoon. Ultimately, however, the commissioned artists were responsible for the final designs. French produced a stiff, classically garbed female figure with both arms raised, the right holding a globe surmounted by an American eagle, the left grasping a pike topped by a liberty cap. The static pose—both feet are planted firmly on the ground—and classical drapery suggested the solid basis upon which the American Republic was founded. Standing on a 35-foot- (10.7-meter-) high pedestal in the middle of the basin, the 65-foot- (20-meter-) tall statue reached well above the cornice line of the buildings and was further set off by its extensive gilding and by a crown of electric lights that glowed in the evening. The Republic may be based on traditions from the past, but not to the exclusion of the technological achievements of the present.

In contrast, MacMonnies produced an elaborate work full of movement and drama. Twenty-eight figures either occupy or surround the central barge. Seated atop a high pedestal is Columbia, bare-breasted, with drapery billowing behind her. An additional eight bare-breasted female figures, representing the arts, sciences, and industries, work the gigantic oars. A female Victory, wreath in hand, stands at the ship's stern while a scantily clad older male figure, representing time, controls the rudder (even in the allegorical world, women need men to steer the boat).

5.18.9 Frederick William MacMonnies: *The Triumph of Columbia* (*The Barge of State*), World's Columbian Exposition, Chicago, 1893 (destroyed).

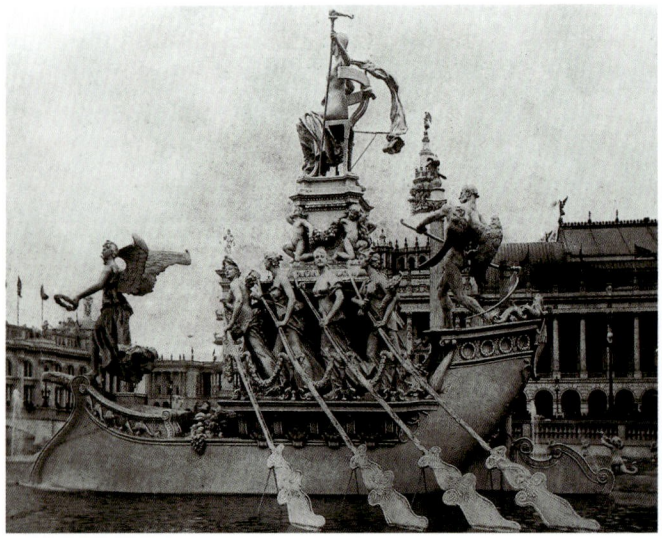

The art historian Judy Sund comments on the reciprocal relation between the sculptures of French and MacMonnies: "Columbia and the Republic might be seen as two aspects of a feminized US: the one emblematic of its physicality (the land, the continent, Columbia), the other of its ideals and/or institutions (i.e. the Republic)." The two personifications could also relate generationally, with the youthful Columbia propelled inevitably forward by Art, Science, and Industry toward the establishment of the Republic. Ultimately, however, these figures were not historical actors. That role was reserved for Columbus himself, who was commemorated in two statues, one on the pavement directly behind MacMonnies's sculptural group, and the other atop a monumental peristyle located behind French's *Republic*.

The fair was filled with similar scantily clothed female allegorical figures, despite the increased presence of women in all aspects of American life and in the organization of the fair itself. Such figures even topped the Woman's Building (1893) [**5.18.10**], designed by Sophia Hayden (1868–?). Hayden was the first woman graduate of the Massachusetts Institute of Technology. She drew on her architectural training to create a simple, two-story Renaissance building with end pavilions, an open arcade in the central section, and a pediment over the main entrance, with steps leading down to the lagoon. Unfortunately, this was to be her only building. The stress of working with too little money, constantly changing requirements, and interference from the all-male Board of Architects led to a nervous breakdown and a retreat from the architectural profession.

The Woman's Building was located at a crucial transition point between the fair proper and the Midway Plaisance. The nature of this transition is described by a character in a contemporary novel by Clara Louisa Burnham:

> In the Midway it's some dirty and all barbaric. It deafens you with noise; the worst folks in there are avaricious and bad; and the best are just children in their ignorance... and when you've come out o' that mile-long babel where you've been elbowed and cheated, and you pass under a bridge—and all of a sudden you are in a great, beautiful silence. The angels on the Woman's Buildin' smile down and bless you and you know that in what seemed like one step you've passed out o' darkness into light.

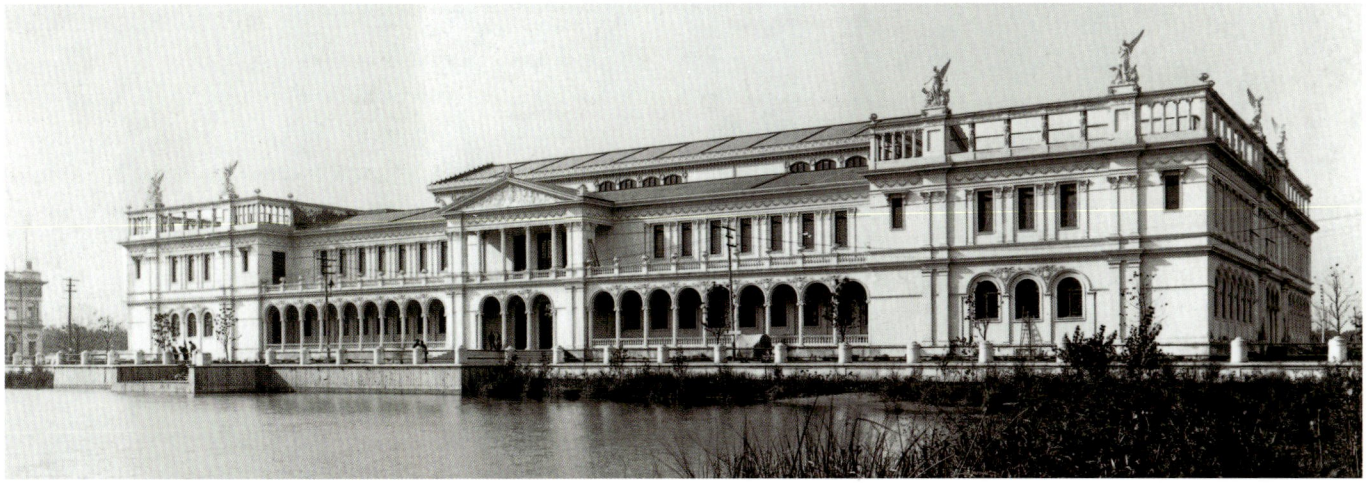

5.18.10 Sophia Hayden: the Woman's Building, World's Columbian Exposition, Chicago, Illinois, 1893 (destroyed).

The Woman's Building was thus a step above barbarism, yet below the buildings in the Court of Honor, designed by leading male architects.

The building was organized and operated by a Board of Lady Managers appointed by the all-male World's Columbian Commission. These one hundred and fifteen white middle- and upper-class women were led by the Chicago socialite Bertha Honoré Palmer. Their goal was to create a building that would function as a meeting-place for women at the fair rather than an exhibition site. The difficulties women faced in getting their work displayed in the main part of the fair, however, meant the building became a showplace for a wide variety of objects, from paintings and sculptures to needlework, industrial goods, and inventions.

The Board of Lady Managers had high aspirations: they wanted to represent the concerns and accomplishments of all women from all races and classes. Their own inherent race and class biases, however, prevented them from fully achieving their goal. For example, they refused to allow African American women to sit on the Board to judge the submissions by African American women. They were also at odds with those who refused to take part in the creation of a separate building and who argued, instead, that women should appear on an equal footing with men throughout the fair.

Whatever its shortcomings, the building provided an unprecedented opportunity to view a wide range of accomplishments by women [**5.18.17**; p. 328]. A visitor could see the advances that had been made not only in painting and sculpture but also in needlework, ceramics, glass, and metalwork. The latter media had experienced a renaissance of sorts during the last half of the nineteenth century, when an increasing number of women entered what have come to be known as the craft professions. One reason for this development, according to the art historian Anthea Callen, was a reduction in the number of men caused by both the Civil War and emigration to the West. Many "respectable" middle-class women were left without the prospect of marriage and a family. Another reason was an increasing sense of independence among women, which led to a conscious choice not to marry. The question then arose: what were these women to do to make a living? How could they, socialized and trained in the roles of domesticity, function in a productive manner in the world outside of the home?

Teaching and the craft professions were seen by many as fitting extensions of the natural roles of women. Craft production, or the applied arts, did not require the kind of "genius" thought necessary for the creation of fine art. Through such schools as the Philadelphia School of Design for Women—the first school of design in the nation, founded in 1844—and the coeducational Cooper Union in New York City, many middle-class women were prepared for entrance into the fields of art education, decorative embroidery or needlework, and pottery.

Women were also central in the growth and promotion of art pottery, setting up societies and schools and planning exhibitions. One of the most important organizations was Rookwood Pottery in Cincinnati, Ohio founded by Maria Longworth Nichols Storer (1849–1932) in 1880. Nichols Storer came from a wealthy Cincinnati family. Her father was a well-known patron of the arts and encouraged his daughter's interest in ceramics, eventually providing her with the money to found Rookwood. In its early years it offered classes in pottery decoration for amateur women. As it became more of a business, the classes were abandoned and an increasing number of men were hired as decorators. Several women remained, however, and produced works that achieved both national and international recognition.

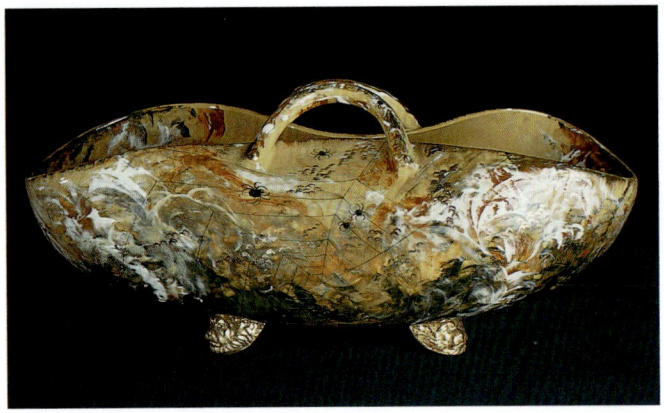

5.18.11 Maria Longworth Nichols Storer: Rookwood Pottery basket, 1882. Painted underglaze decoration and gilt overglaze on clay, h. 8¼ in. (20.6 cm.) Cincinnati Art Museum, Cincinnati, Ohio

5.18.12 Clara Chipman Newton: horn pitcher, 1882. Painted underglaze decoration and gilt overglaze on clay, h. 6½ in. (16.5 cm.) The Brooklyn Museum of Art, New York

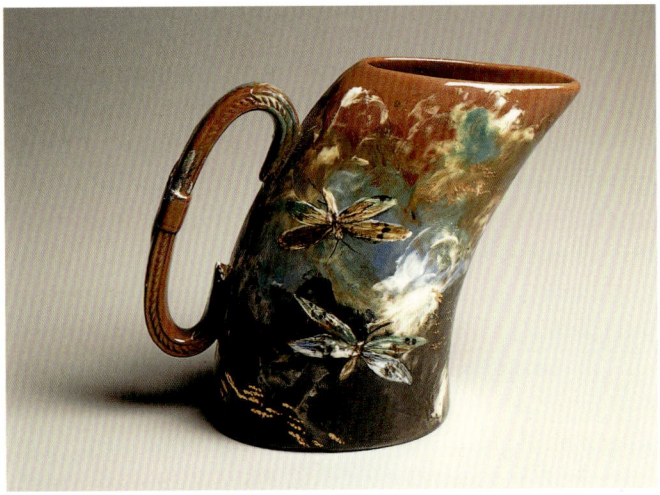

The work of Nichols Storer was included in the Cincinnati Room of the Woman's Building in 1893. Her ceramic basket of 1882 [**5.18.11**] shows evidence of her early interest in Japanese art, which was sparked first by some books of designs given to her in 1875, and then by a display of Japanese ceramics included at the Philadelphia Centennial Exhibition the following year. The basket makes use of motifs often found in Japanese art—spiders, dragonflies, dragons. Its shape, however, and the gilt lion-head feet show the eclecticism that marked much of her work and that of other women ceramists of the period. Among these women was Clara Chipman Newton (1848–1936). Newton was Nichols Storer's personal assistant, but also a pottery decorator in her own right. Her horn pitcher of 1882 [**5.18.12**] features dragonflies on one side and bamboo branches on the other.

Of course, fine craft or applied-art production was not limited to women. The focus on elaborate home decoration at the end of the century grew out of both the Aesthetic Movement (see pp. 300–304)—which promoted interior design and the creation of artistically distinctive functional objects for the home—and the Arts and Crafts Movement. The latter originated in England in the mid-nineteenth century under the leadership of the poet, artist, designer, and social reformer William Morris (1834–1896). Morris celebrated the virtues of handmade objects and the importance of excellence of design and execution as an alternative to the low quality of mass-produced goods. His design principles, as well as his socialist politics, found a sympathetic audience among many American artists. Unfortunately, the expensive, handcrafted objects produced in Arts and Crafts workshops had little impact on the spread of cheap, mass-produced goods.

A demand did arise, however, among more prosperous Americans for fine ceramics, stained glass, mosaics, and silverware. Perhaps the best-known individual who moved to meet this demand was Louis Comfort Tiffany (1848–1933). His father had a flourishing business importing decorative objects from China, Japan, India, North Africa, and Europe, but Louis preferred to study painting, and traveled to Paris in 1868. After limited success as a painter, he turned his attention to interior decoration.

While Tiffany's studio produced objects in metal, ceramics, and wood, he is best remembered for his art glass productions. By the 1880s he had set up a factory in New York. Favrile glass,

5.18.13 Louis Comfort Tiffany: Peacock mosaic, for the entrance hall of the Henry O. Havemeyer House, New York, 1890–91. Iridescent cabochon glass, pottery, and plaster, 52 x 64 x 4 in. (132.1 x 162.6 x 10.2 cm.) University of Michigan School of Art and College of Architecture and Urban Planning, on extended loan to the University of Michigan Museum of Art, Ann Arbor

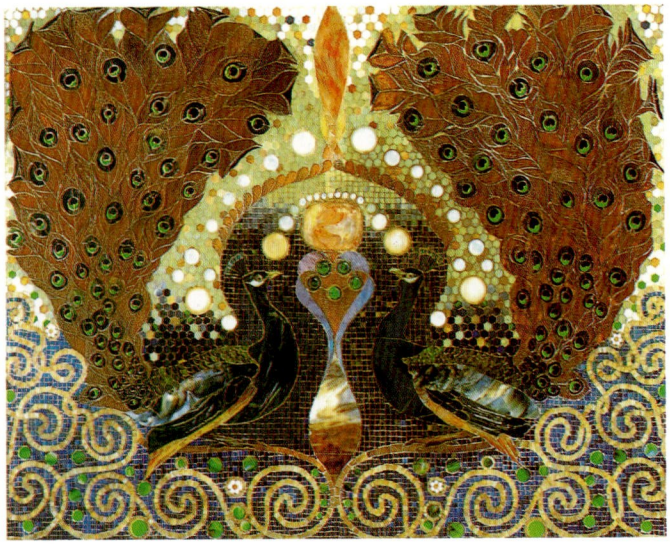

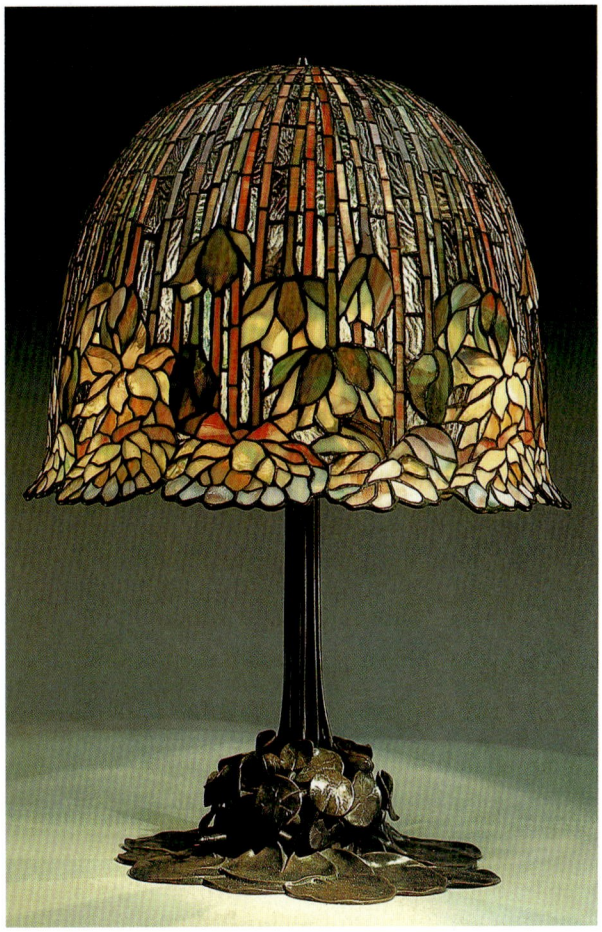

5.18.14 (above) Tiffany Studios: lamp, *c.* 1910. Bronze and leaded glass, h. 14⅝ in. (37.2 cm.) The Metropolitan Museum of Art, New York

5.18.15 (below) Mary Fairchild MacMonnies: *Primitive Woman*, in the Hall of Honor, Woman's Building, World's Columbian Exposition, Chicago, 1893 (destroyed).

5.18.16 (bottom) Mary Cassatt: *Modern Woman*, in the Hall of Honor, Woman's Building, World's Columbian Exposition, Chicago, 1893 (destroyed).

marked by brilliant, iridescent colors, was his own invention. In 1890–91 he used it to create an elaborate mosaic of stylized peacocks for the entrance hall of the industrialist Henry O. Havemeyer's New York mansion [**5.18.13**]. His debt to James Abbott McNeill Whistler and the Aesthetic Movement in general is evident in this work. Thomas Alva Edison's invention in 1879 of the incandescent light bulb, with its unprecedented brilliance, forced designers to rethink the lamp form. Tiffany capitalized on that brilliance to illuminate the extraordinary colors of his glass. As with much of his other glasswork, the lamps are commonly marked by vegetal motifs. The sinuous forms serve to unify the compositions on shade and base [**5.18.14**].

The fine ceramics, glassware, metalwork, needlework, and various commercial products and inventions in the Woman's Building drew much interest among the visiting public. The main focus of attention, however, was the Hall of Honor, with its several paintings and sculptures and, most importantly, its two large murals high up in the tympana at either end [**5.18.17**; p. 328]. At the south end was *Primitive Woman* by Mary Fairchild MacMonnies (1858–1946) [**5.18.15**], who was married to Frederick William MacMonnies [**5.18.9**; p. 324]. It contained women dressed in diaphanous, wind-blown robes arranged across the front of the picture plane. They plow fields, carry water, take care of children, and attend to a man who has just returned from the hunt. Here is not the "primitiveness" of the Midway Plaisance, "some dirty and all barbaric," but the ideal primitive found in the works of Kenyon Cox, Abbott H. Thayer, and Thomas Wilmer Dewing [**5.17.3–5.17.5**; pp. 302–303]. These women are ideal not only because they refer to an ancient Greek past, but also because they engage in activities still deemed most appropriate for women.

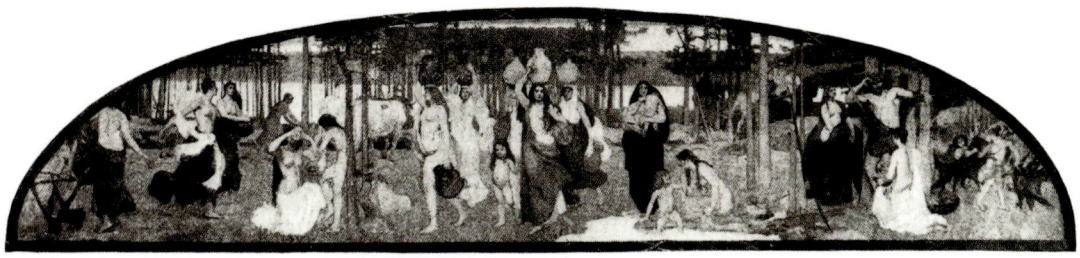

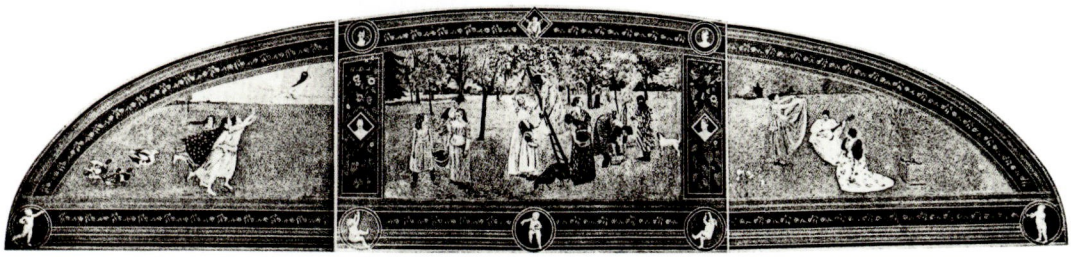

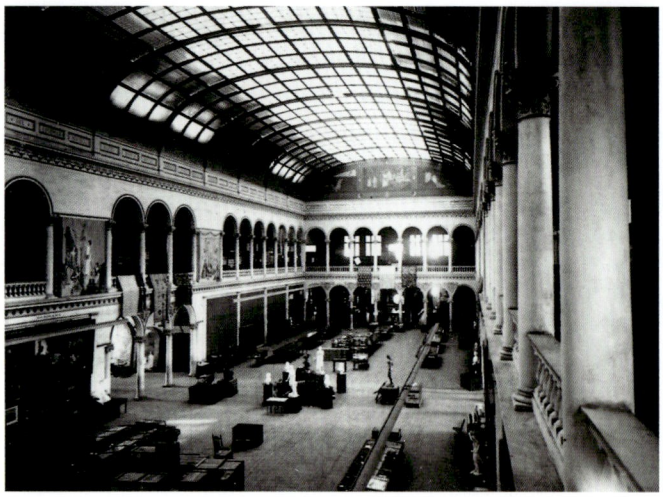

5.18.17 Sophia Hayden: Hall of Honor, the Woman's Building, World's Columbian Exposition, Chicago, Illinois, 1893 (destroyed).

Modern Woman by Mary Cassatt (1844–1926) [**5.18.16**; p. 327], however, which occupied the north tympanum, rejected the ordered, subdued neoclassicism of the fair and included, instead, bright colors and contemporary middle-class dress. On the left, a group of young girls are shown pursuing a winged figure of Fame while being pursued by geese. In the center, women pluck the fruits of knowledge, a revision of the theme of Eve in the Garden of Eden. On the right, women appear not as allegorical figures representing the arts, but actually engaged in creating art, music, and dance. Men are omitted, as well as women as caretakers of children or men. When one of Cassatt's male friends asked if this was not the portrayal of women apart from their relations with men, she wrote:

> I told him it was. Men, I have no doubt, are painted in all their vigor on the walls of the other buildings; to us the sweetness of childhood, the charm of womanhood, if I have not conveyed some sense of that charm, in one word, if I have not been absolutely feminine, then I have failed.

Cassatt thus tried to calm his anxiety by assuring him that her actions, while they might seem to be radical, were really thoroughly "feminine."

The critical response to the two murals was mixed, although most preferred that of MacMonnies. One critic praised it for portraying women in the "more suitable role of domesticity." It was also liked because it conformed to the neoclassicism of the fair, which placed women in the ideal world of myth and allegory. Cassatt's work was most commonly described as cynical and primitive, with a discordant and garish color scheme—all reflections on the "modern" aspects of her style. *Young Women Picking Fruit* of 1891 [**5.18.18**], a study for the mural, gives a sense of its color (neither Cassatt's nor MacMonnies's murals exist today). Perhaps the most telling review of the two murals was a piece by Henry B. Fuller for the *Chicago Record*, which complained:

> Mrs. MacMonnies addresses the eye in a gentle and insinuating fashion; Miss Cassatt does not address the eye at all—she assaults it. Mrs. MacMonnies' tone is light and silvery, while the impudent greens and brutal blues of Miss Cassatt seem to indicate an aggressive personality with which compromise and cooperation would be impossible. Indeed, Miss Cassatt has a reputation for being strong and daring; she works with men in Paris on their own ground.

Thus, Cassatt refused to conform, rejecting the role of gentle wife and occupying, instead, the same ground with men in the art world of Paris. At a time when the nation was turning to art and women to help control confusion and unrest, it is understandable why so many preferred the work of MacMonnies.

5.18.18 Mary Cassatt: *Young Women Picking Fruit*, study for *Modern Woman*, 1891. Oil on canvas, 51½ x 35½ in. (130.8 x 90 cm.)
The Carnegie Museum of Art, Pittsburgh, Pennsylvania

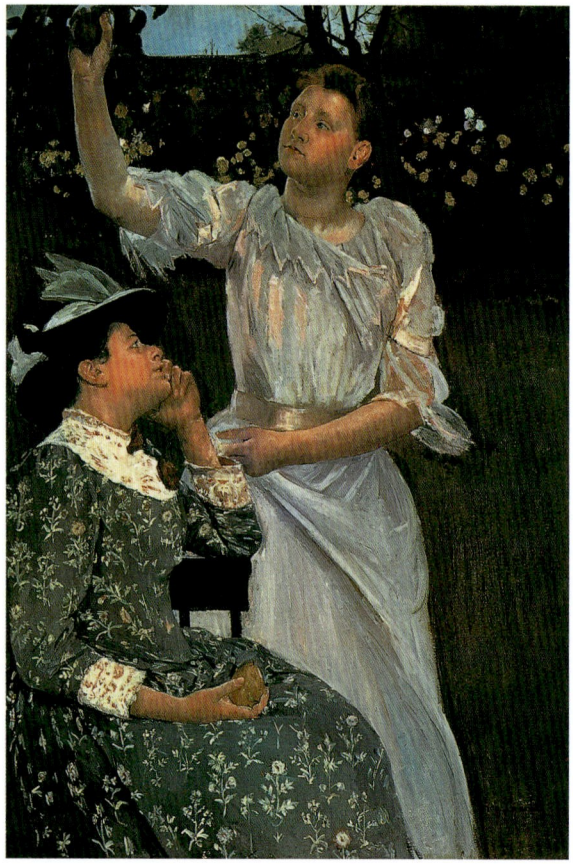

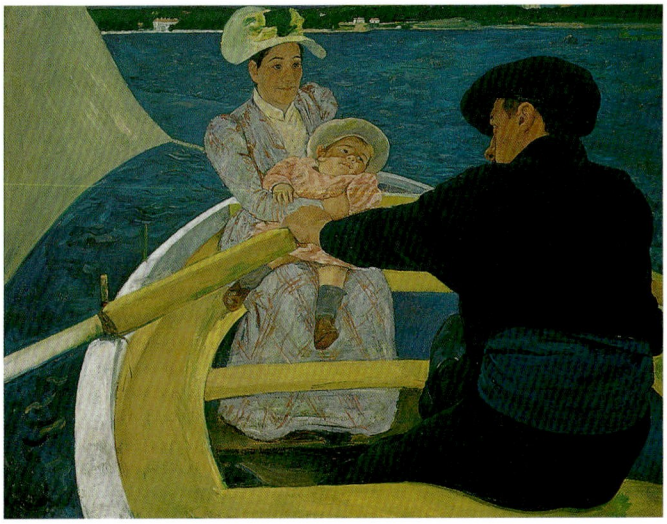

5.18.19 Mary Cassatt: *The Boating Party*, 1893–94.
Oil on canvas, 35½ x 46⅛ in. (90.2 x 117.1 cm.)
National Gallery of Art, Washington, D.C.

While Cassatt omitted references to domesticity in her mural, she did not do so in her easel paintings or prints. Like Whistler and John Singer Sargent (1856–1925), Cassatt spent most of her life in Europe, leaving her home town of Philadelphia in the mid-1860s and settling in Paris in 1866. She joined Dewing, Cox, and Thayer in focusing on women in her paintings. Unlike them, however, her women are often engaged in a particular domestic activity, caring for children. Her subjects are also, as in the work of Cecilia Beaux and Sargent, recognizable people, for she often used her friends and relatives, as well as servants and other working-class women, as models.

Cassatt came from a prosperous Philadelphia family, and the interior settings in her paintings are often marked by comfort and wealth, as are those in the work of Beaux and Sargent. Stylistically, however, she pushed her formal experimentation further than these two artists, perhaps because she was part of the Parisian Impressionist circle. She also took her women out-of-doors, into the streets and parks of Paris and onto the Seine, as in *The Boating Party* (1893–94) [**5.18.19**]. The woman and child so carefully depicted in the center of the composition draw the viewer's attention with their colorful dress and sweet expressions. The broad expanses of blue and yellow that sweep across the painting and anchor the figures in place, also catch the audience's eye. The space is a shallow, Modernist space, one inspired by Japanese prints. The interior of the boat is tipped up to cut off the recession into the distance. Broad areas of flat color—blue, yellow, green—create patterns that, again, emphasize the flatness of the canvas rather than any illusion of three-dimensionality. Cassatt's painting was strikingly different stylistically from the work of many of her American contemporaries who depicted similar subject matter, as can be seen by comparing this work with Thomas Eakins's *Max Schmitt in a Single Scull* of 1871 [**5.16.5**; p. 282].

Cassatt's paintings of mothers and children are not sentimental depictions. Instead they are serious, and often monumental, renditions of the processes of nurturing that were women's socially prescribed tasks. They differed not only from many of the mother and child scenes by late-nineteenth-century artists, but also from common representations of this subject in mass-media publications. For example, her *Mother and Child* (*c.* 1905) [**5.18.20**] departs in significant ways from two earlier treatments of the subject, an engraving in an issue of *Godey's Lady's Book* (January 1867) [**5.18.21**; p. 330] and Lilly Martin Spencer's *Beauty and Barberism* (*c.* 1890) [**5.18.22**; p. 330]. All three images address the socialization of young girls, their introduction into the world of "appropriate" female behavior. In the engraving *The First Party*, the child decked out in her fancy dress with curled hair enters willingly into the game of "womanhood." She gazes approvingly at herself in the mirror while her mother gazes approvingly at her. There is no doubt that she will follow

5.18.20 Mary Cassatt: *Mother and Child*, *c.* 1905.
Oil on canvas, 36¼ x 29 in. (92 x 73.7 cm.)
National Gallery of Art, Washington, D.C.

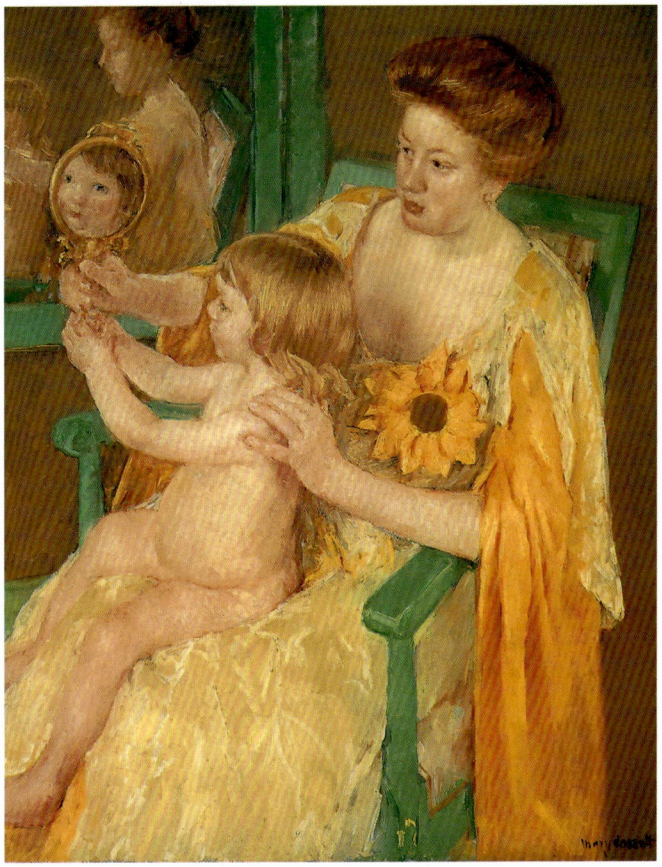

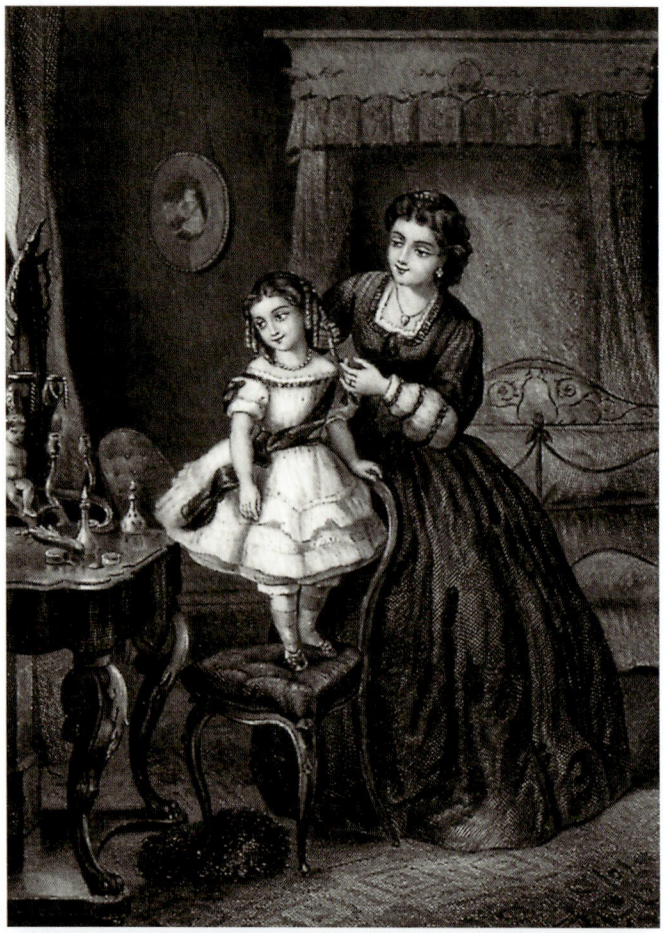

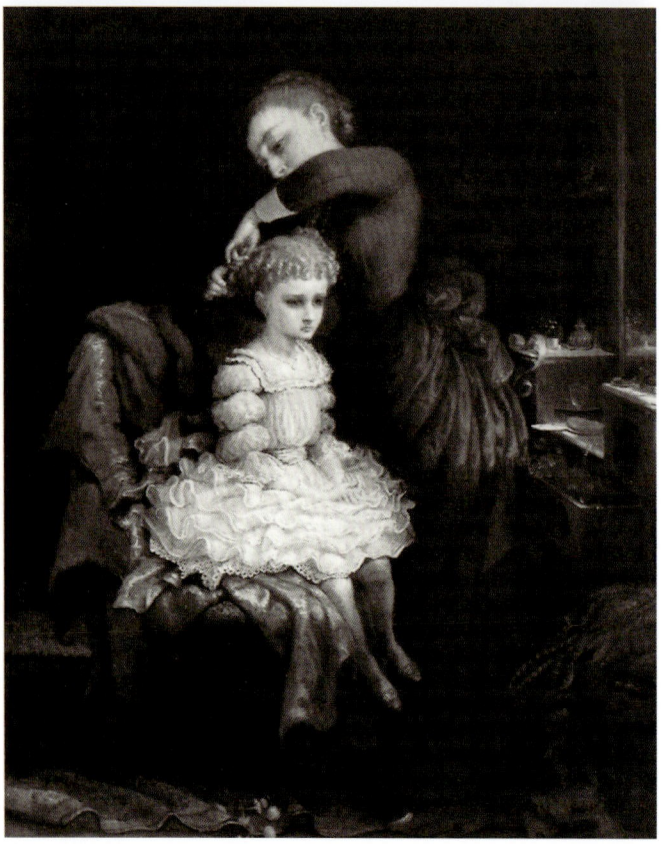

5.18.21 Unknown artist: *The First Party*, engraving from *Godey's Lady's Book*, January 1867.
Library of Congress, Washington, D.C.

5.18.22 Lilly Martin Spencer: *Beauty and Barberism*, c. 1890.
Oil on canvas, 25 x 30 in. (63.5 x 76.2 cm.)
Whereabouts unknown

cheerfully in the footsteps of the older woman and become a wife and mother. Spencer portrays a less willing subject, a child who suffers at the hands of her mother as she is forced to take on the persona of a "respectable" young girl. Spencer reveals her own criticism of this process of socialization, as well as her sense of humor, by titling the painting *Beauty and Barberism*.

Psychologically, Cassatt's painting lies somewhere between what the art historian David M. Lubin calls the "narcissistic self-satisfaction and mother-daughter bonding" of *The First Party* and "the emotional pain and psychic destruction" of *Beauty and Barberism*. Like the mother in *The First Party*, Cassatt's mother watches as her young daughter gazes into the mirror. She is also dressed in elegant, although less formal, attire. Her gaze is more thoughtful, however, as she contemplates her child's future. Cassatt's child, on the other hand, is quite different from those in the other two images. She is younger, and is naked. The moment is one of self-awareness rather than of "narcissistic self-satisfaction" or "emotional pain."

As in *The Boating Party*, Cassatt rejects the detailed three-dimensional space of Spencer and the *Godey's Lady's Book* artist. Instead, she creates a shallow space marked by a series of rectangles—the canvas itself, the chair frame, and the frame of the mirror. Here, the repetitive shapes emphasize the constructed nature of the composition. Cassatt also recasts the mirror, as she earlier recast the Garden of Eden, as the site not of women's vanity but of women's self-consciousness. She presents the child as aware of her separateness from her mother and yet clearly connected to her both compositionally—through the dominant yellows—and psychologically. Cassatt emphasizes the child's face and personality, as well as the role of her mother in initiating her into the realm of femaleness. Her nakedness contrasts with the elaborate dressing gown and coifed hair of her mother. It suggests a blank palette, one that will be filled with both her own thoughts and the expectations of the society within which she will grow up. She will become highly conscious of her appearance, of how people see her. This fact is emphasized by the larger of the two mirrors in the painting, which reflects both figures, and by the very painting itself, which is the product of the artist's gaze.

The mirrors also function as destabilizing elements. Cassatt has built mistakes into the perspective of her painting such that it would be impossible for a viewer positioned in front of the painting to see the figures and mirror images as portrayed. In her analysis of *Mother and Child*, the art historian Harriet Scott Chessman speculates "that the inaccuracy of [Cassatt's] own mirroring invites us to see and understand the inaccuracy of the cultural mirrorings charted with such soberness in this image." The artist also uses the mirrors to implicate the viewer as both object and subject of vision. "She shows us the girl's face in the mirror," notes Chessman, "as if this were the face the girl herself sees; yet we realize that, if we can see an image of the girl's face, the image she can see must, uncannily, be our own." We, as viewers, exist in a world that "impinges on the world of mother and child and determines how the child will be dressed, how her meanings will become figured."

Cassatt also produced at least one image of the relationship between male members of a family, *Alexander Cassatt and His Son Robert* (1884) [**5.18.23**]. This painting is strikingly different from her images of mothers and children, in which the focus is a shared emotional and physical intimacy. Alexander and his son gaze in the same direction rather than at each other. Their physical proximity—they melt into one another in their black suits—heightens the emotional distance between the two. Their connection appears to be at the level of intellect. Their eyes are parallel as they both gaze in the direction of the newspaper held by the father. Yet while the father looks down at the paper, the boy looks past it, and his expression lies somewhere between anxiety and boredom. He perches precariously on the arm of the chair, ready to dismount at a moment's notice. Thus, just as Cassatt's mother prepares her daughter for a world of fashion and self-consciousness, Alexander attempts to prepare his son for the competitive, isolating world of business and commerce, where emotional sensitivity and introspection are liabilities. Their dark suits also suggest a level of social conformity against which many artists in both Europe and the US were already rebelling.

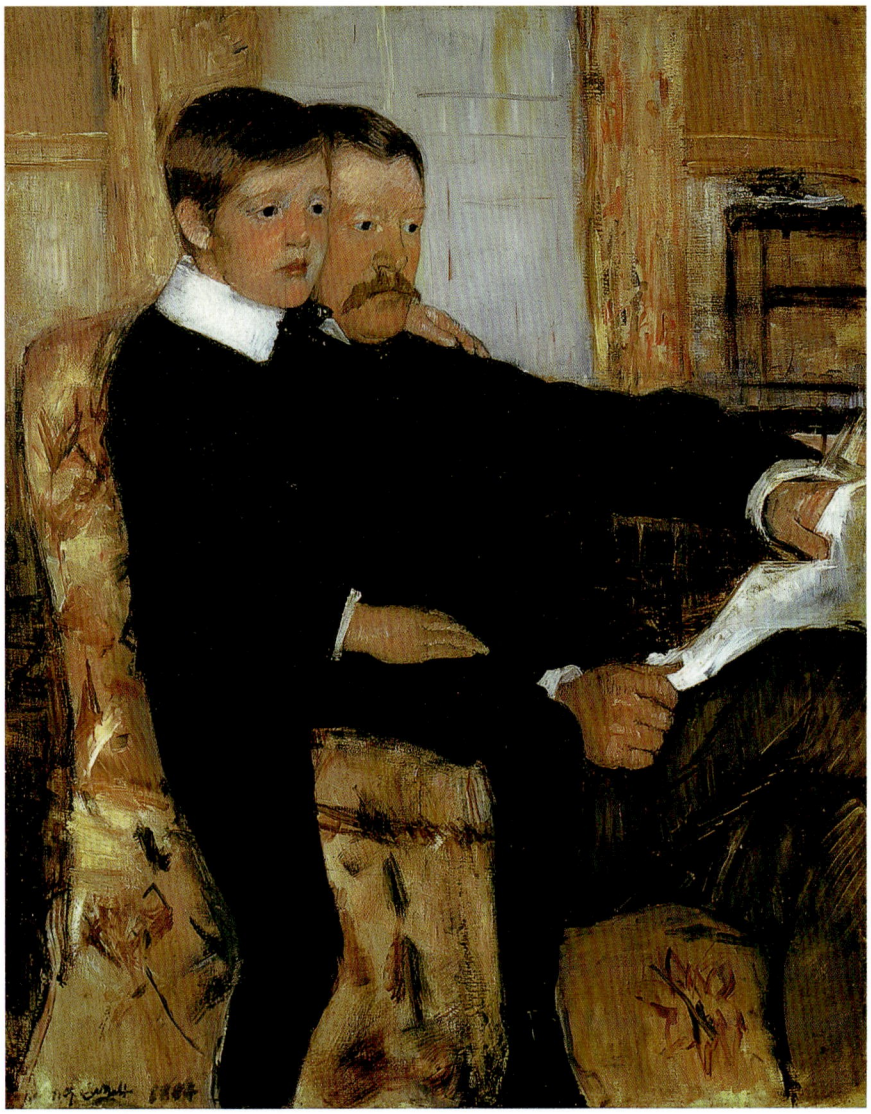

5.18.23 Mary Cassatt: *Alexander Cassatt and His Son Robert*, 1884.
Oil on canvas, 39 x 32 in. (99 x 81.2 cm.)
The Philadelphia Museum of Art, Philadelphia, Pennsylvania

Race and Religion at the Turn of the Century: Henry Ossawa Tanner

While Frederick Douglass and Ida B. Wells were condemning the segregated admission policies of the World's Columbian Exposition and the racist stereotypes contained in its exhibits (see p. 323), another African American was arguing for the significance of the work of African American artists. In a presentation at the Congress on Africa of the World's Columbian Exposition, the artist Henry Ossawa Tanner (1859–1937) pointed out that the actual achievements of African American artists "proved negroes to possess ability and talent for successful competition with white artists." His own career clearly provided an example of such success.

Tanner was born in Pittsburgh and moved to Philadelphia as a child. His father was a minister and later a bishop in the African Methodist Episcopal Church. He instilled in his son a stern belief in the Christian God and in the power of religion as a unifying force in the African American community, one that could help achieve the dignity of all human beings, whatever the color of their skin. The household was a gathering place for many of the country's leading African American intellectuals and politicians.

In 1880, Tanner entered the Pennsylvania Academy of the Fine Arts, where he studied with Thomas Eakins. While he benefited artistically, he could not escape the racism that forced so many artists of color either to abandon their pursuits or to leave the US. In his autobiographical *Adventures of an Illustrator* (1925), Joseph Pennell, who attended the Academy at the same time, described a scene where a young "octoroon, very well dressed...quiet and modest," with short cropped "wool" and a moustache, was tied to his easel in the middle of Broad Street one night by a group of white students "when he began to assert himself." Pennell does not name the victim, but the description matches photographs of Tanner at the time.

Tanner traveled to Paris in 1891, where he entered the Académie Julian and joined the American Art Students' Club. He also made trips to Pont-Aven on the Brittany coast and enjoyed the company of fellow artists in an environment that was substantially less racist than that of Philadelphia. His early paintings were primarily seascapes, landscapes, and animal paintings. It was not until the mid-1890s that he began to take up the theme that would become the major focus of his work in the early twentieth century—religion. In the interim, he created a small number of genre paintings that addressed the life of African Americans.

Tanner's return to Philadelphia in the summer of 1893, his participation in the Congress on Africa, and his inevitable re-encounter with American racism may have prompted him to turn his attention to African Americans as subject matter. He gave a further indication of the reasons for his choice in a statement the following year, in which he referred to himself in the third person:

> Since his return from Europe he has painted many Negro subjects, he feels drawn to such subjects on account of the newness of the field and because of a desire to represent the serious and pathetic side of life among them, and it is his thought that other things being equal, he who has most sympathy with his subject will obtain the best results. To his mind, many of the artists who have represented Negro life have only seen the comic, the ludicrous side of it and have lacked sympathy with and affection for the warm big heart within such a rough exterior.

In writing the last sentence he may well have been thinking of people like John Lewis Krimmel [**4.12.3**; p. 223] and the early Eastman Johnson [**4.12.8**; p. 227].

In 1893 Tanner created his first major painting of African American life, *The Banjo Lesson* [**5.18.24**]. Here is another pairing of an older man (a father or grandfather) and a young boy. Yet the dynamic between the two is very different from that of Cassatt's *Alexander Cassatt and His Son Robert* [**5.18.23**; p. 331]. The boy leans against the old man and is framed by the latter's legs and arms. They both focus on the boy's right hand as its fingers pluck the banjo strings. The overarching effect is one of shared concentration and purpose.

The Banjo Lesson openly addresses and subverts the stereotype of the banjo-playing, high-stepping figure that had become so common over the previous decades in both commercial imagery and fine art. It also undermines the increasingly popular commercial images of "Uncle Tom" or "Uncle Ned." The banjo here is far from a prop. It is central to the passing on of cultural knowledge from one generation to the next, along with the pride and sense of hope and self-fulfillment attached to the acquisition and maintenance of this knowledge.

How does Tanner's painting differ from the work of artists who saw only the "comic" side of African American life? While Johnson drew on the scenes of peasant life painted by seventeenth-century Dutch artists, Tanner looked to another Dutch artist for inspiration—Rembrandt van Rijn (1606–1669). In adopting Rembrandt's looser brushwork and in paring down the objects in the painting, Tanner forces the viewer to focus on the central figures and on their activity. In addition, he uses a golden light entering from the side, which marks so many of Rembrandt's paintings. This light highlights the faces and sharpens the outlines of the figures against the background, adding a sense of solemnity and a religious aura. Tanner would

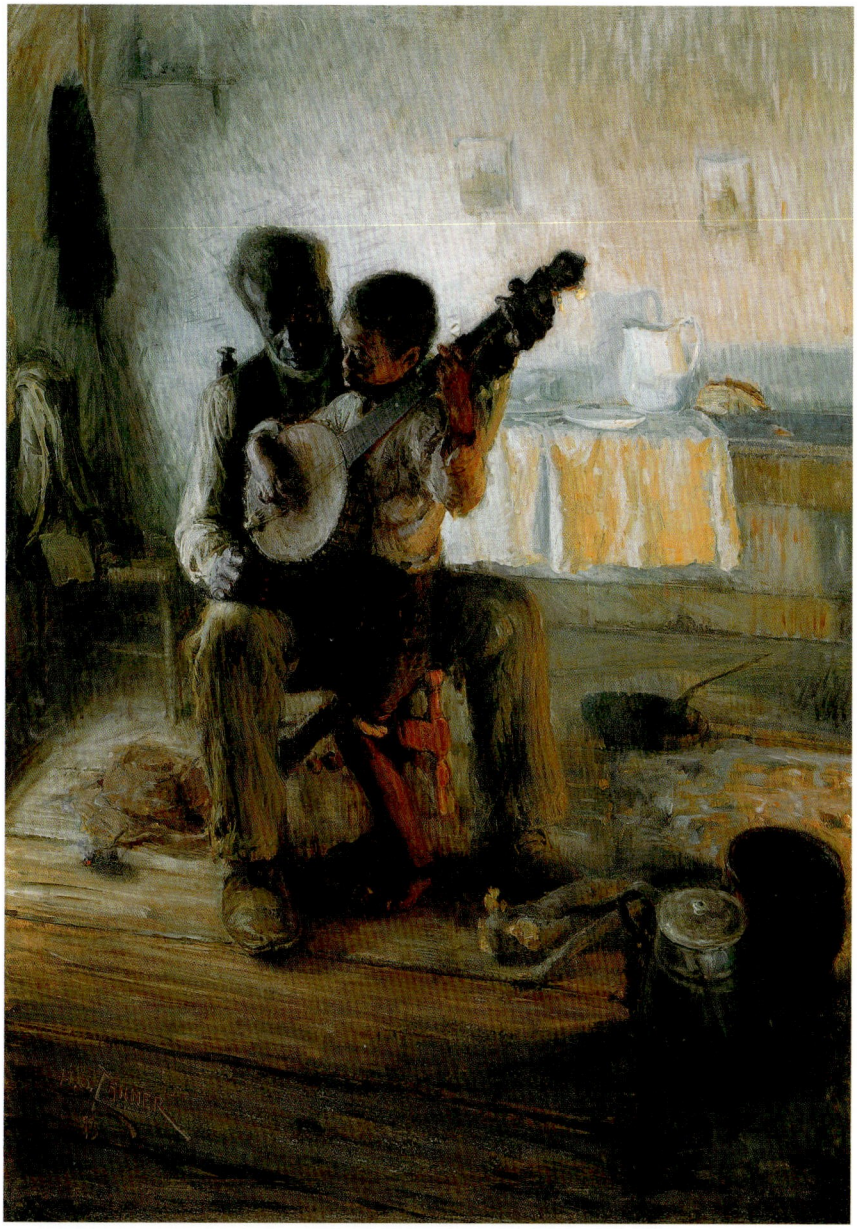

5.18.24 Henry Ossawa Tanner: *The Banjo Lesson*, 1893.
Oil on canvas, 48 x 35½ in. (121.9 x 90.2 cm.)
Hampton University Museum,
Hampton, Virginia

develop this brushwork and use of light even further in his biblical paintings of the subsequent decades.

Tanner portrays the two figures in *The Banjo Lesson* as distinct individuals intensely absorbed in the task at hand. The banjo becomes a conduit, a connection from one generation to the next. It also represents a bridge between Africa and America, for the banjo was developed from a stringed instrument brought over from Africa. In her study of the banjo in American popular culture, Karen S. Linn has traced the changing and conflicting meanings attached to it as a result of its integration into national commercial culture after the Civil War.

Before the Civil War the banjo was seen as primarily an African American instrument. In the later nineteenth century urban entrepreneurs attempted to introduce it into elite white culture and, in the process, to downplay its connections with the lives and culture of African Americans. One way they did this was by promoting a new style of playing. Instead of continuing the downward strokes and chording of minstrel performers whose songs grew out of African American culture, the "new" banjo players plucked the strings separately and upward, like a guitar, in order to play the new parlor music of the day. But African Americans soon mastered this style of playing, and the boy in Tanner's painting has his right hand positioned for that new upward motion. The image could thus have been read as an affirmation both of the banjo as a distinctly African and African American instrument and of the ability of African Americans in this field, as in many others, to adapt to changing techniques and acquire new knowledge.

The Banjo Lesson was exhibited in October 1893 in Philadelphia and the following year in the annual Paris Salon. Robert C. Ogden, a partner in John Wanamaker's dry-goods business and a promoter of African American public education, purchased the painting and donated it to the Hampton Institute (see pp. 260–63). It was appropriate that a school committed to educating African Americans should possess a painting that presented in such a compelling and dignified way the role of education in African American life. Tanner's work is very different from the display of cowboys and Indians in Frances Benjamin Johnston's photograph of a Hampton "class in American history" [**4.14.14**; p. 261]. Rather than an image of assimilation that relegated African (and indigenous) cultural traditions to the past, it is a testimony to the changing and vital nature of these traditions.

Ogden, while a religious man himself, was not fully in favor of Tanner's turn to religious subject matter. He thought the artist would have more influence on African Americans through genre scenes than through more "abstract" religious paintings that were less readily identifiable as the work of an African American artist. Ogden believed, along with the African American educator and political figure Booker T. Washington, that African Americans would improve their lives not through political agitation but through education. The progress of the "race" would be well served by those who became public examples of success. After an encounter with the artist in 1899 in Paris, Washington wrote:

> My acquaintance with Mr. Tanner reinforced in my mind the truth which I am constantly trying to impress upon our students at Tuskegee—and on our people throughout the country, as far as I can reach them with my voice—that any man, regardless of color, will be recognized and rewarded just in proportion as he learns to do something well—learns to do it better than some one else—however humble the thing may be.

Tanner was well aware of the part that his race played in public perceptions of his work, and was seriously committed to combating negative stereotypes of African Americans. But he did not want to be judged by the color of his skin. Ogden wrote of a showing of the artist's *The Annunciation* (1898) in his home:

> I have had a notion that a few people interested in Tanner because of his race might be made useful to him by an opportunity to inspect the picture; I am afraid, however, that this would be offensive to his fine and somewhat sensitive nature, as he has no desire whatever to pose as a professional colored man, preferring to risk his entire success upon his merits as an artist—just as any other man would.

Tanner's light skin opened many doors that were closed to dark-skinned African Americans. Yet the greater ease with which he was able to move through the white world also created a constant reminder of what was always beyond his grasp—the privileges of those whose physical appearance read "white."

Tanner's move to religious subjects may have been motivated by recognition of the fact that they sold better to white audiences than scenes of African American life (little economic support came from the African American community). Yet the paintings also encapsulated much of the radical teachings of his father—the belief that all people were created equal in the eyes of God and that the struggles of the Jews could be seen as parallel to the struggles of African Americans to free themselves from bondage.

His religious pictures are much more somber, less sentimentalized, than many religious works of the time. For example, *Daniel in the Lions' Den* (1907–18) [**5.18.25**] plays with strong contrasts between light and shadow to evoke the deep contemplation and impending liberation of the prophet from persecution. Daniel's ability to calm the lions is subtly suggested by the highlighting that links the lower half of his body and the face of the lion next to him. In 1924, Tanner wrote that he had attempted "to not only put the Biblical incident in the original setting...but at the same time give the human touch 'which makes the whole world kin' and which ever remains the same." One could argue that he was able to embody this notion of the

5.18.25 Henry Ossawa Tanner: *Daniel in the Lions' Den*, 1907–18. Oil on paper mounted on canvas, 41⅛ x 49⅞ in. (104.4 x 126.9 cm.) Los Angeles County Museum of Art, Los Angeles, California

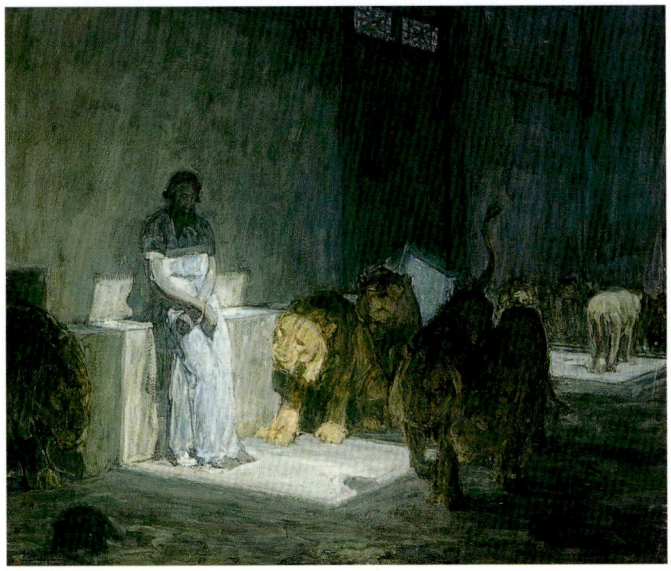

universal in the particular in both his religious paintings and his scenes of African American life. Both are marked by solemn figures engaged in simple acts that speak to noble causes, be they freedom from physical bondage or the maintenance of cultural traditions.

Men at Sea: Albert Pinkham Ryder and Winslow Homer

The connection between the human and the spiritual was expressed in a different way in the paintings of one of Henry Ossawa Tanner's contemporaries, Albert Pinkham Ryder (1847–1917). In *The Flying Dutchman* (*c.* 1887) [**5.18.26**], Ryder takes up the iconography of the storm-tossed boat and its symbolic associations with the struggles between humans and nature, and, in a country where nature is equated with the divine, between humans and God.

Ryder grew up in New Bedford, Massachusetts, which was at that time the greatest whaling port in the world. Art historians often comment on the imaginative or dreamlike quality of Ryder's small seascapes. Yet he was also very familiar with the physical reality of the sea, and the emotional and spiritual turmoil it caused those whose lives depended upon it. This familiarity informed the marine scenes Ryder painted following his move to New York City at the end of the 1860s.

The art historian Elizabeth Broun notes that *The Flying Dutchman* has often been connected to the German composer Richard Wagner's well-known opera of the same name. Yet she

5.18.26 Albert Pinkham Ryder: *The Flying Dutchman*, *c.* 1887. Oil on canvas mounted on fiberboard, 14¼ x 17¼ in. (36.1 x 43.8 cm.) Smithsonian American Art Museum, Washington, D.C.

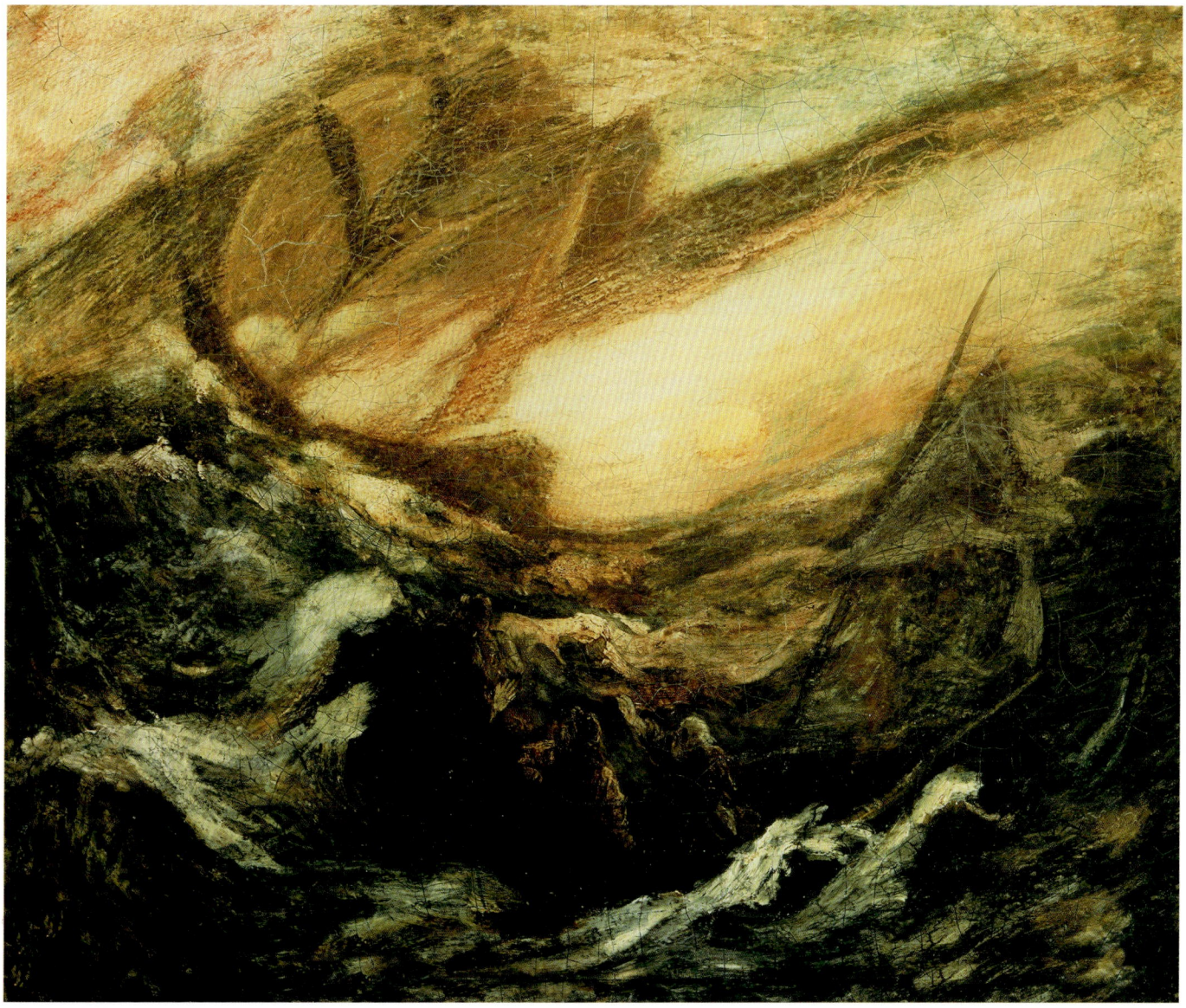

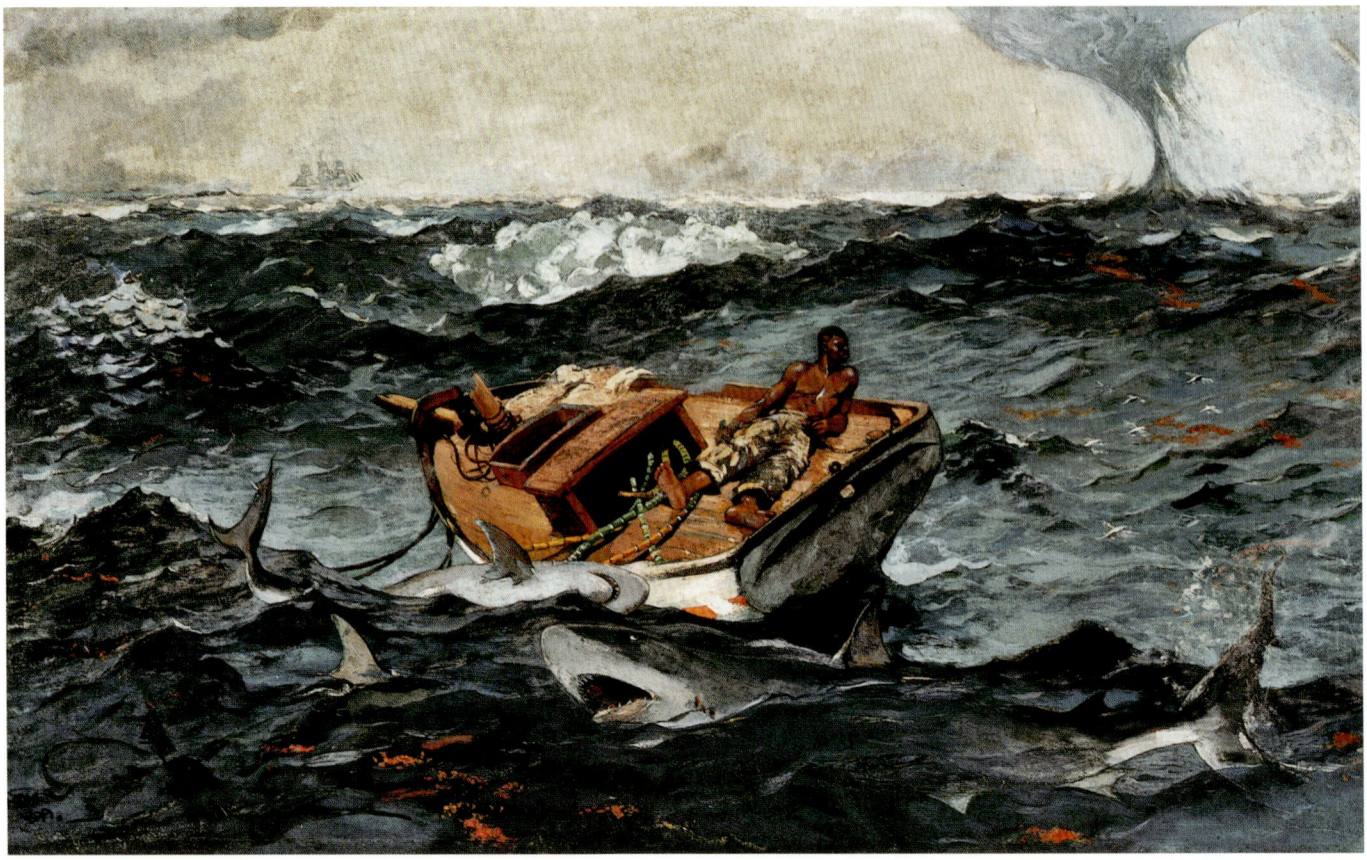

5.18.27 Winslow Homer: *The Gulf Stream*, 1899. Oil on canvas, 28⅛ x 49⅞ in. (71.4 x 124.8 cm.) The Metropolitan Museum of Art, New York

argues that a more likely source is *The Phantom Ship*, a novel by the British officer and writer Captain Frederick Marryat published in 1839 and frequently reprinted. Marryat writes of a Dutch ship captain sailing round the Cape of Good Hope during bad weather. He swears on a relic of the true cross in issuing a challenge that no storm should defeat him. This challenge is taken up by the devil, who condemns him to sail forever in gale-force winds in the cape seas until presented with the relic on which he blasphemed. The captain's son spends the rest of his life trying to track down the phantom ship and present his father with the fragment of the true cross that will set him free. Redemption is available to both father and son only through forgiveness of their enemies, which must be done before the son can succeed in presenting his father with the relic.

Ryder's painting shows the son reaching out to the phantom ship, his old age suggesting that his quest will soon be at an end. The two vessels—those of the father and the son—occupy the center of the canvas, and are rocked by a turbulent sea. The massive cloud that blends with the sails of the father's boat creates an ominous feeling, yet the golden glow of the sun on both boat and cloud points to a sense of optimism. By reducing the level of detail in his painting and by applying the paint in thick, swirling fashion throughout the composition, Ryder enhances the power of the rhythmic forms echoed in both the ships and the sea, making these two aspects of the painting into a single unit. Humans and nature are entwined in one churning mass that has yet to be calmed by the kiss of forgiveness.

Broun rejects the notion that Wagner's opera was the source for Ryder's painting in large part because it omits any mention of the son and the true cross. It replaces the son, instead, with a man who hopes to benefit financially from introducing the Dutchman to his daughter. It is the love of a faithful woman, rather than the forgiveness of one's enemies, that is the source of the Dutchman's salvation. Broun argues that Ryder's focus in this painting, as well as in many other seascapes, was on religious salvation and virtuous characters, rather than mercenary gain. This argument is in keeping with the common assessment of Ryder as a man unconcerned with the material world, who lived the last decades of his life as a recluse in tattered clothes and a run-down apartment and whose energies were directed only toward his art.

The art historian Albert Boime acknowledges that Ryder did not engage in the kinds of material pursuits that marked the lives of many of his well-off patrons. But the artist did demonstrate "his economic awareness in his sensitivity to the prices of his pictures and stated that he would never sell below their current market value and even sell higher in anticipation of their steady increase." He also invested much of his earnings in the stock market. He bought stock in the Pullman Palace Car Company in 1895, a year after the strike by the American Railroad Union against this company over wage cuts had been so violently put down (see p. 322). Thus, while Ryder may have shared with the Dutchman a sense of isolation and loneliness, he was also a participant in a Gilded Age culture and economy marked by excess and inequity.

Winslow Homer (1836–1910) also produced a seascape similar in theme to Ryder's *Flying Dutchman*. In *The Gulf Stream* (1899) [**5.18.27**], a black man occupies a small sailboat whose single mast has broken off. Reclining on the deck, he leans to one side in an attempt to stabilize the boat in the choppy seas. As in Ryder's painting, there is a second boat, but it is a tiny shape on a distant horizon, unseen by the black sailor. While a storm approaches, of more immediate concern to the sailor are the sharks circling the boat. The flecks of bright red on the water suggest that they have already feasted on at least one victim, either human or fish. Homer made several trips through the Gulf Stream in the last three decades of his life. One occurred in late 1898 and early 1899, when he sailed to the Bahamas and Florida. Several preliminary sketches indicate that the *The Gulf Stream* was based, at least in part, on what Homer saw during these trips. But, as with Ryder's seascapes, Homer's work is imbued with broader symbolic value.

The symbolic message of *The Gulf Stream* resonates not only with Ryder's work but even more so with another painting of a black man in a boat surrounded by sharks, John Singleton Copley's *Watson and the Shark* (1778) [**2.5.4**; p. 91]. Copley's painting alluded to the topics of slavery and revolution in the American colonies (see pp. 88–92). Homer's painting, according to the historian Peter H. Wood, "deals in subtle and extended ways with slavery, US imperialism in the Caribbean, southern race wars, and Jim Crow segregation." The association of *The Gulf Stream* with American imperialism is clear in the combination of its title, which points to the major military arena in the Spanish-American War of 1898, and the storm setting. Slavery appears in the figure of the black man and the bamboo that writhes, snake-like, out of the hold of the boat, representing the plantations and sugar industry that fueled the slave trade. The black man's isolation suggests the segregation of the Jim Crow South.

Wood also points to the presence and importance of one particular black man in Homer's life, Lewis Wright. An ex-slave, Wright moved from Virginia to Maine in 1896 to work as the personal servant of Homer's father, Charles Savage Homer. After Charles's death in August 1898, Wright became Winslow's servant. He was approximately the same age as Winslow, and their relationship may well have prompted the artist to reflect more deeply on race relations in both the North and the South. Wright's association with the death of Homer's father may also have contributed to the melancholy nature of the painting, the sense of resignation and isolation in the face of powers beyond one's control. These intimations of mortality are further reinforced by the black cross near the base of the broken mast (in actual fact a cleat, but symbolically funerary), the tomb-like entrance to the hold, and the shroud-like sail across the upper deck. *The Gulf Stream* is thus a complicated painting about personal and national turmoil, one that casts an anxious eye on the coming century.

Review Questions

1 Did the major art museums formed in the late nineteenth century serve the interests of the public? If so, how? If not, why not?

2 What were the characteristics of the Chicago School of Architecture, and what prompted its development in the last three decades of the nineteenth century?

3 How were hierarchies of race, class, and gender embedded in the architecture, sculpture, and overall layout of the World's Columbian Exposition of 1893 in Chicago?

4 How did Mary Fairchild MacMonnies's mural *Primitive Woman* represent the "primitive" and how did Mary Cassatt's mural *Modern Woman* represent the "modern"?

5 How did Henry Ossawa Tanner counter the racial stereotypes of earlier artists, such as John Lewis Krimmel, in his painting *The Banjo Lesson*? How is this painting connected thematically to his later religious works?

Bibliography

Works are divided into a "General works" section, listing titles relevant to more than one chapter, and sections on the individual part introductions and chapters. Within the latter, sources are given first, in the order in which they are referred to in the text, and then suggestions for further reading. Square brackets indicate the original publication date, in instances where a book was reissued after several years of being out of print.

General works

Amaki, Amalia K., ed. *A Century of African American Art: The Paul R. Jones Collection*. Newark: The University Museum, Univ. of Delaware, and New Brunswick, NJ: Rutgers Univ. Press, 2004

Baigell, Matthew *Artist and Identity in Twentieth-Century America*. Cambridge: Cambridge Univ. Press, 2001

—— *Jewish-American Artists and the Holocaust*. New Brunswick, NJ: Rutgers Univ. Press, 1997

Barron, Stephanie, Sheri Bernstein, and Ilene Susan Fort, eds. *Made in California: Art, Image, and Identity, 1900–2000*. Berkeley, Los Angeles, and London: Univ. of California Press and Los Angeles County Museum of Art, 2000

Barter, Judith A., ed. *Art and Appetite: American Painting, Culture, and Cuisine*. Chicago: The Art Institute of Chicago, 2013

Berlo, Janet Catherine, and Ruth B. Phillips *Native North American Art*. Oxford and New York: Oxford Univ. Press, 1998

Boime, Albert *The Unveiling of the National Icons: A Plea for Patriotic Iconoclasm in a Nationalist Era*. Cambridge and New York: Cambridge Univ. Press, 1998

Brown, Steven C. *Native Visions: Evolution in Northwest Coast Art from the Eighteenth Through the Twentieth Century*. Seattle and London: Seattle Art Museum in assoc. with the Univ. of Washington Press, 1998

Burnham, Patricia M. and Lucretia Hoover Giese, eds. *Redefining American History Painting*. Cambridge: Cambridge Univ. Press, 1995

Burns, Sarah *Painting the Dark Side: Art and the Gothic Imagination in Nineteenth-Century America*. Berkeley and Los Angeles: Univ. of California Press, 2004

Burns, Sarah and John Davis, eds. *American Art to 1900: A Documentary History*. Berkeley, Los Angeles, and London: Univ. of California Press, 2009

Calo, Mary Ann, ed. *Critical Issues in American Art*. Boulder, CO: Westview Press, 1998

Caws, Mary Ann, Rudolf Kuenzli, and Gwen Raaberg, eds. *Surrealism and Women*. Cambridge, MA and London: MIT Press, 1991

Chadwick, Whitney *Women, Art, and Society*. 4th edn., London and New York: Thames & Hudson, 2007

Ciucci, Giorgio, *et al.* *The American City: From the Civil War to the New Deal*. Cambridge, MA: MIT Press, 1979

Cohen-Solal, Annie *Painting American: The Rise of American Artists, Paris 1867–New York 1948*. New York: Alfred A. Knopf, 2001

Cooper, Emmanuel *The Sexual Perspective: Homosexuality and Art in the Last 100 Years in the West*. London and New York: Routledge and Kegan Paul, 1986

Corbett, David Peters and Sarah Monks, eds. *Anglo–American: Artistic Exchange between Britain and the USA*. Chichester, West Sussex: Wiley Blackwell, 2012

Crane, Diane *The Transformation of the Avant-Garde: The New York Art World, 1940–1985*. Chicago and London: Univ. of Chicago Press, 1987

Davis, John, Jennifer A. Greenhill, and Jason D. LaFountain, eds. *A Companion to American Art*. Chichester, West Sussex: Wiley Blackwell, 2015

Davis, Keith F. *An American Century of Photography: From Dry-Plate to Digital, The Hallmark Photographic Collection*. 2nd edn., New York: Harry N. Abrams, 1999

Doezema, Marianne and Elizabeth Milroy, eds. *Reading American Art*. New Haven: Yale Univ. Press, 1998

Farrington, Lisa E. *Creating Their Own Image: The History Of African-American Women Artists*. Oxford and New York: Oxford Univ. Press, 2005

Foner, Eric *Give Me Liberty! An American History*. New York and London: W. W. Norton, 2005

Foner, Philip S. and Reinhard Schultz, eds. *The Other America: Art and the Labour Movement in the United States*. London: Journeyman Press, 1985

Foresta, Merry A. *American Photographs*. Washington, D.C.: Smithsonian Institution Press with the National Museum of American Art, 1997

Fort, Ilene Susan, with contributions by Mary L. Lenihan, Marlene Park, Susan Rather, and Roberta K. Tarbell *The Figure in American Sculpture: A Question of Modernity*. Los Angeles and Seattle: Los Angeles County Museum of Art/Univ. of Washington Press, 1995

Fusco, Coco and Brian Wallis, eds. *Only Skin Deep: Changing Visions of the American Self*. New York: International Center of Photography and Harry N. Abrams, Inc., 2003

Gaehtgens, Thomas W. and Heinz Ickstadt, eds. *American Icons: Transatlantic Perspectives on Eighteenth- and Nineteenth-Century American Art*. Los Angeles and Chicago: Getty Center for the History of Art and the Humanities, distrib. Univ. of Chicago Press, 1992

Gelernter, Mark *A History of American Architecture: Buildings in Their Cultural and Technological Context*. Hanover and London: Univ. Press of New England, 1999

Gerdts, William H. *Art Across America: Two Centuries of Regional Painting in America, 1710–1920*. New York: Abbeville Press, 1990

—— and Mark Thistlethwaite *Grand Illusions: History Painting in America*. Fort Worth, TX: Amon Carter Museum, 1988

Goldman, Shifra M. *Dimensions of the Americas: Art and Social Change in Latin America and the United States*. Chicago and London: Univ. of Chicago Press, 1994.

Groseclose, Barbara *Nineteenth-Century American Art*. Oxford and New York: Oxford Univ. Press, 2000

Guerrilla Girls *The Guerrilla Girls' Bedside Companion to the History of Western Art*. London: Penguin Books, 1998

Hammond, Harmony *Lesbian Art in America: A Contemporary History*. New York: Rizzoli International Publications, 2000

Handlin, David P. *American Architecture*. Rev. edn., London and New York: Thames & Hudson, 2004

Harris, Neil *Cultural Excursions: Marketing Appetites and Cultural Tastes in Modern America*. Chicago and London: Univ. of Chicago Press, 1990

Haskell, Barbara *The American Century: Art and Culture, 1900–1950*. New York and London: Whitney Museum of American Art in assoc. with W. W. Norton, 1999

Hayden, Dolores *The Power of Place: Urban Landscapes as Public History*. Cambridge, MA and London: MIT Press, 1995

Heller, Jules and Nancy G. Heller, eds. *North American Women Artists of the Twentieth Century, A Biographical Dictionary*. New York and London: Garland, 1995

Hills, Patricia, ed. *Modern Art in the USA: Issues and Controversies of the 20th Century*. Englewood Cliffs, NJ: Prentice Hall, 2001

Joselit, David *American Art Since 1945*. London and New York: Thames & Hudson, 2003

Johnston, Patricia, ed. *Seeing High and Low: Representing Social Conflict in American Visual Culture*. Berkeley and Los Angeles: Univ. of California Press, 2006

Kasson, Joy *Marble Queens and Captives: Women in Nineteenth-Century American Sculpture*. New Haven: Yale Univ. Press, 1990

Katz, Jonathan D. and David C. Ward *Hide/Seek: Difference and Desire in American Portraiture*. Washington, D.C.: Smithsonian Books in assoc. with the National Portrait Gallery, 2010

Kirkham, Pat, ed. *Women Designers in the USA, 1900–2000: Diversity and Difference*. New Haven and London: Yale Univ. Press, 2000

Kostof, Spiro *A History of Architecture: Settings and Rituals*. Oxford and New York: Oxford Univ. Press, 1985

Langa, Helen and Paula Wisotzki, eds. *American Women Artists, 1935–1970: Gender, Culture, and Politics*. Burlington, VT: Ashgate, 2016

Leja, Michael *Looking Askance: Skepticism and American Art from Eakins to Duchamp*. Berkeley, Los Angeles, and London: Univ. of California Press, 2004

Lewis, Samella *African American Art and Artists*. Berkeley, Los Angeles, and London: Univ. of California Press, 1990

Ling, Amy, ed. *Yellow Light: The Flowering of Asian American Arts*. Philadelphia: Temple Univ. Press, 1999
Loewen, James W. *Lies My Teacher Told Me: Everything Your American History Text Got Wrong*. New York: Touchstone/Simon and Schuster, 1995
Lubin, David M. *Picturing a Nation: Art and Social Change in Nineteenth-Century America*. New Haven and London: Yale Univ. Press, 1994
Maudlin, Daniel and Bernard L. Herman, eds. *Building the British Atlantic World: Spaces, Places, and Material Culture, 1600–1850*. Chapel Hill: Univ. of North Carolina Press, 2016
McCarthy, David *American Artists Against War, 1935–2010*, Berkeley and London: Univ. of California Press, 2015
McElroy, Guy C. *Facing History: The Black Image in American Art, 1710–1940*. San Francisco and Washington, D.C.: Bedford Arts and the Corcoran Gallery of Art, 1990
Meyer, Richard *Outlaw Representation: Censorship and Homosexuality in Twentieth-Century American Art*. Oxford and New York: Oxford Univ. Press, 2002
Mitchell, Mark D. *et al.* *Audubon to Warhol: The Art of American Still Life*. New Haven and London: Yale Univ. Press, 2015
Miller, David C., ed. *American Iconology: New Approaches to Nineteenth-Century Art and Literature*. New Haven and London: Yale Univ. Press, 1993
Morgan, David and Sally M. Promey *The Visual Culture of American Religions*. Berkeley and Los Angeles: Univ. of California Press, 2001
Nabokov, Peter and Robert Easton *Native American Architecture*. Oxford and New York: Oxford Univ. Press, 1989
O'Brien, Mark and Craig Little, eds. *Reimaging America: The Arts of Social Change*. Philadelphia and Santa Cruz, NM: New Society Publishers, 1990
Patton, Sharon *African American Art*. Oxford and New York: Oxford Univ. Press, 1998
Phillips, Lisa *The American Century: Art and Culture, 1950–2000*. New York and London: Whitney Museum of American Art in assoc. with W. W. Norton, 1999
Pierce, Donna and Marta Weigle, eds. *Spanish New Mexico: The Spanish Colonial Arts Society Collection*. 2 vols. Santa Fe, NM: Museum of New Mexico Press, 1996
Poesch, Jessie J. *The Art of the Old South: Painting, Sculpture, Architecture & the Products of Craftsmen, 1560–1860*. New York: Alfred A. Knopf, 1983
Powell, Richard J. *Black Art and Culture in the 20th Century*. London and New York: Thames & Hudson, 1997
Reps, John W. *The Making of Urban America: A History of City Planning in the United States*. Princeton: Princeton Univ. Press, 1997
Rubinstein, Charlotte Streifer *American Women Sculptors: A History of Women Working in Three Dimensions*. Boston, MA: G. K. Hall, 1990
Rushing, W. Jackson, III, ed. *Native American Art in the Twentieth Century: Makers, Meanings, Histories*. London and New York: Routledge, 1999
Scully, Vincent, Jr. *American Architecture and Urbanism*. New York: Henry Holt, 1988
Shohat, Ella and Robert Stam *Unthinking Eurocentrism: Multiculturalism and the Media*. London and New York: Routledge, 1994
Siegel, Katy *Since '45: America and the Making of Contemporary Art*. London: Reaktion Books, 2011
Stiles, Kristine and Peter Selz, eds. *Theories and Documents of Contemporary Art: A Sourcebook of Artists' Writings*. Berkeley and Los Angeles: Univ. of California Press, 1996
Trenton, Patricia, ed. *Independent Spirits: Women Painters of the American West, 1890–1945*. Los Angeles, Berkeley, and London: Autry Museum of Western Heritage in assoc. with the Univ. of California Press, 1995
——— and Patrick T. Houlihan *Native Americans: Five Centuries of Changing Images*. New York: Harry N. Abrams, 1989
Tufts, Eleanor *American Women Artists, Past and Present, A Bibliographic Guide*. New York: Garland, 1984
Wade, Edwin L., ed. *The Arts of the North American Indian: Native Traditions in Evolution*. New York and Tulsa, OK: Hudson Hills Press in assoc. with the Philbrook Art Center, 1986
Wallace-Sanders, Kimberley, ed. *Skin Deep, Spirit Strong: The Black Female Body in American Culture*. Ann Arbor: Univ. of Michigan Press, 2002
Wallach, Alan *Exhibiting Contradiction: Essays on the Art Museum in the United States*. Amherst, MA: Univ. of Massachusetts Press, 1998
Wagner, Anne Middleton *A House Divided: American Art since 1955*. Berkeley and London: Univ. of California Press, 2012
Weinberg, H. Barbara and Carrie Rebora Barratt, eds. *American Stories: Paintings of Everyday Life 1765–1915*. New York, New Haven, and London: The Metropolitan Museum of Art and Yale Univ. Press, 2010
Weinberg, Jonathan *Ambition and Love in Modern American Art*. New Haven and London: Yale Univ. Press, 2001
Zinn, Howard *A People's History of the United States, 1492–Present*. Rev. edn., New York: HarperPerennial, 1995

Preface

Sources

Hauser, Arnold *The Social History of Art*. 4 vols. New York: Vintage Books/Random House, 1951
Clark, T. J. *Image of the People, Gustave Courbet and the 1848 Revolution*. Princeton: Princeton Univ. Press, 1982 [1973]
Corn, Wanda "Coming of Age: Historical Scholarship in American Art," *Art Bulletin* 70 (June 1988): 188–207
Davis, John "The End of the American Century: Current Scholarship on the Art of the United States," *Art Bulletin* 85 (September 2003): 544–80
Wolf, Eric R. *Europe and the People Without History*. Berkeley, Los Angeles, and London: Univ. of California Press, 1982
Levander, Carolyn F. and Robert S. Levine *Hemispheric American Studies*. Piscataway, NJ: Rutgers Univ. Press, 2008
Berlo, Janet Catherine, ed. *The Early Years of Native American Art History: The Politics and Scholarship of Collecting*. Seattle, London, and Vancouver: Univ. of Washington Press and UBC Press, 1992
Kubler, George *Esthetic Recognition of Ancient Amerindian Art*. New Haven and London: Yale Univ. Press, 1991
Henry, William A., III "Beyond the Melting Pot," *Time*, April 9, 1990: 28–31

Part 1: Art and Conquest (*c.* 200 BCE–1821)

Sources

Bartolomé de las Casas *A Short Account of the Destruction of the Indies*. Transl. and ed. Nigel Griffin, with an intro. by Anthony Pagden, Harmondsworth, Middx: Penguin Books, 1992 [1542]
Gould, Eliga H. "Entangled Histories, Entangled Worlds: The English-Speaking Atlantic as a Spanish Periphery," *American Historical Review* 112, no. 3 (June 2007): 764–786
Bucher, Bernadette *Icon and Conquest: A Structural Analysis of the Illustrations of de Bry's "Great Voyages."* Transl. Basia Miller Gulati. Chicago and London: Univ. of Chicago Press, 1981

Chapter 1: Visualizing the Conquest: Colonial Spain and Indigenous Mesoamerica (*c.* 1500–1821)

Sources

Tenochtitlan: Pyramids, Codices, and Monumental Sculpture

Columbus, Christopher *The Journal of Christopher Columbus*. Transl. Cecil Jane; rev. and annotated by L. A. Vigneras, with an appendix by R. A. Skelton. London: The Hakluyt Society, 1960
Cortés, Hernán *Letters From Mexico*. Transl. and ed. Anthony Pagden, with an intro. by J. H. Elliot. New Haven and London: Yale Univ. Press, 1986
Díaz del Castillo, Bernal *The Discovery and Conquest of Mexico*. Transl. A. P. Maudslay. New York: Noonday, 1956
Schwartz, Stuart B., ed. *Victors and Vanquished: Spanish and Nahua Views of the Conquest of Mexico*. Boston and New York: Bedford/St. Martin's, 2000
Gruzinski, Serge *Painting the Conquest: The Mexican Indians and the European Renaissance*. Transl. Deke Dusinberre. Paris: Unesco/Flammarion, 1992

Dürer, Albrecht *Writings*. Transl. and ed. William Martin Conway, with an intro. by Alfred Werner. New York: Philosophical Library, 1958
—— *Diary of his Journey to the Netherlands, 1520–1521*. Transl. from the French by Philip Troutman, with an intro. by J. A. Goris and G. Marlier. Greenwich, CT: New York Graphic Society, 1971
Miller, Mary Ellen *The Art of Mesoamerica from Olmec to Aztec*. London and New York: Thames & Hudson, 1986
Paz, Octavio *Essays on Mexican Art*. Transl. Helen Lane. New York, San Diego, and London: Harcourt Brace, 1993
Loewen, James W. *Lies My Teacher Told Me: Everything Your American History Text Got Wrong*. New York: Touchstone/Simon and Schuster, 1995
Fagan, Brian M. *Ancient North America, The Archaeology of a Continent*. Rev. edn., London and New York: Thames & Hudson, 1995
Todorov, Tzvetan *The Conquest of America*. Transl. Richard Howard. New York: Harper and Row/Harper Torchbooks, 1987 [1982]

Christian Painting, Sculpture, and Architecture in New Spain
Hall, Linda B. *Mary, Mother and Warrior: The Virgin in Spain and the Americas*. Austin: Univ. of Texas Press, 2004
Klein, Cecelia F. "A New Interpretation of Aztec Statue Called Coatlicue, 'Snakes-Her-Skirt'," *Ethnohistory* 55, no. 2 (Spring 2008): 229–50
Weismann, Elizabeth Wilder *Art and Time in Mexico: Architecture and Sculpture in Colonial Mexico*. New York: HarperCollins/Icon Editions, 1995 [1985]

Further Reading
Greenblatt, Stephen, ed. *New World Encounters*. Berkeley and Los Angeles: Univ. of California Press, 1993
Burke, Marcus "Mexican Painting of the Renaissance and Counter-Reformation," in New York, *Metropolitan Museum of Art, Mexican Splendors of Thirty Centuries*. New York and Boston: Metropolitan Museum and Little, Brown and Co., 1990: 286–88
Gruzinski, Serge *Images at War: Mexico from Columbus to Blade Runner (1492–2019)*. Trans. Heather MacLean. Durham, NC and London: Duke Univ. Press, 2001
Householder, Michael *Inventing Americans in the Age of Discovery: Narratives of Encounter*. Burlington, VT: Ashgate, 2011
Mann, Charles C. *1491: New Revelations of the Americas Before Columbus*. New York: Alfred A. Knopf, 2005
Trexler, Richard C. *Sex and Conquest: Gendered Violence, Political Order, and the European Conquest of the Americas*. Ithaca, NY: Cornell Univ. Press, 1995

Chapter 2: Art and Architecture in the Northern Territories of New Spain (c. 900–1821)

Sources

Early Explorations and Fortifications
Fagan, Brian M. *Ancient North America, The Archaeology of a Continent* (above)
Fontana, Bernard L. *Entrada: The Legacy of Spain and Mexico in the United States*. Tucson, AZ: Southwest Parks and Monuments Association, 1994

The Pueblo Cultures
Scully, Vincent *Pueblo/Mountain, Village, Dance*. 2nd edn., Chicago and London: Univ. of Chicago Press, 1989 [1972]
Smith, Watson *When Is a Kiva? And Other Questions About Southwestern Archaeology*. Ed. Raymond H. Thompson. Tucson, AZ: Univ. of Arizona Press, 1990

The Christianization of the Pueblos
Gutiérrez, Ramón *When Jesus Came, the Corn Mothers Went Away: Marriage, Sexuality, and Power in New Mexico, 1500–1846*. Stanford, CA: Stanford Univ. Press, 1991

Church Architecture in the Pueblos
Drain, Thomas A. (text) and David Wakely (photography) *A Sense of Mission: Historic Churches of the Southwest*. San Francisco: Chronicle Books, 1994
Forrestal, Peter P. transl. Benavides' Memorial of 1630. Washington, D.C.: Washington Academy of American Franciscan History, 1954

Church Interiors and Adornments
Cummins, Thomas B. F. "The Indulgent Image: Prints in the New World," in Ilona Katzew, ed., *Contested Visions in the Spanish Colonial World*. Los Angeles/New Haven: Los Angeles County Museum of Art and Yale Univ. Press, 2011
Donahue-Wallace, Kelly "Prints in Eighteenth-century Mexico City," *Print Quarterly* 23, no. 2 (June 2006): 134–54
Donahue, Kelly "Chapter 2: An Odyssey of Images: The Influence of European and New World Prints on Eighteenth-Century Hide Paintings in New Mexico," in Thomas E. Chávez, ed., *A Moment in Times: The Odyssey of New Mexico's Segesser Hide Paintings*. Los Ranchos, New Mexico: Rio Grande Books, 2012
Mather, Christine, ed. *Colonial Frontiers: Art and Life in Spanish New Mexico*. Santa Fe, NM: Ancient City Press, 1983
Pierce, Donna "Chapter 4: 'In the Style of That Country': The History of Hide Painting in New Mexico," in Thomas E. Chávez, ed., *A Moment in Times: The Odyssey of New Mexico's Segesser Hide Paintings* (above)
Gutiérrez, Ramón *When Jesus Came, the Corn Mothers Went Away: Marriage, Sexuality, and Power in New Mexico, 1500–1846* (above)

Texas and Arizona in the Seventeenth and Eighteenth Centuries
Mullen, Robert J. *Architecture and Its Sculpture in Viceregal Mexico*. Austin: Univ. of Texas Press, 1997

Battle Scenes on Hide: Segesser I and II
Hotz, Gottfried *Indian Skin Paintings from the American Southwest: Two Representations of Border Conflicts Between Mexico and the Missouri in the Early Eighteenth Century*. Transl. Johannes Malthaner. Norman: Univ. of Oklahoma Press, 1970
Chávez, Thomas E. ed. *A Moment in Times: The Odyssey of New Mexico's Segesser Hide Paintings* (above)

The California Missions
Monroy, Douglas *Thrown Among Strangers, The Making of Mexican Culture in Frontier California*. Berkeley, Los Angeles, and Oxford: Univ. of California Press, 1990
Lewis, Cynthia Neri "Serra's Painter: José de Páez," *Boletín* 29, no. 1 (2013): 79–98
Moser, Christopher L. *Native American Basketry of Southern California*. Riverside, CA: Riverside Museum Press, 1993
Young, Stanley (text) and Melba Levick (photographs) *The Missions of California*. San Francisco: Chronicle Books, 1988

Further Reading
Antiguo Colegio de San Ildefonso *The Arts of the Missions of Northern New Spain*. Exh. cat. Mexico City: Antiguo Colegio de San Ildefonso, 2009
Jackson, Robert H. and Edward Castillo, eds. *Indians, Franciscans, and Spanish Colonization: The Impact of the Mission System on California Indians*. Albuquerque: Univ. of New Mexico Press, 1996
Kimbro, Edna, Julia G. Costello, and Tevvy Ball *The California Missions: History, Art and Preservation*. Conservation and Cultural Heritage series. Los Angeles: Getty Conservation Institute, 2009
Sands, James A. *Converting California: Indians and Franciscans in the Missions*. New Haven and London: Yale Univ. Press, 2008
Secrest, William B. *When the Great Spirit Died: The Destruction of the California Indians, 1850–1860*. Sanger, CA: Word Dancer Press, 2002

Chapter 3: New France: Contact Zones and Cultural Production (c. 200 BCE–1760)

Sources

Material Exchange: The Impact of Trade on Indigenous Culture
Richter, Daniel K. *The Ordeal of the Longhouse, The Peoples of the Iroquois League in the Era of European Colonization*. Chapel Hill and London: Univ. of North Carolina Press, 1992

Trenton, Patricia and Patrick T. Houlihan *Native Americans: Five Centuries of Changing Images.* New York: Harry N. Abrams, 1989
Ritzenthaler, Robert *Iroquois False-face Masks.* Milwaukee: Milwaukee Public Museum, 1969

France Bringing the Faith: Religious Instruction and Cultural Exchange
Harper, Russell J. *Painting in Canada: A History.* 2nd edn., Toronto, Buffalo, and London: Univ. of Toronto Press, 1977
Monteyne, Joseph "Absolute Faith, or France Bringing Representation to the Subjects of New France," *Oxford Art Journal* 20, no. 1 (1997): 12–22
Davis, Natalie Zemon *Women on the Margins: Three Seventeenth-Century Lives.* Cambridge, MA and London: Harvard Univ. Press,1995
Bailey, Gauvin Alexander "Religious Orders and the Arts of Asia," in Dennis Carr, ed., *Made in the Americas: The New World Discovers Asia.* Boston: Museum of Fine Arts, 2015
Barbeau, Marius *Saintes Artisanes: II – Mille Petites Adresses.* Montreal: Éditions Fides, 1943
Phillips, Ruth B. *Trading Identities, The Souvenir in Native North American Art from the Northeast, 1700–1900.* Seattle and London: Univ. of Washington Press; Montreal and Kingston: McGill-Queen's Univ. Press, 1998

The Influence of Fashion: Painted Caribou-Skin Coats
Burnham, Dorothy K. *To Please the Caribou: Painted Caribou-Skin Coats Worn by the Naskapi, Montagnais, and Cree Hunters of the Quebec-Labrador Peninsula.* Seattle: Univ. of Washington Press, 1992

Monuments to Death: Hopewell and Mississippian Burial Mounds and Effigy Funeral Vessels
Fagan, Brian M. *Ancient North America, The Archaeology of a Continent* (above)

Monuments to Life: Cahokia and the Grand Village of the Natchez
Le Page du Pratz, Antoine S. *The History of Louisiana.* Transl. from the French of M. Le Page. Ed. Joseph G. Tregle, Jr. Baton Rouge: Louisiana State Univ. Press, 1975

Indigenous America in Europe: The Comte d'Artois's Cabinet of Natural History
Vitart, Anne "From Royal Cabinets to Museums: A Composite History," in George P. Horse Capture *et al., Robes of Splendor: Native American Painted Buffalo Robes.* New York: The New Press, 1993
Roscoe, Will *The Zuni Man-Woman.* Albuquerque: Univ. of New Mexico Press, 1991
Berlo, Janet Catherine and Ruth B. Phillips *Native North American Art.* Oxford and New York: Oxford Univ. Press, 1998
White, Richard The Middle Ground: *Indians, Empires, and Republics in the Great Lakes Region, 1650–1815.* Cambridge: Cambridge Univ. Press, 1991

Further Reading

Axtell, James *Beyond 1492: Encounters in Colonial North America.* Oxford and New York: Oxford Univ. Press, 1992
Fitzhugh, William W. *Cultures in Contact: The European Impact on Native Cultural Institutions in Eastern North America, A.D. 1000–1800.* Washington, D.C.: Smithsonian Institution Press, 1985
Greer, Allan, ed. *The Jesuit Relations: Natives and Missionaries in Seventeenth-Century North America.* Boston and New York: Bedford/St. Martin's, 2000

Chapter 4: A Protestant Presence in America—The Arts of the British and Dutch Colonies (c. 1585–1772)

Sources

Picturing the "New World": John White and Theodore de Bry
Fontana, Bernard L. "Chapter 1: Pictorial Images of Spanish North America," in Thomas E. Chávez, ed., *A Moment in Times: The Odyssey of New Mexico's Segesser Hide Paintings* (above)
Nabokov, Peter and Robert Easton *Native American Architecture.* Oxford and New York: Oxford Univ. Press, 1989
Lorant, Stefan, ed. *The New World: The First Pictures of America Made by John White and Jacques Le Moyne and Engraved by Theodore de Bry with Contemporary Narratives of the Huguenot Settlement in Florida, 1562–1565, and the Virginia Colony.* New York: Duell, Sloan, and Pearce, 1946
Hulton, Paul *America 1585: The Complete Drawings of John White.* Raleigh and London: Univ. of North Carolina Press/British Museum Publications, 1984
Morison, Samuel Eliot *The Discovery of America. Vol. 1: The Northern Voyages.* New York: Oxford Univ. Press, 1971
Milanich, Jerald T. and Susan Milbrath *First Encounters.* Gainesville: Univ. of Florida Presses, 1989
Smith, John *The Generall Historie of Virginia, New-England, and the Summer Isles.* Vol. 4. London: J. Dawson and J. Haviland for Michael Sparks, 1624

Early Settlements: Jamestown and Plymouth
Feest, C. F. "Powhatan's Mantle," in Arthur MacGregor, ed. *Tradescant's Rarities.* Oxford: Clarendon Press, 1983
Nash, Gary *Red, White, and Black.* Englewood Cliffs, NJ: Prentice-Hall, 1974
Gould, Eliga H. "Entangled Histories, Entangled Worlds: The English-Speaking Atlantic as a Spanish Periphery," *American Historical Review* 112, no. 3 (June 2007): 764–86
Allen, Paula Gunn *Pocahontas: Medicine Woman, Spy, Entrepreneur, Diplomat.* NY: HarperCollins, 2003
Brickhouse, Anna "Hemispheric Jamestown," in Caroline Field Levander and Robert S. Levine, eds., *Hemispheric American Studies.* New Brunswick, NJ: Rutgers Univ. Press, 2008
Loewen, James W. *Lies My Teacher Told Me: Everything Your American History Text Got Wrong* (above)

Art, Religion, and Politics in Seventeenth-Century New England
Craven, Wayne *Colonial American Portraiture: The Economic, Religious, Social, Cultural, Philosophical, Scientific, and Aesthetic Foundations.* Cambridge: Cambridge Univ. Press, 1986

Displays of Status: Portraiture in New England
Lovell, Margaretta M. *Art in a Season of Revolution: Painters, Artisans, and Patrons in Early America.* Philadelphia: Univ. of Pennsylvania Press, 2005

Displays of Status: Domestic Spaces in New England
Lewis, Michael J. *American Art and Architecture.* London and New York: Thames & Hudson, 2006
Bishop, Robert and Jacqueline M. Atkins *Folk Art in American Life.* New York: Viking Studio Books/London: Penguin Books, 1995
Rhodes, Lynette I. *American Folk Art, From the Traditional to the Naive.* Cleveland: Cleveland Museum of Art, 1978
Clark, Dennis "Chinoiserie in the Colonial Americas," in Dennis Carr, ed., *Made in the Americas: The New World Discovers Asia.* Boston: Museum of Fine Arts, 2015

The Dutch Influence in Architecture and Portraits
Stein, Roger "Thomas Smith's Self-Portrait: Image/Text as Artifact," *Art Journal* 44 (Winter 1984): 315–27

Aristocratic Pretensions in the South
Quinn, Arthur *A New World, An Epic of Colonial America from the Founding of Jamestown to the Fall of Quebec.* Boston and London: Faber and Faber, 1994
Roth, Leland M. *A Concise History of American Architecture.* New York: Harper and Row/Icon Editions, 1979
Vlach, John Michael *Back of the Big House: The Architecture of Plantation Slavery.* Chapel Hill and London: Univ. of North Carolina Press, 1993
Wood, Peter "They Understand Their Business Well: West Africans in Early South Carolina," in Dale Rosengarten *et al.*, eds., *Grass Roots: African Origins of an American Art.* NY: Museum for African Art, 2008
Rosengarten, Dale "By the Rivers of Babylon: The Low Country Basket in Slavery and Freedom," in Dale Rosengarten *et al.*, eds., *Grass Roots: African Origins of an American Art* (above)

Rubinstein, Charlotte Streifer *American Women Artists from Early Indian Times to the Present.* New York: Avon Books, 1982
Chadwick, Whitney *Women, Art, and Society.* London and New York: Thames & Hudson, 2007

Learning Their Stitches and Keeping Warm: Colonial Needlework
Dewhurst, C. Kurt, Betty MacDowell, and Marsha MacDowell *Artists in Aprons: Folk Art by American Women.* New York: E. P. Dutton in assoc. with the Museum of American Folk Art, 1979
Harris, Neil "The Making of an American Culture, 1750–1800," in Charles F. Montgomery and Patricia E. Kane, eds., *American Art: 1750–1800, Towards Independence.* Boston: New York Graphic Society, for Yale Univ. Art Gallery and the Victoria and Albert Museum, 1976

Doors to Eternal Peace: Carved Gravestones
Stein, Roger "Thomas Smith's Self-Portrait: Image/Text as Artifact," *Art Journal* 44 (Winter 1984): 315–27
Bishop, Robert and Jacqueline M. Atkins *Folk Art in American Life* (above)

Foreign Wars and Domestic Unrest: Benjamin West's *The Death of General Wolfe* and Penn's *Treaty with the Indians*
Lord, Barry *The History of Painting in Canada: Toward a People's History.* Toronto: NC Press, 1974
Rather, Susan "Benjamin West, John Galt, and the Biography of 1816," *Art Bulletin* 86 (June 2004): 324–45
Abrams, Ann Uhry "Benjamin West's Documentation of Colonial History: *William Penn's Treaty with the Indians,*" *Art Bulletin* 54 (March 1982): 59–75

Further Reading
Gaudio, Michael *Engraving the Savage: The New World Techniques of Civilization.* Minneapolis and London: Univ. of Minnesota Press, 2008
Mancall, Peter C., ed. *Envisioning America: English Plans for the Colonization of North America, 1580–1640.* Boston and New York: Bedford/St. Martin's, 1995
Miles, Ellen G. *The Portrait in Eighteenth-Century America.* Newark and London: Univ. of Delaware Press and Associated Univ. Presses, 1993
Sloan, Kim *A New World: England's First View of America.* With contributions by Joyce E. Chaplin, Christian F. Feest, and Ute Kuhlemann. Chapel Hill: Univ. of North Carolina Press, 2007
Vlach, John Michael *The Planter's Prospect: Privilege and Slavery in Plantation Paintings.* Chapel Hill and London: Univ. of North Carolina Press, 2002

Part 2: Defining America (*c.* 1765–1850)

Sources

Upton, Dell *Architecture in the United States.* Oxford and New York: Oxford Univ. Press, 1998

Chapter 5: Representing the American Revolution and Its Leaders (*c.* 1765–1810)

Sources

Domestic Production and International Intrigue: The Portraits of John Singleton Copley
Staiti, Paul "Character and Class: The Portraits of John Singleton Copley," in Marianne Doezema and Elizabeth Milroy, eds., *Reading American Art.* New Haven: Yale Univ. Press, 1998: 12–37
Lovell, Margaretta M. *Art in a Season of Revolution: Painters, Artisans, and Patrons in Early America* (above)
Dinnerstein, Lois "The Industrious Housewife: Some Images of Labor in American Art," *Artsmagazine* 55 (April 1981): 109–119
Boime, Albert "Blacks in Shark-Infested Waters, Visual Encodings of Racism in Copley and Homer," *Smithsonian Studies in American Art* 3 (Winter 1989): 18–47
Roberts, Jennifer L. *Transporting Visions: The Movement of Images in Early America.* Berkeley and Los Angeles: Univ. of California Press, 2014

John Trumbull's Canvases of War
Eliot, Alexander *Three Hundred Years of American Painting.* New York: Time Inc., 1957
Trumbull, John *Autobiography, Reminiscences and Letters of John Trumbull from 1756 to 1841.* New York and London: Wiley and Putnam; New Haven: B. L. Hamlen, 1841
Jaffe, Irma B. *John Trumbull: Patriot-Artist of the American Revolution.* Boston: New York Graphic Society, 1975
Burnham, Patricia M. "John Trumbull, Historian: The Case of the Battle of Bunker's Hill," in Patricia M. Burnham and Lucretia Hoover Giese, eds., *Redefining American History Painting.* Cambridge and New York: Cambridge Univ. Press, 1995
Swett, Samuel "Historical and topographical sketch of Bunker Hill battle," in David Humphreys, *An essay on the life of the Honourable Major General Israel Putnam. Addressed to the state Society of the Cincinnati in Connecticut, and first published by their order.* Boston: Samuel Avery, 1818
Kaplan, Sidney *The Black Presence in the Era of the American Revolution, 1770–1800.* New York and Washington, D.C.: New York Graphic Society in assoc. with the Smithsonian Institution Press, 1973
Prown, Jules David "John Trumbull as History Painter," in Helen Cooper *et al., John Trumbull, The Hand and Spirit of a Painter.* New Haven: Yale Univ. Art Gallery, 1982

The Aspirations of Women: Post-Revolutionary Samplers
Bank, Mirra *Anonymous Was a Woman.* New York: St. Martin's Griffin, 1995 [1979]

Money, Beauty, and Rank: Silver in the New Republic
Fairbanks, Jonathan "Paul Revere and 1768: His Portrait and the Liberty Bowl," in Jeannine Falino and Gerald W. R. Ward, eds., *New England Silver and Silversmithing 1620–1815.* Boston: Colonial Society of Massachusetts, distributed by the Univ. Press of Virginia, 2001
Kane, Patricia "Chasers, the Chase, and Other Scenes on Boston Rococo-Style Silver," in Falino and Ward, eds., *New England Silver and Silversmithing* (above)
Falino, Jeannine "'The Pride Which Pervades thro every Class': The Customers of Paul Revere," in Falino and Ward, eds., *New England Silver and Silversmithing* (above)
Bushman, Richard Lyman "The Complexity of Silver," in Falino and Ward, eds., *New England Silver and Silversmithing* (above)

Presidential Poses: Paintings and Statues of George Washington
Eliot, Alexander *Three Hundred Years of American Painting* (above)
Lipman, Jean and Alice Winchester *The Flowering of American Folk Art, 1776–1876.* New York: Viking Press, in cooperation with the Whitney Museum of American Art, 1974
Bishop, Robert and Jacqueline M. Atkins *Folk Art in American Life* (above)
Rubinstein, Charlotte Streifer *American Women Artists from Early Indian Times to the Present.* New York: Avon Books, 1982

Posthumous Portraits of Washington: The Mourning Picture
Dewhurst, C. Kurt, Betty MacDowell, and Marsha MacDowell *Artists in Aprons: Folk Art by American Women* (above)
Rumford, Beatrix, ed. *American Folk Paintings: Paintings and Drawings Other Than Portraits from the Abby Aldrich Rockefeller Folk Art Center.* Boston, Toronto, and London: New York Graphic Society Book; Little, Brown in assoc. with the Colonial Williamsburg Foundation, 1988

From Painting to Print to Embroidery: The History of an Image
Miles, Ellen G., *et al. American Paintings of the Eighteenth Century.* Washington, D.C., New York, and Oxford: National Gallery of Art, Washington, D.C., distrib. Oxford Univ. Press, 1995
Benberry, Cuesta *Always There: The African-American Presence in American Quilts.* Louisville, KY: The Kentucky Quilt Project, Inc., 1992
Fry, Gladys-Marie *Stitched from the Soul: Slave Quilts from the Ante-Bellum South.* New York: Dutton Studio Books in assoc. with the Museum of American Folk Art, 1990

McLeod, Stephen A., ed. *Dining with the Washingtons: Historic Recipes, Entertaining, and Hospitality from Mount Vernon*. Chapel Hill: Univ. of North Carolina Press for the Mount Vernon Ladies' Association, 2011

Further Reading

Barratt, Carrie Rebora *Queen Victoria and Thomas Sully*. Princeton: Princeton Univ. Press in assoc. with The Metropolitan Museum of Art, 2000

Evans, Dorinda *The Genius of Gilbert Stuart*. Princeton: Princeton Univ. Press, 1999

Kamensky, Jane *A Revolution in Color: The World of John Singleton Copley*. New York and London: W. W. Norton and Company, 2016

Kelly, Catherine E. *Republic of Taste: Art, Politics, and Everyday Life in Early America*. Phildelphia: Univ. of Pennsylvania Press, 2016

Sellars, Charles Colman *Patience Wright: American Artist and Spy in George III's London*. Middletown, CT: Wesleyan Univ. Press, 1976

Staiti, Paul *Of Arms and Artists: The American Revolution through Painters' Eyes*. New York and London: Bloomsbury Press, 2016

Chapter 6: Symbols of a New Nation—Architecture and Indigenous Histories (*c.* 1785–1827)

Sources

Home for a President: Thomas Jefferson's Monticello

Roth, Leland M. *A Concise History of American Architecture*. New York: Harper and Row/ Icon Editions, 1979

Upton, Dell *Architecture in the United States* (above)

Thomas Jefferson Foundation, Inc. "Thomas Jefferson and Sally Hemings: A Brief Account" and "Thomas Jefferson and Slavery." www.monticello.org

Gordon-Reed, Annette *The Hemingses of Monticello: An American Family*. New York: W. W. Norton, 2008

Constructing a Capitol: Washington, D.C.

Kostof, Spiro *A History of Architecture: Settings and Rituals*. Oxford and New York: Oxford Univ. Press, 1985

The Louisiana Purchase: New Orleans and Plantation Architecture

Kastor, Peter J. "'What are the Advantages of the Acquisition?': Inventing Expansion in the Early American Republic," in *American Quarterly* 60 (Dec. 2008): 1003–35

Taylor, Joel Gray *Louisiana, A History*. New York and London: W. W. Norton, 1984 [1976]

Ryan, Mary P. "'A Laudable Pride in the Whole of Us': City Halls and Civic Materialism," *The American Historical Review* 105, no. 4 (Oct. 2000): 1131–70

Driskell, David C., with catalog notes by Leonard Simon *Two Centuries of Black American Art*. New York: Alfred A. Knopf and Los Angeles County Museum of Art, 1976

An Architecture of Discipline: Shaker Communities

Nicoletta, Julie (text), Bret Morgan (photography) *The Architecture of the Shakers*. Woodstock, VT: Norfleet Press Book/Countryman Press, 1995

Rhodes, Lynette I. *American Folk Art, From the Traditional to the Naive*. Cleveland: Cleveland Museum of Art, 1978

Dickens, Charles *American Notes for General Circulation*. New York: Harper and Brothers, 1842

An Architecture of Discipline: Prisons

Johnston, Norman *The Human Cage: A Brief History of Prison Architecture*. New York: Walker, 1973

Rothman, David J. *The Discovery of the Asylum: Social Order and Disorder in the New Republic*. Boston: Little, Brown, 1971

Reed, Austin *The Life and the Adventures of a Haunted Convict*. New York: Random House, 2016 [*c.* 1858–59]

Nationhood and Native Americans: The Decoration of the Capitol Building

Fryd, Vivien Green *Art and Empire: The Politics of Ethnicity in the United States Capitol, 1815–1860*. New Haven and London: Yale Univ. Press, 1992

Mills, Robert *Guide to the Capitol and to the National Executive Offices of the United States*. Washington, D.C., 1834

Slotkin, Richard *The Fatal Environment: The Myth of the Frontier in the Age of Industrialization, 1800–1890*. New York: Atheneum, 1985

From Indian Queen to Greek Goddess

Fleming, E. McClung "From Indian Princess to Greek Goddess: The American Image, 1783–1815," *Winterthur Portfolio* 3 (1967): 37–66

Groseclose, Barbara *Nineteenth-Century American Art*. Oxford and New York: Oxford Univ. Press, 2000

Sommer, Frank H. "The Metamorphoses of Britannia," in Charles F. Montgomery and Patricia E. Kane, eds., *American Art: 1750–1800, Towards Independence* (above)

Narratives of Captivity

Truettner, William H. "Picturing the Murder of Jane McCrea," in Andrew Hemingway and Alan Wallach, eds., *Transatlantic Romanticism: British and American Art and Literature, 1790–1860*. Amherst and Boston: Univ. of Massachusetts Press, 2015

Namias, June *White Captives: Gender and Ethnicity on the American Frontier*. Chapel Hill and London: Univ. of North Carolina Press, 1993

Strong, Pauline Turner "Captivity in White and Red: Convergent Practice and Colonial Representation on the British-Amerindian Frontier, 1606–1736," in Dan Segal, ed., *Crossing Cultures: Essays in the Displacement of Western Civilization*. Tucson and London: Univ. of Arizona Press, 1992

Lubin, David "Labyrinths of Meaning in Vanderlyn's *Ariadne*," in *Picturing a Nation: Art and Social Change in Nineteenth-Century America*. New Haven and London: Yale Univ. Press,1994

Portraits and Treaties

Force, William Q. *Picture of Washington and Its Vicinity, for 1848*. Washington, D.C.: William Q. Force, 1848

Jacobs, Paul and Saul Landau, with Eve Pell *To Serve the Devil, Volume 1: Natives and Slaves, A Documentary Analysis of America's Racial History and Why It Has Been Kept Hidden*. New York: Random House/Vintage Books, 1971

Miles, Tiya *Ties That Bind: The Story of an Afro-Cherokee Family in Slavery and Freedom*. Berkeley and London: Univ. of California Press, 2005

Schimmel, Julie "Inventing the 'Indian'," in William Truettner, ed., *The West as America: Reinterpreting Images of the Frontier, 1820–1920*. Washington, D.C. and London: Smithsonian Institution Press, 1991

Trenton, Patricia and Patrick T. Houlihan *Native Americans: Five Centuries of Changing Images*. New York: Harry N. Abrams, 1989

Further Reading

Bellion, Wendy *Citizen Spectator: Art, Illusion, and Visual Perception in Early National America*. Chapel Hill: Univ. of North Carolina Press, 2011

Cosentino, Andrew J. *The Painting of Charles Bird King (1785–1862)*. Washington, D.C.: Smithsonian Institution Press for the National Collection of Fine Arts, 1977

Hall, Gwendolyn Mido *Africans in Colonial Louisiana: The Development of Afro-Creole Culture in the Eighteenth Century*. Baton Rouge: Louisiana State Univ. Press, 1993

Chapter 7: The Schooling of the Nation's Artists (*c.* 1820–1850)

Sources

Improving the Taste of the Nation: Samuel F. B. Morse and the National Academy of Design

Staiti, Paul J. *Samuel F. B. Morse*. Cambridge and New York: Cambridge Univ. Press, 1989

Kloss, William *Samuel F. B. Morse*. New York: Harry N. Abrams, 1988

The Entrepreneurial Spirit and the Production of American Culture: Rufus Porter and the "Valuable and Curious Arts"

Neal, John "American Painters and Painting," *The Yankee and Boston Literary Gazette* 1 (1829): 45

Jaffee, David "'A Correct Likeness': Culture and Commerce in Nineteenth-Century Rural America," in John Michael Vlach and Simon J. Bronner, eds., *Folk Art and Art Worlds*. Ann Arbor, MI: UMI Research Press, 1986

Dewhurst, C. Kurt, Betty MacDowell, and Marsha MacDowell *Artists in Aprons: Folk Art by American Women* (above)

A Plain Likeness: Itinerant Portrait Painters

Neal, John "American Painters and Painting," *The Yankee and Boston Literary Gazette* 1 (1829): 45

Bergengren, Charles "'Finished to the Utmost Nicety': Plain Portraits in America, 1760–1860," in John Michael Vlach and Simon J. Bronner, eds., *Folk Art and Art Worlds* (above)

Jaffee, David "'A Correct Likeness': Culture and Commerce in Nineteenth-Century Rural America," in John Michael Vlach and Simon J. Bronner, eds., *Folk Art and Art Worlds* (above)

Lovell, Margaretta M. *Art in a Season of Revolution: Painters, Artisans, and Patrons in Early America*. Philadelphia: Univ. of Pennsylvania Press, 2005

Patton, Sharon *African American Art*. Oxford and New York: Oxford Univ. Press, 1998

Lewis, Samella *African American Art and Artists*. Berkeley, Los Angeles, and London: Univ. of California Press, 1990

Learning the "Sunbeam Art": The Daguerreotype

Freund, Gisèle *Photography and Society*. Boston: David R. Godine Publisher, Inc., 1980

Arthur, T. S. *Ten Nights in a Bar-Room*. Philadelphia: H. T. Coates and Co., 1882

Sandler, Martin W. *Against the Odds: Women Pioneers in the First Hundred Years of Photography*. New York: Rizzoli International Publications, Inc., 2002

Taylor, Maureen "Nature Caught at the Twinkling of an Eye: The Daguerreotype in Providence," *Rhode Island History*, 42, no. 4 (November 1983)

Trachtenberg, Alan *Reading American Photographs: Images as History, Mathew Brady to Walker Evans*. NY: Hill and Wang, 1989

Further Reading

Gillespie, Sarah Kate *The Early American Daguerreotype: Cross-Currents in Art and Technology*, Cambridge: MIT Press, 2016

Brigham, David R. *Public Culture in the Early Republic: Peale's Museum and Its Audience*. Washington, D.C.: Smithsonian Institution Press, 1995

Johnston, Patricia "Samuel F. B. Morse's *Gallery of the Louvre*: Social Tensions in an Ideal World," in *Seeing High And Low: Representing Social Conflict in American Visual Culture*. Berkeley and London: Univ. of California Press, 2006

Leja, Michael "Mumler's Fraudulent Photographs," in *Looking Askance: Skepticism and American Art from Eakins to Duchamp*. Berkeley and Los Angeles: Univ. of California Press, 2004

National Collection of Fine Arts, Smithsonian Institution, Lois Marie Fink, and Joshua C. Taylor *Academy: The Academic Tradition in American Art*. Chicago: Univ. of Chicago Press, 1978

Rather, Susan *The American School: Artists and Status in the Late Colonial and Early National Era*. New Haven and London: Yale Univ. Press, 2016

Rock, Howard and Diana L. Linden *The City of Promises: The History of the Jewish People in New York, Vol. 1*, ed. Deborah Dash Moore. New York: New York Univ. Press, 2013

Ryan, Mary P. *Civic Wars, Democracy and Public Life in the American City in the Nineteenth Century*. Berkeley and Los Angeles: Univ. of California Press, 1997

Ward, David C. *Charles Willson Peale: Art and Selfhood in the Early Republic*. Berkeley and Los Angeles: Univ. of California Press, 2004

Part 3: Nature and Nation (c. 1000–1863)

Chapter 8: Nature and the Sacred (c. 1000–1863)

Sources

Imagery of Creation and the Vision Quest

Swentzell, Rina "The Sense of Process," in *All Roads Are Good, Native Voices On Life and Culture*. Washington, D.C. and London: Smithsonian Institution Press in assoc. with the National Museum of the American Indian, 1994

Medicine Crow, Joseph "Mysterious Powers," in *All Roads Are Good, Native Voices On Life and Culture* (above)

Ewers, John C. *Entries in Creation's Journey, Native American Identity and Belief*. Ed. Tom Hill and Richard W. Hill, Sr. Washington, D.C. and London: Smithsonian Institution Press in assoc. with the National Museum of the American Indian, 1994

Charles J. Kappler, ed. *Indian Affairs: Laws and Treaties*. Vol. II. Washington, D.C.: Government Printing Office, 1904

The Box that Speaks: The Integration of Form, Content, and Material

Holm, Bill *Northwest Coast Indian Art: An Analysis of Form*. Vancouver and Toronto: Douglas and McIntyre, 1965

Lévi-Strauss, Claude *The Savage Mind*. Chicago: Univ. of Chicago Press, 1966 [1962]

God's Nature as God in Nature

Novak, Barbara *Nature and Culture: American Landscape and Painting, 1825–1875*. London and New York: Thames & Hudson, 1980

Landscape Tourism

Wallach, Alan "Thomas Cole, Landscape and the Course of American Empire," in William H. Truettner and Alan Wallach, eds., *Thomas Cole, Landscape into History*. New Haven, London, and Washington, D.C.: Yale Univ. Press and National Museum of American Art, Smithsonian Institution, 1994

Images of Niagara Falls

Wolf, Bryan "Revolution in the Landscape: John Trumbull and Picturesque Painting," in Helen A. Cooper *et al.*, *John Trumbull, The Hand and Spirit of a Painter* (above)

Boime, Albert *The Magisterial Gaze: Manifest Destiny and American Landscape Painting c. 1830–1865*. Washington, D.C. and London: Smithsonian Institution Press, 1991

Thomas Cole, Federalism, and The Course of Empire

Miller, Angela "Thomas Cole and Jacksonian America: The Course of Empire as Political Allegory," *Prospects* 14 (1990): 65–92

Wallach, Alan "Thomas Cole and the Aristocracy," *Artsmagazine* 56 (Nov. 1981): 94–106

Successors to Cole

Sweeney, J. Gray "The Advantages of Genius and Virtue, Thomas Cole's Influence, 1848–58," in William H. Truettner and Alan Wallach, eds., *Thomas Cole, Landscape into History* (above)

Ketner, Joseph D. *The Emergence of the African-American Artist: Robert S. Duncanson 1821–1872*. Columbia and London: Univ. of Missouri Press, 1993

Edward Hicks and the Peaceable Kingdom

Mather, Eleanore Price and Dorothy Canning Miller *Edward Hicks, His "Peaceable Kingdoms" and Other Paintings*. Newark: Univ. of Delaware Press/New York, London and Toronto: Cornwall Books, 1983

Black, Mary C. "& a Little Child Shall Lead Them," *Arts in Virginia* 1 (Autumn 1960)

Russell, Elbert *The Separation After a Century*. Philadelphia: The Friends Intelligencer, 1928

Frederic Edwin Church: From the Pastoral to the Sublime

Kelly, Franklin *Frederic Edwin Church and the National Landscape*. Washington, D.C. and London: Smithsonian Institution Press, 1988

Christadler, Martin "Romantic Landscape Painting in America: History as Nature, Nature as History," in Thomas W. Gaehtgens and Heinz Ickstadt, eds., *American Icons: Transatlantic Perspectives on Eighteenth- and Nineteenth-Century American Art*. Los Angeles and Chicago: Getty Center for the History of Art and the Humanities, distrib. Univ. of Chicago Press, 1992

Still and Troubled Waters: Luminist Landscapes

Miller, David C. "The Iconology of Wrecked or Stranded Boats in Mid to Late Nineteenth-Century American Culture," in David C. Miller, ed., *American Iconology: New Approaches to Nineteenth-Century Art and Literature*. New Haven: Yale Univ. Press, 1993: 186–208

Novak, Barbara *Nature and Culture: American Landscape and Painting, 1825–1875* (above)

Further Reading

Bedell, Rebecca *The Anatomy of Nature: Geology and American Landscape Painting, 1825–1875*. Princeton and Oxford: Princeton Univ. Press, 2001

Avery, Kevin J. *Treasures from Olana: Landscapes by Frederic Edwin Church*. Ithaca, NY: Cornell Univ. Press, 2005

Bloemink, Barbara *et al.* *Frederic Church, Winslow Homer, and Thomas Moran: Tourism and the*

American Landscape. New York: Bulfinch/Cooper-Hewitt, National Design Museum, 2006
Bracken, Christopher *The Potlatch Papers: A Colonial Case History*. Chicago and London: Univ. of Chicago Press, 1997
Conron, John *American Picturesque*. University Park: Pennsylvania State Univ. Press, 2000
Howat, John K. *Frederic Church*. New Haven and London: Yale Univ. Press, 2005
Jonaitis, Aldona *From the Land of the Totem Poles: The Northwest Coast Indian Art Collection at the American Museum of Natural History*. New York, Vancouver, and London: American Museum of Natural History and Douglas & McIntyre, 1988
LeBlanc, Steven A. *Painted by a Distant Hand: Mimbres Pottery from the American Southwest*. Cambridge, MA: Peabody Museum Press, Harvard Univ., 2004
McKinsey, Elizabeth *Niagara Falls: Icon of the American Sublime*. New York and Cambridge: Cambridge Univ. Press, 1985
O'Toole, Judith Hansen *Different Views in Hudson River School Painting*. New York: Columbia Univ. Press, 2006
Siegel, Nancy, ed. *The Cultured Canvas: New Perspectives on American Landscape Painting*. Durham: Univ. of New Hampshire Press, 2011
Truettner, William H. and Roger Stein, eds. *Picturing Old New England: Image and Memory*. New Haven and Washington, D.C.: Yale Univ. Press and National Museum of American Art, Smithsonian Institution, 1999
Wallach, Alan "Thomas Cole and Transatlantic Romanticism," in Andrew Hemingway and Alan Wallach, eds., *Transatlantic Romanticism: British and American Art and Literature, 1790–1860*. Amherst and Boston: Univ. of Massachusetts Press, 2015
Weekley, Carolyn J., with the assistance of Laura Pass Barry *The Kingdoms of Edward Hicks*. New York: Harry N. Abrams, 1999
Wilmerding, John, ed. *American Light: The Luminist Movement, 1850–1875*. Washington, D.C.: National Gallery of Art, 1980
Wilton, Andrew and Tim Barringer *American Sublime: Landscape Painting in the United States, 1820–1880*. London: Tate Publishing/Princeton: Princeton Univ. Press, 2003
Wulf, Andrea *The Invention of Nature: Alexander Von Humboldt's New World*. New York: Alfred A. Knopf, 2015

Chapter 9: The Occupied Landscape (c. 1830–1863)

Sources

"A City May Rise": Albert Bierstadt's *The Rocky Mountains, Lander's Peak*

Anderson, Nancy K. and Linda S. Ferber *Albert Bierstadt, Art and Enterprise*. New York: Hudson Hills Press in assoc. with the Brooklyn Museum of Art, 1991

Native American Borders: Emanuel Leutze's *Westward the Course of Empire*

Truettner, William H., ed. *The West as America: Reinterpreting Images of the Frontier, 1820–1920*. Washington, D.C. and London: Smithsonian Institution Press, 1991

"The Looks and Modes" of Native American Life: George Catlin and His "Indian Gallery"

Rosaldo, Renato *Culture and Truth: The Remaking of Social Analysis*. Boston: Beacon Press, 1989
Catlin, George *Letters and Notes on the Manners, Customs, and Conditions of North American Indians*, with an intro. by Marjorie Halpin. 2 vols. New York: Dover, 1973 [1844]

George Catlin and the Mandans

Hight, Kathryn S. "'Doomed to Perish': George Catlin's Depictions of the Mandan," *Art Journal* 49 (Summer 1990): 119–24
Fenn, Elizabeth A. *Encounters at the Heart of the World: A History of the Mandan People*. New York: Hill and Wang, 2014
Maximilian of Wied-Neuwied, Prince Alexander Philipp *Maximilian, Prince of Wied's Travels in the Interior of North America during the Years 1832–1834*. London: Ackermann & Co., 1839

Photographic Portraits: Another Take on the Real

Schoolcraft, Henry R. *Historical and Statistical Information Respecting the History, Condition, and Prospects of the Indian Tribes of the United States*. 6 vols. Philadelphia: Lippincott, 1856

The Iconography of Progress: The City and the Train

Lubin, David M. *Picturing a Nation: Art and Social Change in Nineteenth-Century America* (above)
Ketner, Joseph D. *The Emergence of the African-American Artist: Robert S. Duncanson 1821–1872* (above)
Novak, Barbara *Nature and Culture: American Landscape and Painting, 1825–1875* (above)

Human Actors in the Landscape: Genre Paintings of the Yeoman Farmer

Johns, Elizabeth *American Genre Painting: The Politics of Everyday Life*. New Haven and London: Yale Univ. Press, 1991

Human Actors in the Landscape: Genre Paintings of the Westerner

Rash, Nancy *The Painting and Politics of George Caleb Bingham*. New Haven and London: Yale Univ. Press, 1991
Wolf, Bryan J. "History as Ideology or 'What You Don't See Can't Hurt You, Mr. Bingham'," in Patricia M. Burnham and Lucretia Hoover Giese, eds., *Redefining American History Painting*. Cambridge and New York: Cambridge Univ. Press, 1995

Further Reading

Burns, Sarah *Pastoral Inventions: Rural Life in Nineteenth-Century American Art and Culture*. Philadelphia: Temple Univ. Press 1989
Dippie, Brian W. *Catlin and His Contemporaries: The Politics of Patronage*. Lincoln: Univ. of Nebraska Press, 1990
Gurney, George and Therese Thau Heyman, eds. *George Catlin and his Indian Gallery*. Washington, D.C.: Smithsonian American Art Museum/New York: W. W. Norton, 2002

Chapter 10: Domesticated Nature (c. 1818–1860)

Sources

Woman as Nature: The Nude, the Mother, and the Cook

Johns, Elizabeth *American Genre Painting: The Politics of Everyday Life* (above)
Kasson, Joy *Marble Queens and Captives: Women in Nineteenth-Century American Sculpture*. New Haven: Yale Univ. Press, 1990
Wellman, Judith "The Seneca Falls Rights Convention: A Study of Social Networks," in Linda K. Kerber and Jane Sherron de Hart, eds., *Women's America*. 4th edn., New York and Oxford: Oxford Univ. Press, 1995: 203–215
Madsen, Annelise K. "Recipes for Refinement: Art and Sociability in the Mid-Nineteenth Century," in Judith A. Barter, ed., *Art and Appetite: American Painting, Culture, and Cuisine*. Chicago: The Art Institute of Chicago, 2013
Lubin, David M. *Picturing a Nation: Art and Social Change in Nineteenth-Century America* (above)

The Fruits of Art: The Peale Family and Still-Life Painting

Barter, Judith A. and Annelise K. Madsen "'The Symmetry of Nature': Horticulture and the Roots of American Still-Life Painting," in Judith A. Barter, ed., *Art and Appetite: American Painting, Culture, and Cuisine* (above)
Bryson, Norman *Looking at the Overlooked, Four Essays on Still Life Painting*. Cambridge, MA: Harvard Univ. Press, 1990

Tricking the Eye: Raphaelle Peale and the Art of Deception

Ward, David C. and Sidney Hart "Subversion and Illusion in the Life and Art of Raphaelle Peale," *American Art* 8 (Summer/Fall 1994): 97–121
Stein, Roger "Charles Willson Peale's Expressive Design: The Artist in His Museum," *Prospects* 6 (1981)
Lloyd, Phoebe "Philadelphia Story," *Art in America* 76 (Nov. 1988): 154–71, 195–97, 199–201, 203

Gender and the Art of Flower Painting

Hedges, Elaine, Pat Ferrero and Julie Silber *Hearts and Hands, The Influence of Women and Quilts on American Society*. San Francisco: The Quilt Digest Press, 1987

Gerdts, William H. *Painters of the Humble Truth, Masterpieces of American Still Life, 1801–1939.* Columbia and London: Philbrook Art Center with the Univ. of Missouri Press, 1981

Ornithological Paintings as "Nature Morte": Alexander Wilson and John James Audubon

Irmscher, Christoph *The Poetics of Natural History: From John Bartram to William James.* New Brunswick, NJ and London: Rutgers Univ. Press, 1999

Roberts, Jennifer *Transporting Visions: The Movement of Images in Early America.* Berkeley and Los Angeles: Univ. of California Press, 2014

Irmscher, Christoph "Violence and Artistic Representation in John James Audubon," *Raritan* 15 (Fall 1995): 1–34

Further Reading

Audubon, John James *The Audubon Reader.* Ed., with an intro. by Richard Rhodes. New York: Everyman's Library (Alfred A. Knopf), 2008

Danly, Susan and Bruce Weber, eds. *For Beauty and for Truth: The William and Abigail Gerdts Collection of American Still Life.* Exh. cat. Amherst, MA: Mead Art Museum, Amherst College, 1998

Nemerov, Alexander *The Body of Raphaelle Peale: Still Life and Selfhood, 1812–1824.* Berkeley and Los Angeles: Univ. of California Press, 2001

Part 4: A Nation At War (*c.* 1830–1900)

Chapter 11: Images of Mexico and/as America: The Mexican-US War and Its Aftermath (*c.* 1848–1860)

Sources

Learning from the Past: Emanuel Leutze's *The Storming of the Teocalli*

Tyler, Ron "Historic Reportage and Artistic License, Prints and Paintings of the Mexican War," in William Ayres, ed., *Picturing History: American Paintings, 1770–1930.* New York: Rizzoli in assoc. with the Frances Tavern Museum, 1993

Truettner, William H. "Storming the Teocalli—Again, Or, Further Thoughts on Reading History Paintings," *American Art* 9, no. 3 (Fall 1995): 57–95

Life on the Home Front

Husch, Gail "'Freedom's Holy Cause': History, Religious, and Genre Painting in America, 1840–1860," in William Ayres, ed., *Picturing History: American Paintings, 1770–1930* (above)

Wolf, Bryan "All the World's a Code: Art and Ideology in Nineteenth-Century American Painting," *Art Journal* 44 (Winter 1984): 328–37

Life on the Front Lines

Tyler, Ron "Historic Reportage and Artistic License, Prints and Paintings of the Mexican War," in William Ayres, ed., *Picturing History: American Paintings, 1770–1930* (above)

Mexican Culture as American Culture: The *Santeros* of New Mexico

McElroy, Keith "The First Fruits of Isolation: The Arts of the Upper Rio Grand," in Jacinto Quirarte, ed., *Chicano Art History: A Book of Selected Readings.* San Antonio: Research Center for the Arts and Humanities, Univ. of Texas, 1984

Mather, Christine, ed. *Colonial Frontiers: Art and Life in Spanish New Mexico, The Fred Harvey Collection.* Santa Fe, NM: Ancient City Press, 1983

Wroth, William *Images of Penance, Images of Mercy: Southwestern "Santos" in the Late Nineteenth Century.* Intro. to Pt. 2 by Marta Weigle. Norman and London: Univ. of Oklahoma Press, 1991

——— "New Mexican Santos and the Preservation of Religious Traditions," in Mary Ann Calo, ed., *Critical Issues in American Art.* Boulder, CO: Westview Press, 1998

Gonzalez, Deena J. *Refusing the Favor: The Spanish-Mexican Women of Santa Fe, 1820–1880.* Oxford and New York: Oxford Univ. Press, 1999

Pierce, Donna "Chapter 4: 'In the Style of that Country': The History of Hide Painting in New Mexico," in Thomas E. Chávez, ed., *A Moment in Time: The Odyssey of New Mexico's Segesser Hide Paintings* (above)

The Local and the International: New Mexican Furniture and Textiles

Davis, W. W. H. *El Gringo, or New Mexico and Her People.* 1856; repr. Santa Fe, NM: Rydal Press, 1938

Magoffin, Susan Shelby *Down the Santa Fe Trail and into Mexico: Diary of Susan Shelby Magoffin, 1846–1847.* Ed. Stella M. Drumm. 1926; repr. New Haven and London: Yale Univ. Press, 1962

Hill, Tom and Richard W. Hill, Sr., eds. *Creation's Journey: Native American Identity and Belief.* With contributions by Diane Fraher, Ramiro Matos, John C. Ewers, Dorie Reents-Budet, Mari Lynn Salvador, Duane King, Mary Jane Lenz, Eulalie H. Bonar, Nancy Rosoff, and Cécile R. Ganteaume. Washington, D.C. and London: Smithsonian Institution Press, 1994

Further Reading

Reilly, Tom *War With Mexico!: America's Reporters Cover the Battlefront.* Ed. Manley Witten. Lawrence: Univ. Press of Kansas, 2010

Weber, David J. *Myth and the History of the Hispanic Southwest.* Albuquerque: Univ. of New Mexico Press, 1988

Chapter 12: A Nation Divided: Slavery and the Civil War (*c.* 1839–1865)

Sources

Prelude to the Civil War: Representing African Americans and Slavery

Fryd, Vivien Green *Art and Empire: The Politics of Ethnicity in the United States Capitol, 1815–1860.* New Haven and London: Yale Univ. Press, 1992

Hills, Patricia "Picturing Progress in the Era of Westward Expansion," in William H. Truettner, ed., *The West As Images of the Frontier, 1820–1920* (above)

Bennett, Lerone, Jr. *Before the Mayflower: A History of Black America, The Classic Account of the Struggles and Triumphs of Black Americans.* 5th edn., Harmondsworth, Middx.: Penguin Books, 1984

Boime, Albert *The Art of Exclusion: Representing Blacks in the Nineteenth Century.* Washington, D.C. and London: Smithsonian Institution Press, 1990

McElroy, Guy C. *Facing History: The Black Image in American Art, 1710–1940.* San Francisco and Washington, D.C.: Bedford Arts and the Corcoran Gallery of Art, 1990

The Abolitionist Movement and the Challenging of Stereotypes

Powell, Richard J. "Cinque: Antislavery Portraiture and Patronage in Jacksonian America," *American Art* 11 (Fall 1997): 48–73

Driskell, David C., with catalog notes by Leonard Simon *Two Centuries of Black American Art.* New York: Alfred A. Knopf and Los Angeles County Museum of Art, 1976

Parry, Ellwood C., III *The Image of the Indian and the Black Man in American Art, 1590–1900.* New York: Braziller, 1974

Zinn, Howard *A People's History of the United States, 1492–Present.* Rev. edn. New York: HarperPerennial, 1995

Paintings of Fugitives, Contraband, and Soldiers

Simpson, Marc *Winslow Homer: Paintings of the Civil War.* San Francisco: The Fine Arts Museums of San Francisco/Bedford Publishers, 1988

Blight, David W. *Race and Reunion: The Civil War in American Memory.* Cambridge, MA: Harvard Univ. Press, 2007

Photographs of the War

Parry, Ellwood C., III *The Image of the Indian and the Black Man in American Art, 1590–1900* (above)

Trachtenberg, Alan "Albums of War, On Reading Civil War Photographs," in Mary Ann Calo, ed., *Critical Issues in American Art.* Boulder, CO: Westview Press, 1998: 135–54

Lowe, David and Philip Shiman "Substitute for a Corpse," *Civil War Times,* December 2010

Further Reading

McInnis, Maurie D. *Slaves Waiting for Sale: Abolitionist Art and the American Slave Trade.* Chicago and London: Univ. of Chicago Press, 2011

Panzer, Mary *Mathew Brady and the Image of History.* Washington, D.C.: Smithsonian Institution Press, 1997

Wilson, Jackie Napoleon *Hidden Witness: African-American Images from the Dawn of Photography to the Civil War.* New York: St. Martin's Press, 1999

Chapter 13: Reconstruction and Shifting Images of African Americans (*c.* 1866–1900)

Sources

Winslow Homer's *Prisoners from the Front* and *A Visit from the Old Mistress*

Giese, Lucretia H. "Prisoners from the Front: An American History Painting?," in Marc Simpson, *Winslow Homer: Paintings of the Civil War* (above)

Wood, Peter H. and Karen C. C. Dalton *Winslow Homer's Images of Blacks: The Civil War and Reconstruction Years*. Austin: The Menil Collection/Univ. of Texas Press, 1988

Hills, Patricia "Painting Race: Eastman Johnson's Pictures of Slaves, Ex-Slaves, and Freedmen," in Teresa A. Carbone and Patricia Hills, *Eastman Johnson Painting America*. New York: Brooklyn Museum of Art in assoc. with Rizzoli, 1999: 120–65

Pohl, Frances K. "Putting a Face on Difference," *Art Bulletin* 78 (Dec. 1996): 23–28

Bennett, Lerone, Jr. *Before the Mayflower: A History of Black America, The Classic Account of the Struggles and Triumphs of Black Americans* (above)

Cikovsky, Nicolai, Jr. "Winslow Homer's Prisoners from the Front," *Metropolitan Museum Journal* 12 (1977): 155–72

—— and Franklin Kelly, with contributions by Judith Walsh and Charles Brock *Winslow Homer*. Washington, D.C., New Haven, and London: National Gallery of Art and Yale Univ. Press, 1995

Thomas Nast's "Grand Historical Paintings"

Keller, Morton *The Art and Politics of Thomas Nast*. New York: Oxford Univ. Press, 1968

The Freed Slave: Edmonia Lewis's *Forever Free* and Thomas Ball's *Freedmen's Memorial*

Chadwick, Whitney *Women, Art, and Society*. 4th edn., London and New York: Thames & Hudson, 2007

Rubinstein, Charlotte Streifer *American Women Artists from Early Indian Times to the Present*. New York: Avon Books, 1982

Savage, Kirk *Standing Soldiers, Kneeling Slaves: Race, War, and Monument in Nineteenth-Century America*. Princeton: Princeton Univ. Press, 1997

Buick, Kirsten P. "The Ideal Works of Edmonia Lewis: Invoking and Inverting Autobiography," *American Art* 9, no. 2 (Summer 1995): 4–19

Seated Generals, Standing Soldiers: Military Memorials to the Civil War

Savage, Kirk *Standing Soldiers, Kneeling Slaves: Race, War, and Monument in Nineteenth-Century America* (above)

Boime, Albert *Hollow Icons: The Politics of Sculpture in 19th-Century France*. Kent, OH: Kent State Univ. Press, 1987

Further Reading

Dabakis, Melissa "Ain't I a Woman?": Anne Whitney, Edmonia Lewis, and the Iconography of Emancipation," in Patricia Johnston, ed., *Seeing High and Low: Representing Social Conflict in American Visual Culture* (above)

—— *A Sisterhood of Sculptors: American Artists in Nineteenth-Century Rome*. University Park: Pennsylvania State Univ. Press, 2014

Hills, Patricia "Cultural Racism: Resistance and Accommodation in the Civil War Art of Eastman Johnson and Thomas Nast," in Patricia Johnston, ed., *Seeing High and Low: Representing Social Conflict in American Visual Culture* (above)

Johns, Elizabeth *Winslow Homer: The Nature of Observation*. Berkeley and Los Angeles: Univ. of California Press, 2002

Chapter 14: The Indian Wars and the End of the Ghost Dance (*c.* 1869–1900)

Sources

Native Americans in the Popular Press: *Harper's Weekly* and the Washita River Massacre

Parry, Ellwood C., III *The Image of the Indian and the Black Man in America Art, 1590–1900* (above)

The Art of Incarceration: The Fort Marion Ledger Drawings

Szabo, Joyce M. *Howling Wolf and the History of Ledger Art*. Albuquerque: Univ. of New Mexico Press, 1994

Penney, David W. "The Horse as Symbol: Equine Representations in Plains Pictographic Art," in Evan M. Maurer, ed., *Visions of the People, A Pictorial History of Plains Indian Life*. Minneapolis: Minneapolis Institute of Arts, 1992

Berlo, Janet Catherine "Portraits of Dispossession in Plains Indian and Inuit Graphic Arts," *Art Journal* 4 (Summer 1990): 133–41

Berlo, Janet Catherine, ed. *Plains Indian Drawings 1865–1935, Pages from a Visual History*. New York: Harry N. Abrams with The American Federation of Arts and The Drawing Center, 1996

The Battle of the Little Bighorn

Berlo, Janet Catherine "Portraits of Dispossession in Plains Indian and Inuit Graphic Arts," *Art Journal* 4 (above)

Szabo, Joyce M. "Howling Wolf: A Plains Artist in Transition," *Art Journal* 44 (Winter 1984): 367–73

Berlo, Janet Catherine, ed. *Plains Indian Drawings 1865–1935, Pages from a Visual History* (above)

Blume, Anna "In a Place of Writing," in Berlo, ed. *Plains Indian Drawings* (above)

The End of the Ghost Dance

Somma, Thomas P. "The Myth of Bohemia and the Savage Other, Paul Wayland Bartlett's Bear Tamer and Indian Ghost Dancer," *American Art* 6, no. 3 (Summer 1992): 15–35

The Hampton Institute and Lessons in American History

Samuels, Peggy and Harold Samuels *Remington: The Complete Prints*. New York: Crown, 1990

Shapiro, Michael Edward and Peter H. Hassrick *Frederic Remington: The Masterworks*. New York: Harry N. Abrams in assoc. with the St. Louis Art Museum, 1991 [1988]

Sweeney, J. Gray "Racism, Nationalism, and Nostalgia in Cowboy Art," *Oxford Art Journal* 15, no. 1 (1992): 67–80

Petersen, Karen Daniels *Plains Indian Art from Fort Marion*. Norman: Univ. of Oklahoma Press, 1971

Nemerov, Alexander "'Doing the "Old America"': The Image of the American West, 1880–1920," in William H. Truettner, ed., *The West as America: Reinterpreting Images of the Frontier, 1820–1920* (above)

Lindsey, Donal F. *Indians at Hampton Institute, 1877–1923*. Urbana and Chicago: Univ. of Illinois Press, 1995

Slotkin, Richard *The Fatal Environment: The Myth of the Frontier in the Age of Industrialization, 1800–1890*. New York: Atheneum, 1985

Further Reading

Samuels, Peggy and Harold Samuels *Remington: The Complete Prints*. New York: Crown Publishers, 1990

Banner, Stuart *How the Indians Lost Their Land: Law and Power on the Frontier*. Cambridge, MA and London: Belknap Press of Harvard Univ. Press, 2005

Burnham, Patricia M. "Custer's Last Stand: High-Low on Old and New Frontiers," in Patricia Johnston, ed., *Seeing High and Low: Representing Social Conflict in American Visual Culture* (above)

Goetzmann, William N. *The West of the Imagination*. New York: W. W. Norton, 1986

Limerick, Patricia Nelson *The Legacy of Conquest: the Unbroken Past of the American West*. New York: W. W. Norton, 1987

Museum of Fine Arts, Florida State Univ. *Dimensions of Native America: The Contact Zone*. Tallahassee: Museum of Fine Arts, Florida State Univ., 1998

Prown, Jules, *et al.* *Discovered Lands, Invented Pasts: Transforming Visions of the American Frontier, 1600–1860*. New Haven: Yale Univ. Press, 1992

Schekel, Susan *The Insistence of the Indian: Race and Nationalism in Nineteenth-Century Culture*. Princeton: Princeton Univ. Press, 1998

Turner, Frederick Jackson *The Frontier in American History*. New York: R. E. Krieger, 1920

Part 5: Art, Labor, and The Gilded Age (c. 1865–1900)

Sources

Trachtenberg, Alan "Albums of War," in Mary Ann Calo, ed., *Critical Issues in American Art*. Boulder, CO: Westview Press, 1998

Chapter 15: The Art of Industrial Labor (c. 1871–1890)

Sources

One Hundred Years of Independence: Taking Stock of America at the 1876 Philadelphia Centennial Exhibition

Parry, Ellwood C., III *The Image of the Indian and the Black Man in American Art 1590–1900* (above)

Trachtenberg, Alan *The Incorporation of America: Culture and Society In the Gilded Age*. New York: Hill and Wang, 1982

Factory and Foundry: Winslow Homer and Thomas Anshutz

Cikovsky, Nicolai, Jr. and Franklin Kelly, with contributions by Judith Walsh and Charles Brock *Winslow Homer* (above)

Labor Unrest: Robert Koehler's "Strike" and Monuments to Justice and Liberty

Slotkin, Richard *The Fatal Environment: The Myth of the Frontier in the Age of Industrialization, 1800–1890* (above)

Nemerov, Alexander "'Doing the "Old America"': The Image of the American West, 1880–1920," in William H. Truettner, ed., *The West as America: Reinterpreting Images of the Frontier, 1820–1920* (above)

Gladstone, John "Working-Class Imagery in *Harper's Weekly*," *Labor's Heritage* 5, no. 1 (Spring 1993): 42–61

Hills, Patricia *The Painters' America*. New York: Praeger, for the Whitney Museum of American Art, 1974

Foner, Philip S. and Reinhard Schultz *The Other America: Art and the Labour Movement in the United States*. London: Journeyman Press, 1985

Dabakis, Melissa "Martyrs and Monuments of Chicago: The Haymarket Affair," *Prospects: An Annual of American Cultural Studies* 19 (1994): 99–133

Roediger, David "Haymarket Incident," in Mari Jo Buhle, Paul Buhle, and Dan Georgakas, eds., *Encyclopedia of the American Left*. Urbana and Chicago: Univ. of Illinois Press, 1992

Boime, Albert *Hollow Icons: The Politics of Sculpture in 19th-Century France*. Kent, OH: Kent State Univ. Press, 1987

Further Reading

Dabakis, Melissa *Visualizing Labor in American Sculpture: Monuments, Manliness and the Work Ethic, 1880–1935*. Cambridge: Cambridge Univ. Press, 1999

Ott, John *Victorian California: Cultural Philanthropy, Industrial Capital, and Social Authority*. Burlington, VT: Ashgate, 2014

Chapter 16: The Art of Professional and Domestic Labor (c. 1865–1889)

Sources

Celebrating the New Male Professionals: Portraits by Thomas Eakins

Berger, Martin A. *Man Made: Thomas Eakins and the Construction of Gilded Age Manhood*. Berkeley, Los Angeles, and London: Univ. of California Press, 2000

Johns, Elizabeth "*The Gross Clinic* or *Portrait of Professor Gross*," in Marianne Doezema and Elizabeth Milroy, eds., *Reading American Art*. New Haven and London: Yale Univ. Press, 1998: 232–63

—— *Thomas Eakins: The Heroism of Modern Life*. Princeton: Princeton Univ. Press, 1983

Goodrich, Lloyd *Thomas Eakins*. 2 vols. Cambridge, MA: Harvard Univ. Press, 1982

Fryer, Judith "'The Body in Pain' in Thomas Eakins' *Agnew Clinic*," in Laurence Goldstein, ed., *The Female Body: Figures, Styles, Speculations*. Ann Arbor: Univ. of Michigan Press, 1991

Goodbody, Bridget L. "'The Present Opprobrium of Surgery': *The Agnew Clinic* and Nineteenth-Century Representations of Cancerous Female Breasts," *American Art* 8 (Winter 1994): 33–51

Braddock, Alan C. "From Nature to Ecology: The Emergence of Ecocritical Art History," in John Davis, Jennifer A. Greenhill, and Jason D. LaFountain, eds., *A Companion to American Art*. Chichester, West Sussex: Wiley Blackwell, 2015

Middle-Class Masculinity, Mass Production, and *Trompe l'oeil* Painting

Lubin, David M. *Picturing a Nation: Art and Social Change in Nineteenth-Century America* (above)

Whiting, Cécile "Trompe l'oeil Painting and the Counterfeit Civil War," *Art Bulletin* 79 (June 1997): 251–68

Domestic Labor and Cultural Production

Lynes, Russell *The Tastemakers: The Shaping of American Popular Taste*. New York: Dover, 1980 (1949)

Helpful Women: The Evolving Image of the Domestic Servant

O'Leary, Elizabeth *At Beck and Call: The Representation of Domestic Servants in Nineteenth-Century American Painting*. Washington, D.C. and London: Smithsonian Institution Press, 1996

Spaces of Leisure and Labor: Domestic Architecture and Interior Design

Kostof, Spiro *A History of Architecture: Settings and Rituals*. Oxford and New York: Oxford Univ. Press, 1985

Spaces of Leisure and Labor: Parks and Streets

Fein, Albert *Frederick Law Olmsted and the American Environmental Tradition*. New York: Braziller, 1972

Davis, Allen F. *Spearheads for Reform: The Social Settlements and the Progressive Movement, 1890–1914*. New York, London, and Toronto: Oxford Univ. Press, 1967

Trachtenberg, Alan *Reading American Photographs: Images as History, Mathew Brady to Walker Evans*. New York: Hill and Wang, 1989

Lee, Anthony W. *Picturing Chinatown: Art and Orientalism in San Francisco*. Berkeley and London: Univ. of California Press, 2001

Further Reading

Berger, Martin A. *Sight Unseen: Whiteness and American Visual Culture*. Berkeley and Los Angeles: Univ. of California Press, 2005

Braddock, Alan C. *Thomas Eakins and the Cultures of Modernity*. Berkeley and Los Angeles: Univ. of California Press, 2009

Brown, Joshua *Beyond the Lines: Pictorial Reporting, Everyday Life, and the Crisis of Gilded Age America*. Berkeley and Los Angeles: Univ. of California Press, 2002

Cooper, Helen A. *Thomas Eakins: The Rowing Pictures*. New Haven and London: Yale Univ. Press, 1996

Domosh, Mona *Invented Cities: The Creation of Landscape in Nineteenth-Century New York and Boston*. New Haven and London: Yale Univ. Press, 1996

—— *Impressions of California: Early Currents in Art, 1850–1930*. Irvine, CA: Irvine Museum, 1996

Griffin, Randall *Homer, Eakins and Anshutz: The Search for American Identity in the Gilded Age*. University Park: Pennsylvania State Univ. Press, 2004

Le Beau, Bryan F. *Currier & Ives: America Imagined*. Washington, D.C. and London: Smithsonian Institution Press, 2001

Reason, Akela *Thomas Eakins and the Uses of History*. Philadelphia: Univ. of Pennsylvania Press, 2010

Snyder, Joel *One/Many: Western American Survey Photographs by Bell and O'Sullivan*. Chicago and London: Univ. of Chicago Press, 2006

Chapter 17: Gender, the Ideal, and the Real (c. 1871–1900)

Sources

The Rise of Aestheticism

Van Hook, Bailey *Angels of Art, Women and Art in American Society, 1876–1914*. University Park: Pennsylvania State Univ. Press, 1996

Whistler, James Abbott McNeill *The Gentle Art of Making Enemies*. New York, 1890

Anderson, Ross *Abbott Handerson Thayer*. Syracuse, NY: Everson Museum, 1982

Pyne, Kathleen "Evolutionary Typology and the American Woman in the Work of Thomas Dewing," *American Art* 7 (Fall 1993): 12–29

American Impressionism and Consumer Culture: William Merritt Chase's In the Studio

Weinberg, H. Barbara, Doreen Bolger, and David Park Curry *American Impressionism and Realism: The Painting of Modern Life, 1885–1915*. New York: The Metropolitan Museum of Art, 1994

Burns, Sarah "The Price of Beauty: Art, Commerce, and the Late Nineteenth-Century American Studio Interior," in David C. Miller, ed., *American Iconology: New Approaches to Nineteenth-Century Art and Literature*. New Haven: Yale Univ. Press, 1993: 209–38

American Impressionism and the Nostalgic Landscape: J. Alden Weir and John Twachtman

Gerdts, William H. *American Impressionism*. New York: Abbeville Press, 1984

Dawson, Anne E. "J. Alden Weir in Windham, Connecticut, 1882–1919: The Pastoral as Middle Ground," in Anne E. Dawson, ed., *Rare Light: J. Alden Weir in Windham, Connecticut, 1882–1919*. Middletown, CT: Wesleyan Univ. Press, 2016

Weinberg, H. Barbara, Doreen Bolger, and David Park Curry *American Impressionism and Realism: The Painting of Modern Life, 1885–1915*. New York: The Metropolitan Museum of Art, 1994

American Impressionism and Portraiture

Burns, Sarah "The 'Earnest, Untiring Worker' and the Magician of the Brush," in Mary Ann Calo, ed., *Critical Issues in American Art*. Boulder, CO: Westview Press, 1998: 177–98

Hills, Patricia *John Singer Sargent*. New York: Whitney Museum of American Art, with Harry N. Abrams, 1986

Boime, Albert "Sargent in Paris and London: A Portrait of the Artist as Dorian Gray," in Hills, *John Singer Sargent* (above)

Kilmurray, Elaine and Richard Ormond, eds. *John Singer Sargent*. Princeton: Princeton Univ. Press, 1998

Tappert, Tara Leigh *Cecilia Beaux and the Art of Portraiture*. Washington, D.C. and London: Smithsonian Institution Press, 1995

Performing Identity in Photographic Portraits

Smith, Shawn Michelle *American Archives: Gender, Race, and Class in Visual Culture*. Princeton, NJ: Princeton Univ. Press, 1999

Bernardin, Susan *et al.* *Trading Gazes: Euro-American Women Photographers and Native North Americans, 1880–1940*. New Brunswick, NJ and London: Rutgers Univ. Press, 2003

Further Reading

Burns, Sarah *Inventing the Modern Artist: Art and Culture in Gilded Age America*. New Haven: Yale Univ. Press, 1996

Carter, Alice A. *Cecilia Beaux: A Modern Painter in the Gilded Age*. New York: Rizzoli, 2005

Promey, Sally M. *Painting Religion in Public: John Singer Sargent's "Triumph of Religion" at the Boston Public Library*. Princeton: Princeton Univ. Press, 1999

Simpson, Marc, with essays by Richard Ormond and H. Barbara Weinberg *Uncanny Spectacle: The Public Career of the Young John Singer Sargent*. New Haven, London, and Williamstown, MA: Yale Univ. Press and the Sterling and Francine Clark Institute, 1997

Smithgall, Elsa, *et al.* *William Merritt Chase: A Modern Master*. New Haven and London: Yale Univ. Press, 2016

Swain, Kristin *Signs of Grace: Religion and American Art in the Gilded Age*. Ithaca, NY: Cornell Univ. Press, 2008

Chapter 18: Art and Architecture at the End of the Century (*c.* 1885–1900)

Sources

Cultural Institutions and the Public Good: The Metropolitan Museum of Art

Pohl, Frances K. "Art, Education and Labor: The Metropolitan Museum's Workers' Education Program," *Kunst und Politik*, 7 (2005): 41–91

The Chicago School of Architecture and the White City

Pohl, Frances K. "Historical Reality or Utopian Ideal? The Woman's Building at the World's Columbian Exposition, Chicago, 1893," *International Journal of Women's Studies* 5 (Sept./Oct. 1982): 89–311

Rydell, Robert *All the World's A Fair: Visions of Empire at American International Expositions, 1876–1916*. Chicago: Univ. of Chicago Press, 1984

Silkenat, David "Workers in the White City: Working Class Culture at the World's Columbian Exposition of 1893," *Journal of the Illinois State Historical Society*, 104, no. 4 (Winter 2011): 266–300

Women at the Fair: Allegories, Architects, and Artists

Sund, Judy "Columbus and Columbia, Man of Genius Meets Generic Woman, Chicago, 1893," in Mary Ann Calo, ed., *Critical Issues in American Art*. Boulder, CO: Westview Press, 1998

Upton, Dell *Architecture in the United States* (above)

Callen, Anthea *Women Artists of the Arts and Crafts Movement*. New York: Pantheon Books, 1979

Boris, Eileen *Art and Labor: Ruskin, Morris, and the Craftsman Ideal in America*. Philadelphia: Temple Univ. Press, 1986

Zinn, Howard *A People's History of the United States, 1492–Present*. Rev. edn. New York: HarperPerennial, 1995

Pollock, Griselda *Mary Cassatt*. New York: Harper and Row, 1980

—— *Mary Cassatt: Painter of Modern Women*. New York and London: Thames & Hudson, 1998

Lubin, David M. *Picturing a Nation: Art and Social Change in Nineteenth-Century America* (above)

Chessman, Harriet Scott "Mary Cassatt and the Maternal Body," in David C. Miller, ed., *American Iconology: New Approaches to Nineteenth-Century Art and Literature*. New Haven: Yale Univ. Press, 1993: 239–58

Race and Religion at the Turn of the Century: Henry Ossawa Tanner

Boime, Albert "Henry Ossawa Tanner's Subversion of Genre," *Art Bulletin* 75, no. 3 (Sept. 1993): 415–42

Linn, Karen S. *That Half-Barbaric Twang: The Banjo in American Popular Culture*. Urbana: Univ. of Illinois Press, 1991

Mosby, Dewey F. and Darrel Sewell *Henry Ossawa Tanner*. Philadelphia: Philadelphia Museum of Art, 1991

Men at Sea: Albert Pinkham Ryder and Winslow Homer

Broun, Elizabeth *Albert Pinkham Ryder*. Washington and London: Smithsonian Institution Press, 1989

Boime, Albert "Newman, Ryder, Couture and Hero-Worship in Art History," *American Art Journal* 3, no. 2 (Autumn 1971): 5–22

Boime, Albert "Ryder on a Gilded Horse," *Zeitschrift für Kunstgeschichte* 56, no. 4 (1993): 564–75

Conrads, Margaret C. *Winslow Homer and the Critics: Forging a National Art in the 1870s*. Princeton: Princeton Univ. Press in assoc. with the Nelson-Atkins Museum of Art, 2001

Wood, Peter H. *Weathering the Storm: Inside Winslow Homer's "Gulf Stream."* Athens, Georgia: Univ. of Georgia Press, 2004

Further Reading

Brown, Julie K. *Contesting Images: Photography and the World's Columbian Exposition*. Tucson: Univ. of Arizona Press, 1994

Corn, Wanda *Women Building History: Public Art at the 1893 Columbian Exposition*. Berkeley and London: Univ. of California Press, 2011

Kaplan, Wendy *"The Art that is Life": The Arts and Crafts Movement in America, 1875–1920*. Boston: Museum of Fine Arts/Bulfinch Press, 1987

Prelinger, Elizabeth *The Gilded Age: Treasures from the Smithsonian American Art Museum*. Washington, D.C. and New York: Smithsonian Institution Press and Watson Guptil Publishers, 2000

Trapp, Kenneth R., ed. *The Arts and Crafts Movement in California: Living the Good Life*. Oakland, New York, London, and Paris: The Oakland Museum and Abbeville Press, 1993

Glossary

Abstract Expressionism: a term commonly applied to non-geometric abstract art by diverse artists based mainly in New York City and highly active and influential through the 1950s and early 1960s; embraces works in a range of styles, emphasizing spontaneity of expression and individuality; *see* color field painting.

Adobe: a building material of clay mixed with water and a binder, such as straw or manure; used in pueblo architecture of the American Southwest.

Aesthetic Movement: an artistic movement originating in Britain in the 1880s in protest against the idea that art must serve some ulterior purpose and also against the "philistine" taste of the period. Aestheticists denied any moral value in art and argued for the suggestive and evocative over the specific, anecdotal, or didactic.

African Commune of Bad Relevant Artists (AFRICOBRA): a Chicago-based group of African American artists, founded in 1969 by Jeff Donaldson and Wadsworth Jarrell. Promoted a representational style that focused on family, black heroes, and pride in African American culture's roots in black Africa.

Altarpiece: a devotional sculpted and/or painted artwork situated above and behind an altar.

American Abstract Artists (AAA): a group of artists formed in New York in 1936 to promote and foster public understanding of abstract art.

American Impressionism: a style of painting that emerged in the late nineteenth century and drew on the work of contemporary French Impressionists. The movement focused on the ordinary or trivial aspects of everyday modern middle-class life in both the city and country. The movement was concerned with capturing the quality of light and movement with loose brushwork and vivid colors on canvases often painted outdoors.

American Scene Painting: a term applied to artists who painted urban or rural life between World Wars I and II in a narrative manner that was accessible to a broad public. Two main groups included within American Scene Painting were the Social Realists and the Regionalists.

***Américanisme*:** a fascination with America, and specifically American popular culture and industry, among European intellectual circles beginning during World War I.

Amphitheater: a circular or oval structure with rising tiers of seats around a central space.

Anarchism: an ideology that calls for the abolition of government as the key to social and political liberty.

Antebellum: Latin for "before the war"; the period 1820–60 before the American Civil War (1861–65).

Anthropocene: from Greek *anthropos* (human) and *cene* (new or recent). An epoch when human activities started to have a significant global impact on the earth's ecosystems, in particular its climate.

Arcade: a series of arches carried on columns or piers.

Architrave: the lowermost element of a classical entablature.

Armory Show: an international exhibition of modern art held in New York in 1913 at the 69th Regiment Armory, often considered a turning point in American art history for introducing the major French Modernist art movements to the United States.

Art Deco: a decorative style named after the Exposition Internationale des Arts Décoratifs et Industriels Modernes (Paris, 1925) and marked by simplified geometric or stylized forms, strong color contrasts, and textural variety; most popular in architecture and decorative arts during the late 1920s and the 1930s.

Art Nouveau: a late nineteenth- and early twentieth-century style of decoration and architecture that made use of undulating forms of all kinds, especially organic or floral forms.

Arts and Crafts Movement: a movement promoting craftsmanship and a reform of industrial design and industrial labor, initiated in England in the late nineteenth century by William Morris.

Ashcan School: early twentieth-century American movement in painting that focused on a realist depiction of everyday urban scenes. Its name derived from a criticism voiced by the artist Art Young that the members of the group wanted to paint "pictures of ashcans and girls hitching up their skirts."

Assemblage: a three-dimensional work of art made from everyday materials—often found objects—not usually associated with fine art production.

Atrium: an open-aired interior architectural space; also a large and grandiose room in a hotel or public building through which one enters another and more important room.

Augustinian: a Roman Catholic order that follows the Rule of St. Augustine in pursuing a life of poverty, celibacy, and obedience, without withdrawing from the world.

Automatism: the "automatic" use of brush or pencil, without rational control and thus subject to the prompting of subconscious impulses.

Avant-garde: literally "advanced scout" (French). First used by the utopian socialist Henri de Saint-Simon in 1825 to describe the forward-seeing role of artists, and later used to refer to artists who challenge the status quo and stand apart from their peers.

Balustrade: a railing supported by short pillars or ornamental panels.

Baroque: the prevailing style in art commissioned by the European aristocracy and Roman Catholic church from the late sixteenth to the early eighteenth centuries; marked by an interest in dynamic movement and theatrical effect.

***Barrio*:** Spanish word for a district or neighborhood; in the United States, refers most often to neighborhoods inhabited primarily by Spanish-speaking populations.

Bastion: the projecting portion of the outer wall of a fortification.

Bauhaus: a design school founded in 1919 in Weimar, Germany, with the aim of bringing together all the arts under the primacy of architecture, and where teaching methods stressed the need for a rational, practical approach to design problems.

***Baxbe*:** a sacred power in some Native American cultures. It is believed to come from the First Maker or Creator, is granted through an animal emissary, and is obtained by going on a quest.

Beat Movement: a literary movement of the 1950s, characterized by a rejection of materialism, experimentation with drugs and alternative forms of sexuality, and an interest in Eastern religion.

Beaux-Arts: associated with the École des Beaux-Arts in Paris or with the French government's fine art department; in architecture, an academic and eclectic style of the nineteenth and twentieth century practiced by the École des Beaux-Arts and marked by a reuse and recombination of classical Greek and Roman styles.

Belles-lettres: literally "beautiful letters" (French). Refers to literature that is considered light, refined, and purely aesthetic.

Belt Course: a continuous row or layer of stones or another material decorating the face of a wall, such as a molding; also called a string course or band course.

Berdache: literally "male prostitute" (Arabic); term used by anthropologists to refer to Native American gender-mixing individuals.

Black Legend: the large body of anti-Spanish literature that emerged in Europe in the sixteenth century.

Black Power Movement: a political and cultural movement in the United States, most prominent in the 1960s and 1970s, that emphasized racial pride and the creation of black institutions to promote black collective interests.

Blaue Reiter: literally "Blue Rider" (German). Refers to a group of early twentieth-century artists in Germany led by Wassily Kandinsky, August Macke, and Franz Marc. They emphasized child art as a source of inspiration; abstract forms; and the symbolic and psychological aspects of line and color.

Boston Tea Party: a raid on three British ships in Boston Harbor in 1773, in which Boston colonists, dressed as Native Americans, threw the contents of several hundred chests of tea into the harbor as a protest against British taxes on tea.

Brocade: a fabric with a raised pattern created during the weaving process.

Brown v. Board of Education: a decision of the United States Supreme Court in 1954 that struck down earlier "separate but equal" laws for blacks and whites in public facilities and institutions.

***Bulto*:** a carved wooden statue of a holy figure.

Burlesque: a type of popular theatrical entertainment initially marked by parody and humor in the nineteenth century but associated most often with female striptease in the twentieth century.

Buttress: a support built against a wall of a building, either inside or out.

Cabinet: refers to a display of natural historical or anthropological "wonders" and "curiosities" that is often regarded as a precursor to the modern museum.

Calumet: a pipe the stem of which is decorated with feathers.

Camera obscura: literally "dark chamber" (Latin); a darkened box or room with a hole or lens in one side that, when light passes through it, casts an image of an object outside the box onto a ground glass screen or a sheet of paper on the opposite inside wall, which can then be traced. A precursor of the modern-day camera.

Caricature: a picture that exaggerates the physical features of the person or object depicted.

Capital: the sculpted block that crowns a classical column, pier, pilaster, or pillar.

Carpenter Gothic: North American vernacular wooden architecture of the nineteenth century, ornamented with fretwork in Gothic revival style.

***Carte-de-visite*:** small photographic portraits on card stock given out on social occasions as gifts or used as calling cards.

Causeway: a road elevated on a bank of sand, rock, or other material, usually across a body of water.

Chicago School: a group of architects working in Chicago from the Great Fire of 1871 to the mid-1920s; closely connected with the evolution of the skyscraper.

Chicano/a: derived from "Mexicano"; a person of Mexican descent living in the United States. The name was adopted as a public form of self-identification and pride by Mexican American political activists in the 1960s.

***Chinoiserie*:** the iconography, style, and media of Chinese art that filtered through European notions of the exotic East.

Chinese Exclusion Act: federal legislation passed in 1882 prohibiting immigration of all laborers from China for the next decade and excluding current Chinese residents from United States citizenship; extended in 1892, made permanent in 1902, but repealed in 1943.

Chromolithograph: a colored lithograph produced through the use of multiple lithographic stones, one for each color.

Cibachrome: a process for producing photographic color prints directly from transparencies onto photographic paper using azo dyes on a polyester base; it allows for greater image clarity and color purity.

"City Beautiful" movement: an architectural movement in the 1890s and early 1900s that sought to beautify and give monumental grandeur to cities in order to create a moral and harmonious order among urban populations.

Civil Rights Act: legislation of 1964 that outlawed racial discrimination in public schools, at the workplace, and in public facilities.

Clerestory: a row of windows in the upper part of a wall, usually a church, above the adjacent roof, that allows light into the room.

Codex: a folded painting or screenfold usually made of bark paper or deerskin covered with a thin coat of calcium carbonate; produced by the Aztec, Mixtec, and other Mesoamerican peoples before the arrival of Hernán Cortés in 1519; revived in the late sixteenth century by Franciscan friars eager to re-create histories of indigenous populations.

***Colcha*:** an embroidered bed covering produced in New Mexico in the nineteenth century.

***Colchón*:** a folded mattress that functioned as a type of furniture in nineteenth-century New Mexican homes.

Cold War: an ideological rivalry after World War II between the Soviet Union and its satellites on the one hand, and the United States and other capitalist Western countries on the other.

Collage: a technique involving attaching various materials—cardboard, string, fabric, newspaper clippings, etc.—to a canvas or board; sometimes combined with painting or drawing.

Colonnade: a row of columns carrying either an entablature or a series of arches.

Color Field Painting: a style of painting, marked by large fields of flat colors applied with a brush or stained into the canvas, that emerged in the United States in the late 1940s and the 1950s.

Combine: a term coined by Robert Rauschenberg that describes an extension of the principle of collage, in that flat or three-dimensional found objects are attached to the surface of the composition, and are either painted over or left in their natural state.

Communism: a theory or system of social organization based on the communal ownership of all property.

Conceptual Art: art of the 1960s to 1980s that was created according to the following principles: art consists of an idea or concept and does not have to be embodied in a physical form; language is the basic material of art; artistic activity becomes an enquiry into the nature of art itself.

Congregationalist: a Protestant sect in which every local church congregation is independent and self-governing.

Contraband: a term used in the American Civil War to describe escaped slaves who enlisted in the Union Army and, as they were considered property by their owners, were viewed as "confiscated" property by Union officers.

***Contrapposto*:** literally "placed opposite" (Italian); a way of representing the various parts of the body so that they are obliquely balanced around a central vertical axis. First developed by classical Greek sculptors as a means of avoiding stiffness and suggesting impending action (often one leg is straight, while the other is bent, with the upper torso and head rotated to the left or right).

***Coquina*:** shell-limestone that was used to construct fortifications in New Spain.

Corinthian: *see* orders of architecture.

Cornice: the top register of the entablature that includes a projected molding.

Counting Coup: in Native American Plains warfare, the act of touching an enemy during battle with a special coup pole rather than injuring or killing him.

Craft: also referred to as applied arts; a classification of art production that includes needlework, ceramics, metalwork, etc.

Crenellation: a parapet with alternate solid parts and openings.

Cubism: the first abstract art style of the twentieth century. Represents objects, landscapes, and people as many-sided (or many-faceted) solids in an attempt to represent fully and exhaustively on a flat surface all aspects of what the artist saw in three dimensions.

Cult of Domesticity: a nineteenth-century Western understanding of the role of women that anchored their identity in the ability to manage a home and raise children.

Culture Wars: refers to a cultural struggle between political conservatives and liberals in the 1980s in the United States over the legitimacy of certain cultural practices; manifested in the art world by criticism of artists and arts institutions, particularly the National Endowment of the Arts, by members of the religious right and other conservative groups for work they considered indecent or offensive.

Dada: the intentionally meaningless name of an anti-art movement that started in Zurich in 1916 and spread to other European centers and New York City. Dada used techniques of provocation, abstraction, and nonsense to protest the creations of Western civilization that had led to war.

Daguerreotype: the first practicable method of photography made by using light-sensitized metal plates, developed in France by Louis-Jacques-Mandé Daguerre and announced to the public in 1839.

Dawes Act: legislation passed by Congress in 1887 that offered an allotment of land and eligibility for full citizenship to every Native American male who assimilated into European American culture.

Declaration of Sentiments: a document signed by one hundred attendees at the Seneca Falls Convention of 1848. It was modeled after the Declaration of Independence but declared that "all men and women are created equal"; *see* Seneca Falls Convention.

Deconstructivism: a type of architecture that emerged in the mid-1980s and focused on fragmented forms, non-rectilinear shapes, and the manipulation of certain traditional architectural principles—e.g. the relationship between the internal structure of the building and its external envelope—to create unexpected, if not unsettling, structures.

Degikup: Native American artist Louisa Keyser's (Dat So La Lee) original basket shape, which swelled out from a narrow base then curved inward to an open neck slightly wider than the base.

Dome: a hemispheric vault that forms the roof of a building or part of a building.

Dominican: a Catholic order founded in 1216.

Doric: *see* orders of architecture.

Dormer: a structure projecting from a sloping roof, usually housing a window or ventilating louver.

Earthwork: term used from the mid-1960s to describe works of art, either in art galleries or in the open, that make use of such natural materials as earth, rocks, turf, and snow.

Eclogue: an idyllic pastoral poem.

Eight, The: a group of eight American artists who came together in 1907 and, though they painted in different styles, shared a common revolt against Academic art and were determined to bring painting back into contact with ordinary life.

Emancipation Proclamation: a proclamation made by United States President Abraham Lincoln on January 1, 1863, freeing all slaves in the states that were still fighting against the Union Army.

Encaustic: a painting technique that originated in ancient times, using pigments mixed with hot wax as a binder.

Enlightenment: a philosophical movement of the eighteenth century, primarily in Western Europe, influencing intellectual, scientific, and cultural life. Characterized by belief in the power of human reason.

Entablature: the elaborated superstructures carried by the columns in classical architecture, horizontally divided into architrave, frieze, and cornice; may connote similar features in other contexts, such as along the upper portions of walls.

Entasis: the convex curvature, usually very slight, of the shaft of a column.

Episcopal: a Protestant church that originated within the Church of England and that teaches that the roots of Christian belief are the Bible, church tradition, and individual reason.

Equestrian: refers to a painting or sculpture in which the main figure is on horseback.

***Estípite*:** a form that stands in for the shaft of a column but is so extensively carved that its role is purely for decoration, not support.

Executive Order 9066: a presidential order signed and issued on February 19, 1942, by United States President Franklin D. Roosevelt as a response to the bombing of Pearl Harbor, Hawaii, by the Japanese on December 7, 1941. It ordered the removal of Japanese Americans living on the West Coast to internment camps.

Existentialism: a philosophical movement of the nineteenth and twentieth centuries that stresses the unique position of the individual person as a self-determining agent responsible for his/her own choices.

Expressionism: an artistic movement that originated in Germany in the early twentieth century in which the forms arise, not directly from observed reality, but from subjective reactions to reality.

f.64: a group of photographers founded in 1932 who produced pristine, sharp-edged photographs in contrast to the more atmospheric work of the Pictorialist photographers of the time; named for the smallest aperture setting on a camera, which produces the greatest and sharpest depth of field.

Facade: the main face of a building, or the side that is most emphasized architecturally.

Farm Security Administration (FSA): a United States federal agency that existed from 1935 to 1944 as part of President Franklin D. Roosevelt's New Deal administration. The FSA encouraged rural rehabilitation efforts and was well known for its photography program depicting the devastation of the Great Depression.

Fasces: a bundle of rods, often containing an ax with the blade projecting outward, created during the ancient Roman Republic to symbolize Roman political office, and since used to indicate either summary power or strength through unity.

Fascism: a system of government led by a single dictator who forcibly suppresses opposition, controls all industry and commerce, and emphasizes an aggressive nationalism.

Fauvism: refers to the artists of an early twentieth-century French movement characterized by their use of fierce, nonrealistic color and bold, apparently crude draftsmanship.

Favrile Glass: a multicolored iridescent glass invented and manufactured by the American artist Louis Comfort Tiffany in the late nineteenth century; created by mixing together different colors of glass when hot.

Federal Art Project of the Works Progress Administration (FAP/WPA): the federal program that existed from 1935 to 1943 as part of President Franklin D. Roosevelt's New Deal administration. The project was founded to provide support to artists based on financial need.

Federal Style: a streamlined version of neoclassical architecture that flourished in both the East and Midwest of the United States in the late eighteenth and early nineteenth centuries, and was characterized by symmetry and minimal ornamentation.

Federalist: an advocate of a system of government in which power is divided between a central authority and constituent political units.

Feminism: a doctrine advocating rights for women equal to those of men in all spheres of life—social, economic, cultural, religious, political, etc.

***Femme fatale*:** literally "deadly woman" (French); an archetypal female character who is alluring, seductive, and dangerous to men; also known as a siren.

Figurehead: a carved full-length figure or bust built into the bow of a ship.

Fluxus: literally "flow" (Latin); name of an international art movement founded in 1962 to unite members of the extreme avant-garde in Europe and later in America. The group had no stylistic identity and blended different artistic media. Its activities were, in many respects, a revival of the oppositional spirit of Dada.

Folk Art: a term applied to objects produced by individuals who have little or no formal training in the fine arts and who most often reside in rural communities.

Fourteenth Street School: a group of painters who took their subject matter, often the unemployed or low-wage workers, from Union Square in New York City and the neighboring area, including 14th Street.

Franciscan: a Catholic order founded by St. Francis of Assisi that seeks to lead a life of poverty and humility.

Fresco: painting made with mineral or earth pigments on wet plaster.

Frieze: the middle horizontal member of a classical entablature, above the architrave and below the cornice, sometimes decorated with relief sculpture; by extension, any relief or painting used decoratively in a long horizontal format.

Futurism: an early twentieth-century artistic and literary movement founded by the Italian writer F. T. Marinetti. It celebrated speed, war, and the technological world of the future.

Gable Roof: in its simplest form, a symmetrical two-sided roof with one slope on each side. A gable is the generally triangular portion of a wall between the edges of a sloping roof.

Gambrel Roof: a symmetrical two-sided roof with two slopes on each side; the upper slope is positioned at a shallow angle in order to maximize head space while the lower slope is quite steep.

Geneva Convention: a 1949 agreement that updated the standards in international law for humanitarian treatment of victims of war.

Genre Paintings: scenes of everyday life.

Ghost Dance Movement: a late nineteenth-century Native American movement founded by the Paiute visionary Wovoka. Followers prophesized the future non-violent disappearance of white people, and the return of the land to the indigenous peoples.

Gilded Age: term coined by Mark Twain and Charles Dudley Warner in their book *The Gilded Age: A Tale of Today* (1873). Refers to the United States in the period *c.* 1870–98, which was characterized by a greatly expanding economy and the increasing concentration of wealth in the hands of a small number of individuals who exerted strong influence in government and society.

Globalization: the integration of regional economies, societies, and cultures through a global network of communication, transportation, and trade.

Gothic: refers to European art of the twelfth to fifteenth century, but especially describes architecture using pointed arches, rib vaults, and flying buttresses.

Gouache: painting in opaque watercolors, in which the pigments have a gum binder and the filler is invariably some form of opaque white that gives a typical "chalky" look.

Great Depression: the economic crisis in the United States and Europe that began with the stock market crash in October 1929 and continued through the 1930s.

Gulf of Tonkin Resolution: a joint resolution of the United States Congress passed in 1964 that gave President Lyndon B. Johnson the authority to use military force in Vietnam without a formal declaration of war by Congress.

Happening: an art event that synthesizes both planned and improvised theatrical activity with the visual arts and found materials, and often invites audience participation. Happenings began to occur in the late 1950s.

Harlem Renaissance: also known as the New Negro Arts Movement. A literary and artistic movement based mainly in Harlem, New York, in the mid-1920s that sought to combat racism and showcase the range of talents in African American communities.

Hicksite: a sect of the Quaker tradition that emerged in the 1820s in the United States, led by Elias Hicks. Characterized by the resistance to a focus on "correct" interpretation of biblical texts and the life and death of Christ in favor of an emphasis on individual revelation as one's primary spiritual guide.

***Horror vacui*:** literally, "fear of empty spaces" (Latin). Refers to the filling of the entire surface of an artwork with details.

House Un-American Activities Committee (HUAC): also referred to as House Committee on Un-American Activities. A committee of the House of Representatives, active from 1938 to 1975, that investigated and persecuted ostensibly pro-Communist individuals and organizations.

Hudson River School: a mid-nineteenth-century school of American landscape painting influenced by the Romantic movement of the late eighteenth and early nineteenth centuries. Focused on scenes of the Hudson River Valley and surrounding area.

Huguenot: French Protestants, followers of the theologian John Calvin, who reject the sacramental rituals of the Roman Catholic Church and focus on the ability of the individual to gain redemption through faith and study of the Bible.

***Impasto*:** the thick texture produced by heavily applied paint.

Impressionism: a nineteenth-century movement in painting, principally practiced by French artists, that sought to capture a fleeting impression of color and light.

Indian Detour: a joint venture, begun in the 1920s, of the Fred Harvey Company and the Santa Fe Railway that allowed tourists to travel from railroad depots to major Hopi villages to observe the Native American way of life.

Indian Removal Bill: legislation of 1830 that forced the removal of Native Americans east of the Mississippi River to the Plains area to the west, despite treaties guaranteeing them the rights to their lands.

Ionic: *see* orders of architecture.

Japanning: a painted imitation of Japanese lacquer work (lacquer is a liquid made of shellac dissolved in alcohol that dries to form a hard protective coating for wood, metal, or other materials).

***Japonaiserie*:** European imitations of Japanese arts and crafts; also a term that refers generally to the Japanese products that appealed to Europeans after the opening of Japan to trade in the nineteenth century.

***Japonisme*:** refers to the influence of the formal qualities of Japanese art on European art.

Jeffersonian: an advocate of the doctrines of Thomas Jefferson, especially those stressing minimum control by central government, the inalienable rights of the individual, and the superiority of an agrarian economy and rural society.

***Jerga*:** a roughly woven cloth found in nineteenth-century New Mexican homes.

Jesuit: an evangelizing Catholic order founded by St. Ignatius of Loyola in 1534, known particularly for its work in the field of education.

Junk Art: also known as proto-Pop. A variety of assemblages from the late 1950s made out of discarded industrial items and the detritus of modern consumer culture.

Katcina: a supernatural spirit representing the forces of nature (including clouds, rain, animals, and plants) invoked in ritual ceremonies of Pueblo cultures.

Kitsch: mass-produced objects that imitate the aesthetic products of elite culture.

***Kiva*:** a large circular or rectangular underground structure that is the spiritual and ceremonial center of Pueblo cultures of the United States Southwest.

Ku Klux Klan: a group of white Americans founded in 1866 to terrorize African Americans and prevent them from exercising the new freedoms they had achieved as a result of the defeat of the South in the American Civil War.

Land Art: *see* Earthwork.

Landbase: a view of land by Seneca-Tuscarora artist George Longfish as marked by interwoven aspects of place, history, culture, physiology, as well as by a people and their sense of themselves and their spirituality.

***Latia*:** small piece of wood laid between roof beams in Franciscan mission churches.

Ledger Art: drawings made primarily by Native Americans in the Plains regions in the mid- to late nineteenth century, so called because the paper often came from accountants' ledgers.

Liberty Cap: a brimless hat, conical in shape, associated with freed slaves in ancient Rome; also called Phrygian cap. It was used in the late eighteenth and early nineteenth centuries as a symbol of liberty by American and French revolutionaries.

Lintel: a horizontal beam carried by two or more posts or vertical supports to form an architectural opening.

Lithograph: a print made by drawing with a fat- or oil-based medium, such as a wax crayon, onto a smooth stone or metal plate that is then wetted.

Loggia: in both churches and secular buildings, a kind of exterior corridor, communicating with the open air through an arcade or colonnade.

Loyalist: a person who supported the British cause in the American Revolution of 1775–83.

Luminism: name given in the twentieth century to a nineteenth-century style of American landscape painting characterized by a focus on the atmospheric qualities of light and on a mood of calm or tranquillity.

Lynching: punishment carried out by a mob, outside any legal framework, most often by hanging and frequently accompanied by various forms of torture, in order to control and intimidate select groups of people. In the United States, African Americans have been the most common victims of lynchings.

Maltese Cross: a cross in which all four arms are of equal length.

Mammy: also Dinah; a pejorative term that refers to a stereotyped female African American servant, most often represented as fat and sexless, with her head covered by a kerchief.

Manifest Destiny: the nineteenth-century doctrine that it was the destiny and right of the United States to expand westward across the continent.

Mannerism: term coined to describe European art of the sixteenth century typified by stylistic trickery or the contradiction of classical rules and a liking for bizarre effects.

***Manta*:** a blanket or poncho originally made and worn by indigenous peoples of New Mexico.

Marau Society: an all-female society in the Pueblo cultures of the American Southwest, also known as Mamzrautu; *see also* pueblo.

Marginella: a type of small, polished, marine shell.

Marxism: a system of economic and political thought, developed by Karl Marx, that argues that the capitalist system will be overthrown by a socialist revolution resulting in a future classless or Communist society.

Matrilineal: refers to a culture in which property is passed from mother to daughter.

Matrilocal: refers to a culture in which men move to the homes of their wives when they marry.

Medicine Wheel: an important sacred symbol in many Native American cultures that embodies the four directions, as well as the earth, sky, and spirit tree or axis at the center of the world.

***Memento mori*:** any symbol, such as a skull or hourglass, designed to remind the viewer of the transience of human life.

Mestizo: a Spanish term for a person of mixed Native American and European, usually Spanish, racial background.

Methodist: a Protestant sect that stresses both personal and social morality.

Mexican Mural Movement: a movement, originating in Mexico City in the 1920s, in which artists created a new kind of public art throughout the country under the patronage of José Vasconselos, Minister of Education.

Mezzotint: a method of engraving on copper or steel by burnishing or scraping away a uniformly roughened surface, creating pits that can hold ink.

Millennialism: the belief associated with the Second Great Awakening of the late eighteenth and early nineteenth centuries that the thousand years of peace predicted in the Bible were imminent in America.

Minimalism: term coined in the 1960s to describe art that abandons all pretensions either to expressiveness or illusion, and that is generally three-dimensional and often made up of simple geometrical forms.

Miscegenation: the mixing of different racial groups through marriage, sexual relations, or procreation. Anti-miscegenation laws prohibiting "race mixing" between black and white people were passed in colonial America as early as 1691, with the last struck down by the United States Supreme Court in its Loving v. Virginia decision in 1967. Laws were also passed in the United States banning Native American–white and Asian–white marriages, and African American marriage to anyone not African American.

Modernism: general name given to the succession of avant-garde styles in art and architecture that have dominated Western culture from the mid-nineteenth to the late twentieth centuries.

Modernity: most often used to refer to a period, beginning around the sixteenth century, marked by a move from a feudal or agrarian society dominated by religious institutions to a capitalist industrial society where science, reason, and individualism are celebrated and secular institutions have primary importance in the ordering of daily life.

Moldings: decorative strips or edgings, which may be either concave or convex, and plain or patterned.

***Morada*:** Spanish word for a chapel, often decorated with artworks commissioned from *santeros* (*see* santero). In New Mexico, the structure associated with the Catholic confraternities known as the Penitente.

Moravian: a Protestant movement founded in the United States by immigrants from Moravia in the modern-day Czech Republic.

Mormonism: a religious movement founded by Joseph Smith, Jr., in the 1830s. Its beliefs are based on the Book of Mormon, a sacred text on the history of the Americas believed to have been written by an ancient prophet.

Mortar: a device made of a hard substance like stone or wood, with a bowl-shaped bottom that allows substances to be ground to a powder with a pestle or hard round-bottomed utensil.

Mosaic: a design made by cementing small pieces of glass, ceramic, stones, marbles, etc. to a base.

Muckraker: a reporter who writes truthful reports on social issues, often associated with the pro-reform attitudes of the Progressive Era in the late nineteenth and early twentieth centuries.

Mulatto: a person of mixed black and white racial background.

Mural: a painting made directly on a wall, or fastened permanently to a wall.

Nahuatl: the language of the Aztec peoples of central Mesoamerica.

National Endowment for the Arts (NEA): a federal agency founded in 1965 that offers support and funding for artists and art institutions; almost all grants to individual artists ended in 1996.

National Socialism: also Nazism; a German variety of Fascism, espoused by Adolf Hitler's government from 1933 to 1945. Its policies were based on biological racism and anti-Semitism.

***Nature morte*:** French term for still-life painting.

Nave: the long central space of a Christian church.

Négritude: an early twentieth-century philosophy that promoted the unity of peoples of African descent, affirmed black culture, and explored the civilizations of black Africa.

Neoclassicism: a late eighteenth- and early nineteenth-century revival of classical Greek and Roman iconography, style, and decorative motifs; also called classical revivalism.

Neo-Expressionism: figurative art style, largely a revival of early twentieth-century German Expressionist forms, that emerged in the United States, Italy, and West Germany during the late 1970s.

Neogothic: architectural style reviving the Gothic, prominent in England and the United States in the eighteenth and nineteenth centuries.

New Deal: the policies introduced by President Franklin D. Roosevelt in the early 1930s, designed to promote economic recovery from the Great Depression.

New Negro: a term used in the early twentieth century to refer to a new generation of educated and politically astute African Americans who argued eloquently and organized effectively for the rights of black men and women.

New Woman: used in the late nineteenth and early twentieth centuries to describe a woman who pushed against the limits of a male-dominated society and who argued for women's independence and equality with men.

Nineteenth Amendment: an amendment to the United States Constitution, ratified in 1920, granting women the right to vote.

Oculus: a small circular opening in a wall or dome.

Odalisque: a female slave in a Middle Eastern harem, adopted as a subject by nineteenth- and twentieth-century artists as a conventional type of the voluptuous female nude or semi-nude, often with the addition of "Oriental" accoutrements.

One-point Perspective: a method of projecting an illusion of the three-dimensional world onto a two-dimensional surface, in which all parallel lines or lines of projection seem to converge on one point, known as the vanishing point, and associated objects are rendered smaller the further from the viewer they are intended to seem.

Orders of Architecture: a system devised by the Roman architectural historian Vitruvius (first century BCE) to categorize the various types of classical architecture, founded on three standard types of columns, together with their bases, plinths, capitals, and entablature: the Doric order is the oldest, plainest, and sturdiest-looking, with a fluted column and plain circular capital. The Ionic order has a slenderer column and a capital with symmetrical volutes (scroll-shaped ornaments).The Corinthian order has a capital that represents an acanthus (Mediterranean plant) growing in a basket.

Panorama: a wide-angle view of a space that became a popular way to depict landscapes in the nineteenth century; often displayed in a room where the viewer was surrounded by the canvas or in a theatrical setting where the long canvas was slowly unrolled.

Pantograph: a mechanical copying machine.

Papier-mâché: literally "chewed paper" (French). Pulped paper, usually combined with glue, chalk, and sometimes sand, that can be shaped by molding and then baking.

Patrilineal: refers to a culture in which property is passed from father to son.

Patriot Act: legislation of 2001 that reduced restrictions on intelligence gathering by the United States authorities, including the ability to search private records, and broadened the discretion of law enforcement and immigration authorities in detaining and deporting immigrants suspected of terrorism-related acts.

Pattern and Decoration: also known as P + D. A movement in painting and mixed media in which designs drawn from domestic sources, particularly textiles, were self-consciously appropriated and celebrated in large artworks.

Pediment: triangular gable wall above the horizontal cornice of a classically treated building; also a triangular or roughly triangular element, sometimes curved, or broken at the center, surmounting a portico or opening.

Peristyle: a continuous colonnade around a building; also an open court surrounded by a colonnade within a building.

Photorealism: also Superrealism; art of extreme verisimilitude associated with the United States in the 1970s that, in painting, is usually based on the direct copying of photographs.

Photo-Secession: also known as 291. A twentieth-century American photography movement, led by Alfred Stieglitz, that sought to establish photography as an independent and autonomous means of artistic expression.

Phrygian Bonnet: also known as a liberty cap. A soft conical cap with the top pulled forward, used by artists to represent freedom and liberty. It is named for the inhabitants of ancient Phrygia (in modern-day Turkey).

Pictograph: a picture, usually stylized, that represents an idea or conveys a meaning.

Pictorialism: a photographic movement that emerged around 1885 and taught that photography should emulate the techniques found in painting.

Picturesque: a tradition in landscape painting, popular in the eighteenth and nineteenth centuries, that was understood as a balance between the aesthetic ideals of the beautiful and the sublime.

Pier: a large, freestanding, and rectangular pillar.

Pilaster: a pier that is attached to a wall and projects from it only slightly.

Pop art: an art movement originating in the 1950s that makes use of the imagery of consumerism and mass culture, treated with a finely balanced mixture of irony and celebration.

Popular Front: a political coalition of European and American leftist parties in the 1930s organized around an opposition to fascism.

Populism: a political philosophy supporting the rights and power of the people in their struggle against privileged elites.

***Posa*:** a small corner chapel in the mission churches of New Spain.

Post-Impressionism: term used by the British art critic Roger Fry in 1910 to describe the work of a broad range of Western European artists (e.g. Paul Cézanne and Vincent van Gogh) who were moving away from Impressionism's preoccupation with capturing visual appearances.

Postminimalism: also known as Anti-Form. A movement originating in the 1970s that retained the formal simplifications of minimalism but sought to imbue works with a broad range of meaning and reference.

Postmodernism: term used to describe attempts to modify or move beyond the traditions of Modernism in the second half of the twentieth century.

***Po-wa-ha*:** literally "water-wind-breath" (Pueblo/Mimbres); the creative energy or breath of the world.

Prairie Style: architectural style connected most closely with Frank Lloyd Wright. It emphasized the relation of buildings to their sites and the use of natural materials.

Precisionism: an early twentieth-century American movement in painting that was characterized by a simple, formal, and sometimes abstracted representation of industrial and architectural scenes and that avoided human reference.

Pre-Raphaelite Brotherhood: a group of English artists originating in 1848 who sought to turn painting into a moral and political act, to jettison the rules of the Royal Academy, and to return art to a closer relation with nature. Their name derived from the desire to produce work in the spirit that imbued Italian artists before Raphael's move to Rome.

Presbyterian: a Protestant movement that adheres to Calvinist doctrine and stresses the sovereignty of God and the authority of the Scriptures.

Primitive: in early twentieth-century Western art, refers to the art of Africa, Oceania, and Native America, which was often celebrated for its exoticism and innocence or purity and appropriated into Modernist Western art. The term was not applied to art objects from these regions that contained evidence of contact with European cultures.

Progressive Era: the period in the United States, from the 1890s to the 1920s, that was characterized by sweeping reforms in political and social organizations.

Public Works of Art Project (PWAP): a federal program that existed from 1933 to 1934 and was charged with employing artists to create public works of art.

Pueblo: literally "town" or "village" (Spanish). Refers to the cultures or peoples of the Southwestern United States and Northern Mexico—e.g. the Hopi and Zuñi—who lived in multi-story apartment-like structures built of adobe, stone, or other local materials and organized around central plazas.

Pullman Strike: a strike in 1894 by employees of the Pullman Palace Car Company that sparked a nationwide conflict between labor unions and railroad companies and was a pivotal event in the history of labor reform.

Puritanism: a Protestant movement that broke from the Church of England in the sixteenth century, advocating stricter religious discipline and a simplification of doctrine and worship.

Pylon: a tall structure used as a support, to mark a boundary, or as decoration.

Quaker: also the Religious Society of Friends; a Protestant movement that teaches that all members of the religious community are equals, eliminating the hierarchies common in other Christian groups.

Queer: a pejorative term used in the late nineteenth century and later for people in same-sex relationships; it was reclaimed in the late 1980s by those who rejected traditional gender or sexual identities (male, female, heterosexual, homosexual) in favor of more fluid, ambiguous gender/sexual identities.

Readymade: term coined by Marcel Duchamp around 1913 to describe an everyday mass-produced object removed from its normal context and treated as a work of art.

Realism: a style that involves a close investigation of particulars and transmits a sense of concreteness, veracity, and the randomness of the world being depicted.

Reconstruction: the period from 1865 to 1877 following the American Civil War, when the victorious North attempted to "reconstruct" the state and society of the former southern Confederacy, in particular through the abolition of the institution of slavery.

Red Scare: refers to a period from approximately 1947 to 1957 of strong anti-Communist sentiment in the United States that resulted in widespread persecution by the government and several non-governmental organizations of individuals with radical, or even liberal, political views.

Regionalism: the work of a small group of North American artists of the 1930s and 1940s who concentrated on rural Midwestern subject matter and claimed to reject most forms of European influence.

Register: in painting, refers to the ground line on which figures stand in a composition.

Relief: a composition or design made so that all or part of it projects from a flat surface. High relief is carved deeply enough to suggest that the main parts of the design are almost detached from their support; low relief is carved so that the figures project less than half their true depth from the background.

Renaissance: a period of cultural and artistic change in Europe, centered in Italy from the fifteenth to the seventeenth centuries. In architecture, a style characterized by the revival of classical elements, with an emphasis on symmetry, proportion, and geometric forms.

Retablo: Spanish word for a painted or carved altarpiece constructed for monasteries in New Spain.

Robber Baron: a powerful capitalist during the Gilded Age who was considered to have become wealthy by exploiting natural resources and workers, corrupting legislators, or other unethical means.

Romanesque: a term used to describe pre-Gothic art and architecture in Europe from the eighth to the twelfth centuries. Typified by the use of round arches and conspicuously heavy construction.

Romanticism: a cultural movement originating in the second half of the eighteenth century in Europe and influencing American artistic and intellectual life in the early nineteenth century. It constituted the rejection, in part, of the celebration of scientific rationalization in favor of a belief in emotion, often as inspired by nature, as the authentic source of aesthetic experience.

Rotunda: a circular building or interior space, usually covered by a dome.

Salón de recibo: Spanish term for the parlor in nineteenth-century New Mexican homes.

Sampler: a long and narrow strip of cloth containing "samples" of needlework stitches with designs and lettering that vary in complexity; in the mid-eighteenth century in the United States they began to include narrative texts, often drawn from the Bible, and pictorial compositions.

Santa Fe Style: a style in architecture and interior design that combines the celebration of the handcrafted object with the distinct forms of Hopi, Zuñi, and Navajo artistic production.

Santero: literally "saint-maker" (Spanish); a creator of altarpieces depicting Catholic saints.

Sarape: a woven poncho found in New Mexican homes.

Second Great Awakening: a period of great religious revival in the late eighteenth and early nineteenth centuries in the United States.

Section of Painting and Sculpture of the Treasury Department: the federal program that existed from 1933 to 1939 to award employment to artists based on open competitions and commissions.

Seneca Falls Convention: the first women's rights convention, held in 1848 and attended by approximately three hundred men and women.

Shaker: a member of the Millennial Church that originated in England in the middle of the eighteenth century and was brought to the United States in 1774 by Ann Lee. Shakers were so called for the practice of shaking during religious services. They advocated celibacy, common ownership of property, and a strict and simple way of life.

Silhouette: a profile of a human face cut out of black paper.

Sipapu: among Pueblo peoples, a shallow hollow in the center of a *kiva* floor that represented the earth's navel or the place through which the people emerged from the underworld and through which they would return; *see also kiva*, pueblo.

Social Realism: a term used to describe paintings of the life of the lower classes in the twentieth century.

Social Reform Movement: a movement in the last quarter of the nineteenth century in which reformers called for shorter work hours, improved working conditions, and a minimum wage.

Social Surrealism: art created largely during the 1930s and early 1940s that transformed Surrealism by adding explicit references to contemporary political struggles; *see* Surrealism.

Socialism: an economic and political theory that advocates public ownership and cooperative management of a community's means of production.

Socialist Realism: pronounced as a dogma for all Soviet artists in all fields of art in 1934. Refers to art made comprehensible to the masses using realistic and naturalistic artistic traditions and designed to inspire people with admiration for the dignity of the working man and woman and their efforts to build Communism.

Stamp Act: legislation passed by the British Parliament in 1765 authorizing a direct tax on many printed materials in Britain's American colonies; such materials were to be produced on paper made in London and carrying an embossed revenue stamp.

Standing Rock Sioux Protests: organized in the fall of 2016 by a coalition of environmental and indigenous rights activist to protest against the building of an oil pipeline on sacred burial grounds, just north of the Standing Rock Sioux reservation, and across the Missouri River.

Stereograph: a card on which two copies of the same image, usually a photograph, are printed to be viewed through a stereoscope.

Stereoscope: a technology invented in the nineteenth century as a means of looking at two copies of the same image, perceived differently by the right and left eyes so that they appear to be a single three-dimensional image.

Stringcourse: *see* belt course.

Sublime: in art, the creation of a sense of wonder and sometimes terror in the face of an awesome power, whether natural or technological.

Surrealism: a movement founded by the French writer André Breton in 1924 that claimed to liberate the unconscious through dreaming and the suspension of conscious control. Two main types of painting were produced: fantastic or enigmatic dreamscapes, and more abstract images achieved through automatism.

Survey Aesthetic: a way of recording landscapes and cityscapes in the late nineteenth century that contained detailed descriptions of geological formations, architecture, commercial ventures, and the like that were intended to be read as empirical, objective information.

Synchronism: an early twentieth-century American movement that stressed the importance of color, which was believed to be enough in itself to provide the content of an artwork.

Tapestry: hand-woven fabric, usually of silk or wool or a mixture of the two, with a non-repetitive design, usually figurative, which is woven in as it is made.

Tempera: a painting technique in which pigment is mixed with a binder, normally the yolk of an egg or both white and yolk together, thinned with water, and applied to a surface prepared with a gesso (a form of plaster) ground.

Teocalli: a sacred pyramid in Aztec culture.

Tequitqui: literally "one who pays tribute" (Nahuatl). Art produced by Native artists in the service of Christianity that synthesized the imagery and style of their own practice with newly introduced European forms.

Theorem: a style of painting in which the artist uses several stencils to outline the basic shapes of the composition and then adds details.

Thirteenth Amendment: the 1865 amendment to the United States Constitution that abolished slavery.

Tintype: a photograph on a small plate of tinned iron that was cheaper and easier to handle than glass negatives or positives; if used for portrait photography, the resulting print could be handed to the sitter within a few minutes of the exposure being made.

Tlacuilos: literally "painter" or "scribe" (Nahuatl). Refers to an Aztec codex painter, probably from a noble caste and trained in special schools.

Tonalism: an American style of landscape painting that emerged in the 1880s and was marked by an overall tone of colored atmosphere or mist.

Tory: a member of a political party in Britain from the late seventeenth century to about 1832. The Tories sought to preserve the existing social and political order, and believed in royal authority over the power of Parliament.

Totem: an animal that is adopted and identified as the symbol of a clan.

Transcendentalism: a mid-nineteenth-century philosophical and literary movement that believed in contemplation and spirituality as a means of achieving transcendence over the empirical and scientific.

Transept: a part of a building, particularly a church, that lies across or at a right angle to the main axis.

Treasury Relief Art Project (TRAP): a federal program that existed from 1935 to 1938 as part of President Franklin D. Roosevelt's New Deal administration. It was founded to replace the Public Works of Art Project (PWAP) and to provide support to artists based on financial need.

Trefoil: a decorative design with three lobes, particularly a three-lobed shape in Gothic architectural design.

***Trompe l'oeil*:** literally "fools the eye" (French). A type of painting, usually a still life, which by means of various illusionistic devices persuades the spectator that he or she is looking at the actual objects represented.

Truncated Pyramid: a pyramid constructed from a series of step-like platforms.

Tympanum: the triangular area enclosed by a classical pediment.

Unitarian: a religious denomination that teaches that God is one being, rejecting the traditional Christian doctrine of the Holy Trinity.

Ursuline: a Roman Catholic order of nuns founded in Italy in 1535 and dedicated to St. Ursula. The order emphasizes the importance of teaching young girls and caring for the sick and the poor.

***Vanitas*:** an allegorical still life in which all the objects depicted are meant to be reminders of the transience of human life.

***Vaquero*:** a cowboy, typically in the Southwest of the United States.

***Viga*:** a wooden beam used to construct roofs in Franciscan mission churches.

Virtual Reality: a computer-generated, three-dimensional environment that simulates real images and experiences.

Volute: a scroll-shaped architectural ornament, such as those found in pairs on Ionic capitals.

Voting Rights Act: legislation of 1965 that outlawed racist discrimination in United States electoral practice.

Wampum: strings or woven belts made by the Iroquoians and the Algonquians that are composed of white and purple or black shells strung in various designs. They serve most often as reminders of the terms of treaties or trade negotiations.

War Relocation Authority (WRA): the United States Government agency established to handle the internment of Japanese Americans during World War II.

Whig: a member of a political party in Britain from the late seventeenth century to about 1832. The Whigs held liberal principles and favored reform. Also refers to members of the patriotic party during the Revolutionary period.

Wigwam: an oblong- or dome-shaped hut common among the Native peoples of the eastern woodlands of the United States and as far west as the Mississippi River.

Winnowing Basket: a basket made of grass, reeds, or other plant matter used to toss grain into the air so that the wind can separate the grain from the chaff.

Winter Count: an account of a Native American man's life told through one event from each winter that he witnesses.

Women's Suffrage Movement: the reform movement begun in the middle of the nineteenth century that sought the right for women to vote, which was eventually won in 1920.

Works Progress Administration (WPA): a federal agency existing from 1935 to 1943 that was charged with instituting and administering public works during the Great Depression in order to relieve national unemployment.

Yang-na: the site of Tongva village at the time of the arrival of the Spanish. Its geographic location is in present-day Los Angeles.

Ziggurat: a stepped pyramid with a temple built on top.

Zoopraxiscope: an early type of motion-picture projector, invented by Eadweard Muybridge around 1881, which projected images serially onto a screen.

Acknowledgments for Illustrations

The author and publishers are grateful to the individuals and institutions cited in the captions. Additional credits and information are given below.

Page 4 © Jim West/Alamy Stock Photo; **Page 15** Map of North and Central America drawn by Martin Lubikowski; **1.0.1** Beinecke Rare Book and Manuscript Library, Yale University, New Haven; **1.0.2** Drawn by Philip Winton, with reference to Martin Gilbert, *Atlas of American History* (Dorset Press, 1985) for the peoples, and Janet C. Berlo and Ruth B. Phillips, *Native North American Art* (Oxford and New York: Oxford University Press, 1998) for the regions; **1.0.3** Drawn by Philip Winton; **1.1.6** Courtesy Fred R. Kline Gallery & Kline Art Research Associates, Santa Fe, New Mexico; **1.1.7** Colección Hancock Sandoval, Propriedad del Centro de Estudios de Historia de México; **1.1.8** Photo South American Pictures/Tony Morrison; **1.2.1** Library of Congress, Washington, D.C.; **1.2.2** Drawn by Simon S. S. Driver; **1.2.3** Drawn by Sue Cawood; **1.2.4** Photo O. C. Havens, National Geographic Society; **1.2.5** Photo W. Belknap, Boulder City, Nevada; **1.2.6** Drawn by Robert Easton; **1.2.7** Peabody Museum, Harvard University, Cambridge, Massachusetts; **1.2.8** Colorado Springs Fine Arts Center; **1.2.9** Photo David Wakely, San Francisco; **1.2.10** Photo Wittick; **1.2.11** Photo Ernest Knee, Museum of International Folk Art, Santa Fe, New Mexico; **1.2.12** Photo David Wakely, San Francisco; **1.2.13** Museum of International Folk Art, Santa Fe, New Mexico. Fred Harvey Collection. Photo Blair Clark; **1.2.15** Photo David Wakely, San Francisco; **1.2.16** Photo Robert H. Martin; **1.2.17**, **1.2.18** Photo David Wakely, San Francisco; **1.2.19** Photo Sandak; **1.2.20**, **1.2.21** Arizona State Museum, University of Arizona, Photographer Helga Teiwes; **1.2.22** Courtesy the Palace of the Governors Photo Archives, Santa Fe, New Mexico (NMHM/DCA), 149799; **1.2.23** Courtesy the Palace of the Governors Photo Archives, Santa Fe, New Mexico (NMHM/DCA), 152690; **1.2.26**, **1.2.27** Photo David Wakely, San Francisco; **1.3.4**, **1.3.5** Collection des Ursulines de Québec, Musée des Ursulines, Québec; **1.3.11** Chicago Historical Society; **1.3.12** Cahokia Mounds State Historic Site, painting by William R. Iseminger; **1.4.1** The New York Public Library; Astor, Lenox, and Tilden Foundations. Bequest of James Hazen Hyde; **1.4.10** Worcester Art Museum, Massachusetts, Museum purchase, Sarah C. Garver Fund; **1.4.11** Worcester Art Museum, Massachusetts. Gift of Mr. & Mrs. Albert W. Rice; **1.4.12** Society for the Preservation of New England Antiquities, Boston, Massachusetts; **1.4.13** Gilbert Ask Photography; **1.4.14** Photo Sotheby's; **1.4.15** Winterthur Museum. Gift of Henry Francis du Pont, 1957.1084; **1.4.18** Worcester Art Museum, Museum purchase; **1.4.20** Library of Congress, Washington, D.C.; **1.4.21** Virginia Chamber of Commerce, photo Phil Flournoy; **1.4.22** South Carolina Department of Archives and History; **1.4.23** Gibbes Museum of Art, Charleston, 1968.018.0001. Image Courtesy Gibbes Museum of Art/ Carolina Art Association; **1.4.28** Museum of American Folk Art, New York, anonymous gift; **1.4.30** Museum of American Folk Art, New York, photo Daniel Farber; **1.4.31** National Gallery of Canada, Ottawa, transfer from the Canadian War Memorials, 1921 (gift of the 2nd Duke of Westminster, Eaton Hall, Cheshire, 1918); **1.4.32** Courtesy the Pennsylvania Academy of the Fine Arts, Philadelphia. Gift of Mrs. Sarah Harrison (The Joseph Harrison Jr. Collection); **2.5.1** Museum of Fine Arts, Boston, Massachusetts/Gift of the artist's great-granddaughter/Bridgeman Images; **2.5.2** Library of Congress, Washington, D.C., Prints and Photographs Division, LC-DIG-ppmsca-01657; **2.5.4** Museum of Fine Arts, Boston, Massachusetts /Gift of Mrs. George von Lengerke Meyer/Bridgeman Images; **2.5.5** Photo courtesy Mr. and Mrs. Harry Orton-Jones; **2.5.6**, **2.5.7** Yale University Art Gallery, New Haven, Connecticut, Trumbull Collection; **2.5.8** Photo Erik Gould, courtesy the Museum of Art, Rhode Island School of Design, Providence; **2.5.9** Minneapolis Institute of Arts. Tablespoon: Gift of James Ford Bell and his family, and gift of Mr. and Mrs. Byron Wenger; Teapot and ladle: Gift of James F. and Louise H. Bell, Charles H. Bell, and Samuel H. Bell; Teaspoon: Gift of Charlotte Y. Salisbury, wife of Harrison E. Salisbury and great niece of John Templeman Coolidge; **2.5.11** Courtesy the Pennsylvania Academy of the Fine Arts, Philadelphia. Bequest of William Bingham; **2.5.12** Peabody Museum, Harvard University, Cambridge, Massachusetts; **2.5.13** The Museum of the City of New York. Gift of the Seawanhaka Yacht Club; **2.5.15** Undercroft Museum, Westminster Abbey, London, photo courtesy Dean and Chapter of Westminster; **2.5.16** © Americanspirit/Dreamstime.com; **2.5.20** National Gallery of Art, Washington, D.C., Andrew W. Mellon Collection; **2.5.23** Courtesy Mount Vernon Ladies' Association; **2.6.1** Virginia State Library and Archives, Richmond; **2.6.2a** Photo Rieley & Associates; **2.6.2b** © Christopher Stark/Dreamstime.com; **2.6.3**, **2.6.4** Library of Congress, Washington, D.C., Prints and Photographs Division; **2.6.5** Newberry Library, Chicago; **2.6.6** Private collection; **2.6.7** Photo Paul R. Thompson, Mobile, Alaska; **2.6.8** Photo David C. Driskell; **2.6.9** Library of Congress, Washington, D.C., Geography and Maps Division; **2.6.10**, **2.6.11** Bret Morgan Photography, Fairfax, California; **2.6.13** Private collection. Photo courtesy Thomas K. Woodward, American Antiques and Quilts, New York City; **2.6.14** J. Bentham, *Works*, I (Edinburgh, 1843); **2.6.15** Virginia Department of Corrections, Richmond; **2.6.17** *Pennsylvania Journal of Prison Discipline*, XI, April 1856; **2.6.18–2.6.21** Courtesy the Architect of the Capitol, Washington, D.C.; **2.6.24** Wadsworth Atheneum Museum of Art, Hartford, Connecticut. Purchased by the Wadsworth Atheneum, accession no. 1855.4; **2.7.1** Museum of Fine Arts, Boston, Massachusetts/Kristin and Roger Servison Gallery/Bridgeman Images; **2.7.3** Terra Foundation for the Arts, Daniel J. Terra Collection, 1992.51. Photo courtesy Terra Foundation for the Arts, Chicago; **2.7.4** Courtesy the Pennsylvania Academy of the Fine Arts, Philadelphia. Gift of Mrs. Sarah Harrison (The Joseph Harrison Jr. Collection); **2.7.6** Museum of American Folk Art, New York. Gift of William Bernhard and Catherine Cahill; **2.7.8** Photo courtesy Historic Newton; **2.7.12** Museum of Fine Arts, Boston, Massachusetts/Gift of Maxim Karolik for the M. and M. Karolik Collection of American Paintings, 1815–1865/ Bridgeman Images; **2.7.13** Museum of Fine Arts, Boston, Massachusetts /A. Shuman Collection/Bridgeman Images; **2.7.14** National Gallery of Art, Washington, D.C., Andrew Mellon Fund; **2.7.15** The Metropolitan Museum of Art, New York. Gift of Edgar William and Bernice Chrysler Garbisch, 1962; **2.7.18** Private Collection; **2.7.19** Library of Congress, Washington, D.C., Prints and Photographs Division; **3.8.5** Photograph by Dawson; **3.8.7** Wadsworth Atheneum Museum of Art, Hartford. Bequest of Daniel Wadsworth, accession no. 1848.4; **3.8.8** The Art Institute of Chicago. Friends of American Art Collection, 1946.396. All rights reserved; **3.8.10** The Detroit Institute of Arts. Founders Society Purchase, William H. Murphy Fund; **3.8.11**, **3.8.12** Courtesy The New-York Historical Society, New York City. Gift of New York Gallery of Fine Arts; **3.8.16** Cincinnati Art Museum. Gift of Norbert Heerman and Arthur Helbig; **3.8.17** High Museum of Art, Atlanta. Lent by the West Foundation; **3.8.18** Free Library of Philadelphia, Rare Book Department; **3.8.20** Library of Congress, Washington, D.C., Geography and Maps Division; **3.8.23** Photo Sotheby's Picture Library, London; **3.8.25** The Metropolitan Museum of Art, New York. Bequest of Margaret E. Dows, 1909; **3.8.27** Cleveland Museum of Art, 2001, Mr. and Mrs. William H. Marlatt Fund, 1965.233; **3.8.28** Cape Anne Historical Museum, Gloucester, Massachusetts; **3.8.29** National Gallery of Art, Washington, D.C., Gift of Frederick Sturges Jr.; **3.8.30** Amon Carter Museum, Fort Worth, 17.77; **3.9.1** The Metropolitan Museum of Art, New York, Rogers Fund 1907; **3.9.2** After G. B. Tindall and D. E. Shi, *America: A Narrative History* (New York and London: W. W. Norton, 1999), Courtesy W. W. Norton & Company, Inc.; **3.9.4** Photo Art Resource/Scala; **3.9.12** Drawings by Mary Butler, from John Canfield Ewers, *Plains Indian Painting, A Description of an Aboriginal American Art* (Palo Alto, California: Stanford University Press, 1939); **3.9.13** The National Museum of Denmark, Copenhagen, Department of Ethnography; **3.9.18** National Gallery of Art, Washington, D.C., Gift of Mrs. Huttleston Rogers; **3.9.22** National Gallery of Art, Washington, D.C., Patrons' Permanent Fund, 2015.18.1; **3.10.2** Brooklyn Museum of Art, A. Augustus Healy Fund, 70.26; **3.10.3** Private collection. Photo National Museum of American Art, Smithsonian Institution, Washington, D.C.; **3.10.7** Smith College Museum of Art. Purchased with funds given anonymously by a member of the class of 1952; **3.10.10** Ackland Art Museum, The University of North Carolina at Chapel Hill, The William A. Whitaker Foundation Art Fund; **3.10.15** From the Archives of the Museum of Comparative Zoology, Ernst Mayr Library, Harvard University; **4.11.1** Wadsworth Atheneum Museum of Art, Hartford. The Ella Gallup Sumner and Mary Catlin Sumner Collection Fund, accession no. 1985.7; **4.11.5** Drawn by Philip Winton; **4.12.1a** Private Collection; **4.12.1b** Library of Congress, Washington, D.C., Prints and Photographs Division, HABS DC-38-C-3; **4.12.2** Courtesy Architect of the Capitol, Washington, D.C.; **4.12.5** The Detroit Institute of Arts. Gift of Mrs. Jefferson Butler and Miss Grace Conover; **4.12.10** Brooklyn Museum of Art. Gift of Miss Gwendolyn O. L. Conkling, 40.59.B; **4.12.11** The Metropolitan Museum of Art, New York. Gift of Erving and Joyce Wolf, 1982; **4.12.13** The Fine Arts Museum of San Francisco. Gift of Mr. and Mrs. John D. Rockefeller III; **4.12.15** National Archives, Washington, D.C., Audio-Visual Division; **4.12.16** Library of Congress, Washington, D.C., Prints and Photographs Division, LC-B811-2594; **4.12.18** Library of Congress, Washington, D.C., Prints and Photographs Division; **4.12.19** Library of Congress, Washington, D.C., Prints and Photographs Division, LC-DIG-stereo-1s04369; **4.13.1** The Metropolitan Museum of Art, New York. Gift of Mrs. Frank B. Porter, 1922; **4.13.2** Smithsonian American Art Museum. Gift of William T. Evans; **4.13.3** Library of Congress, Washington, D.C., Prints and Photographs Division, LC-USZC6-79; **4.13.5** Wadsworth Atheneum Museum of Art, Hartford. Gift of Mrs. Josephine M. J. Dodge, accession no. 1900.8; **4.13.8, 4.13.10, 4.13.11** Library of Congress, Washington, D.C., Prints and Photographs Division; **4.14.11** National Museum of the American Indian, New York/Bridgeman Images; **4.14.13** Smithsonian Museum of American Art, Washington, D.C., Gift of Mrs. Armistead Peter III; **4.14.14** Library of Congress, Washington, D.C., Prints and Photographs Division, LC-DIG-ppmsca-12031; **5.15.2** Courtesy Architect of the Capitol, Washington, D.C.; **5.15.3** Museum of Fine Arts, Boston, Massachusetts/Henry H. and Zoe Oliver Sherman Fund/Bridgeman Images; **5.15.4** Yale University Art Gallery, New Haven. Bequest of Stephen Carlton Clark, B.A., 1903; **5.15.6** The Fine Arts Museums of San Francisco. Gift of Mr. and Mrs. John D. Rockefeller III; **5.15.8** Photo Bridgeman Images; **5.15.9** Gravure from *Select Chicago* (New York: A. Witteman); **5.15.10** Photo by S. R. Stoddard, 1890. Library of Congress, Washington, D.C., Prints and Photographs Division; **5.16.1** Library of Congress, Washington, D.C., Prints and Photographs Division; **5.16.2** Courtesy the Pennsylvania Academy of the Fine Arts, Philadelphia. Charles Bregler's Thomas Eakins Collection. Purchased with the partial support of the Pew Memorial Trust; **5.16.3** Philadelphia Museum of Art, Philadelphia. Gift of the Alumni Association to Jefferson Medical College in 1878 and purchased by the Pennsylvania Museum of the Fine Arts and the Philadelphia Museum of Art in 2007 with the generous support of some 3,600 donors. 2007-1-1. Photo 2012 The Philadelphia Museum of Art/Art Resource/Scala, Florence; **5.16.4** Courtesy the University of Pennsylvania Art Collection, Philadelphia; **5.16.5** The Metropolitan Museum of Art, New York. Alfred N. Punnett Fund and gift of George D. Pratt; **5.16.6** Wadsworth Atheneum Museum of Art, Hartford. The Ella Gallup Sumner and Mary Catlin Sumner Collection Fund, accession no. 1935.236; **5.16.7** The Metropolitan Museum of Art, New York. Purchase, Henry R. Luce Gift, 1970; **5.16.8** The Fine Arts Museums of San Francisco. Mildred Anna Williams Collection; **5.16.9** Boston Public Library, Print Department; **5.16.11** The Museum of the City of New York. The Harry T. Peters Collection; **5.16.16** Courtesy the Pennsylvania Academy of the Fine Arts, Philadelphia. Gift of Homer F. Emens and Francis C. Jones; **5.16.17** Photo courtesy R. H. Love Galleries, Inc.; **5.16.19** Photo Emily Lane; **5.16.20** Photo Wayne Andrews/Esto; **5.16.21** The Metropolitan Museum of Art, New York, The Richard and Gloria Manney Parlor; **5.16.22** The Museum of the City of New York. The Jacob A. Riis Collection; **5.16.24** Collection of the Birmingham Museum of Art. Gift of the Birmingham Public Library; **5.16.25** Library of Congress, Washington, D.C., Prints and Photographs Division; **5.17.1** National Gallery of Art, Washington, D.C., the Harris Whittemore Collection; **5.17.3, 5.17.4** Photo Art Resource/Scala; **5.17.6** George Eastman House Collection, Rochester, New York; **5.17.7** Brooklyn Museum of Art. Gift of Mrs. Carll H. De Silver in memory of her husband, 13.50; **5.17.10** Photo Smithsonian American Art Museum/Art Resource/Scala, Florence; **5.17.11** Cleveland Museum of Art, 2001. Gift of Mrs. Boudinot Keith, in memory of Mr. and Mrs. J. H. Wade, 1921.1239; **5.17.12** Museum of Fine Arts, Boston, Massachusetts/Gift of Nancy Hale Bowers/Bridgeman Images; **5.17.13** National Gallery of Art, Washington, D.C., Gift of Curt H. Reisinger; **5.17.16** Photo RMN-Arnaudet; Schormans (photographer); **5.17.18** Smithsonian American Art Museum, Washington, D.C., Bequest of Henry Ward Ranger through the National Academy of Design; **5.17.21** National Park Service, Yosemite National Park, California; **5.17.23** Library of Congress, Washington, D.C., Prints and Photographs Division, LC-USZ62-121109; **5.18.1** The Metropolitan Museum of Art Archives, New York; **5.18.2** From H. H. Bancroft, *The Book of the Fair* (1893); **5.18.3–5.18.5** Photo Chicago Architectural Photographing Co.; **5.18.6** Photo Hedrich-Blessing, Chicago; **5.18.7** Chicago Historical Society; **5.18.8** Photograph by C. D. Arnold. The Art Institute of Chicago; **5.18.9** Private collection; **5.18.10** The Art Institute of Chicago; **5.18.11** Cincinnati Art Museum. Gift of Mrs. Roy D. Kercheval; **5.18.12** Brooklyn Museum of Art, Gift of Ethel Brown, 56.32; **5.18.14** The Metropolitan Museum of Art, New York. Gift of Hugh J. Grant, 1974; **5.18.15, 5.18.16** Chicago Historical Society; **5.18.17** Photo by the Souvenir Photo Co., Library of Congress, Washington, D.C., Prints and Photographs Division; **5.18.18** The Carnegie Museum of Art, Pittsburgh. Patrons Art Fund; **5.18.19, 5.18.20** National Gallery of Art, Washington, D.C. Chester Dale Collection; **5.18.21** Library of Congress, Washington, D.C., Prints and Photographs Division; **5.18.22** Photo National Museum of American Art, Smithsonian Institution, Washington, D.C.; **5.18.23** The Philadelphia Museum of Art. The W. P. Wilstach Collection; **5.18.24** Collection of Hampton University Museum; **5.18.26** Photo Smithsonian American Art Museum/Art Resource/Scala, Florence; **5.18.27** The Metropolitan Museum of Art, New York. Catherine Lorillard Wolfe Collection, Wolfe Fund, 1906, acc. no. 06.1234.

Index

Illustrations are indicated by page numbers in *italic*.

Abenaki people 82
abolitionist movement 112, 144, 192, 211, 222, 223–29, 238, 241, 244, 247
Abrams, Ann Uhry 84
abstract art 264
Académie Colarossi (Paris) 292, 309
Académie Julian (Paris) 292, 303, 307, 308, 309, 311, 332
Academy of Fine Arts (Paris) 292, 321
Acadia 55, 82, 114
Acoma Pueblo, NM *32*, *34*, 35
Adam, Robert 105
Adams, Abigail 95, 98
Adams, John 95, 102, 111
Adler, Dankmar 321, *322*
Adler and Sullivan 321
adobe construction 34, 36, 46
Advise, W. W. H. 218–19
Aestheticism 300–313, 326, 327
African Americans: as artists 143–44, 162, 241–45, 332–35; assimilation of 266; basket making 77, *77*; civil rights of 236; and Civil War 125, 221–35, 228–29, 235–48; depicted in art 92, 95, 104, 109, 125, 184, 212, 213, 221–33, 236–48, 312, 337; education of 225, 260–63, 266, 334; as household servants 289–91; medical education of 280; revolts by 226; as soldiers 95, 208, 209, 230–35, 238, 247–48; stereotypes of 222–31, 242, 247, 248, 287, 290–91, 317, 323, 332; at World's Columbian Exposition 323, 325; as writers 185, 323; *see also* slavery; slaves
African House (Natchitoches, LA) 115, *115*
Agnew, Dr. D. Hayes 280, 281, 313
Ahwahneechee people 296
Alaska 31
Albany, NY 51
Albin, W. M. 214
Alexander, Archer 245
Alexander II, Czar of Russia 242
Algonquians 52, 64–66, 85, 307
allegory 52–53, 84, 89, 98, 158, 160, 162, 170, 246, 266, 272, 275; *see also* women, as allegorical figures
Allen, Arthur 75
Allston, Sarah 132
Allston, Washington 131, *132*
Alta California 152
altar frontals 53–54, *54*
Altgeld, John Peter 274
Álvarez de Piñeda, Alonso 29
America (engraving) 124–25, *124*
American Academy of the Fine Arts 126, 134
American Anti-Slavery Society 223
American Art Students' Club (Paris) 332
American Art-Union 191, 192, 202
"American Girl" 303, 311
American Philosophical Society 205; Philosophical Hall 135
American Railroad Union 322, 337
American Renaissance 318
American Revolution 75, 82, 86–87, 88, 99, 110, 112, 122, 124, 131, 158, 212, 213, 276, 288; *see also* revolutionaries; Revolutionary War
American Student of Art 301
La Amistad 224
Anacostia River 112
Anasazi 30–31
Anderson, Ross 302
Andrew, John A. 248
Anglo-American War (War of 1812) 113, 121–22
Annapolis, MD 78
Anne of Austria, Queen Regent of France 52
Anshutz, Thomas 271–72, *271*, 273, 274
Anthony, E. & H. T. 235, 264
anthropology 316
anti-Catholicism 18
Anza, Juan Bautista de 46
Apaches 32, 39, 43; Jicarilla Apaches 32
Apollo Association 191
Apsáalooke (Crow) people 150, 151–52
Aragón, Rafael 216, *217*
Arapaho people 251, 255, 258
Arapoosh (Sore Belly) 150–52, *151*
architecture: church 34–36, 40–43; cultural institutions 318–23; decorative style in 293; domestic 292–94; Gothic 293, 318; Moorish 41; New England 70–71; post-American Revolution 86; prison 118–21; Pueblo 31, 32–33, 34–36; Renaissance 318, 324; Shaker 115–17, 118–21; in southern colonies 75–77
Ariadne, story of 127–28
Arizona 18, 30, 31, 42–43
Arkansas 60
Arkansas River 29, 151
Armstrong, Samuel Chapman 260–61, 263
Art Institute of Chicago 318
Arthur, T. S. 145, 314
Artois, Charles, comte d' (later Charles X, King of France), Cabinet of Natural History 61
Arts and Crafts Movement 326
Athapaskan cultures 31–32
Athore (Timucuan chief) 63
Attucks, Crispus 89
Auburn, NY, state prison 120, *120*
Audubon, John James 204–7, *206*, *207*
Augustinians 27, *27*, 28, 42
"Aunt Jemima" character 291, 323
Austin, John O. 251
Awatovi pueblo, AZ 33, *33*
Aztecs 18, 20–25, 59, 66, 71, 210, 220; art 33; iconography 26; and Powhatan 66; and Puritan town 71; stereotypes of 210

Bachman, John *296*
Bacon, Nathaniel 75
Bacon's Castle (Surrey County, VA) 75–76, *76*
Bailey, Gauvin Alexander 53–54
Baja California 45
Balch, Polly 98
Ball, Thomas 245–46, *245*
Baltimore 144
Baltimore Intelligencer 143
Baltimore and Ohio railroad line 269
Banks, Erastus 71
Baptists 131
Barbara, St. 47
Barbeau, Marius 54
Barclay, Robert 165
Barlow, General Francis Channing 236, 238
Barlow, Joel 126
Barnard, George P. 233
Barré, Major Isaac 83
Barry, James 200
Barter, Judith A. 197, 198
Bartholdi, Auguste 276, *276*, 277
Bartlett, Paul Wayland 260, *260*
Bascom, Ruth Henshaw 138
basketry 46, 48, *48*, 77, *77*, 219, 252
battle painting 209, 236–38
Baur, John I. H. 170
Beadle's Dime Book of Practical Etiquette 194
beadwork 252
Bear's Heart (Cheyenne) 263
"Bears and Pears" artist 136, *137*
Beaux, Cecilia 311–13, *311*, *312*, *313*, 329
Beaux, Etta 313
bed hangings and rugs 80–81, *80*
Beecher, Catherine 285, 309
Beecher, Laban S. 102, *102*
Beecher, Lyman 138, 309
Belknap, Dr. Jeremy 95
Bell, Alexander Graham 268
bell-screens 36, 41
Belter, John Henry 293, *294*
Benavides, Friar Alonso de 34, 39
Benberry, Cuesta 107
Bennett, James Gordon 213
Bennett, Lerone, Jr. 222, 240
Benson, Eugene 237, 304
Bentham, Jeremy 118–19, *119*, 120
Benzoni, Girolamo 16, 18
Bergengren, Charles 140, 141, 144
Berger, Martin A. 278
Berkeley, Bishop George 175
Berlo, Janet Catherine 252, 254, 256
Berlo, Janet Catherine and Ruth B. Phillips 61–62
Bermuda 175
Bernardin, Susan 316
Biard, Father 55, 56
Bienville, Jean-Baptiste Le Moyne, Sieur de 57
Bierstadt, Albert 172–73, *172*, 183, *297*
Big Horn River 150–51
Billings, Hammatt 224–25, *225*
Bingham, George Caleb 188–91, *188*, *189*, *190*, 192
Bingham, William 101
Binney, Amos 210
birch-bark: boxes 54–55, *54*; designs in 56, *57*
bird paintings 203–7
Birmingham, Thomas 275
Birney, James G. 162
Bishop, Robert, and Jacqueline M. Atkins 71, 80, 81
Black Codes 238
Black Kettle (Cheyenne chief) 249
Black Legend 18, 131
Blackburn, Joseph 141–42, *142*
Blake, Lillie Devereux 277
Blight, David W. 232
blood, imagery of 23, 38, 39, 165, 216, 280, 282
Blue Ridge Mountains 110
Blume, Anna 256–57
Bodmer, Karl *180*, 181–82, *181*, 251
Boime, Albert 91, 92, 156, 157, 247, 310–11, 336–37
Bolger, Doreen 304, 307, 308
Bonaparte, Charles-Lucien 204
Bonfield, John 322
Bonnat, Léon 291
Boone, Daniel 123, 126, 128, 175
Borgia, Cardinal Stefano 22
Bosque Redondo 220
Boston, MA 69, 72–73, 78, 88, 89–92, 246–47, 303, 309; Museum of Fine Arts 318
Boston Massacre 89, 98
Boston Newsletter 144
Boston Tea Party 90, 92
Bouguereau, William-Adolphe 300
Boulanger, Gustave-Rodolphe 303, 307
Bourget, Paul 310
Bourke, Captain John Gregory 251, 252
boxes 54–55, *54*, 118, *118*, 152–53, *153*
Brackett, Edward 241
Braddock, Alan C. 283
Brady, Mathew B. 146, *147*, 234
Britain: attack on *Chesapeake* 156; battles with French 81–85, 113; and colonies 29, 89–90, 269; influence on American artists 87; trading expeditions 51, 52, 57, 152; US declares war on (1812) 113
British Columbia 152
Brook, James 153–54
Brooklyn Art Association 231
Broun, Elizabeth 335–36
Brown, David 108
Brown, John 226
Brown University (Providence, RI): University Hall 98
Browne, Lieutenant Henry 83
Bry, Theodore de 16, *17*, 18, 63–66, *65*, 210
Bryant, William Cullen 161, 319
Bryson, Norman 198
Bucher, Bernadette 18
buffalo hide: shields 151–52, *151*; *see also* hide paintings
buffalo hunting 62
buffalo robes 44, 130, 150, *151*, 178–79, *179*, 180, 181, *181*
Buick, Kirsten P. 243
Bulfinch, Charles 113, *113*
Bullard, Laura Curtis 241
Bulman, Mary 80–81, *80*
bultos 39, 216
Bunker Hill, battle of 90–91, 94–95
Bureau of American Ethnology 252
burial mounds 57–58
Burke, Edmund 156
Burlington, Richard Boyle, 3rd Earl of 111
Burne-Jones, Edward 300
Burnham, Clara Louisa 324
Burnham, Daniel H. 320, *321*
Burnham, Dorothy 56

Burnham, Patricia 95
Burns, Sarah 305
Burr, Cynthia 97–98, *97*, 100
Bushman, Richard Lyman 100

Cabanel, Alexandre 300, 302
cabinet cards 314
cabinet of natural history (cabinet of curiosities) 61, 66
Cabot, John 63
Cabrillo, Juan Rodríguez 45
Caddo people 251
Cahokia, IL, mounds 59–60, *59*
Cajetan, St. 216
Calhoun, John C. 175
California 18, 45–48, 211, 226; villages in 46
Callen, Anthea 325
Callender, James T. 111–12
calumet ceremony 61–62
Calvin, John 68, 69
Calvinism 74, 131
Cambridge, MA 91
camera obscura 140
Cameron, Simon 221–22
Canada 52, 82
"Canadian savage" mannequin 61, *61*
Canterbury, NH, Shaker Meeting House 117, *117*
Cany Peale, Harriet 289–90, *290*
Cape Mendocino 45
Cape Spartal 74
Capellano, Antonio *122*, 123
Capen, Rev. Joseph 70
capitalism 135
captivity narratives 126–28
Carey, Edward L. 188
Caribbean 59
caribou-skin coats 55–57, *56*
Caribs 16
Carolus-Duran, Emile-Auguste 309
carpets and rugs 138–39, *139*
Carriera, Rosalba 78
Carrington, Mrs. Edward 107–8
Carson, William M. 293
Cartier, Jacques 49, 52
Cass, Lewis 162
Cassatt, Alexander and Robert 331, *331*, 332
Cassatt, Mary *327*, 328–31, *328*, *329*, *331*, 332
Castañeda, Pedro de 31
Caswell, Zeruah Higley Guernsey 138–39, *139*
Catesby, Mark 203–4
Cathedral of Mexico City 42
Cathedral of St. Francis (Santa Fe, NM) 40
Catholic Rosary 244
Catholicism 18, 52, 67, 68, 84, 127, 131, 135, 210, 212; in Mexico 215, 217; *see also* Christianity; *santeros*
Catlin, George 175–83, *177*, *178*, 189; "Indian Gallery" 176–77, 191; and Mandans 178–81
Catskill Mountain House 157
Catskill Mountains 74, 161, 166
Catskill, NY 157
Catskill people 74
Caughnawaga (on St. Lawrence River) 49–50, *50*
Causici, Enrico *122*, 123, *123*, 126, 128
Cavalry, US 152, 251, 255, 262, 272; 3rd US Cavalry 251
Cayuga nation 50
Cenci, Beatrice 242, *242*
Centennial Board of Finance 266
Centennial Corporation, stock certificate 266–68, *267*, 275
Centennial Exposition (Philadelphia, PA, 1876) 243–44, 245, 266–69, 277, 279, 280, 324, 326
ceramics 30, 252, 325, 326–27; Hopewell pottery 58, *58*; Japanese 326; Mimbres pots 150, *150*
Chaco Canyon, NM 30–31, *30*; Pueblo Bonito *31*
Chadwick, Whitney 78
chair backs 141, 153
Chamberlin, Edward, & Co. *290*, 291
Champlain, Samuel de 50–51, 52, 67, *67*, 81
Chapman, John Gadsby 126
Chapman, Maria Weston 241
Charles I, King 68
Charles III, King of Spain 42
Charles V, King of Spain 22, 28
Charlesfort, SC 63
Charleston, SC 78–79, 132, 134, 232, 233
Chase, William Merritt 304–6, *305*, 308, *308*
chattel slavery 67, 75, 77, 129
Cherokee people 114, 128–29
Chesapeake, USS 156
Chessman, Harriet Scott 331
chests 218, *218*
Cheyenne people 29, 151, 249, 250–51, 253, 255
Chicago: as center of social reform movement 274; Haymarket Square rally 274–77, 277; Police Training Center 276; *see also* World's Columbian Exposition (1893)
Chicago Record 328
Chickasaw people 114
child labor 273
China 45; visual traditions 53–54
Chinese, as immigrants 298
Chinese Exclusion Act 299
chinoiserie 54
Chippewa people 82, 241
Chiswick House (London) 111
Cholula, Mexico, pyramids 59
Christ on the Cross with an Angel (hide painting) 37–38, *38*
Christianity 17–18, 20, 26, 27, 30, 149; art of in New Spain 24–28, 46–48; conversion to 48, 52, 53, 55, 69, 126, 210, 316; as unifying force 318
chromolithography 285, 286, 287
Chumash 46, 47–48
Church of England (Anglicans) 67, 75, 131, 163
Church, Frederic Edwin 166–70, *166*, *167*, *168*, *169*, 172, 185, 293, *293*, 295
Cincinnati, OH 184
Cinque 224, *224*
"city beautiful" movement 295
Civil Rights Act (1875) 236
Civil War 170, 171, 209; African Americans and 125, 221–35, 228–29, 235–48; aftermath of 213, 236–48, 249, 264, 293, 325, 332; photographs of 233–35
Clark, Dennis 72
Clark, William 174, 175, 176–77, 179
Clarke, Thomas (Boston merchant) 69
Clarke, Thomas B. (art collector and dealer) 272
Clarkson, Matthew 85
classicism 86, 99; and African Americans 224, 245; in architecture 110, 113, 115, 119, 318, 320, 321–23; in clothing and settings 124, 300, 304, 324; in history paintings 82, 126; in mourning pictures 105; and Native Americans 180–81, 183; in painting and sculpture 101, 104, 125–26, 160, 180–81, 245, 302, 324, 327
Claude Lorrain 155, 163
Clement XIV, Pope 42
Clérisseau, Charles-Louis 110
Cleveland, Grover 277
Clymer, Mary V. 280–81
Coahuila 40
Coatlicue 22–24, *23*, 26–27
codices, preconquest 21–22, *22*, 24–27, 44
Cogdell, John 134
Cohoe (Cheyenne) 253–54, *253*
colchas 219, *219*
Cold Harbor, Battle of 234
Colden, Cadwallader 103
Cole, James 154, 168
Cole, Thomas 154–63, *158*, 166, 170, 171, 187; historical landscapes 158–60, *159*, *160*; successors to 161–63; views of Niagara Falls 155–57, *157*
Colorado 30
Columbus, Christopher 20, 148, 319, 323, 324
Comanche people 251
commercial art 208–9
"common soldier" monuments 247–48
Comstock, Anthony 301
Confederate Army 230–39
confraternities 216–18
Congregationalists 68
Connecticut colony 68
Connecticut valley 72
La Conquistadora 39–40, *40*
Constable, John 154
Constitution (ship) 102
Constitution of United States 131; Equal Suffrage (Nineteenth) Amendment 192
Constitutional Convention 101
consumption, labor and 287–88
Continental Army 104, 106, 124, 212
Continental Congresses 90, 101
Cook, Captain James 152
Cooper, James Fenimore 158
Cooper, Peter 287
Cooper Union 287, 325
Copley, John Singleton 87, 88–92, *88*, *90*, *91*, 93, 142–43, *144*, 197, 337
Coram, Thomas 76–77, *76*
corporations 268
Cortés, Hernán 20, 21, 23, 24, 29
Cos Cob, CT 308
Cosmopolitan Art Association 191, 192, 194
Couturier, Henri 73, *73*
Covington, Kentucky 184–85
Cox, Kenyon 302–3, *302*, 307, 327, 329
Coyolxauhqui 22, 26
Craven, Wayne 68, 69
Crawford, Thomas 221, 267, *268*
The Crayon 167, 176
creation myths 150
Cree people 56
Cromwell, Oliver 75
Crook, General George 251
Cropsey, Jasper F. 161–62, *161*, 166
Cuauhtémoc 24
Cuba 58
Cuervo y Valdez, Francisco 36
cultural institutions 318–20
Cummins, Thomas B. F. 38
Currier and Ives 286–87
Currier, Nathaniel 286
Curry, David Park 304, 307, 308
Custer, General George Armstrong 249–51, 255–56
Custis, Eleanor Parke 106
Custis, George Washington 106
cut-paper profiles 109, *109*

Dabakis, Melissa 275–76
Daguerre, Louis-Jacques-Mandé 145
daguerreotype 145–47, *146*, *147*, 182, 314
dancing, katcina 33
Danckers, Adrian 73
dark chamber 140
Darley, Felix O. C. 266, 277
Darnall, Henry III 78, *78*, 125
Darwin, Charles 303
Daumier, Honoré 240
David, Jacques-Louis 205, 300
Davis, Jefferson 221
Davis, Natalie Zemon 53
Davis, Robert 72, 72
Davis, Theodore R. 249–50, *250*, 253–54, 255
Dawes Act (1887) 256, 316–17
Dawson, Anne E. 307
Daza, Ignacio 29
death figures 216
Declaration of Independence 91, 92, 95, 98, 110, 192
Declaration of Sentiments 192–93
Degas, Edgar 304
Delaware, Lackawanna, and Western Railroad 185
Delaware people 84, 85, 123
Delaware River 165
Democratic Party 188, 190, 236
Democratic Review 211
Department of the Interior, Bureau of Indian Affairs 316
department stores 305–6
Depew, Chauncey M. 277
Deppe, Ferdinand: *San Gabriel Mission* 46, *46*
Dewey, Rev. Orville 193
Dewhurst, Kurt C., and Betty and Marsha McDowell 80, 105, 138
Dewing, Thomas Wilmer 303–4, *303*, 307, 327, 329
Dexter, Timothy 102
Díaz del Castillo, Bernal 21
Dickens, Charles 112, 118, 120

Dickson, William 81
Digby, Simon, Bishop of Elphin 78
Dinnerstein, Lois 90
Diplomatic Medal 124, *124*, 125
diseases and epidemics 51, 58, 67, 152, 283
domestic service 288–92, 293; by foreigners 288
domesticity, cult of 69, 194, 265, 325, 328, 329
Dominicans 27, 42
Donahue, Kelly 38
Douglass, Frederick 323
Dove of the Holy Spirit (altar frontal) 54, *54*
Drain, Thomas 34, 39, 41–42
Drake, Sir Francis 45
Dred Scott decision 226
Drew, Benjamin 228
Drinker, Catharine Ann 311
Drinker, Henry Sturgis 312–13, *313*
Driskell, David 115
Dryden, John 55, 177
Du Bois, W. E. B. 235, 317, *317*
Duncanson, Robert S. 162–63, *162*, *163*, 184–85, *184*, 185, 224, *225*, 229, 241
Dupré, Augustin 124, *124*
Durand, Asher B. 161, *161*, 167, 168, 183–84, *183*, 186, 267
Dürer, Albrecht 22
Dutch settlers and traders 51, 52, 67, 73–75; influence in architecture and portraits 73–75
Dwight, Rev. Timothy 96, 131, 140

Eakins, Thomas 278–83, *278*, *279*, *281*, *282*, 292, 313, 329, 332
East India Tea Company 90
Easterly, Thomas 182, *182*, 249
Eastern State Penitentiary (Philadelphia, PA) 120, *121*
Eaton, Major Joseph Horace 213
Ecuador 168
Edison, Thomas Alva 327
education: of African Americans 225, 260–63, 266, 280, 334; institutions 86; of women 79, 207, 280
Edward Durant House (Newton, MA) 138, *138*
Edward VII, King (earlier Prince of Wales) 241
Edwin, David 106
Eiffel, Gustave 276
Eliot, Alexander 92
Elizabeth I, Queen of England 64, 68
Emancipation Proclamation 226, 229, 245, 246
embroidery 53–54, 55, 56, 80–81, 104, 138–39, *139*; Ursuline 54
Emerson, Ralph Waldo 171
Enlightenment 61, 112, 177
Epazoyucan, Hidalgo 41; monastery 27–28, *27*
Episcopalians 75
Erie Canal 157
Erie people 50
Esopys people 74
Esther de l'Enfant-Jésus, Mère 55
Esther Lyman Chest 71–72, *72*
estipites 42
ethnography 316
etiquette books 194
Eulate, Juan de 39
evangelical movement 131, 223
Ewers, John C. 151
expansionism 149, 175, 213, 222, 266–67, 300

factories 119, 186, 220, 228, 262, 266–68, 270–75, 278, 283, 284, 287, 307; British 118, 228; glass 326–27; lithography 286–87; in New Spain 17; photography 264; textile 307; women in 265, 288
Fagan, Brian M. 29, 30, 58, 60
Falino, Jeannine 99
False Face masks 51–52
fashion 78, 146, 176, 270, 290, 317, 331; indigenous 55–57
Faux, William 130
Fayolle, M. de 61
Federal Style 100, 117
The Federalist 101
Federalist Party 100, 110, 111, 112, 133, 158–59; *see also* Whig Party
Feest, Christian 66
Félibien, André 196, 197
Fenn, Elizabeth A. 179
Ferber, Linda S. 172–73
Ferdinand II, King of Aragon 20
Ferris, Stephen J. 266, 277
Field, Cyrus 167, 168
Field, Erastus Salisbury 140–42, *141*, 145
54th Massachusetts Regiment 232, *232*, 246–48, *247*
figureheads, ships' 102, *102*
First Great Awakening 131
Fiske, George 315, *315*
Flanders 28
Fletcher, Alice 316
Florentine Codex 24–25, 27, 44
Florida 18, 29, 58, 63
flower paintings 201–3
Fluornoy, Thomas 108
Folwell, Ann Elizabeth 106
Folwell, Samuel 105–6, *106*
Force, William 128
forests 85, 157, 176–78, 229, 306; destruction of 186, 270, 307; Native Americans and 175, 176, 249
Fort Caroline, FL 63
Fort Dodge, KS 251
Fort Mahone, VA 234
Fort Marion, FL (Castillo de San Marcos) 251–55, 262, 263
Fort Nassau (later Albany, NY) 51, 67, 73
Fort Niagara, NY 84
Fort Sumter, SC 228–29
Fort Ticonderoga, NY 95
Fort Wagner, SC 232, 246, 248
Fort William Henry, NY 82
Fox, George 165
Fox people 182
Fox Talbot, William Henry 145
France, gift of Statue of Liberty 276–77
Franciscans 27, 29–30, 33–34, 36, 37, 38, 41–42, 45, 46, 48, 52, 216, 217
Franconia Notch, NH 171
Frank Leslie's Illustrated Weekly 232, 256
Franklin, Benjamin 84
Freake, John, Elizabeth and Mary 69–70, *70*, 140
Free African Society 223
Freedmen's Bureau 261
French in America 18, 44, 49–62, 113; and American Revolution 91, 124; and Louisiana Territory 114; trade with indigenous peoples 49–62
French, Daniel Chester *323*, 324
French and Indian War 82, 89
French Revolution 124, 276
Fresquís, Pedro Antonio 216, *216*
Freund, Gisèle 145
Friends of the Indians 256
Friendship Treaty 152
frontier, myth of 123–24
Fryd, Vivian Green 123, 221
Fryer, Judith 280–81
Fugitive Slave Act (1793) 144, 226
Fuller, Henry B. 328
fur trade 51, 52, 175, 177, 189–90
furniture 101; in New England 71–73; in New Mexico 218–19; nineteenth-century 136–39; Shaker 117–18, *117*

Gaines' Mill, Battle of 234
Gainsborough, Thomas 98
galleons, Spanish 17, 45
Garcia, Father Andrés: *Santo Entierro* 39, *39*
Gardner, Alexander 234
Gardner, Isabella Stewart 309–11, *310*
Garnier, Charles 54
Garrison, William Lloyd 241
Gay, E. Jane 315–17, *316*
Gelert, Johannes 275, *275*
gender: and flower painting 201; identity 194, 284, 315–17; and imaging of women 300; linked with race 9, 244, 286; mixing of 61; of Old and New Worlds 125; and photography 312, 319; in professions and labor 280–81, 283–84, 306; role reversal 275, 315; and sexuality 312; *see also* women
General Coloured Association 223
genre paintings 186–91, 192, 300; Westerner 188–91; yeoman farmer 186–88
George III, King of England 82, 90, 95, 104
Georgia 77, 90; Cherokee in 128–29
Gerdts, William H. 202, 306
Germantown Print Works *164*, 165
Germany 81
Gérôme, Jean-Léon 278, 300, 302
Gevelot, Nicholas *122*, 123
Ghost Dance movement 257–60, *258*
"Gilded Age" 264, 291
Gilmore, General Quincy Adams 247–48
Giroux, Alphonse, and Company 145
Gladstone, John 274
glass 326–27, *326*, *327*
Godey's Lady's Book 329
gold, quest for 29, 298
Gold Rush 314
Golden Gate Bay, CA 175
Goldsmith, Deborah 138, *139*
Goodbody, Bridget L. 282
Gosse, Edmund 309
Gothic style 293, 318
Gould, Eliga H. 18, 66
Goupil 289
Gouraud, François 145, 146
Goya, Francisco de 241
Graham's Magazine 184
"Grand Manner" 131
Grant, General Ulysses S. 235, 241, 266
Graulich, Melody 316
gravestones, carved 81, *81*, 101
Great Exhibition (London, 1851) 193
Great Lakes 57, 59–60, 62, 81, 150, 157
Great Plains 219
Great Serpent Mound (Hopewell, OH) 58, *58*
Great Voyages and *Small Voyages* 16, 64
Greek–Turkish War 193
Greene, Valentine 200, 201
Greenland 49
Greenwich, CT 307–8
Greenwood, Nathan E. 205
Grenville, Sir Richard 63
grid format 71, 77, 112, 115
Grimes, Rev. L. A. 243
Gros, Baron Jean-Antoine 300
Groseclose, Barbara 125
Gross, Dr. Samuel D. 279–82
Grosvenor, Lieutenant 95
Grosvenor, Lord 82
Gruzinski, Serge 22, 26
Guadalupe Hidalgo, Treaty of 214
Guale 29, 30
guilds 28, 268
Guillemard, Gilbert *114*, 115
Gulf of Mexico 18, 60
Gulf of St. Lawrence 49
Gulf Stream 337
Gunn Allen, Paula 67
gunstock clubs 130, *130*
Gutiérrez, Ramón 39

Haberle, John 284, *284*
Haddam, CT 93
Hadley furniture 72
Haida people 152, *153*
Haitian Revolution 114, 144
Hale, Ellen Day 309, *309*
Hale, General John 83
Hale, Nathan 309
Hall, John *164*
Hall, Linda 26, 27
Hampton Institute (Hampton, VA) 260–63, 317, 334
Harnett, William Michael 283, *283*, 284–85, *284*
Harper's Weekly 208, 230, 231–32, 240, 249–51, 253, 262, 270, 272, 274
Harriot, Thomas 64
Harris, Neil 81
Hart, Lydia 80, *80*
Hart, Sidney 199, 200
Hartford, Treaty of 73
Harvard, MA, Shaker settlement 116, *116*
Harvard University (Cambridge, MA) 93, 318
Harvey, George *172*, 202, *202*
Hassam, Childe 304
Havana, Cuba 91
Havell, Robert 205
Haviland, John 120, *121*

Hawaii 260–61
Hawthorne, Nathaniel 241
Hayden, Sophia 324, *325*, *328*
Hayes, Rutherford B. 236, 238, 263
Haymarket Monument (Forest Home, IL) 322–23
Haymarket Riot ("Haymarket Eight") 274, 277, 322
Hazelston, Katherine 315, *315*
Heade, Martin Johnson 170, 171, *171*
Heaten, John 74–75, *75*
Heath, Charles *163*
Hedges, Elaine 201–2
Hemings, Betty 111
Hemings, Sally 111–12
Hendricks, Captain William 95–96
Henrietta Maria, Queen 68
Henry, Patrick 75
Henry VII, King of England 63
Henry VIII, King of England 67
Hicks, Edward 163–65, *164*, *165*
Hicks, Elias 165
Hidalgo y Castilla, Miguel 25
hide paintings 37–39, 43–45, 179, 217, 251, 254, 258–60
Hight, Kathryn 178
Hills, Patricia 236
history painting 82, 88, 91, 93, 97, 122, 126, 132–34, 237–38, 240–41, 304, 311
Hitchcock chair 136–38, *138*
Hitchcock, Lambert 136–38
Hochelaga (later Montreal) 49, *49*
Hogarth, William 223
Hohokam 30
Hokan 46
Holabird, William 320
Holmes, Oliver Wendell 264
Holsaert House (Hancock, NJ) 136, *137*
Holy Week, festivities *217*
home decoration 136–39, 326–27
Home Insurance Building (Chicago, IL) 320, *320*
The Home Journal 214–15
Homer, Charles Savage 337
Homer, Winslow 230–31, *231*, 233, 236–40, *237*, *239*, 240, 241, 245, 269–71, *270*, 273, 304, *336*, 337
Hone, Philip 157
Honeywell, Martha Ann 109, *109*
Hoopes, Clara 311, *311*
Hopewell culture 57–58
Hopi *32*, 33, *33*, 36
horticulture 197
Hosmer, Harriet 241–42, 246, 260
Hotz, Gottfried 43, 44, 45
Houdon, Jean-Antoine 104, *104*, 110
Houlihan, Patrick 130
Houseworth, Thomas, and Company (San Francisco, CA) 314–15, *314*, 316
Howard, John 118
Howling Wolf (Cheyenne) 253
Hudson, Henry 51
Hudson River 51, 74, 120–21, 157, 293
Hudson River School 157, 306
Huejotzingo: monastery 28, *28*
Huguenots 63, 78
Huitzilopochtli 21, 22, 23, 26, 60
Hulton, Paul 65
Humboldt, Baron Alexander von 23, 167
Hunt, Richard Morris 318, *318*
Huntington May, Sibyl 93, *93*
Huron people *49*, 52, 55, 62; Four Nations of 50, *51*
Husch, Gail 212

Iceland 49
Idaho 316
Illinois 57
Illinois River 59
immigration: and assimilation 295; and Central Park 295; and domestic service 288, 289; from China 298; and labor 287; as threat to Anglo-Saxons 304
Impressionism: American 292, 304–14; French 292, 304, 329
Independence, War of 102
"Indian Queen" 124, 125
indigenous people *see* Native Americans
industry and commerce 266–69
Inness, George 185–86, *185*
Innu people 56
Ireland, Irish immigrants 288, 289, 290, 291
Irmscher, Christoph 204, 205, 206, 207
Iroquois League (Six Nations) 101
Iroquois people 50–51, 73, 82, 83–84, 85, 176
Isabella I, Queen of Castile 20
Ives, James Merritt 286, *286*
Iztaccihuatl 21

Jackson, Andrew 102, *102*, 115, 158–59, 160, 174, 186, 187
Jackson Square (New Orleans, LA) *114*
Jaffee, David 135, 140
James, Henry 241, 310
James I, King of England 68–69
Jamestown, VA 66–67, 68
Japan, *Japonaiserie*, *Japonisme* 306, 326, 329; lacquer work 72
japanning 72–73
Jarves, James Jackson 173
Jay, John 121, 319
Jay Treaty Commission 121
Jefferson, Martha 111
Jefferson Medical College 279, 280
Jefferson, Thomas 75, 77, 86, 93, 102, 110–12, *110*, 113, 115, 126, 158, 159, 179, 197, 272; as architect 119, *119*; and slavery 111, 114, 292
Jenney, William Le Baron *320*
jergas 219
Jesuits 42–43, 50, 52–54, 55, 57, 61, 150
Jews 68, 334
Jocelyn, Nathaniel 223–24, *224*
Johns, Elizabeth 186, 187–88, 192, 280
Johns Hopkins University Hospital (Baltimore, MD) 313
Johnson, Andrew 241
Johnson, Eastman 227–28, *227*, 229, *229*, 242, 285, *285*, 332
Johnson, Moses 117, *117*
Johnson, William 84
Johnson (hanged African American soldier) 233, *234*
Johnston, Frances Benjamin 261–62, 263, 317, 334
Johnston, Gideon 78
Johnston, Henrietta Dering 78–79, *79*
Johnston, Joshua 140, 143–44, *144*, 145, *145*
Johnston, Norman 118–19
Journals of Congress 101

Kane, Patricia 99
Kasson, Joy 193, 194
Kastor, Peter J. 114
katcina cult 33–34
Kauffmann, Angelica 105
Kaufmann, Theodor 229–30, *230*, 232
Kaw people 250
Keats, John 300
Keller, Morton 240
Kelly, Franklin 166, 169
Kensett, John Frederick 170, *171*
Keokuk (Watchful Fox) 182–83, *182*
Keres 35
Keresan language 31
Ketner, Joseph D. 184
King, Charles Bird 129–30, 131, 176, 182, *182*
King, Clarence 298
Kino, Father Eusebio 42, 43
Kiowa people 29, 251
Kit Fox Society 251
kivas 30, 32–33, *32*; murals 33, *33*
Klein, Cecelia 26–27
Knirsch, Otto *287*
Koehler, Robert 273–74, *273*
Kokopell Mana 33
Kokopelli 33, *33*
Kostof, Spiro 112, 293
Krimmel, John Lewis 222–23, *223*, 224, 227, 332
Ku Klux Klan 236
Kühn, Justus Engelhardt 78, *78*, 112, 125

La Luzerne, Marquis de 124
La Salle, Robert Cavelier, Sieur de 57, 114
labor: child 273; and consumption 287–88; imagery of 269–72; immigration and 288; organized 264; women's 264, 287
lacquer work 72
Lafitau, Joseph-François 61
Lafosse, Jean-Baptiste-Adolphe 289
Lake Erie 157
Lake George, NY 84
Lakota (Sioux) people 252, 255, 257
Lamy, Jean-Baptiste 217
landscape 148–49, 153–57, 166–70, 183–91; nostalgic 306–8; *see also* forests
landscape tourism 155
Lane, Fitz Henry 170, *170*, 171
Lane, Colonel Samuel 113
Langston, John Mercer 241
Lansdowne, Marquis of 101
Las Casas, Bartolomé de 16, 18
Last Bull (Cheyenne leader) 251, *252*
"last stand" as motif 272
Latrobe, Benjamin 112–13, *113*, *114*, 119, *119*
Laudonnière, René de 63
Laval, Bishop François de 52
Lawrence, George 314
Lawson, Alexander 204, *204*
Le Blond de la Tour, Pierre *114*, 115
Le Brun, Charles 83, 94
Le Jeune, Father Paul 55
Le Moyne de Morgues, Jacques 63, *63*, 64, 65
Le Page du Pratz, Antoine 60, *61*, 114
League of the Iroquois (Five Nations) 50
Leavitt, Sara Allibone 311
ledger art 251–53, 256–57
Lee, Ann 115–16
Lee, Anthony W. 298, 299
Lee, General Robert E. 235, 246, *246*
Lee, William 108
Lefebvre, Jules-Joseph 303, 307
L'Enfant, Pierre Charles 106, 112, *113*
Lenni Lenape (Delaware) people 84, 85
Léon, Alonso de 40
Leutze, Emanuel *149*, 172, 174–75, *174*, 210, *211*, 212, 221–22, 222, 229, 287
Lévi-Strauss, Claude 153
Lewis, Cynthia Neri 45
Lewis, Edmonia 241–45, *243*, 249, *249*, 260
Lewis, Colonel Joseph 95
Lewis, Captain Meriwether 174, 176, 179
Lewis, Michael J. 71
Lexington and Concord, battles of 90, 95
liberty cap 221, 266, 268, 277
Lienzo de Tlaxcala 25
Lincoln, Abraham 228–29, 232, 241, 242; monument to 245–46, *245*, 247; portraits of 245–46
Lindsey, Donal F. 263
Linn, Karen S. 332
Lippincott, William Henry 291–92, *291*
lithography 214, 230, 285–86, 289; chromolithographs 285, 286, 287
Little Bighorn, Battle of the 255–57
Little Bighorn River 255
Little, John 228
Little Wound 259–60, *259*
Lloyd, Edward 200
Loewen, James W. 24, 67
London 103, 121, 129, 131
Lone Dog 252
Long, John D. 263
"The Long Walk" 220
Longfellow, Henry Wadsworth 249
Longsworth, Nicolas 162–63
Los Angeles 45
Louis XIV, King of France 52–53, 62, 78
Louis XV, King of France 60, 78
Louis XVI, King of France 61
Louisburg, Battle of *80*
Louisiana Purchase 113–14, 126, 148, 174
Loup River 44
Louvre (Paris) 319
Lovell, Margaretta M. 69, 88, 142
Lowe, David, and Philip Shiman 235
Lubin, David M. 127–28, 196, 283, 285, 330
Luc, Frère (Claude François) 52, *53*
Luminists 170–71
Lyman, Esther 72
Lynes, Russell 287
Lyon, Pat 269, *269*

McClellan, George 280
McCormick, James: family 144–45, *145*
McCormick Reaper Works 274
McCrea, Jane 125–26, 127, 128
McElroy, Guy C. 223
McElroy, Keith 214, 215
MacFarlane, Lisa 316
McHenry, James 173
McIntire, Samuel 102, *102*
McKim, Charles Follen 247
MacMonnies, Frederick William *323*, 324, *324*, 327
MacMonnies, Mary Fairchild 327, *327*, 328
Madison, James 75, 198
Madsen, Annelise K. 194, 197
"magisterial gaze" 156–57
Magoffin, Susan 219
Mah-To-Toh-Pa (Mandan leader) *177*, 178–81, *178*, 251
Maison Carrée, Nîmes, France 110
La Malinche ("Doña Marina") 24
Mallery, Colonel Garrick 252
Mandan people 44, 176–77, 178–81, 251
Manet, Edouard 312, *312*
Manhattan 67
"Manifest Destiny" 149, 175, 211, 222
Manila 17
manta (skirt) 27, 220
Marau Society 32
Marey, Étienne-Jules 278
María Marta (Lapulimeu), presentation basket 48, *48*
Marie de l'Incarnation, Mère 53, 54
Mariposa Mining Estates 296
Marryat, Frederick 336
Marshall, John 75
Martin, John 154
Martinez, Captain Sebastián 38
Martyr, Peter 22
Mary, Virgin: cult of 45; iconography 26; as Our Lady of the Assumption 38; paintings and sculptures of 2, 20, 21, 23, 37, 38, 39–40, 45, 215–16; as Queen of Heaven (*La Virgencita*) 26–27
Maryland Abolitionist Society 144
masculinity, middle-class 283–85
Mason, John 68
mass production 285, 326
Massachusetts: House of Representatives 98; slavery in 92
Massachusetts Bay Company 68
Massachusetts Institute of Technology 324
Massanet, Friar Damián 40
Mather, Christine 38
Mather, Eleanore Price 163, 165
matrilineal and matrilocal culture 32, 50
Maximilian of Wied-Neuwied, Prince 181
May, Rev. Eleazar 93
Maya 24
Mayer, Mrs. 142–43, *143*
Mayflower 67
Mayo, Sarah Edgerton 202
Meacham, Joseph 116
mechanization 287
Medicine Crow, Joseph 150
medicine wheel motif 151
Meigs, Major Return Jonathan 95
mendicant orders 25, 216
Menéndez de Avilés, Pedro 29, 63
Meramec River 59
Merasty, Angélique: birch-bark bites *57*
Mercié, Antonin 246, *246*
Mesa Verde, CO 31
mestizos 23, 212
Methodists 68, 131
Metoyer, Thomas 115
Mexica 21
Mexico 30, 60, 199, 208, 209–12; culture of 214–18; preconquest cultures 31
Mexico City 21, 22, 34, 210, 214, 215, 217; statue of Santa Maria la Redonda 38
Mexico–US War 210, 211–13
Michoacán 218
Mifflin, Thomas and Sara 90, *90*
Mi'kmaq 55, 82
Miles, Ellen G. 108
Miles, Tiya 129
millennialism (millenarian movements) 131, 257
Miller, Angela 160
Miller, David C. 170, 171
Miller, Mary Ellen 22
Milliken, Dr. Fred 281
millionaires 291
Mills, Robert 123
Mimbres, NM, pottery 150, *150*
Minneapolis Journal 273
Minneapolis School of Fine Arts 273
missionaries 33, 39–43; Californian 45–48; as traders 54
Mississippi River 18, 40, 57, 59, 62, 63, 114, 174, 188, 190
Mississippian culture 58–60, 66
Missouri 190, 191
Missouri River 57, 59, 62, 63, 181, 188, 190
Mitchell, Dr. S. Weir 282
Modernism 260
Mogollon 30
Mohawk people 49–50, 84, 126, 127
Monadnock Building (Chicago, IL) 320–21, *321*
monastic orders, monasteries 25, 27–28, *27*, *28*, 268; *see also* Augustinians; Dominicans; Franciscans; Trappists
Monckton, General Robert 83
Monet, Claude 304
Monks Mound (Cahokia, IL) 59–60, *59*
Monroe, James 75
Monroy, Douglas 45
Montagnais people 52, 56
Montana 151
Montcalm, General Louis Joseph de 82
Monteyne, Joseph 52–53
Montgomery, General Richard 94, 95
Monticello (Charlottesville, VA) 77, 110–12, *111*
Montreal 49, 57
Mooney, James 258
Moore, Almira 140, 141, *141*
Moore, Joseph 140, *141*
Moorhead, Rev. John and Sarah 144
Moorhead, Scipio 144
Moorish architecture 41
Moorish furniture 218
moradas 216, 218
Moravians 68
Morris, William 326
Morrison, Ralph 250–51, *250*
Morse, Jedidiah 131, 133
Morse, Samuel F. B. 131–35, *133*, *134*, 136, 140, 145, 160, 165; and Morse code 146; portrait of 146, *147*; and telegraph system 135, 146
Moser, Christopher 46, 48
Motehcuhzoma II (Montezuma) 20–21, 22, 24
motion pictures 278
Mott, Lucretia 192
Mount, Henry 187
Mount, William Sidney 187–88, *187*, 192, 194
Mount Lebanon, NY 118, 120–22
Mount Vernon, VA 106, 108–9
mourning pictures 104–6
Moustier, Count de 124
Mulberry Plantation (Moncks Corner, SC) 76–77, *76*, 112, 129
multi-figure scenes 177
multi-household complexes 30, 49
multi-story buildings 54, 116
multi-tiered structures 276
Munich 300, 304
murals: Pueblo 33
Murray, Freeman Henry Morris 248
Muslims 20, 37, 41
Muybridge, Eadweard 278, *278*, 314
Mystic River 68

Nahuatl (language) 22, 25–26
Namias, June 126, 127
Napoleon I, Emperor 102, 113–14, 241
Narragansett people 50, 68
Narváez, Pánfilo de 29
Nash, Gary 66
Naskapi people 56
Nast, Thomas 231–32, *232*, 233, 240–41, *240*
Natchez people 60, 114
National Academy of Design 131, 134, 136, 146, 161, 166, 168, 187, 191, 227, 230, 232, 238, 291; Annual Exhibition 231, 236, 262, 272
Native American Grave Protection and Repatriation Act (NAGPRA, 1990) 52
Native Americans: as artists 37–39, 43–45, 179, 209, 251–55; assimilation of 256, 316; colonists dressed as 176; cultural traditions 149–53, 263; depiction of 129–30, *129*, 148, 156, 157, 165, 175–78, 188–90, 249, 266–68; exclusion of 266–68; federal policy on 133; imagery and iconography 150–53, 251–60; imprisonment 251–55, 262; "Indian problem" 255; and Indian Removal Bill 174–75; and industrial unrest 272; and Louisiana Territory 114; as national symbol 124–25; negotiations over land 128–29; in popular press 249–51; portrayed as violent and dangerous 126–27, 174, 175, 188, 250–51, 272; relations with colonists 125–29, 173, 208–9; on reservations 251, 256, 316; seen as doomed to perish 173–77, 222; stereotypes of 244, 254, 287; *see also* "noble savage" concept
Natural Bridge, VA 165
naturalists 204
nature, and religion 153–54, 161, 186
Navajo 32, 219–20
Neagle, John 269, *269*, 272
Neal, John 135, 140
needlework 79–81, 90, 92, 104, 106–9, 201, 266; *see also* samplers
Nemerov, Alexander 262, 272
neoclassicism *see* classicism
Netherlands 67, 81; art of 70; *see also* Dutch
Neutral people 50
New Amstel (New Castle, DE) 73
New Amsterdam 73–74, *73*; *see also* New York
New Bedford, MA 335
New Brunswick 114
New England, visual arts and crafts in 70–75
New England Galaxy and Masonic Magazine 132
New France 49–62
New Haven colony 68
New Jerusalem 71
New Mexico 18, 29, 30, 31, 42, 215, 216–20; churches in 34–43, 46–47; conquest of 36, 43; Spaniards in 36
New Orleans, LA 114–15, *114*; Presbytère and Cabildo 115; St. Louis Cathedral 115; *Vieux Carré* 115
"New Woman" 311
New York City: and appeal of genre painting 186–88; Central Park 167, 295, *296*; Columbian Academy 134; Henry O. Havemeyer House *326*, 327; Metropolitan Museum of Art 318, *318*; Rotunda 132; slums 294–95, *294*; Vanderbilt house, Japanese Room 306, *306*
New York Evening Post 237
New York Evening Telegram 270
New York Herald 213
New York Illustrated News 232
New York Morning Chronicle 107
New York State 50; Woman Suffrage Association 277
Newfoundland 52, 63
Newport, RI 68
Newsom, Samuel and Joseph Cather 293, *293*
newspapers, journals, and magazines 208–9, 213, 249–51, 266
Newton, Clara Chipman 326, *326*
Nez Perce people 316, 317
Niagara Falls 155–57, *155*, *157*, 168, 204
Nichols Storer, Maria Longworth 325–26, *326*
Nicoletta, Julie 116, 118, 121
Niepce, Joseph-Nicéphore 145
Niles' Weekly Register 123
"noble savage" concept 55, 84, 123, 127, 130, 177, 183, 287
Norse sailors and settlers 49
Northwest Coast peoples 152–53
Norton, Charles Eliot 318
Nott, J. C., and George R. Gliddon 245
Nova Scotia 114
Novak, Barbara 154, 170, 186

Nuestra Señora de la Purísima Concepción Mission, Church of (San Antonio, TX) 41–42, *41*
Nutting, M. Adelaide 313, *313*

Oakley, Miss 285
Oberlin College, OH: Young Ladies Preparatory Department 241
Obweebetuck (mountain) 307, *307*
Ogden, Robert C. 334
Oglala Lakota people 259
Ohio River 57, 59, 63, 81–82, 185
Okipa Ceremony 179
Oklahoma 58, 60
Olana (Hudson, NY) 293, *293*, 295
Old State House (RI) 98
Old Tassel (Cherokee leader) 128
O'Leary, Elizabeth 288, 291
Olmsted, Frederick Law 167, 295–96, *296*, 298, 315, 319
Omaha people 130, 316
Oñate, Juan de 33–34
Oneida nation 50, 95, 96
Onondaga nation 50
Ontario 50
Oram, William 154
Ormond, Rose-Marie 309
Ortega, José Benito 216, *217*
Ortiz, Gaspar 219
Osage people 188, 189, 250
Osgood, Rev. Samuel 161
O'Sullivan, John 211
Otomi 220
Otos 44
Ottawa people 62
overmantel paintings 64, 93, 153
Oyster Bay Room (Winterthur Museum, DE) 71, *71*

Páez, José de 45
Paiute people 257
Palladio, Andrea 110
Palmer, Frances Bond 213, *213*, *286*, 287
Pamlico River 64
Panic of 1819 205
Panopticon 118–19, *119*, 120
Paris: artists in 128, 292, 300, 302, 304, 328; Commune (1871) 275; Salon 126, 260, 274, 312, 334; Treaty of 114
parks and streets 295–99
Parlange Plantation, LA 115, *115*
Parry, Ellwood 233
Parson Capen House (Topsfield, MA) 70–71, *71*, 75
Parsons, Lucy 277
Parton, James 287
patrilineal culture 46
patronage of art 68, 87, 88, 140, 158, 160, 200, 203, 272, 283, 309, 318, 325, 336
Patten, Simon 287–88
Patton, Sharon 144
Patuxet (Plymouth) 67, *67*
Pawnee people 44, 130
Paz, Octavio 23, 23–24
"The Peaceable Kingdom" 163–65, *163*, *164*, *165*
Peale, Charles Willson 96, 135, *135*, 146–47, 197, 198, 199, 200–201, 204, 206
Peale, James 197, 198, *198*
Peale, Margaretta Angelica 198–99, *199*
Peale, Raphaelle 197–201, *198*, *200*, 283
Peale, Rembrandt 289
Pecos Pueblo, NM 31
Pecos River 43
Pee Dee River 29
Pelham, Henry 88, *88*, 89
Pelham, Peter 88
Penn, Thomas 84
Penn, William 83, 123, 165
Pennell, Joseph 332
Penney, David W. 251
Pennsylvania 120; University of 280
Pennsylvania Academy of the Fine Arts (Philadelphia, PA) 132, 154, 199, 278, 281–82, 292, 311, 332
penny press 208, 209, 213, 214
Pequot people 50, 68
Peralta, Gastón de 28
Pereyns, Simón 37; *retablo* 28, *28*
Perry, Matthew C. 306
perspective, one-point 148
Peskelachaco (Pawnee leader) 130
Petalesharro (Pawnee leader) 130, 133
Philadelphia Museum (Philadelphia, PA) 135, 318
Philadelphia, PA 84–85, 112, 132, 282–83, 311, 329, 332; First and Second Continental Congresses 90; Jamaican Emancipation Day parade 290; racial tension in 290
Philadelphia Society for Alleviating the Miseries of Public Prisons 120
Philadelphia State House (Independence Hall) (Philadelphia, PA) 135, 266
The Philanthropist 162
Philip II, King of Spain 28, 64
Philippines 45, 306
Phillips, Ammi 140, 142–43, *143*, 144, 145
Phillips, Ruth B. 55
photography 145–47, 208, 209, 264–65; and anthropology 316; cabinet cards and 314; of Chinatown (San Francisco, CA) 298–99; of Civil War 232–35; and gender identity 315–17; of idealized women 304; landscape 296–99, 315; mini-factories 264; Native Americans and 182–83, 233–35, 249, 250–51, 261–62; of New York slums 294–95, *294*; photographic portraits 182–83, 314–17; and racial identity 317; stereoscopic views 233, *233*, 234, 314
phrenology 289
physiognomy (as science) 289–90
Piankashaw people 182
picturesque tradition 156
Pierce, Donna 39, 217
Pilgrims 67–68, 123; *see also* Puritans
Pimeria Baja, AZ 43
Pimm, John 72–73
Pinckney, Thomas 108
Pissarro, Camille 304
Pitcairn, Major John 94, 95
Pitt, William (the Elder), 1st Earl of Chatham 102, 103, *103*
Plains of Abraham, battle of 82, 84
Plains people 44, 61, 62, 151, 152, 174, 179, 251, 254, 257, 259
plantations 76–77, 115, 222, 239, 337
Platte River 44
Pliny the Elder 200
Plymouth Colony 67–68, 73
Pocahontas 67, *68*, 69, 123, 126, 128
Poinsett, Joel 134
Polk, James 211, 213
Ponce de Léon, Juan 29
Pont-Aven, Brittany, France 332
Pontchartrain, Lake 225
Popocateptl 21
population: density *172*; foreign-born 288; growth 149, 264
porcelain, Chinese 54, 199
Porter, Rufus 135, *137*, 140, *140*, 145
portraiture: and American Impressionism 308–13; Dutch influence on 73–74; eighteenth-century 88–89; family 140–43; by itinerant painters 140–45; of male professionals 278–83; of Native Americans 129–30, *129*; in New England 69–70; nineteenth-century 134, 162; photographic 182–83, 314–17; "plain" 142–43, 144; presidential 100–104; in southern colonies 78–79; in wax 102–4
Portuguese, as slave traders 224
Post, George B. 292, *292*
Post, William B. 304, *304*
post-and-lintel construction 35, 36
post-Revolutionary period 100, 102
postal service 213
Potomac River 112
pottery *see* ceramics
Poussin, Nicolas 155
Powder River 151
Powers, Hiram, *The Greek Slave* 193–94, *193*
Powhatan (leader) 66, 67, 69
Powhatan people 66–67, 128
"Powhatan's Mantle" 66, *66*
Prang, Louis, and Co. 230, 285, *285*
Pratt, Captain Richard H. 252, 253–54, 263
Pre-Raphaelite Brotherhood 300
precolonial life 24–26
Presbyterians 68, 131
Prescott, William H. 210
Priest, Charles F. 116 *116*
Prince Edward Island 114
prints 63, 64–65, 69, 73, 78, 82, 84, 88–89, 95–97, 105–9, 124–26, 163, 165, 184, 188, 191, 200–201, 205, 240, 270, 296; images of war 214, 249–51; Japanese 306, 329
Prioleau, Colonel Samuel and Mary 78, *79*
prisons, architecture of 118–21
Procter & Gamble 272
professional workers (male) 278–83; as patrons 283–84; portraits 278–83
Protestantism 29, 214; in New Mexico 217; in North America 63–85, 131; sects 68, 163; and visual arts 68–70
Providence Patriot 136
Providence, RI 68
Prown, Jules 96
Pueblo cultures 30–40, 219; architecture 31, 32–33, 34–36; art 33, *33*, 37–39, 44; Christianization 33–34, 36; church interiors and adornments 36–40; iconography 37; sculpture 39–40
Pueblo Revolt 36, 37, 39
Pujol, Paul 246, *246*
Pullman Palace Car Company, strike 272, 322, 337
Punch 240
Punderson, Ebenezer 105
Punderson, Hannah 105, *105*
Punderson, Prudence 104–5, *105*
Puritans 67–68, 75, 140, 192; clothing and hair 69
Purvis, Robert 224
Pyne, Kathleen 303–4
pyramids 59, 60

Quaker Oats Company 323
Quakers 68, 84, 102, 120, 163–65, 197; Philadelphia Yearly Meeting 165
Quan Quan, Marie Thérèse 115
Quebec 94, 95; fall of 82, 83
Quebec City 52, 54, 55, 57, 81
Quetzalcóatl 21, 24, 26–27
quilting 201–2, 223
Quinn, Arthur 75

racial identity, photography and 317
racial purity (as concept) 317
racism 317, 332
railroads 185–86, 266, 268, 269, 274, 298
Raleigh, Sir Walter 64
Ramusio, Giovanni Battista, sketch of Hochelaga 49, *49*
Rand, John G. 264
Rash, Nancy 190
Rather, Susan 83
Reade, Lieutenant 251
Recollet Order 52
Reconstruction Period 236, 239, 246
Red Horse (Minneconjou Lakota) 255, *255*
Red River War 251
Reed, Austin 120
Reed, Luman 158, 159, 161, 187
Reekie, John 234, *234*
Reformation, Protestant 214, 215
religion: and nature 153–54, 161, 186; and race 332; and visual tradition 215, 217–18; *see also* Catholicism; Protestantism; *santeros*
Rembrandt van Rijn 332
Remick, Christian 89
Remington, Frederic 262, *262*, 272, *272*
Renaissance 28, 68, 71, 72, 110, 131, 216, 293, 305, 318, 324; American 318
Republican Party, republicanism 100, 112, 236, 241
Republicans, Radical 241
reservations 251, 256, 316
retablos 28, *28*, 36, *36*, 39
Revere, Paul 89, *89*, 98–100, *99*
Revillagigedo, Juan Vicente, Count de 23
revolutionaries 90, 92, 94–95, 98–100, 126, 194, 212, 275–77, 289
Revolutionary War 99; paintings 91, 97, 121, 212; *see also* American Revolution
Reynolds, Sir Joshua 82, 196–97

Rhodes, Lynette 118
Ribaut, Jean 63
rice plantations 77
Richter, Daniel 50
Riis, Jacob A. 294–95, *294*
Riley, John 108
Rio Grande Valley 211
Ritzenthaler, Robert 51
River Crow people 150
Rivera, Diego 24
Roanoke settlement, North Carolina 63–64
"Robber Barons" 264, 292
Roberts, Jennifer 88–89, 92, 205
Robertson, Alexander and Archibald 134
robes, painted hide 55, 59, 61–62, 252; buffalo 44, 130, 150, *151*, 178–79, *179*, 180, 181, *181*; canopy 62
Roche, Martin 320
Roche, Thomas C. 234–35, *235*
Rockefeller, John D. 268
Rocky Mountains 298
Rococo Revival 293, *294*
Rococo style 78, 293
Rodin, Auguste 260
Roesen, Severin 202–3, *203*
Rogers, John 226–27, *226*, 244
Rolfe, John 67, 69, 128
Roll, Alfred-Philippe 274
Rookwood Pottery (Cincinnati, OH) 325, *326*
Root, John Wellborn 320, *321*
Rosa, Salvator 131, 156
Rosaldo, Renato 176
Rosengarten, Dale 77
Rossetti, Dante Gabriel 300
Rossiter, Dr. Timothy Wells 104
Roth, Leland 110–11
Rousseau, Jean-Jacques 61, 177
rowing 282–83
Royal Academy (London) 82, 129, 131, 196, 301
Royal Academy (Paris) 196
Royal Society (London) 205
Rubens, Peter Paul 68
Rubinstein, Charlotte Streifer 103
Ruskin, John 162, 168, 264, 300
Russia 152
Ryder, Albert Pinkham 335–37, *335*

Sabbathday Lake prison, ME 121
Sagrario Metropolitano (Mexico City) 42
Sahagún, Bernardino de 26
St. Augustine, FL 29, 263; Castillo de San Marcos 29, *29*, 251
Saint Dominique 114
St. Joachim, New France 52
St. John Nepomuk 37, 215–16
St. John's River 63
St. Lawrence River 18, 49–50, *50*, 56–57, 62, 63, 81
St. Luke's (Isle of Wight County, VA) 75, *75*
Saint-Gaudens, Augustus 209, 246–48, *247*, 324
Salem, MA 102
Salem, Peter 95
Salmon, William 67
saltbox houses 70
Saltillo, Mexico 214, 220
Sambrano de Grijalva, Josefa 39
samplers 79–80, *80*, 97–98, *97*, 100, 153
San Estevan (Acoma Pueblo, NM) *34*, 35, 36
San Francisco, CA 45, 314; Chinatown 298–99
San Francisco de la Espada Mission, Church of (San Antonio, TX) 40–41, *40*
San Francisco de los Tejas Mission 40
San Gabriel Mission, CA 46–47, *46*
San José, Old Laguna Pueblo, NM *35*, 36–37, *36*, 40–41
San Juan Pueblo, NM 33, 38
San Miguel, Santa Fe, NM 37, *37*
San Xavier del Bac (AZ) 42, *42*, 43, *43*
Sandler, Martin W. 145
Santa Anna (General Antonio López de Santa Anna Perez) 210
Santa Barbara Mission, Santa Barbara, CA 46, 47, *47*
Santa Catalina de Guale (St. Catherine's Island, GA) 29–30
Santa Cruz de la Cañada, NM 39
Santa Cruz River 42
Santa Elena, SC 29
Santa Fe, NM 217, 219
Santa Fe Trail 210
santeros 37, 214–18
sarapes 219–20, *219*, *220*
Saratoga, Battle of 126
Sargent, John Singer 309–10, *309*, *310*, 311, 329
Sauk people 182
Savage, Edward 106, *107*, 108, 112
Savage, Kirk 244–45, 246–47, 248
Schimmel, Julie 129–30
Schmitt, Max 282, *282*
School of Design for Women (Philadelphia, PA) 325
Schoolcraft, Henry Rowe 183
Schuylkill River 279, 282, 283
Schwartz, Stuart B. 21
Scientific American 140
Scully, Vincent 31
sculpture 241–46, *243*; Aztec 21, 22, 26–27, *26*; in marble 243; nineteenth-century 101–4; precolonial 26; in wax 102–4; in wood 39, 216; at World's Columbian Exhibition 324; *see also Statue of Liberty*
Searle, William 72
Second American Revolution 232
Second Great Awakening 131, 223
Secoton, NC 64, *64*
Seele, Johann Baptist 222–23
Segesser I and II (hide paintings) 43–45, *43*, *44*, 57
Segesser von Brunegg, Father Philipp von 43–45, 45
Seneca Falls Convention 193, 194, 207, 213
Seneca nation 50
Serra, Father Junipero 45, 52, 128
"servant problem" 288–89
Seven Years' War 82
7th Cavalry 255
sexuality: ambivalent attitudes to 193–95; in Pueblo culture 32, 33
Shackamaxon, PA 84
Shakers 115–18; nesting boxes 118, *118*; prison architecture 118–21
Shakespeare, William 300
Shaw, Colonel Robert Gould 232, 241; monument to 246–48, *247*
shawls 220
shields, buffalo hide 151–52, *151*
shipping 101–2
Shoshone people 173; language 46
Sierra Madre Plateau 43
Sierra Nevada 298
silhouettes 109, *109*
Silkenat, David 322
silver 98–100
Simon, Mary Heidenroder 201–2, *201*
Simpson, Marc 231
Sing Sing prison, NY 120–21
Sioux people 82, 182
Skidegate (Haida village, Queen Charlotte Islands, BC) *153*
Skidi Pawnees 44
slavery 18, 29, 67, 75–76, 89, 208, 209; British opposition to 92, 223; chattel slavery 67, 75, 77, 129; Copley and 92, 337; and Haitian Revolution 114; introduction of 239; Jefferson and 111–12; Lincoln and 242; and new territories 221–22; on plantations 77–78; and Powers' *The Greek Slave* 193; Trumbull and 95; Washington and 106; *see also* abolitionist movement
slaves: as artisans 115, 144; auctions of 226–27, *226*; considered "contraband" 230, 233, 238; depicted in art and crafts 92, 95, 104, 109, 125; as domestic servants 288; escaped 144, 184–85, 226, 229–30, 235; friendships with white women and children 239–40; and liberty cap 277; needlework of 108; as workers 269; *see also* African Americans
Slotkin, Richard 123, 263, 272
slums 266, 287, 294–95, *294*
Small, Major John 94
Smith, John 66, 123, 128
Smith, Joshua B. 246
Smith, Shawn Michelle 314–15, 317
Smith, Thomas 74, *74*
Smith, Watson 33
Smith, William 84
Snider, Denton J. 323
social reform movement 274, 295
Society of American Artists 311
Society of Artists (London) 88
Society of Cincinnatus 104
Society of Faces (False Face Society) 51–52
Somma, Thomas P. 260
Sonora people 43
Soto, Hernando de 58
Soule, William S. 250–51, *250*
South Carolina 29, 58, 77; Academy of Fine Arts 134
Southern Sierra Miwok people 296
Soyer, Paul 274
Spain: Armada 64; leather work 37; and Louisiana 114, 115; trading expeditions 45, 152
Spaniards: and Aztecs 210; in North America 16, 17–18, 20–28, 29–49
Spanish–American War 306, 337
Spencer, Herbert 303–4
Spencer, Lilly Martin 192, 194–96, *195*, *196*, *197*, 288–89, *289*, 329–30, *330*
Spies, August 275
Squanto 67
Staiti, Paul 88, 131, 133
Stamp Act (Britain, 1765) 89
Standard Oil Company 268
Stanton, Elizabeth Cady 192
Statue of Liberty 276–77, *276*
steam engine 213
Stein, Roger 74, 81, 200
stencil (theorem) paintings 203
Stephens, Alice Barber 292, *292*, 295
Stewart, Theodore 284
still-life painting 196–201
Stone, John Augustus 176
Story family 241
Stowe, Harriet Beecher 185, 224–26, 285, 309
strikes and uprisings 269, 273–77, 322, 337
Strong, Pauline Turner 126
Stuart, Gilbert 100–101, *100*, *101*
studios, artists' 305–6
Sturges, Jonathan 161
Stuyvesant, Peter 73, *73*
sublime and beautiful (concepts) 156
suffrage movement 192, 194, 207, 277
sugar trade 92, 114, 224, 337
Sullivan, Louis 321–23, *321*, *322*
Sumner, Charles 241
Sun Dance 151, 179
Sund, Judy 324
Supreme Court 236
surgery 279–82
survey aesthetic 298–99
Sweden 81
Swentzell, Rina 150
syncretism 34, 130

Taber, Isaiah West 298, *299*
Tacoma Building (Chicago, IL) 320, *321*
Taino 16, 20
Tait, Arthur Fitzwilliam *287*
Talcott Family 138, *139*
Talomeco, SC 58
Tanner, Henry Ossawa 332–35, *333*, *334*
Tanner, Henry S. *164*, 165
Tanoan language 31
Tappert, Tara Leigh 311, 313
Tarascans 43, 44
Tatch, Kitty 315, *315*
Tattooed Serpent 60, *60*, 114
Taylor, Joel Gray 114
Taylor, Maureen 146
Taylor, General Zachary 213, *213*
Taylor and Huntington Company 233, *234*
tea sets 99–100
technology, new 316
Telleriano-Remensis Codex 24
Templeman, John and Mehitable 99–100
Tennessee 58
Tenniel, Sir John 240
Tennyson, Alfred Lord 300
Tenochtitlan 20–24, *21*, 24, 60, 71
Teotihuacan, Mexico, pyramids 59

tequitqui 25–26
Ternant, Claude Vincent de 115
territorial growth 215, *215*
Tertiaries 216–17
Teton Sioux people 181
Tewa-Santa Clara Pueblo, NM 150
Texas 18, 40–42, 190, 211
Texcoco, Lake 20
textile production 79–81
textiles, in New Mexico 219–20, *219*
Tezcatlipoca 26, 27
Thayer, Abbott H. 302–3, *303*, 327, 329
Thayer, Mary 302, *303*
Theatine Order 216
Thomas Jefferson Foundation 112
Thoreau, Henry David 167, 171
Thornton, NH 136, *137*
Thornton, William 112–13, *113*
Thorvaldsen, Bertel 268
Three Rivers settlement 54, 57
thunderbird motif 150, *151*
Tiffany, Louis Comfort 326–27, *326*, *327*
Timucuans 29, 63, 65
tlacuilos 22
Tlaloc 21, 60
Tlaltecuhtli 22
Tlaxcalans 24, 33, 44, 220
tobacco (as crop) 67
Tobacco people 50
Todorov, Tzvetan 24
Tohono O'Ohdam (Papago) settlement 42
Toltecs 24, 59
Tonalists 303
Tonkovich, Nicole 316, 317
Tory Party 92
Tours, Ursuline convent 54
Trachtenberg, Alan 146, 147, 234, 264, 268–69, 298
Tradescant, John, senior and junior 66
Trager, George E. 257
Transcendentalists 170–71
Trappist monks 59
Trent, Council of 214, 215
Trenton, Patricia 130; and Patrick Houlihan 50–51
trompe l'oeil paintings 47, 199; and middle-class masculinity 283–85
Truettner, William H. 126
Trumbull, John 87, 92–97, *94*, *96*, 98, 104, 121–22, 131, 132, 134, 140, 154, 168, 212, 233, 267, *267*; views of Niagara Falls 155–56, *155*
Turner, J. M. W. 155
Turner, Nat 226
Twachtman, John 307–8, *308*
Twachtman, Martha 307
Twain, Mark, and Charles Dudley Warner 264
Tyler, Ron 210
typhoid 283

ultra-baroque churches 42–43
"Uncle Tom" label 225–26, 332
Union Army 232, 236, 315
Universal Exposition (Paris, 1900) 261, 317
Upton, Dell 86, 111
Ursuline Order 52–56, 62; convent (Quebec City) 52, 53; decorative art of 53
US Geological and Geographical Survey 252
Uto-Aztecan language 31, 46

Valverde Cosio, Antonio 44, 45
Van Bergen, Marten, house (Leeds, Greene County, NY) 74–75, *75*
van de Passe, Simon *68*, 69
Van Dyck, Anthony 68, 82
Van Hook, Bailey 300, 303
Vanderbilt, Cornelius II 292
Vanderbilt, William H. 306
Vanderlyn, John 125–28, *125*, *127*, 131, 132, 192, 194
Vann, James 129
vaqueros 220
Vásquez de Ayllón, Lucas 29
Vásquez de Coronado, Francisco 29, 31
Vaux, Calvert 293, *293*, 295, *296*, 318
Vaux, Roberts 120
Venice 21, 70
ventriloquism 199–200
Venus de' Medici 193
Verrazzano, Giovanni da 49
Versailles 112, 132
Vespucci, Amerigo 20
Vietnam War 276
"Village Enlightenment" 135
Villasur, Pedro de 44, 45
Viollet-le-Duc, Eugène-Emmanuel 276
La Virgencita del Nuevo Mundo 26–27, *26*
The Virgin (Our Lady of the Assumption) 38, *38*
Virginia 64–67, 69, 73
Virginia Company 66, 75
Virginia Penitentiary (Richmond, VA) 119–20, *119*
Virginia State Capitol (Richmond, VA) 104, 110, 119
vision quests 150, 152
Vitart, Anne 61, 62
Vitruvius 47
Vizcaino, Sebastián 45
Vlach, John Michael 77
Voltaire 177

Wadsworth, Daniel 158
Wagner, Richard 335, 336
Wainwright Building (St. Louis, MO) 321–22, *321*
Waldheim Cemetery (later Forest Home) (Chicago, IL) 275–76
wall paintings 153
Wallach, Alan 154, 155, 158, 160
Walnut Street Jail (Philadelphia, PA) 269
Walter, Thomas Ustick 221, *221*
Wampanoag people 67
wampum belts 50–51, *51*, 82, 96
Wanamaker, John 334
War Eagle (Pawnee leader) 130
War Photograph and Exhibition Company 233, *233*
Ward, Daniel C. 199, 200
Ward, Captain Samuel 95
Ward, Captain William 275
Warren, General Joseph 94
Warren, Robert Penn 204
Washington, Booker T. 334
Washington, Bushrod 108
Washington, George 75, 82, 90–91, 124, 212; and L'Enfant 112; portraits of 100–104, *100*, *101*, *104*, 105–7, *107*, 110, 212, 223, 266; and slavery 106, 108
Washington, Martha 106–9, *107*, *108*
Washington Race Course and Jockey Club 232
Washington state 152
Washington, D.C. 106, 112–13, *113*, 211; Capitol Building 86, 97, 113, 121–23, 128, 132, 135, 175, 221, *221*, 266, 268; Dead Letter Office 315; House of Representatives 132–34, *133*
Washita River, OK, Massacre 249–51, 255
Watkins, Carleton E. 296–98, *297*
Watson, Brook 91–92
Watts, Isaac 80
"Wavy Hem Painter" 18–19
wax sculpture 102–4
Wayles, John 111
weaving 152, 219–20; by men 219, 220
Wedgwood, abolitionist medallion 244, *244*
Wedgwood, Josiah 105
Weinberg, H. Barbara 304, 307, 308
Weinert, Albert 275
Weir, J. Alden 307, *307*
Weismann, Elizabeth Wilder 27
Wells, Ida B. 323
Wells, Rachel 102
West, Benjamin 82–85, *83*, *85*, 87, 88, 93, 94, 95, 100, 129, 135, *164*, 165, 197, 199, 233
Westall, Richard 163, *163*, 165
Western Sanitary Commission of St. Louis 246
Westerner (as type) 188–91
Wheatley, John 144
Wheatley, Phyllis 144
Wheeler, Dora 308–9, *308*
Whig Party 92, 98, 123, 160, 190
Whistler, James Abbott McNeill 264, 300–301, *301*, 304, 306, 308, 309, 327, 329
White, Dr. J. William 282
White, John 64–66, *64*, *65*, 148, 202
White, Joseph 146
White, Lydia B. Webb 146, *146*
White, Richard 62
Whitewater, OH, Shaker Meeting House 117, *117*
Whitney, Anne 241
Whitney, Eli 136
Whitney, Josiah Dwight 298
Whittredge, Worthington 172
Wichita, KS 29
wigwams 64, 67
Wilkes, John 98
Wilkie, David 223
William Carson House (Eureka, CA) 293, *293*
Williams, Eunice 126–27
Williams, Rev. John 126–27
Willimantic Linen Company 307
Wilson, Alexander 204, *204*, 205
Wilson, Joseph 102
Wilson, Martha Stewart 108
Wilson, Mary R. 203, *203*
Wind River 151
Windham, CT 307
Winnebago people 128
Winslow, Isaac and Lucy, and family 142, *142*
Wise, Henry 123
Wo-Haw (Kiowa) 254–55, *254*, 261–62
Wolf, Bryan 156, 191
Wolfe, General James 82–83
women: as allegorical figures 52–53, 98, 266, 275–76, 276–77, 324, 328; as artists 197, 264, 286–87; in artists' studios 305; aspirations of 97–98; black, representation of 238–39, 242–44; and construction work 34; as consumers 284, 305–6; costume design and creation 55–57, 61; depicted as mothers 329–31; as domestic servants 288–92, 293; domesticity and 50, 90, 192, 194–96, 265, 285, 328, 329; education of 79, 207, 280; as educators 285; exclusion of 277, 280, 325; idealization of 302, 304, 328; imaging of 300; and landscape 307–8; men assuming roles of 61; and mourning pictures 104–6; as nature 192–96; and needlework 79–81, 90, 92, 108, 201, 266; nude depictions of 66, 128, 192, 193, 200, 281–82, 300, 301–3, 312, 324; as photographers 145–46, 316–17; place of 194; rights of 192, 207; as sculptors 241–44; suffrage movement 192, 207, 277; as weavers 219; work and occupations of 264, 265, 287, 288, 325–26; at World's Columbian Exposition (1893) 324–26; *see also* gender
women's movement 192, 207, 265
Wood, Peter 77, 337
woodcarving 101–2, 152
woodcuts, European 37–38
Woodville, Richard Caton 212–13, *212*, *213*
World Exposition (Paris, 1867) 236
World's Columbian Exposition (1893) 291, 319–28, 332; Administration Building *323*; Board of Lady Managers 325; Congress on Africa 332; Court of Honor ("White City") *319*, 320, 322, 323, *323*, 324, *325*; Midway Plaisance 323, 324, 327; sculpture at 324; Transportation Building 322, *322*; Woman's Building 324–26, *325*, 326, 327–28; women at 324–26
Wounded Knee, Battle of 257, 260
Wovoka (Paiute) 257
Wright, Joseph 102
Wright, Lewis 337
Wright, Patience Lovell 102–4, *103*
Wyoming 151, 251

Xochimilco, MC 27

Yale College (later University) 96
"Yankee" farmer paintings 187–88
Yellow Nose (Hehúwésse) (Cheyenne) 255–56, *256*, 258, *258*
yeoman farmer (as type) 186–88
Yosemite Valley, CA 296–98, 315, *315*
Young, Stanley 48

Zenobia, Queen of Palmyra 242, *242*
Zuñi 36; language 31